PETER LANG
New York • Washington, D.C./Baltimore • Bern
Frankfurt am Main • Berlin • Brussels • Vienna • Oxford

Media/Cultural Studies

CRITICAL APPROACHES

EDITED BY
Rhonda Hammer & Douglas Kellner

PETER LANG
New York • Washington, D.C./Baltimore • Bern
Frankfurt am Main • Berlin • Brussels • Vienna • Oxford

Library of Congress Cataloging-in-Publication Data

Media/cultural studies: critical approaches /
edited by Rhonda Hammer, Douglas Kellner.
p. cm.
Includes bibliographical references.
1. Mass media and culture—Study and teaching. 2. Popular culture—Study and teaching.
I. Hammer, Rhonda. II. Kellner, Douglas. III. Title: Media cultural studies.
P94.6.M425   302.23071—dc22   2009000284
ISBN 978-1-4331-0701-6 (hardcover)
ISBN 978-0-8204-9526-2 (paperback)

Bibliographic information published by **Die Deutsche Bibliothek**.
Die Deutsche Bibliothek lists this publication in the "Deutsche
Nationalbibliografie"; detailed bibliographic data is available
on the Internet at http://dnb.ddb.de/.

Cover design by Clear Point Designs

The paper in this book meets the guidelines for permanence and durability
of the Committee on Production Guidelines for Book Longevity
of the Council of Library Resources.

■ Table of Contents

From Communications and Media Studies Through Cultural Studies

An Introduction and Overview

Rhonda Hammer and Douglas Kellner

You can't depend upon your eyes when your imagination is out of focus.
Mark Twain, A Connecticut Yankee in King Arthur's Court (1889)

Mark Twain's warning is an apt description of the underlying theme of our book, which attempts to demonstrate the significance of media and cultural studies approaches for interrogating and transforming the many ways in which people "see" the world and relate to media, consumer, and digital culture. The rise of mass media ranging from film to broadcasting was one of the major phenomena of the twentieth century, and, as we shall see, a variety of academic approaches and disciplines emerged to engage the increasing importance of media culture. In the post-World War II era of prosperity and increased consumption, it was perceived by many that a new consumer society was proliferating, and the study of consumption and commodities became a major feature of cultural studies in the second half of the twentieth century. By the 1990s, it was clear that a new digital culture had emerged that was transforming the nature of contemporary culture and society, as well as education, communication, and everyday life.

Our book provides the tools necessary to comprehend and critically analyze our current media, consumer, and digital culture. Unlike texts that separate media studies from cultural studies, our reader combines critical approaches and presents material that will allow students, teachers, and readers to critically engage the many types of media, consumer, and digital culture. This position, found in studies within our text, combines analysis of the production and political economy of media and the emergence of new forms of digital and consumer culture with textual and contextual analysis of a wide range of artifacts—from TV and film to Barbie dolls and YouTube—as well as discussion of audience reception and the social effects of media.

We intend *Media/Cultural Studies: Critical Approaches* to be both practical and theoretical: user-friendly and accessible to both undergraduate and graduate students, as well as to individuals wanting to learn media and cultural studies on their own. The slash in the title signifies the need to combine the media and cultural studies, as done by many of the contributors to our text. Our introduction should make clear that we are combining the traditions of media and communication studies with cultural studies in our book and wish to synthesize these fields, rather than separating them into opposing disciplines. "Critical approaches" in the title indicates that we are providing material that will enable students, teachers, and individuals to analyze, interpret, and critique the artifacts of our media, consumer, and digital culture.

Our text follows in the traditions of those who argue that the development of critical media/cultural studies approaches are so engaging because they "address people, not only intellectuals and academics" (Grossberg, 1997: 268). In fact, leading cultural critic Raymond Williams believed that cultural studies was, foremost, a political pedagogical project that must "always begin where people are" and provide them with knowledge to address issues which are of "real, personal, and immediate concern" to them (Grossberg, 1997: 264, 268). Although some of the chapters in this text employ challenging theoretical conceptualizations, they all focus on relations and practices that inscribe everyday experiences.

Further, the panorama of critical theories incorporated in the writings here is hardly abstract. We realize that to even talk about theory can be the "kiss of death" to a course reader, given the aversion to theory harbored by many students and even some faculty. We argue that theory has received a bum rap due, in part, to the manner in which it is taught in many educational institutions and how it is described in certain academic and popular texts. More often than not, theory is perceived to be tedious ("snoring") and a waste of time, devalued by students and teachers alike. For many, theory's only value is that it is something you have to know to pass a test, use in a paper for a better grade, or even deploy as cultural capital for the publication of scholarly writing.

Theory is thus transformed into a commodity and seen as an object or thing, rather than as a way of describing and interpreting phenomena under inquiry. Theory is too often presented in a decontextualized fashion in which it is divorced from its historical, socio-political, and economic context, as well as from the very relationships it was constructed to explain. Rather than existing in some kind of esoteric vacuum, devoid of any connection to our daily existence, significant theories should be grounded in the real social, political, and cultural relations and experiences of everyday life. To put it more simply, theorizing is often provoked by studying or questioning ideas, experiences, material conditions, or social relationships and then constructing or discovering theories that explain or illuminate the phenomena.[1]

For example, people believed for centuries that our nighttime dreams have meanings with a basis in dimensions of our own experiences, often symbolizing events in our everyday life. It was only in the late nineteenth century, however, that the existence of the unconscious was even acknowledged, positing dreams as expressions of unconscious desires or wishes. Although there are disagreements over who was ultimately responsible for this discovery, Sigmund Freud was the first to develop a theory of the unconscious that provided for not only a cogent examination of the unconscious mind, but a method of investigation which allowed for expressions of the unconscious to surface and be recognized at the conscious level (see Gay, 1989). One of the most important implications of this revolutionary theoretical breakthrough was in relation to our understanding and practical treatment of psychological disorders. Indeed, before Freud, mental illness was believed to be solely biological or physiological in nature.

Freud's theories of dreams and the unconscious provide an apt example of how theories develop from investigations into concrete experiences and can be practically applied to provoke changes in dominant beliefs, values, and behavior. Hence, theorizing about media—much like Freud's interpretation of dreams—can reveal aspects of our own unconscious values and beliefs, as well as the "personality" of the culture that mediates how we think about the world and determines so many of the practical and symbolic realities we often mistakenly perceive as "normal," "natural," or "self-evident." As communications scholar, Paul Watzlawick reminds us:

> our everyday, traditional ideas of reality are delusions which we spend substantial parts of our daily lives shoring up, even at the considerable risk of trying to force facts to fit our definition of reality instead of visa versa. And the most dangerous delusion of all is that there is only one reality. What there are, in fact, are many different versions of reality, some of which are contradictory, but all are the results of communication and not reflections of external, objective truths. (1976: xii)

For decades Karl Marx studied the emergent capitalist society, which he dissected, criticized, and theorized, while a variety of theorists like Emile Durkheim, Max Weber, Georg Simmel, and later Max Horkheimer and T. W. Adorno, Herbert Marcuse, Jean Baudrillard, Michel Foucault, and Jurgen Habermas, all studied modern societies, and controversially, transitions in some of the later cases to a new postmodernity. Others like Frantz Fanon and Paulo Freire studied colonial and post-colonial societies, developing a critical analysis of culture and education. These theories were all of importance to the emergence of cultural studies, and helped provide a context for the study of media and communication.[2]

Other modern theorists like W. E. B. Du Bois concluded that race was the dividing line of the twentieth century and brought critical race theory to bear on American life. Globally, feminist movements and theorists like Simone de Beauvoir began analyzing the oppression of women, and by the 1960s feminist movements often included analysis of how cultural forms marginalized women and reproduced male domination. At the same time, black and brown power movements, indigenous native movements, gay and lesbian movements, and other oppressed groups began theorizing and critiquing how existing dominant Western cultures oppressed and marginalized them.[3]

At their best, critical media/cultural studies approaches introduce us to new ways of thinking about the media and society, to novel forms of critique, and to alternative possibilities for social transformation and construction of a better life, which provokes us to "refocus our imagination." This is why an understanding of the dialectic of theories and practices within critical studies is so exciting and relevant to our everyday life.

In particular, media/cultural studies perspectives assist us to understand, critique, and decode media culture and, hence, generate critical media literacy skills that empower individuals in relation to the images, stories, spectacles, and media that constitute culture and identities, deeply influence politics, and play a crucial role in the economy. However, before we expand further on the significance of this paradigm, we need to discuss some of the problems associated with undertaking both cultural and media studies, as well as some of the key concepts and historical background that characterize these two inter-related arenas of thought. Indeed, as teachers and students of critical media literacy and cultural studies, we find that we are often asked: What is media literacy? What are media and cultural studies? What are some of the key concepts, methods, and subject matters, and how can we learn to do cultural and media studies and teach the concepts, methods, and skills to others?

This book is a response to such questions in that it provides a collection of some of the diverse and fascinating topics that are studied within media and cultural studies today, and it identifies central theories and methods that characterize research in these domains. And because theory is often best explained in terms of practical applications, the contributors to this text provide rich and often complex examples, from a panorama of media and cultural artifacts, to illustrate the usefulness of critical theory in analyzing and interpreting a wide range of cultural forms.

We recognize that there are many textbooks that describe media and cultural studies, their key concepts and debates, and provide an overview of these distinct fields. In fact, there are so many books on these topics that it can be overwhelming. Because both arenas encompass such divergent studies and research, and there is no consensus on either the parameters or definitions of the fields, it is difficult to know where to begin, and as well how to separate the proverbial "wheat" from the "chaff." This is due in large part to the highly profitable and competitive nature of academic publishing in the United States that has identified a lucrative market (i.e., students) for media and cultural studies texts.

Indeed, the label "cultural studies," has become highly fashionable, and publishers are incorporating older bodies of work "into the new category of cultural studies and they have attempted to link cultural studies with their already existing major markets in the largest disciplines of the humanities and social sciences" (Grossberg, 1997: 277). Moreover, what passes for "cultural studies" pales in comparison to what is sometimes categorized as "media studies."[4] Indeed, publishers—as well as many colleges and universities—appear to have appropriated the term to apply to any text or area of study that can be even remotely associated with mass media and media culture. It seems everything from media corporate management to public speaking has been described as part of "media studies." Even celebrity biographies have been included in this category. Furthermore, because some of these books are designed to "cross-over" into the mainstream market (as that is where the real money is to be made), they often offer over-simplified explications of media culture and fail to incorporate any kind of serious analytical or critical perspectives.

To further add to this confusion, it is often difficult to discern between what is called "cultural studies" and that which is described as "media studies," as both traditions seem to share similar perspectives and methodologies, as well as areas of investigation. Yet both media and cultural studies are defined differently and are often highly contested, and relationships between media and cultural studies are highly complex. John Nguyet Erni (2001) argues that this is, in large part, due to the "swift and far-reaching" integration of "theories and methods of cultural studies to the field of media studies" in both the United States and Britain (Erni, 2001: 187). And to complicate the matter even more, it is also difficult to distinguish among what different authors, publishers, and academic departments describe as "media studies" and "communications studies." Given this context, it is hardly surprising that many students are confounded when first introduced to cultural studies and media and/or communication studies.

While we will do our best to provide overviews of the field, within primarily English-language perspectives, we have no illusions that our introduction can provide for any kind of definitive account or topology that will map all of the territories encompassed by these seemingly overlapping but conflicted domains. However, we do contend that there are key writings, ideas, practices, and theories that can help us make sense of media, communication, and cultural studies, as well as reveal the potential for critical and emancipatory work within these arenas.

In the next section we will provide an overview of what we perceive to be some of the central concerns and developments of largely Anglo-American communications and media studies, and then lay out our view of the trajectories of cultural studies. Our goal is to provide a model of media/cultural studies that overcomes the one-sidedness of certain dominant views of social science-based communications and media studies posited in opposition to a text and theory-based cultural studies. It goes without saying that this is a daunting exercise, especially given that these perspectives can be characterized as "contested terrains." And we readily admit that this narrative is mediated by our own experiences, readings, and research, as well as some "chutzpah" on our part, which is indeed a central ingredient of attempts to map out and interrogate the fields of contemporary culture, media, and communication practices.

We will first present our analysis of the rise and trajectory of communications and media studies in North America from the early twentieth century through World Wars I and II, and the post-war period to the present. We will explore origins of the academic disciplines of communications and media studies often overlooked in standard accounts by addressing the often unperceived connection between the development of mainstream mass communications and media research in the United States with government propaganda and corporate and state public relations research, as well as the close connections between mass communications, major corporations, and the government.[5] Next, we discuss the origins and development of British cultural studies into an international enterprise that was exported and that took varying forms throughout the world. We show how cultural studies became a global phenomenon that deeply influenced the study of media, culture, and communication. We describe how conflicts emerged within cultural studies and between it and a social science-based media/communications studies. Dominant in major academic departments, the standard media/communications approach rejected what was perceived as an overly theoretical and highly political cultural studies. We then attempt to overcome this divide and present perspectives on a critical media/cultural studies that transcend existing limitations of certain versions of media/communications and cultural studies as they are currently positioned, often in an unproductive opposition to each other. Many of our contributors to this text share our goal of overcoming sterile divisions between media/communications and cultural studies, as do many recent scholars. Finally, we describe the contents and goals of *Media/Cultural Studies: Critical Approaches,* explaining what is in the various sections of our book and how the specific articles contribute to helping us understand our contemporary media, consumer, and technoculture.

■ The Origins and Trajectory of Communications and Media Studies

Unlike disciplines such as sociology or philosophy, which identify generally accepted schools of thought and ideas, as well as historical figures that help define these domains of study, communications and media studies have no agreed-upon pantheon, canon, or history. Indeed, within the academic domain of "communications studies," departments often bear little similarity to one another due to the plethora of divergent, interdisciplinary areas of focus, which can include journalism, public speaking, public relations, mass media, communication and entertainment law, as well as interpersonal, international, and inter-cultural communications, to name a few.

Communications studies have evolved—and are evolving—in an atmosphere of fervent debate, critique, and divergence, which can often overwhelm students and scholars. Yet if we wade into the "fray," initially as observers, we would suggest that it is through the dialectic of argument and debate that new levels of learning and understanding take place, which often take the form of more complicated and deeper questions and insights, rather than standard conventional accounts. Indeed, it is the contentious nature of research generally associated with media and communication studies that provides for a greater understanding of the development of Anglo-American and global communications/media theory and research, which is characterized by a series of disagreements, power struggles, and acrimonious clashes both theoretical and political in nature. As we will see, many of the divisions and debates persist, which helps to explain the significant differences in contemporary media and communications programs and departments in a variety of colleges and universities.[6]

Long before the emergence of cultural studies in England, a new field of communications studies began unfolding in North America during the first half of the twentieth century, comprising a new academic discipline by the 1940s.[7] This approach, often described as "mainstream communications studies," was primarily concerned with studying and measuring the functions, uses, and effects of mass media in an objective, quantitative, and "scientific" manner. Primarily consisting of sociologists, psychologists, political scientists, and journalists, these researchers advanced relatively simplistic, linear models of communications that attempted to reduce and quantify the complexities of social and cultural relations to behaviorist and mathematical methodologies (McQuail, 2004).

Consequently, the most democratic and progressive dimensions of a rich tradition of U.S. scholarship associated with pragmatism, which recognized "the centrality of communications to a social-philosophical explanation" of American culture and provided for a "sophisticated investigation of media technology in relation to human behaviour, community, education and social change," were pushed aside (Carey, 1989; Hardt, 1992). It was replaced with what sociologist Alvin Gouldner described as a utilitarian social science that tended "towards a theoryless empiricism, in which conceptualizations of problems are secondary and energies are instead given over to questions of measurement, research or experimental design, sampling or instrumentation" (cited in Hardt, 1992: 16). However, it was not only the "Chicago school" of pragmatists of the early twentieth century who were excluded from this field, but a host of other significant communications scholars and critical theorists were essentially erased from what later became known as "mass communications studies."

In fact, the dominance of a largely behaviorist, quantitative, and government and industry-oriented "paradigm" in U.S. mass communications studies owes as much to the American government and commercial corporate interests as it does to the particular visions, expertise, and ambitions of a relatively small but powerful group of intellectuals, who became especially prominent after the Second World War. As critical communications scholar Hanno Hardt explains it:

> The development of [mass] communication research occurred under conditions of social and political upheavals; it coincided with the growth of the United States as an industrial superpower and benefitted from the domestic and foreign consequences of such changes. The production and dissemination of ideologically charged messages in the form of commercial advertising or political propaganda became a major concern; it was supported by industry and successive governments and reproduced in educational systems in the guise of patriotism. (1992: 12)

The early twentieth century was a period of rapid transformations with regard to technological and scientific innovations, major commercial and industrial shifts, radical geopolitical changes in nations, governments, political systems, and international relations. Significant increases in immigration, especially in the United States, and the expansion of urban centers and city populations marked the evolution of the age of mass societies. In this context, there was a burgeoning interest in studying social behavior and control, particularly in relation to the role of emergent mass media.

The development of communications research and the establishment of mass communications studies in the United States were shaped by the dominant beliefs and values of what is often described as the "American Dream," which is framed within a liberal pluralist tradition. Communications were conceptualized within the model of a supposedly democratic society, organized around a normative consensus concerning the common good, in which the plurality of informed citizens participated and interacted in communities, and members were chosen to represent particular concerns and interests. Within the ideal of a democratic and free society, all citizens possess equal opportunities to pursue happiness and prosperity, and should be able to participate in their society. As James Truslow Adams described it in 1931: "it is not a dream of motor cars and high wages, merely, but a dream of a social order in which each man and each woman shall be able to attain to the fullest stature of which they are innately capable, and be recognized by others for what they are, regardless of the fortuitous circumstance of birth or position."[8]

A key to realizing democracy was the manner in which the democratic process might be effected by innovations in, and employment of, mass communications within the current transition of industrial capitalism to a corporate, consumption-based system. Indeed, contentious debates emerged around broadcasting and journalism with regard to the potential of expanding media technologies for advancing or repressing democratic practices in the twentieth century around new media like radio and later television. Debates concerned who should have access to the media, whose interests it served, whether media were serving the common good, and how broadcasting could serve the public interest—debates that determined the structure of the system of U.S. media.[9]

The First World War (1914–1918) was a watershed in the employment and study of mass communications, marking the urgency for research in this area. All participants in the war used the media as instruments of propaganda and used the new techniques of advertising and public relations to manipulate their citizens to follow war aims and to conform to their government's policies. Moreover, it is hardly surprising, given the explosion of new and radical advances in social thought and scientific research, that much of this propaganda research was grounded in psychological and social scientific philosophies and methodologies like behaviorism.

During World War I, the U.S. government, on the executive order of President Woodrow Wilson, established the U.S. Committee on Public Information (also known as the "Creel Commission"), which was, as Stuart Ewen describes it, a "vast American propaganda apparatus mobilized in 1917 to package, advertise and sell the war as one that would 'Make the World Safe for Democracy'" (1996: xxff). During the war, the new techniques of advertising and public opinion manipulation were amply used. In fact, this propaganda campaign was so successful that it astonished even those who had participated in it, including President Wilson who had been elected on the basis of his non-interventionist platform. The Committee had managed to employ "every known device of persuasion and suggestion" to sell the war to an initially pacifist American public (Carey, 1977: 38). Working in conjunction with the British Propaganda Ministry, the Committee quickly moved from presenting factual information to fabricating stories and images of the "Huns," which included depicting German soldiers bayoneting innocent Belgium children and raping nuns. Not only did the committee manage to change public opinion, but provoked what Noam Chomsky (1991) described as "an hysterical war mongering population which wanted to destroy everything German, tear the Germans limb by limb, go to war and save the world."

Americans were also warned that there were spies in their midst, which led to the persecution of many German Americans, as well as the targeting of critics of the government policies as traitors. This mammoth multi-million dollar U.S. propaganda enterprise had over twenty-four bureau divisions in nine foreign counties,[10] as well as establishing its own film and news divisions with a legion of paid and volunteer personnel. These included government officials, Hollywood filmmakers and celebrities, representatives from big business, mass media, journalists, prominent citizens from every community, as well as a number of intellectual and academic scholars. There were also thousands of men who had been involved in what would later be called public relations, who managed to hone and develop revolutionary and highly sophisticated techniques of influencing public opinion.[11]

One of the pioneers of public relations, Edward Bernays, actively participated in this process. Bernays coined the expression the "engineering of consent" to describe the importance of manipulating the public mind to support the status quo, and advanced ways to do this that included government policies, using advertising and commercial interests, and promoting social conformity. Walter Lippmann, the influential journalist, editor, and political commentator, was also associated with applying propaganda and public relations to government and corporate interests. Lippmann's original faith in the capabilities of the American people to be actively and intellectually engaged in the democratic process was eventually replaced by a belief in the innate stupidity of the masses, who he referred to as "ignorant herds"; he harbored serious doubts about the future of American democracy within industrial mass societies (Chomsky, 2003). This radical shift in judgment was apparently provoked by his participation in propaganda research for the U.S. government during World War I. Consequently he believed, as Noam Chomsky explains it, that: "'The public must be put in its place,' Walter Lippmann declared…That goal could be achieved in part through 'the manufacture of consent…' This 'revolution' in the 'practice of democracy' should enable a 'specialized class' to manage the 'common interests' that 'very largely elude public opinion entirely'" (Chomsky, 2003: 6).[12]

Edward Bernays' views were even more elitist, if that's possible, in this regard. In an interview with Stuart Ewen, Bernays "maintained that, while most people respond to their world instinctively, without thought, there exist an 'intelligent few' who have been charged with the responsibility of contemplating and influencing the tide of history" (Ewen, 1996: 6ff). Both Lippmann and Bernays were hardly alone in calling for a radical change in the democratic process that would shift the decision-making powers of the people to a specialized class of experts (although there were significant differences within this elite group). In fact, many intellectuals identified a crisis in democracy, provoked by growing immigrant populations, by technological, scientific, and theoretical advances, and by the escalating number and complexities of issues which had to be addressed by the governing bodies established to "serve the people."

Within this context, the relationship of mass media, social integration, and liberal democracy was of key importance and had been discussed and debated in a variety of forums. In particular, the abilities of the American people to be informed participants in the democratic process were questioned by intellectuals who thought that the people did not have the capacity for self-government and were too easily manipulated by elites, sometimes dangerously so, as was demonstrated during World War I and then in the 1930s with the rise of fascism. Even though advances in media technology, especially during the inter-war years, were considered by many to be a revolutionary means to provide citizens with the information necessary to develop knowledgeable opinions, a number of those in positions of power believed that the masses were too stupid to make "rational" decisions. In fact, experts like Bernays subscribed to dominant "scientific" theories which posited that "the average man" was fundamentally irrational and driven by unconscious forces that could render him dangerous or compliant and could pose a threat to the maintenance of the democratic system. These kinds of prejudices underscored a strand of largely pessimistic studies of mass society and legitimated elitist attitudes toward working and underclass people. They were characterized as passive dupes who were highly susceptible to manipulation and hence could be whipped up into a frenzy. Such behavior was deemed to be especially rancorous and dangerous within crowds, thus requiring that "the masses" had to be protected from themselves.[13]

The rise of fascism and spread of communism in Europe and elsewhere in the 1930s increased concern about using the media to spread democracy and American values and to combat totalitarianism, while at the same time corporate and state institutions calculated how communication media could be used to serve their interests. As academic communications studies started to emerge in the 1930s and 1940s, and as theorists noted the power of propaganda in World War II, a wide range of studies began appearing of the social effects of the media, promoting debate over the media and seeing the media as a social problem. Some of the first empirical studies of the effects of film, for instance, criticized the cinema for promoting immorality, juvenile delinquency, and violence. The Motion Picture Research Council funded the Payne Foundation to undertake detailed empirical studies of the impact of films on everyday life and social behavior. Ten volumes were eventually published and a book *Our Movie-Made Children* (Forman, 1933) sensationalized the Payne findings, triggering debates about the media and how they inflamed social problems like crime, youth problems, sexual promiscuity, and what was perceived as undesirable social behavior (see Jowett, 1976).

The first models of mass communication built on studies of propaganda, film influence, advertising, and other media studies, assuming a direct and powerful influence of media on the audience. This model became known as the "bullet" or "hypodermic" theory, asserting that the media directly shape thought and behavior and thus induce social problems like crime and violence, rebellious social behavior, mindless consumption, or mass political behavior (see Lasswell, 1927 and the presentation of the model in Defleur and Ball-Rokeach, 1989). The propaganda role of the media in World Wars I and II and the growing concern about the social roles of film, advertising, and other media promoted debate about how the media were were intensifying a wide range of social problems ranging from crime to growing teen pregnancies.

A major early communications researcher, Paul Lazarsfeld, pointed out that the field of communications research was initially bifurcated in the 1940s between the "critical school" associated with the so-called Frankfurt School Institute for Social Research (1941),[14] which produced some of the first critical perspectives on mass culture and communications, contrasted to "administrative research," with which Lazarsfeld was associated. Lazarsfeld defined administrative research as work carried out within the parameters of established media and social institutions, which would provide material that was of use to these institutions. "Administrative research" included empirical inquiry into audience tastes and uses of media, demographics of media audiences for different media or programs, and research into existing media organizations. The critical approach, by contrast, looked at the impact of media on society as a whole, in terms of the positive or negative impact of media on values like individuality, critical thought, education, and democracy.

Administrative research that served the interests of dominant corporate and statepowers, who often funded such research, became the hegemonic form of research in the new academic discipline of communications studies. The dominant paradigm was popularized by Wilbur Schramm and others working in a positivist/empiricist tradition of communications studies in the 1940s and 1950s.[15] Schramm founded some of the first departments of communications at the University of Illinois, Stanford, and the University of Hawaii and became a major force in establishing the academic discipline of communication as an empirical, behaviorist, and positivist science. As noted above, what we now recognize as "mainstream communications studies" was largely concerned with studying and measuring the functions, uses, and effects of mass media in an objective, quantitative, "scientific" manner characterized by a rather simplistic and linear sender, message, and receiver model.[16]

It was connected with the new disciplines of information theory and cybernetics that were used by the military in World War II and social planners going into the Cold War.[17] As communication research developed from the 1940s, its major practioners sought corporate and state research money and thus became tied to the interests of media corporations and the state. Lazarsfeld and his associates were also responsible for another pillar of mainstream academic communications studies, "the law of minimal effects" and the "two-step flow" model (Lazarsfeld, Berelson, and Gaulet, 1944). Responding to concerns about the effects of Hollywood films on behavior, propaganda, and the political manipulation of publics during the two World Wars,[18] Lazarsfeld and his colleagues undertook studies of advertising and consumer behavior, the manufacture of public opinion, and election behavior in political campaigns. Their research indicated that direct media effects were quite limited and communication processes took the form of a "two-step flow" where media provide information, but opinion leaders shape and disseminate it and are the main forces in disseminating information.[19]

Lazarsfeld and Elihu Katz expanded this model in *Personal Influence: The Part Played by People in the Flow of Mass Communication* (1955). Their "two-step flow" model claimed that opinion leaders are the primary influence in determining consumer and political choice, as well as attitudes and values. This model holds that the media do not have direct influence on behavior, but are mediated by primary groups and personal influence, thus in effect denying that the media themselves are a social problem because they merely report on issues and reinforce conventional thought and behavior.

The dominant paradigm, as McQuail notes (1994: 41ff), has two dimensions: an analytical modeling of communication as a linear and functional process of transmitting a message from sender to receiver, and a built-in normative model that liberal pluralist societies are the best form of society to allow transparent and democratic communication. Lazarsfeld's "two-step flow" model soon became an important part of the paradigm, which downplayed direct media effects and claimed that "personal influence" intervened. In his model, public opinion leaders were more important in shaping consumer behavior, voting, public opinion, and other key communicative phenomena than the media. This approach downplayed the harmful or manipulative effects of media and kept liberal pluralist society intact as a norm, while also legitimating a relatively passive public that followed wise opinion leaders or, secondarily, the media.

Other schools like the "uses and gratifications" theory postulated an active audience, again suggesting that the effects of the media are benign and in line with the needs of a democratic society.[20] It is highly ironic that after getting major funding from government and corporate sources to help develop methods of manipulation and control of the public through media, advertising, public relations, and other forms of social control, some of the same mainstream communications researchers flip-flopped and now assured the public that it had nothing to fear from the media, which they now identified as a benign and limited force, used and controlled by the people themselves for democratic purposes.

Another way to make a distinction between the two major forms of communications studies is to distinguish between affirmative and critical approaches. The more mainstream administrative and empiricist approach championed by Lazarsfeld and Schramm is largely affirmative of media industries and the social system as they are currently constructed, and is thus largely descriptive or celebratory. Critical approaches, by contrast, usually have a normative ideal of a democratic communications system and criticize the limitations of an approach dominated by corporate or state media. Critical approaches also dissect the ways that journalism and entertainment reproduce the status quo and, as we will see below, in particular criticize the ways that the media fail to adequately provide the news and information necessary to a democracy, as well as to promote sexism, racism, homophobia, and classism, thus reproducing domination, inequality, and injustice.

As Robert McChesney has pointed out (2007), the field of "mainstream" communications studies was never friendly to a critical communications approach, or critical theories, and became a social science of communications in the academic division of labor dominated by empirical research and quantitative methods. To be sure, there were by the 1950s a number of celebrated communication theorists and critical communications researchers like Robert Park, T.W. Adorno and other members of the Frankfurt School, Harold Innis, Marshall McLuhan, Gregory Bateson, Dallas Smythe, George Gerbner, and others.

James Carey (1989), Hanno Hardt (1992), and Larry Grossberg (1997: 42ff, 143ff, passim) point to the importance of pragmatism and the "Chicago School" associated with John Dewey, Robert Park, and others. The Chicago School stressed the importance of the connections between communication, community, and democracy, leading to later work ranging from "symbolic interactionism," to pragmatist theories of communication and the ritual approach of James Carey (1989), Nick Couldry (2003), and others.

In addition, the so-called Frankfurt School, consisting of refugee intellectuals from German fascism who came to work in the United States, began developing systematic critiques of mass media and communication (Kellner, 1989a). The group experienced first-hand Nazi propaganda and the ways that the Nazis used the media system for political manipulation and also had studied the Soviet Union's use of the media for propaganda. When they came to the United States, they discovered that the American media were every bit as propagandistic in promoting capitalism and the "American way of life" as Nazi and Soviet media, thus conceiving of mass culture and communication in the contemporary era as instruments of ideology and domination. One of its members, T. W. Adorno, worked with Lazarsfeld on one of the first radio research projects. The collaboration was difficult, but Lazarsfeld begrudgingly respected Adorno, labeling him and his colleagues an ideal type of "critical communication researcher" who analyzes mass culture and communication within the existing social relations and institutions and criticizes the extent to which they undercut positive values like democracy, individuality, and other progressive ideals.

The Frankfurt School theory of the "culture industry" Chorkheimer and Adorno, 1972 [1948]) posits mass culture as an integrated system of social control, manipulation, and ideology that serves to reproduce the existing system of corporate capitalism. The concept of culture industry signifies the process of the industrialization of mass-produced culture and the commercial imperatives that drove the system. The critical theorists analyzed all mass-mediated cultural artifacts within the context of industrial production, in which the commodities of the culture industries exhibit the same features as other products of mass production: commodification, standardization, and massification. The products of the culture industry have the specific function, however, of providing ideological legitimation of the existing capitalist societies and of integrating individuals into the framework of mass culture and society.

The Frankfurt School also was among the first to develop critical theories of the consumer society. One of the main functions of the culture industries is to shape the needs, attitudes, and behavior necessary to integrate individuals into consumer capitalism. Frankfurt School theorists developed systematic critical reflections on the consumer society as the matrix for new configurations of contemporary capitalism which provided new modes of social integration and control. They anticipated current debates over needs, commodities, and consumer policies and were among the first to see the import of these issues for critical social theory and public policy.

Following Marx and Lukacs, Frankfurt School critical theory from the beginning characterized capitalist society as a commodity-producing society and took the commodity as the basic social unit and key to the functioning of capitalism. In the new configurations of capitalism, everything—goods and services, art, media, politics, and human life—became commodities while commodity exchange became the basic form of relationships in the consumer society. The critical theorists concluded that commodification and consumption were playing fundamental constitutive roles in the contemporary development of capitalist modernity and attempted to theorize its new configurations in the consumer society.

From around the 1920s, the problem of managing consumer demand became an increasingly important challenge to capitalist society. The "captains of industry" had in place an apparatus of mass production and needed to become "captains of consciousness" to manage and administer a new order of mass consumption (see Ewen 1976 and Ewen and Ewen 1982). After World War I, the consumer society began to emerge and developed in North America and other capitalist countries during the roaring 1920s. While during the 1930s depression, consumerism was not an important mode of social integration, it was not until the post-World War II economic boom that consumption became widespread in the more developed capitalist societies. American Soldiers returned from World

War II with savings amassed during the war, and corporations and advertising agencies vied to persuade them to buy new houses, cars, clothes, and other tokens of belonging. As the consumer society developed, it became a major theme in the writings of Adorno, Horkheimer, Lowenthal, Fromm, and Marcuse (see Kellner, 1989a) and their critique of the culture industries were linked with analyses of consumption.

The "Toronto School," associated with Harold Innis and Marshall McLuhan, working in the 1950s and 1960s, investigated forms of media and the history of communication with emphases on how different media carried "biases" of space or time (Innis, 2007 [1950])[21] and the ways that dominant media shaped society. McLuhan later (1964) became famous with his thesis that the "medium is the message," and thus that forms of communication are key influences in structuring society. McLuhan argued that contemporary media societies were evolving from print-oriented societies to ones dominated by electronic forms of mass media, influencing later postmodern theorists like Jean Baudrillard (1983) who, following McLuhan, claimed that emergent technologies were creating dramatically new forms of culture and society (for overviews of Baudrillard, see Kellner, 1989b and 2006a).

Another seminal school, often overlooked, the "Palo Alto School of Communication," and in particular the work of Gregory Bateson (1972),[22] promoted a holistic, multi-leveled and ecological approach to communications studies, advocating a contextual study of relations between communication and society, as well as study of the context of that context. Bateson eschewed reductionist, binary approaches that divide culture from nature and society and called for an integrated approach to all forms of communication.

Further, in the 1960s new approaches to media and communication flourished. Perhaps due to the popularizing influence of McLuhan and the rising awareness of the importance of the media, a field of media studies emerged in the 1960s and 1970s in North America and elsewhere, from communications, English departments, and film and television studies. This form of media studies was often more theory and text based, like the British cultural studies of the same period, which we describe in the next section. In some cases, a critical media studies later merged with cultural studies approaches when the latter began to be a global influence by the 1990s. On the other hand, many in communications and media studies were hostile to cultural studies, which was found to be too textual, political, and multidisciplinary.[23]

In the 1960s and 1970s, scholars in communications and the new media studies took concerns from direct participation in social movements organized around gender, race, class, sexuality, the environment, and war and peace and brought critical consciousness of these issues into the field of communications.[24] New groups appeared like the Union for Democratic Communication and a new school of critical communication and media research emerged. Hence, women, people of color, gays and lesbians, and individuals with a wide range of critical theories greatly expanded the field of communications. To be sure, many used some of the empirical methods employed by the mainstream, but the theoretical, critical, and political orientation produced quite a different kind of communications and media studies, as we shall see below.

In the late 1960s and 1970s as well, many studies of political economy of the media emerged investigating media imperialism, concentration of ownership, and threats to democracy from corporate control of the media. Longtime political economist of the media Dallas Smythe was joined by Herbert Schiller, Thomas Guback, Noam Chomsky and Edward Herman, and younger scholars like Vincent Mosco, Janet Wasko, Eileen Meehan, Robert McChesney, and Dan Schiller.

Marxist and political economy-inspired scholars began criticizing cultural imperialism, especially the imposition of U.S. forms of culture and media on other parts of the world, or creeping Americanization of global media and consumer culture (Schiller, 1971; Tunstall, 1977). Studies in the past decades have researched the impact of global media on national cultures, attacking the cultural imperialism of Western media conglomerates in particular sites and areas. Some later scholars, however, see a growing pluralization of world media sources and hybridization of global and local cultures, with an expanding literature exploring the ways that global media artifacts are received and used in local contexts (Lull, 1995; Canclini, 1995). This literature carries out research into how specific media or artifacts have promoted oppression in local or national contexts, or even globally, and literature that celebrates the democratizing or pluralizing effects of global media.

Some critical research has focused on the political economy and ownership of the media, often perceiving corporate control of the media by ever fewer corporations as a major global social problem. Scholars have argued that in the United States and many Western democracies, the dominant media of information and communication have become largely corporate media, because they are owned by big corporations like NBC/RCA/General Electric, Murdoch's News Corporation, Bertelsmann, ABC/Disney, Sony, or AOL/Time Warner, and tend to advance a corporate point of view (Bagdikian, 1997; McChesney, 2000 and 2007).

Despite the emergence of some theoretical and critical approaches within mainstream communications and media research, the focus within the mainstream was primarily on quantitative and descriptive empirical analysis of the effects of media. As communications departments developed over the decades following World War II, there was also research into interpersonal communications, empirical studies of media organizations, "content analysis" of texts, and studies of audience use of and gratification from media, all of which were often done in uncritical and one-dimensional orientations toward mass media. Further, some communication and media department programs celebrated commercial media and taught students how to become successful in the entertainment industry, becoming adjuncts of media industries.

While alternative theories and schools flourished on the margins, and even had some impact on the mainstream, the academic study of media and communication in leading communications departments maintained a social science-based, empirical approach to their field, rejecting fiercely the theoretical and political approaches of critical media studies and the emergent cultural studies. Further, in the past decades, as John Downing has argued, the field of media and communications studies in the United States and elsewhere became increasingly "segmented" and fragmented. This segmentation, Downing explains, was especially the case with "typically U.S.-originated mainstream approaches, which theorize media as discrete entities in society, and in that way suffer from a frequent failure to integrate their findings even with research on communications in educational institutions, family processes, religious bodies, organized 'leisure' activities or everyday interpersonal communication (not to mention a failure to connect up with political or economic research)" (Downing, 1996: xii).

In this fragmented and conflicted situation, British cultural studies presented itself as a unifying multidisciplinary project. Yet it was also, as we will see, sharply opposed by many in mainstream media and communication studies. Furthermore, cultural studies itself was highly divided and contested from within, as we shall see next.

■ The Moment of Cultural Studies

Cultural studies emerged as a highly popular yet contested project when it began to circulate widely in the English-speaking world and elsewhere in the 1980s. It was inaugurated in the 1960s by the University of Birmingham Centre for Contemporary Cultural Studies, which developed a variety of critical methods for the analysis, interpretation, and criticism of cultural artifacts.[25] Through a set of internal debates, and responding to social struggles and movements of the 1960s and the 1970s, the Birmingham group came to focus on the interplay of representations and ideologies of class, gender, race, ethnicity, and nationality in cultural texts, including media culture. They carried out studies of the nature and effects of newspapers, radio, television, film, and other popular cultural forms on audiences and came to focus on how various audiences interpreted and used media culture differently, analyzing the factors that made different audiences respond in contrasting ways to various media texts.

Under its director, Richard Hoggart, who led the Centre from its opening in 1964 to 1968, and his successor, Stuart Hall, who directed the Centre from 1968 to 1979, the Birmingham group developed a variety of critical perspectives for the analysis, interpretation, and criticism of cultural artifacts, combining sociological theory and contextualization with literary and political analysis of cultural texts. The now classical period of British cultural studies from the late 1960s to the early 1980s adopted a Marxian approach to the study of culture, one especially influenced by Louis Althusser and Antonio Gramsci,[26] which focused on how media culture transmitted ideologies that served the interests of dominant groups. Ideology refers to the dominant ideas in a society that legitimate the ruling institutions, groups, and social relations. Following Marx's critique of ideology as the dominant ideas of the ruling class, British cultural studies expanded the concept of ideology from class to how dominant ideas reproduce domination and subordination in the realms of gender, sexuality, race, ethnicity, religion, and other domains of social life.[27]

From the beginning, British cultural studies systematically rejected high/low culture distinctions and took seriously the artifacts of media culture, thus surpassing the elitism of dominant literary approaches to culture, as well as challenging existing forms of communications and media studies. Likewise, British cultural studies overcame the limitations of the Frankfurt School notion of a passive audience in their conceptions of an active audience that creates meanings and the popular. In his classic article "Encoding/Decoding," Hall (1980b) criticized the dominant paradigm of mass communications, which presented a simplistic, linear model of communications as an objective process comprised of sender, message, and receiver. The receiver, or audience, in this model is a passive receptor. Instead, Hall argued that communication was a complex process that involved audiences' active negotiation of a multiplicity of multi-layered meanings encoded in media texts. His contention was that "media messages are embedded with pre-suppositions about beliefs and practices that shape everyday perceptions of reality" and that "these suppositions operate to reinforce hegemony" (Rojek, 2003: 93).

For Hall, ideological beliefs and values were thus inscribed in dominant media codes. As he puts it: "These codes are the means by which power and ideology are made to signify discourses" (Hall and Birchall, 2006: 169). Hall goes on to argue, however, that not only are audiences active in reading or decoding texts, but viewers' readings are informed by their own experiences and histories, which are often mediated by race, gender, class, sexuality, culture, and other dominant forms of identity and oppression. This move was productive for marginalized audiences to emphasize the specific kinds of readings they can provide from their experiences and social positions (see Bobo, 1995: 55).

Reproducing the activism of oppositional groups in the 1960s and 1970s, the Birmingham Centre was engaged in a project aimed at a comprehensive criticism of the present configuration of culture and society, attempting to link theory and practice to orient cultural studies toward fundamental social transformation. British cultural studies situated culture within a theory of social production and reproduction, specifying the ways that cultural forms served either to further social control, or to enable people to resist. It analyzed society as a hierarchical and antagonistic set of social relations characterized by the oppression of subordinate class, gender, race, ethnic, and national strata. Employing Gramsci's model of hegemony and counterhegemony, British cultural studies sought to analyze "hegemonic," or ruling, social and cultural forces of domination and to locate "counterhegemonic" forces of resistance and contestation. Gramsci and British cultural studies distinguish between different ways that society maintain power and domination, ranging from force such as is exhibited by the police or military, and hegemony, which refers to ways that cultural institutions induce consent to the dominant society. Forces like religion, nationalism, schooling, and the media impose certain values and practices on a society which induce consent to the established society and produce its hegemony, as when individuals submit to capitalist society because they believe it is in their self-interest, or identify as an American because of their schooling, the media, socialization, and cultural values.

British cultural studies aimed at a political goal of social transformation in which location of forces of domination and resistance would aid the process of political transformation. From the beginning, the Birmingham group was oriented toward the crucial political problems of their age and milieu. Their early spotlight on class and ideology derived from an acute sense of the oppressive and systemic effects of class in British society and the movements of the 1960s against class inequality and oppression. The work of the late 1950s and early 1960s Williams/Hoggart/Hall stage of cultural studies emphasized the potential of working-class cultures to promote progressive social change and justice. The Birmingham group then began in the 1960s and 1970s, appraising the potential of youth subcultures to resist the hegemonic forms of capitalist domination (see

Hebdige, 1979 and 1988). Unlike the classical Frankfurt school (but similar to Herbert Marcuse, 1964), British cultural studies looked to youth cultures and social movements as providing potentially fresh forms of opposition and social change.

Some versions of British cultural studies came to center attention on how subcultural groups resist dominant forms of culture and identity, creating their own style and identities. Individuals who conform to hegemonic dress and fashion codes, behavior, and political ideologies produce their identities within mainstream groups, as members of particular social groupings (such as white, middle-class, conservative Americans). Individuals who identify with subcultures, like punk or hip-hop, look and act differently from those in the mainstream, and create oppositional identities, defining themselves against standard models.

As it developed into the 1970s and 1980s, British cultural studies successively appropriated emerging analyses of gender, race, sexuality, and a wide range of critical theories.[28] Its members developed ways to examine and critique how the established society and culture promoted sexism, racism, class prejudice, homophobia, and other forms of oppression, or helped to generate resistance and struggle against domination and injustice. This approach implicitly contained political critique of all cultural forms that promoted oppression, while positively affirming texts and representations that produced a potentially more just and egalitarian social order.

Developments within British cultural studies have been in part responses to contestation by a multiplicity of distinct groups that have produced new methods and voices within cultural studies (such as a variety of feminisms, gay and lesbian studies, critical race studies and multiculturalisms, critical pedagogies, and projects of critical media literacy). The center and fulcrum of British cultural studies at any given moment were determined by the struggles in the present political conjuncture, and their major work was conceived as political interventions. Their studies of ideology and the politics of culture directed the Birmingham group toward analyzing cultural artifacts, practices, and institutions within existing networks of power. In this context, they attempted to show how culture both provided tools and forces of domination and resources for resistance and opposition. This political optic valorized studying the effects of culture and audience use of cultural artifacts, which provided an extremely productive focus on audiences and reception, topics that had been neglected in most previous text-based methods.

Of course, there were many other traditions that studied culture, society, and politics and their interconnections, but by the 1980s British cultural studies already had a small army of committed cadres who produced a stack of globally circulated texts, organized conferences, and published journals. Many of the original Birmingham students got jobs throughout England, and some went to Australia, Canada, the United States, and other sites throughout the world.

Yet cultural studies was an open and multifaceted project and so it took very different forms in varying locales. There was never any strict orthodoxy in theory, method, or concepts, and there were always passionate, sometimes ferocious, debates over concepts, figures, issues, and the field itself. Cultural studies was an idea whose time had come. Culture was increasingly important in the emergent globalized media and consumer societies, and younger people were absorbing identities, styles, looks, and ways of thought and behavior from media culture. Moreover, politics was ever more mediated by the media, and image became central to celebrities' and politicians' popularity, to the positioning of corporate brands, and to individuals' everyday lives. Media spectacle became a determinant feature of contemporary media and politics, with global audiences viewing spectacles like the Gulf War, 9/11 and other terror attacks, destructive hurricanes and tsunamis, or sports events like the World Cup or Olympics (see Kellner, 1992, 2003a and 2003b, 2003b, and 2005).

Cultural studies also became globalized as national and more local forms of cultural studies emerged all over the world. The moment of culture and cultural studies had arrived. Culture was an increasingly important part of an aestheticized realm of commodities and consumption, ever-proliferating computer and technoculture, and style and identities in people's everyday lives. Cultural studies had developed methods to situate culture within relations of power and domination and to relate culture to the economy, the state and politics, the media and culture industries, and to show the many ways in which culture mattered.

Indeed, as Chris Rojek reminds us, "culture counts" in that it can be a force of domination and oppression, as well as enlightenment and emancipation (2007: 1ff). Culture is at once local, national, global, and increasingly hybridized as video, television, and digital culture mutate into emergent spaces like YouTube, as DJs mix varied cultural forms of music from throughout the globe, and as films quote directors and appropriate forms from cinema around the world. Culture counts because it is also a terrain of struggle between different groups and forces, promoting racist or antiracist representations, conflicting images of gender, class, and sexuality, and varying political views.

The very fecundity and omnipresence of culture, its embeddedness in so many domains of life, and its importance for different groups and individuals irresistibly led to a proliferation of versions of cultural studies. Starting off in adult education and then a literature department in Birmingham, England in the 1960s where film, TV, ads, and sports could be read as texts, cultural studies also was taken up by sociology departments that focused on relations between culture and society, a classical theme in modern sociology. Expanding communications departments saw that cultural studies was able to engage dimensions of media culture and consciousness not accessible to the empiricist and reductive theoretical discourses dominant in the field. In film and television departments, some found cultural studies a productive addition to the repertoires of theories that had been proliferating since the 1960s with its roots in political economy, sociology, and philosophy.

Through the efforts of Larry Grossberg, Henry Giroux, bell hooks, and others it was argued that cultural studies was a form of pedagogy and that media literacy should be one of the goals of cultural studies bringing major challenges to education to democratically reconstruct itself and to teach new forms of literacy.[29] Hence, education departments began giving courses in media education and literacy that often included a cultural studies component, a project we have participated in for many years.[30]

Thus, throughout much of the world, cultural studies began emerging in different sites and taking different forms. British cultural studies quickly colonized North America, Australia, and other parts of the English-speaking world. However, cultural studies is not limited to so-called Western or even English-dominant regions. A 1992 Trajectories conference in Taipai, Taiwan, gave rise to an Asian cultural studies group with a journal and conferences, and within Asia different formations have arisen. In Europe, there are forms of cultural studies in Germany, France, Spain, Slovenia, and elsewhere. Indeed, probably somewhere in every Western country someone is doing and teaching cultural studies! Latin American has seen the rise of cultural studies, as have Africa and the Middle East.[31]

However, cultural studies has also been strongly resisted and under attack from the beginning. While the Birmingham Centre originally envisaged a broad and inclusive concept of cultural studies, many academic traditionalists fiercely rejected the proposal to seriously study popular culture in an educational context and eventually many within cultural studies made a populist turn away from so-called high culture. Many English professors, in the tradition of Matthew Arnold or the influential critic F. R. Leavis, both of whom celebrated the ennobling functions of high culture seen by many as essential to British identity and to preserving its core culture, resisted the turn to the popular, often ferociously (see Hall, 1980a and Turner, 1990). Similar responses have taken place elsewhere as defenders of high culture like Harold Bloom celebrate the "classics" as the heart of a genuine liberal education and attack the barbarians of popular culture who would bring in Harry Potter, Stephen King, rap music, or Buffy the Vampire Slayer into the sacred bastions of academia.[32]

In fact, a number of critical scholars have argued that the bias against studying popular culture, in the same spirit as high culture, is related to what has been called the "feminization" of popular culture.[33] Such a gendered characterization implies that popular culture, and its study, is hardly serious and subordinate to more "credible" or "legitimate" cultural forms and academic pursuits. Applying feminine stereotypes to demonstrate inferiority is hardly exclusive to demeaning women but is widely used to signify the inferiority of a diversity of peoples and practices. For example, media representations of Asian men are often feminized. It could be argued that these kinds of prejudices find their basis in philosophical and scientific canonized writings, which argued that women were inherently different from and inherently subordinate to men, and such stereotypes and prejudices have long been circulated in popular culture and media, as well as high culture and theory.

It is interesting to note that many important key studies of popular culture have been initiated by marginalized people, and that there is a strong tendency in much of critical cultural studies toward feminism, critical race theory, and queer theory.[34] Further, critical theorists in these fields have argued for the intersectionality and co-constructedness of domains of class, race, gender, and sexuality. The concept of intersectionality was first developed by critical race and legal theorist Kimberle Crenshaw (1991), who articulated the structural intersectionality of systems of gender, race, and class oppression and the political intersection in terms of overlapping and interconnecting modes of political oppression. The concept has been expanded in women's studies and cultural studies to delineate the interrelation between multiple forms of oppression and identity formation that co-construct, reinforce, and compound each other. For example, an analysis of intersectionality would describe how lesbian black women are co-constructed by all of these major constituents of identity, and are put in positions of marginalization and oppression in ways that cannot be extracted or attributed to solely one domain or another. The texts and representations of media culture also intersect in their construction of discourses and images of race, gender, class, sexuality, and so on to create systems of Otherness and subordination that are co-constructed and intersect with each other in producing intersections of racism, sexism, classism, homophobia, and other forms of oppression.[35] Hence, a critical media/cultural studies articulates the intersection of race, class, gender, and sexuality and attempts to overcome segregation and reductive analyses of disparate area studies, producing more complex analyses that take into account the intersectionality of oppression on social, cultural, and individual levels.

Gloria Anzaldua's (1987) notion of "borderlands" is also useful here. Explicating her own experience of living in the borderlands of race, sexuality, class, and territory, Anzaldua proposed the concept of *mestizaje,* that transcends either/or binary oppositions and the notion of a "new mestiza," which describes an individual aware of conflicting and mixing hybridized identities, ways of seeing, and writing. For a global cultural studies this is immensely productive for articulating work and practices in the borderlands between local, national, and global cultures, as well as the project of using culture to create novel and evolving identities.

The analytical and political embrace of class, gender, race, sexuality, and their co-construction has made cultural studies controversial, especially because these more political tendencies of cultural studies sharply criticize subordination and domination, while championing resistance and struggle. Ironically, opposition toward cultural studies often finds its basis in precisely the central concerns and strengths of the field, involving "the politics of representation" of gender, race, class, sexuality, and other marginalized relations. The embrace of these topics in cultural studies and its critique of classism, sexism, racism, homophobia, and other forms of prejudice have led to accusations of cultural studies being too political, or subversive of academic boundaries, as it takes on issues of power, domination, the university, the state, or corporate media power.

Furthermore, in both England and the United States, many people in mainstream communications departments derided the theoretical and highly textual nature of some versions of cultural studies. Because British cultural studies had Marxist roots that would affirm a primacy of political economy, conservatives scorned this subversive enterprise, while many Marxists in communications studies decried the alleged turn from political economy to text and audience in cultural studies as it evolved into the 1970s and 1980s. In addition, empiricists and conventional academics in a variety of disciplines found the mix of theory and politics too strong a brew and attempted to marginalize the project.[36]

Hence, just as there has emerged a flotilla of books and articles praising and doing cultural studies, so too has a literature emerged attacking and denigrating cultural studies, often producing a "straw man" version. Nonetheless, in every discipline from sociology and political science to philosophy and education, there are those who would promote cultural studies as an important tool in coming to terms with contemporary culture and society. A critical cultural studies investigates the interconnections with economy, politics, society, culture, and everyday life and demonstrates the growing importance of culture, as opposed to those who want to keep their disciplines pure from messy things like theory, culture, and politics. A broad and comprehensive field, versions of cultural studies have developed methods of analysis of texts, audience decoding and construction of meaning, the intertextual system in which texts and audience practices are embedded, the system of production and distribution of media texts, and the broader social context in which texts, audiences, and media are constructed. Such an interdisciplinary optic subverts conventional academic boundaries, and as cultural studies migrated into other disciplines, defenders of disciplinary boundaries and order attacked the interlopers from cultural studies who wanted to deal with ideology, power, representation, class, gender, ethnicity, and sexuality, or audience uses of popular culture artifacts.[37]

Recently, a "new cultural studies" approach has emerged (Hall and Birchall, 2006) that calls for cultural studies to be open to new theories and politics, and that reacts against the assault on theory coming from sectors of the academy and even within cultural studies itself. Yet cultural studies has always been open to and absorbed new theories, just as its politics have always been grounded in the political conjuncture of the era, adopting new theories for new times and seeking new politics when older politics reached an impasse. The Hall and Birchall collection argues for the importance of the new critical theories which have emerged in recent years and that the authors claim have not been adequately made use of by people within cultural studies. Furthermore, new cultural studies are emerging all the time as modes of cyberculture, digital media, and novel cultural forms and spaces emerge, often produced or used by the younger generation, a significant cultural turn as illustrated in studies in Part IV of this book.

Cultural studies has always reinvented itself, as it subverts academic disciplinary boundaries and draws on a wealth of fields, theories, and methods to engage topics that can range from McDonald's or Barbie dolls to the media spectacle of the Iraq war or a U.S. presidential election. Cultural studies also takes on the contentious issue of power and domination and addresses the specific forms of racism, sexism, classism, homophobia, ageism, and other prejudices that are disseminated in media images, discourses, and spectacle. With identities mediated ever more through emergent forms of media culture, dissecting the ways that media promote oppression and domination, and can advance emancipation and empowerment, is an immensely important task.

Cultural studies often positions proponents and practitioners in opposition to mainstream society by challenging forms of oppression, unequal relations of power, and highly offensive forms of culture. Of course, different people will find diverse things offensive, just as people have varying tastes and preferences, hence there are also passionate debates within cultural studies, as well as against its opponents. With so many varieties of cultural studies circulating, one can easily agree with John Hartley (2003: 1) that: "Even within intellectual communities and academic institutions, there is little agreement about what counts as cultural studies, either as a critical practice or an institutional apparatus. On the contrary, the field is driven by fundamental disagreements about what cultural studies is for, in whose interests it is done, what theories, methods and objects of study are proper to it, and where to set its limits."

From the beginning, cultural studies was open to the political movements of the day and as the next section will indicate, was enriched by ideas and energies from a vast array of social movements.

■ Social Movements and the Politics of Representation

The idea that all cultural representations are political is one of the major themes of media and cultural theory of the past several decades. In the 1960s, feminist, African American, Latino, gay and lesbian, and diverse oppositional movements attacked the stereotypes and biased images of cultural representations of their groups. These critiques of sexism, racism, homophobia, and other prejudices made it clear that cultural representations are never innocent or pure, and that they contain positive, negative, or ambiguous representations of diverse social groups. Representations can serve pernicious interests of cultural oppression by positioning certain groups as inferior, thus asserting the superiority of dominant social groups and reproducing their hegemonic position. Studies of representations of women or Blacks on U.S. television, for instance, would catalogue negative representations and show how they produce sexism or racism, or would champion more positive representations.

Early interventions in the politics of representation concentrated on primarily "images of" particular social groups, decrying negative images and affirming more constructive ones. The limitations of such approaches were quickly apparent and already by the 1970s more sophisticated analyses began emerging of how texts position audiences and of how narratives, scenes, and images produce biased representations of subordinate groups. More critical understandings emerged of how textual mechanisms help construct social meanings and representations of specific social groups. Exclusions of groups like Latinos or Asian Americans in the mainstream media, as well as demeaning stereotypes, were emphasized, as were the ways framing, editing, subtexts, and the construction of pictorial images produced culturally loaded and biased representations of subordinate groups. The narratives of media culture were scrutinized to discern how certain (usually socially dominant) groups were represented more affirmatively than subordinate ones. There was also a search for narratives and representations that more positively represented social types that had been excluded or negatively presented in mainstream culture (i.e., working class people, various ethnic groups, gays and lesbians, or members of the deaf community).

The turn toward study of audiences in the 1980s by British cultural studies also created more complex notions of the politics of representation and construction of meaning by stressing how audiences could produce oppositional readings, reacting negatively to what they perceived as prejudiced representations of their own social groups, thus showing themselves to be active creators of meaning, and not just passive victims of manipulation. Reading culture was seen as a political event in which one looked for negative or positive representations, learned how media texts were constructed, and discerned how image and ideology functioned within media culture to reproduce social domination and discrimination, as well as how dominant cultures could be resisted and transformed.

An ethnographic turn in cultural studies moved to examine how diverse audiences appropriated and used cultural texts, sometimes in critical and resistant ways, rejecting dominant encodings.[38] Building on British cultural studies, Jacqueline Bobo (1995) develops a contextual understanding of the significance of the theory of encoding and decoding for understanding how and why varying audiences read a text differently and create their own subversive readings. Bobo notes that: "An audience member from a marginalized group (people of color, women, the poor, and so on) [often] has an oppositional stance as they participate in mainstream media. The motivation for this counter-reception is that we understand that mainstream media has never rendered our segment of the population faithfully" (Bobo, 1995: 55). Bobo goes on to identify another form of oppositional reading which she calls "alternative and subversive": "This alternative reading comes from something in the work that strikes the viewer as amiss, that appears 'strange.' When things appear strange to the viewer, she/he may bring other viewpoints to bear on the watching of the film and may see things other than what the filmmakers intended. The viewer, that is, will read 'against the grain' of the film" (ibid).

The debates over the politics of representation and how best to analyze and criticize problematic images of subordinate groups provided a wealth of insights into the nature and effects of culture and media. Culture was in part conceived of as a field of representation, as a producer of meaning that provided negative and positive depictions of gender, class, race, sexuality, religion, and further key constituents of identity. The media were widely interpreted as potent creators of role models, gender identity, norms, values, and appropriate and inappropriate behavior, positioning audiences to behave in divergent ways. Scholars began perceiving audiences as active and creative, able to construct their own meanings and identities out of the materials of their culture, while contesting dominant ones.

Culture and identity were regarded as constructed, as artificial, malleable, and contestable artifacts and practices and not as natural givens. Representations in turn were interpreted not just as replications of the real, reproductions of natural objects, but as constructions of complex technical, narrative, and ideological apparatuses. The emphasis on the politics of representation called attention to media technologies, as well as narrative forms, conventions, and codes. It was determined that formal aspects of media texts, such as framing, editing, or special effects, could help construct specific representations and that different technologies produced diverse products and opportunities for audience engagement.

In addition, the growing emphasis on the active role of audiences from the 1980s to the present suggested that people could innovatively construct cultural meanings, contest dominant forms, create alternative readings and interpretations, and fashion their own identities and ways of life. Audiences could be empowered to reject prejudicial or stereotyped representations of specific groups and individuals, and could affirm positive ones. The politics of representation focused on both encoding and decoding, texts and audiences, and called for more critical and discriminating responses to the products of media production, and for the production of alternative media.

Consequently, cultural representations were perceived to be subject to political critique and culture itself was conceived as a contested terrain. Film, television, music, and assorted cultural forms were interpreted as an arena of struggle in which representations reproduce the discourses of conflicting political discourses and social movements. Beginning in the 1960s, critical and alternative representations of gender, race, class, the family, the state, the military, the corporation, and additional dominant forces and institutions began appearing in a sustained fashion. More complex and engaging representations of women, for instance, articulated the critiques of negative stereotypes and sexist representations, as well as the demand for more active and positive representations. Calls for alternative voices and the creation of oppositional subcultures were met by increased cultural production by women, people of color, sexual minorities, and others excluded from cultural debate and creation. Giving voice to alternative visions, telling more complex stories from the perspective of subordinate groups, and presenting works of marginalized people shook up dominant systems of cultural production and representation. The process created more variety and diversity but also intensified cultural resistance, as a backlash against oppositional groups of women, people of color, gays and lesbians, and various marginalized subcultures inevitably began and exploded into the so-called "culture wars."[39]

Because of its focus on representations of race, gender, and class, and its critique of ideologies that promote various forms of oppression, media/cultural studies lends itself to a multiculturalist program that demonstrates how culture reproduces certain forms of racism, sexism, and biases against members of subordinate classes, social groups, or alternative lifestyles.[40] A critical multiculturalism affirms the worth of different types of culture and cultural groups, claiming, for instance, that black, Latino, Asian, Native American, gay and lesbian, and other oppressed and marginal voices have their own validity and importance. An insurgent multiculturalism attempts to show how various people's voices and experiences are silenced and omitted from mainstream culture and struggles to aid in the articulation of diverse views, experiences, and cultural forms. This makes it a target of conservative forces which wish to preserve the existing canons of white, male, heterosexual, and Eurocentric privilege and thus attack multiculturalism in cultural wars raging from the 1960s to the present over education, the arts, the limits of free expression, and other issues.

Work on the politics of representation provided insights into how representations of class, gender, race, sexuality, and other key identity markers intersect with each other, work together, and even co-construct each other, as we noted above. Forms of racism, classism, and sexism can work together to oppress people, and movements struggling against oppression developed alliances against common forces of oppression. In this context, cultural studies analyses often made clear how representations of class, gender, race, and sexuality intersect in media and society to promote relations of inequality and oppression. bell hooks (1990), for instance, in a series of books showed how media representations reproduced "white supremacist, patriarchical capitalism" or enabled people to critically perceive sources of oppression and struggle against them. Often, to be sure, there are contradictions and ambiguities in the politics of representation in a given text in which progressive representations of race are undercut by regressive sexist or homophobic representations, showing that texts can be highly contradictory and ambiguous.

A critical media/cultural studies engaging the politics of representation thus promotes a multiculturalist oppositional politics and media pedagogy that aims to make people sensitive to how relations of power and domination are "encoded" in cultural texts, such as those of television or film. It specifies how people can resist the dominant encoded meanings and produce their own critical and alternative readings, cultural texts, and reconstruct their society and everyday lives. Media/cultural studies can show how media culture manipulates and indoctrinates us, and thus can empower individuals to contest the dominant meanings in cultural artifacts and to produce their own meanings and alternative media. It can also point to moments of resistance and criticism within media culture and thus help promote development of more critical consciousness and creation of more progressive cultural forms. In the next section, we shall accordingly suggest how a media/cultural studies approach combines media/communications and cultural studies, and provides resources to engage the full range and effects of a wide range of cultural forms.

■ Toward a Critical Media/Cultural Studies

Cultural and media studies approaches, embodied in many of the articles collected in this reader, help develop concepts and analyses that will enable readers to analytically dissect the artifacts of contemporary media culture and to empower themselves in relation to their cultural environment. By exposing the entire field of culture and society to knowledgeable and critical scrutiny, media/cultural studies provides a broad, comprehensive framework to undertake studies of culture, politics, and society for the purposes of individual empowerment and social and political struggle and transformation.

A media/cultural studies, however, is only a subset or type of the broader project of cultural studies that takes on a wealth of domains from art and so-called high culture to shopping and consumer culture, sports and games, and a multitude of subcultures and cultural practices, always evolving and often quite different in various countries and locales at different times. Further, interpreting the cultural artifacts and practices under scrutiny is always a contested terrain, as is cultural studies itself. Cultural studies thus has an always proliferating diversity of approaches, themes, methods, and projects, and is an open field, subject to dramatic transformations and shifts.

While communications, media, and cultural studies today are as fragmented and contested as ever, we and many of the contributors to this volume propose an inclusive media/cultural studies approach to overcome divisions in the field and to provide perspectives on an open-ended project. This critical approach would keep many of the political, theoretical, and methodological commitments and insights from earlier traditions intact within an ever-evolving communications/media/cultural studies that engages new media, emergent forms of theory, and novel socio-political struggles and hopes. It is a model, we suggest, that is increasingly adopted by a diversity of individuals who want to overcome the fragmentation of the field.

The seemingly never-ending hostility between communications studies and cultural studies has replicated a bifurcation within the fields of communications and culture between competing paradigms. For some time now, however, many, including a large number of contributors to this book and the editors, have declared a truce and have been combining media/communication and cultural studies.[41] In retrospect, the divide was an artificial one, rooted in an arbitrary academic division of labor. The conflicting approaches pointed to a splintering of the field of communications and cultural studies into special-ized sub-areas with competing models and methods, and, ironically, to a lack of com-munication in the field of communications. The split reproduces an academic division of labor which, beginning early in the twentieth century and intensifying since the end of the Second World War, has followed the trend toward specialization and differentiation symptomatic of the capitalist economy. The university has followed this broader trend that some theorists equate with the dynamics of modernity itself, interpreted as a process of ever-greater differentiation and thus specialization in all fields from business to educa-tion. This trend toward specialization has undermined the power and scope of both communications/media and cultural studies and should be replaced, as we and others have been arguing, by a more transdisciplinary position.

A media/cultural studies at its best combines work from communications and media studies with cultural studies, in a genuinely critical transdisciplinary project that transcends the academic division of labor and overcomes divisions between media/communications and cultural studies. Too often the disciplines have been at odds with each other, attack-ing the other discipline's methods; their use, abuse, or failure to use theory; their politics; and their work, as when individuals in communication studies summarily dismiss cultural studies or people in cultural studies attack or ignore the work of communications and media studies.[42]

To be sure, some criticisms of certain versions of communications and media and cultural studies are valid. A number of cultural studies are too textual, theoretical, jargo-nistic, or narrowly focused on audience, and are worthy of critique. Other communica-tions studies are too quantitative, positivistic, and lacking in theory and a critical dimension. Yet it would be an immense mistake for cultural studies and media/communication stud-ies to ignore each other and we are proposing articulations of the various disciplines. Sut Jhally (2006: xiii) recognizes the tensions between critical media studies and cultural studies, juxtaposed against political economy, and himself attempts "to work on both sides of this divide simultaneously, not so much by synthesizing these concerns into a new framework, but by pursuing work located precisely at this boundary, where fields of analysis overlap and intertwine, where purity fuses into an unpredictable hybridity defined by contradictions and complexity." These dimensions can be combined and articulated in different ways in various projects, and our reader has a rich diversity of approaches that contributes to developing the field of critical media/cultural studies.

A critical media/cultural studies takes culture seriously but also forms and technolo-gies of media, the political economy of media industries, media effects and audience uses of media, and the ways that different forms or examples of media and culture function in our society and can be read to provide enlightenment and insight about the society. Our own notion of a critical media/cultural studies also involves studying media culture to gain insight and knowledge about the contemporary world. Reading culture critically via what we call a *diagnostic critique* uses media culture to diagnose problems, hopes, fears, discourses, and social struggles current to the social moment.[43] Diagnostic critique enables one to perceive the limitations and pathologies of mainstream conservative and liberal political ideologies as well as oppositional ones. A critical media/cultural studies thus involves a dialectic of text and context, using texts to read social realities and context to help situate and interpret a wide range of cultural artifacts and to interrogate them about what they tell us about the contemporary world. Scrutiny of McDonald's or Nike can provide knowledge about global capitalism (Kellner, 2003a), while study of the Rambo films, or Tom Cruise's *Top Gun* and *Mission: Impossible* action adventure films, can provide insights into contemporary masculinity and gender politics, as well as the geopolitics of the era. Likewise, 2007 films like *Knocked Up, Waitress,* and *Juno* provide insights into the situation of contemporary young women and the options facing women of different classes concerning jobs, relationships, and having children and families.

A critical media/cultural studies allows us to avoid cutting up the field of media/culture/communications into academic subdisciplines with their own methodologies and boundaries as well as overcoming distinctions between high and low culture, popular versus elite communication, entertainment and information, and to see all forms of media culture and communication as worthy of scrutiny and criticism. A critical media/cultural studies allows approaches to culture and communication that force us to appraise their politics and to make political discriminations between different types of artifacts that have different political effects. Like other multicultural approaches, it brings the study of race, gender, sexuality, and class into the center of the study of media culture and communication. It also adopts a critical approach that interprets culture within society and situates the study of culture within the field of contemporary social theory and political struggle.

■ In This Book

Media/Cultural Studies: Critical Approaches brings together a diversity of areas of research, theories, and methods that capture some of the scope and significance of media/cultural studies with sections on foundational texts, teaching media/cultural studies, doing media/cultural studies, and engaging digital media and culture. Our collection provides material that should enable students, teachers, citizens, and interested individuals to learn some basics of how media and culture functions in their society and how to critically understand, read, and criticize a multiplicity of products of a media, consumer, and digital culture. Various contributors will theorize media and culture differently, but they will all engage important phenomena that will help us better understand present-day experience and give us tools to make sense of our world.

A critical media/cultural studies aims at providing understanding of the role of media and culture in today's societies and producing media literacy that will empower students and citizens to better read, analyze, interpret, critique, and reconstruct their culture and society, as well as to refocus their imaginations to see things differently, from multiple and critical perspectives. Many of our contributors combine theories and methods from cultural studies, media and communication studies, film studies, education, and emergent digital culture studies. Many eschew boundaries of traditional academic practices and provide cutting-edge studies from multidisciplinary perspectives that are sensitive to the politics of representation.

The book is divided into four sections, and each section is prefaced by an introduction that gives an overview of the thematics engaged in the specific articles and the general issues and focuses of each section. We thus offer a diversity of material from media, consumer, and digital culture presented in transdisciplinary perspectives that combine communications, media, and cultural studies. We hope that students and scholars working in diverse fields will see the need for transdisciplinary perspectives and a strong focus on pedagogy that has informed much of the work in this volume. For students and teachers of media education and literacies, we hope that the presentations of media and cultural studies here will provide practical examples of how to engage media and culture and that all of us become more critical readers and participants of/in our culture and society.

Notes

1. The concept of theory derives from the Greek *theoria,* denoting ways of seeing or looking at the world. In the modern era, theories offer perspectives, or ways of seeing, but also ways of explaining and interpreting the world. Of course, theory, like every concept within cultural studies is highly contested, so there are many views of theory and we are offering here our own understanding of the concept.

2. See *The Marx-Engels Reader* (Tucker, 1978) and on modern social theory, see Harrington (2005). On postmodern theory, see Best and Kellner (1991, 1997, and 2001).

3. On Du Bois, see 1903; for overviews of feminism, see Tong (1998) and hooks (2000); and for overviews of queer theory and gay liberation, see Abelove, Barale, and Halperin (1993).

4. For representative textbooks of media studies, see Marris and Thornham (2000) and Valdivia (2003); on communication studies, see the sources in Note 7. In our introduction, we lay out the trajectories of communication and media studies followed by the rise of cultural studies and will argue for a synthesis of the field in following sections.

5. It is important to note, however, that the very label "mass communications" is problematic for a number of reasons, and many contemporary media scholars prefer to define their approaches as communications, media studies, or "cultural studies," which we discuss, in more detail, later on in this introduction.

6. Obviously, we cannot document the development and conflicts of media and communication studies in any great detail here and can only touch upon some of the key issues and debates, as well as mention only a few of the leading protagonists, scholars, and groups or "schools" associated with this contested terrain. It is unfortunate that so many histories or descriptions of communications, media studies, and cultural studies fail to present the colorful characters and conflicts among these scholars as well as the historical contexts in which they took place, as this would reframe and invigorate what are often exceedingly boring classes on "communications theory," or "media studies," which conform to the hegemonic attitudes toward so-called mass media and communication, and often replicate teaching, which privileges standard testing, regurgitation, and memorization rather than critical thinking.

7. For a history and overview of the field of communications studies, largely in the English-speaking world after World War II, see McQuail (1994); for a probing interrogation of the tradition of critical communications studies in a North American context, see Hardt (1992); and for a sharp critique of how mainstream communications has served the interests of dominant corporations, the state and established systems of power in the United States throughout the twentieth century and into the present, see Babe (2006).

8. James Truslow Adams, cited from *http://en.wikipedia.org/wiki/James_Truslow_Adams* (accessed July 7, 2008).

9. On the debates concerning broadcasting and democracy in the United States, see Kellner (1990) and McChesney (1993).

10. "Committee on Public Information" http://en.wikipedia.org/wiki/Committee_on_Public_Information.

11. As journalist and Chairman George Creel described the Committee on Public Information: "it was a plain publicity proposition, a vast enterprise of salesmanship, the world's greatest adventure in advertising..... [This] was not propaganda as the Germans defined it, but propaganda in the true sense of the word, meaning 'the propagation of faith.'" (ibid.)

12. As Chomsky put it (1991): "The 'responsible men' who are the proper decision-makers, Lippmann continued, must 'live free of the trampling and the roar of a bewildered herd.' These 'ignorant and meddlesome outsiders' are to be 'spectators,' not 'participants.' The herd does have a 'function': to trample periodically in support of one or another element of the leadership class in an election..." (2003, p. 6). However, Lippmann was also one of the most vocal critics of the abuse of mass media for the promotion of propaganda, and in 1918 he submitted a blistering report on how the Committee for Public Information "manipulated news to foster national hysteria." After his experiences in World War I he became deeply concerned about the bias of the press corp and editors to manipulate public opinion, which he asserted was "not a free marketplace of ideas, but was channelled and polluted by the managers of news," and hence had serious consequences for the American democratic system as defined in the Constitution (Blumenthal, 2007). Yet, as we shall see, Lippmann also became very concerned about the propensities of the masses to be manipulated and defined the need for an elite corps of experts to help construct public opinion and engineer consent.

13. Prejudices against the "masses" were shared by Bernays, Lippmann, and other propagandists and social scientists drawing on European studies, such as French social scientist Gustave Le Bon whose 1895 book, *The Crowd: A Study of Popular Mind* "soon became the Bible to a growing number of people who were worried by a climate of social unrest" and "had a resounding impact on an entire generation of social thought" (Ewen, 1996: 64). As Ewen put it: "Le Bon's book spoke to the deep fears of a world in which the liberal ideal of natural rights had moved beyond its roots in middle-class life and given rise to more inclusive conceptions of popular democracy" which seriously threatened the status quo and hierarchical structures of power (ibid).

14. On Lazarsfeld and the Frankfurt School, see Hardt (1992); we discuss the Frankfurt School later in the introduction. As Hardt emphasizes (1992: 98ff), Lazarsfeld never engaged or explicated critical traditions, although he tried to incorporate a modicum of "criticism" within empirical and administrative research which became the dominant paradigm.

15. See Schramm (ed) (1948 and 1973), and the discussions in McQuail (1994) and Hardt (1992). Critics claim that Schramm not only worked for the U.S. government but was an informer for the CIA (see Babe 2006: 20f).

16. On the "dominant paradigm," see the presentation and reconstruction in McQuail (1994) and the critiques in Gitlin (1978), Real (1989), and Hardt (1992).

17. Shannon and Weaver's model was especially influential and "is widely accepted as one of the main seeds out of which Communications Studies has grown" (Fiske, 1990: 6; see also Hardt (1992: 89f)). This mathematical model was developed, by engineers, during World War II in the Bell Telephone Laboratories and was designed to maximize and measure the amount of information or signals that could be transmitted through telephone cable and radio wave channels. This simplistic and linear functional model was a variation on the classic "sender-receiver" model of communication in which the source is a "decision maker," in that they choose which messages are to be sent, and the receivers are the passive masses (see McQuail, 1994: 43). Indeed, elite corporate and government claims, backed by some academics, that this model was appropriate for understanding and quantifying all dimensions of human communications was rendered even more ludicrous when information theorists established that the model was severely flawed in that it had not accounted for "noise" in the system (e.g., "static" of crossed lines). Obviously, these esteemed scientists had never played the

once popular children's game "broken telephone," which clearly demonstrated how meanings of messages are often distorted within "channels" or "transmission" of information.

18. Worries about the effects of mass communication were intensified by the dramatic and much-discussed hysterical reaction to Orson Welles' radio broadcast of H. G. Wells' Martian invasion fantasy *War of the Worlds* that created national panic (see Cantril, Koch, Gaudet, and Herzog, 1982 [1940]). A recent article, however, has claimed that the alleged panic over the broadcast was greatly exaggerated; see Michael J. Socolow, "The Hyped Panic over 'War of the Worlds,' *The Chronicle Review,* October 24, 2008 (accessed October 26, 2008).

19. Elihu Katz and Lazarsfeld expanded this model in *Personal Influence: The Part Played by People in the Flow of Mass Communication* (1955). Their "two-step flow" model claimed that opinion leaders are the primary influence in determining consumer and political choice, as well as attitudes and values. This model holds that the media do not have direct influence on behavior but are mediated by primary groups and personal influence, thus in effect denying that the media themselves are a social problem because they merely report on issues and reinforce behavior already dominant in a society. Babe (2006) indicates that Lazarsfeld's research was funded by the Rockefeller Foundation that also channeled funds from the CIA, radio and broadcasting corporations, newspapers, marketing and advertising firms, and polling companies, suggesting that the research was devised to serve interests of dominant media and state elites and alleviate worries about a too-powerful media. The limited effects model has been subjected to withering critique by critical communication research; see Gitlin (1978) and Real (1989), for two examples.

20. A student of Lazarsfeld, Elihu Katz credited Lazarsfeld with initiating uses and gratifications research, and Katz, Gurevitch and Haas (1973) and Blumler and Katz (1974) published books promoting this approach.

21. One of Harold Innis's key insights was that societies and cultures were based on oral forms of communication and hence differed greatly from those in which written communications was the dominant form (Innis, 2007 [1952]). This led to a central tenet of communications and media/cultural studies that communication media play a primary role in shaping culture and society. Innis argued that "concentration on a medium of communication implies a bias in the cultural development of the civilization concerned either toward an emphasis on space and political organization or toward an emphasis on time and religious organization. Introduction of a second medium tends to check the bias of the first and create conditions suited to the growth of empire" (Innis, 2007 [1950]: 196).

    Marshall McLuhan continued Innis' analysis of the form of media with interrogation of a wealth of media ranging from transportation and money to the new electronic media (1964). He became famous as a guru on the explosion of new media in the 1960s; see Stearn, 1967.

22. A true iconoclast and cross-disciplinary figure, Gregory Bateson has been described as a biologist, anthropologist, ethnographer, cybernetics theorist, psychologist and natural philosopher. In Brian Stagoll's description (2005): "Bateson's vision challenged the reductionism, materialism and dualism of Western Science." Instead Bateson (1972) proposed an integrative theory of communication that encompassed nature, human life, culture, and society.

23. The split within the field of communication/media studies was noted in the 1983 issue of the *Journal of Communication* issue "Ferment in the Field" (Vol. 33, No. 3 [Summer 1983]). Some of the participants in this discussion of the state-of-the-art media and communication studies noted a division in the field between a humanities-based culturalist approach that focuses primarily on texts contrasted to more empirical social science-based approaches in the study of mass-mediated communications. The culturalist approach at the time was largely textual, centered on the analysis and criticism of texts as cultural artifacts, using methods primarily derived from the humanities. The methods of communications research, by contrast, employed more empirical methodologies, ranging from straight quantitative research to interviews, participant observation, or more broadly historical research. Some contributors to the *Journal's* 1983 symposium suggested a liberal tolerance of different approaches, or ways in which the various approaches complemented each other or could be integrated, a position that we

are advocating in this introduction and that many of our contributors have been doing in various ways for years.

24. For decades, the fields of communications studies were a white male terrain, although with the rise of new social and political movements it became more diverse; see, for example, van Zoonen (1994); Krolokke and Sorensen (2006); and Sarikakis and Shade (2008).

25. Standard accounts describe how British cultural studies as influenced by Raymond Williams, E. P. Thompson, and Richard Hoggart progressed through adult education programs to forming a center to study contemporary culture that we describe above. On British cultural studies, see Hall (1980b) and Hall et al. (1980); Johnson (1986/1987); Turner (1990); Grossberg (1989); the articles collected in Grossberg, Nelson, and Treichler (1992); Kellner (1995); Hartley (2003); Barker (2008); and Durham and Kellner (2006).

26. The Centre was especially interested in Gramsci's theory of hegemony (1971) and Althusser's theory of ideology (2006 [1971]). See Hall (1992).

27. On the concept of ideology, see the key texts in Durham and Kellner (2006); Kellner (1978, 1979); Centre for Contemporary Cultural Studies (1980); Kellner and Ryan (1988); and Thompson (1990). The Frankfurt School also privileged the study of culture and ideology in their work; on the "missed articulation" between the Frankfurt School and British cultural studies, see Kellner (1997).

28. On race in British cultural studies, see Centre for Contemporary Cultural Studies (1982); Gilroy (1987); and the reader *Black British Cultural Studies* (Baker, Diawara and Lindeborg (eds) 1996);. On gender and British cultural studies, see McRobbie (1994; 1999); Brunsdon (1996); and Nava (1992). In the U.S. context, on the intersections of gender, race and class in cultural studies, see hooks (1990); Hill Collins (1990); and the anthology edited by Dines and Humez (1995). For a Marxist perspective on race and cultural studies, see San Juan (2002). On sexuality in media culture, among many, see Dyer (1993) and Creekmur and Doty (1995). Durham and Kellner (2006) contain "key works" on the politics of representation within cultural studies and other schools on class, race, sexuality, and gender.

29. On connections between cultural studies and pedagogy, see McLaren, Hammer, Sholle and Reilly (1994), and Giroux and Shannon (1997). *The Review of Education, Pedagogy and Cultural Studies* has state-of-the-art publications on the topic.

30. For Douglas Kellner's cultural studies and education website, see http://www.gseis.ucla.edu/faculty/kellner/. For discussion of Rhonda Hammer's cultural studies course and website, see Part II of this reader.

31. For discussion of the global research of cultural studies see material in Miller (2001), Abass and Erni (2005), and the "Special Issue on Cultural Studies and Education" in *The Review of Education, Pedagogy and Cultural Studies,* Vol. 26, Nos. 2–3 (April–September 2004).

32. The redoubtable Champion of the Canon Harold Bloom not only writes series of books on Great Literature, but takes time out periodically to denounce Stephen King's novels, the Harry Potter phenomenon, or other examples of what he considers trivial fiction. A media/cultural studies such as we envisage would engage both Shakespeare and *Star Wars,* and looks at popular fiction or film as indexes of current audience fantasies and interests, as well as indexes to contemporary socio-political reality. Such forms of popular culture may help us understand our world today, as well making apparent key popular pleasures and fantasies.

33. Angela McRobbie writes: "We would need a more developed conceptual schema to account for the simultaneous feminization of popular culture with this accumulation of ambivalent, fearful responses" (Part III) in this book.

34. We discuss feminism, critical race theory, and queer theory in its application to media culture in more detail in the next section on the politics of representation. On the intersection of class, gender, race and sexuality in cultural studies, see the sources in Note 28.

35. For examples, see the texts in this reader by Hant, Henderson, Durham, and Sun, Miezan, and Liberman, among others.

36. For explication of this model, see Kellner (1995) and Chapter 1 of this text, which updates and develops the model.

37. Hall and Birchall (2006) list reasons that cultural studies has been excoriated for being too theoretical and political in neo-liberal academic and conservative political times. Attacks on cultural studies did not just come from conservatives and traditionalists who were allergic to theory or distained engagement with the lowly artifacts of media culture, but also from the Left (see Note 42 below).

38. See Hall (1980b) and the discussion by Rojek in this volume; Morley (1997); and the studies on fans and fandom in Gray, Sandvoss, and Harrington (2007).

39. On the backlash against women and feminism, see Faludi (1991); for one of many books on the culture wars, see Hunter (1991).

40. On the difference between a conservative multiculturalism that adopts a "melting pot" or dominant government perspective, a liberal multicultural approach that accepts a plurality of cultures in the mode of tolerance, as opposed to an insurgent multiculturalism that affirms the positivity of cultural difference and supports struggles of the oppressed for equality and justice (See McLaren, 1997). Zizek (1993) and San Juan (2002), however, dismiss multiculturalism per se as the "cultural logic of multinational" or globalized capitalism (San Juan, 2002: 8). It is true that multiculturalism can serve as an ideology, but it has resistant potential and as this note indicates can also be seen as a terrain of struggle.

41. For a reader that supplements ours, see Durham and Kellner's *KeyWorks* (2006), which contains key classical media and cultural studies texts, with emphasis on the theoretical resources needed to do media/cultural studies and debates in the field. Whereas *KeyWorks* provides crucial theoretical perspectives to do media and cultural studies, this book provides overviews of the field of media and cultural studies and analyses by our contributors that teach how to read, interpret, and critique contemporary culture in concrete studies that also illuminate the contemporary moment. Other readers that combine media/communication and cultural studies include Marris and Thornham (2000); Miller (2001); and Valdivia (2003). Many contributors to a recent symposium in *Television and New Media* (Vol. Ten, Nr. One: January 2009) on "My Media Studies" noted the need for more interdisciplinary work and overcoming limitations of an academic media studies.

42. For a compendium of arguments against cultural studies in communications studies and his own defenses and presentations of cultural studies, often articulated with communications studies and a broad array of theory, see Grossberg (1997). For a recent dismissal of cultural studies from the standpoint of communication studies, see McChesney (2007), who also has his criticisms of the field of communication and himself champions a certain political economy approach. Gitlin attacks cultural studies from a left-liberal position (for a critique of Gitlin's uninformed representation of cultural studies, see Kellner, 2006). We seek to combine humanities and social science approaches in our critical media/cultural studies, drawing on the best of communication and media studies, and cultural studies, rather than pitting these fields against each other, or championing one dimension of cultural or communication theory against others.

43. On diagnostic critique, see Kellner and Ryan (1988) and Kellner (1995: 116–17, and 2003).

References

Abass, Ackbar and John Nguyet Erni (2005) *Internationalizing Cultural Studies: An Anthology.* Oxford: Blackwell.

Abelove, Henry, Michele Aina Barale, and David M. Halperin (eds.) (1993) *The Lesbian and Gay Studies Reader,* New York: Routledge.

Althusser, Louis (2006) [1971] "Ideology and Ideological State Apparatuses: Notes Toward an Investigation" in Durham and Kellner 2006 [1971]: 79–87.

Ang, Ien (1985). *Watching Dallas: Soap Opera and the Melodramatic Imagination.* New York: Methuen.

——— (1996). *Living Room Wars. Rethinking Media Audiences for a Postmodern World*. London and New York: Routledge.

Anzaldua, Gloria (1987) *Borderlands/La Frontera: The New Mestiza*. San Francisco, CA: Aunt Lute Books.

Babe, Robert (2006) "The Political Economy of Knowledge: Neglecting Political Economy in the Age of Fast Capitalism (as Before)," *Fast Capitalism,* Vol. 2, Nr. 1: 1–27 at http://www.uta.edu/huma/agger/fastcapitalism/2_1/babe.html.

Bagdikian, Ben (1997) *The Media Monopoly,* 6th ed. Boston: Beacon Press.

Baker, Houston, Mantha Diawara, and Ruth Lindeborg (eds) 1996. *Black British Cultural Studies: A Reader.* Chicago: University of Chicago Press.

Barker, Chris (2008) *Cultural Studies. Theory and Practice.* Los Angeles and London: Sage; third edition.

Bateson, Gregory (1972) *Steps to an Ecology of Mind.* New York: Ballantine Books.

Baudrillard, Jean. (1983). *Simulations / Jean Baudrillard.* New York: Semiotext(e) Inc.

Best, Steven and Douglas Kellner (1991) *Postmodern Theory: Critical Interrogations.* London and New York: Macmillan and Guilford Press.

——— (1997) *The Postmodern Turn.* New York and London: Guilford Press and Routledge.

——— (2001) *The Postmodern Adventure. Science Technology, and Cultural Studies at the Third Millennium.* New York and London: Guilford and Routledge.

Blumenthal, Sidney (2007) Journalism and Its Discontents," *Salon,* Oct. 25, 2007 at http://www.salon.com/opinion/blumenthal/2007/10/25/walter_lippmann/ (accessed September 6, 2008).

Blumler, Jay G., and Katz, E. (1974). The uses of mass communications: Current perspectives on gratifications research. *Sage Annual Reviews of Communication Research,* Vol. III.

Bobo, Jacqueline (1995) "The Color Purple, Black Women as Cultural Readers" in Dines and Humez: 52–59.

Bogle, Donald (1995) *Toms, Coons, Mulattoes, Mammies, and Bucks: An Interpretive History of Blacks in American Films.* 3rd edition. New York: Continuum.

Brunsdon, Charlotte (1996) "A Thief in the Night: Stories of Feminism in the 1970s at CCCS." In Morley and Chen (eds) 1996.

Brunsdon, Charlotte, and Dave Morley (1978). *Everyday Television: "Nationwide."* London: British Film Institute.

Canclini, N. G. (1995). *Hybrid cultures.* Minneapolis, MN: University of Minnesota Press.

Cantril, Handley, Howard Koch, Hazel Gaudet, Herta Herzog, H. G. Wells (1982 [1940]) *The Invasion from Mars: A Study in the Psychology of Panic.* Princeton, NJ: Princeton University Press.

Carey, James. W. (1977). Journalism and criticism: The case of undeveloped profession. In E. S. Munson and C. A. Warren (Eds.), (1997) *James Carey: A Critical Reader.* Minneapolis, MN: University of Minnesota Press.

Carey, James. W. (1989). *Communication as culture: Essays on media and society.* New York: Routledge.

Centre for Contemporary Cultural Studies (1980) *On Ideology.* London: Hutchinson.

——— (1982) *The Empire Strikes Back: Race and Racism in 70s Britain.* London: Routledge.

Chomsky, Noam (1991) "Early History of Propaganda, Spectator Democracy, Engineering Opinion, Public Relations." Available at Athenaeum Reading Room, http://evans-experientialism.freewebspace.com/chomsky03.htm (accessed September 6, 2008).

Chomsky, N. (2003). *Hegemony or survival: America's quest for global dominance.* New York: Metropolitan Books.

Collins, Patricia Hill (1990) *Black Feminist Thought: Knowledge, Consciousness, and the Politics of Empowerment.* Routledge: New York.

Couldry, Nick (2003) *Media Rituals. A Critical Approach.* New York and London: Routledge.

Creekmur, Corey K. and Alexander Doty (1995) eds. *Out in Culture: Gay, Lesbian, and Queer Essays on Popular Culture.* Durham: Duke University Press.

Crenshaw, Kimberle (1991) "Mapping the Margins: Intersectionality, Identity Politics, and Violence Against Women of Color." Selections for the Third National Conference on Women of Color and the Law. *Stanford Law Review.* July: 43 *Stanford Law Review* 1241.

Defleur, M. and Ball-Rokeach, S. (1989). *Theories of mass communication, 5/e.* White Plains, NY: Longman, Inc.

Dines, Gail and Jean Humez, eds. (1995) *Gender, Race and Class in Media.* Thousand Oaks: Sage.

Doty, Alexander (1993) *Making Things Perfectly Queer: Interpreting Mass Culture.* Minneapolis: University of Minnesota Press.

Downing, John (1996) *Internationalizing Media Theory: Transition, Power, Culture.* London: Sage.

Du Bois, W.E.B. (1903) *The Souls of Black Folk.* Chicago: A.C. McClurg.

Durham, Meenakshi Gigi and Douglas M. Kellner, eds. (2006) *Media and Cultural Studies: KeyWorks.* Malden, MA: Blackwell Publishing; second edition.

Dyer, Richard (1993) *The Matter of Images: Essays on Representation.* New York: Routledge.

Erni, John Nguyet (2001). "Media Studies and Cultural Studies: A Symbiotic Convergence," in Miller 2001: 187–207.

Ewen, S. (1976). *Captains of consciousness: Advertising and the social roots of the consumer culture.* New York: McGraw-Hill.

Ewen, S. and Ewen, E. (1982). *Channels of desire: Mass images and the shaping of American consciousness.* Minneapolis, MN: University of Minnesota Press.

Ewen, Stuart (1996) *PR! A Social History of Spin.* New York: Basic Books.

Faludi, Susan (1991) *Backlash: The Undeclared War Against Women.* Crown: New York.

Ferguson, Marjorie and Peter Golding (eds) (1997) *Cultural Studies in Question.* London: Sage.

Fiske, John (1989a) *Reading the Popular.* Boston: Unwin Hyman.

——— (1989b) *Understanding Popular Culture.* Boston: Unwin Hyman.

——— (1990). *Introduction to Communication Studies.* New York, NY: Routledge.

——— (1993) *Power plays, Power Works.* London: Verso.

Forman, H.J. (1933) *Our Movie-Made Children.* New York: Mellon

García Canclini, Néstor (1995) *Hybrid Cultures: Strategies for Entering and Leaving Modernity.* Minneapolis: University of Minnesota Press.

Gay, Peter, editor (1989) *The Freud Reader.* New York: W.W. Norton and Company.

Gerbner, George (2003) "Television Violence: At a Time of Turmoil and Terror," in Dines and Humez 1995: 339–348.

Gilroy, Paul (1987) *There Ain't No Black in the Union Jack: The Cultural Politics of Race and Nation.* Chicago: University of Chicago Press.

——— (1991) *The Black Atlantic: Modernity and Double Consciousness.* London: Verso.

Giroux, Henry and Patrick Shannon (1997) *Education and Capitalism: Toward a Performative Practice.* New York and London: Routledge.

Gitlin, Todd (1978) "Media Sociology: The Dominant Paradigm," *Theory and Society* 6: 205–224.

——— (2006) *The Intellectuals and the Flag.* New York: Columbia University Press.

Gramsci, Antonio (1971) *Selections from the Prison Notebooks.* New York: International.

Gray, J., Sandvoss, C., and Harrington, C.L. (Eds.) (2007). *Fandom: Identities and Communities in a Mediated World.* New York: NYU Press.

Gross, Larry (2006) "Out in Mainstream Culture: Sexual Minorities and the Mass Media" In Durham and Kellner 2006: 405–423.

Grossberg, Lawrence (1989) "The Formations of Cultural Studies: An American in Birmingham." *Strategies, 22,* 114–149.

———— (1997) *Bringing It All Back Home.* Durham: Duke University Press.

Grossberg, Lawrence, Cary Nelson, and Paula Treichler (1992) *Cultural Studies.* New York: Routledge.

Hall, Gary and Clare Birchall (2006) *New Cultural Studies.* Edinburgh, U.K.: Edinburgh University Press.

Hall, Stuart (1980a) "Cultural Studies and the Centre: Some Problematics and Problems." In S. Hall et al., *Culture, Media, Language.* London: Hutchinson: 15–47.

———— (1980b) "Encoding/decoding." In S. Hall et al. 1980: 128–138.

————(1982) "Cultural Studies and Its Theoretical Legacies" in Grossberg, Nelson and Treichler 1992.

Hall, Stuart et al. (1980). *Culture, Media, Language.* London: Hutchinson.

Hardt, Hanno (1992) *Critical Communication Studies: Communication, History, and Theory in America.* New York and London: Routledge.

Harrington, Austin (ed) (2005) *Modern Social Theory: An Introduction.* Oxford, UK: Oxford University Press.

Hartley, John (2003) *A Short History of Cultural Studies.* London and Thousand Oaks: Sage.

Hebdige, Dick (1979) *Subculture.* London: Methuen.

———— (1988) *Hiding in the Light.* London and New York: Routledge.

Herman, Edward, and Noam Chomsky (1988). *Manufacturing Consent: The Political Economy of the Mass Media.* New York: Pantheon.

Hill Collins, Patricia (1990) *Black Feminist Thought.* Boston: Unwin Hyman.

hooks, bell (1994) *Teaching to Trangress: Education as the Practice of Freedom.* New York: Routledge.

hooks, bell (1990) *Yearning: Race, Gender, and Cultural Politics.* Toronto: Between the Lines.

hooks, bell (2000) *Feminist Theory: From Margin to Center.* London: Pluto Press.

Horkheimer, Max and Adorno, T.W. (1972) *Dialectic of Enlightenment.* New York: Herder and Herder.

Hunter, James Davison (1991) *Culture Wars: The Struggle to Define America.* New York: Basic Books.

Innis, Harold A. (1995 [1951] *The Bias of Communication.* Toronto: University of Toronto Press.

Innis, Harold. *Empire and Communications* (2007/1952). Lanham: Rowman and Littlefield.

Jhally, S. (2006). *The spectacle of accumulation: Essays in culture, media, and politics.* New York: Peter Lang.

Johnson, Richard (1986/1987) "What Is Cultural Studies Anyway?" *Social Text, 16:* 38–80.

Jowett, Garth (1976) *Film: The Democratic Art.* Boston: Little, Brown.

Katz, Elihu and Paul F. Lazarsfeld (1955) *Personal Influence: The Part Played by People in the Flow of Mass Communication.* Glencoe, Ill.: Free Press.

Katz, E., Gurevitch, M., and Haas, H. (1973). On the use of the mass media for important things. *American Sociological Review.*

Kellner, Douglas (1978) "Ideology, Marxism, and Advanced Capitalism." *Socialist Review, 42* (November–December): 37–65.

———— (1979 "TV, Ideology, and Emancipatory Popular Culture. *Socialist Review, 45,* (May–June): 13–53.

———— (1989a) *Critica l Theory, Marxism, and Modernity.* Cambridge, UK and Baltimore, MD: Polity Press and Johns Hopkins University Press.

———— (1989b) *Jean Baudrillard: From Marxism to Postmodernism and Beyond.* Cambridge, UK and Palo Alto, CA: Polity Press and Stanford University Press.

———— (1990) *Television and the Crisis of Democracy.* Boulder, CO: Westview.

———— (1992) *The Persian Gulf TV War.* Boulder, CO: Westview.

———— (1995) *Media Culture. Cultural Studies, Identity, and Politics Between the Modern and the Postmodern.* London and New York: Routledge.

———— (1997). "Critical Theory and British Cultural Studies: The Missed Articulation" in Jim McGuigan (Ed.), *Cultural Methodologies* (pp. 12–41). London: Sage.

————. (2001). *Grand Theft 2000.* Lanham, MD: Rowman and Littlefield.

———— (2003a) *Media Spectacle.* London and New York: Routledge.

———— (2003b) "From September 11 to Terror War: The Dangers of the Bush Legacy." Lanham, MD: Rowman and Littlefield.

———— (2005) *Media Spectacle and the Crisis of Democracy.* Boulder: Paradigm.

———— (2006a) "Jean Baudrillard After Modernity: Provocations on a Provocateur and Challenger," *International Journal of Baudrillard Studies,* Volume 3, Number 1 (January 2007) at http://www.ubish-ops.ca/baudrillardstudies/v013_1/kellner.htm.

———— (2006b) "Education and the Academic Left: Critical Reflections on Todd Gitlin," *College Literature* 33/4 (Fall): 137–154.

———— (2008) *Guys and Guns Amok: Domestic Terrorism and School Shootings from the Oklahoma City Bombings to the Virginia Tech Massacre.* Boulder, CO: Paradigm Press.

Kellner, Douglas, and Ryan, Michael (1988) *Camera Politica: The Politics and Ideology of Contemporary Hollywood Film.* Bloomington: Indiana University Press.

Klapper, Joseph T. (1960) *The Effects of Mass Communication.* New York: Free Press.

Krolokke, Charlotte and Anne Scott Sorensen (2006) *Gender Communication. Theories and Analyses.* London and Thousand Oaks: Sage.

Lasswell, Harold (1927) *Propaganda Technique in the Modern World.* New York: Knopf.

Lazarsfeld, Paul, Bernard Berelson and Hazel Gaulet (1944) *The People's Choice.* New York: Duell, Sloan and Pierce.

Lewis, L. A. (1992). *Adoring Audience: Fan Culture and Popular Media.* New York: Routledge.

Lull, J. (1995). *Communication, culture: A global approach.* London: Polity Press.

Marcuse, Herbert (1964) *One-Dimensional Man.* Boston: Beacon Press.

Marris, Paul and Sue Thornham, editors (2000) *Media Studies: A Reader.* New York: New York University Press.

McChesney, Robert (1993) *Telecommunications, Mass Media, and Democracy: The Battle for the Control of U.S. Broadcasting,* 1928–1935. New York and Oxford: Oxford University Press.

———— (2000) *Rich Media, Poor Democracy.* New York: The New Press.

———— (2007) *Communication Revolution. Critical Junctures and the Future of Media.* New York: The New Press.

McGuigan, Jim (1992) *Cultural Populism.* London and New York: Routledge.

———— (1997) (Ed.), *Cultural Methodologies.* London: Sage.

McLaren, P. (1997). *Revolutionary multiculturalism: Pedagogies of dissent for the new millennium.* Boulder, Colorado: Westview Press.

————, Rhonda Hammer, David Sholle, Susan Reilly. (eds) (1994) *Rethinking Media Literacy: A Critical Pedagogy of Representation.* New York: Peter Lang.

McLuhan, Marshall (1964) *Understanding Media: The Extensions of Man.* New York: McGraw-Hill.

McQuail, Denis (1994) *Mass Communication Theory.* London, Thousand Oaks: Sage; third edition.

McRobbie, Angela (1994) *Postmodernism and Popular Culture.* New York and London: Routledge.

———— (1999) *In the Culture Society: Art, Fashion, and Popular Music.* London: Routledge.

Miller, Toby (2001) *A Companion to Cultural Studies.* Malden, MA and Oxford UK: Blackwell Publishers.

Morley, D. (1986) *Family Television.* London: Comedia.

Morley, David (1997) "Theoretical Orthodoxies: Textualism, Constructivism and the 'New Ethnography'" in Ferguson and Golding 1997: 121–137.

Mosco, Vincent (1996) *The Political Economy of Communication. Rethinking and Renewal.* London: Sage.

Nava, M. (1992). *Changing cultures: Feminism, youth, and consumerism.* Thousand Oaks, CA: Sage.

Radway, Janice A (1983). *Reading the Romance: Women, Patriarchy, and Popular Culture.* Chapel Hill: University of North Carolina Press.

Real, Michael (1989) *Supermedia: A Cultural Studies Approach.* Thousand Oaks: Sage.

Rojek, Chris. (2007) *Cultural Studies.* Cambridge: Polity Press.

——— (2003) *Stuart Hall.* Cambridge, UK: Polity Press.

San Juan, E. Jr. (2002) *Racism and Cultural Studies. Critiques of Multiculturalist Ideology and the Politics of Difference.* Durham, N.C.: Duke University Press.

Sarikakis, Katharine and Leslie Regan Shade (2008) *Feminist Interventions in International Communication.* London and Thousand Oaks: Sage.

Schiller, Herbert (1971) *Mass Communications and American Empire.* Boston: Beacon Press.

Schramm, Wilbur (ed) (1948) *Communications in Modern Society.* Urbana: University of Illinois Press.

——— (1973) *Men, Messages and Media: A Look at Human Communication.* New York: Harper and Row.

Shiach, Morag (ed) (1999) *Feminism and Cultural Studies.* New York and Oxford, UK: Oxford University Press.

Staiger, Janet (1992) "Film, Reception, and Cultural Studies." *Centennial Review, 26*(1), 89–104.

Stagoll, Brian. (2005) "Bateson's Vision Challenged the Reductionism, Materialism and Dualism of Western Science." *Australian and New Zealand Journal of Psychiatry* 2005; 39: 1036–1045. Retrieved Sept. 28/07 from Academic Search Premier Data Base.

Stearn, Gerald Emanuel (1967) (ed) *McLuhan: Hot & Cool.* New York: Signet.

Thompson, John (1990) *Ideology and modern culture.* Cambridge, UK and Stanford, CA: Polity Press and Stanford University Press.

Tong, Rosemarie. 1998. *Feminist Thought: A More Comprehensive Introduction.* Boulder, Colorado: Westview.

Turner, Graham (1990). *British Cultural Studies: An Introduction.* New York: Unwin Hyman.

Tucker, Robert (ed) *The Marx-Engels Reader* (1978) New York: Norton.

Tunstall, Jeremy (1977) *The Media Are American.* New York: Columbia University Press.

van Zoonen, Liesbet (1994) *Feminist Media Studies.* London and Thousand Oaks: Sage.

Wilder, Carol (1978) "From the Interactional View—A Conversation with Paul Watzlawick." *Journal of Communication,* Vol. 28, nr 4:35–45.

Valdivia, Angharad, N. (2003) *A Companion to Media Studies.* Malden, MA and Oxford UK: Blackwell Publishers.

Watzlawick, P. (1976). *How real is real?: Confusion, disinformation, communication.* New York: Random House.

Williams, Raymond (1981) *Culture.* London: Fontana.

Zizek, Slavoj (1993) "Multiculturalism, Or, the Cultural Logic of Multinational Capital," *New Left Review* 225 (September–October): 28–51.

Acknowledgments

We would like to thank the contributors of this volume for their cooperation in the production and editing process and for making available to us and a broader audience their excellent work. For editing of our own articles in the anthology we would like to thank Loran Marsdan and Heather Collette-Derra. Thanks to Kim Mattheussens and Tiffany Current for helping us with permissions and xeroxing. For editorial help in the production process from the Peter Lang side we would like to thank Bernadette Shade and Sophie Appel, and our commissioning editor and good friend, Shirley Steinberg.

The book is dedicated to the memory of Joe Kincheloe who devoted his life to media and cultural studies, to outstanding teaching and work in critical pedagogy, and to making the world a better place. Joe, we miss you already . . .

■ **PART I**

What Is Media/ Cultural Studies?

■ Introduction

Part I, What Is Media/Cultural Studies? attempts to illuminate the field with some chapters laying out basic concepts, approaches, and thematics. In "Toward a Critical Media/Cultural Studies," Douglas Kellner offers critical perspectives on ways to develop a more robust media/cultural studies by engaging the production and political economy of culture; reading and interpreting cultural texts; and studying audience reception and use of cultural artifacts. In an exercise in meta-theory, Kellner explicates key components of a critical media/cultural studies, outlining a field in which a diverse amount of work is possible that may use a wide range of methods, concepts, and theories, engage a wealth of disparate topics, and have a diversity of goals. Hence, his model is not a prescriptive one that indicates requirements that a cultural/media analyst must do in every study, but points to a transdisciplinary project that brings together theories, methods, and concepts from a wealth of disciplines to engage a broad range media and culture forms.

As we have indicated, the terrain of media and cultural studies is highly contested, so there will necessarily be different approaches, highlighted themes, and methods and theories deployed, although readers will see patterns that connect various chapters. Lawrence Grossberg was one of the first to introduce British cultural studies to the United States and then became a distinguished player in cultural studies globally. In his important 1995 study titled "What's in a Name," reprinted here, Grossberg points to the difficulties of defining cultural studies and the need to hold it open as an ever-evolving field of inquiry and intervention. Yet Grossberg seeks to delineate cultural studies as an open-ended and multifaceted project to distinguish it from the ever-proliferating approaches to culture, which have appropriated the term "cultural studies" to diverse and often dissimilar projects. Grossberg stresses the seriousness and disciplinarity of cultural studies that seeks rigorous and objective knowledge of its objects, which are always multiplying and mutating. Crucially, cultural studies is a contextual discipline that situates its object in concrete relations of power and domination.

Cultural studies for Grossberg involves the articulation of its objects of inquiry with the economic, political, social, cultural, and multiple relations that constitute the objects under investigation, using the method of articulation to bring together theories and disciplines to map and interpret its subject matter. Cultural studies is thus theoretical, using theory as a resource, but not tying itself dogmatically to a particular theory, which then becomes the key to interpretation and imposes its own presuppositions on the object of inquiry.

Yet cultural studies is fundamentally, in Grossberg's view, political, getting its projects from the sociopolitical concerns of the moment, taking on the most pressing questions and problems of its era. It draws on a wealth of disciplines, and the particular methods, theories, and concepts used in a particular study depend on the object and project in question. Such a complex project is self-reflexive, constantly scrutinizing its own assumptions, goals, methods, and analyses, transforming them as situations evolve, new questions come to the fore, and new methods and theories appear.

Chris Rojek presents an overview of Stuart Hall's perspectives on representation and ideology and the encoding/decoding of media messages that has been fundamental to British cultural studies and highly influential globally. Stuart Hall is one of the most significant figures in cultural studies and has had an immense influence on a variety of scholars in a diversity of fields throughout the world.

Rojek reminds us that Hall and British cultural studies were reacting against a dominant behaviorist and liberal pluralist tradition of communications studies, and linked representation and ideology in order to imbricate media in the problematics of power and domination and to offer political theorizing of the media. The famous article on encoding/decoding, Rojek suggests, is related to political movements of the 1960s, which saw the empowerment of students and citizens as crucial to emancipatory social change. Hall's re-viewing of media audiences and reception aimed, on one hand, to break with manipulation models that saw audiences as controlled by media and political elites and also wanted to break with liberal pluralist views that the media consumer is king and that audiences themselves primarily create meaning. To break with these dominant paradigms, Hall and other members of British cultural studies insisted that media producers encoded specific meanings in their text, and he carefully distinguished between different types of encoding from uncritically following dominant codes and the "preferred" ideological meanings encoded in the texts, to negotiated and resistant readings, a spectrum of ideal types that show audiences can process media texts in a variety of ways.

Rojek notes that Hall follows certain of Marx's ideas on ideology as the dominant ideas of the ruling class, and indeed one of the major contributions of British cultural studies would be to expand Marx's concept to include gender, race, sexuality, and other key markers of identity which are constructed in media texts. Rojek also notes that Hall draws on Marx's mode of analysis in his 1858–59 *Grundrisse* to avoid economic reductionism and relate production (of media texts in our instance) with their distribution, circulation, and consumption (or reception).

Edward Herman's entry "The Propaganda Model" explicates the model of news and information developed by himself and Noam Chomsky. Their model explains how a set of filters in a corporate-controlled media system produce propaganda in favor of the system comparable to state-controlled media systems. The first filter involves size, ownership, and profit orientation whereby giant corporations control the dominant media system and marginalize smaller media from shaping public opinion and intervening on key issues. Second, an advertising-based media system means that media corporations are likely to present opinions and information congenial to advertisers who in effect are able to filter out strong critiques of the corporate system or the voices of those who oppose it. Third, corporate media tend to rely on established figures as sources of information that usually represent the two dominant parties or major corporations in the United States, who have sophisticated public relations firms to shape information. Fourth, "flak" from organized interest groups puts pressure on media owners and advertisers if they express unpopular opinions, or notions that do not conform to the views and interests of dominant elites. Fifth, a dominant anticommunist ideology filtered out views friendly to socialism and critical of capitalism. With the demise of the Soviet Union, this may have changed, but Herman maintains that the religion of the "free market" remains intact, and we might add that after September 11, 2001, critics of the system or specific policies such as the Iraq war can be labeled friendly to terrorism and thus filtered out of mainstream discussion.

Chomsky and Herman highlight the importance of political economy for media/cultural studies, a theme taken up differently by John Caldwell in "How Producers "Theorize": Shoot-outs, Bake-offs, and Speed-Dating." Caldwell notes that while much cultural studies work has focused on the decoding side of Stuart Hall's distinction and has examined different forms of audience reception of media texts, there has not been as much focus on media production. Caldwell argues that better understanding of contemporary media culture requires grasping changes in production. He proposes examining the microlevel of film and television production in a digital environment to comprehend changes in the media industries. Engaging in analysis of contemporary U.S. film and television production, Caldwell notes growing conflicts and interactions between media corporations, producers, and fans as new digital technologies dramatically transform production, distribution, and reception.

The increased self-referencing of both corporate culture and cultural producers of individual programming has produced, Caldwell suggests, "unruly" work-worlds, technologies, and audiences. As media workers face downsizing and outsourcing, they are becoming increasing mobilized and militant and can use the media and new Internet gossip sites to criticize their bosses. As for audiences, fans can become producers as they recycle popular media for YouTube or digitally edit and produce their own videos, often appropriating materials from dominant media. Media corporations in turn engage in "corporate culture jamming," intervening in chat rooms, blogs, and other sites to promote their programming, counter rumors and misinformation, or spread their own misinformation to keep spoilers from revealing plotlines or program twists. Hence, from Caldwell's perspective, shifts in production and technology require new understandings of cultural production, texts, and audiences. Thus, whereas Herman stresses the filters that ensure corporate hegemony, Caldwell argues that within certain limits there are often conflicts between corporate managers, media producers, and their workers and audiences who now have growing autonomy to critique corporate media and use materials for their own purposes.

Henry Giroux, an eminent theorist and critic of education, explores the intersection of "Cultural Studies, Critical Pedagogy, and the Politics of Higher Education," linking cultural studies with critical pedagogy and radical democratic politics. Giroux envisions cultural studies as a transformative project engaged in the democratic reconstruction of education and society. Hence, Giroux relates cultural studies to transforming both the classroom and education *and* democratizing society, linking cultural studies to social movements and projects of transformation. Giroux calls attention to the responsibility of intellectuals to engage issues of public importance and use their critical faculties in both the classroom and in the broader social and political sphere of their society. Thus, for Giroux cultural studies has an intrinsically political calling.

Robin Mansell, a distinguished communications theorist, highlights the importance of new media and social networks within an expanding digital culture in her London School of Economics inaugural lecture, "The Power of New Media Networks." Mansell argues that gaining access to these networks and developing the capabilities to successfully use and participate in them should be elevated to a right in contemporary technological societies. Mansell argues that more robust media literacy is necessary whereby individuals do not just acquire technological knowledge of how to manipulate new media and technologies but also develop the capacities to find essential information for their lives and well-being, participate in social networks, and engage in political discussion. Her analysis highlights the importance of a contemporary media/cultural studies to reflect upon the emergent digital culture and social networks that are becoming ever more important elements in everyday life, demonstrating the ways that study of media and culture is relevant to contemporary lives.

1

■ Toward a Critical Media/ Cultural Studies

Douglas Kellner

Radio, television, film, and the other products of media culture provide materials out of which individuals in contemporary media and consumer societies forge their very identities, including sense of self, notion of what it means to be male or female, and how people experience class, ethnicity and race, sexuality, age, nationality, and other markers of identity. Media culture helps shape people's view of the world and deepest values, defining good or evil, their positive ideals and sense of who they are as a people, as well as who and what are threats and enemies, often creating sharp divisions between "us" and "them." Media stories provide the symbols, myths, and resources that constitute a common culture and through the appropriation of which individuals become integrated into their culture and society. Media spectacles demonstrate who has power and who is powerless, who is allowed to exercise force and violence, and who is not. They dramatize and legitimate the powers that be and show the powerless that they must stay in their places or face powerful forces of repression.

We are immersed from cradle to grave in a media and consumer society, and thus it is important to learn how to understand, interpret, and criticize its institutions, practices, discourses, images, and spectacles. The media industries are a powerful institution in contemporary societies, and it is essential to comprehend how they work in order to understand, act in, and transform the environment in which we live our lives. The media are an essential economic force, helping manage consumer demand, constructing needs and fantasies through advertising and entertainment which is often an advertisement for the consumer society constructed and reproduced in part by the media. Key instruments of political power, the media provide a terrain upon which political battles are fought and serve as sites of political manipulation and domination. A central force in social life, the media dominate many people's leisure activities and are powerful sources of socialization and ideological domination, as well as a field of struggle, resistance, and the construction of social alternatives.

Media culture is also a profound and often misperceived source of cultural pedagogy, which contributes to teaching individuals how to behave and what to think, feel, believe, fear, and desire—and what not to. The media are forms of pedagogy that teach people how to be men and women. They show how to dress, look, and consume; how to perceive and react to members of different social groups; and how to be popular and successful, as well as how to avoid failure. Media culture dramatizes in advertising, comedies, dramas, and other forms the price of failure to fit in and succeed and celebrates the pleasures and rewards of success.

In sum, media culture teaches individuals how to fit into the dominant system of norms, values, practices, and institutions, and demonstrates punishments for failure to conform. Consequently, the gaining of critical media literacy is an important resource for individuals and citizens in learning how to cope with and act within a seductive cultural environment. Grasping the central functions of the media within society, its roles of power and domination, and the ways that it serves the interests of corporate and state power in reproducing the existing society helps one to become more critical of media culture, able to resist its power and influence, and able to construct one's own meanings and cultural forms. Learning how to read, criticize, and resist sociocultural manipulation can thus help empower one in relation to dominant forms of media and culture. It can enhance individual sovereignty vis-à-vis media culture and give people more power over their cultural environment, as well as the ability to transform their society and create alternative forms of culture and identities.

A critical media/cultural studies also helps teach media consumers and citizens to better read, decode, and critique media culture in order to become literate readers, critics, and ultimately producers of their own culture, society, and individual identity. These critical approaches can thus generate better understanding of contemporary societies and help produce active individual subjects. A critical media literacy can empower individuals to critically engage the images, stories, spectacles, and media that constitute culture and identities, deeply influence politics, and play a crucial role in the economy, as well as to create new identities, cultures, and forms of life.

In this chapter, I discuss the potential contributions of media/cultural studies to understanding the important multiple functions of the media in society and the ways that media culture are caught up with and reproduce power and domination, as well as providing forms of resistance and social alternatives. Drawing on the multiple forms of critical theories, communications, media, and cultural studies that have emerged in the past decades (some of which are described by Rhonda Hammer and myself in the general Introduction to this book), I will set forth here some perspectives on doing media/cultural studies in the contemporary moment.

In presenting my own approach, I want to stress, however, that the field of media/cultural studies is open and evolving and always a subject of contestation and transformation. There are an overwhelming variety of media and cultural studies in a wealth of fields and academic disciplines, national and local cultures, and emergent fields like cyberstudies, which are constantly changing, producing new works, theories, methods, and articulations (see Introduction). As Larry Grossberg usefully reminds us (1997, p. 397):

> There is not, and never has been, a singular thing called British cultural studies. There never even was a thing called the position of the Centre for Contemporary Cultural Studies at Birmingham, which is often mythically and sometimes nostalgically seen as the location of the origin of British cultural studies. Even at the Centre, there were always different and sometimes competing, powerfully invested positions and projects. The differences were both theoretical and political, and they often led to highly charged, emotionally difficult debates. Consequently, even the best histories of the Centre, or of British cultural studies, that have been written manage at best to describe what John Clarke has called "the diversity that won." There are always voices that were part of the discussion that have been excluded (or that excluded themselves) or erased.

Hence, in the following sections, I want to lay out a comprehensive and open, albeit delineated, field of media/cultural studies emerging out of specific theoretical and historical traditions that make possible broad theorizing, contextualizing, and critique of media culture within its field of production, its evolving cultural forms, reception, and uses and effects.[1] The following analysis of components of a critical media/cultural studies provides a broad framework within which work can be done, and an overview of what features of media cultural production, texts, artifacts, practices, and audiences can be engaged in doing media/cultural studies. It also provides my own mapping of the field of contemporary cultural studies, much as Grossberg does in this work, and as other participants in the field such as John Hartley (2003), Chris Rojek (2007), and Chris Barker (2008) have done in recent books. Thus, this chapter is intended as an analysis of some components of the emerging field of media/cultural studies and not a prescriptive model that one must follow, as different projects will require the mixture and articulation of different components, theories, methods, and approaches.

■ Components of a Critical Media/ Cultural Studies

As emphasized in the Introduction to our reader, the concept of a media/cultural studies attempts to overcome one-sided positions in media, communications and cultural studies that focus alone on topics such as text analysis, audiences, political economy, the supposed effects of communication, or other single issues in isolation from constituent economic, political, social and cultural dimensions of the field of culture and society. To be sure, for some projects, one might want to focus on one specific topic in media/cultural studies, such as representations of race or gender in key films, or a question of political economy, such as media ownership and how increased corporate control is producing a homogenization of news and entertainment, especially if one is beginning to study the field. Moreover, students would most likely begin doing media/cultural studies by taking on a specific theme, such as the representations of women, race, and class in a film like

Crash (2005) or *Babel* (2006) (see Kellner, forthcoming), or representations of masculinity in the *Rocky* and *Rambo* films. Other projects might combine analysis of texts and audience reception of popular singers like Madonna, Britney Spears, Hilary Duff, or Kanye West.[2]

Yet as one advances in doing media/cultural studies, the questions of mediations and connections emerge as one sees how production in different sectors of media industries intersects with the construction of specific kinds of texts and audience uses of media. Thus a critical media/cultural studies aims at making connections between texts and contexts, media industries and technologies, politics and economics, and specific texts, practices, and audiences. As one proceeds through the field of media/cultural studies, one can attain a broad framework for contextualizing and analyzing a wide range of cultural artifacts and gain better understanding of the role of the media in contemporary economy, politics, culture, and everyday life. For instance, analyzing the Virginia Tech shootings in April 2007 would require analysis of the role of the media in the spectacle, male rage and the crisis of masculinity that leads young men to become school shooters and construct identity and fame through guns and violence, and an out-of-control gun culture and culture of celebrity in the United States (see Kellner, 2008).

As I have argued (Kellner, 1995), the Frankfurt School and British cultural studies articulate a threefold project of analyzing the production and political economy of culture, cultural texts, and the audience reception and use of those texts and their effects.[3] This tripartite model delineates a specific construction of the field of media/cultural studies, it is not a procrustean bed that every analysis must follow. It provides a framework and overview of a model of media/cultural studies, not necessary components of a complete or ideal work in the field. This approach insists that media/cultural studies should contextualize its object and analysis in the field of socioeconomic and political power (political economy); that cultural representation of a specific object has many dimensions including class, gender, race, sexuality, and other multiple determinants; that the phenomenon under question has multiple and perhaps contradictory effects and will be appropriated and will influence people in various ways according to their own subject position and context of appropriation; and that a cultural studies analysis cannot exhaust its object of study, whose appropriations and meanings may change over time.[4] This model suggests that there are many dimensions to media/cultural studies work ranging from the economic to the political, social, and cultural dimensions; that cultural artifacts have depths and layers of meaning and uses; and that a media/cultural studies must draw on multiple disciplines to adequately engage its objects.

Production and Political Economy

Since the topic has been neglected in many modes of recent media and cultural studies, it is important to stress the significance of analyzing cultural texts within their system of production and distribution, often referred to as "political economy."[5] A political economy approach to media and culture centers more on the production and distribution of culture than on interpreting texts or studying audiences. The references to the terms *political* and *economy* call attention to the fact that the production and distribution of culture take place within a specific economic and political system, constituted by relations between the state, the economy, social institutions and practices, culture, and organizations like the media. Political economy thus encompasses economics and politics and the relations between them and the other central structures of society and culture. In regard to media institutions, for instance, in Western democracies, a capitalist economy dictates that cultural production is governed by laws of the market, but the democratic imperatives mean that there is some regulation of culture by the state. There are often tensions within a given society concerning which activities should be governed by the imperatives of the market, or economics, alone, and how much state regulation or intervention is desirable to assure a wider diversity of broadcast programming, or the prohibition of phenomena agreed to be harmful, such as cigarette advertising or pornography, or the promotion of something positive like "net neutrality" that would guarantee the right to fast wireless Internet access to all (McChesney, 2007).

Political economy highlights that capitalist societies are organized according to a dominant mode of production that structures institutions and practices according to the logic of commodification and capital accumulation. Cultural production and distribution are accordingly profit- and market-oriented in such a system. Forces of production (such as media technologies and creative practice) are shaped according to dominant relations of production (such as the profit imperative, the maintenance of hierarchical control, and relations of domination). Hence, the system of production (e.g., market or state oriented) is important, as suggested below, in determining what sort of cultural artifacts are produced and how they are consumed. "Political economy," therefore, does not merely pertain solely to economics, but to the relations between the economic, political, technological, and cultural dimensions of social reality. The structure of political economy links culture to its political and economic context and opens up cultural studies to history and politics. It refers to a field of contestation and antagonism and not an inert structure as caricatured by some of its opponents.

Political economy should also discern and analyze the role of technology in cultural production and distribution, seeing, as in Marshall McLuhan (1964), how technology and forms of media help structure economic, social, and cultural practices and forms of life. In our era, the proliferation of new technologies and multimedia—ranging from computers to DVDs and iPods to new technologies of digitized film and music—calls attention to the key role of technology in the economy and everyday life and makes clear that technological and economic factors are often deeply interconnected. In a time of technological revolution, the role of technology is especially important, and so analysis of political economy must engage the dominant forms of technology.

In the present stage of capitalist hegemony, political economy grounds its approach within empirical analysis of the actual system of cultural production, investigating the constraints and structuring influence of the dominant capitalist economic system and a commercialized cultural system dominated by powerful corporations. Situating texts into the system of culture within which they are produced and distributed can help elucidate features and effects of the texts that textual analysis alone might miss or downplay. Rather than being an antithetical approach to culture, political economy can contribute to textual analysis and critique. The system of production often determines what type of artifacts will be produced, what structural limits there will be as to what can and cannot be said and shown, and what kind of audience effects cultural artifacts may generate.

Study of the codes of television, film, or popular music, for instance, is enhanced by examining the formulas and conventions of media culture production. These cultural forms are structured by well-defined rules and conventions, and investigation of the production of culture can help elucidate the codes actually in play. Due to the demands of the format of radio or music television, for instance, most popular songs are three to five minutes long, fitting into the format of the distribution system. Network television news on the major corporate media in the United States has traditionally been to fit a small number of stories into short segments totaling about 22 minutes to leave plenty of room for advertising. The cable news networks' emphasis on "breaking news" and the need to fill 24/7 news windows creates a tendency to hype current events into media spectacles, as happened in the 1990s with the O. J. Simpson trial, the Clinton sex and impeachment scandals, and celebrity scandals involving Michael Jackson and others (see Kellner, 2003b). In the early twenty-first century, the 9/11 terrorist attacks created a media spectacle and a resulting "war on terror" that has dominated the epoch (Kellner, 2003b and 2005). Less dramatically, celebrity scandals involving Paris Hilton or Britney Spears, natural disasters like fires, hurricanes, floods, tsunamis, or heinous crimes of the day like the "Virginia Tech Massacre" are hyped into spectacles of the contemporary moment (Kellner, 2008).

Due to their control by giant corporations oriented primarily toward profit, film and television production in the United States are dominated by specific genres such as reality shows, talk and game shows, soap operas, situation comedies, action/adventure series, and so on. This economic factor explains why there are cycles of certain genres and subgenres, sequelmania in the film industry, crossovers of popular films into television series, and a certain homogeneity in products constituted within systems of production marked by rigid generic codes, formulaic conventions, and well-defined ideological boundaries.

Likewise, study of political economy can help determine the limits and range of political and ideological discourses and effects. My study of television in the United States, for example, disclosed that takeover of the television networks by major transnational corporations and communications conglomerates was part of a "right turn" within U.S. society in the 1980s whereby powerful corporate groups won control of the state and the mainstream media (Kellner, 1990). During the 1980s all three major television networks were taken over by corporate conglomerates: ABC was bought out in 1985 by Capital Cities, NBC was absorbed by General Electric, and CBS was purchased by the Tisch Financial Group. All the major U.S. corporate TV networks in the 1980s sought mergers, and this motivation, along with other benefits derived from Reaganism, might well have influenced them to downplay criticisms of Reagan and to generally support his conservative programs, military adventures, and simulated presidency (Kellner, 1990).

Corporate conglomeratization has intensified further, and today AOL and Time Warner, Disney, and other global media conglomerates increasingly control domains of production and distribution of culture (McChesney, 2000; Croteau and Hoynes, 2001; Bagdikian, 2004). In this global context, one cannot really analyze the role of the media in the two U.S./Iraq wars, for instance, without analyzing the production and political economy of news and information, as well as the actual text of the Gulf and Iraq wars and their reception by various audiences (see Kellner, 1992; 2005). Likewise, the ownership by conservative corporations of dominant media corporations helps explain mainstream corporate media support of the Bush/Cheney administration and their policies, such as the wars in Afghanistan and Iraq (Kellner, 2003b and 2005).

Looking toward entertainment, one cannot fully grasp the Madonna phenomenon without analyzing her marketing strategies, her political environment, her cultural artifacts, and their effects (Kellner, 1995). In a similar fashion, younger female pop music stars, such as Carrie Underwood, Avril Lavigne, or Kelly Clarkson, all deploy the tools of the glamour industry and media spectacle, as Madonna, Mariah Carey, Britney Spears, Jennifer Lopez, or N'Sync had in an earlier period. Likewise, one cannot explain the tremendous attention that a non-entity like Paris Hilton or a young actress like Lindsay Lohan receives from the media without grasping how the commercial imperatives of corporate television drive coverage of news and information toward entertainment (it's the ratings, stupid!). Further, in appraising the full social impact of pornography, one needs to be aware of the sex industry and the production process of, say, pornographic films, and not just focus on the texts themselves and their effects on audiences.

In the current conjuncture that is exhibiting a crossing of boundaries and synergy between information and entertainment industries, there have been significant mergers within these sectors. Previous forms of entertainment are rapidly being absorbed within the Internet, and the computer is coming to be a major household appliance and source of entertainment, information, play, communication, and connection with the outside world. The corporate media, communications, and information industries are frantically scrambling to provide delivery for the wealth of information, entertainment, and further services. These include increased Internet access, cellular telephones and satellite personal communication devices, iPods and iPhones, and computerized video, film, and information on demand, as well as Internet shopping and more unsavory services like pornography and gambling, and with strange new phenomena like microchips inserted directly into the body on the horizon. Hence, study of the political economy of media can be immensely useful for describing the infrastructure of the media, information, and communications industry and their effects on culture and society. Yet political economy alone does not hold the key to cultural studies, and important as it is, it has limitations as a single perspective.

Some political economy analyses reduce the meanings and effects of texts to rather circumscribed and reductive ideological functions, arguing that media culture merely reflects the ideology of the ruling economic elite that controls the culture industry and is nothing more than a vehicle for the dominant ideology. It is true that media culture overwhelmingly supports capitalist values, but it is also a site of intense conflict between different races, genders, sexual orientations, political ideologies, and social groups. Thus, in order to fully grasp the nature and effects of media culture, one should see contemporary society and culture as contested terrains and media and cultural forms as spaces in which particular battles over gender, race, sexuality, political ideology, and values are fought.

The conception of political economy proposed here goes beyond traditional, sometimes excessively economistic, approaches that focus on more strictly economic issues such as ownership, gate-keeping, and the production and distribution of culture. While these issues are clearly important, the political and cultural dimensions of products of the media industries are also significant, and political economy should embrace relations between economy and the polity, culture and people, as well as the interconnection between production and consumption, distribution and use. Although some conceptions of political economy are reductive, focusing solely on the economic dimension, far richer notions of political economy are possible.

Moreover, in the present configuration of the emergence of a new global economy, a critical cultural and media studies needs to grasp the global, national, and local systems of media production and distribution. In the 1960s, critics of the global capitalist system described the domination of the world economy by transnational—mostly American and European—corporations as "imperialism" or "neo-imperialism," while its supporters celebrated "modernization." Today, the term "globalization" is the standard concept used to describe the emergent global economy and culture, which is a highly ambiguous and contradictory construct. On one hand, globalization refers to an economy dominated by transnational corporations, global institutions like the WTO or World Bank that are often tools of dominant nation-states, and a homogenized global consumer and media culture. On the other hand, globalization also involves the proliferation of new voices and perspectives on culture and society, as well as the politicization and contestation of forms of culture previously taken for granted. In a global culture, the proliferation of difference and new actors are part of the landscape and the question of representation becomes intensely politicized and contested.

In an era of globalization, one must therefore be aware of the global networks that produce and distribute media culture and spectacle in the interests of profit and corporate hegemony. In addition, the emergence and proliferation of new technologies are constantly creating novel cultural forms and hybrids of previous culture, thus the interconnection of economy and technology is an important component of a critical media/cultural studies. Further, in order to fully grasp the nature and effects of media culture, one needs to develop methods to analyze the full range of its meanings and effects, including textual analysis and audience research, as is indicated in the next two sections.

Textual Analysis

Whereas political economy approaches to the media and culture derive from a social sciences tradition, analysis of the politics of representation in media texts derives from a humanities-based textual approach. Earlier, mass communications approaches to media content ranged from descriptive content analysis to quantitative analysis of references, figures, or images in media texts. The more sophisticated methods of textual analysis, however, derive from more advanced understanding of texts, narratives, and representation, as well as the contributions of critical concepts such as ideology and hegemony, all of which have been developing since the 1960s.

The products of media culture require multidimensional close textual readings to analyze their various discourses, ideological positions, narrative strategies, image construction, and effects. There have been a wide range of types of textual criticism of media culture, ranging from quantitative content analysis that dissects the number of, say, episodes of violence in a text, to qualitative study that examines images of women, blacks, or other groups, or that applies various critical theories to unpack the meanings of the texts or to explicate how texts function to produce meaning. Traditionally, the qualitative analysis of texts had been the task of formalist literary criticism, which explicated the central meanings, values, symbols, and stories in cultural artifacts by attending to the formal properties of imaginative literature texts—such as style, verbal imagery, characterization, narrative structure and point of view, and other formal elements of the artifact. From the 1960s on, however, literary-formalist textual analysis has been enhanced by methods derived from semiotics, a critical approach for investigating the creation of meaning not only in written languages but also in other, nonverbal codes, such as the visual and auditory languages of film and TV.

Semiotics analyzes how linguistic and nonlinguistic cultural "signs" form systems of meanings, as when giving someone a rose is interpreted as a sign of love, or getting an A on a college paper is a sign of mastery of the rules of the specific assignment. Semiotic analysis can be connected with genre criticism (the study of conventions governing established types of cultural forms, such as soap operas) to reveal how the codes and forms of particular genres follow certain meanings. Situation comedies, for instance, classically follow a conflict/resolution model that demonstrates how to solve certain social problems by correct actions and values and thus provide morality tales of proper and improper behavior. Soap operas, by contrast, proliferate problems and provide messages concerning the endurance and suffering needed to get through life's endless miseries, while generating positive and negative models of social behavior. And advertising shows how commodity solutions solve problems of popularity, acceptance, success, and the like.

Semiotic and genre analysis can also be merged with ideology critique and different theories of interpretation. A critical and multidimensional reading of the film *Rambo* (1982), for instance, would show how it follows the conventions of the Hollywood genre of the war film that dramatizes conflicts between the United States and its "enemies" (see Kellner, 1995). Semiotics describes how the images of the villains are constructed according to the codes of World War II movies and how the resolution of the conflict and happy ending follows the traditional Hollywood classical cinema, which portrays the victory of good over evil. Semiotic analysis would also include study of the strictly cinematic and formal elements of a film like *Rambo,* dissecting the ways that camera angles present Rambo as a god, or slow-motion images of him gliding through the jungle code him as a force of nature.

A critically informed reading of the award-winning 2007 film *There Will Be Blood* would investigate the ideological problematics involved in the interaction between capitalism, religion, and the family in the film (see Kellner, forthcoming). Semiotic analysis would engage the representations of oil production and how images of fire and hell suggest that demonic features of the industry, accompanied by analysis of the grating, modernist soundtrack by Radiohead, cut at dramatic moments by classical music from Brahms. A class analysis would engage the highly competitive and individualistic mania for wealth and success and a gender analysis would dissect how the film puts on display patriarchical capitalism and the marginalization of women.

Textual analysis of cultural studies thus combines formalist analysis with critique of how cultural meanings convey specific ideologies of gender, race, class, sexuality, nation, and other themes like religion. Textual analysis is sometimes referred to as "hermeneutics," which interprets the different layers and meaning of texts and uses various methods to unpack myths and symbols, political and ideological meanings, and perhaps individual visions or neuroses of creators, or even social pathologies as a Freudian analysis, such as that practiced by Zizek (2005), would reveal.

Textual analysis should thus deploy a wide range of methods to fully explicate each dimension and to show how they fit into textual systems. Each critical method focuses on certain features of a text from a specific perspective, and each individual perspective illuminates some features of a text while ignoring others. Marxist methods tend to focus on class, for instance, while feminist approaches will highlight gender; critical race theory spotlights race and ethnicity, and gay and lesbian queer theories explicate sexuality, while Freudian analyses reveal a psychological or unconscious dimension. Literary hermeneutics would focus on the literary and aesthetic aspects of texts, as well as engaging philosophical, theological, or moral dimensions.

More sophisticated critical Marxism, feminisms, semiotics, or queer theory articulate their own method with the other approaches to develop multiperspectivist positions that engage multiple levels of the text. Fredric Jameson, who has long developed what might be seen as a Marxian version of cultural studies, has developed methods of analyzing multiple dimensions of a text, including utopian ones that project images of a better world, as well as engaging contemporary forms like postmodernism (1991).

Each specific critical method on its own has its particular strengths and limitations, each with privileged optics but also blind spots. Traditionally, Marxian ideology critiques have been strong on class and historical contextualization and weak on formal analysis, while some versions are highly "reductionist," reducing textual analysis to denunciation of ruling class ideology or economic imperatives. Feminism excels in gender analysis and in some versions is formally sophisticated, drawing on such methods as psychoanalysis and semiotics, although some earlier versions are reductive and the emergence of second-wave feminism in the 1960s and early 1970s often limited itself to analysis of images of gender. Psychoanalysis in turn calls for the interpretation of unconscious contents and meaning, which can articulate latent meanings in a text, as when Alfred Hitchcock's dream sequences in films like *Spellbound* (1945) or *Vertigo* (1958) project cinematic symbols that illuminate his characters' dilemmas, or when the image of the female character in *Bonnie and Clyde* (1967) framed against the bars of her bed suggests her sexual frustration, imprisonment in lower middle-class family life, and need for revolt.

Contemporary interpretive methods often stress the intersectionality of gender, race, class, and sexuality in texts, indicating how they are interconnected or perhaps in tension. Readings of the films *Babel* (2006) and *Crash* (2005), for instance, would stress how representations of race, class, gender, and perhaps sexuality work together in reproducing dominant stereotypes, put them in question, or are highly ambiguous and contradictory, as I would argue (see Kellner, forthcoming). Indeed, while occasionally representations reproduce dominant ideological stereotypes, sometimes they oppose or undermine them, and other times they are contradictory and ambiguous.

Of course, each reading of a text is only one possible reading from one critic's subject position, no matter how multiperspectival, and may or may not be the reading preferred by audiences (which themselves will be significantly different according to their class, race, gender, ethnicity, ideologies, and so on). Because there is a split between textual encoding and audience decoding, there is always the possibility of a multiplicity of readings of any text of media culture (Hall, 1980c; Bobo, 1988; Rojek, 2009). However, there are limits to the openness or polysemic nature of any text, of course, and textual analysis can explicate the parameters of possible readings and delineate perspectives that aim at illuminating the text and its cultural and ideological effects. Such analysis also provides the materials for criticizing misreadings, or readings that are one-sided and incomplete. Yet to further carry through a cultural studies analysis, one must also examine how diverse audiences actually read media texts and attempt to determine what effects they have on audience thought and behavior.

Audience Reception and Use of Media Culture

All texts are subject to multiple readings depending on the perspectives and subject positions of the reader. Members of distinct genders, classes, races, nations, regions, sexual preferences, and political ideologies are going to read texts differently, and a media/cultural studies can illuminate why diverse audiences interpret texts in various, sometimes conflicting, ways. It is indeed one of the merits of British cultural studies to have focused on audience reception in recent years, and this focus provides one of its major contributions, though there are also some limitations and problems with many cultural studies approaches to the audience.[6]

A standard way to discover how audiences read texts is to engage in ethnographic research, in an attempt to determine how texts affect audiences and shape their beliefs and behavior. Ethnographic cultural studies have indicated some of the various ways that audiences use and appropriate texts, often to empower themselves. Radway's (1983) study of women's use of Harlequin novels, for example, shows how these books provide escapism for women and could be understood as reproducing traditional women's roles, behavior, and attitudes. Yet they can also empower women by promoting fantasies of a different life and may thus inspire revolt against male domination. Or they may enforce, in other audiences, female submission to male domination and trap women in ideologies of romance, in which submission to Prince Charming is seen as the alpha and omega of happiness for women.

Media culture provides materials for individuals to create identities and meanings and a media/cultural studies can detect specific ways that individuals use cultural forms. Teenagers use video games and music television as an escape from the demands of a disciplinary society. Males use sports as a terrain of fantasy identification, in which they feel empowered as "their" team or star triumphs. Such sports events also generate a form of community, currently being lost in the privatized media and consumer culture of our time. Indeed, fandoms of all sorts, ranging from *Star Trek* fans ("Trekkies") and devotees of classical soap operas to fans of *Buffy the Vampire Slayer, 24, Lost, Heroes,* or the latest reality TV hit, also form communities that enable people to relate to others who share their interests and hobbies. Some fans, in fact, actively recreate their favorite cultural forms, such as rewriting the scripts of preferred shows, sometimes in the forms of "slash," which redefine characters' sexuality, or in the forms of music poaching or remaking such as "filking" (see examples in Lewis, 1992, and Jenkins, 1992). With a proliferation of new media, audiences today also create their own blogs to comment on cultural texts, perhaps use YouTube to present their own videos, which could involve homage or satire of current popular texts, and might create their own archives of favorite artifacts of media culture with commentary on their Facebook or MySpace sites.

This emphasis on audience reception and appropriation helps cultural studies overcome the previous one-sided textualist orientations to culture. It also directs focus to the actual political effects that texts have and how audiences use texts. In fact, sometimes audiences subvert the intentions of the producers or managers of the cultural industries that supply them, as when astute young media users laugh at obvious attempts to hype certain characters, shows, or products.[7] Audience research can reveal how people are actually using cultural texts and what sort of effects they are having on everyday life. Combining quantitative and qualitative research, current reception studies, including some of the essays in this reader, are providing important contributions into how audiences actually interact with cultural texts (see the studies in Lewis, 1992, and Ang, 1996, and Rojek, 2009, for further elaboration of decoding and audience reception).

Yet there are several problems with audience reception studies as they have been constituted within some versions of cultural studies. First, there is a danger that class will be downplayed as a significant variable that structures audience decoding and use of cultural texts. Cultural studies in England were particularly sensitive to class differences—as well as subcultural differences—in the use and reception of cultural texts, but I have noted many dissertations, books, and articles in cultural studies in the United States and other places where attention to class has been downplayed or is missing altogether. This is not surprising as a neglect of class as a constitutive feature of culture and society is an endemic deficiency in the American academy in most disciplines.

There is also the reverse danger, however, of exaggerating the constitutive force of class and downplaying, or ignoring, such other variables as gender or ethnicity. Staiger (1992) notes that Fiske (1989a, 1989b), building on Hartley, lists seven "subjectivity positions" that are important in cultural reception, "self, gender, age-group, family, class, nation, ethnicity," and proposes adding sexual orientation. All of these factors, and no doubt more, interact in shaping how audiences receive and use texts and must be taken into account in studying cultural reception, for audiences decode and use texts according to the specific constituents of their class, race or ethnicity, gender, sexual preferences, and so on.

Furthermore, I would warn against a tendency to romanticize the "active audience," by claiming that all audiences produce their own meanings, thus denying that media culture may have powerful manipulative effects. Some individuals who do cultural studies reception research distinguish between dominant and oppositional readings (Hall, 1980c), a dichotomy that structures much of Fiske's work. "Dominant" readings are those in which audiences consume texts in line with the interests of the hegemonic culture and the ideological intentions of a text, as when audiences feel pleasure in the restoration of male power, law and order, and social stability at the end of a film like *Die Hard,* after the hero and representatives of authority eliminate the terrorists who had taken over a high-rise corporate headquarters. An "oppositional" reading, by contrast, celebrates the resistance to this reading in audience appropriation of a text. For example, Fiske (1993) observes resistance to dominant readings when homeless individuals in a Madison, Wisconsin, homeless shelter cheered the destruction of police and authority figures in the film, during repeated viewings of a videotape of *Die Hard* (1992) and lost interest near the end when Bruce Willis triumphed over the villains.

Although this can be a useful distinction, there is a tendency in some arenas of cultural studies to celebrate resistance per se without distinguishing between types and forms of resistance (a similar problem resides with indiscriminate celebration of audience pleasure in certain reception studies). For example, resistance to social authority by the homeless evidenced in their viewing of *Die Hard* could serve to strengthen brutal masculinist behavior and encourage manifestations of physical violence to solve social problems. Jean-Paul Sartre, Frantz Fanon, and Herbert Marcuse, among others, have argued that violence can be either emancipatory, when directed at forces of oppression, or reactionary, when directed at popular forces struggling against oppression. Some feminists, by contrast, see all violence as forms of brute masculinist behavior, while those in the Gandhian tradition and many others see it as a problematical form of conflict resolution.

Resistance and pleasure cannot therefore be valorized per se as progressive elements of the appropriation of cultural texts, but difficult distinctions must be made as to whether the resistance, oppositional reading, or pleasure in a given experience is progressive or reactionary, emancipatory or destructive. In fact, Fiske's celebration of *Die Hard* fails to contextualize it within the cycle of male rampage films analyzed by Susan Jeffords in *Hard Bodies* (1993). *Die Hard* was one of a cycle of compensatory male fantasies that responded to the expansion of feminism and the conservative male response that refused to share power with women and that resisted feminist ideas. A series of masculinist ideological extravaganzas starring such ultra-macho men as Sylvester Stallone, Arnold Schwarzenegger, Chuck Norris, and Bruce Willis featured male superheroes as the necessary solution to society's problems, thus promoting an ideology of male supremacy. As the "white male paranoia" and conservative response to feminism intensified, these masculinist fantasies became ever more brutal with three *Die Hard* films (1990, 1995, 2007), the *Young Guns* sequels (1990), or the *Rambo* sequels, doubling or even tripling the acts of redemptive male violence.[8]

Moreover, unqualified valorization of audience resistance to dominant meanings as good per se can lead to uncritical populist celebrations of the text and audience pleasure in its use of cultural artifacts. This approach, taken to the extreme, would lose its critical perspective and would lead to a populist positive gloss on audience experience of whatever is being studied. Such studies also might lose sight of the manipulative and conservative effects of certain types of mass-mediated culture and thus serve the interests of the culture industry as they are presently constituted and those groups who use the corporate media to promote their own interests and agendas.

Earlier British cultural studies wanted to engage both the ideological and the resistant, the hegemonic/dominant and the oppositional. This dialectical vision is evident in Hall's articles "Encoding/Decoding" and "Deconstructing the Popular" (1980c and 1981), which hope to acknowledge the power of the mass media to shape and enforce ideological hegemony, the power of the people to resist ideology, and the contradictory moments and effects of media culture. Cultural studies thus attempts to negotiate the split between manipulation theory, which sees mass culture and society in general as dominating individuals, and populist resistance theory which emphasizes the power of individuals to oppose, resist, and struggle against the dominant culture. Such a dual optic is also evident in the work of E.P. Thompson (1963) which stresses both workers' abilities to struggle against capitalist domination and forms of cooptation, and Dick Hebdige's *Subculture* (1979) which presents subcultural styles and youth culture both as forms of refusal and as commercial modes of incorporation of subcultural resistance into the dominant consumer culture.[9]

Thus one should attempt to avoid the one-sided approaches of manipulation and resistance theory and to mediate these perspectives in analysis. In a way, certain tendencies of the Frankfurt School can correct some of the limitations of cultural studies, just as British cultural studies can help overcome some of the limitations of the Frankfurt School. The Frankfurt School social theory always situated its objects of analysis within the framework of the vicissitudes of contemporary capitalism (Kellner, 1989, 1995). While this sometimes led to reduction of culture to commodities, ideology, and instruments of ruling class domination, it also elucidated the origins of mass-produced cultural artifacts within the capitalist production and accumulation process and thus forced attention to the economic origins and ideological nature of many of the artifacts of media culture. Likewise, the Frankfurt School emphasis on manipulation called attention to the power and seductiveness of the artifacts of the cultural industries and the ways that they could integrate individuals into the established order. The Frankfurt School emphasis on how the cultural industries produce "something for everyone, so that none can escape," suggests how difference and plurality are utilized to integrate individuals into the existing society.

The Frankfurt School emphasis on cooptation—even of seemingly radical and subversive impulses—raises the question of the nature and effects of "resistant readings," beloved by some cultural theorists. It suggests that even production of alternative meanings and resistance to "preferred meanings" may serve as effective ways to absorb individuals into the established society. Producing meanings can produce pleasures that integrate individuals into consumer practices that above all profit media industries. This possibility forces those who valorize resistance to emphasize what sort of resistance, what effects, and what difference does the resistance make?

The Frankfurt School was excellent at tracing the lines of domination within media culture but was less adept at ferreting out moments of resistance and opposition. Yet it always placed its analysis of media and audience within existing relations of production and domination, whereas many studies of the audience and reception often fail to situate the reception of culture in the context of social relations of power and domination. Furthermore, there remain text-centered approaches within cultural studies which engage in theoretically informed readings of texts without considering their production, reception, or anchorage in an institutional organization of culture that takes various specific forms in different countries, or regions, at different times in history—which is to say that textualist approaches often avoid study of the production and political economy of culture and even the historical context of culture.

Although emphasis on the audience and reception was an excellent correction to the one-sidedness of purely textual analysis, in recent years some versions of media/cultural studies have overemphasized reception and textual analysis, while underemphasizing the production of culture and its political economy. While earlier, the Birmingham group regularly focused attention on media institutions and practices, and the relations between media forms and broader social forms and ideologies, this emphasis waned in the ensuing years, to the detriment of much current work in cultural studies. For instance, in his classical programmatic article, "Encoding/Decoding," Stuart Hall began his analysis by using Marx's *Grundrisse* as a model to trace the articulations of "a continuous circuit," encompassing "production-distribution-consumption-production" (1980c, 128ff.). He concretizes this model with focus on how media institutions produce messages, how they circulate, and how audiences use or decode the messages to produce meaning. Hall (1980b, 27) claimed that:

> The abstraction of texts from the social practices which produced them and the institutional sites where they were elaborated was a fetishization....This obscured how a particular ordering of culture came to be produced and sustained: the circumstances and conditions of cultural reproduction which the operations of the 'selective tradition' rendered natural, 'taken for granted.' But the process of ordering (arrangement, regulation) is always the result of concrete sets of practices and relations.

Against the erasure of the system of cultural production, distributions, and reception, Hall called for problematising culture and "making visible" the processes through which certain forms of culture became dominant (ibid).[10] Raymond Williams, one of the formative influences on British cultural studies, called for a "cultural materialism...the analysis of all forms of signification...within the actual means and conditions of their production" (1981, 64–65), focusing attention on the need to situate cultural analysis within its socioeconomic and political relations. Moreover, in a 1983 lecture published in 1985–1986, Richard Johnson provided a model of cultural studies, similar to Hall's earlier model, based on a diagram of the circuits of production, textuality, and reception, parallel to the circuits of capital stressed by Marx, illustrated by a diagram that stressed the importance of production and distribution. Although Johnson emphasized the need for political economy in cultural studies and criticizes the British film journal *Screen* for abandoning this perspective in favor of more idealist and textualist approaches (pp. 63ff.), much work in cultural studies has replicated this neglect. One could indeed argue that much subsequent media/cultural studies have tended to neglect analyses of the circuits of political economy and production in favor of text and audience-based analyses.

Furthermore, there is a danger that media/cultural studies in various parts of the world might lose the critical and political edge of earlier forms of British cultural studies. Cultural studies could easily degenerate into a sort of eclectic populism of the sort evident in the Popular Culture Association which is often celebratory and uncritical of the textual artifacts that it uses. Neglecting political economy, celebrating the audience and the pleasures of the popular, overlooking social class and ideology, and failing to analyze or criticize the politics of cultural texts will make media/cultural studies merely another academic subdivision, harmless and ultimately of benefit primarily to the culture industry itself. Avoiding such a conservative development of cultural studies, I submit, requires a multiperspectivist approach that pays attention to the production of culture, to the texts themselves, and to their reception by the audience within the context of existing social relations of domination and contestation. This requires a variety of disciplinary and critical perspectives and linking cultural studies, ultimately, to critical social theory and radical democratic politics.

■ Toward a Media/Cultural Studies Approach That Is Critical, Multicultural, and Multiperspectival

A critical media/cultural studies approach reads, interprets, and critiques its artifacts in the context of the social relations of production, distribution, consumption, and use out of which they emerge. The dialectic of text and context requires a critical social theory that articulates the interconnections and intersections between the economic, political, social, and cultural dimensions of media culture, thus requiring multiple or trans-disciplinary optics. Textual analysis in turn should utilize a multiplicity of perspectives and critical methods, while audience reception studies should delineate the wide range of subject positions, or perspectives, through which audiences appropriate culture and the key representations that construct the social world. This requires an insurgent multicultural approach that sees the importance of analyzing the dimensions of class, race and ethnicity, and gender and sexual preference, within the politics of representation of texts of media culture and their interconnectedness, while studying their impact on how audiences read, interpret, and use media culture, and in some cases produce alternative cultures.

A critical media/cultural studies attacks sexism, racism, or bias against specific social groups (i.e., gays, intellectuals, youth or seniors, and so on), and criticizes texts that promote any kind of discrimination or oppression. A media/cultural studies that is critical and multicultural provides comprehensive approaches to culture that can be applied to a wide variety of artifacts from pornography to Madonna, from MTV to TV news, or to specific events like the 2001 terrorist attacks on the United States and the U.S. response (Kellner, 2003b) to events like the Columbine High School shootings or Virginia Tech massacre (Kellner, 2008). Its comprehensive perspectives encompass political economy, textual analysis, and audience research and provide critical and political perspectives that enable individuals to dissect the meanings, messages, and effects of dominant cultural forms.

Cultural studies is part of a critical media pedagogy that enables individuals to resist media manipulation and to increase their freedom and individuality. It teaches individuals how to critically read, interpret, and decode media representations and makes readers more critical and informed consumers and producers of their culture.[11] It can empower people to gain sovereignty over their culture and to be able to struggle for alternative cultures and political change, and thus is committed to radical democracy. A media/

cultural studies is thus not just another academic fad but can be part of a struggle for a better society and a better life.

Notes

1. I should make it clear that I am presenting my own construction of a field that is conceived very differently by other individuals in other countries, times, and with different theoretical and political histories. The traditions and literatures I cite will be among those that I have found most useful and influential over the years, and citations to my own texts will signal the theoretical and substantive work that have helped shape my own interventions and views of the field of media and cultural studies.

2. John Fiske (1989b: 72) argues that a cultural studies analysis basically focuses on the meanings encoded in a cultural text such as a Madonna video and the ways that audiences decode and use the text; I am arguing for a more complex model that involves analysis of political economy, politics of an era, technology, and other constituents, such that an analysis of Madonna would need to be contextualized in terms of the Reagan era, the rise of MTV and music video, complex appropriations and packaging of feminism in the era, and other factors (see Kellner, 1995).

3. On the Frankfurt School theory of the culture industry, see Horkheimer and Adorno, 1972 and the discussion of the Frankfurt School approach in Kellner, 1989. For histories of overviews of the Frankfurt School, see Jay, 1973 and Wiggershaus, 1994, and for recent defenses of the Frankfurt School approach to analyzing contemporary media culture, see Gunster 2006 and Steinert 2003.

4. This model was adumbrated in Hall, 1980b and Johnson, 1986/1987 and guided much of the early Birmingham work. Around the mid-1980s, however, the Birmingham group began to increasingly neglect the production and political economy of culture (some believe that this was always a problem with their work) and much of their studies became more academic, cut off from political struggle. I am thus trying to recapture the spirit of the early Birmingham project, reconstructed for our contemporary moment. For a fuller development of my conception of cultural studies, see Kellner 1992, 1995, 2003b, and Durham and Kellner, 2006. On the "missed articulation" between the Frankfurt School and British cultural studies, see Kellner, 1997.

5. The term *political economy* calls attention to the fact that the production and distribution of culture take place within a specific economic system, constituted by relations between the state and economy. For instance, in the United States a capitalist economy dictates that cultural production is governed by laws of the market, but the democratic imperatives of the system mean that there is some regulation of culture by the state. There are often tensions within a given society concerning how many activities should be governed by the imperatives of the market, or economics, alone and how much state regulation or intervention is desirable, to assure a wider diversity of broadcast programming, for instance, or the prohibition of phenomena agreed to be harmful, such as cigarette advertising or pornography (see Kellner, 1990).

6. Cultural studies that have focused on audience reception include Brunsdon and Morley, 1978; Radway, 1983; Ang, 1985, 1996; Morley, 1986; Pribam, 1988; Fiske, 1989a, 1989b; Jenkins, 1992; Lewis, 1992; Bobo, 1999. Some recent audience studies have focused on fans and fandom, which have elicited new energies and ideas for reception studies; see Gray, Sandvoss, and Harrington, 2007.

7. See de Certeau, 1984 and Jenkins, 1992 for more examples of audiences constructing meaning and engaging in practices in critical and subversive ways.

8. Gerbner (1992) noted the acceleration of violence in the initial *Rambo, Die Hard,* and *Young Gun* sequels, a tendency continuing to the present as the 2007 *Rambo* contained more violent episodes than any previous entry in the franchise.

9. For a wide range of studies of contemporary subcultures from different perspectives, see Muggleton, 2003 and Dolby and Rizvi, 2007.

10. Yet in another article from the same period Hall, 1987, rejected the political economy paradigm as reductionist and abstract (46–47). But note that he is rejecting the most economistic base/superstructure "logic of capital" model and not the importance of political economy per se ("This approach, too, has insights which are well worth following through"). Yet from the late 1970s through the present, the dimension of political economy has receded in importance throughout the field of cultural studies, and some have been arguing for reinserting its importance in a reconstructed approach that overcomes the reductionism of some versions of Marxism and political economy; see McGuigan, 1992; Kellner, 1995; and Grossberg, 1997.

11. For more on critical media literacy see Kellner, 1998; Kellner and Share, 2007; and Kahn and Kellner, 2007.

References

Ang, Ien (1985) *Watching Dallas: Soap Opera and the Melodramatic Imagination.* New York: Methuen.

———— (1996) *Living Room Wars. Rethinking Media Audiences for a Postmodern World.* London and New York: Routledge.

Bagdikian, Ben (2004) *The New Media Monopoly.* Boston: Beacon Press.

Barker, Chris (2008; Third Edition) *Cultural Studies. Theory & Practice.* Los Angeles, London: Sage Publication.

Benjamin, Walter (1969) *Illuminations.* New York: Schocken.

Best, Steven and Douglas Kellner (2001) *The Postmodern Adventure. Science, Technology, and Cultural Studies at the Third Millennium,* co-authored with Steven Best. New York and London: Guilford and Routledge.

Bobo, Jacqueline (1988) *"The Color Purple.* Black Women as Cultural Readers," in Pribam, 1988. *Female Spectators: Looking at Film and Television,* edited by E. Dierdre Pribam. London: Verso.

Bobo, Jacqueline and Brantlinger, Patrick (1990) *Crusoe's Footprints. Cultural Studies in Britain and America.* New York and London: Routledge.

Brunsdon, Charlotte and David Morley (1978) *Everyday Television: "Nationwide."* London: British Film Institute.

Centre for Contemporary Cultural Studies (1980) *On Ideology.* London: Hutchinson.

Certeau, Michel de (1984) *The Practice of Everyday Life.* Berkeley: University of California Press.

Croteau, David and William Hoynes (2001) *The Business of Media: Corporate Media and the Public Interest.* Thousand Oaks, CA: Pine Forge.

Dolby, Nadine and Fazal Rizvi (2007) editors, *Youth Moves.* New York: Taylor & Francis.

Durham, Meenakshi Gigi and Douglas Kellner, editors (2006, second edition) *Media and Cultural Studies: KeyWorks.* Malden, Mass. and Oxford, England: Blackwell.

Fiske, John (1989a) *Reading the Popular.* Boston: Unwin Hyman.

Fiske, John (1989b) *Understanding Popular Culture.* Boston: Unwin Hyman.

Fiske, John (1993) *Power Play. Power Works.* London: Verso.

Gerbner, George (1992) "Persian Gulf War: The Movie," in Mowlana, H., Gerbner, G., and Schiller, H. *Triumph of the Image: The Media's War In the Persian Gulf.* Boulder, CO: Westview.

Gramsci, A. (1971). *Selections from the Prison Notebooks.* New York: International.

Gray, J., Sandvoss, C., and Harrington, C.L. (Eds.). (2007). *Fandom: Identities and Communities in a Mediated World.* New York: NYU Press.

Grossberg, Lawrence (1997) *Bringing It All Back Home. Essays on Cultural Studies.* Durham: Duke University Press.

Grossberg, Lawrence, Nelson, Cary and Paula Treichler (1992) *Cultural Studies.* New York: Routledge.

Gunster, Shane (2004) *Capitalizing on Culture. Critical Theory for Cultural Studies.* Toronto: University of Toronto Press.

Hall, Gary and Clare Birchall (2006) *New Cultural Studies.* Edinburgh, U.K.: Edinburgh University Press.

Hall, Stuart et al. (1980) *Culture, Media, Language.* London: Hutchinson.

Hall, Stuart (1980a) "Cultural Studies and the Centre: Some Problematics and Problems," in Hall et al., 1980, 15–47.

Hall, Stuart (1980b) "Encoding/Decoding," in Hall et al., 1980, 128–138.

Hall, Stuart (1981) 'Notes on Deconstructing the Popular' In *People's History and Socialist Theory,* London: Routledge.

Hall, Stuart (1987) "On Postmodernism and Articulation: An Interview," *Journal of Communication Inquiry* 10/2, 45–60.

Hammer, Rhonda and Douglas Kellner (2006) "Review of John Hartley, *A Short History of Cultural Studies. Communication and Critical/Cultural Studies,* Vol. 2, Nr. 1 (March 2005): 77–82.

Harris, David (1992) *From Class Struggle to the Politics of Pleasure. The Effects of Gramscism on Cultural Studies.* London: Routledge.

Hartley, John (2003). *A Short History of Cultural Studies.* London and Thousand Oaks: Sage.

Horkheimer, M., and T. Adorno (2002). *The Dialectic of Enlightenment.* Stanford, CA: Stanford University Press.

Hebdige, Dick (1979) *Subculture. The Meaning of Style.* London: Methuen.

Jameson, Fredric (1979) "Reification and Utopia in Mass Culture," *Social Text:* 1: 130–148.

Jameson, Fredric (1981) *The Political Unconscious.* Ithaca: Cornell University Press.

Jameson, Fredric (1991) *Postmodernism, or the Cultural Logic of Late Capitalism.* Durham, N.C.: Duke University Press.

Jay, Martin (1973) *The Dialectical Imagination.* Boston: Little, Brown and Company.

Jeffords, S. (1993). *Hard Bodies: Hollywood Masculinity in the Reagan Era.* New Brunswick, NJ: Rutgers University Press.

Jenkins, Henry (1992) *Textual Poachers.* New York: Routledge.

——— (2006). *Convergence Culture: Where Old and New Media Collide.* New York: New York University Press.

Johnson, Richard (1986/87) "What is Cultural Studies Anyway?" *Social Text* 16: 38–80.

Kahn, Richard and Douglas Kellner (2006) "Reconstructing Technoliteracy: A Multiple Literacies Approach," in *Defining Technological Literacy,* edited by John R. Dakers. New York and England: Palgrave Macmillan, pp. 253–274.

Kellner, Douglas (1978) "Ideology, Marxism, and Advanced Capitalism," *Socialist Review* 42 (Nov–Dec), 37–65.

Kellner, Douglas (1979) "TV, Ideology, and Emancipatory Popular Culture," *Socialist Review* 45 (May–June), 13–53.

Kellner, Douglas (1989) *Critical Theory, Marxism, and Modernity.* Cambridge, UK and Baltimore, Md.: Polity Press and Johns Hopkins University Press.

Kellner, Douglas (1990). *Television and the Crisis of Democracy.* Boulder, Col.: Westview.

Kellner, Douglas (1992) *The Persian Gulf TV War.* Boulder, Col: Westview.

Kellner, Douglas (1995) *Media Culture. Cultural Studies, Identity, and Politics Between the Modern and the Postmodern.* London and New York: Routledge.

Kellner, Douglas (1997) "Critical Theory and British Cultural Studies: The Missed Articulation," in *Cultural Methodologies,* edited by Jim McGuigan. London: Sage: 12–41.

Kellner, Douglas (1998) "Multiple Literacies and Critical Pedagogy in a Multicultural Society." *Educational Theory,* Vol. 48, Nr. 1: 103–122.

Kellner, Douglas (2001) *Grand Theft 2000.* Lanham, Md.: Rowman and Littlefield.

Kellner, Douglas 2003a) *Media Spectacle.* London and New York: Routledge.

Kellner, Douglas (2003b) *From 9/11 to Terror War: Dangers of the Bush Legacy.* Lanham, Md.: Rowman and Littlefield.

Kellner, Douglas (2005) *Media Spectacle and the Crisis of Democracy.* Boulder, Col.: Paradigm Press.

Kellner, Douglas (2008) *Guys and Guns Amok: Domestic Terrorism and School Shootings from the Oklahoma City Bombings to the Virginia Tech Massacre.* Boulder, Col.: Paradigm Press.

Kellner, Douglas (forthcoming) *Cinema Wars: Hollywood Film and Politics in the Bush/Cheney Era.* Malden, Mass.: Basil Blackwell.

Kellner, Douglas and Michael Ryan (1988) *Camera Politica: The Politics and Ideology of Contemporary Hollywood Film.* Bloomington, Ind: Indiana University Press.

Kellner, Douglas and Jeff Share (2007) "Critical Media Literacy, Democracy, and the Reconstruction of Education," *Media Literacy. A Reader,* edited by Donald Macedo and Shirley R. Steinberg. New York: Peter Lang: 3–23.

Lazarsfeld, Paul (1941) "Administrative and Critical Comunications Research," *Studies in Philosophy and Social Science,* Vol. IX, No. 1: 2–16.

Lowenthal, Leo (1949) (with Norbert Guttermann) *Prophets of Deceit.* New York: Harper.

Lowenthal, Leo (1957) *Literature and the Image of Man.* Boston: Beacon Press.

Lowenthal, Leo (1961) *Literature, Popular Culture and Society.* Englewood Cliffs, New Jersey: Prentice-Hall.

Lewis, Lisa A. (1992) *Adoring Audience. Fan Culture and Popular Media.* New York: Routledge.

McChesney, Robert (2000) *Rich Media, Poor Democracy: Communications Politics in Dubious Times.* New York: New Press.

McChesney, Robert (2007) *Communication Revolution. Critical Junctures and the Future of Media.* New York: The New Press.

McGuigan, Jim (1992) *Cultural Populism.* London and New York: Routledge.

McLaren, Peter (1997) "Unthinking Whiteness, Rethinking Democracy: Or Farewell to the Blonde Beast." *Educational Foundations,* vol. 11, no. 2, pp. 5–39.

McLuhan, M. (1964). *Understanding media: The extensions of man.* Essex, UK: Signet.

Morley, David (1986) *Family Television.* London: Comedia.

Muggleton, David (2003) (ed), *The Post-subcultures Reader,* London: Berg: 299–314.

Pribam, E. Dierdre (1988) (ed) *Female Spectators: Looking at Film and Television.* London: Verso.

Radway, Janice (1983) *Reading the Romance.* Chapel Hill: University of North Carolina Press.

Rojek, Chris. (2009). "Representation and Ideology." In R. Hammer and D. Kellner, *Media/Cultural Studies: Critical Approaches.* Cambridge: Cambridge University Press.

Rojek, C. (2007). *Cultural Studies.* Cambridge, UK: Polity Press.

Staiger, Janet (1992) "Film, Reception, and Cultural Studies," *Centennial Review,* Vol. XXVI, No. 1 (Winter): 89–104.

Steinert, Heinz (2003) *Culture Industry.* Cambridge, UK: Polity Press.

Thompson, E.P. (1963) *The Making of the English Working Class.* New York, NY: Penguin.

Wiggershaus, Rolf (1994), *The Frankfurt School.* Cambridge, UK: Polity Press.

Williams, Raymond (1981) *Communications.* London: Penguin.

Zizek, S. (2005). *The metastases of enjoyment: Six essays on women and causality.* London: Verso.

2

■ Cultural Studies

What's in a Name (One More Time)[1]

Lawrence Grossberg

Defining cultural studies is a risky business. Lots of people are suddenly claiming to do cultural studies while others, nervous about its rather sudden success, are attacking it. Yet the fact is that few people working in cultural studies would agree on a definition and that many who claim to "do" cultural studies might not recognize themselves in such a definition. This is often taken as evidence of the need to avoid offering one. It is sometimes assumed that such definitions, by attempting to police the boundaries, contradict the politics of cultural studies. In the end, the refusal to define it becomes the key to understanding what it is.[2]

But when the range of material being described as cultural studies is expanding exponentially, I believe that cultural studies can be and needs to be defined or delineated, that it is not so broad as to encompass any critical approach to culture nor so narrow as to be identified with a specific paradigm or tradition. This is not a matter of a proprietary definition or of "the proper" form of cultural studies but of holding on to the specificity of particular intellectual trajectories. In the past decade, cultural studies has appeared in a wide range of disciplines. And those disciplines of anthropology, sociology, history, literary criticism, women's studies, Black and ethnic studies, etc., in addition to communication and education, have put something into it, changing its shape and offering new versions of cultural studies. At the same time, cultural studies has appeared in a wide variety of national and ethnic contexts which have also brought different intellectual histories to the task of shaping their own visions of cultural studies. But cultural studies is not equivalent to critical or cultural theory.[3]

There is a wide variety of tropes that currently organize different discourses of culture: aesthetic discourses of discrimination; anthropological discourses of ritual and ways of life; social-psychological discourses of communication; and political discourses of the public sphere. There are also a range of problematics which intersect these tropes: community; ideology; hegemony; identity and subjectivity; the body; and formations of power. But this situation is not so different from other disciplines which similarly constitute themselves in relation to a particular object (e.g., culture) and then struggle to constitute that object.[4]

This paper is, then, an intervention attempting to carve out a limited space for and of cultural studies. Despite my descriptive voice, my intentions are unabashedly prescriptive. Let me begin then by saying something about my understanding of and relation to cultural studies. I have sometimes been described as practicing or advocating British cultural studies in the U.S. I prefer to think of myself as someone partly trained in British cultural studies, attempting to develop a cultural studies appropriate to *fin-de-siècle* America.[5] This is in fact the only way I know of to practice cultural studies: to constantly redefine it in response to changing geographical and historical, political, institutional and intellectual conditions, to constantly make a home for it within a specific discipline even as it challenges the legitimacy of the existing disciplinization of intellectual work. I think of cultural studies as a particular way of contextualizing and politicizing intellectual practices. But cultural studies is not an intellectual panacea nor even a new paradigm attempting to displace all competitors. It is not the only important body of political-intellectual work nor the only approach committed to interdisciplinarity, intervention, etc. It is a particular commitment to a particular style of intellectual work and to its importance both inside and outside of the academy. Unfortunately, cultural studies is too often being used as merely an excuse for disciplines to take on new, usually popular, cultural objects. Too many people in traditional disciplines seem to think that when they start writing about television, or rock music, etc., they are doing cultural studies. Cultural studies is not defined by a particular sort of text; in that sense, you can do cultural studies of almost anything. Nor can it be defined by a particular set of methods although cultural studies does give any method its own particular inflection. I am convinced that if cultural studies is to develop responsibly, we need to find ways to make our methods more rigorous. Without this, cultural studies is too often condemned to repeating the same findings over and over.

■ I.

Any discussion of cultural studies has to locate cultural studies in a variety of contexts in order to describe the forms of its success, the vectors of its dispersion and globalization, and the practices of its transformation, adaptation and institutionalization. Yet I do believe that British cultural studies is a key point of identification even if at the same time, I also believe it is a largely imaginary construction which often overlooks the enormous diversity and contestation within the series of intellectual choices that have given it some shape.[6] However, while I might argue that the link between cultural studies (as a somewhat dispersed intellectual discourse) and British cultural studies should not be ignored, it also cannot be essentialized as if it were the only way into the discourse, the only genealogy, of cultural studies. But the success of various figures and positions of British cultural studies as they followed the vectors of global cultural distribution certainly provided one of the conditions for the emergence of cultural studies as a global field of intellectual practice. Sometimes it enabled scholars and scholarly traditions to constitute and name themselves; other times, it helped to place themselves in relation to other bodies of critical work.

There are lots of conditions—economic, socio-generational, institutional and cultural—that have contributed to the success of, and the excitement generated around, cultural studies. One could obviously write any number of different "cultural studies" of cultural studies itself, constructing them from a number of different narratives: the empowerment of the margins; the emergence of a hegemonic conservatism; the mediatization of culture and the globalization of capital; the theoretical excesses of "critical theory" (as the term was used in the U.S.); the failures of traditional "left" political institutions and movements; the crisis of the humanities (and the social sciences)—a partly self-produced crisis, not only of value but also of representation; and the changing nature of intellectual culture itself (e.g., in terms of its increasing mobility, commodification, professionalization and alienation), the increasing "hybridization" (or postmodernization) not only of cultural practices but of populations and identities as well. None of these narratives offers a singular vision of a homogeneous, progressively developing field. Any story of cultural studies will be as spatially and temporally fragmented as contemporary culture itself.

But any account of the success of cultural studies will also have to reflect on the specificity of cultural studies as an intellectual practice in and for the contemporary context. And, as I shall argue, it is precisely this articulation, this link between context and theory, that somehow defines the possibilities of cultural studies. For if cultural studies is nothing more than the latest name for any attempt to understand the relations of culture and power, then its success is probably little more than the result of its rapid commodification. Certainly cultural studies is, in the first instance, concerned with cultural practices, but only in the first instance, as its entrance into the context of the unequal relations of force and power. But the context itself cannot be separated from those cultural practices and the relations of power, because they articulate the unity and specificity of the context as a lived environment. As a result, cultural studies does not reduce culture to power, nor does it claim that particular relations of power are somehow inherent in, or intrinsic to, specific cultural texts, practices, or relations; rather, it claims that relationship, however contingent and historical it may be, is its focus. It treats culture, then, as more than either a text or a commodity. Moreover, it tends to look at culture itself as the site of the production and struggle over power, where power is understood, not necessarily in the form of domination, but always as an unequal relation of forces in the interests of particular fractions of the population.

One can understand this, perhaps, by looking at the difference between the emergence of cultural studies in Britain and of a cultural theory of communication in the U.S., both of which were intimately bound up with the particular historical and biographical conditions of its producers. One of the possible sources of an "American cultural studies" is the work of the Chicago School of Social Thought.[7] To oversimplify, the Chicago School emerged around the turn of the twentieth century, during a period of rapid modernization (connecting the various parts of the country together and the country with the world), urbanization and immigration; in a sense, it confronted the challenge of a kind of "multiculturalism." The central experience of the Chicago School, most literally embodied in John Dewey, was the move from (oppressive) New England towns to Chicago, where, ironically, they then mourned the disappearance of the community in America. The problem was to find a way to reconstitute community in the nation in the form of the Great Community. The solution depended upon identifying culture with community and communication; the three terms were taken as equivalent processes. The solution was to foster and expand a common culture through communication. But this depended upon the assumption that power, that which prevented the process from working, was an extrinsic factor in the relationship, which had to and could be eliminated. Culture was entirely processual and existed somehow independently of power.

The British context of cultural studies was very different.[8] The question was not the historical loss of community for, as Raymond Williams would write later in his life, "There is more real community in the modern village that at any period in the remembered past."[9] The context immediately after the Second World War did pose a significant social challenge, often understood as the impending threat of Americanization (which was not quite a crisis of multiculturalism—that would take another two decades to appear as such). But the terms within which the question of culture was posed were less those of a perceived social crisis than of a personal experience, immediate and deeply felt, of a distance between community and culture. That distance was the result of spatial and social mobility, as, for example, Raymond Williams and Richard Hoggart (and others, e.g., Doreen Massey) moved from, respectively, a Welsh farming village and working class needs, to Oxbridge. At Oxbridge, they found that the intellectual world denied not merely the quality but the very existence of a culture in the communities from which they had come. Williams described his own experience of this distance as "that border country so many of us have been living in: between custom and education, between work and ideas, between love of place and an experience of change,"[10] and he adds a bit further on, "between fellow-feeling and intelligence, between class and knowledge." The distance between culture as community (labor, family, sentiment, etc.) and culture as knowledge defined the problem of living between cultures and the need for a lived or knowable community, the need to find "a position, convincingly experienced, from which community can begin to be known."[11] Culture then defined a problem of place and belonging or participation; it was the mediation between social position and experienced identity. Or to put it in different terms, that distance was measured in the movement within the class structures of England; hence, culture was not equated to community and communication, and it was not idealized.[12] At least power was not seen as something external, eliminatable, a mere interruption of some idealized image of cultural processes. Instead, they began with an assumed distance between community and culture, with the notion that power always fractures culture. Hence, culture was always more than just a process, for it involved struggles between competing sets of practices and relations, and that sense of struggle meant that it was inevitably tied up with relations of power. This was, of course, partly the result of attempting to operate in the space between aesthetic and "vulgar marxist" responses to culture and cultural change. Increasingly, this placed British cultural studies "on the terrain" of Marxism itself, even if it did not define cultural studies as Marxist.[13]

While locating cultural studies in its biographical or, perhaps more accurately, generational structures of feeling, I do not mean to treat such experiences as some explanatory agent or origin of the different forms of cultural theory that emerged in these different times and places. I am not attempting to actually constitute cultural studies by appealing to the experiences of these founding figures, nor am I attempting to make such experiences paradigmatic. It is not the experiences per se that interest me, but the ways they were articulated and effective.

Obviously, one might question the relevance of such conceptions of culture *and* cultural studies to the present context of work in cultural studies. Or to put it another way, how can the generations born after the Second World War develop a cultural studies appropriate to contemporary America, or to the contemporary global context of culture, by beginning with British cultural studies? In a sense, I want to admit that one cannot, even if also acknowledging that British cultural studies provided me with the best starting point I could find, and even if only as a foil against which to define an alternative vision. Whether this is still true remains to be seen.

Yet it is, in a sense, precisely the link between a culturally defined interpretation of historical events as an experience of spatial and cultural mobility or dislocation and the politics of marginality that continues to direct much of the current work in cultural studies, including the proliferation of cultural studies into postcolonial and diaspora studies: the result is that cultural studies is still often identified with the speaking position of the marginal. Many cultural theories, including cultural studies, have privileged the position of the outside, the marginal, the emigre; they have often argued that such a position enables a uniquely insightful understanding not available to the supposed insider as one who belongs only in this one place. But, as Tony Bennett has argued, this "logic of charismatic closure" too easily reduces knowledge to biography and fetishizes marginality. Such celebrations of the marginal, however, are unnecessary, for the same effect can be achieved through another path. At the heart of contemporary critical theory is the recognition that experience itself is a product of power and that, therefore, that which is the most obvious, the most unquestionable, is often the most saturated by relations of power. The value of the increasingly global milieu of the discourses of cultural studies (and their proliferation along multiple axes) is precisely the possibility of challenging each other's most cherished, and most obvious, assumptions.

While the notion of culture is central to any attempt to delineate the field of cultural studies, it has always been an ambiguous concept in British cultural studies.[14] Raymond Williams traces this ambiguity back to the origins of modern European thought where culture served both as description of the changes resulting from modernization and a normative term by which those changes could be judged. And there is a second dimension of ambiguity that Williams identifies in the notion of culture: it is, on the one hand, a set of specialized practices (emphasized no doubt because of the literary roots of British cultural studies, roots which affirmed the fact that culture matters) and on the other, a whole way of life.

But the terms of this ambiguity—the very assumptions about the meaning of culture—provide the point from which forms of cultural studies more appropriate to the contemporary context may be articulated, even as the terms of this ambiguity are challenged by cultural studies' move into an increasingly global and transdisciplinary context. One can identify at least four different trajectories challenging the dominant conceptions of culture. First, a number of critiques have challenged, not only notions of national cultures and/or whole ways of life but also the possibility of constructing a singular and limited space of a culture. Such notions of culture, it is argued, are the result of the articulation of culture to the colonizing and imperialistic structures of modern Europe. Second, critics have challenged not only nostalgic conceptions of community but also the romantic-aesthetic-ethical conception of culture and criticism. Such notions of culture, it is argued, are the result of the articulation of culture to the disciplinizing and governmental strategies of modern European nation states. Third, various writers have challenged, not only the reduction of culture to the domain of meaning and representation but also, more importantly, the invention and deployment of culture as: (1) the necessary site of differences; (2) the necessary supplement of human existence (by which we compensate for a lack of biological instincts) which transforms the chaos of reality into the ordered sense of a human reality; (3) the necessary mediation by which culture is situated between the person and reality as the realm of experience and knowledge (and through which all reference to the real can be erased); and (4) the necessary historicality or temporality of human existence, both socially and individually. Such notions of culture, it is argued, are the result of the articulation of culture to the changing forms of intellectual and class power of modern Europe. And finally, scholars have begun to explore the ways in which culture functions in the production of "distinctions," thus undermining our ability to assume not only qualitative distinctions (between high and low) within the domain of culture but also the existence of a self-contained category of cultural—creative, textual, signifying—practices such as literature or art outside of their institutional laws of regulation. Such distinctions, it is argued, are themselves the articulation of, and articulated to, specific structures of difference as relations of empowerment and disempowerment.

Such a series of challenges might at first seem to overwhelm the foundations of cultural studies, but this is exactly how cultural studies works. Because the field of culture is always changing, because in this fractured relationship marked by power, culture is always contested and struggled over. Precisely because of that, as Stuart Hall says, it does matter in any particular context how cultural studies is defined.[15] Or, to use Cornel West's terms, cultural studies matters because it is about how to keep political work alive in an age of shrinking possibilities.[16] Consequently, it is necessary to repeat the fact that cultural studies is always open—not just with regard to disciplines, traditions and genealogies, not just with regard to objects, methods, theories and politics—because culture, power and the relations between them are always changing. Thus, while it is the case that there is no single answer, for all places and all times, to the question, what is cultural studies, it is still necessary to constantly define it because it does matter what it is, and because not everything is cultural studies. The answer can only be given in, simultaneously, political and institutional terms, by questioning the conditions of possibility of cultural studies at any moment. But this does not mean that it is sufficient to describe it as a unity-in-difference; it is a network of political and discursive alliances, a discursive space constituted by certain trajectories which enables certain kinds of analyses and knowledges. And the construction of such a space requires precise and disciplined forms of work.

■ II.

I have yet to offer a description of the specificity of cultural studies. I would propose that cultural studies, at any particular time and place, is constructed by articulating its *practice* into particular *projects* and *formations*. Cultural studies always and only exists in contextually specific theoretical and institutional *formations*. Such formations are always a response to a particular political project based on the available theoretical and historical resources. In that sense, in every particular instance, cultural studies has to be made up as it goes along. Thus, cultural studies always reflects on and situates itself and its claims, limits its field, acknowledges its incompleteness.

If we cannot say much in the abstract about the formations of cultural studies, we can, I believe, say something about its *projects*. Cultural studies is interventionist in the sense that it attempts to use the best intellectual resources available to gain a better understanding of the relations of power (as the state of play or balance in a field of forces) in a particular context, believing that such knowledge will better enable people to change the context and hence, the relations of power. Consequently, its project is always political, always partisan, but its politics are always contextually defined. Moreover, it seeks to understand not only the organizations of power but the possibilities of struggle, resistance and change. It takes contestation for granted, not as a reality in every instance, but as an assumption necessary for the existence of critical work and political opposition. I shall return to these issues in a moment.

While the ways this project is actualized depend on its context, we can further specify the nature of cultural studies by reflecting on its *practice,* since I think it is possible to describe cultural studies as a certain kind of intellectual practice, a certain style of doing intellectual work, a certain way of embodying the belief that what we do can actually matter. It is a way of inhabiting the position of scholar, teacher, and intellectual, a way of politicizing theory and theorizing politics. Of course, cultural studies is not the only such practice; it is not the only form of intellectual work attempting to bring politics and theory together, and many of the features or procedures that define the practice of cultural studies are shared with other forms of critical work. The only exception, the feature that I believe is unique to cultural studies, is what I shall identify as its radical contextualism. Moreover, it is, I believe, only cultural studies that exhibits all of these by attempting to enact a particular relationship between context, knowledge and power. The features that, I want to argue, are constitutive of the practice of cultural studies are that it is: disciplined; radically contextual (with three corollaries—anti-re-ductionist; its objects are discursive alliances; its method is articulation); theoretical; political; interdisciplinary; and self-reflective (about its theoretical, political, cultural and institutional site).[17]

i.

First, just as cultural studies is neither monolithic nor pluralistic, so too it is neither authoritarian nor relativist, neither universalist nor particularist. While recognizing that knowledge and power are always inseparable, it refuses to give up either the search for an "objective truth" (always with a small "o" and a small "t") or the claim of the authority of knowledge. Or perhaps more accurately, cultural studies seeks new forms and articulations of authority, built on the effectivities of knowledge (i.e., the possibilities opened up by particular knowledges) rather than the status of the producer.[18] It attempts to produce the best possible knowledge using the most sophisticated intellectual tools. To say that cultural studies is disciplined is to recognize that it does not deny the need for rigorous education, intellectual argument and analysis, and empirical research (built on rigorous methods); it does not deny the existence of traditions that need to be read and contemplated (even if it does refuse to construct them as a canon). Consider the following passage from Stuart Hall:[19]

> Cultural studies' message is a message for academics and intellectuals but, fortunately, for many other people as well. In that sense I have tried to hold together in my own intellectual life, on the one hand the conviction and passion and the devotion to *objective* interpretation, to analysis, to *rigorous* analysis and understanding, to the passion to find out, and to the production of knowledge that we did not know before. But, on the other hand, I am convinced that no intellectual worth his or her salt and no university that wants to hold up its head in the face of the 21st century, can afford to turn dispassionate eyes away from the problem… [to] understand what keeps making the lives we live and the societies we live in, profoundly and deeply antihumane. (Emphasis added)

There is, in this statement, a very real commitment to knowledge, to rigor, and to intellectual discipline, to knowing more than "the other side" as Gramsci put it. Of course, drawing on Foucault, Hall's rhetoric of needing to hold these two poles together appears to be the result of the institutional discourses of the contemporary academy which have produced the apparent rill between always articulated structures of power and knowledge. Cultural studies then can be described as a practice which attempts to maintain the discipline of authority in the face of relativism. Cultural studies, while it has no pretensions to totality or universality, does seek to give a better understanding of where "we" are so "we" can get somewhere else, hopefully somewhere better, leaving open the question of what is better and how one decides, as well as the question of who "we" are.

ii.

Second, and most importantly, the practice of cultural studies is radically contextual-ist, and cultural studies might be described as a discipline of contextuality. Let me begin to explain and explore this by quoting from what is perhaps the classic work of British cultural studies: *Policing the Crisis,* a collective work which first predicted the rise of a new conservative hegemony, Thatcherism. However, *Policing the Crisis* starts off by inves-tigating a specific empirical phenomenon in the 1970s: the appearance of an apparently new crime in England called mugging, and its discovery, not only by the British press but by various state agencies as well. Not surprisingly, according to the press, mugging was a "black on white" crime. *Policing the Crisis* is largely an account of the social construc-tion of this reality through an analysis of the practices of news production and their relations to institutions and structures of social control. This is how the authors described the object of their study—mugging.[20]

> There are, we argue, clear historical forces at work in this period, shaping so to speak, from the outside, the immediate transactions on the ground between "muggers," potential muggers, their victims, and their apprehenders. In many comparable studies, these larger and wider forces are merely noted and cited; their direct and indirect bearing on the phenomenon analyzed is, however, left vague and abstract part of "the background." In our case, we believe that these so-called "background issues" are, indeed, exactly the critical forces which produce "mugging" in the specific form in which it appears.

That is, they argued that the very notion of mugging, its existence as a material and cultural form, could not be defined independently of its existence within the context. An event or practice (even a text) does not exist apart from the forces of the context that constitute it as what it is. Obviously, context is not merely background but the very conditions of possibility of something. It cannot be relegated to a series of footnotes or to an after-thought, to the first or last chapter. It is precisely what one is trying to analyze and it is the most difficult thing to construct. It is both the beginning and the end of cultural studies although the two are not the same point.

The context of a particular research is not empirically given beforehand; it has to be defined by the project, by the political question that is at stake. The context can be as narrow as a neighborhood at a particular moment, or an urban region, or perhaps even some local high school that is having race problems, or it can be as broad as global capi-talism after the cold war. To put it succinctly, for cultural studies, context is everything and everything is contextual.

This contextualism affects every dimension of cultural studies. It affects the most fundamental concepts that define the discourse of cultural studies, which now cannot be defined outside the particular context or field of study and struggle: concepts of cul-ture, cultural text and cultural practice; concepts of power and the dimensions along which it is structured—race, gender, sex, class, ethnicity, generation, etc.; and even the form of the relationship between culture and power. The very relationships between culture and society are contextually specific—the product of power—and hence, they cannot be assumed to transcend particular contexts. Consequently, the commonly held belief that cultural studies is necessarily a theory of ideology, of representation, identity and subjectivity, or of communication (production-text-consumption) is mistaken.[21] While it is true that cultural studies, along with other critical discourses, has struggled to put these questions onto the agenda, it has never asserted that those are the only effects that cultural practices can have or that they are always the relevant questions to be asked. There is no guarantee that, in a particular context, culture works as ideology. Too often, the task of cultural studies is assumed beforehand, independently of the context. To put it another way, the very questions cultural studies asks—its problematics— potentially change in every study. The problematic of one cultural studies investigation is not the same as that of another.

A number of consequences or corollaries follow from this radical contextualism. First, cultural studies is strongly anti-reductionist at all levels. It views cultural practices as the site of the intersection of many possible effects. It does not start by defining culture or its effects or by assuming ahead of time the relevant dimensions within which to describe particular practices. Instead, they are places where different things can and do happen, where different possibilities intersect.[22] Furthermore, cultural studies refuses to reduce reality to culture or to any single dimension or domain of existence: biology, economics, state politics, social and sexual relations, culture—all are a part of human reality. While cultural studies might be seen as a version of "the social construction of reality,"[23] it does not believe reality is entirely constructed by our social and cultural practices, for there are material realities that are being struggled over in various ways, that are being articulated, and that have real, measurable effects. Cultural studies believes that all the different forms of that reality, all of the different kinds of practices that human beings are shaped by, have to be recognized. They cannot be reduced to one another. Hence, cultural studies does not believe that culture can be explained in purely cultural terms, nor does it believe that everything is culture; rather, it believes that culture can only be understood in terms of its relations to everything that is not culture. In this sense, cultural studies is always materialist.

Similarly, it sees power as complex and contradictory, as organized in complex ways, along multiple axes and dimensions which cannot be reduced to one another. One cannot explain gender or sexual relationships through economic and class relationships nor can one explain economic and class relationships through gender and sexual relationships. If gender and sexual relationships are changed, there is no guarantee that class relationships will change (in a similar or comparable way), and if class relationships change, there is no guarantee that gender and sexual relationships will change (in a similar or comparable way). Power is, unfortunately, more complex than we might like. But to be optimistic, power is never able to totalize itself. There are always fissures and fault lines that may become the active sites of change. Power never quite accomplishes everything it might like to everywhere, and there is always the possibility of changing the structures and organization of power. Moreover, while power operates in institutions and in the state, it also operates where people live their lives, in what is sometimes called everyday life, and in the spaces where these fields intersect. Cultural studies is always interested in how power infiltrates, contaminates, limits and empowers the possibilities that people have to live their lives in dignified and secure ways. For if one wants to change the relations of power, if one wants to move people, even a little bit, you must begin from where people are, from where and how they actually live their lives.

A second corollary of cultural studies' radical contextualism involves the definition of its object. Cultural studies is concerned with the role of cultural practices in the construction of the contexts of human life as milieus of power. In other words, it is concerned with how relations of force (effectivity) are organized into relations of power by the discursive practices that constitute the lived world as human. It starts with the assumption that particular cultural or discursive practices do not exist effectively (i.e., as effective) outside of relations, that they are themselves contextual. Thus, rather than practices, cultural studies always constitutes its object as an alliance, a set of relations among practices (not all of which need be textual, symbolic, signifying nor even discursive). Such alliances cannot be identified with texts and certainly not with any particular genre of texts. More accurately, its object is the relations between cultural alliances and contexts, or contexts within contexts, always and already articulated to and by relations of power. An alliance is an event, always constituted with and constitutive of a larger context of relationships. For an alliance is always a set of practices dispersed across a delimited social space. Such relations or dispersions are, however, not random; they are defined by and practices are located within particular trajectories of which particular practices (or texts) are only moments (but not examples or synecdoches). Such trajectories, as well as the alliances they produce, are the product of work; it is an event, comparable perhaps to Mauss' total social phenomenon, which, as Frow and Morris describe it, is a point of intersection and negotiation of radically different kinds of determinations, of temporal and spatial, semiotic and material vectors.[24] Cultural studies then reconstitutes its object by mapping the relations or, more accurately, what I will describe shortly as the lines of articulation. That defines, in a sense, the continuing circularity of cultural studies' practice since it can only produce what it is to analyze through the practice of its analysis. The alliance as context is both a beginning and an end of sorts—but not an absolute end since the analysis can and must continue, mapping the relations of and within contexts.

Radical contextualism also shapes the methodological practice of cultural studies as articulation. Articulation is a particular position in what has been, for many years, the major debate within contemporary cultural and political theory. Perhaps more accurately, articulation is a way of strategically avoiding this debate all together. Let me lay out the terms of this argument. On the one hand, essentialism assumes that things are the way they are because they have to be that way. That is, relationships in history, the relationships that constitute history, are guaranteed, inevitable, intrinsic to the related elements. To be a woman is to have certain experiences. To be black means to have come from Africa. A book has its own proper and correct meaning. The real—intrinsic and essential interests of the working class define an inevitable relationship to socialism. The production or origin of something already defines its possibilities—so, for example, something made within a capitalist mode of production is inevitably a commodity and hence, inevitably alienating and fetishized. Or, the ideology of a text produced by capitalists is necessarily capitalist. In essentialist positions, the answers are guaranteed and everything is sewn up in advance. Identities are fixed. Effects are determined before they are even produced because all the important relations in history are necessary, i.e., necessarily the way they are.

On the other hand, anti-essentialism says there are necessarily no relationships. Relations are an illusion; it is their very appearance that is the product of power, and hence, the only response to a relation is to deconstruct it, to get rid of it, to deny it. A text has no meaning and there are no limits to what it can mean. Perhaps it means whatever a reader wants it to mean. Being a woman has no shared meaning; it does not entail any common experience. And hence, for example, it is difficult to know on what grounds one could organize a "women's movement." There are no relationships in history. Not only are origins (such as capitalist modes of production) not determining, they are themselves not real. The text does whatever it does. The working class has no common interests and certainly no special relation to socialism (or the Left).

Both of these theoretical positions can be found everywhere in the discourses of cultural theory and criticism. But cultural studies takes neither of those positions; it operates in a different space, not exactly between them.[25] It locates everything in relations but assumes that such relations, while always real, are never necessary. Power is both produced as, and produces contexts as, the set of "relations of a nonrelation," to echo Foucault. Articulation as a practice is politically strategically anti-essentialist but it is also anti-anti-essentialist. It says, there are relationships in history but they are not necessary. They did not have to be that way, but, given that they are that way, they are real and they have real effects. A text does not have to mean what it seems to mean to 90% of the people who read it. But in fact it does mean that to 90% of the people who read it because the relationship between those words and that meaning has been produced. Those words, that text, have been articulated to that meaning. The working class does not have intrinsic and essential interests which it carries across contexts and over time, but at any moment, it does have interests. Certain interests are articulated to and taken up by the working class. There is nothing essential about the relationship between labor and socialist parties; they certainly did not have to vote Labour or Democrat. It is not intrinsic to being a worker that one thinks the Labour Party or the Democrats represent one's interests—but for the past fifty years or so, that relationship was real and effective. And now we can understand that Reagan and Thatcher did not dupe the working classes into misunderstanding their own interests but broke (disarticulated) the relationship and created (rearticulated) a new one. That is articulation—the making of a relationship out of a nonrelationship or more often, the making of one relationship out of a different one. (This is, by the way, not the same as mutual constitution, as used in both phenomenology and poststructuralism.) It assumes that there are no necessary relations, but relations are real and have real effects.

Consequently, cultural studies does not believe that you can understand the nature of culture and power by finding origins, by looking for some moment that guarantees the effects of culture. It rejects the notion that because a cultural text is produced as a commodity by capitalism you know ahead of time what its politics are. It rejects the notion that because a text is produced by a racist society you can know ahead of time what the effects of that text are. It rejects the notion that people have some authentic original experience that defines the truth against which power is an external mystifying divine force. Power is there for cultural studies from the very beginning. While it is nice to dream of eliminating power and ideology so that we could get back to some "true" experience as it existed before power reconstructed and misinterpreted it, that is not what power does nor how culture works. That's not how ideology operates. The most basic experiences one has, the things one believes most confidently because they are the most obvious, those are precisely what power and ideology have produced. That which one is sure cannot be doubted, that is what one must doubt, because that is what power is most concerned to produce. What one knows is there because one has seen it, is precisely what ideology and culture are making one see. We see black and white. We see male and female. We see that these matter, that they make a difference. That is what we are being made to see. But if we could challenge and change these structures of perception and experience—by understanding the apparatuses of power that have produced these particular binarisms—we would not get back to some original untainted truth; there is no such thing. There is no experience to which we can appeal as some kind of original justification for the political visions that we have. We can only struggle between different articulations of reality to find one that is more humane for more (all) people.

For cultural studies, articulation is a model—not only of the social formations of power but also of its own practice or method.[26] Articulation is the methodological face of a radically contextualist theory. It describes a non-linear expansive practice of drawing lines, of mapping connections. Of course, different connections will have differing forces in particular contexts and these must be measured; not all connections are equal or equally important. Cultural studies is about understanding the possibilities for remaking contexts through cultural alliances and apparatuses, the very structures of which (and the relations between them) are the product of relations and struggles over power. Cultural studies attempts to construct political and contextual theories of the relations between cultural alliances and contexts,[27] as the milieus of the human relations of power. It is a theory of how contexts are made, unmade, and remade. This is precisely what cultural studies tries to intervene into. It is about the possibilities for remaking the context where context is always understood as a structure of power. But the very structure of the context is precisely where one must go to locate the power that is operating since contexts do not exist independently of power.

Articulation calls for both deconstruction and reconstruction; it places the analyst-critic into the ongoing war of positions fought out through the various apparatuses and practices of articulation. Cultural studies offers an intellectually grounded practice for intervening into the becoming of contexts and power. It attempts, temporarily and locally, to place theory in between in order to enable people to act more strategically in ways that may change their context for the better. Of course, how temporarily and how locally are themselves defined by the project. Insofar as any locale is itself locatable within larger—and even global—contexts, cultural studies can only be advanced and served by the increasing polylogue now taking place along the trajectories of its global dissemination and the local invention of cultural studies. For such a polylogue is predicated on the recognition of the changing face of global relations: that we live in a polycentered world. Theories and problems may travel, but they travel as resources rather than answers and, in the end, the trajectory itself may be a more powerful force than either the departure or the arrival. For travel of any sort, of whatever bodies or practices, can never be entirely one way, and what travels is always remade by the complexities of the journey.

If a context can be understood as the relationships that have been made by the operation of power, in the interests of certain positions of power, the struggle to change the context involves the struggle to understand those relations, to locate those relations which can be disarticulated and to then struggle to rearticulate them. To use the most simple and in some sense the most powerful example, the civil rights movement's attempt to say that black is not evil, that *Black is beautiful* was an attempt to redefine a relationship, to rearticulate it into a different relationship. Cultural studies has to be multiple and changing because the contexts and within them, the political stakes and potential or actual struggles are always fluid, multiple, and contradictory. Cultural studies struggles for space between, on the one hand, absolute containment, closure, complete and final understanding, total domination, and, on the other hand, absolute freedom and possibility, openness, open-endedness. It believes, with Marx, that people make history but in conditions not of their own making.

iii.

I have already said a great deal, at least implicitly, about the next two (the third and fourth) features characterizing the practice of cultural studies. Cultural studies is always theoretical and political, but it is theoretical and political in specific—contextual—ways. Cultural studies' radical contextuality affects its theory and politics, which must be related not only to its historical context but to its institutional context as well.

Cultural studies is always theoretical. It is absolutely committed to the necessity of theoretical work, to what Karl Marx called the detour through theory. It does not assume that the context which it is studying (and constituting) is available in some directly empirical way. Theory is necessary to pin an understanding of the context because the context itself has in part already been constructed by theory, or at least by cultural practices and alliances, which is not to say that the context is in any way reducible to those theoretical or cultural constructions. But its theory is always context-specific in two distinct ways. First, theory is always a response to specific questions and specific contexts; it is measured, its truth and validity judged, by its ability to give a better understanding of the context, to open up new, at least imagined, possibilities for changing that context. Cultural studies refuses to hold to one theory defined in advance. This is, again, not to say that it believes in letting the phenomenon speak for itself, but it does believe that the material and discursive context can speak back as it were (if only as measured in political possibilities). Cultural studies treat theories as hypotheses and resources, to be fitted to, articulated with, its particular project. At the very least, this means that theory is contingent and that one cannot be too invested in particular theoretical paradigms. In a sense, cultural studies refuses to let theory let research off the hook. If someone's theory tells them the answers in advance, because their theory travels with them across any and every context, I do not think they are doing cultural studies. They may be doing interesting and important work, and their answers may offer important truths.[28] But there is little possibility of surprise or discovery here. Theory and context are mutually constituted in cultural studies.

In that sense, you cannot take a theory in cultural studies for example, subculture theory developed in 1970s Britain, or Hall's theory of Thatcherism as a hegemonic formation developed in the 1980s and simply move it to a different context and apply it as if it could work there. Theory and context determine each other. And consequently, as I have suggested, its anti-essentialism is always contextual and political rather than epistemological (as in post-structuralism). Similarly, cultural studies cannot be simply a theory of communication, and the model of encoding and decoding cannot be universalized for it was, after all, a theoretical response to a specific context and a specific political question. Even the earliest statements of British cultural studies distance themselves from a communicational model of cultural studies. Here I might mention Raymond Williams' famous description of cultural studies as the study of all the relations between all of the elements in a whole way of life. While this is admittedly a romantic ideal of totalization, it points, along with Williams' notion of a structure of feeling, to his radical commitment to contextualism: a text could only be understood by locating it with a structured set of contextual relations. Similarly, Richard Hoggart argued that cultural studies is not concerned with what people do with a text but with what relations the complex text has to the imaginative life of its readers.[29]

The second way in which theory is contextual is that cultural studies is never driven by—its agenda is not dictated by—theory, or by a particular theoretical position. It does not take its questions from theory or even from particular academic disciplines. It uses theories to "keep on theorizing," rigorously rearticulating them, strategically constructing theoretical formations in response to its particular projects and alternative formations. Cultural studies operates with a particular relationship between its theoretical work and the historical context in which it is working. It is in this sense that I describe cultural studies as interventionist: not in the sense that it intends to leave the realm of intellection and carry its practice to the streets. Rather, it is interventionist insofar as it is not theory driven, and theory is not its object of study. Where then do its specific research questions come from? Let me quote Stuart Hall again:[30]

> In thrusting onto the attention of scholarly reflection and critical analysis the hurly burly of a rapidly changing, discordant and disorderly world, in insisting that academics sometimes attend where everyday social change exists out there, cultural studies tries, in its small way, to insist on what I want to call the vocation of the intellectual life. That is, cultural studies insists on the necessity to address the central, urgent and disturbing questions of a society and a culture in the most rigorous intellectual way we have available.

Or, to quote Raymond Williams' description of the pedagogical project of cultural studies: it involves "taking the best we can in intellectual work and going with it in this very open way to confront people for whom it is not a way of life, for whom it is not in all probability a job, but for whom it is a matter of their own intellectual interest, their own understanding of the pressures on them, pressures of every kind, from the most personal to the most broadly political."[31]

In another context, Williams described the real power (in the classroom) as the power to ask the questions. Cultural studies begins by allowing the world outside the academy to ask the questions of us as intellectuals. Its questions then are derived from the researchers own sense (admittedly, perhaps commonsensical) of the context and the political questions and possibilities at stake. There is, I am aware, an apparent contradiction here, but I would prefer to see it as another example of the inevitable circularity of cultural studies: the "real" context is both constructed in the analysis and asks the questions before the analysis.[32] I am not claiming, in some naive empiricism, that the context speaks for itself, but I am arguing that cultural studies starts by recognizing that the context is always already structured, not only by relations of force and power but also by voices of political hope and aspiration. If, as I have said, cultural studies must always begin where people are, then it must also begin with already constituted articulations of popular hope and disappointment in everyday life. This is not, of course, to say that the analysis should or will end up in the same place or even using the same terms. Moreover, insofar as cultural studies is materialist, I think it does believe that there are real lines connecting such everyday politics (or their absence) to the real relations of forces (and contradictions) in specific social contexts.[33]

iv.

It is obvious from everything I have said that cultural studies is politically driven, that it is committed to producing knowledge which both helps people understand that the world is changeable and that offers some direction for how to change it. But here too, cultural studies is radically contextual in its vision of politics and political struggle. Cultural studies believes that politics is contextually specific. The sites, goals, and forms of struggle must be understood contextually. One cannot simply assume that because a certain kind of political struggle made sense in the 1980s, it will make sense in the 1990s. One cannot assume that because a certain kind of political struggle made sense in England, it will make sense in America.

But politics must also be understood theoretically. Cultural studies demands a certain distance from the existing constituencies of politics, if for no other reason than its commitment to the absolute necessity of theoretical intervention. It sees the need for a certain autonomy of intellectual work and hence, it cannot be said to produce organic intellectuals. For example, while it may be very reasonable to start with questions of identity in contemporary American politics, it does not follow that we must end up with some form of a politics of identity, We may, instead, chart a trajectory from a politics of identity and difference which leads, through an analysis of the geohistorical mechanisms by which relations have been constructed as differences and politics organized by identities, to a politics organized around singularity and otherness.[34] Cultural studies proposes that we take a flexible, somewhat pragmatic or strategic and often modest approach to political programs and possibilities. Such an approach denies the possibility of a totalizing politics (and hence, of the saliency of political critiques based on the mere fact of the absence of some political issues or constituencies).

Since cultural studies believes that cultural practices have effects but that they are often difficult to find, it also believes that, as a cultural practice, it has effects but they too are difficult to identify. Further, it believes that one can always find possibilities for changing any context. In that sense cultural studies is motivated by a desire to maintain some ground for optimism in the face of the overwhelming and quite reasonable pessimism that confronts anyone looking at the contemporary world. Cultural studies critics are fond of quoting Gramsci: "pessimism of the intellect, optimism of the will." What's the point of being so pessimistic that you cannot find the will to begin to struggle? On the other hand, what's the point of being so optimistic that you cannot find a reason to struggle against the existing structures of power? Thus, while cultural studies often constructs "images of strength, courage, and the will to survive,"[35] and even resist, in the face of overpowering hostility, while it is concerned with people's everyday lives, it does not erase that hostility or the systems of domination that produce it. Its belief that where there is power, there is resistance, is not an assumption about agency but rather, a corollary of its theory of power as always a relation between unequal forces. While it refuses to assume that people are, or to treat them as, cultural dopes, it does not assume that they are always in control, always resisting, always aware, always operating with an informed understanding of the context. This is a crucial misunderstanding, I think. If you assume people are so stupid, cultural dopes, that they have no idea of what is being done to them, then, what's the point of education or critical work? Moreover, it's probably not the best way to try to organize political change to start off by telling people that they're too stupid to understand what's happening to them, that they don't understand their own best interests. That does not mean cultural studies doesn't believe people are often duped by contemporary culture, that they are lied to and sometimes, for a variety of reasons, they either don't know it or refuse to admit it. But above all, cultural studies assumes that power is complex and contradictory, and it is committed to struggling with and within that complexity. For it is committed to contestation, both as a fact of reality, not in every instance, but as a possibility that has to be searched for, and as a description of its own strategic practice. For cultural studies, the world is a field of struggle, a balance of forces, and intellectual work must understand the balance and find ways of challenging and changing it. Of course, it recognizes that survival, change, struggle, resistance and opposition are not the same thing, that the relations among them are not predictable in advance, and that there are many forms and sites of each of them (ranging from everyday life and social relations, to economic and political institutions). In other words, cultural studies does not assume that all politics are cultural; rather the real challenge it faces is, in every instance, to articulate the relationships between what Meaghan Morris has called the politics of culture and the politics of politics.[36]

v.

The fifth feature of the practice of cultural studies, and perhaps the one most commonly cited, is its interdisciplinarity. By describing it as interdisciplinary, I mean to say that it operates at "the frontiers of intellectual life," that it pushes "for new questions, new models, and new ways of study."[37] Cultural studies refuses to be slotted into the existing divisions of knowledge; it cannot avoid a question—say the economic determinations operating—because economics is outside its disciplinary purview. Someone in cultural studies can't use their disciplinary competencies to justify limiting the questions they are willing to take on, merely where they can begin. I do not mean to say that cultural studies does not exist in disciplines; it is precisely the tension that often has made it productive. In that sense, as Richard Johnson describes it, cultural studies' interdisciplinarity is an aggressive counterdisciplinary logic.[38] It involves doing the work necessary to explore and explain the relationships between culture and economy, or history, gender relations, social institutions, etc. It involves doing the work to map out the connections, to see how those connections are being made and where they can be remade.

But too often in the American academy, interdisciplinarity is taken to mean either that you do basically what you have been doing but you add some footnotes to sources, usually theoretical, from outside the discipline; or alternatively, you do basically what you have been doing, but you surround it with allusions or information from outside the discipline which, it is assumed, legitimate the argument. Cultural studies says that interdisciplinarity takes work. For example, Meaghan Morris has criticized[39] the widespread tendency among cultural critics to take a single source, such as David Harvey's widely discussed *The Condition of Postmodernity* as an authoritative analysis of the global conditions of capitalism as if Harvey's theories were uncontestably obvious or commonly accepted. It would be like someone deciding that they needed to know something about cultural studies; so they go off and read articles by someone (perhaps a colleague or someone that a colleague has told them about, or perhaps someone they have heard of), and then quote that person as if his or her positions were the undisputed common sense of cultural studies. In fact, even a little reading in economics shows that there is even less agreement among economists than there is among cultural critics.

If interdisciplinarity takes work, there is not one form that such work must take. It will often involve an individual or collective effort to, as it were, become an economist, not in the disciplinary terms of economics but within the interdisciplinary requirements of cultural studies. But there is, of course, a limit to the extent to which one can re-invent economics for cultural studies. And the question is as much one of deciding and coordinating what work has to be brought into cultural studies from other disciplines. This is, in a sense, no different from work within a discipline: one has to somehow decide what to let in to one's own work. Once again, we have to recognize that cultural studies is not some magical panacea or salvation for the academy. In many ways, it is just like other disciplines (and it often exists within them). As Tony Bennett has pointed out,[40] the current celebration of cultural studies' interdisciplinarity too often assumes that cultural studies is better than other disciplines or practices because it is somehow more totalizing, while they are merely partial. On the contrary, cultural studies is also partial; its difference lies perhaps in the fact that it recognizes its own partiality and hence, constitutes it differently.

vi.

This leads me to the final feature of the practice of cultural studies: it is self-reflective. This is the most difficult to define for it is so dependent upon and integrated into the other features. But it is crucial because it instantiates the recognition that the analyst is also a participant in the very practices, formations and contexts he or she is analyzing (another dimension of cultural studies' circularity). This is not so much, I believe, a question of identity, or of a politics of location, but of reflecting on one's own relation to the various trajectories and dimensions, places and spaces, of the context one is exploring and mapping: theoretical, political, cultural and institutional. As Frow and Morris describe it:

> It is perhaps this 'self-situating' and *limiting* moment of analysis that most clearly distinguishes work in cultural studies from some other modes of analysis on which its practitioners may draw…cultural studies tends to incorporate into its object of study a critical account of its own motivating questions.[41]

It is crucial to recognize the way in which Frow and Morris dissociate themselves here from a psychological notion of self-reflection, for what is involved here is less a matter of a personal ethic, a psychological state, or a laundry list of subject positions than of a form of discursive practice and an analysis of institutional conditions.

vii.

I am aware that my description of cultural studies may seem—and probably is —rather idealistic. While I am not sure that anyone has ever actually done what I have described, there are certainly scholars who have made the project comprehensible. But even the best writers in cultural studies have their problems, and I think they are serious and are only now beginning to be confronted. The first is simple to describe. Consider some of the statements I have quoted and made about how cultural studies addresses people, not only intellectuals and academics. Think of Raymond Williams' notion that cultural studies is a pedagogical project that we bring to people for whom these issues are real, personal and immediate concerns. Cultural studies has not succeeded in doing that very well. Antonio Gramsci said that there are two functions of the political intellectual: the first is to know more than the other side; the second is to share that knowledge. Whatever one may think of the production of knowledge in cultural studies, it remains largely an academic discourse encircled by its theoretical vocabulary. I do not mean to suggest that we as academics and intellectuals should give up that vocabulary. It is necessary to what we do. I find it ironic that we expect car mechanics to have a technical vocabulary; we expect astronomers and physicists to have a technical vocabulary, but we do not expect people describing what is probably the most complex phenomenon we know of, human life, to have a technical vocabulary. The problem is not the elitism of the vocabulary for it is necessary for the production of certain kinds of knowledge, productions which are, in a sense, always elitist. But production and distribution, however closely articulated, are not the same, and it is the second half of Gramsci's prescription that has yet to be realized: to share that knowledge with people who want to do something with it. That, it seems to me, is the problem facing cultural studies—as well as many other forms of intellectual discourse. It is a problem facing those of us in communications more than in any other discipline, not only because communications is such an important political issue in the contemporary world, but also because we are the people who most directly deal with the media by which communication and education have to be accomplished in the contemporary world. And this will no doubt require reconstituting pedagogy in the face of such critical tasks as cultural studies poses. However, it should also be clear that there is no necessary reason why those charged with communicating knowledge have to be the same as those producing it; this is certainly one of the lessons that the New Right has taught us. Perhaps we need to think about educating a generation of students who are more comfortable with both sides of the political function, or perhaps we need to think about educating and training students who consciously think of themselves as the translators of knowledge into the public realm, as cultural workers in a variety of institutional sites. Is it not peculiar that we have journalists trained to report science but none trained to report social and cultural knowledge?

A second problem is more serious and difficult, and I have already touched on it earlier. Recent work in postcolonial studies, and in certain traditions of cultural studies, has begun to challenge some of the most fundamental concepts and assumptions of cultural studies on the grounds that they are themselves implicated in particularly powerful structures and technologies of power.[42] Many of the categories that we continue to use, not only in cultural studies but in cultural criticism more broadly—categories of the nation, culture, society, race, gender, identity, institutions—were not coincidentally invented or significantly rearticulated at about the same time as the rise of modern society and modern systems of power. Culture, as Raymond Williams points out, was first used in a context outside of agriculture in the early 18th century with the rise of industrial society. As Paul Gilroy has argued, race itself as a category was invented in the 19th century.[43] To the extent that culture is always implicated in relations of power, then cultural studies has to begin to examine its own cultural categories. It has to question the concepts that have founded its own critical practices. It must begin to ask, to what extent are we, as cultural studies analysts, locked into the very systems of power that we are attempting to get out of because we use the cultural practices, categories and concepts of that system of power? There is no easy way out of this dilemma, and I refuse to resign myself to it by saying that it is simply the fate of intellectuals. I think that is the lazy way. Instead, what is demanded of us is that we begin to accept the possibility that we can rearticulate (which is not to say escape) our own social and cultural determinations, that we can begin to rearticulate our cultural and historical identities, that we can challenge our inherited philosophical commonsense, in the name of the political struggles that must be carried on if we are to contribute as intellectuals to the creation of a better world in the face of the pressing challenges posed by the global conditions in which we are all living, albeit in different ways and places. We have to begin to describe and theorize the ways in which, in our present circumstances, culture often operates as both the site and the weapon of other—economic and political— struggles, even as these struggles appear to be always and already cultural. I believe cultural studies can be useful for this task; it will have to avoid the easy answer that once again simply puts the economic in the leading position as the machine of history in order to find a new and more sophisticated model of the contemporary articulations of cultural and economic practices.

It is, I hope, clear, that my vision of cultural studies defines its task somewhat differently from others: the task of cultural studies is not to somehow map aesthetics onto the social or theory onto the textual. It is not about tracing the trajectory of desire and/or power or the inscription of the social in the text. It does not take theory as a metaphor for social or textual processes, nor does it take social or textual processes as metaphors of theory. Cultural studies is not about rediscovering what we already know—whether in the structures of domination or the possibilities of resistance—about the relations between the text and the subject, or between the subject and the social. Cultural studies is not about communication, ideology, desire or pleasure, although all these may enter into it. It is not about the ethnographic documentation of the local. Cultural studies is about mapping the deployment and effects of discursive practices and alliances within the context of specific social spaces and milieus. It is about the relations or articulations between: (1) discursive alliances as the configurations of practices which define where and how people live specific practices and relations; (2) the practices and configurations of daily life (as the sites of specific forms of determinations, controls, structures of power, struggles, pleasures, etc.); and (3) the apparatuses of power that mobilize different practices and effects to organize the space of human life and the possibilities of alliances. And that means that cultural studies must avoid reducing power to the simple terms of domination, subordination and resistance, and locating power only within culture and/or everyday life. It must struggle, in a sense, to escape culture—if it is to discover the powers of culture.

Notes

1. An earlier version of this paper was delivered as the B. Aubrey Fisher Memorial Lecture at the University of Utah in October 1993. It was published by the Department of Communication as "Cultural Studies: What's in a Name?" I would like to thank the Department of Communication at the University of Utah and especially Len Hawes for the invitation and the honor. 1 would also like to thank Tony Bennett, Cameron McCarthy, Carol Stabile, John Clarke and Ellen Wartella for their comments and criticisms of that version.

2. I want to emphasize that the name "cultural studies" applies to works and not people. Not everything that someone identified with cultural studies writes must necessarily be cultural studies. This confusion of individuals with work is all too common, and the result is that experiences are substituted for practices, and ethics for politics. This is dangerously close to "political correctness." The real questions, however, are (1) whether and how one can generalize from the experience of the individuals involved to the structural conditions of the institution, and (2) what such experiences have to do with the constitutions of a field of intellectual practice.

3. While cultural studies has been influenced by many of these positions, including structuralism, post-structuralism, certain traditions in feminism, Marxism, and postmodernism, it cannot be identified with any one of them or with the field of theory in general. Such theories travel as resources

rather than answers, and they are rearticulated by their appropriation into particular projects in the course of their travels.

4. In this, I would like to argue that the situation of cultural studies is somewhat akin to that of phenomenology. Since intellectuals are always studying phenomena, it might be fairly argued that we are all doing phenomenology. But that loses the specificity of the practice of phenomenology, a specificity that yet leaves a great deal of latitude for disagreement and difference.

5. Speaking as I do from within the U.S. academy, I am aware of the difficulty of trying to describe cultural studies in terms general enough to have some relevance to those in very different institutional and geographical conditions.

6. There is not, and never has been, a singular thing called British cultural studies. There never even was a thing called position of the Centre for Contemporary Cultural Studies at Birmingham, which is often mythically and sometimes nostalgically seen as the location of the origin of British cultural studies. Even at the Centre, there were always different and sometimes competing, powerfully invested positions and projects. The differences were both theoretical and political, and they often led to highly charged, emotionally difficult debates. Consequently, even the best histories of the Centre, or of British cultural studies, that have been written manage at best to describe what John Clarke has called "the diversity that won." There are always voices that were part of the discussion that have been excluded (or that excluded themselves) or erased.

7. The Chicago School has had an enormous impact on a wide range of disciplines and perspectives in North America. We need at the very least to distinguish its influence on social theory—particularly as the source of symbolic interactionism—from its continuing presence as one of the early articulations of pragmatism (visible in the work on such diverse writers as Richard Rorty and Cornel West). In a more complete analysis of the Chicago School's theory of culture, one would also need to distinguish and compare the work of John Dewey, the philosopher, and the sociologists such as Robert Parks.

8. Bill Schwarz has described the geographical determinations of British cultural studies, connecting the fact that it was "decentered and mis-placed" from the "metropolitan culture of imperial Britain" to its "structural ambiguity." See Bill Schwarz, "Where is Cultural Studies?" *Cultural Studies,* 8, in press.

9. Raymond Williams, *The Country and the City,* New York, Oxford University Press, 1973, p. 195.

10. Raymond Williams, Ibid., p. 197 and 207.

11. Raymond Williams, Ibid.

12. This is not entirely accurate, since in Williams' earlier theoretical writings, there is certainly an image of an idealized culture which depends upon the projection of a time when culture and community would be equivalent. In fact, the rhetoric of *The Long Revolution* is remarkably similar to that of John Dewey at times. However, this idealized image ("the community of process") was never assumed to be the reality and was always juxtaposed to another, less ideal, concept (the structure of feeling, the community of culture). Moreover, the development of British cultural studies depended as well on the work of E.P. Thompson, and in particular, on Thompson's critique of Williams: E. P. Thompson, "The Long Revolution," *New Left Review,* no. 9 (pp. 24–29) and no. 10 (pp. 34–39).

13. See Stuart Hall, "Cultural studies and its theoretical legacies," in Lawrence Grossberg, Cary Nelson and Paula Treichler, eds., *Culture Studies,* New York, Routledge, 1992.

14. Thus, for example, James Carey creates a cultural studies by bringing together the Chicago School and the work of Harold Innis. Similarly, an anthropological cultural studies emerges when the anthropological model of culture is critiqued by, and juxtaposed with, emergent notions of culture in postcolonial studies.

15. Stuart Hall, op. cit.

16. Cornel West, quoted in Joel Pfister, "The Americanization of cultural studies," *Yale Journal of Criticism,* 4 (1991).

17. Following Tony Bennett, I want to emphasize that I am trying to describe a set of procedures which can be empirically discriminated, and not a set of biographical or psychological characteristics of the intellectuals practicing them. Bennett has argued that this distinction results from a choice between Foucault and Gramsci as different bodies and styles of theory and politics. Alternatively, I see it as a decision about how Foucault is to be brought into and allowed to reconfigure cultural studies. Or in other words, which Foucault, what part of Foucault, is central to the projects of cultural studies? Foucault, after all, might himself be described as a founder of a discourse: does one read Foucault as a theorist of: knowledge/power? effectivity, the body and the critique of ideology? genealogies? archaeologies? discipline? governmentality? the constitution and care of the self? the micropolitics, mechanisms and apparatuses of power? My own reading emphasizes questions of effectivity and of the particular deployments of power, i.e., the organizations and machineries producing particular unequal relations of force and power. See Tony Bennett, "Useful culture," *Cultural Studies,* 6 (1992).

18. Tony Bennett has criticized the way in which the commitment to discipline is often contradicted in practice by a "specific political technology of the intellectual" which he describes as "charismatic authority and closure," often constructed by the apparatuses of cultural studies. Such a technology conflates intellectual work and biography, so that someone's ideas are read and judged through their life, and their life is read and judged as the embodiment of their ideas. For Bennett, this is the result of the moral-aesthetic tradition out of which British cultural studies arose. Obviously, the existence of such a technology in the U.S. cannot be assigned to the same history, as education always functioned in more pragmatic and political terms. While such authoritative voices may be useful in particular contexts, for certain ends, they are not, Bennett argues, particularly useful in defining the intellectual enterprise of cultural studies. Tony Bennett, "Being 'in the true' of cultural studies," *Southern Review,* 26–2 (1993).

19. Stuart Hall, "Race, culture and communication: Looking backward and forward at cultural studies," *Rethinking Marxism,* 5 (1992).

20. Stuart Hall, Chas Critcher, Tony Jefferson, John Clarke and Brian Roberts, *Policing the Crisis: Mugging the State, and Law and Order.* New York, Holmes and Meier, 1978.

21. Here I am obviously distancing myself from Richard Johnson's "What is Cultural Studies?" *Social Text,* 16 (1986/87), which defines cultural studies by articulating a model of culture as communication (sender-message-receiver) to Marx's model of the cycle of production (production-distribution-consumption). Johnson would make cultural studies into a combination of political economy, textual analysis and ethnographic audience studies, although how this is to be accomplished remains something of a mystery. I am also distancing myself from, e.g., Patrick Brantlinger, *Crusoe's Footprints,* New York, Routledge, 1990.

22. John Frow and Meaghan Morris, "Introduction," John Frow and Meaghan Morris, eds. *Australian Cultural Studies,* Urbana, University of Illinois Press, 1993.

23. Actually, I would argue that the assumption of the social construction of reality defines the continuing modernist basis of cultural studies. Consequently, if we are to find a form of cultural studies appropriate to its contemporary global situation, we must renounce this assumption in order to articulate a different-spatial-form of materialism.

24. Frow and Morris, "Introduction."

25. Eve Sedgewick, *Epistemology of the Closet,* Berkeley, University of California Press, 1990.

26. Cultural studies' methods vary widely. Sometimes, articulation is the only way to describe what the critic is doing. More often, however, the method is derived from another disciplinary methodology—ethnography, textual analysis, survey research—but the way it is enacted and interpreted changes significantly as a result of the commitment to articulation.

27. For cultural studies, the context might be better thought of as specific bits of daily life, positioned between (culture as a specific body of practices and social forces/institutions/apparatuses.

28. I think this describes the work of such important critics as Fred Jameson, discovering once again the class struggle (or the third world struggling against the colonizers), as well as a large number of identity critics discovering once again, apparently to their surprise, that the latest Hollywood production is sexist and racist.

29. Richard Hoggart, "Contemporary cultural studies: An approach to the study of literature and society," Centre for Contemporary Cultural Studies Occasional Paper, Birmingham, 1969.

30. Stuart Hall. "Race, culture and communications."

31. Raymond Williams, "The future of cultural studies," in *The Politics of Modernism,* London, Verso, 1989.

32. I am aware that I am also leaving unremarked the issue of who, if anyone, can claim to "speak for the context."

33. The question of the "empirical" reality of contexts and power cannot be addressed here. I believe it can only be answered by a serious reconsideration of the foundations of contemporary cultural theory, and of the relations between ontology and epistemology. See Gilles Deleuze, *Foucault,* Minneapolis, University of Minnesota Press, 1988.

34. See Giorgio Agamben, *The Coming Community,* trans. Michael Hardt, Minneapolis, University of Minnesota Press, 1993.

35. David A. Bailey and Stuart Hall, "The critical decade," *Ten 8,* 2–3, 1992.

36. Meaghan Moths Morris, "Tooth and Claw: Tales of Survival and *Crocodile Dundee,*" in *The Pirate's Fiancée: Feminism, Reading Postmodernism,* London, Verso, 1988.

37. Stuart Hall, "Race, culture and communications."

38. Richard Johnson, "What is cultural studies anyway?"

39. Meaghan Morris, "The man in the mirror: David Harvey's 'condition' of postmodernity," in Mike Featherstone, ed., *Cultural Theory and Cultural Change,* London, Sage, 1992.

40. Tony Bennett, "Being 'in the true' of cultural studies."

41. Frow and Morris, p. xvii-xviii.

42. Gauri Viswanathan, "Raymond Williams and British Colonialism," *Yale Journal of Criticism,* 4–2 (1991). Viswanathan argues that there is a serious problem with the notion of culture as it is used in cultural studies and, in particular, in the work of Raymond Williams. He challenges the notion of English culture (and, by extension, of any national culture) and argues that, in fact, significant aspects of the English culture of the 19th and 20th centuries were actually developed by colonial regime in India (as forms of regulation and control) and then exported back to England (also as forms of regulation and control). For example, pedagogical practices that Williams assumes to have been constructed in the English educational system were actually developed as strategic weapons in the struggle to "civilize the colonial masses" and were then brought back to England in order to civilize the working masses. Eventually, they worked their way up into the middle class where they were not only normalized but nationalized as well. What became English culture was not English, but part of a global colonial culture that Williams has erased. The very complexity and contextuality that cultural studies is supposedly committed to have been ignored.

43. Paul Gilroy, *The Black Atlantic: Modernity and Double Consciousness,* Cambridge, Harvard University Press, 1993.

3

■ Stuart Hall on Representation and Ideology

Chris Rojek

Ideology and representation are central concepts in Cultural Studies. The notion that identity, action and belonging are coded and represented in particular ways opens up the fundamental questions of who does the coding and representing and why? The classical Marxian expression of the concept of ideology is generally regarded as faulty. This is because it suggests that ideology is the product of the ruling class who code and represent the paramount sense of social, economic and cultural reality in order to engineer popular consent. It might be objected that this criticism is itself defective since it is directed against a version of vulgar Marxism associated with a bipolar model of class ('the ruling class' and the 'proletariat'). In his own writings, especially in *The Eighteenth Brumaire of Louis Napoleon (1851–52)* and *Grundrisse* (1857–61) Marx presents a much more sophisticated analysis of how multiple layers of stratification and the interplay between contesting groups produce the voluntary consent of the masses.

Stuart Hall's discussion of ideology and representation takes up these ideas, via an engagement with more contemporary, largely European authors, of whom the most significant is Antonio Gramsci. He provides a way of analyzing the operation and inter-connection of coding and representation along 'many fronts' of engagement. The organized manipulation of behaviour is presented as part of a 'complex whole' in which ruling groups are themselves subject to forces that are beyond their control. The result is a seminal contribution to the study of culture, power, repression and resistance.

Born in Kingston, Jamaica in 1932, Stuart Hall was a Rhodes Scholar in Oxford University in the 1950s. He went on to work with Richard Hoggart, the founder of the Birmingham Centre for Contemporary Cultural Studies. Hall eventually succeeded Hoggart as the Director of the Centre and presided over what is widely regarded as the most fruitful moment in the Birmingham School approach to culture. Hall left the University of Birmingham to accept the Chair of Sociology at the Open University. In the 1980s he emerged as one to the leading critics of the neo-liberal revival and 'authoritarian populism' (Thatcherism). His thought has moved away from an emphasis on the centrality of class in cultural studies to a focus on multi-ethnicity, multi-culturalism, identity and post-identity. Hall is generally regarded to be one of the giants of Cultural Studies.

The concepts of representation and ideology are pivotal in Hall's approach to the analysis of society and culture. Hall proposes first, that points of enunciation are always implicated by the practices of representation, and second, that representation bears a subsidiary relationship to ideology. By the term 'enunciation' Hall means not merely speaking and writing, but all modalities through which agency is expressed in what Marx and Engels (1965) called 'man's double relation' to nature and other wo/men. For Marx, wo/man intervenes upon nature and, with the help of certain instruments and tools, adapts nature to reproduce the material conditions of human existence. As Hall observes in one of his first important essays on ideology (1977a: 315), Marx understood that from an early.point in the history of the human intervention into nature, labour is socially organized. The generation of surplus wealth extends the forms through which wo/man's mediation with nature is conducted and eventually supports a complex, multilayered set of distinctions between and within manual and mental specialization in the division of labour.

At this juncture, there is no need to go into the complexities that Hall, following Marx, locates in manual and mental specialization and the various ensembles, sub-ensembles and sedimentations in the process of ideology in social reproduction. It is enough to note two things. Firstly, Hall submits that there is no space of representation, including theoretical space, which exists outside ideology (1984:11). As we shall see later, this proposition exists in some tension with other approaches to culture which prefigure embodiment, emplacement and sensuality in man's 'double relation' with nature and other wo/men (Willis 1977; Turner 1984). In addition, it drives a coach and horses through the argument of academics situated outside the 'organic intellectual' tradition, who submit that principled academic labour proffers a 'detour via detachment' (Elias 1956).

Secondly, Hall reiterates his antipathy to essentialism by rejecting models of ideology that posit false consciousness in favour of an approach that presents and analyses representation and ideology as a mobile *field* of relations. This is consistent with Gramsci's understanding of culture as striated, constituted through relations of reciprocity and conflict, and always 'in process.' Hall's construction of the concepts of representation and ideology is elaborated through close readings of certain key texts in Marx, notably *The German Ideology* and the 1857 Introduction to the *Grundrisse,* and the writings of Gramsci, Althusser and, to a lesser extent, Volosinov. But his initial written confrontation with the problem was through his early work in Birmingham on the media.

In particular, the faults he perceived in the American behaviourist model of mass communications led him to postulate ideology as central in analysing the media and mass communications. Hall has convincingly argued that media and communication studies constitute a 'regional' rather than a 'self-sustaining' discipline (1989: 43). That is, they are ineradicably bound up with the theoretical efficacy or lacunae of the general social sciences that take as their subject matter the social and economic formation as a whole. Hence, the problematic of 'the ideological effect' that Hall first ventured in relation to media and communication studies inevitably reflects the whole social formation and requires an encounter with the general social sciences entrained upon questions of communication and power. However, to begin with, the problematic is addressed in short-range terms. Hall's much cited paper on encoding and decoding targets television discourse (1973a), although it is apparent throughout that the issues raised in relation to the representation of facticity in the media are connected with wider questions of privilege and power. However, in this paper the questions are substantially undertheorized, a condition rectified by Hall in his published work on representation and ideology between the mid-1970s and mid-1980s.

■ Encoding and Decoding

As Hall notes elsewhere (1989; 1993), the origins of the encoding/decoding paper are partly polemical. His immediate target is the Centre for Mass Communications Research at the University of Leicester. Hall regards the Leicester School as representing the dominant paradigm of the day in media and communication studies in the UK, namely behaviourism.[1] The crux of Hall's dissatisfaction with it is his contention that reception isn't the open-ended, perfectly transparent thing at the other end of the communication chain. (1993: 254). On this reading, behaviourism assigns too much freedom to the individual and exaggerates the transparency of the communication process. It is insufficiently reflexive about the context of identity formation and communication exchange, postulating transcendental naturalism where historical specificity should go and hypothesizing communication processes as technical, apolitical effects of modernization rather than regarding them as the phenomenal forms of capitalist power.

Hall's contention is that media messages are embedded with presuppositions about beliefs and practices that shape everyday perceptions of reality. Further, these presuppositions operate finally to reproduce hegemony. The effect of his argument is to topple the behaviourist claim of transparency in communication and objectivity in media research and to replace it with a thoroughly politicized approach to the media. Thus the behaviourist proposition that the media message is a transcription of social reality is challenged with a redefinition that attributes ideological transformation to the media process. Hall's concern is not merely to focus on the relationship between ideology and communication. He also seeks to establish the principle that decoding is an ordinary accomplishment of audiences through the practices of reflexive assimilation and critical exchange.

The emphasis on the active audience is consistent with the intellectual mood of the early 1970s. Terry Eagleton (1996) observes that Hall's most persistent political strength is a deep-seated belief in popular democracy. With hindsight, the early 1970s, building on the counterculture movement of the 1960s, constituted a 'democratizing moment' in a variety of areas in academic life. For example, ethnomethodology succeeded in challenging the positivist assumptions of structural functionalism by focusing on the tacit knowledge and members' methods in constructing social reality. For its part, semiology demonstrated the importance of sign economies in agency and culture, and argued that meaning is subject to infinite semiosis that is beyond the control of any social agent.[2] Similarly, feminism revealed the disturbing extent of patriarchy in the Academy, and generated a serious debate about the politics of identity. All three offered the Left the prospect of revival after the battering taken by Marxism following the fiasco of the May 1968 'revolution' in Paris.

Hall's appropriation of these influences was connected with a recasting of his relationship with Marxism. Of fundamental importance there was his close reading of Marx's 1857 Introduction to the *Grundrisse* (Hall 1973b). As we shall see presently, Hall used this work to overcome the productivist bent that he castigated in classical Marxism. In the 1857 Introduction he found a classical pretext in Marxism for emancipating consumption and culture from their subaltern status to production. The encoding/decoding paper and the remarks on the 1857 Introduction were published in the same year: 1973. Much of the theoretical élan exhibited in the encoding/decoding piece can be put down to Hall's exploits in Marxist revisionism.

Hall understands encoding and decoding to operate in complex ways. As usual with his analysis of representation, multiple layers of meaning and circuits of communication are posited as integral to the encoding and decoding process, and the Gramscian notion of 'unstable equilibria' is implicit. In large measure, Hall's criticism has become the conventional wisdom in the field. As such it perhaps obscures nuances in the position of the Leicester School that Hall omitted to recognize in his scene-changing piece. James Halloran (1970) and his colleagues at Leicester were certainly aware of the effect of distortion in media communication, and they recognized that the manipulation of meaning was logically compatible with the assembly and transmission of media messages. However, they conceptualized these matters in terms of negotiated transaction between the audience and the producer, a liberal-pluralist interpretation that fails to hold water for Hall. He rejects the Leicester School approach because it neglects to base the question of media distortion in the Marxist theory of power and agency, opting instead, as was the field convention of the day, to pursue media and communication studies as a self-sustaining discipline. For Hall, Leicester was therefore insufficiently political in its representation of culture and power and inadequately theoretical. The encoding/decoding paper was his response to this impasse.

The paper is organized into three broad sections. First, Hall refutes the proposition that the media merely reflect facts. Instead he redefines the media as producers of messages or transmitters of 'sign vehicles.' The media 'effect' is to place a particular gloss on social reality. Hall acknowledges that meaning is polysemic in its nature. However, the effect of ideology is to seek to negate polysemy. As he explains:

> I use ideology as that which cuts into the infinite semiosis of language. Language is pure textuality, but ideology wants to make a particular meaning…it's the point where power cuts into discourse, where power overcuts knowledge and discourse; at that point you get a cut, you get a stoppage, you get a suture, you get an overdetermination. The meaning constructed by that cut into language is never permanent, because the next sentence will take it back, will open the semiosis again. And it can't fix it, but ideology is an attempt to fix it. (1993: 263–4)

Hall's wording here is slightly misleading, since it implies that ideology exists outside of discourse and knowledge. As his wider writings on ideology and representation affirm, it is more accurate to regard discourse and knowledge as always and already inscribed with ideology. However, leaving that aside, the passage reveals both Hall's understanding of the force of ideology in constructing meaning as 'obvious' or 'natural' and his conviction that the role of intellectual labour is to expose and unpack this force. Hall's interest in the media is partly based on his recognition that it is axial in the construction of meaning in advanced capitalist society. He regards its professional codes and technological practices as making a decisive 'cut' or 'overcut' into the semiosis of language in the culture at large. This brings me to the second section of the paper.

Much of the impetus in the encoding/decoding paper is directed towards confirming the notion of 'the active audience' as an antidote to the blank social subject constructed by behaviourism.

However, Hall is also concerned to demonstrate that the media play a constructionist role in advancing some narratives and meanings at the expense of others. The process of encoding and decoding is clearly very complex. It functions as a mixture of conscious and unconscious levels and involves perpetual struggle over the specific type of representational practices. Gramsci's notion of dominance as a structured field of relations in which relations of force constitute 'unstable equilibria' informs Hall's analysis throughout. Hegemony is therefore never irreversible or univocal. Rather, it always involves a balance of power that is contested, redressed and opposed through ordinary agency. These are significant caveats, but they should not be allowed to obscure the fact that Hall regards media representation as finally operating through determinate codes which anchor semiosis and ultimately enhance 'the dominant cultural order' (1973a: 13).

Hall's position on this matter is nuanced and sophisticated. Elsewhere, he has criticized the 'conspiracy theory' of vulgar Marxism that portrays the media as the simple ideological instrument of capital (Hall, Connell and Curti 1976: 51). Hall is an implacable opponent of the notion of 'false consciousness' since the term implies that the goal of analysis should be to elucidate the so-called reality underlying ideological distortion. Instead he submits that the notion of social reality is always discursively constituted, and further, that representation inevitably bears the inflections of class, gender, race and status. For these reasons Hall refuses to countenance a version of the dominant ideology thesis which hypothesizes class control over the popular. On the contrary, for Hall, the popular is always contested terrain, cultural space in which resistance and opposition foment and evolve as ordinary accessories of agency. As he advises in another place:

> In the study of popular culture, we should always start here: with the double-stake in popular culture, the double movement of containment and resistance, which is always inevitably inside it…I think there is a continuous and necessarily uneven and unequal struggle, by the dominant culture; to enclose and confine its definitions and forms. There are points of resistance; there are also moments of supersession. This is the dialectic of cultural struggle. In our times, it goes on continuously, in the complex lines of resistance and acceptance, refusal and capitulation, which make in the field of culture a sort of constant battlefield. A battlefield where no once-and-for-all victories are obtained but where there are always strategic positions to be won and lost. (1981: 227,233)

At the same time Hall is at pains to pre-empt the inference that society is a completely open discursive field in which all readings or 'battle reports' are of equivalent analytic value. His remedy is to introduce the vexatious notion of 'preferred readings.' The notion is vexatious because both the criteria for determining preferred readings and the consequences that follow from it have proved to be mercurial. I will take up this point in more detail later.

The third section of Hall's paper examines the concrete mechanisms through which media representations are constructed by producers and assimilated by audiences. To this end he constructs a typology of four codes by which, he contends, audiences read media messages.

(1) The dominant hegemonic code. When audiences assimilate media messages as 'straight' reflections of reality they are operating in the code of the dominant or hegemonic order. This is a state of 'transparent communication' in which the critical reflexivity of the audience is suspended or at least decisively checked. Given Hall's emphasis on the 'active audience,' he stresses that transparent communication is an ideal-type case. Nonetheless, because he is concerned to demonstrate that the media operate within the field of dominant ideology, he is required to nominate closure in the dominant code as a logical possibility in the communication process.

(2) The professional code. The professional code refers to the techniques and practices deployed by media personnel to construct and transmit messages. A good deal of the encoding/decoding paper is devoted to nullifying the self-image of impartiality and objectivity cultivated by media professionals. Hall does not wish to impute bad faith to them. On the other hand, he attributes 'over-defensiveness' to them on the question of bias (1974: 24). For Hall, media professionals are not autonomous agents. This is a proposition that ruffles media feathers. Hall understands that impartiality and neutral reporting of the 'facts' have totemic significance in the self-image of media professionals. Against this, he argues that the concepts of impartiality and neutrality already presuppose a 'natural' order in which notions of justice, difference and inclusion reflect dominant values. It is not a matter of positing media conspiracy, although rather contrarily Hall claims that media professionals are organically linked with dominant elites through the structural position of the media as an 'ideological apparatus' and their privileged access to elite constructions of reality (1973a: 17).[3] Rather it is at the level of connotative 'metacodes' that Hall identifies complicity between elites and the media. This is not necessarily a conscious complicity. Rather Hall maintains that it typically operates through unspoken shared understandings of the 'common ground' of debate and agency, so that 'ideological reproduction therefore takes place here inadvertently, unconsciously, 'behind men's backs' (1973a: 17). Hall therefore theorizes the professional code as compliant with

the hegemony of the dominant code. It transmits a staged version of reality to the consumer that is inscribed with the 'cut' of dominant ideology.

(3) The negotiated code. This is the most common code in assimilating media messages. It recognizes that media messages are dominantly defined and professionally signified. As such, it might be said to constitute a reflexive engagement with the media. Reflexivity is understood to comprise a mixture of adaptive and oppositional elements. For example, it acknowledges the legitimacy of hegemonic definitions of the national interest, while simultaneously reading these definitions in relation to habitus and experience. Hall uses the term 'situated logics' to describe the operation of this code (1973a: 18). By this term he means that media messages are assimilated according to the particular life circumstances of the audience. The negotiated code reflects high levels of ambivalence and inconsistency about political, economic and cultural matters. For example, Hall mentions that agreement with the hegemonic mantra that it is in the national interest to practice pay restraint as a hedge against inflation does not necessarily carry over into a readiness to accept a low pay offer on the shopfloor (1973a: 18). The ambivalence intrinsic to the negotiated code makes it a fruitful space in political agency. For the mismatches between the hegemonic code and the situated logic of lived experience potentially expose the hiatus between fact and bias which ideology labours to disguise.

(4) The oppositional code. When audiences respond to media messages as mere ideology they operate in the oppositional code. Here the literal and connotative inflection given to a particular event is understood by the audience but read in a converse way. The audience decodes the preferred code of referencing and presenting an event and 'retotalizes' it in an alternative framework. The oppositional code may be a continuous way of reading media messages for some strata. These strata may have developed lifestyles with values that are inimical to hegemonic order and therefore automatically discount and oppose the media messages through which this order is represented. Willis's study of 'profane culture' in the habitus and practice of bikers and hippies (1978) may be referred to as an example of the inimical values at issue here. The people he studied maintain a highly conditional relation with hegemonic culture. They transgress it through their means of material and symbolic subsistence, inhabiting, so to speak, a self-validating ring of culture within the universe of hegemony, Moreover, their discourse about the latter is often automatically dismissive and carnivalesque in form, hence Willis's choice of the label 'profane' to describe it.

However, Hall's interest in oppositional readings is primarily relating to class, status, gender, race and generation. Privileged access refers to the availability of politicians, business leaders and celebrities to the media. Hall's point is that media professionals move easily in elite circles and therefore have a higher risk of contamination with elite ideology. However, this point is not empirically developed in Hall's work. One profitable area of research might be to compare patterns of recruitment into the media and key elite institutions focusing on factors of class directed towards conjunctures of instability in hegemony which are conducive to the articulation of transformative intervention. As he concludes, 'one of the most significant political moments (they also coincide with crisis points within the broadcasting organizations themselves for obvious reasons) is the point when events that are normally signified and decoded in a negotiated way begin to be given an oppositional reading' (1973a: 18).

The encoding/decoding paper was not based on empirical research. It was left to David Morley, an associate of Hall's in Birmingham, to test the propositions. He showed episodes of the BBC current affairs programme *Nationwide* to social groups representing the middle and working classes and asked them to comment on the output (Morley 1980). Broadly speaking, his findings confirm Hall's fourfold typology. However, he also discovered significant anomalies in the audience response which cross-cut class, status, race and gender lines. Following the discourse theorist Michel Pecheux, Morley argues that the operation of codes must be understood in relation to *interdiscourse,* a term designed to render the interpellation of social subjects as involving a multiplicity of discourses. The inference is that the closure denoted in Hall's fourfold typology is untenable. To some extent, Hall's readiness to acknowledge ambivalence and slippage in the coding process anticipates this manoeuvre. All the same, Morley's intervention suggests that Hall did not go far enough in clarifying the dialectics of ambivalence and slippage.

Morley's critics responded by submitting that he himself did not go far enough in practising what he preached. In particular, Lewis (1983) complains that Morley underestimated the autonomy of media professionals and caricatured them as agents of 'primary definitions.' This again raises difficult empirical questions relating to the class backgrounds, education history and lifestyle practices of media professionals and elite members in business, the state and the celebrity sector that remain substantially underresearched in the field. On this basis Lewis queries the validity of the concept of 'preferred reading' in Morley's research, observing that the verification of the concept is always a matter of empirical research and never theoretical fiat. The import of this remark is that Morley, and implicitly Hall, are overdependent on theoretical categories to support their claims in respect of the ideological effectivity of the media.

Jordin and Brunt (1988) offer a countervailing view, criticizing Morley's methodology for replicating positivist assumptions in its application of quantitative analysis. *Contra* Lewis they hold that preferred readings can be established textually prior to empirical research. The empirical task that derives from this is to establish the range of decodings attached to encoded preferred readings. As empirical tasks go it is a daunting prospect, since the range of encoded and decoded readings is potentially infinite. Nor is the ideological pretext governing preferred readings adequately explained.

Morley himself became dissatisfied with the ethnographic limitations of his original research, forsaking the controlled ambience of his research for investigation into audience responses in 'natural settings' (Morley 1986; 1980). This involved a loosening of the ideological problematic formulated in the original encoding/decoding model in favour of a more diversified reading which embraced factors of age, race, gender and generation as well as class in the 'viewing context.' Morley argued that the subject is split both psychologically and sociologically, so that it is a mistake to impute identity to audience responses. The result is a more multilayered model of coding than envisaged in the original encoding/decoding paper.

Underlying these various reformulations is dissatisfaction with the criteria of encoding and decoding elaborated by Hall (1973a). Jim McGuigan gets to the nub of the matter with his observation that Hall's insistence on ideological effectivity and audience activity is 'flexible almost to the point of incoherence' (1992: 131). Hall's criteria of audience activity in decoding and ideological effectivity in encoding are undersubstantiated. The encoding/decoding model strives to defend relative autonomy in the negotiated and oppositional codes but is nebulous on the question of the route or passport that audiences use to achieve this end. Simultaneously, he wants to retain two arguments that point in contrary directions.

In an important interview (1993), Hall recognizes that the original encoding/decoding paper is faulty in at least four respects. Firstly, the distinction between signification at the level of society, culture and politics, and encoding at the level of the media message, is not adequately adumbrated. The dialogue between hegemonic reproduction and the encoding practices of media professionals is poorly enunciated. Other traditions regard reflexivity to be a general characteristic of communication (Beck, Giddens and Lash 1994). In contrast Hall's fourfold typology posits a polarized view of reflexivity in which reflexive consciousness is concentrated at the end of the negotiated and oppositional pairing and is virtually absent in the dominant and professional codes.

Secondly, the formulation of the encoding/decoding paradigm suggests that signification works in the real world. The analytic task becomes to determine how a preferred reading is attempted through the encoding process and how a preferred meaning is achieved by the audience.[4] However, the distinction between signification and the real world overturns Hall's thesis on ideology, which is that ideology 'pre-signifies' or 'over-determines' the 'natural' world, thus making 'the real' a dubious category. As Hall attests:

> I really create problems for myself by looking as if there is a sort of moment there. So you read the circuit as if there is a real world, then somebody speaks about it and encodes it, and then somebody reads it, then there's a real world again. But of course, the real world is not outside of discourse; it's not outside of signification. It's practice and discourse like everything else is. (1993: 260–1)

Thirdly, the dynamics of preferred meaning and preferred reading are obscure. Hall wants to use the terms in order to get away from any connotation of determinism. Both the active agent and the active audience are consistent with his view of ideology as positioning actors in situations. The criteria of preferred meaning and preferred reading cannot be simply inferred from hegemony. As Morley's work demonstrated (1980; 1986), preference in the polysemy of the TV broadcasting process can only be established by assigning diligence to the particular context in which communication messages are assembled and assimilated. Preference cannot be predesignated or inferred since its efficacy is a matter of the specific exchange of reflexivity between the producer of the communication message and the audience. Because this is the case, Hall's conflation of preferred reading and meaning with ideology needs to be much more carefully expressed. No one would seriously quibble with the argument that communication operates within the force of normative coercion and that the media constitute a central institution of normative coercion. The question is the nature of coercion. For Hall, coercion tends to operate to reproduce the rules of capital. But this requires more explication than is achieved in the encoding/decoding paper.

Fourthly, the paper continuously begs the question of the relationship between the real and the discursive in the capitalist mode of production. The encoding/decoding paper ends up framing everything as discourse. But as Hall recognizes (1993: 267–8), this is unsatisfactory because it dissolves the question of the relationship between discourse and history. Hall's approach aims to avoid assigning determinacy to discourse. However, the analytical edge of his work is the proposition that discourse operates to reinforce the rule of capital. Understandably, Hall does not want to produce a reading that turns the media message into pure polysemy. But in avoiding doing so he is forced to connote the media message with material levels of power and history. The problem is that these levels are precluded by his insistence that power and history are discursively constituted. Hall's effort to wrestle with this difficulty raises more dilemmas than it solves. He writes:

> I simply can't think 'practice' without touching ground, with each practice always touching ground as the necessary but not sufficient element—its materiality, its material registration. Somewhere. What that, however, pushes me to is what 1 would call the historically real, which is not philosophically real but which has a good deal of determinacy in it. So the historical structures may not be long lasting, they may not be forever, cannot be transcendental, but while they are going, they do structure a particular field. (1993: 268)

Elsewhere, Hall has complained of his frustration at lacking a language to express his argument adequately (1995: 68). The remark is made in relation to his attempted exegesis of the politics of difference and interrupted identity. However, it is also relevant to the passage cited above. Thus, in one sentence Hall proposes that history is not 'philosophically real' but confusingly invokes the 'historically real,' which, he adds, 'has a good deal of determinacy in it.' What Hall hopes to gain from the concept of the 'historically real' in preference to 'history' is puzzling. Perhaps the overweening confidence of some left-wing writers, *après* Marx, that history is on their side troubled him, and he sought to put distance between himself and them by adopting the concept. Be that as it may, it is not clear that the rejection of 'history' is required to refute historicism. In another sentence, the 'historically real,' which he submits exists 'somewhere,' is adduced as exerting 'structure' over a particular 'field,' albeit structure that may not be 'long lasting' and 'cannot be transcendental.' Nor is the calibre of determinacy specified, which somewhat weakens its analytic purchase. Most historians would regard the proposition that historical forces are variable as unexceptional.

However, it reprises the question of why Hall discards 'history' in favour of the 'historically real.'

To be fair, Hall is cognizant of the problem. 'I suppose,' he writes, 'in moving away from the real or the extradiscursive as a kind of transcendental signifier outside of the system, I try to reintroduce it back as an element of tendential structuralism' (1993e: 268). This is perhaps another example of the slippage that critics argue is a general problem with Hall's work. But it is also evidence of the structural opacity between discourse and the extradiscursive that runs right through his writings.

The encoding/decoding paper represents one of Hall's first significant contributions to the investigation of ideology in capitalist society. It has been rightly appreciated as a notable intervention in politicizing the study of the media and communication. Hall's method of syncretic narrative fusion of elements from Marxist theory, structuralism and semiology is imaginative. It generated both critical discourse and a programme of research, conditions that Jeffrey Alexander (2001) proposed as requirements of knowledge in the human sciences to possess canonical status. In as much as this is the case, Hall's paper should be regarded as an addition to the canon. However, the paper was constrained by a focus on the media. Hall's real interest is in how the phenomenal form of ideology functions to organize subjects and to mask the real foundations of capitalist society. Throughout, it is evident that he is straining to stop himself from losing his audience in media and communication studies by delving deeper into the societal mechanics of this process. His work between the mid-1970s and 1980s returns repeatedly to the question of the form and functions of ideology in capitalist society. The analysis of authoritarian populism may be regarded as the climax of these efforts.

I shall now turn to this work, leaving aside the subject of authoritarian populism, as it is more apposite to consider it in relation to Hall's position on the state and society, Hall's thought on ideology is best approached via an examination of his use of Marx, especially the 1857 Introduction to the *Grundrisse,* Gramsci, Althusser, Laclau and Mouffe. Other influences are formative in Hall's thought on ideology, notably Levi-Strauss, Barthes and Eco. However, I think that Marx, Gramsci, Althusser, Laclau and Mouffe can properly be attributed as seminal influences.

Hall's writing has a tendency towards didacticism. In his publications on ideology he is at his most didactic, frequently pulling up others for misreading key texts and conjunctures, and setting readers right, often in somewhat lapidary terms, about what constitutes 'good sense' in the analysis of culture and society.[5] Hall is not a sanctimonious writer, although he possesses a strong moral conscience that occasionally comes over as priggishness. For example, his accounts of the Birmingham tradition in Cultural Studies and the wrong turn taken by Cultural Studies in America (1989b; 1992; 1996) have a certain holier-than-thou quality which grates with some readers. His writings on ideology abound with a sense of delineating the terrain of cultural studies as distinct from sociology, politics and economics. They have an embattled quality as Hall struggled to open up new space, often in opposition to critics who doubted the very legitimacy of his enterprise. This problem loomed large in Hall's revision of culture in the Marxist tradition. The significance that he attached to this revision is evidence of his desire to remain identified with the Left. Later, as the linguistic turn in Hall's thought became pronounced, he grew more comfortable in professing Marxism 'without guarantees.' But in the work on ideology between the mid-1970s and mid-1980s, he is plainly struggling to achieve a new modus operandi within the Marxist legacy.

Notes

1. Hall's conflation of behaviourism with the Leicester School is arguably unfair. Although James Halloran and his colleagues were influenced by the behaviourist tradition in American media research, they were always more critical about the notion of transparent communication and the 'scientism' of media research than perhaps Hall allows. In a later contribution to ideology and

communication theory, Hall (1989) clarifies his position by arguing that the individualism and naturalism of behaviourist research in media and communications are the American tradition.

2. Although Hall does not refer directly to the work of Harold Garfinkel and his associates, he would have been aware of its significance. The influence of semiotics is more overt. In an interview published twenty years after the encoding/decoding paper, Hall cites the work of the early Barthes, notably *Elements of Semiology* and *S/Z,* and also Marx's 1857 Introduction to the *Grundrisse* as formative influences (1993: 254). Umberto Eco is also clearly standing in the shadows. Althusser is another influence. Indeed, Hall observes that the paper is 'founded on the Althusserian notion of the over-determined, complex totality' (1993: 261)

   The aetiology of the encoding/decoding paper is interesting. The level of analysis is far more sophisticated than Hall's paper on 'Innovation and decline in cultural programming on television' (1971), which he prepared as part of a report to UNESCO on Innovation and Decline in the Treatment of Culture on British Television. Hall may have felt hamstrung in the latter paper by the need to write in a style suitable for an official report. Certainly the discussion is largely descriptive, with little of the theoretical risks and inspiration demonstrated in the encoding/ decoding paper. Hall's citation of Marx's 1857 Introduction is significant. The importance that Hall attaches to the 1857 Introduction is evidence of a major shift in his engagement with the Marxist tradition. It freed him from the base-superstructure dilemma in Marxism, a dilemma from which his anti-essentialist soul would recoil. The liberation that Hall feels in finding consumption and culture taken seriously by Marx is evident in the theoretical range and confidence exemplified in the encoding/decoding paper.

3. His work with Ian Connell and Lidia Curti (1976) at the Birmingham Centre on the construction of current affairs programmes related power and signification at the heart of the broadcasting process. Hall and his associates argued that broadcasters gather, select and prearrange topics by mobilizing a variety of verbal and visual codes. Programme transmission is defined as an 'audio-visual discourse' involving systems of signification which encode 'preferred readings.' The broadcaster's professional encoding practices are geared to bringing the encoding and decoding moments into alignment in order to establish ideological closure and, *ipso facto,* to achieve a preferred reading of the topic. At the same time, polysemy means that absolute closure in the construction and reception of messages is impossible. Audiences are reflexive and decode meaning as an ordinary condition of the viewing process. The parameters of decoding are defined in fairly conventional sociological terms, as relating to class, status, gender, race and generation. Privileged access refers to the availability of politicians, business leaders and celebrities to the media. Hall's point is that media professionals move easily in elite circles and therefore have a higher risk of contamination with elite ideology. However, this point is not empirically developed in Hall's work. One profitable area of research might be to compare patterns of recruitment into the media and key elite institutions focusing on factors of class background, education, marital alliances and leisure practice. But this is not examined in Hall's work.

4. Achievement here is a double-edged sword. It refers to the unreflexive assimilation of the preferred reading, a condition that Hall describes as 'harmony' between the encoding and reception 'moments.' However, achievement also refers to the decoding of the encoded reading by working through the negotiated or oppositional codes to disable ideology.

5. The term bears a characteristically Gramscian inflection. Gramsci distinguished between 'common sense' and 'good sense.' Because he regarded common sense to be saturated with bourgeois values, he tended to scorn it. Good sense refers to the working-class consciousness that the mode of production in which they are enmeshed is limiting. As Hall put it: 'Working people have known that their ways of being in the world would always be different and would find forms of cultural expression, kinds of relationships, ways of building values into the day-to-day, which sets limits to the degrees to which the logic of capital could impose itself. That is good sense. It is the sense of what Lenin called "the class instincts" without which no political and intellectual work can be done' 1978: 10).

* An earlier version of "Representation and Ideology" was published in Chris Rojek, *Stuart Hall* (Polity Press: Cambridge, 2002), which he has revised for this text.

References

Alexander, J. (ed.) (2001) *Mainstream and Critical Social Theory.* 8 vols, London: Sage.

Beck U., Giddens, Al and Lash, S. (1994) *Reflexive Modernization.* Cambridge: Polity.

Eagleton, T. (1996) 'The hippest'. *London Review of Books,* Mar., pp. 3–6.

Easthope, A. (1991) *British Post-structuralism since* 1968. London: Routledge.

Elias, N. (1956). 'Some problems of involvement and detachment.' *British Journal of Sociology,* 7, no. 3: 226–52.

Hall, S. (1971) 'Innovation and decline in cultural programming on television.' Paper for UNESCO report.

Hall, S. (1973a) 'Encoding and decoding in the television discourse.' Stencilled Occasional Paper, Birmingham Centre for Contemporary Cultural Studies.

Hall, S. (1973b) 'A "reading" of Marx's 1857 Introduction to the *Grundrisse.' CCCS Occasional Papers* (Birmingham): 1–70.

Hall, S. (1974) 'Media power: the double bind.' *Journal of Communication,* 24, no. 4: 19–26.

Hall, S. (1977) 'Culture, media and the "ideological effect"'. In *Mass Communication and Society,* edited by J. Curran, M. Gurevitch and J. Woollacott, London: Edward Arnold: 315–48.

Hall, S. (1978) 'Marxism and culture.' *Radical History,* no. 18: 5–14.

Hall, S. (1981) 'Notes on deconstructing "the popular"'. In *People's History and Socialist Theory,* ed. R. Samuel, London: Routledge and Kegan Paul: 227–40.

Hall, S. (1984) 'The narrative construction of reality: An interview with Stuart Hall' *Southern Review, 17, no. 1:* 3–17.

Hall, S. (1989) 'Ideology and communication theory.' In *Rethinking Communication,* vol. 1: *Paradigm Issues,* ed. B. Dervin, London and Thousand Oaks: Sage: 40–52.

Hall, S. (1990, Summer). The emergence of cultural studies and the crisis of the humanities. *The humanities as social technology,* 53: 11–23.

Hall, S. (1992) 'Cultural Studies and its theoretical legacies.' In *Cultural Studies,* ed. L. Grossberg et al., London: Routledge: 277–86. Reprinted in Morley and Chen 1996.

Hall, S. (1993) Reflections upon the encoding/decoding model: An interview with Stuart Hall.' In *Viewing, Reading, Listaning: Audience and Cultural Reception,* ed. J. Cruz and J. Lewis. Boulder: Westview: 253–74.

Hall, S. (1995) Fantasy, identity, politics.' In *Cultural Remix,* ed. E. Carter, J. Donald and J Squires, London: Lawrence and Wishart: 63–9.

Hall, S. (1996) 'The formation of a diasporic intellectual: Interview with Kuan-Hsing Chen.' In *Stuart Hall: Critical Dialogues in Cultural Studies,* ed. D. Morley and K.-H. Chen, London: Routledge: 484–503.

Hall,S., Connell, I. and Curti, L. (1976) 'The "unity" of current affairs television.' Working Papers in Cultural Studies 9, Birmingham.

Halloran J. (1970) *The Effects of Television.* London: Panther.

Jordin, M. and Brunt, R. (1988) 'Constituting the television audience—a problem of method.' In *Television and Its Audience,* edited by P. Drummond and R. Patterson, London: British Film Institute.

Lewis, J. (1983) 'The encoding/ decoding model: criticisms and redevelopments for research on decoding.' *Media, Culture & Society,* 5 211–32.

Marx, K. (1971) *Gruindrisse* (1857). Edited by D. McLellan. New York: Harper and Row

Marx, K. and Engels, R. (1965) *The German Ideology.* London: Lawrence and Wishart.

McGuigan, J. (1992) *Cultural Populism.* London: Routledge.

Morley, D. (1980) *The 'Nationwide' Audience.* London: British Film Institute.

Morley, D. (1986) *Family Television.* London: Routledge.

Turner, B. (1984) *Body and Society.* Oxford: Blackwell.

Willis, P. (1977) *Learning to Labour.* London: Saxon House.

Willis, P. (1978) *Profane Culture.* London: Routledge and Kegan Paul.

4

■ A Propaganda Model

Edward Herman

In countries where the levers of power are in the hands of a state bureaucracy, monopolistic control over the media, often supplemented by official censorship, makes it clear that the media serve the ends of a dominant elite. It is much more difficult to see a propaganda system at work when the media are private and formal censorship is absent. This is especially true when the media actively compete, periodically attack and expose corporate and governmental malfeasance, and aggressively portray themselves as spokespersons for free speech and the general community interest. What is not evident (and remains undiscussed in the media) is the limited nature of such critiques, the huge inequality in ability to command resources, and the effects of such limitations both on access to a private media system and on its behavior and performance.

A propaganda model focuses on this inequality of wealth and power and its multilevel effects on mass media interests and choices. It traces the routes by which money and power are able to filter out the news fit to print, marginalize dissent, and allow the government and dominant private interests to get their messages across to the public. The essential ingredients of the propaganda model, or set of news "filters," fall under the following headings: (1) the size, concentrated ownership, owner wealth, and profit orientation of the dominant mass media firms; (2) advertising as the primary income source of the mass media; (3) the reliance of the media on information provided by government, business, and "experts" who are funded and approved by the primary sources and agents of power; (4) "flak" (negative and constraining feedback) as a means of disciplining the media; and (5) anticommunism as a national religion and control mechanism.[1] These elements interact with and reinforce one another. The raw material of news must pass through successive filters, leaving only the cleansed residue fit to print. The filters fix the premises of discourse and interpretation and the definition of what is newsworthy in the first place, and they explain the basis and operations of what amount to propaganda campaigns.

■ The First Filter: Size, Ownership, and Profit Orientation of the Mass Media

In their analysis of the evolution of the media in Great Britain, James Curran and Jean Seaton describe how a radical press emerged in the first half of the nineteenth century that reached a national working-class audience. This alternative press was effective in reinforcing class consciousness: it unified the workers because it fostered an alternative value system and framework for looking at the world and because it "promoted a greater collective confidence by repeatedly emphasizing the potential power of working people to effect social change through the force of 'combination' and organized action."[2] This was deemed a major threat by the ruling elites. One member of Parliament asserted that the working-class newspapers "inflame[d] passions and awaken[d] their selfishness, contrasting their current condition with what they contend to be their future condition—a condition incompatible with human nature, and those immutable laws which Providence has established for the regulation of civil society."[3] The result was an attempt to squelch the working-class media by using libel laws and prosecutions, by requiring an expensive security bond as a condition for publication, and by imposing various taxes designed to drive out radical media by raising their costs. These coercive efforts were not effective, and by midcentury they had been abandoned in favor of the liberal view that the market would enforce responsibility.

Curran and Seaton show that the market did successfully accomplish what state intervention failed to do. Following the repeal of the punitive taxes on newspapers between 1853 and 1869, a new daily local press came into existence, but not one new local working-class daily was established through the rest of the nineteenth century. Curran and Seaton note that

> Indeed, the eclipse of the national radical press was so total that when the Labour Party developed out of the working-class movement in the first decade of the twentieth century, it did not obtain the exclusive backing of a single national daily or Sunday paper.[4]

One important reason for this was the increase in scale of newspaper enterprise and the associated growth in capital costs from the mid-nineteenth century onward, which were based on technological improvements and owners' increased stress on reaching large audiences.

Thus the first filter—the ownership of media with any substantial outreach limited by the requisite large size of investment—was applicable a century or more ago, and has become increasingly effective over time.

■ The Second Filter: The Advertising License to Do Business

In arguing for the benefits of the free market as a means of controlling dissident opinion in the mid-nineteenth century, the Liberal Chancellor of the British Exchequer, Sir George

Lewis, noted that the market would promote those papers "enjoying the preference of the advertising public."[5] Advertising did, in fact, serve as a powerful mechanism that weakened the working-class press. Curran and Seaton give the growth of advertising a status comparable with the increase in capital costs as a factor that allowed the market to accomplish what state taxes and harassment failed to do. They note that these "advertisers thus acquired a de facto licensing authority since, without their support, newspapers ceased to be economically viable."[6]

Before advertising became prominent, the price of a newspaper had to cover the costs of doing business. As advertising grew, papers that attracted ads could afford a copy price well below production costs. This put papers that lacked advertising at a serious disadvantage: their prices would tend to be higher, which would curtail sales, and they would have less surplus to invest in changes that would improve the salability of the paper (features, an attractive format, promotion, etc.). For this reason, along with the economies of scale based on high first-copy costs,[7] an advertising-based system tends to drive out of existence or into marginality the media companies and types that depend on revenue from sales alone. With advertising, the free market does not yield a neutral system in which final buyer choice decides. The advertisers' choices influence media prosperity and survival.

■ The Third Filter: Sourcing Mass-Media News

The mass media are drawn into a symbiotic relationship with powerful sources of information by economic necessity and reciprocity of interest. The media need a steady, reliable flow of the raw material of news. Economics dictates that they concentrate their resources where significant news often occurs, where important rumors and leaks abound, and where regular press conferences are held. The White House, the Pentagon, and the State Department in Washington, D.C. are central nodes of such news activity. On a local basis, city hall and the police department are the subject of regular news beats for reporters. Business corporations and trade groups are also regular and credible purveyors of stories that are deemed newsworthy. These bureaucracies turn out a large volume of material that meets the demands of news organizations for reliable, scheduled flows. Mark Fishman calls this "the principle of bureaucratic affinity: only other bureaucracies can satisfy the input needs of a news bureaucracy."[8]

Government and corporate officials are also credible sources by virtue of their status and prestige. This is important to the mass media. As Fishman notes,

> Newsworkers are predisposed to treat bureaucratic accounts as factual because news personnel participate in upholding a normative order of authorized knowers in the society. Reporters operate with the attitude that officials ought to know what it is their job to know…In particular, a newsworker will recognize an official's claim to knowledge not merely as a claim, but as a credible, competent piece of knowledge. This amounts to a moral division of labor: officials have and give the facts; reporters merely get them.[9]

Another reason for the heavy weight given to official sources is that the mass media claim to be "objective" dispensers of the news. Partly to maintain the image of objectivity, but also to protect themselves from criticisms of bias and the threat of libel suits, they need material that can be portrayed as presumptively accurate. This is also partly a matter of cost: taking information from sources that may be presumed to be credible reduces investigative expense, whereas material from sources that are not prima facie credible, or that will elicit criticism and threats, requires careful checking and costly research.

■ The Fourth Filter: Flak and the Enforcers

Flak refers to negative responses to a media statement or program. It may take the form of letters, telegrams, phone calls, petitions, lawsuits, speeches and bills before Congress, and other modes of complaint, threat, and punitive action. It may be organized centrally or locally, or it may consist of the entirely independent actions of individuals.

If flak is produced on a large scale, or by individuals or groups with substantial resources, it can be both uncomfortable and costly to the media. Positions have to be defended both inside and outside the organization, sometimes before legislatures and possibly even in courts. Advertisers may withdraw patronage. If certain kinds of fact, position, or program are thought likely to elicit flak, this prospect can be a deterrent.

Freedom House, an example of a well-funded flak organization that dates back to the early 1940s, has had interlocks with Accuracy in Media (AIM), the World Anti-Communist League, Resistance International, and U.S. government bodies such as Radio Free Europe and the CIA, and has long served as a virtual propaganda arm of the government and international right wing. It has expended substantial resources to criticize the media for insufficient sympathy with U.S. client states. Its most notable publication of this genre was Peter Braestrup's *Big Story,* which contended that the media's negative portrayal of the Tet Offensive helped lose the Vietnam war. The work is a travesty of scholarship, but more interesting is its premise: that the mass media not only should support any national venture abroad, but should do so with enthusiasm, as such enterprises are by definition noble.

■ The Fifth Filter: Anticommunism as a Control Mechanism

A final filter is the ideology of anticommunism.[10] Communism as the ultimate evil has always been the specter that haunts property owners, as it threatens the very root of their class position and superior status. The Soviet, Chinese, and Cuban revolutions were traumas to Western elites, and the ongoing conflicts and the well-publicized abuses of communist states have contributed to the elevation of opposition to communism to a first principle of Western ideology and politics. This ideology helps mobilize the populace against an enemy, and because the concept is fuzzy it can be used against anybody who advocates policies that threaten property interests or supports accommodation with communist states and radicalism. It therefore helps fragment the left and labor movements and serves as a political control mechanism. If the triumph of communism is the worst imaginable evil, then the support of fascism abroad can be justified as a lesser evil. Opposition to social democrats who are too soft on communists and "play into their hands" is rationalized in similar terms.

Liberals at home, often accused of being procommunist or insufficiently anticommunist, are kept continuously on the defensive in a cultural milieu in which anticommunism is the dominant religion. If they allow communism, or something that can be labeled communism, to triumph in the U.S. sphere of influence while they are in office, the political costs are heavy. Most of them have fully internalized the religion anyway, but they are all under great pressure to demonstrate their anticommunist credentials.

■ Conclusion

The five filters narrow the range of news that passes through the gates, and even more sharply limit what can become "big news" that is subject to sustained news campaigns. By definition, news from primary establishment sources meets one major filter requirement and is readily accommodated by the mass media. Messages from and about dissidents and weak, unorganized individuals and groups, both domestic and foreign, are at an initial disadvantage in terms of sourcing costs and credibility, and they often do not comport with the ideology or interests of the gatekeepers and other powerful parties that influence the filtering process.

Notes

1 For an extension of this ideological control mechanism to a faith in the market, see "The Propaganda Model Revisited," chapter 18. *The Myth of the Liberal Media. An Edward Herman Reader.* (New York: Peter Lang, 1999).

2 James Curran and Jean Seaton, *Power Without Responsibility: The Press and Broadcasting in Britain,* 2nd ed. (London: Methuen, 1985), 24.

3 Ibid., 23.

4 Ibid., 34.

5 Ibid., 31.

6 Ibid., 41.

7 This factor is stressed in C. Edwin Baker, *Advertising and a Democratic Press* (Princeton: Princeton University Press, 1994), 21–22.

8 Mark Fishman, *Manufacturing the News* (Austin: University of Texas Press, 1980), 143.

9 Ibid., 144–45.

10 As I pointed out earlier, this final filter is readily extended to include belief in the "miracle of the market" as an ideological control mechanism.

5

■ How Producers "Theorize"

Shoot-outs, Bake-Offs, and Speed-Dating

John T. Caldwell

As scholars pursued Stuart Hall's field-forming call for studies of media "encoding-decoding," much of the scholarship that resulted focused on the backend of that equation. That is, cultural studies became a pervasive and influential field by mining a rich and extensive spectrum of cultural practices related to either consumption (viewing, reception, end-use, re-use, fandoms, marginalization, resistance, identity formation, media-cultural politics, social relations, etc.); or to textual practice (as it relates to those cultural activities). Far less work has emerged around the first site for Hall's model, media encoding, arguably because of industrial and legal obstacles to fieldwork and access, including corporate conglomeration.[1] Yet the industry is not as monolithic as we sometimes make it. In fact, as fewer and fewer media conglomerates seem to own everything in sight, the actual work-worlds intersecting the super-companies now churn with an incredibly complex array of production modes, social interactions, cultural practices, and contention. Far from being a hardened monolith, therefore, "the industry" is actually a very porous political-economic phenomenon, comprised of hundreds of very different work sectors and conflicted social communities, locked in temporary alliances of willed affinity. Cultural studies would do well to acknowledge the complex, heterogeneous nature of these new risk-averse, flexibility-focused media conglomerates. Doing so would allow scholars to study industrial communities (not just audience or fan communities) "from the ground up" as lived, cultural phenomena. Far from being antithetical to political-economic approaches, studying media industry as a set of micro-social "cultures of production"—rather than as the engine behind the macroscopic "production of culture"—actually provides a complex array of evidence that supports many macroscopic political-economic critiques.

This chapter examines a range of current cultural activities among and between media workers and media corporations. This approach means confronting a reality that problematizes any cultural-studies-of-production methodology: namely, that contemporary film and television obsessively invest in, produce, and distribute self-analysis and critical knowledge about themselves to anyone looking in from the outside. In essence, the film and television industries already station a wealth of *preemptive "self-ethnographic"* accounts in the path of any ethnographer seeking to uncover "what is really going on" in the new media industries. Viewing such commercial reflexivity as lies or subterfuge is less productive than considering how this kind of workaday self-analysis and preemptive marketing is relevant for the maintenance and economic exploitation of both cultures of production *and* cultures of consumption. Before offering a critical theory about how the industry works, therefore, I first want to consider how producers and media workers themselves "theorize."

A great deal of what viewers see in film/TV critically mediates or deconstructs other forms of film/TV content. This obsessive self-scrutiny may suggest that the newly convergent industry now leads by hyping its theoretical and critical sophistication to viewers. But this is not always the case. In fact, although self-reflexive onscreen forms and genres—DVD bonus tracks, directors' commentaries, film festival retrospectives, making-of documentaries—show a constant churn of critical and theoretical ideas among practitioners, actual spoken disclosures by industry players, *in public,* commonly deny or disavow any agency or intellectual pretense. Far from being crass movers-or-shakers who exploit critical trends or cultural ideas, industry players tend to talk about themselves as simple, honest, and direct men; screenwriters in touch with the universalism of Aristotle's three-part drama and well-rounded characters; producers responsively creating what the common person wants; executives couching even lowest-common denominator programming as opportunities for reflection, consensus, and therapeutic escape. In trade talk, screenplays and films are never ideological, television shows are never racist or about race, and producer-creators never have a cultural axe to grind. Remarks by veteran writers, producers, and directors demonstrate one resilient way the industry poses rhetorically. Spoken denials of intention, relevance, and profundity, that is, rule retrospective trade talk. One senior writer dismisses the significance of the many edgy, intellectual references in his series with a standard explanation: "People think it's mostly a result of some deep effort. Mostly it's just about trying to be funny."[2] One film studio executive mocks intellectual pretension by defining producing in bodily, visceral terms: "as a zoo…as zoo-keeping"; as an emotional situation that "connects the producer's 'eureka' with the audience's epiphany." He then shares an "insider's" key to success in film/television: "You have to know when to kiss, and when to bite. Sometimes you need a public hanging." An agent and film executive mimics tragic, Nietzschean "hubris" in his approach to production: "I am not relying on the Gods to come down and give me an Academy Award. I am going to make my own destiny." Another producer likens producing to dangerous "high-stakes gambling," based on intuitive "hunches." Then goes on to define the multi-million dollar producing process in the most simplistic, Forrest Gump-like terms possible: "You're the guy who turns on the lights at the beginning of the project. And turns the lights off at the end."[3] Strangely, this same executive's *own* publicity underscores the producer's Ivy

League status as a graduate of "Harvard" to situate him industrially in the pantheon of prestige creators.

Consider the favored metaphors spoken here by film/TV executives to explain the feature filmmaking skill-set: animal husbandry, touchy-feely facilitation, gut instincts, kissing-biting, public lynching, meditative simplicity, mythic hubris, and simple care-and-feeding. I would argue that this metaphorical litany of "serious" explanations and disclosures is precisely why studying the industry from the top-down—that is, from the vantage point of above-the-line executives in interviews—can be so useless. At least if one wants to get past the cultural flak of personal branding in order to examine actual production activities. In this way, above-the-line self-disclosures can stand as interpretive cul-de-sacs, especially if one hopes to get beyond cultural expressions to understand deeper critical dimensions of industrial practice and daily work. Even as creative practitioners assume their formulaic but effaced, "it-was-nothing" posture, many of the films and series that these executives have produced have generated immense amounts of critical writing that exposes the dense cultural and intellectual intertexts that form the very fabric of many productions.The practitioner disavowal systematically deployed in executive rhetoric here can also be found in other film/video production sectors. In some cases, producer disavowals tame industrial complications and so cover-over economic and ideological dimensions of media. In other cases practitioner disavowals legitimate long-standing, tightly held industrial mythologies.[4]

As public-relations and producer rhetoric announce that the industry is only about basic human values, "emotional transport" and "entertainment," however, the deep texts, socio-professional networking, new technologies, and stylistic methods all suggest something very different. Even though administrative hierarchies, bottom-line thinking, legal constraints, and producers' *overt rhetorical disclosures* may underscore self-sufficiency, creative intuition, moral integrity, and mystique, various *embedded texts and practices* may demonstrate the importance of cooperative work. This avowal/disavowal habit regularly inflects public events. Advertisements for a L.A. event honoring one distinguished screenwriter promised that the featured speaker "will try not to be boring," and publicized the event with the subtitle: "Why People Who Suck Make It Big. AKA: More Hollywood Gas-Bags Yak About Themselves."[5] This *Beavis-and-Butthead* posture of feigned disinterest and self-contempt frequents public appearances and Q&As. Yet the same pose is dramatically undercut by endless DVD bonus tracks intended to "prove" the opposite: the acute intentionality of practitioners in all aspects of production. Former executive Martin Kaplan notes that in Hollywood "both sides of transaction(s) assumed that rank insincerity was baseline behavior; everyone also understood that 'yes' could just as easily mean 'no.'"[6] This habitual duplicity he linked psychologically to the "imposter syndrome, in which people have nightmares that they will be discovered to have no credentials for their job."

Despite such denials of significance, production cultures publicly act-out their critical abilities on a daily basis as part of a new industrial and commercial imperative.[7] The conflicted industry habits just described and in the sections ahead—disclosure/non-disclosure, avowal/disavowal, habitual duplicity—can be understood not as any "essential" affect in Hollywood, therefore, but as arbitration mechanisms used to manage industrial change. Analytical and critical disclosures, that is, are fundamental parts of this organizational process. Universal Pictures Chairwoman Stacey Snider, for example, "educated" her new "old business" partners in the GE/NBC conglomerate with what she termed her "movie business 101 primer," which explains Hollywood terminology such as "tent-pole pictures and franchise strategy."[8] Snider's theoretical disclosures about film proved crucial ways that employees from film (whose "business is built on relationships" and mystique) could enable employees from GE (whose "plastic business is based on how many contracts they can get in China") to productively co-exist within a single multimedia conglomerate. Detailed critical, analytical disclosures are increasingly part of the fabric of film/television work.

Some work sectors establish critical analysis by the group as a winnowing "gate" before allowing products to surface as candidates for industry-wide attention. Every year, for example, the Motion Picture Editors Guild hosts the AMPAS sound branch's annual group ritual of competition—and artistic disclosure—entitled "The Bake-Off." As part of the process, the Editors Guild provides its members a detailed list of artistic criteria to use in judging the films that had been pre-nominated by effects editors ("sub-woofer rumble does not a profound reel make," "louder is not better," "recognize subtle, tasty, thought-provoking work under 96 SPL," etc.).[9] Another example of this kind of Geertzian "focused gathering" occurs at the trade gathering and technical "camp" called "HD Expo." The women coordinators of 2005 HD Expo in Los Angeles facilitated intense personal disclosures by practitioners by organizing what it termed an "HD Speed Dating with Industry Experts" event. Lucky participants got 5 minutes of "face-time" to ask a succession of 20 individual experts their "burning questions, get insider tips, how-tos, and knowledge of new trends." A bell gonged every 5 minutes, sending each solicitor on to the next in a long line of interpersonal "hook-ups."[10] The industry also stimulates disclosure—by rigidly controlling it—in the form of the semi-annual "Television Critics Association" meetings in Los Angeles. The TCAs were launched to provide journalists with important insights and behind-the-scenes realities behind each season's primetime programming. Rather than the unfettered gateway to industry access that the concept may presuppose, the TCAs now unfold as a frenzied interactive ritual choreographed by programming executives and publicists who deftly know how to sway and influence critics by strictly managing access to stars and to a succession of meeting-related parties. The TCAs' own website underscores how tightly journalistic standards are now bound to industry access and even conglomeration: "Set visits…may be coordinated not by individual presenters but by corporate partnerships inspired by industry consolidation."[11] The TCAs are one of the most explicit examples of how the industry's ostensible sharing, openness, and disclosure function more like a publicist's tightly coordinated dog-and-pony show. Even though reviewers resent being carefully led around by the nose, they must "play by the rules" if they want to continue with the kind of access and industry snapshots that their media editors expect of them.

Even professional interactions that appear to be benign, therapeutic opportunities for personal development are frequently designed, instigated, or overseen by corporations. Screenwriting software companies, for example, sponsor professional "user-groups," and bulletin boards to facilitate "community" and critical "feedback" among writers. In building its professional community, one enabling company announced: "We welcome new people...no reservations required."). [12] In a related vein, Los Angeles Center Studios sponsors what it terms "weekend shootouts" for various "aspiring" film workers employed by any company renting production space on its lot and sound-stages. Shoot-outs are essentially no-budget filmmaking opportunities. Writers write scripts on Fridays, based on 2 arbitrarily selected words (a verb and an adjective). 30 volunteer film workers, light, shoot, edit and mix a film in two days. The "final" shoot-out film is screened Sunday evening, and a party is thrown on the lot to celebrate. Many regional film festivals mount the same kinds of manic, no-budget filmmaking shootouts to lure filmmakers out into the provinces. LA Center Studios uses shootouts to market itself to potential renters as a film "campus," while regional festivals (Sundance wannabes) use shootouts to build "edgier" fest circuit brands.

A peculiar industrial logic lies behind the kinds of imaginative, ostensibly creative group self-disclosures that unfold at weekend shoot-outs, screenwriter/therapy workshops, new technology camps, pitchfests, critics meetings, and professional speed-dating events. Each of these implicitly enabling initiatives: 1) cost relatively little; 2) produce either free on-screen content or buyers/renters for commercial products/services; 3) exploit LA's acute oversupply of production labor; and 4) facilitate orgies of smart, personal self-disclosures without having to pay for them, even as the companies hosting such events largely control of the results (for either marketing or direct financial gain). The theatricalized group self-disclosures at the heart of these activities represent only the tip of the disclosure/non-disclosure iceberg. Each labor sector has numerous mechanisms which facilitate the exchange of critical insider knowledge: media lab researchers with Ph.D.s promulgate new standards for the field at Siggraph or in the *SMPTE Journal;* CNN brands its research-driven prowess with specific affluent, educated demographic groups for ad-buyers and programmers; SCRI sells annual "Global Trends Reports," and "Brand Awareness and Ratings Reports" to time- and resource-stretched broadcasters; and semi-exclusive trade publications are invented "to educate television and station network owners, management and engineering talent on the opportunities and challenges presented by the latest technological developments." [13] As in any industry, these latter forms of basic critical knowledge about new technologies, methods, trends, markets, and buyers necessarily pervade trade discourses in film/television as well. Unlike other industries, however, film/television seems particularly adept at staging and dramatizing critical industrial self-disclosures as bracketed artistic or entertainment experiences for its professional members.

Couching or theatricalizing trade knowledge as personal, cultural sophistication in this way proves an efficient way to stimulate workers to innovate while keeping any tangible labor or legal responsibilities for them at arm's length. Cultural relationship building in the trades helps move the process along. One videographer explained the key to the quintessential meta-text of below-the-line workers, a good demo tape: "If they cry, they'll buy...a good demo should show emotion." [14] For film/television workers, establishing this kind of emotional relationship with other practitioners is arguably as important as establishing such a bond with consumers. Mass media audiences are positively influenced by what economist De Vany terms film marketing's "information cascade," but professional practitioners depend upon more nuanced forms of community building and different kinds of reflexivity.[15] Excessive, critical therapeutic sharing among industrial workers may make the industry's systematically regulated disclosures to consumers particularly effective.

■ Reflexivity as Industrial Culture Jamming

The recent explosive growth and popularity of self-referencing, self-disclosure, and organizational transparency in film/TV have been stimulated by at least four general factors: by the wide-ranging breakdown of traditional barriers between media professionals and audiences; by new digital technologies that have animated the cross-cultural leaks and blurred borders that once distinguished lay and professional media worlds; by the increasingly dense clutter of multimedia markets which require self-referencing meta-texts for effective viewer navigation; and by increased competition and task uncertainty which triggers pressures to symbolically value craft distinction and innovation in public ways.

Given the scale and diversity of the film and television industries—a world with at least 250 different "official" job categories, far more unofficial ones, and a quarter million workers in Southern California—discerning general principles may seem myopic, wishful, or misguided.[16] Yet several trends have recurred across the discrete production sectors.[17] In the model I have used in this chapter, top-down self-referencing (or reflexivity) *by corporations* makes sense as an outgrowth of two contemporary corporate goals: first, to "level industrial distinctions" in the production/labor chain; and second, to "level hierarchical distinctions" in the market/distribution chain. While the immediate, abstract goal of the first strategy is to lower corporate costs and eliminate costly labor "entitlements," something more profound and unsettling unfolds alongside these benefits. Leveling and confusing long-standing labor distinctions and job titles in the production workforce—between colorists and timers, DPs and directors, producers and executives, editors and sound-designers, story editors and screenwriters, reality PAs and union editors, production designers and visual effects supervisors—keeps much of the workforce off-balance and stirred up with inter-craft contention. The manic pace of production today—in union and non-union work, on location and in post-production work—reflects this objective. Desperate filmmaking increases productivity, and, some now argue, creativity. The erosion of job classifications also helps drive down production costs and scale, as production companies unintentionally emulate the reform ethos of the outsider's *Scratchware Manifesto* in order to create innovative titles with small teams for affordable purchase.[18] Such tactics reinforce what I now consider to be the new uber-fantasy and goal of Hollywood: *to acquire content for little or no cost and to get everyone to work for free.*

While the second strategy—leveling hierarchies in the market/distribution chain— aims to cultivate direct and efficient economic relations with media consumers (by cutting out middlemen), it too has a more lasting cultural impact. Endless publications hail the new consumer power that now ostensibly drives film and television in the United States due to digital interactivity. Fewer accounts acknowledge that Internet-driven media, blogging, and uploading also provide ideal conditions within which the media conglomerates succeed in utterly traditional business activities (like cutting out the middlemen) and direct-to-consumer marketing. The collapse of the barriers between media producers and consumers, then, is less about democracy than it is about facilitating two specific tactical film/TV goals: first, the creation of information cascades on multiple platforms (a publicity-driven viral process needed to maximize buzz around exceptional, blockbuster franchises); and second, the cross-promotion of less exceptional conglomerate properties (advertising-driven promotions needed to raise mundane, syndicated content above the media market clutter). The shrinkage of the box-office distribution window from 6 months to 4 months before DVD release, and in some cases the release of content on all media platforms simultaneously, has made finding the audience a chaotic industrial free-for-all. The new direct-to-consumer imperative makes self-referencing and hyper-marketing a necessary corporate skill set. The deer-in-the headlights assault of YouTube by Sumner Redstone in March 2007 illustrates the business logic of unsettling the distribution chain. By suing YouTube for $1 billion at the same time that its corporate partner CBS struck a major deal with YouTube, Viacom's schizophrenic relations placed chains on the uploaders even as the company opened its own distribution floodgates. As the majors wring their hands about no longer "owning" distribution, they textually carpet-bomb video-sharing sites thereby making every uploader and downloader a potential distributor.

One contradiction of this dynamic is that the industrial leveling of distinction in both the labor chain and the market chain occurs even as the same conglomerates generate excessive degrees of distinction in the form of abundant and ever-narrower consumer niches. Job categories blur. Taste mutates endlessly. Corporate reflexivity provides one effective way to proliferate the sense of distinctiveness among consumers. Distinction-invoking texts dominate *external* corporate and consumer discourses. At the same time, however, managers drag out an array of *internal* distinction-reducing rituals to "enable" workers to multi-task, distribute cognition, disperse authority, share competencies, inspire the workplace community, and convert labor itself into artistic expression. Management tomes praise the benefits of non-hierarchical workplace "sharing" but attempt to precipitate it by creating agitated, adrenalin-driven "hot-spots" within companies. Good for management, perhaps, but alarming for most workers.[19] Others conflate this unstable leveling and sharing with a corporation's moral "purpose" and "altruism."[20] Throughout *Production Culture* I have described how these sorts of two-faced organizational contradictions help conglomerates move light-and-fast on their feet. The major conglomerates remain profitable, despite their institutional and fiscal inertia, by pursuing the two fundamental requirements of post-Fordist business: to effectively externalize risk (through co-productions, presales, crowd-sourcing, merchandizing, and ancillary markets); and to effectively cultivate flexibility (through outsourcing, contract labor, short-term labor commitments, and rapid project-based incorporation cycles). Wooing *consumers* in this kind of cluttered market requires sophisticated meta-textual abilities and corporate transparency. NBC, CBS, and Fox can no longer expect young viewers to "find" them in the clutter, so now send some screen content to as many media-sharing sites as possible. At the same time, soliciting *workers* reeling from industrial flux demands as much in the way of innovative self-referencing and self-disclosure.

The collision of self-reflexive corporate strategies and self-reflexive worker counter-measures can be gauged in three arenas in which the contest unfolds, each governed by informal principles of reflexivity. Specifically, corporate activities generate *unruly work-worlds, unruly technologies,* and *unruly audiences.* The picture of corporate-versus-worker warring I've sketched thus far may look too causal, top-down, and deterministic. In practice, any fieldwork in the world of production shows that there is as much ground-up worker agency and resistance as there is top-down corporate control and acquiescence. Reconsidering the three "unruly" industrial spaces just described—but now from "below"—proves this point. First, in the off-balance, increasingly division-less, unruly workworld of crews, worker reflexivity constantly negotiates and resuscitates technical and craft identities for vocational survival. Much reality programming is nonunion, and all reality shows are scripted, the majority surreptitiously by story editors and members of produc-ers' staffs. Fearing the networks' plans to use reality shows as warehoused "filler" to circumvent the unions if labor strikes ensued, the WGA and IATSE went after CW's top show *Top Model* by asking the NLRB to intervene in 2006. The NLRB sided with the unions, prompting IATSE president Thomas Short to draw out the moral: "This election points up the importance of bottoms-up organizing and grass-roots representation…these (types of) employees have always belonged in the IA, and we are pleased to bargain on their behalf."[21] This was a warning shot across the bow to networks everywhere against collapsing job descriptions. It succeeded by critically challenging the industrial genre theory that had made spurious aesthetic/labor distinctions between fiction and reality screen content. *From labor's perspective, the reflexive principle of unruly workworlds means that the histories, hierarchies, and cultural rhetoric of crafts increase in prominence and intensity as the oversupply of labor increases.*

Second, in response to the disruptiveness of new and unruly digital technologies, worker reflexivity is deployed to legitimize one technical or craft group over another, usually by establishing superior competence and thus exclusivity. ABC, Fox, and NBC opened up the new digital technology gates in Fall of 2006 to allow viewers to freely download expensive primetime programs, like *Heroes, Prison Break,* and *Ugly Betty,* imme-diately after airing. One problem. In the networks' giddy embrace of video sharing and video iPods, half-century-old precedents for paying screenwriters syndication royalties or "residuals" on the shows they'd written was thrown out the window. "We've learned from history that when these new technologies emerge we can be left behind," said one union spokesman.[22] Again, only critical legal arguments from the unions—these were syndicated end-uses, not just marketing—forced the networks to back away from the digital free-for-all. Once again, labor had to make convincing arguments that the new portable and mobile technologies fit the old definition of syndication and distribution windows. Industry's well-managed confusion between self-referential marketing and content was at the root of the conflict. *From labor's perspective, the reflexive principle behind these unruly technologies is that craft and worker theorizing, self-referencing, and collective cultural activities increase as the pace of technical obsolescence accelerates.* Distinctions between workers do in fact matter.

Third, worker reflexivity also churns in response to the unruly audiences that now threaten the lucrative job guarantees once securely held by organized production labor.

Users, fans, and digital uploaders increasingly share production and aesthetic competencies with film/TV workers. What makes production workers distinctive and economically valuable, therefore, now matters a great deal. As one wearied, middle-aged videographer complained, "The sad part is that…a lot of good, talented people will suffer.…It seems that (our profession) is constantly being undermined by wannabes."[23] *From labor's perspective, the reflexive principle of unruly audiences is that worker claims of "professionalism" increase as the popularity and circulation of user-generated-content increases.* Dismissing amateurs, independents, and outsiders is a time-honored cultural habit in Hollywood, one that goes hand-in-hand with high-production values and the cult of technical superiority. Behind the trade harangues against amateur uploaders and 1-person crews, however, many film/TV workers in the lesser ranks are also quietly migrating to the lower-stakes world of the Internet. Break.com now pays pros to produce uploads; YouTube compensates the best of its uploaders from ad schemes, and Jack Black and his Hollywood "entourage" pose as outsiders who—with actual outsiders from Channe1101.com—co-produce "TV pilots" for the VH1 series *Acceptable TV* (part of the giant Viacom conglomerate).

In Los Angeles, some forms of industrial self-reflexivity circulate around the interpersonal ground-zero of disenchanted employees, who "de-fame" their producer/executive bosses at "DeFamer.com," who take-down former on-set celebrities at "TMZ.com," or who bitch and moan anonymously online about horrible conditions caused by specific producers on the set. Remember that for every fan "spoiler" who ruins future plot episodes of *Lost* through cultural espionage, there are crewmember spoilers who sabotage series story-arc secrets and skewer showrunner hubris by "leaking" episode info before broadcast. But it gets even more complicated than that. Fans, lay critics, and production employees are not the only ones launching cynical criticisms and unauthorized "snarking" against shows and producers on "Televisionwithoutpity.com" (TWOP). Producers and executives themselves anonymously wade through this site, facing critical deconstructions of their shows, in order to monitor reception and, if possible, influence it positively. By 2007 Bravo, a network in the Universal-NBC conglomerate, purchased TWOP precisely in order to harness the churning, agitated buzz of worker and corporate reflexivity as part of the industrially incestuous programming flow that has come to define the Bravo brand.

Dozens of my students in Los Angeles (having recently fled from alienated positions as burned-out producer's assistants, interns, and PAs in order to return to graduate school) vouch that if producers or executives themselves do not produce positive preemptive disinformation about their shows and films on these sites, then their employee minions at lower levels do. It's easy enough to see production worker online rants as "resistant" forms of reflexivity, but what is one to make of gangs of anonymous PAs and interns posing as fans on faux-blogs and MySpace.com? As one "desk slave" (AKA producer's assistant) marveled: "I watched firsthand as [he] high-jacked the Hollywood subculture and used its obsessive information sharing network for personal gain. The machinery of fame was waiting. I just had to turn it on."[24] Once you open this can of worms—recognizing industry's pervasive presence inside online fandom—it's difficult to imagine that anything could be truly "unruly" here. The producers and agents behind industrial lurkers are of course "workers" too, but the systematic self-referencing going on when they weigh in online makes their "personal expressions" far more like corporate than worker reflexivity. Higher-up still on the continuum are marketing department professionals who systematically generate viral buzz campaigns as part of what is now called "crowd-sourcing" or "hive-sourcing." At this level, individual self-referencing by workers has given way almost entirely to the institutional parameters and corporate reflexivity that set them in motion in the first place. This suggests that highly publicized recent attempts by Stephen Bochco to retool his tightly scripted, A-List primetime persona for the "unscripted," "distracting" and "spontaneous" aesthetic of uploading culture are merely the tip of a much bigger, but submerged, producer iceberg.[25]

This kind of coercive practice should change how we describe and address online agency and cherished academic notions of audience "resistance." Alternative media producers, DIY activists, and scholars have made convincing arguments for "culture-jamming." This counter-media anti-conglomerate strategy essentially updates for the information age Luddite calls for individual workers "to throw a wrench into the machine." The Internet and digital media now provide optimum conditions for realizing the culture-jamming imperative, since access to the master's "machine" is now ostensibly available to everyone. Being effective in culture jamming, however, should also require being aware of the bigger picture unfolding inside the networked machine. I would argue that the industrial reflexive activities detailed in this book demonstrate that there are many media employees as well as fans systematically throwing textual wrenches into the machine as a systematic part of *corporate culture jamming*.

Two examples of corporate culture jamming are instructive in this regard, one successful, the other a failure. After the positive "up-front" hype that greeted NBC's elite new signature show by Aaron Sorkin, *Studio 60* in May 2006, the network created a fake fan blog-site called Defaker.com to preemptively generate viral buzz about the show. Problem was, the half-hearted attempt to have NBC employees fake fan amateurism by simply paraphrasing studio press-releases and posting production stills as surveillance photos was quickly read by real fans as a deception—and an insult at that. NBC paid the price. The same fans (spurred on by Defamer.com) that were to have turned the show into a viral phenomenon instead loaded up the NBC website with damning critiques of the naïve amateurism of NBC and its office minions, which forced the site to shut down. Six months later, another studio plant by the producers of the CBS series *How I Met Your Mother,* "The Robin Sparkles" MySpace page, pulled off the same kind of lie, but this time to raves from both the online community and respected journalists as well.[26] The difference? The CBS/Robin Sparkles page was deftly integrated into the content of the show, so that primetime episodes raised significant narrative questions (flashbacks, references to memories) that could only be answered on the MySpace page, and developed a system of cues whereby fans knew when to turn to the website to complete the narrative. Site hits spiked from 100 to more than 5000 hits in the first day, prompting the showrunners to deem the stunt an "online brush fire," and a way to "activate the fan base, to turn them into advocates for your show."[27] As the budgets of standard reflexive "making-of" documentaries for any feature film regularly now run into the millions of dollars, fake blog and websites by studios and networks only seem to work if there is a considerable critical, theoretical, *and* economic investment in creating complex, challenging narrative and screen forms that fans want to deconstruct in a multimedia environment. Industrial culture jamming like this, therefore, is not for the faint of heart, the under-capitalized corporation, or the low-budget crowd.

On one level, the distinction between corporate and worker reflexivity can be expressed as follows. Corporate initiatives circulate meta-texts to conceptually manage instabilities and unruliness once labor and consumption distinctions are leveled. In effect, corporate reflexivity plays on the blurring of consumer identities *and* job descriptions in order to mine the economic confusion that follows on both ends of the spectrum. By contrast, worker reflexivity tends to resuscitate many of the leveled distinctions in the production/labor and market/distribution chains. In the world of industrially leveled distinctions, jobs, craft legitimacy, and careers are clearly always at stake. Workers know this, and seldom limit themselves to the physical job at hand. Along with online and on-set griping, self-defining statements and meta-commentaries continuously issue from the labor unions, guilds, and professional gatherings in an attempt to manage the volatility from the ground-up.

Yet the politics of worker-versus-corporate reflexivity are not as clear and unproblematic as the top-down versus ground-up model may imply. At least in union production, worker reflexivity emerges from professional communities that make their craft, association, or guild self-perpetuating through a quasi-medieval system requiring protracted mentoring. In Los Angeles, such groups still codify Taylorist efficiencies in order to maximize the degree to which production tasks and sub-routines are divided and distributed across department areas and crew. Given the nomadic system of rapid start-up/shut-down production incorporation, workers need to network in order to survive the unending cycles of unemployment. These instabilities provide the groundwork from which many of production's cultural activities described in this book are launched. As social and economic problem-solving operations, production culture now persistently cultivates ideals of unified industry in collusion with management in order to protect incomes after contracts are signed; converts work into cultural capital, via socio-professional rituals, demonstrations of craft ancestry, and meritocracy; and buffers underemployment by showing-off and leveraging cultural capital via credits and demo reels. From this perspective, the industry uses aesthetic and cultural capital to shortchange workers. But, given the yearly incomes of many in the industry, including below-the-line workers, it is difficult to explain this short-changing as a form of victimization. Yes, organized labor is under attack, and jobs threatened. But even as the old labor system slips, slides, and regroups, many of its practices remain exclusionary. Labor's old guard—which is still predominantly white, male, and upper middle-class—seldom gets much sympathy from tens of thousands of non-union workers, industry aspirants, women, and people of color in Los Angeles. The resilience of the old system results in part because production labor maintains high-costs of entry and exclusivity. As such, production's cultural rhetoric preaches collectivity, even as it bars aspirants and outsiders from entry. Yes, production is anxious. But it is anxious for many more invisible aspirants and underemployed individuals off the set and outside the studio as well.

■ Segregating and De-Segregating Cultures of Production and Consumption

The growing confusion about what the industry now is, and is not, begs larger social questions. Several current industrial tendencies can be understood as defensive responses to this rising confusion over identity and limits. The relationship building and collective rituals described at the start of this chapter (shoot-outs, bake-offs, and speed-dating), make sense as part of two general tendencies: regeneration (keyed to the logic of the group); and legitimation (keyed to the logic of career and craft). These tendencies tend to *segregate* professional practices from audience activities, spotlighting their differences, by continuously redefining and re-valuing the otherwise uncertain futures of creative communities through expressions of professionalism.

From the perspective of *regeneration,* many cooperative activities of film/video workers can be understood as socio-professional forms of consensus-building or dissensus-making. These unification and segregating tendencies tend to emerge in response to broader institutional and industrial changes. Effectiveness at these processes proves crucial in the formation, survival, and recreation of production groups, firms, and associations. Both consensus and dissensus activities enable the diverse and heterogeneous coalition of craft communities to constantly redefine and regenerate themselves—through cultural expressions of willed affinity—as a temporarily unified industry. Such identity boundaries hold at least until competition or economic and technological change threatens consensual relationships and temporary tactical affinities. Practitioner networks also participate in broader social and professional processes, through rituals and events that define the industry in a symbolic and public relations sense. Members of unions and guilds, that is, don't just participate interactively in the technical tasks that define production in the work place. They also represent different groups that constantly cultivate either a sense of professional autonomy (when needed) or common cause and industry-wide consensus (when coalition is needed to crossover craft and company lines). Rapid technological change—and the threat of obsolescence that comes with it—has destabilized the traditional ways that tasks are distributed during a production. In response to these instabilities, companies regularly stage handholding events. One studio hosts holiday "tree-lighting ceremonies," to forge common "studio family" identities. Yet many who attend are transient producers and contract employees soon to be replaced by other migratory tenants on the lot when productions fold.[28] Without the "real" long-term employee "family" that defined and profited the studios in the classical era, contemporary companies work overtime to concoct imaginary families for their brands, in ways that cover over the depersonalizing churn of tenants and contract employees on the lot.

Industrial changes also animate the social rituals that are used to cultivate a craft or trade group's legitimacy. These *legitimizing activities* frequently seek to underscore the ostensibly "necessary" role the given craft or trade group plays within a common industry (even though this consensus and commonality can be largely symbolic). The production stories that practitioners tell are not just narratives about "what happened," they also function to sanction careers and crafts. As I suggest elsewhere, allegories are also arguments, and sometimes parables, that legitimize one or more perspectives even as they discredit others. I include in this proposition not simply the stories and anecdotes one finds in trade publications, or the career "war stories" that film/video professionals tell in public appearances, but also the icons, images, demo tapes, and self-representations that practitioners make across a wide range of formats. Invariably, by telling stories or making demos practitioners individualize industrial phenomena for career reasons. This tendency to personalize is fairly common in almost any field of work, since stories are among the most efficient ways to anchor more complicated ideas about any industry.[29] My research has been focused on both the career and institutional logics of trade narratives, iconographies, rituals, and spaces. Such forms and practices serve as self-reflections, or group self-portraits, thus providing scholars with evidence of workplace analysis and self-interrogation that is frequently as provocative as the films or series that the group produces for the public at large. Trade stories are told to value and resuscitate careers, but they are also emblematic expressions of trade group cultural preoccupations as well.

Two other tendencies—producers-as-audiences and consumerism-as-production (or producer-generated-users)—are antithetical to regeneration and legitimation, since they *blur lines* between producer and consumer. These trends operate systematically at a broader cultural level even though they are based on very local work practices. They are fueled by the need to *desegregate* professional and audience activities. This makes these last three tendencies particularly effective in popularizing the kinds of self-referencing that are at the heart of my argument. Professional knowledge about film/TV production now functions as a widespread cultural competence *and* consumer activity.

First, we seldom acknowledge the instrumental role that *producers-as-audience* members play or the role that the industry-as-cultural-interpreter plays. Film/video makers are also audiences and film/video encoders are also decoders. Media scholarship tends to disregard the inevitability of maker-viewer multi-tasking, and the industry's competence as an interpretive "audience."[30] Many favored binaries fall by the way when one recognizes the diverse ways that those who design sets, write scripts, direct scenes, shoot images, and edit pictures also fully participate in the economy, political landscape, and educational systems of the culture and society as a whole. Above-the-line producers, directors, and executives are especially good at intentionally confusing the audience/producer split. Executives frequently invoke hard numbers from research departments when useful—but ignore them when the data contradict their personal hunches or intuitions. To break this research/intuition quandary (and the managerial conflict that necessarily follows from it), executives employ one favored tactic. They master the pose of "speaking for the audience" in order to get their way in contentious production, development and programming meetings. In the final analysis, arguments that the "audience wants this" or "that" trump all others—at least if the person saying it has enough institutional power to ignore conflicting evidence to the contrary.[31] Production personnel also design productions vis-à-vis the parameters and constraints of consumer electronic and home viewing environments that they personally know. Media conglomerates, in turn, have shifted to direct audience merchandising and the DVD as the key to delivering features, given the inability of ratings and advertising systems to accurately track the multichannel flow in the home.[32]

Directors/editors use split screens and frenetic editing to keep apace of viewers' sensory acceleration, while producers design online components to engage the multi-tasking activities of increasingly distracted viewers.[33] To exploit these new digital options, TV creators develop mobile content and "snack TV" for hand-held "third screens"[34] and insert Internet referrals for the audience within screenplay dialogue and primetime scenes.[35] At the same time, online blogs "by" series characters help viewers solve fictional crimes before sending them back to view the next episode.[36] Finally, production personnel circulate publicly in consumer culture, and most film/television professional organizations seldom shy away from public exposure. Many associations and guilds have "speaker's bureaus," "educational divisions," and publicized "internship opportunities." Other companies cultivate and interact with the public through timely topical media events or by co-sponsoring local quasi-Sundance film festivals. Colleges host alumni meetings in L.A. for industry networking (AKA fund-raising) and mount "Alumni in Hollywood" issues for alumni magazines. Far from L.A. and New York film/television professionals circulate as short-term artists-in-residence, while film/video equipment companies, star DPs, editors, and directors travel widely to participate in regional production workshops and technical demonstrations.[37] All of these producer-as-audience initiatives work to merge audience identification with industrial identity.

Finally, although much has been made recently about *user-generated content* (UGC), far less attention has been focused on two other trends: what I term UGC's evil twin *producer-generated-users* (PGU); and the many ways that production analysis serves as a form of hyper-consumerism. Audiences themselves frequently function as self-conscious media producers and critics even as production theory and media aesthetics now circulate widely in and as consumer discourses. More than simply a technology-driven phenomenon, many popular press and websites now promulgate film/TV theory as fan discourses. As discussed earlier, metacritic.com and televisionwithoutpity.com compile second-order reflections on critical trends and biting deconstructions of film/TV style and content.[38] *Entertainment Weekly* and newspapers formulate film/TV "canons" through annotated lists of the "most important DVDs, films, TV shows you should own."[39] "Making-ofs" and behind-the-scenes documentaries promote "production thinking" as staples on many channels and networks (AMC, The Sci-Fi Channel, HBO, Bravo, Discovery, TNT, IFC, etc.). Plus, through reality television, "making-ofs" and "makeovers" have become entertainment programs. We don't just get *Extreme Make-over: Home Edition,* we get "The Making-of" *Extreme Make-over Home Editions: How'd They Do That.* We don't just get MTV's *Making of the Band* (about music video production), we get ABC's *Next Action Hero,* (blockbuster casting and acting), Jon Favreau's *Dinner for Five* (critical debates about cinema), AMC's *Shoot-out* (industry trends and film development), and HBO's *Project Greenlight.* (producing, directing, and managing a feature film). Given this televised cineastic milieu, the IFC Channel's series *Film School* (2004), *Film Festival* (2005), and Fox Movie Classics *After Film School* (2006) are actually fairly unremarkable exercises, since production pedagogy is *constantly* churning on many other channels as well. The theorizing bent also spills over into blockbuster films where some journalists pull out their philosophy 101 *Cliff Notes* to score smug big-screen references to "metaphysics," "ontological" inquiry, the "psychoanalytic id," "ancient philosophical conundrums about the nature of free will," and celebrity "intellectuals" from Columbia, Harvard, and Princeton.[40] Others paint a far darker picture of onscreen theoretical exhibitionism: "This summer, millions of teenagers have been invited to experience *the tedium and pedantry of graduate school in Dolby-surround,* accompanied by the latest special effects."

The Pretentious Summer Superhero

By A. O. SCOTT

The industry also solicits and "welcomes" contact with viewers. Test screenings "in Glendale" or "Peoria" have been a part of the Hollywood mystique for decades. But current economic conditions have made the solicitation of viewers for service as focus groups, online, or test screening participants even more intense.[41] These public solicitations posture audience research less as a "deal with the devil" than as a unique opportunity to change culture and "serve the entire viewing public" by building personal relationships with producers, who are (apparently) standing by, waiting for each viewer's every command. Critical acumen about production, therefore, doesn't just travel from Los Angeles to the heartland. It supposedly surges back to Hollywood, in an ecstasy of shared, staged critical analysis from the provinces as well.[42] Viral multimedia marketing and PGU strategies also employ numerous new media formats to perpetuate production's conceptual frameworks as viewing frameworks.[43] The widespread network/studio practices discussed earlier of planting faux personal videos by "fans" on MySpace.com and YouTube.com in order to virally market forthcoming features, or of harvesting antagonistic personal video "mashes" on the same sites as part of anti-marketing campaigns, provide merely the latest evidence that lines between producers and consumers have irrevocably clouded.[44] Producers generate faux-amateur content, buy and distribute amateur content professionally, provide online learning in film/video aesthetics, spin blogs and online discussions, spoil ostensible secrets as stealth marketing, snark and defame competitors, pose as fans, award fans, and are fans. Welcome to the brave new world of PGU.

Scholars have tended to fall back on a series of classic, totalizing binaries used to separate culture industry-and-citizenry, producer-and-consumer, and ideological perpetrator-and-victim. Yet these handy and neat binaries in no way reflect media industry activities today in the age of digital and conglomeration. That is, they fail to explain the complex cultural-industrial confusions that media industries now systematically pursue as strategic parts of their business plans. Certainly the heightened forms of self-analysis, deconstruction, and self-interpretation by film/video professionals examined in this chapter—together with the audience's ever-increasing awareness and sophistication with film/video production nuance—provide a space for critical interrogation every bit as complex as the onscreen, textual, or fan spaces typically isolated and targeted by scholars and professional critics. Given this state of affairs—the widespread bilateral infiltration of cultures of media production with cultures of media consumption—we would all do well to pay more than obligatory lip-service to the "encoding" side of Stuart Hall's classic cultural studies formulation. After all, the cultures of production are very much a part of the cultures of consumption that we live in each day.

* Excerpted, extensively revised, and reprinted by permission of Duke University Press from: Caldwell, John T., *Production Culture: Industrial Reflexivity and Critical Practice in Film and Television* (2008)

Notes

1. This disciplinary tilt to one side resulted less from any innate intellectual predisposition against analyses of media production than it did from two broad-based societal trends. First, media corporations like Viacom and Newscorp are exceptionally proprietary and guarded and seldom grant easy access to scholars for research or fieldwork. When access is achieved, blanket "confidentiality" and "non-disclosure agreements" effectively muzzle much that can be legally said or revealed. Second, the massive movement toward multimedia conglomeration following de-regulations over the past two decades has created the illusion that our media fates are now in the hands of fewer and fewer companies. Political-economy scholars have rightly excavated the incestuous corporate ties and collusion that now drive contemporary film and television through inside-dealing. Yet political economists and cultural studies scholars alike fail if they conflate the move and "reduction" toward fewer and fewer super-conglomerates, as evidence that media industries are more and more monolithic. Even casual contact with the human work force inside of these conglomerates shows that while boardroom activity may have become more totalizing and top-down, the actual activities that churn inside of and between these super companies are far from reductive.

2. When discussing the overt meta-critical and intellectual dimensions of *The Simpsons,* senior writer Tom Martin assumes a suspect pose by disavowing any meaningful intent on the part of the creators. In rejecting the notion that anything profound was engineered into or intended by the series, Martin suggests that most of the critical-theoretical barbs in the 12-year history of the series were purely the result of "accident." "People think it's mostly a result of some deep effort. Mostly it's just about trying to be funny."

3. These comments, from a studio executive, agent, and executive producer come from interviews at UCLA, December 7, 2005. (Persons are anonymous by request. University alumni affiliation of interview subjects also changed.)

4. One important issue to consider is "disclosures, but on whose terms?" Yours, mine? AMPAS and ATAS both have extensive "oral history" archives. This includes interviews with hundreds of below-the-line cinematographers and editors at AMPAS, and hundreds of on-camera, above-the-line, and below-the-line talent at ATAS. This is all very valuable stuff. But the questions have been asked, and the topics framed, by someone else, usually a non-scholar, for lots of different reasons. Invariably, these pre-packaged collections of interviews are created to ensure a given legacy. Usually, a labor or advocacy group is behind the recordings and collections. Using them for scholarship inevitably begs the question about how and why they were gathered, and for what purpose. And this broader question makes it important to consider the cultural politics of the advocacy organization (the union, guild, or honorary association). Once again, that status of these artifacts becomes an issue that must be addressed upfront in any study. Sponsorship or advocacy does not mean that the information is not valuable, rather, it means that an additional level of analysis must be brought to bear in understanding the insights made available.

5. These statements are from an announcement for an event celebrating the screenwriting of Ed Solomon, "The John Zakin Chair in Screenwriting," held at the James Bridges Theater in Los Angeles, April 4, 2005.

6. See Martin Kaplan, "Love Ya. Loved the Pitch. We'll Do Lunch. I'll Call," commentary in the *Los Angeles Times,* February 25, 2005.

7. Industrial reflexivity circulates through onscreen forms (making-ofs, show-biz reports or DVD director's tracks), and collective, critical interactions (in the deep texts and work spaces of film/video work worlds proper).

8. Snider's statement, and the anonymous comment that follows are from Richard Verrier and Claudia Eller, "Universal, GE Getting Acquainted," *Los Angeles Times,* May 6, 2005, c1, c5.

9. From Mark Mangini, *The Motion Picture Editors Guild Newsletter,* Vol. 18, N0.2, March/April 1997, reprinted at http://www.editorsguild.com/newsletter/MarApr97/bakeoff.html.

10. I observed and visually documented the "Speed Dating with Industry Experts" event, which was also publicized in "HD/High Def Expo" flyers and signage at the Los Angeles Center Studios, March 3, 2005.

11. The full text reads: "Current trends in the TV business are quickening the pace of change. Hotel-based interview sessions are now supplemented by set visits and other remote activities, some of which may be *coordinated not by individual presenters but by corporate partnerships inspired by industry consolidation.* As new business alignments emerge, and as tighter economics challenge us all, TCA strives to keep its members' coverage ahead of the curve." This statement is from http://tvcritics. org/interview2.htm (italics mine.)

12. See "The Dramatica Writers Group—Free!" posted at http://www.dramatica.com/community/writer_group/index.html.

13. For these traditional forms of industrial knowledge-exchange, see John A. Watlington and V. Michael Bove, Jr., "Stream-Based Computing and Future Television," *SMPTE Journal,* April 1997, 217–224. Direct mail and trade ads entitled "Buy CNN: Get Light Viewers," stated that the network was quantifying its "reach with more light viewers [affluent, educated], more than any other news network"), and were distributed by CNN in Fall 2004. See also "Welcome to the SCRI Website" at http://www.seri.com/index2/html. The final quote is from "Letter from the Publisher," posted Spring 2005 on the website for the trade *Broadcast Engineering.*

14. This quote by videographer Jenny Lehman, is from Geoff Daily, "Reel 'Em In: An Essential Part of Any Videographer's Marketing Materials Is an Effective Demo Reel," *EventDV,* January 2005, 24–29, 25.

15. See Arthur De Vany, *Hollywood Economics: How Extreme Uncertainty Shapes the Film Industry.* New York: Routledge, 2003.

16. This figure of 250 "craft classifications" is for film, video, and CGI only, not for television, broadcasting, or the music industry, and is from the definitive text by William E. Hines, SOC, *Job Descriptions for Film, Video, and CGI,* Los Angeles: Ed-Venture Books, 1999.

17. These persistent tendencies can be mapped on a wide continuum, ranging from institutionalized corporate reflexivity on one end to inter-personalized worker reflexivity on the other. (See "Appendix 3" in my book *Production Culture.*) Corporate reflexivity involves top-down self-referencing, organizational relations, and is closely related to marketing. By contrast, worker reflexivity can be understood via more local forms of self-referencing, socio-professional relations, and individual expression. Corporate reflexivity encompasses a world of branding, marketing, making-ofs, meta-texts, franchises, DVD extras, EPKs, and conglomeration, while worker reflexivity includes mentoring, how-to panels, trade stories, technical retreats, and craft meritocracies. While it may be tempting to force this corporate-versus-worker continuum into the long-standing mold that opposes macro political economies and micro sociologies of work, I have tried to show how both extremes involve a rich array of cultural self-representation and visual expression. Cultural texts, that is, are fundamental parts of both corporate practices and labor activities. Attempting to understand the industry's economy without understanding these cultural textual practices provides only part of the picture of film/TV workworlds. Likewise, attempting to understand production culture's reflexive texts without also understanding the economy that animates them is shortsighted as well. It is difficult,

furthermore, to mark precisely where human agency ends and corporate control begins on the continuum.

18. Greg Costikyan's *Scratchware Manifesto* is praised in Jared Newman, "Rogue Leader," *Wired,* Jan. 2007. P. 70.

19. See Lynda Gratton, *Hot Spots,* London: Berrett-Koehler, 2007.

20. See Nikos Mourkogiannis, *Purpose: The Starting Point of Great Companies,* London: Palgrave Macmillan, 2007.

21. This quote and account are from Carl DiOrio, "'Model' a Step Closer to Unionization,"www. Hollywoodreporter.com/hr/content_display/news, posted Dec. 5, 2006.

22. This quote is from Richard Verrier, "Residuals Debate: Old Script on New Set," *Los Angeles Times,* Nov. 27, 2006. A1.

23. This is from a letter to the editor of *TV Technology,* April 2, 2007. p.4.

24. See Nick Confalone, "Revenge of the Desk Slaves," *Los Angeles Times,* April 22, 2007. M8.

25. The Emmy-winning creator of *Hill Street Blues* and *LA Law* moved from the hour-long format of his primetime dramatic series to the 60-second format of the Internet on his new show *Cafe Confidential,* which premiered online at Metacafe.com on March 19, 2007. The point about the difference between the old, scripted Bochco, and the new, unscripted Bochco, is from Alex Phram, "To Make a Long Story Short," *Los Angeles Times,* March 19, 2007. C1, C6.

26. Even the *New York Times* appreciated the sophistication of this stunt. See Joe Rhodes, "A Fictional Video on MySpace Puts a TV Show's Promotion into Hyperspace," www.nytimes.com/2007/04/09/business/media/09sparkles.html , April 9, 2007.

27. The "online brush fire" analogy is from show producers Craig Thomas and Carter Bays. The comment about fans as "advocates" is from Steven Melnick, Senior VP of Marketing at 20th Century Fox Television, as quoted in Rhodes.

28. At the December 2005 "holiday tree lighting" at Paramount, for example, studio executives celebrated and thanked the "Paramount family," even though many of those gathered were transient producers and independent company employees who would soon be gone and replaced by other tenants on the lot in a matter of weeks or months. This account is from a television producer on the lot, describing the odd ethnic/religious contradictions of such an event, which was staged the week of December 5, 2005 in Los Angeles.

29. In fact Angela McRobbie makes a key distinction between careers in the old industries, which were based on managing career "narratives," and the new creative industries which are driven by what she terms "portfolio careers." Hollywood workers show that trade story-telling is almost as important as the demos they make and use to professionalize and manage their careers.

30. Film and television have never been produced in a vacuum that completely walls off "the industry" from "the audience." The general journalistic and academic tendency to segregate industry and culture methodologically, therefore, is shortsighted and problematic at the least.

31. No matter how disingenuous this rhetoric can be at times, this kind of assertion is commonplace in everything from production meetings to "Q&As" with producers after public screenings. The "producer as audience" trope also percolates through various behind-the-scenes genres, such as ABC's mid-1970s hour-long primetime news special entitled *ABC News Close-up: Primetime TV, The Decision Makers.* See PVA#2340T at the UCLA Film and Television Archives.

32. 60% of revenues for films comes from electronic media, and DVD merchandise is now by far the most lucrative of these home delivery formats. As a result, DVD opportunities are exploited during all major film productions in Los Angeles, both in terms of what the film/video looks like, but also in terms of all of the meta-texts and making-ofs that will be produced and packaged with the DVD. Perhaps the best example of this domestication of film studio thinking, is the first release of the boxed set of *King Kong* in December 2005—which consisted almost entirely of making-ofs, and was released simultaneously with the feature film premiere.

33. A consortium of major studios established the DCI (the "Digital Cinema Laboratory") to conduct various comparative tests of new digital projection systems with test audiences. DCI underscored to the public the fact that "engineering knowledge is NOT required," even as it stroked the egos of viewers who had the "opportunity to participate in an historic test that will influence the way motion pictures will look on the screen for the next 50–100 years!" (This statement and solicitation are from an "email blast" sent by Charles Schwartz, CEO of the Entertainment Technology Center, April 26, 2004.) Far from dismissing "amateur" technical knowledge, DCI enjoined the public to critically participate in the development of media consumption technologies. Finally, companies like GoldPocket Interactive provide television producers and network programmers with "turnkey" interactive systems to augment programming. In providing an easy way "to connect internet audiences to your TV broadcast" via "competitions, chat sessions, (and) streaming audio/video," the one-stop service allows programmers to "reach millions of people," in order to "get the audience to reach back to your programming—before they go somewhere else." From GoldPocket Interactive, direct marketing brochure. Los Angeles, 2003.

34. With television viewing and box-office declining many entertainment providers began developing content that could be efficiently dispersed to mobile phone users. The use of cell-phones for film/TV consumption follows concerted industrial efforts to find and harness a "third screen" in the viewer's hands. This is sometimes referred to as "snack TV." The TV and PC/Web are deemed the other 2 screens. Fox Television, for example, developed *24: Conspiracy* to launch the new season of primetime's *24*. Verizon cell-phone users in the U.K. and U.S. received 24 1-minute "mobisodes" that corresponded to the primetime series albeit with a different cast. A mobile division of NBC produces up to 20 news stories per day for mob-casting. Fans can also watch updates from CNN, regular sports reports, or out-takes from *The Simple Life*—all custom produced to work effectively on the small 2-inch screens of cell-phones. One marketing analyst described the efficient financial logic of mobile phone usage: "You're not necessarily looking to channel surf…you've got five to 10 minutes to kill." This quote is from Linda Barrabee, senior analyst at the Yankee Group, a market research firms, as quoted in Matea Gold, "I Can't Talk, I'm Watching My Cellphone," *Los Angeles Times,* May 7, 2005, A18.

35. This characterization of NBC's *Crossing Jordan* is from the "TV Reaches Millions of People" advertisement in the *Hollywood Reporter,* February 6–12, 2001, 19.

36. This "circular" strategy is discussed further in Chris Gaither, "The Plot Thickens Online," *Los Angeles Times,* February 25, 2005, A1, A26. In this way, television creators now design stories that directly target the audience's "second-shift" life outside of primetime, through multitasking technologies that mirror increasingly accelerated lifestyles. Contemporary on-the-run consumers are deemed too unpredictable and migratory for traditional television programmers and advertisers. Largely circumventing the problem of content clutter and grazing, pod- and mob-casting promise cost-effective ways to find and grab transient viewers with bursts of customized niche programming.

37. Examples include HDCamp, and DVExpo/Chicago/Dallas, Film/television associations also regularly host production award shows that function as primary forms of onscreen consumer entertainment.

38. See http://www.televisionwithoutpity.com/ and http://www.metacritic.com.

39. See, for example, the "Special Edition: Overwhelmed by Extras and Specials and Extra, Extra Specials at your Local Video Store? We Make It Easy with This Guide to 50 New and Revisited Titles," *Entertainment Weekly,* April 15, 2005, 37–50.

40. The 2003 arrival of the features *The Hulk* and *Matrix Reloaded* and their references to film theorist James Schamus and Harvard/Princeton philosopher Cornel West generated endless "think pieces," along with concept- and name-dropping throughout the popular press. These phrases and the quotation that follow are from: A.O. Scott, "The Pretentious Summer Superhero," *New York Times,* July 13, 2003, reprinted at *http://www.nytimes.com/2003/07/13/movies/13SCOT.html.* (ital. mine).

41. The following promise strokes the viewers' awareness of their role in production: "Your participation in a Television Preview screening will serve the interests of the entire viewing public, as you

will be providing direct feedback to producers, directors, sponsors, and other people behind television, who in turn will be better able to understand and respond to your viewing preferences." This statement begins with "You have been selected…," and is included in printed correspondence (direct mail) to the author from G. B. Edwards, Director, Audience Selection Staff, Television Preview, Inc., Hollywood California, Spring 2004.

42. Admittedly, film/video production cultures do not always approximate or mirror the cultures of consumption. Yet there are many significant overlaps between the two cultural sets. When one finds marked differences between cultures of film/video production and cultures of consumption, important and/or problematic issues can be found and critical questions raised. Racial politics, for example, offers a classic, recurring example in this regard. Racial representations produced by the progressive, white liberal Hollywood establishment seldom mirror the actual degree of racial diversity in American society at large; or align easily with public pressures to achieve ethnic and racial diversity in the industry. As a result, public activists emerge every few years in repeated attempts to pressure Hollywood to change and diversify. Many of these confrontations end in a kind of headscratching or disbelief in Hollywood, mostly because industry employment still does not reflect the racial diversity of society at large. Even so, the question of industrial status and autonomy in this racial "mismatch" is not an either/or question.

43. Bonus tracks and making-ofs function like film appreciation or intro production courses. Hidden DVD "Easter-eggs" facilitate film/TV production pedagogy among consumers. Choosing multiple shot-angles or endings to films on DVD cultivates production competencies among users. Director's tracks encourage viewers to see production as a working process from its maker's point-of-view.

44. In August 2006, I was asked by a marketing staffer at Columbia Tri-Star studios if I could provide film students who would be willing to produce "their own" unpaid "amateur" videos for YouTube. com that would have the effect of marketing the studio's "professionally" produced, forthcoming feature film.

6

■ Cultural Studies, Critical Pedagogy, and the Politics of Higher Education

Henry A. Giroux

■ Introduction

Within the last few decades, a number of critical and cultural studies theorists such as Stuart Hall, Lawrence Grossberg, Douglas Kellner, Meaghan Morris, Toby Miller, and Tony Bennett have provided valuable contributions to our understanding of how culture deploys power and is shaped and organized within diverse systems of representation, production, consumption, and distribution. Particularly important to such work is an ongoing critical analysis of how symbolic and institutional forms of culture and power are mutually entangled in constructing diverse identities, modes of political agency, and the social world itself. Within this approach, material relations of power and the production of social meaning do not cancel each other out but constitute the precondition for all meaningful practices. Culture is recognized as the social field where goods and social practices are not only produced, distributed, and consumed but also invested with various meanings and ideologies that are implicated in the generation of political effects. Culture is partly defined as a circuit of power, ideologies, and values in which diverse images and sounds are produced and circulate, identities are constructed, inhabited, and discarded, agency is manifested in both individualized and social forms, and discourses are created which make culture itself the object of inquiry and critical analyses. Rather than viewed as a static force, the substance of culture and everyday life—knowledge, goods, social practices, and contexts— repeatedly mutates and is subject to ongoing changes and interpretations.

Following the work of Antonio Gramsci and Stuart Hall, many cultural theorists acknowledge the primacy of culture's role as an educational site where identities are being continually transformed, power is enacted, and learning assumes a political dynamic as it becomes not only the condition for the acquisition of agency but also the sphere for imagining oppositional social change. As both a space for the production of meaning and social interaction, culture is viewed by many contemporary theorists as an important terrain in which various modes of agency, identity, and values are neither prefigured nor always in place but subject to negotiation and struggle and open for creating new democratic transformations, though always within various degrees of iniquitous power relations. Rather than dismissed as a reflection of larger economic forces or as simply the "common ground" of everyday life, culture is recognized by many advocates of cultural studies as both a site of contestation and as a site of utopian possibility, a space in which an emancipatory politics can be fashioned which "consists in making seem possible precisely that which, from within the situation, is declared to be impossible" (Badiou, 1998, p. 11).

Cultural studies theorists have greatly expanded our theoretical understanding of the ideological, institutional, and performative workings of culture, but, as important as this work might be, it does not go far enough—though there are some exceptions as in the work of Stanley Aronowitz, bell hooks, and Nick Couldry—in connecting the most critical insights of cultural studies with an understanding of the importance of critical pedagogy, particularly as part of a larger project for expanding the possibilities of a democratic politics, the dynamics of resistance, and the capacities for social agency. For too many theorists, pedagogy often occupies a limited role theoretically and politically in configuring cultural studies as a form of cultural politics.[1] While many cultural studies advocates recognize the political importance of pedagogy, it is often acknowledged in a very limited and narrow way. For instance, when invoked as an important political practice, pedagogy is either limited to the role that oppositional intellectuals might play within academia or it is reduced almost entirely to forms of learning that take place in schools. Even when pedagogy is related to issues of democracy, citizenship, and the struggle over the shaping of identities and identifications, it is rarely taken up as part of a broader public politics—as part of a larger attempt to explain how learning takes place outside of schools or what it means to assess the political significance of understanding the broader educational force of culture in the new age of media technology, multimedia, and computer-based information and communication networks. Put differently, pedagogy is limited to what goes on in schools, and the role of cultural studies theorists who address pedagogical concerns is largely reduced to doing or teaching cultural studies within the classroom.

Within this discourse, cultural studies becomes available as a resource to educators who can then teach students how to look at the media (industry and texts), analyze audience reception, challenge rigid disciplinary boundaries, critically engage popular culture, produce critical knowledge, or use cultural studies to reform the curricula and challenge disciplinary formations within public schools and higher education. For instance, Shane Gunster (2000) has argued that the main contribution that cultural studies makes to pedagogy "is the insistence that any kind of critical education must be rooted in the culture, experience, and knowledge that students bring to the classroom (p. 253)." While this is an important insight, it has been argued in enormously sophisticated ways for over fifty years by a host of progressive educators that include John Dewey, Maxine Greene, and Paulo Freire. But the problem lies not in Gunster's unfamiliarity with such scholarship,

but in his willingness to repeat the presupposition that the exclusive site in which pedagogy becomes a relevant object of analysis is the classroom. If he had crossed the disciplinary boundaries that he decries in his celebration of cultural studies, he would have
found that educational theorists such as Roger Simon, David Trend, and others have
expanded the meaning of pedagogy as a political and moral practice and extended its application far beyond the classroom while also attempting to combine the cultural and the
pedagogical as part of a broader notion of political education and cultural studies.

Many cultural studies theorists, such as Lawrence Grossberg, have rightly suggested
that cultural studies has an important role to play in helping educators rethink, among other
things, the nature of pedagogy and knowledge, the purpose of schooling, and how schools
are impacted by larger social forces.[2] And, surely, Gunster takes such advice seriously, but
fails to understand its limits, and in doing so repeats a now familiar refrain among critical
educational theorists about connecting pedagogy to the histories, lived experiences, and
discourses that students bring to the classroom. In spite of the importance of bringing matters of culture and power to the schools, I think that too many cultural studies theorists are
remiss in suggesting that pedagogy is primarily about schools and by implication that the
intersection of cultural studies and pedagogy has little to do with theorizing the role that
pedagogy might play in linking learning to social change outside of traditional sites of
schooling.[3] Pedagogy is not simply about the social construction of knowledge, values, and
experiences, it is also a performative practice embodied in the lived interactions among
educators, audiences, texts, and institutional formations. Pedagogy, at its best, implies that
learning takes place across a spectrum of social practices and settings in society. As Roger
Simon (1995) observes, pedagogy points to the multiplicity of sites in which education
takes place and offers the possibility for a variety of cultural workers

> to comprehend the full range of multiple, shifting and overlapping of sites of learning that exist
> within the organized social relations of everyday life. This means being able to grasp, for
> example, how workplaces, families, community and institutional health provision, film and
> television, the arts, groups organized for spiritual expression and worship, organized sport,
> the law and the provision of legal services, the prison system, voluntary social service organi-
> zations, and community based literacy programs all designate sets of organized practices within
> which learning is one central feature and outcome (p. 109).

In what follows, I will argue that pedagogy is central to any viable notion of cultural
politics and that cultural studies is crucial to any viable notion of pedagogy. Moreover, it
is precisely at the intersection at which diverse traditions in cultural studies and pedagogy
mutually inform each other that the possibility exists of making the pedagogical more
political for cultural studies theorists and the political more pedagogical for educators.

■ Rethinking the Importance of Cultural Studies for Educators

My own interest in cultural studies emerges out of an ongoing project to theorize the
regulatory and emancipatory relationship among culture, power, and politics as expressed
through the dynamics of what I call public pedagogy. Such a project concerns, in part,

the diverse ways in which culture functions as a contested sphere over the production, distribution, and regulation of power and how and where it operates both symbolically and institutionally as an educational, political, and economic force. Drawing upon a long tradition in cultural studies work, I take up culture as constitutive and political, not only reflecting larger forces but also constructing them; in this instance, culture not only mediates history, it shapes it. I will argue that culture is the primary terrain for realizing the political as an articulation of and intervention into the social, a space in which politics is pluralized, recognized as contingent, and open to many formations.[4] I also argue that it is a crucial terrain in order to render visible both the global circuits that now frame material relations of power and a cultural politics in which matters of representation and meaning shape and offer concrete examples of how politics is expressed, lived, and experienced. Culture, in this instance, is the ground of both contestation and accommodation, and it is increasingly characterized by the rise of mega corporations and new technologies which are transforming the traditional spheres of the economy, industry, society, and everyday life. Culture now plays a central role in producing narratives, metaphors, and images that exercise a powerful pedagogical force over how people think of themselves and their relationship to others. From my perspective, culture is the primary sphere in which individuals, groups, and institutions engage in the art of translating the diverse and multiple relations that mediate between private life and public concerns. It is also the sphere in which the translating possibilities of culture are under assault, particularly as the forces of neoliberalism dissolve public issues into utterly privatized and individualistic concerns.

Central to my work in cultural studies is the assumption that the primacy of culture and power be organized through an understanding of how the political becomes pedagogical, particularly in terms of how private issues are connected to larger social conditions and collective forces; that is, how the very processes of learning constitute the political mechanisms through which identities are shaped, desires mobilized, and experiences take on form and meaning within and through collective set conditions and those larger forces that constitute the realm of the social. In this context, pedagogy is no longer restricted to what goes on in schools, but becomes a defining principle of a wide ranging set of cultural apparatuses engaged in what Raymond Williams (1967) has called "permanent education." Williams rightfully believed that education in the broadest sense plays a central role in any viable form of cultural politics. He writes

> What [permanent education] valuably stresses is the educational force of our whole social and cultural experience. It is therefore concerned, not only with continuing education, of a formal or informal kind, but with what the whole environment, its institutions and relationships, actively and profoundly teaches....[Permanent education also refers to] the field in which our ideas of the world, of ourselves and of our possibilities, are most widely and often most powerfully formed and disseminated. To work for the recovery of control in this field is then, under any pressures, a priority (pp. 15, 16).

Williams (1967) argued that any viable notion of critical politics would have to pay closer "attention to the complex ways in which individuals are formed by the institutions to which they belong, and in which, by reaction, the institutions took on the color of individuals thus formed" (p. 14). Williams also foregrounded the crucial political question of how agency unfolds within a variety of cultural spaces structured within unequal relations of power.[5] He was particularly concerned about the connections between pedagogy and political agency, especially in light of the emergence of a range of new technologies that greatly proliferated the amount of information available to people while at the same time constricting the substance and ways in which such meanings entered the public domain. The realm of culture for Williams had taken on a new role in the latter part of the twentieth century because the actuality of economic power and its attendant networks of control now exercised more influence than ever before in shaping how identities are produced, desires mobilized, and everyday social relations take on the force and meaning of common sense (Williams, 1977). Williams clearly understood that making the political more pedagogical meant recognizing that where and how the psyche locates itself in public discourse, visions, and passions provides the groundwork for agents to enunciate, act, and reflect on themselves and their relations to others and the wider social order.

Following Williams, I want to reaffirm the importance of pedagogy in any viable understanding of cultural politics. In doing so, I want to comment on some very schematic and incomplete elements of cultural studies that I think are useful for thinking about not only the interface between cultural studies and critical pedagogy but also for deepening and expanding the theoretical and political horizons of critical pedagogical work. I believe that pedagogy represents both a mode of cultural production and a type of cultural criticism that is essential for questioning the conditions under which knowledge is produced, values affirmed, affective investments engaged, and subject positions are put into place, negotiated, taken up, or refused. Pedagogy is a referent for understanding the conditions for critical learning and the often hidden dynamics of social and cultural reproduction. As a critical practice, pedagogy's role lies in not only changing how people think about themselves, their relationship to others and the world, but also in energizing students and others to engage in those struggles that further possibilities for living in a more just and fairer society. But like any other body of knowledge which is constantly struggled over, pedagogy must constantly enter into dialogue with other fields, theoretical domains, and emerging theoretical discourses. As diverse as cultural studies is as a field, there are a number of insights it provides that are crucial to educators who use critical pedagogy both in and outside of their classrooms.

First, in the face of contemporary forms of political and epistemological relativism, a more politicized version of cultural studies makes a claim for the use of highly disciplined, rigorous theoretical work. Not only does such a position reject the notion that intellectual authority can only be grounded in particular forms of social identity, it also refuses an increasing anti-intellectualism that posits theory as too academic and complex to be of any use in addressing important political issues. While many cultural studies advocates refuse to either separate culture studies from politics or reject theory as too complex and abstract, they also reject theory as a sterile form of theoreticism and an academicized vocabulary that is as self-consciously pedantic as it is politically irrelevant. Matters of language, experience, power, ideology, and representation cannot make a detour around theory, but that is no excuse for elevating theory to an ethereal realm that has no referent outside of its own obtuseness or rhetorical cleverness. While offering no guarantees, theory in a more critical perspective is seen as crucial to attending to questions of politics power and public considerations. Moreover, theory in this view is called upon as a resource to do the important bridging work in which cultural studies is connected to those sites and spheres of contestation in which it becomes possible to open up rhetorical and pedagogical spaces between the actual conditions of dominant power and the promise of future space informed by a range of democratic alternatives (Fritsch, 2002).

Underlying such a project is a firm commitment to intellectual rigor and a deep regard for matters of compassion and social responsibility aimed at deepening and extending the possibilities for critical agency, racial justice, economic democracy, and the just distribution of political power. Hence, cultural studies theorists often reject the anti-intellectualism, specialization, and methodological reification often found in other disciplines. Similarly, such theorists also reject both the universalizing dogmatism found in some strands of radical theory as well as a postmodern epistemology that enshrines difference, identity, and plurality at the expense of developing more inclusive notions of the social that bring together historically and politically differentiated forms of struggles. The more progressive strains of cultural studies do not define or value theory and knowledge strictly within particular interests as much as they define their political currency and promise as part of a more generalized notion of freedom that combines democratic principles, values, and experiences with the rights and discourses that build on the histories and struggles of those excluded others. For instance, cultural studies theorist Imre Szeman (2002) has looked at the ways in which globalization opens up not only a new space for pedagogy but "constitutes a problem of and for pedagogy" (p. 4). Szeman looks at the various forms of public pedagogy at work in the rhetoric of newspapers, TV news shows, financial service companies, advertising industries, and the mass media, and how such rhetoric fashions a triumphalist view of globalization. He then offers an analysis of how alternative pedagogies are produced within various globalization protest movements that have taken place in cities such as Seattle, Toronto, and Genoa—movements that have attempted to open up new modes and sites of learning while enabling new forms of collective resistance. What is particularly important about Szeman's analysis is how new pedagogical practices of resistance are being fashioned through the use of new media, such as the Internet and digital video, to challenge official pedagogies of globalization.

Second, cultural studies is radically contextual in that the very questions that it asks change in every context. Theory and criticism do not become an end in themselves but are always engaged as a resource and method in response to problems raised in particular contexts, social relations, and institutional formations. This suggests that how we respond as educators and critics to the spheres in which we work is conditioned by the interrelationship between the theoretical resources we bring to a specific context and the worldly space of publicness that produces distinct problems and conditions particular responses to them. Politics as an intervention into public life is expressed, in this instance, as part of a broader attempt to provide a better understanding of how power works in and through historical and institutional contexts while simultaneously opening up imagined possibilities for changing them. Lawrence Grossberg (1996) puts it well in arguing that cultural studies must be grounded in an act of doing, which in this case means "intervening into contexts and power....in order to enable people to act more strategically in ways that may change their context for the better" (p. 143). For educators, this suggests that pedagogy *is not* an a priori set of methods that simply needs to be uncovered and then applied regardless of the contexts in which one teaches but is the outcome of numerous deliberations and struggles between different groups over how contexts are made and remade, often within unequal relations of power. At the same time, it is crucial for educators to recognize that, while educators need to be attentive to the particular context in which they work, they cannot separate such contexts from larger matters and configurations of power, culture, ideology, politics, and domination. As Doug Kellner and Meenakshi Gigi Durham (2001) observe, "pedagogy does not elide or occlude issues of power.... Thus, while the distinctive situation and interests of the teachers, students, or critics help decide what precise artifacts are engaged, what methods will be employed, and what pedagogy will be deployed, the socio-cultural environment in which cultural production, reception, and education occurs must be scrutinized as well" (p. 29).

The notion that pedagogy is always contextual rightly points to linking the knowledge that is taught to the experiences that students bring to their classroom encounters. One implication for such work is that future and existing teachers be educated about the viability of developing context-dependent learning that takes account of student experiences and their relationships to popular culture and its terrain of pleasure, including those cultural industries that are often dismissed as producing mere entertainment. Despite the growing diversity of students in both public schools and higher education, there are few examples of curriculum sensitivity to the multiplicity of economic, social, and cultural factors bearing on students' lives. Even where there is a proliferation of programs such as ethnic and black studies in higher education, these are often marginalized in small programs far removed from the high-status prestige associated with courses organized around business, computer science, and Western history. Cultural studies at least provides the theoretical tools for allowing teachers to recognize the important, though not unproblematic, cultural resources that students bring to school and the willingness to affirm and engage them critically as forms of knowledge crucial to the production of the students' sense of identity, place, and history. Equally important, the knowledge produced by students offers educators opportunities to learn from young people and to incorporate such knowledge as an integral part of their own teaching. Yet, there is an important caveat that cannot be stated too strongly.

I am not endorsing a romantic celebration of the notion of relevance or the knowledge and experience that students bring to the classroom. Nor am I arguing that larger contexts that frame both the culture and political economy of the schools and the experiences of students be ignored. I am also not suggesting that teaching be limited to the resources that students already have as much as I am arguing that educators need to find ways to make knowledge meaningful in order to make it critical and transformative. Moreover, by locating students within differentiated sets of histories, experiences, literacies, and values, pedagogical practices can be employed that not only raise questions about the strengths and limitations of what students know but also grapple with the issue of what conditions must be engaged to expand the capacities and skills needed by students to become engaged global citizens and responsible social agents. This is not a matter of making a narrow notion of relevance the determining factor in the curriculum. But it is an issue of connecting knowledge to everyday life, meaning to the act of persuasion, schools and universities to broader public spheres, and rigorous theoretical work to affective investments and pleasures that students use in mediating their relationship to others and the larger world.

Third, the cultural studies emphasis on transdisciplinary work is important because it provides a rationale for challenging how knowledge has been historically produced, hierarchically ordered, and used within disciplines to sanction particular forms of authority and exclusion. By challenging the established academic division of labor, a transdisciplinary approach raises important questions about the politics of representation and its deeply entrenched entanglement with specialization, professionalism, and dominant power relations. The commitment to a transdisciplinary approach is also important because such work often operates at the frontiers of knowledge and prompts teachers and students to raise new questions and develop models of analysis outside of the officially sanctioned boundaries of knowledge and the established disciplines that sanction them. Transdisciplinarity in this discourse serves a dual function. On the one hand, it firmly posits the arbitrary conditions under which knowledge is produced and encoded, stressing its historically- and socially-constructed nature and deeply entrenched connection to power and ideological interests. On the other hand, it endorses the relational nature of knowledge, inveighing against any presupposition that knowledge, events, and issues are either fixed or should be studied in isolation. Transdisciplinary approaches stress both historical relations and broader social formations, always attentive to new linkages, meanings, and possibilities. Strategically and pedagogically, these modes of analysis suggest that, while educators may be forced to work within academic disciplines, they can develop transdisciplinary tools to make established disciplines the object of critique while simultaneously contesting the broader economic, political, and cultural conditions that reproduce the academic division of labor. This is a crucial turn theoretically and politically because transdisciplinary approaches foreground the necessity of bridging the work educators do within the academy to other academic fields as well as other public spheres. Such approaches also suggest that educators function as public intellectuals by engaging in ongoing public conversations that cut across particular disciplines while attempting to get their ideas out to more than one type of audience. Under such circumstances, educators must address the task of learning the forms of knowledge and skills that enable them to speak critically and broadly on a number of issues to a vast array of publics.

Fourth, in a somewhat related way, the emphasis on the part of many cultural studies theorists to study the full range of cultural practices that circulate in society opens the possibility for understanding a wide variety of new cultural forms that have become the primary educational forces in advanced industrial societies. This seems especially important at a time when new electronic technologies and the emergence of visual culture as a primary educational force offer new opportunities to inhabit knowledge and ways of knowing that simply do not correspond to the long-standing traditions and officially sanctioned rules of disciplinary knowledge or of the one-sided academic emphasis on print culture. The scope and power of these new informational technologies, multimedia, and visual culture warrant that educators become more reflective about engaging both the production, reception, and situated use of new technologies, popular texts, and diverse forms of visual culture and how they structure social relations, values, particular notions of community, the future, and varied definitions of the self and others. Texts in this sense do not merely refer to the culture of print or the technology of the book, but to all those audio, visual, and electronically mediated forms of knowledge that have prompted a radical shift in the construction of knowledge and the ways in which knowledge is produced, received, and consumed. Recently, my own work has focused on the ways in which Disney's corporate culture—its animated films, radio programs, theme parks, and Hollywood blockbusters—functions as an expansive teaching machine which appropriates media and popular culture in order to rewrite public memory and offer young people an increasingly privatized and commercialized notion of citizenship.[6]

Contemporary youth do not simply rely on the culture of the book to construct and affirm their identities; instead, they are faced with the daunting task of negotiating their way through a decentered media-based cultural landscape no longer caught in the grip of either a technology of print or closed narrative structures.[7] I do not believe that educators and other cultural workers can critically understand and engage the shifting attitudes, representations, and desires of new generations of youth strictly within the dominant disciplinary configurations of knowledge and practice and traditional forms of pedagogy. Educators need a more expansive view of knowledge and pedagogy that provides the conditions for young people and adults to engage popular, media, and mass culture as serious objects of social analysis and to learn how to read them critically through specific strategies of understanding, engagement, and transformation. Informing this notion of knowledge and pedagogy is a view of literacy that is multiple and dynamic rather than singular and fixed. The modernist emphasis on literacy must be reconfigured in order for students to learn multiple literacies rooted in a mastery of diverse symbolic domains. At the same time, it is not enough to educate students to be critical readers across a variety of cultural domains, they must also become cultural producers, especially if they are going to create new alternative public spheres in which official knowledge and its one-dimensional configurations can be challenged. That is, students must also learn how to utilize the new electronic technologies, how to think about the dynamics of cultural power and how it works on and through them so that they can build alternative cultural spheres in which such power is shared and used to promote non-commodified values rather than simply mimic corporate culture and its underlying transactions.

Fifth, cultural studies provocatively stresses analyzing public memory not as a totalizing narrative, but as a series of ruptures and displacements. Historical learning in this sense is not about constructing a linear narrative but about blasting history open, rupturing its silences, highlighting its detours, acknowledging the events of its transmission, and organizing its limits within an open and honest concern with human suffering, values, and the legacy of the often unrepresentable or misrepresented. History is not an artifact to be merely transmitted, but an ongoing dialogue and struggle over the relationship between representation and agency. James Clifford (1992) is insightful in arguing that history should "force a sense of location on those who engage with it" (p. 129). This means challenging official narratives of conservative educators such as William Bennett, Lynne Cheney, Diane Ravitch, and Chester Finn for whom history is primarily about recovering and legitimating selective facts, dates, and events. A pedagogy of public memory is about making connections that are often hidden, forgotten, or willfully ignored. Public memory in this sense becomes not an object of reverence but an ongoing subject of debate, dialogue, and critical engagement. Public memory is also about critically examining one's own historical location amid relations of power, privilege, or subordination. More specifically, this suggests engaging history, as has been done repeatedly by radical intellectuals such as Howard Zinn and Noam Chomsky, by analyzing how knowledge is constructed through its absences. Public memory as a pedagogical practice functions, in part, as a form of critique that addresses the fundamental inadequacy of official knowledge in representing marginalized and oppressed groups along with, as John Beverly (1996) points out, the deep seated injustices perpetrated by institutions that contain such knowledge and the need to transform such institutions in the "direction of a more radically democratic nonhierarchical social order" (p. 354).

Sixth, cultural studies theorists are increasingly paying attention to their own institutional practices and pedagogies (Giroux & McLaren, 1993). They have come to recognize that pedagogy is deeply implicated in how power and authority are employed in the construction and organization of knowledge, desires, values, and identities. Such a recognition has produced a new self-consciousness about how particular forms of teacher authority, classroom knowledge, and social practices are used to legitimate particular values and interests within unequal relations of power. Questions concerning how pedagogy works to articulate knowledge, meaning, desire, and values to effects not only provides the conditions for a pedagogical self-consciousness among teachers and students but also foregrounds the recognition that pedagogy is a moral and political practice and cannot be reduced to an a priori set of skills or techniques. Rather, pedagogy in this instance is defined as a cultural practice that must be accountable ethically and politically for the stories it produces, the claims it makes on public memories, and the images of the future it deems legitimate. As both an object of critique and a method of cultural production, critical pedagogical practices cannot hide behind claims of objectivity, and should work, in part, to link theory and practice in the service of organizing, struggling over, and deepening democratic political, economic, and social freedoms. In the broadest sense, critical pedagogy should offer students and others—outside of officially sanctioned scripts—the historically and contextually specific knowledge, skills, and tools they need to both participate in, govern, and change when necessary those political and economic structures of power that shape their everyday lives. Needless to say, such tools are not pregiven but are the outcome of struggles, debate, dialogue, and engagement across a variety of public spheres.

While this list is both schematic and incomplete, it points to a some important theoretical considerations that can be appropriated from the field of cultural studies as a resource for advancing a more public and democratic vision for higher education. Hopefully, it suggests theoretical tools for constructing new forms of collaboration among faculty, a broadening of the terms of teaching and learning, and new approaches toward interdisciplinary research that address local, national, and international concerns. The potential that cultural studies has for developing forms of collaboration that cut across national boundaries is worth taking up.

■ Where Is the Project(s) in Cultural Studies?

Like any other academic field, cultural studies is marked by a number of weaknesses that need to be addressed by educators drawn to some of its more critical assumptions. First, there is a tendency in some cultural studies work to be simply deconstructive; that is, there is a refusal to ask questions about the insertion of symbolic processes into societal contexts and their imbrication with the political economy of power. Any viable form of cultural studies cannot insist exclusively on the primacy of signification over power, and in doing so reduce its purview to questions of meaning and texts. An obsession in some cases with cultural texts results in privileging literature and popular culture over history and politics. Within this discourse, material organizations and economic power disappear into some of the most irrelevant aspects of culture. Matters of fashion, cultural trivia, isolated notions of performance, and just plain cultural nonsense take on the aura of cultural analyses that yield to the most privatized forms of inquiry while simultaneously "obstructing the formulation of a publically informed politics" (Dirlik, 2002, p. 218).[8] In opposition to this position, cultural studies needs to foreground the ways in which culture and power are related through what Stuart Hall calls "combining the study of symbolic forms and meanings with the study of power," or more specifically the "insertion of symbolic processes into societal contexts and their imbrication with power" (Osborne & Segal, 1998, p. 24). Douglas Kellner for years has also argued that any viable approach to cultural studies has to overcome the divide between political economy and text-based analyses of culture.[9] But recognizing such a divide is not the same thing as overcoming it. Part of this task necessitates that cultural studies theorists anchor their own work, however diverse, in a radical project that seriously engages the promise of an unrealized democracy against its really existing forms. Of crucial importance to such a project is rejecting the assumption that theory can understand social problems without contesting their appearance in public life. At the same time, it is crucial to any viable notion of cultural studies that it reclaim politics as an ongoing critique of domination and society as part of a larger search for justice. Any viable cultural politics needs a socially committed notion of injustice if we are to take seriously what it means to fight for the idea of the good society. I think Zygmunt Bauman (2002) is right in arguing that, "If there is no room for the idea of *wrong* society, there is hardly much chance for the idea of good society to be born, let alone make waves" (p. 170). Cultural studies advocates need to be more forceful, if not committed, to linking their overall politics to modes of critique and collective action that address the presupposition that democratic societies are never too just or just enough, and such a recognition means that a society must constantly nurture the possibilities for self-critique, collective agency, and forms of citizenship in which people play a fundamental role in critically discussing, administrating, and shaping the material relations of power and ideological forces that shape their everyday lives. Moreover, the struggle over creating an inclusive and just democracy can take many forms, offers no political guarantees, and provides an important normative dimension to politics as an ongoing process of democratization that never ends. Such a project is based on the realization that a democracy that is open to exchange, question, and self-criticism never reaches the limits of justice; that is, it is never just enough, and it is never finished. It is precisely the open-ended and normative nature of such a project that provides a common ground for cultural studies theorists to share their differences and diverse range of intellectual pursuits.

Second, cultural studies is still largely an academic discourse and as such is often too far removed from other cultural and political sites where the work of public pedagogy takes place. In order to become a public discourse of any importance, cultural studies theorists will have to focus their work on the immediacy of problems that are more public and that are relevant to important social issues. Such issues might include the destruction of the ecological biosphere, the current war against youth, the hegemony of neoliberal globalization, the widespread attack by corporate culture on public schools, the ongoing attack on the welfare system, the increasing rates of incarceration of people of color, the increasing gap between the rich and the poor, or the dangerous growth of the prison-industrial complex. Moreover, cultural studies theorists need to write for a variety of public audiences, rather than for simply a narrow group of specialized intellectuals. Such writing needs to become public by crossing over into sites and avenues of expression that speak to more general audiences in a language that is clear but not theoretically simplistic. Intellectuals must combine their scholarship with commitment in a discourse that is not dull or obtuse and expands the reach of their audience. This suggests using opportunities offered by a host of public means of expression, including the lecture circuit, radio, internet, interview, alternative magazines, and the church pulpit, to name only a few.

Third, cultural studies theorists need to be more specific about what it would mean to be both self-critical as well as attentive to learning how to work collectively through a vast array of networks across a number of public spheres. This might mean sharing resources with cultural workers both within and outside of the university such as the various groups working for global justice or those activists battling the ongoing destruction of state provisions both within and outside of the United States. This suggests that cultural studies become more active in addressing the ethical and political challenges of globalization. As capital, finance, trade, and culture become extraterritorial, removed from traditional political constraints, it becomes all the more pressing that global networks and political organizations be put into play to provide an effective response to the reach and power of neoliberal globalization. Engaging in intellectual practices that offer the possibility of alliances and new forms of solidarity among cultural workers such as artists, writers, journalists, academics, and others who engage in forms of public pedagogy grounded in a democratic project represents a small, but important, step in addressing the massive and unprecedented reach of global capitalism.

Critical educators also need to register and make visible their own subjective involvement in what they teach, interact in the classroom and other cultural sites, and locate, mediate, and defend the political nature of their work as teachers and cultural workers, but not exclusively in individualized terms, which refuse to link commitment, scholarship, and pedagogy. Such a task points to the necessity for educators and cultural theorists to define intellectual practice "as part of an intricate web of morality, rigor and responsibility" (Roy, 2001, p. 6) that enables them to speak with conviction, enter the public sphere in order to address important social problems, and demonstrate alternative models for what it means to bridge the gap between higher education and the broader society. One useful approach is for educators to think through the distinction between a politicizing pedagogy, which insists wrongly that students think as we do, and a political pedagogy that teaches students by example the importance of taking a stand without standing still while rigorously engaging with the full range of ideas about an issue. Political pedagogy connects understanding and critical engagement with the issue of social responsibility and what it would mean to educate students to not only critically engage the world but also be responsible enough to fight for those political and economic conditions that make its democratic possibilities viable. Such a pedagogy affirms the experience of the social and the obligations it evokes regarding questions of responsibility and social transformation by opening up for students important questions about power, knowledge, and what it might mean for them to critically engage the conditions under which life is presented to them and simultaneously work to overcome those social relations of oppression that make living unbearable for those who are poor, hungry, unemployed, refused adequate social services, and under the aegis of neoliberalism, viewed largely as disposable. What is important about this type of critical pedagogy is the issue of responsibility and what it would mean for cultural studies educators to encourage students to reflect on what it would mean to connect knowledge and criticism to becoming an actor, buttressed by a profound desire to overcome injustice and a spirited commitment to social agency. Political education teaches students to take risks, challenge those with power, and encourage them to be reflexive about how power is used in the classroom. Political education proposes that the role of the public intellectual is not to consolidate authority but to question and interrogate it, and that teachers and students should temper any reference for authority with a sense of critical awareness and an acute willingness to hold it accountable for its consequences. Moreover, political education foregrounds education not within the imperatives of specialization and professionalization, but within a project designed to expand the possibilities of democracy by linking education to modes of political agency that promote critical citizenship and engage the ethical imperative to alleviate human suffering. On the other hand, politicizing education silences in the name of orthodoxy and imposes itself on students while undermining dialogue, deliberation, and critical engagement. Politicizing education is often grounded in a combination of self-righteousness and ideological purity that silences students as it imposes "correct" positions. Authority in this perspective rarely opens itself to self-criticism or for that matter to any criticism, especially from students. Politicizing education cannot decipher the distinction between critical teaching and pedagogical terrorism because its advocates have no sense of the difference between encouraging human agency and social responsibility and molding students according to the imperatives of an unquestioned ideological position. Politicizing education is more religious than secular, more about training than educating, and it harbors a great dislike for complicating issues, promoting critical dialogue, and generating a culture of questioning.

Finally, if cultural studies theorists are truly concerned about how culture operates as a crucial site of power in the modern world, they will have to take more seriously how pedagogy functions on local and global levels to secure and challenge the ways in which power is deployed, affirmed, and resisted within and outside traditional discourses and cultural spheres. In this instance, pedagogy becomes an important theoretical tool for understanding the institutional conditions that place constraints on the production of knowledge, learning, and academic labor itself. Pedagogy also provides a discourse for engaging and challenging the production of social hierarchies, identities, and ideologies as they traverse local and national borders. In addition, pedagogy as a form of production and critique offers a discourse of possibility, a way of providing students with the opportunity to link meaning to commitment and understanding to social transformation—and to do so in the interest of the greatest possible justice. Unlike traditional vanguardists or elitist notions of the intellectual, cultural studies should embrace the notion that the vocation of intellectuals be rooted in pedagogical and political work tempered by humility, a moral focus on suffering, and the need to produce alternative visions and policies that go beyond a language of critique. I now want to shift my frame a bit in order to focus on the implications of the concerns I have addressed thus far and how they might be connected to developing an academic agenda for teachers as public intellectuals in higher education, particularly at a time when neoliberal agendas increasingly guide social policy.

■ The Responsibility of Intellectuals and the Politics of Education

In opposition to the corporatizing of everything educational, educators need to define higher education as a resource vital to the democratic and civic life of the nation. At the heart of such a task is the challenge for academics, cultural workers, and labor organizers to join together and oppose the transformation of higher education into commercial spheres, to resist what Bill Readings (1997) has called a consumer-oriented corporation more concerned about accounting than accountability (pp. 11, 18). As Zygmunt Bauman (1999) reminds us, schools are one of the few public spaces left where students can learn the "skills for citizen participation and effective political action. And where there are no [such] institutions, there is no 'citizenship' either" (p. 170). Public and higher education may be one of the few sites available in which students can learn about the limits of commercial values, address what it means to learn the skills of social citizenship, and learn how to deepen and expand the possibilities of collective agency and democratic life. Defending education at all levels of learning as a vital public sphere and public good rather than merely a private good is necessary to develop and nourish the proper balance between democratic public spheres and commercial power, between identities founded on democratic principles and identities steeped in forms of competitive, self-interested individualism that celebrate selfishness, profit making, and greed. This view suggests that public and higher education be defended through intellectual work that self-consciously recalls the tension between the democratic imperatives and possibilities of public institutions and their everyday realization within a society dominated by market principles. If the public and higher education are to remain sites of critical thinking, collective work, and social struggle, public intellectuals need to expand their meaning and purpose. As I have stressed repeatedly, academics, teachers, students, parents, community activists, and other socially concerned groups must provide the first line of defense in defending public and higher education as a resource vital to the moral life of the nation, open to people and communities whose resources, knowledge, and skills have often been viewed as marginal. Such a project suggests that educators and cultural studies theorists develop a more inclusive vocabulary for linking politics and the tasks of leadership. In part, this means providing the language, knowledge, and social relations for students to engage in the "art of translating individual problems into public issues, and common interests into individual rights and duties" (Bauman, 2002, p. 70). Leadership demands a politics and pedagogy that refuses to separate individual problems and experience from public issues and social considerations. Within such a perspective, leadership displaces cynicism with hope, challenges the neoliberal notion that there are no alternatives with visions of a better society, and develops a pedagogy of commitment that puts into place modes of literacy in which competency and interpretation provide the basis for actually intervening in the world. Leadership invokes the demand to make the pedagogical more political by linking critical thought to collective action, human agency to social responsibility, and knowledge and power to a profound impatience with a status quo founded upon deep inequalities and injustices.

One of the most crucial challenges that educators and cultural studies advocates face is rejecting the neoliberal collapse of the public into the private, the rendering of all social problems as biographical in nature. The neoliberal obsession with the private not only furthers a market-based politics that reduces all relationships to the exchange of money and the accumulation of capital, it also depoliticizes politics itself and reduces public activity to the realm of utterly privatized practices and utopias, underscored by the reduction of citizenship to the act of buying and purchasing goods. Within this discourse, all forms of political solidarity, social agency, and collective resistance disappear into the murky waters of a biopolitics in which the pursuit of privatized pleasures and ready-made individual choices are organized on the basis of marketplace pursuits and desires that cancel out all modes of social responsibility, commitment, and action. The current challenge intellectuals face is to reclaim the language of the social, agency, solidarity, democracy, and public life as the basis for rethinking how to name, theorize, and strategize a new kind of politics, notions of political agency, and collective struggle.

This challenge suggests, in part, positing new forms of social citizenship and civic education that have a purchase on people's everyday lives and struggles. Academics bear an enormous responsibility in opposing neoliberalism—the most dangerous ideology of our time—by bringing democratic political culture back to life. Part of this effort demands creating new locations of struggle, vocabularies, and subject positions that allow people in a wide variety of public spheres to become more than they are now, to question what it is they have become within existing institutional and social formations, and "to give some thought to their experiences so that they can transform their relations of subordination and oppression" (Worsham & Olson, 1999, p. 178). One element of this struggle could take the form of resisting attacks on existing public spheres such as the schools while creating new spaces in clubs, neighborhoods, bookstores, trade unions, alternative media sites, and other places where dialogue and critical exchanges become possible. At the same time, challenging neoliberalism means fighting against the ongoing reconfiguration of the state into the role of an enlarged police precinct designed to repress dissent, regulate immigrant populations, incarcerate youth who are considered disposable, and safeguard the interests of global investors. As governments globally give up their role of providing social safety nets, social provisions, and regulating the excesses of corporate greed, capital escapes beyond the reach of democratic control and marginalized individuals and groups are left to their own meager resources to survive. Under such circumstances, it becomes difficult to create alternative public spheres that enable people to become effective agents of change. Under neoliberalism's reign of terror, public issues collapse into privatized discourses and a culture of personal confessions, greed, and celebrities emerges that sets the stage for depoliticizing public life and providing the grounds for turning citizenship and governance into a form of consumerism.

The growing attack on public and higher education in American society may say less about the reputed apathy of the populace than it might about the bankruptcy of old political languages and orthodoxies and the need for new vocabularies and visions for clarifying our intellectual, ethical, and political projects, especially as they work to reabsorb questions of agency, ethics, and meaning back into politics and public life. In the absence of such a language and the social formations and public spheres that make democracy and justice operative, politics becomes narcissistic and caters to the mood of widespread pessimism and the cathartic allure of the spectacle. In addition, public service and government intervention are sneered at as either bureaucratic or a constraint upon individual freedom. Any attempt to give new life to a substantive democratic politics must address the issue of both how people learn to be political agents and what kind of educational work is necessary within what kind of public spaces to enable people to use their full intellectual resources to provide a profound critique of existing institutions and struggle to make the operation of freedom and autonomy possible for as many people as possible in a wide variety of spheres. As critical educators, we are required to understand more fully why the tools we used in the past feel awkward in the present, and thus often fail to respond to problems now facing the United States and other parts of the globe. More specifically, educators face the challenge posed by the failure of existing critical discourses to bridge the gap between how society represents itself and how and why individuals fail to understand and critically engage such representations in order to intervene in the oppressive social relationships they often legitimate.

Against neoliberalism, educators, cultural studies theorists, students, and activists face the task of providing a language of resistance and possibility, a language that embraces a militant utopianism while constantly being attentive to those forces that seek to turn such hope into a new slogan or punish and dismiss those who dare look beyond the horizon of the given. Hope is the affective and intellectual precondition for individual and social struggle, the mark of courage on the part of intellectuals in and out of the academy who use the resources of theory to address pressing social problems. But hope is also a referent for civic courage which translates as a political practice and begins when one's life can no longer be taken for granted, making concrete the possibility for transforming politics into an ethical space and public act that confronts the flow of everyday experience and the weight of social suffering with the force of individual and collective resistance and the unending project of democratic social transformation.

There is a lot of talk among social theorists about the death of politics and the inability of human beings to imagine a more equitable and just world in order to make it better. I would hope that, of all groups, educators would be the most vocal and militant in challenging this assumption by making it clear that at the heart of any form of inclusive democracy is the assumption that learning should be used to expand the public good, create a culture of questioning, and promote democratic social change. Individual and social agency becomes meaningful as part of the willingness to imagine otherwise "in order to help us find our way to a more human future" (Chomsky, 2000, p. 34). Under such circumstances, knowledge can be used for amplifying human freedom and promoting social justice, and not for simply creating profits. The diverse but connected fields of cultural studies and critical pedagogy offer some insights for addressing these issues, and we would do well to learn as much as possible from them in order to expand the meaning of the political and revitalize the pedagogical possibilities of cultural politics and democratic struggles. The late Pierre Bourdieu (2000) has argued that intellectuals need to create new ways for doing politics by investing in political struggles through a permanent critique of the abuses of authority and power, especially under the reign of neoliberalism. Bourdieu wanted scholars to use their skills and knowledge to break out of the microcosm of academia, combine scholarship with commitment, and "enter into sustained and vigorous exchange with the outside world (especially with unions, grassroots organizations, and issue-oriented activist groups) instead of being content with waging the 'political' battles, at once intimate and ultimately, and always a bit unreal, of the scholastic universe" (p. 44).

At a time when our civil liberties are being destroyed and public institutions and goods all over the globe are under assault by the forces of a rapacious global capitalism, there is a sense of concrete urgency that demands not only the most militant forms of political opposition on the part of academics, but new modes of resistance and collective struggle buttressed by rigorous intellectual work, social responsibility, and political courage. The time has come for intellectuals to distinguish caution from cowardice and recognize the ever fashionable display of rhetorical cleverness as a form of "disguised decadence" (Roy, 2001, p. 12). As Derrida (2000) reminds us, democracy "demands the most concrete urgency…because as a concept it makes visible the promise of democracy, that which is to come" (p. 9). We have seen glimpses of such a promise among those brave students and workers who have demonstrated in Seattle, Genoa, Prague, New York, and Toronto. As public intellectuals, academics can learn from such struggles by turning the university and public schools into vibrant critical sites of learning and unconditional sites of pedagogical and political resistance. The power of the existing dominant order does not merely reside in the economic or in material relations of power but also in the realm of ideas and culture. This is why intellectuals must take sides, speak out, and engage in the hard work of debunking corporate culture's assault on teaching and learning, orient their teaching for social change, connect learning to public life, link knowledge to the operations of power, and allow issues of human rights and crimes against humanity in their diverse forms to occupy a space of critical and open discussion in the classroom. It also means stepping out of the classroom and working with others to create public spaces where it becomes possible to not only "shift the way people think about the moment, but potentially to energize them to do something differently in that moment" (Guinier & Smith, 2002, pp. 34–35), to link one's critical imagination with the possibility of activism in the public sphere. This is, of course, a small step, but if we do not want to repeat the present as the future or, even worse, become complicitous in the dominant exercise of power, it is time for educators to mobilize collectively their energies by breaking down the illusion of unanimity that dominant power propagates while working diligently, tirelessly, and collectively to reclaim the promises of a truly global, democratic future.

Notes

1. For instance, in a number of readers on cultural studies, the issue of critical pedagogy is left out altogether. Typical examples include: During, 1999; Miller, 2001; Storey, 1996.
2. For instance, see Grossberg, 1994, pp. 1–25.
3. I take this issue up in greater detail in Giroux, 2000a, 2000c.
4. On the importance of problematizing and pluralizing the political, see Dean, 2000, pp. 1–19
5. See especially Williams, 1977, 1983.
6. Giroux, 2000b. Also see Giroux, 2000a, 2002.
7. See, for instance, Durham & Kellner, 2000.
8. Other examples of such work can be found in Garber, 1997, 2000.
9. See, for example, Kellner, 1995.

References

Badiou, A. (1998). *Ethics: An essay on the understanding of evil.* London: Verso.

Bauman, Z. (1999). *In search of politics.* Stanford: Stanford University Press.

Bauman, Z. (2002). *Society under siege.* Malden: Blackwell.

Beverly, J. (1996). Pedagogy and subalternity: Mapping the limits of academic knowledge. In R.G. Paulston (Ed.), *Social cartography* (p. 354). New York: Garland.

Bourdieu, P. (2000). For a scholarship of commitment. *Profession,* p. 44.

Chomsky, N. (2000). Paths taken, tasks ahead. *Profession* (p. 34).

Clifford, J. (1992). Museums in the borderlands. In M. Tucker (Ed.), *Different voices: A social, cultural, and historical framework for change in the American art museum* (p. 129). New York: Association of Art Museum Directors.

Dean, J. (2000). The interface of political theory and cultural studies. In J. Dean (Ed.), *Cultural studies and political theory* (pp. 1–19). Ithaca: Cornell University Press.

Derrida, J. (2000). Intellectual courage: An interview. (P. Krapp, Trans.). *Culture Machine, 2,* p. 9

Dirlik, A. (2002). Literature/identity: Transnationalism, narrative, and representation. *Review of Education/ Pedagogy/Cultural Studies, 24*(3), p. 218.

Durham, M.G. and Kellner, D.M. (2000) Adventures in media and cultural studies: Introducing KeyWorks. In M.G. Durham and D.M. Kellner (Eds.) *Media and cultural studies: KeyWorks.* (p. 29) Malden: Blackwell.

During, S. (Ed.). (1999). *The cultural studies reader* (2nd ed.). New York: Routledge.

Fritsch, M. (2002). Derrida's democracy to come. *Constellations, 9*(4), p. 579

Garber, M. (1997). *Dog Love.* New York: Touchstone Press.

Garber, M. (2000). *Sex and real estate: Why we love houses.* New York: Anchor Press.

Giroux, H., & McLaren, P. (Eds.). (1993). *Between borders: Pedagogy and the politics of cultural studies.* New York: Routledge.

Giroux, H. (2000a). *Impure acts: The practical politics of cultural studies.* New York: Routledge.

Giroux, H. (2000b). *The mouse that roared: Disney and the end of innocence.* Lanham: Rowman and Littlefield.

Giroux, H. (2000c). *Stealing innocence: Corporate culture's war on children.* New York: Palgrave.

Giroux, H. (2002). *Breaking into the movies: Film and the politics of culture.* Malden: Blackwell.

Grossberg, L. (1994). Introduction: Bringin' it all back home—Pedagogy and cultural studies. In H. Giroux & P. McLaren (Eds.), *Border crossings: Pedagogy and the politics of cultural studies* (pp. 1–25). New York: Routledge.

Grossberg, L. (1996). Toward a genealogy of the state of cultural studies. In C. Nelson & D.P. Gaonkar (Eds.), *Disciplinarity and dissent in cultural studies* (p. 143). New York: Routledge.

Guinier, L., & Smith, A.D. (2002). Rethinking power, rethinking theater. *Theater, 31*(3), pp. 34–35

Gunster, S. (2000). Gramsci, organic intellectuals, and cultural studies. In J. Frank & J. Tambornino (Eds.), *Vocations of political theory* (p. 253). Minneapolis: University of Minnesota Press.

Kellner, D. (1995). *Media culture: Cultural studies, identity, and politics between the modern and the postmodern.* New York: Routledge.

Miller, T. (Ed.). (2001). *A companion to cultural studies.* Malden: Blackwell.

Osborne, P., & Segal, L. (1998). Stuart Hall: Culture and power. *Radical Philosophy, 86,* p. 24

Readings, B. (1997). *The university in ruins.* Cambridge, MA: Harvard University Press.

Roy, A. (2001). *Power politics.* Cambridge, MA: South End Press.

Simon, R. (1995). Broadening the vision of university-based study of education: The contribution of cultural studies. *Review of Education/Pedagogy/Cultural Studies, 12*(1), p. 109

Storey, J. (Ed.). (1996). *What is cultural studies?: A reader.* New York: Arnold Press.

Szeman, I. (2002). Learning to learn from Seattle. *The Review of Education, Pedagogy, and Cultural Studies, 24*(1–2), p. 4.

Williams, R. (1967). Preface to second edition. *Communications* (pp. 14–16). New York: Barnes & Noble.

Williams, R. (1977). *Marxism and literature.* New York: Oxford University Press.

Williams, R. (1983). *The year 2000.* New York: Pantheon.

Worsham, L., & Olson, G.A. (1999). Rethinking political community: Chantal Mouffe's liberal socialism. *Journal of Composition Theory, 19*(2), p. 178.

7

■ The Power of New Media Networks

Robin Mansell

■ Introduction[1]

In this chapter I reflect on some of the implications of the new media that are associated with substantial changes in the social, political and economic power relationships embedded in social networks. There are many claims about the multiple ways in which the intensification of such relationships can become empowering for citizens. References in the literature to empowerment generally imply that relationships facilitated by new media can equip citizens with the knowledge they need to make choices about how they want to live their lives, and more specifically, to participate more effectively in democratic processes.[2] It is often assumed that this holds even for the most culturally, politically or economically marginalised people. I argue here that policy makers, business leaders and citizens must become more aware of the many different ways that relationships mediated by the new media may be altered, not always for the better. When it is simply assumed that these technologies are always a 'good' thing, there is little that can be done to use new media in ways that may help to avert social exclusion when this is already a feature of people's lives. One means of encouraging reflection on the full range of implications of new media is by focusing on citizen's rights and entitlements in an intensely mediated world.

Despite the fact that for those who do have access to new media, these technologies are becoming relatively routine 'everyday technologies,'[3] the availability of email, video, instant messaging, blogs, wikis, personal websites, listservs, and social networking websites such as Facebook and MySpace, continues to give rise to debate about how their use by citizens is influencing on and offline practices. It is known, for example, that users of mobile phones, instant messaging, and social networking websites in the United States communicate primarily with small groups of well-known friends and family (Walther 1996, 2006). While empirically grounded research is providing some understanding of the dynamics of mediated relationship of this kind, we do not have sufficient insight to assume, as some observers do, that these relationships are necessarily empowering. This is especially so in places where little or no empirical research has been conducted. What we do know is that, as Silverstone argues, '…the world of globally mediated communication offers and to a degree defines the terms of our participation with the other' (Silverstone, 2007, p. 27). It therefore matters what is said and how what is said is interpreted and understood. This means that it also matters whether citizens are able to develop critical evaluative skills to assess how to value their communicative relationships and the information that they both produce and consume. The capabilities or critical evaluative skills in question are often labelled media literacies. Research has shown that the capabilities for making sense of various types of online spaces are unevenly spread across populations even in the wealthy countries (Berker et al., 2005).[4] Information or media literacies are difficult to define, but generally are said to involve the following.

> …at a minimum these skills include the abilities to access, navigate, critique and create the content and services available via information and communication technologies (Livingstone and Van Couvering, 2008).

Participation in education, the workplace and society depends increasingly on these kinds of skills (Livingstone, 2004; Livingstone et al., 2007). This means it is very important to give consideration to the implications of a growing dependency on new media in terms of citizen's rights and entitlements.

It is also important to focus on both the potentially enabling power of new media which support social networks and on the circumstances in which a growing dependency on these networks may be disabling or disempowering. Such networks become the mediators of our responses to human and natural disasters wherever they occur (Chouliaraki, 2006). It can be very difficult to make sense of this mediated environment, not only because of the quantity of network relationships, but also because of the absence of clarity as to the provenance of information. In this environment the empowering or disempowering character of new media is ambiguous at best.

I indicated almost a decade ago in an assessment of the potential of new information and communication technologies (ICTs), that issues relating to capabilities would be very important even as efforts were being made to reduce disparities in access to them.

> In some parts of the world ICTs are contributing to revolutionary changes in business and everyday life. Other parts of the world, however, have hardly been touched by these technologies. There is little question that their social and economic potential is enormous, but so too are the risks that those without the *capabilities* to design, produce and use the new products and service applications may be disadvantaged or excluded from participating actively in their local communities… (emphasis added) (Mansell and Wehn, 1998: 266).[5]

The potential for exclusion as a result of difficulties in acquiring certain capabilities, notwithstanding the spread of access to new media (including the evermore ubiquitous content available via mobile phones) is just as great almost a decade after this observation was made. More affordable access to new media has been achieved in some parts of the world, but the greater reach of global networks and new media applications has been accompanied by a situation in which '…they have provided few or no resources to understand and respond to…difference, nor do they necessarily represent it adequately. And the consequences of that representation have tended to produce either worldly indifference or hostility, both strategies for denial' (Silverstone, 2007, p. 28). This suggests that the issue of media literacy and the acquisition of relevant capabilities must be taken very seriously if informed public discussion is to be encouraged. Is it possible to imagine how the contradictory power of new media can be employed in a manner that is enabling for most citizens—and therefore for society as a whole? It is feasible to do so but changes of this kind require a consideration of the wider framework of human rights, entitlements and the dynamics of social development (Mansell, 2006).

The remainder of this chapter is structured around four questions. First, why should we be concerned about the new media and the power of the networks of relationships that they sustain? Second, is there a case for a change in new media policy to ensure that citizens have the right to acquire certain kinds of capabilities? Third, why can we not leave it to teachers to address the ways in which these capabilities should be acquired? And, fourth, what grounds are there for optimism that the emphasis of policy will shift in the direction I advocate in this chapter?

■ New Media and the Power of Networks

Why should we be concerned about new media and the power of the networked relationships they facilitate? Silverstone (1999) suggests that we need to be concerned because of the way the media contribute to the exercise of power in late-modern society. The focus of most policy with respect to new media is on markets and regulation, on access to technology, and on the costs of reducing social exclusion. However, as indicated above, it is increasingly clear that people need to acquire certain new media literacies if they are to be able to make choices in an intensely mediated world. Such literacies go far beyond being able to read or understand the content of new media. If people are to have the freedom to achieve the livelihoods that they want, they must be able to acquire the necessary literacies. Without the ability to achieve these literacies, problems of alienation, poverty, or ignorance, and terrorism are likely to worsen and the empowering potential of new media will be substantially reduced.

For some, the new media are encountered in situations where they are able to acquire the capabilities to use the new applications in ways that strengthen their chances of making choices about how to live their lives. They do so, for example, by accessing or sharing information about treatments for illness, exploring websites that enable learning and skill development, or simply by searching for like-minded people with whom they can establish online relationships. For those who are unable to do so, however, it can be argued that their human rights are being infringed. There are grounds therefore for policy action to ensure that new media spaces are available to enable citizens to acquire the capabilities that will assist them in managing their lives.

The capabilities that are at stake here are not simply those necessary for acquiring skills to surf the Internet, or the ability to use the web, discussion lists, or email. Nor is this matter concerned solely with access to new electronic government or commerce services. The capabilities that are at stake are those associated with the acquired cognitive abilities to discriminate between alternative choices. As Sen (1999) suggests, these capabilities are the foundation of freedoms that allow an individual's needs to be met, needs such as remaining healthy and interacting with others in ways that are valued.

If new media electronic spaces can be developed in ways that will augment these kinds of capabilities, then arguably there is a public obligation to do so. Much has been written about the need to reduce or eliminate so-called 'digital divides,' an issue that is too often characterised by the documentation of the uneven diffusion or affordability of telephones, computers, or Internet access (Norris, 2001; Warschauer, 2003). In this chapter I argue that a radical step is needed to ensure that the spread of new media does not simply exacerbate social and economic disparities. New media policy must be developed in such a way as to give a much higher priority to the creation of electronic spaces to facilitate the acquisition of capabilities in Sen's meaning of the term. Castells (2001: 158) suggests that 'rather than strengthening democracy by fostering the knowledge and participation of citizens, use of the Internet tends to deepen the crisis of political legitimacy by providing a broader launching platform for the politics of scandal.' New media are becoming 'the new, and most effective, frontier for the exercise of power on the world stage' (Castells, 2001, p. 161). In this context, media literacies are essential if people are to achieve what they value through their capacity for critical evaluation. In the context of older media, similar issues have been raised. Williams (1974) linked the structure and content of older media to questions about equity and the organisation of society. However, Thompson's (1995) analysis of the social organisation of the media suggests that there has been a profound neglect of how specific forms of media—including the new media spaces—influence the way people choose to live their lives. Much discussion about new media is not about how or even whether they might augment people's abilities to change their lives. There is a growing body of research on strategic uses of new media by activists and civil society groups (Rogers, 2004; Axford and Huggins, 2001; and Chadwick, 2006), but it offers little insight into the cognitive capabilities for critical evaluation that are the concern of this chapter (see, for example, Latham and Sassen, 2005; McCaughey and Ayers, 2003; Olesen, 2005 and Van de Donk et al., 2004). Instead, much of this work is completely divorced from a consideration of the conditions of citizens' everyday lives or of their freedom (knowledge and other resources) to create positive changes in their lives (Golding and Murdock, 2001).

Thompson (1995) writes about the 'double bind of mediated dependency.' By this he seems to mean that just when the process of identity formation is being potentially enriched by new media's symbolic content and by the multiple identities people are able to adopt, citizens are becoming more dependent on new media networks that seem to be largely beyond their control. The majority of citizens have no control over what new media systems are developed, how they are structured, or whether they are consistent with enabling people to acquire capabilities for living their lives more effectively. He suggests, for example, as do Giddens (1991) and Beck (1992), that the kinds of mediated experiences associated with new media tend to disempower local forms of political organisation, rendering traditional fora for democratic dialogue very difficult to sustain. Thompson (1995, p. 10) concludes that a new form of 'publicness' is needed. He does not indicate, however, just where the responsibility for achieving this might lie.

Like Habermas's (1989) advocacy of the need to create arenas for public discourse and Thompson's (1995, p. 255) appeal to strengthen 'deliberative democracy' (see also Held, 1987), most theoretical treatments of this issue say little about what might be done. There are, of course, debates about the need for regulation to achieve a reduction in the concentration of the media industries and many discussions about new media regulation or self-regulation as practiced by organisations such as the Internet Watch Foundation in the United Kingdom or the Free Press in the United States.[6] However, discussions within the context of regulation often appear to have little bearing on questions of democracy and whether or not new media can contribute to the empowerment of citizens.

It is necessary to consider questions about new media policy and democracy alongside problems created by inequitable development. Melody (2007) argues that hardware, software, and human capital are becoming the replacements for capital and raw materials as well as traditionally skilled workers (see also Romer, 1995). Economic growth depends increasingly on being able to reap the benefits of organising one's life within densely interconnected networks (Mansell et al., 2007). However, the main focus of discussions about emerging knowledge societies is usually on issues of economic growth and the diffusion of technology (Quah, 2001). Rarely is attention given to matters of equity, human rights or social development. Where issues concerning capabilities are addressed, the focus is often mainly on technological capabilities for designing networks and services or on institutional capabilities for making policy, regulating and governing in areas such as intellectual property protection, electronic commerce or broadcasting (Mansell, 2002). A consideration of the capabilities that may be understood as citizens' entitlements in the new media context calls for a different starting point.

■ Acquiring New Media Capabilities

What is the case for changing new media policy to encourage new media capabilities? Sen (1999, p. 75) offers a helpful way of thinking about issues of rights and entitlements that can be applied with very practical results in the new media field. He calls for an examination of certain capabilities as a basic human right. In building his idea of capabilities, he is concerned about 'functionings' understood as what 'a person may value doing or being.' Functionings may be very basic like being free from hunger or illness. They can also be complex such as 'being able to take part in the life of the community and having self-respect' (Sen, 1999, p. 75). Capabilities are therefore the combinations of functionings that citizens are able to achieve for themselves.

In applying his argument in the context of new media, it is essential to ask what an individual's 'realised functionings' might be or, in other words, 'what can a person do'? It is necessary to consider what capability set is available to each individual. There also must be some means to evaluate and decide upon the capability set that a person is entitled to. As Sen (1999, pp. 78–79) puts it, this evaluation process is 'a "social choice" exercise, and it requires public discussion and a democratic understanding and acceptance.'

The social choice is not only concerned with capabilities for encouraging social or human capital development for effective participation in the economy. As Sen points out, these capabilities tend to emphasise the agency of human beings in augmenting the production of goods and services and they are mainly concerned with the economic problem of growth in the economy, that is, with productivity or efficiency. While this dimension is important, Sen's (1999, p. 293) approach emphasises 'the substantive freedom—of people to lead the lives they have reason to value and to enhance the real choices they have, in other words, the freedom to critically assess the information available to them in both their offline and online everyday lives.

His argument begins with a concern for human well-being and from a view that choice and the freedom to act are essential. Sen explicitly rejects the neo-classical proposition that human welfare can best be served by market exchange or that such exchange produces a measure of well-being.[7] This framework offers the foundation for a needs-based approach to the evaluation of appropriate new media entitlements. Garnham (1999) applied this approach to issues of telecommunication access, emphasising that entitlements are unrelated to merit or absolute wealth. The metric for deciding who is entitled to what is not money or pleasure (utility), but, instead, a judgement about whether citizens should be entitled to develop a capability set that will enable them to achieve what they value.

For example, following Sen, those who lack food, safety, love or esteem are likely to need food more than other things, but when their physiological needs are relatively satisfied, another set of needs, for instance, for stability, security, protection, freedom from fear, anxiety or chaos, may be highly valued. The emphasis on the individual's capacity for well-being downplays considerations about the self in relation to others, but this framework is useful in drawing attention to a capability set that involves cognitive capacities and learning. As we move towards a more intensely mediated society, arguably it is the cognitive capacity for critical evaluation of encounters within new media spaces that becomes increasingly essential for well-being.

Predictions that the new media will offer new capacities for improving social connectivity which, in turn, will lead to profound social changes are probably correct, notwithstanding the fact that they suffer from hyperbole. However, such predictions often overlook the fact that the offline world of things and relationships still matters (Orgad, 2007). Nevertheless, in the light of the global reach of new media networks, the potential is there for providing open spaces for learning in ways that could enable critical reflection on a host of pressing issues that affect citizens everywhere.

In the absence of capabilities for critical reflection it is likely to be difficult, if not impossible, for the majority of people to take advantage of the potential offered by new media in terms of augmenting their freedoms in Sen's terms. Silverstone argues that there is a need for all contributors to these spaces to be accountable. This means that contributors to new media spaces must have the right to acquire the capabilities that will enable them to be accountable both to themselves and others.

> Accountability must be systemic, and as such dependent on the work of audiences and media users as participants, who are media literate enough to make their own judgements on what is being presented to them or in what they are participating. Our trust therefore must be conditional, critical. Our participation must be knowing participation: proper distance must be informed by proper scepticism. Trust can neither be blind nor passive. The media are both institutions and discourses. Both need to be trustworthy (Silverstone 2007: 127).

The availability of software- and hardware-based technical tools (such as Privacy Enhancing Technologies and encryption) intended to support trusted mediated relationships has given rise to the hope that citizens' privacy can be protected and that they will be able to regard their mediated environments as being trustworthy (Borking and Raab, 2001; Collins and Mansell, 2005). As new media applications have become more pervasive, there are similar aspirations for the tools for managing and organising information and online modes of communication. The personalisation of digital services using 'intelligent' search engines that learn individual preferences and content-rating systems is the most obvious example. However, none of these technical solutions detracts from the need for citizens to acquire capabilities for making judgements about whom and what to trust or to value. Therefore, it does seem appropriate that the policy agenda for new media should focus on the right of citizens to acquire capabilities to enhance their 'functioning' with respect to their participation in society.

Sen (1999) observes that modern communication networks require basic education and training although he does not outline specifically what this should entail. Social justice arguably requires that, if they choose to do so, citizens can take part in decisions that affect their lives. Sen argues that the capabilities of reading and writing are important, as are being well informed and able to participate freely in society. Arguably these become more complicated in new media spaces as demonstrated by those who, for example, have researched the use of language in computer-mediated discourse (Herring, 2004). Increasing reliance on new media spaces means that, as Silverstone (2007, p. 147) puts it, '...access to, and participation in, a global system of mediated communication is a substantive good and a precondition for full membership of society, and...the distribution of such a right must be fair and just.'[8] The difficulty is that we do not have a sufficiently detailed consideration of what measures would encourage the broadest development of capabilities for informed choice making. Without detailed consideration of this, it is difficult to imagine what policy action would be feasible or, indeed, realistic.

■ Acquiring a New Capability Set

Why can we not leave it to teachers to address the ways in which these capabilities should be acquired? Moving beyond exhortations that more new media spaces should be established to encourage the capabilities for critical reasoning strongly suggests the need to strengthen the capabilities of all citizens to participate in mediated environments in ways that they choose (Couldry, 2007). This means that there is a need to re-imagine the roles that new media can play in society and the associated cognitive capabilities that are needed. This is not an issue that can be left solely to those concerned with pedagogical development for ICT skills in educational settings. Formal education is very rarely organised to encourage a diverse dialogue about entitlements and social or political purposes. A focus on human rights and entitlements in the new media age raises the question of whether the new media spaces that are available are sufficiently oriented towards this kind of learning.

The problem is not simply one of access and affordability. At present, new media spaces arguably are overwhelmingly oriented away from fulfilling their potential in this way. An Internet search quickly yields large numbers of information intermediaries on the World Wide Web. Industry sectors from publishing to automobiles, and from insurance to banking are populated by dozens of web sites, many claiming to offer support for commercial transactions. However, the majority of these sites are walled or closed sites for members only. Even when they are open, they are not always what they seem. Claims are made about offering business support services like logistics or about providing help for producers to meet industry standards for quality or environmental protection and to verify the identities of firms, but few sites that make such claims deliver on them without requesting registration and sometimes payment. The notion of the trusted intermediary in the commercial world of new media is valid in practice only for a minority of employees of firms who are members of relatively closed clubs (Humphrey et al., 2004).

The commercialisation of new media spaces is creating pressures to close up the public online spaces so that they are more trustworthy for commercial purposes and to mitigate security threats (Lessig, 1999; Mansell and Collins, 2005). As this pressure increases it is likely that the open spaces for learning the capabilities that will facilitate critical reflection will recede or become closed to some segments of the potential population (as a result of security measures). Hence, if new media literacies or capabilities are to be fostered, there needs to be a consideration, not only of the architectures and platforms (the artefacts), but also of the activities, practices and social arrangements that are encouraged by new media intermediaries. For instance, there is a need for empirical analysis of whether new media developments are encouraging open spaces that support citizens in acquiring the capability set involved in discriminating between alternative choices with respect to information and with respect to mediated communicative relationships. From the health sector to the education sector, and on issues of environmental protection or globalisation and, indeed, anti-globalisation, there are huge numbers of web sites. Those sites that are embedded in established institutions—governments, education establishments, or development organisations—provide people with highly structured, authoritative information, at least in terms of the institutional creators' view. Some support interactivity, but few allow citizens to contribute their own information, or indeed, to acquire the capability of deciding how that information should be valued or acted upon.

Apart from institutional sites, there are growing numbers of individual home pp, blogs, and text and video spaces such as MySpace. Many of the thousands of English-language blogs on political issues contain citizens' views, albeit in a highly unstructured format. Organisations representing various segments of civil society have set up blogs such as MySociety.org, and, at the time of writing, the United Kingdom government was assessing how to take advantage of 'the phenomenon of internet advice sharing sites' so as to '...empower people with information that could help improve their lives.'[9] The status of these sites as trusted intermediaries is established by these organisations. Although 'sharing' is assumed, most sites mainly offer information *to* citizens, only rarely providing the means for acquiring the capabilities to critically assess information that is provided.

What new media intermediaries generally do is to keep track of information the online visitor has viewed, or they may enhance information with annotations and personalisation features. Putting an intermediary between the originator of the information and the online visitor can make Internet surfing more efficient. However, these developments do not address the issue of capabilities in Sen's meaning of the term. Nor do they suggest the extent to which progress is being made on the wider issue of human rights and entitlements to acquire these capabilities.

One means of beginning to address this issue may be the development and free availability of toolkits for producing and sharing information in open new media spaces. There are examples of this type of website. For instance, the Internet Scout project supported by the National Science Foundation and the Mellon Foundation in the United States has developed a toolkit that simplifies the technical hurdles involved in creating and sharing web-based information and discussions. The availability of blogging software has opened up new opportunities, but there is little evidence about which voices are represented or about which views are being taken into account by those in the position to do so.[10]

In addition, even when citizens are given the tools to make contributions to public discussion or to share information, many of these sites are inadequately funded (Latham and Sassen, 2005). The contributors struggle to maintain their work and to manage their new media spaces. Most publicly sponsored sites and most sites of civil society organisations are designed mainly to be authoritative information providers in a familiar 'broadcast' or 'advertising' mode. Even when account is taken of the unstructured blogs, it is not clear that they are encouraging the majority of citizens to acquire new media literacies (Cammaerts and Carpentier, 2006; Hemer and Tufte, 2005).

Any assessment of the capabilities for critical assessment of new media environments also needs to take into account the unequal power and contested relationships in the offline world. These relationships constrain what views can be published in the online world. This is so notwithstanding the potential for anonymity and claims about the empowering and libertarian features of new media. If, for example, the constraints confronting reporters in countries where governments do not encourage press freedom are considered, it is clear that even where improved access to new media is possible and media producers have the necessary capabilities for critical reflection, the offline world constraints can be substantial.

Regardless of their capacities for critical reflection, what journalists choose to report can be constrained in many different ways. For example, Philip Ocheing, a reporter for *The Nation* in Kenya, comments in an interview with a researcher that, 'we still have a lot of problems with NGOs working in the media sector. I don't agree with their vision of the world, especially with that of a free flow of information....Free flows of ideas are only moving in one direction, all the ideas are coming from the West. The West is not paying attention to ours. If I have any idea about democracy, it won't reach you in London.'[11] The availability of new media and the appropriate skills for critical assessment can do little themselves to counter this perception.

The realities of political contexts and power relations informing what can be voiced are visible again in a comment by Jusef Gabobe, Editor of the *Somaliland Times* and *Hatuuf*, to the effect that 'we are hostages of peace.' Jailed and subsequently released, his comment was offered in the light of the fact that he and others had fought for peace. To maintain it, he argued that sometimes journalists would have to censor themselves so as not inflame potential tensions. This would apply to online new media spaces as well as to the hardcopy of the newspaper, highlighting again that critical reflection, whether on or offline, needs to be politically contextualised. The voice of Lucy Orieng, Managing Editor of *The Nation* in Kenya, points to politics and power relations more directly. 'There is nothing more political than women rights. Talking about women rights in Kenya is talking about power. But when you raise issues like that, people try to silence you'—this is likely to be so regardless of where such issues are raised.

Offline power relations have an economic dimension as well that can limit which voices will be heard regardless of whether older or newer media are used. Drake Ssekeba, an experienced Ugandan journalist, observes that 'we journalists come to serve people. We don't serve ourselves. When politicians come to government, they're actually pretending that they are serving you but actually they are serving their own interests. When I come to write a story, I don't expect a reward from the public. I just expect my employer to give me a salary at the end of the month or week.' Without a means of obtaining an income, critical evaluation of what should be reported in the online world is no less difficult than it is in the case of the older media.

Notwithstanding these reflections by several media practitioners, the under-resourcing of efforts to develop the capabilities for critical evaluation still needs to be addressed. Finding better ways to encourage such developments through sustainable funding mechanisms is one way of enabling improved conditions for learning and for more people to participate in choices about their lives. Policy measures encouraging sensitivity to offline power relations and to the need to learn the skills of critical reflection could be facilitated by a needs-based approach to new media policy, a policy that takes citizens' entitlements and human rights into account.

■ Potential for Radical Change

Are there any grounds for optimism about a radical change in new media policy? The relationship between technical change and social development is a key theme in social science inquiry historically. In the 1930s Lewis Mumford (1934, p. 6) wrote, for instance, that 'technics' and civilisation as a whole are the result of human choices and aptitudes and strivings, deliberate as well as unconscious.' A needs-based approach was called for but little progress was made. Arguably, it will be more difficult to achieve now that the scale of the challenge is global and it is complicated by a world fragmented by multiple networks.

Nevertheless, since the new media have profound implications for society, the implications of the 'new' media for the distribution of knowledge and for democracy need to be considered (Innis 1951). While today's new media offer spaces for new kinds of mediated dialogues, it is becoming clear that the mediation of the conflicts and tensions experienced by others is not experienced in the same ways as in the past and can lead to misperceptions of many different kinds (Chouliaraki, 2006; Cohen, 2001; Silverstone, 2007). It is also clear that online spaces will not foster dialogue aimed at building trust and understanding if citizens have limited capabilities for contributing, for discerning the provenance of information, or for deciding how to value the new media's content or those they meet online.

As indicated above, there are economic incentives as well as growing concerns about human and information security that are favouring closed new media spaces, 'broadcast' modes of communication are still common, and advertising is becoming interwoven with non-commercial information provision. All these developments work against the potential for learning and the acquisition of the capability set discussed in this chapter. Nevertheless, the networked world is malleable, and greater effort could be given to developing policies that will encourage the acquisition of these new media capabilities. If this should happen, there is a chance that as, Lévy (1997, p. xxi) observes, the new media could play an important role in enabling citizens to acquire the essential capabilities to which they are arguably entitled. The new media might then become instrumental in reshaping 'the structure of the social bond in the direction of a greater sense of community and help us resolve the problems currently facing humanity.' To achieve this there will be a need to divert existing public support for new media developments into establishing open new media forums for debate and for learning. These issues are being addressed to some extent by those who are critical of media and communication researchers' efforts to tackle these issues. McChesney (2007) argues for example, for greater attention to media criticism by scholars. My argument is intended to go beyond the realm of scholarship to consider how more concrete efforts might be made to enhance capabilities for critical reflection by all those who encounter our mediated environment.

It might be argued that policy intervention of this kind is inconsistent with a libertarian stance towards new media developments. Castells (2001, p. 183) argues that 'there is an unsettling combination in the Internet world: a pervasive libertarian ideology with an increasingly controlling practice.' Any policy intervention is often interpreted as being contrary to the libertarian ethos and as a controlling effort to shape nascent markets. However, diverting a proportion of the spending that is allocated to promoting access to the new technologies, to underwriting the costs of regulating the media conglomerates, and to developing means of digital rights management, towards support for new media spaces that foster capabilities consistent with citizens' entitlements is not likely to jeopardise spending in other areas to support innovation. Instead, it may well stimulate a growing interest in new media dialogues that are valued by broader segments of the global population, at least by those for whom access is affordable.

It may also be argued that a policy enabling more citizens to acquire capabilities for discriminating between alternative information and communicative relationships could have unintended consequences. It might, for instance, heighten the risk that new forums for deliberative debate, with potentially global participation, will become unstable, thereby weakening the capacities for governance on a global scale. However, the risk associated with inaction is arguably greater. Deepening inequalities in new media literacies are likely to compound the complexities of governing and weaken capacities for addressing problems arising as a result of inequality in many other spheres of life. The potential of the new media to be used in ways that help to address social problems associated with marginalisation and poverty would then be substantially reduced.

■ Conclusion

This application of Sen's capability set approach to questions about appropriate policy interventions with respect to new media suggests that new media policy centred around legal issues and regulation on the supply side of the industry needs to be complemented by policies that address the capabilities or new media literacies that all citizens should be entitled to acquire. The key issue is the freedoms that people should have in the new media age. In the formal education arena, new media skill development tends to focus on information technology-related skills, and most training initiatives aim to enable people to be more productive in the workplace. Most initiatives do not entail a needs-based assessment with respect to the functionings of citizens in society more generally. In addition, they are often driven by what the technology has the potential to do, rather than by what citizens may need to do with it. Public investment in new media intermediaries charged with developing toolkits and resources for learning the skill of critical reflection would go some way towards enabling citizens to acquire capabilities to become informed participants in democratic debate, whether on or offline.

Most importantly, there is a need for an evaluation of the capability set that citizens should be entitled to acquire. This evaluation should not be limited to the main capabilities associated with human capital development for the workplace. The commercial sector is unlikely to have an incentive to encourage the development of the kinds of tools and new media spaces that are needed to foster well-being (unless revenues can be generated). It therefore must fall to the public sector and to civil society organisations to create and mobilise these kinds of spaces. There is a need for debate about what capabilities specifically are required. All those involved in teaching and learning will be aware of how difficult it is to inculcate capacities for critical reflection in the offline spaces of learning as the 'student as consumer' culture becomes more entrenched; the challenge of doing so for citizens and new media spaces is arguably even greater. Evaluation is necessary, not with a view to reducing the conventional understanding of the 'digital divide' in terms of access and technical skills, but to provide the foundation for meeting the citizen's entitlement to become an informed participant in society.

As Silverstone (2007, p. 181) argues, 'media literacy is, or should be, a skill and capability of all those who participate in the mediapolis.'[12] He insists that '…media literacy is a matter for individual competence and that it will only be once it becomes so that it will emerge as a matter of societal capacity' (Silverstone, 2007, p. 182). This applies as much to citizens who contribute to new media spaces as it does to those who consider themselves to be members of the journalism profession. With respect to the latter, '…. media literacy at this level, that is among journalists and their editors,…is a matter of informed and reflexive understanding of the nature of mediation as a practice and of the mediapolis as a social, cultural and political environment, in which their activities have significant moral consequences' (Silverstone 2007, p. 183). In this paper, I have suggested that citizens must be entitled to the extent they chose to do so, to acquire capabilities for reflexive understanding too.

Following this line of argument, it is clear that claims about the potential of new media spaces to empower citizens need to be critically assessed in the light of whether measures are being taken to augment their capabilities for critical reflection. New media technologies are Janus-faced in the sense that they may be empowering but they may also be disempowering. The implications of new media depend partly on the capability set that citizens can acquire for participating in mediated societies and partly on the offline power relationships within which they are embedded. If media literacies are being encouraged that are consistent with capabilities for critical reflection then there is the potential for those who both produce and consume media to affect their circumstances through deliberation and action that may be empowering. If they are not able to do so, then the new media will be allied with the compounding of disparities in power relationships in social networks both off and online.

Notes

1. A shorter version of this chapter was presented 23 October 2001 as the First Dixons Public Lecture, 'New Media and the Power of Networks,' London School of Economics and Political Science.

2. The literature in question is often produced by organisations concerned with development, gender equity, education, etc. It is too voluminous to cite here.

3. Lievrouw and Livingstone (2006: 2) define new media as 'information and communication technologies and their associated social contexts,…as infrastructures with three components' (artefacts, activities and practices, and social arrangements).

4. And see for the UK, Ofcom (2006).

5. "Revolutionary" refers here to the potentially disruptive nature of the technology following Freeman (2007), not necessarily to the magnitude of change in society.

6. See http://www.iwf.org.uk/ and http://www.freepress.net accessed 30 March 2008.

7. It is acknowledged that there may be concerns about the standpoint from which well-being is assessed, see White and Pettit (2006).

8. This issue should not be confused with questions concerning codes of practice to foster civility in the new media blogging environment, see Freedland (2007).

9. See Cabinet Office (2007).

10. See http://scout.cs.wisc.edu/ accessed 30 March 2008.

11. Journalists in this section were interviewed in 2006 with by Iginio Gagliardone, then employed by UNESCO, and currently a doctoral student in the Media and Communications Department, London School of Economics. The author of this paper is grateful for permission to use these quotations.

12. Mediapolis is defined as 'the mediated public space where contemporary political life increasingly finds a place, both at national and global levels, and where the materiality of the world is constructed through (principally) electronically communicated public speech and action)' (Silverstone, 2007, p. 31).

References

Axford, B. and Huggins, R. (Eds) (2001) *New Media & Politics.* London: Sage.

Beck, U. (1992) *Risk Society: Towards a New Modernity.* London: Sage, translated by M. Ritter, first published in German in 1986.

Berker, T., Hartmann, M., Punie, Y. and Ward, K. (2005) *Domestication of Media and Technology.* New York: McGraw-Hill.

Borking, J. and Raab, C. (2001) 'Laws, PETs and Other Technologies for Privacy Protection,' *The Journal of Information Law and Technology,* 1, elj.warwick.ac.uk/jilt/01–1/borking.html accessed 12 April 2007.

Cabinet Office (2007). 'The Power of Information Review: online advice sites could improve citizen empowerment,' Press Office, London, 5 April, http://www.cabinetoffice.gov.uk/newsroom/news_releases/2007/070405_power.asp accessed 12 April 2007.

Cammaerts, B. and Carpentier, N. (Eds) (2006) *Reclaiming the Media: Communication Rights and Democratic Media Roles,* Bristol: Intellect.

Castells, M. (2001) *The Internet Galaxy: Reflections on the Internet, Business and Society,* New York: Oxford University Press.

Chadwick, A. (2006) *Internet Politics: States, Citizens, and New Communication Technologies,* New York: Oxford University Press.

Chouliaraki, L. (2006) *The Spectatorship of Suffering.* London: Sage.

Cohen, S. (2001) *States of Denial: Knowing About Atrocities and Suffering,* Cambridge: Polity Press.

Collins, B. S. and Mansell, R. (2005) 'Cyber Trust and Crime Prevention,' in R. Mansell and B. S. Collins (eds) *Trust and Crime in Information Societies,* Cheltenham: Edward Elgar, pp. 11–55.

Couldry, N. (2007) 'Communicative Entitlements and Democracy: The Future of the Digital Divide Debate,' in R. Mansell, C. Avgerou, D. Quah and R. Silverstone (eds) *Oxford Handbook of Information and Communication Technologies,* New York: Oxford University Press, pp. 383–403.

Freedland, J. (2007). 'The blogosphere risks putting off everyone but point-scoring males,' *The Guardian,* 11 April, accessed 12 April 2007.

Freeman, C. (2007) 'The ICT Paradigm' in R. Mansell, C. Avgerou, D. Quah and R. Silverstone (eds) *Oxford Handbook of Information and Communication Technologies,* New York: Oxford University Press, pp. 34–54.

Garnham, N. (1999)'Amartya Sen's 'Capabilities' Approach to the evaluation of welfare: Its application to communications,' in A. Calabrese and J-C Burgelman (eds) *Communication, Citizenship and Social Policy.* Lanham, MD: Rowman and Littlefield, pp. 113–124.

Giddens, A. (1991) *Modernity and Self-identity: Self and Society in the Late Modern Age.* Cambridge: Polity Press.

Golding, P. and Murdock, G. (2001) 'Digital Divides: Communications Policy and Its Contradictions,' *New Economy,* 8: 110–115.

Habermas, J. (1989) *The Structural Transformation of the Public Sphere: An Inquiry into a Category of Bourgeois Society,* trans. By Thomas Burger with Frederick Lawrence. Cambridge: Polity Press.

Held, D. (1987) *Models of Democracy.* Cambridge: Polity Press.

Hemer, O. and Tufte, T. (Eds.). (2005). *Media and glocal change: Rethinking communication for development.* Buenos Aires, Argentina: Clacso.

Herring, S. C. (2004) 'Computer-mediated discourse analysis: An approach to researching online behavior,' in: S. A. Barab, R. Kling, and J. H. Gray (eds) *Designing for Virtual Communities in the Service of Learning.* New York: Cambridge University Press, pp. 338–376.

Humphrey, J., Mansell, R., Paré and Schmitz, H. (2004) 'E-commerce for Developing Countries: Expectations and Reality' (with J. Humphrey, D. Paré and H. Schmitz), *IDS Bulletin,* 35(1): 31–39.

Innis, H. A. (1951). 'Minerva's Owl' in *The Bias of Communication,* Toronto: University of Toronto Press.

Latham, R. and Sassen, S. (Eds) (2005) *Digital Formations: IT and New Architectures in the Global Realm.* Princeton NJ: Princeton University Press.

Lessig, L. (1999) *Code and Other Laws of Cyberspace.* New York: Basic Books.

Lévy, P. (1997) *Collective Intelligence: Mankind's Emerging World in Cyberspace,* Cambridge MA: Perseus Books, translated by R. Bononno.

Lievrouw, L. and Livingstone, S. (2006) 'Introduction to the Updated Student Edition,' in L. Lievrouw and S. Livingstone (eds) *The Handbook of New Media—Updated Student Edition,* London: Sage, pp.1–14.

Livingstone, S. (2004) 'Media literacy and the challenge of new information and communication technologies,' *Communication Review,* 7: 3–14.

Livingstone, S., Van Couvering, E., and Thumim, N. (2007) 'Converging traditions of research on media and information literacies: Disciplinary, critical and methodological issues.' in D.J. Leu, J. Coiro, M. Knobel and C. Lankshear (Eds) *Handbook of Research on New Literacies.* Mahwah, NJ: Lawrence Erlbaum Associates, ch. 4.

Livingstone, S. and Van Couvering, E. (2008), 'Information Literacy' in W. Donbach (ed) *The International Encyclopaedia of Communication,* New York: Wiley-Blackwell.

Mansell, R. (ed.) (2002) *Inside the Communication Revolution: New Patterns of Technical and Social Interaction,* Oxford University Press.

Mansell, R. (2006) 'Ambiguous Connections: Entitlements and Responsibilities of Global Networking' *Journal of International Development,* 18(4): 1–13.

Mansell, R. and Wehn, U. (eds) (1998) *Knowledge Societies: Information Technology for Sustainable Development,* prepared for UN Commission for Science and Technology for Development, New York: Oxford University Press.

Mansell, R., Avgerou, C., Quah, D. and Silverstone, R. (eds) (2007) *Oxford Handbook of Information and Communication Technologies,* New York: Oxford University Press.

Mansell, R. and Collins, B. S. (eds) (2005) *Trust and Crime in Information Societies.* Cheltenham: Edgar Elgar.

McCaughey, M. and Ayers, A. (Eds) (2003) *Cyberactivism: Online Activism in Theory and Practice.* London: Routledge.

McChesney, R. W. (2007) *Communication Revolution: Critical Junctures and the Future of Media.* New York: The New Press.

Melody, W. H. (2007) 'Markets and Policies in New Knowledge Economies,' in R. Mansell, C. Avgerou, D. Quah and R. Silverstone (eds) *Oxford Handbook of Information and Communication Technologies,* Oxford University Press, pp. 55–74.

Mumford, L. (1934) *Technics and Civilization, London:* Routledge & Kegan Paul.

Norris, P. (2001) *Digital Divide: Civic Engagement, Information Poverty, and the Internet Worldwide.* Cambridge: Cambridge University Press.

Ofcom (2006) *Media Literacy Audit: Report on Adult Media Literacy,* London: Ofcom, http://www.ofcom. org.uk/advice/media_literacy/medlitpub/medlitpubrss/medialit_audit/medialit_audit.pdf accessed 12 April 2007.

Olesen, T. (2005) 'Transnational Publics: New Space of Social Movement Activism and the Problem of Long-Sightedness,' *Current Sociology,* 53(3): 419–440.

Orgad, S. (2007) 'The Interrelations between Online and Offline: Questions, Issues, and Implications,' in R. Mansell, C. Avgerou, D. Quah and R. Silverstone (eds) *Oxford Handbook of Information and Communication Technologies,* Oxford University Press, pp. 514–536.

Quah, D. (2001) 'The Weightless Economy in Economic Development,' in M. Pohjola (ed) *Information Technology, Productivity, and Economic Growth: International Evidence,* New York: Oxford University Press, pp. 72–96.

Rogers, R. (2004) *Information Politics on the Web.* Cambridge, MA: MIT Press.

Romer, P. (1995b) 'Increasing returns and long-run growth,' *Journal of Political Economy,* 98(5, Pt. 2): 1002–1037.

Sen, A. (1999) *Development as Freedom,* New York: Oxford University Press.

Silverstone, R. (2007) *Media and Morality: On the Rise of the Mediapolis,* Cambridge: Polity Press.

Silverstone, R. (1999) *Why Study the Media?* London: Sage.

Thompson, J. B. (1995), *The Media and Modernity: A Social Theory of the Media.* Stanford, CA: Stanford University Press.

Van de Donk, W., Loader, B. D., Nixon P. G., and Rucht, D. (Eds) (2004) *Cyberprotest: New Media, Citizens and Social Movements.* London: Routledge.

Walther, J. B. (1996) 'Computer-mediated communication: Impersonal, interpersonal, and hyperpersonal interaction,' *Communication Research, 23,* 1–43.

Walther, J. B. (2006) 'Nonverbal dynamics in computer-mediated communication, or : (and the net : ('s with you, :) and you :) alone,' in V. Manusov and M. L. Patterson (Eds) *Handbook of nonverbal communication* (pp. 461–479). Thousand Oaks, CA: Sage.

Warshauer, M. (2003) *Technology and Social Inclusion: Rethinking the Digital Divide:* Cambridge, MA: MIT Press.

White, S. and Pettit, J. (2006) 'Participatory Approaches and the Measurement of Human Well-Being' in M. McGillivray (ed) *Human Well-being: Concept and Measurement,* London: Palgrave, pp. 240–267.

Williams, R. (1974) 'Communications as cultural science,' *Journal of Communication,* 24(3): 17–25.

■ PART II

Teaching Media/ Cultural Studies

■ Introduction

While some of the texts on media and cultural studies presented in this book give an overview of the field and perhaps delineate specific methodologies and theories, or new fields of study, we want also to offer practical pedagogical approaches to the topic that focus on how to teach media and cultural studies on different levels ranging from K–12 to the college and university level. Part II on "Teaching Media/Cultural Studies" focuses on the literacies and pedagogies that are necessary to teach media/cultural studies to students of different ages and to empower students and citizens to become media literate, active participants in their society. Students can then become teachers and citizens, helping their peers, teachers, and parents understand media and become media literate, while using media to express themselves and to transform their society and culture.

In his study, "Young Children and Critical Media Literacy," Jeff Share explores the potential of teaching critical media literacy to young children from preschool to first grade, between the ages of three and seven. While critical media literacy is a subject that is seldom considered with young students, Share argues that it is essential for educators to begin teaching critical thinking and media literacy as early as possible, especially in relation to media and social justice. Since the first public pedagogy that most children encounter comes right into their own homes and surrounds them in society in the form of cartoons, songs, toys, food packaging, clothing, home decorations, and so on, social researchers should investigate the best ways to help students understand and negotiate these multimodal messages, ubiquitous media and consumer culture, and new information communication technologies.

Share argues that critical teachers need skills to help them question and understand the highly constructed, mass-mediated messages that are too often embraced as merely entertainment, all the while positioning, framing and shaping viewer's perceptions of themselves and world. Exploring classroom examples of work in critical literacy and multimedia literacy with preschool and kindergarten children by two teachers working on the front lines with young students, Share frames his interpretation of their work within the context of theoretical work by Carmen Luke, Alan Luke, Peter Freebody, Douglas Kellner, David Buckingham, Marsha Kinder, and others. His inquiry aims to expose theoretical as well as practical possibilities for building some of the first steps toward critical media literacy with young children.

Ernest Morrell's "Teaching Popular Music" builds on his own experience as a high school teacher using popular music to teach poetry and motivate students to become critics of their culture. Recognizing the important role of popular music in young people's lives, Morrell experimented with mixing and matching rap music with canonical poetry in his classes to engage students in both their own culture and broader streams of Western culture. In particular, Morrell adopted critical pedagogy to get the students to develop their analytical, interpretive, and discursive skills in learning to discuss and write critically about both hip-hop texts and canonical literature. Following Freirean pedagogy, Morrell and his students related their classroom material to broader social and political issues and the ways that education could make a difference in their everyday lives.

Rhonda Hammer's "'This Won't Be on the Final': Reflections on Teaching Critical Media Literacy" draws upon her experience teaching critical media literacy and production in university settings in Canada and the United States. Opening with a discussion of the corporatization of the university, she notes how courses that teach critical thinking and literacies are being marginalized in a corporatized university in which grades and jobs are the overriding concerns. She argues, however, that teaching courses in critical media literacy empower students to better participate in their societies. While new technology and production are often taught by technicians, Hammer argues for a critical media literacy approach that includes theoretical and critical readings of film, broadcasting, and a diversity of media in order to overcome the limitations of a technical approach. She argues that teaching critical media literacy through learning codes of production and applying them to actually producing their own media texts is one of the best ways to gain a critical media literacy and become empowered to participate in the media society. Describing in detail her course on critical media literacy through production at UCLA, Hammer illustrates some ways in which critical media literacy can help students gain the skills to navigate within a highly complex media society and become participants in it.

In her chapter "As Seen on TV or Was that My Phone? 'New' Media Literacy," Carmen Luke provides an overview of emergent media and the need to provide new forms of literacy. She argues for the need to combine traditional media literacy studies with information and communication literacies to deal with the convergence of media and new media that require complex reading and critical skills as well as technical ones. Luke makes the important point that critical media literacy does not just read forms of entertainment, but also engages politics, using as examples terrorist attacks, presidential elections, and natural disasters like the 2004 Asian tsunami as media events that combine images, spectacle, narrative, and discourses, often transmitted through new digital media that require a multitude of new literacies. In a networked and global world, Luke suggests, students and teachers are participants in local, national, and global cultures and need the tools and literacies that will allow them to be intelligently informed and active.

Richard Beach, in his chapter, "Digital Tools for Collecting, Connecting, Constructing, Responding to, Creating, and Conducting Media Ethnographies of Audience Use of Media Texts," also explores emergent digital media and the need for new pedagogies to engage the proliferation of images, information, news, entertainment, and research material. Beach argues that a critical media literacy involves proficiency in multimodality, as media migrates from site to site and words are accompanied by sounds, images, video, and multimedia spectacle. The new digital culture also involves hypertextuality and interactivity, requiring students to be able to collect media texts from disparate sources, make connections between these texts and shared topics, and critically analyze this material as it pertains to race, gender, and class, or hot-button news topics such as presidential elections or war. Additionally, Beach articulates pedagogies of constructing responses to media texts through blogs, Wikis, online chat sites, or virtual game sites. Students can also be encouraged to create their own media texts through digital story-telling, vlogs (video blogs), on-line newspapers or 'zines,' or satire and parody. Beach also argues for the importance of conducting media ethnographies of audience use of digital media texts to discern how different individuals and groups use digital culture and its possible effects on and applications by diverse audiences.

Together, these chapters thus provide a broad range of pedagogies for teaching critical media literacies in a variety of contexts and sites.

8

■ Young Children and Critical Media Literacy

Jeff Share

Most children born in the United States in this millennium have never known a time without the Internet, cellular phones, or television.[1] More than 98% of U.S. households have at least one television set[2] and about one third of young children live in households where the TV is on "always" or "most of the time" (Rideout, Vandewater & Wartella, 2003, p. 4). Before most children reach six years of age, they spend about two hours per day with screen media,[3] something that doubles by age eight, and before they are 18 they spend approximately six and a half hours daily with all types of media (Rideout, Roberts & Foehr, 2005).[4] It is also estimated that nearly all young children in the United States, "have products—clothes, toys, and the like—based on characters from TV shows or movies" (Rideout et al., 2003, p. 4). The implications for the amount of media enveloping today's youth is significant when one considers current research about literacy acquisition that suggests "the early childhood years—from birth through age eight—are the most important period for literacy development" (IRA & NAEYC, 1998, p. 1).

Technological innovations, expansion of global media empires, and unrestricted commercial targeting of children have all contributed to an environment where today's kids are growing up in a mediated world far different than that of any previous generation. While the technological advancements have created new possibilities for the free flow of information, social networking and global activism, there is also the potential for corporations or governments to restrict the flow of information and appropriate these new tools for profit and control at the expense of free expression and democracy. Now more than ever, young children need to learn how to critically question the messages that surround them and how to use the vast array of new tools available to express their own ideas and concerns. Since television programs, video games, computers, cell phones, music, and even toys have become our current transmitters of culture—tellers as well as sellers of the stories of our time—it has become imperative to teach critical media literacy to children as early as possible. Numerous examples and analyses of media education with college students and teenagers are now available, but very little has been written about critical media literacy with young children in preschool, kindergarten, and first grade. It is with these young children, between the ages of three and seven, that I explore possibilities of critically analyzing and creating alternative messages.

■ Critical Media Literacy

Critical media literacy is a pedagogical approach that promotes the use of diverse types of media and information communication technology (from crayons to webcams) to question the roles of media in society and the multiple meanings of the form and content of all types of messages (Kellner & Share, 2007). Analysis of media content is combined with inquiry into the medium, the codes and conventions, the media industries, and the sociocultural contexts within which capitalism and media function to shape identities and empower and disempower individuals and groups. This approach is both hermeneutical and skills-based; critical media literacy pedagogy integrates production activities with the process of critical inquiry. The potential of critical analysis increases when questioning is conducted through production activities that encourage students to examine, create and disseminate their own alternative images, sounds, and thoughts (Share & Thoman, 2007).

Media education has evolved from many disciplines, such as communication theory, media studies, and the multidisciplinary field of cultural studies. Critical media literacy emanating from cultural studies is defined less as a specific body of knowledge or set of skills and more as a framework of "conceptual understandings" (Buckingham, 2003). Many people and organizations around the world have generated their own lists of concepts[5] that vary in numbers and wording, but for the most part they tend to coincide with at least five basic elements: (1) recognition of the construction of media and communication as a social process, as opposed to accepting texts as isolated neutral or transparent conveyors of information; (2) some type of textual analysis that explores the languages, genres, aesthetics, codes, and conventions of the text; (3) an exploration of the role audiences play in negotiating meanings; (4) problematizing the process of representation to uncover and engage issues of ideology, power, and pleasure; and (5) examination of the productions and institutions that motivate and structure the media industries as corporate profit-seeking businesses (see Kellner & Share, 2005).

Critical media literacy offers the potential for young children to develop multiple literacies, engage with popular culture, media, and new information communication technologies in ways that are meaningful to them, experience the excitement of creating their own messages in many formats, and participate as productive citizens empowered to confront their problems and to transform society. Critical media literacy involves a progressive pedagogy that combines an expanded notion of literacy (including all types of media, technology, popular culture, advertising, as well as print) with a deep analysis of communication (exploring the relationships between media and audiences, information and power). Issues of race, class, gender, and power can be addressed through a multiperspectival approach that integrates ideas from cultural studies, critical pedagogy, and media literacy (Kellner, 1995). Following Paulo Freire's (1970) "problem-posing pedagogy," critical media literacy involves praxis, reflection, and action to transform society.

■ Obstacles

Often, false assumptions about children, society and media keep many educators from exploring this new pedagogy. Popular ideas about what is and is not appropriate often prevent the possibility of discovering the potential of critical media literacy to engage young children in meaningful learning that develops their cognitive, social, emotional, moral, and political abilities. A large number of educators in the United States consider teaching a neutral and unproblematic activity, something Henry Giroux asserts is based upon an instrumental ideology which is tied to the culture of positivism and "the various modes of technocratic rationality that underlie most school practices" (2001, p. 209). Kathy Hall (1998) warns that this perspective is not actually apolitical as is claimed, instead "many practicing teachers' political naiveté concerning literacy, teaching and schooling, serves to perpetuate the status quo" (p. 187). Howard Zinn calls this common confusion the myth of objectivity and insists that "[o]ur values should determine the *questions* we ask in scholarly inquiry, but not the answers" (1990, p. 10).

Critical media literacy helps students ask deeper questions about information and its relationship to power, teaching students how to critique, analyze, and express their own ideas in multiple formats. Hall writes, "even quite young children can understand matters of equity, including matters like, say, sexist language practices and discriminatory social organisation. Young children's sense of fairness is usually acute" (p. 187). Determining what is appropriate education for young children is a complex task that requires understanding cognitive abilities, considering social and cultural contexts, and scaffolding teaching to meet individual needs and differences. Barbara Nicoll states, "Teachers who use developmentally appropriate practices are doing more to promote critical thinking than traditional teachers who believe children are too young to think well" (1996). Examples provided in this chapter demonstrate that critical media literacy can be taught to young children.

■ Children and Media

In today's mass mediated culture in which young children need skills for interacting with new media and technologies, educators should be considering which sensory motor and cognitive abilities will be most needed and what are the best developmentally appropriate practices for facilitating their growth. This is especially important when literacy is understood as a social, as well as a developmental, process of assimilation and accommodation. Rogoff and Morelli write that the role of "social interaction provides an essential context for development itself" (1989, p. 346). Marsha Kinder states, "Piaget claims that 'in order to know objects, the subject must act upon them, and therefore transform them'; in turn, the subject is transformed, in a constant process of 'reequilibration'" (1991, p. 4). As an example, Kinder asserts that video games "not only accelerate cognitive development but at the same time encourage an early accommodation to consumerist values and masculine dominance" (p. 119).

Victoria Carrington (2005) writes that the emergence of new media texts, "situate contemporary children in global flows of consumption, identity and information in ways unheard of in earlier generations . . ." (p. 22). Understanding media more as a flow than as separate texts is essential to understanding the culture in which today's children are growing up. Tania Modleski describes Raymond Williams' concept of flow as the complex interactions and interrelations between various television programs and commercials (1982, p. 100). Beverle Houston explains, "The flow of American television goes on for twenty-four hours a day, which is crucial in producing the idea that the text issues from an endless supply that is sourceless, natural, inexhaustible, and coextensive with psychological reality itself" (1984). Houston states that this flow is one of desire and consumption in which the structured interruptions only enhance the desire for endless consumption.

■ Transmedia Intertextuality

Much of commercial children's television programming has advertising breaks every 5 to 10 minutes. During a typical half-hour show on Cartoon Network, a child watches about 20 commercials. This advertising often uses the same cartoon characters from the program she/he is watching (*Scooby Doo* hawking Gogurts) or current movies (*The Simpsons* toys at Burger King) and other popular culture to sell products. These crossovers and merchandising relationships are examples of what Kinder refers to as transmedia intertextuality. Kinder writes that Saturday morning television and "home video games, and their intertextual connections with movies, commercials, and toys, help prepare young players for full participation in this new age of interactive multimedia—specifically, by linking interactivity with consumerism" (p. 6). However, this is no longer just Saturday morning cartoons, the flow is now constant with Nickelodeon, Cartoon Network, Disney Channel, and the Internet (that now offers programming and accompanying games); children's television is available all the time, for those who can afford it.

Children's transmedia intertextuality reaches from the bedroom to cyberspace, as everything from cartoons to junk food is available 24-7, with games to play and merchandise to buy. Children have become a multibillion-dollar consumer market; they are bought and sold, observed and analyzed by some of the largest corporations in the world (Kanner, 2006; Buckingham, 2000). Merchandising and mass marketing construct a flow that links everything together: television, movies, music, Internet, toys, food, clothing, and sometimes even school. The system functions so well that it often goes unnoticed as a natural part of the cultural environment. This normalization veils the historical construction and corporate planning of highly sophisticated marketing strategies and techniques targeted at children. While this may seem commonplace, it is important to remember that advertising to children is a relatively new concept. Jyotsna Kapur points out that "[i]n the early 1900s, there was a certain embarrassment in profiting off childhood" (1999, p. 128).

■ Cultural Ritual

Ideas of media flow and transmedia intertextuality supplement Horace Newcomb and Paul Hirsch's notion of television as a cultural ritual. Newcomb and Hirsch (1983) write that television functions as a cultural ritual and "ritual must be seen as a process rather than as a product" (p. 505). They focus on the cultural role of entertainment and TV as they quote James Carey about the ritual view of communication that is directed toward, "the maintenance of society in time; not the act of imparting information but the representation of shared beliefs" (p. 504). Herbert Marcuse (1991) and other theorists from the Frankfurt School (Horkheimer & Adorno, 2002) stress that while media are imparting information, they are also perpetuating ideologies, shaping epistemologies, and socializing consumers. The common experiences children have with their media encounters at home are then acted out and shared in schools and playgrounds and interconnect with other media texts in the private and public spheres. By contextualizing media as a cultural ritual, the focus moves away from a specific television program or episode to focus on media as a whole system, the flow, the viewing strip as text. This notion of media as ritual and flow offers a larger contextual framework for analysis to situate media in relation to other social influences such as parents, schools, government, church, and so on. A broader vision can also reveal the manner in which media *position* audiences. Using this "culturalist" approach, Buckingham suggests:

> Rather than attempting to measure the effectiveness of news in communicating political information, we should be asking how it enables viewers to construct and define their relationship with the public sphere. How do news programmes "position" viewers in relation to the social order—for example, in relation to the sources of power in society, or in relation to particular social groupings? How do they enable viewers to conceive of the relations between the "personal" and the "political"? How do they invite viewers to make sense of the wider national and international arena, and to make connections with their own direct experience? How, ultimately, do they establish what it means to be a "citizen"? (2000, p. 175)

These changes in society and media require a paradigm shift in education from a purely cognitive psychological model to one in which psychology embraces sociology in the understanding of literacy as a social process (Luke & Freebody, 1997). While children are growing, their cognitive abilities are not isolated from their social and moral development, therefore literacy should be taught as a social process in which critical questioning becomes a regular strategy for engaging with all texts, as early as possible.

■ Protection

Another factor that often prevents educators and parents from engaging young children in questioning and creating media is an excessively protectionist attitude toward young children and media that overvalues the power of media and undervalues children's abilities. Ellen Seiter (2002) found this fear of media and popular culture greatest with preschool teachers and childcare providers at middle and upper class economic levels. She writes, "the media are deemed most powerful by those working and living in situations of relative privilege; in the poorest centre the media are seen as only one factor—less significant than the part played by poverty, by parental absence, and by violence" (pp. 59–60).

I am not arguing that media have no effects and that children are all-powerful and should be allowed to view any media any time. Media representations can have direct effects causing nightmares, anxiety, and even trauma when children are exposed to images or content that are too scary or disturbing for them. All children have the right to live free of fear and violence and they need to be protected from dangerous influences, both in fiction and nonfiction. Some media experiences are more pernicious to children when encountered in nonfiction, such as news programs, than when viewed in fictional entertainment (Buckingham, 2000, p. 136).

However, most media effects are indirect and long-term (such as reinforcing male privilege within a patriarchal society or contributing to eating disorders in a culture obsessed with body image), repeated as transmedia intertextual flows that permeate society in the information age. This process cannot be censored; the best protection we can provide children is education that will empower them with critical autonomy[6] (Masterman, 1994) and prepare them to participate as active citizens in critical solidarity[7] (Ferguson, 2001) with the world around them.

■ The Earlier the Better

While I agree that children need to be protected from inappropriate experiences and representations, in this chapter I am suggesting that most children have the ability to begin questioning their media much earlier than often occurs. The work I have done teaching in elementary schools and working with elementary school teachers has demonstrated that both students and teachers have the ability to understand many of these complex ideas when they are taught through active media production and developmentally appropriate analytical activities (Share, 2006). Experiences with my own son have also demonstrated that from a very early age[8] some children can understand many basic media literacy concepts of media construction, multiple perspectives, and commercial motivations.

I am also arguing that young children not only have the ability, but for the sake of developing critical teenagers and active citizens, it is essential that we start as early as possible to plant these seeds of inquiry. Rather than denying young children opportunities to explore controversial ideas about media because of assumptions about children's inabilities and deficiencies or fears about the dangers of media, I propose we investigate with children the possibilities for connecting their personal experiences and concrete ideas with critical questioning about their lives and the mediated culture in which they are growing up.

Critical media literacy can also make abstract ideas more concrete when students create their own media and experience constructing their own representations. Learning through doing allows children to apply theoretical concepts through hands-on activities. When teachers create the space for students to experiment in multiple modalities with issues of representation, audience theory, political economy and social justice, then students will be better prepared to understand these ideas later in greater depth. Teaching critical media literacy to young children is by no means an easy project, yet, as the reader will see in the examples provided, it is feasible for many children much earlier than most adults realize.

■ Two Directions

Teaching critical media literacy requires epistemological movement in two directions; a horizontal expansion and a vertical deepening. The horizontal motion entails a broadening of the definition of literacy to include multiple ways people read and write, view and create information and messages. This expansive notion of literacy consists of a serious study of popular culture, advertising, photographs, phones, movies, video games, the Internet, and of the many hand-held devices and information communication technologies (ICTs) available, as well as print. Along with analysis, it involves production, as students learn to create messages with different media and technology. Many of these ideas can be found under various labels, such as: multimedia literacy (Daley, 2003), new literacies (Kist, 2005), multimodal literacy (Kress, 2004), multiple literacies (Kellner, 1998), information literacy (American Library Association, 2006), technology literacy/computer literacy (Thomas & Knezek, 1995) and visual literacy (Debes, 1969).[9]

Some of the horizontal expansion of literacy also inclines to the vertical movement toward a sociological deepening that frames literacy as more than a purely cognitive thought process. Critical media literacy understands reading and writing as social practices embedded within social contexts. It is this sociocultural framing that requires vertical movement to deepen the questioning of the interconnections between information, knowledge and power.

■ Critical Thinking

According to a definition created by a panel from the American Philosophical Association (Facione, 1990), critical thinking involves both cognitive skills ("interpretation, analysis, evaluation, inference, explanation, and self-regulation") and affective dispositions ("a critical spirit, a probing inquisitiveness, a keenness of mind, a zealous dedication to reason, and a hunger or eagerness for reliable information"). This cognitive/affective definition provides an important part of understanding critical thinking, however, it lacks a socio-logical understanding of communication and information.

Meanings are not only created inside an individual's head, they are also dependent on historical, social, political, economic, cultural, and numerous other contexts in which the text is created and in which the text is received. The social construction of knowledge makes it impossible for information to ever be neutral, it always connotes values and ideologies. In addition, the concept of an active audience suggests that individuals and groups of people negotiate meanings similarly or differently depending on the experi-ences, values, feelings, and many other influences that shape their group and individual identities. Adding this sociological understanding to a cognitive/affective definition of "critical thinking" opens up new possibilities to embrace the many social dimensions of how we think (Luke & Freebody, 1997).

The vertical movement in critical media literacy unites the skills and dispositions of critical thinking with a social consciousness and an understanding of knowledge as socially and historically constructed within hierarchal relationships of power. The rejection of the notion that education or information can be neutral and value-free is essential for critical inquiry to address social injustice and inequality through transformative pedagogy based on praxis (reflection and action). Giroux writes, "Education is not training, and learning at its best is connected to the imperatives of social responsibility and political agency" (2001, p. xxiv). This type of pedagogy can be found under many labels, such as: critical literacy (Luke & Freebody, 1997), critical pedagogy (Darder, Baltodano & Torres, 2003), critical reading (NCTE & IRA, 1996) and critical multiculturalism (Cortés, 2000).

■ Linking the Two Approaches

For critical media literacy, the horizontal expansion of literacy and the vertical deepening of analysis are intrinsically connected, but for many educators they are often separated, as teachers working within one approach do not consider the need to link with the other. It is not uncommon that teachers doing excellent work in media production fail to engage their students in critical analysis of the very media they are creating. At the same time, many progressive educators have their students critically deconstruct the power relations in historical documents and books but fail to apply those same critical questions to popular culture, technology, or mass media. These myopic perspectives are even more shortsighted when working with young children because of the preconceived limitations that many educators have internalized.

Viewing these two educational approaches as separate can be helpful in understand-ing their differences and similarities, but critical media literacy is built on the integration of multiple media and production with critical inquiry and social justice. To demonstrate the differences between the horizontal and the vertical movement, I provide examples from two teachers, each working primarily out of one of the two approaches. Both teach-ers demonstrate excellent examples of developmentally appropriate teaching practices that are child-centered, promote active learning, and encourage deep understanding (Geist

& Baum, 2005). While the pedagogy of both teachers is exceptional and does occasionally overlap the broadening of literacy with the deepening of critical inquiry, only occasionally do they unite the two ideas into a critical media literacy framework.

■ Technology

One of the easier routes for horizontally expanding literacy is available via information communication technologies and the current interest in technology literacy. Carmen Luke (2004) suggests that if media literacy can enter schools through "the 'backdoor' into computer literacy education" then it will have a better chance of being accepted. However, computer literacy is different from media literacy since the former is primarily a positivistic approach that appropriates new tools to unproblematically transmit content, while the latter requires problematizing media and technology to explore how the content and the audience are affected by the communication process. Recognizing the differences can help educators take advantage of the support and funding available for technology literacy to expand the notions of literacy on the path to critical media literacy.

■ Patty Anderson: Expanding Literacy

The first example comes from a public charter elementary school in the Los Angeles Unified School District (LAUSD) in which the teacher, Patty Anderson, had the same students for kindergarten and first grade. Working with 20 bilingual children for two years, Anderson created a multimedia classroom that integrated technology and media into her core curriculum. During both years my son was a student in her class and I regularly observed and assisted the students and teacher.

Due largely to the conservative political climate and backed by requirements of the federal No Child Left Behind law, the present expectations for early childhood education have become more academic and skills-based. In the LAUSD, like many other school districts in the United States, the majority of kindergarten classes are full-day programs and are expected to have students reading before first grade. This movement is also ratcheting up academic expectations for children between the ages of three and five as most states have now adopted early learning standards in literacy, language, and mathematics (Neuman & Roskos, 2005a). Even Head Start, the longest running federally funded school readiness program, has been legislated to ensure literacy growth with several goals, including letter recognition and phonemic awareness (Dickinson, 2002).[10] The focus on print literacy and phonics-based instruction has forced many kindergarten teachers to minimize art activities, playtime, and experiential learning for more standardized and often scripted phonics programs (Hemphill, 2006; Miller, 2005; Tyre, 2006). According to Susan Neuman and Kathleen Roskos, the skill and drill routine in early literacy instruction, "may inevitably consign children to a narrow, limited view of reading that is anti-thetical to their long-term success not only in school but throughout their lifetime" (2005b, p. 2). They assert that reading achievement is less about sounds and letters and more about *meaning*. Neuman and Roskos write, "It is the higher order thinking skills, knowl-edge, and dispositional capabilities, encouraging children to question, discover, evaluate, and invent new ideas, that enable them to become successful readers" (p. 4). Since Anderson teaches at a charter school that runs a full bilingual program in Spanish and English, she has more flexibility and control over her curriculum than most teachers in her district who are required to follow the scripted phonics-based Open Court Reading program and the district pacing plan.

■ Taking Pictures

Anderson is a young teacher who enjoys using media and technology in her daily life and recognizes the importance of teaching her students to become technologically literate as early as possible. In kindergarten, Anderson began teaching her four- and five-year-old students how to take photographs and use photography to communicate. She comments, "I think a lot of us use pictures in our daily teaching, but I think it's more powerful to use pictures that the kids actually take." She explains how most kindergarten teachers she knows purchase commercial packets of photographs that illustrate specific themes or concepts, but through working with her students to create their own images, she finds that abstract ideas become more concrete and the students take more ownership of their learning.

Her students began kindergarten studying the theme of "caring," so Anderson had them discuss how they could visually show this idea. Once a student was able to act out caring, another student would photograph one moment that the class all agreed conveyed the idea of caring. Using a digital camera, Anderson then downloaded the images that the children took and printed them out as mini-books with just the pictures and the title in Spanish, "cariño." Each child was able to take home their own book that same day to reinforce their learning and encourage a love of books. During math, Anderson had her students take the digital camera around the classroom and the school to photograph all the different shapes they could find. By searching for shapes in their everyday environment through the lens of a camera, they were connecting math to their real world and seeing the familiar with a new set of eyes. These pictures were printed for the students to cut out and sort according to different attributes. The students' experiences with photography were also supported by mini-lessons about photography that I provided, which can be found online at the Center for Media Literacy Web site (Share, 2005).[11] Throughout their year in

kindergarten and much more in first grade, the students were allowed to use the digital camera often as another instrument in their literacy tool kit.

Anderson teaches in a low socioeconomic area and has many students who begin their education in kindergarten, without any preschool experience. Therefore, one of her first goals in kindergarten is to teach the children how to recognize and form letters. One activity that supported this learning required the students to lay down outside on the grass so that they could be photographed from above as they used their bodies to form different letter shapes. These photographs were displayed in the classroom and printed on homework pp as friendly graphic reminders. Along with the use of photography, Anderson utilized her own laptop computer and an LCD projector to visually demonstrate concepts whenever the lesson warranted it. Her school has a broad vision of literacy and the arts; therefore all the students have an art and music teacher visiting their classrooms on a regular basis. During kindergarten, Anderson videotaped all of her students for a movie they presented to the parents at the end of the year. Repeating this project in first grade allowed students to play a much greater role in the production process.

■ Using Computers

In first grade, Anderson moved into a room with four computers and was able to finally implement her desire to have her students create multimedia projects. During that year, I was able to volunteer a couple of days each week and work with small groups of four to eight children at a time. Most of the children had no experience with a computer and took considerable effort to learn the most basic concepts, like how to double-click and drag and drop. Since the children were already familiar with photography and visual imagery, we began teaching them PowerPoint. We scaffolded the teaching of new computer skills incrementally: the first writing they did was with Word Art and then later they learned to insert a text box. Inserting pictures and animation was simple and fun so it made it easier for them to learn about folders and subfolders. As their skills progressed, the tasks became more sophisticated, and the students began to create more computer projects that addressed the themes and content from their core curriculum. They used Microsoft Word to publish their writer's workshop stories and PowerPoint to create posters and presentations. The Internet was occasionally used with adult guidance but the students were not permitted to surf the Web alone. Anderson's incorporation of ICTs into the core curriculum added to student's literacy development but did not replace other experiential and developmental activities, such as drawing, painting, printing, acting, singing, discussing, experimenting, playing, and socializing.

While the school had a computer lab, other students rarely had the opportunities that Anderson's students did to use technology to communicate and create. This is in large part because of Anderson's philosophy that media and technology should be tools used to empower students. Unfortunately, her school administration viewed media and technology as neutral conveyers of content for transmission, as opposed to teaching students to analyze these new tools and use them to create their own messages. At Anderson's school, most of the computers in the lab did not have a writing program but they all had a math game. While the kids loved to play it and the teachers saw their student's math skills and spatial reasoning improve, it would be a mistake to assume that this was computer literacy. Each child logged onto their own computer for 30 minutes to an hour and answered math questions with plenty of audio and visual stimulation. While students did indeed interact with this computer game, it was a closed type of interaction, one in which choices were limited by the few options provided. This contrasts greatly with Anderson's classroom where the projects that students created on the computers entailed much more open interactivity and student control as the children had many more choices about both content and form.[12]

At the beginning of first grade, each student created a guide book about another student, in which they had to photograph and interview a classmate. Anderson gave each child a blank book in which to record their interview and attach the photographs to accompany the text. The four- to six-page books were shared with the class and passed around during reading time. The series of photographs each student took of his or her partner were archived in all four classroom computers for use in other literacy and art projects. These archives grew as students photographed every field trip and guest speaker, and numerous class activities. They also began using the teacher's mini-DV camera to document their interests with sound and motion.

One of the obstacles keeping many teachers from even considering these types of activities is the fear that young children cannot behave responsibly with expensive equipment. Anderson states, "It's true that a lot of the fear I think that teachers have, that probably I had at the very beginning of kindergarten, is that they're going to ruin these things and that they're going to drop them or they're going to not be safe with them. But obviously, teaching them from the very early age how to handle that, then you get past that." Beginning in kindergarten, Anderson taught her students to always wear the strap around their neck and treat the camera as an important tool, not a toy. Since the technology has become so simple, no longer does the photographer have to set the light meter or even focus the lens. The old Kodak slogan, "you press the button and we do the rest" has been surpassed as now any child who can press a button can take a picture and see the results immediately. In the twenty-first century, any school or teacher that can afford a digital camera can easily make photography a valuable literacy tool for young children.

Visual media also bring an aesthetic component to education, something that is often overlooked or downplayed as unimportant. According to Ray Mission and Wendy Morgan (2006), by engaging aesthetics in education, teachers can create new opportunities for students to access different truths, provide a broad range of personal development, and make learning more fulfilling and entertaining. They write, "The aesthetic may only be one among many ways of knowing that human beings have, but it is a significant one because it acknowledges the breadth, diversity, and even contradictoriness of human experiences, as well as the drive to make sense of it" (p. 226).

■ Project-based Learning

Throughout the two years, Anderson had her students create many projects, individually and collaboratively. The use of technology in the classroom was greatly facilitated by group work and peer teaching. A type of "interthinking" occurred as students collaboratively used language for thinking together to create media and solve problems (Mercer, 2000). The final culminating projects that Anderson's first graders produced included a movie about first grade and a PowerPoint presentation on endangered species. The purpose of their movie was to reflect on and document their learning and also to show new students what to expect when they began first grade. Because of technology limitations (only one camera and no editing software in the classroom), the students could not physically edit their movie. While they were able to film most of the scenes, narrate voiceovers, and discuss planning and editing choices, Anderson did most of the editing work herself.

For the final PowerPoint presentation, students were able to do all the production work themselves. They worked in pairs to create between four and eight slides about an endan-gered animal of their choice. They researched about the animal in books and Web sites, and then discussed why the animals are in danger of extinction and what can be done about it. They explored issues of global warming, habitat destruction, poaching, and contamination of the oceans and discussed ways they could help by minimizing pollution, encouraging their parents to drive less, and not dumping trash down drains that lead to the ocean.

Each team inserted photographs, Word Art titles, and text boxes with information into their PowerPoint slides. Following the writing process, they shared, revised, edited, and published their work with the help of their partner and other students. The process required considerable work to make sure the photographs and the words worked well together, a literacy skill important for reading and writing. Anderson reflects on this process, "I hear them having this conversation about, 'well, we shouldn't put a picture of an animal that's playing around when we're talking about something that's bad,' which I think is really good. And I've heard other pairs talk about the kind of pictures they want to include and where." After one pair discovered a mistake or something new, they would share it with others and before long everyone was making similar changes. The sense of ownership and exploration that students felt while working on this project led some to take the project beyond the teacher's expectations. On their own, one pair discovered symbols and inserted a red circle with a slash through it, and soon others began inserting different symbols to accompany their photos and text. Working with the music teacher, the students wrote their own song about protecting endangered animals and performed it for their parents.

■ Real Audiences Beyond the Teacher

Another important aspect of both culminating projects was that the students were creating their presentations for real audiences beyond the teacher. Presenting their PowerPoint shows to other students and their parents gave the first graders a strong sense of purpose as well as genuine feedback. By reading the text they had written in each PowerPoint slide, the students had the opportunity to read and present publicly to an audience, thus meeting many state standards for Language Arts. Creating and presenting projects for a real audience is one of Foxfire's[13] Eleven Core Practices and is an important element of good pedagogy because it motivates students and provides deeper learning opportunities that are less likely to arise otherwise. After presenting to a kindergarten class, Anderson's first graders returned to their classroom and debriefed the presentation. The students were disturbed by the reaction of the kindergarteners to a photograph in the show of a dead whale with red blood in the water. They discussed the picture further and talked about the reasons for the presentation and the seriousness of the topic. While some students expressed their dislike of the picture and felt it shouldn't be in the show, others discussed the importance of saving the animals and the need to have a serious photograph, like that one, to communicate to others that animals are dying. The discussion that evolved from a real audience response to their work and picture choices took these six- and seven-year-olds into an analysis of the power of visual imagery and the appropriateness of their choices for specific purposes and particular audiences. This inquiry linked their concerns and use of different media with much deeper theoretical concepts of semiotics, audience theory, and the politics of representation. Neuman and Roskos (2005b) state, "Literacy development is not just a matter of learning a set of technical skills. It is a purposeful activity involving children in ways of making, interpreting, and communicating meaning with written language" (p. 5). Anderson's students accomplished Neuman and Roskos' purposeful content-rich literacy description and bumped it to a higher level by expanding the notion of literacy beyond just written language.

■ Discussing and Questioning

While Anderson did not design her class around critical literacy principles, she did engage her students in many critical concepts through questioning, discussing, and taking action by creating their own media messages. The atmosphere of open inquiry that Anderson created encouraged the autonomy and curiosity necessary for the development of critical thinking. Nicoll (1996) asserts that "Critical thinking skills can only be taught in an environment that encourages the children to ask questions, to devise ways of answering those questions, to make decisions about how to proceed, and to evaluate the quality of their answers." Engaging with the students' popular culture and asking questions (such as who created the message, how, and why) encourages students to critically reflect on the media they use and the media they create. Anderson also used interactive journaling, where she could correspond one on one with students, to encourage critical reflection.

For young children, posing questions that aim to reveal the construction of media messages can help them start to think about media differently and consider different ways of knowing. While it is important not to negate children's media culture nor destroy the pleasures they get from it, the denaturalization of media is necessary for children to be able to ask different questions. For example, when a movie is considered just entertainment and not understood as a construction of reality, then the questions that one can ask tend to be limited to the content of the movie. Anderson mentions:

> I think in this age group, they have a tendency to think they know the difference between fantasy and reality, but a lot of the times, they struggle with it, they really don't know what is true and what isn't true. In a movie like *Ice Age*, there are elements of it that are true, that are based on the fact that there was an Ice Age, but what about the animals and what is created and what isn't. I think we talked that day about, someone had to write the movie, someone had to animate it and draw the pictures, because of the cartoons, so we kind of got into a conversation about that.

Many of the mandated standards that teachers are expected to follow in elementary school cover media literacy concepts such as the California State Content Standards for Language Arts that state that kindergarten students should be able to "Distinguish fantasy from realistic text" and "Identify types of everyday print materials (e.g., storybooks, poems, newspapers, signs, labels)."[14]

Anderson clearly demonstrated that integrating media literacy concepts and technology skills into a kindergarten and first grade curriculum is not only feasible but can be highly successful. While she faced many obstacles in terms of limited resources and difficulty in negotiating time constraints, she managed to make the lessons developmentally appropriate for her students and provided numerous opportunities for them to communicate with different ICTs. The deficit thinking and protectionist fears that keep many administrators and educators from engaging young children in these types of activities are the wrong issues. Administrators must let go of these misconceptions and place their time and energy in training teachers (not only on how to use the new tools but more importantly how to teach *with* them and *about* them), providing ongoing teacher support, purchasing and maintaining ICTs, and allowing teachers and students to use these new tools as components of an integral literacy program. Educators, like administrators, also need to relinquish old fears and embrace these new tools and new pedagogies as exciting opportunities to link classroom learning to students' life experiences. Technology must not replace drawing and other experiential activities, instead it should expand children's full capacities by providing more developmentally appropriate opportunities to communicate and create (Miller, 2005).

Anderson's engagement with media and technology expands her literacy pedagogy horizontally yet only occasionally deepens her teaching vertically into a more profound analysis and critical action. For this type of critical literacy and sometimes critical media literacy, Vivian Vasquez offers some excellent examples and advice.

■ Vivian Vasquez: Deepening Literacy

Vasquez is a teacher who has written methodically about her experiences in teaching young children critical literacy. She builds her curriculum on social justice concerns with an affirmative approach that seeks to empower students to confront injustice. Vasquez asserts that critical work with students "does not necessarily involve taking a negative stance; rather, it means looking at an issue or topic in different ways, analyzing it, and hopefully being able to suggest possibilities for change or improvement" (2004, p. 30). In line with Paulo Freire's (1970) problem-posing pedagogy and Robert Ferguson's (1998, 2004) concept of productive unease,[15] Vasquez writes, "A critical perspective suggests that deliberate attempts to expose inequality in the classroom and society need to become part of our everyday classroom life" (p. xv).

Through posing critical questions, Vasquez aims to disrupt authorial power and problematize social situations. Exposing the social construction of information and knowledge is necessary to unveil power inequalities. Vasquez follows the theoretical work of Alan Luke and Peter Freebody (1999) in Australia who developed the Four Resources Model promoting a sociological emphasis in literacy education. Vasquez writes:

> Luke and Freebody assert that reading should be seen as a nonneutral form of cultural practice, one that positions readers in advantageous and disadvantageous ways. They argue that readers need to be able to interrogate the assumptions and ideologies that are embedded in text as well as the assumptions that they, as sociocultural beings, bring to the text. This leads to asking questions such as, Whose voice is heard? Who is silenced? Whose reality is presented? Whose reality is ignored? Who is advantaged? Who is disadvantaged? These sorts of questions open spaces for analyzing the discourses or ways of being that maintain certain social practices over others (2003, p. 15).

■ Action

When a child raises a question about issues that are unfair or unjust, Vasquez explains that a teacher has basically three ways to respond. The teacher can take a traditional *banking* (Freire, 1970) educational approach by treating the student's question as a fact; thereby positioning the teacher as expert and the student as a passive recipient of a seemingly "objective" factual answer. This response often ends the child's inquiry and curiosity with the false notion that information is neutral and memorization is the goal. A more constructivist teacher can turn the question back to the student and ask her or him what she or he thinks. This was a common response that Anderson used to encourage her students to be more independent and reflective. While re-posing a question cognitively can be a useful strategy to stimulate cognitive critical thinking, it does little to transform the problem or the student. The critical response that Vasquez uses moves the student further toward empowerment as she challenges her students to collaboratively take action by asking them: "What can we do to change the situation?" (2004, p. 98). Encouraging students to take action is an essential component of transformative pedagogy and a necessary element of critical media literacy. The editors of *Rethinking Our Classrooms* (Bigelow, Christensen, Karp, Miner & Peterson, 1994) explain:

> If we ask the children to critique the world but then fail to encourage them to act, our classrooms can degenerate into factories of cynicism. While it's not a teacher's role to direct students

to particular organizations, it is a teacher's role to suggest that ideas need to be acted upon and to offer students opportunities to do just that (p. 5).

During the 1996–1997 school year, Vasquez taught a half-day "junior kindergarten" in Toronto, Canada, with 16 students between the ages of three and five. For 10 months the students and teacher worked together to develop a critical literacy curriculum based on everyday texts and issues from their school and community. They created an audit trail, a bulletin board with artifacts and commentary that visually documented their learning and the way incidents and themes flowed from one issue to another. Even though junior kindergarten is voluntary, the school board had a required curriculum from which Vasquez departed, yet she was careful to ensure that the curriculum she negotiated with her students exceeded the requirements of the mandated program.

Rather than just adding social issues to a predetermined curriculum, Vasquez worked with her students to build their own course of study as they went; a dynamic approach that allowed them the flexibility to flow with student interest and connect ideas as they arose naturally. Barbara Comber (2001a) asserts that centering teaching on the concerns of the students and engaging local realities are crucial aspects of critical literacy. Some critics suggest that promoting a social justice agenda necessarily contradicts a student-centered curriculum. While this can be a bit of a balancing act, since negotiating curriculum with students requires listening as well as guiding, that does not mean that the two are contradictory. Carole Edelsky (1999) explains, "What makes a critical direction for a topic seem like an imposition of the teacher's agenda but a noncritical direction seem like neutral guidance is that the former disrupts prevailing ideologies" (p. 4).

■ Pleasure

Kathy Hall supports the idea of critical literacy playing a role in early childhood education, yet fears that if it dominates instruction it could "take the joy out of learning and living" and lead to cynicism (1998, p. 191). However, taking the pleasure out of learning is a problem that is more likely to occur when education fails to engage with students' interests, does not connect with their lived experiences, and provides them little opportunity to act on their learning. Vasquez's transformative pedagogy empowers children to actively engage with meaningful problems for the purpose of improving the situation. She writes, "The conversations that we had and the actions we took, although often serious, were very pleasurable. We enjoyed our work because the topics that we dealt with were socially significant to us" (pp. 30–31).

This freedom to allow the curriculum to evolve in negotiation with the students is a luxury that Anderson and many teachers in the United States do not have without risking their employment. Especially now in the United States, as No Child Left Behind promotes stringent accountability and high-stakes standardized testing, many teachers are mandated to teach from commercially produced scripted curriculum with predetermined pacing plans that aspire to have all children on the same page, on the same day, throughout a district. While integrating social issues into a core curriculum may be the only option many teachers have to bring progressive ideas to their students, Vasquez's work demonstrates an ideal situation. According to John Dewey (1938/1963), a defining characteristic that distinguishes progressive education based on experience from traditional banking education, is that children's experiences are problematized and become the basis for learning. Dewey writes, "The new facts and new ideas thus obtained become the ground for further experiences in which new problems are presented. The process is a continuous spiral" (p. 79).

■ Eliciting Student Concerns

It is because of the current state of affairs in public education that the work Vasquez has done with young children is so important, to demonstrate alternative pedagogy and the value of critical literacy. Vasquez organized her class around a daily meeting chaired by a student who followed an agenda of interests and concerns that students listed before the meeting began. Read-aloud literature was also shared daily and often generated topics for class discussion. At the beginning of the year, a children's book that Vasquez read prompted student interest in the rain forest, which led to letter-writing action and the production of a rain forest play that highlighted the need to save the animals by not cutting down trees. On another occasion, an advertisement brought from home sparked media literacy analysis of the construction of advertising, which led to an inquiry of gender stereotypes and inspired some students to create alternative Halloween costumes.

During the year, different literature experiences and personal incidents set the students off on many critical inquiries and actions. Their exclusion from the French Café (a school event that most of the other students were able to enjoy) provoked feelings of anger and injustice. To protest their exclusion, they observed and surveyed other students to learn who else was not allowed to attend the French Café. Then they discussed their findings and considered having all the excluded students write letters to complain. Vasquez explained to the students that if all the letters were going to say the same thing, then a quicker option was to create a petition. Their interest in using literacy to solve a problem demonstrates the motivational power of an audience beyond the teacher and the value of having a genuine purpose for literacy activities. The students circulated their petition and included an audio tape of their discussion about the French Café for the event organizers. Through their investigation and action, these young children exposed the power structure of the school and repositioned themselves within the hierarchy by using their collective voice. Vasquez writes, "My role was not to tell the children what to think or how to act, but based on their inquiries, to offer alternative ways of taking action and a way of naming their world within the stance they chose to take" (2004, p. 101).

Vasquez's stated goals of fairness and equality, along with the encouragement to problematize issues, built a strong sense of social justice in her students. When the class discovered after the annual school barbecue that one of their peers was not able to enjoy the food because only meat was available and he was a vegetarian, they moved into action. They began with a textual analysis of the flyer inviting people to the barbecue. The three- and four-year-old students challenged the use of the word "our" in the beginning of the text, "Join us for our Annual School Barbecue." Since the choice of hamburgers and hotdogs excluded vegetarians, the students insisted that the organizers were not being fair. This incident became a powerful opportunity for the students to apply the discursive analytic strategies that Vasquez had shown them before. She explains that previously they "had done some analysis of the words used in magazine ads and how pronouns work to position readers in particular ways" (p. 104). In the letter to the chair of the school barbecue committee, the student chosen to write it decided to begin the letter using "we" instead of just mentioning the one vegetarian. When Vasquez questioned her about this choice, the young girl reminded her of the petition and explained to Vasquez about the strength in numbers. This understanding and application of pronouns go well beyond most state standards for language arts skills in the upper grades.

The interests in the marginalization of vegetarians led the students to discover the complete absence of books about vegetarians in their school library. This, and curiosity about how other schools treat vegetarians, led Vasquez's students to send out many letters promoting vegetarian rights. She states that the letter-writing campaign, "demonstrates what happens when young children begin to unpack the relationship between language and power by engaging in some form of discourse analysis" (p. 111).

Teaching critical literacy involves vertical movement that encourages students to think more critically and analyze deeper the relationships between knowledge and power. Critical media literacy moves in this direction while also expanding horizontally to engage with many different forms of media and technology. The lessons about the French Café and the marginalization of vegetarians are excellent examples of critical literacy's vertical movement but barely expand the analysis horizontally to analyze and use different media and technology. In the next two examples, Vasquez engages her students with more of a critical media literacy perspective.

■ Engaging Media

The first lesson began when one of her students spoke to the class about a news report she had seen on television the night before. She told the other children about how pollution being dumped into a river was endangering the beluga whales that lived there. Based on this new knowledge, Vasquez decide to revisit the picture book and song, *Baby Beluga,* by Raffi (1992), "to see whether they would read the book differently given what they had just learned" (2004, p. 113). The students compared the two texts and charted the different words used to describe the whales in the news report and the words used in the song. Vasquez explains, "In essence, what I was trying to do here was to get at the dominant themes and discourses of each text" (p. 115). This comparison triggered a student to ask "which one is real?" demonstrating how difficult it is for some children to distinguish between fantasy and reality. Vasquez used this problem to discuss different perspectives and how the construction of a text shapes the way we think. The students decided to rewrite Raffi's song to present more perspectives about belugas. During the process of rewriting the song, Vasquez led the students to explore issues of voice (who was speaking?), audience (who were they speaking to?), and construction (how were they using words to position the audience?). They experimented by swapping pronouns and changing all the verses of the song to read "you" instead of "I" or "we." This activity demonstrated how easily they could change the voice of the author and the positioning of the audience by simply switching pronouns.

The students continued to research the plight of the beluga whales and performed their song for other students as a way to create awareness of the dangers of pollution. They also raised money from their class store to donate to the World Wildlife Fund of Canada that was doing research to help the belugas. This critical media literacy activity began from student interest and involved analyzing different media representations as well as creating an alternative song. Vasquez explains that the power of this learning went well beyond just learning about whales, "[d]econstructing the book text and the everyday media text provided a space to explore the social construction of truth and reality" (p. 121).

By the time spring arrived, all of the three-year-old students had turned four and many of the four-year-olds were five. They were also becoming better versed at critically interrogating texts as was apparent during a discussion about McDonald's Happy Meal toys. A small group of students began discussing the way McDonald's has different toys for boys and girls. The students shared how the people working at McDonald's expected boys to prefer cars and girls to prefer dolls, but that they didn't always agree with that. This discussion about the gender bias of McDonald's and the students' ability to transgress it, began a bigger critique of consumerism. The children discussed how McDonald's continually changes toys in order to lure kids to buy the Happy Meal in order to collect the new toy. One boy spoke with his father about this and later told the class that McDonald's claims that the toy is free but actually charges for it in the price of the Happy Meal. Through their discussions, the students were recognizing ways McDonald's targets them as consumers. They also questioned the fairness of McDonald's marketing strategies for children who do not have access to Happy Meal collectables.

Vasquez encouraged the students to explore the construction of a consumer identity and worked with them to deconstruct the Happy Meal as a text. She drew a web with the golden arches in the center and then wrote the student's first responses in a circle around it to the question: "What makes up a Happy Meal?" After listing their initial comments (hamburger, French fries, bag, toy, and drink), she pushed them to think about all the things that are part of those items. The second concentric circle grew larger and more profound as the students mentioned advertising, designers, packaging, materials, and so on. This activity brilliantly addresses the essential media literacy concept that all media messages are constructed. Vasquez continued with a third concentric circle to expand further all the items related to those mentioned in the second circle. With each circle, the students were peeling away the unseen layers to reveal the complexity and subtexts of something as seemingly simple as a Happy Meal. Vasquez asserts that through critically questioning issues of gender and consumerism, her students were "disrupting taken-for-granted normality to consider how things could be different" (p. 131). This use of the students' culture and questions to deconstruct a media text, like the Happy Meal, is an excellent example of how critical media literacy can be taught through developmentally appropriate practices to young children. As experts in early childhood literacy assert, children learn literacy best not by working in isolation but through actively constructing meaning in an interactive and purposeful process (Neuman & Roskos, 2005a & 2005b).

■ Conclusion

Barbara Nicoll (1996) states, "From a developmental perspective, the process of growing toward being a critical thinker occurs very early in life. A necessary characteristic of critical thinkers is autonomy. As infants move into the autonomous stage of toddlerhood the seeds of critical thinking have the potential to grow." Barbara Comber (2001b) asserts that when young children can learn to not only admire an author's crafting, but also disrupt it and see different possible representations, this can help children, who might not even be code-breakers, to start seeing texts as constructions and engage texts with deeper questions about the form as well as the content.

Unfortunately, many educators do not attempt to teach young children critical thinking skills and even fewer teach critical media literacy. The vast majority of U.S. educators have no idea what media literacy is and would not know how to begin to teach it. For the few who do know about critical media literacy, many do not teach it to young children because of the assumption that it is inappropriate. Yet the pedagogies used by Anderson and Vasquez are far more developmentally appropriate than many currently mandated phonics-based curricula. Some teachers might resist exposing young children to media out of fear that it is too dangerous and young children are too vulnerable; while other teachers might avoid critical pedagogy believing that teaching is a neutral activity and literacy just a technical competence. The primary goal of this chapter is to dispel those misconceptions and demonstrate through the outstanding work of two practicing teachers just how successful young children can be with multimedia literacy, computer literacy, critical literacy, and especially when it all comes together as critical media literacy. In a paper presented on critical thinking in K-3 education, Nicoll (1996) concludes:

> Children need to develop an ability to recognize differing points of view and a willingness to explore alternatives. They need to be organized in their problem solving and have good communication skills. The teacher's role is to create an atmosphere which encourages these attitudes. The teacher models open-mindedness, encourages differences of opinion, and asks for reasons for conclusions. Primary children will then be able to develop critical thinking skills and more importantly, critical thinking dispositions.

Some of the real challenges for critical media literacy are to encourage educators to see media and popular culture as productive tools and texts for critical inquiry into issues of social justice as well as the opportunity to bridge the gap between "the real world" and the classroom. Key findings from research conducted in England with parents and early years practitioners, suggest that both parents and early childhood educators feel that media education should be taught to young children. These researchers also found that "[t]he introduction of popular culture, media and/or new technologies into the communications, language and literacy curriculum has a positive effect on the motivation and engagement of children in learning" (Marsh, Brooks, Hughes, Ritchie, Roberts, & Wright, 2005, p. 6).

However, as we have seen, this type of pedagogical change is not easy with the current neoliberal policies that mandate accountability through high-stakes standardized testing and back-to-basics through skill-and-drill banking education. The challenge is significant but can be overcome when the obstacles are correctly identified. The real obstacles impeding critical media literacy are not children's deficiencies or media's danger, instead, they are the lack of backing and funding for the training and resources necessary to support teachers' exploration and implementation of critical media literacy pedagogy. The obstacles also include the lack of understanding and commitment to social justice and the development of empathy, empowerment, curiosity, and autonomy.

Mandates from above are needed to create space in the overcrowded curriculum for these ideas, and support at the school site is necessary to train and assist teachers in their efforts to integrate and transform their teaching practices to become more critical and inclusive. As Vasquez demonstrated from her teaching that flowed from student interests, critical media literacy needs official endorsement, but it cannot become a scripted cookbook of lessons. Vasquez writes:

> …there is no one-size-fits-all critical literacy…we need to construct different critical literacies depending on what work needs to be done in certain settings, contexts, or communities, and… it needs to be negotiated using the cultural and linguistic resources to which children have had access (2003, p. 56).

This mandate must be accompanied by funding to pay for training and to purchase the tools for students to create in multiple formats so that their voices and ideas can be heard and seen beyond the classroom. Anderson offered many examples of the production possibilities that five- and six-year-olds are capable of creating. If we expand literacy beyond print to include popular culture, media, and technology and immerse that broader understanding of communication into a critical literacy framework, we have the potential to create transformative education for children from preschool on up. It is not enough to begin teaching critical media literacy to teenagers, we must start as early as possible, even if we are just planting seeds. Building awareness of how media operate, how we interact with ICTs, how ideas and culture are socially constructed, and how power is linked to all these processes is essential if we hope to create a world of media literate citizens who can participate in the struggle to recover democracy and transform society into a more equal and just place to live.

Notes

1. While all people born in this millennium have been alive since the invention of the Internet, cellular phones, and television, this does not mean that everyone can access this technology. Since approximately one third (about 2 billion) of the world's population still live without electricity, it is important to remember that billions of people are being left behind the so-called technological revolution and that the digital divide is real.

2. The U.S. Census Bureau reports that 98.2% of all U.S. households had at least one television set in 2001. Statistics available online: http://www.census.gov/Press-Release/www/releases/archives/facts_for_features/001702.html

3. This data is based on random telephone interviews in 2003 with 1,065 parents of children between six months and six years of age. "Screen media" refers to watching TV, watching videos/DVDs, using a computer and playing video games. This research was reported in the Kaiser Family Foundation's *Zero to Six* study.

4. The number of hours spent with media is based on questionnaires from a 2004 national sample of 2,032 students between eight and eighteen years of age, as well as 694 media-use diaries, as reported in the Kaiser Family Foundation's *Generation M* study. The figure of 6½ hours per day includes one quarter of that time spent multitasking with several different media at the same time, thereby increasing media exposure to an estimated 8½ hours per day.

5. Canada's Ontario Ministry of Education's Eight Key Concepts, British Film Institute's Signpost Questions, The Center for Media Literacy Five Core Concepts, Masterman (2001), etc.

6. Len Masterman (1994) describes critical autonomy as the ability and desire of students to think critically about media when they are on their own.

7. Critical solidarity, according to Robert Ferguson (2001), involves recognition of the interconnections between people and information as well as empathy to be in solidarity with those marginalized or oppressed by these connections.

8. At three years of age, my son was able to explain that advertising was trying to make a product look more fun to trick him into wanting to buy it.

9. Kathleen Tyner (1998) offers insightful analysis of many types of literacies in *Literacy in a Digital World: Teaching and Learning in the Age of Information.*

10. In spite of this mandate and research supporting the effectiveness of early childhood education, the United States is still under-funding these programs. According to an article in *Business Week,* Head Start's "$6.5 billion-a-year budget means it can't accommodate three of five eligible children" (Starr, 2002).

11. I wrote a set of 25 media literacy lessons for children of different ages. Activities 2A and 2B are photography lessons that I taught to these kindergarten students: http://www.medialit.org/pdf/mlk/02_5KQ_ClassroomGuide.pdf

12. For three years I worked as an occasional substitute teacher in this school and had the opportunity to see how most of the teachers were using technology.

13. http://www.foxfire.org/teachi.html

14. Available online at: http://www.cde.ca.gov/be/st/ss/engkindergarten.asp

15. The disruption or denaturalization of media representations is something Robert Ferguson suggests can create a place of liminality or unease that can become productive when teachers and students begin asking "what if" questions about media and society (1998, 2004).

References

American Library Association. (2006). *Information Literacy Competency Standards for Higher Education.* Retrieved 14 Aug, 2006 at http://www.ala.org/acrl/ilcomstan.html

Bigelow, B., Christensen, L., Karp, S., Miner, B., & Peterson, B. (Eds.) (1994). *Rethinking Our Classrooms: Teaching for Equity and Justice.* Milwaukee: Rethinking Schools.

Buckingham, D. (2000). *After the Death of Childhood: Growing Up in the Age of Electronic Media.* Cambridge: Polity Press.

Buckingham, D. (2003). *Media education: Literacy, learning and contemporary culture.* Cambridge: Polity Press.

Carrington, V. (2005). New Textual Landscapes, Information and Early Literacy. In Marsh, J. (Ed.). *Popular Culture, New Media and Digital Literacy in Early Childhood.* London: RoutledgeFalmer. (pp.13–17).

Comber, B. (2001a). Critical Literacies and Local Action: Teacher Knowledge and a "New" Research Agenda. In Comber, B., & Simpson, A. (Eds.) (2001). *Negotiating Critical Literacies in Classrooms.* Mahwah, New Jersey: Lawrence Erlbaum Associates. (pp. 271–282).

Comber, B. (2001b) Classroom Explorations in Critical Literacy. In Fehring, Heather & Green, Pam. (Eds.). (2001). *Critical Literacy: A collection of articles from the Australian Literacy Educators' Association.* International Reading Association: Newark, Delaware. (pp. 90–102).

Cortés, C. (2000). The Children Are Watching: How the Media Teach About Diversity. New York: Teachers College Press.

Daley, E. (2003, March/April). Expanding the Concept of Literacy. In *Educause Review.* (pp. 33–40) Retrieved August 14, 2006 at http://www.educause.edu/ir/library/pdf/ERM0322.pdf

Darder, A., Baltodano, M., & Torres, R. (Eds.) (2003). *The Critical Pedagogy Reader.* New York: RoutledgeFalmer.

Debes, J. (1969). "The Loom of Visual Literacy." In *Audiovisual Instruction.* Vol. 14, No. 8. (pp. 25–27).

Dewey, J. (1938/1963). *Experience and Education.* New York: Collier Books.

Dickinson, D.K. (2002). Shifting Images of Developmentally Appropriate Practice as Seen Through Different Lenses. In *Educational Researcher.* Vol. 31, No. 1.

Edelsky, C. (Ed.) (1999). *Making Justice Our Project: Teachers Working Toward Critical Whole Language Practice.* Urbana, Illinois: NCTE.

Eggen, P., & Kauchak, D., (1994). *Educational Psychology: Classroom Connections.* New York: Macmillan College Publishing.

Facione, P.A. (1990). *Critical Thinking: A Statement of Expert Consensus for Purposes of Educational Assessment and Instruction.* Research findings and recommendations prepared for the committee on pre-college philosophy of the American Philosophical Association. Retrieved August 13, 2006 at http://www.insightassessment.com/pdf_files/DEXadobe.PDF

Ferguson, R. (2004). *The Media in Question.* London: Arnold.

Ferguson, R. (2001). Media education and the development of critical solidarity. In *Media Education Journal, 30,* 37–43.

Ferguson, R. (1998). *Culture, communication and contradiction: (media) education and the pursuit of productive unease.* Unpublished manuscript dated June 3, 1998.

Freire, P. (1970). *Pedagogy of the Oppressed.* New York: Seabury Press.

Geist, E. & Baum, A.C. (2005). Yeah, But's That Keep Teachers from Embracing an Active Curriculum: Overcoming the Resistance. In *Beyond the Journal.* Journal of the National Association for the Education of Young Children. Retrieved August 10, 2006 from http://www.journal.naeyc.org/btj/200507/03Geist.pdf

Ginsburg, H., & Opper, S. (1969). *Piaget's Theory of Intellectual Development, an Introduction.* Englewood Cliffs: Prentice-Hall.

Giroux, H. (2001). *Theory and Resistance in Education: Towards a Pedagogy for the Opposition.* Westport: Bergin & Garvey.

Hall, K. (1998). Critical Literacy and the Case for it in the Early Years of School. In *Language, Culture and Curriculum.* Vol. 11, No. 2. (pp. 183–194).

Hemphill, C. (2006, July 26). In Kindergarten Playtime, a New Meaning for "Play." *The New York Times.* Retrieved August 2, 2006 at http://www.nytimes.com/2006/07/26/education/26education.html?_r=1&oref=slogin

Horkheimer, M., & Adorno, T. (2002). *Dialectic of Enlightenment.* Stanford: Stanford University Press.

Houston, B. (1984). Viewing Television: The Metapsychology of Endless Consumption. In *Quarterly. Review of Film Studies* 9(3).

International Reading Association (IRA) & National Association for the Education of Young Children (NAEYC). (1998). Learning to read and write: Developmentally appropriate practices for young children. A joint position statement of the International Reading Association and the National Association for the Education of Young Children. In *Young Children* (July 1998). Vol. 53, No. 4. (pp. 30–46). Retrieved August 13, 2006 at www.naeyc.org/about/positions/pdf/PSREAD98.PDF

Kanner, A.D. (2006 summer). The Corporatized Child. In *Independent Practitioner: Bulletin of Psychologists in Independent Practice*. Phoenix, AZ: American Psychological Association. Vol. 26, No. 3. (pp. 135–136).

Kapur, J. (1999). Out of Control: Television and the Transformation of Childhood in Late Capitalism. In Kinder, M. (Ed.). *Kids' Media Culture*. Durham & London: Duke University Press.

Kellner, D. (1995). *Media Culture: Cultural Studies, Identity and Politics Between the Modern and the Postmodern*. New York: Routledge.

Kellner, D. (1998). Multiple Literacies and Critical Pedagogy in a Multicultural Society. *Educational Theory*. Vol. 48. (pp. 103–122). Retrieved September 1, 2006 at: http://www.gseis.ucla.edu/faculty/kellner/essays/multipleliteraciescriticalpedagogy.pdf

Kellner, D., & Share, J. (2005). Toward critical media literacy: Core concepts, debates, organizations and policy. In *Discourse: Studies in the cultural politics of education* Vol. 26, No. 3 (pp. 369–386). The University of Queensland, Australia: Routledge.

Kellner, D., & Share, J. (2007). *Critical Media Literacy, Democracy, and the Reconstruction of Education*. In *Media Literacy: A Reader*. Eds: Donaldo Macedo and Shirley R. Steinberg. New York: Peter Lang Publishing. (pp. 3–23).

Kinder, M. (1991). *Playing with Power in Movies, Television, and Video Games*. Berkeley: University of California Press.

Kist, W. (2005). *New Literacies in Action: Teaching and Learning in Multiple Media*. New York: Teachers College Press.

Kress, G. (2004). *Literacy in the New Media Age*. New York: Routledge.

Luke, A. & Freebody, P. (1999). Further Notes on the Four Resources Model. *Reading Online*. Retrieved February 12, 2006, at http://www.readingonline.org/research/lukefreebody.html

Luke, A. & Freebody, P. (1997). Shaping the Social Practices of Reading. In S. Muspratt, A. Luke, & P. Freebody (Eds.). *Constructing critical literacies: Teaching & Learning textual practice*. Sydney: Allen & Unwin; and Cresskill, NJ: Hampton Press.

Luke, C. (2004). Re-crafting Media and ICT Literacies. In Alvermann, D.E., (Ed.). *Adolescents and Literacies in a Digital World*. New York: Peter Lang Publishing. (pp. 132–146).

Marcuse, H. (1991). *One-Dimensional Man: Studies in the Ideology of Advanced Industrial Society*. Boston: Beacon Press.

Marsh, J., Brooks, G., Hughes, J., Ritchie, L., Roberts, S., & Wright, K. (2005). *Digital beginnings: Young children's use of popular culture, media and new technologies*. University of Sheffield: Literacy Research Centre. Retrieved September 6, 2006 from http://www.digitalbeginnings.shef.ac.uk/DigitalBeginningsReport.pdf

Masterman, L. (1994). A rationale for media education (First Part). In L. Masterman, & F. Mariet, *Media Education in 1990s' Europe* (pp. 5–87). Strasbourg: Council of Europe.

Masterman, L. (2001). *Teaching the media*. New York: Routledge.

Mercer, N. (2000). *Words and Minds: How We Use Language to Think Together*. New York: Routledge.

Miller, E. (2005, November). Fighting Technology for Toddlers. In *Education Digest*. Vol. 71, No. 3. (pp. 55–58).

Mission, R., & Morgan, W. (2006). *Critical Literacy and the Aesthetic: Transforming the English Classroom*. Urbana, Illinois: NCTE.

Modleski, T. (1982). *Loving with a Vengeance: Mass Produced Fantasies for Women*. New York: Routledge.

National Council of Teachers of English (NCTE) & International Reading Association (IRA). (1996). *Standards for the English Language Arts.* Published by both NCTE & IRA.

Neuman, S. & Roskos, K. (2005a, second quarter). The State of State Pre-Kindergarten Standards. In *Early Childhood Research Quarterly.* Vol. 20, No. 2. (pp. 125–145).

Neuman, S. & Roskos, K. (2005b, July). Whatever Happened to Developmentally Appropriate Practice in Early Literacy? In *Beyond the Journal.* Journal of the National Association for the Education of Young Children. Retrieved August 10, 2006 at http://www.journal.naeyc.org/btj/200507/02Neuman.pdf

Newcomb, H. & Hirsch, P.M. (1983, summer). Television as a Cultural Forum. In *Quarterly Review of Film Studies.* Taylor & Francis. (pp. 503–515).

Nicoll, B. (1996, January). *Developing Minds: Critical Thinking in K-3.* Paper presented at the California Kindergarten Conference, San Francisco, CA.

Raffi. (1992). *Baby Beluga.* Toronto, Canada: Crown Publishers.

Rideout, V., Roberts, D.F. & Foehr, U.G. (2005). *Generation M: Media in the Lives of 8–18-Year-olds.* Washington: Kaiser Family Foundation. Retrieved May 14, 2005 at http://www.kff.org/entmedia/entmedia030905pkg.cfm

Rideout, V.J., Vandewater, E.A., & Wartella, E.A. (2003). *Zero to Six: Electronic Media in the Lives of Infants, Toddlers and Preschoolers.* Washington: Kaiser Family Foundation.

Rogoff, B., & Morelli, G. (1989, February). Perspectives on Children's Development from Cultural Psychology. In *American Psychologist.* Vol. 44, No. 2.

Seiter, E. (2002). *Television and New Media Audiences.* New York: Oxford University Press.

Share, J. (2005). *Five Key Questions That Can Change the World: Classroom Activities for Media Literacy.* Center for Media Literacy. Available online at: http://www.medialit.org/pdf/mlk/02_5KQ_ClassroomGuide.pdf

Share, J. (2006). *Critical media literacy is elementary: A case study of teachers' ideas and experiences with media education and young children.* Unpublished doctoral dissertation, University of California, Los Angeles.

Share, J., & Thoman, E. (2007). *Teaching Democracy: A Media Literacy Approach.* Los Angeles: National Center for the Preservation of Democracy. Available online at: http://www.ncdemocracy.org/sites/ncdemocracy.org/files/docs/D+Dweb_educators_guide.pdf

Starr, A. (2002, April 29). Does Universal Pre-School Pay?. *Business Week.* Retrieved August 14, 2006 at http://www.businessweek.com/magazine/content/02_17/b3780100.htm?chan=search

Thomas, L.G. & Knezek, D.G. (1995). *Technology Literacy for the Nation and for Its Citizens.* Technology Literacy White Paper. Retrieved August 14, 2006 at the International Society for Technology in Education (ISTE) web site: http://www.iste.org/Content/NavigationMenu/Research/Reports/Technology_Literacy_White_Paper_1995_/Technology_Literacy_for_the_Nation_and_for_Its_Citizens.htm

Tyner, K. (1998). *Literacy in a Digital World: Teaching and Learning in the Age of Information.* Mahwah, NJ: Lawrence Erlbaum Associates.

Tyre, P. (2006, September 11). The New First Grade: Too Much Too Soon?, In *Newsweek Magazine.* Retrieved September 6, 2006 at http://msnbc.msn.com/id/14638573/site/newsweek/

Vasquez, V. (2004). *Negotiating Critical Literacies with Young Children.* Mahwah, NJ: Lawrence Erlbaum Associates.

Vasquez, V. (2003). *Getting Beyond "I Like the Book": Creating Space for Critical Literacy in K-6 Classrooms.* Newark: International Reading Association.

Zinn, H. (1990). *The Politics of History.* (2nd ed.). Urbana: University of Illinois Press.

9

■ Teaching Popular Music

Vignettes from Practice

Ernest Morrell

Vignette #1:
A group of four high school students enter the Student Union building at a nearby university. Wanda and Camille are carrying their notebooks. Charles trails behind with the digital video camera. Francisco stays close to Charles as the two will switch off with the filming. Once they have refined their questions and gained confidence, they begin approaching the college students who are eating lunch, shopping, or hanging out. Wanda explains to potential interviewees that she and her colleagues are conducting research relating to the impact of hip-hop culture on the lives of youth. Most of the college students are willing to participate and the group collects a multitude of data to use in their report.

Vignette #2:
It has been several minutes since the bell has rung releasing students for break, yet the classroom is still crowded with students who are discussing the most recent group presentation from the Poet in Society unit. The specific topic of debate is an interpretation that V offered of a line from a Goodie Mob song which states, "Look out for the man with the mask on the white pony." V and her class-mates argue back and forth over whether the man and his horse represent the government, corporate America, or whether he represents racism in general. References are made to former CIA agent William Cooper's *Behold a Pale Horse*, which chronicles government conspiracies and cover-ups. The end of break finds these students still defending their respective interpretations until they are sent off to their third period classes.

■ Popular Music in the Lives of America's youth

There is no doubt that popular music plays a preeminent role in the lives of America's youth. One need look no further than the amazing success of MTV or the sheer number of CDs that are sold to young people annually. Popular music also has a clear and prominent impact on fashion, hairstyles, youth language, and youth attitudes toward authority and dominant institutions. This chapter makes the legitimate case that, for today's youth, hip-hop is the popular music. It is a genre whose popularity transcends race, class, and gender. In a 1999 *Time* magazine article entitled "Hip-hop Nation," it was reported that more people purchase hip-hop CDs than any other genre of music in any time in history. Further, though the music and culture are frequently associated with urban America and with youth of color, more than 70% of hip-hop CDs are purchased by white middle class teens. Hip-hop is a genre whose motifs of oppression and resistance resonate with a large national and increasingly international audience. For this reason, I have focused in this chapter on the teaching of hip-hop culture though these examples could easily be changed or expanded to include any other genre of popular music. In the conclusion, I talk more about strategies for incorporating other forms of popular music.

This chapter lays out the history and background of hip-hop music and culture, explaining its origins in urban, post-industrial America. It also explains how hip-hop music has gained importance as a counter-cultural voice of resistance even as it has become co-opted by mainstream, corporate interests. The heart of the chapter presents and analyzes an intervention that used hip-hop as a bridge to canonical poetry in an urban secondary English classroom. I explain the rationale for the unit, the various goals and objectives, the class activities, and share classroom vignettes, samples of student dialogue and student work, and excerpts from interviews conducted with students at the unit's conclusion. I also examine a research project where a team of high school students from the South Bay Project investigate the impact of hip-hop culture on youth in America. I describe the project, its context as part of a larger seminar on youth research, and present examples of the students in action along with excerpts from their final presentation and report.

As an English teacher at North Bay High, I witnessed the impact of hip-hop music and culture on all of my students. I saw at the same time that the culture's influence seemed to transcend race as students from a variety of ethnic backgrounds were strongly influenced by the culture (Mahiri, 1998). At the same time, through looking at the literacy practices (Barton and Hamilton, 2000) associated with engagement with hip-hop, I also saw that students in this non-mainstream cultural practice (Ferdman, 1990) were exhibiting the critical and analytical skills that we wanted them to bring to academic texts from the canon. I ultimately decided that I could utilize hip-hop music and culture to forge a common and critical discourse that was centered upon the lives of the students, yet transcended the racial divide, and allowed me to tap into students' lives in ways that promoted academic literacy and critical consciousness.

Baker (1993), Farley (1999), and George (1999) all argue that the creative people, who are talking about youth culture in a way that makes sense, happen to be rappers and the youth are responding in many ways. Hip-hop artists sold more than 81 million CDs, tapes and albums in 1998, more than in any other genre of music. Taking their cue from the music industry, other major corporations are creating advertising schemes that cater to the "hip-hop generation." Even mainstream Hollywood, with films such as Warren Beatty's *Bulworth,* has dealt with issues related to hip-hop. Although the music is largely criticized by politicians, religious groups, and some women's groups, its proponents claim that it is here to stay as it represents a resistant voice of today's youth through its articulation of problems that the young people of this generation and all Americans face on a daily basis.

Rose (1994) and Tabb Powell (1991) argue strongly that hip-hop music is the representative voice of urban youth as the genre was created by and for urban youth. Tabb Powell states:

> [Rap] emerged from the streets of inner-city neighborhoods as a genuine reflection of the hopes, concerns, and aspirations of urban Black youth in this, the last quarter of the 20th century. Rap is essentially a homemade, street-level musical genre…Rap lyrics concentrate primarily on the contemporary African American experience…Every issue within the Black community is subject to exposition in the rap arena. Hit rap tunes have broached touchy subjects such as sex, sexism, racism, and crime…Rap artists, they contend, 'don't talk that love stuff, but [rather] educate the listeners.'(p. 245)

Many rappers consider themselves as educators and see at least a portion of their mission as promoting consciousness within their communities. (Lipsitz, 1994; Rose, 1994) As articulated by Freire, the raising of critical consciousness in people who have been oppressed is a first step in helping them to obtain critical literacy and, ultimately, liberation from oppressive ideologies. The influence of rap as a voice of resistance and liberation for urban youth proliferates through such artists as Lauryn Hill, Pras, and Wyclef Jean of the Refugee Camp, Public Enemy, Nas and Mos Def who endeavor to bring an accurate, yet critical depiction of the urban situation to a hip-hop generation.

I further argue that hip-hop texts are literary texts and can be used to scaffold literary terms and concepts and ultimately foster literary interpretations. Hip-hop texts are rich in imagery and metaphor and can be used to teach irony, tone, diction, and point of view. Also, hip-hop texts can be analyzed for theme, motif, plot, and character development. It is very possible to perform feminist, Marxist, structuralist, psychoanalytic or postmodernist critiques of particular hip-hop texts, the genre as a whole, or subgenres such as gangsta rap. Once learned, these analytic and interpretative tools developed through engagement with popular cultural texts can be applied to canonical texts as well (Lee, 1992). If one goal of critical educators is to empower urban students to analyze complex literary texts, hip-hop texts can be used as a bridge linking the seemingly vast span between the streets and the world of academics.

Hip-hop texts, given their thematic nature, can be equally valuable as springboards for critical discussions about contemporary issues facing today's youth. Provocative rap texts can be brought into the classrooms, and discussion topics may be produced from a listening/reading of the text. These discussions may lead to more thoughtful analyses which could translate into expository writing, the production of poetic texts or a commitment to social action for community empowerment.

Teaching hip-hop as a music and culture of resistance can facilitate the development of critical consciousness in all youth. Analyzing the critical social commentary produced by the Refugee Camp, Public Enemy, or Nas may lead to consciousness-raising discussions, essays, and research projects attempting to locate an explanation for the current state of affairs for adolescents today. The knowledge reflected in these lyrics could engender discussions of esteem, power, place, and purpose or encourage students to further their own knowledge of urban sociology and politics. In this way, hip-hop music should stand on its own merit in the academy and be a worthy subject of study in its own right rather than necessarily leading to something more "acceptable" like a Shakespeare text. It can, however, serve as a bridge between urban cultures and the literary canon.

Given the social, cultural and academic relevance of hip-hop music and culture, a colleague and I (Morrell and Duncan-Andrade, 2002) designed a classroom unit with three objectives:

1. To utilize our students' involvement with hip-hop culture to scaffold the critical and analytical skills that they already possess
2. To provide students with the awareness and confidence they need to transfer these skills into/onto the literary texts from the canon.
3. To enable students to critique the messages sent to them through the popular cultural media that permeate their everyday lives

The unit was designed to incorporate hip-hop music into a "traditional" senior English poetry unit. Our desires were to increase motivation and participation in discussions and assignments and to teach critical essay writing and literary terminology in the context of, among other types of poetry, rap music. We also wanted to situate hip-hop historically and socially and discuss its inception as a response to urban post-industrialism. Further, we wished to encourage youth to view elements of popular culture through a critical lens and to critique messages sent to them through popular media and to help students understand the intellectual integrity, literary merit, and social critique contained within elements of their own youth culture.

There were several goals and objectives for this unit that combined our simultaneous agendas of tapping into popular culture and facilitating academic and critical literacy development. To accomplish this, we needed to cover the poetry of the Elizabethan Age, the Puritan Revolution, and the Romantics which was a part of the district-mandated curriculum for 12th grade English and which they would be expected to have knowledge of for the Advanced Placement exam and college English. It was also important to learn about the poets in the context of the literary and historical periods in which they wrote to gain a greater understanding of the role poetry plays as a critique of its contemporary society.

In addition to a critical exposure to the literary canon, we felt it important to concentrate on the development of issues and ideas presented in poetry and song as a vehicle to expository writing. Our objectives were:

- ❑ To develop oral and written debate skills,
- ❑ To facilitate the ability to work in groups,
- ❑ To help students to deliver formal public presentations.
- ❑ To teach students how to critique a poem/song in a critical essay,
- ❑ To help students to develop note-taking skills in lectures and presentations; and
- ❑ To help students to become comfortable writing in different poetic forms such as the sonnet, elegy, and ballad

We began the unit with an overview of poetry in general attempting to re-define poetry and the role of a poet in society. We emphasized the importance of understanding the historical period in which a poem was written to come to a deep interpretation of the poem. In the introductory lecture, we outlined all of the historical/ literary periods that would be covered in the unit (Elizabethan, Puritan Revolution, Romantics, and Metaphysical Poets from England, and the Civil War, Harlem Renaissance, Civil Rights Movement, and Post-Industrial Revolution in the United States). It was our intention to place hip-hop music—as a post-industrial art form—right alongside these other historical periods and poems so that the students would be able to use a period and genre of poetry they were familiar with as a lens with which to examine the other literary works and also to encourage the students to re-evaluate the manner in which they view elements of their popular culture.

The second major portion of the unit involved a group presentation of a canonical poem along with a hip-hop text. The groups were commissioned to prepare a justifiable interpretation of their texts situating each within its specific historical and literary period while also analyzing the linkages between the two. There were eight groups for this portion who were, after a week of preparation, each given a day to present to the class and have their arguments critiqued by their peers. The groups were assigned as follows:

Group	Poem	Song
1	"Kubla Khan," Coleridge	"If I Ruled the World," Nas
2	"Love Song of J. Alfred Prufrock," Eliot	"The Message," Grand Master Flash
3	"O Me! O Life!," Whitman	"Don't Believe the Hype," Public Enemy
4	"Immigrants in Our Own Land," Baca	"The World Is a Ghetto," Geto Boys
5	"Sonnet 29," Shakespeare	"Affirmative Action," Nas
6	"The Canonization," Donne	"Manifest," Refugee Camp
7	"Repulse Bay," Chin	"Good Day," Ice Cube
8	"Still I Rise," Angelou	"Cell Therapy," Goodie Mob

* Other poems used for this unit were "Let America Be America Again" by Langston Hughes and "Elegy Written in a Country Churchyard" by Thomas Gray.

In addition to the group presentations, students were asked to complete an anthology of ten poems that contained an elegy, a ballad, a sonnet, and a poem that described a place with which they were familiar. The title of the poem was to be the place that was featured. Also, the students were asked to write a poem that conveyed a mood, a poem that dealt with a political, social, or economic problem that was important to them (i.e., racism, teen pregnancy, drug abuse, police brutality, poverty, homelessness, etc.), a love poem, a poem that celebrated a particular facet of life (first date, summertime, graduation, etc.), and two open poems that dealt with whatever subject students wanted and written in any style they desired. Following the group presentations, we held a poetry reading where each student selected five of his/her original poems to read for the class giving brief comments on each poem such as the context or a special meaning. For the outside-of-class assignment, students were allowed to pick any song of their choice and write a 5–7-page critical essay on that song. They were also required to submit a transcription of that song.

The unit held consistent with the original goals of being culturally and socially relevant, critically exposing students to the literary canon, and facilitating the development of college-level expository writing. The positioning of hip-hop as a genre of poetry written largely in response to post-industrialism was a concept with which the students were able to relate. The issues of joblessness, poverty, rage, and alienation all had resonance to the urban youth culture of which the students were all a part. The foregrounding of hip-hop as a genre of poetry also helped to facilitate the transition to understanding the role individual poets may have played in their own societies.

The students were able to generate some excellent interpretations as well as make interesting linkages between the canonical poems and the rap texts. For instance, one group articulated that both Grand Master Flash and T.S. Eliot gazed out into their rapidly deteriorating societies and saw a "wasteland." Both poets were essentially apocalyptic in nature as they witnessed death, disease, and decay. Also, both poems talk about a message, indicating the role of a poet in society as a messenger or prophet. Another group discussed the role of allegory in their two texts where both John Donne and the artists from the Refugee Camp utilize relationships with lovers to symbolize the love and agony poets can feel for their societies.

The unit was consistent with the basic tenets of critical pedagogy in that it was situated in the experiences of the students (as opposed to those of the teacher), called for critical dialogue, a critical engagement of the text, and related the texts to larger social and political issues. The students were not only engaged and able to use this expertise and positionality as subjects of the post-industrial world to make powerful connections to canonical texts; they were also able to have fun learning about a culture and a genre of music with which they had great familiarity. Ultimately, our experiences introducing hip-hop and other elements of popular culture into traditional curricula lead us to believe that there are countless possibilities for literacy educators who jump outside of the box and tap into the worlds of their students in order to make more powerful connections with traditional academic texts and affirm, in meaningful ways, the everyday lives of their students.

■ The Hip-Hop Research Project

In partnership with the South Bay Unified school district, a major research university offered an introductory summer seminar for South Bay High school students in the field of the sociology of education, ED 001—Special Topics in Sociology of Education. The seminar invited a group of working class Latino and African American youth to read seminal works in sociology of education and participate in a set of mini-research projects around the broad theme of "Race, Class, and Access in American Education." While all of the student participants had recently completed 10th grade at a local high school, they represented a fairly broad range of academic backgrounds. Over the course of three intensive weeks of study, the high school students worked in five-member teams to produce a piece of original research that they presented to a panel of university faculty members with expertise in the area of educational sociology.

One research group in particular studied the impact of hip-hop music and culture on high school students in America and the implications of this impact on how teachers approach the standardized curriculum. This group created and disseminated a survey to high school students and conducted interviews with teachers, friends and family, and undergraduates at a nearby university. During the three weeks of the seminar, student participants spent an hour with the whole group and two hours in the small groups with their research team advisor, which in this case, happened to be me. During the two-hour research team meetings, the students discussed concepts and readings relating to the sociology of education, learned the various aspects of the research process, prepared interview protocols and surveys, analyzed transcripts, and prepared presentations of their findings. On the final day of the seminar, the students presented their work to a group of university faculty involved in research relating to the sociology of education, parents, and other interested parties.

The summer seminar sought to place high school students in the role of legitimate *peripheral participants* within the broader community of practice of sociology of education research focused on the theme of access and equity (Lave and Wenger, 1991). Lave and Wenger define legitimate peripheral participation as an approach to learning and membership where beginners have full access to full membership within a community without having full responsibility for membership. That is, the community establishes a process of changing participation over time that will result in becoming full participants. According to two educational sociologists that were interviewed, becoming a full participant in the field entailed developing competence in the literature, the research process, and the important issues. Novices in educational sociology (usually advanced undergraduates or graduate students) begin to demonstrate competence in several ways. They recognize critical questions in the field and identify answerable questions. They also demonstrate an understanding of difficult concepts by applying them to everyday situations.

Students in the summer seminar manifested emerging competence along these lines throughout the course of their research. Importantly, these demonstrations of competence arose in the process of being inducted into the research university's community of practice. The seminar students' participation changed over the course of the seminar on three levels—each of which speaks to their induction into the broader community of practice as well as their emerging 'readiness.' First, they appropriated the tools and culture of the research community. I mean by this that the students understood and internalized the language, culture, and purpose of research as they synthesized existing literature and ideas with their own burgeoning research projects. Second, students took on new identities through these new forms of participation. They began to see themselves not merely as passive objects but as participants, questioners and investigators with something to contribute to the world of ideas. Third, they asserted more of a sense of ownership and control over the entire practice. Students, in the seminar presentations, commanded the center of attention in assuming the authority of research "experts" who were able to present findings, make recommendations, evaluate the viability of research alternatives, and set agendas for follow-up research.

■ The Presentation of the Hip-Hop Project

On the day of the final presentations, the project is occupying a room that is reserved for special meetings and presentations. Called the Reading Room, it is adorned with tall solid oak bookshelves that contain bound volumes of scholarly writings from journals and other distinguished literature. Also in the room are two long oak tables that are often put together during meetings to make the room more cozy, a lectern, and fluffy La-Z-Boy-type chairs that are usually situated in the nooks between bookshelves but, for now, are placed in the back of the room behind several rows of "convention" seats. One oak table sits in front of the rows. On the table sit three binders that contain a program of the presentation, the summer seminar readers and proposals for the various research projects. There are also copies of the "Hip-Hop Project," a paper completed by the hip-hop group, and copies of the PowerPoint presentations from the language, family, and resistance groups. Behind the great oak table are three tall wooden chairs reserved for the professors who are the distinguished guests of the presentation. All three professors are located in the school of education, and their research on students of color and urban education is nationally renowned. Behind the professors are some forty chairs filled with friends and family of students, officials from the students' home school district, university faculty and staff, and a group of ACLU attorneys and their (student) clients that the resistance team had interviewed.

There is a general buzz throughout the room as groups and advisors huddle together, plan last-minute strategies and situate the room to their liking. Between setting up and greeting early arrivals with programs and papers, the advisors try to offer words of encouragement to students as they continue to pace and rehearse. Charles wants to go over the methodology section one more time so he approaches his advisor in the front of the room to make sure that his talk is fine. He is also worried because Wanda, another member of his group, is a few minutes late and audience members are already beginning to arrive. I assure him that Wanda will show up and tell him not to worry.

In the hip-hop group presentation, Camille begins by introducing the group as Tanya retrieves her posters that are displayed around the room. Charles and Francisco stand behind Camille.

> Camille: Our group is researching hip-hop music and its impact on teens and how it can be used in the school's curriculum. The problem that our research project addresses is the inequality that is promoted through the school's curriculum. The inequality is manifested through the fact that not everybody has a fair shot and that there is unequal achievement. The ways that inequalities are promoted through the curriculum are: 1) It justifies oppression and 2) Different people's cultures are excluded from the school's curriculum. Our research is important, because by studying hip-hop culture, people can learn about their own experiences so that they can become critical of the world.

Camille has a schema for the research process of a question stemming from a problem and inspiring a study that seeks to find answers or provide further explanation of that problem.

> Charles: Our research question is what is the impact of hip-hop culture on high school students in urban America and our research group has came up with a definition of hip-hop culture. It's urban Americans expressing their struggles in Urban America where they are forced to deal with poverty and alienation. This expression occurs through rap, R&B, and language, and how they dress and their attitude toward authority and society.

Charles and Wanda have developed this definition of hip-hop culture themselves and take great pride in predicating the research upon a culture that they have had the power to define.

During his discussion of methodology, Charles refers to the hip-hop cohort not as a group but as a research team. These are his classmates from high school, yet, in this arena, they are working together on an ambitious three-week research agenda. This language usage points to the ability of the new space to create room for new identities and allows Charles to see himself and his peers in a different light.

> Charles: To find a solution to our research problem, each member of our research team took pictures of things in our community that represent hip-hop. We also interviewed teachers that were here in a summer institute. We also distributed 24 surveys to high school students that were here for a technology program. We also walked around the university campus with a video camera, and we had questions that we asked like did they think that hip-hop had a big impact on our youth, and some of them were like kinda camera shy and they would agree to answer our questions, but when they saw the camera they were like, they got scared off and wouldn't answer our questions. But I don't understand how teachers…teachers say students of color never do anything positive, but when we do something positive, they don't help us out.

Throughout the hip-hop group's presentation, my sole task is to switch the overheads. The students are in control here. They are actually the instructors at this point. They have legitimate sociological knowledge to impart about the intersection of reproduction theory, critical pedagogy, and hip-hop music. They have control of the mechanical tools of research such as the overheads and posters, but they are also able to navigate the discourse and terminology of qualitative research, which they employ to serve their purposes. At this point, these young students are the experts at where this theory intersects with practice. This process also has amazing consequences for the students' development of academic literacy skills. They learn how to conduct and transcribe interviews, how to analyze survey data, and write a professional quality report that was disseminated to university faculty and graduate students. For the remainder of their high school tenure, these students would continue to reference and push upon the hip-hop research that started in this seminar. For example, Wanda was one of several students who presented the hip-hop research to the English department at South Bay High. She, Camille, and Charles all presented this research to a statewide literacy organization. Some of the teachers these students addressed decided to incorporate hip-hop culture and music into their English curricula as a direct result of the powerful presentation.

■ Considerations When Teaching Popular Music

Given that popular music changes so rapidly and that there are so many popular songs at any given time, the task of making appropriate musical selections can be daunting for English teachers. By contrast, there are only a handful of films that teachers would have to consider in a given year compared to hundreds of songs. There are, of course magazines and shows such as MTV's "Total Request Live" that crown the song and the star of the moment. There are also the icons that transcend particular moments that teachers will have no trouble identifying. On the other hand, there are important lesser known and underground musicians to consider. One may ask whether these musicians are even popular if they are not widely known. Based on the criteria I offered in *Linking Literacy and Popular Culture: Connections for Lifelong Learning*, I can say most definitely that artists can be considered popular and worthy of study even if they are relatively obscure within the mainstream media.

Certainly teachers should consult with their students early and often about the artists, songs, and genres that have had and are having a big impact on their lives, but this does not let teachers off the hook. Teachers must understand that, although all of their students listen to music, they are not all equally tapped into the popular culture. Teachers need to find informants; students who are intimately connected to multiple genres of popular music and can give them the expert advice they require. These are the students who play in bands, are president of the hip-hop society, or write lyrics in little notebooks that they carry everywhere. These students can prove invaluable in identifying trends, spotting visionaries, providing a detailed history of a particular genre, and locating hard-to-find music. They can also help with the processes of decoding, translating, and interpreting, though the teacher must ultimately find her own way. In my experience, these closet artists and musicians have been happy to play this role.

Teachers also have a responsibility to highlight themes and generate topics for opening and facilitating discussions. They can also work collaboratively with students to create assignments and rubrics that simultaneously honor students' interests while providing access to relevant academic skills. Sharing ownership of the classroom space and incorporating popular culture does not mean letting go or adopting a hands-off policy. Teachers definitely need to keep their hands on; it's still their class. Students need them to help illuminate the bigger picture, to monitor the classroom space, and to make explicit the connections between students' strengths and literacies and cultures of power . Sometimes this means saying no to particular texts or selecting songs that may not have the largest appeal but are important for the larger goals of the class. It certainly means working diligently to develop a sophisticated understanding of popular music and to maintain an affirming, yet critical stance toward popular texts that enables them to challenge students in their beliefs and interpretations.

It is important to note that the how of teaching popular culture is just as important as the "what." Simply inserting popular selections into a teacher-dominated classroom will not change outcomes. The effective teaching of popular music must occur in a dialogic space that acknowledges student voice and encourages student action. Students must be given permission to engage popular music in ways that respect them as critical cultural consumers as opposed to ignorant partakers of a base and common culture. Critical teachers of popular music will find ways to simultaneously affirm and challenge while maintaining a problem-posing environment where students feel free to challenge each other and the teacher as well. These teachers will also create spaces that enable students to come to their own readings of musical texts while learning from the readings of their peers and trying on critical lenses that force them to read from marginalized positions. Teachers should feel confident using popular music in conjunction with poetry, by itself, as part of theme-based multi-genre units or as part of larger research on youth and popular culture. The possibilities are virtually endless for the teacher who wants to bring popular music into her or his English classroom.

* Reprinted from Ernest Morrell, *Linking Literacy and Popular Culture: Connections for Lifelong Learning,* Norwood, MA: Christopher-Gordon Publishing, 2004.

References

Baker, H.A. (1993). *Black studies, rap, and the academy.* Chicago: University of Chicago Press.

Barton, D., & Hamilton, M. (2000). Literacy practices. In D. Barton, M. Hamilton, and R. Ivanic (Eds.), *Situated literacies: Reading and writing in context* New York: Routledge, 7–15.

Farley, C. (1999). Hip-hop nation: There's more to rap than just rhythms and rhymes. After two decades, it has transformed the culture of America. *Time,* 153, 5, 55–65.

Ferdman, B.M. (1990). Literacy and cultural identity. *Harvard Educational Review,* 60, 2, 181–204.

George, N. (1999). *hiphopamerica.* New York: Penguin Putnam Inc.

Lave, J. and Wenger, E. (1991). *Situated learning: Legitimate peripheral participation.* Cambridge, UK: Cambridge University Press.

Lee, C. (1992). *Signifying as a scaffold for literary interpretation: The pedagogical implications of an African American discourse genre.* Urbana, IL: NCTE Press.

Light, A. (Ed.) (1999). *The Vibe history of hip-hop.* New York: Three Rivers Press.

Lipsitz, G. (1994). History, hip-hop, and the post-colonial politics of sound. *Dangerous crossroads: Popular music, postmodernism, and the poetics of place.* New York: Verso, 23–48.

Mahiri, J. (1998). *Shooting for excellence: African American and youth culture in new century schools.* New York: Teachers College Press.

Morrell, E., & Duncan-Andrade, J. (2002). Toward a critical classroom discourse: Promoting academic literacy through engaging hip-hop culture with urban youth. *English Journal,* 91, 6, 88–94.

Powell, C.T. (1991). Rap music: An education with a beat from the street. *Journal of Negro Education,* 60, 3, 245–259.

Refugee Camp, The. (1996). *The Score* [Compact Disc]. New York: Columbia Records

Rose, T. (1991). Fear of a Black planet: Rap music and black cultural politics in the 1990s. *Journal of Negro Education,* 60, 3, 277–291.

Rose, T. (1994). *Black noise: Rap music and Black culture in contemporary America.* Hanover, NH: University Press of New England.

10

■ "This Won't Be on the Final"

Reflections on Teaching Critical Media Literacy[1]

Rhonda Hammer

Everyone's been there. The professor has just explained a central idea to the class and asked if there are any questions. There is that awkward silence, interrupted by a few coughs. Even the sound of text messaging has disappeared. Then a student raises her hand. Everyone hopes that s/he is going to ask something which will provoke the professor to further clarify dimensions of the lecture or generate a discussion. But, instead, it is that insidious question which punctuates so many undergraduate classes—at the most inappropriate of times—"Will this be on the final?"

Nothing can be more deflating to an instructor's ego—especially when you are on a "roll"—or hijacks an animated class discussion faster than these kinds of queries. Yet this escalating obsession with grades is understandable given the pressures experienced by so many 21st-century students, especially in relation to acceptance to more advanced programs, a radically declining job market, certain forms of financial assistance and sometimes unreasonable expectations and demands by parents.

Although this scenario has happened to me on too many occasions to count, it never fails to catch me off guard. It is not only disconcerting but is also a glaring reminder of the nature of "knowledge" as a commodity, which seems to be no longer measured by learning but almost solely by "grades." And it is these grades, regardless of whether they are earned or not,[2] which constitute the dominant currency of many students' experience in and relationship to education in contemporary universities.

Indeed, the commodification of grades has reached such epic proportions that new businesses have evolved,[3] such as the *Campus Buddy Site* which provides its customers with the grade distributions of courses and professors from over 32 California universities and community colleges. It seems that it is not enough to just rate professors in regard to the effectiveness of their teaching style and the rigors of the course but to assess them in relation to what really counts: how easily they grade. Unfortunately, this focus on grades as the goal of the course reduces the quality of higher education to what Karl Marx and Friedrich Engels described as "commodity fetishism," the process in which social relationships are transformed into objects or commodities, often translated into monetary terms. This fetishism is especially apparent in how the creators of Buddy Site advertise their service: they assert that, "As students you don't get paid. Your salary's your grade" (quoted in: Fung, 2008).

Although this "truism" is, in fact, largely fallacious—given that potential employers rarely, if ever, require the inclusion of grade transcripts in job applications[4]—it is an indication of what many describe as a crisis in education which threatens the rights of students and faculty to pursue the kinds of critical learning needed to participate in a contemporary media and technological culture. In fact, this increasing fixation on grades reflects what many experts have described as the reduction of the complex and emancipatory process of higher education into a commodity product which is measured solely on the basis of its market value, especially in relation to job opportunities.

While grades may not matter to potential employers, the diploma and, even more importantly, its "brand" are now a prerequisite for most jobs, except for those that simply involve manual labor or "service industry" work, the majority of which fail to provide their workers with a "living wage."[5] As Stanley Aronowitz (2008) makes painfully clear:

> Ours is an era when 'higher education' credentials have become the new mantra of public schooling. The rationale for the need for credentials is the technological imperative, the material basis of which is deindustrialization. The days when a teenager could drop out of high school and get a decent-paying factory job or go into retailing or wholesaling with a prospect of eventually earning enough to support self and family with dignity are, it seems, long gone.(10)

Given the ever-increasing off-shore outsourcing of blue- and white-collar jobs and industries, which under the rubric of so-called "free trade" allowed corporations to cut their operating costs and increase their profits, a college or university diploma is now considered a mandatory requirement for a relatively decent paying job in the United States (especially given the shrinking job market and rising unemployment rates).[6]

Within this context, "learning" has been largely replaced by "vocational training" in American universities and colleges (Aronowitz, 2000). Even though some would argue that this mode of education trains graduates to meet the needs of many private and corporate employers, in its most vulgar form it deprives students of participation in what many scholars contend is the mainstay of post-secondary education: to "develop skills of critical analysis," to "engage differences of opinion," as well as to "imagine alternative futures, decide on their intended careers, and consider their larger life's work of contributing to the common good" (AAC&U, 2006).

Moreover, given the massive downsizing and bankruptcy of so many corporations and businesses and the escalating numbers of unemployed, authoritarian training which "favors a series of measures that hold students accountable for passing standardized tests and for a definite quantity [rather than quality] of education" is actually detrimental. Such education deprives students of the critical and creative abilities which are now a prerequisite for their own survival, as well as for a collective democratic reshaping of a social system which has proven to be completely dysfunctional (Aronowitz, 2008: 16).

As Giroux and Giroux (2008) point out, the devastating failures of "free market fundamentalism," or what is often referred to as "neo-liberalism," have provoked many to demand a radical restructuring of the economic system and a return to "a form of governance that assumed a measure of responsibility for the education, health and general welfare of its citizens (ibid.)." However, what many of these critics are failing to include is that this kind of reform presumes that "we have on hand and in stock generations of young people and adults who have somehow been schooled in an entirely different set of values and cultural attitudes…and who are not only intellectually prepared but morally committed to the staggering challenges that comprehensive reform requires" (ibid.). However, due in large part to the cooptation of US public education by the "standards movement"—which Aronowitz describes as "a euphemism for the subordination of pedagogy to tests"—many lack the necessary abilities to even understand or constructively criticize the pathological consumption-based ideology and practices which have wreaked such devastating havoc on the national and global economy and ruined the lives of so many people (2008: xviii).

In fact, the massive cut-backs in government support of our public education and the consequent endorsement of so-called standardized testing, dubbed by the Bush administration as the "No Child Left Behind" program, have contributed to alarming increases in illiteracy as well as the deteriorating quality of education in the United States. The realities and outrageous consequences of this have been demonstrated in a "2006 study supported by the Pew Charitable Trust [that] found that *50% of college seniors scored below 'proficient' levels on a test that required them to do such basic tasks as understand the arguments of newspaper editorials or compare credit-card offers*" (Nemko, 2008; *emphasis mine*). Moreover, according to the same study only 20% had basic quantitative skills, while a 2006 federal commissioned report found that: "Over the past decade, literacy among college graduates has actually declined.…According to the most recent National Assessment of Adult Literacy, for instance, the percentage of college graduates deemed proficient in prose literacy has actually declined from 40 percent to 31 percent in the past decade" (ibid).

Our best hope of democratizing society is through what Thomas Jefferson defined as an educated and "informed citizenry." However, corporate and privatized media which have tremendous influence over our citizens are systematically misinforming and miseducating our students and citizens, as Chomsky, Herman, and others have long pointed out. In this situation, we have the need to make critical thinking and media literacy a fundamental part of contemporary education. This has become decidedly more urgent in light of the toxic effects of what Naomi Klein (2007) describes as "disaster capitalism" whereby corporate elites manipulate the system for their own power and profit, while systematically undermining democracy.

In this chapter, I argue for the importance of developing critical media and cultural studies courses for all levels of schooling—and especially within post-secondary institutions—as a necessary requirement for reclaiming participatory democracy. In the following discussion, I will first argue for the necessity of the adoption within educational institutions of a radical form of media literacy which finds its foundations in an insurgent pedagogy which is critical, humanizing, and empowering. Indeed, as Aronowitz so cogently explains it: "any reasonable concept of democratic citizenship requires an individual who is able to discern knowledge from propaganda, is competent to choose among conflicting claims and programs, and is capable of actively participating in the affairs of the polity" (2008: 17). Hence, a critical education needs to give students the power to question authority, express their own views and provide them with the skills and time for self-reflection and creativity. This also entails the promotion of a lifestyle change which celebrates and prioritizes the pleasures of "thinking" and learning, eschewing the time-consuming and mind-numbing practices mediated by a politics of greed and obsession with consumption which distracts us from critical engagement in our everyday lives. Yet, this is an arduous and challenging task, given that it involves our recognition, and even condemnation of the ideology of neo-liberalism, "the political philosophy that dogmatically equates generating profits with generating maximum human happiness," which pervades all of our social, political and economic institutions as well as the cultural standards which mediate our collective and individual values and beliefs, to various degrees.

In the second part of this chapter, I will describe my own efforts at UCLA and elsewhere to create courses in critical media literacy in which students are encouraged to exercise their creative potential and critical thinking through the production of media projects. One of the goals of these courses is to reshape student visions so that they can become informed and active participants in multiple dimensions of social life and provoke and engage in the advance of participatory democracy.

■ Radical Pedagogy and Critical Media Literacy

Part of the problem with contemporary university education is that an obsession with grades and training for jobs is facilitated by a pedagogy that treats students as passive objects of indoctrination. In his classic 1970 text, *Pedagogy of the Oppressed,* Brazilian educator and activist Paulo Freire identified and critiqued a dominant educational form of teaching, which he argued restricted and "annulled" students' capacities for creative thought and critical consciousness. He described this as the "banking concept of education," in which students are treated as empty accounts, in which teachers deposit educational currency which is stored, filed, and later withdrawn. Freire goes on to argue that this dehumanizing practice, for both students and teachers, encourages students to accept the "passive roles imposed on them" as well as "the fragmented view of reality" which has been deposited in their cerebral accounts (2001: 73).

One of the most repressive and debilitating aspects of this banking system of education is that it teaches us to never question authority and to therefore treat socially constructed hierarchical relations of power as if they are inherent and natural. It is within this type of oppressive pedagogy that commercial values and market logic supersede fundamental democratic principles of education, which demand exploration of diversities of ideas, including those which elicit us to question conventional wisdom and so-called truths, including our own. In other words, a key dimension of higher education is to promote "self-reflexivity" which is loosely described as on-going conversations with yourself, in relation to the wide range of experiences which have shaped your identity(ies) and provoke you to examine and interrogate your own unconscious biases and perceptions of the world. Yet, such critical education is at odds with a key function of educational institutions in the United States, which is to train students to "define themselves as consumers rather than as multifaceted social actors" (Giroux, 2003: 173).

This alienated consumption-based relationship between student and teacher is one in which students are evaluated by their abilities to memorize and repeat the "knowledge" which has been imparted to them by their teacher and/or texts. Further, the instructor's worth is largely gauged by the students on how well s/he trains or prepares them to excel on standardized course tests and assignments that are designed to "evaluate the student's ability to imbibe and regurgitate information and to solve problems according to prescribed algorithms" (Aronowitz, 2008: 17). Hence, although Freire's critique of the banking method is over 40 years old, it is still an apt description of the prevailing mode of teaching in many contemporary colleges and universities.

In fact, many argue that the primary purpose of this training/banking mode of education is "to help the student adapt to the prevailing order" and "to identify with social and cultural authorities" (Aronowitz, 2000: 1). Or as David Nasaw more bluntly puts it, this training model "rob[s] students of their individuality" and trains them to become "cogs in the corporate machine" (cited in Aronowitz, 2000: 3). [7] A common critique of the conformist standardized banking education is that it does not adequately prepare students for the contemporary world that demands skills in cognitive thinking, multiple literacies in media and technology, and the ability for autonomous thought and action.

This is not to say that courses which focus on technical education and particular dimensions of job training have no place within the academic domain. However, as Henry and Susan Giroux assert: "while the university should equip people to enter the workplace, it should also educate them to contest workplace inequalities" (2004: 10). Progressive education should also challenge injustices which mediate students' own personal experiences as well as contribute to a globalized corporate mentality which promotes a politics of greed within an atmosphere of moral panic and a culture of fear. Sociologist Barry Glassner (2003) contends that: "In the U.S, our fears are so exaggerated and out of control that anxiety is the number one mental problem in the country."

I would argue that the kinds of growing anxieties which typify university and college experiences personify the increasing diversities of manufactured and inflated fears and terror which characterize contemporary American life. And it is largely through transnationally controlled mainstream media—in conjunction with other hegemonic institutions, such as big business, government, education, and organized religion—that these kinds of largely unfounded and overstated dangers are promulgated (Glassner, 1999).

Such fears, both real and imaginary, prevent us from criticizing our socio-political and economic system and contribute to the ideological blinders that distract us from questioning the authority and decisions of those who are in the positions of power and who are responsible for a variety of our social problems. Glassner and many others, such as Pulitzer prize-winning investigative reporter Naomi Klein, argue that the escalation and repeated employment of fear mongering by those in power (such as the Bush Administration) have managed to induce a kind of collective psychological shock on the American people, which can leave us traumatized, deeply disoriented, far more open to suggestion and often incapable of rational thought or protecting our own self-interests (Klein, 2007: 16).

Recently, the media and those in positions of power have been promoting some justifiable fears about the future of the United States and anxieties about our financial well-being and future. However, the media and government's unrelenting practice of employing "shock and awe" tactics to intensify our panic, rarely if ever explain how our tax dollars are being spent, or that radical shifts in priorities and the redistribution of these allocations, could resolve our current crisis. Indeed, instead of berating us with double-speak and incomprehensible explanations of economics, bail-outs, speculative stocks, budget deficit balloons, national debts, complicated investment practice and so on, they should be addressing and examining the failures of our current so-called free market, neo-liberal system, which is loosely described as a "grim alignment of the state, corporate capital and transnational corporations" (Giroux and Giroux, 2008).

It is within this context that mainstream corporate media provoke us to believe that the government and corporations are offering the only possible solutions and always include a variety of so-called "experts" to justify these positions. Yet, they omit to report on the kinds of contextual information which would better inform the public in regard to these decisions. In fact, many find it outrageous that the media never indicate that the economic crisis could be alleviated if, for example, the government stopped investing so much in war and militarism. There is never any questioning of why 42 percent of our tax dollars are spent directly or indirectly on defense. "Even nonwar military expenditures have soared. With so much money spent on weapons that don't work against enemies that don't exist, there is ample room to increase security at the same time that we cut defense expenditures" (Stiglitz, 2008). Indeed, Joseph Stiglitz, who won the Nobel Prize in economics in 2001, has documented that the direct and indirect costs of the Iraq war have been three trillion dollars! (ibid.).

Although the U.S. can spend $3 trillion on wars of choice and can recommend a bailout program for big corporations that could cost trillions, we are told that there is not enough money for basic needs of education, health care, social services or our deteriorating infrastructure. Scandalously, students are being forced to pay even higher tuition and increase their already escalating student loans (many of which are privatized with high interest rates) for a declining quality of education, due, in large part to increasing cut-backs in state funding, which many governors, like California's Arnold Schwarzenegger, threaten will be even further reduced in light of the financial crisis. And even though the new Obama administration has promised to address some of these concerns, it is unlikely—given the priorities of the new administration and the horrendous economic mess he has inherited—that we will see the kinds of radical reforms necessary for the reinstitution of the "widespread calls for 'participatory democracy,' a vision of society administered collectively by—and according to the needs of—its various constituents . . ." (Ewen, 1996: 405).

Yet, why do we rarely question the solutions proposed by those in positions of power, or demand more progressive alternatives? It is in part because we have been indoctrinated to believe that, in Robert McChesney's words: "there is…no alternative to the status quo [that] will improve matters" (2004: 10).[8] It is in this sense that the corporate media are a primary vehicle of promoting the often false and exaggerated fears that are embroidered into the fabric of every domain of life, from the university to the political system, while not providing alternative views that challenge the existing power structure.

The ubiquity of media in a multiplicity of forms and the prominent roles they play in our everyday experiences demand that media become a compulsory area of critical inquiry and investigation in all levels of educational curricula. This kind of critical thinking would liberate the majority of Americans to "think outside of the box" of the dominant ideology and corporate system and look for new political and social alternatives.

As Richard Beach points out, according to recent studies 8-year-olds to 18-year-olds are devoting 8 and a half hours a day to media-related activity, while college students aged 18 to 24 spend "an average of 11 hours a day involved in some sort of media or digital communications" (2009, pg. 206). Given the nature of our contemporary society and global world, it is crucial that all citizens become literate in media culture, emergent new media, and related developing technological, computer, and web 2.0 digital forms. Many argue that universities in particular have a responsibility to provide students with multiple techno-literacy and critical pedagogical skills to overcome the limitations of purely technical media production or computer literacy courses which are becoming the norm within a variety of educational institutions (see Jhally and Earp (2006: 232ff). As Carmen Luke argues: "Most universities include these new info- or techno-literacies in their lists of promised graduate outcomes. Yet they remain conceptually and practically grounded in an instrumental end user rationale rather than a critical analytic approach" (Luke, 2009: pg. 194).[9] However, many colleges and universities in the U.S. are cutting back on even those courses and workshops which teach students the necessary rudimentary technological skills they need for pursuing critical media literacy projects.

I argue for the importance of teaching critical media literacy from a perspective that seeks to empower students by giving them abilities to read, critique, and produce media, which in turn, teaches them to become active participants rather than "sophisticated consumers" in a highly hyper*media*ted culture and society (Jhally and Lewis, 2006: 225). Given the power of the contemporary media and consciousness industry in that it shapes "virtually every sphere of public and political life" (Jhally and Earp, 2006: 244), it is more important than ever to "understand media," as McLuhan (1965) pointed out. Since, as Douglas Kellner reminds us, we are "immersed from cradle to grave in a media and consumer society," (2009: pg. 5) it is essential that we privately and publicly interrogate the multidimensional and complex nature of mainstream and alternative media in a contextual manner. This demands that we take into account the political/economic dimensions and implications of media production and decode dominant and resistant values encoded in these texts. Yet we should also become literate in the technical codes which are employed in media productions, and, of course, in examining how and why divergent active audiences read texts differently.

In relation to film, for example, bell hooks explains that: "Movies not only provide a narrative for specific discourses of race, sex, and class, they provide a shared experience, a common starting point from which diverse audiences can dialogue about these charged issues" (1996: 2). Media texts dealing with such issues can provoke animated and passionate discussions and inspire students to actively engage in further research, writing, media productions, and activism.[10] Within this context, the essential dialectical nature of critical media literacy, which eschews binary oppositional notions that posit various forms of media as either good or bad becomes apparent. Popular media, like texts of high culture, are "polysemic" in that they often encode multiple and even paradoxical meanings as well as being open to a variety of interpretations. In fact, numerous perspectives are often expressed which can include "incredibly revolutionary standpoints merged with conservative ones" (hooks, 1996: 3). The contradictory and multidimensional nature of media culture, which can induce our greatest pleasures, can thus also generate important discussions and provide crucial insights into our society and culture.

It is important to note that there is no fundamental contradiction between pleasure and critique, as critique can provide its own pleasures, and cultural studies attempts to understand popular pleasures rather than denounce them.[11] Moreover, as the astute film critic Pauline Kael described it, criticism can, in fact, enhance pleasure. As she explains:

> Readers of *The New Yorker,* where my reviews have appeared for the past twenty years, frequently ask if I don't sometime just go to the movies for pleasure. My answer is that I always do. I got hooked on movies at an early age…and I am still a child before a moving image. I want to watch it; I want to see what comes next. This desire to be caught up—to be entranced—doesn't interfere with my critical faculties. If anything, it sharpens them. My hopes make my disappointments all the keener; my hopes make the pleasure keener, too. (1985: xv)

Cultural criticism of media texts "illuminates, enabling us to see a work in a new way" (hooks, 1996: 5). As Jhally and Earp remind us, when advocating the significance of "conceptualizing media education as crucial to democratic citizenship," it is important to note that in no way should one assume "that all media are bad, or that young people and the public more generally must be protected from the so-called evil influences of media images and messages" (2006: 242). On the other hand, a critical media literacy questions representations and stories that promote sexism, racism, classism, homophobia, and other oppressive and bigoted forces, a well as the underlying values which mediate and inscribe media culture. In my experience, I have found that students are especially interested in examining the "politics of representation" in a multiplicity of media forms. This enterprise explores positive, negative or ambiguous representations of class, gender, race, sexuality, and other determinants of identity and social stratification (see Hammer and Kellner, 2009: Introduction).

Student engagement with the politics of representation and difference is hardly surprising given the ascendancy of "colorblindness" in much of our contemporary public and private discourse which, like allegations of "political correctness," curtails dialogues about real hierarchies of power and privilege.[12] Patricia Hill Collins asserts that this color-blind mentality, which claims that racism no longer exists, is in fact a racist ideology.[13] The paradoxical nature of this "new racism," as she calls it, "which relies heavily on the manipulation of ideas within mass media," has been especially successful because it characterizes any racial language (or interrogations about race or ethnicity) as perpetuating racism. As Hill Collins explains it: "Despite protestations to the contrary, this new colorblind racism claimed not to see race yet managed to replicate racial hierarchy as effectively as the racial segregation of old" (2006: 3).[14]

John Downing and Charles Husband describe the insidious manner in which racism has "evolved" and continues to permeate our dominant values and beliefs despite the myth of its extinction. As they so eloquently and emphatically assert: "Racism is a poisonous ideology and a destructive practice. It is predominantly anathemized by states, politicians and populations as a stain on civilized society. And yet, it is virtually endemic. The discourses which vilify racism are more than amply countered by the many other discourses through which racism is made invisible, normative and even virtuous" (2005:1). Hence, the consequences of what Stuart Hall refers to as inferential racism have been especially evident in educational institutions in the United States where the term "political correctness" has been employed by right-wing pundits and mainstream media to demonize and trivialize "those people who were trying to create a more respectful and inclusive environment on campus for groups which have largely been excluded" (Glassner, 1999: 10). According to cultural critic and education scholar Ellen Seiter, "the 'color-blind' model imposed by so many teachers effectively shuts down discussion of a topic—race and racism—that students are struggling with on a daily basis" (2005: 24). She goes on to argue that:

> It is a disservice to students to exclude from classroom discussions issues of class and race that they are negotiating throughout their everyday lives. Instead whiteness is embedded in "colorblindness" discourse, which is "universally framed and has thus sidestepped the issues of racial imbalance implicit in colorblindness."[14] (ibid.)

Unfortunately, this "disservice" is hardly particular to issues of race but also includes the multiple dimensions of identity and culture which necessarily include, but are not exclusive to, relations of class, gender, sexuality, age, and other forms which often intersect with race as well as with one another.[15] Hence, teaching critical media literacy can be, as bell hooks (1994) describes it, a liberatory experience for both teachers and students. Yet, ironically, the dearth of culturally critical media literacy classes, especially those that involve media production, which I will shortly describe, owes much to the general lack of support in regard to the credibility afforded such courses as well as to limited technological resources which are often only available within specialized programs. As noted media and cultural studies scholar David Buckingham puts it:

> I am frustrated by the fact that teachers of media education still seem to be insufficiently recognized and supported. Despite the generally inhospitable climate, there is a great deal of excellent work being done in the field by highly dedicated teachers and committed students. Media education generates a degree of enthusiasm and enjoyment that is all too rare in contemporary schooling; and it offers a form of educational practice that is not just engaging for students, but also intellectually rigorous, challenging and relevant to their everyday lives.
>
> Without being at all uncritical of what goes on, I believe this is something we should affirm and celebrate. (2003: x)

■ Teaching Critical Media Literacy Through Production: Where Theory Meets Praxis

It is within this context that I will discuss a critical media literacy course which I have been teaching for eight years at the University of California, Los Angeles, as well as some of my earlier pedagogical and production experiences which have informed much of its form and content. My current course is a unique one for UCLA, as it is one of the only courses outside of the film school which incorporates a practical component in which students produce a group media project. One of the underlying tenets of the course is to provide students with the opportunities and skills to recognize and speak out against the exclusion of marginalized and progressive voices (which often includes their own) within the mainstream media as well as the dominant factory system of education.

To even attempt to address the politics of representation through a media literacy course, however, necessitates a dialectic of relevant theory and praxis in which students study scholarly critical cultural studies writing as well as historical and analytic interrogations of a variety of media and new media forms to develop a critical media literacy. It also involves utilizing more technically oriented literature and media on production techniques as well as hands-on instruction in video, webpage, and sometimes PowerPoint production. The emphasis on watching and discussing media texts both inside and outside of the classroom is also a key feature of theoretical and practical exercises which promote media literacy. In fact, my love of film and video—especially documentaries—has shaped many of my own personal and academic choices and pursuits. And even though the seemingly never-ending impediments and sheer unmitigated hassles associated with teaching production-based critical courses (especially this one) can be overwhelming, I think that I persist due to the profound pleasure I take in introducing students to a different way of looking at and thinking about media. It is in this sense that I try to adopt an approach which Buckingham (2003) describes as "making the familiar strange" in which students are asked to look closely at how media texts are constructed as well as how and why they think they were made.

In addition, the course breaks with the dominant university codes which promote individualism and competition and is completely at odds with the "banking system of education." Indeed, a hegemonic, standardized approach to this kind of teaching and learning would destroy the critical, creative and activist dimensions provoked by these kinds of courses. Instead, the pedagogy is based on cooperation, debate, argument and respecting the voices of other members of the group (at least in theory, but like in any collaborative project, differences of opinion can sometimes become acrimonious, although these tend to be resolved on completion of the final production).

Group projects require articulation of difference and then consensus (rather than acquiescence), which provide students with exercises in democratic practice. The class also seeks to enable students to reshape the way they see the world through reading, discussing, producing, and watching critical media. Much of this material is "counter-hegemonic" and contradicts many of the dominant societal beliefs and media codes. One of the most significant aspects of the course is to discuss and investigate how ideological codes can be subverted. Rather than being restricted to more classical or vulgar explications of ideology, we attempt to instead recognize its complexities and multidimensional nature in that it is inscribed both consciously and unconsciously in all of our experiences of everyday life. As Stuart Hall describes it, "the concept of ideology 'are those images, concepts and premises...through which we represent, interpret, understand and 'make sense' of some aspect of social existence." For critical media theorists the study of ideology is intimately connected to the study of media texts, because they play a major role in producing and reproducing ideologies" (Dines and Humez, 2003: 4). And one of the ways to do this is to celebrate how the production of alternative and oppositional media often gives voice and agency to subaltern people, including marginalized students and allows them to "talk back."

The development of this course was based on a number of classes I had taught at other universities in the late 1980s and early 1990s as well as my own experiences as a grassroots and educational video producer. It is also informed by my transdisciplinary academic background and research, which includes communications, sociology, feminism, education, critical race and queer theory, as well as cultural studies and critical media literacy, and it is these kinds of experiences which inform my classes. Hence, the dialectical and radical nature of critical media courses, I would argue, indicates that they do not and cannot conform to a predesigned syllabus but rather are ultimately determined by the lived and scholarly experiences of the specific instructor. Thus each course is framed by the individual instructors' own "personalities," and therefore no critical media literacy courses are alike. For example, the different courses in media literacy described in this section of the book all reflect the specific interests, experiences, and expertise of the professor in question. There is thus no one curriculum, teaching plan, or model for critical literacy courses which, like cultural studies, engage the issues of the day and interests and goals of the students. As Carmen Luke so aptly describes it:

> A major challenge in developing critical media literacy, however, results from the fact that it is not pedagogy in the traditional sense with firmly established principles, a canon of texts, and tried and true teaching procedures. It is a democratic pedagogy that involves teachers sharing power with students as they join together in the process of unveiling myths and challenging hegemony. Moreover, the material of media culture is so polymorphous, multivalent, and polysemic, that it necessitates sensitivity to different readings, interpretations, perceptions of the complex images, scenes, narratives, meanings, and messages of media culture, which in its own ways is as complex and challenging to critically decipher as book culture (cited in Kellner and Share, 2007: 17).

Regardless of different approaches, however, critical media literacy is always related to the "project of radical democracy and concerned to develop skills that will enhance democratization and civic participation" (Kellner and Share, 2007: 17). It is in this sense that I will attempt to summarize my experiences and the ways that I've developed my own critical media literacy courses. I first discovered video in the early '70s through a non-credit workshop and communications course at Simon Fraser University in Vancouver (although I had used video for a supplementary school project at York University in Toronto the year before...and became hooked!). In those days, portable video systems (called porta-paks[16]) were state of the art and were being used by many diverse groups and individuals who had not previously had access to this kind of inexpensive media equipment. The porta-pak was hardly portable by today's standards and was comprised of a bulky video reel-to-reel deck which you had to thread by hand and a rather large camera, tripod, battery, and sometimes a separate microphone. Moreover, this early video system only recorded in black and white, and editing was done using reel-to-reel tapes and a grease pencil,[17] which was later replaced by a rudimentary linear computer editing system, which was primarily designed for assemble editing, and cassette videotapes, which we found absolutely miraculous.

Many argue that the field of media production became democratized with the advent of portable videos in that film production was often financially prohibitive (and demanded more sophisticated training and expertise). Artists, dancers, musicians, activists, documentary producers, teachers, and even filmmakers, to name a few, took advantage of this new accessible media form. In fact, the Yippies[18] (a 60s political and social movement, the Youth International Political Party) used video for their campaign to run a pig for president in 1968. Video production classes were also incorporated into many schools including universities. Much of my own video experiences were the result of the availability of this equipment through educational forums.

I taught video in the community and in the university in Canada and worked on a number of grants producing educational videos for many years. I found that doing video often clarified and gave new meaning to many of the theoretical notions I was studying—not only communications, media theory, and cultural studies but also sociological, pedagogical, and feminist concerns. In fact I spent some years in graduate school studying and writing about the complex nature of "ideology," and discovered that critical studies of media and video production helped me to better understand this multileveled process and how deeply it is embedded in the media of everyday life.

For example, the technical codes of film and video production are rarely (if ever) objective and often communicate ideological values and beliefs. High and low camera angle shots can symbolize positions of domination and subordination (for example, *film noir* of the 40s and 50s was infamous for the manner in which it depicted women as evil, employing technical codes of lighting, camera movements, angles, music, and/or sound effects). News magazine programs such as *60 Minutes* often use camera and editing techniques to manipulate audience readings of interviewees (for example, zooming in on a subject's face, especially when they are sweating, can make the interviewee appear to be nervous and dishonest). Richard Nixon learned this lesson the hard way during his unsuccessful presidential campaign against John Kennedy in the 60s. Moreover, I have found that employing these kinds of examples is an essential component of effective critical media pedagogy, and the advent of new media, such as YouTube, for example, makes these especially accessible and provides for far more expansive levels of decoding texts.

Thus, it is crucial that critical media literacy pedagogy identify the ideological codes and dominant and resistant social values and beliefs embedded in media texts in both form and content. Understanding that these kinds of codes often operate at unconscious levels, through symbolic forms, becomes imperative. For example, "semiotics" (the study of signs and codes) also greatly assisted me in my understanding and past and present teaching of media literacy and practice as well as the significance of the symbolic dimensions of media. I began to include these various theoretical ideas and concepts into courses I taught in video production in the late 1980s and mid-'90s in Canada, as well as in those I have been teaching at UCLA for the past eight years, which promote critical media literacy through the dialectics of production and the study of critical theory.

As Steve Goodman (2003), a ground-breaking scholar and activist in education and progressive media, argues: "Such a critical literacy gives students the analytic tools to read a commercial or a movie, and also to understand the big picture: how the media's overriding objective of getting and satisfying an audience tends to convert politics, warfare, religion, crime, and all aspects of our society into branches of show business" (7). This should also involve "creating spaces and modes of communication that are alternatives to the ratings-driven show business model of media making" (ibid.)

It is within this context that I have tried to teach my students to produce counterhegemonic video using popular forms like the documentary, advertisements, and commercial and progressive entertainment media, to assist them in recognizing and understanding dominant genre and ideological and technical production codes and to employ or subvert these in their productions of alternative media projects. However, there appears to be a growing opposition in many film and video schools to the production of oppositional or alternative media although we are currently witness to an astonishing rise in radical documentary production by progressive individuals and organizations.[19] Hence, in my courses the theoretical and practical dimensions of critical media literacy, geared towards progressive and resistant forms of portable video production, are of central importance.

For example, I began teaching a course on video production in the 1980s which included theory and praxis and encouraged the students to produce progressive projects which reflected their own "voice," and I have continued to incorporate and expand upon this dialectical pedagogical approach throughout the years. In this earlier course, some of the student assignments, which included the production of anti-commercials and/or anti-"rock videos" (as they were called at the time), demanded that we study technical and popular media's representative symbolic and narrative codes and try to subvert them. Crucially, we must be fortunate enough to have the critical and production resources, which necessarily include, for most of us, technical support—often in the form of paid student or professional "I.T." assistants—as "one of the most effective strategies for teaching critical literacy is for students to create their own media" (Goodman, 2003). It is through this process that they can better understand the multiple layers of data and information which make up the television, videos, magazines, blogs, video/computer games, social networks, wikis, interactive sites and other new media forms which mediate so much of their everyday lives. In this kind of hands-on creative process:

> They can see for themselves how words can be deleted or added to sentences and made to seem as if they had originally been spoken that way; how causes and effects can be made into their opposite; and how perceptions of time, space, power, and history can all be altered without seeming to be. With a critical appreciation, students can understand how the media acts as a frame and a filter on the world while appearing to be a clear window (ibid.)

It was in fact, through my involvement in this production-oriented pedagogical process that I discovered that this practice is one of the most effective, exciting and pleasurable practices of critical media studies for both students and teachers. In particular, I strongly focus on teaching students documentary production, which is a great format for presenting unconventional, critical or resistant perspectives on a diversity of issues. During the 1960s, a counter-hegemonic documentary movement evolved which often provided the public with alternative views, visions and factual information which was completely at odds with the status quo and "establishment" views. This tradition of alternative documentary engendered by anti-racist, feminist, civil rights, gay and lesbian (and later queer), social activist and other progressive groups has been attempting to transform our views and facilitate humanistic change of contemporary U.S. and global society and was and continues to be a seminal component of my course and encourages students to produce short documentary style projects.

I was so amazed by the commitment and enthusiasm of many of the students and the innovation and creativity of their video projects in the courses I originally taught that I encouraged them to work on a longer project which we viewed as a kind of "scholarly MTV-style video." Many students and teachers have become convinced that an adapted music video format, which employs highly diverse and complex edits, is one of the most effective genres of progressive educational videos. (Indeed, many of the most brilliant Media Education Foundation [MEF] productions, which produce and distribute some of the most entertaining and innovative progressive media employ this kind of format. [*http:// www.mediaed.org.*]) To encourage critical video production of this more extensive project, I arranged for the students to get course credit to attend and videotape sessions of the annual Popular Culture Studies conference which was held in Toronto in 1990. This annual scholarly conference had, at the time, literally thousands of participants who presented on a diversity of themes and topics related to popular culture. Since then, its numbers have increased.

Despite a multiplicity and diversity of challenges, we managed to capture a lot of useable footage and presented, a year later at the PCA 1991 conference, a 100-minute montage of highlights of various sessions of the 1990 meetings, which actually took close to a year to complete. (We also won a conference award for the video.) This experience, although highly stressful and incredibly frustrating at times, convinced me of the significance of progressive student media production within the context of critical approaches like cultural studies.

Moreover, introducing undergraduate students to academic pursuits like scholarly conferences—especially those which explore critical themes—is often a revelatory experience for them. Many of the students, for the first time, understood the empowering nature of education, which was at odds with what Paulo Freire characterized as the banking system of education, which, as I've previously discussed, continues, unfortunately, to characterize the dominant pedagogical approach in too many schools and universities.

Many of the students employed rapid, montage style editing and other production techniques specific to music videos and television ads in their media projects, which was considered quite innovative at the time, and this became an important part of my own productions, research, and teaching. (Indeed, this kind of editing was an extremely time-consuming and intensive process, given that we were limited to linear editing systems, and sophisticated edit programs, like "final cut pro" were just a figment of our nerdish imaginations at the time.) It was, however, largely though this practical process that we began to notice and examine the multiple ideological and technical codes and levels being employed in the semiotics of media texts as well as the multiplicity of ways that meaning could be constructed both consciously and unconsciously. Thus, many of the student exercises, which I developed then and continue to employ, involved watching media without the sound, and in contrast, listening only to the audio dimensions of a variety of media forms. These kinds of assignments are especially useful in learning about iconic and symbolic codes, camera techniques, lighting, etc. as well as the integral and significant role of music and sound effects in different film and video genres. This, in turn, leads us to further examine the hierarchical relations and levels of meaning encoded in media texts. For example, we might ask how important was the music and sound track in meta-communicating about, or providing meaning to the iconic text? Such exercises can thus lead to new kinds of more sophisticated questions about the relationship of technical and ideological forms and substantive meaning encoded and decoded in media culture.

In fact, semiotics, which is loosely described as the study of signs, or the social production of meanings by systems of signs—especially those employed in media texts—continues to be an important component of my current classes on media literacy and cultural studies. And although we can only touch upon it within the larger constraints of the quarter system's 10-week course, some of the most exciting classes have involved group semiotic analyses of media and film. For instance, identifying and decoding some of the technical and ideological codes and symbols in relation to cultural meanings, using examples of *film noir*[20] and advertisements for example, have proved revelatory for demonstrating the complexities and multiplicity of meanings both conscious and unconscious encoded in a diversity of media forms. It is within this context that the realities of the existence of what has been called "the grammar" of television make sense in that media includes its own set of technical, symbolic, and ideological codes. Moreover, these kinds of exercises not only make these often hidden and unconscious codes and meanings apparent, but lead to further discussions and debates about the social construction of media—including the political, economic, and ideological or "counter-hegemonic" dimensions of media texts and/or oppositional forms. These often passionate and intense conversations also make evident and demonstrate the active role of viewers and how audiences read, or decode, texts differently. bell hooks makes clear the pedagogical rewards of these kinds of non traditional, insurgent practices. As she puts it:

> I have found that students are much more engaged when they are learning how to think critically and analytically by exploring concrete aspects of their reality, particularly their experience of popular culture…teaching theory, I find that students may understand a particular paradigm in the abstract but are unable to see how to apply it to their lives. Focusing on popular culture has been one of the main ways to bridge the gap. (hooks, 1990: 6)

hooks' advice has continued to serve as a mandate for my pedagogical approach to teaching, which I resumed in the late 1990s after finally completing my Ph.D. dissertation (which I had somehow forgotten to complete), pursuing further scholarly research and relocating to Los Angeles where I gained employment as a part-time lecturer in Women's Studies and later Communications, Sociology, Education and Film & Digital Media, at UCLA.[21]

Although, as part of my course load, I had developed an exciting course for women's studies and communications called "Media: Gender, Race, Class and Sexuality" which employed a critical media/cultural studies approach to the study of media culture, I began to consider the possibilities of teaching a critical media course which incorporated both theory and production, as I had done 10 years earlier. This seemed especially relevant, given the importance of. the computer and technological revolutions which characterize the new millennium, and the kinds of new media which were evolving in conjunction with these escalating new developments. Given the pervasiveness and influence of media culture many schools and universities were ignoring the very real needs of students to become critically media literate and provide them with the necessary practical skills which would empower them to be media producers as well as consumers. Although some schools have been teaching critical media and production courses to their general undergraduate population, UCLA, for instance, continues to largely restrict television, film, and digital computer media production to its film and television schools. Indeed, at most universities, especially in the U.S. it seems as if "there is an elephant in the room" when it comes to addressing these kinds of urgent and relevant needs.[22] I hadn't realized at the time that for the majority of students and educators in the United States critical media literacy "was not an option." As Jeff Share (2009) explains it: "Unlike educators in Canada, Great Britain, and Australia, many in the U.S. are not informed enough about media literacy to even consider it" (37).

For those of you who want to be involved in teaching critical media literacy which incorporates media production, be forewarned that although some universities and colleges have one separate, self-contained instructional media and/or AV center, many have a number of separate media resource centers which are often administrated by different departments, schools, or divisions. In the case of UCLA, most of them appeared to know very little about each other as they were all administered by different divisions, schools, and departments. This came as a real shock for me, as I had been used to working in departments which either had their own resources and or in a centralized audio/visual or instructional media center which could provide all of the production and/or computer resources, as well as technical support. And even though I thought I was especially cognizant of "Murphy's Law"[23] when it came to teaching and doing media production, especially within the university, I have to admit I was not prepared for the multitude of problems associated with the implementation of this course. These kinds of issues are hardly particular to my case but are, unfortunately—as many critical media professors and instructors can attest to—are simply the "nature of the beast."

Moreover, "planned obsolescence is the guiding principle of the new technological industries, and educational institutions are poorly situated to bear the costs of constant replacement and upgrading" (Seiter, 2005: 102). Indeed, I have found that this is one of the major impediments to teaching critical media production to students in the university, and—I have to add—the cause of the frustrations so many of us experience in using computers or media technology in the classroom. It is also hardly surprising that given massive cutbacks in education, researchers have found that "computers drain resources from basic education and require so much attention and maintenance that teachers are distracted from working with students" (Goodman, 2003: 12). Furthermore, for some bizarre reason, many schools and universities assume that most everyone is technically literate, especially teachers and students. Yet as Siva Vaidhy Anathan (2008) asserts:

> As a professor, I am in the constant company of 18–23 year olds. I have taught at both public and private, and I have to report that levels of comfort with, understanding of, and dexterity with digital technology vary greatly within every class. Yet it has not changed in the aggregate in more than 10 years…Every class has a handful of people with amazing skills and a large number who can't deal with computers at all.

She goes on to argue that these kinds of assumptions are also incredibly elitist in that they presume that all students have access to and or experiences with digital technology. In the "olden days," even before the invention of digital technology, the university or college offered technical support, usually in the form of students, who were paid for their services (indeed, this is one of the many jobs I had to support my studies). We knew that even with what we would now perceive as relatively user friendly instructional resources, like VCRS, there would likely be some kind of problem, which would necessitate hands-on assistance. However, in many contemporary universities, including UCLA, technical support staff have been radically downsized. Indeed, although many of the universities continue to fund expensive corporate computer and digital resources, many have decided to cut one of the most indispensable and relatively inexpensive support systems which is mandatory for the effective employment of instructional technology. Investing instead in so-called 'smart classrooms,' and developing costly on-line tutorials have undermined many of the benefits of digital instructional resources, which are deemed no longer necessary. This has become a serious problem at UCLA, especially in relation to my critical production course. Indeed, given the budgetary crisis, it appears that even instructional workshops, taught by student experts will be radically reduced, or cease to exist. That there is a critical need for progressive teaching and expert technical assistance speaks for the future of critical media literacy courses, at all educational levels. Yet, without a progressive approach to pedagogy, which eshews standardized methods and employs digital instructional resources in interactive and democratic manners, new technologies can actually further advance and make more expedient the promotion and maintenance of the banking system of education, which has proven to impede the kinds of critical thinking abilities which contemporary students so desperately require. As, Steven Goodman insists:

> Despite the exaggerated claims that have historically been made about the power of technology in the classroom, it has made a marginal difference to instruction in most schools due to the prevalent teacher-centered pedagogy and 'factory' like institutional structures (2003: 13).

Further, as Jhally and Lewis (2006) so insightfully explain it, we have to distinguish between media literacy, which can tend to celebrate the institutions of commercial media and the emphasis of alternative modes of production which provoke critical thinking and empowerment: "It is sometime assumed, for example, that a practical knowledge of video production on its own will help demystify the world of television, necessarily promoting a more analytical, critical perspective. There is, however, little evidence to support such an assumption. On the contrary, we have found that students are apt to be seduced by the form, to try to imitate commercial television and, when their efforts fall short, to regard the work purely in terms of their aesthetic or technical prowess" (232).

Without doubt, introducing new technologies into the classroom to empower students to produce their own works involves ongoing challenges, as I discovered in organizing my present course. After some effort, I managed to find a few digital 8 and mini-dv cameras from the university's Audio Visual Department as well as from the Educational Technology Unit (ETU) at UCLA's Graduate School of Education and Information Studies. Fortunately, having the course cross-listed with education and women's studies had major benefits in that it allowed me to utilize resources from a number of support centers which would ordinarily be exclusive to those disciplines which fund them. I also discovered an amazing facility called the Instructional Media Production Lab (IMPL), which was part of the Office of Instructional Development (OID), which is not to be confused with the Instructional Media Lab (IML) which houses an incredible film and video library and facility where students can study these media. The IMPL was a godsend and one of the most valuable facilities on campus. Unbelievably, this resource center was a combined lab and classroom directed by a highly experienced educator and producer which provided the students with portable hard-drives (to store video), computer editing systems and a variety of softwares, including professional microphones and soundproof rooms for voice overs and narration. Moreover, it employed student experts to teach and assist the students with web page production and editing programs as well as a diversity of other media production systems. Furthermore it served all undergraduate and graduate students at UCLA (including the film and TV schools!). After many meetings and description of technical assignments, students were taught Dreamweaver for webpage production and Final Cut Pro for editing. The lab could accommodate about 20 students and I scheduled a one-hour lab for each week, plus students could work on their productions in this facility at other times. However, what was bizarre was that the facility did not provide cameras, and these had to be separately booked through AV, although they did eventually take on the responsibilities of checking out cameras. They did however assist the students with basic camera set up and the director personally taught a session on shooting skills.

The three-hour seminar component of the course was taught in the Ed school; however, there were some problems with the playback facilities, at least for me, as the DVD/VCR and monitors were bolted to the ceiling of the room, which made access especially difficult for those of us who are "height challenged." But this was a minor impediment. Later on, the Ed department designed a media "smart" classroom, which I continue to use, although due to various "quirks" in the system it was, initially, a nightmare and required constant technical assistance, which was readily available.

Unfortunately, thanks in large part to Arnold Schwarzenegger's California state educational cutbacks, the Instructional Media Production Center was, to my horror, "disappeared" in 2003. After a series of complex negotiations I did manage, to employ the resources of the Computer Library Instructional Computing Commons (CLICC) in UCLA's College Library for the production labs, although CLICC's mandate was designed to facilitate a multiplicity of computer needs. They did however provide me with computers and laptops, as well as some paid student assistants who were available to advise some of the students on their projects, although they were not allowed to teach the labs. And many of these assistants, provided excellent advice and help in regards to technological problems, when they were available. CLICC did, however, provide regularly scheduled workshops in a variety of areas, which included Dreamweaver (for web page production) I-Movie (a much easier and more user-friendly editing software program) as well as photoshop, to name a few, which were open to all students and faculty. Some of the staff also set up some special tutorial times to meet with students outside of the class.

Given that I lacked familiarity with these programs, having missed the computer transformation in digital editing, I managed to solicit the services of two of the leading technicians, who were employed by ETU (the Educational Technology Unit) to teach Dreamweaver and I-Movie in the CLICC labs, over a three-week period. Needless to say, this was not part of their job description, and they did so, often on their own time and as a favour. These techs were brilliant instructors who had the capacities to clearly explain and demonstrate these programs and designed their labs in a manner which provided the students with the technical expertise they required to successfully complete their projects. Although, a number of people have the expertise in these areas, teaching others how to employ them takes special talents. Unfortunately, one of the techs was no longer available to teach the Dreamweaver lab, but to my amazement I was directed to another media resource center (which I had no idea existed) which served Information Sciences, and due to their affiliation with Education, one of the technicians agreed to take over this class.

Initially, CLICC did not own or provide fire wire (hard drives) on which the productions depended and I somehow convinced OID (the Office of Instructional Development) to loan me theirs. Eventually, CLICC did purchase fire wire drives, although they cannot accommodate all of their production courses simultaneously. Hence, those of us involved in production try to schedule our courses in different quarters. Moreover, this is also the case with the finite number of cameras available through AV. CLICC has also purchased a large number of laptop computers which can be checked out by any UCLA students, and the students in my class can also work in the CLICC labs when they are not being used for other classes. They can also use the computers and work on their productions in the ETU labs (although this is not always feasible given the constant updating of programs, which means that often the different computers in different labs, as well as those owned by students, don't have compatible software).

I later discovered that there were instructional equipment grants available for full time faculty (which like most grants, required very specific information and were quite time consuming to prepare). It was only due to the assistance of staff members of Women's Studies that we were able to complete and submit them. Given that I am a part-time lecturer, the Chair(s) of Women's Studies co-sponsored these applications and I was awarded 3 of these, within a 5-year period, which allowed me to purchase one professional and two inexpensive consumer quality cameras, a desktop computer for women's studies and funding for a Teaching Assistant who has both theoretical and practical experiences and shares in the many complex responsibilities associated with the multiple dimensions involved in this complicated course. AV also replaced its outdated 8 video cameras with similar camcorders which I had purchased through the grant. And Women's Studies independently purchased 2 more camcorders for use in this class. Indeed, the course had become impossible to teach and organize without a Teaching Assistant and is no longer feasible without TA support. Thus, I have been especially fortunate in that they all have been exceptional, and dedicated to the class, its students, and mandate. Moreover, all of these TAs have continued to pursue or complete their graduate degrees as well as be actively involved in alternative and independent media productions. Regrettably, OID rejected my last grant application and it is highly unlikely that they will support any others. However, Women's Studies provided me with part-time TA support for the course last year.

Initially, the Social Science Computing Center (SSC) also provided services to teach student web page production and are largely responsible for assisting me in the design of my course web page as well as streaming all of the student videos for online viewing. Indeed, many of the administrators and resource people in the various technical centers, and staff of the departments which co-sponsor the course have been incredibly supportive of the class and often attend the screenings of the student final presentations.

However, the limited resources do constrain enrollment and also time constraints and access to equipment reduce the amount of original footage the students can produce. Hence, I encourage them to use media to critique media, and many of the videos and web sites employ these kinds of techniques.[24] However, although Women's Studies in particular has committed to on-going support of this course, cutbacks seriously threaten the future of this and other kinds of courses. Indeed, a number of universities are no longer replacing or increasing the kinds of educational resources which provide for interactive, creative and critical student productions. Instead, it appears that many universities are investing in highly expensive technology designed for pod-casting standardized lectures. As Henry Giroux describes it, "The turn toward downsizing and deskilling faculty is also exacerbated by the attempts on the part of many universities to expand upon the profitable market of 'distance education' whose online courses reach thousands of students" (123). Many experts have argued that higher education is being radically restructured "under the imperatives of the new digital technologies and the move into distance education" (ibid.).

I find it astonishing that, given all of the dramas associated with this course and the corporate universities' decisions to cut back on particular kinds of instructional technology, that I have managed to survive and maintain its standards for 8 years. Student feedback indicates that the course has become increasingly popular and the demand increases with each year. While it is difficult to describe all of the complex and multi-leveled dimensions of the course, I believe that its success and importance are best communicated through the student productions themselves. Hence, I am including a link to the course web site which includes the course syllabus, and some of the student projects. http://www.sscnet. ucla.edu/08W/womencm178–1/.

In regards to format, the course has a a three-hour seminar and a one-hour lab each week. Due to the nature of the assignments (especially the counter-hegemonic critical group media production) students spend a large amount of time on the projects. I have, however, only had one person drop out of the course since its tenure, although I do lose a few students after the first class when they hear what is involved and the amount of time it takes to produce a media project. This is even more astounding given that I just recently learned, after consulting with a number of students, that they spend about 80 hours outside of the class, on their productions, and how, when challenged and offered the opportunities to engage in these kinds of creative, oppositional projects, their obsession with grades is suppressed by their pride and passion for learning. Because I believe so strongly in the dialectic of theory and practice, the students are required to do particular readings from the course reader as well as produce a short analytical final paper in which they discuss their group project within the context of critical media literacy. They are asked to incorporate course readings, guest lectures, and films presented in the class. Notions of ideology and hegemony as well as the "politics of representation" in media (which includes dimensions of sexism, racism, classism and homophobia, to name a few) are central concerns. Also the ideas and realities of resistance, social and political change, and agency are emphasized.

The assignments include a camera technique and editing exercise, a basic web page, and a brief storyboard, as well as the final take-home paper and group alternative media project. The three-hour seminar is comprised of short lectures and discussions related to the required readings, guest lectures, and presentations of excerpts from a variety of different genres of media—primarily alternative and usually documentary style. Different genres of films are also discussed and analyzed.

Some of the films and or videos I have shown include excerpts from classic cinéma vérité such as Frederick Wiseman's *High School* (1968) and Albert and David Maysles' *Gimme Shelter (1970)* ; feminist/labor documentaries, which embrace dimensions of oral history, like Barbara Kopple's *Harlan County, USA* (1977) and Julia Reichert, James Klein and Miles Mogulescu's *Union Maids* (1977). I also lecture and discuss the significance of the new cinema or cinéma vérité movement, and how it has influenced more contemporary alternative documentaries and films. Excerpts are presented from some National Film Board of Canada (NFB) documentaries; music videos like the classic Michael Jackson *Thriller* (1982); mockumentaries like Rob Reiner's *This Is Spinal Tap* (1984); Mark Lewis's satirical classic *Cane Toads: An Unnatural History* (1988); and Cheryl Dunye's *The Watermelon Woman (1996)* to name a few. I always include excerpts from a variety of Michael Moore films, Errol Morris television and film productions, as well as a diversity of media from alternative media organizations, such as MEF (Media Education Foundation) and Women Make Movies (WMM, which have included Chyng Sun's remarkable *The Mickey Mouse Conspiracy: Disney, Childhood and Corporate Power* (2001); Sut Jhally's and Jackson Katz's *Tough Guise: Violence, Media and Masculinity* (2001) and, of course, Jean Kilbourne's *Killing Us Softly 3: Advertising's Image of Women* (2001) as well as such independent films as Ngozi Onwurah's *And Still I Rise* (1993), *Slaying the Dragon* (1988) and *The Bronze Screen: 100 Years of the Latino Image in Hollywood Films* (2002) and some of the works of Marlon Riggs (to name a few).

There are approximately 50 films and videos on reserve for the course, which students can watch on campus or online due to the wizardry of the UCLA Instructional Media Library Collections and their video furnace (although they have limited me to 30 for the online portion of the class) as well as present (or invite students to present) student videos from previous courses. In addition, I present some of my own work if there is time and also show some instructional production videos on camera techniques, lighting, sound, and editing. I try to keep up with new cutting-edge works and am constantly updating the films used in the course as well as those I put on reserve. Some of my more recent favorites include Errol Morris's 2008 *Standard Operating Procedure*, about the Abu Ghraib scandal; Jonathan Caouettes' 2004 video *Tarnation* (which was edited entirely on I-Movie and was produced for a total cost of $218.32, incorporating super 8, home videos, photographs, and found images); Mark Achbar, Jennifer Abbot and Joel Bakan's *The Corporation*, (2003) Robert Greenwald's *Outfoxed: Rupert Murdoch's War on Journalism* (2005), as well as excerpts from a number of his *Brave New Films* Productions and Morgan Spurlock's *Supersize Me* (2004), as well as some of his other docs. I try to include a diversity of films which are produced by and present marginalized peoples and their particular standpoints. Needless to say, these films have promoted many provocative discussions.

In particular, I stress the importance of editing and show examples from classic films, like Sam Peckinpah's *The Wild Bunch* (1969), to demonstrate the significance of good editing as well as how editing constructs meaning. In this session are included an example of the effectiveness of clever editing which was posted on the Internet, a subversive edit of George Bush's 2003 State of the Nation address at *http://fuckitall.com.*

Guest speakers and presentations have included a number of the contributors to this book including Jeff Share (UCLA), who has constructed a provocative PowerPoint presentation on media literacy (he is a former student of the class); Douglas Kellner (UCLA) on Emile de Antonio, alternative public access television, and blogging; Leah Lievrouw (UCLA) on alternative and activist New Media. We are incredibly fortunate that a number of progressive film and video makers have agreed to generously share their expertise and offer advice as well as present excerpts from their own works throughout the years, especially given that I can offer them very little, if any, remuneration. These have included Joan Sekler, the co-producer, director, and writer for the award-winning 2002 documentary *Unprecedented: the 2000 Presidential Election,* feminist documentary filmmaker Sara Mora Ivicevich, who is associated with a number of independent media forums, including Women Make Movies, and is also a graduate of this course; Tommy Palotta, independent producer, director, and writer who has worked, in a variety of capacities on such cult classics as *Slacker* (1991); *Waking Life* (2001), and *A Scanner Darkly* (2006). Last quarter multitalented and award-winning major director, producer, writer, actor writer and producer Stuart Gordon presented excerpts from his films, and discussed a diversity of fascinating topics related to commercial and independent media and production techniques, as well as the role of documentary formats in a variety of films.

Since the course incorporates such a multiplicity of areas I put together a reader that organizes critical media/literacy according to four major sections (which was in itself a daunting exercise). Supplemental readings both recommended and required are included on the course website under online readings and are regularly updated. I assign what I believe to be a manageable amount of pages of readings, given the real kinds of time constraints, and what I believe to be often unrealistic volume of readings required for other courses, and number of assignments which characterize most undergraduates' experiences. The total average of required readings for my course is generally 300–350 pages over a 10-week period, and I find that the majority of my students manage to complete most if not all of the required readings as well as a large percentage of the recommended texts. Since the lectures, guest lectures, seminars, discussions, media presentations and technical and production techniques reference the course texts, it is essential that the students be adequately prepared. Due to the nature of the course and multiple dimensions of cultural studies and critical media literacy addressed the course reader is broken down into four interrated sections:

"Foundational Readings" includes key theoretical readings on critical media literacy and cultural studies. The text includes articles by bell hooks, Stuart Hall, Robert McChesney, Douglas Kellner, Zillah Eisenstein as well as some of my own. There are also a number of articles on semiotics, the internet, cyberspace, political economy of media as well as various dimensions of media criticism in this section.

The second section is called "Film/Video Makers: Practical Dimensions" is comprised of articles about cinéma vérité, feminist documentaries, and particularly activist filmmakers such as Emile de Antonio and Frederick Wiseman.

The third section of the reader addresses "Practical/Technical Skills" and contains readings on production techniques.

The Final Section is called "Critical Media Literacies and Cultural Studies: Selected Topics." It is designed to help students in formulating topics for their group productions. It includes articles on a diversity of topics related to media culture, including writings on cyberschooling, music videos, Barbie, Disney, and McDonald's as well as fan and hate sites on the internet.

Student projects have included websites as well as a number of short video montages which interrogate representations of gender, race, and heterosexism in a variety of media forms. They produce different documentary genres which include interviews, narrations and voice-overs (see http://women.ucla.edu/faculty/hammer/cm178/) and use media to critique media and produce their own alternatives. This course provides the opportunity to incorporate a diversity of student "voices" into media production, as well as to apply critical thinking to dominant media forms and contemporary social life. The goal is therefore to empower students and to provoke them to become informed, democratic citizens who can question hegemonic corporate media and society and produce their own alternative cultural forms. This course thus enables students to be active participants in their society and serves the ends of participatory democracy.

Indeed, as Aronowitz argues: "Redefining power democratically entails, at its core, interrogating the concept of 'representation'" (2008: 178). Hence, it is hardly surprising that many of the students choose to present their own standpoints and "voice" in regards to the politics of representation, in their media productions, which often include critiques of dominant institutions, media and ideology. Moreover, the enthusiasm and pride they take in their productions are contagious. And it is within this context that there is a revolutionary shift in student and faculty attitudes, which transform the classroom into a challenging, provocative and entertaining forum. As bell hooks describes it, to take "pleasure in teaching is an act of resistance countering the overwhelming boredom, uninterest, and apathy that so often characterize the way professors and students feel about teaching and learning, about the classroom experience" (1994:10)

Although teaching courses in critical media literacy that involve production can be stressful to say the least, I encourage others to consider teaching courses which incorporate theory and practice and and teaching media literacy through production. From my own experience, it is clear that student appreciation makes teaching critical media literacy through production extremely gratifying. It is also valuable to the students in that experience in media production is becoming a mandatory requirement for many jobs, as well as work in teaching and the community which requires that one be experienced in media production and literacy. Many of the students who have taken my course are presenting their work in classes, conferences and festivals. Some have employed their media productions in their graduate research which further qualifies them for academic positions which increasingly require expertise in new media literacies. Others have successfully pursued careers in both mainstream and alternative media. Thus, critical media literacy courses can assist students in many intellectual and practical ways.

Finally, critical media/cultural studies empowers us to recognize and interrogate the highly persuasive powers of media culture in shaping public opinion and reinforcing dominant ideological values and beliefs. At the same time, an activist media/cultural studies demonstrates the potential of alternative, critical and oppositional media to promote democratization and global social justice.

Notes

1. I would like to especially thank Douglas Kellner and also Loran Marsan for her critical reading of this chapter, as well as the valuable insights she provided in this regard. I'd also like to acknowledge all of her contributions to the critical media literacy course I am discussing later on in this chapter, in her capacities as teaching assistant (and/or associate) for this class.

2. Many would argue that grades have become almost meaningless in that studies reveal that grade inflation is escalating in both private and public institutions (Notebook, 2003). One such report by professors Henry Rosovsky and Mathew Hartley demonstrates that there is no correlation between higher grades, which have now become the norm, and the quality of the student's work, through their analysis of "trends in SAT scores and grade point averages over the last 40 years" (Lee, 2002). Indeed, there was some cause for alarm when 91 percent of Harvard University's class of 2001 graduated with honors" (Roarty, 2004). Linguist chair Stephen Anderson, who has taught at both Yale and Harvard, asserts that: "There was a feeling that everyone who was [at Harvard] deserved an 'A.' It was much more automatic to give people high grades at Harvard" (Lee, 2008). Changing values and attitudes and increasing emphasis on competition and credibility through material commodity products (including high grades and a brand name degree)which underlie our educational system, have created an atmosphere in which "[f]or many students, being average in the classroom is unacceptable. Receiving mostly A's and B's not only have become the norm, but it's become an expectation…(Roarty, 2004).

3. The market logic which has transformed public education into a commercial enterprise has proven incredibly profitable for particular individuals (such as the upper echelons of college and university administrators), as well as a variety of business enterprises, which not only include multiple sites which evaluate faculty and academic institutions, but also a diversity of organizations which "rank" universities. However, it is the so-called "standards movement," which is based on high-stake tests and exams (such as SATs) which has become an exceedingly lucrative business. Ironically, while we are witnessing draconian cut-backs to, and downsizing of, resources necessary to address basic educational standards, and hence a scandalous escalation of illiteracy in the United States, *"there is no shortage of money for private corporations that are making huge profits on school systems. High stakes testing, a form of privatization, transfers huge amounts of public money to publishers, testing organizations, and large consulting companies"* (ibid. 21–22 *emphasis mine).*

4. This is not to say that grades are not important, as they continue to be a key consideration for scholarships and acceptance to graduate programs and professional schools. However, in contemporary corporate culture and a highly competitive job market, the quality of one's education is

determined almost exclusively by one's school's 'credentials,' or "rank" rather than grades. And within an econometric model, where the quality of a credential is measured in "the number of jobs and salaries offered to recent graduates," then Harvard, Yale, and other Ivy League schools are the best. As Stanley Aronowitz explains it: "The credential, rather than the various standards of academic evaluation, thus becomes the crucial criterion of the worth and standing of a university." (Aronowitz, 2000: 58). It is within this context that services like Campus Buddy, which attempt to quantify education in monetary terms, have it completely wrong, for it would be the "diploma" rather than grades which would more accurately personify the salary allegory. Barbara Ehrenreich (2007) has a more specific but prescient explanation of why both the corporate university and the businesses they cater to prefer this vocational training model of education. As she puts it: "My theory is that employers prefer college grads because they see a college degree chiefly as a mark of one's ability to obey and conform. Whatever else you learn in college, you learn to sit still for long periods while appearing to be awake. And whatever else you do in a white collar job, most of the time you'll be sitting and feigning attention. Sitting still for hours on end—whether in library carrels or office cubicles—does not come naturally to humans. It must be learned—although no college has yet been honest enough to offer a degree in seat warming."

5. See, for example, Barbara Ehrenreich's brilliant investigative report and memoir *Nickel and Dimed: On (Not) Getting by in America* in which she describes this horrifying reality within the context of 1998.

6. As Nemko notes: "Perhaps worst of all even those who do manage to graduate too rarely end up in careers that require a college education. So it's not surprising that when you hop into a cab or walk into a restaurant, you're likely to meet workers who spend years and their family's life savings on college, only to end up with a job they could have done as a high school dropout" (Nemko, 2008). Even before the 'great depression' of 2008, for the majority of jobs available to graduates "a liberal arts, business, or administration degree provides no special qualifications which relieve the employer of the obligation to train. Most employers say they want school-leavers to have a degree, be able to read and write, follow oral and written instructions, and be fairly articulate. From their perspective, the B.A. signifies that the candidate can tolerate boredom and knows how to follow rules, probably the most important lesson in postsecondary education" (Aronowitz, 2008:10).

    Moreover, as Barbara Ehrenreich (2007) insightfully notes, there is yet another factor which makes a graduate even more appealing to these kinds of employers: "maybe what attracts employers to college grads is the scent of desperation. Unless your parents are rich and doting, you will walk away from commencement with a debt averaging $20,000 and no health insurance. Employers can safely bet that you will not be a trouble-maker, a whistle-blower or any other form of non-'team-player.' You will do anything. You will grovel." (Ehrenreich, ibid.) In fact, the deleterious consequences of the mounting debt facing so many graduates forces them to reject low-paying but vital professions, like teachers, social workers, journalists, pro bono lawyers, environmentalists, artists, secondary medical professionals and community workers, because they can't earn enough to pay back their loans (Von Hoffman, 2006).

7. Indeed, Aronowitz and others argue that this kind of banking system of education renders invisible the real nature of a neoliberal, corporate system, which is predicated on a "politics of greed," which is fundamentally at odds with a democratic system which finds its basis in the "common good." As he explains it, "the American workplace has virtually no room for dissent and individual or collective initiative not sanctioned by management. The corporate factory, which includes sites of goods and symbolic production alike, is perhaps the nation's most authoritarian institution" (2008: 17). He goes on to argue, as do a number of other experts, that contemporary corporatized schooling is predicated on an ideology of authoritarianism and intimidation. "Children of the working and professional and middle classes are to be molded to the industrial technological imperatives of contemporary society. Students learn science and mathematics not as a discourse of liberation from myth and religious superstition but as a series of algorithms, the master of which is presumed to improve the student's logical capacities, with no aim other than fulfilling academic requirements. In most places the social studies do not emphasize the choices between authoritarian and democratic

forms of social organization, or democratic values, particularly criticism and renewal, but instead are disseminated as bits of information that have little significance for the conduct of life" (ibid: 16).

8. This kind of complacency, which seems to characterize the majority of the citizens of the United States, is especially puzzling, given the active and successful collective challenges to government policies in the past, as was the case with the civil rights and anti-Vietnam War movements in the 1960s and 1970s. Many would argue that the generally defeatist attitudes, of so many of us, in relation to the escalation of criminal and anti-democratic policies and practices, especially since 9/11, and the current collapse of our economic system are provoked, in large part by what Naomi Klein (2007) has described as the rise of disaster capitalism, "the rapid-fire corporate restructuring of societies" engineered by a neo-conservative elite, who made it appear as if "the global free market triumphed democratically" (np). And one of the most ominous consequences of this has been the obliteration of many of our constitutional rights, including the guarantees of a free press. As leading communications and economics scholar and activist Robert McChesney (2001) explains it: "Over the past two decades, as a result of neoliberal deregulation and new communication technologies, the media systems across the world have undergone a startling transformation. There are now fewer and larger companies controlling more and more, and the largest of them are media conglomerates, with vast empires that cover numerous media industries. Hence, "many of our most trenchant critics warn that the most serious threat to democracy is coming from the very press charged with protecting it" as media are "ruled by the agenda-setting power of privately owned media corporations" (Schechter, 2005: 16). Yet, this is an issue which is hardly ever discussed in the media, nor is the collaboration of politicians and political agencies, who are responsible for this kind of corporate concentration. Indeed one of the "core problems of the media system" which has been identified as "inadequate journalism and hypercommercialization" is, in fact, "linked to the commercial structures of the media and how these structures are directly and indirectly linked to explicit government polices" which have been implemented in "the public's name but without the public's consent" (McChesney, 2004: 11).

9. In fact radical increases in government and corporate spending on "technological literacy" in universities are having dire consequences for humanities programs. For example, a 1998 mission statement called "Engaging the Future" at George Mason University in Virginia "calls for increasing investment in information technology and tightening relations between the university and northern Virginia's booming technology industry" (Press and Washburn, 2000). By the end of 1998, the president had "added degree programs in information technology and computer science, poured money into the 125-acre Prince William Campus, whose focus is biosciences, bioinformatics, biotechnology, and computer and information technology, and suggested that all students pass a 'technology literacy' test. Amid the whirlwind of change, however, other areas fared less well. Degree programs in classics, German, Russian and several other humanities departments were cut." (ibid.) Nationwide, funding and support for the humanities, the liberal arts, and the social sciences have been neglected, while there has been an escalating increase in support for information and computing sciences, as well as business and "the hard sciences." And even though there have been mass demonstrations and protests from students from all over the United States opposing the growing corporatization of the university and demanding democratic participatory rights, we rarely hear about this in the mainstream academic or popular media. (see, for example, SDS http://studentsforademocraticsociety.org/home/).

10. See, for example, the fascinating discussions of students on different dimensions of media posted at http://www.youtube.com/watch?v=1GC4QCrp8xs which is part of the exciting project of Professor Mark Auslander's and the Cultural Production Program at Brandeis University's new media channel at http://hk.youtube.com/culturalproduction.

11. As black feminist cultural critic bell hooks so insightfully explains it: "If we were always and only 'resisting spectators,' to borrow a literary phrase, then films would lose their magic. Watching movies would feel more like work than pleasure. Again and again I find myself stressing to students,

to nonacademic readers, that thinking critically about a film does not mean that I have not had pleasure in watching the film" (1996: 4).

12. For an excellent analysis of how "political correctness," or "PC," was used to silence progressive critics of sexism, racism, homophobia, and other forms of prejudice, see Glassner (1999: 9ff.)

13. Patricia Hill Collins describes *ideology* as "a body of ideas reflecting the interests of a particular social group. Racism, sexism, and heterosexism all have ideologies that support social inequality. Ideologies are never static and always have internal contradictions" (2005: 351). And as Bill Nichols so aptly describes it: "Ideology uses the fabrications of images and the processes of representation to persuade us that how things are is how they ought to be and that the place provided for us is the place we ought to have" (1981:1) .

14. The Seiter quotation is drawn from black feminist Audrey Thompson's 1996 article "Not the color purple: Black feminist lessons for educational caring."

15. "Intersectionality" is a notion and theoretical framework which is central to any understanding of the politics of representation. Briefly put, intersectionality is an "analysis claiming that systems of race, economic class, gender, sexuality, ethnicity, nation and age form mutually constructing features of social organization." (Hill Collins, 2005: 351)

16. http://en.wikipedia.org/wiki/Portapak.

17. For an explanation of this form of editing, please see: http://books.google.com/books?id=vIgN0vF sI4cC&pg=PA5&lpg=PA5&dq=video+editing,+grease+pencil&source=bl&ots=BOtTuzb3qj&sig= stsYd_j8xFakztAN2h259uXZkSg&hl=en&sa=X&oi=book_result&resnum=7&ct=result.

18. On the Yippies, see http://en.wikipedia.org/wiki/Yippies.

19. Recent progressive documentaries include the work of Michael Moore; the Media Education Foundation [MEF]; Robert Greenwald's Brave New Films; Women Make Movies; PBS programs like *Frontline* and *Independent Lens,* as well as a wealth of documentaries available on a variety of cable channels and web sites and through mainstream services like Netflicks and even Blockbuster.

20. See http://en.wikipedia.org/wiki/Film_noir.

21. As Stanley Aronowitz (2008) explains it, "The part-timer is typically not a regular member of the tenure-bearing faculty. She is hired on a semester or at best a yearly, basis and except where collective bargaining has provided some continuity of employment, may be discharged at the will of a department chair or other academic officer....Now at a time when only 20 percent of of recent faculty positions are tenure track, the [part-timer, sometimes described as] adjunct has become the bedrock of the curriculum. In some public and private universities and colleges alike, 40–60 percent of courses are taught by part-timers. In turn, since adjunct rates are not prorated to full-time salaries, in order to make a living the part-timer teaches more than a full load, frequently racing from department to department of campus to campus to make a living [if they can find enough work](xv).... In no way would I deny the quality of adjunct teachers or their dedication to the educational enterprise. In the overwhelming majority of instances, finding oneself in the subaltern position of part-time instructor has nothing to with ability or even achievement. Many part-timers are superb teachers, accomplished authors, and skilled mentors. If about 70 percent of those who seek employment as professors are destined for part-time status, their fate is not chiefly their own doing except for the decision to remain in college teaching regardless of the circumstances that reduce them to poorly paid contractors..." (xvi). Needless to say, this varies, as the status and salaries of part-timers are largely dependent upon the strength of their unions (if they have one at all). For example, in Canada, although hardly ideal, part-timers have far greater security and better wages–due in large part to their unions—than most of those of us in the United States.

22. The *New York Times* published an article, by Elizabeth Van Ness, "Is Cinema Studies the New MBA?," May 6, 2005, which addresses the significance of media literacy for contemporary students.

23. Murphy's law is an adage in Western culture that broadly states, "if anything can go wrong, it will." It is also cited as: "If there's more than one possible outcome of a job or task, and one of those

outcomes will result in disaster or an undesirable consequence, then somebody will do it that way"; "Anything that can go wrong, will," the similar "Whatever can go wrong, will go wrong," or, "Whatever can go wrong will go wrong, and at the worst possible time, in the worst possible way." (http://en.wikipedia.org/wiki/Murphy's_law).

24. Unfortunately, many universities in the United States are no longer purchasing media equipment for student or instructional use, usually citing budgetary constraints. Ironically, these constraints have not curtailed the acquisition of highly sophisticated and obscenely expensive media and information technology which allows for the "pod casting" of courses for registered students to access these classes on line. As Aronowitz notes: "If this trend gains momentum, we may witness in our lifetimes an educational regime in which only a tiny minority of students and professors enjoy the luxury of classroom learning while the immense majority earns credentials without seeing a single live professor or conversing in person with fellow students" (2008: 80).

References

AAC&U Board of Directors Statement. Jan. 6, 2006. "Academic Freedom and Educational Responsibility" Association of American Colleges and Universities. Available Online at http://www.aacu.org/About/statements/academic_freedom.cfm. (accessed 7/30/2008)

Aronowitz, Stanley. 2000. *The Knowledge Factory: Dismantling the Corporate University and Creating True Higher Learning*. Boston: Beacon.

Aronowitz, Stanley. 2008. *Against Schooling: Toward An Education That Matters*. Boulder: Paradigm.

Beach, Richard. 2009. "Using Web 2.0 Digital Tools for Collecting, Connecting, Constructing, Responding to, Crating, and Conducting Media Ethnographies of Audience Use of Media Texts" In *Media/Cultural Studies: Critical Approaches*. Edited by Rhonda Hammer and Douglas Kellner. Chapter 12. New York: Peter Lang.

Becker, Jo, Sheryl Gay Stolberg and Stephen Labatan. "White House Philosophy Stoked Mortgage Bonfire. *New York Times,* Dec. 20, 2008. Available at: "http://www.iht.com/articles/2008/12/21/business/21admin.php

Buckingham, David. 2003. *Media Education: Literacy, Learning and Culture*. Cambridge: Polity.

Dines Gail and Jean Humez. 2003. "Part 1: A Cultural Studies Approach to Gender, Race, and Class in Media." In *Gender, Race and Class in Media*. Edited by Gail Dines and Jean Humez. 1–7. Thousand Oaks: Sage.

Downing, John, and Charles Husband. 2005. *Representing Race: Racisms, Ethnicity and the Media*. Sage: London.

Dreyfuss, Robert. Jan.7, 2009. "Hey Obama, Don't Let Afghanistan Be Your Quagmire" *Alternet*. Available at: http://www.alternet.org/module/printversion/117816.

Ehrenreich, Barbara. 2007. "Higher Education Conformity" *AlterNet,* May 2, 2007. http://www.alternet.org/story/51316, Accessed: 1/27/08.

Ewen, Stuart. 1996. *PR! A Social History of Spin*. New York: Basic Books.

Freire, Paulo. 2001. *Pedagogy of the Oppressed*. New York: Continuum.

Fung, Allison. 2008. "Site Reveals Grades By Professors." *Daily Bruin,* Tues., Feb. 12.

Giroux, Henry. 2003. "Kids for Sale: Corporate Culture and the Challenge of Public Schooling" In. *Gender, Race and Class in Media*. Edited by Gail Dines and Jean Humez. 171–175. Thousand Oaks: Sage Publications.

Giroux, Henry. 2007. *The University in Chains*. Boulder: Paradigm.

Giroux, Henry, and Susan Giroux. 2004. *Take Back Higher Education: Race, Youth, and the Crisis of Democracy in the Post-Civil Rights Era*. New York: Palgrave Macmillan.

Giroux, Henry and Susan Giroux. 2008. "Beyond Bailouts: On the Politics of Education After Neoliberalism" *truthout*. Available at: http://www.truthout.org/123108A.

Glassner, Barry. 2003. "Professor Barry Glassner, The Man Who Knows About Fear in American Culture" A BuzzFlash Interview, April 10. Available at http://www.buzzflash.com/interviews/03/04/10_glassner.html (Accessed 6/17/2008).

Glassner, Barry. 1999. *The Culture of Fear.* New York: Basic Books.

Goodman, Steven. 2003. *Teaching Youth Media.* New York: Teachers College Press.

Herman, Edward and Noam Chomsky. 1988. *Manufacturing Consent: The Political Economy of The Mass Media.* New York: Pantheon.

Hill Collins, Patricia. 2005. *Black Sexual Politics: African Americans, Gender, and the New Racism.* New York: Routledge.

Hill Collins, Patricia. 2006. *From Black Power to Hip Hop: Racism, Nationalism, and Feminism.* Philadelphia: Temple University Press.

hooks, bell. 1990. *Yearning: Race, Gender, and Cultural Politics.* Toronto: Between the Lines.

hooks, bell. 1994. *Teaching to Transgress: Education and the Practice of Freedom.* New York: Routledge.

hooks, bell. 1996. *Reel to Real: Race, Sex, and Class at the Movies.* New York: Routledge.

Jhally, Sut, and Jeremy Earp. 2006. "Empowering Literacy: Media Education as a Democratic Imperative." In Sut Jhally's *The Spectacle of Accumulation: Essays in Culture, Media, & Politics.* Pp. 239–267. New York: Peter Lang.

Jhally, Sut, and Justin Lewis. 2006. "The Struggle for Media Literacy." In Sut Jhally, *The Spectacle of Accumulation: Essays in Culture, Media, & Politics.* 225–227. New York: Peter Lang.

Kael, Pauline. 1985. *Hooked.* New York: E.P. Dutton.

Kellner, Douglas. 2005. *Media Spectacle and the Crisis of Democracy.* Boulder: Paradigm.

Kellner, Douglas. 2007. *Guys and Guns Amok: Domestic Terrorism and School Shootings from the Oklahoma City Bombing to the Virginia Tech Massacre.* Boulder: Paradigm.

Kellner, Douglas. 2009. "Toward a Critical Media/Cultural Studies" In *Media/Cultural Studies: Critical Approaches.* Edited by Rhonda Hammer and Douglas Kellner. pp. New York: Lang.

Kellner, Douglas and Jeff Share. 2007. "On Critical Media Literacy, Democracy, and the Reconstruction of Education." In D. Macedo and S. Steinberg, editors. *Media Literacy: A Reader.* pp. 3–23. Peter Lang: New York

Klein, Naomi. 2007. *The Shock Doctrine: The Rise of Disaster Capitalism.* New York: Metropolitan Books.

Kristoff, Kathy. "Students Learn Too Late the Costs of Private Loans." *LA Times,* Dec. 27, 2008

Lee, Brian. (Feb, 2002) "Grade Inflation Debate Extends Beyond Ivies." *Yale Daily News.* Available at: http://www.yaledailynews.com/articles/printarticle/3264.

Lee, Felicia. 2003. "Academic Industrial Complex." *New York Times,* Sept 3. Available at http://query.nytimes.com/gst/fullpage.html?res=9E02E4D81E38F935A3575AC0A9659C8B63 (accessed 7/31/08).

Leistyna, Pepe. 2008. "Teaching About and with Alternative Media." *Radical Teacher,* Spring 2008. Available at http://muse.jhu.edu/journals/radical_teacher/v081/81.11eistyna02.html.

LiAnna, D., 2009. "Bush Administration at Fault for Financial Crisis." *Care2 Action Alerts* [actionalerts@care2.com].

Liddell, Jean and Valerie Fong (2005) "Faculty Perceptions of Plagiarism." *Journal of College and Character.* Available at: http://www.collegevalues.org/articles.cfm?a=1&id=1417.

Liddell, Jean and Valerie Fong. (2007) "Honesty, Integrity and Plagiarism: The Role of Student Values in Prevention." *Plagiary: Cross-Disciplinary Studies in Plagiarism, Fabrication and Falsification, 3 (1).* Available at http://www.plagiary.org/2008/student-values.pdf.

Luke, Carmen. 2009. "As Seen on TV or Was That My Phone? New *Media* Literacy." In *Media/Cultural Studies: Critical Approaches.* Edited by Rhonda Hammer and Douglas Kellner. Chapter 10. New York: Lang.

McLuhan, Marshall. 1965. *Understanding Media: The Extensions of Man.* New York: McGraw-Hill.

McChesney, Robert. Oct. 2001. "Policing the Thinkable" *OpenDemocracy.* Available at: http://www. opendemocracy.net/media-globalmediaownership/article_56.jsp

McChesney, Robert. 2004. *The Problem of the Media: U.S. Communication Politics in the 21ˢᵗ Century.* New York: Monthly Review Press.

Mooney, Nan. Nov.12, 2008. "College Loan Slavery: Student Debt Is Getting Way Out of Hand. Alternet. Available at: http://www.alternet.org/workplace/106445/college_loan_slavery:_student_debt_is_ getting_way_out_of_hand/

Nemko, Marty. May 2, 2008. "America's Most Overrated Product: the Bachelor's Degree." *The Chronicle of Higher Education.* Available at: http://chronicle.com/free/v54/i34/34b01701.htm

Nichols, Bill. 1981. *Ideology and the Image: Social Representation in the Cinema and Other Media.* Bloomington: Indiana University Press.

Notebook. Feb. 2003. "Professor Compiles GPA Database to Confront Grade Inflation." *The Chronicle of Higher Education.* Available at http://chronicle.com/weekly/v49/i23/23a03702.htm

Press, Eyal, and Jennifer Washburn. March 2000. "The Kept University." *The Atlantic Monthly: Digital Edition.* Available at http://www.theatlantic.com/issues/2000/03/press.htm

Roarty, Megan. 2004. "Dumbing Down A's: GW, Universities Rife with Grade Inflation. *The Hatchet.* Available at: http://media.www.gwhatchet.com/media/storage/paper332/news/2004/10/25/Style/ Dumbing.Down.As-779324.shtml

Schechter, Danny. 2005. *The Death of Media and the Fight to Save Democracy.* Hoboken: Melville House Publishing.

Seiter, Ellen. 2005. *The Internet Playground: Children's Access, Entertainment, and Mis-Education.* New York: Peter Lang.

Share, Jeff. 2009. *Media Literacy Is Elementary: Teaching Youth to Critically Read and Create Media.* New York: Peter Lang.

Stiglitz, Joseph. Dec 22, 2008. "The Seven Deadly Deficits: What the Bush Years Really Cost Us" *Mother Jones.* Available at: http://www.motherjones.com/news/feature/2008/11/the-seven-deadly-deficits. html

Vaidhy Anathan, Siva. Sept. 2008. "Generational Myth: Not All Students Are Tech-Savvy" *The Chronicle of Higher Education.* Available at: *http://chronicle.com/weekly/v55/i04/04b00701.htm*

Von Hoffman, Nicololas von. March 13, 2006. "Student Debts, Student Lives" *The Nation.* Available at: http://www.thenation.com/doc/20060327/vonhoffman

Von Hoffman, Nicholas von. June 18, 2007. *The Nation. Available at:* http://www.thenation.com/ doc/20070702/howl

11

■ As Seen on TV or Was That My Phone?

'New' Media Literacy

Carmen Luke

Information literacy, media literacy, technology literacy or computer literacy are current 'must-have' skill repertoires and curriculum components whether in schools or higher education. In a broad sense, these 'new' literacies are tied to issues of globalization, global connectivity enabled by new media, new information and communication technologies (ICTs). The vast banks of knowledge, information and data bases on virtually any topic that are available to anyone, anytime, anywhere—as long as they are connected to a phone line and have the requisite software, memory and power—have pushed educators to recognize the urgent need for critical skills with which to discern misinformation, disinformation, truth from fiction, trustworthy from unauthenticated information (Burbules & Callister, 2000). Most universities include these new info- or techno-literacies in their lists of promised graduate outcomes. Yet they remain conceptually and practically grounded in an instrumental end user rationale rather than a critical analytic approach. For example, at my university, computer literacy consists of the "ability to use computers for information retrieval, processing and presentation to levels comparable with workplace expectations" Most other Australian universities claim to provide similarly vague and generic definitions: the ability to identify, use and critically evaluate information technology including choosing appropriate technology for a task; retrieving information, manipulating data using technology, using technology to present information; to identify, gather, retrieve and operate on textual graphical and numerical information. Melbourne University takes a slightly different, job-oriented, tack by promising "receptiveness to the expanding opportunities of the information revolution."

Such a simplistic utilitarian approach ignores important issues critical to our understanding of and mediated access to knowledge/information sources: the commercialization of search engines that track our searches, pepper our screens with banner ads, pop-ups and pop-unders, dead ends and mouse-traps; increasing privatization and access costs to published research in the wake of corporate mergers and take-overs among a handful of the world's publishing giants. In short, ICT literacy, however defined or taught, has to contend with 'new media,' multimedia *and* convergence, and current drifts toward privatization and commercialization of knowledge which stands in stark contrast to promises only a decade ago of the information revolution as heralding a new dawn in the democratization of knowledge. If anything, universities should be the final frontline in giving the next generation of future community leaders, policy makers, scientists, politicians, researchers, educators, the critical lenses with which to identify and scrutinize, challenge or change the politics embedded in the current knowledge/information revolution. In this paper I argue for an expanded form of media literacy that applies the critical analytic foundation of 'old-style' media literacy to 'new media' in the context of the politics of globalization. I scope a few high profile geopolitical, global media events to illustrate and support the case for a new media literacy that must engage in critical social and cultural analysis of representation and politics of new times.

■ Media literacy

As language, knowledge, communication have become technologised, digitized and globalized, traditional print-based notions of literacy have been the focus of considerable critique and reconceptualization for the last decade (Alvermann, 2002; Burbules & Callister, 2000; Cope & Kalantzis, 2000; Kress, 2003; C. Luke, 2002; Snyder, 2002). Cellphones, personal digital assistants (PDA) or the internet and networked computers are both media and digital technologies that demand new hybrid forms of visual and print literacy, internet and information literacy, technology *and* media literacy. And yet there remains a substantive divide between the long established critical and analytic tradition of media literacy and new comers such as information or computer literacy. For the most part, the scholarly literature on internet, computer, or information literacy in schools has done little more than provide a simplistic pedagogy of front end user skills—a kind of 'how-to' navigation license consisting of skill mastery of the most rudimentary keyboarding, text editing 'cut and paste' and 'save' skills, or the effective use of spreadsheets or web browsers (e.g., Kearsley, 2000). Where a 'critical' information literacy component is present, it usually amounts to little more than calls for students to be able to recognize and utilize a range of data sources (data searching and collection), to incorporate a range of information sources into an assignment or project (design/ production), or—at best—to 'critically evaluate' hypertext documents (critical literacy) (e.g., Grabe & Grabe, 1998a, 1998b). This often means not much more than verifying a web page date of last updating, or noting the number of 'hits' a page has received in a specified time frame. The more hits and the more recent the last updating of a web page, the more we should be able to trust it to be 'authentic,' 'reliable,' and legitimate. How web page design—the strategic use of print, font selection, colors, imagery, sound, graphics, link cartography—shapes a message system, entices target audiences to 'enter' viewer-readers to that shape of a message system—is usually not addressed in information or media literacy instruction. And yet, semiotic and representational decisions, or the central narratives—whether at nasa.com or gap.com—are as much an ideological cultural product governed by established and emergent medium-specific rules and possibilities as any TV program or ad, billboard or movie all of which have long been objects of critical deconstruction.

Media studies, by contrast, has always focused on the critical deconstruction of 'mass' or 'broadcast' media texts such as popular magazines, TV programs and advertising, movies, billboards, and related forms of media representations. The usual analytic focus is on the study of genre, narrative structures, persuasive appeals, medium-specific production features, and semiotic analyses of imagery (Buckingham, 1998; Buckingham & Sefton-Green, 1994; Hart, 1991; A. Luke, 1993; C. Luke, 1997; Lusted, 1991). Media literacy, or 'media studies,' has a long and chequered history. During the late 1970s and 1980s media studies focused heavily on 'critique'—both of texts and the cultures that form around them. A preoccupation with 'ideology critique' assumed that students were 'duped' consumers of mass culture, unable to read 'through' and 'between' the lines. Teachers, on the other hand, were assumed to be able to rescue students from 'naïve readings' by providing students the analytic tool box with which they would produce ideologically correct, and teacher-preferred text meanings and interpretations. In the 1990s, spearheaded by the work of British media studies scholars (e.g., Buckingham & Sefton-Green, 1994; Lusted, 1991) this focus on students' 'self-critique' was abandoned in favor of analysis of the politics of pleasure, and a focus on production (of media texts) rather than a sole focus on critique and deconstruction. Rather than getting students to critique the very texts and images that they like and from which they derive a fair amount of pleasure, this shift toward encouraging students (and teachers) to reflect on what kinds of pleasure people derive from various media forms and texts, enabled a move toward problematizing the 'politics of location,' of differences in 'reading position.' I think this point is often overlooked in current debates about literacy and this generation of digi-kids. That is to say, academic and social commentary tend to be alarmist and disparaging of alleged drops in lexico-grammatical and (online) social conduct standards, instead of coming to terms with forms of creativity and pleasure children derive from working the web, producing web content, text messaging, or even internet or console gaming. Arguably, the textbook or cursive handwriting 'standards' we inherited are a generational legacy, not an ahistorical and universal standard against which to measure and judge new and different—not 'worse'—forms of social connection, literacy, communicative competence.

School based media literacy studies arose in earnest during the 1980s and has its theoretical and analytic roots in neo-Marxist ideology critique through the work of the Birmingham Centre for Critical Cultural Studies. It also has its roots in the media of the day—that is, TV—seen as purveyor of false consciousness, ideological indoctrination and, not least, mindless consumerism. Film study was always an integral component but here the analytic focus was more literary which fit well with the English curriculum. In short, media literacy then and now is strongly associated by teachers, parents, students, teacher educators, with cultural and literary critique, cinema studies, or else the study of popular culture and 'old-style' broadcast media. Social critics and commentators, educators, even the media themselves have long produced a litany of disparaging and dismissive comments about schools or universities wasting time on the 'study of Madonna,' Power Rangers, The Incredibles, Harry Potter or Barbie. Media literacy has received a bad rap. And yet, the critical analytic, deconstructive task of media literacy is based on a strong established theoretical foundation that is sorely lacking in the rhetoric and skills-orientation of the 'new' information or technology literacy. Indeed, it lacks any self-reflective understanding of its historical and cultural place in the history of media and the history of communication.

■ Convergence

In light of the rapid pace toward towards media convergence and the accelerated shift toward electronically mediated communication and social exchange in almost every facet of everyday life, the need for an expanded form of media literacy is more crucial than ever. By media convergence I mean three levels of convergence: (i) convergence of functions—cellphones, for example, now function as messaging device, camera, MP3 player, radio, games console, internet and email portal as well as a phone—(ii) provider convergence which extends beyond bundled services offered by cable, fixed line or mobile phone providers to the new corporate behemoths of print and online scholarly publishing, and (iii) as a consequence of function-device, 'soft'ware-services and provider convergence, a much tighter synergy between previously disparate industries, between knowledge and information, consumerism, popular culture, entertainment, communication, and education. If anything, the sophisticated visual, interface, and multimedia menu on the many screens we activate all day provides a lavish consumer fest where connectivity, knowledge, information, consumption, and pop culture all melt into one common denominator of the market. There are many social, political, and cultural issues at stake in the 'information revolution' including changes in language, communication structures and processes, social relations, and the (re)organization, privatization and access to public knowledge consequent of the shift from print to cybertextuality (C. Luke, 2000), from page to screen (Snyder, 1998), from civil to cyberian society (Lukes, 2000). These are crucial lessons for students—they are about a critical and self-reflexive analysis of the role of ICTs in society, how culture, politics, and social subjects shape and are shaped by technological change.

A critical media literacy relevant to today's users of new media and ICTs can no longer afford to fixate on broadcast media or print text-image analysis (whether genre, narrative or semiotics), but must engage with the politics of representation in ways that move beyond politics as equivalent to analysis of textual or image stereotyping, in- or exclusions, reading paths or positions, media bias, and so forth. The politics of representation has long been one of several curriculum components in any media studies syllabus—alongside the study of 'industries' (political economy of ownership, censorship, etc.), audience, and so forth. The study of representation deconstructs text-image to reveal how youth, gender, age, conflict, family, indigenous groups, news, etc. are represented; which socio-demographic groups are included or excluded; how text-image shapes certain reading paths at the exclusion of others; how consumer desires are textually and semiotically shaped, etc. Politics looks at sociocultural issues of power: how and why text-images serve particular (ruling class and corporate) interests and ideologies.

However, politics *and* representation have taken on a new powerful global role in the last few decades in tandem with, first, the advent, development and broad public access to broadband cable, the internet, and high speed computing; second, the spectre of global media monopoly-mergers (e.g., Newscorp, Viacom, Time-Warner); and, third, the proliferation of global cable TV networks (FOX, SKY, BBC, CNN) that are not only the world's most-watched, and 'defining' news programs (depending on political vantage point), but that follow us on demand to our cellphones, laptops, PDAs, or desktops. In a world of connectivity, there is no escape from the online information deluge—voicemail, email, text or photo or multimedia messages on our phones, PDAs, computers at home, work, or on our laps. Mobile TV service is the current development frontier already trialed in Korea between SK Telecom and Toshiba, Nokia in the US, and fixed line operators Deutsche Telekom, Verizon, and British Telecom are rushing to add TV to telephone and internet access on digital phone lines or fiber optic networks. As *The Economist* put it: "In recent years the mobile phone has become the jack-of-all-trades, the remote control for everyday life, a digital equivalent of the Swiss Army knife" (2005b, p. 56)

High speed computing and the internet have lured millions from newspapers and free-to-air TV to cable and the web. The world was glued to CNN during and after 9/11 and the 2004 Boxing Day tsunami in South Asia, not to national newspapers, newsmagazines or broadcast TV. Although TV remains globally the most powerful advertising medium, more and more consumers "watch cable or satellite channels rather than the main networks;...the web now accounts for $USD 8.7 billion of America's ad spending... mostly at the expense of newspapers and magazines" (Economist, 2005a, p. 53). Clearly, if we are to talk about critical media literacy or media studies, the analytic and pedagogic focus must include, alongside study of traditional established broadcast media and media culture, analysis of a range of 'new' media, among them the multifunction, bluetooth, triband, 175 gram camera, MP3player, soon-to-include TV cellphone. A whole new grammar and literacy—alphabetic, iconic, semiotic, multimedia mixes—have sprung up on cellphones and, as usual with new technologies, kids are leading the way in 'writing/ tapping' the new literacies, let alone in speed texting.

Language change rolls out as fast as communications technologies change (cf. Shortis, 2000) and such collateral effects ought to be part of a critical media literacy. Consider how quickly computing discourse has generated linguistic convergence and functional shifts and infiltrated everyday language use: acronyms (PDF, ftp, www, http, url, html, CD, RAM, ROM, etc.) have taken on the function of nouns, new words emerge (emoticon, hypertext, email, autobot), and old words are imbued with new meanings (boot, browse, button, flame, etc.). Linguistic hybrids reflect a merging of the language of ICT and the book: 'click' or 'scroll' have replaced 'turn the page,' 'bookmark' means to put an electronic marker where there is no 'book'; websites consist of 'documents' or hypertext which consist of paperless 'pp.' What started out as 'electronic mail,' quickly became 'E-mail,' then 'e-mail,' and today, as verb and noun, the hyphen is dropped and we are 'on email,' 'doing email,' or 'emailing.' Reading is undergoing subtle shifts from the exclusively bookish horizontal direction of left to right text chunking to vertical scanning as we scroll and fix on key words. What began as 'smilies' to signify emotional context to text messages has expanded into a much larger acronym based mode of communication initially developed and used in online chat, but now taken-for-granted script on cellphones that force us to write more economically within message character limits. Electronic reading and writing practices are framed within these meaning systems that suggest not only new symbolic languages but also new forms of social interaction and communication (C. Luke, 1996). Parents and educators may lament the alleged erosion of literacy standards, the demise of the subject-verb-object rule, but postmodern textual hyper-reality of life on line *is* the real lifeworld of kids today just as readers, radio, TV or comic books were to previous generations. Just as 'old media' (including 'The Book') shaped a generation's politics, worldviews, literacy, consumer and communications behaviours then, so do 'new media' today shape this and coming generations' understanding of self and other, local and global politics, social and communicative practices.

■ Politics and representation

'Wall to Wall Dallas' (Ang, 1985) speaks of another age—today we are immersed in relentless 24/7 live politics and representation. And while my argument here is not a purist's lament of some golden media age of innocence—which the 1960s, 70s, 80s or even 50s never were—my point is that globalization and new technologies are already and will be the dominant future force of politics. What we know of the world we learn from the innumerable screens that saturate our everyday lives from shopping malls to hospitals and airports, from cellphones in our pockets to our laptops or desktops at home and at work, from buses to planes and trains. Kids are not exempt from this new world and communication order. Post 9–11, kids of all ages and from everywhere flooded newly constructed memorial websites, email, chatrooms, and text messaged their anxieties, fears, words of support and condolence, sent US flag icons or put them on their own websites or screensavers.

To expand briefly on the points I have raised so far, let me revisit some well-trodden territory in order to make a few points about politics, representation, and the politics of representation. Few of us have witnessed first hand the live events of 9/11, the US invasion of Afghanistan or Iraq, or the carnage in Bosnia, Kosovo, the first or second Gulf War. Yet we share the vivid images of cockpit cam vaporization of targets, deserts on fire, close-ups of human pathos and misery, the WTC meltdown, insect-like B52s streaking across the Afghan skies delivering destruction and freedom. Alongside immediate global calls for a global coalition to mount the war on terror, and a near global (i.e., western) emotional response to the 'loss,' the 'attack' on a global icon, a new powerful 'them and us' divide emerged from the layers of media replay, commentary, speculation, investigation which temporarily halted the porous flows and expansive metaphors of globalization. New boundaries emerged around home, homeland, the nation state, freedom-loving people here and 'evil doers' over there. New vocabularies circulated about immigration, borders, others, security, including new visa categorizations for overseas or 'foreign' students. In short, the media—particularly the neocon-friendly cables—immediately seized this new nodal point to construct a public pedagogy of 'the enemy' (the evil doers) and a 'them-us' discourse reminiscent of the Cold War and Vietnam. Images of heroism alongside close-ups of personal grief and loss tied together by the symbolism of the flag blanketed the media and the nation. The dissolutions of old boundaries are the very hallmarks of globalization and 9/11 temporarily reversed the popular mantra that globalization equals the subtle demise of the nation state. Doug Kellner (2002) calls this the "ambiguity of globalization" although I would argue that it isn't all that ambiguous but more of a clear cut 'both/and' contradiction in the classic Hegelian sense; that is, a perpetual tension and dynamics around difference and sameness, heterogeneity and homogeneity.

The educational fallout from 9/11 meant that parents and teachers everywhere had to deal with the impact on kids of the visual shock of endlessly repeated images, as well as the politics behind kids' incomprehension of "why?" Trauma counseling was available immediately in U.S. schools and elsewhere, widely covered by the media. Muslim schools, families, kids and teachers reacted just as quick with strategies to counter a rapidly escalating racism against any visible associations with what might appear as 'Islamic,' 'Arab,' 'Middle Eastern.' In Australia as elsewhere, fire-bombing of mosques, Muslim schools or racist slurs against head-scarf wearing Muslim women accelerated at alarming rates—all duly reported by all media. In short, most of the world witnessed 9/11 and the continuing aftermath on our screens, and yet the politics of a new cultural/religious divide impacted on the everyday lives of millions on both sides of that divide including kids. A critical media literacy that responds to the political economy of a 'new world order,' simply has to begin from acknowledgement of what Held (Held, 2000; Held & Koenig-Archibugi, 2003) calls "overlapping communities of fate"—that is, people's multiple affiliations, new forms and sensibilities of local/national *and* global citizenship. Global media connectivity shapes new kinds of collectivities as much as they incite politics of difference, hierarchy, and exclusion. And these transnational collectivities and differences sit side by side in millions of classrooms around the world. My point is that a truly democratic education for citizenship in new times must provide students with the tools for critical analysis of the politics of the new world order they see on their multiple screens, in which they are growing up and will inherit as adults.

The following examples illustrate three recent (and ongoing) 'events' and political issues that provide a rich text-image base from which to engage students in political analysis of and dialogue about media globalization and new world orders. First, I look briefly at one aspect of the ambiguity of globalization—the public media's tacit collusion with government tactics of silencing public debate, failing in their civic and professional duty to investigate and question governments' political agendas. Next I look at the Abu Ghraib prison scandal in relation to the power of 'alternative media' (i.e., Al-Jazeera), and then turn to discuss at some length the evolving media spectacle of the Boxing Day 2004 tsunami disaster and the politics of aid and consumerism generated in its wake.

Following 9/11, the discourse of fear spearheaded by Bush Inc. and the coalition—including a very vulnerable Australia—was propagated by the cable and network media, as well as thousands of private and commercial internet news sites. The fear factor and sense of urgency enabled the passing of the US Patriot Act with virtually no public debate or input, and no media commentary on the government's muzzle. Even the most basic high school social studies course has taught us that the first principle of a democratic society is press freedom which includes the public media's moral and ethical responsibility to inform, to question, to investigate, to make public any government meddling through media blackouts or off limits coverage. In Australia, we fare no better. The media duly report but do not question or set up studio or community debates about the new vocabularies and immigration policies for asylum seekers, the government's xenophobic and racist position on Australian identity, how our tax dollars are spent on the 'Pacific solution'—shipping asylum seekers into detention camps on remote Pacific islands. We might ask then—and provide the space for our students to ask—what we, 'the west,' are peddling to the world as a shining model of a democratic public sphere, a democratic polity? What is politically silenced and what is privileged by media representations? I have repeatedly argued elsewhere that the baseline of a critical multimedia and multiliteracy pedagogy insists that educators engage students in a critical dialogue with capitalism, globalization, commodity culture, cultural difference and diversity, patriarchy and gender politics, and so forth (e.g., Luke in Cope & Kalantzis, 2000). It's about getting students to look at themselves (identity) and others in self-reflexive and critical ways: how text/image creates preferred and counter 'reading' positions; how it teaches us lessons about others (e.g., the global roll-out of a virulent 'them' and 'us' discourse following the 9/11 terrorist attacks); how we use text/image to position others, represent ourselves, to get things done, etc.

The newsflash about the Abu Ghraib atrocity, the Iraqi prisoners in detention scandal, first broke on the web followed by extensive global media coverage. Many around the world may well have read the details in newspapers or newsmagazines but most of the world received the startling shock and awe images from western TV via the feeds provided by the now globally infamous Al-Jezeera TV station in Qatar—the conduit of communication between Al-Quaeda and the west and, for 35 million viewers, a credible alternative to CNN or BBC (Miles, 2005). Perhaps not surprising in light of the global focus on Middle East politics during the last few years, Al-Jazeera was voted the fifth most influential global brand for 2004 (www.brandchannel.com), topped by Apple (ipod), Google, Ikea, and Starbucks. There is already a long history of the media as principal conduit and global megaphone of radical politics such as the 1970s and 1980s middle east hijackings where all demands for prisoner release or exchange were made exclusively through TV. It is a well established military axiom that the first target in any assault is a nation's communication infrastructure—a media blackout is a powerful political blindfold. There is no question that globalization and new technologies are already and will be the dominant future forces of politics—whether in the form of packaged political candidates or debates, pre- or post-election spectacles, interactive digital voting or opinion polling, natural or military/political disasters.

On a final note, there are other lessons to be learned by looking at the flipside of representations of interventionist politics such as the Afghanistan and Iraq invasions, Kosovo, or 9/11 which were so heavily cloaked in selective representation ('embedded' journalists, moratorium on media images of body bags returning home). Large scale natural disasters such as famine, earthquakes, bush and forest fires, hurricanes, flooding and landslides have long been popular media fare that usually generate national government and global aid support. Let me illustrate and focus on the most recent 2004 Boxing Day tsunami catastrophe in the Indian Ocean which was reported by CNN within the hour, without local feeds, and a reported initial estimated death toll of 2,000. Here, unlike 9/11, politics followed after the event. The magnitude of population loss, geographic scope, and unimaginable images of destruction not seen in living memory captured the world's attention, sympathy and 'good will.' Charts, maps, graphs and death toll statistics alone would not have had the dramatic impact on the world and the subsequent 'tidal wave' of aid dollars without the powerful images captured on people's camcorders   itself testimony to the global electronic consumer whether the 'third world local' or cashed up tourist. A week after 24/7 blanket coverage of what many called an unimaginable disaster of 'epic' or 'biblical' proportions, countries started lining up in the political aid stakes. Links to aid agencies proliferated on commercial and private websites next to warnings of internet aid scams. Aid updates tickered on newsbars and bizbars alongside death, missing and injured updates. Within a week, after the UN chided affluent countries for their paltry contribution, the aid race was on.

On 27 December, one day after the tsunami struck, Australia pledged AUD $10 million (AUD $9m strategically allocated for Indonesia, undoubtedly to soften a longstanding 'frosty' relationship). Two days later, another AUD $25 million was added to the relief package. By January 5th, the Prime Minister announced an additional AUD $1 billion over five years, positioning Australia as the world's largest donor. As the magnitude of the devastation rolled across the world's TV screens alongside daily increases in body count deaths, missing, and injured, the aid dollar trickle turned into a torrent. Under the guise of humanitarian generosity, political cache accrued exponentially especially among western countries that saw political capital in reaching out to the world's largest Muslim nation state. In the context of Australia's geographic proximity to the affected region and virtual next-door neighbor to Indonesia, our socio-demographic profile as the only 'Anglo-Saxon' nation in this region and this latitude with a largely unprotected border, a small population of 20 million rolling in relative economic affluence, coupled with our trade relationship with Indonesia (which importantly includes education), the residual tension over East Timor, asylum seeker flows which originate in Indonesia, the harsh lesson of the Bali and embassy bombings in Jakarta—all factor into a political and economic mix that, arguably, accounts for Australia's top spot on the global aid scorecard.

Strategically and economically these countries were undoubtedly of little interest to most, especially western, donor countries and most people probably had no idea where the Thai west coast, Sri Lanka, or the northern tip of Sumatra are until TV screened regional maps on which to pinpoint Aceh, Phuket or the Adamans. As with 9/11 this was a monumental event without precedent—or visual record—in living memory. Tens of thousands of 'eye witnesses' perished, yet billions around the world have been moved by global media coverage of survivors' camcorder clips to mobilize aid. Young kids are lining up with their parents at impromptu aid agency donor stands in cities and markets to donate their bit of piggy-bank or pocket money savings. The politics of representation, in this case as with 9/11, clearly reach down to the preschool set. Expanding the media loop, celebrity telethons and music benefit concerts were organized on short notice, televised nationally and generating record breaking audiences and donations. In Australia 'Wave Aid' went live at the Sydney Opera House two weeks after Boxing Day, raised AUD $15 million, is now available on CD, and gets consistent airplay on radio and cable music channels. Melbourne hosted a tsunami relief cricket match on 10th January which was watched by a billion viewers in 122 countries and raised $14 million. Within weeks, the rest of the cricket world in the Commonwealth was organizing similar benefit matches scheduled throughout 2005.

I have elaborated a few recent events, and the tsunami disaster in particular, to highlight the synergy between politics and media representation, and to point to relevant and current examples with which to engage students in analysis of capitalism, globalization, politics, and representation: how flows of images and capital converge and meld on global mediascapes and financescapes. That is, how we are collectively as nations represented by government action (donor hierarchies), how media representations can shape our individual actions (from donations to consumerism), how media function as public pedagogies, teaching us geography lessons about places, oceanography dynamics or islands (e.g., Nias) we never knew existed, about the politics of global aid predicated on the predatory affluence and show-case 'generosity' of the west to the rest. These are important political lessons for students about the role, content, and politics of 'new' and 'old' media in a globalized media(ted) world.

■ Concluding comments

We participate in local events half a world away through our connections to online, cabled, wired or wireless media that mediate content and our response—kids can donate at the Red Cross, we can buy the aid benefit CD, we can organize a donation campaign in our schools or put together lessons on 'tsunami' which teachers around the world prepared for the start of the school year in January. The magnitude and complexity of the disaster dovetail into almost every content area from geography, science, politics and social studies, to maths, media and language studies. The word 'tsunami' literally washed over the global media within hours and has since become a new word in the vocabulary of millions. The Global Language Monitor tracks words in the global print and electronic media and internet, and its web headline in the first week of January 2005 read: "Tsunami cascades in worldwide media: South Asian tragedy featured in over 20,500,000 media appearances"—a 700% increase over any typical previous year. They note that "there were some 88,000 stories involving the tsunami since December 26th, compared to 15,000 stories mentioning the word tsunami over the prior two years." The term *ground zero* has a similar history of global media diffusion and uptakes, its transition from being used principally as a business cliché to its current popular meaning as epicenter of destruction treated as sacred ground. GLM observes that, "in the same manner, we envision that the word tsunami will be the subject of considerable discretion before being used in anything other than a most serious manner." (http://www.languagemonitor.com/wst_page19.html)

Since so much of students' entertainment, leisure, school or university work is today conducted online, political engagement with media culture and content, broadly defined, is non-negotiable in any educational agenda that claims a truly critical and democratic education for citizenship in new times where all our everyday affairs and 'life politics' are connected to local and global events, politics, and re-presentations. Educators cannot afford to carry on with business as usual, hammering away at content without attending to the media and politics of representation that also channel content to students, and make up the background media(ted) life world that informs students' engagement with their world. Rather, educators "need to take account of emerging synergies among cultural formations and practices, new technological initiatives, and emerging populations and markets" (Green, Reid, & Bigum, 1998, p. 22).

In light of the issues I have raised about literacy, new media convergence and proliferation, the undoubtedly irreversible commercialization of the internet and public knowledge goods, the homogenization, differentiation, and contradictions of emergent (geo) politics of representation, and the increasing amount of classroom and leisure time spent on-line, we need now more than ever a strong critical literacy component structured across the curriculum and grade levels. Beyond school, so much of everyday life has already migrated on-line. Clearly educators have a responsibility to teach this and subsequent generations to ask the critical questions of the politics, form and content that mirror the world back to us from our multiple screens. Media of communication, sociality, and information are today and will invariably become more central in all our lives. Students have a right to be equipped with evolving meta-analytic skills with which to consider what they are taught and how they are being positioned and taught by media's public pedagogies, how their consumer-learner identity is crafted, what their consumer and information choices are, how pathways to and the form and content of knowledge are shaped by commercial interests, how *they* are reshaping literacy into new lexico-semiotic grammars, and how connectivity is transforming all our identities into a much more cosmopolitan experience of global citizenship. In that regard, I would argue that we cannot look at literacy, pedagogy, or curriculum independent of issues around the politics of globalization, the rapid metamorphoses of new media and the staying power and hybridization of old media. What this requires is a critical social and cultural literacy—a cultural analysis of the politics of new times.

* Reprinted from Carmen Luke's "As Seen on TV or Was That My Phone?" in *Policy Futures* 5 (1) 2007.

References

Alvermann, D. (Ed.). (2002). *Adolescents and literacies in a digital world.* New York: Peter Lang.

Ang, I. (1985). *Watching Dallas: Soap opera and the melodramatic imagination.* New York: Methuen.

Buckingham, D. (Ed.). (1998). *Teaching Popular Culture.* London: University College London Press.

Buckingham, D., & Sefton-Green, J. (Eds.). (1994). *Cultural studies goes to school.* London: Taylor & Francis.

Burbules, N., & Callister, T. (2000). *Watch IT: The risky promises and promising risks of new information technologies in education.* Boulder, CO: Westview Press.

Cope, B., & Kalantzis, M. (Eds.). (2000). *Multiliteracies: Literacy learning and the design of social futures.* Melbourne: Macmillan.

Economist, T. (2005a, Jan. 1–7, 2005). Back on the up. *The Economist.*

Economist, T. (2005b, January 15–21). TV on your phone. *The Economist,* 56.

Grabe, M., & Grabe, C. (1998a). *Integrating technology for meaningful learning.* New York: Houghton Mifflin.

Grabe, M., & Grabe, C. (1998b). *Learning with Internet tools: A primer.* Boston: Houghton Mifflin Co.

Green, B., Reid, J., & Bigum, C. (1998). Teaching the Nintendo generation? Children, computer culture and popoular technologies. In S. Howard (Ed.), *Wired-up: Young people and the electronic media.* London: UCL Press.

Hart, D. (1991). *Understanding the media: A practical guide.* London/New York: Routledge.

Held, D. (2000). Regulating globalization? In D. Held & A. McGrew (Eds.), *The global transformations reader* (pp. 405–419). Cambridge, UK: Polity.

Held, D., & Koenig-Archibugi, M. (2003). *Taming globalization: Frontiers of governance.* Cambridge, UK: Polity.

Kearsley, G. (2000). *Online education: Learning and teaching in cyberspace.* Belmont, CA: Wadsworth Thompson Learning.

Kellner, D. (2002). Technological revolution, multiple literacies, and the restucturing of education. In I. Snyder (Ed.), *Silicon literacies* (pp. 154–170). London/New York: Routledge.

Kress, G. (2003). *Literacy in the new media age.* London/New York: Routledge.

Luke, A. (1993). Social construction of literacy. In L. Unsworth (Ed.), *Literacy learning and teaching language as social practice in the primary school.* Melbourne: Macmillan Education Australia.

Luke, C. (1996). ekstasis@cyberia. *Discourse, 17*(2), 187–208.

Luke, C. (1997). Media literacy and cultural studies. In S. Muspratt, A. Luke & P. Freebody (Eds.), *Constucting critical literacies* (pp. 19–50). New York: Hampton Press.

Luke, C. (2000). Cyber-schooling and technological change: Multiliteracies for new times. In B. Cope & M. Kalantzis (Eds.), *Multiliteracies: Literacy learning and the design of social futures* (pp. 69–91). Melbourne: Macmillan.

Luke, C. (2002). Re-crafting media and ICT literacies. In D. Alvermann (Ed.), *Adolescents and literacies in a digital world.* (pp. 132–146). New York: Peter Lang.

Lukes, T. (2000). Governance. In T. Swiss (Ed.), *Unspun* (pp. 73–87). New York: New York University Press.

Lusted, D. (1991). *The media studies book: A guide for teachers.* New York: Routledge.

Miles, H. (2005). *Al-Jazeera: How Arab TV news challenged the world.* London: Abacus.

Shortis, T. (2000). *The language of ICT.* New York/London: Routledge.

Snyder, I. (1998). *Page to screen—Taking literacy into the electronic era.* London: Routledge.

Snyder, I. (Ed.). (2002). *Silicon literacies: Communication, innovation and education in the electronic age.* London/New York: Routledge.

12

■ Digital Tools for Collecting, Connecting, Constructing, Responding to, Creating, and Conducting Media Ethnographies of Audience Use of Media Texts

Richard Beach

Picture Jill, a high school senior, multitasking with different digital media in her bedroom. With music playing in the background, she is listening to a podcast of a lecture from her history class on her iPod as she views the latest YouTube videos. She then switches over to Facebook, seeking help on an assignment from others in her media studies class, as well as setting up a time to meet with friends on Friday night.

As documented on the Public Broadcasting Service Frontline documentary *Kids Online* (www.pbs.org/wgbh/pp/frontline/kidsonline), Jill is immersed in a world mediated by digital media. And she is not alone. A January 2007, report by the Pew Internet and American Life Project (Lenhart & Madden, 2007) found that more than half (55%) of all adolescents aged twelve to seventeen who are online use social networking sites such as MySpace and Facebook; 48% visit these sites daily or more often; 70% of girls aged fifteen to seventeen have created profiles. An August 2007, study reported that an even higher percentage, 96% of adolescents, use social networking sites (National School Boards Association, 2007). And, about half of all online users over 18 have visited a video-sharing site such as YouTube (Rainie, 2008). Further, a December 2007 report found that 64% of online adolescents create some form of online content (Lenhart, Madden, Macgill, & Smith, 2007).

This use of online media is enhanced by the mobility of digital media tools, which allows adolescents to listen, view, and create media according to their own time schedule. Moreover, given the multiplicity of available media, multitasking could be viewed as what Lee Rainie (2008) refers to as "continuous partial attention" (p. 12) driven by the need to continually select incoming media that is the most engaging or useful in terms of their own social agendas.

dana boyd (2007) argues that adolescents find online social networking to be an appealing alternative to their highly regulated lives in school and at home, as well as a public arena that fosters identity construction, given their need:

> to be situated within the social world they see, and then attempt to garner the reactions to their performances that match their vision...By allowing us to have a collective experience with people who are both like and unlike us, public life validates the reality that we are experiencing...Social network sites have complicated our lives because they have made this rapid shift in public life very visible. Perhaps instead of trying to stop them or regulate usage, we should learn from what teens are experiencing. They are learning to navigate networked publics; it is in our better interest to figure out how to help them (p. 138).

These online public spaces function as what Konrad Glogowski (2006) describes as "third spaces" similar to restaurants, bars, parks, malls, or even deviant "carnival" worlds where people interact in public differently than in "first space" home and "second space" work and school spaces. In these "third spaces," students can experiment with adopting different identities and stances through creating profiles on social networking sites or creating and responding to digital videos on sites such as YouTube, Ourmedia, UnCut, and ClipShack (for descriptions of 150 digital video sites: mashable.com/2007/06/27/video-toolbox/).

■ Web 2.0 Digital Media

So what does this participation in online media have to do with critical media literacy? In the past, studying media primarily involved analyzing cinematic techniques or ideological representations in films or television programs in terms of journalism practices and political biases in newspapers or magazines, or the manipulative techniques of advertising and branding. With the rise of new "read-write" Web 2.0 digital media—blogs, social networking sites, podcasts, online virtual worlds—everything has changed (Richardson, 2006). Rather than being the passive recipients of media, audiences are now assuming an active role, responding to and producing media, and this plays a central role in their social identity construction.

Web 2.0 digital media involve users as active participants and even contributors of Web-based media texts. As described in Michael Wesch's YouTube screen cast "The Machine is Us/ing Us" (youtube.com/watch?v=NLlGopyXT_g), Web 2.0 audiences are constructing their own online blogs, Web sites, videos, or wikis for general consumption. Users can now create their own television "channels" by downloading their videos to OneTrueMedia.com, adding a musical soundtrack, getting a password, and sharing that password with TiVo owners who can watch the videos on the creator's TiVo "channel" (Pogue, 2007) (for links to information about Web 2.0 theory: digitalwriting.pbwiki.com/Web2Theory).

The advent of Web 2.0 digital media has served to "re-mediate" traditional television, radio, and print media (Bolter & Grusin, 2000) by giving audiences more control over how and when they consume media. Audiences can now watch television or listen to the radio according to their own schedules, with thousands of options available. To respond to these shifts, traditional media are using Web 2.0 tools to engage audiences interactively. Television networks are producing online "webumentaries" and fan sites to accompany their drama programs to foster audience participation. After broadcasts of the CBS show *Jericho,* audiences were able to view short documentaries online that included interviews about topics such as radiation or disaster preparation portrayed on the show (Gold, 2007). The teen soap opera program *Gossip Girl* is broadcast online and audiences can also chat with their peers about the show (Gold, 2008).

Moreover, users do not have to seek out media texts. Rather, by using RSS feeds that trap information according to automatic keyword searches or "tags," users automatically receive the media texts they want (Calishain, 2006). This has served to create a vast virtual network of users with a "collective intelligence, turning the Web into a kind of global brain, the blogosphere is the equivalent of constant mental chatter in the forebrain, the voice we hear in all of our heads" (O'Reilly, 2005, p. 2).

All of this has created what Henry Jenkins (2006, p. 3) describes as a "participatory culture" in which students are not simply responding to media, but also creating media through active use of various digital literacies (Black, 2005) that engage students through social participation. As Jeff Utecht (2006) notes:

> Morning after morning my middle school students come in and head to one Web site…YouTube. YouTube is the new entertainment center for teens, and I don't blame them. Spend some time there and you soon find the minutes flying by as you get deeper into viewing what people have created and contributed to this social network….
>
> Watching this day after day, I decided to harness this power of creativity and have my students create digital stories. Using the free Microsoft application Photo Story 3 and the tutorials created by David Jakes, my students taught themselves how to use the program to create their stories for class. Then using the K–12 group within YouTube that Miguel Guhlin created, the students uploaded the videos to share with a worldly audience. Students as creators contributing their new knowledge to the world (p. 1).

■ Features Of Web 2.0 Digital Texts

Responding to and producing these Web 2.0 digital texts involves use of them following features.

Multimodality

Web 2.0 tools foster creation of multimodal texts that draw on and combine different media—images, audio, music, and text—to communicate ideas and engage audiences through visual rhetoric (Kress, 2003; Wysocki, 2004). By responding to and creating multimodal media texts, students focus on how best to combine texts, images, audio, and/or video designed to craft a visual argument in which "the visual elements [that] overlie, accentuate, render vivid and immediate, and otherwise elevate in forcefulness a reason or set of reasons offered for modifying a belief, an attitude or one's conduct" (Blair, 2004, p. 50). Students therefore benefit from instruction related to digital design, layout, and use of navigation links associated with framing visual arguments. At Stanford University, students are now required to take a second composition course that focuses on multimodal digital presentation and delivery of their writing (Lunsford, 2006). Their first assignment requires them to translate a brief text from one presentation form to another (e.g., a print text to a blog), analyze the different rhetorical strategies used in these different forms, and present their analysis to their class. Their next assignment requires the creation of a multimodal argument involving extensive writing and collaboration and a presentation in several media. For their final assignment, students reflect on their writing in the course in terms of how the use of different media influenced their writing.

Hypertextuality

Web 2.0 tools also involve the use of hypertextual links to other Web sites, blog posts, videos, pdfs, or, in hypertext literature, links to optional narrative paths in a digital story, and so on (Samuels, 2005). In navigating and creating hyperlinks, students need to consider their own or their audiences' need for relevant information and clear navigation cues based on a "rhetoric of expectations and arrivals" (Bolter and Grusin, 1998, p. 10) so that audiences know where certain links may take them and how they should respond when they arrive at certain destinations. Hypertextuality affords endless possibilities for making connections with the vast network of the Web, connections that foster student thinking about the relationships between interrelated texts.

Interactivity

Another feature of Web 2.0 tools involves interactivity with audiences as active participants with and contributors to digital texts (Kress, 2003). For example, successful blogs employ comments, syndication, blogrolls, and "pingbacks" to involve audiences in social conversations through blogging (Du & Wagnera, 2006). Media or music fan sites create forums for audiences to share responses to media or music. Because audiences are contributing content, they then perceive themselves as active members of a particular online community.

■ Using Web 2.0 Tools to Study and Construct Media Texts

The development of Web 2.0 tools has led to media literacy that involves responding to and constructing new media texts through the use of multimodality, hypertextuality, and interactivity. This chapter describes five media literacies afforded by the use of Web 2.0 tools: collecting, connecting, constructing responses to, creating, and conducting media ethnographies of audience use of digital media texts. For further information on each of these topics, links are provided to relevant sections from two resource sites (Beach, 2007): teachingmedialiteracy.com and digitalwriting.pbwiki.com (Beach, Anson, Breuch, & Swiss, 2008), as well as a media literacy wikibook (teachingmedialiteracy.pbwiki.com).

Collecting Media Texts

For studying and constructing media texts, students need to know how to collect texts by searching for relevant information, images, video clips, print texts, or ideas. For non-copyrighted images, students can use Flickr (www.flickr.com), Google Images (images.google.com), Picasa (picasa.google.com), or Shutterfly (www.shutterfly.com) to store, search, organize, and share images. They can also find video clips at YouTube, CurrentTV, Veoh, BlipTV, Jaman, CinemaNow, Joost, GreenCine, Amazon, NetFlix, BitTorrent.com, iTunes, Xbox Live, National Geographic Channel video, or Unitedstreaming, a commercial distributor of some 40,000 clips. (About 1,000 of the Discovery Education Streaming videos are "royalty-free," which means that teachers can splice and edit them for their own use.) The Library of Congress mounts online exhibits such as the American Memory exhibit (memory.loc.gov/ammem/index.html) and Cartoon America (www.loc.gov/exhibits/cartoonamerica). The Association of Public Television Stations is also working on an "American Archive" project that is designed to make public television video available for students in classrooms.

Students also need to know how to employ search tools to find relevant information on topics related to media or to collect media texts. Rather than relying simply on Google or Yahoo, students need to know how to employ specific kinds of search tools to obtain certain kinds of information. The following is a list of resources for various specific content:

- ❑ Scholarly material: Librarians' Internet Index, Blackboard Scholar, Virtual LRC, ResourceShelf, Google Scholar, INFOMINE, Academic Search Premiere, LexisNexis
- ❑ Current news: Google News, NewsNow, Yahoo News, CNN News, MSNBC, World News Network, FindArticles, Feedster, Syndic8, NewsisFree, or subject indexes such as RSS or RSS Network
- ❑ Opinions on current issues: Yahoo News, HeadlineSpot Opinion/Editorials, PollingReport, Social Issues, Public Agenda

❑ Blogs: Google Blog Search, Technorati, Blogdigger, Bloglines, Del.icio.us, Feedster, IceRocket, Sphere
❑ Podcasts: Yahoo! Podcasts, Odeo, iTunes, Internet Archive, or Juice
❑ Online research communities: Carmun, Conntea, or PennTags

Students can also conduct their own automatic searches so that the computer is collecting data through RSS feeds, which Tara Calishain (2006) describes as "information trapping." By "trapping" information in advance, students receive the information they need without having to continually conduct separate searches. As suggested by the notion of "feeds," users are fed relevant information or images from sites or blogs based on topics or keywords that are addressed in their writing.

When students go to a site or blog, they can subscribe to receive feeds by subscribing to "feed readers" such as Bloglines, Google Reader, RSSReader, SharpReader, My Yahoo, Newsburst, NetNewsWire (for Mac) or NewzCrawler (for PC). These tools keep track of various sites and blogs and send feeds to the student's computer (Holzner, 2006). To collect texts, students should use "tags" as key terms to categorize specific sites, blog posts, or images and video clips. For example, on the popular tagging site Flickr, students tag photos based on perceived similarities in what is portrayed in the images, leading users to apply "folksonomies" or categories they have found useful to label different images. Once they have developed a collection, they can search their own collections and those created by other users by keyword or date. They can also label other users' images using their own labels, as well as visit the most popular tag categories. (For further resources related to collecting media texts, see http://digitalwriting.pbwiki.com/GeneratingInformation).

Connecting Media Texts

Once students collect media texts, they can then define connections between those texts based on shared topics, themes, or issues common to them. Jody Shipka (2005) cites the example of a student, Maggie, collecting material for a hometown history project, which involved collecting various kinds of data from classmates, researching hometown Web sites, scripting "live" news reports, traveling to hometown locations, filming the reports, and putting her report on the Web (p. 286). In this project, Maggie defined connections between these materials in ways that portrayed the culture of her hometown.

Defining connections between texts leads students to perceive patterns that serve as the basis for critical analysis of media representations. For example, in his classes for preservice English teachers, James Trier (2007a; 2007b) has his students collect YouTube clips to analyze their messages. In studying the topic of cultural jamming, which is the parodying of popular media, students located videos that represented examples such as a video of McDonald's billboards on which the words "Double Cheeseburger" had been changed to "Double Bypass" (p. 411).

Trier's students searched YouTube videos according to keywords to create playlists and then critiqued the themes or ideas portrayed. He modeled the process for his students:

> While thinking about a seminar focusing on racist representations constructed in media texts I happened upon a racist cartoon with the YouTube title *Banned Cartoons You're a Sap Mr. Jap,* which is a Popeye cartoon shown during World War II. Subsequent searching with the tag phrase "banned cartoons" led to dozens more of these racist cartoons, and I created a playlist of videos to use during class. The cartoons not only provide a visual–aural representation to critique, but also many of them are accompanied by viewer comments, and arguments typically emerge among viewers about whether the cartoons are really racist (p. 601).

Once students create YouTube playlists, teachers can assign papers based on analysis of specific topics, themes, or keywords that include links to videos on their playlists. Students can also organize collections of digital texts found through search engines based on certain themes, topics, or concepts. For example, Jeff Rice (2004) asked students to create a "handbook of cool" based on images of dress, behavior, artifacts, consumer goods, as well as texts from the 1950s to the present as a way of encouraging them to examine different cultural attitudes towards what has been considered "cool" in different decades.

Students can also envision themselves as curators creating exhibits based on collections of media texts. Geoff Sirc (2004) cites the example of creating an "arcades project" about different aspects of hip-hop culture. His students begin by searching academic databases and sites related to the topic of hip-hop and rap. Students then take notes on the material they find. Sirc responds to these notes by posing inquiry questions about their topic or suggesting other links and resources. Then, by examining how museums present their physical and digital exhibits, students mount their own arcades project. Sirc encourages his students to continually reflect on how their connections between texts serve as:

> a vehicle of reverie, an object that would enrich the imagination of the viewer. The model of college writing, then, becomes the contemporary DVD—a compendium of "finished" text, commentary, selected features, interviews, alternative versions, sections initially deleted…our new classroom genre might best be called a diary journal, repository laboratory, picture gallery, museum, sanctuary, observatory, key…inviting us to see things in a light in which we do not know them, but which turns out to be almost that one in which we have hoped one day to see them bathed (p. 146).

Using Connections to Analyze Media Representations

Students could also define connections between media texts in terms of media representations of certain phenomena or topics, representations that are often part of how children and adolescents are socialized as consumers (Montgomery, 2007) (for supplementary videos and teaching resources on media representations, see the Education Media Foundation Web site, www.mediaed.org).

To study these representations in my media studies classes, I have students work in small groups to collect images to create collages using magazine ads or online images based on a specific topic: masculinities, femininities, race, class, urban/suburban/rural worlds, school, vacations, and so on. They then put these images on a poster board, online slideshow, PowerPoint, blog, wiki, or iMovie, and add comments or categories describing underlying patterns or oppositions. They also use VoiceThread.com to add audio voice-over or text commentary to image slideshows. Students can also create digital documentaries. (For examples of such documentaries developed by students in Bettina Fabos's journalism class at Miami University of Ohio, see www.centerforsocialmedia.org/videos/sets/critical_media.)

In analyzing these representations, students ask the following questions: "Where do these representations come from?" "Who produces these representations?" "Why are they producing these representations?" "How is complexity limited by these representations?" and "What is missing or how is it silenced in these representations?" (Hall, 1997). Posing these questions can lead to a critique of how media corporations have the power to frame and promote their agendas through socializing audiences around commodity values (Kellner & Share, 2007). As Prior et al. (2007) have noted:

> think of Disney, which is populating our world with t-shirts, stuffed animals, pajamas, coffee cups, TV shows, films, DVDs and CDs, mall stores, theme parks, books, and so on. When Disney wants to promote the next Britney Spears or the next *Lion King,* they do not have to make an isolated argument for a single product. They are working in a world populated with Disney artifacts that naturalize Disney, that incline people to attend favorably to whatever Disney offers next (p. 24).

To model this process for my students, I share examples of media representations of teachers in Hollywood films found on YouTube, noting that teachers are often portrayed in ways that deviate from traditional pedagogical methods. For example, in *School of Rock,* the Jack Black character draws on rock music to engage students. In the film *History Boys,* a gay history teacher builds personal relationships with his private school students to motivate them to learn. One student in the class analyzed representations of homelessness in the media, noting that the media often portray the homeless as drug addicts, panhandlers, or "beggars" living on the streets in urban areas. Another student examined the portrayals of sisters in media, poetry, and literature. She found that sisters were portrayed in a binary way, either as "best friends," as evidenced in Barbie-doll sisters, or as "enemies," with little alternative variation, such as the student's relationship with her own sisters. Another student, who examined clips of representations of feminists, found that feminists are portrayed as "loud," as evidenced in a comedy sketch, as "working against the institution of the family," and as "unpopular," given that people "don't believe that feminism is good or necessary."

Students were asked to critique media representations using the following topics and guidelines.

Gender. Students could analyze how females are frequently represented in terms of their femininity and sexuality—as being married, or as mothers, or as sex objects. For example, female athletes are often described in terms of their appearance or relationships, while male athletes are represented more in terms of their physical strength and skills. Females are also represented as consumers, particularly in terms of consuming products associated with domestic roles such as homemaker, cook, and cleaner. And, females are represented according to idealized images of feminine beauty that objectify women in ways that deny their unique qualities (Wysocki, 2004).

Students in Rhonda Hammer's Critical Media Literacy and the Politics of Gender: Theory and Practice course at UCLA create final projects related to representations of females in the media (www.sscnet.ucla.edu/07W/womencm178–1/studentprojects2007. php). For example, one project, "Commodifying Lolita: The Hypersexualization of 'Tweens' in America," portrays the influence of the hypersexualization of celebrity females on tween adolescent females. Another project, "Are You Black Enuf? The Politics of the Black Female Identity," examines stereotypes of black women in the media around notions of "blackness."

Students may also examine representations of masculinity portrayed in sports, ads, and action-detective TV programs and films in terms of physical violence and toughness. For example, in the Education Media Foundation video *Tough Guise,* (www.mediaed.org/ videos/MediaGenderAndDiversity/ToughGuise), masculinity is equated with power over women through bullying or violence against women. Students may also discuss the portrayals of homophobic attitudes in films such as *Brokeback Mountain* (Lee, 2005) that limit male identity construction (Stuckey & Kring, 2007).

Racial/Ethnic Groups. Students may also define connections in terms of how certain racial and ethnic groups are represented in the media in which "whiteness" often operates as the invisible norm, positioning people of color as the "other" (Roediger, 2002). Few if any African Americans or Latinos assume roles as news anchors, main characters in drama shows, talk show guests, characters in ads, or organizational spokespersons. Students could create slideshows of images of these representations of race; for an example, David Segal (2007) created a slide-show essay for *Slate Magazine* (www.slate.com/id/2164062) that examined how racist portrayals of characters are used to pitch certain products— Aunt Jemima (pancakes), Uncle Ben's (rice), Frito Bandito (Fritos corn chips), Crazy Horse (Crazy Horse malt liquor), and Chief Wahoo (Cleveland Indians baseball team). And, students could examine media representations of Middle Eastern and Muslim people, who are often portrayed as suspicious and exotic (Kramer, Vittinghoff, & Gentz, 2006). (For a Project Sharp curriculum: Media Construction of the Middle East: www.ithaca. edu/looksharp).

Class. Students could also examine patterns in representations of social class related to assumptions about valued practices in working- versus middle- versus upper-middle-class worlds. For example, students may note how working-class people are represented in the news, political ads, or prime-time shows as "good, hard-working, salt-of-the-earth" people who differ from knowledge-economy workers. These representations shift the focus away from analysis of an economic system in which blue-collar wages have remained flat since the 1980s and that pits working-class people in opposition to "government bureaucrats" in political campaigns (Frank, 2004). Thus, the issue of increases in social network support for poor people is represented in terms of the need for higher taxes and poor people's lack of initiative due to their dependency on "government handouts," while corporation tax subsidy programs receive little attention (Chomsky, 2002). (A useful resource for examining class is the PBS documentary, *People Like Us*).

Urban, Suburban, and Rural Communities. Students could also examine how different places such as urban, suburban, and rural communities are represented. While urban communities are often portrayed as problematic, dangerous, and blighted, suburbia or exurbia is often represented in more positive ways, particularly in terms of a discourse of "whiteness," representations that fail to portray the challenges now facing suburbs as well as the cultural diversity of suburbia. Representations of rural communities also fail to provide accurate portrayals of the problems that citizens face in rural America, such as the control of agribusiness that relegates farmers to the role of sharecroppers.

War. Representations of war are often driven by the need to demonize the enemy and glorify one's own army, as illustrated in media portrayals of both the Gulf War and the Iraq War as a visual spectacles associated with vitriolic terms such as "shock and awe" (Kellner, 2005). (For a Project Sharp curriculum: Media Construction of War www.ithaca.edu/looksharp).

Political Media Representations. Students could detect certain patterns in how political candidates and issues are represented in the media by going to Web sites for specific candidates or advocacy organizations. They could examine how politicians and issues are represented in terms of their ties to either corporate interests (often in the form of public relations "front groups") or advocacy groups that make large contributions to campaigns.

News Topics. Students could also collect the titles of news stories from the Web sites of different newspapers and/or television networks (Fox, NBC, CBS, ABC, CNN, etc.) and compare the types of stories being covered in terms of what topics or issues are represented, for example, how Fox News often represents issues from a conservative perspective. Students could also view parodies of the news on *The Daily Show* or *The Colbert Report* and discuss the blurring of entertainment and "news" in newspapers and television, in which news focuses more on entertainment and celebrity news than on substantive political or economic news. This can be discussed in light of the fact that entertainment news may be less expensive to produce than more expensive, high-quality journalism (Trier, 2008). They may also discuss reasons for the decline in the depth and amount of original reporting given a shift in ownership of news outlets to large corporations who are often more interested in bottom-line profits than on quality journalism.

Media Genres. Students could also identify connections in terms of shared genre characteristics related to film genres such as action, thriller, comedy, romance, detective, science fiction, or horror, and television genres such as talk shows, reality TV, news, sports, cooking, drama, sit-coms, or documentaries. For example, by going to the Internet Movie Data Base (www.imdb.com), Rotten Tomatoes (www.rottentomatoes.com), Jahsonic (www.jahsonic.com/FilmGenre.html), or MovieGoods (www.moviegoods.com), students can find specific examples of films within certain genres and then define the prototypical characteristics shared by these films.

Music Genres. Playlists can be created on iTunes based on common features of popular music genres, such as rock, soul, blues, country, Cajun, calypso, gospel, punk, heavy metal, hip-hop, and rap. In my media studies class, we identify the characteristics of particular music genres by sampling 10-second clips from the genre catalogue on iTunes. We also explore the relationships between certain music genres and the historical and cultural forces influencing the development of these genres, for example, how the blues, and later rock, evolved from African American experiences with slavery.

For further resources on defining connections between media texts, see material on media representations, www.tc.umn.edu/~rbeach/linksteachingmedia/chapter5/index.htm, and on media genre www.tc.umn.edu/~rbeach/linksteachingmedia/chapter7/index.htm

Constructing Responses to Media Texts

In collecting and connecting media texts, students can also share their responses to collections of media texts with peers and other online audiences through use of blogs, wikis, online chat sites, digital storytelling, and podcasts (Beach, Anson, Breuch, & Swiss, 2008; Richardson, 2006; Solomon & Schrum, 2007). These tools readily foster use of links to media texts in ways that foster multimodality, hypertextuality, and interactivity. And students are more likely to voice their responses to media if they know that they can share with other online audiences as "affinity groups" (Gee, 2003).

Blogs

In my media studies class, students keep individual blogs using Blogger in which they share their analysis of media texts with "blog partners" (for an example of these blogs go to http://teachingmedialiteracy.pbwiki.com and click on "student blogs"). Students are given specific assignments to analyze use of film technique; examples of media representations of race, class, gender, and age; film and television genres; advertising images; news; and documentaries. In creating their blog posts, students import images and links to video clips of the media texts they have analyzed, allowing them to directly comment on these images and clips in their posts. The "blog partners" then comment on their peers' responses.

Students can create blogs using any number of different blog platforms: Blogger, LiveJournal, Vox, TypePad, WordPress, Movable Type, Edublog, or Tumblr. For working with K–12 students in districts concerned with security, teachers may want to consider Elgg (elgg.net) or Imbee.com, and for secondary students Moodle (moodle.org), Drupal (drupal.org) (VanDyk & Westgate, 2007), or Joomla (www.joomla.org) all centralized sites that provide a lot of security, interactive features, and secure storage space.

In setting up their blogs to access other blogs using RSS feeds previously noted, students can use Bloglines, Google Reader, Squeet, or Technorati to subscribe to others' blogs. By using these feed aggregators, students then automatically receive new posts for their subscribed blogs.

There are several advantages to using blogs to foster responses to media. Students can do the following:

- ❏   Present their writing in an appealing manner, drawing on use templates and other design features to readily create attractive, polished layouts associated with a professional, magazine-like appearance

- ◻ Embed images or YouTube video clips into their posts to illustrate their ideas or to engage in analysis of those images or clips
- ◻ Access and link to each other's blog posts as well as bloggers throughout the blogosphere. For example, in accessing Blogher (www.blogher.com) which contains links to thousands of women's blogs, students are able to make connections with other women according to shared interests.
- ◻ Provide and receive comments to blog posts that serve to bolster students' confidence in writing and foster further dialogue about a media text.
- ◻ Adopt a more natural, informal voice than is usual when writing formal academic papers (Watrall & Ellison, 2006)

Because they may adopt a particularly unique voice, students may then become known in the blogosphere in terms of their particular perspective or style, which defines their online identity (boyd, 2006). By voicing their opinions based on a particular perspective, students become known as the persona associated with "who we think the blog writer *is:* what they are like, how they want to think of themselves, and how they want us to think of them" (Knobel and Lankshear, 2006, p. 12).

Wikis

Teachers can also employ wikis in media studies classrooms to encourage collaborative writing about media texts by using media literacy links in Wikipedia, (en.wikipedia.org/wiki/Media_literacy).

In my media studies class, I use the Teaching Media Literacy site as the class Web site. I post links to resources, announcements, the syllabus, students' blogs/projects, teaching activities, and so on. Working in pairs with their blog partners, students write chapters on various aspects of media, drawing on text and images as well as their blogs. Each class adds new material to this wiki site. One advantage of using a wiki is that it fosters a sense of collaboration in constructing and sharing knowledge in the class. For example, a group of elementary students used a wiki to create an online encyclopedia about pop culture topics such as anime and X-Men (Borja, 2006). Students in a tenth-grade computer class in Georgia and an eleventh-grade computer class in Bangladesh used a wiki to work on what they described as the Flat Classroom Project (flatclassroomproject.wikispaces.com) to examine the role of Web 2.0 tools in fostering globalization. For a course on politics and the mass media, Anne Crigler of the University of Southern California used a class wiki as a news portal that contained RSS feeds to a range of different news sites so that students could access news based on a range of political perspectives (Higdon, 2006).

To create wikis, students and teachers can go to free wiki hosting sites such as Wikicities (www.wikicities.com), WikiSpaces (www.wikispaces.com), PBWiki (http://pbwiki.com), JotSpot (www.jot.com), UseMod (www.usemod.com), Project Forum (projectforum.com/pf/), or TikiWiki, (tikiwiki.org/). For example, to enter material with PBWiki, students click on the "edit" option on a page to enter text and format it as they would in a word processor. By clicking on "insert plug-ins," students can embed YouTube clips, videos, or image slideshows from their media text collections.

Online Chat Sites

Students can also share their responses to media texts on chat sites. Some examples follow.

- ❑ Course management systems such as Blackboard, Tapped In, Moodle, Drupal
- ❑ Google Talk (www.google/talk), Yahoo Messenger (messenger.yahoo.com/chat.php), PalTalk (www.paltalk.com), YackPack (www.yackpack.net), or Twitter (www.twitter.com) allow brief text messages to be used to provide peers with momentary, diary-like comments about their responses to or uses of media texts. (Students could be asked to keep a "Twitter" log of their daily media use and reactions to that media to share with peers.)
- ❑ Virtual world and game sites such as Second Life or Palace Planet multi-user virtual environment sites in which participants often adopt avatars, language, and practices mediated by popular culture texts (Thomas, 2004).
- ❑ Collaborative fiction writing sites such as New Worlds Project (rpgnewworlds.net) based on a science fiction world in which participants grapple with issues of peace in the midst of a world war in 2051.
- ❑ Online community journalism sites such as Wikinews, current.com news broadcasts, or the Assignment Zero project site (zero.newassignment.net/) established by Jay Rosen at New York University designed to foster what is known as "crowdsourcing" (Carr, 2008). This project supports online collaborative construction of news stories by large groups of people which are then edited by journalists.

Podcasts

Students can listen to podcasts that focus on the media listed in various podcast directories, such as iTunes (www.apple.com/itunes), Juice (www.podcastdirectory.com/podcasts/10101), Podcast Alley (www.podcastalley.com), Happyfish (happyfish.info/blog), Podcast.net (www.podcast.net), and The Podcast Network (www.thepodcastnetwork.com). For example, for podcasts on Web 2.0 technology tools, they could subscribe to the EdTechTalk podcasts (www.edtechtalk.com).

Students can then create podcasts in which they record and edit their perceptions of media texts and then edit those podcasts using Audacity (audacity.sourceforge.net), Garageband (www.apple.com/ilife/tutorials/garageband), or QuickTime Player (apple.com/quicktime/download/mac.html).

In creating podcasts, student can also employ free telephone software such as Skype (www.skype.com) to conduct long distance interviews. For example, in the global podcast project Rock Our World project (www.rockourworld.org), students create and share podcasts and videos about music across seven continents. And, based on their listening to news podcasts, such as CNN Student News (www.cnn.com/studentnews/) and BlogTalkRadio (www.blogtalkradio.com), students can create their own classroom or school news podcasts as a radio broadcast similar to the Radio WillowWeb (www.mpsomaha.org/willow/radio), produced by students at the Willowdale Elementary School in Omaha, Nebraska.

For further resources on sharing responses to media using blogs, see the PBwiki digital writing Web pp.

Creating Media Texts

Given the importance of learning about media through creating media, students can employ Web 2.0 tools to create their own media texts.

Digital Storytelling

Students can create digital storytelling texts that combine language with images, sounds, and video to communicate multimodally (Ohler, 2007). Students in the Digital Underground Storytelling for Youth community project program in Oakland, California, created digital storytelling texts that drew heavily on popular culture texts that mediate their portrayals of their lives in urban Oakland neighborhoods (Hull & Katz, 2007). For example, one student, Randy, created "Lyfe-N-Rhyme" (oaklanddusty.org/videos.php), described by Hull and Katz (2007):

> Randy narrates the movie, performing his original poem/rap to the beat of a Miles Davis tune playing softly in the background. He illustrates, complements, or otherwise accompanies the words and the message of his poem/rap, along with the Miles Davis melody, with approximately 80 images. Most of these images are photographs taken by Randy of Oakland neighborhoods and residents, while others he found on the Internet, and a few screens consist solely of typed words...He enacts himself as artist, not just directly through his artful use of poetic and aesthetic techniques, but by implicitly connecting himself with works of art and African-American icons, past and present...removing them from their particular historical contexts, and recenters them, recontextualizing them in his own creative universe of this digital story and his own social world of Oakland, California (p. 58).

Students can use any number of different tools to create digital stories. They can use the Mac program, ComicLife, to transform written stories into online comic books using templates to create dialogue balloons, boxes, and characters. They can make their own short videos (Bell, 2005) by creating a script and then using digital storyboards using Atomic Learning's Video StoryBoard Pro, Directors Board free storyboard software, Ian Pegler's free storyboard and scriptwriting software, or Interactive Storyboard. Once they have shot their video, they can use online editing sites such as Eyespot, JumpCut, One True Media, Pinnacle Studio, or Ulead VideoStudio as well as iMovie, Windows Movie Maker, Adobe Premiere, or Final Cut Pro to collaboratively edit and remix their own video or online clips.

Vlogs

Students can also create vlogs, which are blogs with video content (Bryant, 2006; Verdi & Hodson, 2006). Students can use vlogs to critically analyze selected media clips in terms of, for example, gender, race, and class media representations as noted earlier. Steve Garfield, John Barth, Jason Crow and Four Eyed Monsters have created a useful vlogging tutorial (projectnml.org/exemplars/06vlog). My own tutorial on creating vlogs can be accessed at digitalwriting.pbwiki.com/Vlog+production+tutorials. Students can view or share their vlogs on sites such as MeFeedia (mefeedia.com), iTunes (www.apple.com/itunes), FireAnt (fireant.tv), dailymotion (www.dailymotion.com), or BlipTV (bliptv/).

In her Feminist Film Studies course, Rachel Raimist (2007) has students post vlog reactions to representations of women in films (see blog.lib.umn.edu/raim0007/wost3307/). For one of her assignments, she asked students to analyze women's vlogs in terms of their personal experience as a spectator observing the lives of others. Viewing these vlogs provided her students with ideas for creating their own.

Classroom Newspapers and Newsletters

As part of a community or critical journalism project, students could also create their own online class newspaper or newsletter using blogs or wikis, or, for a polished look, Google Page Creator, Apple's iWork Pp 2, Bricolage, or Typ03. Students in Jim Hatten's journalism class in Edina, Minnesota, used Google Page Creator to create their own online newspaper (edinajournalism.googlepp.com/gazette).

In a program sponsored by the American Society of Newspaper Editors, 470 schools now publish online editions available at HighSchoolJournalism.org. In creating online periodicals, students learn about story selection, layout, design, blocking, and use of images to illustrate the key ideas in their stories. Adolescent Harry Potter fans manage an online "school newspaper," *The Daily Prophet* (www.dprophet.com). Students can also use the *ByLine* epistemic game to write news articles in science classes (Hatfield & Shaffer, 2006) or the *Harperville Gazette* game in which students write articles about a train derailment that led to a spill of anhydrous ammonia (www.jcvr.org/products/index.php).

Electronic Literature

Students can also create electronic literature (Hayles, 2003; Morris & Swiss, 2006) by reading examples at the Electronic Literature Organization sites (eliterature.org), Word Circuits (www.wordcircuits.com), and the Electronic Poetry Center at the University of Buffalo (epc.buffalo.edu). Based on their experiences with electronic literature, students can then create their own digital stories or poems using PowerPoint, digital video, or Flash technology.

Parodies of Media Texts

Students can create parodies of media texts, in what is known as culture jamming—expropriating, altering, or remixing existing media texts to ridicule or calls attention to the original text's problematic meanings (Dery, 1993; Knobel & Lankshear, 2003; Lievrouw, 2006). Students can employ Web 2.0 tools to alter or remix texts as a form of cultural critique, as reflected in Adbuster's parodies of ads. They can also embed statements or new messages into media texts that serve to counter the original message, as in "subvertisements," where people add messages to billboards or subway ads (for an example of subvertisements, see the YouTube video, "An Ad Busters Intervention" www.youtube.com/watch?v=vPMFdpfRzLI; for a unit on teaching satire, see http://teachingsatire.pbwiki.com).

From viewing parody videos on YouTube, students learn how producers copy, combine, and remix video clips in ways that reframe the original meaning of these texts by recontextualizing and interrogating the original meaning of that text (Beach & O'Brien, 2007). For example, in an MTV cable show, *The N,* students can stream the programs on the Web using the MTV broadband player, The Click (Olsen, 2007). When they are on this online site students use a "video mix masher" to comment on a scene from a show and then add another scene. Participants can then comment on each other's work so that students from different parts of the country can share their views of the remixing and reconstructing of texts (Olsen, 2007).

Younger students enjoy going to My Pop Studio (www.mypopstudio.com) developed by the Media Education Lab, Temple University, to engage in remixing material available in a reality television, music, magazine, or digital studio. For example, in creating their own version of a reality television show featuring adolescents coping with relationships, they can reflect on how changing the characters or order of events resulting in different meanings.

Students also alter online literary texts by inserting dialogue bubbles or hyperlinks, creating what Kathleen Yancey (2004) describes as "pop-up" writing based on the *Pop-Up Video* show on VH1 in which music videos are continually interrupted by visual pop-up bubbles that contain interpretations, background contexts, or critiques of the music video. Yancey notes that use of these pop-ups applied to a text invites connections across different texts:

> Collectively, pop-ups on or in a single text can create a random metatext, and it is equally possible that collectively pop-ups can create a series of parallel texts, or, perhaps, multiple stories prompted by, but not necessarily limited to, a "primary" text...[they] allow both composer and consumer to engage in intellectual *interplay* of both visual and verbal varieties (p. 65)

E-zines

Students also use e-zines for remixing texts to challenge status quo sexist and racist norms in the culture, as reflected in the feminist ezine (Knobel & Lankshear, 2002). One study of three adolescent girls who published their own 'zine *Burnt Beauty,* identified creative ways that they expropriated online popular culture to parody gender representations (Guzzetti & Gamboa, 2004). To gain a sense of the layout and style of e-zines, students could study some e-zines such as *Brain Event, Bamboozled,* or *Respect E-Zine.* Based on analysis of her students' e-zines, Tobi Jacobi (2007) notes that she values:

> the chaos it inspires, and "zine" terminology has come to symbolize the kind of exploration, collaboration, and debate I want to encourage in students. They need to be mired in conversations about wordplay, document design, and context just as I need to have my expectations about Standard English and genre challenged. Such issues inevitably deepen our classroom conversations and our collective understanding of what it means to be writers whose words circulate in the public sphere (p. 47).

For further resources on creating digital media texts, see the following:

◻ Digital literature and storytelling: http://digitalwriting.pbwiki.com/Digital Literature

❏ Video: www.tc.umn.edu/~rbeach/linksteachingmedia/chapter3/index.htm

❏ Newspapers and e-zines: http://digitalwriting.pbwiki.com/EditingDigitalWriting

Conducting Media Ethnography of Audience Use of Digital Media Texts

Finally, students can use Web 2.0 tools to conduct media ethnography studies of how audiences construct the meaning of digital media texts (Beach, 2004; Dicks, Mason, Coffey, Atkinson, 2005; Hine, 2005; Pink, 2004, 2006). Rather than simply assuming that the meaning of digital meaning is *in* media texts or making assumptions about how audiences *may* construct this meaning, it is important for students to study how audiences *actually* construct their own unique meanings of digital media texts given their particular purposes, needs, knowledge, interests, attitudes, and social agendas constituting the context of media use. In my media studies class, students conduct media ethnography studies by observing audiences responding to or constructing digital media texts: playing online video games, constructing Facebook/MySpace profiles, participating in music-group fan sites as part of participation in a music "scene" (Bennett & Peterson, 2004), and so on. Projects are similar to those conducted by members of the Digital Youth Research Project (digitalyouth.ischool.berkeley.edu/node/5) at the University of California, Berkeley.

Media ethnographers are also interested in determining disparities between intended meanings versus actual meanings of audiences' responses to media texts. For example, Bud.TV (www.bud.tv), the online entertainment network, consists of short, well-made videos such as parodies of Reality TV shows. The producers of this network wanted to design their video content to project an image of coolness that may then be associated with Bud Light or Michelob beer. As Lorne Manly (2007) notes:

> Attach a brand name to something cool, something entertaining, and that elusive young man (and to a lesser extent, young woman) may check out Bud.TV's offerings again and again, send them along to friends, even take a stab at creating his own minifilm for the site. Cultivate that warm, fuzzy feeling about Budweiser, and the company may cement the loyalty of the existing customer, or better, woo the uncommitted or hard-to-reach drinker to a Bud Light or a Michelob or a Peels malt-liquor beverage (p. 28).

For a media ethnographer, this begs the question as to how audiences actually respond to this marketing ploy. Students could interview their peers about their responses to the Bud.TV content by asking questions such as: Do they perceive it as cool? Do they equate the content with the Bud Light brand? Do they adopt any critical responses?

Students could also examine how their peers are being rhetorically positioned by media texts. Online adolescent teen magazine sites address readers as "you" in an attempt to create a "synthetic sisterhood" of imaginary communities of consumption based on the need to acquire group norms as to what it means to be popular (Currie, 1999, p. 65). Ellen Seiter (2005) noted that "The World Wide Web is a more aggressive and stealthy marketeer to children than television ever was, and children need as much information about its business practices as teachers and parents can give them" (p. 100). As documented in the PBS program, *Merchants of Cool,* (www.pbs.org/wgbh/pp/frontline/shows/cool)

marketers themselves employ these ethnographic methods to study adolescents' perceptions of what is considered to be "cool," information useful for branding and marketing products.

Students can study how audiences construct their identities or interact with others on these sites. For example, the online virtual site, Barbiegirl (www.barbiegirls.com) invites tween females to enjoy the experience of "fashion, fun, friendship" by creating their own avatars and talking or shopping with other tweens in this virtual site. Or the Stardoll (stardoll.com) site that involves tween females in dressing up paper dolls. They might also examine how tweens react to the idea that their talk is being monitored on the Barbiegirl site. Parents visiting the Barbiegirl site are told, to "review reports of chatting in the environment and adjust the word filters as needed to block or allow new words or phrases" (Newitz, 2007), something that would typically be a turn-off for tweens.

Students can also use Web 2.0 tools to record these experiences and interviews. In her study of undergraduates' disclosure of "private" versus "public" information in their construction of FaceBook profiles, Debbie Weismann (2007) found that IM'ing participants served as a useful, informal interview tool. Students in the Digital Ethnography project at Kansas State University (www.mediatedcultures.net/ksudigg) headed by media anthropologist Michael Wesch employ digital video to capture participants' experiences with sites such as YouTube, allowing them to include both YouTube content and audience participation in their videos for online sharing of their results. Students study why audiences participate in and what they post on YouTube as part of their need for social connections. In her course taught at Vassar College, Anthropology Goes to the Movies: Film, Video, and Ethnography, Collen Cohen (computing.vassar.edu/news/faculty/facultyfocus/cohen.html) uses digital video to revise and remix clips from Cohen's video fieldwork of audience responses to films to create their own studies of audience film response. Students also remix documentaries and then reflect on how these changes alter their responses to the remixed version.

Topics for Media Ethnography Studies
Students could conduct media ethnographies of the following:

❑   Online advertising. Students could examine the ways in which advertisers increasingly employ online advertising (en.wikipedia.org/wiki/Online_advertising) using "spam" or "push" messages or uses of animation or flashing signals or "ad bots" that inhabit chat rooms and respond to trigger words (see the Media Awareness Network: Online Marketing Strategies: www.podcastdirectory.com/podcasts/10101 as well as online advertisers site, Clickz (www.clickz.com/showPage.html?page=resources/adres). Google derives much of its revenue from ads that appear on the right side of the Google sites as well as its ads that appear in blogs. Media conglomerates purchase Web 2.0 sites, which leads to an increase in the use of these sites to promote their product. For example, eBay now owns Skype, which they hope to use to mesh videos of eBay auction items with voice-over descriptions of those items on Skype. Given its ownership by News Corporation,

MySpace could increasingly become a primary space for youth marketing and acquiring data on consumption trends.

- ◻ Political/advocacy group sites. Politicians and advocacy/think-tank groups are using Web 2.0 tools such as Facebook or MySpace profiles or blogs to promote their causes, campaigns, and agendas, particularly given the high costs of television advertising. It is often difficult to determine the credibility of the information available on these sites, so that much of the information provided is part of politicians' or organizations' spin campaigns (Jackson & Jamieson, 2007). Students could study whether audiences as potential voters can detect instances of misinformation or the underlying economic and political agendas driving these sites. They can also go to sites such as lijit.com, snopes.com, or factcheck.org to acquire accurate information that may challenge the inaccurate content on these sites, as well as adding critical annotations on Getoutfoxed.com. Students could also contrast audience responses to commercial news sites with nonprofit sites such as FreeSpeechTV (community.freespeech.org).

- ◻ Video gaming. Students could study game players' social participation in their game playing (Gibson, Aldrich, & Prensky, 2006), as well as their acquisition of problem-solving strategies (Gee, 2003) and scenarios or narratives for coping with challenges or conflicts (Jenkins, 2004). Students could also study gamers' creation of their own training videos on how they learn to play a game.

- ◻ Online news. Students could study how readers respond to online news sites. They could identify the kinds of information readers seek out and acquire related to the question as to whether readers only seek out information that reifies their knowledge and beliefs or whether they are exposed to information that might alter their knowledge and beliefs. Students could also determine whether readers are aware of the influence of nonlocal versus local corporate ownership on the selection of stories and editorial perspectives on, for example, Foxnews.com versus the LATimes.com (see the Frontline documentary, Trouble at the *Los Angeles Times* (www.pbs.org/wgbh/pp/frontline/newswar/part3/latimes.html). In one study, locally owned TV stations presented an average of 5 and a half minutes more local news than did stations owned by nonlocal corporate owners (Klinenberg, 2007), differences that may also be evident in their sites.

- ◻ Online fan clubs/fan-fiction. Students could also study online fan clubs associated with television programs, films, music groups, or sports teams, as well as groups on Flickr or YouTube organized around shared interests in, for example, images of Hollywood movie stars.

- ◻ Fan-fiction groups. Participants at fanfiction.net create their own fictional versions of characters' lives (Black, 2005). IMing, blogs (anyaka.blogspot.com), or trailers can also be used create fan fiction (Thomas, 2004).

Through conducting these media ethnographies, students critically examine how audiences' responses are often shaped by merchandizing forces, as well as how and why audiences resist these forces. For further resources on media ethnography, see http://www.tc.umn.edu/~rbeach/linksteachingmedia/chapter6/index.htm

■ SUMMARY

As students use various Web 2.0 tools for collecting, connecting, constructing responses to, creating, and conducting media ethnography studies, they are learning not only *about* media, but they are also learning to use these tools *as* digital media. In doing so, they acquire various digital literacies that will foster their development as critical thinkers and citizens in a world mediated by digital media. Hopefully, this will lead students to go beyond simply reacting to media and produce media as a means of voicing their opinions about the world.

References

Beach, R. (2007). *Teachingmedialiteracy.com: A web-based guide to links and activities.* New York: Teachers College Press.

Beach, R. (2004). Researching response to literature and the media. In A. Goodwyn & A. Stables (Eds.)., *Learning to read critically in language and literacy* (pp. 123–148). Thousand Oaks, CA: Sage.

Beach, R., Anson, C., Breuch, L., & Swiss, T. (2008). *Engaging students in digital writing.* Norwood, NJ: Christopher Gordon.

Beach, R., & O'Brien, D. (2007). Using popular culture texts in the classroom. In D. Leu, J. Coiro, M. Knobel, & C. Lankshear (Eds.)., *Handbook on New Media Literacies.* Mahwah, NJ: Lawrence Erlbaum.

Bell, A. (2005). *Creating digital video in your school: How to shoot, edit, produce, distribute and incorporate digital media into the curriculum.* Worthington, OH: Linworth.

Bennett, A., & Peterson, R. A. (Eds.). (2004). *Music scenes: Local, translocal, and virtual.* Nashville, TN: Vanderbilt University Press.

Black, R. W. (2005). Access and affiliation: The literacy and composition practices of English language learners in an online fanfiction community. *Journal of Adult and Adolescent Literacy, 49*(2), 118–128.

Blair, J. A. (2004). The rhetoric of visual arguments. In C. A. Hill, & M. Helmers (Eds.)., *Defining visual rhetorics* (pp. 41–61). Mahwah, NJ: Erlbaum.

Bolter, J. D., & Grusin, R. (2000). *Remediation: Understanding new media.* Cambridge, MA: MIT Press.

Borja, R. R. (2006). Educators experiment with student-written wikis. *Education Week, 25*(30), 10.

boyd, d. (2006). A blogger's blog: Exploring the definition of a medium. *Reconstruction 6*(4). Retrieved March 3, 2007, from http://reconstruction.eserver.org/064/boyd.shtml

boyd, d. (2007). Why youth social network sites: The role of networked publics in teenage social life. In D. Buckingham (Ed.)., *Youth, identity, and digital media* (pp. 119–142). Cambridge, MA: The MIT Press. Retrieved February 28, 2008 from http://www.mitpressjournals.org/toc/dmal/-/6

Bryant, S. (2006). *Videoblogging for dummies.* Indianapolis: Wiley.

Calishain, T. (2006). *Information trapping: Real-time research on the web.* Thousand Oaks, CA: New Riders Publishing.

Carr, N. (2008). *The big switch: Rewiring the world, from Edison to Google.* New York: W. W. Norton & Co.

Chomsky, N., Schoeffel, J., and Mitchell, P. (2002). *Understanding power: The indispensable Chomsky.* New York: New Press.

Currie, D. (1999). *Girl talk: Adolescent magazines and their readers.* Toronto: University of Toronto Press.

Dery, M. (1993). Culture jamming: Hacking, slashing and sniping in the empire of signs. *Open Magazine Pamphlet Series.* Retrieved May 15, 2007 from http://www.levity.com/markdery/jam.html

Dicks, B., Mason, B., Coffey, A. C., Atkinson, P. A. (2005). *Qualitative research and hypermedia: Ethnography for the digital age.* Thousand Oaks, CA: Sage

Du, H. S., & Wagnera, C. (2006). Weblog success: Exploring the role of technology. *International Journal of Human-Computer Studies, 64*(9), 789–798.

Frank, T. (2004). *What's the matter with Kansas? How conservatives won the heart of America.* New York: Metropolitan Books.

Gee, J. P. (2003). *What video games have to teach use about learning and literacy.* New York: Palgrave Macmillan.

Gibson, D., Aldrich, C., & Prensky, M. (Eds.). (2006). *Games and simulations in online learning: Research and development frameworks.* Hershey, PA: IGI Global.

Glogowski, K. (2006). Classrooms as third space. Teach and Learn. Retrieved January 5, 2007 from http://www.slideshare.net/teachandlearn/classrooms-as-third-places

Gold, M. (2007). "Countdown" a leap for TV news's Susan Zirinsky. *The Los Angeles Times.* Retrieved May 15, 2007 from http://www.latimes.com/entertainment/news/tv/cl-et-zirinsky16mar16,1,1382344.story?coll=la-headlines-entnews

Gold, M. (2008, January 27). The buss on Gossip Girl. *The Los Angeles Times.* Retrieved January 30, 2008 from http://www.latimes.com/entertainment/la-ca-gossip27jan27,1,6293924.story?ctrack=2&cset=true

Guzzetti, B., & Gamboa, M. (2004). Zines for social justice: Adolescent girls writing on their own. *Reading Research Quarterly, 39*(4), 408–436.

Hall, S., (Ed.). (1997). *Representation: Cultural representations and signifying practices.* Thousand Oaks, CA: Sage.

Hatfield, D., & Shaffer, D. W. (2006). Press play: designing an epistemic game engine for journalism. Paper presented at the Paper presented at the International Conference of the Learning Sciences (ICLS), Bloomington, IN. http://epistemicgames.org/cv/papers/hatfield_shaffer_icls_2006.pdf

Hayles, N. K. (2003). *Writing machines.* Chicago: University of Chicago Press.

Higdon, J. (2006). Wikis in the academy. In S. Mader (Ed.), *Using wikis in education.* Retrieved April 18, 2007, from http://www.wikiineducation.com/display/ikiw/Home

Hine, C. (Ed.). (2005). *Virtual methods.* Oxford, UK: Berg.

Hollzner, S. (2006). *Secrets of RSS.* Berkeley, CA: Peach Pit Press.

Hull, G., & Katz, M. (2007). Crafting an agentive self: Case studies of digital storytelling. *Research in the Teaching of English, 41*(1), 43–81.

Jackson, B., & Jamieson, K. H. (2007). *unSpun: Finding facts in a world of disinformation.* New York: Random House.

Jacobi, T. (2007). The zine project: Innovation or oxymoron? *English Journal, 96,* 4.

Jenkins, H. (2004). Game design as narrative architecture. In N. Wardrip-Fruin, & P. Harrigan (Eds.)., *First person: New media as story, performance, and game.* Cambridge: MIT Press. Retrieved from http://www.electronicbookreview.com/v3/servlet/ebr?essay_id=jenkins&command=view_essay

Jenkins, H. (2006). Confronting the challenges of participatory culture: Media education for the 21st century. The MacArthur Foundation. Retrieved October 25, 2006, from http://www.digitallearning.macfound.org/site/c.enJLKQNlFiG/b.2108773/apps/nl/content2.asp?content_id={CD911571–0240–4714-A93B-1D0C07C7B6C1}&notoc=1

Kellner, D. (2005). *Media spectacle and the crisis of democracy: Terrorism, war, and election battles.* Boulder, CO: Paradigm Publishers.

Kellner, D., & Share, J. (2007). Critical media literacy is not an option. *Learning Inquiry, 1*(1), 59–69.

Klinenberg, E. (2007). Breaking the news. Mother Jones, March/April. Retrieved May 15, 2007 from http://www.motherjones.com/news/feature/2007/03/breaking_the_news.html

Knobel, M., & Lankshear, C. (2002). Cut, paste, publish: The production and consumption of zines. In D.E. Alvermann (Ed.), *Adolescents and literacies in a digital world* (pp. 164–185). New York: Peter Lang.

Kramer, S., Vittinghoff, N., and Gentz, N. (Eds.). (2006). *Globalization, cultural identities, and media representation.* Albany, NY: SUNY Press.

Kress, G. (2003). *Literacy in the new media age.* New York: Routledge.

Lee, A. (Director). (2005). *Brokeback Mountain.* [Motion picture]. United States: Paramount Pictures.

Lenhart, A., & Madden, M. (2007). Social networking Websites and teens: An overview. Pew Internet & American Life Project. Retrieved February 28, 2008 from http://www.pewinternet.org/PPF/r/198/report_display.asp

Lenhart, A., Madden, M., Macgill, A. R., & Smith, A. (2007). Teens and social media: The use of social media gains a greater foothold in teen life as they embrace the conversational nature of interactive online media. Pew Internet & American Life Project. Retrieved February 28, 2008 from http://www.pewinternet.org/PPF/r/230/report_display.asp

Lievrouw, L. (2006). Oppositional and activist new media: Remediation, reconfiguration, participation. Retrieved May 20, 2007 from http://polaris.gseis.ucla.edu/llievrou/LievrouwPDC06Rev2.pdf

Lunsford, A. A. (2006). Writing, technologies, and the fifth canon. *Computers and Composition, 23*(2), 169–177.

Manly, L. (2007). BrewTube. *The New York Times Magazine.* Retrieved May 12, 2007 from http://www.nytimes.com/2007/02/04/magazine/04BudTV.t.html?ex=1179720000&en=a7c2122ad74faea0&ei=5070

Montgomery, K. C. (2007). *Politics, commerce, and childhood in the age of the Internet.* Cambridge, MA: MIT Press. Retrieved February 1, 2008 from http://mitpress.mit.edu/catalog/item/default.asp?ttype=2&tid=11125

Morris, A., & Swiss, T. (Eds.), (2006) *New media poetics: Text, technotext, theories.* Cambridge, MA: MIT Press.

National School Boards Association (2007). Creating & connecting: Research and guidelines on online social and educational networking. Retrieved February 28, 2008 from http://onlinepressroom.net/nsba/new/

Newitz, A. (2007). MySpace + SecondLife / Ponies!1 = BarbieGirls. *Wired Magazine.* Retrieved May 20, 2007 from http://blog.wired.com/underwire/2007/05/myspace_secondl.html

Ohler, J. B. (2007). *Digital storytelling in the classroom: New media pathways to literacy, learning, and creativity.* Thousand Oaks, CA: Sage.

Olsen, S. (2007, January 22). A new crop of kids: Generation We. *CNET News.com.* Retrieved May 15, 2007 from http://news.com.com/A+new+crop+of+kids+Generation+We/2009-1025_3-6151768.html?tag=nefd.lede

O'Reilly, T. (2005, Sept. 30). What is Web 2.0? Design patterns and business models for the next generation of software. Retrieved 5 February 2009 from: http://www.oreillynet.com/pub/a/oreilly/tim/news/2005/09/30/what-is-web-20.html?page=1

Pink, S. (2004). *Working images: Visual research and representation in ethnography.* New York: Routledge.

Pink, S. (2006). *The future of visual anthropology: Engaging the senses.* New York: Routledge.

Pogue, D. (2007). TiVo plays a trump card: Web smarts. *The New York Times.* Retrieved May 12, 2007 from http://www.nytimes.com/2007/04/05/technology/05pogue.html?pagewanted=2&ei=5070&en=f025705903b2a443&ex=1178337600

Prior, P. et al. (2007). Re-situating and re-mediating the canons: A cultural-historical remapping of rhetorical activity. *KAIROS, 11*(3). Retrieved February 30, 2008 from http://kairos.technorhetoric.net/11.3/binder.html?topoi/prior-et-al/index.html

Raimist, R. (2007). Blog: Women's Studies 3307, Feminist Film Studies, University of Minnesota. Retrieved May 12, 2007 from http://blog.lib.umn.edu/raim0007/wost3307/

Rainie, L. (2006). Life Online: Teens and technology and the world to come. Pew Internet & American Life Project. Retrieved February 27, 2008 from http://www.pewinternet.org/PPF/r/63/presentation_display.asp

Rainie, L. (2008). Increased use of video-sharing sites. Pew Internet & American Life Project. Retrieved February 28, 2008 from http://www.pewinternet.org/PPF/r/232/report_display.asp

Rice, J. (2004). *Writing about cool: Hypertext and cultural studies in the computer classroom.* New York: Longman.

Richardson, W. (2006). *Blogs, wikis, podcasts, and other powerful web tools for classrooms.* Thousand Oaks, CA: Corwin Press.

Roediger, D. R. (2002). *Colored white: Transcending the racial past.* Berkeley, CA: University of California Press.

Segal, D. (2007). Uncle Ben, CEO? The strange history of racist spokescharacters. *Slate Magazine.* Retrieved May 18, 2007 from http://www.slate.com/id/2164062/

Seiter, E. (2005) *The Internet playground: Children's access, entertainment, and mis-education.* New York: Peter Lang.

Shipka, J. (2005). A multimodal task-based framework for composing. *College Composition & Communication, 57*(2), 277–306.

Sirc, G. (2004). Box-logic. In A. Wysocki, J. Johnson-Eilola, C. Selfe, & G. Sirc (Eds.), *Writing new media: Theory and applications for expanding the teaching of composition* (pp. 111–146). Logan: Utah State University Press.

Solomon, G., & Schrum, L. (2007). *Web 2.0: New tools, new schools.* Eugene, OR: International Society for Technology in Education.

Stuckey, H., & Kring, K. (2007). Critical media literacy and popular film: experiences of teaching and learning in a graduate class. *New Directions For Adult And Continuing Education, 115,* 25–33.

Thomas, A. (2004). Digital literacies of the cybergirl. *E-Learning, 1*(3), 358–382.

Trier, J. (2007a). "Cool" engagements with YouTube: Part 1. *Journal of Adolescent and Adult Literacy, 50*(5), 408–412.

Trier, J. (2007b). "Cool" engagements with YouTube: Part 2. *Journal of Adolescent and Adult Literacy, 50*(7), 598–603.

Trier, J. (2008). *The Daily Show* with Jon Stewart: Part 1. *Journal of Adolescent and Adult Literacy, 51*(5), 424–427.

Utecht, J. (2006). A problem with blogs. *Techlearning.* Retrieved March 24, 2007 from http://www.tech-learning.com/blog/2007/03/a_problem_with_blogs.php

VanDyk, J., & Westgate, M (2007). *Pro Drupal development.* New York: APress.

Verdi, M., & Hodson, R. (2006). *Secrets of videoblogging.* Berkeley, CA: Peachpit Press.

Watrall, E. & Ellison, N. (2006). Blogs for learning: A case study. Retrieved 5 February 2009: http://www.higheredblogcon.com/teaching/watrall/blogs-for-learning2/player.html

Weismann, D. (2007). Assessing boundaries of speech in FaceBook. Unpublished paper. University of California, Los Angeles.

Wysocki, A. (2004). Open new media to writing. In A. Wysocki, J. Johnson-Eilola, C. Selfe, & G. Sirc (Eds.), *Writing new media: Theory and applications for expanding the teaching of composition* (pp. 1–41). Logan: Utah State University Press.

Yancey, K. (2004). *Teaching literature as reflective practice.* Urbana, IL: National Council of Teachers of English.

Doing Media/ Cultural Studies

■ Introduction

Part III, "Doing Media/Cultural Studies," offers practical examples that teach how to "do" media and cultural studies. All of the contributions in this section are by practitioners of media/cultural studies in a wide diversity of arenas and with different optics, methods, and approaches. While these chapters engage a range of subject matters and take varying approaches, they share an impetus to take culture seriously and to contextualize cultural artifacts within contemporary cultures and societies. All the studies included help to provide knowledge of the contemporary era and show how we can learn more about our present day world through the study of the media and culture.

Long-time cultural and media theorist and critic Toby Miller, in his chapter "Children and the Media: Alternative Histories," points to a large number of historical attempts to demonize youth and to blame the media for problems of youth and society. Moral panic concerning youth has been fuelled, he claims, by the "psy" function, in which a shifting field of psychoanalysis and psychology, psychiatry, pseudo-pharmacology, and other psy-enterprises teamed up with government agencies, academic institutions, and medical and other research groups to discern causes of youth pathology and prescribe solutions. From the Payne Foundation that claimed that films were producing juvenile delinquency and violent and promiscuous youth in the 1930s through demonization of comic books in the 1950s and then attacks on television, rock music, and other forms of youth culture, culminating in our time with the demonization of the Internet, government and academic agencies have blamed media for the corruption of youth. Miller acknowledges that there have been growing problems with youth violence, crime, and even suicide; yet he argues that political and legal policies have mightily contributed to these social problems but are invisible in the popular and academic discourses that demonize the media or youth. Miller notes another discrepancy in that corporations take youth as a main consumer target, assuming they are rational and competent consumers, yet they bombard them with advertisements that are often highly contradictory.

Educator and practioneer of cultural studies Joe Kincheloe, in "Capital, Ray Kroc, and McDonald's: The World's Lovin' It," lays bare the way McDonald's sells its burgers to children and families by associating their product with family values, good times, and America itself. In particular, Kincheloe emphasizes how McDonald's produces a children's culture with the evocative name that recalls a popular song ("Old McDonald Had a Farm…") and exploits its well-liked clown, Ronald McDonald, its association with toys and popular culture, and its marketing of fun and good times. Part of McDonald's marketing appeal has been to associate the corporation with America and, in a global age, McDonald's is a potent vehicle of cultural imperialism and "soft power," producing global desires for Americanized fast food and corporate values.

Educator, author, and cultural critic Shirley Steinberg's "Barbie: The Bitch Still Has Everything" takes on the Barbie doll phenomenon, producing an inventory and analysis of the various manifestations of the popular Barbie doll in its multiple incarnations. Not only does Barbie celebrate whiteness—especially blonde whiteness—as the standard for beauty, but her shape combines anorexic thinness with large breasts, thus creating sexually fetishized images for young girls. In addition, Barbie is associated with and sells a variety of fashion products, making fashion and commodity possession the ideals of a young girl's life. Why, Steinberg exclaims, "the bitch has everything," inspiring girls to buy as much as they can of all the stuff that Barbie owns. Barbie also sells corporate America through her association with an astonishing array of corporations that promote Barbie products, as she promotes their wares. Barbie also colonizes history; Barbie dolls feature stories and figures from all arenas of American history, properly sanitized, of course. Hence, Barbie sells the United States itself, just as Barbie herself becomes an iconic princess of Americana.

Educators and cultural critics Kathalene A. Razzano, Loubna H. Skalli, and Christine M. Quail's "The Spectacle of Reform: Vulture Culture, Youth, and Television" explores how so-called "reality television" presents youth out of control and in need of discipline, surveillance, and punishment. Noting how the "teens-out-of-control" genre emerged in the late 1990s in shows like *Maury* and *Montel,* the authors point out that the out-of-control teen is often female, sexually promiscuous, rebellious, and a petty criminal while the media at-large vilifies a group of "superpredators" who are violent, dangerous, and usually boys of color. The authors elicit calls for reform and remediation of what the media portrays as a serious social problem. They are characterized by the authors as examples of a "vulture culture" that preys on people's problems and suffering for media entertainment and to legitimize the legal and police systems of dealing with youth.

Reading some recent reality TV shows as spectacles of reform that portray youth as out-of-control and offer only individualized solutions to the problem, the authors carry out an in-depth study of MTV's *Juvies* and A&E's *Intervention. Juvies* features girls who are undergoing rehabilitation at an Indiana juvenile center, presenting out-of-control girls who require surveillance and discipline. *Intervention,* by contrast, is a spectacle of confession and redemption in which individuals admit their addictions or aberrant behavior, perceive the pain it brings to their families, and struggle to solve their problems. The authors claim that these reality shows present purely individualized problems and do not explore the determinants of race, gender, and class or how social institutions produce or aggravate the problem. They present the fantasy that existing institutions are capable of solving social problems. The authors conclude, however, by noting that scholars and media commentators are beginning to note that incarceration provides neither rehabilitation nor solutions to the problems that caused the incarceration and are now looking for better understanding and solutions to those problems.

In "Gideon Who Will Be 25 in the Year 2012: Growing Up Gay Today," Larry Gross, professor at the Annenberg School of Communications, explores the differences between growing up gay in the not-so-distant past compared with the present. Whereas gays and lesbians were until some decades ago either invisible in the mainstream media or presented in extremely negative stereotypes, today news and entertainment in broadcasting, films, and the Internet are making queerness increasingly visible and exploring multiple gay and lesbian experiences and identities. Increased visibility, however, creates new problems, challenges, and terrains of struggle as gays and lesbians come out at increasingly early ages and still face intense discrimination, sometimes even violence. This has resulted in lawsuits in high schools and the formation of gay-straight alliances to promote acceptance of homosexuality. Younger gays also have magazines, Web sites, and access to chat rooms and social networking sites that help them in coming out, finding acceptance and communities, and dealing with the ongoing problems of bigotry and prejudice. Thus, growing up gay in a media culture in which gays and lesbians are visible creates a dramatically different situation and new, positive possibilities; nonetheless, prejudices and challenges remain.

Distinguished author and educational video entrepreneur Sut Jhally has for years been a major analyst and critic of advertising. In "Advertising, Gender and Sex," Jhally investigates the gendered nature of advertising and how gender and sex are used to sell a variety of products and life-styles. He notes the power of advertising and that ads are obsessed with gender and sexuality. In his view, ads should be seen as hyper-ritualized presentations of the dominant codes of gender and sex that function as part of social reality, and not simply as representations. Ads play off of conventional expectations concerning gender and sex and associate the product with these features, thus reproducing hegemonic gender and sexual codes and relations at the same time it sells products.

Rejecting wholesale denunciations of advertising as pure manipulation, Jhally indicates that to comprehend its power we must understand the pleasures of advertising and what attracts consumers to its images and messages. While representations of gender and sexuality in advertising often objectify women, Jhally insists that such representations embody a legitimate dimension of sexuality that points to real desires and pleasures; it must be understood, not simply denounced. Every ad, Jhally notes, is different and must be addressed on its own terms. While ads that objectify women's sexuality in offensive and violent ways should be sharply criticized, we should discuss the extent to which gender representation and the use of sexuality are or are not offensive. While acknowledging that advertising is a highly undemocratic discourse controlled by advertisers and the media, we need to have an engaged discussion of advertising that is open to its appeal and does not just denounce it out of hand.

Feminist cultural critic Elayne Rapping's "The Magical World of Daytime Soap Operas" counters a sometimes rejective and denunciatory form of cultural criticism that is often leveled against soap operas and women's daytime television to try to understand the utopian appeal of the genre and how it deals with real problems. Opening with reflections on how her conversations with her daughter over the years about their shared soap opera *Guiding Light* have allowed articulation of a variety of social and gender issues, Rapping suggests that soaps can be a cultural forum in which to discuss issues of concern to women and families.

Moreover, Rapping argues that soaps present a utopia of community and compassion, and "good" characters who can serve as models of social norms or ideals. Bringing to bear a wealth of feminist thought on the subject of soap operas, Rapping suggests that the genre embodies many feminist ideals and values and shares positive features embodied in Marge Piercy's utopian novel *Woman at the Edge of Time* (1985). Of course, there is a fantasy dimension to soap operas. Problems are often solved magically, covering over a social system torn by racial, class, and gender oppression. Yet, although soaps ultimately uphold the values and institutions of the status quo, they articulate many problems and issues of interest to their audiences and embody a wide range of feminist values and concerns.

Cultural critic and educator Pepi Leistyna's "Social Class and Entertainment Television: What's So Real About Reality TV?" carries out a systematic historical survey of the presentation of the working class in popular U.S. entertainment shows, followed by a survey of the depiction of workers on so-called reality TV. Leistyna's analysis of TV entertainment from the 1950s to the present indicates that during the 1950s U.S. television tended to create a utopia of idealized middle-class families, while the few working-class characters were presented as buffoons and butts of jokes. When people of color began appearing in situation comedies in the 1970s, they tended to be portrayed in racial stereotypes and were often typecast as working class or underclass. There have only been a handful of working-class women characters, and they are often presented as single mothers, with the exception of *Roseanne,* which many critics praise for raising class and gender issues. Yet, on the whole, television entertainment rarely, if ever, depicted working-class oppression and struggle or realistically explored class issues.

Leistyna argues that TV cop shows tend to villainize lower class whites and communities of color, while rural areas were never seriously depicted in TV series, and country folks were often butts of jokes. The rise of "trash TV" in the 1980s and 1990s continued and even intensified extremely derogatory presentations of working-class characters of all races and genders. Leistyna raises the question of whether reality TV has diversified and improved such representations and finds that class and racial stereotypes abound in the most popular reality-TV series. As one countervailing tendency, he sees some attempts to depict the reality of labor on Discovery Channel shows about work, although here, too, the focus is on spectacle and drama, not exploring working-class life or problems. Leistyna concludes with a plea for media literacy to detect classist as well as racist, sexist, and homophobic representations and a media reform movement that will struggle for more realistic representations and serious dealing with social issues and struggles of working people.

Cultural critic Myrna Hant's "African American and Jewish Mothers/Wives on Television: Persistent Stereotypes" demonstrates how both African American and Jewish women have been "othered" in derogatory stereotypes that present them as inferior to non-Jewish white women and deviating from societal norms. While Jewish mothers were idealized in an early TV show, *The Goldbergs,* by the 1970s Jewish mothers and wives were stereotypically and negatively portrayed in many TV series as loud-mouthed, domineering, and obnoxious. From the early days of TV, African American women were put in the "mammy" role as exemplified in *Beulah,* which in Hant's words "personified the 'slave' coming to the TV sit com." A surprising amount of later TV shows perpetuate the "mammy" stereotype, accompanied by representations of black women as overweight, loud-mouthed, and perhaps oversexed.

While sons in many sitcoms are deferential to African American mothers, they are often oppressed and denigrated by Jewish mothers. Hant argues for the need to decode the mythologies of women and race in television entertainment and critically engage the misrepresentations of stereotypes. Television writers and producers, she suggests, perpetuate these stereotypes because audiences recognize and laugh at familiar ethnic humor. But audiences should demand a wider range of representations of diverse social groups and women, so as to capture the true variety and diversity of people in the United States.

TV writer and producer and cultural critic Felicia D. Henderson's "Successful, Single and 'Othered': The Media and the 'Plight' of Single Black Women" undertakes a systematic exploration of multiple media representations of unmarried African American women. Looking at a set of representations of African American professional women in a De Beers Corporation "Right Hand Ring" campaign, a set of *Washington Post* articles on dating between single black men and women, and the 2006 interracial romantic comedy *Something New,* Henderson explores how single African American women are marginalized and "othered" and how at the same time the dominant white and patriarchal power structure is reproduced.

The De Beers' "Right Hand Ring" campaign shows four women with their left hand ready for that all-important marriage ring and, while the white women are shown in close-ups, attractive clothing, and confident smiles, the lone single black woman is shot in a long shot, wearing a nightgown and without much prospect of getting that magic ring on her finger. The *Washington Post* series on relations between single black men and women is one of a large number of similar series, Henderson notes, all of which include shocking statistics concerning the large numbers of single African American women and the desperate measures women are driven to in order to find a mate—in the case of the *Washington Post* series, cyberspace dating. Henderson decodes the cultural representations and meanings found in this cyber-dating site, which reinforce, she claims, the marginalized situation of African American women. In a concluding section, Henderson interrogates the 2006 Hollywood romantic comedy *Something New* to show how the culture recommends interracial romance as the solution to black women's plight, reinforcing patriarchal norms and suggesting that if black women want to be "normal," they must pursue marriage, thus strengthening a white, male-dominated institution and ideology.

Feminist cultural critic Merri Lisa Johnson's "Ladies Love Your Box: The Rhetoric of Pleasure and Danger in Feminist Television Studies" presents a survey of new cable television programming that deals with gender and sexuality in much more open and mature forms than previous television programming, which stereotyped women, people of color, and gays and lesbians. Johnson's clever play on the multiple meanings of "box" in her title reminds one of the relationship between television and sexuality, and especially representations of women, in TV programs. Her study identifies a controversial debate in feminist media studies—as well as within some communications theory and cultural studies—which is often referred to as the "pleasure debates," or "porn wars." Against critiques that question women's pleasure in popular-culture forms that may contain problematic representations of women and sexuality, Johnson counters that many recent TV shows contain feminist themes and should be seriously scrutinized by cultural theorists.

In an extended version of a now-classic article that has become a key reference point in feminist theory on the question of post-feminism, the distinguished cultural theorist Angela McRobbie argues in "Post Feminism and Popular Culture" that a distinctive strategy in contemporary popular culture (and confirmed elsewhere in political culture) finds feminism taken into account, referred to as though it has been effective and is, as a result, no longer necessary. According to this post-feminist discourse, women, especially young women in the West, have gained their freedom and equality. This process of taking feminism into account is also, McRobbie argues, a way of undoing feminism, since it is deemed as belonging absolutely in the past. In films like *Bridget Jones's Diary,* this process can be seen with clarity. While feminism haunts the edges of the film's narrative, it is constantly disavowed, though in these very acts of disavowal its ghostly status signals a loss that is nevertheless registered.

Cultural and literary critic Kathleen McHugh's "Women in Traffic: L.A. Autobiography" reflects on a series of Hollywood films that depict women in automobiles, opening with reflections on the simultaneous rise of the automobile industry and film industry. While traveling on public transportation was in the nineteenth and early twentieth centuries highly dangerous to women, the automobile offered a private and protective space for travel—at least for upper-class women who could afford cars. McHugh notes that the films and genres that feminist theory used to illustrate Hollywood's positioning of women as objects of the gaze also emphasized their mobility in various modes and sites. Observing that women's mobility seemed to operate as a threat to be contained in certain classical Hollywood genres, McHugh turns to contemporary Hollywood films to interrogate some examples of women in traffic.

McHugh chooses four films from different genres to illustrate how women's auto-mobility operates in relation to their visual objectification in contemporary Hollywood films. This relation dramatizes both the empowerment of women to occupy spaces previously dominated by men and the elements of their continued gender oppression. The fantasy of *The Terminator* features Sarah Connor's transformation from waitress to woman warrior, her strength deriving from her pregnancy and her salvation from a photograph that travels through time. The film leaves her alone and in an ambiguous situation. *Thelma and Louise* uses the buddy and road film genres to explore the oppression of women, depicting their liberation as a fantasy of visual transcendence captured in the final freeze frame of their driving over a cliff, in a notoriously ambiguous and controversial ending. F. Gary Gray's *Set It Off* uses the caper genre to explore the gender, class, and racial oppression of four African American women who decide to rob banks to solve their problems, triggering an urban outlaw road movie. In each, the women's agency and mobility clash with the traditional constraints of women's passive role and visual representation. In a coda, McHugh turns to an indie melodrama, Todd Haynes' *Safe,* reading it as an allegory of the good girl, a married, domestic, white, middle-class woman, whose very contained auto-mobility nevertheless exposes her to the public sphere beyond her home. She loses her protective cocoon and suffers a nervous breakdown, trying to find comfort in self-help regimes and her reflection in the mirror.

Film professor and cultural critic Chon Noriega's "'Waas Sappening?' Narrative Structure and Iconography in *Born in East L.A.*" interrogates Cheech Marin's 1987 film *Born in East L.A.* to illuminate the situation of Chicano culture and life in the contemporary United States. While the film did not receive much national critical attention, it was extremely popular, especially in the Southwest, upon its release and was acclaimed in film festivals throughout Latin America. Engaging in a close reading of the film's narrative while contextualizing it within the situation of the contested positions of Chicanos within contemporary U.S. culture, Noriega shows how the film encodes the complex history of generations of Chicano immigrants negotiating their dual Mexican and American cultural heritage and histories.

The film opens with the main character arguing with his mother in front of the background of a rich mise-en-scène tapestry of cultural symbols. Although Rudy Robles (Cheech Marin) is a third-generation immigrant who does not speak Spanish, he is rounded up and deported to Mexico, and the film's adventure portrays his comic attempts to re-cross the border and return to his home. Along the way, he interacts with a variety of figures who illustrate, in Noriega's reading, the Chicano people's Mexican American history, heritage, and historical challenges. Full of complex symbolism and multiple levels of meaning, Noriega demonstrates that *Born in East L.A.* is a highly complex and engaging work that illuminates the situation of Latinos and immigrants in the United States today.

In a selection from their book *The Hollywood War Machine* (2007), "American Militarism, Hollywood, and Media Culture," with an added postscript and update, educators and film critics Carl Boggs and Tom Pollard explore the relations between Hollywood films, militarism, and recent U.S wars. Boggs and Pollard argue that over the past decades, many Hollywood war films, which were often made in cooperation with the Pentagon, served as outright propaganda for U.S. military intervention. Moreover, the celebration of the U.S. military and demonization of its enemies contribute to a culture of militarism, where war is naturalized and shown as the solution to conflicts and military values and a warrior ethic are celebrated.

In a detailed postscript to their book, Boggs and Pollard indicate how Hollywood war films of the last years confirm their theses. They also answer their critics by arguing that rather than advance a mechanistic model that claims that war films cause violence and war, they use a dialectical model that affirms films as reflecting and influencing social reality.

Cultural critic Meenakshi Gigi Durham's "Ethnic Chic and the Displacement of South Asian Female Sexuality in the U.S. Media" explores the ways that cultural forms from South Asia are largely appropriated by white women in U.S. culture, but in ways that erase the ethnic origins, cultural significance, and bodies of the women whose artifacts are appropriated, while constructing as the norm or ideal of beauty the white women's bodies that appropriated the artifacts. In turn, Durham looks at how Asian women's bodies are displaced and reconstituted in Western media texts as highly sexualized and orientalized "others," objects of an erotic gaze without voice or subjectivity, or are simply not visible. Using Rony's concept of the "third eye," Durham notes that South Asian women in media representations are denied a gaze on those who perceive women in terms of an orientalized and sexualized spectacle, and are denied positions as subjects and agents in dominant Western media constructions.

The appropriation of symbols and fashion from South Asian women in the youth subculture is often a quite different thing, Durham notes, as young people construct hybridized and globalized identities and styles. While this appropriation could be significant in enlarging the cultural understanding and possibilities of the society at large, the Western media tend to trivialize such appropriation or to code it negatively in ways that construct the hegemony of white Western culture. Consequently, it is important to explore the implications of these issues for South Asian women and other women of color, as well as white women. Further, Durham argues that new ways to theorize and represent South Asian women's femininity, sexuality, and culture need to be opened up.

Education professor and cultural theorist Allan Luke's "Another Ethnic Autobiography? Childhood and the Cultural Economy of Looking" uses his own childhood and the experiences of his actor father, Edwin Luke, and his uncle Keye Luke to reflect on the constructedness of childhood and ethnic identities. Raising questions about previous forms of ethnic narratives, like those of liberation that seek a cultural authenticity and of displacement that seek recovery and continuity within a situation of displacement, Luke posits narratives of simulation that construct the ways in which different traditions, cultural experiences, and forms of media and culture can construct hybridized and highly mediated identities. Arguing that in a postmodern media culture, identities are more mediated than ever, Luke reflects on his own family history and immersion in media to explicate emergent types of hybridized identities, a project facilitated by Luke's own family's imbrication in the film and television business and his generation's immersions in these forms of media culture. Hence, Luke presents not only a fascinating and new kind of cultural autobiography but one that is an exercise in metatheorizing about cultural identity, the role of media, blended and hybridized identities, and the emergence of a highly mediated postmodern culture and society.

The study by cultural theorists Chyng Sun, Ekra Miezan, and Rachael Liberman, "Model Minority/Honorable Eunuch: The Dual Image of Asian American Men in the Media and Everyday Perception" inquires into how the media and U.S. society have perpetuated a stereotype of Asian American men. The authors carry out a research project with college students from multi-racial groups to investigate how media representations of Asian American men influence how the subjects see and interact with Asian American men in real life. The authors explore how the stereotype of Asian Americans as the "model minority" arose, accompanied by stereotypes of Asian American men as asexual, nerdy, and highly domesticated, an "honorary eunuch" in the authors' provocative phrasing. Investigating the historical roots of Asian American immigration to the United States and the resultant media stereotypes, the authors note that after cinematic stereotypes like "good" Charlie Chan and "bad" Fu Manchu emerged in Hollywood cinema, dominant media were by the 1960s discussing and presenting Asian Americans as a "model minority," a presentation that was used to further political agendas at that time.

The authors call for the need for new representations of Asian Americans but warn against the dangers of falling prey to the hegemonic and misogynistic masculinity that they see emerging in some Asian rap music and films. With a broader range of representations, they conclude, the hegemonic stereotypes would dissolve in importance, and the public would see the Asian American community, including men, in its variety and diversity.

Educator, cultural critic and gender activist Jackson Katz's "'Politics Is a Contact Sport': Media, Sports Metaphors, and Presidential Masculinity" carries out investigations of the role of sports metaphors in presidential politics. Noting that there has been neglect of analysis of the role of sports and masculinities in presidential politics, Katz undertakes a study of how sports, gender, and class play out together in recent U.S. presidential elections. After inquiry into "sports studies, cultural studies, and the electoral gender gap," Katz analyzes sports and class politics and zeroes in on the violent sports of boxing and football as major sources of metaphors for presidential politics that appeal largely to men. This raises the question of the role of masculinity in presidential elections and whether women candidates can make use of sports metaphors, calling for the need for gender analysis of presidential politics, as well as class and race analysis.

13

■ Children and the Media

Alternative Histories[1]

Toby Miller

Media audiences provide crucial conceptual links between individuals and the wider social world. Why? Because reading, playing, viewing, and listening involve both solitary interpretation and collective conduct. This dynamic captures solitude, yet also community, in an oscillation that can entail harmony and dissonance in contrapuntal form. It should come as no surprise then, that many constituencies invoke the audience: Media-production executives do so to measure their success, via ratings or sales, and to claim knowledge of what consumers want in order to attract advertisers. Regulators do so to create and administer laws of ownership and control to encourage or restrict diversity, obscenity, commercialism, and politics. Psychologists do so to undertake research into how the media change people's minds, and lobby groups do so to change content in the name of the representation of particular groups or to improve their access to the means of communication. Hence, the links between panic and media concerning education, violence, and apathy, which has supposedly been engendered by the media, and routinely investigated by the state, psychologists, communication studies, Marxism, conservatism, the church, liberal feminists, and others, through the "psy-function" (Foucault, 2006). The psy-function is a shifting field of knowledge and power, occupied by psychoanalysis, psychology, psychotherapy, psychiatry, social psychology, criminology, and psychopharmacology. It makes dual claims, that it can both describe and manage the mind.

The psy-function emerged in the nineteenth and twentieth centuries around the figure of the child and has stood ready ever since to "plug in, rush in, when an opening gapes in familial sovereignty" (Foucault, 2006: 85–86). In both commercial and governmental forms, the psy-function exercises authority over young people, those "socially deictic" pointers to shifts in cultural norms and anxieties. It has done so ever since British protests against the Industrial Revolution were metaphorized in a rash of child-abduction stories, through U.S. worries about lost generations that had no birthright after the Great War, through movements *contra* 1970s fascist "disappearances" of children in Argentina, and through post-industrial Yanqui concerns about Satanism rampant in the cornfields (Durham, 2004: 589, 591). In this chapter, I seek to trace how the discourse of children and the media operates and bring it into question, suggesting that it serves as part of a broader assault on children in the United States by reactionary forces. I do so by interrogating the media-effects audience-research tradition, illustrating how it fits into centuries of anxiety about the spread of literacy, and the control of young people.

The audience as consumer, student, felon, voter, and idiot engages public policy and civil society via the psy-function, and religious and familial iconophobia, the sense that young people lie beyond the control of the state and the ruling class, and may be led astray by popular texts. Moral panics and the psy-function combine in media critique via a caricature of the audience as a "cultural dope," who supposedly "produces the stable features of the society by acting in compliance with pre-established and legitimate alternatives of action that the common culture provides." The "common sense rationalities... of here and now situations" used by ordinary people are obscured and derided by such categorizations (Garfinkel, 1992: 68). When the audience is invoked by the psy-function, the media, critics, or regulators, it frequently becomes such a "dope," for example, via the assumption that "[c]hildren are sitting victims; television bites them" (Schramm et al., 1961: 1). The assumption is that the media *do* things *to* people, with the citizens understood as audience members at risk of becoming a "dope," and abjuring interpersonal responsibility (see Comstock and Scharrer, 1999; Cooper, 1996; Surgeon General's Scientific Advisory Committee on Television and Social Behavior, 1971).

The effects model offers analysis and critique of education and civic order. It views the media as forces that can either direct, or pervert, the citizen-consumer. John Hartley refers to the youth version of this process as "juvenation" (1998: 15). Entering young minds hypodermically, the media both enable and imperil learning; they may even drive the citizen to violence through aggressive and misogynistic images and narratives. The model is found at a variety of sites, including laboratories, clinics, prisons, schools, newspapers, psy-function journals, media organizations' research and publicity departments, everyday talk, program-classification regulations, conference papers, political debates, advertising agencies, and state-of-our-youth or state-of-our-civil-society moral panics. The focus is on the cognition and emotion of individual human subjects, as studied via observation and experimentation. The media are deemed to make people well- or ill-educated, wild or self-controlled, as measured electronically or behaviorally. The effects model is spectacularly embodied in the nation-wide U.S. media theatrics that ensue after mass school shootings, questioning the role of violent images (not hyper-Protestantism, straight white masculinity, a risk society, or easy access to firearms), in creating violent people (more routinely, it is crucial to the claims made by marketers about the efficacy of their work).

As Bob Dylan puts it, recalling the 1960s in Greenwich Village, "sociologists were saying that TV had deadly intentions and was destroying the minds and imaginations of the young—that their attention span was being dragged down." The other dominant site of knowledge was the "psychology professor, a good performer, but originality not his long suit" (2004: 55, 67). They still cast a shadow across that village, and many others. Consider Dorothy G. Singer and Jerome L. Singer's febrile twenty-first-century call for centering media effects within the study of child development:

> For the first 60 years of the twentieth century, conceptions such as Freud's...theory of a fundamental aggressive drive or instinct predominated....[C]ritical analyses and careful research on social learning...and literally scores of psychophysiological and behavioral empirical studies beginning in the 1960s have pointed much more to aggression as a learned response....[C]an we ignore the impact on children of their exposure through television and films or, more recently, to computer games and arcade video games that involve vast amounts of violent actions? (2001: xv)

The psy-function's effects model is dominant in the United States and has been exported around the world. It originated and has thrived here because of some very particular factors: an extremely violent state internationally that repeatedly invades other lands, an astonishingly high rate of interpersonal violent crime, a domestically violent state embarked on unprecedented rates of execution for a First-World nation, minimal rehabilitation for prisoners, the world's greatest uptake of audiovisual media, a risk society of moral panic around socialism, racial difference, and language, ongoing anxiety about educational attainment and commitments to a science of selling and propaganda. Those who are concerned enough to mount psychological, rather than political-economic accounts of social problems, draw correlations between these things. Despite this very specific background, the effects model is typically applied without consideration of place or time, while its latter-day export correlates with the export of neoliberal U.S. policies, such as disinvestment in education, welfare, the redistribution of income upwards, and a scratching of the head by pundits as misery and violence surround them.

The media-effects model suffers from all the disadvantages of ideal-typical psychological reasoning. It relies on the philosophy of individualism and fails to account for cultural norms and politics, as well as the arcs of history that establish patterns of text and response inside politics, war, ideology, and discourse. Each costly laboratory study seems to be based in "a large university in the mid-West" and is countered by a similar experiment, with conflicting results. As politicians, grant-givers, and complaining pundits call for more and more research to prove that the media makes you stupid, violent, and apathetic—or the opposite—academics line up at the trough to indulge their contempt for popular culture and ordinary life and their rent-seeking urge for public money. The model rarely interrogates its own conditions of existence—namely, that governments, religious groups, and the media themselves use it to account for social problems, and it satisfies those authorities who desire surveillance of popular culture. To leaven this lack of reflexivity, some historical background to the emergence of effects study is needed.

With the Industrial Revolution, the extension through societies of the capacity to read had, as its corollary, the possibility of a public beyond a group of people physically gathered together—and hence the prospect of a politics beyond the local. As a consequence, great concern was expressed about public "stimulation of the passions" by popular romances and plays (the "liturgy of the devil") in sixteenth- and seventeenth-century

Western Europe. Typography was thought to disrupt ecclesiastical authority via a trio of crimes: "heresy, sedition, or immorality." At the same time as this dystopic gloom hung all around, there was a ray of hope that the new technology represented aesthetic and political innovation—new forms of personal pleasure and social participation. But when books began to proliferate across Western Europe in the mid-eighteenth century, people frequently skim-read, generating anxious critiques that a plenitude of text was producing a simplistic level of comprehension that lacked profundity and erudition—the down-side of a *Leserevolution* that displaced the continuing study of a few important, hermeneutic texts with chaotic, permissive practices of reading. Nineteenth-century U.S. and European societies saw spirited debate over whether new popular media and genres—newspapers, crime stories, and novels—would breed anarchic readers, who lacked respect for the traditionally literate classes, and might become independently minded and informed, perhaps even distracted from the one true path of servitude. So white slave-owners terrorized African Americans who taught themselves and their colleagues to read. And when unionists in the nineteenth-century Cuban cigar industry organized mass readings of news and current affairs to workers, management and the state responded brutally. The advent of outdoor reading, and the appearance of the train as a site of mobile public culture, led to new anxieties about more open knowledge and debate, with the railway terminus a key site of anxiety, as a sales point for sensationalist novels and non-fiction (Manguel, 1996: 110–11, 141, 280, 284; Briggs and Burke, 2003: 2–3, 18, 49, 64; Miller, 1998).

The sexual side to the new openness through mass literacy became the heart of numerous campaigns against public sex and its representation, most notably the Comstock Law in the United States, which policed sex from the late nineteenth-century. The Law was named for the noted Post Office moralist Anthony Comstock, who ran the New York Society for the Suppression of Vice. Comstock was exercised by "EVIL READING." He avowed that before the Fall, reading was unknown. In the early twentieth century, opera, Shakespeare, and romance fiction were censored for their immodest impact on the young. Throughout the history of U.S. media regulation since that time, both governments and courts have policed sexual material, based on its alleged impact on young people, all the way from the uptake of Britain's 1868 *Regina v. Hicklin* decision's anxieties about vulnerable youth, through to the U.S. Supreme Court's 1978 *Federal Communication Commission v. Pacifica* (Heins, 2002: 9, 23, 29–32).

There was reinforcement from academic experts who, by the early twentieth century, had decreed media audiences to be passive consumers, thanks to the missions of literary criticism (distinguishing the aesthetically cultivated from others), and psychology (distinguishing the socially competent from others) (Butsch, 2000: 3). The origins of the psy-function can be traced to nineteenth-century anxieties about "the crowd" in a suddenly urbanized and educated Western Europe, which raised the prospect of a long-feared "ochlocracy" of "the worthless mob" (Pufendorf, 2000: 144), able to participate in politics and share popular texts. Elite theorists emerged from both right and left, notably Vilfredo Pareto (1976), Gaetano Mosca (1939), Gustave Le Bon (1899), and Robert Michels (1915). They argued that newly literate publics were vulnerable to manipulation by demagogues. The Latino, James Truslow Adams, who invented the term the "American Dream," saw "[t]he mob mentality of the city crowd" as "one of the menaces to modern civilization";

he was particularly severe on "the prostitution of the moving-picture industry" (1941: 404, 413). Tests of beauty (in the humanities) and truth (in the social sciences) were finding popular culture wanting.

As working-class U.S. immigrants and their children learned to read, the middle class sought ways of managing this rapidly-changing population. With civil society growing restive, the wealth of radical associations was explained away in social-psychological terms, rather than political-economic ones. Within academia, Harvard took charge of theorizing the great unwashed, Chicago the task of meeting them, and Columbia their statistical enumeration (Staiger, 2005: 21–22). Such tendencies moved into high gear with the sociological Payne–Fund studies of the 1930s, which were animated by the realization that "[m]otion pictures are not understood by the present generation of adults" but "appeal to children" (Charters 1933: v). This research juxtaposed the impact of films on what were known as "superior" adults—young college professors, graduate students, and their wives—versus their effects on children, frequently from juvenile centers, who were easily corraled due to their "regular régimes of living" via the collection of "authoritative and impersonal data which would make possible a more complete evaluation of motion pictures and their social potentialities" to answer: "what effect do motion pictures have upon children of different ages?," especially on the many young people who were "retarded" (Charters, 1933: 8, iv–v, 12–13, 31). These pioneering scholars boldly set out to see whether "the onset of puberty is or is not affected by motion pictures," especially given what were called 'The Big Three' narrative themes, of love, crime, and sex (sound familiar from today?). They gauged audience reactions through "autobiographical case studies" that asked such questions as whether "All Most Many Some Few No Chinese are cunning and underhand," and pondered the impact of "demonstrations of satisfying love techniques" for fear that, "[s]exual passions are aroused and amateur prostitution…aggravated." This was done, *inter alia,* through "[l]aboratory techniques" that used such sensational machinery as the psychogalvanometer, and beds wired with hypnographs and polygraphs to measure children's restlessness at night, after being required to drink multiple cups of coffee, versus watching Hollywood films (Charters, 1933: 4, 10, 15, 25, 32, 49, 54, 60; Staiger, 2005: 25).

The notion of the suddenly enfranchised being bamboozled by the unscrupulously fluent has recurred throughout the modern period. It inevitably leads to a primary emphasis on the number and conduct of audiences to audiovisual entertainment: where they came from, how many there were, and what they did as a consequence of being present. The example set by the Payne Fund has led to seven more decades of obsessive attempts to correlate youthful consumption of popular culture with anti-social conduct. The pattern is that whenever media technologies emerge, children are immediately identified as both pioneers and victims. Simultaneously endowed by manufacturers and critics with immense power and immense vulnerability, they are held to be the first to know, and the last to understand, the media—the grand paradox of youth, latterly on display in the "digital sublime" of technological determinism, as always with the super-added valence of a future citizenry at risk (Mosco, 2004: 80). Each media technology and genre has brought with it a raft of marketing techniques focused on young people, even as concerns about supposedly unprecedented and unholy new risks to youth recur: cheap novels during the

1900s, silent, then sound, film during the 1920s, radio in the 1930s, comic books of the 1940s and 1950s, pop music and television from the 1950s and '60s, satanic rock as per the 1970s and 1980s, video cassette recorders in the 1980s, and rap music, video games, and the internet since the 1990s. Recent studies totalize 8- to 18-year olds as "Generation M," for "media." The satirical paper *The Onion* cleverly satirized the interdependent phenomena of moral panic and commodification via a *faux* 2005 study of the impact on U.S. youth when seeing Janet Jackson's breast in a Super Bowl broadcast the year before (Kline, 1993: 57; Mazzarella, 2003: 228; Roberts, et al., 2005; "U.S. Children," 2005).

Of course, things *have* changed for young people thanks to the commercial media, though not in the way the psy-function's epistemology allows it to address. *Popular Science* magazine coined the word "teenager" in 1941, and *Seventeen* magazine appeared on newsstands three years later. Youth became simultaneously a "mass movement and mass market" in the post-War period, and both left and right in politics were alarmed by the "commercial child" (Liljeström 1983: 144–146). Prior to the televisualization and suburbanization of the United States that began after World War II, toys were exclusively advertised to the trade, with 80% of sales made each December. When Disney began the Mickey Mouse Club on TV in 1955, product placement and commercials centered children as consumers for the first time, and on a year-round basis: "children began their training as consumers" at the age of four or five (Riesman et al., 1953: 120, 122). The white-picket family and home were deemed to be under threat from this newly enfranchised shopper, who formed communities outside the family. Congressional hearings into juvenile delinquency heard again and again from social scientists, police, parents, and others, that the emergent mass media were diverting offspring from traditional values. The hearings promoted psy-function denunciations of comic books, for example, as causes of nightmares, juvenile delinquency, and even murder (Mazzarella, 2003: 230; Malkki and Martin, 2003: 217–18; Gilbert, 1986: 3; Park, 2004: 114; Heins, 2002: 52–54).

Today, young people have textual and consumer value as never before. Viacom, Time Warner, and Disney identify them as key sources of TV profit, because advertising, programming, and merchandising have such an effortless organic connection. By 1999, young people were estimated to account for $300 billion a year (measured in U.S. dollars) in expenditure by parents across the United States, and marketing was working with the slogan "Kids Getting Older Younger." Children themselves were spending upwards of $20 billion annually. In 2003, Nickelodeon sold $3 billion of consumer products, up one-fifth from the previous year. That made it the fastest-growing part of Viacom. In 2004, U.S. industry allocated twice as much money to targeting children as a decade earlier. PBS launched Sprout for 2- to 5-year-olds in 2005, and BabyFirstTV, aimed at six-month-old viewers, began in 2006. Companies like Posh Tots offer a bewildering array of personalized bedroom furnishings and ambience for the billion-dollar child via poshtots. com. No wonder that when the "stars" come to life in *Toy Story* (Lasseter, 1995) and *Toy Story 2* (Lasseter & Brannon, 1999), they proceed to converse about their "parent" companies and brand identities (Mickenberg, 2006: 1221; Kapur, 2005: 2, 29, 33, 31; Stephens, 1995: 14; Watson, 2004: 14; "Kids & Cash," 2004; "Children's Television," 2004; DeFao, 2006).

State, church, and commerce commodify youth culture, even as they demonize it (Hartley, 1998: 14); for example, Jacques Gansler, Bill Clinton's Assistant Secretary of Defense for Acquisition and Technology, declared teen hackers a "real threat environment" to national security (quoted in Bendrath, 2003: 53). In 1997, Clinton announced that the nation had "about six years to turn this juvenile crime thing around or our country is going to be living in chaos," even as youth crime had dropped by almost 10% in a year (Glassner, 1999: xiv). Republican Party front organizations such as the Parents Television Council (2005) undertake obsessive content analyses of media output. Its Entertainment Tracking System is designed to "ensure that children are not constantly assaulted by sex, violence, and profanity on television and in other media…along with stories and dialogue that create disdain for authority figures, patriotism, and religion." William Bratton, the much-heralded former chief of police in New York City, celebrated his first term in charge of the Los Angeles Police Department by denouncing "a youthful population that is largely disassociated from the mainstream of America," even as the average age of violent criminals in his city was well on the increase, and rates of arrest for local youth had plummeted (Males, 2006). Needless to say, such mendacity was rewarded by a second term in office. However ridiculous these assessments may be, they neatly index the state's contempt for its young, and the symbolic power of popular culture. Young people incarnate adult terror in the face of the popular. They provide a *tabula rasa,* onto which can be placed every manner of anxiety about new knowledges, technologies, and tastes (Hartley, 1998: 15).

Such obsessions divert attention from the material infrastructure of children's lives. For reasons entirely unrelated to reading comic books, watching video, or listening to music backwards, the supposedly idyllic world of the *bourgeois* U.S. family simply does not work. By the 1980s, just 12% of children lived with their biological parents, while only 7% lived with an employed father and "home-duties" mother. And the 2000 Census disclosed that married couples with children were only 25% of the population. Clearly, the family is "a contingent form of association with unstable boundaries and varying structures" (Shapiro, 2001: 2). Ideologies, institutions, and policies predicated on "tradition" were threatened in the face of major social change. On the one hand, children had to cope with the extended working hours and diminished spending power of harried, often single, parents. On the other, they were interpellated by corporate advertising and entertainment as competent, knowledgeable consumers who should not be cowed into submission by authoritarian parental or educational will. Problems such as child abuse, which correlate quite clearly with poverty, were scrupulously defined as unrelated to the economy by government and the psy-function—the response was to psychologize rather than politicize. By 2003, more money was being spent on stimulants and antidepressants for children than antibiotics or asthma medications (Steinberg and Kincheloe, 1997: 2–3, 16–17; Hacking, 1995: 64–65; Albright, 2006: 170).

Basically, moral panics about children and the media have displaced attention from the horrific impact on the young by deregulation, and the cessation of vital social services that characterized the catastrophic presidencies of Ronald Reagan, George Bush the Elder, and George Bush Minor. The data on youth welfare demonstrate the centrality of big government to the family solidity that these hegemons rhetorically pined for but programmatically undermined through massively eroded expenditure on health, nutrition, foster care, and a raft of other services for young people. The outcome of decades of policies exacting a toll upon the young, through distributing money away from them, is that U.S. citizens over the age of forty are the wealthiest group in world history, with the lowest tax payments in the First World. Child poverty is at unprecedented levels—20% of the population, which is three times the figure for northern Europe—and half of all children experience poverty at some point. Whereas very few teenaged children in the United States worked for money in the first half of the twentieth century, almost 50% had to do so by its end. One in eight children has no health coverage (Romer and Jamieson, 2003; Putnam, 2000: 261–63; Gillham and Reivich, 2004: 152).

Meanwhile, a succession of judicial decisions has further disenfranchised the young, with conservative justices contemptuous of privacy rights for children. Only two countries deny children rights, other than to counsel and due process in criminal cases. One is Somalia. You are encouraged to guess the identity of the latter, with the following hints to help you: the Kansas Juvenile Code incorporates parental rights as part of creepy Christianity's horror, in the face of children's citizenship. The United States repeatedly establishes new records amongst developed countries for the execution of people under 18. Half the Supreme Court favored killing those aged below fifteen until a 2005 decision. Young people lost free-speech protection when the Court differentiated youthful from adult citizens, permitting state governments to legislate in ways that would be unconstitutional if applied to adults. Today's capacity of the FBI and the Customs Service to utilize body-language profiling to identify potential terrorists, with agents trained to notice "exceptional nervousness" via visible carotid arteries, chapped lips, "fleeting smiles," "darting eyes[,] and hand tremors," derives from a 1968 decision of the Court, which established that young people could be arrested because they "didn't look right" to officials. And while the law protects adults from being treated with psychotropics against their will, this protection does not exist for youth in the majority of United States jurisdictions, who have also been subject to genetic testing on the grounds that it can disclose future classroom disobedience (Davis et al., 2002; Males, 1996: 7, 35; *Ginsberg v. New York* 390 US 629; Albright, 2006: 171; Rose, 2007: 119; Watson, 2004: 5, 18 n. 5; Minow, 2002: 262).

Key social measures of unhappiness correlate with youth today in a way that they did not, up to the mid-1970s. Suicide is the eleventh largest cause of death in the United States, but it is third amongst the young; the rate for 15- to 19-year-olds quadrupled between 1950 and 1995. Perhaps to cope with their feelings of helplessness, 135,000 teenagers packed a gun with their sandwiches and school books each day in 1990, while by 2004, eight children and teenagers died by gunshot per day. This in turn relates to marketing. With the white-male market for fire-arms saturated, and attempts to sell to women falling short of the desired numbers, manufacturers turned to young people in the 1990s. At the same time, powerful antipsychotic drugs are being used on them as never before, increasing five times over between 1993 and 2002 (Lewis, 1992: 41; Children's Defense Fund, 2004; Glassner, 1999: xxi, 55; Ruddick, 2003: 337, 348; Hacker, 2006: 32; Foundation for Child Development, 2004; Liebel, 2004: 151; Ivins, 2005; Carey, 2006).

For all this disenfranchisement and peril, the little beasts must be prevailed upon for yet more sacrifices: Reagan education bureaucrat, pop philosopher, and secret serial gambler William Bennett calls for young people to respect the law and the individual, and George W. Bush introduced a "Lessons of Liberty" schools program to ideologize them into militarism. In 2004, 83% of U.S. high schools ran community-service programs, up from 27% two decades earlier, and some required anti-leftist ideology (Westheimer and Kahne, 2004; "Kids' Role," 2004). In 2002, George W. Bush promulgated policies to "improve students' knowledge of American history, increase their civic involvement, and deepen their love for our great country," and he went on to require that children learn "America is a force for good in the world, bringing hope and freedom to other people." Senator Lamar Alexander, previously Federal head of education and a university bureaucrat, sponsored the American History and Civics Education Act "so our children can grow up learning what it means to be an American" (Bush and Alexander quoted in Westheimer, 2004: 231). Meanwhile, progressive political activism by young people led to sanctions. In West Virginia, a high-school pupil was suspended for inviting her colleagues to join an anti-war club in 2002, as were a ninth-grader in Maryland, for marching against the invasion of Iraq in 2003, and a high-school student in Colorado for posting peace flyers (Westheimer, 2004: 232); wrong knowledge of "American history," wrong type of "civic involvement."

But there are signs of hope. Despite such propaganda, whereas three-quarters of school-leavers thought the United States was the best country in the world in 1977, only half were sufficiently narcissistic and deluded to believe this in 2000. They are less likely than their self-satisfied elders to proclaim U.S. culture superior to all others or to oppose immigration. Globally, preferences for European over U.S. influence on international relations see young people appalled by Yanqui imperialism. In the 2004 presidential contest, the young were the only age group that favored the Democrats, and they were solidly Democratic in the 2006 mid-term elections. Plus they are the least religious sector among the U.S. population by far (Center for Information & Research on Civic Learning & Engagement, 2004; Pew Research Center for the People & the Press, 2004; Globescan/ Program on International Policy Attitudes, 2005; Baylor Institute for Studies of Religion, 2006).

These mild-mannered signs of a critical, skeptical attitude are interpreted by their elders and betters with shock and awe, in keeping with the latter's belief in severe moral decline among the young. A 1997 Public Agenda report disclosed that two-thirds of U.S. adults regarded young people as out of control and irresponsible, with parents seeking to shield children from news that covers international and domestic social conflict. And whereas half the adult population in 1952 was convinced that young people knew the difference between good and evil, only 19% believed so 50 years later (Giroux, 2000: 15; Galston, 2002: 280–81; Lemish, 2007: 13).

Caught by the psy-function's "production and marketing of the idea that the inevitable alienation, dispossession and injustice inherent in consumer capitalism is an individual and personal…problem," youth's grand paradox is to be simultaneously "the most silenced population in society" and "the noisiest" (Hansen et al. 2003: 15; Grossberg, 1994: 25). Media-effects audience research, under the sign of the psy-function, plays a vital part in this mystification. On the one hand, the effects tradition argues that the interaction of children and the media explains all manner of social problems. On the other, it argues for an entirely individual model. Cultural studies must present a counter-history to these narratives, one that brings back the specificities of space and time, to what has been a sorry story of misrecognition.

Notes

1. Thanks to Rhonda Hammer for her helpful remarks on an earlier version.

Works Cited

"Children's Television: Too Much of a Good Thing?" (2004, December 18). *Economist:* 97–98.

"Kids & Cash." (2004, November/December). *Mother Jones:* 28–29.

"Kids' Role in Securing USA." (2004, August 10). *USA Today.*

"U. S. Children Still Traumatized One Year After Seeing Partially Exposed Breast on TV." (2005, January 26). *The Onion.*

Adams, James Truslow. (1941). *The Epic of America.* New York: Triangle Books.

Albright, Jennifer. (2006). "Free Your Mind: The Right of Minors in New York to Choose Whether or Not to be Treated with Psychotropic Drugs." *Albany Law Journal of Science & Technology* 16: 169–194.

Baylor Institute for Studies of Religion and Department of Sociology, Baylor University. (2006). *American Piety in the 21st Century: New Insights to the Depth and Complexity of Religion in the US.*

Bendrath, Ralf. (2003). "The American Cyber-Angst and the Real World—Any Link?" *Bombs and Bandwidth: The Emerging Relationship Between Information Technology and Security.* Ed. Robert Latham. New York: New Press. 49–73.

Briggs, Asa and Peter Burke. (2003). *A Social History of the Media: From Gutenberg to the Internet.* Cambridge: Polity Press.

Butsch, Richard. (2000). *The Making of American Audiences: From Stage to Television, 1750–1990.* Cambridge: Cambridge University Press.

Carey, Benedict. (2006, June 6). "Use of Antipsychotics by the Young Rose Fivefold." *New York Times.*

Center for Information & Research on Civic Learning & Engagement. (2004, November 3). *Youth Turnout Up Sharply in 2004.*

Charters, W. W. (1933). *Motion Pictures and Youth: A Summary.* New York: Macmillan.

Children's Defense Fund. (2004, July 13). *The State of America's Children 2004: A Continuing Portrait of Inequality Fifty Years After* Brown v. Board of Education.

Comstock, George and Erica Scharrer. (1999). *Television: What's on, Who's Watching, and What It Means.* San Diego: Academic Press.

Cooper, Cynthia A. (1996). *Violence on Television: Congressional Inquiry, Public Criticism and Industry Response—A Policy Analysis.* Lanham: University Press of America.

Davis, Ann, Joseph Pereira, and William M. Bulkeley. (2002, August 15). "Security Concerns Bring New Focus on Body Language." *Wall Street Journal:* A1, A6.

DeFao, Janine. (2006, September 11). "TV Channel for Babies? Pediatricians Say Turn it Off." *San Francisco Chronicle.*

Durham, Deborah. (2004). "Disappearing Youth: Youth as a Social Shifter in Botswana." *American Ethnologist* 31, no. 4: 589–605.

Dylan, Bob. (2004). *Chronicles: Volume One.* New York: Simon & Schuster.

Foucault, Michel. (2006). *Psychiatric Power: Lectures at the Collège de France, 1973–74.* Ed. Jacques Lagrange. Trans. Graham Burchell. Basingstoke: Palgrave Macmillan.

Foundation for Child Development. (2004). *Index of Child Well-Being (CWI), 1975–2002, with Projections for 2003.*

Galston, William A. (2002). "Participación ciudadana en los Estados Unidos: Un análisis empírico." *Deonstruyendo la Ciudadanía: Avances y Retos en el Desarrollo de la Cultura Democrática en México.* Mexico: Secretaría de Gobernación/Secretaría de Educación Publica/Instituto Federal Electoral. 279–293.

Garfinkel, Harold. (1992). *Studies in Ethnomethodology.* Cambridge: Polity Press.

Gilbert, J. (1986). *America's Reaction to the Juvenile Delinquent in the 1950s.* New York: Oxford University Press.

Gillham, Jane and Karen Reivich. (2004). "Cultivating Optimism in Childhood and Adolescence." *Annals of the American Academy of Political and Social Science* 591: 146–163.

Giroux, Henry A. (2000). *Stealing Innocence: Youth, Corporate Power, and the Politics of Culture.* New York: St. Martin's Press.

Glassner, Barry. (1999). *The Culture of Fear: Why Americans Are Afraid of the Wrong Things.* New York: Basic Books.

Globescan/ Program on International Policy Attitudes. (2005). "In 20 of 23 Countries Polled Citizens Want Europe to Be More Influential than US."

Grossberg, Lawrence. (1994). "The Political Status of Youth and Youth Culture." *Adolescents and Their Music: If It's Too Loud, You're Too Old.* Ed. J. S. Epstein. New York: Garland. 25–46.

Hacker, Jacob S. (2006). *The Great Risk Shift: The Assault on American Jobs, Families, Health Care, and Retirement and How You Can Fight Back.* New York: Oxford University Press.

Hacking, Ian. (1995). *Rewriting the Soul: Multiple Personality and the Sciences of Memory.* Princeton: Princeton University Press.

Hansen, Susan, Alec McHoul, and Mark Rapley with Hayley Miller and Toby Miller. (2003). *Beyond Help: A Consumer's Guide to Psychology.* Ross-on-Wye: PCCS Books.

Hartley, John. (1998). "'When Your Child Grows Up Too Fast': Juvenation and the Boundaries of the Social in the News Media." *Continuum: Journal of Media & Cultural Studies* 12, no. 1: 9–30.

Heins, Marjorie. (2002). *Not in Front of the Children: "Indecency," Censorship, and the Innocence of Youth.* New York: Hill and Wang.

Ivins, Molly. (2005, February 17). "Screw the Children." *AlterNet.org.*

Kapur, Jyotsna. (2005). *Coining for Capital: Movies, Marketing, and the Transformation of Childhood.* New Brunswick: Rutgers University Press.

Kline, Stephen. (1993). *Out of the Garden: Toys, TV, and Children's Culture in the Age of Marketing.* London: Verso.

Le Bon, Gustave. (1899). *Psychologie des Foules.* Paris: Alcan.

Lemish, Dafna. (2007). *Children and Television: A Global Perspective.* Malden: Blackwell.

Lewis, Jon. (1992). *The Road to Romance & Ruin: Teen Films and Youth Culture.* New York: Routledge.

Liebel, Manfred. (2004). *A Will of Their Own: Cross-Cultural Perspectives on Working Children.* Trans. Colin Boone and Jess Rotherburger. London: Zed.

Liljeström, Rita. (1983). "The Public Child, the Commercial Child, and Our Child." *The Child and Other Cultural Inventions.* Ed. Frank S. Kessel and Alexander W. Siegel. New York: Praeger. 124–152.

Males, Mike A. (1996). *The Scapegoat Generation: America's War on Adolescents.* Monroe: Common Courage Press.

Males, Mike. (2006, September 17). "It's a Crime How We Misjudge the Young." *Los Angeles Times:* M6.

Malkki, Liisa and Emily Martin. (2003). "Children and the Gendered Politics of Globalization: In Remembrance of Sharon Stephens." *American Ethnologist* 30, no. 2: 216–224.

Manguel, Alberto. (1996). *A History of Reading.* New York: Viking.

Mazzarella, Sharon R. (2003). "Constructing Youth: Media, Youth, and the Politics of Representation." *A Companion to Media Studies.* Ed. Angharad N. Valdivia. Malden: Blackwell. 227–246.

Michels, Robert. (1915). *Political Parties: A Sociological Study of the Oligarchical Tendencies of Modern Democracy.* Trans. Eden and Cedar Paul. London: Jarrold & Sons.

Mickenberg, Julia L. (2006). "American Studies and Childhood Studies: Lessons from Consumer Culture." *American Quarterly* 58, no. 4: 1217–1227.

Miller, Toby. (1998). *Technologies of Truth: Cultural Citizenship and the Popular Media.* Minneapolis: University of Minnesota Press.

Minow, Martha. (2002). "About Women, About Culture: About Them, About Us." *Engaging Cultural Differences: The Multicultural Challenge in Liberal Democracies.* Ed. Richard A. Schweder, Martha Minow, and Hazel Rose Markus. New York: Russell Sage Foundation. 252–267.

Mosca, Gaetano. (1939). *The Ruling Class.* Trans. Hannah D. Kahn. Ed. Arthur Livingston. New York: McGraw-Hill.

Mosco, Vincent. (2004). *The Digital Sublime: Myth, Power, and Cyberspace.* Cambridge, Mass.: MIT Press.

Parents Television Council. (2005). <www.parentstv.org>.

Pareto, Vilfredo. (1976). *Sociological Writings.* Trans. Derick Mirfin. Ed. S. E. Finer. Oxford: Basil Blackwell.

Park, David W. (2004). "The Couch and the Clinic: The Cultural Authority of Popular Psychiatry and Psychoanalysis." *Cultural Studies* 18, no. 1: 109–133.

Pew Research Center for the People & the Press. (2004). *A Global Generation Gap: Adapting to a New World.*

Pufendorf, Samuel. (2000). *On the Duty of Man and Citizen According to Natural Law.* Trans. Michael Silverthorne. Ed. James Tully. Cambridge: Cambridge University Press.

Putnam, Robert D. (2000). *Bowling Alone: The Collapse and Revival of American Community.* New York: Simon & Schuster.

Riesman, David with Nathan Glazer and Reuel Denney. (1953). *The Lonely Crowd: A Study of the Changing American Character.* Garden City: Doubleday Anchor.

Roberts, Donald F., Ulla G. Foehr, and Victoria Rideout. (2005). *Generation M: Media in the Lives of 8–18 Year-Olds.* Kaiser Family Foundation.

Romer, Daniel and Patrick Jamieson. (2003). "Introduction." *American Behavioral Scientist* 46, no. 9: 1131–1136.

Rose, Nikolas. (2007). *The Politics of Life Itself: Biomedicine, Power, and Subjectivity in the Twenty-First Century.* Princeton: Princeton University Press.

Ruddick, Sue. (2003). "The Politics of Aging: Globalization and the Restructuring of Youth and Childhood." *Antipode* 35, no. 2: 334–362.

Schramm, Wilbur, Jack Lyle, and Edwin B. Parker. (1961). *Television in the Lives of Our Children.* Stanford: Stanford University Press.

Shapiro, Michael J. (2001). *For Moral Ambiguity: National Culture and the Politics of the Family.* Minneapolis: University of Minnesota Press.

Singer, Dorothy G. and Jerome L. Singer. (2001). "Introduction: Why a Handbook on Children and the Media?" *Handbook of Children and the Media.* Ed. Dorothy G. Singer and Jerome L. Singer. Thousand Oaks: Sage Publications. xi–xvii.

Staiger, Janet. (2005). *Media Reception Studies.* New York: New York University Press.

Steinberg, S. R. and J. L. Kincheloe. (1997). "Introduction: No More Secrets—Kinderculture, Information Saturation, and the Postmodern Childhood." *Kinderculture: The Corporate Construction of Childhood.* Ed. S. R. Steinberg and J. L. Kincheloe. Boulder: Westview Press. 1–30.

Stephens, Sharon. (1995). "Children and the Politics of Culture in "Late Capitalism."" *Children and the Politics of Culture*. Ed. Sharon Stephens. Princeton: Princeton University Press. 3–48.

Surgeon General's Scientific Advisory Committee on Television and Social Behavior. (1971). *Television and Growing Up: The Impact of Televised Violence*. Report to the Surgeon General, U.S. Public Health Service. Washington: U.S. Government Printing Service.

Watson, Alison M. (2004). "Seen but not Heard: The Role of the Child in International Political Economy." *New Political Economy* 9, no. 1: 3–21.

Westheimer, Joel. (2004). "Introduction." *PS: Political Science & Politics* 37, no. 2: 231–234.

Westheimer, Joel and Joseph Kahne. (2004). "Educating the "Good" Citizen: Political Choices and Pedagogical Goals." *PS: Political Science & Politics* 37, no. 2: 241–248.

14

■ Capital, Ray Kroc, and McDonald's

The World's Lovin' It

Joe L. Kincheloe

Cameron was a counter. He vomited nineteen times on his way to San Francisco. He liked to count everything that he did. This had made Greer a little nervous when he first met up with Cameron years ago, but he'd gotten used to it by now.

People would sometimes wonder what Cameron was doing and Greer would say, "He's counting something," and people would ask, "What's he counting?" and Greer would say, "What difference does it make?" and the people would say, "Oh."

People usually wouldn't go into it any further because Greer and Cameron were very self-assured in that big relaxed casual kind of way that makes people nervous now. (*The Hawkline Monster: A Gothic Western*, Richard Brautigan 1974, 11)

I can relate to Cameron, for I too, am a counter. McDonald's counts—and like the people who noticed Cameron's peculiar proclivity, most Americans don't go very far in analyzing the company's obsession for counting, or, for that matter, anything else about the fast food behemoth. Like Greer and Cameron, McDonald's self-assurance—its power—should make people a little nervous.

I was destined to write about McDonald's, as my life has always intersected with the golden arches. As part of my undergraduate comedy shtick, I told my listeners (truthfully) that I had consumed 6,000 McDonald's hamburgers before graduating from high school.

In junior high and high school we were allowed to go off campus to eat. My friends and I (before we had driver's licenses) would tromp through the Tennessee woods rain or shine to McDonaldland—then in high school we drove. After six years of three-hamburger lunches, not to mention three more on Wednesday nights with my parents, and several on weekend nights after cruising with friends—the count began to mount. A secondary bonus for my fifteen-cent burgermania involved the opportunity to count my cholesterol numbers as they crept higher and higher. Ray Kroc, the man who made McDonald's a household name, would have been proud.

Somewhere in my small-town-Tennessee adolescent consciousness, I understood that McDonald's was the future. I couldn't name it, but the standardized hamburger was a symbol of some vague social phenomenon. Like any immigrant of another place and time, I was ethnic—a hillbilly. And like all children of traditional ethnic parents, I struggled for an American identity free from the taint of my ethnicity. Though it hadn't yet assumed the mantle of All-American symbol around the world, I knew that McDonald's of the early 1960s was mainstream American. As such, my participation in the burger-fries ritual was an act of shedding my ethnic identity. Understanding McDonald's regulation of customer behavior, I complied readily, knowing the menu in advance and placing my order quickly and accurately. My parents, on the other hand, raised in the rural South of the early twentieth century, were lost at the ordering counter—lost to the Hamburger Patch. Never understanding the menu, always unsure of the expected behavior, the effort to shape their consumer conduct was a disaster.

On a very different level, however, my parents were seduced by McDonald's. Students of cultural studies have come to understand that readings of film, TV, and commercials are idiosyncratic (Steinberg 2007), differing significantly from individual to individual. So it was in my home. As victims of the Great Depression in southern Appalachia, my mother and father came to see excessive spending as a moral weakness. Eating out, when it was possible to prepare food at home, was especially depraved. My father entered a McDonald's only if he was convinced of its economic "good sense." Indeed, advertisers struck an emotional chord when they pitted McDonald's fifteen-cent hamburgers and twelve-cent fries as an alternative to the extravagant cost of eating out. To my self-identified working-class father, eating at McDonald's was an act of class resistance. He never really cared much for the food—he would rather eat my mother's country ham and cornbread. But as we McDined, he spoke with great enthusiasm about how McDonald's beat the price of other burgers around town by fifty or sixty cents. Such statistics made him very happy.

Like others in peculiar social spaces around the world, my father consumed a democratic egalitarian ethos. French teenagers accustomed to the bourgeois stuffiness of French restaurants could have identified with my father's class-resistant consumption, as they revel in the informality and freedom of McDonald's "American atmosphere." The inexpensive fare, the informal dress, the loud talk are class signifiers (Leidner 1993). Such coding is ironic in light of McDonald's right-wing political history, its manipulations of labor, and its cutthroat competition with other fast food enterprises. That McDonald's continues to maintain an egalitarian image is testimony to the power and expertise of its public relations strategists. And here we find the major questions raised by this chapter:

What is the nature of these PR strategies? What do they tell us about McDonald's? And how do they affect American culture—particularly what Shirley Steinberg and I have defined as *kinderculture* (Steinberg and Kincheloe 2004).

■ Shaping Culture, Shaping Consciousness

Few Americans think about efforts by powerful interests in the large society to regulate populations to bring about desired behaviors. In America and other Western societies political domination shifted decades ago from police or military force to cultural messages. Such communications are designed to win the approval or consent of citizens for actions taken by power elites (Giroux 1988). Those engaged in cultural studies, in their own ways are involved in efforts to expose the specifics of this process of cultural domination (often labeled hegemony). The process takes place in the everyday experience of our lives. The messages are not sent by a clandestine group of conspirators or devised by some secret ministry of propaganda; neither are they read by everyone in the same way. But some people understand their manipulative intent and rebel against their authority (Goldman 1992). The company's role in these power dynamics illustrates the larger process. If any organization has the power to help shape the lives of children, it is McDonald's.

The construction of who we are and what we believe cannot be separated from the workings of power. Americans don't talk much about power; American politicians don't even talk about power. When power is broached in mainstream sociology, the conversation revolves around either the macro level, the political relations of governments, or the micro level, the personal relations between two people (Abercrombie 1994). Power, as the term is used in this chapter, is neither macro nor micro, nor does it rely on legality or coercion. Power, as it has evolved in the first decade of the twenty-first century, maintains its legitimacy in subtle and effective ways.

Consider the power generated by McDonald's use of the media to define itself not simply as an American institution but as America itself. As the "land we love" writ small, McDonald's attaches itself to American patriotism and the cultural dynamics it involves. Ray Kroc understood from the beginning that he was not simply selling hamburgers—he was selling America a vision of itself (Luxenberg 1985). From the All-American marching band to the All-American basketball and football teams, to the All-American meal served by All-American boys and girls, the All-American of the Year, Ray Kroc, labored to connect the American signifier to McDonald's. The American flag will fly twenty-four hours a day at McDonald's, he demanded. Using the flag as a backdrop to highlight the hamburger count, Kroc watched the burger numbers supplant the Dow Jones closing average as the symbolic statistical index for America's economic health. In the late 1960s and early 1970s, Kroc saw the perpetually flying flag as a statement to the war protesters and civil rights "kooks" that McDonald's (America) would not stand for anyone criticizing or attempting to undermine "our" country (Kroc 1977).

One of the reasons Americans don't talk much about power is that it works in a subtle, hard-to-define manner. Ask Americans how McDonald's has shaped them or constructed their consciousness, and you'll draw blank stares. What does it mean to argue that power involves the ability to ascribe meanings to various features of our lives? Return to the McDonald's All-American ad campaign. Kroc and the McDonald's management sanctioned the costliest, most ambitious ad campaign in American corporate history (Boas and Chain 1976). All this money and effort were expended to imbue the hamburger—the McDonald's variety in particular—with a star-spangled signification. And it worked in the sense that Americans and individuals around the world began to make the desired connection. Described as the "ultimate icon of Americana," a "cathedral of consumption" where Americans practice their "consumer religion," McDonald's, like Disneyland, transcends status as mere business establishment (Ritzer 1993). When McDonald's or Disney speaks, they speak for all of us. How could the Big Mac *or Pirates of the Caribbean* mislead us? They are us.

Just as Americans saw mystical implications in Thomas Jefferson and John Adams both dying on July 4, 1826—the fiftieth anniversary of the Declaration of Independence—contemporary Americans may see mystical ramifications in the fact that Ray Kroc and Walt Disney were in the same company in the U.S. Army. Having lied about their age, the two prophets of free enterprise-grounded utopian Americana fought the good fight for the American way. It takes nothing away from the mystery to know that Kroc described Disney as a "strange duck" because he wouldn't chase girls (Kroc 1977).

No expenses were spared, no signifiers were left floating freely in the grand effort to transfer reverence for America to McDonald's. The middle-class cathedral was decorated as a shrine with the obligatory plastic eagle replete with powerful wings and glazed, piercing eyes. A banner held in the bald eagle's beak read "McDonald's: The American Way" (Boas and Chain 1976). These legitimation signifiers work best when they go unnoticed, as they effectively connect an organization's economic power to acquire property, lobby Congress, hire lawyers, and so on to its power to ascribe meaning and persuade. In the process the legitimated organization gains the power to create and transmit a view of reality that is consonant with its larger interests—American economic superiority as the direct result of an unbridled free enterprise system.

One ad campaign painted a nostalgic, sentimentalized, conflict-free American family pictorial history. The purpose of the ad is to forge an even deeper connection between McDonald's and America by creating an American historical role for McDonald's where none ever existed. You can almost hear the male voice-over: "Though we didn't yet exist, we were there to do it all for you—McDonald's then, McDonald's now." We're all one big, happy family with the same (European) roots. "We" becomes McDonald's and America—"our" family (Goldman 992). The only thing left to buttress the All-American image would be Santa Claus connection. Kroc's PR men quickly made their move, introducing Kroc himself to distribute hamburgers to Chicago's street corner Santas and Salvation Army workers. Newspapers noticed the event. The legend grew when the PR men circulated a story about a child who was asked where Santa had met Mrs. Santa. "At McDonald's," the child reportedly said. Wire services picked up the anecdote, sending it to every town in the country (Boas and Chain 1976). Whether with big ad campaigns or bogus anecdotes, McDonald's has used the media to create an American mythology.

Like other contemporary giant international corporations, McDonald's has used the media to invade the most private spheres of our everyday lives. Our national identifications, desires, and human needs have been commodified—appropriated for the purposes of commerce (Giroux 1994; Kellner 1992). Such media usage grants produce a level of access to human consciousness never imagined by the most powerful dictator. Such power is illustrated in the resistance McDonald's elicits as signifier for America. Time and time again in McDonald's brief history, neighborhood organizers have reacted to the firm's efforts to enter their communities. Seeing McDonald's as a form of cultural colonization that overwhelms locally owned businesses and devours local culture, individuals fought to keep McDonald's out. In the 1970s opposition became so intense in New York City that Kroc ordered high walls built around construction sites to keep them hidden from local residents. At the same time in Sweden, radicals bombed two restaurants in hopes of thwarting "creeping American cultural imperialism" (Boas and Chain 1976). In various demonstrations against the World Trade Organization in the early years of the twenty-first century demonstrators smashed McDonald's windows and vandalized stores (Kincheloe 2002). For better and for worse, McDonald's has succeeded in positioning itself as America.

■ McDonald's, Globalization, and Hegemony

Ironically, as McDonald's became America it outgrew U.S. borders. By the last quarter of the twentieth century the golden arches represented a global enterprise. In this trans-national process, the company became the symbol of Western economic development. Often McDonald's was the first foreign corporation to penetrate a particular nation's market. Indian social critic Vandana Shiva (1997) found dark humor in the symbolism of the golden arches. They induce the feeling that when you walk into McDonald's, you are entering heaven. The corporate marketers want children around the world to view the "McDonald's experience" as an immersion in celestial *jouissance*—while they are actually eating junk. In terms reminiscent of the outlook of the Pentagon in the second Iraq war, McDonald's executives refer to their movement into foreign markets as the company's "global realization" (Schlosser 2001). When statues of Lenin came down in East Germany after reunification, giant statues of Ronald McDonald took their place almost overnight. Driving through the former East Germany in the late 1990s and the first decade of the twenty-first century, I imagined cartoon bubbles coming out of each Ronald's mouth as the clown proclaimed: "No, Nikita, we buried you—the West has won." A couple of months ago, as we disembarked our flight to Amsterdam, turning into the large and ultramodern Schiphol Airport, Ronald McDonald's ceramic wave greeted us, our first sight of The Netherlands.

In the city of Santos, Brazil, several schoolteachers told me that they worried about the impact of McDonald's on their pupils. One teacher contended: "The danger of McDonald's imperialism is that it teaches children to devalue Brazilian things and to believe that Americans are superior to all of us poor South Americans." The anger these women directed at McDonald's and the company's ideological impact on Brazilian children was inscribed on each word they spoke. Western societies and the United States in particular have set up this corporate colonialism via the construction of corporatized governments (Kincheloe 1999) over the past twenty-five years. Particular types of consciousness are needed for such political economic reforms to work. Individuals in Brazil, Mexico, Malaysia, and the United States need to dismiss from their consciousness questions of social justice, egalitarianism, and environmentalism. Corporatized, globalized governments and their corporate allies need well-managed, socially regulated, consumption-oriented children and adults who understand that economic growth demands "good business climates," antiunion perspectives, and low wages for those lower in the hierarchy.

To gain the ability to introduce these ideas to children in the United States and around the world, corporations such as McDonald's continue to refine their appeal to the affective dimension. Their ability to produce entertainment for children that adults deem inappropriate is central to this enterprise. After decades of marketing research over the years, the best sellers are items which parents eschew: Ugly Stickers, Wacky Packs, Toxic High stickers, Garbage Pail Kids, Mass Murderer cards, and McDonald's cuisine. Producers of kinderculture understand part of the appeal of children's consumer products lies in vociferous parental disapproval of them (Spigel 1998). Indeed, the more subversive the kinderculture, the better. Schools not only ignore the power of such influences on children but have allowed McDonald's and other marketers into their hallways and classrooms (Molnar 1996; Kenway and Bullen 2001).

In addition to selling its products in school cafeterias, McDonald's has almost unlimited ideological access to elementary and secondary students by way of such ploys as, for example, "job interview seminars." Analysis of such seminars reveals that they are less about the interviewing process and more about inculcating particular beliefs about the social benefits of McDonald's and the unregulated free enterprise system. Creating a positive affective valence with the subversive kinderculture, McDonald's goes in for the knockout punch with its ideological treatises. In my research I found that students who were savvy enough to recognize the covert ideological dimensions of McDonald's seminars and brave enough to expose them to the school community were often punished for such "misbehavior" by school officials (see Kincheloe 2002 for an expansion of this theme).

A critical pedagogy of childhood cannot ignore these political, economic, social, and ideological dynamics. It is important for children around the world to understand the ways commercially produced children's culture (Kenway and Bullen 2001) in general, and the subversive kinderculture in particular wins their consent to positions that serve the interests of multinational corporations and their allies, not young people or anybody else. Children are directly affected by corporate hegemonization and globalization—forces that are central players in the social construction of childhood in hyperreality (Kincheloe 2002). As always in discussions of these hegemonic dynamics, it is important to outline the complex issues of the production and reception of ideology. Daniel Cook (2004) offers valuable insights in this context that are important in the reading of McDonald's impact on children. Arguing that we must reject the dichotomy of the exploited child and the empowered child, Cook maintains that children are inevitably positioned in market relations and are always empowered to make decisions in this context.

Researchers of childhood must always maintain a delicate balance between structure and agency. We cannot understand contemporary childhood(s) outside of its/their relation to the market, and children always make decisions in this context. Importantly, they are not free to make any consumption or ideological decision they want—they must make decisions based on their social, political, economic, and cultural terrain. In the twenty-first century, that terrain cannot be understood outside of the commodification of children's culture. The market does not snatch children from the innocent garden of childhood and transform them into crazed consumers. Concurrently it does not simply have to do with providing empowerment for self-sufficient agential children. Corporate producers and marketers must be exerting economic and ideological effects by their efforts, since they keep pouring billions of dollars into advertising directed at children from New Orleans to Nigeria, from Jacksonville to Jakarta. While children construct their own meanings, the corporate culture of power does exploit them—the corporate effort to ideologically construct children's consciousness is a cold reality.

Social scholars who do not value the importance of studying the effects of dominant power on the lived world often slam more critical takes on the effects of political economic structures on the lives of children. They often interpret critical charges of ideological exploitation with the assertion that the dominant power of McDonald's, for example, produces standardized and homogenized "corporate children." (See Kincheloe 2002 for examples of this dynamic in anticritical scholarship from various disciplines.) This is not what McDonald's and other producers of kinderculture do. Producers of commercial children's culture reshape everyday places and activities in ways that resonate with corporate economic and ideological interests. In this context, as parents of young children often describe, the relationship of children to, say, eating is reconfigured as children cry out for McDonald's hamburgers. For example, as I sat in the waiting room of a doctor's office I observed a young mother of a restless, frightened six-year-old boy struggle to contain him as they waited to see a pediatrician:

MOTHER: Would you please sit still and stop crying. Stop it! Now! I'm not going to take you to McDonald's if you don't stop it.

CHILD: (screaming) I want to go to McDonald's. Let's go, Mommy. Please…let's go now. (crying) I want to go to McDonald's.

MOTHER: I'm going to brain you. Now you just stop it.

CHILD: I want a coke and a cheeseburger. Please (screaming) McDonald's, McDonald's, McDonald's. Cheeseburger!

MOTHER: (slapping child's face) You're not going to McDonald's, young man!

CHILD: (louder screams and hysterical crying) McDonald's, McDonald's, McDonald's.

McDonald's advertisers have tapped into this child's affect at a level that transcends rational understanding. In his time of stress in the pediatrician's office the little boy seeks the comfort of his provider of pleasure. To seek pleasure from the pain of a doctor's visit, he wants to visit the golden arches. Reading her child's reactions, the mother appeals to the most severe threat she can formulate in the situation—the threat of not going to McDonald's. As the child breaks free from the mother's restraint, he runs around the waiting room, screaming, crying, and flailing his arms. She chases him for several moments, finding it difficult to corral him. Finally catching him, she carries him back screaming, crying, and flailing to her seat. Panting for breath, she reassesses her strategy in her attempt to get control of the situation:

> MOTHER: I'm going to buy you two cheeseburgers and one of them hot apple pies.
>
> CHILD: (immediately calmed by the prospect of consumption at McDonald's) You are?!
>
> MOTHER: Yes, and I'm going to get you some of those animal cookies you like. Hippo-hippo-hippopotamus.
>
> CHILD: I love those cookies. I LOVE THEM! Cheeseburgers and cheeseburgers.

Everyday places and activities have been reshaped by McDonald's-mediated kinderculture. There are no standardization and homogenization processes at work here. A new relationship has emerged that will be acted on in diverse ways by different children and parents. The complexity of the relationship between corporate producer and child consumer is so powerful that I cannot produce a final interpretation of what this vignette means. Though meaning here is loose and slippery, it does not mean that my readings are irrelevant. I stand ready to argue their contribution to the effort to understand McDonald's social power and resulting impact on contemporary childhood. It could be argued that the vignette is a micropolitical reflection of a new knowledge order that decenters parents' roles as the primary providers of aid and comfort to their children. It may tell us that a new set of material realities, ideological assumptions, and configurations of power have made an impact on contemporary childhood. The little boy in the doctor's office possessed a detailed, if not expert, knowledge of McDonald's product line that he had learned via TV. Such knowledge shaped his behavior and his relationship to his mother. Undoubtedly the child's cultural identifications and affect had been rerouted by corporate marketers.

Consumption and pleasure are intimately connected in the life of this young boy and millions of other children. Corporate power has entered domains of life once free from market influences. Without their conscious awareness such children may eventually find that this power and the connections it forges exert a significant impact on their life choices. Young boys in China, for example, fantasize about opening chains of McDonald's restaurants in Beijing (Yan 1997). In a communist country such dreams are ideologically significant and alter the relationship between the young boy and Chinese politics. Like the U.S. military in Vietnam and Iraq, corporations work to win the hearts and minds of young consumers; the only difference is that corporate methods are more sophisticated and work much better than the military strategies. Subtle kinderculture is amazingly intrusive, working twenty-four hours a day to colonize all dimensions of lived experience (Kenway and Bullen 2001; Cook 2004).

■ McDonald's Is a Kids' Kind of Place

Contrary to the prevailing positivist wisdom, we begin to understand in more detail that childhood is not and never has been an unchanging developmental stage of humanness. Rather, it is a social and economic construction tied to prevailing perceptions of what constitutes the "natural order" (Polakow 1992). Forces such as urbanization and industrialization have exerted significant influences on the nature of childhood—as have the development of media and the techno power it produces. By "techno power" I mean the expansion of corporate influence via the use of recent technological innovation (Kellner 1989; Harvey 1989). Using techno power, corporations like McDonald's have increased their ability to maximize capital accumulation, influence social and cultural life, and even help mold children's consciousness. Since childhood is a cultural construction shaped in the contemporary era by the forces of this media-catalyzed techno power, the need for parents, teachers, and community members to study it is dramatic. Let us turn now to McDonald's and the construction of childhood in contemporary globalized society.

Even the name, "McDonald's," is kid-friendly, with its evocation of Old MacDonald and his farm-E-I-E-I-O. The safety of McDonald's provides asylum, if not utopian refuge, from the kid-unfriendly contemporary world of child abuse, broken homes, and childnapping. Offering something better to escape into, McDonald's TV depiction of itself to children as a happy place where "what you want is what you get" is very appealing (Garfield 1992). By the time children reach elementary school, they are often zealous devotees of McDonald's who insist on McDonaldland birthday celebrations and surprise dinners. Obviously McDonald's advertisers are doing something right, as they induce phenomenal numbers of kids to pester their parents for Big Macs and fries. The creation of McDonald's playlands, with enormous brightly colored climbing toys and tunnels… complete with parents' watching tables has made Mickey D's the favored destination of parents without anywhere to go.

McDonald's and other fast food advertisers have discovered an enormous, previously overlooked children's market. Children aged five to twelve annually spend almost $5 billion of their own money. They influence household spending of an additional $140 billion each year, more than half of which goes to soft drinks and fast food. Every month nineteen out of every twenty kids aged six to eleven visit a fast food restaurant. In a typical McDonald's promotion, where toys with movie tie-ins (*Batman, Spiderman, Kung Fu Panda*), Hot Wheels, Barbies, and Beanie Babies accompany kids' meals, company officials can expect to sell over 30 million to child customers. By the time they barely reach two, over four out of five children know that McDonald's sells hamburgers. As if this level of child consciousness colonization were not enough, McDonald's, along with scores of other companies, has targeted the public schools as a new venue for child marketing and consumption. In addition to hamburgers for A's programs and advertising-based learning packets for science, foreign language, and other subjects, McDonald's and other fast food firms have gained control of school cafeterias, much to the consternation of many advocates of child health (Hume 1993; Ritzer 1993; Giroux 1994; Kincheloe 2002).

Make no mistake about it, McDonald's and its advertisers want to transform children into consumers; indeed, they see children as consumers in training (Fischer, et al. 1991). Ellen Seiter (1993), however, warns against drawing simplistic conclusions about the relationship between advertisers and children, as have, she says, many well-intentioned liberal children's advocacy groups. The leading voice against corporate advertising for children, ACT (Action for Children's Television), fails to capture the subtle aspects of techno power and its colonization of childhood, the complicated interactions of structure and agency. Seeing children as naive innocents who should watch only "good" TV, meaning educational programs that portray middle-class values, the ACT has little appreciation of the complexity of children's TV watching. Children are not passive, naive TV viewers. As advertising professionals have learned, children are active, analytical viewers who often make their own meanings of both commercials and the products they sell. These social and psychological dynamics between advertiser and child deserve further analysis.

One important dynamic is advertisers' recognition that children feel oppressed by the middle-class view of children as naive entities in need of constant protection. By drawing on the child's discomfort with middle-class protectionism and the accompanying attempt to "adjust" children to a positivist "developmentally appropriate" norm, advertisers hit on a marketing bonanza. If we address kids as kids: a dash of anarchism and a pinch of hyperactivity—they will love our commercials; even though parents (especially middle-class parents) will hate them. By the end of the 1960s, commercial children's TV and advertising were grounded on this premise. Such media throw off restraint, discipline, and old views that children should be seen but not heard. Everything, for example, that educational TV embraces—earnestness, child as an incomplete adult, child in need of correction—commercial TV rejects. In effect, commercial TV sets up an oppositional culture for kids.

One doesn't have to look far to find that children's enthusiasm for certain TV shows, toys, and foods often isolates them from their parents. Drawing on this isolation, children turn it into a form of power—they finally know something that Dad doesn't. How many dads or moms understand the relationship between Mayor McCheese and the French Fry Guys? Battle lines begin to be drawn between children and parents, as kids want to purchase McDonald's hamburgers or action toys. Conflicts in lower-middle-class homes may revolve around family finances; strife in upper-middle-class homes may concern aesthetic or ideological concerns. Questions of taste, cultural capital, or self-improvement permeate child-adult interactions in such families. The child's ability to negotiate the restrictions of adult values is central to the development of an independent self. A common aspect of this developing independence involves the experience of contradiction with the adult world. Children of upwardly mobile, ambitious parents may find it more difficult to negotiate this experience of contradiction because of the parents' strict views of the inappropriateness of TV-based children's culture. Thus the potential for parent-child conflict and alienation may be greater in this familial context. Adding to this, with the growing propensity for bourgeois-bohemian parents to go "green" and to avoid many prepared foods—eating at McDonald's can prove to be a political minefield. I recall last year when two of our closest friends, parents to a sixteen-year-old girl, told us that their worst fights with Sadie have centered around her insistence to stop training and eat fast food.

■ The Colonialization of Fun

In this context, play is placed in cultural conflict. Over the past several decades psychologists and educators have come to recognize the importance of play in childhood and child development. With this in mind, our examination of McDonald's opens a window into what can happen when the culture and political economy of play begin to change. With a changing culture of play, we begin to discern different effects of play on the construction of children's identities and with their cognitive development. New forms of play may accelerate particular forms of intellectual development while concurrently limiting the imagination—a dynamic that holds interesting implications for universalist perspectives on child development. With the corporate colonization of play in hyperreality, play begins to lose its imaginative dimensions. Contemporary children's play occurs in the same public spaces as adult labor, as children enter into cyberspace using the same hardware and software that their parents use in their professional lives.

McDonald's is, of course, just one producer in an expanding children's commercial culture. Again, it is important to note that children in their interactions with McDonald's and other manifestations of this commercial kinderculture use its symbolic and material dimensions in often unique ways. McDonald's and other corporations worry about this idiosyncratic agential dynamic of childhood play. Like other marketers McDonald's wants children to engage its products and company-produced meanings in an "appropriate" manner. Such engagement would not include "playing" with environmental and health concerns by developing cyber communities of like-minded children calling for corporate responsibility. McDonald's and other corporations do not want power-savvy children, such as the ones who formed the organization Children Against McDonald's, engaging in socially conscious use of their products. Corporate marketers and other protectors of the status quo fear the agential, empowered child. Media corporations and companies like McDonald's work hard to control and structure the way consumers interact with their products. Indeed, child consumers do not experience the freedom and empowerment some advocates of the agential childhood claim for them. Play as political resistance must be opposed at all costs (DuBois-Reymond, Sunker, and Kruger 2001; Hengst 2001; Nations 2001; Cassell and Jenkins 2002; Mouritsen 2003; Jenkins 2003).

A covert children's culture has always existed on playgrounds and in schools. The children's culture of the past, however, was produced by children and propagated through child-to-child contact. Children's culture of today is increasingly created by adults and dispersed via television for the purpose of inducing children to consume. (The use of the Internet may provide a countervailing trend in this context.) As they carefully subvert middle-class parents' obsession with achievement, play as a serious enterprise, and self-improvement oriented "quality time" (a subversion that in my opinion probably contributes to the public good), advertisers connect children's culture to their products. McDonald's commercials reflect these themes although less blatantly than many advertisers.

In attempts to walk a tightrope between tapping the power of children's subversive culture and offending the middle-class guardians of propriety—a walk that has become increasingly difficult in the first decade of the twenty-first century—McDonald's developed a core of so-called "slice-of-life" children's ads. Casting no adults in the commercials, advertisers depict a group of preteens engaged in "authentic" conversations around a McDonald's table covered with burgers, fries, and shakes. Using kid's slang to describe toys in various McDonald's promotions, children discuss the travails of childhood with one another. Twenty-first century McDonald's ads declare: *I'm lovin' it.* Global ads proclaim the slogan in every language, creating the ultimate hyperreal tie-in between desire and consumption. Hip hop artists and dancers move to the groove of the mchappiness on 30-second spots.

In many commercials children make adults the butt of their jokes or share jokes that adults don't get (Seiter 1993; Goldman 1992). McDonald's subtly attempts to draw some of the power of children's subversive culture onto their products without anyone but the kids knowing. Such slice-of-life ads are opaque to the degree that adults watching them don't get it—they don't see the advertiser's effort to connect McDonald's with the subversive kinderculture. This "oppositional aesthetic" (Jenkins 1998) has fueled numerous aspects of children's commercial culture (*Malcolm in the Middle,* Hannah Montana*, Family Guy, The Simpsons,* etc.) that play on children's differences from adults. It is a key weapon in the corporate construction of childhood.

■ The Bloody Fight for Conformity, Courtesy, and Established Virtue: McDonaldland, Ronald, and Ray

TV ads often serve as hyperreality's myths, as they resolve cultural contradictions, portray models of identity, and glorify the status quo. While all McDonald's ads accomplish these mythic functions to some degree, none does it better than ads and promotions involving McDonaldland. To understand the mythic dynamics of McDonaldland, one must appreciate the psychological complexity of Ray Kroc. Born in 1902 in a West Side Chicago working-class neighborhood into what Kroc called a "Bohunk" (Bohemian) family, Kroc was obsessed throughout his life with proving his worth as both a human being and a businessman. Having failed in several business ventures in his twenties and thirties, Kroc had much to prove by the time the McDonald's opportunity confronted him at the age of fifty-two (Boas and Chain 1976). Kroc defined McDonaldland the same way he defined himself—through consumption. Driven by an ambition to own nice things, Kroc's autobiography is peppered with references to consumption: "I used to comb through the advertisements in the local newspaper for notices of house sales in the wealthier suburbs…I haunted these sales and picked up pieces of elegant furniture . . ." (Kroc 1977, 27). Watched over by the messianic Ronald McDonald, McDonaldland is a place (your kind of place) where consumption functioned as the means through which its inhabitants gained their identities.

McDonaldland is a kid's text fused with Kroc's psyche that emerges as an effort to sell the system, to justify consumption as a way of life. As central figure in McDonaldland, Ronald McDonald emerges as a multidimensional clown deity, virgin-born son of Adam Smith, press secretary for free enterprise capitalism. He is also Ray Kroc's projection of himself, his ego creation of the most-loved prophet of utopian consumption in the McWorld. Ronald's life history begins in Washington, D.C., with Willard Scott, the former *Today Show's* weatherman. Struggling to make it as a junior announcer at WRC-TV in D.C. in the early 1960s, Scott agreed to play Bozo the Clown on the station's kid show. When Scott donned the clown suit, he was transformed from bumbling Willard to super-clown. The local McDonald's franchises recognized Scott's talent and employed Bozo as a spokesperson for McDonald's. When the Bozo show was canceled by WRC, McDonald's lost a very effective advertiser. The local D.C. McDonald's owners worked with Scott to create Ronald McDonald (Scott's idea), debuting him in October 1963. Ronald created traffic jams every time he appeared in public, and local operators suggested to the Chicago headquarters that Ronald go national (Love 1986).

After a lengthy debate over whether they should employ Ronald McDonald as a clown, a cowboy, or a spaceman, corporate leaders and advertisers settled on the clown Ronald. Dumping Scott because he was deemed too fat for the image they wanted to promote, the company in 1965 hired Coco, an internationally known clown with the Ringling Bros. and Barnum & Bailey Circus. Beginning with his first national appearance in the Macy's Thanksgiving Day parade on November 25, 1966, the deification of Ronald began. The press releases on Ronald issued by the McDonald's Customers Relations Center are sanctification documents cross-pollinated with frontier tall-tale boasting. "Since 1963, Ronald McDonald has become a household name, more famous than Lassie or the Easter Bunny, and second only to Santa Claus" (McDonald's Customer Relations Center 1994).

The other characters in McDonaldland, the company's promotional literature reports, revere Ronald (Kroc's alterego). He is "intelligent and sensitive…he can do nearly any-thing…Ronald McDonald is the star." If children are sick, the promos contend, Ronald is there. Even though he has become an "international hero and celebrity," Ronald is the same friend of children he was in 1963. Ninety-six percent of all children, claimed a bogus "Ronald McDonald Awareness Study" fed to the press, can identify this heroic figure (Boas and Chain 1976). Ronald was everything Kroc wanted to be: a beloved humanitarian, an international celebrity, a philanthropist, a musician (Kroc made his living for a while as a piano player; Ronald has cut children's records). Even the sophisticates loved Ronald, Kroc wrote in his autobiography—a group whose affection Kroc sought through-out his life. Unfortunately he had to settle for it vicariously through Ronald. Abe Lincoln too was rejected by the sophisticates of his day; as a twentieth-century Lincoln, Kroc prominently displayed the bust of Ronald adjacent to the bust of Lincoln on a table behind his desk at the Chicago headquarters (McCormick 1993; Kroc 1977).

According to the promotional literature designed for elementary schools, Ronald "became a citizen of [the McDonald's] International Division" in 1969 and soon began to appear on TV around the world. Kroc was propelled to a new level of celebrity as the corporation "penetrated" the global market. Now known everywhere on Earth, Kroc/Ronald became the grand salesman, the successful postindustrial Willie Loman—"they love me in Moscow, Belgrade, and New York." Stung by a plethora of critics, Kroc was obsessed with being perceived as a moral man with a moral company that exerted a wholesome influence on children around the world. Kroc wrote and spoke of his noble calling, establishing his "missions" with the golden arches as part of his white man's burden. "I provide a humanitarian service," Kroc proclaimed: "I go out and check out a piece of property [that's] not producing a damned thing for anybody," he wrote in his epistles from California. "The new franchise provides a better life for scores of people: out of that bare ground comes a store that does, say, a million dollars a year in business. Let me tell you, it's great satisfaction to see that happen." Kroc/Ronald personified the great success story of twentieth-century capitalism. The fortunes that were made by Kroc and his franchises came to represent what happens when one works hard in the free enterprise system. McDonaldland and the McWorld—signifiers for the McDonaldization of the planet. The convergence of the growth of international mega-corporations with the expanding technological sophistication of the media has prompted a new era of consumption. Students of cultural studies often argue that the central feature of the hyperreal lifestyle revolves around the act of consuming. As a free enterprise utopia, McDonaldland erases all differences, all conflicts; social inequities are overcome through acts of consumption.

Life in McDonaldland is free of conflict—the Hamburger Patch is a privatized utopia. It is contemporary America writ small, corporate directed and consumer oriented. Questions such as distribution of income among classes, regulation of corporate interests, free trade, minimum wage, and collective bargaining traditionally elicited passion and commitment—now they hardly raise an eyebrow. The political sphere where decisions are made concerning who gets what and who voted for what is managed by a small group. Their work and the issues they confront are followed by a shrinking audience of news watchers tuned to CNN and the Internet news. Politics, Americans have concluded, is not only useless but, far worse in the mediascape, boring. It can't be too important; it gets such low ratings.

The benign nature of capitalist production with its freedom from serious conflict of any type portrayed by McDonaldland and Kroc/Ronald is a cover for a savage reality. Business analysts, for example, liken McDonald's operations to the Marine Corps. When a recruit graduates from basic training (Hamburger University), he believes that he can conquer anybody (Love 1986). Motivated by an econo-tribal allegiance to the McFamily, store operators express faith in McDonald's as if it were a religion. Kroc openly spoke of the Holy Trinity—McDonald's, family, and God in that order (Kroc 1977). Released from boot camp on a jihad for a success theology, Ronald and Ray facilitated thousands of independent restaurant owners out of business (Luxenberg 1985). Competing fast food franchises tell of their introduction to recent Hamburger University graduates and other

McDonald's managers with amazement. "We will run you out of business and bury you."

No matter how ruthless business might become, there is no room for criticism or dissent in McDonaldland. "I feel sorry for people who have such a small and wretched view of the system that made this country great," Kroc (1977) wrote in his autobiography. The "academic mobs" who criticized McDonald's tapped a sensitivity in Kroc's psyche that motivated counterattacks until the day he died. This love-it-or leave-it anti-intellectualism was championed by Kroc who never liked books or school and saw little use for advanced degrees: "One thing I flatly refuse to give money to is the support of any college" (Kroc 1977, 199). Intellectuals don't fit into the culture of the Hamburger Patch.

The Kroc influence is alive and well in the gender dynamics of the corporation. Referring to himself in the third person as Big Daddy, Kroc expressed a sometimes disturbing misogyny in his handling of company affairs. Ray's personality, one colleague observed, would never allow a woman to gain power (Love 1986). To Kroc, women were to take care of frills, leaving the important work to men:

> Clark told me I should hire a secretary. "I suppose you're right," I [Kroc] said. "But I want a male secretary…I want a man. He might cost a little more at first, but if he's any good at all, I'll have him doing sales work in addition to administrative things. I have nothing against having a pretty girl around, but the job I have in mind would be much better handled by a man.… My decision to hire a male secretary paid off when I was hospitalized for a gall bladder operation and later for a goiter operation. [The male secretary] worked between our office and my hospital room, and we kept things humming as briskly as when I was in the office every morning." (Kroc 1977, 48–49)

June Martino was a very talented woman who had been with Kroc from the earliest days of his involvement with McDonald's. Corporate insiders described her as a gifted businesswoman whose expertise often kept the company going during difficult times. Kroc's view of her reflected his view of women in general: "I thought it was good to have a lucky person around, maybe some of it would rub off on me. Maybe it did. After we got McDonald's going and built a larger staff, they called her 'Mother Martino.' She kept track of everyone's family fortunes, whose wife was having a baby, who was having marital difficulties, or whose birthday it was. She helped make the office a happy place." (Kroc 1977, 84)

This attitude at the top permeated all levels of the organization, expressing themselves in a variety of pathological ways. Management's sensitivity to sexual harassment was virtually nonexistent well into the 1980s. Interviews with women managers reveal patterns of sexual misconduct involving eighteen- and nineteen-year-old women employees being pressured to date older male managers. Reports of sexual harassment were suppressed by the company bureaucracy; women who complained were sometimes punished or forced to resign. One successful manager confided that after she reported harassment, company higher-ups stalked her both and off the job. She was eventually forced to leave the company. Not surprisingly, such an organization was not overly concerned with women's complaints about the exaggerated gender roles depicted in McDonald's commercials and promotions. (Hume 1993). Even in the twenty-first century, one must travel to scores of McDonald's to find a female manager or even floor manager.

McDonald's perpetuates what Allen Shelton (1993) referred to as a hegemonic logic—a way of doing business that privileges conformity, callously defends the middle-class norm, fights to the death for established virtue, and resists social change at all costs. As a passionate force for a Warren G. Harding "normalcy," McDonald's is the corporation that invites the children of prominent civic, military, and business leaders to the opening of its first McDonaldland Park—but leaves the daughters and sons of the not so rich and famous off the list. This hegemonic logic holds little regard for concepts such as justice or morality—McDonald's morality is contingent on what sells. This concept is well illustrated in McDonald's emphasis on the primacy of home and family values in its advertising.

■ Home Is Wherever Ronald McDonald Goes

Kroc and his corporate leaders understood their most important marketing priority: to portray McDonald's as a family kind of place. As they focused on connecting McDonald's to America and the family, they modified the red and white ceramic take-out restaurants to look more like the suburban homes that sprang up throughout America in the late 1950s and 1960s. Ad campaigns proclaimed that McDonald's was home, and that anywhere Ronald goes "he is at home." Like many other ads in American hyperreality, McDonald's home and family ads privilege the private sphere, not the public sphere, as the important space where life is lived. As an intrinsically self-contained unit, the family is removed from the public realm of society; such a depiction, however, conceals the ways that politics and economics shape everyday family life. The greatest irony of these ads is that even as they isolate the family from any economic connections, they promote the commodification of family life. A form of double-speak is discernible in this situation: The family is an end in itself; the family is an instrumental consumption unit whose ultimate purpose is to benefit corporate profits and growth.

McDonald's ads deploy home and family as paleosymbols that position McDonald's as the defender of "the American way of life." Kroc (1977) never knew what paleosymbols were, but he understood that McDonald's public image should be, in his words, a "combination YMCA, Girl Scouts, and Sunday School." Devised to tap into the right-wing depiction of the traditional family under attack from feminists, homosexuals, and other "screwballs," these so-called legitimation ads don't sell hamburgers—they sell social relations. Amid social upheaval and instability, McDonald's endures as a rock of ages, a refuge in a world gone mad. McDonald's brings us together, provides a safe haven for our children. The needs the legitimation ads tap are real, but the consumption panacea they provide is false (Goldman 1992). After its phenomenal growth in the 1960s, McDonald's realized that it was no longer the "cute little company" of the 1950s (Love 1986). The antiwar, civil rights, and other social movements of the late 1960s were repugnant to Kroc's American values. Such views, when combined with the marketing need for McDonald's to legitimate itself now that it was an American "big business," made home and family the obvious battle field in the legitimation campaign. As the public faith in corporations declined, McDonald's used the paleosymbols to create an environment of confidence. Going against the grain of a social context perceived to be hostile to big business, the ads worked. The lyrics of accompanying music read:

> You, you're the one.
> So loving, strong, and patient. Families like yours made all the states a nation. Our families are our past, our future and our pride. Whatever roots we come from, we're growing side by side. (quoted in Goldman 1992, 95)

The world of home and family portrayed by the McDonald's legitimation ads is a terrain without conflict or tension. McDonald's ads are created for demographics; for example, in Atlanta, television ads are almost 100% African American. Urban areas tap into hip hop for commercials, and middle America has ads which reflect the "heartland." The genius of McDonald's ads creates a seamless union between Rockwellian American life and the hyperreal pulse of house or hip hop music. Declaring family values and love with every breath, McDonald's has globally become everyone's safe haven.

The grand irony of McDonald's family ads reveals that under the flag of traditional family values McDonald's actually undermines the very qualities it claims to promote. The McDonald's experience depicted in ads does not involve a family sharing a common experience—each market segment experiences it in a different, potentially conflicting way. In terms of everyday life McDonald's does not encourage long, leisurely, interactive family meals. The seats and tables are designed to be uncomfortable to the point that customers will eat quickly and leave. In the larger scheme of things, family values, America, and home are nothing more than cynical marketing tools designed to legitimate McDonald's to different market segments. (Kroc made his feeling about family very clear—work comes first, he told his managers. "My total commitment to business had long since been established in my home" (Kroc 1977, 89). The cynicism embedded in ads by McDonald's and scores of other companies undermines the social fabric, making the culture our children inhabit a colder and more malicious place. Such cynicism leads corporations to develop new forms of techno power that can be used to subvert democracy and justice in the quest for new markets. Such cynicism holds up Ronald McDonald/Ray Kroc as heroes, while ignoring authentic heroes—men and women who struggle daily to lead good lives, be good parents, and extend social justice. As students of culture, we wait and watch, as McDonald's recreates itself through the decades to replicate its original mandates—set in place by the man himself.

---

* Portions of this chapter also appeared in *Kinderculture: The Corporate Construction of Childhood*, 2004, Boulder, Co: Westview Press.

References

Abercrombie, N. 1994. "Authority and Consumer Society." In R. Keat, N. Whiteley, and N. Abercrombie, eds., *The Authority of the Consumer.* New York: Routledge.

Boas, M., and S. Chain. 1976. *Big Mac: The Unauthorized Story of McDonald's.* New York: Dutton.

Brautigan, R. 1974. *The Hawkline Monster: A Gothic Western.* New York: Pocket Books.

Cassell, J., and H. Jenkins. 2002. "Proper Playthings: The Politics of Play in Children." web.media.mit. edu/-andrew_s/andrew_sempere_2002_politics_of_play.pdf

Cook, D. 2004. *The Commodification of Childhood: The Children's Clothing Industry and the Rise of the Child-Consumer.* Durham, N.C.: Duke University Press.

DuBois-Reymond, M., H. Sunker, and H. Kruger, eds. 2001. *Childhood in Europe.* New York: Peter Lang.

Fischer, P.M., et al. 1991. "Brand Logo Recognition by Children Aged 3 to 6 Years." *Journal of the American Medical Association* 266, no. 22: 3145–3148.

Garfield, B. 1992. "Nice Ads, but That Theme Is Not What You Want." *Advertising Age* 63, no. 8: 53.

Giroux, H. 1994. *Disturbing Pleasures: Learning Popular Culture.* New York: Routledge.

———. 1988. *Teachers as Intellectuals: Toward a Critical Pedagogy of Learning.* Granby, Mass.: Bergin & Garvey.

Goldman, R. 1992. *Reading Ads Socially.* New York: Routledge.

Harvey, D. 1989. *The Condition of Postmodernity.* Cambridge, Mass.: Basil Blackwell.

Hengst, H. 2001. "Rethinking the Liquidation of Childhood." In M. DuBois-Reymond, H. Sunker, and H. Kruger, eds., *Childhood in Europe.* New York: Peter Lang.

Hume, S. 1993. "Fast Food Caught in the Middle.*" Advertising Age* 64, no. 6: 12–15.

Jans, M. 2002. "Children and Active Citizenship." www.surrey.ac.uk/education/ etgace/brussels-papers/ march-paper—jans. doc.

Jenkins, H. 2003. "The Poachers and the Stormtroopers: Cultural Convergence in the Digital Age." web. mit.edu/21fms/www/faculty/henry3/pub/stormtroopers.htm.

Keat, R., N. Whiteley, and N. Abercrombie. 1994. Introduction to R. Keat, N. Whiteley, and N. Abercrombie, eds., *The Authority of the Consumer.* New York: Routledge.

Kellner, D. 1989. *Critical Theory, Marxism, and Modernity.* Baltimore: Johns Hopkins University Press.

———. 1992. "Popular Culture and the Construction of Postmodern Identities." In S. Lash and J. Friedman, eds., *Modernity and Identity.* Cambridge, Mass.: Blackwell.

Kenway, J., and E. Bullen. 2001. *Consuming Children: Entertainment, Advertising, and Education.* Philadelphia: Open University Press.

Kincheloe, J. 1999. *How Do We Tell the Workers? The Socio-Economic Foundations of Work and Vocational Education.* Boulder: Westview.

Kincheloe, J. 2002. *The Sign of the Burger: McDonald's and the Culture of Power.* Philadelphia,PA: Temple University Press.

Kroc, R. 1977. *Grinding It Out: The Making of McDonald's.* New York: St. Martin's Paperbacks.

Leidner, R. 1993. *Fast Food, Fast Talk: Service Work and the Routinization of Every-day Life.* Berkeley: University of California Press.

Love, J. 1986. *McDonald's: Behind the Arches.* New York: Bantam.

Luxenberg, S. 1985. *Roadside Empires: How the Chains Franchised.* New York: Viking Penguin.

McCormick, M. 1993. "Kid Rhino and McDonald's Enter Licensing Agreement." *Billboard* 105, no. 8: 10–11.

McDonald's Customer Relations Center. 1994. Handout to Schools.

Molnar, A. 1996. *Giving Kids the Business: The Commercialization of America's Schools.* Boulder: Westview.

Mouritsen, E. 2003. Project Demolition: Children's Play-Culture and the Concept of Development. www. hum.sdu.dk/projekter/ipfu.dk/online-artikler/mouritsendemolition.pdf.

Nations, C. 2001. "How Long Do Our Children Have to Wait? Understanding the Children of the Twenty-first Century." pt3.nmsu.edu/edu621/cynthia 2001.html.

Polakow, V. 1992. *The Erosion of Childhood. Chicago:* University of Chicago Press.

Ritzer, G. 1993. *The McDonaldization of Society.* Thousand Oaks, Calif.: Pine Forge.

Schlosser, E. 2001. *Fast Food Nation: The Dark Side of the All-American Meal.* Boston: Houghton Mifflin.

Seiter, E. 1993. *Sold Separately: Parents and Children in Consumer Culture.* New Brunswick, N.J.: Rutgers University Press.

Shelton, A. 1993. "Writing McDonald's, Eating the Past: McDonald's as a Post-modern Space." *Studies in Symbolic Interaction* 15: 103–118.

Shiva, V. 1997. "Vandana Shiva on McDonald's Exploitation and the Global Economy." www.mcspotlight. org/people/interviews/vandanatranscripts.html.

Steinberg, S. 2007. "Reading Media Critically." In Macedo, D. and S. Steinberg (eds.) *Media Literacy: A Reader.* New York: Peter Lang.

Steinberg, S. and J. Kincheloe (eds.). 2004. *Kinderculture: The Corporate Construction of Childhood.* Boulder, Co: Westview Press.

Yan, Y. 1997. "McDonald's in Beijing: The Localization of Americana." In J. Watson, ed., *Golden Arches East: McDonald's in East Asia.* Stanford: Stanford University Press.

15

■ Barbie

The bitch still has everything

Shirley R. Steinberg

This is the book of the generations of Barbie. (1) In the day that Ruth created her, in the likeness of Ruth's daughter and a German whore, she made Barbie. (2) Female first she created her, and blessed her and called her name Barbie after her firstborn. (3) And Barbie lived three years and Ruth created Ken, male and female she created them both. (4) And Barbie begat Skipper and friends, by the year of our lord nineteen hundred and sixty-four, they were three. (5) And Barbie lived fifty years until this record. Within those years, ten friends were created for Skipper; Midge was created to be Barbie's best friend. (6) And in the year nineteen hundred and sixty-eight, Christie was created. Christie was unlike any other creation; her skin was black. (7) And these are the years and days of Barbie, the days of Barbie and the Rockers; the days of Barbie and her pets, including puppy Sachi and horse Rosebud; and the years of Barbie's family, cousins Francie and Jazzie; siblings Tutti, Todd, and Stacie. (8) And through Stacie, friends were born, Whitney and Janet. (9) And through Ken, multiple male friends were born, and like Ken, none of them ever married, and verily their manhood was always in question. (10) However, Barbie was most plentiful with friends, by the year 2009, having multitudes of girlfriends with whom to shop. Among them Cara, who was also black, Teresa, who was made Hispanic, and Kira, who was Asian. (11) Hence Barbie was known through the land as diverse, multicultural, and virtual—having become cyber-connected. (12) And these were the days of Barbie; and it came to pass, when Barbie and her friends began to multiply on the face of the earth, little girls began to buy, as verily, one doll was never enough.

I am taking an artist's license in rewriting scriptures. It only seemed appropriate, as Mattel has been rewriting history and children's play for years.

Playing Barbies in the fifth grade consisted of lugging plastic cases laden with "outfits" to the playground and constructing scenarios around Barbie and "getting" Ken. I knew at this early age that Barbie (as a female) must have an "outfit" for every occasion and that wearing the same thing within some unspoken frame of time was just not done.

When I was twelve or thirteen I began meticulously recording what I wore each day on a calendar. I made sure that at least a month went by before I wore an outfit again. While a high school teacher, my students called attention to my idiosyncrasy by applauding the first day that I duplicated an outfit in the classroom. Did Barbie construct this behavior, or do I just love clothes?

Where does the text of Barbie begin? Fifty years ago, Mattel invested in the production of a slim, blonde doll who (that?) wore a variety of coordinated "outfits." While on vacation in Europe, Mattel co-founder Ruth Handler discovered Lily. Lily was a prominent star of comics—a sexy blonde with loose morals who adorned dashboards throughout Germany and Switzerland. Her origin is not well documented, although her lineage has been traced back to a *Lily* comic strip. Handler decided to take the model of Lily back to the States and create a doll that could wear multiple outfits. She named her Barbie, after her daughter, Barbara. The promotional "hook" that Handler cited was the possibility that the doll could have multiple outfits and girls could just own one doll.

Physiologically, Barbie had perfect breasts (although no nipples), a tiny waist and long, slender legs. Much has been written in a feminist framework about Barbie, discussing the unrealistic body shape, and so on. I won't "go there." Barbie was made slim so that layers of designer fabric would flow nicely and realistically on her body. She was, first and foremost, a model—fabric by Dior, designs by Mackie, nothing was beyond reach for her. I am not offended by her figure; I do wonder, however, about her poorly constructed private parts.

Speaking of private parts, four years later, Barbie was given a boyfriend, Ken—he had no genitals. Ken's crotch was (and is) as flat and smooth as Barbie's. I remember specifically my disappointment in disrobing my first Ken—nothing to see. Possibly that physical defect is in line with the personality that Ken has displayed throughout the years (although Earring Ken had a certain flair). Ken and Barbie have gotten as far as their wedding but never past it. The couple has never had a wedding night and Barbie is always seen pushing a stroller of cousins, younger siblings, or friends. Only Ken's friends of color, Derek and Steve, radiate any machismo sexuality—still crotchless.

Within months of her creation, Barbie was a sensation. Mattel had transformed toys, especially dolls, and Barbie became "us." Little girls were frenzied to own a Barbie, each one coming in her own long, thin box, wearing a black-and-white striped swim suit. Barbie had a blonde ponytail and earrings. She was a teen model. Girls moved from cradling baby dolls to demanding the latest in haute couture à la Mattel. Barbie was sexy, although most of her owners were not even aware of the genre of sexiness—they just loved their Barbies.

Barbie is not only literal, she is virtual. Dozens of websites are devoted to her: everythinggirl.com, and Barbie.com are cyber environments where fans can log on: *Enter the world of Barbie products. You can browse, buy, and even create a wishlist to email.* Sites encourage shopping, beauty products, princess-ness, and pink.

■ From Research to Obsession

I take my work seriously. Indeed, I think I am a superb researcher. I love the challenge of finding strange and wonderful factoids of trivia in little known academic nooks and crannies. However, this chapter has caused havoc in my life. Four years ago, I became fascinated with Barbie's effect on little girls. I started to pick up Barbies, Barbie furniture, Barbie comics, Barbie books, Barbie jewelry, and Barbie toys wherever I went. I even found the Benetton Barbie in the Istanbul airport (under the sign featuring the Marlboro man).

In order to do thorough textual analyses of Barbie and Barbie accoutrements, I needed to purchase my artifacts. I sit now, with great embarrassment, in an office with no less than forty Barbies, ten Kens, several Skippers (including a beauty princess and a cheerleading Skipper), and a plethora of "ethnic" and "special edition" Barbies. I have three Barbie watches, a $300 Barbie jacket from F.A.O. Schwartz, a Barbie McDonald's playset, Christmas playset, and bakery set. I have two Barbie board games, one computer game—Barbie Goes Shopping—and a floppy disk game, Barbie Design Studio. My life is out of control. I am only thankful that this research came long after my children stopped playing with toys—consequently I am the only one in the family who lays claim to this Mattel treasure trove. However, when children come to visit, they plow through my Barbies in an hour and then inquire, "Do you have anything else?" Obviously I don't have enough. What kid law was written which expressed the need to have multiples of any and every toy and object? Even the cyber-conscious Webkins fanatics are not happy with one, or two, or three…they must have every one made. Barbies are that way: you can never have enough.

My ownership of Barbies and paraphernalia qualifies me as an expert. I am a consumer and a scholar; there is no better combination. Historically, I come by the expertise naturally: I have had Barbies since she was invented. However, as I trace my Barbie autobiography, I am only able to single out my fetish for outfits as a permanent influence à la Barbie. I remain untouched from other taint…unless one looks at my research.

■ What Barbie Doesn't Have

Discussing what Barbie doesn't have is easier than what she does have. The list is much shorter. Barbie doesn't have a locomotive, a battleship (although she is a sailor), a rocket (although she is an astronaut), or an Uzi (although she is a soldier). Thematically Mattel still has not invented the Homeless Barbie, the Abortion Barbie, the Alcoholic Barbie, or the S&M Bondage Barbie. As far as special editions, Barbie still has not come out as a criminal—she has, however, come out in special editions of fairy tales (never a witch), "true" history, careers, and in different ethnicities—different from white, that is. There is no northern Barbie, but the Southern Beauty Barbie features "today's Southern belle with charm and style!"

Barbie doesn't have holes in her clothes (unless placed there by Bob Mackie); she doesn't ever walk because she has a plane, boat, Corvette, bicycle, horse, roller blades, and Ken. Barbie doesn't have a favorite color other than hot pink; she has one logo and no last name. Actually, I once heard her last name is Roberts; so, where are her people from? Barbie does not have holiday sets for Chanukah or Ramadan, although she does have them for Easter and Christmas. Kmart does not have a Kmart Barbie, but there is a Wal-Mart, Saks Fifth Avenue, Gap, Bloomingdale's, Avon, and Nichole Miller Barbie (the designer whose ties cost $60).

It is also easier to look at what Barbie isn't. Barbie is never sad, is always available, and "saves the day" in every story written about her. Barbie is timeless; she existed in the days of the *Mayflower,* she was in Oz as Dorothy, and has run for president in several U.S. elections. She has never been a cook but has been a chef; has never been a construction worker but has been a fashion designer. She has been a soloist, a rock star, and the mythical tooth fairy. Barbie is exclusively thematic; Ken, Christie, and the rest are occasionally given professions.

■ The Bitch Has Everything

She does. From the pink condo, to the swimming pool, to the RV, to the recording stage, to more friends than anyone. Everyone loves Barbie and Barbie loves everyone. Barbie proves to us that if we try hard enough, we can own anything and everything. Barbie always succeeds. She becomes whatever she sets her mind to—she influences generations of children and adults and is a perpetual reminder of all that is good, wholesome, and pink in our lives. Barbie is a true American. She stands for the family values that our country holds dear. She is strictly heterosexual, self-providing, philanthropic, and moral. She is also ready to bring "other" people into her life, no matter what color or ethnicity.

Barbie moves in and out of social circles with ease. Her plate is always filled with charity organizations and doing "good." The "Love to Read" Barbie comes with two children (one black and one white) and a book; for every LTR Barbie sold, Mattel donates a dollar to the Reading Is Fundamental organization. As consumers, we are able to support reading by purchasing this doll. That makes all the difference.

■ Intercourse Barbie

As much as Barbie is a virgin in sexual relationships, she is a whore in the corporate world. Barbie has "been in bed" with more Fortune 500 members than anyone. She has worked in and owned her own Pizza Hut and McDonald's, she is a special Wal-Mart edition; she is also the star of *Baywatch* and a perennial guest in Happy Meals. Disney's Epcot Center features a Magical World of Barbie show, complete with dancers, singers, and fireworks. Avon regularly offers a special edition Barbie, and Hallmark has Barbie Christmas ornaments, a new one issued each year. I already mentioned the Benetton Barbie, my unlikely find in a broken-down Turkish airport. eBay is filled with bidding searchers for the rare Holiday Barbie each year. Barbie wanders in and out of corporate headquarters with ease. Companies know that if they tap into her resources, it is a quick ride to higher profits. No one really wants the tiny hamburger in the child's meal; they all are looking for the Barbie—which one is she? the Kenyan? the ballerina? or the wedding Barbie? As a professional, Barbie chooses from her cellular phone, her video camera, and numerous pink briefcases for "just the right thing" for breaking that glass ceiling.

As a professional, Barbie has set records for changing vocations. In the early days, she was featured as a nurse, a baby-sitter, and a secretary. Within months of political correctness, she became a doctor, a pilot, and a businesswoman. Naturally, many of her careers still smack of nurturing; how can one avoid it with a perpetual pink motif? One of my favorite fashion sets is the Caring Careers Fashion Gift Set. These "play pieces for Barbie at work" include a firefighter suit with pink trim, a teacher set, and a veterinarian's smock. Dr. Barbie is a pediatrician with a little black child and a little white child, all adorned in pink and blue. Astronaut Barbie came out in the 1980s and reappeared in the late 1990s. As a part of the Career Collection, this Barbie first appeared as a space pioneer. A newer version highlights Space Week and NASA and "encourages children of all ages to discover the past and future of the exploration in space." All of the boxes featuring careers have the slogan We Girls Can Do Anything! ribboned across the front. Police Officer Barbie is a "friend to all in the community! In her glittery evening dress, Police Officer Barbie shines with pride at the Police Awards Ball. Everyone applauds as she receives the Best Police Officer Award for her courageous acts in the community." PO Barbie comes with a badge and a short formal gown for the ball.

No group of careers could be complete without acknowledging our armed forces. As sergeants and majors, these booted girls march to the beat of proud, patriotic America. Choosing a favorite would be hard, but, well, okay, I guess mine was the Desert Storm Barbie. "Wearing authentic desert battle dress uniforms" of camouflage material—Sergeant Barbie is a medic, and she's ready for duty! Staff Sergeant Ken is ready too! Their berets bear the distinctive 101st Airborne unit insignia with the motto: Rendezvous with Destiny. Both are proud, patriotic Americans serving their country wherever they are needed."

Rounding up the professions, 1992 ushered in the Barbie for President Gift Set. This was a Toys R Us limited edition. "Barbie hits the campaign trail in spectacular style! Dressed in her winning red and gold suit she's the picture perfect candidate to get out the vote. Then, at her inaugural ball, the festive crowd cheers as Barbie enters in a sensational sparkling gown sprinkled with silver stars!" We girls can do anything. How about the $75 Statue of Liberty Barbie? Holding the torch of freedom, this golden-haired doll stands perched on a plastic island, adorned with a shimmery crown, beckoning all who will listen to join her in liberty and justice for all. Of course, it may be the only way we can see Lady Liberty, as all visits to her shores are now forbidden.

■ Herstory

Barbie's other identities lie in ethnic and historical roots. Not satisfied with the existential Barbie, Mattel allowed Barbie to revisit, ergo, rewrite the past through a series of historical dolls. Each doll belongs to a collector's set, usually priced from $5 to $100 more than a regular Barbie. A collector's doll should be kept in her box, appreciating in value as the ages tick by.

One must take a little boat down *It's a Small World* in Disneyland or Disneyworld to understand how ethnicity is defined by a corporation. Sailing down that channel, listening to hundreds of little dolls sing—constantly—we see different peoples grouped together on their continents. Northern countries show a preponderance of buildings and clothing—countries from south of the equator seem to exhibit dolls wearing scant clothing, selling vegetables, taking a siesta, or climbing trees. No buildings are evident in Africa, and only huts appear in the South American countries. Taking It's a Small World seriously as a metaphor for The World, we are able to understand the consciousness that constructed Mattel's line of ethnic Barbies.

Imagine we are sailing through our own small world and meeting these diverse Barbies; we hear their words describing their heritage. Each Barbie is distinct in native dress and manner. The Jamaican Barbie comes with large hoop earrings and a red bandanna. Many exclaim how like Aunt Jemima or a slave she looks. Jamaican Barbie claims that her people speak patois, "a kind of Jamaica talk" filled with English and African words. She also insists Jamaicans are a very "happy" people and are "filled with boonoo-noonoos, much happiness." Culturally, this Barbie teaches us that her country is filled with higglers (women merchants) who sell their food in open markets. Along with pictures of Bob Marley, sugar cane, and palm trees, the Jamaican Barbie is prettily packed in hot pink.

In keeping with the island theme, we move to the Polynesian Barbie. The box never mentions which island she is from, somewhere within the thirteen groups of tropical islands. We are told that people live closely together and are kind to one another. Polynesians like luaus and like to eat.

Another Barbie "of color" is the Indian Barbie. Unlike her island cousins, her box shows a picture of a building, the Taj Mahal. We are reminded that India is a very old country and that most people eat only vegetables and rice "with their fingers." It is not mentioned whether or not Indians are happy or kind. None of these Barbies discuss their skin color or hair texture, and there is no mention of physical attributes. Naturally, they are all standing on tiptoe. Puerto Rican Barbie is dressed all in white as she readies herself for, dare I say? Her confirmation. No self-respecting Puerto Rican girlfriend I have has ever done anything but shriek in horror at this plastic sista.

As we visit northern Europe, we do not meet amalgamated Barbies. For instance, there are no British Isles Barbies or Scandinavian Barbies. Each has her own country. The German Barbie looks splendid in her milkmaid's outfit with long blonde braids. We are welcomed to a country that is known for its "breathtaking beauty and hard-working people." Evidently the south of the equator Barbies do not work, or at least not hard.

Mentioned on the box are modern cities, museums, art galleries, and industries. The Norwegian Barbie tells us of her mythological tradition and describes her people as "tall, sturdy, fair-skinned, blonde and blue eyed." Food is not mentioned nearly as often on northern Barbies as on the southern counterparts. Evidently the farther north one moves, the less people talk or think about food.

There is no specifically American Barbie. However, there is a Native American Barbie in the Dolls of the World Collection. NA Barbie is a part of a "proud Indian heritage, rich in culture and tradition." Long ago her people belonged to a tribe. Her dress is that of a Plains Indian, yet she describes homes like those constructed by eastern Indians. Three times she mentions her pride in her people.

What's going on here? Mattel has defined ethnicity as other than white. Regular blonde Barbie is the standard from which the "others" come. As it emulates the dominant culture, the norm is Barbie, without a title. All other Barbies are qualified by their language, foods, and "native" dances. Attempting to be multicultural, parents buy these dolls for their children to teach them about "other" people. No "regular" Barbie ever talks about her regular diet, the personality of "her" people, and her customs. Only the designated "ethnic" dolls have those qualifications. Much like the sign in the local Kmart that designates the location of ethnic hair products, Barbie has otherized dolls into dominant and marginal cultures. Barbie's whiteness privileges her to not be questioned; she is the standard against which all others are measured.

■ The New Social Studies

A couple of years after the ethnic Barbie line, Mattel introduced the American Stories Collection, which featured a Civil War Nurse Barbie, a Pilgrim Barbie, a Pioneer Barbie, and an American Indian Barbie (there she is again). Each doll comes with a storybook that places Barbie in the middle of essential historical action. Each book ends with Barbie "saving the day" and changing history for the better.

As you have probably guessed, the Pilgrim Barbie meets Squanto and he teaches her how to plant corn: "he wasn't savage at all." She grows a successful crop of corn and decides to share it with her neighbors; hence, the first Thanksgiving. And Barbie was there. Conveniently neglected are the Pilgrims' grave robbing, confiscation of Indian lands, and, yes, the sticky matter of genocide.

Since Betsy Ross already made the flag in 1776, Colonial Barbie decides to make a quilt to celebrate the thirteen colonies. The quilt was embroidered "Happy Birthday America," and Barbie and her female helpers were congratulated for it and treated "with great respect." Western Barbie cleverly brings dried apples on the long journey during the westward expansion. When her friends get hungry, the apples are produced to make a delicious apple pie. American Indian Barbie takes care of a papoose, parentage unknown, and tells stories to the little Indian villagers. I will stop here, fearing an overload of saccharine.

Each book is signed on the back with a personal note from the author. History becomes firm in the eyes of the reader as it is legitimized by the author. Here are a few excerpts:

> During my research for Western Promise, I learned a lot about pioneers. The more I read, the more I admired these courageous, self-reliant people.

> Even though it's fun to read books, I still love to hear someone tell a good story! In the early days of the American Indians, there were no books or schools like there are today.

> In writing this story for you, I have learned so much! What I noticed most about the story of the Pilgrims and Thanksgiving is how the Native Americans became their friends and helped these strangers in a new land.

> I hope you enjoyed imagining Barbie as a colonial girl. Perhaps you will think of her on the next 4th of July and what it must have been like during the early days when America was first "born."

Consumers are told that history is being taught in a friendly way through Mattel. Children now place Barbie within historical contexts in order to understand what *really* happened.

Fairy tales and fiction are not immune from Mattel's rewriting. The Children's Collection Series features heroines from different stories. "Childhood favorites 'come to life' with Barbie. Play out the story of Rapunzel." Barbie as Scarlett O'Hara promises to be one of the most successful dolls of the decade. Promoted in a thirty-minute infomercial by Cathy Lee Gifford (a TV Barbie), the doll is sold as essential for anyone who was affected by the novel or movie version of *Gone with the Wind:* "See Barbie as your favorite character, Scarlett," Cathy Lee advises us. She recalls that when she was a little girl, Barbie was her favorite doll and there is nothing more special than having her best friend become Scarlett. The line between reality and fantasy is blurred. Barbie acting as a character?

■ Barbie as Literary Text

In its merchandising Mattel recognizes the importance of reading and education, creating hundreds of types of reading materials that feature Barbie. Not satisfied with the toy market, Mattel has branched out to themes in magazines, books, newspapers, and film.

The Adventures with Barbie book series features a set of paperback books in which "Barbie stars in her own series of fabulous adventures that tie inspiring messages in with action, suspense and fun with friends—and set an example of independence, responsibility and kindness for young girls everywhere." *Barbie,* the magazine for girls, gives fashion tips, promotes new Barbie themes, teaches fun crafts, and gives beauty advice. The comic market promotes *Barbie Fashion* and *Barbie.* Both comics are monthly and tell "stylish stories" and give "trend-setting tips." Little Golden Books for toddlers include several Barbie titles, including *Very Busy Barbie* (Barbie as a model who gives up her career), *A Picnic Surprise* (Barbie finding an old lady's puppy instead of having fun), and *Barbie, the Big*

Splash (Barbie's photo shoot is spoiled, but she is able to take disappointment). We constantly are bombarded by the altruistic blonde (in the books she is usually monocolored) giving up something sensational for the good of all humankind. Little girls are taught at an early age that it is more important to give up one's own goal than to disappoint someone else. Disney did it well with *The Little Mermaid* and *Beauty and the Beast.* It is a female's place to sacrifice for the good of others. What about Pocahontas? Esmeralda? You get the point.

Not to be outdone by three-foot-tall competitors, adults have their own Barbie literature: *Barbie Collector's Magazine* and several weekly and monthly newspapers, the most circulated paper being *Miller's Market Report: News, Advice and Collecting Tips for Barbie Doll Investors.* The tabloid features Barbie events; in an April issue, nineteen "don't miss" gatherings were advertised, including the Great Barbie Show of Southern California, Barbie Comes to Bloomingdale's, Seventh Annual Barbie Grants-A-Wish, and many regional conventions. Barbie clubs adorn the United States from sea to sequined shining sea. There is an annual Barbie world convention, classes on Barbie, and, a couple of years ago, a Barbie summit in New York. To emulate a global consciousness, Mattel organized this summit for women and girls to caucus about their needs and desires from Mattel for the twenty-first century. Always the educator, Barbie proves to us that reading and schooling cannot be left behind. Math becomes essential in order to add up the values of vintage dolls and collectors' items. Barbie, for many, is a full-time occupation. Barbie is the only non-human figure in the famed wax museum of Hollywood. Naturally, she has her own Barbie Boutique on Fifth Avenue adjoining F.A.O. Schwartz, a store that provides myriads of books, magazines, videos, and objects devoted to Barbie. The market flourishes.

What could possibly be next?

Are Barbies good for children? Should our girls play with them? How many Barbies should a child own? Do the dolls teach us what true beauty is? Can a child have self-esteem and not look like Barbie? Should we bend to peer pressure and allow our children to reside in pink-trimmed junior condos, dreaming of far-away places and exotic men? Does Barbie assist in constructing childhood, consciousness? Do Barbie-centered websites increase the obsession with pink consumerism and girlishness?

Of course she does—just like any other feature of kinderculture. The effect of the Barbie curriculum is idiosyncratic—for some it facilitates conformity; for others, it inspires resistance. Multiple readings aside, Barbie does operate within the boundaries of particular cultural logics. She does celebrate whiteness, blonde whiteness in particular, as a standard for feminine beauty; she does reify anorexic figures coupled with large breasts as objects of male desire. She does support unbridled consumerism as a reason for being. She never questions American virtue and supports the erasure of the colonial genocide in America's past. Make no mistake, she is a Christian, not a Jew, and certainly not a Muslim—mainstream and not countercultural. No poor girl is Barbie as she repetitively displays her upper-middle-class credentials. Again, the curriculum may not take, no effect is guaranteed, but we must be aware of the terrain on which Barbie operates.

Barbie enthusiasts feel great anticipation about the next line of Barbies. Having featured professions, movie stars, stories, sports, and fashion, could Barbie ever run out of themes? By maintaining authenticity, Mattel is able to continue rewriting history and life. Re-invention of Barbie is a constant in Mattel world. As Barbie adapts to current lifestyles and girl-fads, cross-marketing with Disney and Hollywood gives her extra earning power.

I'd like to see Barbie a bit more realistic: in keeping with real-life professions, wouldn't we be wise to wait for a factory worker Barbie, a prostitute Barbie, a drug pusher Barbie—can a pimp Ken be far behind? What about more politically active Barbies? Protest Barbie, chained to her dream house, Bisexual Barbie, complete with both Ken and Midge (or Steve and Christie)? Green Barbie? Bo-ho Barbie? Neo-Marxist Barbie?

The mind wearies with the possibility. One knows for certain, however, Barbie is with us: (13) Yea, verily, she who is known as Barbie will walk the earth through the millennium, being praised by both women and men and ushering in a new day for all humankind.

* Parts of this chapter also appeared in *Kinderculture: The Corporate Construction of Childhood* (2004). Ed: Shirley R. Steinberg and Joe L. Kincheloe. Boulder, CO: Westview Press.

16

■ The Spectacle of Reform

Vulture Culture, Youth, and Television

**Kathalene A. Razzano, Loubna H. Skalli,
& Christine M.Quail**

After running away from her foster parents, Karissa went on a two-week partying binge. When the cops came to break up the party, Karissa was arrested and thrown into juvenile detention. In juvie, Karissa played tough. But on the stand, she realized what was important, and the judge let her go home. Has Karissa cleaned up her act once and for all?

—*Life After Juvies: Karissa and Nathan, 2007*[1]

Reality television is increasingly interested in the spectacle of youth in trouble—drug addiction, running away, teen sex, disrespect for authority, theft, vandalism, reckless driving, assault. Many daytime television talk shows, MTV's *Juvies,* and A&E's *Intervention* each devote considerable air time to the representation of youth in trouble. Each show offers ways to reform, rescue and/or reconcile youth to their families, their schools, and their communities. However, these promises of reform are formulated around the logic of the media spectacle and the profit imperatives of the entertainment industry.

The logic of the media spectacle is one of commodification and representation, as well as detachment, fragmentation, and isolation. The spectacle works to reinforce the hegemony of the ruling economic order through the commodification of knowledge, image and subject, and then through the subsequent fragmentation of that knowledge, image and subject. According to Debord, the spectacle as commodification and fragmentation "is both the outcome and the goal of the dominant mode of production....In form as in content the spectacle serves as the total justification for the conditions and aims of the existing system"[2] The concept of the media spectacle has most recently been nuanced by Douglas Kellner who addresses spectacles ranging from political events and sports contests, to famous trials and "breaking" news events.[3] According to Kellner "media produce spectacles around events and controversies of social and everyday life, often providing forums through which major political issues and social struggles are negotiated and debated."[4]

As a media spectacle, the televisual spectacle of reform is mobilized through popular culture, political and professional discourses, but in the end, isolates and villainizes young women and men of color.[5] It mirrors and plays into the moral panic of the 1990s that centered around the perceived rising incidences of youth crime. In order for the spectacle of reform to be effective, it must present the individual as separated from larger socioeconomic processes. This task falls to the "specialized science of domination," which is itself fragmented into areas such as sociology, psychology, criminology, etc.[6] These areas of professional knowledge work to situate individuals as separate from the means of economic and social production. The spectacle of reform relies heavily on the expertise and participation of professionals who represent the justice/welfare system, including probation officers, juvenile court judges, social workers, psychologists, family counselors, intervention specialists, drill sergeants/police officers, and public defenders.

In addition to that expert knowledge, are principles of control, surveillance, confinement, confession, and atonement of the youth in trouble. All of this is staged, packaged, and sold to us as information and entertainment—"infotainment" is the driving force behind "vulture culture."[7] Vulture culture is the result of media's continuous, persistent process of scavenging the personal narratives and professional discourses that make up everyday knowledge and common sense. Vulture culture then (re-)presents these narratives and discourses back to us as spectacle, entertainment, and information.[8]

Using the examples of the daytime television talk shows and *Juvies,* and *Intervention,* we explore the construction of youth in trouble and how the logic of reform used by these television programs echoes—as well as reinforces—the logic found in the juvenile justice system, the welfare system, and rehabilitation/addiction discourse. We demonstrate how these parallels provide a rationale for the televisual spectacle of punitive, bodily confinement solutions for youth in trouble. Each of these programs mirrors the ways in which youth are incorporated into and treated in the juvenile justice and welfare systems. Perhaps most striking initially are the differences in the presentation and experiences between sexes. By examining some of the academic literature concerning women, men, and the justice/welfare system, we may better understand the ways youth are positioned in society, especially youth in trouble.

An overwhelming amount of research on women in the justice/welfare literature finds that girls are more often punished for status (read moral) offenses than are boys. For instance, Meda Chesney-Lind, a leading scholar on women in the justice system, examines the role of the criminal justice system in the maintenance of patriarchy. She offers substantial evidence that women are most often convicted of status offenses and petty crimes such as minor property crimes, forgery, and prostitution. They are rarely convicted for serious property crimes and violent crimes, which "parallels their assigned roles in straight society."[9] This research may point to the reasons why the talk show's "teen-out-of-control" is usually female, and why most of the girls featured on *Juvies* are either charged with being runaways or with theft. Further, what is striking in this research is that women who are convicted of crimes are mostly women living in poverty.[10]

In contrast to girls and young women, boys and young men are seen as violent and dangerous "super-predators,"—"a 'generational wolfpack' of 'fatherless, Godless, and jobless' youth."[11] The super-predator is a conservative political and cultural construct that links male youth of color to the inevitability of crime and violence. In mobilizing this concept, politicians have helped create a "youth control complex,"[12] wherein youth are suspects across a range of cultural spaces, including the justice system, the street, school, and family. A system that assumes youth's criminality works to "manage, control, and incapacitate black and Latino youth."[13] In so doing, the possibilities, real and imagined, for these youth are severely curtailed. This legacy is evident in both public policy and in the television programs we are analyzing in this chapter.

We understand that the category of youth encompasses significant race, gender, and class differences. These differences are important to underline because they inform dominant trends, on and off the television shows, of policing, punishing, and reforming youth in trouble. Race and poverty continue to be two determining features of popular representations and conceptions of criminality. This should come as no surprise, given the decades-long hostility toward the gendered, racialized welfare state and the racist dimensions of the War on Drugs.[14] Indeed, race, class and gender have always been central in shaping youth experiences with the justice/welfare system.

■ Youth-in-Trouble: Conflict, Surveillance and Confession

Our initial interest in youth in trouble was sparked by the over-representation of "teen-out-of-control" talk shows in the late 1990s and the early 2000s. In programs such as *Maury* and *Montel,* teen and pre-teen girls exhibit behavior that does not conform to gender norms—essentially making a "spectacle of themselves." Hence, the talk show becomes a space for reforming and realigning them with "acceptable" modes of dress and behavior. This reform usually focuses on the body. This raises questions about the logic of such punishment/reform solutions. Where did these solutions come from? Who suggested them? And why do talk shows use them? How are these solutions reproduced in other entertainment programs? These initial questions pointed us to further questions about the institutions and discourses that define youth in trouble, measures of reform, and rehabilitation.

The youth-in-trouble theme on talk shows is grounded in moments of conflict. The focus of these programs is particularly on "teen-out-of-control" and the hyper-spectacularization of their deviance. In contrast to the seemingly chaotic, conflict-ridden atmosphere of the talk show, *Juvies* stages youth in trouble in a more disciplined environment. Here, the televisual presentation of youth replicates the rigidity of the juvenile detention center where the program is filmed. While the spectacle of reform ends at the age of eighteen on talk shows and *Juvies,* it begins at precisely that age on *Intervention.* Though it does not exclusively focus on youth, *Intervention* is a more confession-oriented, atonement-focused show, where individuals are encouraged to submit to rehabilitation, expert guidance, and treatment programs. Thus, we can see the spectacle of reform in three ways—conflict on the talk shows, surveillance on *Juvies,* and confession on *Intervention*—although elements of conflict, surveillance, and confession are present on each program. The punitive logic behind the spectacle of reform becomes more visible when we look at each show in detail. So let's begin by looking at the teen-out-of-control talk show.

In any given week, one is likely to stumble across a talk show with titles such as *Maury*'s "If My Teen Gets Paid for Sex…She's Going to Boot Camp," *Montel's* "Out of Control Daughters" or *Dr. Phil*'s "The Young and the Reckless."[15] On these programs you can "meet a twelve-year-old who gets so drunk, she blacks out"[16] or hear the story of "five desperate mothers" and see the talk show aid them in trying "to tame their daughters' wild, violent ways."[17]

What these programs make clear is that "teen" is not a gender-neutral term. The "teen-out-of-control" is female and characterized primarily by sexual behaviors, profane language, and disrespect toward authority. Occasionally, she may also be violent, and use drugs and/or alcohol. (Rarely, the talk show may include a boy on a teen-out-of-control episode. In contrast to the girls featured on these programs, the male "teen-out-of-control" is characterized by his violence, not by his promiscuity.) The goal of these types of programs is to both punish and reform the girl out-of-control through and on the body. Depending on the degree of the out-of-control behavior, the girls' punishments/reforms can range from a make-over to public humiliation[18] to a day in boot camp or jail. A *Sally* episode is a bit more straightforward—"Send My Wild Teen to Boot Camp!"; *Jenny Jones* recruits the help of a drill instructor to send her "guests" to boot camp; and, *Ricki Lake* "enlists the experts for some on-the-spot counseling."

One wonders why the boot camp is taken to be a logical form of punishment, why the social workers and counselors on the show allowed children as young as seven to be subjected to stereotypically in-your-face drill sergeants—usually large, loud, intrusive men, and only occasionally large, loud, intrusive women. If we understand these programs as vulture culture, we can see the connections between these punishments, these professionals, and the spectacle of reform. As a form of vulture culture, talk shows rely on "expert" knowledge. This use of expertise allows us to understand how normal and deviant behaviors are defined and constructed in talk show narratives. These narratives both inform and are informed by popular discourses coming out of criminology, psychology, social work, fashion, and other forms of popular culture. Furthermore, these discourses have a history of defining girls, in particular, in terms of their sexuality and offer punishment/reform solutions that focus on the body.

Juvies' spectacle of reform is less a spectacle of conflict and more a spectacle of surveillance. Where the daytime talk show devotes roughly one-fourth of its screen-time to showing the girls during their punishment/reform exercise (boot camp, jail, makeover),

Juvies takes place at Indiana's Lake County Juvenile Center (LCJC). The show follows teen-age boys and girls as they are processed into and through the center, which includes detention facilities (intake holding rooms, cells, lunchroom), as well as court-rooms. Most of the youth profiled are first-time offenders. The opening sequence to each episode includes images of the teens to be profiled, the judge, shots of the juvenile center, surveillance monitors and re-enactments as well as the following text on the screen: "Every day teenagers get into trouble. Some end up here. One judge. One verdict. Will they stay… or go home?"

A typical episode's chronology includes the youth's arrival at the facility, the call to their parent(s), changing out of their street clothes into the detention center uniform, social time with other youth, a visit from the parents, confessional moments, bed time, court appearance, and either return to detention or release to the home. These moments are chronicled not only by the *Juvies* camera crew, but also by what we will call the "institutional camera." Interwoven into the program are shots from the LCJC's central control center cameras. We watch, or rather surveil, these youth as they walk down a hall, meet with their parents, and sit in the common area. Between the institutional camera and the *Juvies* cameras, the show creates a sense that the youth is confined and, in that very confinement, also exposed. For example, a common camera shot on the show is to film the youth through the small window in their cell's door. Even behind closed doors, there is no place where they can escape surveillance. Thus, a crucial feature of the spectacle of reform is the ever-present surveillance apparatus—a twenty-first century form of the panopticon.

Whereas the talk show is focused mainly on the teenage girl, *Juvies* profiles youth of both genders, of varied class backgrounds, and of different races. However, as we will demonstrate, boys and girls are treated differently within the juvenile system, both as a product of the justice system and in the televisual representation of that system. Further, where the "institutional" figures on talk shows are often intimidating drill instructors, on *Juvies,* the comparable institutional figures are the intake and detention officers who offer calm, yet firm, words of caution, encouragement, and advice to these youth.

We argue that the difference here is related to the spectacle of reform and surveillance. The talk show defines the girls as out-of-control. The actions of the institutional figures are to bring them under control. In contrast, the youth at LCJC are already under the control of the institution. As such, the officers at LCJC can mobilize their authority without physical and verbal intimidation. In the tradition of vulture culture, we are encouraged to view these confinement and surveillance practices as benevolent, legitimate, and effective.

Intervention provides us with a hybrid site combining elements of the talk show with elements of *Juvies*. According to the program's website:

> *Intervention* is a powerful and gripping television series in which people confront their darkest demons and seek a route to redemption. The *Intervention* television series profiles people whose dependence on drugs and alcohol or other compulsive behavior has brought them to a point of personal crisis and estranged them from their friends and loved ones. Each *Intervention* episode ends with a surprise intervention that is staged by the family and friends of the alcohol of [sic] drug addict, and which is conducted by one of four *Intervention* specialists: Jeff VanVonderen, Candy Finningan, Ken Seeley and Tara Fields.[19]

Presented in a documentary-style similar to *Juvies,* this show features one or two stories each episode. It begins with an interview-style, medium-range close-up of the featured addict and is followed by shots of the addict performing their addictive act (i.e., shooting up, purging, taking pills). We are then introduced to the concerned family and friends (also shot in medium close-up). In these initial interviews, we are inevitably referred back to the addict-as-child. Thus, *Intervention* not only offers us a site to explore youth as young adult, but also a site to see the future of the teens on the talk shows and LCJC. The narratives of the addicts' childhoods echo the talk show and *Juvies* narratives. And, in some ways, the addicts are the embodiment of the teens' parents' fear as well as the failure of juvenile reform measures.

As the program progresses, we follow the addict's out-of-control behavior and bear witness to the concern and pain of the family who often both enable and detest the addiction. Most of the program involves confessional moments from the addicts as well as their family and friends, interspersed with footage of the addicts again succumbing to their addiction or of interactions with family and friends. The addicts confess their addiction, discuss their addictive behavior, regret their lost or wasted opportunities, and show remorse for the pain they have caused their family and friends. The family and friends discuss their failures as parents and spouses, their fears and concerns, and the effects addiction has had on their other relationships. Once we have witnessed the addiction and heard the confessions, the intervention takes place. Indeed, the program sets up the intervention moment as the climax: the opening of the program includes the following text on the screen, "The addicts in this show have agreed to be in a documentary about addiction. They do not know they will soon face an intervention. Millions of Americans struggle with addiction. Most need help to stop."

Intervention thus centers on the spectacle of reform and confession. The intervention moment is the means to end the "struggle with addiction" and provide the "help to stop." However, the intervention is also presented as a moment managed and structured by expertise using professionals with backgrounds in social work, counseling, psychology, and, in some cases, who are recovering addicts themselves. This combination of the spectacle, the personal narratives of the dangers and destruction of drug addiction, and the reliance on expert knowledge for legitimatizing the program as well as its solutions culminates in a product of vulture culture. While the program itself has altruistic goals, its presentation of race, class, and gender should force us to acknowledge the different experiences, possibilities, and consequences for people with varied backgrounds and histories. Instead, this program falls flat in its refusal to address these very issues that point to systemic and systematic injustice.

As we can see, the devices of conflict, surveillance, and confession are integral to the construction of the youth in trouble as the modes through which the spectacle initiates commodification and fragmentation. It is also important to analyze experiences of youth with(in) justice and welfare systems, and the relationship between these experiences and these modes of the spectacle. These experiences are framed as a process of fragmentation/isolation, control and reform/repentance. This three-step process also plays out in the televisual world as the spectacle of reform.

■ Fragmentation and Isolation of Youth-in-Trouble

The spectacle of reform depends on both the deviance of youth as well as the possibility of their reform. As such, the youth in trouble has to be framed as "reformable." The first step in this approach is to isolate the youth in trouble from the broader historical, social, political, and economic context that has shaped their lives. This is part of the spectacle's process of fragmentation. Indeed what most television programs succeed in doing is stripping the youth in trouble of the tensions resulting from class, race, and gender differentials. The spectacle of reform needs the youth to take full responsibility for their own acts while denying any claim to the other important factors shaping their lives, "such as lack of education and skills, unemployment, housing conditions, crime and poverty."[20] In this way, individual choices and behaviors become a distraction and focal point. If we can transform issues of education, crime, and poverty into individual problems, then punishment/reform can be extracted on an individual and the "problem" is contained.[21]

A real-world example of how teen-age girls experience this shift from social problem to individual problem is seen in Kerry Carrington's ethnographic study on female delinquency. She explores a case from her research where a teenage girl has repeatedly run away from home, has been orphaned, has been sexually abused by relatives, has admitted to being sexually active, and has attempted suicide. The psychologist's assessment of the girl was that she had an inability to cope in the community and, for her own safety, ought to be institutionalized. In Carrington's analysis of the case material she concludes, "By making Judy appear individually responsible for the social and familial world in which she inhabited, the rationale provided for punitive intervention masked as benign expertise."[22] As we will see, cases like Judy's abound in televisual representations of youth in trouble.

In terms of social welfare and youth in trouble, this individualist isolation exposes youth, especially girls, to greater surveillance and censure. This is a key point of tension between individualism and the state. In seeking the help of state welfare agencies, talk shows, or altruistic reality shows, the parents/guardians define their children as deviant, in need of reform. Instead of examining the institutional structures that create the youth's "world," professional knowledge bases and the television format seek to reconcile the youth back to their (potentially hostile) environments.

A key feature in the fragmentation of the individual is the life story. The role of the life story takes different forms. On shows that feature youth under eighteen years old, the life story is only alluded to, while conflict and surveillance are emphasized. For example, on the talk shows and *Juvies*, the reasons for running away, getting in a fight, stealing, doing drugs, or having sex usually have something to do with abuse in the home. We need only to look back to Carrington's essay where "teen-out-of-control" Judy was repeatedly sent back to a home where she was being sexually abused to understand the importance of life stories in contextualizing youth with troubling behaviors.

In contrast, the life story on *Intervention* is a featured part of the confessional and is crucial to the youth's eventual redemption. Here, the life story provides one justification or explanation why the subject is worthy and in need of reform, quite different from other trouble narratives where the life story is not a factor. The emphasis on confession often reveals the addict's own experiences as a youth in trouble. For instance, in the case of methamphetamine addict Ashley, we learn that she comes from a Christian household but always felt like an outsider. At an early age, she started doing drugs and having sex. In short, she was a "teen-out-of-control." We are provided with her story of deviance and her history of addiction. However, this history is left without critique, and thus her experiences with earlier rehabilitative institutions such as the church and the juvenile justice system remain unexplored and unquestioned and therefore still valid and legitimate. Her life-story constructed as individual, familial problems erase the failures of earlier rehabilitation institutions. *Intervention* reveals a life story as a part of its confessional thrust but only as a means to further the spectacle and make the redemption more spectacular.

Such programs featuring youth in trouble rarely interrogate the roles of institutions in the life stories of the girls featured on the "teen-out-of-control" shows or the youth in *Juvies*. In fact, the programs rarely open an honest investigation into the power differentials and the forces of oppression that characterize the youth's experiences. This is, in part, due to the structural constraints of reality television itself. For instance, a traditional talk show format usually consists of a brief introduction to the show's topic of the day, followed by the introduction of the guests and the telling of their stories, a short discussion with the host and audience, and concludes with the expert giving advice to the guests. Guests are allotted roughly five-minute segments in which they are to share their story. This structure of talk shows works to individualize these social problems. The talk show does not have time to explore the girls' life-stories; it is a here-and-now format, decidedly situated in the present with the goal of the future. However, the inevitable failure of this approach to make a constructive critique (or to radically alter the lives of the youth on these programs) is situated in the erasure of the past. As with all these shows, there is a need to stay on task because of the capitalist nature of television time.[23]

The reality television genre offers a made-to-order format allowing repetition of similar narratives and character types(stereo-types)—the faces and names are different but the roles are the same. On talk shows and on *Juvies*, the life stories aren't mentioned because they complicate and interfere with the pre-existing format. One can only fit so much information into a five-minute segment. On *Intervention*, the life story is a part of the prefigured narrative. In all three cases, however, the implications of race and class for these life stories remain unacknowledged. Thus, the life story, both in its absence and presence, works to further individualize social problems and therefore does not acknowledge individual experience as linked to the larger gendered, raced, and classed histories.

■ Control: Policing the Self, Policing the Body

Once the social problem is reframed as an individual failing, the spectacle of reform can then move forward with rationalizing its reform goals. An individualized problem calls for an individualized solution. Hence, the promotion of self-control and/or bodily control by the experts involved with these programs. Self-control implies a policing of one's attitudes and behaviors, as well as appearance, in order to conform to social and institutional definitions of what is normal and acceptable. In terms of sexuality and sexual behavior, women/girls are responsible for policing their own sexuality as well as the sexuality of men. So, if a woman gets pregnant, it is her own fault because she did not stop the man or use birth control. While we all ought to know better, a Ricki Lake expert once said, "Women allow themselves to be taken advantage of."

The above discussion on individualism, professional knowledge, and self-control illustrates that these forms of punishment/reform are not arbitrary. They are, in fact, rooted in institutionalized discourses. When youth get in trouble, systems of discourse rise up to treat, reform, and recuperate them back within normative bounds. Foucault suggests, "in our societies, systems of punishment are to be situated in a certain 'political economy' of the body...it is always the body that is at issue—the body and its forces, their utility and their docility, their distribution and their submission."[24] Throughout time and across cultures, women's bodies have been sites where domination and control have been enforced.[25]

In terms of the teen-out-of-control talk show, we see self-control working on two levels. The first level is the girl herself. Chances are the girls who are on the talk shows do not have the self-control expected of them and in this way, self-control becomes a morality issue. The second level is related to this expectation of self-control. This is what is implicitly, and sometimes not so implicitly, implied in talk show discourse. Teen-out-of-control guests are on the show because they have been unable or unwilling to police themselves. The above quote from the talk show expert implies that women are the controllers of not only their own sexuality and behavior, but also that of men. This has become a taken-for-granted assumption with dramatic ramifications for women and their views of themselves and their experiences.[26]

Research demonstrates that girls are more likely than boys to be questioned by the courts about their sexual activity.[27] Furthermore, girls' offenses are more likely to be viewed "as an aspect of sexual promiscuity, and more likely to lose their liberty for activities which would not be against the law if committed by an adult."[28] It is interesting that on talk shows, chastity is no longer an issue. The women and girls aren't there to prove their chastity. Rather, the focus is on issues of pregnancy, drug use, disease, and paternity, although this is a paternity with a decided focus on exposing the mother's sexuality. The "teen-out-of-control's" reform is one centered primarily on the young female body that must be controlled, contained, and made over. It has to be contained because it is seen as overly sexualized and, therefore, a threat to social order. In its perceived excesses and exuberance, the female body takes center stage in this spectacle of reform.

In *Juvies*, the narrative is framed as a bad choice or decision, which marks the youth's lack of self-control. Running away, theft, drug use, and assault suggest that these teens are not in line with the institutions of family, school, and community. Because their actions suggest a rejection of these institutions, containing them is seen as the logical solution. Thus, of the seven girls profiled on the program, three are charged as runaways, two with theft, and two with assault/attempted murder. Of the ten boys profiled on the program, three are charged with burglary, two with battery, one with hit-and-run plus drug possession, one with resisting arrest plus underage drinking, one with auto theft, one with criminal recklessness, and only one charged as a runaway. The differences in the violations by gender and by race fall along (stereo)typical lines. All of the youth arrested for assault/battery are black. Of the four youth arrested as runaways, all are white and three are girls. Given the historical trend of charging girls with status offenses, it is surprising that two girls are arrested for assault. However, the televisual narrative positions these two as acting in self-defense.

Juvies presents all the above cases as the result of a poor decision. For instance, Jeff is arrested on charges of criminal recklessness. According to the show, a friend brought a BB gun to Jeff's apartment, and the boys decided to shoot the gun off the balcony. When the apartment complex manager saw Jeff shooting the gun, he thought it was real and called the police. In this narrative, it is Jeff's mother who frames the action as a decision. She says, "You've got your whole life ahead of you. It's in your hands. It's based on what you do. You were charged with reckless endangerment...You're a good kid. You're smart. But all of that can go down the drain just like that." In another instance, Steve is arrested for resisting arrest and underage drinking. After his first night at LCJC, he says, "I'd have to say I made a number of bad decisions."

In *Juvies*, such a spectacle takes the notion of bodily confinement to the next level. Premised on surveillance, the confined body is at once a site of spectacular discipline and display. While the spectacle is built around sexualized female bodies on talk shows, the spectacle in *Juvies* involves the over-protection of the young female bodies and the over-exposure of the young males' bodies. This difference is seen most clearly in the intake and bedtime rituals. All of the youth presented on *Juvies* seem to follow the same intake procedure: they are imaged, stripped, deloused, showered, then re-clothed in the inmate uniform. However, this process, as presented in the program, is structured by gender norms that treat male/female bodies differently. Virtually none of the girls' bodies are seen during the delousing/shower scene. Instead, we see a guard standing in front of the shower area door, blocking our view. In contrast, the boys' bodies are exposed from the waist up during the same process. Again, at bedtime, the boys must strip to their briefs, in front of the camera's eye, before we see them, framed in a long shot, walking down the hall, still only in their briefs, to their cell. The girls, on the other hand, are only seen wearing full-length, long-sleeved, over-sized nightgowns. What this suggests is that boys' bodies are disciplined and punished through the very act of bodily exposure over which they have no control. The same system of surveillance disciplines the girls' by covering their bodies.[29]

On the other hand, *Intervention* features the body as incapable of self-control, and thus in need of rehabilitation and reform. Unlike on *Juvies* and the talk show, addiction is not framed as a bad choice or an unwillingness to enact self-control. Rather, the very nature of addiction is an inability to resist the compulsion. As a result, the addicted body is out-of-control, abused and abusing. For instance, Ricky, a heroin addict and former Marine, is shown after shooting up some heroin, scratching his skin uncontrollably, shaking, and pacing. Self-control is not only compromised during the addictive act, but also in everyday life as the addicted individual is compelled to seek means to support the addiction. As Ricky confesses, "The hard part is what you gotta do to get it." It is not uncommon for women to become strippers and/or trade sex. The men steal, and may also trade sex, although this is less common. While the addicts may recognize that their behavior is deviant and sometimes criminal, they are doing it to satisfy their addiction. And yet, their recognition that the behavior is wrong is also the foundation for their ability to change it. For example, Jessie, a bulimic who chronically binges and purges, has become a stripper to support her food addiction. She has kept her stripping secret from her parents. During one of her confessional moments she says, "I've done a lot of really bad things with this and I am a bad person, but I hope to be a good person." Jessie recognized that her stripping is not socially acceptable in her family's middle-class world. However, she does it anyway and accepts the definition of herself as "bad" because she strips. She also expresses her hope that once she conquers the bulimia, she will be able to be a "good person."

Jessie's story also demonstrates a notion of self-control heard repeatedly on *Intervention*. The addiction itself is often a response to an attempt by the individual to control the world around them. For instance, Jessie's bingeing is her response to a feeling of emptiness inside of her, a void she is trying to fill. In another instance, Laurie uses prescription pain medication to numb her sense of failure. And Ashley says, "When horrible, messed-up things happened to me, when I shoot up, I don't care." The addictive act is viewed by the addicts as a form of self-control, as a way to determine how they experience, or dull, emotions and events.

Intervention is premised on the confessional mood. The spectacle of reform must offer hope, and the hope comes in the form of medicalized discourses promoting bodily control. This control involves subjecting the body to detoxification, routine drug screenings and ultimately confinement in rehabilitation facilities. The intervention is positioned as the last opportunity for redemption before the addict is (re)incorporated into the justice system or dead. But, this opportunity itself is an attempt to circumvent the justice system, to define the addiction as medical rather than criminal. Failure to police the body to this strict regime transitions the addict from medical institutions to the justice system.

■ Repentance and Reform

In talk shows, the "out-of-control" girls are sent to boot camp or prison. When they return, they come on stage and hug the hosts, their mothers and the boot camp authority figures. This plays out as what we call repentance themes. Once the punishment/reform has been carried out, there is a need to assess its effectiveness. Research on youth in the justice system has revealed that girls are more often given cautions, instead of prosecution, if they appear sorry—that is, if they cry. Furthermore, they are more likely to get cautions if their parents seem concerned and involved. Interestingly, the same is true of boys.[30]

This resonates with the "teen-out-of-control" shows, especially on *Maury*. After their prison/boot camp experience, the girls come out and give Povich a hug, thanking him for his help. Some appear more grateful than others, who seem forced into this affectionate display.[31] Regardless, the action itself is meant to symbolize realignment with, or at least recognition of, authority—in much the same way that crying to the police officer indicates the same realignment and recognition (although one has to wonder exactly whom the talk show reconciliation is for). This is a convenient resolution because the spectacle of reform depends on the tears and fears of the young girls. For instance, on the "teen-out-of-control" shows, the girls giving hugs and thanking the hosts and the drill sergeants for their discipline indicates that the girls recognize authority and are submitting to it. Furthermore, this repentance also reinforces the erasure of the life story. Although the experience itself temporarily removes the girl from the environment that created her, she will return to an unaltered home life. Without altering the girl's permanent environment, the impetus of change is put on the girl to accept her life situation, which often includes abuse and neglect. While there will be mention during the talk shows of parental drug addiction, violence, and sexual abuse, these issues are essentially confined to the home and are rarely continued or factored into the talk show narrative and resolution. However, because the talk show rarely explores this life story, the girls' repentance in the final segment of the show works to legitimate the boot camp solution and gain of bodily control. This type of punishment comes to be seen as reasonable and effective. The disciplines and discourses of professional knowledge and the talk show format have worked simultaneously to legitimate bodily control.

In *Juvies* the moment of repentance is presided over by the authoritative figure of the court judge. The same confession-remorse-tears ritual seen on talk shows is rewarded by the release to parental custody. In all of the cases on *Juvies,* the spectacle of reform ends with the youth's promise of future conformity and obedience. However, this promise is not enough to secure the child's release because parents must demonstrate their willingness to recuperate their children. On the show, there were three instances where the youth were forced to remain at LCJC when their parents expressed an inability or unwillingness to control them at home. For the youth who are released, the discipline and authority were extended to not only the parents but the school authorities as well. Mandatory school attendance is another condition for release.

While *Juvies* surrenders the youth back to the family and the larger community, *Intervention* removes and isolates the addict from the family and community. The intervention is not just about rehabilitating the addict but also about rehabilitating the family which has enabled the addiction. One of the show's interventionists, Candy Finningan, makes this clear during the pre-intervention, "[Laurie] has to know that you as a family are not going to love her to death." On *Intervention,* repentance and resolution climax at the actual intervention itself. In this program, every aspect of the spectacle culminates in the moment where the confessor has nothing more to confess. The televisual narrative, woven from a series of confessions, takes us to where all confessions ultimately lead—the redemptive moment. The entire episode builds to this moment of intervention, which revolves around the spectacle of confession. The result is the addict's voluntary submission to a confinement/treatment facility.

One of the most striking features of the redeemed addicts on the show is their whiteness. Most of the people profiled for *Intervention* are white, though not all from the same social class. This should not be surprising, however, because white drug use has historically been constructed as an "illness," whereas black drug use has been constructed as "criminal." As a sickness, it is curable with the aid of specialists (read interventionists). As a crime, on the other hand, it calls for punishment under the expertise of the legal system.[32]

■ Conclusion: The More It Changes, the More It Stays the Same

The media's fascination with youth in trouble is not new or limited to the programs mentioned above. More and more entertainment programs build their popularity on the promises of reforming deviant youth, assisting parents, and saving families. Perhaps the most recent manifestation of the youth in trouble can be found on *Dr. Phil* with Dr. Phil House. Heavily advertised, Dr. Phil House's three-part series on the "Heroin Twins" features twenty-five-year-old Sarah and Tecoa, who have struggled with heroin and crack addiction, prostitution, pregnancy, homelessness, and incarceration. The three-part series, which aired in the 2006–2007 season, follows the twins on their journey toward intervention with a storyline devoted to their reform and "rescue." What the "Heroin Twins" reveals is that, although the program titles change, and the names change, and the faces of the experts change, the shows remain fundamentally committed to the logic of the reform/punishment institutions. The same logic of reform used in "teen-out-of-control" talk shows, *Juvies* and *Intervention,* is clearly apparent in the treatment of the heroin twins. This consistency is one of the striking features of how vulture culture constructs youth in trouble through the spectacle of reform.

Understanding youth in trouble through the spectacle of reform reveals the commodification and the fragmentation of the youth themselves. These youth, fragmented into individual cases, are on display for our consumption. But what should be clear from the above discussion is that the televisual spectacle of reform is not solely a creation of the entertainment industry. Rather, it is the result of a complex interaction between political, professional, educative, and economic forms of knowledge. Each of these programs is informed and structured by psychology, sociology, and criminology, on the one hand, and the logic of commodification and economic exploitation on the other hand.

If we understand the spectacle as "the image of the ruling economic order,"[33] then we are forced to ask how, and in what ways, these televisual representations of youth in trouble work. We conclude that the process of fragmentation/isolation, control and reform/repentance work to frame the possibilities and options for imagining youth in trouble. The rationale behind the punitive solutions offered by these programs is solidified through the spectacle of reform. Alternative rehabilitative solutions are erased.

The televisual youth-in-trouble comes at a time when we have seen a dramatic increase in the number of youth being incarcerated. Further, an alarming percentage are being tried as adults, many for non-violent offenses.[34] And, an overwhelming proportion of these youth are boys and girls of color. Indeed, perhaps the most striking feature of *Intervention* is the possibility of a medicalized treatment for their mostly white drug addicts, while research shows that, "For young people charged with illicit drug-related offenses, *black youth were 48 times more likely than white youth to be sentenced to time inside juvenile correctional institutions.*"[35] The logic of punishment and reform is raced and gendered—it can be medicalized and/or criminalized. The conflict, surveillance, and confession modes further work to disenfranchise youth in trouble and reinforce the punitive measures to get them under control. As a result, the justice and welfare institutions remain unchallenged. They may continue to perpetuate racial, gendered, and class biases without challenge because the spectacle of reform has isolated the individual from these institutions. Further, the spectacle itself commodifies and makes entertainment of these injustices.

However, the spectacle of reform does not necessarily have to reinforce punitive measures. Media spectacles are laden with contradictions and tensions. For those who are looking, these contradictions can speak volumes and can provide us with the means by which we can challenge the very logic of punitive reform. Furthermore, academics as well as media sources are beginning to challenge the incarceration of youth. Recent commentaries, most notably in *The New York Times* Op/Ed pages,[36] are questioning the rationale and the rehabilitation behind the rampant incarceration of juveniles, noting increased incarceration of girls as well as the general increased youth-adult facilities. The televisual presentation of youth in trouble and the associated spectacle of reform may begin to change as discourses about the efficacy and validity of reform measures are critiqued and questioned.[37]

Notes

1. *Life After Juvies: Karrisa and Nathan.* http://www.mtv.com/overdrive/?type=1405&id=1553134&vid=135127 Date Accessed: 6–25–07.

2. Debord, Guy (1995). *The Society of the Spectacle.* New York: Zone Books. 13.

3. Kellner, Douglas. *Media Spectacle.* New York: Routledge, 2003. Also, Kellner. *Media Spectacle and the Crisis of Democracy: Terrorism, War and Election Battles.* Boulder, CO, 2005. Kellner. *Guys and Guns Amok: Domestic Terrorism and School Shootings from the Oklahoma City Bombing to the Virginia Tech Massacre.* Boulder: Paradigm, 2008.

4. Kellner, Douglas. *Guys and Guns Amok: Domestic Terrorism and School Shootings from the Oklahoma City Bombing to the Virginia Tech Massacre.* Boulder: Paradigm, 2008.

5. According to the 2007 report from The Campaign for Youth Justice, "the Central Park Jogger provided an opening for conservative politicians to agitate fears about youth and violence. As a result, the federal government, as well as numerous states, began introducing punitive legislation to charge children as adults." The report cites former Representative Bill McCollum (R-FL) as saying "Brace yourself for the coming generation of superpredators." (p. 1) The Campaign for Youth Justice. The Consequences Aren't Minor: The Impact of Trying Youth as Adults and Strategies for Reform." Eds. Liz Ryan and Jason Ziedenberg. http://www.campaignforyouthjustice.org/Downloads/NEWS/National_Report_consequences.pdf. Date Accessed 6/16/07.

6. Debord, 29.

7. The concept of vulture culture is fully explored in Quail, Razzano, and Skalli's *Vulture Culture: The Politics and Pedagogy of Daytime Television Talk Shows.* New York: Peter Lang, 2005. This chapter expands upon the teen-out-of-control discussion in *Vulture Culture.*

8. Quail, Razzano, Skalli, 2005.

9. Chesney-Lind, Meda "Women and Crime: The Female Offender" in *Gender, Crime and Feminism,* ed. Ngaire Naffine (Brookfield, VT: Dartmouth, 1995), 8.

10. Ibid.

11. The Campaign for Youth Justice, 1.

12. Rios, Victor. "The Hypercriminalization of Black and Latino Male Youth in the Era of Mass Incarceration." *Racializing Justice, Disenfranchising Lives.* Eds. Manning Marable, Keesha Middlemass and Ian Steinberg. New York: Palgrave Macmillan, 2007. 17–32.

13. Ibid., 17.

14. For a detailed account of race, the welfare state, and the justice system, see *Racializng Justice, Disenfranchising Lives,* especially Manning Marable's introductory chapter. See also, Emily Gaarder and Joanne Belknap "Tenuous Borders: Girls Transferred to Adult Court." *Criminology.* 40:3, 2002. 481–517.

15. These titles come from the following programs and air dates—*Maury* 6/26/07, *Montel* 4/6/07, and *Dr. Phil* 6/26/07, respectively.

16. Weekly Show Schedule. www.jennyjones.warnerbros.com. Date Accessed 10–14–01.

17. Episode Guide. www.studiosusa.com/maury. Date Accessed 10–08–01.

18. In a few episodes, the girls are forced to walk around a city wearing placards stating their out-of-control behavior.

19. *Intervention: About the Show.* http://www.aetv.com/intervention/int_about_the_show.jsp. Date Accessed: 6/19/07.

20. Kenneth Thompson, *Moral Panics.* New York: Routledge, 1998. 85.

21. Thompson illustrates this idea through the notion of illegitimacy and family in Britain where conservative politicians used the notion of illegitimate children as the cause of the moral and social decline of the traditional community and increase in crime. Thompson and others suggest instead that we look at illegitimacy as a symptom rather than the locus of a problem.

22. Kerry Carrington, "Feminist Readings of Female Delinquency" in *Gender, Crime and Feminism,* ed. Ngaire Naffine. Brookfield, VT: Dartmouth, 1995. 140.

23. Quail, Razzano, Skalli, 2005.

24. Michel Foucault, *Discipline and Punish.* trans. Alan Sheridan. New York: Vintage, 1995. 25.

25. Judith Allen, "Men, Crime and Criminology: Recasting the Questions" in *Gender, Crime and Feminism,* ed. Ngaire Naffine. Brookfield, VT: Dartmouth, 1995. 99–120. Perhaps one of the most powerful explorations of bodily control comes from Judith Allen's "Men, Crime and Criminology: Recasting the Questions." Allen argues for a return to examinations of the "sexed-body," recognizing it as a site of coercion and control. Allen makes an important argument. The research clearly shows that there is more to the social control of women than notions of masculine and feminine. This social control is being carried out on women's bodies, not men's (as much). In more recent times, the recent reinstitution of virginity testing in South Africa as a means of deterring the AIDS epidemic is alarming. The logic is that by monitoring girls' virginity, they will be less likely to have sex and bring shame on themselves and their families. While this testing is not mandated by the state, girls are often pressured or forced into the testing by their families. The virginity testing requires a pelvic examination, and if a girl passes, she gets a stamp of approval. There is no equivalent test for boys. What is perhaps even scarier (for lack of a better word) is that virginity testing is being done in places such as schools and community centers where the girls receive their badge and then go home. In a country where there is a widely held superstition that sleeping with a virgin will cure AIDS, virginity testing puts these girls at grave risk of rape. Turkey is also considering instating virginity testing. For another sociological and historical account see Nanette J. Davis and Clarice Statz, *Social Control of Deviance: A Critical Perspective.* New York: McGraw-Hill, 1990. 232.

26. See Davis and Statz, 1990.

27. James Messerschmidt, "Feminism, criminology and the rise of the female sex 'delinquent,' 1880–1930" in *Gender, Crime and Feminism*, ed. Ngaire Naffine. Brookfield, VT: Dartmouth, 1995. 51–72. Messerschmidt offers an historical context of bodily control.

28. Ibid., 51.

29. This televisual representation of the incarcerated male and female body plays out in other "journalistic" treatments of men and women in prison. For instance, on June 16, 2007, the National Geographic Channel featured two programs on the California prison system. The first was part of the *Explorer* series titled "Surviving Maximum Security." In this episode, journalist Lisa Ling followed two men being processed into the California Sacramento State prison. The intake procedure was similar to that of *Juvies*. The men were stripped and exposed full-rear nudity to the *Explorer* camera. In contrast, the second program was part of the *Lockdown* series titled "Women Behind Bars." In contrast to the conspicuously nude male body, in *Lockdown*, the female body is carefully guarded and clothed. The only skin exposure is during a pregnant inmate's sonogram.

30. Lorraine Gelsthorpe, "Towards a Sceptical Look at Sexism" in *Gender, Crime and Feminism*, ed. Ngaire Naffine. Brookfield, VT: Dartmouth, 1995. 23–50. Gelsthorpe's analysis has been most useful in understanding the repentance themes in talk shows. She examines the use of sexism as a determining ideology in the criminal justice system by conducting ethnographic research with a British Juvenile Liaison Office.

31. A similar scene also plays out almost daily on *The Dr. Phil Show*, where the episode ends with guests thanking Dr. Phil for his assistance.

32. Ricki Solinger makes a similar case regarding unwed mothers. She argues that black unwed mothers are portrayed as highly sexual, promiscuous breeders and women who have children to get more money from the welfare system. On the other hand, white unwed mothers are seen as mentally ill but able to be rehabilitated. In this context, black illegitimate children are seen as drains on society. White illegitimate children are seen as valuable commodities on the adoption market. As such, blackness gets positioned with immorality. See Ricki Solinger. *Beggars and Choosers: How the Politics of Choice Shapes Adoption, Abortion, and Welfare in the United States.* New York: Hill and Wang, 2002.

33. Debord, 15.

34. Marable, Manning. "Racializing Justice, Disenfranchising Lives: Toward an Antiracist Criminal Justice." *Racializing Justice, Disenfranchising Lives.* Eds. Manning Marable, Keesha Middlemass and Ian Steinberg. New York: Palgrave Macmillan, 2007. 1–14.

35. Ibid., 8, italics Marable.

36. See "Saving, Not Victimizing, Children," *The New York Times,* May 9, 2007, p A24; "Juvenile Injustice," *The New York Times,* May 11, 2007, p A26; "Giving Juvenile Offenders a Chance," May 24, 2007, A26; "Back Where They Belong," *The New York Times,* July 5, 2007, p A12; "Juvenile Justice," *The New York Times,* July 12, 2007, p A22. See also Clyde Haberman, "The Young and Exploited Ask for Help," *The New York Times,* June 12, 2007, p B1 and Avi Salzman, "Redefining Juvenile Criminals," *The New York Times,* April 2, 2006, p 14CN1.

37. See Grossberg, Lawrence. *Caught in the Crossfire: Kids, Politics, and America's Future,* Boulder, CO: Paradigm Publishers, 2005. Grossberg argues that there are two views of childhood/youth that exist in twentieth century American politics and culture. One view argues that the child is love and as such, is vulnerable and in need of protection. The other view is that children are "troublesome." He writes, "Kids are then seen as troublesome and threatening, and when they are in trouble, it is their own fault; it is because they are trouble. How these two views are balanced determines how the country treats its kids at any particular moment." p 3.

17

■ Gideon Who Will Be 25 in the Year 2012

Growing Up Gay Today

Larry Gross

This is one of those "half empty, half full" stories. It's not the worst of times, and it's certainly not the best of times, but the story I'm interested in here is one of remarkable progress as well as often depressing challenges. In the 1976 film by Alain Tanner (written with John Berger), *Jonah Who Will be 25 in the Year 2000* (*Jonas—Qui Aura 25 Ans en l'An 2000*), a character notes wistfully that "men wish history would move as fast as time." History rarely grants that wish, but in the past half century the circumstances of gay people in the United States and around the world have transformed in ways that would have been unimaginable at the middle of the twentieth century.

■ That Was Then

A half century ago homosexuality was still the love that dared not speak its name. It was a crime throughout the United States and officially defined by the medical establishment as a mental illness. In the fervor of the Cold War that gripped the country, homosexuals were targeted along with Communists (Johnson, 2004), appearing in newspapers and magazines only in the context of police arrests or political purges, as in a 1953 headline: "State Department Fires 531 Perverts, Security Risks." Hollywood operated under the Motion Picture Production Code, which prohibited the presentation of explicitly lesbian or gay characters and ensured that any whose homosexuality was implied would be villains or victims.

Throughout the 1950s and into the 1960s the "homophile movement," as it was then called, expanded and deepened the self-awareness of lesbian and gay people as a distinct, self-conscious, and embattled minority. The movement was born behind a veil of pseudonyms and secrecy at the height of the Cold War, and its members, defined as criminal, mentally ill, and immoral, attempted to effect social change by persuading experts—mostly progressive psychologists and liberal clergy—to speak on their behalf. With the advent of television, several brave activists appeared on the new medium using pseudonyms, but this did not protect them from being recognized and promptly fired.

By the early 1960s, leaders inspired by the civil rights movement emerged, proclaiming "gay is good!" They took their struggle to the streets, demonstrating in front of government buildings, demanding an end to the laws that criminalized gay people while promoting ones that protected them from discrimination and harassment.

The Stonewall riots in June 1969 harvested a crop that had been planted by a decade of political and social turmoil. This new movement was founded on the importance of coming out as a *public* as well as an individual act. The open avowal of one's sexual identity, whether at work, at school, at home, or before television cameras, symbolized a shedding of the self-hatred that gay men and women had internalized. To come out of the closet quintessentially expressed the fusion of the personal and the political that the radicalism of the late 1960s exalted.

"The most momentous act in the life of any lesbian or gay person is when they proclaim their gayness—to self, to other, to community. Whilst men and women have been coming out for over a hundred years, it is only since 1970 that the stories have gone very public." (Plummer, 1995, p. 82)

The experience of coming out is at the center of the story I am concerned with here. That is, the experience of coming to terms with an identity that is not what everyone— parents, peers, preachers and teachers, even oneself—expects or welcomes. All too often, even today, to quote Andrew Hodges and David Hutter, "we learn to loathe homosexuality before it becomes necessary to acknowledge our own" (1974). In the early part of the twentieth century, and even in the first decade or so following Stonewall, young men and women came to this realization in an environment of pervasive public and private invisibility.

Among the earliest appearances of the topic of homosexuality on television that I have located is a Miami local news report of a crackdown on homosexuals in the city's parks from 1966. The program includes an appearance by police vice officers before an audience of eighth graders. The officers warn the embarrassed and uncomfortable teenagers of the dangers of becoming involved with adult homosexuals, lest they "become queer" and their lives "become a living hell." [See clip of the program—the quality is poor but the message is clear].

The occasional encounter with a queer image or actual person would likely be greeted with undisguised hostility. In 1972, when he was ten years old, Aaron Fricke's mother warned him that a man might ask him up to his house and, "If I went, terrible things would happen to me. The man might cut me up into little pieces. When I asked her why someone would do this to me, she paused and said, 'Because they are what you call homosexuals.' She had no idea what impact that admonishment would have on me" (1981, p. 17–18). Fricke had by that age begun to consider that he might be gay, but now he knew he was, "in the eyes of my mother and many others, something more vile."

The early gay liberation moment of the 1970s broke through the wall of silence that had been eloquently captured by Adrienne Rich:

> Whatever is unnamed, undepicted in images, whatever is omitted from biography, censored in collections of letters, whatever is misnamed as something else, made difficult-to-come-by, whatever is buried in the memory by the collapse of meaning under an inadequate or lying language—this will become, not merely unspoken, but unspeakable. (1976/1979, p. 199)

In the 1970s, the unspoken began to speak as coming-out stories flooded out. Julia Penelope Stanley and Susan Wolfe's collection, *The Coming Out Stories* (1980) was representative of the new genre: forty women (or, as they mostly wrote, "wimmin") telling their stories of lies, secrets, oppression, and liberation. These were mostly stories of growing up queer in earlier decades. C. J. Martin's opening is representative:

> The day I accepted my label I still didn't know the word lesbian. The label I accepted was homosexual. Still, I had problems with even that since what little I could find in the literature that was available to me in 1950 was about men or about women in prison. Since neither of those categories included me—I was alone in my affliction—so horribly deviant there were no others like me. (Martin, 1980, p. 56).

Growing up gay meant coming to terms with a stigmatized sexuality in an environment of public invisibility. Although U.S. society was increasingly dominated by broadcast media—television was well ensconced in the nation's living rooms and was rapidly overshadowing other forms of public culture—we were rarely to be seen on the tube or, for that matter, on the pages of newspapers or at the movies. Lesbians and gay men were usually ignored altogether, but when we did appear, it was in roles that supported the "natural" order. Gay people made it on stage, in the roles generally offered to minority groups, as villains or victims. In unfriendly shows, queers were a threat to be contained; in friendly ones, we sparked surprise that someone apparently *normal* could be, gasp!, gay, and offered the *real* characters the opportunity to demonstrate tolerance. The familiar stereotypes were always present, if only implicitly, as when gay characters were depicted in a carefully "anti-stereotypic" manner that drew our attention to the absence of the "expected" attributes—thus setting up the surprise or joke. Richard Dyer has pointed out that, "What is wrong about these stereotypes is not that they are inaccurate." They are, after all, often more than a little accurate, at least for some gay people, some of the time. Dyer continued, "What we should be attacking in stereotypes is the attempt of heterosexual society to define us for ourselves, in terms that inevitably fall short of the 'ideal' of heterosexual society (that is, taken to be the norm of being human), and to pass this definition off as necessary and natural" (1977). Sexual minorities are not, of course, unique in this regard—one could say the same for most media images of minorities. But our general invisibility makes us especially vulnerable to the power of media images (Gross, 2001).

Despite the rapid advances made by the gay liberation movement in the 1970s—advances real enough to spur a fervent backlash (headlined in the mid-70s by Anita Bryant) that continues until the present—most queer teens were only dimly aware of the changes being advocated and even achieved, mostly in a few large cities. The daily experience of queer youth remained one of public invisibility and private isolation.

■ "I'm Scared to Death"

As late as the early 1990s, the reality of this experience was illustrated by the responses of audiences to a soap opera story thread. In the summer of 1992, the daytime TV serial *One Life To Live* (OLTL) began what was at the time the longest and most complex television narrative ever to deal with a lesbian or gay character. When Billy Douglas, a star high-school athlete and class president, confides to his best friend and to his minister that he is gay, he sets off a series of plot twists that differ from the usual soap opera complications in that they expose homophobia and AIDS phobia and thus offer the characters—and the audience—an opportunity to address topics that daytime serials, along with the rest of U.S. mass media, have generally preferred to ignore.

Billy Douglas was played by Ryan Phillippe, in his first professional role, and he found himself at the center of a great deal of media and audience attention. He received an unusually large amount of mail even for a good-looking young soap opera actor (see Gross, 1996). Even more unusual was the fact that so many of the hundreds of letters he received during the months that he appeared on OLTL came from young men, most of whom identified themselves as gay. In one interview, Phillippe reported getting two thousand letters, "a good 45 percent...from homosexual teenagers" (Mallinger, 1993, p. 14). Among the most frequent expressions were those of isolation from family and friends, and desperation:

> My favorite scene was when Billy told Joey that he was gay. I like this so much because it was like a scene from life. Ever since this storyline began I have not been able to think of anything else, but what's going to happen next...I feel the same way your character does about my parents finding out. I'm scared to death about that happening, because my family doesn't like gay people. I just don't want my family to hate me or be embarrassed or ashamed of me. I'm writing this letter to you because I think you can relate to what I'm talking about. Ryan, I would like to know if we can become pen pals.

> I'm 19 years old and I live in XX, Colorado, and I'm gay. This is the first time I have ever told someone that... Some of my closest friends say prejudiced things about gays and it hurts me very deeply because I am pretty sure they would have nothing to do with me if they knew about me. I hope that you aren't like that in real life; I'm pretty sure that you aren't but one never really knows...If it's alright with you maybe we could write each other every so often? I would really like that!!

> I begin this letter by being blunt and upfront. I am a 22-year-old homosexual male... Life has been so hard for me. I've tried suicide, I was threatened with expulsion from my high school, I ran away and I was nearly stabbed by some people at my college. Storyline may be fiction,

but mine was not—it was an ugly reality. I write this letter in hopes I can get help and need any advice you can give me. Ever since I was 13, I've been scared and alone.

While it is not difficult to imagine that African American, Asian American, or Latino actors would get letters from teenagers who identify with and appreciate their representation of an under-represented group on the public media stage, it is inconceivable that they would receive letters like the ones quoted above, let alone similar letters from adults:

> Your performance has been 'right on.' I am a happily married, successful father of two teenagers (one, your age, equally good looking as you)… You see, I lived the character you are playing, and still live it, although in the 'closet.' I've never been a victim of homophobia, because no one knows I'm a life-long, born-that-way homosexual, comfortable with who I am, but not comfortable with living as a gay person. Still your character has created an empathy in me, because I can relate so well to your character. You are doing a service to millions of people, whether you know it or not, just by bringing the subject to a mass audience. Keep up the good work. Sorry, I can't sign this letter.

■ This Is Now

Over the past three decades the circumstances facing queer youth have changed radically. Thanks in part to AIDS—if the expression of thanks isn't too obscene—gay people have overcome many of the last vestiges of public invisibility. Today, few can remain unaware of the existence of lesbian and gay people, and young people grow up reading words and seeing images that previous generations never encountered. By the final years of the twentieth century, lesbian, gay, bisexual, and transgendered people entered the ranks of our culture's permanent cast of characters, even though rarely in leading roles and almost never permitted to express physical affection. We can confidently expect to show up as the subject of news stories, even some that do not presume that our existence is controversial or that simple equality is a special right (although the current same-sex marriage struggle pretty much guarantees a flood of these stories for the foreseeable future). And, in a further demonstration of the emergence of gay people onto the American landscape, we are receiving the ultimate recognition that this country can bestow: being included in advertising. Gay and lesbian Americans have been identified as a certifiable market niche, one well-heeled enough to warrant targeted ads, especially ones that wink at us over the heads of straight people.

Those growing up queer at the turn of the new century are facing new circumstances, both good and bad, as well as the familiar challenges of the past. In their 1993 study of gay youth in Chicago, *Children of Horizons,* Gilbert Herdt and Andrew Boxer defined four age cohorts of gay people in twentieth century America. Their first cohort comprised those coming of age after World War I, and their fourth cohort came of age in the era of AIDS, since the early 1980s. Unlike previous cohorts, this fourth cohort includes a "great majority [who] come of age self-identifying as gay or lesbian, and thus expecting not only to live their lives openly, but to tell all their family and friends, and their employers, of their desires and lifestyles" (1993, p. 12). A decade later it's clear that a fifth cohort has emerged, a generation of queer youth who have come of age in the era of media visibility and of the Internet. Thus, while much remains the same, much has changed.

We need to reconsider ways of thinking about queerness based on the experiences of pervasive invisibility in order to comprehend the experiences of today's and tomorrow's kids growing up in a culture that acknowledges queerness by attempting to integrate it into the commercialized array of cultural products, niche-marketed demographic slices, and political voting blocks. Most lesbigay (pre-queer) theorizing presupposed invisibility and rare stereotypic representations as a limiting and distorting condition of growing up. What do we say now about growing up with a reasonably common news and entertainment presence and with the opportunities for exploration and contact offered by the Internet?

One option is to deny the meaningfulness of identity and theorize the problem away. The 1990s were also the era of what British social scientists Paul Flowers and Katie Buston call the "metropolitan blossoming of both queer theory and queer politics." But, as they point out in the context of their interviews with young gay men in Northern England, while these theories "shatter and fragment the apparent unity of ideas of gay identity," the stories told by "these working class men all articulate a distinct and familiar coming-out story" (2001, p. 61). The story is one of isolation, vulnerability, and deception, followed, if they are lucky, by telling others, self-acceptance, and connection to a community.

Today's stories start at a younger age. Savin-Williams (1998) summarized a body of research on the stages of the coming-out process conducted over more than two decades and concludes that ages at which these "developmental milestones are reached… have been steadily declining from the 1970s to current cohorts of youths… awareness of same-sex attractions has dropped from the onset of junior high school to an average of third grade" (p. 16). He attributes this reduction in the age of self-definition to the "recent visibility of homosexuality in the macro culture (such as in the media), the reality of a very vocal and extensive gay and lesbian culture, and the presence of homosexuality in their immediate social world" (p. 122).

Coming out earlier is hardly a guarantee of smooth passage. Most kids still find themselves growing up in enemy territory, in a country where heterosexuality is the love that needn't speak its name, because it's taken for granted, and where *gay* is a term of abuse to rival *faggot* or *queer.* But in contrast to the experience of most kids in the past, there are ways to fight back, and public schools have become battlegrounds for new civil rights struggles.

A young man named Jamie Nabozny made news in 1996 when he successfully sued a Wisconsin school district for failing to stop the anti-gay abuse he suffered for years. Other pupils realized Nabozny was gay when he was in the seventh grade. In later years a classmate pushed him to the floor and simulated raping him as other pupils watched; another time he was knocked into a urinal by one boy while another urinated on him. When he sought help from the principal, he was told "boys will be boys." During another assault, ten students surrounded Nabozny while a student wearing boots repeatedly kicked him in the stomach. Nabozny attempted suicide several times and, like many gay teen-agers in similar situations, dropped out of high school. But Jamie Nabozny also fought back in federal court, and won. The school district agreed to a $900,000 settlement. "That case opened the floodgates to lawsuits—and, perhaps more important, to *threats* of lawsuits—from other gay students who said their complaints about harassment had been ignored. School officials saw the potential for liability" (Jones, 1999).

More common than lawsuits has been the emergence of supportive organizations within schools, starting in 1984 with the founding of Project 10 in a Los Angeles high school, and growing slowly for the next decade. In the aftermath of Matthew Shepard's killing, the number of gay-straight alliances (GSAs), as most of these groups are named, rose dramatically, reaching approximately 750 nation-wide by 2001 (Platt, 2001). In November 2006 more than 2500 GSAs were registered with the national organization GLSEN, or Gay, Lesbian and Straight Education Network (http://www.glsen.org/cgi-bin/iowa/chapter/home/index.html). The clubs often meet resistance from school officials, but they have an effective weapon, courtesy of the religious right. In 1984, in order to force public schools to permit bible study clubs, Senator Orrin Hatch spearheaded the passage of the federal Equal Access Act, which makes it illegal for a school to ban some extracurricular clubs if it allows others. In 1995, when the Salt Lake City Board of Education refused to permit a GSA to meet at a public high school, they were forced to ban all extra-curricular clubs. Salt Lake City stuck by its principles and sacrificed the interests of all students in order to deny gay students the right to a club, before finally relenting in 2000. In other localities as well, the Equal Access Act has served to open school doors to GSAs (Platt 2001; Barovick, 2001).

The existence of GSAs is an important achievement, but even 2500 schools are only a small fraction of the nation's local schools, and LGBT students remain at risk of harassment and bullying. In many ways, of course, the growing visibility of gay people and the political prominence of gay-related issues contributes to the hostility directed at LGBT folk, especially in school environments where "Gay"—meaning stupid or worthless—has become an epithet of choice. In April 2006, GLSEN released the results of a survey of over 1700 LGBT students between the ages of thirteen and twenty. Three-quarters of the students had been taunted as "faggot" or "dyke" and over a third had experienced physical harassment on the basis of sexual orientation. Nearly one-fifth had been physically assaulted because of their sexual orientation and over a tenth because of their gender expression (http://www.glsen.org/cgi-bin/iowa/chapter/library/record/1927.html).

■ Queer Teens as Demographic Niche

The changing circumstances of gay people in the 1990s led to the emergence of media products not only produced by gay people themselves, which had been the case since the start of the gay liberation movement (then called the homophile movement) in the 1950s but targeted at segments not previously addressed so directly. Notable among these are gay youth, who have been generally avoided—both as customers and subjects—by media wary of the accusation of "recruiting" or seducing the innocent.

XY, a San Francisco-based magazine for gay male teens was founded in 1996; by 2002 it boasted: "We sell over 60,000 copies per issue and have more than 200,000 readers from all over the world. Our average reader age is twenty-two, according to our last reader survey, and *XY* is officially targeted toward 12–29 yo young gay men." The magazine's twenty-four-year-old editor told the *San Francisco Chronicle,* "I don't think there's a magazine in the country that means more to its readers. I say that because we're dealing specifically with a demographic of gay teenagers who are not living in L.A. or New York, or some place where being gay is accepted. There's really no other forum for them to read about that experience" (Vaziri, 1999). The magazine's price—$7.95 per issue and $29 for a six-issue subscription, in 2002—might be a deterrent to many in the magazine's target audiences.

If the success of magazines for lesbian and gay teens is limited by steep prices and prying parents, the Internet offers most young people readier access and greater privacy (those without access to computers and the Internet are also less likely to have the money for a subscription to *XY*). The website for *XY,* in fact, offers much more than enticements to subscribe to the magazine, buy back issues or such tempting merchandise as "glamourous laminated cardboard containers to neatly store your *XY* issues…only $12."

The section called *Bois* contains personal "profiles"—called "peeps"—posted by young men after they submit their name, e-mail address, and age (the site pledges that complete privacy will be maintained). In August 2002, there were 13,559 profiles listed on the site;by March 2004 there were 92,440, many of them containing personal photographs. Scanning through the lists—it is possible to specify a location and to limit oneself to seeing profiles containing pictures—it is clear that the listings are far from evenly distributed across the United States and beyond. Still, the numbers are often impressive, as is the geographical dispersion. Alabama listed 637 "peeps," thirty-five with photos, and Montana had 127 (sixty-three photos), whereas Los Angeles boasted 2,284, of which 1,461 had pictures. Outside the United States the patterns are predictable, with Toronto offering 565 "peeps" (358 photos), London 251 (138 photos), and Australia 408 listings (182 with photos). Leaving the English-speaking world the numbers fall off. There are 123 listed in Germany (sixty-four with pictures), thirty-five in France (twelve photos, and some of these would appear to be older than the target age), twenty-four in Japan (fifteen photos), and only twelve in China (three pictures).

While there is no lesbian equivalent of *XY,* the most successful lesbian magazine, *Curve,* includes on its website extensive "personals" listings, with and without photographs, that specify ages beginning at eighteen and going up to ninety. In the section called "community," discussions are posted under many group and topic headings, including "Baby Dykes—Youth Hangout."

However, sites run by magazines are only the tip of the Internet iceberg when it comes to opportunities to post personal ads and engage in conversation. Despite a slant towards the interests of those old enough to get into bars and spend more money, the major gay Websites appear to be accessible to teens. *PlanetOut,* the largest commercial gay site, boasting over 600,000 personal ads that range from fifteen to the early sixties, is likely to attract the attention of teenagers looking for information, connections, and no doubt, sex. In addition, there are sites specifically developed for gay youth, such as

OutProud, Oasis, Blair, and *Mogenic* (located in Sydney), that combine support, counseling, and information with news and links to other youth-oriented sites (Addison and Comstock, 1998).

■ Growing Up Gay in Cyberspace

In contrast to the world of earlier decades, young people today grow up reading words and seeing images that previous generations never encountered, and few can remain unaware of the existence of lesbian and gay people. But despite the dramatic increase in visibility of gay people in nearly all domains of our public culture, most young lesbian, gay, bisexual, and transgender people still find themselves isolated and vulnerable. Their experiences and concerns are not reflected in the formal curricula of schools or in our society's informal curriculum, the mass media. For these teenagers the Internet is a god-send and thousands are using computer networks to declare their homosexuality, meet and seek support from other gay youths.

"Does anyone else feel like you're the only gay guy on the planet, or at least in Arlington, Texas?" When seventeen-year-old Ryan Matthew posted that question on AOL in 1995, he received more than 100 supportive e-mail messages (Gabriel, 1995). The stories that fly through the ether make all too clear that the Internet can literally be a lifesaver for many queer teens trapped in enemy territory:

☐ JohnTeen Ø (John Erwin's AOL name) is a new kind of gay kid, a sixteen-year-old not only out, but already at home in the online convergence of activists that Tom Rielly, the co-founder of Digital Queers, calls the "Queer Global Village." Just ten years ago, most queer teens hid behind a self-imposed don't-ask-don't-tell policy until they shipped out to Oberlin or San Francisco, but the Net has given even closeted kids a place to conspire. Though the Erwins' house is in an unincorporated area of Santa Clara County in California, with goats and llamas foraging in the backyard, John's access to AOL's gay and lesbian forum enables him to follow dispatches from queer activists worldwide, hone his writing, flirt, try on disposable identities, and battle bigots—all from his home screen (Silberman, 1994).

☐ Kali is an eighteen-year-old lesbian at a university in Colorado. Her name means "fierce" in Swahili. Growing up in California, Kali was the leader of a young women's chapter of the Church of Jesus Christ of Latter-day Saints. She was also the "Girl Saved by E-mail," whose story ran last spring on CNN. After mood swings plummeted her into a profound depression, Kali—like too many gay teens—considered suicide. Her access to GayNet at school gave her a place to air those feelings, and a phone call from someone she knew online saved her life. Kali is now a regular contributor to *Sappho,* a women's board she most appreciates because there she is accepted as an equal. "They forgive me for being young," Kali laughs, "though women come out later than guys, so there aren't a lot of teen lesbians. But it's a high of connection. We joke that we're posting to 500 of our closest friends" (Silberman, 1994).

◻ Jay won't be going to his senior prom. He doesn't make out in his high-school corridor the way other guys do with their girlfriends. He doesn't receive the kind of safe-sex education at school that he feels he should. He can never fully relax when he's speaking. He worries that he'll let something slip, that the kids at his Long Island high school will catch on. He'd rather not spend his days at school being beaten up and called a faggot. It's not like that on the Internet. "It's hard having always to watch what you say," said Jay, which is not his real name. "It's like having a filter that you turn on when you're at school. You have to be real careful you don't say what you're thinking or look at a certain person the wrong way. But when I'm around friends or on the Net, the filter comes off." For many teenagers, the Internet is a fascinating, exciting source of information and communication. For gay teenagers like Jay, seventeen, it's a lifeline. The moment the modem stops screeching and the connection is made to the Net, the world of a gay teenager on Long Island can change dramatically. The fear of being beaten up and the long roads and intolerant views that separate teens lose their impact (McAllester, 1997).

◻ Jeffrey knew of no homosexuals in his high school or in his small town in the heart of the South. He prayed that his errant feelings were a phase. But as the truth gradually settled over him, he told me in a phone conversation punctuated by nervous pauses to make sure no family member was listening in, he became suicidal. "I'm a Christian—I'm like, how could God possibly do this to me?" he said. He called a crisis line for gay teenagers, where a counselor suggested he attend a gay support group in a city an hour and a half away. But being fifteen, he was too young to drive and afraid to enlist his parents' help in what would surely seem a bizarre and suspicious errand. It was around this time that Jeffrey first typed the words "gay" and "teen" into a search engine on the computer he'd gotten a few months before and was staggered to find himself aswirl in a teeming online gay world, replete with resource centers, articles, advice columns, personals, chat rooms, message boards, porn sites and—most crucially—thousands of closeted and anxious kids like himself. The discovery changed his life (Egan, 2000).

◻ Without unfettered access to the Internet at Multnomah County Public Library, sixteen-year-old Emmalyn Rood testified, she might not have found courage to tell her mother she was gay. "I was able to become so much more comfortable with myself," Rood told a special three-judge panel weighing the constitutionality of the Children's Internet Protection Act. "I basically found people I could talk to. I didn't have anybody I could talk to in real life." In the summer of 1999, Rood was a freshman at Portland's Wilson High School confused about her sexual identity but eager to learn. Today, she is attending a Massachusetts college and is a determined plaintiff in a lawsuit aimed at scuttling the new federal law, which she said would have hindered her search (Barnett, 2002).

Similar accounts abound, not only in the United States but in many other parts of the world. In the case of the gay Israeli teenagers interviewed by Lilach Nir (1998), online discussions offered them contact and confirmation unavailable in their "real" environments of smaller cities, rural villages, and kibbutzim. While one of the clichés of computer-mediated communication is that one can hide one's true identity, so "that nobody knows you're fifteen and live in Montana and are gay" (Gabriel, 1995), it is also true, as Nir's informants told her, that in their IRC conversations they "are unmasking the covers they are forced to wear in the straight daily lives" (Nir, 1998).

In the past few years social networking sites such as Friendster, MySpace, and most recently, Facebook, have attracted millions of "members" and have become the hottest phenomenon in the growing universe of online communities. On November 11, 2006, there were 33,745 "gay, lesbian or bi" groups on MySpace, according to the Web site, and 3000 were listed. The largest of these, "Support Gay Marriage" (founded in July, 2004) had 102,446 members. The most recent, "Gay Kids: you can just like hook up or do w/e with gay kids on myspace," had been formed that day, and had one member.

For LGBT youngsters, however, MySpace might not be an entirely safe space. On *Curve*'s "Baby Dykes—Youth Hangout" bulletin board there was a discussion in August 2005 about the dangers of being open on MySpace:

A: man...I've gotten in real shit on Myspace...My warning is be careful what you say because you never know who's watching.

B: What do you mean by that, because i have some stuff on mine that could be a little incriminating. Did u get in trouble w/ good old johnny law???

A: nope... try good old parents...not much difference, though...☺My best friend's sister's best friend told my step-sister's mother some things I said online and my step-sister's mother's husband stalked me on myspace...One day a folder full of everything I said on it showed up on my front door...and I had stayed home sick...FUN

C: On myspace, since pretty much anyone from my school and sports teams etc can look me up I put that I was straight, just because if I want someone to know I will tell them myself. And I also erase my internet history so as to not let the parentals know I am on a site such as this. ☺

D: I know how myspace can get you in trouble. So many people have one now, and sooner or later (if you blog) some secrets can get around. Whoopsie. ☺ I've learned to be very careful what I write there. I only write exactly what I'm feeling in my secret livejournal that's not all that live. 🎎

■ Beyond the Anecdotes

The stories recounted above, and others readily found in news accounts, can be seen as exceptional or extreme instances. However, there is more representative data on the role of the Internet in the lives of queer kids. In the September and October of 2000 an online survey was conducted by two of the largest websites serving lesbian, gay, bisexual, and transgendered youth: OutProud, an arm of The National Coalition for Gay, Lesbian, Bisexual and Transgender Youth, founded in 1993 to provide advocacy, information, resources and support to in-the-closet and openly queer teens through America Online and the Internet, and *Oasis* Magazine, founded in December 1995. The survey, authored by OutProud director Chris Kryzan, was advertised on the two sponsoring sites, as well as on several other youth-oriented Websites and, as it turned out, two sites devoted to gay and lesbian erotica. The survey was completed by 7,884 respondents, of whom 6,872, aged twenty-five or under, constituted the primary sample.

The survey permitted respondents of any age to complete the form, thus hoping to discourage older respondents from presenting themselves as younger in order to participate. Obviously, respondent age, like anything else queried over the Internet is subject to falsification, but there seems little reason to imagine that many people would be moved to spend an average of thirty-eight minutes pretending to be something they're not. Nearly 60% of those who started the survey completed it. As the researchers discovered midway, slightly more than half of the respondents (60% of the males) entered the survey from a gay erotica Web-site. Although there were no systematic differences in respondents corresponding to the point of entry, this pattern does tell something about the importance of sexual content sites for gay youth, who aren't likely to find similar material in mainstream media, as well as giving further evidence of the centrality of pornography to the appeal of the Internet. For queer youth, of course, pornography is often the only available source of the sort of sexual imagery and information widely available in the media for heterosexual youth.

The respondents clearly do not constitute a probability sample from which one can generalize about queer youth. Indeed, no such sample can ever be obtained for gay people, who remain largely hidden from the survey researcher's sampling frames. However, the size and diversity of the group do offer illuminating insights into the lives of queer youth and their relationships to the new communications technologies that came into the world as they were being born. Most (77%) of the respondents were from the United States, with the next largest number from Canada (8%), the United Kingdom (5%), and Australia (4%); seventy-two other countries contributed less than 1% each. In general, few differences seemed to follow geographical origin, suggesting that many of those responding from other countries might not have been of local origin (e.g., children of diplomats or overseas businessmen).

A somewhat similar, more qualitative survey was conducted by the Australian Research Centre in Sex, Health and Society (Hillier et al., 2001). The sample of respondents included 5310 males, 1412 females, and 150 who identified as transgendered. The median age of respondents was eighteen (the mode was seventeen), and the median age reported for realizing that they were gay was thirteen, while the median age of accepting that they were gay was fifteen. There were significant correlations between their reported position on the Kinsey scale ('0' being completely heterosexual, while '6' being completely homosexual), the age of becoming aware of their sexuality (-.06), and the age of accepting their sexuality (-.20). The more strongly they identified as gay, the earlier they recognized and accepted their sexual orientation (these correlations are controlling for gender). Needless to say, causality may run in either direction.

As might be expected, this is a group of young people who are familiar with the Internet: nearly half of those sixteen and under and two-thirds of those twenty and over had been online for at least three years; fewer than 10% had been online less than one year. Over 90% of respondents reported going online at least once a day, nearly half said several times per day. About 50% reported spending more than two hours online each day. The usage figures reported in the survey put these young people well above the average of 9.8 hours per week found in the 2001 UCLA Internet Report, *Surveying the Digital Future.*

The most frequent activities online included: looking at specific sites, 28% (more males than females cited this—presumably this includes the erotica site from which so many respondents came to the survey); chatting, 24%, and e-mail, 20% (these two were cited by females more than males). Unspecified surfing absorbed 20%, reading message boards, 2%. Downloading music, the RIAA would be relieved to learn, only accounted for 5% of reported time.

Given the makeup of this sample it would be expected that their online experiences would be related to their sexuality. Two-thirds of the respondents said that being online helped them accept their sexual orientation; 35% said that being online was crucial to this acceptance. Not surprisingly, therefore, many said they came out online before doing so in "real life"—this was much more the case for males (57%) than for females (38%)— and more for those who had spent more time online.

Connections online sometime lead to real life meetings: about half of the respondents report such meetings, and 12% of the males (but only 4% of the females) said they met someone off-line for the purpose of having sex. About a quarter of both males and females met someone "with the hope that we might become more than friends." In general, a quarter of the respondents said that they met the people they've dated online. It is good to know that 83% report having enough knowledge of STDs to follow safer sex practices; nearly a third cite the Internet as their primary source for this information.

Queer youth often feel isolated and rarely have access to a supportive queer community in their vicinity. Sixty percent of the respondents said they did not feel as though they were part of the gay, lesbian, bisexual and transgendered community, but 52% said they felt a sense of community with the people they've met online. Mass media, even minority media, do not necessarily provide a great deal of contact and support for these young people. Only 47% have bought a gay or lesbian magazine, and only two of these, the *Advocate,* the largest U.S. gay magazine, and *XY,* for young gay males, are read by as many as a fifth of the sample. Even fewer report familiarity with *Oasis,* the longest running online magazine for queer youth.

A frequent concern regarding the isolated and vulnerable situation facing many queer youth is that they are peculiarly vulnerable to suicide, and, indeed, it is commonly reported that the rate of attempted and completed suicides is disproportionately high among this group. Among the online survey respondents, 40% of the females and 25% of the males reported seriously thinking about suicide sometimes or often; 30% of the females and 17% of the males said they had in fact tried to kill themselves (the median age for these attempts was fourteen). For queer teens the Internet can often be a lifeline: 32% of the females and 23% of the males say they've gone online when feeling suicidal, so that they would have someone understanding to talk to. Among those who report frequent suicidal thoughts, 53% of the females and 57% of the males say they've gone online for this reason.

■ Gideon Who Will Be 25 in the Year 2012

In late 2000, the twelve-year-old son of a colleague of mine told his mother that he was gay. Gideon told his mother that he had known this since he was about six years old, and that he was telling her now because he wanted to see the American version of *Queer as Folk,* which was about to debut on the subscription cable channel Showtime.

While American viewers were wondering when Will would get a date, let alone get laid, Britain's Channel 4 made television history in 1999 with something completely different. *Queer as Folk* centered on three gay men in Manchester who spend most of their non-working hours in the bars of Manchester's trendy gay neighborhood. The three men include two twenty-nine-year-olds—Stuart, a sexy, heartless Don Juan who wants to "die shagging," and Vince, his shy best friend, hopelessly yearning to shag Stuart, and Nathan, a golden-haired fifteen-year-old who is bursting out of the closet. In the first episode Nathan is picked up (or vice versa) by Stuart, and we are shown the boy being introduced to rimming and anal sex.

At least as much as the explicit sex *Queer as Folk* was a novelty for mainstream media because the dramatic lens was focused on the gay characters and their world, with only token straight characters, and no effort made to explain things to or wink at the audience. "Most of the gay drama we've had on British television has dealt with big statements: victimization, the political agenda, AIDS," Channel 4's head of drama Gub Neal said to the *New York Times.* "But this group of characters doesn't think they're victims at all. They're not even aware that they're a minority. They simply exist and say, 'Hey, we don't have to make any apologies, and we're not going away.' The series has given us a chance to simply reveal gay life, to some extent, in its ordinariness" (Sarah Lyall, "Three Gay Guys on British TV: What's The Fuss?" *The New York Times,* April 15, 1999).

It didn't take long for the series to attract Hollywood's attention, and Showtime began to produce an American version, set in Pittsburgh. "I thought this show was unique," said Jerry Offsay, Showtime's president of programming. "I had never seen characters like these on television. The characters were unapologetic, they lived their lives the way they wanted to. There were great twists and turns and reverses in the storytelling. This show will be as edgy as any television series has ever been in America." Edginess has its limits, however. Unlike the British Nathan, who is fifteen, the youth in the American version, named Justin, will be nearly eighteen. "The boy is on the cusp of being the legal age," said Tony Jonas, one of the executive producers of the series. "The idea is, kids who are seniors in high school are being sexual. We can't deny that. It's the reality" (Bernard

Weinraub, "A controversial British series seduces Showtime," *The New York Times,* May 14, 2000).

High-school seniors are, indeed, being sexual, and their sexuality is at the center of the peculiarly American fertility ritual known as the senior prom. The prom is officially defined as a celebration of young love and coming of age, but for many teens it is a painful reminder of social hierarchy and exclusion. For queer teens, even more than most, the prom is likely to be an occasion for suffering rather than joy, and most queer adults probably look back on theirs—if they went at all—as a low point of their high-school years. But there are exceptions.

In 1981 Aaron Fricke went to federal court to force his high school to permit him to bring a male date to his senior prom. The court case and the prom drew national attention, and in subsequent years many lesbian, gay, bisexual and transgender youth have braved parental, peer, and official disapproval in order to participate in their preferred fashion in this rite of passage.

In bigger cities across the country, there are special proms for queer teens: in May 2003, Denver held its tenth Queer Prom in a local college student union. "Most of the kids who attend the prom come from the Denver area, but we see people from all over the region—Wyoming, Utah, Montana," says Julie Voyles, director of youth services at Rainbow Alley. "We're the biggest GLBT youth group in the western states, and for a lot of the rural youth we're it." (Lesley Kennedy, "Queer Prom Night; Alternative dance a haven for gay students," *Rocky Mountain News,* May 19, 2003, 3D.). Other teens follow in Aaron Fricke's footsteps, although they rarely need to go to court these days. Some of them even run for prom queen or king, and sometimes they succeed. Seventeen-year-old Catherine Balta wanted to be prom queen of Lincoln High School in Omaha because if her fellow Lincoln High seniors elected her prom queen, it would prove she was accepted. And if an out lesbian could be prom queen, "I just felt it would be something that would be cool for everybody" ("Prom tiara is more than a crown," *Omaha World Herald*, June 6, 2003, 1b), and elected she was, wearing a mismatched tuxedo with a red fedora over her short hair. Brenda Melton, president of the American School Counselor Association told *Newsweek*/MSNBC that "it has become almost commonplace in urban and suburban areas for a student to bring a date of the same sex to the prom—and that in most schools, it's really no big deal" (Scelfo, 2003).

After Gideon's mother told me about his coming out, and the reason for it, I offered to tape *Queer as Folk* for him, and I subsequently passed on copies of the program.

The final episode of the first season—the series turned the British eight-episode series into an open-ended soap opera that ran for five seasons—climaxed at Justin's high school prom. The creators of the program, Ron Cowen and Daniel Lipman, two gay men who are life as well as work partners, gave their fictional eighteen- year-old a prom that would fulfill every queer high-school boy's dream fantasy. Having gone to the prom with his straight female best friend, Daphne, Justin is surprised when 30-year-old Brian appears, gorgeous in a tuxedo. The crowd clears a space in the center of the floor, the band begins to play "Save the last dance for me," spotlights shine down on the couple as they twirl and spin, ending in an extended romantic kiss. Immediately following this, in the parking garage, a high school bully comes up behind and hits Justin in the head with a tire iron.

Brian knocks the bully out, and cradles Justin in his arms. The season ends with Brian sitting in a hospital corridor, holding a bloodied silk scarf.

Here, in a dramatically effective nutshell, we have the situation of queers in America today. We are able to live our lives openly and fully to a degree that would have been unimaginable a few decades ago, and at the same time we are targeted for gay-bashing, whether in high school parking lots or by Republican and Democratic politicians who wish to deny us full equality as citizens. History may not move as fast as time, but I trust that Gideon will live in a freer world by the time he reaches twenty-five.[1]

* To see video clips referenced in this article, download the previously published online version of this essay, in *International Journal of Communication 1* (2007), 121-138, at http://ijoc.org/ojs/index.php/ijoc/issue/view/1.

Note

1. In November 2006 Gideon was in the cast of a new musical, *Spring Awakening*, that transferred to Broadway after a successful Off-Broadway opening. Gideon played a gay teen who kisses another boy. Gideon has since played an openly gay teenager in the Off-Broadway play *Speech/Debate*.

References

Addison, J., & Comstock, M. (1998). Virtually out: The emergence of a lesbian, bisexual, and gay youth cyberculture. In J. Austin and M. Willard, (Eds.), *Generations of youth* (pp. 367–378). New York: New York University Press

Barnett, J. (2002, March 27). Gay teen testifies against law on Internet. *The Oregonian.*

Barovick, H. (2001, February 21). Fear of a gay school. *Time Magazine* .

Dyer, R. (1977). Stereotyping. In Richard Dyer (Ed.), *Gays and film* (pp. 27–39), London: British Film Institute; reprinted in Gross and Woods, eds., 1999, 297–301.

Egan, J. (2000, December 10). Lonely gay teen seeking same. *The New York Times Magazine.*

Flowers, P., & Burston, K. (2001). 'I was terrified of being different': Exploring gay men's accounts of growing up in a heterosexist society. *Journal of Adolescence, 24,* 51–65.

Fricke, A. (1981). *Reflections of a Rock Lobster: A story about growing up gay.* Boston: Alyson.

Gabriel, T. (1995, July 2). Some on-line discoveries give gay youths a path to themselves. *The New York Times,* p. 1.

Gross, L. (1996). You're the first person I've ever told: Letters to a fictional gay teen. In M. Bronski (Ed.), *Taking liberties: Gay male essays on politics, culture, and art* (pp. 369–386). New York: Kasak Books.

Gross, L. (2001). *Up from invisibility: Lesbians, gay men, and the media in America.* New York: Columbia University Press.

Gross, L., & Woods, J. (1999). *The Columbia reader on gay men and lesbians in media, society and politics.* New York: Columbia University Press.

Herdt, G., & Boxer, A. (1993). *Children of horizons: How gay and lesbian teens are leading a new way out of the closet.* Boston: Beacon Press.

Hillier, L., Kurdas C., & Horsley, P. (2001). *'It's just easier': The internet as a safety-net for same sex attracted young people.* Australian Research Centre in Sex, Health and Society. La Trobe University, Australia.

Hodges, A., & Hutter, D. (1999). With downcast gays. In Gross and Woods, (Eds.), *The Columbia reader on gay men and lesbians in media, society, and politics* (pp. 551–561). New York: Columbia University Press. (Original work published in 1974).

Johnson, D.K. (2004). *The lavender scare: The Cold War persecution of gays and lesbians in the Federal Government*. Chicago: University of Chicago Press.

Jones, R. (1999). 'I don't feel safe here anymore': Your duty to protect gay kids from harassment. *American School Board Journal*.

Mallinger, M.S. (1993). I'm not a homosexual, but I play one on TV. *Au Courant, 11*(19), 11–17.

Martin, C. J. (1980). Diary of a queer housewife. In Stanley, J.P., & Wolfe, S.J. (Eds.), *The coming out stories* (pp. 56–64). Watertown, MA: Persephone Press.

McAllester, M. (1997, January 28). What a difference a modem makes. *Newsday*.

Nir, L. (1998). A site of their own: Gay teenagers' involvement patterns in IRC and newsgroups. International Communication Association 48th Annual Meeting. Jerusalem.

Platt, L. (2001). Not your father's high school club. *The American Prospect, 12*(1),

Plummer, K. (1995). *Sexual stories: Power, change and social worlds*. London: Routledge.

Rich, A. (1976/1979). It is the lesbian in us. In *On lies, secrets, and silence* (pp. 199–202). New York: Norton.

Savin-Williams, R. (1998)....*And then I became gay*. New York: Routledge.

Scelfo, J. (2003, August 19). *Out at the prom*. Newsweek Web Exclusive. Retrieved from http://msnbc. msn.com/id/3068938/.

Silberman, S. (1994, December 13). We're teen, we're queer, and we've got e-mail. *Wired,* , 1–3.

Stanley, J.P., & Wolfe S.J. (1980). *The coming out stories*. Watertown, MA: Persephone Press.

Vaziri, A. (1999, June 13). A voice for gay teens. *San Francisco Chronicle*.

18

■ Advertising, Gender, and Sex

What's Wrong with a Little Objectification?

Sut Jhally

I start this paper with an assumption: Advertising is a very powerful form of social communication in modern society. It offers the most sustained and most concentrated set of images anywhere in the media system. The question that I wish to pose and attempt to give an answer to from this assumption is what lies behind the considerable power that advertising seems to have over its audience. Particularly, I wish to do this without reverting back to one-dimensional explanations of manipulation and the use of sophisticated techniques by advertisers. I do not want to deny this element (there is, of course, a huge amount of accumulated knowledge in the advertising industry concerning persuasion), but I wish to probe culturally rather than technically.

Erving Goffman, in his book *Gender Advertisements* (1979), was concerned with similar types of questions, although he did not phrase them in the same way. He instead asked another question: Why do most ads not look *strange* to us? Goffman believes that, when we look at ads carefully, they are, in fact, very strange creations, particularly in regards to their portrayals of gender relations. He shows us that, in advertising, the best way to understand the male–female relation is to compare it to the parent–child relation in which men take on the roles of parents, whereas women behave as children normally would be expected to. In advertising, *women are treated largely as children.*

Goffman supports his argument by pointing to a number of aspects of gender relations in advertising. For instance, in examining the portrayal of hands, he finds that women's hands are usually shown just caressing an object or just barely touching it, as though they were not in full control of it, whereas men's hands are shown strongly grasping and manipulating objects. Goffman is concerned with what such social portrayals say about the relative social positions of men and women. Beds and floors, for example, are associated with the less clean parts of a room; also, persons using them will be positioned lower than anyone who is sitting or standing. A recumbent position also leaves people in a poor position to defend themselves and thus puts them at the mercy of others. These positions are of course also a "conventionalized expression of sexual availability" (1979, p. 41). Goffman's sample of ads shows that women and children are pictured on beds and floors much more than are men. In addition, women are constantly shown drifting away mentally while under the physical protection of a male, as if his strength and alert-ness were enough. Women are also shown in the finger-to-mouth pose, directly reminiscent of children's behavior. Furthermore, when men and women are shown in physical contact, invariably, the woman is snuggling into the man in the same way that children solicit protection and comfort from their mothers.

If grown women are largely treated as children in ads, why does this not look strange to us? Goffman comments that, indeed, the most negative statement that we could make of advertisements is that, *as pictures of reality,* they do not look strange to us. To answer this question, he reverts back to the vocabulary of social anthropology, particularly the concepts of ceremony, display, and ritual. These are actions or events that seek to give structure and stability to a shared social life, to communicate the system of meaning within which individuals are located and within which they must be viewed. It is the use of this cultural resource that makes ads resonate with meaning for the audience. Ad maker Tony Schwartz has given the most eloquent expression of this *resonance theory* of communication, whereby "the critical task is to design our package of stimuli [ads] so that it resonates with information already stored within an individual and thereby induces the desired learning or behavioral effect" (1974, p. 25) Schwartz's concern is not with the message itself as a communicator of meaning but rather with the use-value of the mes-sage for the audience:

> The meaning of our communication is what a listener or viewer *gets out* of his experience with the communicator's stimuli. The listener's or viewer's brain is an indispensable component of the total communication system. His life experiences, as well as his expectations of the stimuli he is receiving, interact with the communicator's output in determining the meaning of the communication. (p. 25)

The job of the advertiser is to understand the world of the segmented audience, so that the stimuli that are created can evoke the stored information: It has to resonate with information that the listener possesses. However, we should not confuse this *resonance* with *reflection.* As adman Jerry Goodis says, "Advertising doesn't always mirror how people are acting, but how they're dreaming….In a sense, what we're doing is wrapping up your emotions and selling them back to you" (Nelson, 1983, p. C2).

Thus, advertising draws its materials from the experiences of the audience, but it reformulates them in a unique way. It does not reflect meaning but rather constitutes it. Advertisers, according to Schwartz, should be in the business of "structured recall." The purpose is to design commercials that create pleasurable emotions that will be triggered when the product is viewed in the marketplace. As Schwartz says, "I do not care what number of people remember or get the message. I am concerned with how people are affected by the stimuli" (1974, p. 69).

Goffman is particularly interested in how advertisers use the cultural resource of gender and how they reconstitute what gender means in social terms. While *sex* refers to the biological distinction between males and females, *gender* is the culture specific arrangement of this universal relationship. Specific relations between men and women are very different around the world and can be given many different definitions depending upon the specific cultural pattern that exists in any society. Of course, there is nothing *natural* about gender relations—they are socially defined and constructed. As such, any culture must constantly work to maintain existing gender relations. This is achieved during the course of social life by *gender displays*—conventionalized portrayals of the culturally established correlates of sex. In our daily interactions, we are constantly defining for ourselves and other people what it means to be male and female in this society. From the way we dress, the way we behave, and the structure of our interactions to things such as body postures and ceremonial activities (opening doors, giving up chairs, etc.), we are communicating ideas about gender by using culturally conventionalized routines of behavior. These displays, or *rituals of gender behavior,* help the interpretation of social reality; they are guides to perception. It is from these conventionalized portrayals of gender that advertising borrows so heavily, and that is the reason why, according to Goffman, most ads do not look strange to us, for they are an extremely concentrated reflection of one aspect of our social lives—they are a reflection of the realm of gender displays. Advertisers largely do not *create* the images they depict out of nothing. Advertisers draw upon the same corpus of displays that we all use to make sense of social life. "If anything, advertisers conventionalize our conventions, stylize what is already a stylization, make frivolous use of what is already something considerably cut off from contextual controls. Their hype is hyper-ritualization" (1979, p. 84).

This, however, is not merely a simple reflection of reality—ads are neither false nor true. As *representations,* they are necessarily abstractions from what they reflect. Indeed, all communication is an abstraction at some level. For too long, the debate on gender has been focused on the extent to which advertising images are true or false. Ad images are neither false nor true reflections of social reality, because they are in fact *a part of social reality.* Just as gender displays are not true or false representations of real gender relations, neither are ads true or false representations of real gender relations or of ritualized gender displays—they are *hyperritualizations* that emphasize some aspects of gender displays and deemphasize others. As such, advertisements are part of the whole context within which we attempt to understand and define our own gender relations. They are part of the process by which we learn about gender.

In as far as our society defines sex as gender through culture (and not through biology or nature), we are not fundamentally different from any other past or present society. All cultures have to define gender for their own purposes, and they all have conventionalized forms to accomplish this socialization. Gender relations are social and not natural creations in any setting.

However, I believe that our culture is different in one very important sense. Gender is only one aspect of human individuality; political, occupational, educational, creative, artistic, religious, and spiritual aspects, among others, are also very important elements of individuals' lives. Human existence is potentially very wide and very varied in the experiences it offers. In our culture, though, advertising makes the balance between these things very different—indeed, everything else becomes defined through gender. In modern advertising, gender is probably the social resource that is used most by advertisers. Thousands of images surround us every day of our lives and address us along gender lines. Advertising seems to be *obsessed* with gender.

There are two reasons for this obsession. First, gender is one of our deepest and most important traits as human beings. Our understanding of ourselves as either male or female is the most important aspect of our definition of ourselves as individuals. It reaches deep into the innermost recesses of individual identity. Second, gender can be communicated at a glance (almost instantly) because of our intimate knowledge and use of the conventionalized codes of gender display. Advertisers are trying to present the world in ways that could be real (Goffman calls ads "commercial realism"), and so they are forced to draw upon the repertoires of everyday life and experience. What better place to draw upon than an area of social behavior that can be communicated almost instantly and that reaches into the very core of our definition of ourselves? As Goffman writes,

> one of the most deeply seated traits of man, it is felt, is gender; femininity and masculinity are in a sense the prototypes of essential expression—something that can be conveyed fleetingly in any social situation and yet something that strikes at the most basic characteristics of the individual. (1979, p. 7)

While every culture has to work to define for its members what gender relations should be, no other culture in history, I believe, has been this obsessed with explicit portrayals of gender relations. Gender and (because of the way in which gender has been narrowly defined) sex have never been as important as they are in our culture. Never in history has the *iconography* of a culture been so obsessed or possessed by questions of sexuality and gender. Through advertising, questions of sex and gender have been elevated to a *privileged* position in our cultural discourse.

The reasons why this should be the case are not mysterious. First, the discourse through and about objects that is a part of the cultural discourse of any society comes to be defined largely through marketplace information in the consumer society. That is, it fills the void that is left when the traditional institutions that provided this meaning decline in influence (see Jhally, 1987). Within the domain of advertising, imagistic modes of communication historically have become more important, as has the need for concentrated or instant forms of communication (see Leiss, Kline, & Jhally, 1986). Gender communication meets the needs of advertising very nicely here.

This may also offer an answer as to the source of the power of advertising. The representations of advertising are part of the context within which we define our understanding of gender. Advertising draws us into *our* reality. As Judith Williamson writes on this point,

> Advertising seems to have a life of its own; it exists in and out of other media, and speaks to us in a language we can recognize but a voice we can never identify. This is because advertising has no "subject." Obviously people invent and produce adverts, but apart from the fact that they are unknown and faceless, the ad in any case does not claim to speak from them, it is not their speech. Thus there is a space, a gap left where the speaker should be; and one of the

peculiar features of advertising is that we are drawn in to fill that gap, so that we become both listener and speaker, subject and object. (1978, pp. 13–14)

We do not *receive* meaning from above, we constantly recreate it. It works through us, not at us. We have to do the work that is not done by the ad, "but which is only made possible by its form." We are drawn "into the transformational space between the units of the ad. Its meaning only exists in this space; the field of transaction; and it is here that we operate—*we are this space*" (Williamson, 1978, p. 44). This crucial mediation by the audience is the basis of what Schwartz calls *partipulation,* whereby the ad does not manipulate the audience but invites their participation in the construction of meaning. It is also behind Marshall McLuhan's notion that the audience works in the consumption of the television image. These systems of meaning from which we draw the tools to complete the transfer are referred to by Williamson as *referent systems.* They constitute the body of knowledge from which *both* advertisers and audiences draw their materials. As such, mass media advertising literally plays the role of a mediator. For the audience to properly *decode* the message (transfer meaning), advertisers have to draw their materials from the social knowledge of the audience and then transform this material into messages (*encode*), developing appropriate formats and shaping the content in order that the process of communication from *audience to audience* be completed (Hall, 1980).

The question is what gets changed in this process? For clearly advertising does not and cannot *reflect* social reality. As hyperritualistic images, commercials offer an extremely concentrated form of communication about sex and gender. The *essence* of gender is represented in ads. That is the reason why advertising is relatively immune from criticism about its portrayals of gender. The existing feminist critiques, those based on the content analysis of occupational roles in ads and those that focus on the forms of the objectification of women, are pitched at an intellectual level that does not recognize the emotional attraction of the images. We cannot deny the messages of advertising; we cannot say that they are false, because they bear some resemblance to ritualized gender relations. Furthermore, we cannot deny them, because we define ourselves at our deepest level *through the reality of advertising.* We *have* to reach a socially accepted understanding of gender identity in some way. It is not an option one can refuse. If we do not cope at this level, then the evidence suggests that it is very difficult to cope at any level. Gender confusions cloud the entire domain of social identity for individuals. To completely deny the messages of advertising is to deny our definition of ourselves in gender and sexual terms—it is to deny ourselves as socially recognizable individuals in this culture. As Wendy Chapkis writes in her book *Beauty Secrets,* "The most important function of gendered appearance is to unambiguously distinguish men from women" (1986, p. 129). If the dominant definitions of gender are not accepted, deviant individuals are relegated to the perverted section of our culture (e.g., transsexuals and transvestites). I believe that is the reason why the feminist critiques concerning regressive representations in advertising have not been very successful; they have not recognized the basis of its *attraction.* The attraction for both men and women is important to recognize, although it is, of course, varied in its specific focus: In terms of the representation of women, men want possession of what they see, whereas women identify with it.

If the critique does not recognize this attraction, then the attack on advertising becomes an attack on *people*. People thus feel guilty about being attracted to the images of advertising while being told that they should not find them attractive. Much of the best feminist writing on sexual imagery has, of course, been directed at pornography rather than advertising (or the two have simply been equated as the same). Ellen Willis writes of this for pornography:

> Over the years I've enjoyed various pieces of pornography—some of the sleazy Forty-second Street paperback sort—and so have most women I know. Fantasy, after all, is more flexible than reality, and women have learned, as a matter of survival, to be adept at shaping male fantasies to their own purposes. If feminists define pornography, per se, as the enemy, the result will be to make a lot of women ashamed of their sexual feelings and afraid to be honest about them. And the last thing women need is more sexual shame, guilt and hypocrisy—this time served up as feminism. (1983, p. 462)

Similarly, film theorist Annette Kuhn in her book *The Power of the Image* comments on the pleasures of reading the film text:

> Politics is often thought of as one of life's more serious undertakings, allowing little room for pleasure. At the same time, feminists may feel secretly guilty about their enjoyment of images they are convinced ought to be rejected as politically unsound. In analyzing such images, though, it is possible, indeed necessary, to acknowledge their pleasurable qualities, precisely because pleasure is an area of analysis in its own right. "Naive" pleasure then, becomes admissible. And the acts of analysis, of deconstruction and of reading "against the grain" offer an additional pleasure—the pleasure of resistance, of saying "no": not to "unsophisticated" enjoyment, by ourselves and others, of culturally dominant images, but to the structures of power which ask us to consume them uncritically and in highly circumscribed ways. (1985, p. 8)

A critique of advertising has to start by giving people permission to recognize the pleasure, the strength, of the images of advertising and of where that power rests. From that, we can start to unfold the exact role that advertising plays in our culture from a critical perspective. There is, of course, a great danger involved in this move, for the recognition of pleasure becomes a distorted conception if it is not simultaneously contextualized within the context of power relations (in this case, patriarchal). Pleasure can be used against people under the guise of freedom.

Now, defining gender and sexual identity is a difficult activity at the best of times; in modern consumer society, this difficulty is compounded by individuals being bombarded by extremely concentrated images of what gender is about. Advertising, it seems, has a privileged place in the discourse on gender in consumer societies due to its prominence in our daily lives. As a result, what advertising says about gender is a very important issue to understand. Gender could be defined in many ways (achievement, control of our lives, independence, family, creativity, etc.). It is a multidimensional aspect of human individuality. In advertising, however, gender is equated almost exclusively with sexuality. Women especially are defined primarily in sexual terms: What is important about women is their sexual behavior. As the debate on pornography has indicated, viewing women from this narrow and restricted perspective can result in treating women as less than truly human. The concentration on one aspect of behavior detracts from seeing people as people. Rather, they are seen as standing for something or being associated with one thing. As Judith Williamson notes on this point,

> If meaning is abstracted from something, from what it "means," this is nearly always a danger signal because it is only in material circumstances that it is possible to "know" anything, and looking away from people or social phenomena to their supposed abstract "significance" can be at worst an excuse for human and social atrocities, at best, a turning of reality into apparent unreality, almost unlivable while social dreams and myths seem so real. (1978, p. 169)

This is the basis of the feminist critique of objectification, of course. When subjectivity is denied, then one need not worry about people as people but only about how they may further your ends. Objects have no interest, no feelings, and no desires other than the way they affect yours. Women become defined as an object for the other. Within advertising, this is reflected in four basic ways in terms of the representations of women: (a) as *symbols* for an object and, thus, as exchangeable with it; (b) as a *fragmented* object made up of separate component parts that are not bound together in any coherent way to create a personality; (c) as an object to be *viewed;* and (d) as an object to be *used.*

I want to stress that gender identity is constructed in part through social representations of which the most pervasive and powerful forms in the consumer society are those associated with advertising (for women especially, representations in advertising are much more powerful than those of pornography). The social construction of gender identity is not an option, it is a necessity. Judith Williamson writes more broadly on this:

> Advertising may appropriate, not only real areas of time and space, and give them a false content, but real needs and desires in people, which are given a false fulfillment. We need a way of looking at ourselves: which ads give us falsely…we need to make sense of the world: which ads make us feel we are doing in making sense of them. (1978, p. 169)

The radical feminist literature has drawn a conclusion from this analysis of contemporary patriarchy and its representations. Feminism requires the articulation of new types of gender relations and new types of sexuality. In rejecting standard notions of beauty and sexuality (vital in a patriarchal culture for the construction of female identity), others have to be provided. Within the debate on pornography, this has led to calls for *erotica* versus pornography or a sexuality that focuses on relationships. Again, Ellen Willis has commented insightfully on these issues in relation to pornography and the women's movement:

> In the movement's rhetoric pornography is a code word for vicious male lust. To the objection that some women get off on porn the standard reply is that this shows how thoroughly women have been brain-washed by male values.…And the view of sex that most often emerges from talk about "erotica" is as sentimental and euphemistic as the word itself: lovemaking should be beautiful, romantic, soft, nice, and devoid of messiness, vulgarity, impulses to power, or indeed aggression of any sort. Above all, the emphasis should be on relationships, not (yuck) organs. This goody-goody concept of eroticism is not feminist but feminine. (1983, p. 464)

That is, in the political battle with the standard forms of patriarchal sexuality (and of course representations) there has to be an *alternate,* a different option, defined. This cannot be left to talking about the future and not basing our present actions on utopian possibilities. In the battle over gender, we have to have that alternative vision *now.* The problem for feminists who reject the standard notions is to build a positive one that will *attract* people (both men and women). It is to recognize that culture is a battlefield, a site of contestation of visions and definitions of social relations (both real and imagined). I think that, up to now, that alternative has simply not been one around which to rally people. The cultural battle has been lost. Even a radical feminist such as Susan Brownmiller can recognize the problem. She says,

> On bad days, I mourn my old dresses, I miss the graceful flow of fabric…and pretty colors. Sensible shoes announce an unfeminine sensibility.…Sensible shoes aren't fun.…Sensible shoes aren't sexy.…They are crisply efficient. As a matter of principle I stopped shaving my legs and underarms several years ago, but I have yet to accept the unaesthetic results.…I look at my legs and know they are no longer attractive, not even to me. They are simply legs, upright and honest and that ought to be good enough, but it isn't. (Chapkis, 1986, p. 131)

Wendy Chapkis also asks how women's liberation ended up on the sensible side over the sexual, the "efficient, upright and honest" over the colorful and fun: ultimately, of how the choice came down to one *between* principle and pleasure.

> What a grim post-revolutionary world is envisioned. Artifice-free functional clothing is gender-less and often comfortable. It is also unquestionably sensible attire for many activities. But what would functional clothing look like if our intended activity is sex. Mightn't a lacy bra or sheer stocking have erotic appeal less because they are symbols of female powerlessness and more because they are familiar symbols of female sexuality. (1986, p. 133)

If gender symbols have a legitimate erotic role, then the challenge seems to be to find a way to allow for gender play without gender privilege. As Wendy Chapkis's eight-year-old sister says about this in relation to her future life, "Wendy is a feminist. When I grow up, I am going to be just like her except I'll dress better" (1986, p. 7). As mentioned previously, Judith Williamson refers to advertising as providing a false way of looking at ourselves, a false fulfillment of real needs and desires. I also want to argue that ads give us a false way to look at ourselves, but I wish to establish *where* precisely falsity lies. It does *not* lie in the individual advertisement. There is nothing necessarily false about the consumption of individual messages. That is what draws us in. Individually, each message communicates a certain meaning. Each individual ad is produced for a certain strategic purpose in terms of communication. Conventionalized sexual imagery (e.g., high heels, slit skirts, and nudity) draws us in and makes an ad attractive for us. It is very difficult to criticize a single ad in isolation, unless it is blatantly sexist or violent. Even the ones that explicitly objectify women become attractive or draw us in, because objectification is a *pleasurable part* of sexuality. More and more of the feminist literature is starting to recognize this quite fundamental point that we all objectify men and women in some way at some time, that it can fulfill a socially positive function. As Ann Snitow notes in commenting upon objectification and pornography,

> The danger of objectification and fragmentation depend on context. Not even in my most utopian dreams can I imagine a state in which one recognizes all others as fully as one recognizes oneself.…The antipornography campaign introduces misleading goals into our struggle when it intimates that in a feminist world we will never objectify anyone, never take the part for the whole, never abandon ourselves to the mindlessness or the intensities of feeling that link sex with childhood, death, the terrors and pleasures of the oceanic. Using people as exten-

sions of one's own hungry will is hardly an activity restrained within the boundaries of pornography. (1985, p. 116)

Wendy Chapkis recognizes that

there is something impossibly earnest about the demand that we feel sexual attraction only in
a non-objectified, ungendered fashion. It may be impossible not to objectify an attractive
stranger. Until one learns enough to fill in the blanks, the attraction can't help but be built on
the image s/he chooses to project and the fantasy which the observer then creates. (1986, p.
134)

Recognizing that gender play and variation are difficult in a mainstream heterosexual
world, Chapkis gives some pertinent examples from her lesbian experiences of how
objectification may be used in creative and pleasurable ways (for both, not just one side),
where power is not so rigidly exercised:

I slowly press myself against the fading pretense of butch restraint and then withdraw. She
wants feminine, I'll give her feminine: promising but deliberately delaying her release. Now I
lead this subtle dance. My painted nails flash a message that has nothing to do with passivity.
Those fingers dipped in blood and red lacquer can penetrate her depths....These are symbols
of control and surrender. But they are fluid; mouth and fingers, sheer underwear and leather
ties, teasing out a woman's desire. (p. 136)

Similarly, Cynthia Peters and Karen Struening write in *Zeta* magazine,

Although there are important insights in the work of those theorists who challenge and repudi-
ate men's objectification of women, there is a moment in the objectification process that must
be saved. We are all sexual objects, and it is a good thing that we are. Sexual interactions require
that we be able to see the other as a source of pleasure and sexual gratification....We must ask
ourselves, do we want a world where the gaze is always evaded, in which words are never
used to tease and flirt, in which the body is never seen as an object of sensual desire? Must
sexuality be barred from the theater of public spaces? (1988, p. 79)

Parts of daily life do have to do with sexuality, and, thus, there is nothing wrong with
individual messages that focus on sex and gender. (That is, unless one took a moralistic
stance on advertising in which some messages are inherently unacceptable for public or
private viewing. Groups on the political right criticize advertising from this perspective.
Similarly, some radical feminist theorists would argue against these images on the basis
that all representations of heterosexual sex are representations of patriarchal domination.)
Some parts of sexuality have to do with objectification, so that individual ads in that
sense are not false. The falsity arises from the *system of images,* from the ads as a totality
and from their cumulative effect. All (or at least many) messages are about gender and
sexuality. It seems that, for women, it is the *only* thing that is important about them. The
falsity then arises from the message *system,* rather than individual ads. It arises from the
institutional context within which ads are produced and suggests that attempts to modify
its regressive features should be concentrated at this level.

The argument I have made depends wholly on an understanding of the context of
social phenomenon. While there is nothing wrong with a *little* objectification, there is a
great deal wrong and dangerous with a *lot* of objectification—that is when one is viewed
as *nothing other than an object.* Peters and Struening again write the following:

Many women walk through public spaces fearing the gazes, gestures and words directed at them. Although many women bring sexuality into the streets with fashion and body language, they do not think of the street as an entirely safe place for sexual play. They can (and do) seek the gaze of the other, but most women are aware of the attendant dangers. They know they cannot be objects of sexual attention with impunity. Many women have ambivalent responses to being addressed as sexual objects. While some women experience the gratification and pleasure…many others recount feelings of humiliation, anger, outrage, and diminished self-esteem. (1987, p. 79)

Commentating from a lesbian perspective, Wendy Chapkis recognizes not only the pleasure, but also the danger of sexual play in a world of male violence, "where sexually provocative means asking to be attacked" (1986, p. 138). It is little wonder that many women simply withdraw from the standard conceptions of beauty, especially in public spaces.

Escapes from this situation are difficult to imagine, but imagined they must be, because, despite all I have said about pleasure and objectification, we cannot forget that the advertising system offers us the most negative and dangerous set of images of sexuality and gender anywhere in our culture. Battles can take place on all kinds of individual levels over definitions concerned with the meanings of gender and the body. But they will be relatively meaningless unless one can affect the overall context of their interpretation. The discourse through and about objects (of which advertising sexuality is a part) is, at the present time, a profoundly *undemocratic* discourse. It is controlled only by advertisers and media. What is needed is not monitoring of individual images but a restructuring of the total system of images, so that sexuality can be separated from objectification, and objectification can be separated from patriarchal power. We need to take *back* the erotic, not construct a new eroticism using none of the symbols of the past: to redefine, for example, silk stockings as symbols of female sexuality rather than to expel them from the lexicon of a new female sexuality. Wendy Chapkis writes,

Sex, like its sister appearance, should be made more fun not more of a burden. Playing with the way we look, creating a personally or sexually provocative image has pleasures of its own. Denying ourselves those pleasures because they have been used against us in the past is understandable but hardly the final word in liberation. (1986, p. 146)

Within Marxist social theory, it has been recognized that whatever comes after capitalism will depend on the development of productive forces under capitalism, that there are progressive tendencies and movements within the belly of the beast. Could a similar case be made with regard to the cultural realm? Can the progressive elements of contemporary culture be rescued and recontextualized in the transition to a more egalitarian society? Can we base a cultural politics on some of the products and outcomes of the contemporary cultural marketplace? Or will a future society involve a total overthrowing of capitalist social and cultural relations?

Some objects, phrases, and images have a deep connotative meaning that makes them incredibly powerful symbols of identification. We cannot simply give them away to the forces of reaction. One way to accomplish this would be to force new voices of liberation, new erotic images of the diversity of female beauty, into the present totalitarian discourse, to intervene at the level of the system of images, "to dissolve the commercial monopoly on sex appeal" (Chapkis, 1986, p. 146).

* This essay first appeared in *Working Papers and Proceedings of the Center for Psychological Studies,* vol. 29, ed. R. Parmentier and G. Urban (1989). Reprinted by permission.

References

Chapkis, W. (1986). *Beauty secrets.* Boston: South End Press.

Goffman, E. (1979). *Gender advertisements.* New York: Harper and Row.

Hall, S. (1980). Encoding/decoding. In S. Hall, D. Hobson, A. Lowe, & P. Willis (Eds.), *Culture, media, language.* London: Hutchinson.

Jhally, S. (1987). *The codes of advertising: Fetishism and the political economy of meaning in the consumer society.* New York: St. Martin's Press.

Kuhn, A. (1985). *The power of the image.* London: Routledge & Kegan Paul.

Leiss, W., Kline, S., & Jhally, S. (Eds.). (1986). *Social communication in advertising.* London: Methuen.

Nelson, J. (1983). As the brain tunes out, the TV ad-men tune in. *Globe and Mail.*

Peters, C., & Struening, K. (1988, February). Out on the street. *Zeta.*

Schwartz, T. (1974). *The responsive chord.* New York: Anchor.

Snitow, A. (1985). Retrenchment versus transformation: The politics of the antipornography movement. In V. Burstyn (Ed.), *Women against censorship.* Vancouver: Douglas & McIntyre.

Williamson, J. (1978). *Decoding advertisements: Ideology and meaning in advertising.* London: Boyars.

Willis, E. (1983). Feminism, moralism, and pornography. In A. Snitow, C. Stansell, & S. Thompson (Eds.), *Powers of desire: The politics of sexuality.* New York: Monthly Review Press.

19

The Magical World of Daytime Soap Operas

Elayne Rapping

"For only in art has bourgeois society tolerated its own ideals and taken them seriously as a general demand. What counts as utopia, phantasy, and rebellion in the world of fact is allowed in art. There affirmative culture has displayed the forgotten truths over which 'realism' triumphs in daily life."

Herbert Marcuse (1968, p. 114)

"A work of art opens a void where…the world is made aware of its guilt."

Michel Foucault (1965, p. 278)

It's Sunday night and my daughter is calling: "I hate that they have to kill off Eve," she moans, "although I don't blame her for wanting out of her contract—the show is definitely going downhill. And at least they're using her death to make a point about experimental drugs. The gay groups should be happy about that, if any of them are watching. Probably not. Even the rec.arts.tv.soaps.cbs crowd on the Internet seem to hate her, which I really don't get. She's the only interesting woman left on the show, and by far the most feminist. I mean once she goes, who will be left to really live a life that centers around female bonding and support? Her relationships with Harley and Lucy are just so neat. And she was the only one in the hospital who stood up for that poor nurse who was being sexually harassed by that creepy doctor what's-his-name and got the jerk fired. What do you think?"

We are having our usual weekly check-in call about *Guiding Light,* the soap opera of choice among Pittsburgh women in the 1970s, when she was growing up, and the one to which we have remained loyal for almost three decades, through good times and bad. Neither of us lives in Pittsburgh now, but when we watch and discuss our soap opera, we still share a common community and a set of friends and neighbors about whom we care deeply, even as we laugh at their often ridiculously implausible lives.

But what's this about AIDS? The dying doctor, as you may know if you are a fan yourself, has died of a rare disease with no links to sex, drugs or blood transfusions. She has, it seems, picked up this virus while working as selflessly as Mother Teresa (and with as little political sophistication), as a doctor in a war-torn fictional nation.

Nonetheless, as Alison and I both understand, having followed and discussed the murky, contradictory, often subtextual politics of daytime soaps for so long, there is something progressive, in the most utopian sense of that word, about the conclusion of the storyline. The dying woman has made contact by way of the Internet with a colleague doing research on this disease and has been secretly medicating herself with an untested drug. Her fiancé, a physician of the more usual, conservative variety, is adamantly opposed. But lo and behold, the cyber-researcher she has hooked up with is an old med school pal of his—a woman who is representative of the many admirable examples of female bonding, both professional and personal, in soap operas. This brilliant woman, for whom he has the utmost respect, convinces him—in a series of inspiring speeches of the kind Alison and I love to savor—of his fiancée's courage, her intuitive scientific acumen and her right to choose her own treatment. Men on soap operas often, and admirably, take moral and professional leadership from the wonderful women they love and/or work with. Eve even improves for a while on the treatment, but it is too little, too late, and she finally succumbs—as the contract of the actress who plays the role demands (and as we who follow the cyber-chat gossip have long known she would)—amidst sobbing friends, flashback clips of better days and a eulogy in which it is predicted that her final act of medical courage will lead to an early cure for the disease. In Soapville, this is credible. For soap operas—and this is the quality that elicits the most derision from detractors and the most pleasure in fans—are highly unrealistic in a way that is, remarkably, often delightfully utopian.

The idea that bourgeois culture incorporates utopian visions and values, moments during which we are liberated from the constraints of realism and can glimpse in the distance a vision of that better world in which our often unarticulated heart's desires are fulfilled is not, of course, new. Media scholars have been aware of this since Fredric Jameson's (1990) seminal essay on "Reification and Utopia in Mass Culture." Nor is it news that popular culture, being taken so much less seriously than high art forms, has been the most powerful site of imaginative utopian protest. For as Jameson (1975) has written elsewhere, it is in times like ours, when "our own particular environment—the total system of capitalism and the consumer society—feels so massively in place and its reification so overwhelming and impenetrable that the serious artist is no longer free to tinker with it that popular forms—forms that are less 'serious,' less 'massively in place'"— assume "the vocation of giving us alternate versions of a world that has elsewhere seemed to resist even *imagined* change" (p. 64).

While Jameson does not specifically mention soap opera, feminist media theorists have written extensively and insightfully about the utopian element in daytime soaps. Feminists have discovered in soaps a representation of "a world in which the divine functions"; a world which "exhorts the [real] world to live up to [women's] impassioned expectations of it," as Louise Spence (1995, p. 193) nicely puts it. And John Fiske (1987), taking a somewhat different perspective, has described soap opera as a genre in which "feminine culture constantly struggles to establish and extend itself within and against a dominant patriarchy…to whittle away at patriarchy's power to subject women and… establish a masculine-free zone from which a direct challenge may be mounted" (p. 197). Other feminist theorists have pointed to any number of specific soap conventions and teased out their utopian implications. It is often noted, for example, that through the incorporation of multiple subjectivities and points of view and the use of multiple, open-ended narrative lines, readers are potentially empowered to question dominant patriarchal assumptions about family and gender norms and to resist hegemonic readings.

But most of this work has focused on the way soaps represent and negotiate the traditionally feminine sphere of private life—the home, family and gender relationships, marriage and maternity, presenting their implicitly utopian social and political vision. Raymond Williams (1973) has written that "community is the keyword of the entire utopian enterprise" (p. 212). And it is the sense of community—but of a feminized community closer to feminist visions of the future than to classic, literary utopias—that makes soaps so seductively addictive to so many women.

"The personal is political" is a classic, feminist slogan, and its meaning is particularly important to an understanding of what a feminist vision of community—and of women's roles with in that community—would be. Barbara Ehrenreich and Dierdre English (1978) eloquently articulated the vision and demands of that utopian world view: "There are no answers left but the most radical ones," they wrote:

> We cannot assimilate into a masculinist society without doing violence to our own nature, which is of course *human* nature. But neither can we retreat into domestic isolation, clinging to an archaic feminine ideal. Nor can we deny that the dilemma is a social one…The Woman Question in the end is not a question of *women*. It is not we who are the problem and it is not our needs which are the mystery. From our perspective (denied by centuries of masculinist "science" and analysis) the Woman Question becomes the question of how shall we all—women and children and men—organize our lives together. (p. 323)

This statement still resonates for feminists—and still, unfortunately, remains unrealized. But on soap operas, in often bizarre, always complicated and highly contradictory ways, it is realized in ways which are often surprisingly satisfying.

How is it possible, in a form in many ways so hokey and even reactionary, for such progressive ideas to regularly appear? For one thing, soaps are presented from a female perspective which is, by its very nature, alterior. The private sphere, as has so often been noted, is privileged and valorized on soaps, and the things women do in that sphere are seen as central to the maintenance and proper functioning of human life. But what is less often noted is the effect this valorizing of private, feminine experience has on the representation of the public sphere. Soaps portray a world in which reality, as we know it, is turned on its head so that the private sphere becomes all important. But there is more to it than that. For in so privileging private values, soaps also construct a highly unrealistic but nonetheless prominent and important public sphere in which all institutions are forced to conform to private, feminine values.

The feminist idea that "the personal is political" is, of course, a critique of what had, since the rise of the industrial world order, been a sharp delineation between the male-driven public sphere, in which work, business and public affairs were handled, and the female-driven domestic sphere—the haven in a heartless world—in which the work of caring for and maintaining family relations, the socializing of children and the negotiation of emotional and spiritual matters, took place. In this scheme, issues of morality, and emotional and spiritual health were designated "female" concerns relevant primarily, if not exclusively, to the home and family life. The male world, by contrast, was understood to be ruled by the competitive, individualist values of the marketplace in which ruthless-ness and greed and self-interest were largely accepted as inevitable, if not necessarily desirable. The need for men to return to the caring, nurturing, hearth and home where values such as caring, emotional openness and mutual support and concern for the welfare of the group—in this case, of course, the nuclear or, at best, extended family or immediate neighborhood community—was understood to be necessary.

Most popular culture genres elide this contradiction by foregrounding one sphere and hinting, usually only indirectly, at the contradictions between the values which prevail in those different worlds. Thus, westerns and crime genres focus on the male world of competition, aggression and violence and hold up, symbolically, an image of the personal, feminine sphere as a reminder of what has been sacrificed in the transcendence of male-driven public values. By contrast, family melodrama foregrounds the private sphere of marriage and family, even as it refers to the family-destroying values which inform the public sphere and which must be overcome (and this is rarely seen as possible) for personal happiness to be achieved. Soap operas handily elide this contradiction and manage not to acknowledge or deal with it at all by ingeniously mapping out an entire public realm of political, economic and legal events and institutions, as prominent as the personal, in which women and the concerns of the feminine operate as visibly and importantly as in the domestic. By so blurring the distinctions between the concerns of the two spheres, they alter the traditional representation of male figures—heroes and villains—and draw their male characters more fully into the life of the family and the emotions than other genres. Thus, even murderers and schemers are seen to be driven by obsessive love or family loyalties, just as are good doctors and lawyers. In this way, soaps create a world in which women are free to take their concerns for such values as compassion, coopera-tion, the valorization of spiritual and emotional concerns and perspectives into the mar-ketplace, the workplace and the arenas in which law, justice, public health and welfare and the business of maintaining democratic institutions are negotiated. And by extension, men themselves—now forced to operate in so feminized and humanized a public sphere—have no choice but to bring home the values by which they run their public lives.

In discussing feminist utopias, Fran Bartkowski (1989) notes that unlike most tradi-tional male utopias, they incorporate "tacit rather than reified models of the state" (p. 15). What is "tacit" in feminist utopias, she suggests, and what distinguishes them from their male-defined counterparts, is a "discourse on the family" which sees the family as the "place where the inhabitants of the projected utopian state [are] formed" (p. 15). It is just such a discourse on the family, as the foundational root of social and political ideology, that informs the vision of community and public life on soap operas. If home is where the heart is, on soaps, home is located everywhere. The gathering spots of soap geography—the restaurants, the health clubs, the diners and malls, even the hospital nurses stations and corporate office buildings—all serve as "homelike" environments. This is a world of public space which is family-driven in every arena. Its laws and policies are imbued implicitly with the values—"interconnectedness...nurturance, responsibility, and mutual respect" (Gilligan, 1982, p. 57)—which Carol Gilligan has defined as informing the feminist moral universe which girls are socialized to maintain. On soaps, the binary split between private and public is virtually dissolved.

Thus, it is standard on soaps for police officers, district attorneys and lawyers—and they tend to be equally divided between genders—to view their work in fighting crime, for example, as an extension of their roles as parents, keeping the city safe for their children, or wives and sisters and mothers. So thoroughly blurred are the sphere distinctions that there is *never* a contradiction between the two roles, never any possibility that one's role as a family member might clash with one's duty to defend a client or uphold the law. In fact, it is not uncommon, on soaps, for characters in these kinds of positions of authority to willfully ignore the law when their own sense of what is best for the safety of their loved ones is involved. And they are always, inevitably, judged to have been right—even heroic—in their judgment. On soaps, one's instincts about what is right for the family—no matter what the law might say—are always validated since the laws themselves, in their utopian idealism, are assumed, implicitly, to be in the service of such values.

Soaps, then, conform nicely to Angelika Bammer's (1991) description of feminist utopia. "Utopia," she notes, "identifies society as the site of lack." Unlike ideology, she explains, which "represents things as they are from the perspective of those in power... utopia is the opposing view of how things could and should be different" (p. 44). Soaps construct a world in which women—who do not, in any meaningful sense, participate in public policy formulation in reality—are allowed to "play house" with the world, to set up a public sphere informed by the values they are, in reality, enjoined to maintain and pass on (but only within the home and family of course). Simone de Beauvoir (1961) once said that women were most grievously disempowered in not being allowed to "take responsibility for the world" (p. 49). On soaps, they are allowed to do just that. This is what is most empowering about the genre, because it is most at odds with the "common sense" to which women—and children—are otherwise exposed.

Of course, this is a somewhat unorthodox view of soaps. It is usually assumed that romance and the rituals of mating and marriage are what draw and hold women viewers. But while this is certainly a factor, I have always thought it was misleading to focus so heavily on these elements of soaps and to ignore what, to me, has always seemed so much more compelling—the sense of community. Men in soap operas—the good ones in their good phases, anyway—are wonderfully nurturing and caring. They become totally obsessed with the needs of the women in their lives and seem to devote every waking moment of work and leisure time to them. It is all too common, for example, to see a lawyer, doctor or cop stare soulfully into the eyes of a woman character in deep trouble and say, "I'm going to drop all my other cases and devote myself entirely to your case, because I care about you so much." And somehow, this becomes possible to accomplish without total destruction of the man's career or business.

In a storyline on the *The Guiding Light,* for example, a CEO of a major corporation (one of the stereotypical presences on all soaps) disappeared for weeks at a time from his job when his fiancée was being held by a psychopath who previously had raped her. Even before her abduction, when the poor girl was *merely* suffering the post-traumatic stress of the rape, her lover seemed to leave his office continuously at the merest hint that she was feeling down, in order to take her out for a special treat, or whisk her to his palatial penthouse where she could be pampered and coddled, and allowed to weep, talk about her ordeal or not, as the need arose, or simply sleep. Every woman who has ever complained that her male partner had no time for her because of work, or had no understanding of what she was going through after a traumatic experience, could only drool in envy.

Such are the common characteristics and behaviors of good men—and even the worst of them, if they become regulars, are periodically good—on soaps. But, as wonderful as they are, like their real-life counterparts, these men come and go. The sorrows and joys they bring are always fleeting. The marriage vows and family structures to which they commit themselves are always already disintegrating even as their Friday afternoon wedding vows are being said. Thus, crisis and trauma are always imperiling the sexual and family lives of even the most fortunately partnered women. At the very moment when things seem, at last, to be blissfully perfect in a marriage, every viewer knows that catastrophe looms. In fact, if any marriage goes untroubled for too long, it is a sure sign that the characters will soon be written out, shipped off to another town or country to return, perhaps years later, in different bodies and with new threads of chaos and tragedy ominously looming.

To avoid such annihilation, it is customary on soaps for even the best of longstanding characters to periodically undergo serious character lapses, if not outright transformations, in which they abandon or lose their wives and families, in order to free them up for new storylines. One of the very best of the many extraordinarily caring, compassionate, feminized men on soaps, has, in his long career on *The Guiding Light,* gone through many such periodic marital lapses. Indeed, there is hardly a longstanding, regular character on a soap who has not been through countless marriages and other romantic involvements, each of which, invariably, includes vows of undying love which are—as every fan knows—as easily forgotten as last year's hairstyle.

Marital and romantic upheaval and disaster, then, rather than family stability, are the norm in the lives of the most prominent and regular members of soap communities. But through all this family turmoil and crisis, the community itself always remains stable and solid. This is what really holds the women and children together. Every soap character—no matter how battered, how evil, how hopelessly fallen—can always rely on the emotional and material safety net of the soap community of extended family, social and political relationships. No sooner has crisis struck than the character suddenly has more friends and attention than ever before. Suddenly, new career and social opportunities came from all quarters and once more her life is filled with adventure. Marriage, while always longed for—indeed, often schemed for—is in actuality far from the "happily ever after" event it symbolizes for soap characters. Actors—who do not know the fates of their characters very far in advance and therefore watch for telltale signs in their scripts that they are about to be written out of a show—grow nervous as their characters' weddings approach, for this is generally a sign of less visibility if not total annihilation.

Weddings, then, do not signal the kind of narrative closure one finds in romantic comedies or fairy tales. Nor do they even focus, primarily, on the bride and groom as the central figures. Rather, as in other public events on soaps, weddings offer an opportunity for the entire community to gather and celebrate as a group. It is traditional, on soap weddings for example, for the camera to pan to one character after another, as the vows are read, so that the particular dramas of each of their storylines can be highlighted. A character whose own marriage is in trouble, for example, will look appropriately anxious as the vows are said. And characters involved in extra-marital affairs will typically eye each other furtively as the lines about fidelity are repeated by the marrying couple. Even characters involved in shady business deals or political intrigue will be given a chance to remind viewers of their plights during the service in some, never very subtle, way. In this way, viewers' thoughts are kept directly on the real action, the plotlines of those characters—and there are always many of them—who are engaged in the meaty issues that involve the community as a whole, as the marrying couple is swept gracefully out of sight and mind.

Thus weddings, far from focusing on personal romantic closure and family stability, are a site of community unity and festivity, an anchor which reinforces the sense of unity and cohesion within the community itself. As such, they are also among the most anticipated of delights for viewers, not only because they allow for the largest number of cast members to be seen collectively, but because they present visions of luxury and pleasure which, again, mark the genre's resemblance to feminist utopian visions. Soaps' characters all live in relative luxury, have an endless supply of always up-to-date furniture, clothing and (it seems) hairdressers. For example, they have at their disposal gourmet cooking from places with names like "The Pampered Palate" that deliver at a moment's notice. Nor are the poorer characters excluded from such treats. Sharing is endemic in Soapville, and, in fact, the first hint that a "bad" character is about to be converted may well be when a wealthy character invites her or him—out of compassion or an instinct that they are save-able—to share in some celebration or luxury.

And, as the "Eve" story line that so intrigued my daughter and me illustrates, soaps, also offer the strongest portrayal of what we used to call "sisterhood"—female bonding and solidarity—of any genre on TV today. Women matter to each other on soaps in a way that rarely is the case elsewhere in the media and not in some sugary, unbelievably cartoonish way. In a surprisingly realistic way, friendships between women are often, as in life, put to the test. They sometimes falter and, in many cases, bitterly end (temporarily) over moral disagreements or serious betrayals. But the love that women friends and colleagues share invariably moves them to resolve their differences, forgive each other, and retrieve the loss of closeness they had shared. Women are not perfect on soaps, but they are rarely as unredeemably evil as are many minor, male characters whose evil doings become so unforgivable they must be killed off.

In a recent storyline, for example, a woman increasingly bored with her longstanding marriage becomes involved with a sleazy but sexy sportscaster and almost—but not quite—has an affair with him before coming to her senses with the help of her best friend's sound advice. The advice comes too late for the marriage, however, and her husband leaves her. The friend then succumbs to the sportscaster's charms herself and sleeps with him, destroying her own marriage. For most friendships, this would be a real deal-breaker. But while both marriages gradually were saved; the heart of this story line was in the break-up of such a long-standing friendship, the way in which each woman suffered the agonies of the loss, and how they came together, over many a tearful cup of coffee or tea, to repair their relationship. The repair of the marriages was much less emotional. There was no real talking out of what had gone wrong but rather a more contrived and predictable process by which the couples, over time, simply gravitated back together. To fans, in fact, it was clear that the writers had no plans to give either couple new front-burner love stories and that the resolution of their marital problems was actually a way of putting all four characters on the back burner for the time being, as other story lines and characters took center stage. But the depth of the seriousness with which the women worked though their problems and resumed their friendship was, while shorter lived, far more intense and moving.

Female bonding and sisterhood are not only, or most interestingly, played out in such one on one negotiations between friends. In fact, the most utopian aspect of the way in which sisterhood is portrayed on soaps often involves groups of women—many times women who were not necessarily close before, or who even disliked each other for various reasons—who find themselves in terrible situations engineered by unredeemably evil males who must, ultimately, be killed off. For example, three women on an episode in *As the World Turns* found themselves kidnapped and trapped in a bizarre clinic where they were being drugged into near helplessness. All three of these women had in one way or another antagonized each other in the past and were far from close. But finding themselves in a common predicament, they pulled together, the stronger helped the weaker to fight off the effect of the drugs, and eventually managed to escape. They are now the best of friends. In fact, all three had, when first introduced as new characters, been seen as placing more value on careers and men than female friendships. But living through a male-imposed ordeal had taught them what so many female characters on soaps already know: that women friends are, in the end, the ones you can really count on. Now, all three are long-running, major characters who regularly come to each other's rescue.

Soaps, then, are in many ways similar to the utopias envisioned in many feminist science novels. And not only because of the bonding and strength of women characters. Marge Piercy's (1985) Mattapoisett, the utopian community of *Woman on the Edge of Time,* in fact, offers a similar vision of community, abundance, pleasure and community bonding across race, gender, ethnic and other differences. Here, technology is fueled by collective decision-making to produce the very best food and clothing for all, shared in communal dining and recreation areas or—as on soaps—alone if one chooses. Among the most delicious features, for example, of what a socialist-feminist imagination would do with technology in the service of pleasure and beauty—one which soaps mimic constantly—is Piercy's idea of disposable garments called "flimsies," which can be whipped up instantly, cheaply and to one's personal taste and measurement, for special occasions where formal attire or costumes are required. After wearing, the flimsies are easily disposed of and recycled.

A number of soap conventions resemble this kind of fantasized world of pleasure and beauty. Every soap periodically presents elaborate celebrations—masked balls, weddings and so forth—at which everyone, rich and poor, seems to magically acquire the most elaborate, gorgeous evening wear immediately upon hearing of the occasion, even if it is scheduled for the next evening, as it often is. Here too, the costumes seem to magically disappear, never to be worn again, come the stroke of midnight. On soaps, in fact, the entire community seems to coordinate their attire in ways which allow for the whole event to take on a particularly collective, communal flavor. Such things do not normally appear in traditional male utopias, but Piercy's feminist world answers real women's dreams, as any proper, technologically advanced, post-scarcity utopia should.

In fact, the inclusion of complex interpersonal factors not usually allowed in legal and political procedures is one of the most politically interesting aspects of the form. For in creating characters who live and interact with each other, sometimes over decades, and who are thrust into so wide a variety of storylines and conflicts and crises, viewers are allowed to see characters as contradictory, complex and changeable. A good mother can be a terrible friend, or adulteress, or worse. A terrible tyrant in one sphere can be a doting godfather in another. A personally selfish, conniving woman can be a leading figure in a political or legal battle for a progressive cause. One often ruthlessly self-serving matriarch in *As the World Turns,* for example, dotes on the younger members of her dynasty and acts as a good and loyal friend to several other women characters, some decidedly beneath her socially. She is also often among the most welcoming and supportive characters to newcomers to the community, even as she ruthlessly schemes to rob and cheat her business and political opponents. Through complex narrative story lines, it is possible to portray a variety of women characters as being far from perfect but truly admirable in many ways rarely seen in American media.

But even when women characters are at their worst, when they are, for example, telling off an enemy or business opponent in the most outspokenly harsh way, there is often something gratifying to many women viewers in these outbursts of anger and vitriol. In fact, the tough women in soap communities are often most likable to fans when they are least "ladylike" and "nice." There is something refreshing, I would argue, in hearing women lash out in ways most of us would never dream of allowing ourselves to do. What seems "strong" in male leaders is so often seen as "abrasive" in women. And while viewers know—or should know—that behaving professionally in this way is not a good idea, there is a vicarious pleasure for many of us in seeing our own socially repressed urges acted out on the small screen with positive rather than negative results. That's why so many "villainesses" are among fan favorites: they seem to speak for all of us silenced women, even when what they are saying is not always commendable.

But the complexity of soaps' structures and characters, and their open-endedness, serve more than a merely personal, psychological function. There is also a truly utopian vision of a feminized, radically democratic political process in which difference and subtlety are recognized and honored within a community structure. To give one example, in one storyline developed over months of endless intrigue and complication in *All My Children,* a woman accused her ex-lover—who was actually her husband's son—of acquaintance rape. As the community discussed the case, taking sides, reviewing in detail her past sins, and recalling bits of their own histories and those of other characters in an effort to come to terms with the moral nuances of this case, an ongoing "community meeting" of sorts took place around this publicly charged issue.

As the trial itself played out, things—quite realistically in this case—looked bad for the defendant. Her checkered past and recent adultery with the accused made it difficult to imagine a jury believing her. But then the defendant, having witnessed a gang rape which suddenly put his own act in a new perspective, confessed, entered counseling and volunteered, upon release from prison, to work in a rape crisis center. In this way, viewers were taken through the experience in real time, in all its subtlety and nuance, and allowed to digest the emotional and political strands gradually, as one would indeed do in an ideal political setting in which all parties had adequate counsel and access to all the time and resources needed to locate and sift evidence, find and bring in witnesses, and deliberate. Soap operas, in this way, open a discursive space within which the characters and the audience form a kind of community. The experience is especially intense since the characters involved are so familiar to viewers and are "visited" virtually every day, for years on end.

The often bizarrely unconventional family and living arrangements which arise from the extended families and community relationships on soaps provide a similarly rich and complex representation of political structure and process. Again, Piercy's Mattapoisett is brought to mind in these utopian projections of a community which honors and accommodates the needs of all members for emotional and material support and security. Piercy's utopia articulates a private family realm in which various choices of sexual and child-care arrangements are allowed, to suit the varied and often changing tastes and inclinations of citizens. Children in Piercy's world have three biological parents and do not necessarily live with any. They may choose households that suit them, just as those who remain childless may find ways to relate to the children of the community that do not involve custodial care or biological connection.

Similar things happen on soaps. For example, a typical custody decision might, as was the case on *The Guiding Light,* rule that two single mothers—one the birth mother, who was a stylist at a low-rent salon, and the other the adoptive mother, the CEO of a major corporation—share custody in a way which gave the child two homes and mothers linked by a common community of support.

But parenting isn't the only problem for which soap communities provide utopian solutions. It is also common, on soaps, for people to move in and out of relationships and households often. The end of a relationship does not involve the kind of trauma and agony that today sends so many desperate people searching far and wide—even into cyberspace—in search of "support groups." Not on soaps. Support groups come to you. They find you sitting alone somewhere, or being beaten by a boyfriend, and they invite you to live with them or with some other character in need of just the service you can provide. Characters who are originally derelicts, ex-convicts or worse often wander into town and are immediately recognized for some wonderful character trait or talent and given a home and work.

Most theorists who have discussed utopia in popular or feminist works have described the engines of state as implicit. Richard Dyer (1985), in his analysis of Hollywood musicals, describes the ways in which popular commercial texts attempt—not always successfully—to work through and resolve the contradictions inherent in their efforts to suggest a utopian world within a system of representation very much tied to and dependent upon the existing order. For him, the solution involves a substitution of emotion for detailed political mapping. "Entertainment does not…present models of utopian worlds, as in the classic utopias of Sir Thomas More, William Morris, et al.," he says. "Rather the utopianism is contained in the feelings it embodies" (p. 229). Nonetheless, there is something much closer to an actual social model in the soap representation of community than Dyer finds in Hollywood musicals, although the soap model contains the same contradictions and "gap[s] between what is and what could be" (p. 229) that Dyer rightly attributes to all commercial forms.

To see how this is done, it is useful to compare Piercy's Mattapoisett with the soap imaginary. Mattapoisett, as a socialist-feminist utopia, includes detailed, discursive blueprints for ownership and decision-making processes. The political and economic foundations of soap institutions, while elaborately laid out, are far more contradictory and implausible. The most important difference is in the portrayal of ownership and property issues. Where Mattapoisett's public hearings and trials, elections and economic negotiations, family and child-care polices all grow organically out of its radically democratic and collectivized ownership and decision-making structures, soap operas simply impose a retrograde, almost medieval—and insanely implausible—structure of ownership and power relations upon their idyllic communities. In every soap, two or three corporate lords own virtually everything in the town and so provide all the employment and control all the media and other institutions. Nepotism and monopoly are givens in these realms.

Nonetheless, while these powerhouses are often the most "evil" of villains, things always work out in the interest of democracy, humanity and justice because justice and virtue always magically triumph. The corporate, patriarchal tyrants, at the proper moment, invariably undergo an always temporary period of conversion to "goodness" which allow them, despite all their evil deeds and ways, to remain a part of the community. The date rape trial and resolution are typical. But such things happen regularly to even the most powerful male figures. The most evil of corporate despots, for example, will have moments of moral rehabilitation, only to revert to their wicked ways until, yet again, caught, chastised and transformed.

Thus, "good" always emerges out of the "goodness" of human nature, a human nature which has no relation whatever to the social conditions in which it thrives. Race and gender and class never play a role in one's fate here—at least not for long. A "good" person—white or black, male or female, well born or orphaned—simply prospers through the goodness of her soul, as do the equally "good" power brokers and owners who provide material security and mete out perfect justice. If soaps are informed by a feminist set of values, then, it is a set of values based, in its root, on the most hopelessly essentialist assumptions, if not about gender difference, certainly about human nature. And even this essentialism is not consistent. Characters transform themselves from "good" to "bad" at the drop of a hat in accord with producers and sponsors, who have myriad considerations of their own in making these things happen.

It is by presenting so patently absurd a view of money and power that soaps manage to wholly elide the "Procter and Gamble" problem—the problem, that is, of how to present a world in which gender justice reigns without challenging the corporate structure that sponsors this fantasy world. Things happen on soaps in the same "magical" way—to use Raymond Williams's (1980) term—that they happen on commercials where, as Williams has shown, happiness, justice, freedom and so on are seen—quite magically—to arise out of the consumption of commodities which, in fact, have not the slightest ability to provide them. Similarly, on soap operas, justice and freedom and goodness and bliss arise quite magically out of a system which, if realistically portrayed, would inevitably thwart, by its very foundational principles, the very happiness it is shown to promote. The date rape trial is again a perfect example. A legal system in which, somehow, characters are compelled to act on principle, even if their very lives, fortunes or reputations are at stake, is a system very different from the one in which O.J. Simpson, for example, was tried and acquitted. For in the real world, money, class position and the gender biases that inform all institutions are driving forces not only in legal proceedings but also in the molding of a defendant's character and his decision-making processes.

Soaps are a bit like extended version of commercials, then, in which the "magical" thinking of sponsors is drawn out into long, equally implausible storylines. A social system in which an elitist ruling class runs every institution in it own interest somehow is presented as capable of meting out perfect justice and equity, even as commodities such as breakfast foods, fast food restaurants, shampoos and cars are seen as capable of smoothing the fault lines of a capitalist, post-industrialist world and bringing family and romantic harmony and joy to their consumers. The relation between commercials and dramas, after all, is integral. Dr. Cliff Warner of *All My Children*—late of the commercial "I'm not a doctor, but I play one on television" fame—shamelessly sold aspirins to a TV audience that wished to believe the medical and pharmaceutical industries operate by the humane and ethical principles that drive the doctors and hospitals on the soaps.

The feminist-informed public world of soaps, then, is one which bears absolutely no relationship to economic and political reality. Nonetheless, a fairly elaborate set of laws, rituals and policies, unmoored from economic and political reality, govern the social world of soaps. The trials follow actual legal practice, to a point. The board meetings and nurses stations and police procedures, for all their clumsy gaffes and goofs in the interest of plotline, operate according to a logic and system which are relatively coherent. If it is difficult to recognize these images of public life as "political," it may be because the melodramatic conventions of soaps render their political vision so unrealistic. But it is, in fact, the very use of melodramatic conventions that allows soap operas to so easily incorporate and transform traditional male political, legal and economic matters into an essentially feminine—and implicitly feminist—world view. Again, the date rape trial serves as a perfect example. It followed understandable, recognizable procedures of testimony from witnesses and principals, arguments from defense and prosecution, and sentencing hearings and decisions. The way in which characters were allowed to testify, however, was often unbelievably absurd. Characters, for example, were allowed to simply rise up and demand to be heard because of the "urgency" of the testimony they were suddenly moved to share or the events they were suddenly driven by conscience to reveal. No real court of law would allow such irregularities. Similarly, hearsay, personal opinion about motives and character, and so on, were included with no objections if they were crucial to a feminist-informed understanding of the issues in the case. The rapist's confession, for example, would have demanded any number of hearings and rulings to be permitted, once he had plead innocent. In soaps, however, doing the right thing, from a feminine, humane, point of view, is all that is needed for testimony to be considered relevant, or even crucial.

I have mentioned Carol Gilligan's (1982) moral vision as an implicit aspect of the soap imaginary. Similarly, Kathleen Jones (1988) applies feminist moral assumptions to traditional male theories of public sphere politics and suggests how they might lead to a radically transformed version of justice and political authority. "The standard analysis of authority in modern Western political theory begins with its definition as a set of rules governing political action, issued by those who are entitled to speak," she writes. But these rules, she notes "generally have excluded females and values associated with the feminine" (p. 119). Moreover, she argues, the "dominant discourse on authority," in placing "strict limits on the publicly expressible, and limit[ing] critical reflection about the norms and values that structure 'private' life and which affect the melodies of public speech," further ensures that female values will be marginalized within a private realm. Thus, "compassion, and related emotions" are rendered "irrelevant to law and other policy matters," she explains (pp. 130–131).

This is hardly the case on soaps. Compassion, especially, is always relevant. Because of this, all hearings and procedures arbitrate public matters in ways which implicitly, if implausibly, echo the political ideals of feminists. The 1960s model of consciousness-raising meetings and public speak-outs in which women linked private emotional suffering to public institutions and policies offers a useful comparison. In both, there is an effort to correct for the failings of the masculinist public sphere by recognizing the subjective and emotional realities of women's experience and demanding that they be included in official notions of justice and the common good. The custody hearing mentioned above, for example, was interrupted by the birth mother herself who, for love of the child, suddenly offered—without benefit of counsel—the compromise suggestion about shared mothering which the judge, a woman herself, accepted as ideal based on a shared notion of what was best for the child rather than issues of property, money or paternal rights. The key was the wrenching, heart-breaking sincerity of the two obviously deeply loving women. Nor was there ever any mention—and this would be unthinkable in the real world—of the financial arrangements between the two very differently propertied and positioned women or any of the other social or material issues which, in real life, dominate custody hearings.

That soaps are excessively melodramatic and emotional—and therefore highly *un*realistic—is, from a feminist viewpoint, affirmative. In feminist theory, it is the exclusion of the values of the private, domestic sphere from issues of justice and equality that must be addressed and corrected. But, of course, in aggressively injecting such values into the portrayal of every sphere of life and flagrantly rejecting the conventions of esthetic realism valorized in our culture, soaps risk the laughter and derision of those who maintain the artistic and literary canons.

The (gender- and class-based) shame that fans feel in watching soaps is therefore understandable. But it is based on a faulty psychological assumption that fans too often internalize: that pleasure in soap amounts to taking them at face value. This is hardly the case. In fact, laughter and ridicule are very much a part of the viewing experience of fans. Fans understand and laugh about the contradiction and "gaps" of the form. This is in fact among the most sophisticated pleasures of viewing. This aspect of viewership became an important part of my pleasure in the viewing session I shared with my children. As they grew older and more sophisticated about politics and narrative, the issue of "realism" periodically arose in contexts that engendered increasingly vexed relationships between social reality and what is filtered through the lens of popular culture texts.

Nor are our conversations as one-dimensional as when we were simply looking for "positive images." Today we are likely to jumble together, in any conversation, in ways which make perfect sense to us, facts and tidbits from soap narratives, actual social issues, personal issues and our knowledge of behind the scenes information about why plot lines and characters are being done in the ways they are done, and many other things.

Michel Foucault (1965), in writing about in writing about the relationship between art and madness credits art with "interrupting" the tyranny of bourgeois reason and allowing for the return of the repressed. The work of art "opens a space where the world is made aware of its guilt." But soaps go further. They offer a glimpse of a world in which the guilty may be redeemed. And when we laugh at the absurdity of this vision, we are, at the very least, acknowledging the distance between our dreams and our reality in a way that those whose tastes run only to the more fashionably cynical forms may be able to avoid.

Bibliography

Ang, I. (1985).*Watching Dallas: Soap opera and the melodramatic imagination.* New York: Methuen.

Bammer, A. (1991). *Partial visions: Feminism and utopianism in the 1970s.* New York: Routledge.

Bartkowski, F. (1989). *Feminist utopias.* Lincoln, Neb.: Nebraska University Press.

de Beauvoir, S. (1961). *The second sex.* New York: Bantam Books.

Dyer, R. (1985). Entertainment and utopia. In B. Nichols (Ed.) *Movies and methods: Vol. II.* Berkeley: University of California Press.

Ehrenreich, B. & English, D. (1978). *For her own good: 150 Years of the experts' advice to women.* New York: Anchor.

Fineman, M. & McCluskey, M. (1996). *Feminism, media and the law.* Oxford: Oxford University Press.

Fineman, M. & Thomadsen, N. (1991). *At the boundaries of law: Feminism and legal theory.* New York: Routledge.

Fiske, J. (1987). *Television culture.* New York: Methuen.

Foucault, M. (1965). *Madness and civilization.* New York: Random House.

Gilligan, C. (1982). *In another voice: Psychological theory and women's development.* Cambridge, MA: Harvard University Press.

Gledhill, C. (1987). *Home is where the heart is: Studies in melodrama and the womens' film.* London: BFI.

Hansen, K. & Philipson, I. (1990).*Women, class and the feminist imagination.* Philadelphia: Temple University Press.

Jameson, F. (1990). Reification and utopia in mass culture. In *Signatures of the visible* (pp. 9–34). New York & London: Routledge.

Jameson, F. (1975). World reduction in LeGuin: The emergence of utopian narrative. *Science Fiction Studies,* 2(3), 221–230.

Jones, K. (1988). On authority: Or, why women are not entitled to speak. In I. Diamond & L. Quinby (Eds.) *Feminism and Foucault: Reflections on resistance.* Boston: Northeastern University Press.

Marcuse, H. (1968). *Negotiations.* Boston: Beacon Press.

Modleski, T. (1982). *Loving with a vengeance: Mass-produced fantasies for women.* New York: Methuen.

Nochimson, T. & M. (1992). *No end to her: Soap opera and the female subject.* Berkeley: University of California Press.

Piercy, M. (1985). *Women on the edge of time.* New York: Fawcett Books.

Schatz, T. (1991). *Hollywood genres: Formulas, filmmaking and the studio system.* Philadelphia: Temple University Press.

Spence, L. (1995). They killed off Marlena, but she's on another show now. In R. Allen (Ed.) *To be continued…: Soap operas around the world.* New York: Routledge.

Williams, R. (1980). Advertising: The magic system. In *Problems in materialism and culture.* London: Verso.

Williams, R. (1973). *Key words: A vocabulary of culture and society.* Oxford: Oxford University Press.

20

■ Social Class and Entertainment Television

What's So Real and New about Reality TV?

Pepi Leistyna

Corporate bodies take the fact that culture shapes our sense of political agency very seriously and mediates the relations between everyday struggles and structures of power. In fact, in this age of postmodern technologies that can saturate society with media messages, elite private interests have worked diligently to monopolize the means of production and distribution of information and ideas so as to be able to more effectively circulate, legitimate, and reproduce a vision of the world that suits their needs (Allan & Hill, 2004; Bourdieu, 1996; Carey, 1995; Durham & Kellner, 2001; Hall, 1997; Parenti, 1992).[1] While there is a plethora of ways in which agencies of knowledge production like schools, houses of faith, and the media, are strategically used to engineer history and shape public consciousness, one of the pedagogical forces that needs to be watched more closely is entertainment television.[2]

Television in the United States is largely controlled by five massive transnational corporations: Time Warner (which among its many assets, owns and operates CNN, Turner Classic Movies, HBO, Court TV, TNT, TBS, and the Cartoon Network); Disney (owns ABC, ESPN, the Disney Channel, The History Channel, A&E, Biography, Military History, Lifetime, E, The Style Network, and Soapnet); News Corporation (owns Fox, National Geographic Channel, Direct TV, FX, and STAR); General Electric (owns NBC, Telemundo, Bravo, MSNBC, CNBC, Sci Fi, Paxon, the USA Network, and Sundance—which is a joint venture with CBS); and Viacom (owns CBS, MTV, Showtime, Comedy Central, BET, TV Land, VH1, CMT, Nick at Nite, Spike TV, and Nickelodeon). It's important to look critically at the stories these corporate-managed media channels script and ask:

whose interests are served by such representations, and what alternative visions of the world are available to the public?

When it comes to labor in the United States, network television has a long history of constructing tales about the lives of working people that reinforce classist, racist, and sexist stereotypes that serve to justify the inequities inherent in capitalism's class structure. The following chapter explores what images the recent wave of reality TV has brought to the entertainment table. Does this ubiquitous genre break away from, or simply reinforce, the network mold of denigrating working-class identities?

■ What's Been the Norm?

The working class has always found its image on entertainment television. In the early years of broadcasting, working-class and immigrant families appeared regularly on shows like *I Remember Mama* (1949–1957), *The Goldbergs* (1949–1955), and *Life with Luigi* (1952–1953), which featured Norwegian, Jewish, and Italian families.[3]

As TV evolved as a commercially sponsored medium, advertisers took the reins in steering the creation and production of programs, including script writing and hiring of talent (Barnouw, 1978). Advertisers worked diligently to redefine the meaning of the American Dream from the search for a better life, to the pursuit of a consumer lifestyle. Working together, producers and advertisers understood that associating products with middle- and upper-class lifestyles would increase both ratings and sales. They effectively perpetuated the myth that buying products would bring about class mobility (Lipsitz, 2002). Unlike on radio, where many of the earlier shows got their start, on television you can really see what the assimilation process is supposed to look like, according to the advertising-driven media. It's the acquisition of consumer goods, becoming less ethnic, and looking more like middle-class American families with aspirations. The stark contrast between the gritty image of working-class life, and the shiny sanitized world of consumer advertising, proved to be irreconcilable (Barnouw, 1978). As television became more consolidated in the late 50's and the early 60's, working-class and immigrant families would gradually disappear. On the contrary, programs that could provide a pristine setting for product placement and articulate the needs of a healthy, successful middle-class family living the American dream would take center stage—shows such as: *I Married Joan* (1952–1955), *The Adventures of Ozzy and Harriet* (1952–1966), *Make Room for Daddy* (1953–1965), *Father Knows Best* (1954–1960), *Leave it to Beaver* (1957–1963), *Dennis the Menace* (1959–1963), and *The Dick Van Dyke Show* (1961–1969).[4]

In the 1950s as the white working class was disappearing into the classless middle, African Americans and other racially subordinated groups continued to endure the horrors of white supremacy, coupled with the exploitative logic of capital.[5] Disregarding these harsh realities, TV's fantasy land only allowed people of color to be visible as happy servants or entertainers on programs like *Beulah* (1950–1953) and *The Nat "King" Cole Show* (1956–1957) (Riggs, 1991; Gray, 1995).[6]

In order to gain broader access to television, blacks and other marginalized groups would have to learn to play by TV's rules—namely to have faith in the American Dream.[7] While this logic has served television's commercial imperatives, it has also reduced struggles for economic justice and social equality to a simple matter of inclusion.

In the post-civil rights era, the arrival of African Americans onto primetime television with shows like *Sanford and Son* (1972–1977), *Fat Albert and the Cosby Kids* (1972–1980), *Good Times* (1974–1979), *Grady* (1975–1976), *What's Happening* (1976–1979), and *That's My Momma* (1974–1975), suggests that there is no need for the redistribution of wealth and power because on TV, there is plenty of room for everyone. As Marlon Riggs (1991) notes in his documentary film *Color Adjustment,* in large part these sitcoms cast ghetto life in a happy light where opportunity was simply a question of initiative. He also reveals how *Good Times* showed real potential to take on some of the harsh realities of class exploitation and racism—potential that was quickly extinguished because of the transparent political content of some of the earlier episodes. And of course, in the spirit of the American Dream and meritocracy, by the last episode—as with so many of these programs, the family escapes the ghetto and moves into the middle class.[8]

The other storyline running through black sitcoms during this period dealt with this idea of "moving on up," but these shows didn't address economic hardship at all. The best known example is *The Jeffersons* (1975–1985) with the self-made man, George Jefferson. George's hard work and entrepreneurial spirit ensure the success of his dry cleaning business and consequently allows his family to "move on up" to the East Side. As Robin Kelly argues:

> He proves that black people are successful, so therefore the Civil Rights Movement is over. He proves that there is no need for affirmative action because he is a self-made man. He proves that there is no need for welfare because these people can make it on their own. (interview in *Class Dismissed,* 2005)

The Cosby Show (1984–1992) was also controversial in this respect. While the sitcom provided an important non-stereotypical image of a black family that countered the overwhelmingly pejorative representations that preceded it, the show nonetheless disregarded the harsh realities faced by poor and working-class people of color, and it made it look like the middle class is open to anyone (Dyson, 1993; Jhally & Lewis, 1992; Riggs, 1991). It's important to note that, while still very popular, the show went off the air the year of the Los Angeles uprisings.

This same ideology of openness and arrival is embedded in more recent shows that feature African Americans such as *Martin* (1992–1997), *The Hughleys* (1998–2002),[9] *The Bernie Mac Show* (2001–present), *My Wife and Kids* (2001–2005), *All of Us* (2003–present), and *That's So Raven* (2003–present). While these shows depict the everyday lives of people, they are scripted outside of the reality that 30.4% of black workers and 39.8% of Latino/a workers earn low wages (Economic Policy Institute, 2004/2005). The median income of racially subordinated families is $25,700, as compared with white families—$45,200 (Dollars & Sense & United for a Fair Economy, 2004). The unemployment rate for African Americans and Latino/as over the years has remained more than double that of whites. While about 10% of white children live in poverty in the United States, over 30% of

African American and Latino/a kids experience economic hardship. Representations that capture these realities are at best few and far between.

There have been some black working-class characters on situation comedies; for example, the *Fresh Prince of Bel Air* (1990–1996). This character played by actor Will Smith is having some trouble in the ghetto, so he's shipped off to live with his rich relatives in Bel Air—leaving his single mom behind in the hood. In this post-Cosby world, there is no need for government programs to provide much-needed social services and economic support because there are wealthy black families that can rescue troubled youth and offer them all of the necessities for social advancement.[10]

There are other shows like *Eastside Westside* (1963), *Frank's Place* (1987–1988), and *Roc* (1991–1994) that have taken up some of the complexities of race and class politics. However, either because of the controversial nature of the material, or the fact that networks have done such a poor job of promoting these shows and building audiences for them, they don't last long.

With the exception of a few prominent roles (featuring middle- and upper-middle-class characters) on shows like *ER* (1994–present), *Law & Order: Special Victims Unit* (1999–present), and *Grey's Anatomy* (2005–present), Asian Americans are still largely excluded from prime time, or relegated to bit parts (Hamamoto, 1994). And while the growing importance of the Latino/a demographic has resulted in a small increase in representations [e.g., *The Brothers Garcia* (2000–2004), *Resurrection Blvd.* (2000–2002), and *American Family* (2002–2004)], most Latinos are still confined to cable and Spanish-language networks, and are overwhelmingly middle class (Davila, 2001; Negrón-Muntaner, 2004; Rodriguez, 1997).[11] The only show to feature a working-class Latino character since *Chico and the Man* (1974–1978) is *The George Lopez Show* (2002–present).[12] But unlike the characters of the ghetto sitcom era who are trying to move out of the working class, George Lopez has already left it behind and moved up to the comfortable familiarity of the middle-class family sitcom.

The George Lopez Show is a perfect example of how the American dream is supposed to work. A former assembly line worker, George is promoted to manager of the factory. Suddenly he has no problems. He lives in a beautiful space. His family has no problems other than what typical American middle-class families supposedly go through. And the only thing that marks him as working class is his mom and his buddies back at the factory that refer to him as "Mr. Clipboard."[13] It's pretty comical that the producers chose to use *Low Rider* as the theme song for the show. While this is a song about urban Latino/a culture, there's a total disconnect between the song and who this middle-class character is—there's nothing *Low Rider* about George Lopez. In fact, if anything, the show eclipses the reality that the overwhelming majority of Latino/as in the United States suffer the abuses of immigration discrimination, labor exploitation, unemployment, and racism.[14]

■ Women with Class

While they have never been excluded like other underrepresented groups, television largely ignores the economic realities faced by so many women in this country (Bettie,

2003; Douglas, 1995; Press, 1991). Across the board, women earn less than men regardless of education, and they often work a double shift as part of the paid labor force, and as unpaid caretakers of the home and family. On average, women make 77 cents to a man's dollar. Median income for men in the United States is $40,800; for women, it is $31,200. The leading occupations for women are all lower-middle and working-class jobs. In addition, the majority of jobs at the bottom of the economic scale are held by women, especially women of color. In 2003, "33.9% of Black women and 45.8% of Latinas earned low wages" (Economic Policy Institute, 2004/2005, p. 130). Not only does television disregard these realities, it rarely even depicts work as an economic necessity. This is evident in older shows that feature female characters such as *Bewitched* (1964–1972) and *The Brady Bunch* (1969–1974) (where even Alice, the family maid, is happy and carefree),[15] and in more recent programs like *Friends* (1994–2004) and *Sex & the City* (1998–2004).

In the last three decades, the number of households headed by single moms has remained fairly constant, at around 80%. With an average income of only $24,000, single moms experience poverty at a rate that is substantially higher (28%) than the national average (13%) (U.S. Census Bureau, 2003). Single moms, in shows like *Julia* (1968–1971), *The Partridge Family* (1970–1974), *One Day at a Time* (1975–1984), *Murphy Brown* (1988–1998), *Ally McBeal* (1997–2002), *Judging Amy* (1999–2005), *The Parkers* (1999–2004), *The Gilmore Girls* (2000–present), and *Reba* (2001–present) don't reflect the reality of single mothers' lives.

We've only seen a handful of working-class female characters on entertainment television. Most women, even single moms, have been middle-class characters in career jobs where money isn't paramount. The few shows that have portrayed women struggling economically don't deal directly with class issues. These are women who are simply down on their luck [e.g., *Alice* (1976–1985)], they've lost their husbands, or they've made a really bad choice for a husband. A perfect example of this is *Grace under Fire* (1993–1998); she's divorced with two kids and a recovering alcoholic. Her ex-husband Jimmy, also an alcoholic, offers the family very little support. While she deals with serious issues, what this show is really about is one woman's determination to not make the same mistakes that she's made in the past. So in other words, her obstacles are self-imposed, and so it's her responsibility to transcend them.

Really the only show to put gender and class together is *Roseanne* (1988–1997).[16] It aired in the late 1980s at a time when network ratings were down, and ABC was willing to take a chance on it. It's important to note that the decision to air the show was not made in order to democratize the air waves by finally including the realities and struggles of a working-class family. With ratings down, the corporate media were simply desperate for new and attractive ideas. In addition, as Rhoda Zuk (1998) reveals, the production company responsible for putting the program together was able to hire non-union workers for all aspects of the show:

> Such activity gives the lie to an apparently well-meaning production designed to communicate the affective life of a large group materially disadvantaged by the overriding of workers' organization. (p. 3)

Roseanne also appears in the midst of a feminist backlash where the ideology is essentially that women have won equal rights; they've arrived, and they don't need feminism anymore. But what was really going on at the time was an attack against all working women, who were being blamed for the disruption in the family for going to work.

Regardless of the pressures to tone down the program and her public political persona, Roseanne insisted that her sitcom be a feminist show about a working-class family and address issues that are basic to feminism: the division of labor in the family, and the need for good childcare and employment. Barbara Ehrenreich adds: "Now and then it would actually follow Roseanne into her workplace, her confrontations with her bosses; that's a rare event on TV—might give people ideas I guess so they don't show it too often" (interview in *Class Dismissed,* 2005). *Roseanne* was also revolutionary in that it didn't use the father figure to reinforce the stereotype that working-class men are all a bunch of buffoons (Freed, 2002).[17]

■ Class Bozos

In order to reinforce its middle-class ideology, television must account for the members of the working class who haven't made it. TV has reproduced the deeply ingrained belief that worker's inadequacies are to blame for their lack of advancement. In reality, most Americans do not change their class position, and the boundaries of social class are now more restrictive than ever. Television representations either perpetuate the idea that the cream always rises to the top, or they reinforce stereotypes about workers' failure to succeed due to their inferior qualities such as bad taste, lack of intelligence, reactionary politics, poor work ethic, and dysfunctional family values (Aronowitz, 1992; Butsch, 2002).[18]

One of the flaws that is supposedly characteristic of the working class that is widely circulated in popular culture, and in which TV plays an important role in that circulation, pertains to taste, lifestyle, and leisure. A stereotypical image that we get is a bunch of slobs sitting around on some cheesy couch drinking beer, preferably brown bottle or can beer, and starring endlessly at the tube. Given their love of junk culture, we don't get the sense that they are deserving of the finer things in life—they wouldn't appreciate them anyway. On entertainment television, we don't get the idea that working-class characters are economically deprived; rather, their low tolerance and limited access to the 'virtues of high culture' are attributed to personal taste and choice.

When working-class characters do try to move out of this space and hob-knob with the middle and upper classes, it's made really laughable because they're so awkward in this new environment—they don't have the cultural capital to navigate it. TV plays on this, in particular sitcoms [e.g., older shows like *Laverne & Shirley* (1976–1983) and more recent programs such as *The Nanny* (1993–1999)].[19]

Another debilitating characteristic of this group of people, according to the stereotype, is that working-class men lack intelligence. It's obvious they weren't good students. They often fumble the language and a lot of basic stuff just goes right over their heads. The classic character of the lovable but laughable buffoon that is still very much with us today was played by Jackie Gleason in *The Honeymooners* (1955–1956), in the character of Ralph

Cramden (Aronowitz, 1992; Butsch, 2002). This show was preceded by *Life of Riley* (1945–1950), where Gleason played the bumbling father.[20]

In *The Honeymooners,* Gleason is a city bus driver who hates his job. He's loud and blustery and always coming up with ridiculous money-making schemes, and the real joke is that we know that he's not that smart. He has this sidekick, Ed Norton, who's this dimwitted, but lovable, happy-go-lucky sewer worker. While eating, Ed tells Ralph, "Man, I'm telling you, if pizzas were manhole covers, the sewer would be a paradise!"

These class clowns get reproduced in the 1960s with *The Flintstones* (1960–1966). Even though it's set back in the Stone Age, Fred is the direct descendant of Ralph Cramden and Barney is definitely the son of Ed Norton. And what follows is a whole parade of dumb working-class guys whose stupidity is the brunt of the joke (e.g., *Gilligan's Island* (1964–1967), *Welcome Back Kotter* (1975–1979), *Taxi* (1978–1983), *Working Stiffs* (1979), *Cheers* (1982–1993), *Momma's Family* (1983–1990—which was taken from a skit on *The Carol Burnett Show* (1967–1978)], *Married with Children* (1987–1997), *The Simpsons* (1989–present), *Dinosaurs* (1991–1994), *The Drew Carey Show* (1995–2004), *The King of Queens* (1998–2007), *King of the Hill* (1997–present), *My Name Is Earl* (2005–present), and *Lucky Louie* (2006–present)).[21]

The Honeymooners is also an important prototype for a particular gender dynamic.[22] Because these guys are so lacking in common sense, and the wives are obviously smarter, it's the women who end up ruling the roost (Butsch, 2002; Riggs, 1991). What we end up with is a reversal of traditional gender roles where these guys are essentially incapable of taking their place at the head of the household.

It's not just the wives. In a typical working-class household, even the kids are smarter than the dad. This is really evident in shows like *The Simpsons* (1989–present), in the father son relationship in *Married with Children* (1987–1997), and in *Still Standing* (2002–present).

The working class is being blamed for not being educated enough to compete in a global economy, and yet we have one of the most educated workforces in the world, regardless of the fact that our public education system is highly class based. It's also ironic that given this claim of lack of education, corporations are moving to 'third world' countries where there is enormous illiteracy in order to find "cheap" labor.

On corporate-run TV, there is a recurring representation that the working class has no interest in education as they wallow in anti-intellectualism. They have no interest in reading, unless it's the sports page, the comics, or a tabloid of some sort. The history of the working class fighting for public education is nowhere to be found. There's a reason for these stereotypes: they distract us from the structural realities, especially the unequal distribution of resources in public education that inhibit people's lives. But what's worse is they disregard the fact that the overwhelming majority of working-class parents really do care about their kids' education.

The working class is also represented as being disinterested in politics, which is ridiculous if you think about working-class history, and the struggle for basic rights and a living wage. When we do get characters that are interested in politics, they're almost always staunch conservatives, bigots, and closed-minded. The archetypal figure here is Archie Bunker from *All in the Family* (1971–1979), a character that for a long time was a stand-in for working-class guys.

Perhaps the most blatant representational crime against the working class by this corporate media is this image of this lazy, incompetent worker, who's complacent and not interested in improving his or her lot in life.[23] These characters have no leadership skills and they are in constant need of supervision. In this era of globalization with enormous job loss, outsourcing and off-shoring, corporations need a scapegoat for their avarice activity, and the scapegoat is the working class who is not working hard enough and yet, since 1975, productivity is way up (163%); who's asking for too much money, and yet wages are stagnant (115%) and profits are through the roof (758%).

When it comes to family values, in the late 1980s and early 1990s there's a dramatic shift away from the omnipresent image of the happy, homogenous, nuclear family. This era that is often referred to as "Loser TV," gave birth to shows like *Married with Children, The Simpsons, Jerry Springer* (1991–present), and *Beavis and Butthead* (1993–1997). These shows appear at the tail end of eight years of Ronald Reagan, when the country was going through some serious economic turmoil. But instead of looking at downsizing, layoffs, unemployment, and corporate greed, these working-class couples are seen as the poster child of bad parenting, and hence the source of all society's ills. They certainly don't have the wisdom, discipline, and morality of the middle-class parents of other shows.[24]

These families give rise to a couple different kinds of children, either they are smart and talented, which reinforces the myth of meritocracy—these kids are going to make it out regardless of the circumstances, or they are deviant in a number of ways—the Bart Simpson type.[25]

The two biggest troublemakers are definitely Beavis and Butthead. These guys celebrate stupidity, and they live for sex and violence. The show plays on a generation of youth raised on a media-saturated society of junk culture, commodity, and alienation where the parents are driven out of the home and into the labor force, and where the TV becomes the babysitter and the role model (Kellner, 1997). As Doug Kellner notes, there surely is an element of working-class revenge for these two guys who come from broken homes in a disintegrating community, where school and work in the fast-food industry are meaningless, and where they are downwardly mobile with a bleak future, if any. Shows like *The Simpsons* and *Beavis and Butthead* do offer a critique of our corporate-driven society. These guys know that something is wrong. But the problem is that their actions are just individualized acts of rebellion—their response is to trash stuff. As a consequence, such behavior ends up being self-destructive, rather than transformative.

■ Race, Deviance, and Class

Outside of the comic frame, there is a different and more threatening image of the working class on crime shows. Because this genre does not use class as a lens to view criminal behavior, deviance is most often framed in racial or cultural terms. The 70s and 80s are filled with cop shows that criminalize the black culture.[26] The more recent incarnation of such shows [e.g., *Cops* (1989–present), *Homicide: Life on the Street* (1993–1999), *NYPD*

Blue (1993–2005), *Oz* (1997–2003), *The Shield* (2002–present), and *Dog the Bounty Hunter* (2004–present)] continue to do important ideological work. They justify the growing prison system that now has a record 2.1 million people behind bars—over 70% of whom are non-white. African American males make up the largest number of those entering prisons each year in the United States. Racially subordinated women are also being incarcerated in epidemic proportions. As Loic Wacquant (2002) states, "The astounding upsurge in Black incarceration in the past three decades results from the obsolescence of the ghetto as a device for caste control and the correlative need for a substitute apparatus for keeping (unskilled) African Americans in a subordinate and confined position—physically, socially, and symbolically" (p. 23).[27] And of course, these images are scripted outside of any analysis of racism and the poverty caused by capitalism. 37 million people in this country live in poverty, a number that is up 1.1 million from 2003. According to the U.S. Department of Agriculture, there are 25.5 million people who rely on food stamps to avoid hunger—a number that is up 2 million from 2004. 6.8 million families live in poverty. 17% of the nation's children, or about 12 million kids, are compelled to endure inhumane economic conditions. An Urban Institute study recently revealed that about 3.5 million people are homeless in the U.S. (a number projected to increase 5% each year), and 1.3 million (or 39%) of them are children (National Coalition for the Homeless, 2002).

The largest group of poor people in the United States is white. Yet we have a very limited understanding of who they are, because their images historically have been so few and far between. And because whiteness is associated with a dominant culture, poor and working-class whites are usually portrayed as cultural outcasts or a subculture. And while TV mocks their condition, it gladly uses their image to entertain us.

The rural working class is nearly invisible in mainstream culture. What we find on television are these twisted comedic images, which, like the ghetto sitcoms, really pastoralize poverty. The earlier images were of hillbilly characters popularized on shows like *Ma & Pa Kettle* (1954) and *The Real McCoys* (1951–1963). And these are followed by the 'idiot sitcom era,' with country bumpkin shows like *The Beverly Hillbillies* (1962–1971), *Andy Griffith* (1961–1968), *Gomer Pyle* (1964–1970), *Green Acres* (1965–1971), and *Petticoat Junction* (1963–1970), which featured characters who were simple-minded, non-threatening, and really easy to laugh at. These shows would be followed by *Hee-Haw* (1969–1993), *The Dukes of Hazard* (1979–1985), *Newhart* (1982–1990), *Enos* (1980–1981), and *The Dukes* (1983–1984).[28]

The guy who resurrected the hillbilly and has given it new life as "redneck pride," is Jeff Foxworthy. From comedy tours to films to a cable show, *Blue Collar TV* (2004–present), being a redneck seems like a lifestyle which includes NASCAR and country music. What Foxworthy has done, is to take what in reality is an economic position and make it look like a lifestyle choice.

As the effects of the economic downturn become more visible, so is this more threatening image of the white poor who're being popularized as white trash. All these types, the hillbilly, the redneck, and white trash are racially coded terms to describe a genetic subset of white people—lowlifes. So Jerry Springer, who introduces his show with a television in the trashcan, is where all the qualities associated with white trash are on display: a lack of desire to work, sexual perversion, incest, and so on. In a similar spirit, *Geraldo* (1987–1998—hosted by Geraldo Rivera), created a perverse spectacle that was described by *Newsweek* as "trash TV." It's interesting because this is a multiracial world— it's a sort of equal opportunity spectacle. The common link that brings them all together is social class.

While presented with a touch of seriousness and professionalism, there is a similar entertainment strategy used on talk shows such as *Sally Jesse Raphael* (1985–2002), *Montel Williams* (1991–present), *Jenny Jones* (1991–2003), *Riki Lake* (1993–2004), and *The Maury Povich Show* (1998–present). They often have programs about working-class children who are out of control. A popular response is to send these deviant youth to military boot camp or prison and televise the spectacle.

Courtroom series also play a role in reproducing the image of working-class cheats and buffoons [e.g., *Judge Judy* (1996–present) and *Judge Joe Brown* (1998–present)].

■ What's Reality TV Got to Offer?

Unfortunately, reality TV on the networks is a spitting image of the past, in that they generally provide a stock working-class character who is presented as crass and dysfunctional [e.g., *The Real World* (1992–present), *The Amazing Race* (2001–present), *Big Brother* (2000–present)]. In its first year, *Survivor* (2000–present)[29] drew a great deal of attention because of Susan Hawk, a Midwestern truck driver whose accent and etiquette epitomized the stereotype of the tacky, abrasive, working-class character. Hawk's gender is also important as working-class women have long been bombarded with the stereotype of being trashy, especially "fake blonds." *The Anna Nicole Smith Show* (2002–2003) is an egregious recent example of this, as we have the movement of a woman from Texas, where she was abandoned by her father and was raised by her mother and aunt, to exotic dancer, to billionaire. What she brings to her new class status is from the gutter.[30]

Reality TV has played a significant role in perpetuating the myth that one way for the working class to fit into this upper-class world, is to get a personal makeover. There are a slew of reality shows that are dedicated to this process. In the opening credits of *I Want to Be a Hilton* (2005), a "poorly dressed" young woman is standing in front of her trailer-like home and says into the camera, "I want to trade in my blue-collar life." This is followed by all the contestants on the show proclaiming "I want to be a Hilton," that is, a member of the wealthy hotel family, as they prepare themselves for the etiquette classes and challenges that the multi-millionaire matriarch will put them through in order to win this status.

Joe Millionaire (2003–2004) is another prime example of this make over process where you take these working-class guys and you give them the necessary social skills and etiquette to pass as moneyed.

There are a number of other shows that are about physical transformation and class advancement. The idea that bodily perfection leads to upward mobility is reinforced on shows like *The Swan* (2004) and *Extreme Makeover* (2003–2005), where people even go under the knife in order to change the way they look.[31] And not only that, now you can make over your house on shows like *Trading Spaces* (2000–present) and *Design on a Dime* (2003–2006), as well as your junk box car—on *Pimp My Ride* (2004–present). Then there's *Queer Eye for the Straight Guy* (2003–present) that goes for the whole package—the body and the house.[32]

This ideological thread has been woven into Web TV as well. The new program, *Brawny Academy.com* (2006) is an attempt to clean up sloppy men.[33]

None of this actually changes a person's class position or the economic conditions that have created their situation in the first place. If you want a real class makeover you are going to have to radically change the economic system. Now that would make for a really interesting reality show. That was supposed to be the intent of the new program *Kid Nation* (2007), where a bunch of kids are dropped off in an old western town in order to create a new and better world. While the show stresses the difficulty in creating a viable society, one of the rules of the town is that there is a class hierarchy: the rich, the managerial class, and the workers. Capitalist social relations undergird the process as if it were natural and inevitable; however, it is precisely this economic logic—which never gets named in the show—that makes equity and survival within this budding world impossible.

But, when it comes to reality TV, it's not all bad news. An independent, international cable company has recently been selling the public new images of labor. With 1.5 billion subscribers across 170 countries, Discovery Communications Inc.—owned by Discovery Holding Co., includes the Discovery Channel, the Learning Channel, Animal Planet, the Science Channel, and Discovery Health. Ranked the number one nonfiction television and media brand globally, what do its reality TV shows *Dirtiest Jobs, Miami Ink, American Chopper, Deadliest Catch,* and *Lobster Wars* have to offer?

Dirtiest Jobs was piloted in 2003 and has run as a series since 2005. Aired internationally, and one of the most popular shows on the Discovery Channel, this program is based on former opera singer Mike Rowe—a clean-cut, articulate TV personality with a witty sense of humor—getting down and dirty with real workers doing undesirable, often dangerous, but vital jobs. What's refreshing here is that Rowe and his camera crew show respect for the people showcased and how they make a living. Even the music selected for the program reveals a sense of dignity—*We Care a Lot* by the band "Faith No More" has been used as the theme song.

Miami Ink is a reality show about life in a tattoo shop in Miami Beach, Florida. Now in its third season, and aired worldwide, the basic premise of the show is to follow the stories of people getting tattoos in a newly established business that is co-owned by two artists. Beyond being innovative in its content and format, *Miami Ink* works to rupture a number of deeply embedded stereotypes about tattooing and the kinds of people who engage in this practice. The workers on this show take their trade very seriously, and they demand that their labor-intensive efforts be portrayed as an artistic endeavor that deserves respect.

American Chopper, which recently moved from the Discovery Channel to the Learning Channel, chronicles life inside a father and son motorcycle business in Orange County, New York. Already in its fifth season, this popular series is built around Paul Teutul, Sr.

and his son Paul Jr. building custom choppers on a tight schedule. Each episode follows the team as they design and build a dream bike for an eagerly waiting customer. The show's primary tension is built on two very different visions of the world of work: there's Paul Sr. who is a neatness freak and a workhorse, and then there's the more creative Paulie, who enjoys life at a very different pace.

Deadliest Catch is a documentary-style television series that chronicles life on the Bering Sea aboard fishing boats that are in search of Alaskan king crab. Created from two short documentaries on the same subject, the series first aired in 2005. With cameras mounted on the fishing boats, the audience gets a bird's eye view of the trials and tribulations of life on the high seas. Viewers also get a taste of the working relationships that develop between the captains and their crew as they brave the insane conditions that Mother Nature has to throw at them, in order to make enough money during the short fishing season for their families and businesses to survive for the entire year. As Mike Rowe, who also narrates this show, constantly reminds the viewer, this is the most dangerous job on the planet—a fact according to the Bureau of Labor Statistics. It's evident that these guys are willing to work really hard under the worst of conditions, and they are deeply committed to their trade, their vessel, their co-workers, and their families.

The show, which commands a huge audience, was nominated for four Primetime Emmy Awards this year, and a number of other prestigious honors including Outstanding Nonfiction Series.

Now in its first season, *Lobster Wars* is a spin-off of *Deadliest Catch.* Following the same general motif, the program explores the culture of lobster fishing off George's Bank in the North Atlantic. The show features five crews, and focuses on the difficulties of making a living at sea in the middle of winter when fishing is at its peak, and the struggles of keeping operations running in such a fickle industry. Like the crew members featured on *Deadliest Catch,* these workers are portrayed as having a serious work ethic and a deep respect for the traditions and practices that make up their trade.

One of the most refreshing features of Discovery's reality TV shows is that they actually depict working-class people on the job. What's also unusual here, in particular on *Dirtiest Jobs, Miami Ink,* and *Lobster Wars,* is that real women are shown working side-by-side with the men.

Now there's certainly plenty of testosterone and macho nonsense flying around these shows, and room for a lot more stories of working women, but featuring working-class women on the job is atypical in TV land, regardless of the fact that women make up 52% of the population and a large part of the workforce. Tattoo artist Kat Von D, who appeared on *Miami Ink* for a short stint, is featured in the spin-off *LA Ink* which opened this season. Unfortunately, her show is all about chasing men, and her example of a strong woman is Jenna Jameson, a porn star.

While Discovery's shows do a far better job than primetime television when it comes to including working-class women, they too are in need of more economic and political contextualization. Even though the shows are intended to be educational, they offer very little in the form of teaching about survival within current labor conditions. *Dirtiest Jobs,* for example, would be far more interesting and educational if it were to discuss how workers currently face a declining standard of living, and the loss of job security. The reality is that within the inhumane conditions of capitalism, the average income in the United States is shrinking and workers are earning less, adjusting for inflation, than they did a quarter century ago. Real wages are falling at their fastest rate in 14 years, as both blue collar and white collar jobs have been, and continue to be, exported by U.S. corporations to nations that pay below a living wage, and that ensure that workers have no protection under labor unions and laws that regulate corporate interests and power. Meanwhile, the ratio of average CEO pay in the U.S. to the average blue-collar pay in the same corporation is 470 to 1. Part-time, temp, or subcontracted jobs currently make up 30% of the workforce and this number is rapidly increasing. 71.4% of minimum-wage workers are over the age of twenty and even though they work fulltime they live just a click above the federal poverty threshold. Meanwhile, over 50 million people in this country lack access to adequate healthcare. Showing people working hard, taking risks, and getting dirty on TV is certainly an important step for television, but the potential educational impact of this kind of programming is greatly limited without the rest of the story.

The working class—especially people who are employed to do the kinds of undesirable tasks as those showcased on *Dirtiest Jobs*—is also experiencing a fierce effort by corporate America to dismantle organized labor. While workers in unions earn 30% more than non-union people doing the same job, and get far more guaranteed benefits such as a pension and healthcare, unions have been under attack for decades regardless of the federal law (Section 7 of the National Labor Relations Act) that states that:

> Employees shall have the right to self organization, to form, join or assist labor organizations, to bargain collectively through representatives of their own choosing and to engage in other concerted activities for the purpose of collective bargaining or other mutual aid or protection....

The harsh reality is that those who try to organize often face serious repercussions. Human Rights Watch has recorded that ten to twenty thousand people a year are fired or punished for trying to unionize. None of the Discovery programs mention, let alone discuss and engage, the trials and tribulations of unions and organizing labor—subject matter that would certainly relate to most people's lives and make an interesting reality show.

Instead, Discovery's programs focus on the duties at hand, the eccentricities of the job, and the drama that manifests in the personality wars that emerge among the cast. As such, it's unclear whether or not the audience is really being enlightened or simply entertained. Data from online chat room commentary suggest the latter. "My favorite episodes usually deal with him [Rowe] working with animals. The funniest I have seen was the Llama episode." "I love your show. I am watching it right now!! Right now you are checking cow poop! I think you should clean something dirty like a rabbit farm! I don't like when you get hurt but it is so cute!"

Miami Ink suffers from a similar problem. Its promotional clips describe the show as being about a group of people living and working together to establish and maintain a business. But, other than a few superficial shots in the opening credits of cleaning and getting the shop ready for service, any substantive issues dealing with the actual operations are eclipsed by the usual soap opera-style content of jokes, fights, gossip, and drama—

content that is perhaps entertaining, but not necessarily educational. While there are plenty of intriguing stories from customers about why they are getting tattoos, there is virtually no commentary on work and survival.

For that matter, the show offers little to no historical insight into the evolution of tattoos within popular culture in the U.S. In an effort to argue that tattoos are for everyone, the show fails to take up how these symbols have been part of working-class history and identity in the United States—in particular for sailors, bikers, and prison inmates. The series frames tattooing as a serious art, but the bottom line is that most people get them now because it's in fashion. Almost one in three adults age twenty-five to thirty-four, from across the professional spectrum, has tattoos. Instead of being an educational show about the politics of art and labor, *Miami Ink* risks becoming a piece of commodified popular culture, and what one online chat room participant describes as, "just an excuse for them to charge exorbitant prices for their work."

The other reality missing from reality TV is how small businesses are taking a beating in this country. With capital flight, global outsourcing, and trade policies that favor massive corporations, small businesses are finding it impossible to compete. A reality show about the Teutuls could surely deal with the toils of surviving within this neoliberal atmosphere. But this is precisely where this particular show becomes problematic: the men not only don't actually make much of the bike on screen, but they generally rely on pre-made parts—from where, the audience doesn't know. What's educational about the program is questionable given that it isn't really about learning how custom choppers are made, nor is it about what it takes to operate a small business in the current economic climate. Many viewers dislike what they perceive as simply a soap opera filled with macho drama as the two men bicker constantly; a prevalent criticism that got the show moved from the Discovery Channel over to the Learning Channel in 2006—an odd reconciliation. As one blogger explains:

> I hate this show! Wow! What ever happened to Discovery airing educational programming? Not only does this show contain no educational value to it what-so-ever, it actually makes me feel dumber for watching it. It would be one thing if this show actually showed step by step how these machines are made. But no, it stoops to the lowest common denominator by showing how despicable these sell-out, corporate blow-holes act.

Insight into what future episodes might explore is no more encouraging; sadly the show is currently being used to promote Sunoco gas and has been turned into two popular video games. With the newest wave of racism from father Teutul, the show now works to perpetuate the stereotype that only "white trash" is racist.

Deadliest Catch certainly has plenty of room for educating viewers about the fishing industry; unfortunately, it also relies far too much on the action and spectacle aboard the ships. Each season promotes the show as being even more treacherous than the year before. The subtleties of the program that allude to the difficult economic issues that are faced in commercial fishing and the heroic efforts involved in making a living for these workers are eclipsed by the spectacle of crews competing and fighting the elements. As one viewer comments online:

> As I was watching, I couldn't help but wonder why any sane person would subject themselves to this kind of a job. I mean, it is Alaska, and I'm sure there is no shortage of work there…I guess the real answer is greed. What's worse, is some of the crew members especially the rookies (green horns) joined on because they wanted some adventure . . .

Anyone in the audience concerned with labor conditions within capitalist relations will probably be irritated by the way that the show focuses a great deal on the competition among boats. This is also evident in *Lobster Wars,* which, from its title, emphasizes competition rather than camaraderie—which in reality is an essential element for the survival of fishing communities.

While Discovery's shows are certainly a step up from network television's narrow, unrealistic images that conceal the corporate assault on the workforce of this country, there is nonetheless room for improvement. But these shows are definitely worth watching—as long as it's with a critical eye. The ability to ask hard questions about the role that TV images play in shaping our understanding of the world—what's commonly referred to as critical media literacy—is especially important for youth. It's vital that people take their entertainment seriously, not so they can't have a good laugh, but rather so they can develop a more profound sense of the world around them. Shouldn't that be the goal of any kind of television programming that claims to be about discovery, teaching, and learning?

■ Class Action

While television has long used the image of the working class to entertain us, current labor conditions are no laughing matter. Today's workers face a declining standard of living and the loss of job security. They also risk falling victim to corporate greed and malfeasance such as the recent atrocities of Enron, Tyco, Walmart, Worldcom, or any of the other over 20,000 acts of corporate lawbreaking that are documented annually.

Regardless of the neoliberal promise of prosperity for all, it's more than obvious that the structural dimensions of social class within this economic logic remain profoundly in place. In fact, economic conditions for millions of people in the United States, and for billions of people worldwide, are worsening as a direct result of privatization, deregulation, and restructuring; as well as by the ways in which elite private powers have been successful in using the State to protect corporate interests and dismantle many of the rights and protections achieved locally and internationally by grassroots activists, organized labor, and social democracies.

Corporate media's narrow, unrealistic images conceal the extent of this assault on America's workforce, so we can no longer afford to ignore TV's framing of the working class or see it as just entertainment.[34]

The media reform movement has already begun to educate the general population about the political economy of the mass media—that is, ownership and regulation of this industry—and challenge the FCC and Congress to democratize the airwaves and new technologies, and to diversify representations that reflect both the new realities of work and the changing face of the working class in the United States.

A key component of any activist effort should be to encourage the wide-spread development of critical media literacy, that is, the ability to read the values and beliefs embedded in the knowledge that is circulated throughout society, so as to be able to defend ourselves from propaganda and participate in its eradication. A critical model of media literacy is primarily concerned with the kinds of theories and practices that encourage people to develop an understanding of the interconnecting relationships among ideology, power, meaning, and identity that constitute *culture*. Literacy of this sort entails understanding culture as a pedagogical force in which the multiplicity of aural and visual signifying systems that people are inundated with every day, through language, TV, advertising, radio, print journalism, music, film, and so on, are ideological and formative rather than merely vehicles for expression or reflections of reality. They are the conduits through which values and beliefs that work to shape how people see, interpret, and act as socialized and political beings are promoted.

Critical media literacy encourages us to not only think about culture politically, but also to think about politics culturally, and is thus rooted in a democratic project that emphasizes new theories and languages of critique, resistance, and possibility capable of engaging the oppressive social practices that maintain the de facto social code in the United States. These new theories and languages provide the necessary analytic stepping stones for realizing a truly democratic process through which we can better identify the sociopolitical realities that shape our lives, and where necessary, transform our practices. In any battle for economic justice and racial and social equality, TV in the hands of the public can play a pivotal role.

Notes

1. This process is far more complicated than simply a bunch of media moguls and corporate heads sitting around making these decisions together—which needless to say, does happen. Someone like Rupert Murdoch is very clear about his political agenda, and that agenda is evident in the representations circulated by FOX. The same goes for the rest of the so-called liberal media, which in reality is also in favor of monopolizing the airwaves, and circulating corporate logic (Herman & Chomsky, 2002). This is no conspiracy. These people are simply protecting their own best interests. At the same time, while major decisions are made by bigger power brokers, writers and producers don't really need big brother around to monitor their work. In most cases, they have been properly educated so as to know what is appropriate and what isn't. At the same time, writers and producers may not be conscious of the fact that they are reproducing oppressive ideologies. They, too, are the product of representation, and their sense of humor, for example, is constructed within accepted discourses and circulated through society's institutions—they've already been called into that ideological space, and thus know what will make people laugh or cry. In the end, whether they are conscious of it or not, they play a central role in reproducing discriminatory images and social practices.

2. It is also important to look at how the news media and Hollywood frame the working class. For information about the ways that labor is depicted in the news media, see: Puette, William (1992). *Through Jaundiced Eyes: How the Media View Organized Labor*. Ithaca, NY: Cornell University Press; Buckingham, David (2000). *The Making of Citizens: Young People, News and Politics*. New York: Routledge, and Martin, Christopher (2004). *Framed: Labor and the Corporate Media*. Ithaca, NY: Cornell

University Press. For an analysis of Hollywood films and their depiction of the working class, see: Booker, Keith (1999). *Film and the American Left: A Research Guide*. Westport, CT: Greenwood Press; Buhle, Paul & Wagner, Dave (2002). *Radical Hollywood*. New York: The New Press; Ross, Steven (1998). *Working-Class Hollywood*. Princeton, NJ: Princeton University Press, and Horne, Gerald (2001). *Class Struggles in Hollywood: 1930–1950*. Austin, TX: University of Austin Press.

3. While it wasn't a regularly scheduled program, *Marty* (1953), the story of the everyday life of a butcher living in an urban environment, provided an interesting image of the working class.

4. In part, the reason that the working class seems to disappear from public discourse, and from the world of entertainment television, is because there was a real economic boom going on at the time. Within this post-WWII economic climate, many workers, especially white workers, did achieve a better standard of living. This was due to organizing and collective bargaining, as well as to government programs that provided a real safety net. But there is also an ideological reason for the disappearance of class from the public eye. The country was moving into the cold war—the McCarthy era, and what's ironic is that unions, the very organizations that enabled workers to achieve a better standard of living, are seen as a real threat now. Any effort to further democratize industry, technology, economic and social relations gets branded as communist and has to be crushed.

5. While racism can't simply be conflated with the economic base of capitalism, we certainly need to look at the ways in which it is used to exploit diverse groups within capitalist social relations. It is also crucial to look at the ways in which historically racism, and sexism for that matter, has served an important role in keeping at bay working-class unity and maintaining a system of labor exploitation.

6. A classic example of this is the character "Rochester" on *The Jack Benny Program* (1951–1965). It's important to note that *The Nat "King" Cole Show* ran up against racist sponsors, which ultimately led to its premature death.

7. This can be seen in shows like *Julia* (1968–1971) and *I Spy* (1965–1968), which featured a young Bill Cosby.

8. Fred and Lionel get out of the ghetto and move to Arizona, and in 1977 a spin-off of *Sanford and Son* is released—*The Sanford Arms*. The storyline is about turning the old rooming house into a successful hotel. Archie Bunker also makes it out of his working-class neighborhood and opens a bar. The featured characters on *What's Happening* either escape the ghetto or enter the middle class therein.

9. As in the typical format, the family moves form the inner-city to the suburbs.

10. *704 Hauser Street* (1994) is a show with African-American, working-class characters. They live in Archie Bunker's old house in Queens, NY. While the two parents are portrayed as, "typical working-class, blue collar liberals," their son is very conservative, and fancies a Jewish girl from the neighborhood. While this may be Norman Lear's attempt to make up for pigeon-holing the working class through the earlier depiction of Archie Bunker as a working-class yahoo, the show only lasted for 6 episodes. In 1996, Bill Cosby initiated and co-produced the show *Cosby*. The short-lived sitcom was based on a retired old man who loses his job and searches for another. Most of the episodes are preoccupied with this character driving his wife crazy. What's interesting is that the show was based on the English program *One Foot in the Grave* (1990–2001), which entertained some serious political criticism. On the contrary, Cosby lightened the humor and thus the content of his version. *The PJs* (1999–2001), an animated show created by actor Eddie Murphy, offered insight into life in a housing project and the chief superintendent, but it was more about comical adventures than any explicit critique of the formation of such projects. *The Tracy Morgan Show* (2003) is built around the life of an African-American family in a tiny Brooklyn apartment, and while Tracy struggles while working as an auto mechanic, the show, in its short life, was preoccupied with trying to fulfill his dream of expanding his business. *Everybody Hates Chris* (2005–present) is based in Brooklyn, New York during the early 1980s. Chris is sent to a primarily white middle school, and so while it has the potential to reveal some of the realities of that world, it is more about coming of age.

11. Latino/a characters have appeared on shows like *Norm* (1999–2001), *Walker, Texas Ranger* (1993–2001), (1999–2001), *Gideon's Crossing* (2000–2001), *Third Watch* (1999–2005), *Nash Bridges* (1996–2001), *That 70's Show* (1998–2006), and Latino/a characters have appeared in secondary roles on such shows as *ER* (1994–present), *Jag* (1995–2001), *Felicity* (1998–2002), and *Family Law* (1999–2002). Many of the Latino shows are soap operas. Soap operas in general are interesting places for doing class analysis as the hierarchy is so evident in these programs. Working-class characters are almost always trouble in soap operas, or they are gold diggers, or they move up the economic ladder very quickly, but carry with them their cultural capital from the past as they continue to be marked as working class.

12. The show *CHIPS* (1977–1983) did feature Erik Estrada as Officer Frank "Ponch" Poncherello.

13. In this racialized space, his father is missing and is assumed to have abandoned the family.

14. There are no programs that take up the conditions of persons with disabilities. Disability is also a class issue in that two-thirds of people with disabilities are unemployed. The material conditions of the elderly are also neglected by the corporate media. When they are included, it's in drug commercials, retirement success stories on advertisements, or on shows where money isn't an issue, such as *The Golden Girls* (1985–1992).

15. All of the maids/housekeepers/butlers/servants on television are depicted as complacent, without serious worries, and often empowered to question the boss; e.g., *Beulah, Hazel* (1961–1966), Mr. French on *A Family Affair* (1966–1971), Florence on the *The Jeffersons*, Bentley, Florida on *Maude*, Geoffrey on *The Fresh Prince of Bel Air*, Paul Hogan on *Joe Millionaire*. There are no scenes of them scrubbing toilets and taking abuse.

16. The show *Maude* (1972–1978) did provide a good deal of feminist critique, but it was coming from an upper-middle-class white woman who had a housekeeper.

17. While *Roseanne* was a breath of fresh air, the show was more about working-class moms getting the recognition that they deserve, than what would need to change in order to democratize wealth and power in this country. When I asked Ehrenreich about this critique of the show, she responded with a giggle, "these are capitalist media, they're supported by sponsors…You're gonna have to make those shows if that's what you want."

18. Advertising also relies on these stereotypes. The strategy is to use humor to create fear by showing the audience what they should avoid.

19. It's interesting how these shows often assume class integration in neighborhoods; and unlike the rather bleak household settings depicted in some of the earlier shows, today's working-class families usually live in very comfortable homes that are equipped with all the modern amenities associated with the good life.

20. An interesting show that needs further attention when it comes to these representations is *The Three Stooges* (1930–2006).

21. Comedy shows like *Saturday Night Live* (1975–present), *In Living Color* (1990–1994), and *MADtv* (1995), all have characters and skits that mock the working class. While they also poke fun at the rich, the impact is surely not the same.

22. Fonzie on *Happy Days* (1974–1984) is a break from this. But the Fonze is never in need of help, and gets what he needs with a click of his fingers, or the bump of his hip. He's the typical 'salt of the earth' working-class guy who makes it on his own, and is thus revered.

23. The new, award-winning show *Ugly Betty* (2006–present), has an ambitious character—an ordinary girl from Queens trying to fit into the world of high fashion—but her ability to move up is based on her good values and work ethic. The fact is that she got the job because she is ugly, and therefore wouldn't be enticing for her boss. At least the audience is occasionally made aware of her struggle with family, a sick father, and little resources. The cartoon, *As Told by Ginger* (2000–2004), offered an interesting perspective of a working-class girl living with her single mom. Ginger's mom is a nurse who is on strike and works for her own cleaning business. While the show is by no means radical, it does move a bit beyond the typical television content. The characters in the reality show

Hell's Kitchen (2005–2007) are also shown working hard, but their survival is based on having thick skin as the show's sales pitch is that it's "served with a side of sarcasm" as "contestants endure Ramsay's hellishly intense culinary boot camp." What's amazing about this show is that there is no mention of restaurant unions that would not put up with the chef's unwarranted abuse—the spectacle of the program.

24. One of the most fascinating examples of shows that romanticize the virtues of family, even in the worst of conditions, is *The Waltons* (1972–1981). Taking place during the Depression, the family survives the hard times because of the caring and dedication of the entire family. In the mythology, this is what pulled the country out of trouble, not F.D.R.'s socialist response in the form of the New Deal, as well as the economic revitalization caused by the war.

25. While the shows *Nanny 911* (2004–present), and *The Super Nanny* (2005–present) help fix families from most diverse backgrounds, the majority of the troubled families screaming for help are working class.

26. The crime shows of the 70s and 80s include: *Streets of San Francisco* (1972–1977), *The Rookies* (1972–1976), *Kojak* (1973–1978), *Police Woman* (1974–1978), *Starsky & Hutch* (1975–1979), *Baretta* (1975–1978), *S.W.A.T.* (1975–1976), *Hunter* (1984–1991), *Hill Street Blues* (1981–1987), *Miami Vice* (1984–1991), and *21 Jump Street* (1987–1991).

27. *Law and Order* (1990–present) occasionally provides some interesting political commentary about race, class, and gender discrimination, as do the shows *Cold Case* (2003–present), and *CSI* (2000–present, *CSI Miami*, 2002–present). What's unfortunate about police shows is that, while the class hierarchy is readily apparent with judges, district attorneys, lawyers, chiefs of police, and street cops, the class differences are rarely explored.

28. For a long time now, cartoons such as *Deputy Dog* (1959–1972), have often played off of this country-bumpkin stereotype.

29. The most recent edition of *Survivor* is in China—what's supposed to be a Communist regime but what in fact is a totalitarian regime based on state capitalism, a kind of Walmart with an army, has worked economically to the extent that China now owns over one trillion dollars of the over 8.7 trillion dollar U.S. national debt; interesting that you'll never see such a program in Cuba.

30. The dumb blonde stereotype finds its way into *The Simple Life* (2002–2003) with Paris Hilton and Nicole Richie. While the show works to mock everyone as the two rich women find themselves doing menial jobs, it is nonetheless preoccupied with the two Hollywood rich 'girls' trying to make-over the working-class cast.

31. This myth is also perpetuated by the slew of talk shows like *Oprah* (1986–present) that dedicate enormous amounts of airtime transforming guests with the help of hair, make-up, and style experts.

32. Since the early 1990s, television has cautiously opened the door to a few gay and lesbian characters (e.g., *The Real World* (1992–present), *Ellen* (1994–1998, and her newest talk show (2003)), *ER* (1994–present), *Spin City* (1996–2002), *The View* (1997–present), *Will & Grace* (1998–2006), *Queer as Folk* (2000–2005), *Survivor* (2000–present), *Six Feet Under* (2001–2005), *The Amazing Race* (2001–present), *The L-Word* (2004–present), and in many soap operas. Queer visibility on primetime, as with other marginalized groups, is due in part to changing social conditions, and also when the networks need to spice up existing repertoires with small variations but at the exclusion of working-class, gender variant, and other non-conforming individuals.

33. Reality shows like *Wife Swap* (2004–present) also play this role.

34. While this chapter and research are not about audience reception, that is, how people interpret these messages, we would argue that workers themselves often internalize this stigma. They may see themselves as working men and women, working families, but they reject the label working class. As a result they don't have a sense of class solidarity, or class-consciousness.

References

Allan, Robert & Hill, Annette (Eds.) (2004). *The Television Studies Reader.* New York: Routledge.

Aronowitz, Stanley (1992). "Working-Class Culture in the Electronic Age." In: *The Politics of Identity: Class, Culture, Social Movements.* New York: Routledge.

Barnouw, Erik (1978). *The Sponsor: Notes on a Modern Potentate.* New York: Oxford University Press.

Bettie, Julie (2003). *Women without Class: Girls, Race, and Identity.* Berkeley: University of California Press.

Bourdieu, Pierre (1996). *On Television.* New York: The New Press.

Butsch, Richard (2002). "Ralph, Fred, Archie and Homer: Why Television Keeps Recreating the White Male Working-Class Buffoon." In: *Gender, Race and Class in Media.* (Eds.) Gail Dines and Jean Humez. Thousand Oaks, CA: Sage.

Carey, Alex (1995). *Taking the Risk out of Democracy: Corporate Propaganda Versus Freedom and Liberty.* Chicago: University of Illinois Press.

Class Dismissed: How TV Frames the Working Class (2005). A project by Pepi Leistyna, narrated by Ed Asner, co-written and produced with Loretta Alper, executive producer Sut Jhally, directed by Loretta Alper. Northampton, MA: Media Education Foundation. (All of the interview references are from this source.)

Davila, Arlene (2001). *Latinos Inc.: The Marketing and Making of a People.* Berkeley, CA: University of California Press.

Dollars & Sense and United for a Fair Economy (Eds.) (2004). *The Wealth Inequality Reader.* Cambridge, MA: Economic Affairs Bureau.

Douglas, Susan (1995). *Where the Girls Are: Growing Up Female with the Mass Media.* New York: Three Rivers Press.

Durham, Meenakshi Gigi & Kellner, Douglas (2001). *Media and Cultural Studies: KeyWorks.* Malden, MA: Blackwell.

Dyson, Michael Eric (1993). *Reflecting Black: African-American Cultural Criticism.* Minneapolis: University of Minnesota Press.

Economic Policy Institute (2004/2005). *The State of Working America.* Ithaca, NY: ILR Press.

Freed, Rosanna (2002). "The Gripes of Wrath: Roseanne's Bitter Comedy of Class." *Television Quarterly.* Available at: www.emmyonline.org/tvq/articles/30–2–15.asp

Gray, Herman (1995). *Watching Race: Television and the Struggle for "Blackness."* Minneapolis: University of Minnesota Press.

Hall, Stuart (Ed.) (1997). *Representation: Cultural Representations and Signifying Practices.* London: Sage.

Hamamoto, Darrell (1994). *Monitored Peril: Asian Americans and the Politics of TV Representation.* Minneapolis: University of Minnesota Press.

Herman, Edward & Chomsky, Noam (2002). *Manufacturing Consent: The Political Economy of the Mass Media.* New York: Pantheon.

Jhally, Sut & Lewis, Justin (1992). *Enlightened Racism: The Cosby Show, Audiences, and the Myth of the American Dream.* Boulder, CO: Westview.

Kellner, Douglas (1997). "Beavis and Butt-Head: No Future for Postmodern Youth." In: *Kinderculture: The Corporate Construction of Childhood.* (Eds.) Steinberg, Shirley & Joe Kincheloe. Boulder, CO: Westview.

Lebowitz, M. A. (2006). *Build it now: Socialism for the twenty-first century.* New York: Monthly Review Press.

Leistyna, P. (2004). Introduction: Youth as a category through which class is lived. *Workplace: A journal for academic labor,* 6, 1. Retrieved 5 February 2009 from: http://www.cust.educ.ubc.ca/workplace/issue6p1/leistyna.html

Lipsitz, George (2002). "The Meaning of Memory: Family, Class and Ethnicity in Early Network Television." In: *Gender, Race and Class in Media* (Eds.) Gail Dines & Jean Humez. Thousand Oaks, CA: Sage.

National Coalition for the Homeless (1999). Available at: www.nationalhomeless.org/jobs.html

National Coalition for the Homeless (2002). Available at: www.nationalhomeless.org/who.html

Negrón-Muntaner, Frances (2004). *Boricua Pop: Puerto Ricans and the Latinization of American Culture.* New York: New York University Press.

Parenti, Michael (1992). *Make-Believe Media: The Politics of Entertainment.* Belmont, CA: Wadsworth.

Press, Andrea (1991). *Women Watching Television: Gender, Class, and Generation in the American Television Experience.* Philadelphia: University of Pennsylvania Press.

Riggs, Marlon (1991). *Color Adjustment.* San Francisco: California Newsreel.

Rodriguez, Carla (Ed.) (1997). *Latin Looks: Images of Latinas and Latinos in the U.S. Media.* Boulder, CO: Westview.

U.S. Census Bureau (2003). "Poverty in the United States: 2003."—report issued 15 September.

Wacquant, Loic (2002). "Deadly Symbiosis: Rethinking Race and Imprisonment in Twenty-first-century America." *Boston Review: A Political and Literary Forum.* 27(2) (April/May): 23–31.

Zuk, Rhoda (1998). "Entertaining Feminism: *Roseanne* and Roseanne Arnold." *Studies in Popular Culture.* Available at: http://pcasacas.org/SPC/spcissues/21.1/kuk.htm

21

■ African American and Jewish Mothers/Wives on Television

Persistent Stereotypes

Myrna A. Hant

Since the early days of television, depictions of certain character types have conditioned the audience to expect predictable behavior. One icon is the Jewish wife/mother who has remained, throughout television's history, almost consistently a devouringly negative, albeit loving presence in her family's life. Counter to the common Jewish wife/mother stereotype is the seemingly more positive evolutions of portrayals of the African American maternal figure, originally stereotyped as *Beulah* (1950–1953)[1] and Sapphire's mother in *Amos 'n Andy* (1951–1953)[2] where, "blacks were lazy, conniving, emotional and uneducated inferiors" (MacDonald, 1992, p. xvi), evolving to the contemporary Rochelle in *Everybody Hates Chris,* a savvy and definitely not inferior female. A feminist cultural studies textual analysis of these two types, who may seem to be outwardly quite disparate, reveals a schema of similarities that promotes racial and ethnic prototyping. A cursory analysis of the African American wife/mother depictions reveals what appear to be positive traits, but similar to the Jewish wife/mother she too, has largely remained fixed in problematic representations.

In order to deconstruct these representations, cultivation analysis (that is, the exploration of "common assumptions and ways of understanding the world—not by overt attempts at persuasion, but simply by privileging some kinds of images, representations, or facts over others") can be utilized (Lewis, 2002, p. 7). Developed in the 1960s by George Gerbner, dean of the Annenberg School for Communication at the University of Pennsylvania, cultivation analysis is the study of television content and cultural indicators with the assumption that, "television is the source of the most broadly shared images and messages in history" (Gerbner et al., 2002, p. 4). Gerbner et al. hypothesize that television promotes, "the continual repetition of stories (myths, ideologies, "facts," relationships, etc.) that serve to define the world and legitimize a particular social order." He goes on to argue that this promotes homogeneous thinking, thought processes that are orchestrated by the political and social powers in society. The power of television is often disguised because many viewers assume that it is only an entertainment medium, exclusive of influencing viewers' perspectives of the world (Leistyna and Alper, 2007, p. 54).

This leads one to ask how the politics of representation, especially the dominant media stereotypes of African American and Jewish mothers, reproduce a social reality? According to Kellner, "images and representations are never innocent or pure," but are politically motivated portrayals, be they positive or negative. They often, "serve pernicious interests of cultural oppression," by conditioning the audience to the inferiority of, or concomitantly, the superiority of specific groups (Kellner and Durham, 2001, p. 24).

I am not arguing that representations of Jewish and black women are the same, as this would symmetrize hierarchically different existences. "There is much evidence substantiating the reality that race and class identity create differences in quality of life, social status, and lifestyle that take precedence over the common experience women share—differences that are rarely transcended" (hooks, 2000, p. 40).

However, we can contend that both icons are "the other." The "other," a term popularized by Simone de Beauvoir in her book, *The Second Sex* (1977), is the nonessential, inferior, and subordinate. Man is the essential being, and woman is "the other." More specifically, the definition of personhood is male, so that woman defines herself in terms of the male. Audre Lorde uses the term "mythical norm," that set of standards in American culture that is normative—"white, thin, male, young, heterosexual, Christian" (Lorde, 1984, p. 116). Similarly, we can extrapolate that the essential being or standard of womanhood in American culture is white and Gentile, and thus both African American and Jewish women are "the other."

As Stuart Hall argues, otherness is often signified by race and gender for African American women. It can then be proposed that ethnicity and gender are "signifiers" for Jewish women. Or, more precisely, both are women who define themselves or are defined by differences, black not white, Jewish not Gentile. Each wife/mother prototype is also frequently mediated by male power and patriarchal definitions of womanhood. Consequently, as in most stereotypes, the African American, as well as the Jewish mother, is used to represent a mythography in which entire belief systems are reinforced, merely by watching their TV portrayals.

■ Differences

One need only look at the myriad array of Jewish mothers, from Molly Goldberg in *The Goldbergs* (1949–1955)[3] to contemporary types such as Susie in *Curb Your Enthusiasm* (1999–2007) to validate the notion of shifting representations of Jewish women. The lovable and peace-making Molly is the personification of the "shtetl mother,"[4] warm, motherly, resourceful, nurturing and problem-solving…and overbearing and inescapable" (Pearl and Pearl, 1999, p. 86). But because Molly is so likable, many critics view her and her clan as excellent ambassadors for acceptance of Jews as different, but trying desperately to become Americanized, thus like Gentiles, in the 1950s. According to Friedman, "Gentiles perceive them as 'good Jews' who give them no reason to worry; they just make them laugh. Their exaggerated mannerism and quaint customs encourage a patronizing attitude toward America's Jews" (Friedman,1982, p. 163).

But the relatively benign image of the Jewish mother on television is not adopted when she resurfaces in the 1970s. These TV mothers represent disharmony in the home, disjointedness between parent and child. "She was not the Yiddishe Mama of the Old World, to whom immigrants longingly turned with sentimental songs and harsh comparisons to American sweethearts and wives. Rather, this representation of New World prosperity was an American-born Jewish mother who pushed, wheedled, demanded, constrained, and was insatiable in her expectations and wants. The guilt induced by the Old World was not her siren song; rather she demanded loyalty to herself and her impossible New World expectations" (Prell, 1999, p. 143) to be accepted by the majority culture.

Numerous examples of the Jewish mother's failed efforts at acceptance can be seen throughout the span of television shows from the 1970s to the present. For instance, when Rhoda (1974–1978)[5] marries Joe, a Gentile, in the October 18, 1974 episode of *Rhoda,* she laments how Mother Ida has instilled her with insecurity, food-obsession, and oversensitivity. Ultimately, Rhoda turns to Joe and says, "I feel sorry for you," essentially for entering a family with a meddlesome mother-in-law who will never behave in a normal fashion. Another pathetic example of the Jewish mother is Sylvia in *The Nanny* (1993–1999). Here the Jewish mother becomes even more of a caricature, an exaggeration of materialism, consumerism, whininess and poor taste. Fran is in her 30s, working as a nanny for the three children of her employer, an unmarried British producer named Maxwell Sheffield. And Mother Sylvia is convinced that Mr. Sheffield, an upper class Brit, is the appropriate mate for her loud and brash daughter. In one episode entitled "Hurricane Fran," Sylvia descends upon Mr. Sheffield, hugs him and cries out, "hold me, don't be such a Gentile," and later proclaims, "why, why don't you marry my daughter?" The obvious absurdity of such a match only emphasizes the "otherness" of Sylvia and Fran.

Another in the panoply of Jewish mother images that has persisted is Sheila, Kyle Broslovski's mother in *South Park* (1997–present). In the "Mr. Hanley, the Christmas Poo" episode on December 20, 1997, Sheila announces her difference emphatically by going to the mayor to protest Christmas celebrations because "our family doesn't celebrate Christmas." Kyle's mother succeeds in stopping all celebrations allowing only non-Santa and non-Jesus Christmas songs. And the show ends by Mr. Hanley yelling, "Jews, you bastards, ruined Christmas."

The discourse on African American mothers, like Jewish mothers, can also be centralized around the concept of "otherness," a denigration of one image (black) and a glorification of the other (white). Patricia Hill Collins categorizes these dichotomous positions as object and subject: "as objects, one's reality is defined by others, one's identity created by others, one's history named only in ways that define one's relationship to those who are subjects" (Collins, 1998, p. 122). Consequently, "much of the psychic pain that black people experience daily in a white supremacist context is caused by dehumanizing oppressive forces, forces that render us invisible and deny us recognition" (hooks, 2001, p. 434). It can be argued that with a denial of human viability, control of that person, that type, can be facilitated.

Although the politics of representation are vastly diverse for the Jewish wife/mother, and the African American wife/mother, the outcomes produce similar dehumanizing images. The TV Jewish mother, whose "otherness" is manifested in a destructive and uncontrollable character, does not verbalize in shows the extent of her outsidedness; the African American mother is often overtly verbal about her differences. The Jewish mother is not forced to deny her heritage but becomes a caricature of that heritage because her behavior is so inappropriate in a Gentile world. And because of her excesses she psychically cripples those around her. But black women must contend with the mythology of "dark Others whose cultures, traditions, and lifestyles may indeed be irrevocably changed by…racist dominations" (hooks, 2001, p. 427). Paradoxically, both types are invisible women, not understood for their uniqueness.

In the early days, *Beulah* personified the "slave" comes to television sitcom. Donald Bogle labels her a "warm and winning hefty, full-figured and good-hearted 'colored gal' with a deep hearty laugh" (Bogle, 2001, p. 19). As he describes it, she exemplifies the good servant, the one who is oblivious to her own needs, unaware of politics and change, a maid whose sole purpose in life is to be sure that the life of the Hendersons is as problem-free as Beulah can make it. She willingly serves her bosses, and ultimately as "earth mother" maintains order in the household. Her buffoonish cleverness, wisdom, and astuteness are admired, because she never forgets that she's the smiling servant. One of the many examples of her prowess is an episode in which Donny goes to school and has been called a "sissy." Beulah decides that Donny's manliness can be rescued by showing the bully at school that Donny and Dad can go camping and take care of themselves. Unfortunately, though, Mr. Harry is not adept as an outdoorsman and must call on Beulah and her friend, Bill Jackson, to set up the camp and prepare the meal. Although ridiculous in her fishing outfit, Beulah resuscitates Donny's self-esteem and Mr. Harry's by catching a fish and even making Harry look like he did it. Beulah is quick to point out that, "if this fish was a man fish I never would have landed him." Beulah, although self-deprecating, self-confident, and nurturing, is less than a white woman in her acceptance of her desexed demeanor. Most egregious of all though, is that she performs her tasks willingly and with devoted love for her "masters."

This ultimate Mammy figure serves the needs of the white viewer, reifying the comfortable stereotype of the "'domesticated African Americans'…the slaves who exhibited behaviors that made them suitable to serve whites. To justify the exploitation of domestic servants, white elites created controlling images of Uncle Tom and Mammy as prototypes of asexual, safe, assimilated and subordinated black people" (Collins, 2005, p. 57). In this caricature of a black woman, she is not even remotely considered a threat to white womanhood but rather another fixture in the household, established to maintain the status quo of racial hierarchies.

"White men, including those who ran the entertainment industry, did not ordinarily look at black women as competitors or adversaries. As the white male saw things, it was black men, not black women, who might plot revolt, take over white men's jobs, or violate white men's women....It was the white woman who supposedly sought to ensnare the male in the web of domesticity, or who, in the role of mother, wife, or mother-in-law, might try to order his life, restrain his behavior, and limit his options. The black woman made no such demands on him" (Ely, 1991, p. 106).

In *Good Times* (1974–1979), Esther Rolle, as Florida Evans, is the black mother trying to help her children, J. J., Thelma, and Michael, navigate the exigencies of a Chicago inner-city ghetto. The themes of the shows center on the perseverance of a black family, and their ability to stay together despite dealing with poverty and the frequent unemployment of James, the father. Florida maintains admirable values as she struggles with such ubiquitous occurrences as muggings, assaults, and the proliferation of guns. Mama's wisdom is a basic part of the show, and she warns J. J. that, "those streets are just full of bad habits waiting to be picked up." When James takes a job on the Alaska pipeline, Florida laments, "we've been poor all of our lives and we got through it without you leaving the family." Florida is represented as unquestionably black as she consistently uses such expressions as "ain't" and "Lord, have mercy." Thus, "the other" is perpetuated in each episode through language, neighborhood, and situations. When Mama doesn't feel well, she exclaims that there's been, "too much toting that barge and lifting that bale." When Mama finds out that James is insisting that she go to a private hospital rather than County Hospital to have her operation, she admonishes James, "let's not pretending we somethin' we ain't."

The catchy theme song of *The Jeffersons* (1975–1985), "Movin' on Up" immediately alerts the audience that this family is trying to separate themselves from the prevailing stereotype of the black ghettoized family. Coming from Harlem to the Eastside, they "finally got a piece of the pie." Mother Louise (Weezie) never seems to lose her fear that the family will "fall," and once again be consumed by what is characterized as the typical black family's surroundings, poverty and violence. George frequently admonishes Louise when she interferes with George's business decisions, "I don't want to go back to the ghetto." The ghetto has no redeeming qualities. Louise, who had been a maid herself, spars with her own newly acquired maid, Florence, a sassy, sardonic representation of how difficult it is to really "tame" the black female.

Black/white issues are a predominant theme in the series, issues that are no longer covert or implied as in *Beulah* and *Good Times*. When Weezie is frightened about George's expansion plans of his dry cleaning stores, he lectures her that, "all these years Whitey using us, it's about time we use him," or "the only way to fight white power is with black power." Although George is the mouthpiece for racial discrimination, Louise is constantly supportive of him and does not thwart his attempts at "business revenge" on whites. Louise is not white, and she knows it as she struggles gracefully to maintain her highly ethical and moral approach to all the bigotry she encounters.

With the introduction of some later shows such as *What's Happening* (1976–1979), *The Cosby Show* (1984–1992), *The Parkers* (1999–2004), and *My Wife and Kids* (2001–2005), overt race-related comments are largely absent, but prototyping is translated into body language, dress, and physical appearance. "Although often staged from a black normative universe, these shows seldom presented black subjectivities and cultural traditions as alternative perspectives on everyday life. That is to say, as a cultural and experiential referent, blackness was seldom privileged or framed as a vantage point for critical insights, guides to action, or explanations for what happens to African American people in modern American society" (Hunt, 2005, p. 164).

Mabel King in *What's Happening* lives in a lower class neighborhood raising two children alone. Although few race-related plots are promulgated, everything about the comedy reflects racial stereotypes. Mabel, hugely obese, wears vividly colored tent-like dresses. Although wise and respected by her children, she is a laughable clown as she pursues a handsome, fellow night school student, Todd, only to find out that he shows interest in her so that she will write his term paper. She perpetuates the ingrained beliefs that black women are "earth mothers" with innate wisdom but not schooled and definitely not sexual beings.

Much has been written about *The Cosby Show* and its incredible popularity in the 1980s and early 1990s. By presenting a benign black family, with all the inherent problems of families of means, the audience is introduced to diversity in the black community that had not previously been emphasized. It is lauded for its presentation of an impressive upper middle class family that happens to be black. The "discourse seeks to limit white advantages through denial of racial differences" (Winant, 2004, p. 59). Clair Huxtable, an attorney, belies the female stereotype of the black, large, "earth mother" so prevalent in TV black families both before and after *The Cosby Show*. Clair, however, is basically portrayed as a wife and mother in the early shows, smartly dressed but often wearing an apron. She's an equal partner with her husband.

An analysis of the show broadly fits into two categories. Either it is considered "racially progressive," or a perpetrator of a racist system blaming the individual for his lack of success (Jhally and Lewis, 1992, p. 3). Not surprisingly though, criticism of the show centers on its refusal to tackle the issues of the day pertinent to blacks—continued racism, AIDS, poverty, and class diversity. Beloved by white America, *The Cosby Show* allows the populace to extol the virtues of a long-sought color-blind country, supporting the conservative views that racial tension has long ago been eradicated and thus reforms, based on racial discrimination, are no longer necessary. Concomitantly, "black Americans who had not achieved the American Dream had only themselves to blame" (Hunt, 2005, p. 15).

With the creation of such contemporary shows as *The Parkers, My Wife and Kids,* and *Everybody Hates Chris* (2005–present), black-themed sensitivities and stereotypes are altered. In *The Parkers,* once again Nikki Parker, the uneducated but resilient mother, is childlike in her constant eating and her often embarrassing pursuit of Professor Stanley Oglevee. But the issues are not overtly racial ones, even though Nikki cannot be decoded as a white woman either. In her risible efforts to attract men, she is depicted as fat, clumsy, crude, and despite incorrect grammar, archetypically wise. Thus, she is a dichotomous figure, one that is black, not white, but comfortable in her "otherness," not striving to be white.

My Wife and Kids has been loosely compared to *The Cosby Show,* a show about an upper middle class family residing in a suburban, and not an urban area, as with most previous comedies about African American families. However, despite the setting, the mother, Jay Kyle, is a somewhat heavyset, "moved on up" kind of woman, who chides her husband's humor about her weight with a "you don't look like no damn walrus" or a quip to her son when she finds out his girlfriend is pregnant with a "boy, you crazy. What we gonna do?" Thus, the Kyles may be economically in the upper middle class, but they are tagged with blackness and a lower class consciousness. Once, again, the mother figure is clearly not white, but she revels in who she is, rather than laments her differences from whites.

Rochelle, in *Everybody Hates Chris,* represents the ambitious mother who's not ashamed of blackness, as much as she's a snob who's convinced she can get her family out of the ghetto. Her issues are more related to class than to color. Chris goes to a white school because "my mother thought I was learning all kinds of things." The school is riddled with racists like the gay white principal who is convinced that Chris has a hard life having been born a crack baby with no father and a mother on drugs. Chris' teacher is sure that Chris can't study because he has to care for all those half-brothers and sisters of his. But Rochelle, who acts and speaks in a stereotypical black manner, scolds anyone who interferes with her family and her goals of achieving middle class status. Chris proclaims that there's "nothing worse than a mad black woman in an all white school." What Rochelle wants is respectability, not whiteness. She is obsessed with what others think and meticulous about not presenting herself, or her family, as poor. "Girl, whatchoo talkin' 'bout food stamps? Who's sellin' food stamps? I ain't sellin' no food stamps!" And that's why when son Drew asks for a new suit for the school talent show, and she knows they can't afford it, she relents because "my baby's not going to look ratty."

In the early years of the nineteenth century in the United States, the Cult of True Womanhood or the Cult of Domesticity was popularized for the promotion of certain desirable qualities for white women (Welter, 1966, pp. 151–174). The four major characteristics of the "Cult" are piety, purity, submissiveness, and domesticity. These traits, particularly submissiveness and domesticity, have had a particularly long-lasting effect on television's depictions of Jewish and African American wives/mothers. The portrayals of the Jewish mother are warnings to women about how not to behave. Depictions of African American mothers are far more complex, involving both the continuation of the Mammy image, and the matriarch, dualities that often are counter-hegemonic to the Cult of True Womanhood.

Because Jewish TV wives/mothers have notoriously been unwilling to submit to males, their sons and husbands have become unwilling hostages to their unending demands and complaints. She demasculates her husband and her son, infantilizing them in the pursuit of power and control, thus personifying what women should not try to emulate. Some would argue that the Jewish mother image on TV and other media gets transformed from a laughable caricature into a, "kind of pathology" (Friedman, 1998, p. 10). "Being a Jewish Mother is not only no honor, it is really a disease...without a cure" (Prell, 1999, p. 163). "Jewish women were excluded from the 'heart' of traditional Orthodox Judaism, from the mandatory communal prayer and study which is the Jew's primary mode of expression and commitment, and therefore from an active religious role" (Roith, 1987, p. 89).[6] Consequently, she needs to fulfill her religious and intellectual requirements largely by living vicariously through her sons and husbands. "The fact that legal, political, and religious authority resides in the men, together with the concomitant assumptions about women, ensures that the power of the woman is often a more subtle affair which, under certain unfavorable circumstances, may be comprised of emotional and psychological pressures: that is manipulative stratagems, such as emotional blackmail and masochistic threats mobilizing guilt, anxiety, and other pathological defenses" (Roith, 1987, p. 103). The men married to these Jewish mother types are often portrayed as weak willed, defeated, and often, as Frank Barone in *Everybody Loves Raymond* (1996–2005), somewhat demented.

Thus, the TV Jewish mother becomes the anti-purveyor of the tenets of the Cult of True Womanhood. Ida in *Rhoda,* Sylvia in *Mad About You* (1992–1999), and Susie in *Curb Your Enthusiasm* (2000–present) are obvious Jewish mothers. Estelle Costanza in *Seinfeld,* Marie Barone in *Everybody Loves Raymond,* and Livia Soprano in *The Sopranos* (1999–2007), all supposedly Italian matriarchs, are honorary members of the Jewish motherhood club.

In the 1993 *Mad About You* episode, "Bedfellows," Sylvia goes to visit her son, Paul and daughter-in-law Helen. They are so distraught when they hear she's coming that they both push a bureau to the door so they can "mom-proof" the room from her invasion. When Sylvia's husband is admitted to the hospital and needs to wear a heart monitor, both Paul and his sister Sharon agree that when Sylvia is in the room, her husband's heart monitor goes wild. Sharon exclaims, "oh my God, she's going to kill him and she'll come live with me."

Esther Costanza in *Seinfeld* has been described as a "fingernail scrapping against the scattered life of her son, George" (Antler in Gabler, 2000, p. 65). In the famous "Outing" episode, Seinfeld and George are mistakenly assumed to be gay by a New York University reporter. Estelle Costanza, while sitting on the toilet, reads the article about them in the paper. Estelle is so shocked she falls off the toilet and her back goes out. When George visits her in the hospital, she blames him again for her condition, and cries, "every day it's something else with you. I don't know anything about you anymore. Maybe you're making porno films!" In "The Contest," Estelle, prone to falling and guilt-tripping, once again lands in the hospital when she collapses after witnessing George in the act of masturbating. From her hospital bed she laments, "you have nothing better to do at 3:00 in the afternoon. You treat your body like an amusement park. Too bad you can't do that for a living. You'd be a big star!" Thus, not only is George infantilized, but he is humiliated constantly by his mother regarding his manhood. Susie, in *Curb Your Enthusiasm,* continues the expected portrayal of Jewish wives/mothers into the twenty-first century as she frequently excoriates her husband, Jeff Greene, with her favorite epithet, "you dumb f…k."

In seemingly great contradiction to the Jewish wife/mother's castrating, and exasperating relationship to the males in her life, is the African American mother in which so much sanctification surrounds black motherhood that, "the idea that mothers should live lives of sacrifice has come to be seen as the norm" (Collins, 2000, p. 174). Consequently, in the portrayals of African American mothers on television, sons are particularly deferential to mother's advice and wisdom. And in her, "devotion, self-sacrifice and unconditional love," she is apparently a model for the Cult of Domesticity. But because she'll "brook no bull from anyone," (Bogle, 2001, p. 429), she is unquestionably not submissive to men, often being portrayed as a virago whose men have long accepted her dominant role (*What's Happening, The Parkers, Everybody Hates Chris*). Frequently labeled as the "matriarch image," she "represents the sexually aggressive woman, one who emasculates black men because she will not permit them to assume roles as black patriarchs" (Collins, 1998, p. 127). The matriarch is represented far more subtly, and in a much more sophisticated manner, in such shows as *Good Times, The Jeffersons,* and *My Wife and Kids.*

From the early stages of black mothers on TV, defined character types are typical: the desexed "Mammy," the matriarch, and emerging after WWII a sexually aggressive, uncontrollable, and often welfare mother whose runaway sexuality is the reason for her impoverishment. "While the Mammy typifies the black mother figure in white homes, the matriarch symbolizes the mother figure in black homes (Collins, 1998, p.124–125). bell hooks explicates the reasons for the creation of the black Mammy figure, so intertwined with sexism and racism. "Considering white male lust for the bodies of black females, it is likely that white women were not pleased with young black women working in their homes for fear that liaisons between them and their husbands might be formed, so they conjured up an image of the black nanny" (hooks, 1981, p. 8), a fat, unclean, desexed sub-human who is programmed to serve the master willingly and effectively. Beulah is the ultimate example of the Mammy, but remnants of the heavy-set caricature remains in the mamas of *Good Times, What's Happening, The Jeffersons,* and even in such contemporary shows as *The Parkers.* Hefty black mothers on television are the norm into the twenty-first century (*My Wife and Kids, Everybody Hates Chris*).

Just as the Mammy represents the "good" black mother, the matriarch symbolizes the "bad" black mother (Collins, 2000, p. 75), wrenching control from her hapless husband or lover. The infamous Sapphire in *Amos 'n' Andy,* and her mother, were prototypical matriarchs, shrews who never ceased terrorizing the unfortunate men in their lives, Kingfish, Amos, and Andy. Mama admonishes Andy Brown in "Cousin Effie's Will," by declaring that he "don't got sense enough to come in out of the rain." This image is still replayed in such shows as *The Parkers* when Nikki, the obese, clumsy, and crude mother never ceases to pursue as her paramour, the sophisticated Professor Oglevee, or Rochelle in *Everybody Hates Chris,* a woman completely in control, and insisting on obedience or she'll " slap the caps off your knees!"

The TV Jewish mother is an icon that has basically remained immutable. Since the 1970s, she is a cloying nuisance in the lives of her husband and children. The African American mother on the other hand, is consistently presented as revered by her sons and daughters and often only tolerated by her male companions, be they husbands or lovers. She is still Mammy in her typically hefty appearance, often in unfashionable, bright clothing, with an overlay of the matriarch, a no-nonsense woman in control to the detriment of the adult men in her life. Thus, African American mothers have not shed the stereotypical images that began in 1950; they merely have been transformed to be more acceptable to audiences that no longer expect the blatant racism of *Beulah.* hooks (1998, p. 117) contends that there has been, in American culture, an understanding that the roles of black and white women are different; blacks serve, and whites are served. In contemporary times, the Mammy doesn't clean the white woman's house, but rather "caretakes her soul." In the sexual competition for women, white women are considered more desirable and thus more worthy of respect.

■ Decoding the Mythography

Is the key to the Jewish mother her Jewishness? Many writers have explained the longevity of the image, by emphasizing the need for the Jewish writer (largely male) to shed his shame for not being a Gentile, onto the Jewish mother who has locked him into an eternal struggle with his Jewishness. By portraying her in often such a disgusting fashion he can explain to his audience, but mainly to himself, that it really isn't his fault that he's so neurotic, a reductive explanation that suggests only one of several explanations.

As the Jewish male struggles for assimilation into the longed-for Gentile world, "these stereotypical women represent the anxiety, anger and pain of Jewish men as they negotiate an American Jewish identity. Jewish women, in these stereotypes, symbolize elements of 'Jewishness'…to be rejected" (Fishman, 1998, p. 5). And the men who portray these women can use them as "cultural decoys," (Fishman, 1998, p. 7) so that they can not only deal with their own paradoxes and ambiguities as to what their identity is, but they can also be free to jettison the deplorable traits onto women.

According to Paula Hyman, "faced with the need to establish their own identities in societies in which they were both fully acculturated and yet perceived as partially Other because they were Jews, Jewish men were eager to distinguish themselves from the women of their community, whom they saw as guardians of Jewishness. The negative representations of women that they produced reflected their own ambivalence about assimilation and its limits" (Fishman, 1998, p. 5). The male writer may be projecting onto the Jewish mother all the characteristics that he hates himself. Davidman reiterates the anguish that the third generation Jewish sons feel about assimilation and what responsibilities they have to carry on their heritage (Davidman and Tenenbaum, 1994). By vilifying their mothers, some of the burdens of these religious and cultural demands can be alleviated.

It has traditionally been up to the Jewish mother to promote and maintain in the family a Jewish way of life, an attachment not only to religious practices, but to cultural practices as well. What could account for Jews increasingly marrying out of the religion and rejecting their Judaism? The Jewish mother is an easy target as experts blame her in "her suburban world for many crises American Jews faced" (Prell, 1999, p. 151). The Jewish mother is too domineering, thus causing the poor father and children to submit to all of her demands, both emotionally and economically

Herman Gray (Gray, 2001, pp. 439–461) categorizes the evolving images of African Americans on television into three discursive practices: assimilationist, pluralist, and multi-culturalist. In such programs as *Julia* (1968–1971), black is invisible and Julia's problems are just the problems of an individual trying to raise her son. There is not a socio-economic or political dimension to the program, but rather a concentration on individuals, regardless of ethnicity or race or religion, navigating the vicissitudes of life. Shows such as *Good Times* and *What's Happening* are classified as pluralist, that is separate but equal. These families experience the same kinds of situations as whites, but they are separate from white society and largely do not represent the inherent struggles and diversity that either exists within the black community or the interracial conflicts that are occurring at the time. A bridge between Gray's pluralist and multi-culturalist (black middle class cultural viewpoints) perspectives is *The Jeffersons* (1975–1985), in which blacks and whites spar with each other, particularly represented by George in such episodes as "The First Store" (April 6, 1980) when George is convinced that he's dealing with a bigoted white banker. When Martin Luther King, Jr. is assassinated, he expresses his fury at whites by throwing a chair and shattering the window of his prospective new cleaning establishment.

In looking at more contemporary African American shows such as *The Parkers, My Wife and Kids,* and *Everybody Hates Chris,* the message promulgated is that racism is over. The hegemonic ideology is that it's up to the African American alone to improve his or her status. Nikki, in *The Parkers,* has her opportunity to start over again by becoming a student at Santa Monica College. Jay, in *My Wife and Kids,* is a modern day revised resuscitation of Clair Huxtable in *The Cosby Show,* who makes it because of her good middle-class values of work and perseverance, and Chris, in *Everybody Hates Chris,* is the vessel for his mother's credo that if Chris only associates with whites he will succeed. Societal structural change is not necessary because it's really the responsibility of the individual, not society, to cope with racism.

The African American mother though, on television, may actually not be a transformative archetype but a disguised one. "The image of Mammy, the loyal female servant created under chattel slavery, has been resurrected and modernized as a template for middle-class black womanhood. Maneuvering through this image of the modern Mammy requires a delicate balance between being appropriately subordinate to white and/or male authority yet maintaining a level of ambition and aggressiveness needed for achievement in middle class occupations" (Collins, 2005, p. 140). Patricia Hill Collins proposes that Mammy is not gone but has assumed new forms. "Within each segment of the labor market, the low-paid jobs at fast-food establishments, nursing homes, day-care centers, and dry cleaners that characterize the secondary sector, the secretaries and clerical workers of the primary lower tier sector, or the teachers, social workers, nurses, and administrators of the primary upper tier sector, U.S. black women still do a remarkable share of the emotional nurturing and cleaning up after other people" (Collins, 2000, p. 40). In that sense, black mothers from Beulah to Rochelle in *Everybody Hates Chris,* are still Mammies. By keeping African American mothers strong, and basically emasculating, the television power managers are using her as a "cultural decoy" to explain the African American male's position in society.

The Jewish mother has largely maintained her image as the "long-suffering Jewish mother, a role that quickly degenerated into a comic cliché…Celluloid Jewish mothers worry most of the time, they sigh and cry a lot. They protect their children" (Friedman, 1982, p. 162). The Jewish mother remains a one-dimensional figure, easily recognized not only by her behavior, but by her dress, and her nasally voice that always deteriorates into a whine. Hers is motherhood of denigration, and the African American mother is motherhood of sanctification. "Motherhood glorification is especially prominent in the works of U.S. black men who routinely praise black mothers, especially their own" (Collins, 2000, p. 174). However, Jewish women are often demonized by Jewish men. The Jewish mother becomes a cultural construct of negative mothering, and the African American mother, a construct of positive mothering. Are they both manifestations of the inherent ambiguities males feel towards mothers? In either case, males are threatened by these Amazon women who have the audacity to demand agency.

Television writers have perpetuated the formulaic caricature of the Jewish and African American mothers, precisely because they elicit specific, inalterable, and prejudiced reactions from the audience. Through the guise of humor, many otherwise painful and best hidden interactions between mother and child can be safely navigated and ignored. By presenting her as an icon, be it positive or negative, she is relegated to a form of powerlessness in the public sphere, a predictability that can be controlled. We can laugh at her and keep her somewhat manageable, as she cleverly manipulates her own miniature environment.

It is incumbent on all viewers to become "media literate," in an effort to counter the manipulations that television programming promulgates. Stereotypes are comfortable for the audience and project a false sense of benignity, but "when exposed to negative, stereotypic depictions of blacks, whites reported higher levels of negative evaluations of blacks compared with non-stereotypical depictions" (Greenberg et al., 2002, p. 344). What is so insidious about the portrayals of the black mother is that she possesses so many seemingly positive characteristics, but despite this she is still a recognizable type, not individualized. After conducting focus group sessions on attitudes about Jewish women gleaned from TV, the Morning Star Commission found that most saw "Jewish women as pushy, controlling, unattractive, materialistic, high maintenance, shallow, and domineering….cheap bargain hunters who nagged their husbands and spend all their time shopping and cooking." Physically, they are even more repulsive, "overweight and big-nosed, sharp tongued and arrogant, scolds and henpeckers" (Antler in Gabler, 2000, p. 54). Thousands of words have been written about why Jewish men do not want to marry Jewish women, a view that is obviously understandable given the propagandizing about her many undesirable traits. By perpetuating these images, the powerful (usually white males) can continue to maintain hierarchical control over all women by pitting woman against man, race against race, and class against class.

Notes

1. *Beulah* was originally a radio show that began in 1945 and became a television show from 1950–1953. The show is a situation comedy about an African American housekeeper and cook who serves in the household of the white Henderson family. Beulah is a stereotypical Mammy figure who inevitably solves the problems in the family.

2. *Amos 'n' Andy* began as a radio show in 1928 with white actors who promoted the minstrel traditions of the time. The show was adapted for television and shown from 1951–1953, and this time used African American actors. *Amos 'n' Andy* details the life of poor African Americans living in Chicago. The three main characters are Amos, honest and a dedicated worker, Andy, lazy and a

dreamer, and Kingfish, their lodge leader who's always trying to convince the two that his schemes will make each one of them rich. Because this situation comedy egregiously promoted despicable racial stereotypes, the NAACP spearheaded a protest, and was eventually successful in having the show canceled in 1953.

3. *The Goldbergs* began on the radio as a daily show in 1931, and eventually became a TV show off and on from 1949 to 1959. The show relays the exploits of a poor Jewish immigrant family in New York, learning how to become good Americans.

4. A "shtetl" refers to a little village or small town in the Jewish communities of Eastern Europe. "The Jews of the shtetl were poor folk, fundamentalist in faith, earthy, superstitious, stubbornly resisting secularism or change" (Rosten, 1968, p. 373). The Jewish mother from the shtetl was often idealized as the perfect, self-sacrificing woman, who protected her children from the real-life threats to their very existence.

5. *Rhoda,* on television from 1974–1978, is a spin-off from *The Mary Tyler Moore Show. Rhoda* tells the story of a young Jewish woman who tries to escape her upbringing and the demands of her mother Ida, by moving from New York to Minneapolis. Eventually she returns to New York and marries Joe Girard, a relationship that ends in divorce.

6. Orthodox Jewish women are not allowed to read the Torah (the first five books of the Bible) in the synagogue, cannot be a part of a religious quorum for worship which requires ten men, cannot become rabbis, cannot start divorce proceedings, cannot be a witness in a Jewish court of law, and must maintain distance from men during menstruation. (Roith, 1987)

References

Antler, J. (2000). Problematics. In N. Gabler, F. Rich and J. Antler (Eds.) *Television's Changing Images of American Jews* (pp. 43–75) . Los Angeles: American Jewish Committee.

Bogle, D. (2001). *Prime Time Blues: African Americans on Network Television.* New York: Farrar, Straus and Giroux.

Collins, P. H. (1998). Mammies, Matriarchs, and Other Controlling Images. In R. Adkins et al., (Eds.) *Placing Women's Studies* (pp. 121–134). New York: McGraw-Hill.

Collins, P. H. (2000). *Black Feminist Thought.* New York: Routledge.

Collins, P. H. (2005). *Black Sexual Politics.* New York: Routledge.

Davidman, L. & Tenenbaum, S. (Eds.). (1994) *Feminist Perspectives on Jewish Studies.* New Haven: Yale University Press.

Ely, M. P. (1991). *The Adventures of Amos 'n' Andy: A Social History of an American Phenomenon.* New York: The Free Press.

Fishman, S. B. (1998) *I of the Beholder. Jews and Gender in Film and Popular Culture.* Waltham, MA: Haddassah Research Institute on Jewish Women.

Friedman, M. (1982). *Capitalism and freedom.* Chicago, IL: University of Chicago Press.

———— (1998). *Two lucky people: Memoirs.* Chicago, IL: University of Illinois Press.

Gerbner, G. et al., (2002) Growing Up with Television: Cultivation Processes. In J. Bryant & D. Zillmann (Eds.) *Media Effects: Advances in Theory and Research* (pp. 43–63). Mahwah, NJ: Lawrence Erlbaum Associates.

Gray, H. (2001). The Politics of Representation in Network Television. In M. G. Durham & D. M. Kellner (Eds.) *Media and Cultural Studies: KeyWorks* (pp. 439–461) Malden, MA: Blackwell Publishers Ltd.

Greenberg, B.S., et al. (2002). Minorities and the Mass Media: Television Into the 21st Century. In J. Bryant & D. Zillmann (Eds.) *Media Effects: Advances in Theory and Research* (pp. 333–351). Mahwah, N.J.: Lawrence Erlbaum Associates.

hooks, bell. (1981). *Ain't I A Woman.* Boston: South End Press.

hooks, bell (1998). Where Is the Love? Political Bonding Between Black and White Women. In R. Adkins et al. (Eds.) *Placing Women's Studies* (pp. 116–119). New York: McGraw-Hill.

hooks, bell. (2000). *Feminist Theory. From Margin to Center.* Cambridge, MA: South End Press.

hooks, bell. (2001) Eating the Other: Desire and Resistance. In M.G. Durham & D. M. Kellner (Eds.) *Media and Cultural Studies: KeyWorks* (pp. 424–438). Malden, MA: Blackwell Publishers Ltd.

Hunt, D. M. (2005). Making Sense of Blackness on Television. In D. M. Hunt (Ed.). *Channeling Blackness* (pp. 1–24). New York: Oxford University Press.

Jhally, S. & Lewis J. (1992). *Enlightened Racism.* Boulder, Co.: Westview Press.

Kellner, D.M. & Durham, M. G. (2001) Adventures in Media and Cultural Studies: Introducing the KeyWorks. In M.G. Durham & D.M. Kellner (Eds.) *Media and Cultural Studies: KeyWorks* (pp. 1–29) Malden, MA: Blackwell Publishers. Ltd.

Leistyna, P. & Alper, L. (2007). Critical Media Literacy for the Twenty-First Century. In D. Macedo and S. Steinberg (Eds.) *Media Literacy* (pp. 54–78). New York: Peter Lang.

Lewis, Justin (2002). Mass Communications Studies. In T. Miller (Ed.). *Television Studies* (pp. 4–7). London: British Film Institute.

Lorde, Audre (1984). *Sister Outsider.* Berkeley: Crossing Press.

MacDonald, J. F. (1992) *Blacks and White TV.* Chicago: Nelson-Hall Publishers.

Pearl, J. & Pearl, J. (1999). *The Chosen Image: Television's Portrayal of Jewish Themes and Characters.* Jefferson, NC: McFarland & Co., Inc.

Prell, R. E. (1999). *Fighting to Become Americans. Assimilation and the Trouble Between Jewish Women and Jewish Men.* Boston: Beacon Press.

Roith, E. (1987). *The Riddle of Freud: Jewish Influences on His Theory of Female Sexuality.* New York: Tavistock Publications.

Rosten, L. (1968). *The Joys of Yiddish.* New York: Pocket Books.

Welter, Barbara. (1966). The Cult of True Womanhood: 1820–1860. In *American Quarterly* 18 (Summer 1966): pp. 151–174.

Winant, H, (2004). *The New Politics of Race.* Minneapolis, MN: University of Minnesota Press.

22

■ Successful, Single, and "Othered"

The Media and the "Plight" of Single Black Women

Felicia D. Henderson

[In 2005], the federal government reported that 44 percent of black men and 42 percent of black women had never been married. Black men and women surveyed this year in a national poll conducted by *The Washington Post*, the Henry J. Kaiser Family Foundation and Harvard University said they believe the top reasons for the decline are the high incarceration and murder rates for young black men.[1]

Washington Post

While finding Mr. Right can be tough for women of all races, black women in Pittsburgh find it especially hard. If statistics show anything, it quantifies the situation facing unmarried black women. Gaps in education, high unemployment and incarceration rates among black men and lack of workplace diversity have created a dating dilemma.[2]

Pittsburgh Tribune

40 years ago marriage and children were a given in most women's lives, today many of us are entering our thirties and forties with no prospects. We have our degrees, we've scaled a few rungs on the career ladder and we're finally ready to settle down. But we find ourselves confronted with a relatively new reality—that we may never marry at all.[3]

Essence Magazine

Go to any Friday night to Lola's Cajun eatery in Los Angeles and you'll find a weekly gathering of what could easily be dubbed "the black, beautiful, accomplished but can't find a mate club." In bars, colleges and other gathering spots across America, the question is much the same: where are the decent, desirable black men?[4]

Newsweek Magazine

Cover stories in magazines that cater to black women, mainstream magazines, countless newspaper articles, and *The Oprah Winfrey Show* have bemoaned the "plight" of single, black women. According to these reports, the situation is dire for the single black woman hoping to be married: She is too accomplished and black men are too few. In interview after interview, black women themselves participate in the critical unpacking of their "plight." The black woman also laments the aberrant nature of her singlehood and how terrified she is about her future as an unmarried woman. The media then further validate her terror by reminding her that not only do black women outnumber black men, those black men that do exist are not marriageable.

For example, on one hand, a 2003 *Newsweek Magazine* series praises the strides black professional women have made, complete with a photograph of several female veterinary students in lab coats—signs of the educational strivings of young, black women.

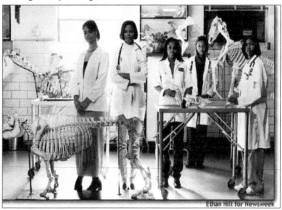
Ethan Hill for Newsweek

Then, in a later photograph, four attractive friends are posed to illustrate maximum hopelessness while sharing an evening together. The photograph is a wide, full-body shot, and the women are arranged in a manner that suggests empty space surrounds their lives. The caption reads, "What's love got to do with it?"

A third photograph is of a mother solemnly hugging one young daughter as another teenaged daughter stands nearby. All three women forlornly stare into the camera. The copy that

accompanies the photograph explains that this mother is preparing her daughters for the possibility of ending up alone.

This juxtaposition of images—the rising professional class of black women and the accomplished but lonely black woman—is only one example of a theme that occurs often in the media.

It is not only the print media that reinforce the "plight" of the single black woman. In 2007, the feature film, *Something New,* further reinforced the lack of marriage-able black men by depicting the dating options of a black female accountant whose best hope for love is a white landscape architect she hires for a home improvement project. After all, if "forty-two percent of black women might never marry because of the dearth of marriageable black men," then black women had better expand their horizons if they want to marry. Media messages that can be described as a schizophrenic bombardment of images that frame black women as social misfits simultaneously praise the accomplish-

Ann States for Newsweek

ments of these women while depicting them as unmarriageable for being accomplished.

At least two disturbing messages are being regularly disseminated: 1) The black woman may be smart, but she will be alone because of her intelligence; and 2) If she is alone in a culture where heterosexual marriage is still the dominant lifestyle, she is a freak of nature who should feel dejected, even depressed about her apparent abnormality. These messages, along with the often-reported statistics on the number of unmarriageable black males, serve to create a new stereotype of black women.

According to Stuart Hall, "stereotyping reduces, essentializes, naturalizes and fixes 'difference.' It is part of the maintenance of social and symbolic order. It sets up a symbolic frontier between the 'normal' and the 'deviant,' the 'normal' and the 'pathological,' the 'acceptable' and the 'unacceptable,' what 'belongs' and what does not or is 'Other.'"[5] It is this Othering, or categorization based on difference, that is at the root of yet another addition to the list of stereotypes of black women. The mammies, matriarchs, welfare recipients, and hot mommas so meticulously deconstructed by black feminist Patricia Hill Collins have not disappeared. However, these stereotypes have taken a back seat to the new racialized Other—the single, desperate and lonely, educated black woman whose purpose is to reinforce a socio-cultural system that is white, male-dominated, and married.

As depicted in the mass media, this group of women is desperately attempting to attain what is unattainable. Rather than attempting to redefine normal for themselves, black women continue to buy into and be defined by a system that is dominated by white males and invested in the institution of marriage that must Other *Singleness, Blackness,* and *Femaleness* in order to perpetuate itself. As noted by Hill Collins, "Black women's lives are a series of negotiations that aim to reconcile the contradictions separating our own internally defined images of self as African-American women with our objectification as the Other."[6] If this is so, the contradictions between self-definition and objectification require black women to become media literate in order to interrupt the media's messages about who and what they are.

By utilizing close textual analysis and a critical media literacy approach—a multiperspectival interrogation of mass media messages in print advertising, popular press, and feature filmmaking—a diagnostic critique emerges of how a media culture driven society uses class, race, and gender to Other single black females and reinforce America's dominant patriarchal power structure. By critically analyzing media images of single black women, the need for media literacy becomes clear. How differently would the messages be received if the primary subjects—black women—were well informed about how to read media texts in order to interrogate and decode them and to reject what is false and/or detrimental and what prevents the self-definition of "normal"?

More specifically, this project will be approached from multiple points of entry to examine various mass media: 1) print advertising—the De Beers Corporation's *Right Hand Ring* campaign; 2) the popular press—a *Washington Post* multipart series on blacks and dating; and 3) a feature film—*Something New*—an interracial romantic comedy. Such an approach will address several questions: Why are the media so invested in crafting the single black woman's image as that of a social outcast who is fearful and desperate as a result of her attempts to find a marriageable man? Do black women really "lack" families or simply "opt against" them? How do the media use singlehood to negate the historical strides made by educated, successful black women?

■ Ring Finger Blues: What's Wrong with the "Right Hand Ring" Campaign?

Media culture scholar Douglas Kellner defines a diagnostic critique as one that uses history to read texts and texts to read history. Kellner argues that such a dual optic allows insight into the multiple relations between text and contexts, between media culture and history.[7] The media have often painted the single black woman as desperate to find a marriageable man. In print advertising this stereotype or Othering is reinforced through De Beers Corporation's *Right Hand Ring* campaign.

> In 1947, a maiden copywriter at N.W. Ayer, Frances Gerety, created the most durable advertising slogan in history: A diamond is forever. Within three years of creating the 'diamonds are forever' slogan, an estimated eighty percent of wedding engagements in America were consecrated with diamond rings. The true genius of De Beers lies in having created a connection, and sustaining in the popular imagination a connection between something that has no value at all and something that is extremely valuable, which is human love. They created that connection—they made it up—and they've sustained it.[8]

De Beers was founded over one hundred years ago in South Africa. The company dominates the world's diamond market by controlling supply and aggressive marketing. Through its marketing arm, the Diamond Trading Company, De Beers continues to increase the diamond's growth in the marketplace. Besides the highly influential, *Diamonds Are Forever* campaign, De Beers has been very successful with other advertising campaigns, including: *Journey Diamond Jewelry*—"celebrating the journey and growth of love": For example, *The Trilogy Ring* "represent[s] the past, present and future of a relationship," and

The Right Hand Ring "symboliz[es] a woman's independence" (and is primarily purchased by women).[9]

The *Right Hand Ring* marketing campaign is what Kellner calls "the text." This campaign provides rich and complicated material through which a critical examination of the relationship between the media and "the history" (educational, financial, and professional status) of black women can be conducted. Further, this relationship can be decoded counter-hegemonically to explore class, gender, and race in the United States. The De Beers "Diamonds Are Forever" *Right Hand Ring* ads began to appear in the fall of 2003. The copy for the ad that features a black woman reads:

> *Your left hand plans ahead. Your right hand plans for anything. Your left hand gets it done. Your right hand shows the world how it's really done. Women of the world, raise your right hand.*

This campaign encourages the black woman to celebrate her independence by buying herself a diamond ring for her right hand. The mere fact that the woman in the advertisement is black does not necessarily suggest that the product is being sold to this segment of the population. However, the ad was placed in *Essence Magazine,* a preeminent black woman's magazine. Therefore, the advertisement is directed at this segment of the population.

The popular press and scholarly research report that black women are experiencing greater educational, economic, and political gains than at any other time in American history. According to *Newsweek,* "Once consigned to mostly menial work, black women (24 percent, compared with 17 percent of black men) have ascended to the professional-managerial class.…College-educated black women already earn more than the median wage of all black working men—or, for that matter, of all women. And as women, in general, move up the corporate pyramid, black women increasingly are part of the parade."[10] It is this parade that is reinforced in the "Diamonds Are Forever" ad campaign. In the print ad, an obviously affluent black woman sits on a well-appointed emerald sofa, in an expensive formal gown, and casually, confidently, *raises her right hand* (see *Appendix A* for a larger image). On that right hand is a substantial diamond, digitally enhanced to emphasize the diamond's *bling*—the ultimate hip-hop inspired symbol of an ostentatious attitude about one's affluence. In other words, what the hip-hop generation refers to as "ghetto fabulous" goes upscale here. However, the image is problematic on many levels.

If the *Newsweek* statistics are accurate, 24 percent of black women have reached professional-managerial class. This indicates that, conversely, 76 percent of black women still labor at a socio-economic level below that of the Right Hand Ring woman. Through this ad, these women, the clear majority of black women, are exposed to more schizophrenic messages by the diamond industry's marketing machine: 1) If you are not this woman, an accomplished young beauty with an abundance of disposable income, this ad is not for you. You are of little value to us and by extension to the larger society that sets the rules by which your worth is judged. 2) Through presenting the woman in the ad as the definition of success, 76 percent of the black female population, which includes a large number of working-class and poor women, is encouraged to emulate the woman in the ad. The message is: If this woman represents what is valuable in society, I want what she has, which includes the right hand ring. By wearing such a ring, like the woman in the ad, I will be successful, beautiful, and self-confident. Even if it means purchasing an item I can't afford. As quoted by Sut Jhally, one advertising executive best described the ideas explicated above: "Advertising doesn't always mirror how people are acting but how they're dreaming. In a sense what we're doing is wrapping up your emotions and selling them back to you."[11]

Even for the affluent black women, the ad's message is problematic. Given that single black women experience a constant barrage of mass media messages about their desperate matrimonial prospects, this ad is additional reinforcement for the idea that the probability of her getting married is so slim that she may never get a diamond placed on her left-hand ring finger, so she had better buy her own diamond for her right hand. As the ad claims, "Your left hand plans ahead. Your right hand plans for anything." In other words, the bare ring finger on her left hand indicates that she is not married. Therefore, she should "plan" for this by purchasing herself a diamond for her right hand as a symbol of her acceptance of her singlehood. The deconstruction of this ad reveals that the diamond industry has found yet another means of increasing the market for its product by creating another reason to purchase diamonds, and, as is not the case for engagement and anniversary diamonds, the marketing is not dependent on getting the attention of men.

Through the Right Hand Ring campaign the diamond industry is able to sidestep male consumer-centered marketing campaigns and market its product directly to women by giving them an emotional-social reason to buy a diamond ring for themselves. This is not to say that men are not encouraged to buy these rings for the independent women—mothers, sisters, and lovers—in their lives. Although it is not the project of this argument, given that gay couples have traditionally worn commitment rings on their right hands, there is much to be said about the subtle ways in which this Right Hand Ring campaign is targeting them without having to announce to the dominant heterosexual culture that it is doing so.

Through the media's discussion of and marketing to black women, a construction of stereotypes of black accomplished women emerges. However, a critical media approach to an analysis of the construction of such stereotypes is incomplete without juxtaposing the images of black women with those of white women. In the *Right Hand Ring* campaign three print ads that feature white women are similar, in many ways, to the ad that features a black woman. A dominant reading of this marketing campaign suggests that purchasing a diamond ring for oneself is a feminist act that signifies independence from the need to be given a ring by a male. However, if one reads the ads oppositionally, such ads fortify the hegemonic institution of marriage.

Of the four *Right Hand Ring* ads analyzed here (see *Appendix A for larger images*), the model's left hand (and her ring or "marriage" finger) is hidden in two of the ads and the ring or "marriage" finger is bare in the two ads in which it was visible. In other words, each woman's "marriage" finger is still available and ready to have an engagement ring placed on it. But while she waits, the independent woman has the financial means to purchase her own diamond for her right hand. This message in what Jhally calls a "commodity image-system" provides a particular vision of the world—a particular mode of self-validation that is integrally connected with what one has rather than what one is. In the sense that every ad says it is better to buy than not to buy, we can best regard advertising as a propaganda system for commodities. In the image-system as a whole, happiness lies at the end of a purchase.[12] Although the financially independent woman can purchase her own diamond as depicted in the ad, independence equals aloneness, a woman who is unable to find a mate.

This message is strongly reinforced by the fact that all of the women in the ads are single. The message of being independent and alone is even more pointedly made in the ad that features the single black woman. All four of the models are beautiful, appealing brunettes who are photographed in dramatic, romantic lighting. The fact that all three white women are brunettes reinforces another media-perpetuated stereotype—blondes are for fun and brunettes are for marriage. Although the brunettes in the ads are all single, by virture of their hair color, they are marriage-ready. However, it is how the three ads featuring white women differ from the ad featuring the black woman that is most significant:

Right Hand Ring Ad #1   **Right Hand Ring Ad #2**   **Right Hand Ring Ad #3**   **Right Hand Ring Ad #4**

- All of the white women in the ads have blue eyes; the black woman's eyes are dark brown.

- The copy on the ads that feature the white women begins with lines that refer to romance and marriage. However, the ad featuring the black woman begins with a line about planning her [lonely] life. Ad #1: *Your left hand dreams of love...* Ad #2: *Your left hand sees red and thinks roses...* Ad #3: *Your left hand says you're taken...* The copy on the ad that features the black woman begins, *Your left hand plans ahead.*

- The white women are photographed in medium and three-quarter length close-ups; The black woman is photographed in a long shot.

- The white women are conservatively dressed; the black woman is dressed in a skin-baring dress that is either a formal gown or an expensive nightgown (lingerie).

All of these factors constitute visually reinforced methods of Othering the black woman. Blue eyes further emphasize the preferred "whiteness" of the women in the ads. The copy in the ads that feature the preferred women attests to their desirability. They are romantics who are or soon will be in relationships, while the left hand of the black woman simply "plans ahead." Her future is that she will take care of herself, so she does not entertain romantic notions. Additionally, all of the white women are photographed in close-ups. Close-ups are more intimate shots, and this intimacy invites the reader to get to know the women behind the blue eyes.

The black woman is photographed in a long shot. This shot is more impersonal in that she is farther away from the reader/viewer, the photograph and the statement it makes are that of the aloof, unattainable stranger. Additionally, long shots are designed to highlight the mise-en-scene or surroundings in which the subject is placed and makes the subject appear small in comparison to her "world." In the ads that feature the white women, the background and the furniture on which the women sit are barely discernible. The black woman sits on a sofa that is green, the color of money, and a symbol of her affluence. Also, because it is a long shot, one can easily determine that she is alone on a sofa that has room for another person, but that person, her potential mate, does not exist. Her clothing is more sensual, making her more sexually appealing, yet she is photographed in a manner that depicts her aloneness and therefore her Otherness.

Why is Otherness, in this case racial difference, such a compelling object of representation? What do the differences in how single white women and single black women are depicted in the ads mean? As argued by British cultural theorist, Stuart Hall:

> Meaning is established through dialogue—it is fundamentally dialogic. Everything we say and mean is modified by the interaction and interplay with another person. Meaning arises through the "difference" between the participants in any dialogue. The "Other," in short, is essential to meaning.[13]

Stuart Hall further illuminates the dialogue on meaning by pointing out that it cannot be fixed, and one group can never be completely in charge of meaning. In the case of these ads, De Beers desires to sell diamond rings to single women who otherwise might not be able to justify having one. Through a marketing campaign, this purchase is given meaning: It signifies independence and success. However, in a media-dominated society, when a segment of the population is empowered through the media in a manner that is counter to the hegemonic power structure, the representations that do not reinforce that power structure are contained through Othering those being represented. Anthropologist Mary Douglas and others argue that cultural order is disturbed when things turn up in the wrong category or when things fail to fit any category. As paraphrased by Hall, what unsettles culture is 'matter out of place'—the breaking of our unwritten rules and codes. Dirt in the garden is fine, but dirt in one's bedroom is 'matter out of place,' a sign of pollution, of symbolic boundaries being transgressed, of taboos being broken. We must sweep up this 'matter,' throw it out, restore the place to order, and bring back the normal state of affairs.[14]

Because the growing population of affluent black women cannot be merely swept out the door, they are marginalized and contained by becoming the racialized Other in the process of purification and restoration of the white, male-dominated power structure. In other words, a single black woman is invited to consume the products of the rich and powerful, but she is not truly accepted as one of them. In fact, in the De Beers ad her conspicuous consumption reinforces the media's depiction of her as alone. Lacking marriageable black men, she must buy the diamonds; an effective marketing campaign has convinced her, as she accepts her aloneness.

■ "Point & Click": Media Obsession with Single Black Women Goes Interactive

In October 2006 the *Washington Post* published a multipart series that explored the complex relationship between single black men and black women. It is not the first such series.

In fact, it is merely part of a mass media obsession. In the past several years, *Newsweek Magazine, Essence Magazine, USA Today,* and the *Washington Post,* are among the many mainstream print outlets that have participated in the obsession. Most of the articles begin similarly, with the shocking statistics. The focus of such statistics is usually the dearth of black men who are marriage material; the educational, economic, and professional gains of single black women; and why this combination of "facts" necessarily leads to a black woman considering dating outside of her race.

As Kellner points out, the media are a profound and often misperceived source of cultural pedagogy. They educate us on how to act and what to think, feel, believe, fear, and desire—and what not to want. Therefore, critical media literacy is important if individuals are learning how to cope with a seductive cultural environment.[15] Given how often the media focuses on the "plight" of single black women, particularly middle and upper-middle-class black women, society receives a continuous bombardment of what to "think, feel, believe, and fear" about this segment of the population. As consumers of media, single black women are also being taught what to think of themselves and their place in this society.

When considering the *Washington Post* piece through a cultural pedagogical lens, one idea is clear—the representation of single black women as a group of desperate citizens in search of mates that do not exist has been extended to include the interactive capabilities of cyberspace. The series of articles printed in the *Washington Post* were then posted on *Washington Post.com* with an additional feature—the ability to point and click. Through the posting on the newspaper's website, the printed piece was no longer just one of the many articles that crop up in the press about the plight of single black women. The media-perpetuated idea of single black women as desperate "Others" now becomes an interactive game. In short, the interactive world of cyberspace is a highly seductive and potentially manipulative environment—one that is ideal for reinforcing dominant ideologies.

All you have to do is point and click on subject titles: a) The Importance of Marriage; b) Marrying a Black Man; and c) Interracial Dating to find yourself transported inside the single black woman's mind and inside her dilemma. The dominant ideology being reinforced through *Washington Post.com*—the set of beliefs, values, and opinions that shapes the way America sees single black women—becomes even more powerful via the interactivity component. By clicking on "The Importance of Marriage" or "Marrying a Black Man" one can peruse multiple responses to the questions being posed (see *Appendix B* for a larger image of the interactive page of the article). By this interactive act, the patriarchal norms of the United States are reinforced.

By interviewing single black women, posting their responses, and giving readers the ability to surf the site for the many examples (provided by black women) of desperation experienced by these women, the *Washington Post* has made the subordination through "Othering" of single black females appear natural and just. The dominant ideology is reinforced—the institution of marriage is still celebrated; black women are still outperforming black men, educationally and financially; and interracial dating may be a single black woman's only hope.

As evidenced on the home page photograph of this interactive story (see *Appendix B),* single black women come in all shapes, sizes, and shades of brown and black. In other words, ideological domination casts a wide net in ensuring that all of the members of the subordinated group are represented. If, as Hall suggests, ideological work is the winning and securing of hegemony over time, the fact that one more media outlet (the Internet) has been secured for presenting the multi-media reinforced representation of the "plight" of single black women suggests a strengthening of dominant American ideologies. As discussed earlier, black women themselves participate in the reinforcement of their dire plight. However, it is not only consumers who participate in this reinforcement. Another manner in which dominant American ideologies are privileged is through an unlikely place—the black women who have the opportunity to create their own images. This idea is counter-intuitive if you consider the work of Jacqueline Bobo and others who argue that black women offer the best opportunity to provide more accurate portrayals of themselves.

■ Something Old in Something New: Interracial Dating and Desperation

To offer opposition to the dominant American ideologies, in *Black Women as Cultural Readers,* Jacqueline Bobo argues that effective counters to black women's representation in mainstream media are the works by black women themselves. According to Bobo, "Black women's perspective on their material conditions has impelled them to value the ways in which they represent themselves, for others' characterizations have distorted their history and attributes."[16] Bobo connects black women's history of resistance to social domination to their resistance to cultural domination. In the 2006 feature film *Something New,* the complicated nature of the politics of representation is on full display. Historically, since the revolting and racist representations of blacks in 1915's *Birth of a Nation,* blacks have contested their depictions at the hands of non-blacks. The National Association for the Advancement of Colored People (NCAAP) and other civil

rights organizations have protested negative media portrayals and stereotypes for nearly a century. Such organizations have consistently bemoaned the scarcity of people in positions of power who look like those being depicted in terms of race and gender. The logic being that if more women and racial minorities were "behind the scenes" creating images, those images would be less harmful and offensive and more positive and authentic. However, the politics of representation are not that simple. As found in *Something New,* some negative stereotypes are diminished when the images on screen are created or controlled by people who are of the group being represented. However, other stereotypes can be brought to the fore. As argued by Kellner:

> The products of media culture require multidimensional close textual readings to analyze their various forms of discourses, ideological positions, narrative strategies, image construction, and effects…qualitative study examines images of women, blacks, or other groups or applies various critical theories to unpack the meanings of the texts to explicate how texts function to produce meaning.[17]

A qualitative analysis of character development and narrative structure in *Something New* demonstrates how meaning is produced through verbal and nonverbal signs and symbols and the binary use of race.

In *Something New,* Kenya McQueen (Sanaa Lathan) is a successful, single black accountant who is a workaholic. Urged by her friends to let go of her dream of the "Ideal Black Man" (or "IBM"), she accepts a blind date with Brian, a landscape architect (Simon Fuller). However, Kenya abruptly ends the date upon discovering that Brian is white. The two meet again at an engagement party and Kenya hires Brian to landscape her backyard. When the two find themselves romantically interested in the other, it is a case of opposites attract: she is a prissy neat-freak who is wound too tightly; he is a grungy everyman who travels with his dog. Yet the two find themselves attracted to each other. When they begin dating Kenya's friends make inappropriate jokes about the couple, and her brother threatens to tell their parents that she has been "sneaking off to the O.C."

From there, the romantic comedy about finding love in the least likely places further reinforces what other mass media texts continue to dictate—affluent black women are lonely and desperate, have no marriage possibilities among black men, and therefore must continue to purchase expensive toys, cars, and homes in an effort to consume their way to happiness. Or, as in *Something New,* she can decide to accept the inevitable road to contentment—interracial dating. The message is that a single black woman can only be happy in the arms of someone who is the embodiment of everything she is not—a culturally and socially dominant white male.

Something New begins with a nightmare. It is Kenya's wedding day; everything is perfect, including the bride. At the moment that she is about to kiss her new husband, a handsome black male, alarm sirens sound as if the wedding party is about to come under aerial assault. As everyone runs away screaming, Kenya bolts awake. She is back to her plight-ridden reality. She is successful, single, and alone on Valentine's Day. Within the first thirty minutes of the film Kenya receives a phone call from her father urging her not to give up on finding a mate; her best friends (a pediatrician, a banker, and a judge) share drinks to lament their plight as professional, single black women; Kenya greets several "unacceptable" working-class black men on the street as she takes her morning power walk; and one of her co-workers, an attractive, young white woman, asks for Kenya's help in choosing the perfect wedding dress. Over and over, the narrative reminds the audience that Kenya is single, accomplished, bright, and alone—a representation that is found throughout various forms of media texts and reinforces the idea of the single black woman as desperate and lonely.

Characterizations associated with class politics also reinforce the ideas expressed in the narrative. Kenya is a well-educated accountant; her only brother is a film studio attorney, and her father is a neurosurgeon. She has just purchased her first home in an affluent suburb of Los Angeles and is about to be made partner at her firm. Her love interest is not only a white male, he is a blue-collar entrepreneur. Therefore, Kenya's brother feels justified in being rude to Brian when he meets him. When Kenya brings her brother's unacceptable behavior to his attention, he is incredulous and defends his behavior by declaring, "he's the help!"

There are competing problematic issues here. On one hand, affluent single black women are encouraged to separate themselves from others who are not equally economically advantaged. All the black men who signify working-class status (a security guard, a cook, and a gardener) are depicted as being interested in Kenya, but she is not interested in them. For an upper-class black woman, such a black man is not marriageable. On the other hand, however, when Kenya finally gives up on finding an acceptable black man and dates a white man, race and class politics conflictingly intersect. Brian is a member of the dominant culture's privileged race—a white man—but he is also a landscaper—working class. Because of the value placed on whiteness, he does not have to meet the same standards that she set forth for a black man as a potential mate. What is most interesting about these narrative signs of the marginalized single black woman's desperation is that these problematic issues are depicted in a film written by Kriss Turner, a single black woman.[18]

When this film was released Turner, Lathan, and the film's director (Sanaa Hamri) appeared on ABC's late night news broadcast, *Nightline,* and on *The Oprah Winfrey Show.* Both interviews celebrated the fact the film starred a black woman (Lathan), was written by a black woman (Turner), produced by a black woman (Stephanie Allain), and was directed by a woman (Hamri), who, although she is not black, is a woman of color. Somehow this emphasis on the creative team's race and gender is supposed to sooth the sensibilities of single black women like the one depicted in the film. At least her story, in the body of Kenya, is being told by those sensitive to who she is. What complicates this assumption is well stated in bell hooks' work on racism and feminism, "American women, irrespective of their education, economic status, or racial identification, have undergone years of sexist and racist socialization that has taught us to blindly trust our knowledge of history and its effect on present reality, even though that knowledge has been shaped by an oppressive system."[19]

As further argued by hooks in her essays on black filmmakers, "The essentialist belief that merely the presence of larger numbers of visible black filmmakers would lead to a more progressive and/or revolutionary cinematic representation of blackness has been utterly challenged by the types of films that are being made."[20] Although hooks was not referring to *Something New,* specifically, and, in fact, was speaking to more traditional and insidiously ingrained stereotypes of blacks and women, her argument is applicable to the "new and improved" stereotype of the middle-class black woman that depends on her upward mobility and her marital status to further the ideologies of a white, male-dominated America.

In *Something New* the story's dialogue, although written by a black woman, reinforces the idea that there is something wrong with being black and single. Kenya's beautiful, young, engaged to be married, and white co-worker tells her, "We've got to get you married," as if being single is a disease. While Kenya goes out for drinks with her friends, a lawyer, doctor, and judge, one of them says, "We may not have everything we want at the moment, but we have each other." They are depicted as a sad and lonely crew of educated, upwardly-mobile women who appear to have everything except the one thing that will make you whole—a husband. This is the problematic part of the depiction of successful black women by a creative team of black women. It is not necessarily damaging to the psyche of black girls and black women to see cinematic representations of their lives as single and successful. What is damaging, however, is the added characterization of their lives as incomplete because they are not married and the reinforcement of mass media's obsession with the supposed lack of marriageable black men.

Together these messages—from a black female writer and producer—tell black women that they are incomplete if they are not married and that they have few choices for marriage within their own community. Therefore, if they want to be "normal" (married), they had better seek mates outside of their race. Such messages are further supported by *Something New*'s conclusion. Kenya and Brian break up because of their inability to understand each other's point of view on race issues. But remember this is a romantic comedy. The two eventually become a couple again, and the film ends with a "coming out" of sorts when Kenya takes Brian to a black society function (debutante ball) and dances with him in front of everyone. This scene dissolves into the couple's wedding day. The successful, single, black woman is finally "complete" and her "plight" is arrested. By accepting that she is deficient and will remain so unless she dates outside of her race, she is contained. By containing her, this film strengthens a white, male-dominated, marriage as normal, American ideology. For, as hooks points out, all women have undergone years of sexist and racist socialization. This socialization includes our conscious and unconscious responses to mass media cultural, economic, and social representations of race and gender. It also partly explains why the essentialist belief that the presence of black creative artists necessarily leads to more progressive and/or revolutionary representation is faulty. Black writers, directors, producers, and actors have lived within the sexist and racist society that has oppressed them. It is unreasonable to expect that this system's ideologies are not, at least partially, embedded in the minds of the artists it has oppressed and that the same ideologies would not be manifested in the work these artists do.

■ Reading Media Critically

As previously argued, given the power of hegemonic ideologies, whether mass media texts are read from dominant, negotiated, or oppositional points of view, having black women create images in film (*Something New),* host television talk shows (*The Oprah Winfrey Show),* or edit magazines aimed at black women (*Essence Magazine*) is no guarantee that these images will not simply reinforce dominant ideologies perpetuated in mainstream mass media. How can single black women and women in general resist social and cultural domination that continues to influence and define them, even in their own work? How would the messages be received if the primary subjects were interrogating and decoding it in order to reject whatever is false and/or detrimental and prevents self-definition of "normal"?

Putting the work of women, specifically women of color, in dialogue with critical media literacy, is a good place to start. If creators of such work can separate themselves from the dominant system's definition of them, then they can define themselves even while working within the dominant system. As Bobo points out, "as cultural producers, critics, and members of an audience, women are positioned to intervene strategically in the imaginative construction, critical interpretation, and social condition of black women."[21] This intervention can better affect the politics of representation and democratic social change if the black women who are interrupting mainstream representations with representations of their own, do so with the understanding that, from a critical cultural studies perspective, power, domination, and information are always linked. Therefore, from a critical media literacy perspective, producers and consumers must question the images they create and consume. They must treat all mass media—advertising, print media, radio, television, film, the Internet—simply as mass media, not as truth. Then, they must further interrogate the information that is being presented: How accurate is the content? Is this ad trying to reach a particular audience? Who is invisible in that television series? Why? Are multiple histories being told? What is the impact on society if multiple histories exist? How do these representations of race and gender make me feel?

By interrogating media is this manner, cultural producers and critics cannot so easily manipulate consumers with texts that reinforce the ideologies of the dominant power structure. More to the point, with this understanding, single black women who are cultural producers, critics, and members of the audience will not unquestioningly participate in a system of media representations that use their educational and economic gains, gender, class, and intraracial politics to paint them as desperate and lonely in order to Other and marginalize them.

As hooks argues, "Changing how we see images is clearly one way to change the world."[22] By changing how they see images, single black women can define their own experiences as normal by re-signifying them. When not comparing their experiences to and judging them based on what a media culture dominated society tells them they are supposed to be, single black women are less likely to negatively interpret their own experiences simply because they are not parallel to mainstream America's. Creative work, such as writer/director Kasi Lemmons' 1997 feature film, *Eve's Bayou;* Maya Angelou's *"Phenomenal Woman,"* a poem that celebrates a black woman's empowering self-image; and the much-analyzed television comedy series, *The Cosby Show,* all depict black female characters that do not rely on dominant ideologies to define them. This is not to say that all such characters are perfect, but they are celebrations of difference as normal and therefore liberatory.

In her examination of black filmmakers, hooks asks what is required to imagine and create images of blackness that are liberatory. When speaking of director Spike Lee's mocking artistic accountability by suggesting that he is merely documenting life "as is," hooks points out that, "His unwillingness to engage critically with meaning and messages that his work conveys (whether the content does or does not reflect his belief system) undermines the necessity for both critical spectatorship and critical thinking about representation."[23]

As shown in this essay, it is not only the creative community that must participate in critical spectatorship and critical thinking about representation. The fact that, despite their varied target markets, print media as disparate as *Essence Magazine* and *Newsweek Magazine* or as *USA Today* and the *Washington Post,* and television series with such different target audiences as *The Oprah Winfrey Show* and *Nightline,* all participate in reinforcing a problematic representations of race and gender in the body of a successful, single black woman, is further proof of the need for media literacy among producers and consumers of such media. For, as Kellner notes, "We are immersed from cradle to grave in a media and consumer society and thus it is important to learn how to understand, interpret, and criticize its meanings and messages."[24] It is the only way to interrupt the process of power and domination and its harmful consequences when media is unquestioningly consumed and to informatively separate the actual information being presented from the "truth" media makers want readers and viewers to accept.

■ Appendix A

De Beers Corporation's "Diamonds Are Forever"
1   Campaign

■ APPENDIX B

Artwork from Washington Post.com Multipart Series
"Singled Out: In Seeking a Mate, Men and Women Find Delicate Imbalance"

■ APPENDIX C

Movie Posters from
Something New

Still

Photography from *Something New*

Notes

1 Williams, Krissah, "Singled Out: In Seeking a Mate, Men and Women Find Delicate Imbalance," *Washington Post,* October 8, 2006.

2 Williams, Darice, "Where Have All the Good Men Gone?" *Pittsburgh Tribune,* August 22, 2005.

3 Jones, Charisse, "Living Single—Unmarried Black Women," *Essence Magazine,* May 1994.

4 "The Black Gender Gap," *Newsweek Magazine,* February 26, 2003.

5 Hall, Stuart, ed., *Representation: Cultural Representations and Signifying Practices,* London: Sage, 2003, p. 258.

6 Collins, Patricia Hill, *Black Feminist Thought: Knowledge, Consciousness, and the Politics of Empowerment,* New York: Routledge, 1991, p. 95.

7 Kellner, Douglas, *Media Culture: Cultural Studies, Identity, and Politics Between the Modern and the Post Modern,* London: Routledge, 2003, p. 116.

8 Lynden, Jacki & Michael Montgomery, "Diamonds Are Forever," *http://americanradioworks.publicradio. org/features/diamonds/mystique2.html.*

9 http://www.adiamondisforever.com/

10 "The Black Gender Gap," op. cit.

11 Jhally, Sut, "Image-Based Culture: Advertising and Popular Culture," in *Gender, Race, and Class in Media: A Text Reader,* ed. Gail Dines and Jean M. Humez, Thousand Oaks: Sage, 2003, p 252.

12 Ibid.

13 Hall, Stuart, ed., op. cit.,, chap. 4.

14 Hall, Stuart, *Race, the Floating Signifier,* The Media Foundation Presents, Media Education Foundation, Northampton, MA, one-hour video-taped lecture, 1997.

15 Kellner, Douglas, "Cultural Studies, Multiculturalism, and Media Culture," in *Gender, Race, and Class in Media: A Text Reader,* ed. Gail Dines and Jean M. Humez, Thousand Oaks: Sage, 2003, p. 9.

16 Bobo, Jacqueline, *Black Women as Cultural Readers,* New York: Columbia University Press, 1995, p. .205.

17 Kellner, Douglas, "Cultural Studies, Multiculturalism, and Media Culture," op. cit., p. 14.

18 Kriss Turner is a writer/producer I worked with when I was a consulting producer on the television comedy, *Everybody Hates Chris.* We remain good friends and I am a fan of her writing. My relationship with Ms. Turner as well as other relationships I have with writers, directors, actors, and producers in Hollywood make writing about the media, critically, a particular challenge for me. I think Ms. Turner is a very gifted writer and *Something New*'s star, Sanaa Lathan, is a talented, nuanced actress. Additionally, the film's producer, Stephanie Allain, is someone I've always admired very much. She has thoughtful taste in creative material and a well-deserved reputation for supporting the vision of filmmakers. Ironically, I once met with Ms. Allain and an executive at Focus Features (a subsidiary of NBC/Universal) to be considered to direct this film. In the interest of constructive scholarly analysis and a commitment to media literacy, I find myself in the position of critically discussing artists I respect and whose work I enjoy. This will probably continue to be a challenge for me as a working writer/producer/director employed in Hollywood and a new scholar writing about what interests me concerning the business that employs me.

19 hooks, bell, *Ain't I a Woman,* Boston: South End, 1981, p.121.

20 hooks, bell, *Reel to Real,* New York: Routledge, 1996, p. 6.

21 Bobo, Jacqueline, *Black Women as Cultural Readers,* New York: Columbia University Press, 1995, p. .27.

22 hooks, bell, *Reel to Real,* op. cit., , p. 6.

23 Ibid., p., 9.

24 Kellner, Douglas, "Cultural Studies, Multiculturalism, and Media Culture," op. cit., p. 9.

■ Ladies, Love Your Box

The Rhetoric of Pleasure and Danger in Feminist Television Studies

Merri Lisa Johnson

In a 2003 promotion for a new show on Comedy Central, comedian Wanda Sykes offered a characteristically pointed observation about the "reality romance" genre of television. Commenting on the wildly popular *Joe Millionaire* as its season finale neared, Sykes announced the show ought to be called *Bitches Love Money.*

She cocked her head and asked, "Are all the feminists in a coma?"

I was watching television alone in my apartment, but I looked back and forth at the imaginary people seated to my left and right. *Is she talking to me?* A sharp sound burst from between my lips, something between a laugh and a squawk. Ha! The television addresses my feminist commitments once again.

Yes, again.

I had been enjoying a secretly feminist relationship with my television for many years. I started watching *The Sopranos* and *Six Feet Under* around the spring of 2001, during that uniquely painful part of the academic career between getting my Ph.D. and securing a tenure-track position. Florence Dore sings a country song about spending all her money on wine and three-dollar stamps, an ode to the despair of the academic job search. I hummed along to her CD as I dialed the number to the cable company and requested that they close my account. Having just read bell hooks's *Class Matters,* I thought of this budgeting decision as a gesture of "solidarity with the poor." I determined not to rent another movie until I had read every book I owned. In her own gesture of solidarity with the poor, my Aunt Cheryl started lending me tapes of these HBO original series. I could not believe my eyes: Brenda's ambivalence towards marriage on *Six Feet Under*—her insistence on getting a proposal from Nate mixed with her diatribes against romance and monogamy—dramatized the very debates in feminism over the marriage mystique about which I had recently been writing. Tony Soprano's anxiety complex—his fears of being undone by psychiatry and cunnilingus, combined with cold gangster justice—illustrated the mottled surface of masculinity theorized in all the hot books on gender performativity.

I was being hailed as a feminist—by my television!

Cut off from the feminist connections of graduate school and back in my hometown for a temporary teaching post, I cherished the time I spent with these characters as they grappled with feminist-influenced conflicts over gender, sex, desire, and power. The measure of what constitutes a "feminist enough" character or series—a common gauge in feminist television and film studies—varies depending on the viewer's particular situation. While nowhere close to radical revolution, these shows were nevertheless feminist enough to get me through the day, filling a void of conversation in my life away from art theaters and research universities.

One of the ways conservative cultural pundits criticize contemporary life, post-sexual revolution, is to decry the entry of white middle-class women into the workforce by announcing with despair that we now have a generation of Americans who were raised by television. The assumption behind this statement is that television is doing something bad to the children it raises—teaching them violence and promiscuity, shortening attention spans and lowering shock thresholds—but television can also provide kids with a rare source of insight into alternative ways of living in the world. The small screen paradoxically provides a broader horizon. For rural adolescents, television can be the sole window into big-city subjects like homosexuality, singlehood-by-choice, multiculturalism, and, I'm not kidding, existentialism—my philosophy minor may well have stemmed from a certain episode of *Family Ties* in which Alex's little sister Jennifer reads Kierkegaard at the kitchen table.

Yet television is denounced by conservatives and progressives alike. For the latter, it is not progressive enough. *Where are the positive images of women and people of color?*, many critics want to know. Or if the images are positive, maybe they are *too* positive: the Cosbyfication of racial imagery that erases the poverty and urban despair of many African-American families, or the choiceoisie of liberal feminism that ignores the pressures on and implications of women's choices, masking a "new traditionalism" as television shows from *thirtysomething* to *Sex and the City* reposition women inside the home as if such a return marked the apex of feminist social transformation.[1] But as riddled with stereotypes as it may be, television taught me a lot about life beyond my own living room in the hills of North Carolina and the church-going, manners-instilling, but sufficiently sixties-inspired nuclear family that plopped me down in front of *Different Strokes* and *Facts of Life* as a convenient babysitter. Born with a temperament that naturally resonated with the idea that "it takes different strokes to move the world," I was utterly receptive to stories of cross-racial adoption and the struggle for harmony despite remaining biases within the dominant culture. I can still remember dancing in front of the television while the theme music played, hopping from floor to blue stool to couch and then floor again before the first scene began. I felt overwhelmed, filled to bursting with this new world of birds and bees and high-rise buildings. I listened closely as Ann Romano pronounced her status as divorcee on *One Day at a Time* with a reminder to her superintendent—it's *Ms.* Romano—the feminist marker reverberating between her teeth with an instructive buzz.

As a single woman supporting myself, I think back fondly to these images and still watch television with an eye towards its feminist content. There is, of course, a Marxist-inflected analysis to be made of the fact that I turn to television to mitigate the "on the treadmill quality" of my life (Bordo 59). The use of television as "indispensable to the reconstitution of the labour-power of the wage-earner" (Althusser 87) would seem, from this angle, to be an instance in which leisure is not "free" time but rather a holding pattern for the worker as she recharges for another day in the academic salt-mines. In such an analysis, the television screen functions as opiate and anodyne, diversion and cheap date.

Ironies abound.

In my first book, *Jane Sexes It Up: True Confessions of Feminist Desire,* I scrutinized the guilty pleasures of romance with great urgency. Eventually those pleasures dried up, and I saw them as deep-seated illusions; in Marxist terms, they constitute a fantasy structure designed "to mystify the social contradictions and material conditions of women's exploitation in patriarchal capitalism" (Ebert 9). Now I spend the evening with my television instead, experiencing this "primetime panacea" (Pender, "Kicking Ass" 167) as a space free from the hassles of romantic negotiations: what to watch, whether to watch, where to set the volume (familiar codes for control in many relationships). Like Miranda on HBO's *Sex and the City,* I have traded Steve-o for TiVO. Taking in the television as "feminist comfort food" (Pender 166), I am fully cognizant of replacing one opiate of the masses (romance) with another (media culture). Fully cognizant, too, of the irony of using television to get away from work and then writing an academic book about it. Within this imbrication of lures and illusions, I am once again asserting what might be perceived as a problematic desire.

Wanting to watch television anyhow.

Wanting to watch television as stress relief, as a small gesture of control over my time and mind. In one sadly mismatched romantic relationship, I closed myself into my bedroom each evening after dinner to watch television; the activity created a magical space around me, a box that protected me from the intrusions of fraught conversation. In this role, the television functioned to enlarge the available space in which I could rest, despite the problematic context of a bad relationship and the economic and emotional limits that kept me from moving out sooner. This minor improvement in my situation calls to mind John Fiske's work on "[t]he politics of popular culture," which he argues "is progressive, not radical":

> It is concerned with the day-to-day negotiations of unequal power relations in such structures as the family, the immediate work environment, and the classroom. Its progressiveness is concerned with redistributing power within these structures toward the disempowered; it attempts to enlarge the space within which bottom-up power has to operate. It does not, as does radicalism, try to change the system that distributes that power in the first place. (*Understanding Popular Culture* 56)

The television was my escape route from these "day-to-day negotiations," and, eventually, once I became ready for more radical change, I moved out—and took the TV with me.

* * *

In the introduction to *Feminist Television Criticism: A Reader,* Charlotte Brunsdon, Julie D'Acci, and Lynn Spigel assert a positive relationship between feminism and television, noting a progression in feminist cultural studies away from simplistic dismissals of popular culture:

> Since the 1970s, feminists have become increasingly interested in television as something more than a bad object, something that offers a series of lures and pleasures, however limited its repertoire of female roles. For its part, over the last twenty-five years, television too has engaged with the themes and tropes of feminism....Indeed, much of the current entertainment output of television features strong women, single mothers, and female friends and lovers—that is, female types who are integral to feminist critique and culture. (1)

With its focus on "the contradictions and reciprocities of the relationships between feminism and television," *Feminist Television Criticism* defines the field in terms of dialogue and possibility, yet the phrase, "since the 1970s," gestures discreetly to a history of feminist film theory that continues to trouble feminist critics. The reception of "television as something more than a bad object" is an opening in the conversation I want to pick up and run with, but something drags at my heels.

Those "lures and pleasures" recall an unresolved debate in feminism over the politics of pleasure: the problem of bad pleasures lurking and lulling women into false consciousness, complicity with patriarchy, masochistic submission. "[O]ne of the crucial concerns of feminist film theory," writes Jane Gaines in "Women and Representation: Can We Enjoy Alternative Pleasure?," "intersects with a burning issue in women's movement politics—correct pleasure" (86). It is not entirely clear what correct pleasure is, but its opposite in feminist discourse is masochistic pleasure. In "Pleasure under Patriarchy," Catherine MacKinnon concludes, "Masochism insures that pleasure in violation defines women's sexuality, so women lust after self-annihilation" (42). This statement, echoed in the work of Sandra Lee Bartky, Andrea Dworkin, and other separatist feminists, casts women's desire in a suspect light—what becomes, in feminist television studies, the lurid glow of the television screen—and wanting to watch television appears, in this framework, to be merely another outlet of women's lust for self-annihilation. This distrust of female (and feminist) desire joins feminist film theory and feminist theories of sexuality at the hip.

In a series of debates, or "sex wars," originating at the Barnard Scholar and Feminist conference in 1982, feminists fought doggedly over the problem of women licking the boot of patriarchy.[2] Porn, sex work, intercourse, butch/femme role-play—these were key sites of struggle between separatists and sex radicals. Separatists wrote angrily against women who participated in these male-identified practices. Sex radicals responded with matching fury at the perceived insult and prescriptivism, scoffing at the notion of "politically correct sex," a vision of mutuality often pictured as two women lying side by side, matching each other's rhythms stroke for stroke. Freedom, agency, power, and pleasure were put under the microscope to be examined for the faint line between socially constructed desire (what feminists should disavow) and reconstructed sexuality (a state feminists allegedly should achieve—our behaviors, fantasies, and longings lining up smoothly with our political ideals).

These debates had already occurred in feminist film studies several years earlier, constituting what we might think of as the *pleasure wars,* a philosophical debate reaching back to Plato and Aristotle, and drawing on rich tributaries from Marxist and Freudian criticism. Laura Mulvey's heavily cited thesis on the abolition of pleasure in the cinema, "Visual Pleasure and Narrative Cinema," mirrors separatist treatises in the sex wars. She is the Ti-Grace Atkinson, the Andrea Dworkin, the Catherine MacKinnon of film theory. Mulvey writes, in exhilarating manifesto style,

> It is said that analysing pleasure, or beauty, destroys it. That is the intention of this article. The satisfaction and reinforcement of the ego that represent the high point of film history hitherto must be attacked. Not in favour of a reconstructed new pleasure, which cannot exist in the abstract, nor of intellectual unpleasure, but to make way for a total negation of the ease and plenitude of the narrative fiction film. The alternative is the thrill that comes from leaving the past behind without simply rejecting it, transcending outworn or oppressive forms, and daring to break with normal pleasurable expectations in order to conceive a new language of desire. (8)

After being criticized for neglecting the female spectator, Mulvey more directly addresses the question of "whether the female spectator is carried along, as it were, by the scruff of the text, or whether her pleasure can be more deep-rooted and complex" ("Afterthoughts," 29). Of the latter option, she is doubtful:

> [I]t is always possible that the female spectator may find herself so out of key with the pleasure on offer...that the spell of fascination is broken. On the other hand, she may not. She may find herself secretly, unconsciously almost, enjoying the freedom of action and control over the diegetic world that identification with a hero provides. It is *this* female spectator that I want to consider here. (29)

As a result of this focus, the name "Mulvey" has come to serve as shorthand for total-izing disavowals of visual pleasure in cinema. Her attack on satisfaction consistently rankles many third wave feminist media critics.

Yet her call "for a total negation of the ease and plenitude of the narrative fiction film" and her invitation "to break with normal pleasurable expectations in order to conceive a new language of desire" tempt my latent revolutionary leanings. Film *does* warrant feminist intervention. "Normal" pleasure often requires serious "troubling." I find I want to take her dare. In analyzing contemporary televisual pleasures, I can't leave the radical feminist psychology of Laura Mulvey entirely behind. Her condemnation of cinematic pleasure calls for a hard look at my own truant thumb resting on the remote control. Marxist critique, too, crowds me on the couch. I settle in for a pleasant evening of television viewing—fleece blanket, hot chocolate, HBO on Demand—and in the exhalation of rest and leisure, Terry Eagleton's words catch in my throat: "pleasurable conduct is the true index of successful social hegemony, self-delight the very mark of social submission" (21). Just when the television show starts to feel really good, when it holds my attention and dramatizes the very feminist debates that compel me, am I to understand that this moment is the measure of my submission to the status quo? That I am sufficiently entertained, lulled into false contentedness? I am not only "caught looking," I am *caught liking.* "The pleasures of the aesthetic are in this sense masochistic," Eagleton reasons, and "the delight that matters is our free complicity with what subjects us, so that we can [in Althusserian terms] 'work all by ourselves'" (25). From this angle, the feminist subject matter of television is precisely the pleasure quotient that guarantees third wave feminists' participation in an otherwise patriarchal media culture. We lean in towards the complex images on the screen—masochistic mobsters, sadistic vampire slayers, network harem fantasies, lesbian tutor texts—and we are goners.

The pleasures of reading Eagleton and Mulvey are at least as masochistic as the pleasures against which they warn us in aesthetic and cinematic products, in that both theorists require us to trash the delight that doubles as complicity.

All pleasure is masochistic?, third wavers ask with raised eyebrows. Destroy our *own* pleasure?, we query. Put our*selves* back into a pre-orgasmic, pre-Kinsey relationship to pleasure?

Tall order.

As the call for collective anti-climax comes down from above, I am torn between pleasures: the pleasure of petulantly resisting the call (I'll watch what I want to watch) and the pleasure of performing feminist self-restraint (corseted in theory, sitting in a straight-backed chair, facing away from the screen in flawless self-abnegation). It is difficult to imagine wanting to hold all pleasure at arm's length like a good social critic. Laura Mulvey, my critical dominatrix, cracks the whip of feminist consciousness and I submit on certain gray afternoons to her strict guidance.

I'd like to make much of Brunsdon's above-cited "more than," but I can't rest easy in it, for in exceeding its status as bad object, television does not negate its bad-objectness. The lures and pleasures and limited female roles blur into a single image on the screen.

How to tell them apart?

* * *

Many taxonomies of the female spectator have appeared in feminist film studies, toying with the gender and sexuality of watching. She is, in most accounts, giving something up, in thrall to the flickering images of patriarchy. Picture her down on her knees, redefining her pleasure in terms of the available subject position of subordination, very much like the female spectator in Daphne Gottlieb's poem, "Her Submissive Streak," a title that harkens back to Mulvey's theory of narrative pleasure as masochistic for women. The female persona goes down on her boyfriend in a leather Barcalounger, her back to the television screen, a figure of subservience and self-denial. Her chaps and whips and corset have been stored in the closet so that she can take on the more traditional, less playful version of feminine submission: the role of wife. "It's like that sometimes, / I guess," ponders the poem's narrator, who mourns this transformation from the kinkiness of "youthful / foolishness" to the truly perverse rationalizations of nonreciprocal sexuality:

> She's right. It's kinky,
> the way he doesn't look away
> from the TV,
> as her head bobs

in his lap
like a fisherman's float
on a nature program,
hectic
with the pace
his breath sets.
His crotch swells
under her mouth's
prowess. He's such
a sweetheart
he waits
until the
commercials
to come.

In this image, male pleasure takes precedence over female pleasure. He enjoys a preponderance of stimuli, "with one of his hands wrapped around a remote, / the other, a bottle of beer," and an agreeable girl bobbing hectically in his lap. The closest she comes to pleasure is the sweetness of his timing, which really has nothing to do with her since she's not watching the program anyway. This "submissive streak"—taking pleasure in his nonchalance, "the way he doesn't look away / from the TV"—affirms male sexual dominance and works as a metaphor of the female spectator, who may also be seen as contorting herself to frame her relationship to mass media as sweet or kinky or otherwise pleasurable. I bring this image into play here to keep myself honest, as feminist and television aficionado, to remember the horror of the media (sluts die first, as another of Gottlieb's poems reminds us) and the blowjobs in the glow of late-night television—all the ways that women's pleasures in popular culture are undeniably intertwined with our learned submission to existing power structures and limited female imagery. I want to address in some way the submissive streak in the feminist spectator without redrawing her as always or utterly masochistic. To ask if the woman in this poem would be any better off sitting in the leather Barcalounger watching television; to ask whether watching television is in some sense, frankly, like sucking the dick of patriarchy.

In *Outlaw Culture,* bell hooks writes about the need to transform the structure of our desire as women in patriarchy and to "actively construct radically new ways to think and feel as desiring subjects" (112–13). Her assessment of heterosexual women's residual attachment to conventional masculinist erotic desire could be productively applied to the feminist viewer of television culture. In enjoying certain television series, we must, in hooks's words, ask ourselves if we are drawn to the "usual 'dick thing'" of media culture, as self-defeating fans of problematic female characters, consumers of violent plots and conservative romantic imagery. Do we need, as feminist viewers, to come up with radically new ways to watch television as desiring subjects? Or is there something kinky about liking television, something worth preserving? What does it mean to like television, or to like men, or to like sex, once feminists have mounted crippling critiques of these sexist cultural segments? What does it mean to experience feminism as a forbidding voice, marking must-see-TV as the concentration camp orgasm of media culture? Feminist film theory, in wrestling with television as lure and pleasure, may well have fallen into the same pattern Amber Hollibaugh noted with dismay in the feminist sex wars: "Our collective fear of the dangers of [television] has forced us into a position where we have created a theory from the body of damage done to us."[3]

One might usefully recast feminist attraction to television imagery in the same terms Ellen Willis once used to describe women's pleasure in rock music: "This was not masochism but expediency" (170). In other words, we take what we need from the available culture, sieve out the rest. This "negotiated reading" is not, as some third wave feminists have argued, an instance of turning away from the hard work of personal and cultural transformation. It is, rather, an acknowledgement that incremental shifts in power may be the most we can hope for, and that the kinds of pleasure available to women in the current media culture include the pleasures of oppositional reading as well as the pleasures of seeing feminist concepts dramatized on television. The least compelling pleasure on hand is, however, "the wry pleasure of recognizing patriarchy up to its tricks yet again" (Fiske, "British Cultural Studies," 266).

In a recent roundtable discussion of film feminisms in *Signs,* Linda Williams explains her reluctance to participate in terms of "the burdens of what feels like orthodox feminist position taking" in the field (1264). Williams, well known for her unorthodox feminist analysis of porn, argues against "the paradigms of seventies feminist film theory" in their "singular and perhaps too clearly identifiable patriarchal villain" (1270–71). In her resistance to "a moralizing feminism" and simultaneous rejection of the "postfeminist" label (1271), Williams paves the way for a third wave feminist television studies and calls for "a more relaxed understanding of gendered fun" (1266–67). The need for this more relaxed feminist stance arises directly from the tight grind of teeth and clamp of jaws at work in much feminist cultural studies, the fret and sweat of feminist anxiety.

Reading ideological critiques of various films and television shows provides excellent exercise in seeing through the structures of sexism and racism and can therefore be incredibly useful in the feminist classroom. Returning to this sort of work, like a musician practicing her scales, refreshes and renews the key principles and commitments of feminist critique, and I take genuine intellectual pleasure in reading the best practitioners of these critiques: the thrilling triple threat of bell hooks, Susan Bordo, and Tania Modleski. There is pleasure to be had in being put through the feminist paces in Modleski's essays on postfeminist film; take, for instance, her analysis of *Gorillas in the Mist* as a problematic instance of postfeminist ideology in which a strong female lead is softened in predictable ways and killed off in the end. Dian Fossey (played by Sigourney Weaver), as Modleski demonstrates, is presented as a tenacious underdog with whom audience members sympathize in the face of insurmountable obstacles to progressive environmentalist research and policy formation. Then Fossey's feminism—her self-sufficiency, her radical ideals—is neutralized by the film as its narrative structure "takes it all back." The story of what can happen to a woman when she goes off on her own and takes matters into her own hands, the cautionary tale most of us know all too well, lingers and obscures the progressive energies the story almost galvanizes.

True enough, but the problem with the analytical formula of *Feminism without Women* is that it boils every text down to its patriarchal capitalist white supremacist skeleton as if revealing something new. This structure is why the text works so well for students, but for the feminist scholar it may feel rote after a while. I begin reading Modleski's "thuses" in the muffled lilt of Charlie Brown's teacher: "Thus the black man [in *Clara's Heart*] comes to serve as the white male's oedipal scapegoat, and the black woman is positioned, as in so many popular representations (like Spielberg's *The Color Purple*) as sexual victim" (131). That generalization-as-aside ("as in so many popular representations") can feel wearying. In describing the misogynist implications of the Tom Hanks film, *Big* (directed by Penny Marshall), Modleski concludes, "Thus once again we see woman presiding over her own marginalization, participating in a nostalgia for a time in which human relationships are felt to have been relatively uncomplicated, although the cost of this simplicity is her own repression" (98–99). The forced march through a landscape marked by sexism is the "once again" which many third wave feminists avoid as we seek a rhetorical strategy designed to liberate other kinds of meanings from media texts. Our redirection does not constitute a turning away from the skepticism and critique Modleski encourages, but a thoroughgoing acceptance of skepticism and critique as the givens of our approach, joined with a desire to go beyond them, into some as-yet unformed level of discourse, drawing on the intersectionality of black feminism, the subversive identifications of queer theory, and a post-sexual revolution longing to locate unexpected conclusions in feminist media theory.

For example, to return to Wanda Sykes's joke about *Joe Millionaire,* the implied feminist critique behind renaming the show *Bitches Love Money* is based on a reading of the show as sexist because it reproduces stereotypes of conniving gold-diggers, and because it deploys the motifs of romance—red roses, special meals, lingering gazes, unexpected gifts—in the service of a conservative backlash against women's independence of feminist critiques of "wifework" under patriarchy. This is the set of associations beneath my own groan at the popularity of reality romance. But to say the show is sexist is like saying the sky is blue. Yeah, it's sexist. And? All the feminists are not in a coma, but our alertness does not predispose us to a particular stance on reality romance or anything else on television.

Perhaps I am revealing a self-incriminating postmodern blasé, the "nothing shocking" of grunge lyrics circulating in my subconscious—a mood characteristic of Generation X—but the pervasiveness of racism and sexism, their presence "in so many popular representations," is both a cause of dismay and, basically, business as usual in this Reagan era redux of the second term for George W. Bush. "[T]hird wavers," Helene Shugart asserts, "are in no doubt about the significance of sexism and the consequent role of feminism." At the intersection of third wave and Gen X, Shugart traces an awareness of sexism as a commonplace fact of life. There is nothing shocking here. No new intellectual turns. We already know, as Susan Gubar notes in "What Ails Feminist Criticism," that "racism, classism, sexism, and homophobia reign supreme," and our hearts rise up at her call for "more mirthful scholarly lexicons" (891).[4] There is still work to be done in the direction of raising consciousness and instilling critical media literacy, but for those of who already get it, we want to know, *What else is there to say?* What is the most useful work for feminist media critics nowadays? Is it still about revealing the internalized racism of sit-coms on UPN? Or tracing new permutations of the marriage plot on the fall line-up of the WB? Flipping through these by-now formulaic feminist analyses, I look up from the book in my lap and wonder, *What else is on?*

···   ···   ···

Both sides of the pleasure/danger debate reside in the analyses of third wave feminist media critics. This is our inheritance, even as we experience mixed feelings over the rhetoric of "pleasure" and "danger." This dichotomy continues to fragment women's studies, operating as an additional fracture (in addition to generation), splitting peers from peers and generating cross-generational alliances. Perhaps the pleasure/danger divide is *what was always at stake,* masked by the diversionary rhetoric of generations and waves.[5]

Many third wave feminists emphasize "danger," seeing only the always-already-ness of patriarchal capitalist white supremacist media manipulation and commodification. Cristina Lucia Stasia's essay on female action heroes, for instance, foregrounds the danger of being "seduced by images": "My concern is that these new female action heroes provide images of an equality that has not been achieved and that they mitigate their viewers' interests in exploring inequalities. It is easy to be seduced by images of strong women fighting, but these images capitalize on a basic belief in feminism evacuated of any consciousness of why girls still *need* to 'kick ass'" (181–82). This language of seduction replays the terms of debate in the feminist sex wars, reaching all the way back to the social purity doctrines of nineteenth-century feminism, positing media culture as a threatening man and the female spectator as vulnerable maiden. We might call this group *separatist feminist media critics* because they ultimately encourage women to turn off the television, give pop culture the cold shoulder. Consider Rebecca Munford's critique of Girlie culture, "Wake Up and Smell the Lipgloss," in which the media are presented as an "insidious form of indoctrination" (142) and the focus is deliberately shifted from the agency and playfulness of Girlie to its "dangerous paradoxes" (147), "[t]he dangers of colonization and recirculation" (148), the "risks" and "problem[s]" of Riot Grrrl (149). This language departs significantly from the earlier (and I would argue definitive) characterization of Girlie by Jennifer Baumgardner and Amy Richards in *Manifesta: Young Women, Feminism, and the Future* as "girls in their twenties or thirties who are reacting to an antifeminine, antijoy emphasis that they perceive as the legacy of Second Wave seriousness" (80). These two attitudes towards Girlie culture can be mapped neatly on to the pleasure/danger divide in feminism.

Susannah Mintz's treatment of feminism and television in her essay, "In a Word, *Baywatch,*" likewise focuses on danger with a bland totalizing formula we might call the "stating the obvious" moments in feminist media criticism, redirecting a phrase she uses to describe Lieutenant Van Buren's role on *Law and Order.* Like "Debbie Downer" on recent seasons of *Saturday Night Live,* this feminist voice interrupts us mid-hilarity to set the record straight:

> While the preponderance of women represented as smart and capable is meant to prove TV's
> 'feminist' leanings, marking its transcendence of the sexism that drove *Charlie's Angels* or *Three's*

Company, television nonetheless demonstrates the way in which misogyny can go underground, asserting its force through less visible—and therefore more difficult to combat—avenues. This makes television an enormously effective tool with which to sustain patriarchal ideology. (59)

Jane Gaines asserts provocatively that the priority of sexual correctness in film practice and gaze theory "offer[s] feminists a rather tight-lipped satisfaction" (87), an image that captures well the limited pleasures produced by this focus on danger in third wave feminist television studies.

Other third wave feminists more strongly identify with the "pleasure" side. These media critics—who have not enjoyed much air time to date—import sex radical theories into television studies, valuing fantasy as a space of free play, advocating acceptance of our darker drives, and indulging in fascination with imagery that queers gender, decenters heterosexuality, and valorizes the erotic. We might call this group *sex radical media critics* or *visual pleasure libertarians* because of their positive attitudes towards viewer agency and productive pleasures. They conduct negotiated readings, rife with creative identifications between viewer and text, often motivated by a sense of the text as polymorphously perverse, offering sites of pleasure all over the textual body. This third wave feminist media theory engages regularly with what may seem to be politically incorrect television— the "should-not-be-looked-at-ness" delineated by positive-images criticism.[6]

This perspective thus counters the trend in feminist television studies of reading for the wry pleasures of catching patriarchy at its old tricks once again. As is the case in feminist sexuality studies, there is not enough work being done to articulate what we like about television, what it does for us, what we do with it—while always taking note of where it fall shorts, as well as where we do. Certain television series perhaps require what Patrocinio Schweickart calls "a dual hermeneutic: a negative hermeneutic that discloses their complicity with patriarchal ideology, and a positive hermeneutic that recuperates the utopian moment—the authentic kernel—from which they draw a significant portion of their emotional power" (619). Schweickart seeks to complicate the "resisting reader" of feminist literary criticism, and in the same spirit, I would like to complicate the resisting viewer of film theory, asking, with Schweickart, "Where does the text get its power to draw us into its designs? Why do some (not all) demonstrably sexist texts remain appealing even after they have been subjected to thorough feminist critique?" (618). In television studies, as in literary criticism, "The usual answer—that the power of male texts is the power of the false consciousness into which women as well as men have been socialized—oversimplifies the problem" (618). The viewer's "authentic liberatory aspirations" (619) must be taken into account. Here I would agree with Tania Modleski in *The Women Who Knew Too Much: Hitchcock and Feminist Theory* that "the female spectator need not occupy either of the two viewing places typically assigned her in feminist film theory: the place of the female masochist, identifying with the passive female character, or the place of the 'transvestite,' identifying with the active male hero" (25). Modleski resists the "denial of pleasure to the female spectator," reminding us that "other pleasures remain possible," including the pleasure of "analysis itself, in understanding how the joke works even when it works against women" (27). In this view, watching television after work is not merely the cultural trap of alleviating the on-the-treadmill quality of life under patriarchal capitalism. It can be a genuinely feminist activity that allows women to pause and reflect on their own fears, anxieties, and desires mid-revolution.

Although the presence of our own pleasure in television culture often provides the "opaque moment" through which we enter a discussion of various series, third wave feminist television criticism must refrain from participating in the either/or of the pleasure/ danger debate, or what Patricia Pender calls the "Good Buffy/Bad Buffy" model of feminist television studies. Like Pender, we must strive "to rethink the terms of the debate staged around [various characters' genders] by questioning the logic of the transgression/contain-ment model":

> The model of feminist agency usually employed to analyze *Buffy* dictates that Buffy is "good" if she transgresses dominant stereotypes, "bad" if she is contained in cultural cliché. Yet the binary logic itself works to restrict a range of possible viewing positions and to contain *Buffy*'s political potential. ("Postmodern Buffy," 38)

Instead, Pender advocates a less totalizing analysis, one that focuses on how the particular images of femininity on this show articulate with the ambiguous sexual politics of parody. The kinds of questions Pender poses model the intricately textual and contex-tual approaches to pop culture to which third wave feminist media theory might aspire: "How, for instance, does the exaggerated or cartoonish representation of Buffy's feminin-ity mediate its 'earnestness'? Does Buffy's femininity in fact *require* amelioration? And how does an understanding of her 'over-the-top girliness' as 'necessary' to her makeup challenge the very political judgments that are frequently made about her character?" (38).

Another good example of this sort of work appears in Kristyn Gorton's recent analysis of the *Ally McBeal* phenomenon, in which women across America became avid Ally fans, and feminists raised the question, *What does this mean?* They raised this question franti-cally, fearing the implantation of more anorexic logic in our young girls, scoffing in horror at the micro-mini-skirts this lawyer donned for court in every episode. The show itself raised the questions, *What is the relationship of Ally McBeal to feminism, to young women, and to cultural debates over gender and power, in response to the infamous* Time *magazine cover that featured Ally as the face of a problematic new (post)feminism?* (apologies all around—I may vomit if I hear about that cover one more time). Gorton moves instructively from the question "Should women enjoy a character like Ally McBeal with all her sniveling, whin-ing and man problems?" to "Or maybe we should ask *why* women enjoy a character like Ally McBeal?" (160). Her answer may be applicable to a wide range of images of women on television: "programmes such as *Ally McBeal* become pleasurable insofar as they offer play with some of the conflicting inheritances of feminism: desire for both independence and companionship" (161). Gorton draws on the work of Ien Ang, whose theory of the melodramatic imagination acknowledges the cultural work of primetime television in assisting women in working out their feelings of insecurity that cannot be divulged in the florescent light of the workday. "[I]t can be argued that Ally, as a character," explains Gorton, "allows women to explore their feelings of anxiety about their position within a male-dominated workplace, about being thirty-something and about marriage and children" (161). Far from a reactionary text or backlash against feminism, *Ally McBeal* points up the remaining conflicts in women's lives in this period of troubled entitlement.

"Some women enjoy Ally's fantasies, in part, because the demands of the second wave have *not* yet been met," says Gorton, and furthermore, "while *Ally McBeal*'s success has generally been read within the academy as a representation of the triumph of postfeminism, the contention here is that it demonstrates the continuing salience of the demands of second wave feminism to modern women" (162).

Gorton's work coincides with key tenets of postfeminist television criticism as delineated by Amanda Lotz, and of this list I will highlight one in particular as central to the project of third wave feminist televison studies: critical attention to *"the way situations illustrating the contemporary struggles faced by women and feminists are raised and examined within series"* (116). One important element of an effective third wave feminist media theory is the dialogical reading of televisual texts in light of feminist theory and of feminist theory in light of certain televisual texts; that is to say, such critics would not only offer a close reading of a specific series, invoking feminism as a frame of reference, they would explore a less familiar approach in cultural studies by reading the televisual text not merely as the *object* but as the *source* of theory.[7] Reading television as theory opens up the possibility of granting media culture a more important role in contemporary conversations about gender and sexuality; each show is a performance of theory, a dramatization of its insights and impasses. Television is, as Linda Williams once said of pornography and Colin McArthur of gangster films, one of the ways our culture talks to itself about itself.[8]

The shortcomings of "primetime feminism," as Bonnie J. Dow articulates them—"a white, middle-class, heterosexual bias, an assumption that a 'seize the power' mindset and more vigorous individualism will solve all women's problems, and a conflation of feminist *identity* with feminist *politics*" (207)—give reason for serious pause. Dow cautions, "we need to appreciate media for what it can do in giving us images of strong women; yet, at the same time, we need to maintain a very keen sense of the limitations of media logic" (214). This balance between appreciation and skepticism, or pleasure and danger, shapes the third wave feminist media theory I am proposing. The progressive moves of most television shows are all, I concede, intercut with moments of containment, flashes of stereotypes, plot crutches, and predictable jokes, yet they constitute a significant and sustained effort at writing outside the box of essentialism (the idea that femininity and masculinity are natural inborn identities) and beyond the walls of identity politics (the idea that our identity categories are rigid, stable, and directly related to our political orientation). For this reason, this approach focuses on the conversations made *possible* by various series without feeling the need to subordinate this positive approach to an obligatory deprecation of television culture. This perspective does not therefore ask, *Is the show feminist or not?,* or *Is it feminist* enough *or not?,* but rather takes for granted that all the shows on television today are a mixture of feminist, postfeminist, antifeminist, and pseudofeminist motifs.

Within this context of competing energies, third wave feminist television critics should ask more precise contextual questions:

- ❑   Why is this show popular right now?
- ❑   What specific desires and fears are being addressed by it?

- ◘ What material concerns in women's lives are being sublimated, resolved, mystified, alleviated in this fantasy?

- ◘ How do these shows reflect and participate in the unresolved feminist sex wars?

- ◘ In what ways does it respond to, contest, misinterpret, or translate feminist concerns about romance, marriage, family, desire, sexuality, and money?

- ◘ How are women (contestants, viewers, feminists) *using* it?

In response to anticipated criticisms of *this approach,* let me be clear about the politics of this third wave feminist media theory: I am in no way interested in uncritically embracing television; I am under no delusions that television or any other media outlet in contemporary culture is primarily feminist in content or intention; I am not diametrically opposed to the insights of second wave feminist film theory regarding pleasure, false consciousness, and the female spectator. For these reasons, "postfeminist" (rehabilitations notwithstanding) probably does not apply to my perspective. As a third wave feminist media critic, I recognize that pop culture is a ubiquitous part of many women's lives. It is therefore necessary to address it, to develop a reading practice that attends to its contradictions in content, in its role in our lives, and in its attitudes towards feminism.

Once again, the poetry of Daphne Gottlieb provides a set of images through which to conceptualize this theoretical move in feminist television studies. One of her most provocative books of poems explores the concept of the "final girl" in horror films, creatively interacting with Carol Clover's work in *Men, Women, and Chainsaws.* Clover's analysis of splatter films posits the heroine as a transgendered figure, a masculinized girl with whom male and female spectators can both identify. Gottlieb expands this figure into a wide context of American culture, imagining a range of situations in which girls face horrific social conditions in the media and in real life, from Mary Rowlandson, whose captivity narrative is a staple of colonial American literature, to Patty Hearst, kidnapped in 1974 and becoming infamous for identifying with her kidnappers and developing Stockholm Syndrome. In "Final Girl II: The Frame," Gottlieb writes a sort of handbook for heroines of horror films:

> You are here because you are in danger
> and you are in danger because you are here.
> You've got a bad case
> of the captivity narrative.

I imagine this "bad case of the captivity narrative" as one way of explaining women's pleasures in popular culture. Yet the poem ends with an image of survival:

> The story runs all the way
> to daybreak, when you can be a girl
> again and everything will be returned home.
> Until then, everything
> is electric projection
> and we are
> your captive audience.

There is a throat-ripping harshness to Gottlieb's "tits and scream" poems, but even in this angry voice, the feminist spectator can imagine her way into a more powerful position. In "Gone to Static," she is not the one on her knees sucking off some guy holding a remote control in one hand and a beer in the other, but the one facing the television and calling up the images she desires:

> the whisky is open
> the vcr is on.
> I'm running
> the film backwards
> and one by one
> you come back to me

Rather than watching the women walk one by one into the slaughterhouse of film history, I am calling them back to us, pausing at the line break between "I'm running"—the flight response, the fear, the urge to turn off the television—and "I'm *running the film* backwards," an image of control and desire and the rewriting of history, a "writing beyond the ending" that transforms the arc of these captivity narratives so that all the girls come back. Post-horror, post-static, post-frame—where "everything / is electric projection"—we might consider the feminist spectator as a sort of "final girl" and feminist television studies as a space of camaraderie and survival: "it's just you and me / and the bourbon and movie / flickering together."

Ultimately, third wave feminist media studies of television are most engaging when they address the experience of liking television without being duped by it, adopting a differential consciousness that allows us to move around inside our responses, between what we like and what we critique, balancing on the shifting grounds between hegemony and agency in which every text is "an inevitable site of ideological struggle" (Fiske, "British Cultural Studies," 259) and every reading is "interested in the latent possibility of alternative viewpoints erupting" within the text (White, 163). The third wave feminist media theory imagined here accommodates both the joyful, playful exuberance women feel when we see feminist influences in contemporary television, as well as the incendiary refusals and revisions women make in the face of the media as captivity narrative. The discontinuity readers might feel in moving from the *liking* parts of such an analysis to the *disliking* parts is precisely the point of third wave feminist media theory: the pleasure and danger of women's relationships to television have yet to be reconciled.

In the meantime—against all the anxieties that lead third wave feminist media critics to "mak[e] speech[es] about [televisual] pleasure taboo" and against our tendency to experience television as the new "great guilty secret among feminists," and because, as Carole Vance has forcefully argued, "Feminists are easily intimidated by the charge that their own pleasure is selfish" (7)—I offer this slightly modified version of Germaine Greer's famous exhortation as a brief respite from ruthless self-scrutiny:

Ladies.

Love your box.

---

* An earlier version of "Ladies Love Your Box: The Rhetoric of Pleasure and Danger" appeared in the "Introduction" to Merri Lisa Johnson's *Third Wave Feminism and Television: Jane Puts It in a Box* (I.B. Taurus: London, 2007), which she revised for this text.

Notes

1. Elspeth Probyn describes several television shows from the late 80s that participate in "a sort of 'vulgarization' of feminist discourses" (127). Probyn focuses on *thirtysomething* as "a post-feminist vision of the home to which women have 'freely' chosen to return" (128), arguing that this "new age of 'choiceoisie'" (130) obscures the politics of particular choices (134). Beth Montemurro revisits the rhetoric of choice in *Sex and the City*, arguing that the position of liberal feminism is indicted by the show, as one character insists that leaving career for husband and family is her feminist-guaranteed choice, and the other three main characters variously question and condemn her. Jhally and Lewis addressed a parallel problem with *The Cosby Show*: "Black viewers are thus caught in a trap because the escape route from TV stereotypes comes with a set of ideologically loaded conditions. To look good, to look 'positive,' means accepting a value system in which upper middle class status is a sign of superiority. This is more than crude materialism; for a group that has been largely excluded from these higher socioeconomic echelons, it is cultural and political suicide" (122).

2. While the term "sex wars" has been problematized by many feminists as reductive and sensationalistic, it remains the most familiar and recognizable way to reference these debates. To avoid the unwieldiness of excessive quotation marks, this endnote should function as a knowing wink at our readers any time the phrase, "sex wars," appears.

3. The original text reads, "Our collective fear of the dangers of sexuality has forced us into a position where we have created a theory from the body of damage done to us" (227). The ease with which "sexuality" can be replaced by "television" in many key statements from the sex wars underscores the continuity of the pleasure/danger divide across these two fields of feminist debate.

4. In her 1998 essay, "What Ails Feminist Criticism?" Susan Gubar asserts that many feminists

    make obeisance to the necessity of considering (without subordinating) race, class, gender, sexuality, and nation in litanies that often translate into depressingly knee-jerk essays rejecting out-of hand the speculations of a given literary or theoretical work simply because it neglects to discuss *x* (fill in the blank—bisexual Anglo Pakistani mothers; the heterosexual, working-class, Jews-for-Jesus community of Nashville, and so forth). Too often, each text becomes grist for a mill that proves the same intellectually vapid—though politically appalling—point that racism, classism, sexism, and homophobia reign supreme (891).

5. A significant pattern is emerging in discourse on third wave feminism in which women who are chronologically third wave are renouncing the wave model as a diversion and distortion. Lisa Maria Hogeland, in "Against Generational Thinking; or, Some Things That 'Third Wave' Feminism Isn't," writes, "There is, I argue, nothing specifically generational about any of these feminisms; they are political stances with particular histories in the movement. They may be differently nuanced for women of various age groups, historical experiences, and geographical or institutional locations—but these differences in nuance do not add up to generational difference, not least because the nuances themselves are so uneven. The effect of using claims of generational difference is to reify ageism in the movement—on both sides of a putative generational divide" (np). Her argument "that generational thinking pushes emotional buttons" strikes me as convincing. Lisa Jervis, the cofounder and publisher of *Bitch: Feminist Responses to Pop Culture*, pronounces "The End of Feminism's Third Wave," making the particularly relevant argument that "third wave" and "second wave" are labels that mask ideological disagreements, especially pertaining to "the issues motivating both sides of the '80s sex wars" (np). She concludes: "I want to see these internal disagreements continue. I want to see as much wrangling over them as ever. But I want them articulated accurately. And that means recognizing the generational divide for what it is—an illusion" (np). Despite these disavowals, it is still useful to invoke "third wave" in certain contexts. For instance, Deborah L. Siegel notes the emergence of "third wave" as "a response to what one might call the cultural dominance of 'post-feminism,'" and in this case denotes "a stance of political resistance to popular pronouncements of a moratorium on feminism and feminists" (np).

6. I take this term from Ellis Hanson, who outlines the problematic models of feminist and gay film criticism and offers queer film theory as a possible unsettling of these models.

7. For the idea of reading television as theory ; I am indebted for this idea to the work of Jane Gallop in *Living with His Camera*. She writes, "The book for the third chapter—Kathryn Harrison's *Exposure*—is not a text of theory but a novel. I find it nonetheless to be a substantial contribution to understanding photography, and so I read it as theory....The view of photography and the photographer in this novel is very much in keeping with Sontag's view, but as a novel it allows us to explore the personal, familial, and psychological dimensions of photography that Sontag's essay only gestures toward" (14).

8. Invoking Fredric Jameson's work on medieval romance and Colin McArthur's work on gangster film as her models, Williams writes, "We can therefore ask of the current hard-core genre, What problems does it seek to solve? What is it 'talking to itself' about?" (*Hard Core* 129).

Works Cited

Althusser, Louis. *Lenin and Philosophy and Other Essays*. Trans. Ben Brewster. New York: Monthly Review, 2001.

Ang, Ien. "Melodramatic Identifications: Television Fiction and Women's Fantasy." Brunsdon et al., 155–66.

Baumgardner, Jennifer and Amy Richards. *Manifesta: Young Women, Feminism, and the Future*. New York: Farrar, Straus and Giroux, 2000.

Bordo, Susan. *Twilight Zones: The Hidden Life of Cultural Images from Plato to O.J.* Berkeley: U Cal P, 1997.

Brunsdon, Charlotte, Julie D'Acci, and Lynn Spigel, eds. *Feminist Television Criticism: A Reader*. Oxford: Clarendon, 1997.

Clover, C. (1993). *Men, women, and chain saws: Gender in the modern horror film*. Princeton, NJ: Princeton University Press.

Dow, Bonnie J. *Prime-time Feminism: Television, Media Culture, and the Women's Movement since 1970*. Philadelphia: U of Pennsylvania P, 1996.

Eagleton, Terry. "The Ideology of the Aesthetic." *The Politics of Pleasure: Aesthetics and Cultural Theory*. Ed. Stephen Regan. Buckingham: Open UP, 1992. 17–31.

Ebert, Teresa. *Ludic Feminism and After: Postmodernism, Desire, and Labor in Late Capitalism*. Ann Arbor: U of Michigan P, 1996.

Fiske, John. *Understanding Popular Culture*. London: Routledge, 1989.

———. "British Cultural Studies." *Channels of Discourse: Television and Contemporary Criticism*. Ed. Robert C. Allen. Chapel Hill: U of North Carolina P, 1987. 254–89.

Gaines, Jane. "Women and Representation: Can We Enjoy Alternative Pleasure?" *Issues in Feminist Film Criticism*. Ed. Patricia Erens. Bloomington: Indiana UP, 1990.

Gallop, Jane. *Living with His Camera*. Durham: Duke UP, 2003.

Gillis, Stacy, Gillian Howie, Rebecca Munford, eds. *Third Wave Feminism: A Critical Exploration*. New York: Palgrave, 2004.

Gorton, Kristyn. "(Un)fashionable Feminists: The Media and *Ally McBeal*." Gillis, Howe, and Munsford, 154–63.

Gottlieb, Daphne. *Why Things Burn*. New York: Soft Skull, 2001.

———. *Final Girl*. New York: Soft Skull, 2003.

Greer, Germaine. "Lady Love Your Cunt." *The Madwoman's Underclothes: Essays and Other Occasional Writings*. New York: Atlantic Monthly, 1986.

Gubar, Susan. "What Ails Feminist Criticism?" *Critical Inquiry* 24 (1998): 878–902.

Hanson, Ellis. *Out Takes: Essays on Queer Theory and Film.* Durham: Duke UP, 1999.

Heywood, Leslie and Jennifer Drake, eds. *Third Wave Agenda: Being Feminist, Doing Feminism.* Minneapolis: U Minnesota P, 1997.

Hogeland, Lisa Maria. "Against Generational Thinking; or, Some Things That 'Third Wave' Feminism Isn't." *Women's Studies in Communication* 24.1 (2001): Infotrac.

Hollibaugh, Amber. "Desire for the Future: Radical Hope in Passion and Pleasure." Vance 401-10.

Jeffreys, Sheila. "How Orgasm Politics Has Hijacked the Women's Movement." *On the Issues.* http://www.echonyc.com/~onissues/s960rgasm.html (Accessed August 1, 1999).

Jervis, Lisa. "The End of Feminism's Third Wave." *Ms. Magazine.* Winter 2004. http://www.msmagazine.com/winter2004/thirdwave.asp (Accessed January 3, 2004)

Jhally, Sut and Justin Lewis. *Enlightened Racism: The Cosby Show, Audiences, and the Myth of the American Dream.* Boulder, CO: Westview, 1992.

Johnson, Merri Lisa, ed. *Jane Sexes It Up: True Confessions of Feminist Desire.* New York: Four Walls Eight Windows, 2002.

Kellner, Douglas. *Media Culture: Cultural Studies, Identity, and Politics between the Modern and the Postmodern.* London: Routledge, 1995.

Lotz, Amanda. "Postfeminist Television Criticism: Rehabilitating Critical Terms and Identifying Postfeminist Attitudes." *Feminist Media Studies* 1.1 (2001): 105–21.

MacKinnon, Catherine A. "Pleasure under Patriarchy." *Sexuality and Gender.* Eds. Christine L. Williams and Arlene Stein. Malden, MA: Blackwell, 2002. 33–43. Rpt. 1989.

Mintz, Susannah B. "In a Word, *Baywatch.*" *Catching a Wave: Reclaiming Feminism for the 21ˢᵗ Century.* Eds. Rory Dicker and Alison Piepmeier. Boston: Northeastern UP, 2003. 57–80.

Modleski, Tania. *Feminism without Women: Culture and Criticism in a "Postfeminist" Age.* New York: Routledge, 1991.

———. *The Women Who Knew Too Much: Hitchcock and Feminist Theory.* New York: Methuen, 1988.

Montemurro, Beth. "Charlotte Chooses Her Choice: Liberal Feminism on *Sex and the City.*" *The Scholar and Feminist Online* 3.1 (2004):   http://www.barnard.edu/sfoline/hbo/montemurro_01.htm.

Mulvey, Laura. "Visual Pleasure and Narrative Cinema." *Screen* 16.3 (1975): 6–18.

———. "Afterthoughts on 'Visual Pleasure and Narrative Cinema' inspired by King Vidor's *Duel in the Sun* (1946)." *Visual and Other Pleasures.* Bloomington: Indiana UP, 1989.

Munford, Rebecca. "'Wake Up and Smell the Lipgloss': Gender, Generation and the (A)politics of Girl Power." Gillis, Howie, and Munford, 142–53.

Pender, Patricia. "'I'm Buffy and You're…History': The Postmodern Politics of *Buffy.*" *Fighting the Forces: What's at Stake in* Buffy the Vampire Slayer. Eds. Rhonda V. Wilcox and David Lavery. Lanham, MD: Rowman & Littlefield, 2002. 35–44.

———. "'Kicking Ass Is Comfort Food': Buffy as Third Wave Feminist Icon." Gillis, Howie, and Munford, 164–74.

Probyn, Elspeth. "New Traditionalism and Post-Feminism: TV Does the Home." Brunsdon, d'Acci, and Spiegel, eds. 126–37. Rpt. *Screen* 31 (1988): 147–59.

Schweickart, Patrocinio. "Reading Ourselves: Toward a Feminist Theory of Reading." *Feminisms: An Anthology of Literary Theory and Criticism.* Ed. Robyn Warhol and Diane Price Herndl. New Brunswick: Rutgers UP, 1997. 609–34.

Shugart, Helene A. "Isn't It Ironic?: The Intersection of Third-Wave Feminism and Generation X." *Women's Studies in Communication* 24.2 (2001): 131–69. Infotrac.

Siegel, Deborah L. "The Legacy of the Personal: Generating Theory in Feminism's Third Wave." *Hypatia* 12.3 (1997): Infotrac.

Stasia, Cristina Lucia. "'Wham! Bam! Thank You Ma'am!': The New Public/Private Female Action Hero." Gillis, Howie, and Munford, 175–84.

Vance, Carole S., ed. *Pleasure and Danger: Exploring Female Sexuality*. London: Pandora, 1989.

White, Mimi. "Ideological Analysis." *Channels of Discourse: Television and Contemporary Criticism*. U of North Carolina P, 1987. 134–71.

Williams, Linda. *Hard Core: Power, Pleasure, and the "Frenzy of the Visible."* Berkeley: U California P, 1989.

———. "Why I Didn't Want to Write This Essay." *Signs: Journal of Women in Culture and Society* 30.1 (2004): 1264–71.

Willis, Ellen. "Rock, etc." *The New Yorker*. Oct. 23, 1971. 168–75.

24

■ Post-Feminism and Popular Culture

Bridget Jones[1] and the New Gender Regime.

Angela McRobbie

■ Introduction: Complexification of Backlash?

This chapter presents a series of possible conceptual frames for engaging with what I refer to as post-feminism. Broadly I envisage this as a process by which feminist gains of the 1970s and 1980s are actively and relentlessly undermined. I propose that through an array of machinations, elements of contemporary popular culture are perniciously effective in regard to this undoing of feminism, while simultaneously appearing to be engaging in a well-informed and even well-intended response to feminism. I then propose that this undoing, which can be perceived in the broad cultural field, is compounded, unexpectedly perhaps, in those sociological theories, including the work of Giddens and Beck, which address themselves to aspects of gender and social change, but as though feminist thought and years of women's struggles had no role to play in these transformations. I also argue that by means of the tropes of freedom and choice which are now inextricably connected with the category of young women, feminism is decisively aged and made to seem redundant. Feminism is cast into the shadows, where at best it can expect to have some afterlife, where it might be regarded ambivalently by those young women who must, in more public venues, stake a distance from it, for the sake of social and sexual recognition. I propose here a complexification of the backlash thesis (which, again, will be examined in more detail in the chapter that follows).

Faludi refers to a concerted, conservative response to challenge the achievements of feminism (Faludi 1992). Her work is important because like that of Stacey and others it charts anti-feminist interventions that are coterminous with feminism more or less as it happens. My argument is rather different, which is that post-feminism positively draws on and invokes feminism as that which can be taken into account, to suggest that equality is achieved, in order to install a whole repertoire of new meanings which emphasise that it is no longer needed, it is a spent force. This was very apparent in the (UK) *Independent* newspaper column *Bridget Jones's Diary,* then in the fantastically successful book and the films which followed. The infectious girlishness of Bridget Jones produces a generational logic which is distinctly post-feminist. Despite feminism, Bridget wants to pursue dreams of romance, find a suitable husband, get married and have children. What she fears most is ending up as a 'spinster.' Bridget is a girl who is 'once again' re-assuringly feminine. She is not particularly career-minded, even though she knows she should be. She makes schoolgirl errors in her publishing house, not knowing that the literary critic F. R. Leavis is long dead, she delivers an incoherent speech at a book launch; her head seems to be full of frivolous thoughts, though she is clever and witty in her own feminine way. But most of all she is desperate to find the right man. The film celebrates a kind of scatterbrain and endearing femininity, as though it is something that has been lost. Thank goodness, the film seems to be saying, that old-fashioned femininity can be retrieved. Post-feminism in this context seems to mean gently chiding the feminist past, while also retrieving and re-instating some palatable elements, in this case sexual freedom, the right to drink, smoke, have fun in the city, and be economically independent.

Broadly I am arguing that for feminism to be 'taken into account' it has to be understood as having already passed away. The pushing away which underpins the passing away is very much the subject of this book. This is a movement detectable across popular culture, a site where 'power…is remade at various junctures within everyday life (constituting) our tenuous sense of common sense' (Butler 2000a: 14). Some fleeting comments in Judith Butler's short book *Antigone's Claim* suggest to me that post-feminism can be explored through what I would describe as a 'double entanglement' (Butler 2000b). This comprises the co-existence of neo-conservative values in relation to gender, sexuality and family life (for example, George Bush supporting the campaign to encourage chastity among young people, and in March 2004 declaring that civilisation itself depends on traditional marriage), with processes of liberalisation in regard to choice and diversity in domestic, sexual and kinship relations (for example, gay couples are now able to adopt, foster or have their own children by whatever means, and in the UK at least, have full rights to civil partnerships). It also encompasses the existence of feminism as at some level transformed into a form of Gramscian common sense, while also fiercely repudiated, indeed almost hated (McRobbie 2003). The 'taken into accountness' permits all the more thorough dismantling of feminist politics and the discrediting of the occasionally voiced need for its renewal.

■ Feminism Dismantling Itself

The impact of this double entanglement which is manifest in popular and political culture coincides however, with feminism in the academy finding it necessary to dismantle itself.

For the sake of periodisation we could say that 1990 marks a turning point, the moment of definitive self-critique in feminist theory. At this time the representational claims of second wave feminism come to be fully interrogated by post-colonialist feminists like Spivak, Trinh and Mohanty among others, and by feminist theorists like Butler and Haraway who inaugurate the radical de-naturalising of the post-feminist body (Spivak 1988, Trinh 1989, Mohanty 1999, Butler 1990, Haraway 1991). Under the prevailing influence of Foucault, there is a shift away from feminist interest in centralised power blocks, e.g., the State, patriarchy, law, to more dispersed sites, events and instances of power conceptualised as flows and specific convergences and consolidations of talk, discourse, attentions. The body and also the subject come to represent a focal point for feminist interest, nowhere more so than in the work of Butler. The concept of subjectivity and the means by which cultural forms and interpellations (or dominant social processes) call women into being, produce them as subjects whilst ostensibly merely describing them as such, inevitably means that it is a problematic 'she,' rather than an unproblematic 'we,' which is indicative of a turn to what we might describe as the emerging politics of post-feminist inquiry (Butler 1990, 1993). In feminist cultural studies the early 1990s also mark a moment of feminist reflexivity. In her article 'Pedagogies of the Feminine' Brunsdon queried the (hitherto assumed) use value to feminist media scholarship of the binary opposition between femininity and feminism, or, as she put it, the extent to which the 'housewife' or 'ordinary woman' was conceived of as the assumed subject of attention for feminism (Brunsdon 1991, re-printed 1997). Looking back we can see how heavily utilised this dualism was, and also how particular it was to gender arrangements for largely white and relatively affluent (i.e., housewifely) heterosexual women. While at the time both categories had a kind of transparency, by the late 1980s these came under scrutiny. Not only was there a homogenising force on both sides of the equation, but it also became apparent that this binary permitted a certain kind of useful, feminist, self-definition to emerge, particularly in media and cultural studies where there was an interest in the intersections of media with everyday life, through conceptualisations of the audience. In this case the audience was understood to comprise of housewives who would be studied empathetically by feminists. The concept of the housewife in effect facilitated a certain mode of feminist inquiry, but we were at the time inattentive to the partial and exclusive nature of this couplet. The year 1990 also marked the moment at which the concept of popular feminism found expression. Andrea Stuart considered the wider circulation of feminist values across the landscape of popular culture, in particular magazines where quite suddenly issues which had been central to the formation of the women's movement like domestic violence, equal pay, workplace harassment, were now addressed to a vast readership (Stuart 1990). The wider dissemination of feminist issues was also a key concern in my own writing at this time, in particular the intersection of these new representations with the daily lives of young women who as subjects (called into being) of this now-popular feminism, might then be expected to embody more emboldened (though also of course failed) identities. This gave rise to the idea of feminist success. It suggested that forms of popular mass media like magazines were in fact more open to change than had previously been thought, and this gave rise to a brief tide of optimism. What could have an impact inside the academy in terms of the feminist curriculum could also have some impact beyond the academy, indeed in the commercial world. Of course no sooner is the word success written than it is queried. How could this be gauged? What might be the criteria for judging degrees of feminist success?

■ Female Success

Admittedly there is some extravagance in my claim for feminist success. It might be more accurate to remark on the keen interest across the quality and popular media (themselves wishing to increase their female readers and audiences) in ideas of female success. As feminist values are indeed taken on board within a range of institutions, including law, education, to an extent medicine, likewise employment and the media, high profile or newsworthy achievement of women and girls in these sectors shows the institutions to be modern and abreast with social change. This is the context then within which feminism is acknowledged, and this is what I mean by feminism taken into account. The kind of feminism which is taken into account in this context is liberal, equal opportunities feminism, where elsewhere what is invoked more negatively is the radical feminism concerned with social criticism rather than with progress or improvement in the position of women in an otherwise more or less unaltered social order. But across the boundaries of different forms of feminism, the idea of feminist success has, so far, only been described sporadically (for accounts of girls' achievement in education see Arnot and Weiner 1999 and also Harris 2004). Within media and cultural studies both Brunsdon and myself have each considered how with feminism as part of the academic curriculum, (i.e., canonised), then it is not surprising that it might also be countered, that is feminism must face up to the consequences of its own claims to representation and power and not be so surprised when young women students decline the invitation to identify as a 'we' with their feminist teachers and scholars (Brunsdon 1997, McRobbie 1999a). This interface between the feminist academy and the student body has also been discussed in US feminist journals particularly in regard to the decline of women's studies, and this is a subject I return to in the concluding chapter of this book (Brown 2005). Back in the early 1990s (and following Butler) I saw this sense of contestation on the part of young women, and what I would call their distance from feminism as one of potential, where a lively dialogue about how feminism might develop would commence (Butler 1992, McRobbie 1994). Indeed it seemed in the very nature of feminism that it gave rise to dis-identification as a kind of requirement for its existence. But still, it seems now, over a decade later, that this space of distance from feminism and those utterances of forceful non-identity with feminism have consolidated into something closer to repudiation rather than ambivalence, and it is this vehemently denunciatory stance which is manifest across the field of popular gender debate. This is the cultural space of post-feminism.

In this context it requires both imagination and hopefulness to argue that the active, sustained and repetitive repudiation or repression of feminism also marks its (still fearful) presence or even longevity (as afterlife). What I mean by this is that there are different kinds of repudiation and different investments in such a stance. The more gentle denunciations of feminism co-exist however with the shrill championing of young women as a metaphor for social change on the pages of the right wing press in the UK, in particular the *Daily Mail*.[2] This anti-feminist endorsement of female individualisation is embodied in the figure of the ambitious TV blonde (McRobbie 1999b). These so-called 'A1' girls are glamorous high-achievers destined for Oxford or Cambridge and are usually pictured clutching A level examination certificates. We might say these are ideal girls, subjects *par excellence,* and also subjects of excellence. Nor are these notions of female success exclusive to the changing representations of young women in the countries of the affluent west (Spivak 1999, 2002). Young women are a good investment; they can be trusted with micro-credit; they are the privileged subjects of social change. But the terms of these great expectations on the part of governments are that young women must do without more autonomous feminist politics. What is consistent is the displacement of feminism as a political movement. It is this displacement which is reflected in Butler's sorrowful account of Antigone's life after death. Her shadowy, lonely existence, suggests a modality of feminist effectivity as spectral; she has to be cast out, indeed entombed for social organisation to once again become intelligible.

■ Unpopular Feminism

The media has become the key site for defining codes of sexual conduct. It casts judgement and establishes the rules of play. Across these many channels of communication feminism is routinely disparaged. Why is feminism so hated? Why do young women recoil in horror at the very idea of the feminist? To count as a girl today appears to require this kind of ritualistic denunciation, which in turn suggests that one strategy in the disempowering of feminism includes it being historicised and generationalised and thus easily rendered out of date. It would be far too simplistic to trace a pattern in media from popular feminism (or 'prime-time' feminism including TV programmes like *LA Law*) in the early 1990s, to niche feminism (BBC Radio 4, *Women's Hour,* and the Women's Page of the *Guardian* newspaper), in the mid 1990s, and then to overtly unpopular feminism (from 2000 onwards), as though these charted a chronological 'great moving right show' as Stuart Hall once put it in another context (Hall 1989). We would need a more developed conceptual schema to account for the simultaneous feminisation of popular media with this accumulation of ambivalent, fearful responses. We would certainly need to signal the seeming enfranchisement of women in the west, of all ages as audiences, active consumers of media and the many products it promotes, and by virtue of education, earning power and consumer identity, a sizeable block of target market. We would also need to be able to theorise female achievement predicated not on feminism, but on 'female individualism,' on success which seems to based on the invitation to young women by various governments that they might now consider themselves free to compete in education and in work as privileged subjects of the new meritocracy. Is this then the New Deal for New Labour's modern young women; female individualisation and the new meritocracy at the expense of feminist politics?

There are various sites within popular culture where this work of undoing feminism with some subtlety becomes visible (see also Brunsdon 2003). The Wonderbra advertisement showing the model Eva Herzigova looking down admiringly at her cleavage enhanced by the lacy pyrotechnics of the Wonderbra, was through the mid 1990s positioned in major high street locations in the UK on full size billboards. The composition of the image had such a textbook 'sexist ad' dimension (the 'male gaze' is invited and encouraged by the gaze of the model herself to look towards her breasts) that one could be forgiven for supposing some ironic familiarity with both cultural studies and with feminist critiques of advertising (Williamson 1986). It was, in a sense, taking feminism into account by showing it to be a thing of the past, by provocatively 'enacting sexism' while at the same time playing with those debates in film theory about women as the object of the gaze (Mulvey 1975) and with female desire (De Lauretis 1987, Coward 1984). The picture is in *noirish* black and white and refers explicitly through its captions (from 'Hello Boys' to 'Or Are You Just Pleased To See Me?') to Hollywood and the famous lines of the actress Mae West. Here is an advertisement which plays back to its viewers well known aspects of feminist media studies, film theory and semiotics. Indeed, it almost offers (albeit crudely) the viewer or passing driver Laura Mulvey's theory of women as object of the gaze, projected as cityscape within the frame of the billboard. Also mobilised in this advertisement is the familiarity of the term political correctness, the efficacy of which resides in its warranting and unleashing such energetic reactions against the seemingly tyrannical regime of feminist puritanism. Everyone and especially young people can give a sigh of relief. Thank goodness, the image seems to suggest, it is permissible, once again, to enjoy looking at the bodies of beautiful women. At the same time, the advertisement also hopes to provoke feminist condemnation as a means of generating publicity. Thus generational differences are also produced, the younger female viewer, along with her male counterparts, educated in irony and visually literate, is not made angry by such a repertoire. She appreciates its layers of meaning, she gets the joke.

When in a TV advertisement (1998/9) supermodel Claudia Schiffer takes off her clothes as she descends a flight of stairs in a luxury mansion on her way out of the door towards her new Citroen car, a similar rhetoric is at work. This advert appears to suggest that yes, this is a self-consciously sexist ad. Feminist critiques of it are deliberately evoked. Feminism is taken into account, but only to be shown to be no longer necessary. Why? Because it now seems that there is no exploitation here, there is nothing remotely naïve about this striptease. She seems to be doing it out of choice, and for her own enjoyment. The image works on the basis of its audience knowing Claudia Schiffer to be one of the world's most famous and highly paid supermodels. Once again the shadow of disapproval is evoked, (the striptease as site of female exploitation) only instantly to be dismissed as belonging to the past, to a time when feminists used to object to such imagery. To make such an objection nowadays would run the risk of ridicule. Objection is pre-empted with irony. In each of these cases a spectre of feminism is invoked so that it might be undone. For male viewers tradition is restored or as Beck puts it there is 'constructed certitude,' while for the girls what is proposed is a movement beyond feminism, to a more comfortable zone where women are now free to choose for themselves (Beck 1992).

■ Feminism Undone?

If we turn attention to some of the participatory dynamics in leisure and everyday life which see young women endorse (or else refuse to condemn) the ironic normalisation of pornography, where they indicate their approval of and desire to be pin-up girls for the centrefolds of the soft porn so-called lad's mags, where it is not at all unusual to pass young women in the street wearing T shirts bearing phrases such as 'Porn Queen' or 'Pay To Touch' across the breasts, where in the UK at least young women quite happily attend lap-dancing clubs (perhaps as a test of their sophistication and 'cool'), and where *Cosmopolitan* magazine considers how empowering it is for young women to 'flash ' their breasts in public, we are witness to a hyper-culture of commercial sexuality, one aspect of which is the repudiation of a feminism which is invoked only to be summarily dismissed (see also Gill 2003, 2006). As a mark of a post-feminist identity, young women journalists refuse to condemn the enormous growth of lap-dancing clubs. They know of the existence of the feminist critiques and debates (or at least this is my claim) through their education, since as Shelley Budgeon describes in her study, most girls these days are 'gender aware' (Budgeon 2001). Thus the new female subject is, despite her freedom, called upon to be silent, to withhold critique in order to count as a modern sophisticated girl. Indeed this withholding of critique is a condition of her freedom. There is quietude and complicity in the manners of generationally specific notions of cool, and more precisely, an uncritical relation to dominant commercially produced sexual representations which actively invoke hostility to assumed feminist positions from the past, in order to endorse a new regime of sexual meanings based on female consent, equality, participation and pleasure, free of politics.

■ Female Individualisation

By using the term female individualisation I am drawing on the concept of individualisation which is discussed at length by sociologists including Giddens (1991), Beck and Beck-Gernscheim (2001) as well as Zygmunt Bauman (2000, 2001). This work is to be distinguished from the more directly Foucauldian version found in the work of Nikolas Rose (2000). Although there is some shared ground between these authors, insofar as they all reflect on the expectations that individuals now avidly self-monitor and that there appears to be greater capacity on the part of individuals to plan 'a life of one's own,' there are also divergences. Beck and Giddens are less concerned with the way in which power works in this new friendly guise as personal advisor and instead emphasise the enlarge-ment of freedom and choice, while in contrast Rose sees these modes of self government as marking out 'the shaping of being,' and thus the 'inculcation of a form of life' (Rose 2000). Bauman bewails the sheer unviability of naked individualisation as the resources of sociality (and welfare) are stripped away, leaving the individual to self-blame when success eludes him or her. (It is also possible to draw a political line between these authors, with Bauman and Rose to the left, and Giddens and Beck 'beyond left and right'). My emphasis here is on the work of Giddens and Beck, for the very reason that it appears to speak directly to the post-feminist generation. In their writing there are only distant echoes (if that) of the feminist struggles that were required to produce the new-found freedoms of young women in the west. There is no trace whatsoever of the battles fought, of the power struggles embarked upon, or of the enduring inequities which still mark out the relations between men and women. All of this is airbrushed out of existence on the basis that, as they claim, 'emancipatory politics' has given way instead to life politics (or in Beck's terms the sub-politics of single interest groups). Both of these authors provide a sociological account of the dynamics of social change understood as 'reflexive modernisation.' The earlier period of modernisation (first modernity) created a welfare state and a set of institutions (e.g., education) which allowed people in the second modernity to become more independent and able for example to earn their own living. Young women are as a result now dis-embedded from communities where gender roles were fixed. And, as the old structures of social class fade away, and lose their grip in the context of late or second modernity, individuals are increasingly called upon to invent their own structures. They must do this internally and individualistically, so that self-monitoring practices (the diary, the life plan, the career pathway) replace reliance on set ways and structured pathways. Self-help guides, personal advisors, lifestyle coaches and gurus and all sorts of self-improvement TV programmes provide the cultural means by which individualisation operates as a social process. As the overwhelming force of structure fades, so also, it is claimed, does the capacity for agency increase.

Individuals must now choose the kind of life they want to live. Girls must have a life-plan. They must become more reflexive in regard to every aspect of their lives, from making the right choice in marriage, to taking responsibility for their own working lives and not being dependent on a job for life or on the stable and reliable operations of a large scale bureaucracy, which in the past would have allocated its employees specific, and possibly unchanging, roles. Beck and Giddens each place a different inflection on their accounts of reflexive modernisation, but overall these arguments appear to fit very directly with the kinds of scenarios and dilemmas facing the young women characters in the narratives of contemporary popular culture (chick lit). There is an evasion in this writing of social and sexual divides, and of the continuing prejudice and discrimination experienced by black and Asian women. Beck and Giddens are quite inattentive to the regulative dimensions of the popular discourses of personal choice and self improvement. Choice is surely, within lifestyle culture, a modality of constraint. The individual is compelled to be the kind of subject who can make the right choices. By these means new lines and demarcations are drawn between those subjects who are judged responsive to the regime of personal responsibility, and those who fail miserably. Neither Giddens nor Beck mounts a substantial critique of these power relations which work so effectively at the level of embodiment. They have no grasp that these are productive of new realms of injury and injustice.

■ Bridget Jones

The film *Bridget Jones's Diary* (a worldwide success) draws together many of these socio-logical themes. In her early 30s, living and working in London, Bridget is a free agent, single and childless and able to enjoy herself in pubs, bars and restaurants. She is the product of modernity in that she has benefited from those institutions (education) which have loosened the ties of tradition and community for women, making it possible for them to be disembedded and to re-locate to the city to earn an independent living without shame or danger. However this also gives rise to new anxieties. There is the fear of loneli-ness, the stigma of remaining single and the risks and uncertainties of not finding the right partner to be a father to children. In the film, the opening sequence shows Bridget in her pyjamas worrying about being alone and on the shelf. The soundtrack is *All By Myself* by Jamie McNeal and the audience laughs along with her, in this moment of self doubt. We immediately know that what she is thinking is 'what will it be like if I never find the right man, if I never get married?' Bridget portrays the whole spectrum of attri-butes associated with the self-monitoring subject, she confides in her friends, she keeps a diary, she endlessly reflects on her fluctuating weight, noting her calorie intake, she plans, plots and has projects. She is also deeply uncertain as to what the future holds for her. Despite the choices she has, there are also any number of risks of which she is regu-larly reminded, the risk that she might let the right man slip from under her nose, so she must always be on the lookout, prioritising this over success in the workplace, the risk that not catching a man at the right time might mean she misses the chance of having children (her biological clock is ticking), there is also the risk that, without a partner she will be isolated, marginalised from the world of happy couples.

With the burden of self-management so apparent, Bridget fantasies about very tradi-tional forms of happiness and fulfilment. Flirting with her boss during office hours, Bridget imagines herself in a white wedding dress surrounded by bridesmaids, and the audience laughs loudly because they, like Bridget, know that this is not how young women these days are meant to think. Feminism has intervened to constrain these kinds of conventional desires. But it is surely a relief to escape this censorious politics and freely enjoy that which has been disapproved of, and this is what the film not only allows but absolutely encourages and enjoys. Feminism was anti-marriage and this can now to be shown to be a great mistake. Feminism is invoked, in order to be relegated to the past. But this is not simply a return to the past, there are, of course, quite dramatic differences between the various female characters of current popular culture from *Bridget Jones* to the girls in *Sex and the City* and to *Ally McBeal,* and those found in girls' and women's magazines from a pre-feminist era. These new young women are confident enough to declare their anxieties about possible failure in regard to finding a husband, they avoid any aggressive or overtly traditional men, and they brazenly enjoy their sexuality, without fear of the sexual double standard. In addition they are more than capable of earning their own living, and the degree of suffering or shame they anticipate in the absence of finding a husband is coun-tered by sexual self confidence.

With such light entertainment as this, suffused with irony and dedicated to re-inventing highly successful women's genres of film and TV, an argument about feminism being so repudiated might seem heavy handed. Indeed *Bridget Jones's Diary* is exemplary as a women's genre film, re-invented to bring back romance in a specifically post-feminist context. Neither it, nor *Ally McBeal* nor *Sex in the City* are rabid anti-feminist tracts, instead they have taken feminism into account and implicitly or explicitly ask the question what now? There is a strong sense in all three that young women somehow want to reclaim their femininity, without stating exactly why it has been taken away from them. These young women want to be girlish and enjoy all sorts of traditional feminine pleasures without apology, although again, quite why they might feel they have to apologise is left hanging in the air. But it seems we the audience, like they the characters, are meant to know the answer to this question because it is so obvious. Feminism, it seems, robbed women of their most treasured pleasures, i.e., romance, gossip and obsessive concerns about how to catch a husband, indeed as I write this I am reminded of being right back there in the land of *Jackie* magazine, where I myself implicitly scolded readers for falling into these traps especially the fantasies of romance and marriage. It is as though this is the vengeance of the younger generation who had to put up with being chided by feminist teachers and academics at university for wanting the wrong things. (This well-educated female demographic is factored into the narrative, littered as it is with references to Germaine Greer, Jane Austen, Salman Rushdie, post-modernism and literary theory.) The post-feminist moment of *Bridget Jones's Diary* also coincides with the new popularity once again, massively promoted by consumer culture, of weddings, including gay and lesbian weddings and all the paraphernalia that goes with them. The cultural references and the humour in this particular 'rom-com' are up-to-the moment, girls now get so drunk they tumble out of taxis, they have sex when they feel like it, without always being prepared with the best underwear and so on. But, as we know, relations of power are indeed made and re-made within texts of enjoyment and rituals of relaxation and abandonment. These young women's genres are vital to the construction of a new 'gender regime,' based on the double entanglement which I have described. They endorse wholeheartedly what Rose calls 'this ethic of freedom,' and young women have come to the fore as the pre-eminent subjects of this new ethic. These popular texts normalise post-feminist gender anxieties so as to re-regulate young women by means of the language of personal choice. Despite all of this planning and diary keeping even 'well regulated liberty' can backfire (the source of comic effect), and this in turn gives rise to demarcated pathologies (leaving it too late to have a baby, failing to find a good catch, etc.) which carefully define the parameters of what constitutes liveable lives for young women without the occasion of re-invented feminism.

Bridget Jones's Diary celebrates the return of romance in a soft rather than hard post-feminist framing. Bridget is endearingly plump and reminiscent of any number of literary predecessors, but most obviously Jane Austen's Elizabeth Bennet. She is self-mocking, self-disparaging, and her witty observations of the social life around her create a warmth and an audience that is almost immediately on her side, as she negotiates the codes of contemporary sexual relationships. Although she constantly defines herself as a failure, and even plays dumb, messing up the chances that come her way to shine at work, and saying the wrong thing in public places, she is also aware of every wrong step she takes, scolding herself along the way. Much of the comic effect evolves around her daily attempts to become the sort of woman who she thinks will be the kind of woman men want to marry, hence the crucial romantic moment in the film when Mark Darcy says he likes her just the way she is. There is of course poignancy here, since who does not want to be liked for just who one is, whoever that may be? *Bridget Jones's Diary* speaks then to female desire, and in a wholly commercialised way, to the desire for some kind of gender justice, or fairness, in the world of sex and relationships. Here too the ghost of feminism is hovering. Bridget deserves to get what she wants. The audience are wholly on her side. She ought to be able to find the right man, for the reason that she has negotiated that tricky path which requires being independent, earning her own living, standing up for herself against demeaning comments, remaining funny and good humoured throughout, without being angry or too critical of men, without foregoing her femininity, her desires for love and motherhood, her sense of humour and her appealing vulnerability.

* An earlier version of this article was published by Taylor and Francis Group as "Post-feminism and popular culture" in *Feminist Media Studies*, 4, 3: 255-264. Taylor and Francis Group permitted the reprint of this article.

Notes

1. *Bridget Jones's Diary* appeared first as a newspaper column in the UK newspaper *The Independent* in 1996, its author Helen Fielding then published the diaries as a book, and the film, *Bridget Jones's Diary* directed by Sharon McGuire, opened in 2001. The sequel *Bridget Jones: The Edge of Reason* directed by Beebron Kidron opened in November 2004.

2. The newspaper *The Daily Mail* has the highest volume of female readers in the UK. Its post-feminist stance is unambiguous; it frequently commissions recanting feminist journalists to blame feminism for women's contemporary complaints. E.g. in 23/11/2003: 12–13 the famous novelist Fay Weldon wrote a piece called 'Look What We Have Done'…arguing that all feminists created was ' a new generation of women for whom sex is utterly joyless and hollow'.

References

Arnot, M., David, M. and Weiner, G. (1999) *Closing the Gender Gap,* Polity Press, Cambridge.

Bauman, Z. (2000) *Liquid Modernity,* Polity Press, Cambridge.

Bauman, Z. (2001) *The Individualised Society,* Polity Press, Cambridge.

Beck, U. (1992) *Risk Society: Towards a New Modernity,* Sage, London.

Beck, U. and Beck-Gernscheim, E. (2001) *Individualization,* Sage, London.

Brown, W. (2005) ' The Impossibility of Women's Studies' in W. Brown, *Edgework: Critical Essays on Knowledge and Politics,* Princeton University Press, 116–136, New Jersey, first published in *Differences: A Journal of Feminist Cultural Studies, 9* (5): 79–102 , 1997.

Brunsdon, C. (1991/1997) 'Pedagogies of the Feminine' in C. Brunsdon, *Screen Tastes: Soap Opera to Satellite Dishes,* 172–189, Routledge, London.

Brunsdon, C. (2004) 'Taste and Time on Television' *Screen* 45 (2): 115–129.

Brunsdon, C. (2003) 'Lifestyling Britain: The 8–9 Slot on British Television' in *International Journal of Cultural Studies* 6 (1): 5–23.

Budgeon. S, (2001) 'Emergent Feminist (?) Identities: Young Women and the Practice of Micropolitics' in *European Journal of Women's Studies,* 8 (1): 7–28.

Butler. J, (1990) *Gender Trouble: Feminism and the Subversion of Identity,* Routledge, New York.

Butler, J. (1992) 'Contingent Foundations: Feminism and the Question of the Postmodern' in (eds) J. Butler and J.W. Scott *Feminists Theorise the Political,* 3–22, Routledge, New York.

Butler, J. (1993) *Bodies That Matter: The Discursive Limits of Sex,* Routledge, New York.

Butler, J. (2000a) *Antigone's Claim: Kinship Between Life and Death,* Columbia University Press, New York.

Butler, J. (2000b) 'Agencies of Style for a Liminal Subject' in (eds) P. Gilroy, Coward, R. (1984) *Female Desire,* Paladin, London.

De Lauretis, T. (1987) *Technologies of Gender: Essays on Theory, Film, and Fiction,* Macmillan, Basingstoke.

Faludi, S. (1992) *Backlash: The Undeclared War Against Women,* Vintage, London.

Giddens, A. (1991) *Modernity and Self Identity,* Polity Press, Cambridge.

Gill, R. (2003) 'From Sexual Objectification to Sexual Subjectification: The Resexualisation of Women's Bodies in the Media' in *Feminist Media Studies,* 3 (1): 100–106.

Gill, R. (2006) *Gender and the Media,* Polity Press, Cambridge.

Hall, S. (1989) *The Hard Road to Renewal,* Verso, London.

Haraway, D. (1991) *Simians, Cyborgs and Women,* Free Association Books, London.

Harris, A. (2004) *Future Girl,* Routledge, London.

McRobbie, A. (1994) *Postmodernism and Popular Culture,* Routledge, London.

McRobbie, A. (1999a) 'All the World's a Stage, Screen or Magazine,' in *In the Culture Society,* Routledge, 22–31, London.

McRobbie, A. (1999b) 'Feminism v the TV Blondes,' Inaugural Lecture, Goldsmiths College University of London.

McRobbie, A. (2003) 'Mothers and Fathers: Who Needs Them? In *Feminist Review* no 73.

Mohanty, C.T. (1999) 'Under Western Eyes' in Ashcroft B., Griffin, G., Tiffin, H. *The Postcolonial Studies Reader,* Routledge, London.

Mulvey, L. (1975/1989) *Visual and Other Pleasures,* Macmillan, Basingstoke.

Rose, N. (2000) 'Genetic risk and the birth of the somatic individual,' *Economy and Society, Special Issue on Configurations of Risk,* 29 (4): 484–513.

Spivak, G. C. (1988) In *Other Worlds; Essays in Cultural Politics,* Routledge, New York.

Spivak, G.C. (1999) *A Critique of Postcolonial Reason,* Harvard University Press, Cambridge, Mass.

Spivak, C.G. (2002) 'Resident Alien' in (ed) D.T. Goldberg and A. Quayson, *Relocating Postcolonialism,* Blackwell, Oxford: 47–65.

Stuart, A. (1990) 'Feminism Dead or Alive' in (ed) J Rutherford, *Identity, Community Culture Difference,* Lawrence and Wishart, London.

Trinh, T. M. (1989) *Woman Native Other,* Indiana University Press, Bloomington.

Williamson, J. (1986) *Consoling Passions: The Dynamics of Popular Culture,* Marion Boyars, London.

25

■ Women in Traffic

L.A. Autobiography

Kathleen McHugh

> To be content with the easy pleasures of the feminine is to lose a fundamental opportunity: an opportunity to precisely use our material experiences to map out the changing relationships between identity, ideology and gender within the historical moment in which we live.
>
> *Elsbeth Probyn[1]*

Identity-oriented approaches to films and to representation in general have been both necessary and problematic. Necessary as a corrective to an objective, exclusive, elitist critical stance, such approaches insist upon the importance of the critic's location, upon the place and power dynamics from within which s/he speaks. Yet to signify that place within the self (as "identity"), however socially marked by gender, ethnicity, race, or sexuality, is to invoke the conventions of bourgeois subjectivity (interiority, authenticity, sentimentality) and to subsume those socially marked constructions within those conventions. Thus, in order to avoid issues of who I am or what the feminine is and to investigate instead how gender works, I would like to take up Probyn's suggestion and bring one aspect of my material experience—I live in L.A. and I commute—to bear upon another—my profession as a feminist film critic. As the title indicates, my essay fashions elements of my autobiography (my gender, the city I live in and one of its most striking material conditions) to reconsider cinematic representations of women in relation to the trope of automobility.[2]

It is my contention that the socio-geographic particulars of any given location can provide provocative metaphors for the construction of an enigmatic and generative political self, a self whose evocation incorporates material experiences. Such invented selves obviate problematic universal or essentialist assertions (such as those that trouble many varieties of identity politics), while also grounding theoretical explorations in a specific environment or situation. This approach can produce surprising and inventive models for thinking an environmentally and politically appropriate(d) self. To live and work in L.A. is to be in traffic; the fortuitous initials "LA" invoke both the city and femininity, the two coupled at the intersection of autobiography and automobility. My chapter uses the automobile—a ubiquitous figure and feature of life in Southern California—to literalize and remotivate a metaphor inherent in theoretical discourse about women, articulated most cogently in Gayle Rubin's watershed piece "The Traffic in Women." I will make use of the actuality and the metaphor of women's automobility to contextualize and nuance the other dominant gender metaphor that rises out of L.A. and the film industry— women as objects of the gaze.

■ I. Sadism Demands a Story: "Don't Let Her Get Away!"

The research trope of "women in traffic" quickly pays off. In the article that inaugurates psychoanalytic feminist film theory, "Visual Pleasure and Narrative Cinema," the films that Laura Mulvey uses to illustrate women's role in spectacle and narrative share another feature she doesn't mention: they all depict and more or less depend upon women's movement, upon their self-motivated *traffic* through the diegesis. While von Sternberg's *Morocco* (1930) culminates in Marlene Dietrich/Amy Jolly's barefoot trek into the desert, *Dishonored*'s (1931) plot depends upon Dietrich/Magda's travel behind enemy lines. In the more domestic *Blonde Venus* (1932), Helen Faraday's attempt to keep her son involves their travel around the country in trains, on foot, and on a hay wagon, chased by an army of private detectives and anonymous men out for reward money. The Hitchcock *oeuvre* shares the same insistent motif. In *Vertigo* (1958), Madeleine is tailed by Scottie as she aimlessly drives the streets and environs of San Francisco. The main character in *Marnie* (1964) travels from city to city, changing her luggage, clothing and haircolor to evade detectives as she deceives one gullible mark after another; in *Psycho* (1960), Marion Crane, having stolen forty thousand dollars, hightails it out of town in her car, stopped and later followed by a very suspicious police officer. In each of these narratives, women in traffic, in movement through the diegesis, stir up the interest of the law and its agents who pursue, surveil and attempt to stop them.

Mulvey chooses her films well, avoiding more gender specific genres such as the western, where the narratives concern men on the move, and the women's melodrama, where the claustrophobic space of the home provides the compression necessary for plots that are usually without any significant geographic movement at all. Indeed, D.W. Griffith, whose name, films and Victorian ideologies designate one beginning of the cinema, distinguished between the genders precisely around the question of movement: "Man is a moving animal. It isn't so with women."[3] The adventure/thrillers that "Visual Pleasure and Narrative Cinema" focuses on illustrate clearly the anxiety and the sadism instigated when the Victorian binary "men move/women stay home" is violated, when women attempt to move, to travel, to fend for themselves, unattended and unprotected, outside the law. Thus the narratives that found the psychoanalytic theorization of gender and sexuality in the cinema actually constitute a liminal body of films unlike those genres—the western and the melodrama—whose narratives were clearly gendered according to a class-based status quo inherited through Griffith from nineteenth-century Victorianism. In boy genres, such as the western, women are neither consistently specularized nor are they necessarily the objects of narrative sadism. As often as not, it is the gunfighter himself who is subjected to sadistic treatment (*The Man Who Shot Liberty Valance, One Eyed Jacks, A Man Called Horse, Fistful of Dollars, The Good the Bad and the Ugly,* etc.), while if there are women in the films at all, they are often there just long enough for their frailty to motivate the plot. As regards women's genres, many feminist critics (Mary Ann Doane, Linda Williams) have commented on the insufficiency of Mulvey's model to address the narrative and specular dynamics of the women's melodrama.[4]

The films Mulvey chooses render exceptional cases of women who move through the diegesis, working and attempting to be single mothers (*Blonde Venus*), to rectify class inequities (*Psycho*), to make their way as career grifters (*Marnie*), as spies (*Dishonored*) or, alternatively, women who have the time and money to just cruise around aimlessly (*Vertigo*). My precis of these films exaggerates the economic situations of these women in order to make a point—that these films overtly raise *class* issues that are then mystified by their intensely oedipalized gender narratives. Marnie is the daughter of a prostitute who caters to sailors; her mother routinely wakes her up to send her to the living room when the men in the white uniforms come to the door; unlike her mother, Marnie grows up to prey on very *rich* men, bankers and businessmen, to whom she never grants sexual favors. In *Vertigo,* the distinction between the elegant and elusive Madeleine, who doesn't have to work at all, and cheap, sluttish Judy, a working-class shop girl, turns out to be both real and an "act," a sleight of hand accomplished by proper clothes and posture in the vertiginous dynamics of the film. This false distinction is only enhanced by the girl in the middle—the middle-class professional woman, pragmatic and sexless Midge.[5] *Dishonored* and *Blonde Venus* both feature women who prostitute themselves for a good cause—the nation and maternity, respectively. In *Psycho,* the class angle is presented and simultaneously mystified by its oedipalized framing. In the first office scene, the wealthy Tom Cassidy leers at Marion Crane as he tells her he can ward off unhappiness, flipping in her face the forty thousand dollars that he is going to use to buy his daughter a house for her wedding present.

In each of these films, the plots wed motifs concerning women, money, class, agency and, frequently, *prostitution* to women's literal diegetic movement or transportation. Though seemingly a coincidence, these apparently unrelated concerns are signified very precisely in the word "traffic" whose meanings include prostitution, as in "the traffic in women," and all forms of pedestrian and vehicular transportation. Originally referring to trade—

buying, selling, dealing, communication, and business—an early usage of the word *traffic* (1561) also included trade in sexual favors. Not until the nineteenth century, with many developments in transportation technologies, does "traffic" also come to mean "the passing to and fro of persons, or of vehicles or vessels along a road, railway, canal, or other route of transport."[6] Thus, the term references both bodies as property, as objects of trade, and bodies as subjects capable of autonomous movement, whether self-animated or vehicular or both. The distinction between these two kinds of bodies (objects or subjects of movement) is obviously an *economic* distinction which informs the construction of differences in social identities—racial, class and gender.

In this chapter, I would like to investigate the possible relations between women's gender identity, the types of movement of which they are capable, and the economic aspects of feminine gender construction as represented in popular and independent films. Mulvey's articulation of gender and sexuality *exclusively* in relation to castration ("the female form...speaks castration and *nothing else*"[7]) marks this formulation historically as class limited, in that class (labor, material relations) is what gender and sexual difference cannot speak; it is the "nothing else" besides castration, the structuring absence of modern sex/gender systems.[8] Significantly, Mulvey does not theorize women's movement and the economics of that movement in the films she examines. However, the films themselves crystallize another aspect of female sexuality as it is represented in the movies: that women's literal and social movement is the impetus for the sadism directed at them. That is, that in their plots, women are in traffic and the law is after them, to stop them, to not let them get away.

■ II. From Objects of Exchange to Auto Motivation

Published in 1975, the same year as Mulvey's article, Gayle Rubin's landmark piece, "The Traffic in Women: Notes on the 'Political Economy' of Sex," engages exactly those issues that Mulvey's psychoanalytic approach precludes—sexuality and gender difference in relation to political economy. Rubin's article investigates the nature and genesis of women's oppression and social subordination from a more materialist and historical standpoint. She summarizes the structure and the evolution of this oppression with the term "the traffic in women."

Rubin argues that the source of women's subordination to men lies in those social relations which constitute a society's sex/gender system:

> Every society has a sex/gender system—a set of arrangements by which the biological raw material of human sex and procreation is shaped by human social intervention and satisfied in a conventional manner, no matter how bizarre some of the conventions may be.[9]

The sex/gender system of kinship, based on the incest taboo and the exchange or traffic in women, once organized all other social relations—political, economic, and educational. Now, Rubin observes, sex/gender systems only organize and reproduce themselves, as the development and evolution of the state has generally superceded kinship in organizing political and economic relations.[10] Thus, sex/gender systems now *complement* economic systems, and it is this division that is symptomatic of modern social organization in the West. While economic systems transform raw natural resources into objects of human consumption, sex/gender systems "take up females as raw materials and fashion domesticated women as products."[11] Seizing upon what had been women's preeminent social functions as wives and mothers, Rubin underscores the exploitive character of these roles by conflating women's conventional social location ("the domestic sphere") with their invisible labor (as "domestics") and with an oppressive relation (as "domesticated"). She also stresses the economic implications of women's domestication, noting the instance of housework, but finds Engels's famous investigation of gender, sex and labor provocative, yet ultimately outdated.[12] She uses Freud to help explain why it is that women do housework.

The feature of Rubin's work that helps reinterpret the films I have cited above concerns her point about women's static social location (the home) and the particular circumstances, historically, under which they moved through the socius—in marriage and in other forms of exchange between men. Rubin observes, "The relations of such a system are such that women are in no position to realize the benefits of their own circulation."[13] This perception must be nuanced by several points implied by Rubin's analysis. One, that the category "woman" and the modes of exchange that have distinguished the genders have never been homogeneous across cultures. Second, the traffic in women that structured kinship systems has changed dramatically, and women in the West have a very different relation to social exchange and movement now than they did in kinship societies or in the eighteenth and nineteenth centuries. In historicizing sex/gender systems and insisting they be culturally specific, Rubin provides a frame for historicizing the disparities between her approach and Mulvey's. Our social organization is predicated on the illusory but insistent distinction between economic and political systems (the public sphere) and sex/gender systems (the private sphere), a distinction that was itself frequently reproduced in feminist and other methodologies in the humanities and social sciences in the 1970's and 80's.[14] Tending to emphasize either materialist or symbolic concerns, these methods produced different and seemingly incompatible research objects, "real" women versus representations of women.

I propose then the notion of "women in traffic" as both a literalization and a metaphor for our historical moment when certain women have been and are entering into social relations as agents rather than objects—that is, when they have much more autonomy over their literal and their social and sexual movement. The notion of women in traffic allows for a synthesis of material and symbolic research objects. In order to implement this synthesis methodologically, I would like to compare the history of the cinema to that of the automobile, considering their singular and interrelated effects on gender and sex constructions that presumably have no class.[15] Both are industries that create private space within the public sphere, a very significant feature of their gendered function in relation to certain women. Overall, I am trying to approach gender construction outside its usual containment within identity and subjectivity and instead look at its industrial context, bringing that context back to bear on women in traffic in the cinema.

▪ III. Moving Pictures, Moving Vehicles

As might be expected, the history of the automobile from its speculative pre-history to its Fordist organization bears a striking resemblance to that of the cinema. Roger Bacon in the 13th century and Leonardo da Vinci in the 16th dreamed of self-propelled vehicles.[16] These two thinkers also speculated on the implications and possibilities posed by the *camera obscura*.[17] Like the cinema, prototypes of the automobile were developed throughout the nineteenth century for sport, as curiosities and, particularly in relation to the automobile, as playthings for the wealthy. The technological developments that led to the invention of the automobile, like those contributing to the cinema, came from machines that were analogous in function to the automobile, such as the bicycle and the locomotive, and those that were not, such as the sewing machine and the electric cash register. As with the Kinetograph, Kinetoscope and Cinematographe, various formats vied for dominance of the automobile market once the demand for the product caught on— specifically gasoline, electric and steam engines. The 1890's were crucial years for both the cinema and the automobile, the Lumiere's first public screening of December 1895 occurring during the same period that the automobile industry in Europe engaged in regular commercial production.[18] While inventors in the U.S. and Europe developed cinematic technologies in conjunction with one another, the U.S. was ten years behind the Europeans in the development of the automobile, although America would come to dominate production in both industries after World War I. Beyond the organizational, financial and technological similarities between the cinema and the automobile industries, what I would like to stress here are the imbrications of class and gender interests crucial to the "distinctly American achievement" of both.[19] Historians of both industries note that the success of each in the years between 1905 and 1915 hinged on their respective abilities to appeal to middle- and upper-class women.

While film historians have explained the complex factors leading to mass spectatorship, a vital component of which was the development of plots and venues appropriate to middle-class women, in the automobile industry the gender angle took a slightly different form.[20] The electric versus internal combustion engine became the terms of automotive sexual difference, with the industry carefully marketing electric cars to women, internal combustion engines to men. Electric cars only had limited, local range; they were clean, quiet, and slow and they didn't have to be cranked to start. In the same year Henry Ford developed the Model T, he bought an electric car for his wife Clara; if she wanted to travel longer distances, she relied on her husband or her son Edsel to drive her in a combustion engine.[21] Gasoline-powered combustion engines were powerful, complicated, fast and capable of long-distance runs. They were also dirty, loud, and their crank starter mechanisms were notoriously difficult to operate. As John Rae observes, "The electric starter…was a major factor in promoting widespread use of the gasoline automobile, particularly because it made the operation of gasoline engines more attractive to women."[22]

The development of the electric starter signals the end of the electric car and its gendered appeal, but the specific nature of that appeal indicates the social and economic concerns that were wrapped up in gendered marketing strategies for automobiles. For instance, a December 1910 *Motor* ad stated:

> To the well-bred woman, the Detroit electric has a particular appeal. In it she can preserve her toilet immaculate, her coiffure intact. She can drive it with all desired privacy, yet safely—in constant touch with traffic conditions all about her.[23]

To be well-bred, a woman had to maintain both her appearance and a certain level of privacy, gender values widely purveyed in nineteenth century America by the cult of domesticity. The cult had introduced an ideal of femininity predicated on an array of class-exclusive parameters, among which were a delicate, fragile, *unlabored* appearance; the restriction of social movement to the home and appropriate private environs by rigid moral codes; and a related moral sensibility characterized by excessive modesty and needs for privacy. While working-class women did not have the economic means to adhere to any of these strictures (to stay home, to appear fragile, to maintain strict codes of privacy), they were nevertheless held to the morally sanctioned modes of dress, appearance and social behavior of middle-class women. For example, in 1895, a working-class woman in New York City, who was attempting to find her sister's house after dark, asked two men for directions. She was subsequently arrested and convicted for disorderly conduct, the presumption being that any woman out alone at that hour was a "public woman" or a prostitute. (She was only released after a doctor's examination proved she was a "good" girl.)[24]

The Victorian ideology of separate spheres fostered a generalized, yet tacitly class-based, anxiety about women venturing beyond the private sphere, both metaphorically and literally. Public transportation in the early twentieth century was unreliable, annoying, inconvenient, sometimes dangerous, and utterly lacking in privacy. Virginia Scharff writes of the social outcry and political action at the turn of the century, which focused on the problem of mass transit and the protection of female virtue: "Beneath the welter of political conflicts, there lurked the idea that the very character of mass transit set it on a collision course with bourgeois ladyhood."[25] The automobile saves the day, providing the well-bred American woman initially limited, privatized transportation (such that she could fulfill her increasingly important cultural role as a consumer) while preserving her immaculate toilet and coiffure. The automobile thus protects a feminine appearance standard and code of behavior vested with explicitly moral and tacitly class-based distinctions.

Though many historians of the American automobile point to its function in ameliorating class differences, their analyses are usually related to men.[26] The relationship of women, specifically upper and middle-class women, to public transportation in the early twentieth century casts the automobile and its relation to gender and class concerns in a very different light. While the automobile threatened nineteenth-century America's preeminent gender distinction—that men move and women stay home—the needs of the economy demanded a more mobile feminine consumer. The automobile preserved the class-exclusive character of the specific kind of femininity idealized by a social order that has used gender, from the nineteenth century onwards, to privatize and mystify class inequity. Unlike public transportation, which was rife with threats to a woman's "well-bred appearance" and privacy, the automobile, once the problems with the combustion engine were worked out, allowed middle-class women to be auto/mobile without ever having to rub shoulders or any other body parts with strangers on the subway, the trolley, the bus or the train.

■ IV. The Gaze, the Girls and the Drive: Four Films about Women and Cars[27]

Because of its complicated and cathected functions involving money, class, agency, gender, social geography, and the mercurial demands of late capitalism, it is not surprising that the relationship between women and automobiles is highly charged. Stereotypes of woman as bad drivers versus actuarial statistics that prove that, for all age groups, women are much better drivers than men indicate the ambivalence at stake in women's automotive agency, their ability to move freely through public space. In the cinema, this type of contradiction surfaces in a slightly different way. Though focused primarily on domesticity, the private sphere, and emotions, the cinema contains very few representations of domestic labor. Instead, women's domestic function is frequently secured in narratives by way of contrast with "bad" women in traffic. Some obvious examples include: Ingrid Bergman in *Notorious* (1946) whose reckless drunken driving and impetuous agency at the beginning of the film are contrasted with her helplessness at the end when Cary Grant literally carries her, near death, out of the house where she has been operating as a spy. In *Written on the Wind* (1956), Dorothy Malone as Marylee Hadley drives her own sportscar and picks up men, her "fast" behavior set against the demure domesticity of Lauren Bacall who lets the men drive and gets Rock Hudson for her troubles. Women are frequently threatened, struck down, blinded or blown up by or in automobiles (*Suspicion* 1941, *Magnificent Obsession* 1954, *The Big Heat* 1953, *The Postman Always Rings Twice* 1946, 1981, *The Godfather* 1972, etc.), each of these films' narratives using the car to threaten or destroy romance, domesticity or reproduction.

As these examples and those with which I opened my essay suggest, Mulvey's attempt to anchor gender representation in the gaze is not wrong; it simply exists within a much larger dynamic. Her focus interiorizes gender distinctions, while the films themselves locate this type of interiority within narratives that both literalize women's "movement" and attempt to contain it. As the century has progressed and the demands of the economy have resulted in many more middle-class women working, gender representations, as would be expected, have become increasingly insecure. Given the role of traffic and automobiles in negotiating an apparently immaterial feminine gender identity and the economic needs of late capitalism, it would seem that many "insecure" representations of femininity in the cinema would rely heavily on the motif of women in traffic, on their autonomous movement, a motif that would exist in some tension with the (class-based) appearance standard that generally subtends representations of women. An array of recent films present "brave new girls" precisely in narratives where concerns with appearances and the gaze coincide with and are sometimes overridden by women, automobiles and agency. From many possibilities that range from *Tank Girl* to *Basic Instinct,* I will discuss four films from very different genres—Sci Fi, Action and Independent—each of which foregrounds, both formally and narratively, the relationship between the gaze and the drive as it relates either to apparently liberatory representations of women or more self-reflexive considerations of this relationship. The films are: *The Terminator* (1984), *Thelma and Louise* (1991), *Set It Off* (1996) and *Safe* (1995).

James Cameron's *The Terminator* was a breakthrough film in several ways. It made Arnold Schwarzenegger a star. With Ridley Scott's 1979 *Alien* and 1982 *Blade Runner,* it completed the rebirth of science fiction film inaugurated by *Star Wars* (1977). Unlike their blockbuster predecessors, however, the two later films (*Blade Runner* and *The Terminator*) actually *sexualize* their Oedipal narratives. On the other hand, *The Terminator,* like *Alien,* has a female protagonist, one who ultimately triumphs over the monster cyborg that has been programmed to track her down and kill her no matter what the cost.[28] The story is actually her story, despite Schwarzenegger's post-film triumph, a literal and psychic odyssey that converts teenage waitress into futurist warrior mother. She enters the film on a scooter, leaves it in a jeep, having learned to make and throw bombs and drive getaway cars in between. In the elegant time-loop narrative that structures this sci-fi action thriller, Sarah Connor becomes warrior to protect her unborn child and, by inference, the future of the human race.

The film emphatically separates domesticity and maternity, but in its closing scene, it reasserts the importance of the woman's image, even as this particular woman, visibly pregnant, heads for safety in Mexico, her rifle and her German shepherd by her side. At a gas station just the other side of the border, a young boy, proclaiming her beauty, takes a Polaroid snapshot of Sarah and then sells it to her. Within this film all about a naive young woman becoming a superhero, it is finally this still, this image, upon which the whole narrative depends. Kyle Reese, unknowing father, receives the image from his unborn son, John Connor; he travels through time because of this photo, his desire insinuated in the two types of reproduction it represents—photographic and biological. The time-loop narrative inverts the logical relationship between the two, the reproductive bodies retrospectively following the path of the image. Our entry point into this temporally regressive narrative is marked specifically by the reproductive value of Sarah Connor's body and the danger her autonomous and unprotected agency poses to her and, by inference, to the whole human race. Kyle subdues her and her independence, convincing her, with ample support from the Terminator, that she needs him. It is not until after her body has been inseminated that she begins to fight and take charge. (This same equation between maternity and physical prowess structures the *Alien* trilogy with increasing insistence and, of course, informs Sarah's characterization in *T-2*).[29]

Finally, it is the photo, and not Sarah's agency and mobility, that seals the ideological relationship between present and future, one in which an apocalyptic vision of mass destruction is ultimately contained and subsumed within the brief but intense romance between Kyle and Sarah. As Sarah drives off, the film leaves us not with the future she or the rest of humankind faces, but rather with the tragic loop of love, desire, and loss figured in the photograph's inception, that moment when the narrative both begins and ends—in the still, frozen image of a woman. The dynamism of the film and the kinetic prowess of Sarah Connor who, despite a severe wound in her thigh, destroys the Terminator with the words "You're terminated, fucker" suggest that we are in a whole new realm of gender construction. In that context, the still, which formally and narratively equates Sarah and the film's reproductive bodies, also acts to contain Sarah, to return her to a more conventional femininity, her strength, her autonomous movement through the diegesis, and her motivation finally subject to reproductive logics, both her own and that of the image.

Though of a very different genre, Ridley Scott's *Thelma and Louise* seems to develop a similar relationship between its protagonists' narrative movement and the images of them produced within and finally as the diegesis. Several critics of the film have pointed out that the narrative of these two women in traffic unfolds between two stills, the first the Polaroid that Louise takes when she and Thelma set out on their vacation and the second the freeze frame that ends the film, women and automobility suspended between the law behind them and a very hard place beyond.[30] The first photo documents the women's frivolity in "setting off," their faces made-up, femmed-up, to-be-looked-at in very conventional terms. But their idyll in Louise's Thunderbird convertible, the terms of their getaway are utterly transformed when Louise kills a man who attempts to rape Thelma. Further down the road, a good-time boy pleasures Thelma and then steals Louise's stash, compelling Thelma to take up armed robbery as the solution to their economic woes.

In order to continue to move, to not go back to their stultifying lives, Thelma and Louise have to have money. Feminist critics of the film have indicated the explicit connection it makes between movement, money and the conventional containments of gender, especially conventions of appearance. As the story progresses, as their flight becomes more and more determined, Thelma and Louise shed lipstick and other accoutrements of their femininity. And rather than sentimentalizing their actions with a maternal or romantic angle, the film points instead to male aggression, economic limitations and the constraints of their feminine roles (wife and waitress) as their motivation to keep on going.[31] The police chase the two to the Grand Canyon, where faced with going back or going forward together, the two drive off the cliff. The diegesis freezes, the Thunderbird in flight.

Unlike the grim tourist photo that ends *The Terminator* or the more cheery one that begins the travels of *Thelma and Louise,* the freeze frame at the end of this film denotes a very different kind of travel. The narrative reaches a limit where it has nowhere else to go—as far as feminine gender construction goes, it has expended all its options. In relinquishing the usual affective and narrative tropes that define and confine femininity, either at rest (spectacle) or in motion (romance and maternity), the film seems to push the association between women and cars beyond conventional subjective anchors by refusing to name or resolve the social contradictions it invokes, as exemplified by the freeze frame. Yet the moment before the car lifts off, we get a shot of the Polaroid that documents the journey's beginning as it blows out of the back seat. Immediately after the freeze frame, the film begins running again, recycling an array of glamorous clips of Thelma and Louise before take-off. In a move formally identical to that of *The Terminator,* the photo in the back seat seals this film's time-loop, one articulated solely around images, both still and moving, of Thelma and Louise. In its last moments, the film refers its lack of resolution back to its own reproductive capacities—the images are preserved, they can be *re*-run. Thelma and Louise, seemingly gender outlaws par excellence, become myth, returning once again to be looked at.

In both *The Terminator* and, to a much greater degree, *Thelma and Louise,* narrative and iconographic tensions between feminine appearance and automobility organize issues concerning class and gender such that class difference *disappears* within that of gender. Sarah Connor, like Louise Sawyer, is a waitress in a cheap restaurant chain. The narrative transforms her from a waitress to the mother and savior of the future human race. In the latter film, the two protagonists are working class: Louise waits tables in a diner, while Thelma keeps house in a dismal tract home for her car salesman husband. Their lack of mobility and the stultifying quality of their lives have as much to do with money as with men. However, by shifting the emphasis to men, the film keeps gender problems "in the family," in the private sphere, and out of the arena of money, class and opportunity.

The material constraints and claustrophobic spaces that limit Thelma and Louise's lives melt away as they take to the road, their working-class accents and preferences dispersed into a country-western regionalism. Thus, the film partakes of a myth that is archetypally American, archetypally male, archetypally white: that in the wide-open spaces of the territories, the west, the frontier, a man can escape any social barrier or constraint—domesticity, family, class limitations, a criminal or dubious past, any social markings (except race or gender), any dead end. The automobile, made for this myth, modernizes the fantasy of lightin' out for the territories.[32] Adjusting the road movie to accommodate female protagonists, Ridley Scott uses a convertible to feminize the story, pitting spectacle against mobility. As the women's journey progresses, Scott makes ample use of Davis and Sarandon's beauty, their hair, their cheekbones, their bodies, sculpting their faces in the rust-red hues and shadows of the panoramic landscapes that provide the locations for the second half of the film. Yet he consistently does so with the car, either stopped or in motion, using it to frame the women with the windshield, to capture their hair blowing in the wind, to provide a prop for their bodies in an array of compelling poses.[33] Their automobility is ultimately subordinated to their appearance.

While *The Terminator* and *Thelma and Louise* make welcome and important changes in gender representation, the more dramatic and threatening implications of female agency— those that have to do with literal and economic autonomy and with the role of traditional femininity in mystifying class in America—are posed and defused in the films' symptomatic play between mobility and spectacle. F. Gary Gray's *Set It Off* tells the story that these earlier films cannot tell, realigning femininity, romance, maternity and spectacle in relation to money, mobility and opportunity. The film both solicits and alters the generic elements of the road/outlaw movie, as well as the gangster film, the female friendship film and the 'hood flick, by explicitly or implicitly referencing *Thelma and Louise, Bonnie and Clyde* (1967), *The Godfather, Body Heat* (1981), *Point Break* (1991), and *Boyz in the Hood* (1991). Alluding to these films in its dialogue, gesture, mise-en-scene and/or dramatic situation, *Set It Off* adjusts and corrects the genres they represent, most notably for race and gender, but most insistently for class. Described alternately by critics as a "Girlz in the Hood" or a "black Thelma and Louise," *Set It Off* tells the story of four African American women who, out of anger, desperation or inspired frustration, decide to rob banks. The four protagonists—Cleo (Queen Latifah), Stony (Jada Pinkett), Frankie (Vivica A. Fox) and Tisean (Kimberly Elise)—"go way back together" and each of them, save Cleo, has strong motivations for striking back at the system: Stony's brother Stevie, whom she has protected and fostered since their parents died in a car accident, is killed by the police who mistake him for someone else; the managers of the bank Frankie works for fire her after a violent robbery solely because she happens to know one of the gunmen from the projects; protective services takes Tisean's child from her after he has an accident at her workplace where she has taken him because she can't afford childcare.

Cleo's motivations are less melodramatic and more unequivocally self-motivated and economic—she wants money and a cool lowrider. She works in a dead-end janitorial job, has an abusive and incompetent boss to whom she is clearly superior, and keeps her girlfriend on a pager. Unlike the characters in almost any female friendship or lesbian film, *Set It Off*'s Latifah plays Cleo, with relish and without apology, as a very convincing and compelling butch, the most rare sexual creature in contemporary American cinema.[34] Latifah is also the "real" outlaw (and the real hero), the one who does it for fun.

Set It Off's director Gray and writers Kate Lanier and Takashi Bufford do not transform class issues into gender issues because they refuse to implement the conventions by which this transformation is accomplished. *Set It Off* does not use the iconography of wide-open spaces or female spectacle, nor does it employ a romance narrative to resolve the thorny issues of women, race, money and opportunity that the film raises. This outlaw road movie, set in Los Angeles, never leaves the city. The heroines, save one, never get out of town. In fact, they have never been out of town. The claustrophobic, rundown urban iconography of the 'hood—the projects, the industrial skyline, small cramped apartments—contrasts sharply with the luxury and expansiveness of the heroines' workplaces where they clerk and clean: a very upscale bank, plush corporate headquarters, an enormous private home. Gray focuses on the labor they do, setting scenes in workplaces, garages, and the streets as opposed to the women's homes. In fact, the only home we see, and then only briefly, is Stony's.[35]

Similarly, the heroines' mobility is not unfettered. Only Cleo owns a car. The women steal cars to use in their bank heists. At their first bank job, Tisean is separated from the other three and takes a bus back to the projects. After their last job has gone horribly awry, Cleo's car breaks down as they are trying to make their getaway. Stony finally gets out of town on a tour bus. These instances of constrained automobility exist in tension with the film's representation of the women's femininity, sexuality, and relationships, all of which are subsumed by their economic situations. It is noteworthy that the only one of the four women with a successful romance is Cleo. The other women are each personally cathected to "troubled" black masculinity—Stony's dead brother, Frankie's 'hood friend turned bank robber, Tisean's vulnerable child—while professionally they have verbally and sexually abusive employers or potential employers (Luther and Nate). The film suggests that the only relationships working-class black women can have with black men are political and economic. Conventional romance, predicated on leisured, protected, delicate femininity, depends upon economic privilege. The film emphatically makes these points in a subplot which involves a bank manager's romantic pursuit of Stony.

As Stony cases the first bank the women intend to rob, the bank's handsome new manager Keith Weston (Blair Underwood) approaches her, wanting her phone number. She plays along, gets his number, and has a brief but intense romance with him, marked by her understanding and insistence that the relationship between them will never work because of the difference in their class backgrounds. On their first date, Stony arranges to meet Keith at his condo. As he shows her into the spacious, elegant and richly appointed loft, saying "It's not much but it's home," we wince with her at his utterly distorted frame of reference and the dramatic contrast between his space and those in which she lives and moves. Stony and the film refuse to endorse Keith's liberal humanist racial solidarity. Whereas he would like to believe that his upper-class, Harvard-educated background is completely compatible with hers, she acerbically mocks his illusions, indicating that that humanist perspective is itself always privileged—only people who have money can pretend it really doesn't make a difference.

The film skillfully uses this subplot to extend its engagement with economic constraints beyond a racialized dichotomy, ultimately providing an astute critique of the fairy tale of romance, class rise and femininity as it is usually construed. Keith takes Stony to a formal bank party, directing their limo driver to a fancy boutique in order to buy her a beautiful dress since her own party clothes would never fit in. She has an idyllic evening with him; she loves him, but she does not buy the Cinderella story that he obviously believes in and which informs classical narrative. The *Chicago Tribune* film review makes this point even more cogently, if unwittingly: "When Stony begins dating a suave bank executive...who buys her pricey dinners and clothing, you hope she'll ask whether he has three friends so the women can lay off the gunplay."[36] Beyond the fact that the reviewer apparently misses Cleo's sexuality, the notion that romance can solve any woman's economic woes is precisely the myth that this film so brilliantly exposes. Indeed, reviewers of the film consistently missed its economic themes, some even protesting that the dramatic difference in mise-en-scene between Stony's world and Keith's was a flaw in the production design, unrealistic and jarring.[37]

What really jars in this dramatic difference, though, is what the film lacks—representations of the women as spectacle that would take away all the other jarring differences that have to do with class. While all four women are stunning, across butch/femme registers, their beauty never becomes the iconographic or narrative axes whereby their auto/mobility is reassuringly transformed into feminine spectacle. Photographic images of the women do figure in the plot of the film, just as they do in *The Terminator* and *Thelma and Louise*. But significantly, in *Set It Off*, the images are not personal snapshots nor do they ever achieve meta-narrative status, two connected features of the earlier films that utilize feminine spectacle and nostalgia to override the political elements of their plots. Rather, in *Set It Off*, the images are mug shots, surveillance photos, that Detective Strode uses to prove that the four women know each other, that they are collaborators in crime. In addition, the film's ending makes its avoidance of feminine spectacle particularly apparent. Cleo's death functions as spectacle—a masculine one where, grossly outnumbered and outgunned, she is momentarily unstoppable, larger than her inevitable mortality.[38]

Her death contrasts sharply with Stony's humble escape on a bus, her mobility utterly functional and unspectacular.

In its closing moments, the film finds Stony in a cheap motel room, cutting off her dreds, packing her money in a backpack and remembering her friends. Unlike the film clips at the end of *Thelma and Louise,* the scenes of the four women that are re-run here are clearly anchored to Stony's subjectivity and to her bonds with her friends. Signifying memory rather than spectacle, they do not serve to reproduce the four protagonists' spectacular and enticing images.

Following in the tradition of *Body Heat,* Stony ends up in a tropical milieu, pulling off the road momentarily to make a phone call to Keith. She doesn't speak, but he knows it's her. He tells her he's glad she's safe. She says "thank-you," hangs up and takes off in her red jeep down a mountainous road, the surf below. Unlike the ending of *Body Heat,* where the femme fatale sips a pina colada, waited on by the polite and crisply uniformed locals, Stony ends up with a rustic independence, her tropical paradise consisting of dusty roads and thatched shelters. *Set It Off*'s final fantasy does not have to do with luxury and conspicuous consumption, with indulged and pampered femininity, but with freedom and autonomy. The film completely undercuts a formulaic, if foundational, representation of white, middle-class femininity, knowing all the while that what even begins to make this possible is a racialized class representation that cannot be reduced to or subsumed by gender.

■ Coda

And what of good girls whose automobility never exceeds the constraints of appropriate middle-class femininity? I would like to end with an entirely different rendering of women and cars, one which addresses this question within the more claustral, interiorized gender dynamics of melodrama. Todd Haynes's *Safe* works in a much more self-reflexive and knowing way than either *Thelma and Louise* or *The Terminator* and approaches women and automobility from a different generic perspective than *Set It Off.* While the characters in *The Terminator* and *Thelma and Louise* finally function allegorically as universalized gender types, Haynes uses his protagonist, the very aptly named Carol White, to represent a very particularized race and class of women. Thus, *Safe* is similar to *Set It Off* in that the cultural, social and economic specificity of their main characters limits their audience appeal. Mainstream cinema's need for mass identification has led to an insistent and pervasive use of gender to universalize characters, to maximize their potential for mass appeal. What the very different women in *Set It Off* and *Safe* indicate quite clearly is that class and race produce significantly different variants of "femininity," differences mainstream culture works very, very hard to efface. Haynes's film takes on a woman, an upper middle-class white housewife, who might be a suitable subject for melodrama, were her socioeconomic contours not so painstakingly drawn.

Carol White lives in the Valley; she always speaks softly and wears pastels. She is a very nice person. Her house, her friends, her children and her lifestyle are relentlessly insipid. One day, after a lunch date, a workout and a trip to the dry cleaners, Carol has a breakdown in traffic. As she is running errands, her own automobility proves too much for her. Carol White becomes overwhelmed by the public exposure that even her very hermetically sealed and protected lifestyle demands. Staring at the exhaust fumes pouring out of the truck in front of her, she starts to cough. She rolls up the windows of her luxury automobile, turns on the air conditioner, her panic rising, her coughing growing ever more hysterical. Frantically driving into a parking garage, her screeching tires an apt objective correlative for her panic, Carol stops the car, collapsing out of it, panting and gasping for breath.

Carol's breakdown takes the form of a radical sensitivity to the environment, specifically to commercial, urban spaces, which she goes to more and more extreme measures to control. She completely withdraws from her social world; she sees doctors and therapists who cannot help her. Ultimately, she ends up at a retreat in the desert, living in an antiseptic igloo and going through recovery. Having very carefully plotted its course through the lifestyle and concerns of a leisured, privileged L.A. housewife, the film ends by savagely documenting the symbolic outcome of an affluent white femininity whose only standards are appearances. In the film's final moments, Carol sits in her igloo, inhaling deeply from an oxygen tank. She gets up, approaching a mirror on the wall. In the reverse shot that ends the film, Carol White looks into the mirror/camera, faces her own image and says, "I love you. I really love you." That outcome? A wounded and anemic narcissism whose self-focused interiority ultimately arrests all movement.

* An earlier version of this article was published by Duke University Press as "Women in Traffic: LA Autobiography" in *The South Atlantic Quarterly*, 97, 2. Duke University Press permitted the reprint of this article.

Notes

I would like to thank Lisa Duggan, David James, Katherine Kinney and Chon Noriega for their insights and thoughtful feedback, all of which greatly enhanced this chapter.

1. Elsbeth Probyn, *Sexing the Self: Gendered Positions in Cultural Studies,* (London and New York: Routledge, 1993), 57.

2. I take inspiration from Gregory Ulmer's method of mystory, laid out in chapter 3 of *Teletheory: Grammatology in the Age of Video* (New York and London: Routledge, 1989), 82–112, and from teaching autobiography, where I have students convert aspects of their own identities into abstracted research tropes. Thus identity is directed not to programmatic or fixed ideological positions or problems but rather to the more properly epistemological—that which is not yet known, without, however, the latter being bereft of political grounding. Such research tropes—like women in traffic— frequently necessitate interdisciplinary work, disciplines being another way of fixing knowledge programmatically within identity.

3. Quoted in Michael Rogin, "'The Sword Became a Flashing Vision': D.W. Griffith's *The Birth of a Nation,*" *Representations* 9, Winter 1985, 185.

4. Mary Ann Doane, *The Desire to Desire* (Bloomington: Indiana University Press, 1987) and Linda Williams "Something Else Besides a Mother" in *Issues in Feminist Film Criticism,* edited by Patricia Erens (Bloomington: Indiana University Press, 1990), 137–162.

5. Virginia Wright Wexman discusses *Vertigo* in relation to class and race in "The Critic as Consumer: Film Study in the University, *Vertigo,* and the Film Canon," in *Film Quarterly* 39:3, Spring 1996, 32–41.

6. Virginia Scharff, *Taking the Wheel: Women and the Coming of the Motor Age* (New York: Macmillan, 1991), 3–4.

7. Laura Mulvey, "Visual Pleasure and Narrative Cinema," *Screen* 16 # 3 (1975), 8.

8. Such an assertion is warranted historically. In Europe and the U.S., emphatic gender distinctions permeate all economic strata at the same time that class differences become mystified by the public/private split, though in the U.S. this mystification was fundamental to this country's (ostensible) resistance to aristocratic privilege and, as such, has been much more pervasive. See Nancy Armstrong's *Desire and Domestic Fiction,* especially the introduction (New York and Oxford: Oxford University Press, 1987), 3–27, and Kathleen McHugh's *American Domesticity: From How-To Manual to Hollywood Melodrama* (New York and Oxford, Oxford University Press, 1999).

9. Gayle Rubin, "The Traffic in Women: Notes on the 'Political Economy' of Sex," *Toward an Anthropology of Women,* edited by Rayna Reiter [Rapp], (New York: Monthly Review Press, 1975), 199.

10. Ibid., 165.

11. Ibid., 158.

12. Ibid., 163–64. See Frederick Engels' *The Origin of the Family, Private Property and the State* (New York: International Publishers, 1972), 94–147.

13. Ibid., 174.

14. Economic hierarchy certainly pervades households in the case of maids, nannies and other domestic employees. Yet mainstream cultural narratives continually serve up the image of the domestic as the best friend, confidante, and advisor to the woman of the house or, in negative portrayals, as a sexual or maternal competitor (*The Hand that Rocks the Cradle*). The economic relation is generally not articulated.

15. Kristen Ross's *Fast Cars, Clean Bodies: Decolonization and the Reordering of French Culture* (Cambridge: MIT Press, 1996) discusses the very different history of French culture and the automobile, focusing on the crisis between traditional and modern social organizations precipitated by the automobile and other industrial developments in France after World War II. Ross's book, which stops short of May '68, nevertheless provides a cogent context for this strike which brought a government down. France, like other European countries, differs from the U.S. in that gender construction has never functioned to obfuscate and mystify class relations to the degree it has in the U.S.

16. John B. Rae, *The American Automobile* (Chicago: University of Chicago Press, 1965), 1.

17. Jonathan Crary, "Modernizing Vision," *Viewing Positions: Ways of Seeing Film,* edited by. Linda Williams (New Brunswick: Rutgers University Press, 1995), 24.

18. Rae, *The American Automobile,* 8.

19. Ibid., 1.

20. Lary May, *Screening Out the Past* (Chicago: University of Chicago Press, 1980), 43–96, and, for more nuanced accounts of how this process related to morality, class and spectatorship, see Tom Gunning, *D.W. Griffith and the Origins of American Narrative Film* (Urbana: University of Illinois Press, 1991), 85–187, and Miriam Hansen, *Babel and Babylon: Spectatorship in American Silent Film* (Cambridge, MA: Harvard University Press, 1991), 23–89.

21. Virginia Scharff, "Gender, Electricity, and Automobility," *The Car and the City,* edited by Martin Wachs and Margaret Crawford (Ann Arbor: University of Michigan Press, 1991), 77.

22. The electric starting device was invented by Henry M. Leland and Charles F. Kettering; Leland was prompted to devote his efforts to this invention because a friend of his, Byron Carter, broke his jaw, contracted gangrene and died as a result of a cranking accident. He had gone to assist a lady and the cranking mechanism of her car kicked back, causing the fatal injury. Rae, *The American Automobile,* 47–48.

23. Quoted in Scharff, "Gender, Electricity and Automobility," 77.

24. Glenna Matthews, *The Rise of Public Woman* (New York and Oxford: Oxford University Press, 1992), 3.

25. Scharff, *Taking the Wheel*, 6–7.

26. See David Gartman's *Auto Opium: A Social History of American Automobile Design* (New York and London: Routledge, 1994), xiii-xvi, and John B. Rae, *The American Automobile*, 1–15.

27. Among the many puns that shape or haunt this article, the "drive" is one of the more substantial, necessitating another approach. An altogether different draft of this chapter investigates the questions of gender, trauma, fatality, the gaze and automobility in relation to the drive. For an excellent collection of essays on the pun, its implications and applications, see *On Puns,* edited by Jonathan Culler (New York: Basil Blackwell, 1988).

28. Vivian Sobchack's "Child/Alien/Father: Patriarchal Crisis and Generic Exchange," *Close Encounters: Film, Feminism and Science Fiction,* edited by Constance Penley, Elizabeth Lyon, Lynn Spigel and Janet Bergstrom (Minneapolis: University of Minnesota Press, 1991), 3–30 and "The Virginity of Astronauts: Sex and the Science Fiction Film," *Alien Zone: Cultural Theory and Contemporary Science Fiction Cinema,* edited by Annette Kuhn (London & New York: Verso, 1990), 101–114, discuss, respectively, the regressive, patriarchal and problematic qualities of films like *The Terminator* and the threat that women pose in the science fiction film, a threat 'acted out' in a film like *Alien.*

29. See Constance Penley's comments on the use of maternal affect in *The Terminator* and *Alien(s)* in "Time Travel, Primal Scene and the Critical Dystopia," *The Future of an Illusion: Film, Feminism and Psychoanalysis* (Minneapolis: University of Minnesota Press, 1989), 130–133.

30. Jack Boozer, "Seduction and Betrayal in the Heartland: Thelma and Louise," *Film Literature Quarterly* vol 23 # 3, 1995, 192 and Sharon Willis, "Hardware and Hardbodies, What Do Women Want?: A Reading of *Thelma and Louise,*" in *Film Theory Goes to the Movies* (New York: Routledge, 1992), 124.

31. Cathy Griggers's "*Thelma and Louise* and the Cultural Generation of the New Butch-Femme" in *Film Theory Goes to the Movies,* 129–141, contains an inspired account of the relationship the film develops between sexual preference and material and social conditions.

32. The phrase and many of these ideas in relation to American literature come from chapter 12 in Leslie Fiedler's *Love and Death in the American Novel* (New York: Stein and Day, 1975).

33. He inverts the conceit of the car show, where women's bodies highlight the automobile bodies on which they are draped and posed.

34. More rare now than in the classical cinema, observes Judith Halberstam in her comprehensive and insightful "Looking Butch: A Rough Guide to Butches on Film" in *Female Masculinities* (Durham: Duke University Press), 304–306. See also her discussion of Cleo as butch, 313–314.

35. Cleo lives in a garage—her car is her life. But she cannot imagine living anywhere but the 'hood. To Stony's repeated injunctions that they leave town, Cleo says "Can you imagine me in Thousand Oaks or Hollywood?" For her, getting out of town never involves leaving L.A.

36. Mark Caro, "Alarming Failure," *Chicago Tribune,* Tempo Section 5, 6 November, 1996, 1 & 7.

37. Vicky Allan, "*Set It Off,*" *Sight and Sound* #3, March 1997, 62.

38. Frankie's death is ultimately imbricated in Stony's escape because she prompts Detective Strode's guilt. Kneeling over Frankie's body, he sees Stony in the window of a bus and lets her go.

26

■ "Waas Sappening?"

Narrative Structure and Iconography in *Born in East L.A.*[1]

Chon A. Noriega

"The best way to make a statement is you slip it in the coffee so they don't taste it, but, they get the effect."

Richard "Cheech" Marin[2]

Coffee? When, on August 21, 1987, Universal Studios released Cheech Marin's directorial debut, *Born in East L.A.,* it seemed as if the studio did not know what to do with the film. After all, it was unlike the sex, drugs and rock-n-roll, and more drugs, of the Cheech and Chong "occasions-on-film" that had earned almost $300 million since *Up in Smoke* (1978). Even so, Marin's past reputation conflicted with the "just say no" ethos of the Reagan era.[3] To make matters worse, Universal changed studio heads mid-film, which all but guaranteed a lackluster promotion, since the film's success would accrue to the old, and not the new person in charge. And so, *Born in East L.A.* was dumped on the national market without the usual advance press screenings.

Caught off guard, the local press nonetheless responded favorably to the film, particularly in the Southwest, where the *Los Angeles Times* critic even concluded: "It has more drive and energy than *La Bamba.*"[4] Coming one month after the box office success of Luis Valdez's *La Bamba,* statements such as these fueled speculation about the emergence of a "Hispanic Hollywood."[5] But in the national press, *Born in East L.A.* hit a brick wall, receiving only two reviews. *People Weekly* dismissed the film as "a string of uneven skits," while *Cineaste* prefaced its interview with Marin with the high-minded assessment that the film was "well-intentioned," "progressive," but little more than "loosely strung together shticks and vignettes," and, in the final analysis, "politically naive."[6] These very different publications—one popular and conservative, the other elite and "left-of-center"—nonetheless shared a common assumption: namely, that the film lacked a coherent narrative when judged against the correct aesthetics and politics.

Still, *Born in East L.A.* was the second highest grossing film in its first week and would be the number one film in the Southwest for nearly four weeks.[7] But aside from the "surprise" box office revenue, the film's social impact was not spoken about outside the Chicano and Spanish-language press. When the film premiered in East L.A., the *barrio* newspaper *La Opinión* described the event as the reclamation of a ceremonial ritual and a collective reunion.[8] *La Opinión, Unidad,* and *Americas 2001* also praised the film as an alternative and risky look at a "highly controversial issue" then dominating the news: the expiration on September 1, 1987, of the "grace period" for undocumented workers to apply for "amnesty" under the new immigration law.[9] Indeed, the film represents a calculated use of humor to respond to the Simpson-Rodino Immigration Reform Act and California's successful English-Only Initiative (both 1986). But if the Hollywood film's political significance did not register outside of the Hispanic press in the United States, it did become a turning point for reconsidering oppositional cinema in Latin America.

In December 1987, *Born in East L.A.* won four major awards at the Ninth International Festival of New Latin American Cinema in Havana, Cuba, including, ironically enough, the Glauber Rocha award, given by Prensa Latina, an international press organization based in Havana.[10] The irony is two-fold insofar as New Latin American Cinema represented a counter-cinema vis-a-vis both Hollywood and the national industries in Latin America that followed in its footsteps. Furthermore, New Latin American Cinema did not just speak *to* an underlying issue of underdevelopment, it transformed underdevelopment into an aesthetic logic aimed at *concientización* and cultural decolonization. In this manner, Glauber Rocha, an early filmmaker and theorist of Cinema Novo in Brazil, spoke of an "aesthetics of hunger" and an "aesthetics of violence" as revolutionary responses to colonial oppression: "The moment of violence is the moment when the coloniser becomes aware of the existence of the colonised."[11] In the 1960s and 1970s, such an aesthetics stood outside commercial industrial production, outside humanist, rationalist discourse, and outside a strictly nationalist politics.

But, by the time the festival was established in 1979, New Latin American Cinema had entered into a crisis, brought on by military coups and repression, crippling international debt, and the limits of social transformation in the face of the mass media. The festival represented an attempt on the part of Cuba to provide an institutional mooring and industrial model for New Latin American Cinema that—in some ways—brought the movement into alignment with the national industries. From the start, Chicanos were part of this vision, with Chicano cinema understood as a "national" category, allowing a paradoxical situation when Chicano filmmakers were able to work within *their* national industry, Hollywood. Thus, the awards received by *Born in East L.A.* were at once a sign of a strategic shift within New Latin American Cinema toward more popular and commercial forms, and of the continuing presence of "Chicano cinema" within Latin American film festivals since the 1970s. What the awards suggested, then, was that the political ideals and goals of New Latin American Cinema could now be expressed through Hollywood, with the troubling implication that perhaps the opposite could also be true.[12]

Since its release and appearance at the festival, *Born in East L.A.* has generated considerable interest among Chicano scholars, who have elucidated Cheech Marin's role as the *pelado* and "Chicano Moses" of American popular film.[13] Why, then, has *Born in East L.A.* been all but forgotten in the U.S. mainstream—in fact, Marin and Valdez have been unable to direct other feature films in the intervening two decades—while it has such resonance within the Chicano community (and the New Latin American Cinema Festival)? Can this resonance itself be explained as a cultural sensibility that allows Chicano audiences to fill in the narrative gaps; that is, to make exceptions for the film in the absence of other Chicano-themed or -produced feature films? Or, does the film have a coherent structure, after all? While the emphasis so far has been on narrative structure or coherence, the iconography of the Chicano Movement (especially in murals and graphic arts) has had a significant impact on Chicano film and video and provides an important key with which to answer these questions. *Born in East L.A.,* for example, lampoons the Immigration Reform Act and English-Only Movement but does so by situating its critique through bicultural iconography within the *mise-en-scène.* Thus, while the industry genre classification—comedy, musical—provides some sense of the episodic structure, it is iconography and *mise-en-scène* that provide an overall logic with which to assign meaning to the narrative.

In *Born in East L.A.,* Rudy Robles (Cheech Marin) is deported to Mexico, although he is a third-generation Chicano who does not speak Spanish. The film's premise is based on a newspaper account that Cheech Marin read in the *Los Angeles Times,* as he also listened to Bruce Springsteen's "Born in the U.S.A." on the radio.[14] Thus the narrative is first and foremost about the ephemeral status of Chicano citizenship and not, as many non-Latino critics assumed, "wetbacks" and "illegal aliens." But unlike the earlier accommodationist politics among Mexican-Americans in which American citizenship and Mexican immigration were placed in opposition, *Born in East L.A.* conflates Chicano nationalism (which is inherently pro-immigration) with the national ideology of America as a land of immigrants.[15] As a critique of the English-Only Movement, *Born in East L.A.* reveals race and not language to be the underlying factor, especially insofar as official language movements often walk hand-in-hand with immigration politics. As Dennis Baron notes in *The English-Only Question,* "so central is language to political organization that in many societies defining language has become tantamount to defining nationality."[16] But this itself often obscures an implied equivalence between language, nation, and race/ethnicity. As Baron concludes, "Americanism evidenced by the adoption of English is not always enough," since official language legislation "inevitably [expresses] a nativism which rejects certain groups of Americans no matter what language they speak."[17] In some respects, Chicano nationalism made an end-run around such nativism insofar as its pro-immigration stance is based on prior claims to the Southwest that are rooted in pre-historical myths as much as in the Mexican nation. In this manner, Chicanos are equated with the Southwest in a move that places them outside of history in order to proclaim the rights of U.S. citizenship.[18]

In the final analysis, *Born in East L.A.* places these issues about the relationship between race and citizenship within a spatial logic more than a narrative one. In other words, the emphasis is on being somewhere (East L.A.) rather than becoming someone (a good citizen). After Rudy is deported, the film depicts his various attempts to reason, purchase and sneak his way back across the border. Like the deracinated character of another musical fantasy, Rudy pleads on several occasions, "I just want to go home now, okay?" I refer, of course, to Dorothy in *The Wizard of Oz* (1939). But the allusion is not entirely facetious, since it foregrounds the role of "home" within the otherwise picaresque adventures, and——in the end——reveals these two spaces (home and exile) to be one and the same. As a picaresque hero, Rudy experiences a number of unrelated adventures without an essential transformation of character. Instead, through his romance with Dolores, a would-be border crosser from El Salvador, Rudy—like Dorothy—makes a series of simple realizations that empower him to cross the border through sheer will power or desire. In between deportation and return, Rudy comes to realize that (1) American society views him as more Mexican than American, (2) Mexicans see him as American or *pocho,* and (3) his attitudes toward women and immigrants have been callous. The latter act of lateral identification follows upon the first two realizations and leads to Rudy's return. What organizes these picaresque scenes——or, "loosely strung together shticks and vignettes"—is an overarching satire on the paradox that Rudy must struggle to return to a position that remains a birthright. In this sense, he is like Dorothy in that he never left "home," since he never stopped being an American. But it is a birthright that is both entrenched (acculturation) and tenuous (citizenship), adding a racial dimension to Springsteen's working class lament on citizenship in a post-industrial economy.[19] In effect, the picaresque or "loose" nature of the narrative mirrors the protagonist's own ambiguous status as citizen, while the iconography and *mise-en-scène* continually frame these scenes within a bi-national logic that works against stereotypical expectations. Insofar as the lost "home" is also a literal domicile shared with his mother, sister, and her children, Rudy's status and birthright as the "man" within the family are also called into question. His deportation, then, signals a crisis of citizenship and patriarchy within the *barrio.*

Because *Born in East L.A.* questions space or location, it places more attention on constructing "borders" that will frame events than it does on character and plot development. In the remainder of the chapter, I will focus on the opening and closing scenes of the film as well as a comedic framing device that separates these from the narrative proper. These brief scenes use a highly charged *mise-en-scène* in order to provide an interpretive structure with which to read the "body" of the film. In the end, the "loosely strung together shticks and vignettes" are neither incoherent nor "politically naive" but rather over-determined by the paradoxes and contradictions of Chicano birthright.

In its establishing shot, *Born in East L.A.* challenges Hollywood conventions of the *barrio,* initiating a shift from public to private space as the source for Chicano representation in Hollywood films. The film begins with a shot of the Los Angeles skyline, pans to the left to East L.A., tilts down and—through a series of dissolves—comes to rest on a house beside a church. Thus the home, with its fence, well-kept yard and a tree, becomes the defining unit for the *barrio,* rather than—as in *Colors* (1988) et al.—a montage of graf-fiti, gangs, drug deals and so on that signify "problem space." In essence, East L.A. is identified as an appropriate site for the American Dream. Similar shot sequences are used to locate the *barrio* within Los Angeles in social problem films since the 1950s, but these work against either metonymic or metaphoric associations between East Los Angeles and Los Angeles (and America).[20] Instead, these films impose mimicry as a model for Chicanos, who are not seen as a part of or equivalent to American but rather as "like but not quite" American.[21] As I have argued elsewhere, this supports an argument for ideo-logical assimilation coupled with *barrio* segregation, both of which are depicted as choices made by the male protagonists.[22]

In its next shot, however, *Born in East L.A.* moves beyond a mere alternative to the usual external depictions of the *barrio,* when it zooms in and cuts to the interior of the home. Inside, we see a household that cuts across several "borders" in terms of language usage, generation, popular culture, and cultural identity *vis-à-vis* Mexico and the United States.[23] These "borders" are represented as a gentle conflict between Rudy and his mother, initially over her baroque interior decor, then over his duties to extended family members. The two argue as Rudy eats breakfast in the dining room. Rudy's mother wants him to pick up his cousin Javier, an undocumented worker who has recently arrived in the United States, since she and Rudy's sister are going to Fresno for the week. Rudy refuses, reveal-ing that he doesn't speak Spanish and making several snide remarks about Mexican immigrants, but eventually he relents. Throughout the scene, the full shots of Rudy and his mother register details of the interior decor: devotional items, family photographs, kitsch lamps and other objects, a home altar. Once Rudy relents, the camera frames him at the table in a medium close up in which the background consists of a home altar atop a bookcase filled with an encyclopedia set. Here in one concise image we see their argu-ment both expressed and resolved within the *mise-en-scène:* Below, the encyclopedias represent the immigrant's rite of purchase into the objective knowledge of American society; while above, the altar with lit *velas* (candles) is an active and personal engagement of spiritual belief. In this scene, the *mise-en-scène* establishes a hierarchical conflict between mother and son that works on a number of levels: gender, generation, class, and culture of origin. But it also suggests a resolution that favors the mother's side of the equation.

This is literally acted out in their initial struggle over cultural expression within the home when Robles gets into an argument with his mother over her placement of a len-ticular print of Jesus Christ in front of the telephone niche. It is this humorous, playful struggle between the mother's *rasquachismo* and her son's middle class disdain that estab-lishes the Chicano family and community as the initial context for the narrative conflict. Tomás Ybarra-Frausto defines *rasquachismo* as "an underdog perspective...rooted in resourcefulness and adaptability yet mindful of stance and style."[24] Here, making do with what's at hand upends middle class notions of good taste, decorum, and pragmatism, expressing instead a highly baroque decorative style. Given its working-class sensibilities, "*rasquachismo* suggests vulgarity and bad taste, a sense of being *cursi* (tacky),"[25] rather than its subversive potential. Indeed, Rudy responds to his mother's decorative style with an exasperated roll of the eyes.

But Rudy is not without his own contradictions. In the next scene, he leaves for work in a lowrider fashioned from a pink Volkswagen bug with the license plate "Pink Luv." Thus, Rudy parodies even as he partakes of the masculine expressive culture that stands as a counterpart to that of his mother. But whereas his mother places belief over knowledge and technology (literally) within a *rasquache* aesthetic, Rudy conflates the two within a second- or third-degree kitsch. In other words, for Rudy objects no longer index and interrelate the ineffable (God) and the alienated (mass society) but become either self-referential commodities or acts of postmodern recycling and hybridity within an assimilationist discourse.[26] The conflict between mother and son, then, expresses itself as a split between private and public, sincere and parodic, form and function, resistance and assimilation. Thus, the film poses much more than the question, "How will Rudy get home?"[27] Instead, home itself is at first called into question, until the film "de-territorializes" Rudy, re-figuring home as his object of desire. The film then asks, "How will Rudy be reconciled to domestic space?" This question places the issue of his relationship to women—initially, his mother and sister—within a familial context in which the absent father and wife suggest a failure on Rudy's part to perform his expected gender role. The parodic lowrider, then, marks Rudy's simultaneous *machismo* and assimilation as a threat to the home, one that is acted out and must be resolved in the public sphere.

In between the first and last scenes—the home and a Cinco de Mayo parade—and the narrative itself is a sequence in which a "sexy" French woman walks through the *barrio*.[28] These two sequences overlap with the opening and closing credits and coincide with the two times in the film in which Rudy occupies the public space of the United States. Thus, despite the brevity of her appearances, the French woman plays a complex allegorical function that frames the picaresque narrative, prefiguring Rudy's deportation and return on sexual, political, and cultural levels. Her appearance marks a shift in Rudy's behavior between home (mother's *rasquachismo*) and the public sphere (son's kitsch), and between the familial and the sexual. As he drives to work, Rudy pursues the French woman in his pink lowrider, issuing catcalls out of earshot. Whenever he loses sight of her, he stops to ask men on the corner if they have seen a red-headed woman in a green dress. In unison the men point the way. The scene, modelled after the opening sequence in *The Girl Can't Help It* (1956) with Jayne Mansfield, reveals the woman's effect as an uncontrollable "object of desire" on both Rudy and the entire male *barrio*, who—as such—become paralyzed and objectified by their own "gaze" at the woman. Two brief scenes with lowriders provide a doubling with Rudy and his parodic lowrider, blurring the boundaries between the lowrider as cultural identity, nationalist icon, and object of parody. In the first, we see the French woman walk alongside a mural, passing an approving *vato* (dude) squatting in front of a lowrider painted on the wall. In the next, an "authentic" lowrider with four *vatos* bounces up and down in an excited phallic manner as the French woman crosses the street in front of them. This doubling reveals the limits of Rudy's parody, suggesting class-based assimilation and not masculinity as its real object.

The sequence ends with the French woman walking toward the camera and into Rudy's car shop. Behind her is a spray paint mural of the Mexican and United States flags with lowriders beneath them heading toward the Mexican side of the mural. As she approaches, her body increasingly occupies the space between the two flags, acting as the border. Both the border symbolism and the woman's allegorical status are reinforced in her iconographic coding. She has white, almost alabaster skin, red hair and a green dress: the colors of the Mexican flag. These colors, in addition to her heavy French accent and reappearance during the Cinco de Mayo parade at the end of the film, link her to the French occupation of Mexico in the 1860s. Cinco de Mayo, after all, celebrates the battle that initiated Mexico's overthrow of the French on May 5, 1862. The allusion works on two levels. First, it posits an historical connection between the Chicano *barrio* and Mexico on the basis of colonialism, with the French woman serving as an allegorical figure for French colonialism in Mexico and, by extension, internal colonialism in East L.A.[29] Second, Cinco de Mayo celebrations in the United States speak directly to the history of deportation as well as civil rights struggles since the 1930s. During Depression-era repatriation, the Mexican consulates sponsored Cinco de Mayo celebrations as fundraising activities for their efforts to represent the Mexican and Mexican American communities.[30] Since the 1960s, these celebrations, along with Day of the Dead and Mexican Independence Day, have become symbolic expressions of *Chicano* cultural affirmation, resistance and maintenance within the United States.

The French woman functions as a border symbol, embodying the dual or double-edged notion of "liberty" the French acted out in the Americas in the mid-1800s. In addition to the occupation of Mexico, of course, the French also presented the Statue of Liberty to the United States as a gift of freedom to the world (dedicated in 1886). On an iconographic level, the French woman shares the "exaggerated and slightly vulgar" stride of the statue; while her position between the two flags and her red-white-and-green color scheme imply that for Chicanos and Mexicans the colonial experience still prevails over notions of universal liberty.[31] Thus the French woman negotiates a complex relationship between Mexico and the United States, one that calls into question the symbolic purity of the Statue of Liberty in identifying the United States as a nation of immigrants. Within four years of the statue's dedication, the U.S. Census Bureau would declare the frontier closed, the borders set. Those borders, however, had been reached at the expense of Mexican and Native American lands, a fact which set in motion the contradiction between a Jeffersonian sense of Liberty spreading around the globe and an American expansion and exceptionalism that took liberties with other peoples' sovereignty. In referencing the period between 1862 and 1886, *Born in East L.A.* shifts the discourse on Chicano citizenship from its usual origins in the Mexican-American War and the Treaty of Guadalupe Hidalgo (1848). As I discuss later, this places emphasis on the politics of immigration within an international and multiracial context rather than on the counter-nativist claims of Chicano nationalism.

After approaching Rudy's garage (and the camera) against the backdrop of the mural, the French woman turns and leans against her car. Situated on the right side of the screen, the car is on the U.S. side of the mural. With her legs spread, her left hand folded across her waist, and her right hand raised to the side of her head with a burning cigarette, the French woman strikes a pose similar to the Statue of Liberty with its tablets and torch. Here, positioned in front of the two flags, she suggests a welcome to Mexican immigrants in which the original invitation to assimilate is framed in sexual terms, seemingly addressed to *male* Mexican nationals. But, contrary to this reading, the bottom portion of the mural itself depicts Chicano lowriders driving from the United States to Mexico, with the *mise-en-scène* implying that they have passed between the woman's legs. It is at this point—in the film's most vulgar sight gag—that the *mise-en-scène* foreshadows Rudy's deportation and the terms of his eventual return. Rudy, who had been working beneath the car, slides out on his back in such a way that his head emerges between the French woman's feet. Taken as an allegory of citizenship, Rudy passes beneath the Statue of Liberty on his way to Mexico.[32] The joke here is that the Statue of Liberty does not face Mexico, but Europe, hence the mutual surprise of Rudy and the French woman, captured in shot/reverse-shot to show his pleasure and her shock. Passing beneath the Statue of Liberty against the backdrop of the mural, then, presages Rudy's deportation and precludes his return within the usual terms of immigration and assimilation.

When linked with the lowriders in the earlier scenes (including Rudy's), this scene establishes a causal relationship between desire (for white women, for lowriders) and deportation (from citizenship). Chicano masculine desire is figured as a contrarian form of assimilation in which the desire to "consume" is freed from the object's ostensible function within a Protestant family and work ideology: procreation (woman), transportation (car). The film conflates these two objects of desire around an idea of the foreign-ness of "American" public status symbols (lowriders, white women) in the *barrio*. After he emerges from beneath the car, Rudy leaves the French woman for a moment in order to pick up his guitar from a friend standing next to Rudy's pink lowrider. In response to a question about what he will do over the weekend, Rudy responds, "Probably just sit home and 'Wang Chung,' man." The suggestion of masturbation (and womanlessness) is spoken over a full shot of the red-headed woman leaning against the hood of her black Peugeot. Opposite her on the left half of the frame is a poster of a Zoot Suiter dressed in black and standing in front of a red lowrider; the poster reads: "In East L.A.—where every car is a foreign car." As a symbol of defiance, the image of the Zoot Suiter coopts and exaggerates American popular culture itself, making the car and clothing into a sign of foreign-ness. This symbolic use of the Zoot Suiter provides a counter-discourse drawn from the militarism of the Zoot Suit Riots (voiced by sailors and journalists), while the red-and-black colors posit a genealogy of resistance from the Aztec warrior to the United Farm Workers.[33] Thus, the juxtaposition of these two red-and-black tableaux, and Rudy's earlier pun contrasting the woman's "black Peugeot" (pubic hair) with her red-headedness, constructs a Chicano masculine ideal of a defiant stance and its rewards that Rudy desires, yet cannot replicate: due to a continuity error in the film, his much smaller, pink (as in less red) lowrider even disappears in the final shot of the scene with the French woman. Rudy never does get to "Wang Chung" at home, since he is deported in the next scene, when he attempts to pick up his cousin after work. The last scene of the film, which depicts Rudy's return "home," provides the second half of this narrative frame. While in Mexico, Rudy had taught a group of "Indian" and "Chinese" workers—called OTMs for Other Than Mexican—how to pass as Chicano in order to avoid deportation. In addition to the obvious irony that Rudy himself could not "pass" as Chicano (and that many of the OTMs are played by Latino actors), these scenes, which are punctuated by stereotypical "Chinese" music, allude to the Chinese Exclusion Act of 1882, which lasted until 1943 (the same year as the Zoot Suit Riots), and represented the first denial of the right of free migration to the United States as well as one of the first victories of the emergent labor movement (as it sought to define its working class agenda in racial terms as "white"). The Chinese Exclusion Act and subsequent laws prohibiting foreign contract labor resulted in a decisive shift within the unskilled labor force from Chinese to Mexican migrants. Mexican nationals—exempted as "foreigners *temporarily* residing in the U.S."—provided a cheap labor pool for the rapid industrial development in the Southwest; and, between 1880 and 1920, the Mexican population in the United States would increase ninefold, while the national population would double.[34] Given that Rudy identifies himself as the third-generation born in the United States, he places his family history at the tail end of this period. In this manner, *Born in East L.A.* establishes the limits of U.S. immigration policy and ideology with respect to racial others, revealing a hidden dynamic at the level of the working class that places various racial and ethnic groups in competition with each other.

In the end, Rudy leads a massive multi-racial and -national assault on the border. The scene visualizes Anglo-Americans' worst fear about illegal aliens swarming across the border to take away jobs, drain welfare funds, overburden social services, and increase urban crime. Marin, however, undercuts these associations, visually coding the scene as humorous, and using music as an added counterpoint. Neil Diamond's "America," which played at the rededication ceremonies for the Statue of Liberty, describes these new immigrants: "Got a dream they come to share. They come to America…." As with Marin's parody of "Born in the U.S.A.," the sincerely ironic use of Diamond's "America" does not so much shift the discourse as expand it to include non-European-descent citizens and immigrants. It is noteworthy, then, that the rededication of the Statue of Liberty occurs in the same year in which the Immigration Reform Bill and California's English-Only Initiative passed into law. Likewise, "America" replaces—literally, in the 1986 rededication—the Emma Lazarus lines inscribed on the statue's base in 1903:

> Give me your tired, your poor,
> Your huddled masses yearning to breathe free,
> The wretched refuse of your teeming shore.
> Send these, the homeless, tempest-tos't to me,
> I lift my lamp beside the golden door!

The status of these earlier immigrants suggested that they brought nothing with them. Their names were changed, and like empty ciphers, they were expected to acculturate; that is, to acquire the "American" language and culture. Diamond's song, especially in the context of *Born in East L.A.,* reveals a different set of expectations on the part of immigrants as well as inevitable cultural hybridity. For example, Dolores does not want to cross the border until she has saved enough money to be independent—i.e., not on welfare. In cross-referencing "American" popular culture, the film constructs its argument out of contradictions and conflicts within the "mainstream" itself.

While "America" adds an ironic twist to the border crossing, the next scene further undermines the great fear of the mid-1980s, often expressed in the mainstream press as the fear of "latinization." Rudy and the OTMs are shown running down a hill into the United States, only to emerge in the next scene from a sewer hole into the *barrio* of East

L.A. In other words, they move directly from the Mexican border to the Chicano *barrio*, invisible in the social space in between, which includes "white flight" suburbs and the military industrial complex. While immigration discourses often invoke and contend over a generic, "American" public space and its attendant rights, the actual struggle is more geographically specific, as the film suggests. After all, it is because the Mexicans and OTMs (Asian and Central American) will have to adapt and fit into the *barrio* and avoid other social spaces that Rudy is able to earn money in Tijuana teaching the OTMs *rasquache* coping strategies.

Having stormed the border, in the next shot, Rudy reemerges from a sewer amidst the Cinco de Mayo parade in East L.A. with Dolores and the OTMS. The Chinese OTMs quickly blend in as Chicanos—at least as far as the police are concerned. It is at this point that the French woman re-appears, causing the parade watchers—men, women, children—to freeze.[35] Does this scene reveal a culture paralyzed by the gazed-upon "white" woman, a sexual-political Medusa who represents the promises and pitfalls of *barrio* aspirations vis-a-vis citizenship, cultural maintenance, and racial difference? Does her final look (and smile) into the camera freeze us, make us complicit, or free us from the gaze? The next and final shot of the film suggests the latter: Rudy and Dolores are animated, embracing in front of a priest upon a church float. But if her look frees us from the gaze that she constitutes—that is, from one particular sexual-cultural positioning—on what terms? On an obvious level, the French woman is the whore to Dolores's Madonna. In fact, "dolores" means "pains" or "sorrows" in English. The film conflates the sexual dichotomy with cultural nationalism, so that the whore also tempts Rudy with assimilation (pleasure), while the Madonna ensures cultural affirmation (pain). Although that conflation leads to Rudy's apparent reform, it also relieves him of responsibility. As a *pícaro,* Rudy does not change as much as his circumstances change around him. It is Dolores, after all, who baptizes Rudy with a pail of water after a sexist remark, and who stands in silent witness to his subsequent acts of charity toward two women, a young, single *mother,* and an older *wife.* These characters mirror or double Robles's own sister and mother—not just in terms of their familial characterization (Rudy's sister also has two children), but also in the scant screen time given to each. What these brief scenes allow, then, is for Dolores to act as the "witness" or mediation point for Robles to resolve his Madonna/whore complex, first toward (working class) Mexican women, then, by extension and implication, toward the (middle class) Mexican-American women in his own family and community. This is most apparent in the scene with the poor single mother and her two children. After Rudy gives the woman his cart of oranges, the rack-focus pulls back to reveal Dolores watching Robles's act of charity on the other side of the street. Dolores, however, stands in an awkward posture that accentuates both her breasts and buttocks: facing away from the camera, she twists her torso toward Rudy. In other words, for the viewer, she is framed in order to be seen watching Robles. Rather than act as a point of moral identification, Dolores becomes the site of an acceptable sexual gaze, but only *after* her role as a moral guardian has been established—first for the viewer, then for Rudy. In the end, Dolores makes it possible for Rudy's spiritual return to the domain of the family, which he had taken for granted, if not ridiculed, in the opening scene. In addition to the mother's religious belief, Dolores facilitates a *latinidad* or pan-ethnic "Latino" identity characterized by her insistence that Rudy learn Spanish.

In this manner, the first and last scenes in the film provide a narrative frame that moves from the private to the public symbols of the *barrio:* the home and the Cinco de Mayo parade. Both spaces are defined in relationship to the church. This shift in social space brings about a corresponding shift in the configuration of familial relations, from mother-son-sister to "father"/priest-son-wife.[36] But this is not necessarily a shift from private to public as defined by Richard Rodriguez in *Hunger of Memory* or as represented in *The Ring.*[37] That is, a shift from the language of a minority culture to that of the political and economic "mainstream." Instead, the film constructs East L.A. as an alternative public sphere in its own right, one that stands between the ethnic family and dominant culture.[38]

The overall message, as Marin notes, was *chicanismo,* often translated as Chicano pride.[39] According to Marcos Sánchez-Tranquilino,

> Chicanismo was a complex of nationalist strategies by which Chicano origins and histories, as well as present and future identities, were constructed and legitimized. Furthermore, it provided a context for historical reclamation of the self through the affirmation of Chicano cultural narratives while resisting Anglo models of assimilation.[40]

Sánchez-Tranquilino goes on to connect the initial articulations of *chicanismo* through activism, scholarship, literature and the arts to the concurrent call for a Chicano homeland based on Aztlán, the mythical Aztec homeland: "The renaming of the American Southwest as Aztlán within the national Chicano community [in 1969] was an important initial step in reclaiming the land-base upon which further development of this Chicano world view [*chicanismo*] could take place."[41] In *Born in East L.A.,* there is not a call for a nationalist "homeland" that exists within and against the United States itself as an ideological overlay, but rather an attempt to make "East L.A." synonymous with "U.S.A." and, hence, with citizenship. This is achieved through a rhyme that establishes metonymy between *barrio* and nation, "I was born in East L.A.," and thereby signifies two seemingly opposite birthrights: Mexican descent and U.S. citizenship.

While negotiating between nationalist and assimilationist conceptions of social space, *Born in East L.A.* attempts to solve its problems of space through a "conservative" cultural politics at the level of gender. Thus, if *Born in East L.A.* stresses *chicanismo,* it is a message that is structured around female allegories (French woman) and stereotypes (Dolores) and the threat of homosexual rape (in prison), and ultimately leads to traditional Latino gender roles.[42] It could be argued, however, that *Born in East L.A.* is not a realist drama, but a comedy, and "[c]omedy always and above all depends upon an awareness that it is fictional."[43] Indeed, it is hard to explain several scenes in terms of realism or non-fictional narrative conventions. Did the mariachi performance of Jimi Hendrix's "Purple Haze" *really* happen, or was it a fantasy on the part of the protagonist? The film repeatedly collapses not just narrative space, but geographical space, as well. First of all, *Born in East L.A.* collapses the space from Tijuana to the south in its representation of Dolores, who works three jobs in Tijuana but lives in a trailer in El Rosario about two hundred miles south. Next, the border crossing scene that ends the film, and which recalls the fatal crossing in *El Norte,* humorously collapses the hundred-plus mile distance between Tijuana and East L.A. Herein lies the film's logic: In collapsing the space between Dolores's and Rudy's homes, and between Tijuana and East L.A., the film draws attention to the erasure of history (how people get from one space to another) within public discourse and the popular imagination. When one considers the fact that Rudy's mother and sister are visiting family in Fresno—about two hundred miles north of Los Angeles—the film can be seen to map out a generic Chicano family history that moves from Mexico (underemployed) to the agricultural belt (working class) to the urban center (middle class).[44] But, at the same time, the film constructs desire within these very same terms, conflating space and history around the French woman who enters the *barrio,* symbolizing assimilation and internal colonization.[45]

If anything, then, *Born in East L.A.* manifests the ways in which Chicano expressions have understood cultural resistance and affirmation within oppositional terms that center on the role of women, family and the home as sites of either redemption or betrayal. Ultimately, what the film argues is a familial, collective identity over and against a masculine, individual one, presenting this shift in nationalist terms as an alternative between assimilation with deportation versus cultural maintenance within the *barrio.*[46] While this itself is framed within the patriarchal terms of a madonna/whore dichotomy, the film also uses these terms to register a subtle shift from Chicano nationalism to a pan-Latino identity. The implication of marriage between an assimilated Chicano and an "illegal alien" reveals how the immigration continuum both sustains and diversifies *barrio* culture. The fact that Dolores is from El Salvador alludes to the impact of recent Central American refugees while Rudy's repeated utterance of Ronald Reagan's name in Tijuana serves as a reminder that it was his Central American and immigration policies that are, in large part, responsible. In the end, to be born in East L.A. is no longer equated with Mexican descent (let alone descent from a single country of origin, if we imagine that Rudy and Dolores have children). The fact that the Spanish-language float is for an Evangelist church suggests other recent changes in the *barrio.* The reference to Evangelical Christianity first occurs in the prison scenes in Tijuana, where the jail guard Feo ("ugly") uses evangelical-style sermonizing to frighten the inmates.[47] This keeps the inmates from raping Rudy, a "favor" that Feo uses to exploit Rudy for financial gain. These two references (prison and float), then, establish a complex counterpoint to Catholicism and Liberation Theology *within* the representation of Latino cultural politics. These cracks in the image of a monolithic Chicano/ Mexican-descent culture may, in fact, explain the film's progressive appeal for Chicana and Chicano critics: it is seen to de-stabilize the essentialist underpinnings of Chicano nationalism while still offering a critique of dominant culture.[48] But while the film de-stabilizes internal and external stereotypes of the *barrio* in terms of culture, language, religion and country of origin, it does so through traditional gender roles that reproduce the *barrio* as *barrio,* while equating that space with citizenship.

Returning to Marin's coffee metaphor, it is fitting, then, that David Avalos, one of the original founders of the Border Arts Workshop/Taller Arte Fronterizo (BAW/TAF), extends the metaphor to account for *mestizaje* as well as the use of comedy for hidden messages. In his installation piece *Café Mestizo,* which rejects the notion that "two halves makes less than a whole," Avalos depicts that process as coffee and cream poured side by side into a cup, while a caption reads, "A grind so fine…you give in to the pleasure."[49]

Unlike other Chicano writers and artists, Avalos extends *mestizaje* both as metaphor (cultural hybridity) and as literal act (miscegenation) in locating Chicanos within the United States. Interestingly, though, *Born in East L.A.* argues against *that* pleasure from the perspective of the state and of the *barrio*. Indeed, Rudy taught the OTMs how to be Chicano by way of a *posture* of desire for the white women (two blonde tourists) who entered *their* public space. But when the OTMs actually run after these women, rather than cruise them from a street corner or lowrider, Rudy stops the OTMs. This is his contradiction, which becomes defined as that which paralyzes the entire *barrio,* and is resolved (if also transformed) only through a Latino marriage. Thus, the picaresque—with its emphasis on the material aspects of existence and its parody of social institutions— finds its resolution within the terms of melodrama wherein religious devotion and couple formation overcome the "outside" threat to the home.[50] While this process registers cultural shifts within the *barrio* itself, the film is unable to pose this in either ambiguous or intercultural terms vis-a-vis the national culture. In other words—despite Marin's contention that "American culture and Latino culture are inextricably bound, and there is no history of one without the other"—these cultural shifts must nonetheless be re-contained within the *barrio* or risk moral ambiguity about de-territorialization.[51] In the end, Rudy's trademark question remains a rhetorical one: "Orale vato, waas sappening?"

Notes

1. Reprinted from *Studies in Latin American Popular Culture,* vol. 14 (1995). A much shorter version of this article appeared in the media arts issue of *Tonantzin* (February 1991), a tabloid magazine published by the Guadalupe Cultural Arts Center in conjunction with its annual CineFestival. I want to thank Tomás Ybarra-Frausto, Mary Louise Pratt, Kathleen Newman, and Ana M. López for their insightful comments on earlier versions of this essay.

2. Ruben Guevara, Interview with Cheech Marin, *Americas 2001* (June-July 1987): 18–21, p. 18.

3. According to Pat Aufderheide, "Cheech Marin says, Universal Studios funded *Born in East L.A.* to clear up his doper image at a time when antidrug hysteria has gripped American culture." "Reel Life," *Mother Jones* (April 1988): 24–26, 45–46; p. 46.

4. Kevin Thomas, "'East L.A.' Gets the Green Card," *Los Angeles Times,* August 24, 1987, sec. F, pp. 1, 4.

5. See Chon A. Noriega, "Chicano Cinema and the Horizon of Expectations: A Discursive Analysis of Film Reviews in the Mainstream, Alternative, and Hispanic Press, 1987–1988," *Aztlán: A Journal of Chicano Studies* 19.2 (Fall 1988–1990): 1–32.

6. Tom Cunneff, "Born in East L.A.," *People Weekly* (September 14, 1987): 14; and Dennis West and Gary Crowdus, "Cheech Cleans Up His Act," Interview, *Cineaste* 16.3 (1988): 34–37. *Cineaste* at least provided a forum for Marin to express his views, although the preface to the interview uses later questions as statements that in no way engage, let alone acknowledge Marin's responses.

7. Information gathered from *Variety:* August 26, 1987; September 2, 1987; September 9, 1987; September 16, 1987; and September 23, 1987.

8. Juan Rodríguez Flores, "En el estreno de la película 'Born in East L.A.,'" *La Opinión,* August 22, 1987, sec. 3, p. 1.

9. Maggie Cardenas, "Born in East L.A.," *Unidad/Unity,* October 12, 1987, p. 12; and *Americas 2001* (cited above). On the end of the "grace period," see: Marita Hernandez, "Amnesty—The First Wave Battles Red Tape," *Los Angeles Times,* September 1, 1987, pp. A9, A16; and Jess Bravin, "No Mass Firings of Aliens Seen as Exemption Ends," *Los Angeles Times,* September 1, 1987, pp. B3, B16.

10. This included: "Tercer Premio Coral" (third prize) in fiction, the "Premio Coral" in screenwriting, the "Premio Coral" in set design, and the Glauber Rocha award. Teresa Toledo, *10 años del nuevo cine latinoamericano* (Madrid: Verdoux, S.L., 1990), p. 575. Also, Paul Lenti, "Broad U.S. Presence at Havana's New Latino Fest," *Variety,* December 23, 1987, p. 5.

11. Glauber Rocha, "The Aesthetics of Hunger," trans. Julianne Burton, in *Twenty-Five Years of the New Latin American Cinema,* ed. Michael Chanan (London: British Film Institute/Channel Four Television, 1983), p. 13.

12. For an extensive discussion of these historiographic issues, see Ana M. López, "An 'Other' History: The New Latin American Cinema," in *Resisting Images: Essays on Cinema and History,* ed. Robert Sklar and Charles Musser (Philadelphia: Temple University Press, 1990), pp. 308–330.

13. See Rosa Linda Fregoso, "Born in East L.A. and the Politics of Representation," *Cultural Studies* 4.3 (October 1990): 264–280; Eddie Tafoya, "Born in East L.A.: Cheech as the Chicano Moses," *Journal of Popular Culture* 26.4 (Spring 1993): 123–129; and Christine List, "Self-Directed Stereotyping in the Films of Cheech Marin," and Víctor Fuentes, "Chicano Cinema: A Dialectic of Voices and Images of the Autonomous Discourse Versus Those of the Dominant," in *Chicanos and Film: Representation and Resistance,* ed. Chon A. Noriega (Minneapolis: University of Minnesota Press, 1992), pp. 183–194, 207–217.

14. Interview by author with Richard "Cheech" Marin, October 16, 1990, Malibu, California.

15. On the split between Mexican American and Chicano politics, see Carlos Muñoz, Jr., *Youth, Identity, Power: The Chicano Movement* (New York: Verso, 1989). In many ways, this dichotomy has been a self-serving one within Chicano historical revisionism, and does little to explain, for example, the combined Mexican nationalism and anti-immigration politics of the United Farm Workers Union. For my purposes here, I want to show how immigration functions as a trope around which *Born in East L.A.* conflates cultural nationalism and structural assimilation. In his case histories of the Mexican American Generation, Mario García complicates the above initial assessment, which reduced the wide range of political activism to a question of accommodation. See *Mexican Americans: Leadership, Ideology, & Identity, 1930–1960* (New Haven: Yale University Press, 1989). See also, David G. Gutiérrez, "Sin Fronteras?: Chicanos, Mexican Americans, and the Emergence of the Contemporary Mexican Immigration Debate, 1968–1978," *Journal of American Ethnic History* 10.4 (Summer 1991): 5–37.

16. Dennis Baron, *The English-Only Question: An Official Language for Americans?* (New Haven: Yale University Press, 1990), p. 6.

17. Ibid., p. 62.

18. For example, see Rosa Linda Fregoso's contention that the U.S. conquest of the Southwest as a result of the Mexican-American War was *illegal,* and, therefore, Mexican immigrants must be given the *legal* status of citizens. Without recourse to some notion of international law, Fregoso makes a reified "historical standpoint"—the fact the California was part of the Mexican nation between 1821 and 1848—the basis for a law (and citizenship) that stands outside of history and historical processes. The "law" that she conjures can only exist within the realm of moral discourses, while the laws that do exist—such as the Treaty of Guadalupe Hidalgo—are never examined as a way to deconstruct the U.S. legal system. *The Bronze Screen: Chicana and Chicano Film Culture* (Minneapolis: University of Minnesota Press, 1993), pp. 85–90.

19. On the political ambiguity of the song's lyrics and reception, see John Lombardi, "St. Boss: The Sanctification of Bruce Springsteen and the Rise of Mass Hip," *Esquire* (December 1988): 139–154, esp. 146.

20. In *The Ring* (1952), the film begins and ends with a montage sequence centered on another public *barrio* space, Olvera Street, a tourist market that becomes the preferred symbol of social contact between Anglos and Chicanos (rather than boxing). In the Chicano gang film *Boulevard Nights* (1979), the opening sequence stops briefly on a house, where two Chicano youths emerge (depicted in long shot) and walk down into the nearby L.A. riverbed to meet other gang members (with the camera tracking after them). See also Ilene S. Goldman's discussion of the opening sequence in

Stand and Deliver in her article in *The Ethnic Eye: Latino Media Arts,* ed. Chon A. Noriega and Ana M López (Minneapolis: University of Minnesota Press, in press).

21. Homi K. Bhabha, "On Mimicry and Man: The Ambivalence of Colonial Discourse," *October* 28 (1984): 125–133.

22. Chon A. Noriega, "Internal 'Others': Hollywood Narratives 'about' Mexican-Americans," in *Mediating Two Worlds: Cinematic Encounters in the Americas,* ed. John King, Ana M. López, and Manuel Alvarado. (London: British Film Institute, 1993), pp. 52–66.

23. In defining "border culture," Guillermo Gómez-Peña states, "Whenever and wherever two or more cultures meet—peacefully or violently—there is a border experience." "The Multicultural Paradigm: An Open Letter to the National Arts Community," *High Performance* 12.3 (Fall 1989): 18–27, p. 20. In *Born in East L.A.,* "border culture" is first depicted as operative *within* the Chicano home, then between Chicanos and Mexicans, and, finally, between Chicanos (and Mexicans/OTMs) and Anglos (and the state). For a critical overview of Gómez-Peña's work, see Claire Fox, "Mass Media, Site-Specificity, and the U.S.-Mexico Border: Guillermo Gómez-Peña's *Border Brujo* (1988, 1990)," in *The Ethnic Eye,* ed. Noriega and López.

24. Tomás Ybarra-Frausto, "Rasquachismo: A Chicano Sensibility," in *Chicano Art: Resistance and Affirmation, 1965–1985,* ed. Richard Griswold del Castillo, Teresa McKenna, and Yvonne Yarbro Bejarano (Los Angeles: Wight Art Gallery/UCLA, 1991): 155–162, p. 156.

25. Ibid.

26. While I borrow Celeste Olalquiaga's distinction between the three degrees of kitsch, I do not want to suggest the class-based historicism that is implicit in the way she privileges postmodern recycling and hybridity. *Megalopolis: Contemporary Cultural Sensibilities* (Minneapolis: University of Minnesota Press, 1992), pp. 36–55.

27. Fregoso, *The Bronze Screen,* pp. 55–56. Fregoso continues, "The film poses an even more scathing question: what type of society deports its citizens merely on the basis of the color of their skin?" While Fregoso focuses attention solely on the role of "institutional racism," I want to show how the film interrelates questions about the Chicano home and U.S. citizenship.

28. The woman steps from a bus marked "Civic Center" and crosses a bridge over the Los Angeles River, which separates downtown from East L.A. [The bus route (35) terminates in Beverly Hills.]

29. For a review of internal colonialism, see Tomás Almaguer, "Ideological Distortions in Recent Chicano Historiography: The Internal Model and Chicano Historical Interpretation," *Aztlán: A Journal of Chicano Studies* 18.1 (Spring 1987): 7–28.

30. Francisco E. Balderrama, *In Defense of La Raza: The Los Angeles Mexican Consulate and the Mexican Community, 1929 to 1936* (Tucson: University of Arizona Press, 1982), pp. 45–46.

31. On the statue's stride, see Marina Warner, "The Monument (New York)," *Monuments and Maidens: The Allegory of the Female Form* (London: Weidenfeld and Nicolson, 1985): 3–17, p. 8. Warner captures the bipolar terms of the statue's symbolism: "Perceived either as a lie, or as a statement of truth, the claim that the Statue of Liberty makes on behalf of the United States defines the nation's self-image" (p. 11).

32. Consider Warner's sexualized description of a visit to the Statue of Liberty: "…when we enter into her, we are invited to merge with her, to feel at one with her." She concludes: "The female form tends to be perceived as generic and universal, with symbolic overtones; the male as individual, even when it is being used to express a generalized idea." Hence, citizens can be *represented* by (as well as occupy, possess) the Statue of Liberty, but *identify* with Uncle Sam. Warner, "The Monument," pp. 11–12.

33. The UFW banner is a red-and-black Thunderbird. For an account of the militaristic discourses of the Zoot Suit Riots, see Mauricio Mazón, *The Zoot Suit Riots: The Psychology of Symbolic Annihilation* (Austin: University of Texas Press, 1984).

34. Rodolfo Acuña, *Occupied America: A History of Chicanos,* Third Edition (New York: HarperCollins, 1988), p. 127; and James D. Cockcroft, *Outlaws in the Promised Land: Mexican Immigrant Workers and*

America's Future (New York: Grove Press, 1986), pp. 47–48. According to Cockcroft, "the migration of Mexicans during the first third of the twentieth century shifted an estimated one-eighth of Mexico's population north of the border—one of the largest mass movements of a people in human history."

35. The television broadcast of the film contains an additional fifteen minutes with a "cloak-and-dagger" subplot that takes place after the parade scene. Since the standard movie length for a two-hour broadcast is one hundred minutes, shorter films often contain extra footage not included in the theatrical release and video versions.

36. This contrasts with an earlier film such as *Bordertown* (1935), in which the padre (church) and mother (home) frame the protagonist's return. See my article, "Internal 'Others'" (cited above).

37. Richard Rodriguez, *Hunger of Memory: The Education of Richard Rodriguez* (New York: Bantam Books, 1982).

38. Ricardo Romo and others describe the barrio as both a culture in its own right and as a mediation point between two national cultures that allows recent immigrants to adapt to "American life" on their own terms. Romo, *East Los Angeles: A History of a Barrio* (Austin: University of Texas Press, 1983).

39. See West and Crowdus interview in *Cineaste,* p. 37 (cited above).

40. Marcos Sánchez-Tranquilino, "Murales del Movimiento: Chicano Murals and the Discourses of Art and Americanization," in Eva Sperling Cockcroft and Holly Barnet-Sánchez, eds., *Signs from the Heart: California Chicano Murals* (Venice, CA: Social and Public Art Resource Center, 1990), p. 90.

41. Ibid.

42. In fact, in response to questions about the "sexist images of women" in the film, Marin argues that his message was about *chicanismo* and not about women, suggesting that issues of gender and cultural affirmation are two different things. See West and Crowdus interview cited above. See also the discussion of *chicanismo* in Ramón Gutiérrez, "Community, Patriarchy, and Individualism: The Politics of Chicano History and the Dream of Equality," *American Quarterly* 45.1 (March 1993): 44–72, p. 46.

43. Stephen Neale, *Genre* (London: British Film Institute, 1980), p. 40.

44. These movements to the north and south leave the house empty, except for Javier (Paul Rodriquez), who must mediate between the mother and son's contradictory configuration of the home: the Jesus Christ picture over the phone versus Rudy's beer and cable television (Playboy channel). When Rudy calls home for help, Javier mistakes him for Christ and covers the television. On the spatial contrast between Rudy and Javier, see Fregoso, *The Bronze Screen,* p. 57.

45. The film reinforces this conflation of spatial and historical references through an ambiguous time frame for the narrative. While Rudy's brief time in the United States is defined by a 9-to-5 workday which ends in deportation, it is unclear how many days he is in Tijuana.

46. This is implicit in Tafoya's reading of the film in light of Latin American Liberation Theology. In *The Bronze Screen,* Fregoso explicitly links this "political/religious metaphor" with a "sense of collectivity" that "resists ideology of individual heroism" (p. 61).

47. See Tafoya, "Cheech as the New Moses," p. 127.

48. In *"Born in East L.A.* and the Politics of Representation," for example, Rosa Linda Fregoso stresses the film's cultural affirmation and critique of dominant ideologies but chooses not to raise gender issues in the non-Chicano publication *Cultural Studies* (1990). In *The Bronze Screen,* Fregoso takes up the iconographic elements and gender critique that I raised in *Tonanztin* but sets these "apart" from the film's "effective indictment of dominant official discourse" (p. 54). See also Tafoya's article (cited above) and Sandra Peña-Sarmiento's "Pocha Manifesto #1," *Jump Cut* no. 39 (June 1994): 105–106. Peña-Sarmiento, who speaks for a new generation of Chicano and Chicana filmmakers, identifies *Born in East L.A.* as the only feature film to question "The Chicano Experience."

49. David Avalos, *Café Mestizo,* exhibition catalogue (New York: Intar Gallery, 1989).

50. In this respect, *Born in East L.A.,* like the slave narrative, "is a counter-genre, a meditation between the novel of sentiment and the picaresque, oscillating somewhere between the two in a bipolar moment." Henry Louis Gates, Jr., *Figures in Black: Words, Signs, and the "Racial" Self* (New York: Oxford University Press, 1987), p. 81. Insofar as this is also "set in motion by the mode of the confession," the film becomes a site of quasi-autobiography. Indeed, the film represented a decisive break in Marin's career, albeit one that was negotiated within the generic limitations and expectations of Hollywood.

51. Quotation from West and Crowdus interview, *Cineaste,* p. 35. See Gates, *Figures in Black* , p. 87.

27

■ American Militarism, Hollywood, and Media Culture

Carl Boggs and Tom Pollard

The steady growth of a militarized society in the United States cannot be understood apart from the expanded role of media culture in its different forms: TV, radio, Internet, publishing, video games, and film. An unsurpassed source of information, opinion, and entertainment, the corporate media have become the main linchpin of ideological hegemony in the United States, a repository of values, attitudes, and myths that shapes public opinion on a daily basis. Transnational media empires such as Disney, Time-Warner, Viacom, News Corporation, and General Electric, which are bulwarks of privilege and power, routinely celebrate the blessings of a "free-market economy," the virtues of personal consumption, the wonders of a political system built on freedom and democracy, a benevolent and peace-loving U.S. foreign policy, the need for a globalized permanent war system to protect against imminent foreign threats, and of course old-fashioned patriotism. A wide panorama of militaristic images and discourses infuses media culture today, probably nowhere more so than in Hollywood cinema, helping to legitimate unprecedented Pentagon budgets and U.S. armed interventions abroad. If elements of the mass media can be viewed as outright propaganda, for the most part we are talking about something entirely different here. Not deliberate propaganda, but something even more effective in molding public opinion: deeply ingrained traditions within the popular and political culture that by the 1990s had come to permeate every corner of American life.

Given the century-long influence of Hollywood movies, and with it the power of related newer media such as TV, video games, and the Internet, it might be useful to adopt Norman Denzin's reference to the United States as something akin to a "cinematic society"(Denzin, 1995). Within this conceptual framework we have set out to analyze a cultural phenomenon we identify as the "Hollywood War Machine," an integral part of the film industry and media culture that produces dozens of motion pictures yearly featuring combat, warfare, and various other violent high-tech spectacles. The corporate studios release on average 450 films each year, drawing hundreds of millions of viewers from every class, income, age, ethnic, and gender category—and from every part of the world. Mainstream cinema in general exerts a unique impact on public discourse, in great measure owing to its visual power and entertainment appeal. The American culture industry cannot be understood apart from what George Ritzer refers to as "cathedrals of consumption" and Guy Debord long ago identified as the "society of the spectacle" (Debord, 1995; Ritzer, 1999). We argue that these dynamic tendencies converge within an increasingly militarized society, both reflecting and feeding into an ensemble of beliefs and attitudes that help sustain the U.S. empire and the war system that protects it.

As Denzin observed, "American cinema created a space for a certain kind of communal urban life [just as] Americans entered the public realm," providing a terrain of fantasies, myths, and illusions that would take hold of the popular imagination (Denzin, 1995, p. 14). Film "became a technology and apparatus of power that would organize and bring meaning to everyday lives"(Denzin, 1995, p. 15). He adds: "Within this birth American society became a cinematic culture, a culture which came to know itself, collectively and individually, through the images and stories that Hollywood produced" (Denzin, 1995, p. 24). This facet of the motion picture industry has grown steadily from the period of its supposed peak popularity in the 1930s and 1940s to an omnipresent cultural force, flexing its power internationally as well as domestically. Today, as Denzin suggests, "the everyday is now defined by the cinematic. The two can no longer be separated. A single epistemological regime governs both fields" (Denzin, 1995, p. 36). As movies have come to simultaneously reflect and shape reality, their trajectory is inseparable from that of the expanding megacorporations, which bind the lives of ordinary citizens to an assortment of fantasies, myths, and illusions churned out by the most far-reaching culture industry ever known. The patriotic war experience, embellished and glorified within this culture industry, best captures the essence of the Hollywood War Machine. With this in mind, we mention here that our media explorations in our book *The Hollywood War Machine* have been strongly influenced by earlier seminal works on the media/culture industry, including those of the Frankfurt School, Marshall McLuhan, Guy Debord, the Noam Chomsky–Edward S. Herman work, Jean Baudrillard, Douglas Kellner, Robert McChesney, and others.[1] At the same time, we have embarked on some new journeys as our investigations take us into a rapidly changing universe.

By the 1990s the American media had become little more than an extension of gigantic corporate interests, its power increasingly concentrated, global, and, especially after the Telecommunications Act of 1996, far more deregulated and commercialized. Through mergers, consolidations, worldwide operations, and sheer scope of activity, media culture grew more pervasive, oligarchical, and profit-driven. At the same time, it became more profoundly *conservative*—a trend evident from even the most superficial glance at the content of TV programs, talk radio, popular magazines and tabloids, and the endless parade of blockbuster movie extravaganzas.[2] The studios became more commodified as the increasingly few media empires competed ever more fiercely for consumer markets, which meant that advertising, sales, and marketing took center stage. Robert McChesney writes: "The clear trajectory of our media and communications world tends toward ever-greater corporate concentration, media conglomeration, and hypercommercialism. The notion of public service—that there should be some motive for media other than profit—is in rapid retreat, if not total collapse" (McChesney, 1999, p. 77). Under such circumstances, the "public" was transformed into a depoliticized mass of atomized, fragmented, and largely passive spectators, while the notion that the media ought to inform, educate, or simply furnish space for open debates, appeared more and more archaic, made obsolete by the workings of "market forces."

Yet if media culture is synonymous with corporate power and is a crucial pillar of ideological hegemony, then "market forces" surely do not equate with cultural or political neutrality but rather coincide with the dominant interests and values. The film studios, despite their unwarranted liberal reputation, are an integral part of this structure and its well-planned agendas. As profit-making enterprises first and foremost, the studios favor definite "products"—typically high-tech, fast-paced, violent extravaganzas driven by conventional narratives, heroic deeds, and happy endings. The combat genre itself has been visible in Hollywood since the time of D.W. Griffith, but currently this same (though broadened) format extends to other fare including science fiction, thrillers, horror pictures, and action/adventure movies. It is a format that resonates with the desires of studio executives, producers, and directors attuned to the world of technological wizardry, celebrity actors, and narrative devices (battlefield clashes, car chases, wild shootouts, etc.) appealing to mass audiences already immersed in video games, MTV, and computer technology.[3] The result is a perfect matrix for the familiar convergence of entertainment and propaganda, which accounts in part for both the box office success and ideological influence of the Hollywood War Machine. Beyond a particular "cycle" or "genre" of films, we refer here to a more general media *commodity* structure that exists also as *spectacle,* reflecting what audiences can expect to see in the sequels to *Star Wars, The Terminator,* and *Batman, War of the Worlds* as well as in the *Rambo* series, *Top Gun, Saving Private Ryan,* and other easily identified combat pictures.

It is a truism that film audiences today, as in the past, seem little aware of movies as business or political enterprises, oriented as they are to what appears as simple, unmediated entertainment. The average filmgoer does not read *Variety* or other trade periodicals. Of course studios do publicize gross box office receipts shortly after a picture's release, but they rarely divulge vital information about sources of investment, preproduction budgets, casting, shooting, editing, distribution, and marketing—allocations that can determine success or failure. For many years the film industry was confined to a small group of studios that included Columbia, MGM, Paramount, Twentieth Century Fox, and Warner Brothers, places where executives wielded nearly absolute control over every aspect of production. By 1988, when Neal Gabler's book *An Empire of Their Own* was published, the old studio system had undergone such radical transformation that Gabler was able to conclude it had become essentially defunct (Gabler, 1988). At the start of the twenty-first century, just a few of the old studios remain, although even these have been taken over by such conglomerates as Gulf and Western, General Electric, Viacom, Sony, and News Corporation. Controlled mostly by big-time corporate entrepreneurs, investment bankers, and lawyers, the reincarnated studios are more obsessed than ever with profits and marketability, and less interested in the quality and originality of what is produced. Today studio executives face entirely new challenges, such as competition from TV, the Internet, and cable outlets such as HBO and Showtime, and they have responded with new business methods that would have been unrecognizable to Golden Age executives.

Given the astronomical budgets of many first-run movies, projects soon bring large and risky investments for megacorporations looking furtively at profit-and-loss statements. Production strategies are clearly linked to financial agendas and involve some combination of bankers, investment brokers, wealthy entrepreneurs, and celebrity investors, not to mention possible creative profit-sharing with distribution outlets or kindred entertainment firms. The daunting task of bringing motion pictures to the big screen, especially blockbusters, means that "development"—financing, production, distribution, marketing—is bound to consume ever-greater human, material, and technological resources dependent on an army of professionals, technicians, temp workers, agents, and lawyers not to mention the usual stable of investors. Filmmaking depends on continuous, but always fragile, interaction among studios, banks, talent agencies, unions, insurance companies, lawyers, and consultants, each input presumably leaving some mark on the final product. Delays in filming, unforeseen problems on the set, and cost overruns can prove devastating. Severe difficulties can further arise from code struggles with the Motion Picture Association of America, an industry-run regulatory body responsible for rating film content.

In the "new" Hollywood, limited partnerships, institutional loans, foundation grants, government loans, distribution arrangements, and profit-sharing contracts along with celebrity backing influence filmmaking strategies in ways unheard of in previous decades. Fast-rising production costs, including rich contracts for star actors and technical personnel, account for what are commonly labeled "monster budgets" that by 2004 had reached an *average* of $63.6 million per film. Certain blockbusters have far exceeded this amount: *Poseidon* at $175 million, *Pirates of the Caribbean* parts one and two at $200 million each, *King Kong* at $207 million. By the late 1990s major studios such as Fox and Paramount had begun combining their resources to minimize financial risk—for example, with the costly ($200 million) production of *Titanic*. "Blockbusters" of an earlier period, such as *Gone with the Wind, Cleopatra,* and the early *Star Wars* episodes were made for a tiny fraction of such budgets. Given such bloated costs, investors are predictably less willing to risk their money on innovative, creative, or otherwise outside-the-mainstream projects, especially material that might be regarded as too "political" or "controversial." A studio executive famously lamented this state of affairs when he observed: "Rupert Murdoch isn't looking at the quality of script, I promise you. He's looking at the quality of return."[4] Intense aversion to financial risk can be disastrous for any ambitious Hollywood venture intent on challenging mainstream, formulaic approaches to filmmaking.

This predicament turns out to be even more daunting for producers of combat movies and related fare, which often require special assistance and expertise: access to military bases and equipment, use of warships, airplanes, and vehicles, Pentagon advice, stock footage, and so forth. Cost reductions made possible by this kind of support can be substantial, literally the difference between success and failure. It is difficult to imagine pictures such as *Saving Private Ryan, Black Hawk Down,* or *Pearl Harbor,* for example, coming to fruition without Pentagon support. As Lawrence Suid notes, the well-known partnership between Hollywood and the Pentagon, despite its inevitable twists and turns, has solidified over the years, with big-budget combat films depending more and more on provision of troops, equipment, technology, and historical resources (Suid, 2002, p. 2). In return for this largesse, of course, the military insists upon special treatment for its all-important operations and personnel—treatment vital to its public image and its ability to secure budgetary requests and recruitment quotas. With few exceptions, the Pentagon has supported only movies that depict courageous American troops fighting (and winning) noble wars against hated enemies—a maxim that applies, though less strictly, to comparable genres. Films that have departed from this modality—*From Here to Eternity, Apocalypse Now,* Oliver Stone's Vietnam trilogy, *Memphis Belle*—have been deprived of military support, explaining why most filmmakers today, with their swollen budgets, tend to embrace "good war" motifs and shy away from antiwar messages of the sort found in *All Quiet on the Western Front* and *Born on the Fourth of July.* Whether the advent of digital technology can relieve such pressures on producers and directors who wish to capture more "realistic" images and narratives of modern warfare remains to be seen.

Given the huge budgets needed to make high-profile mainstream films, the odds against projects with distinctly antiwar themes or narratives that focus on Pentagon misconduct, strategic blunders, misuse of funds, or botched war planning—not to mention possible atrocities or war crimes committed by U.S. forces—have risen dramatically. (Such *critical* motifs are restricted to lower-budget documentaries and small independent movies, viewed by much smaller "art-house" audiences.) After World War I a few Hollywood pictures appeared that questioned the warrior mentality and conventional ways of thinking about combat—for example, *The Big Parade* and *All Quiet on the Western Front,* both of which reached mass audiences. A similar cycle followed the intensely unpopular Vietnam War, including *The Deer Hunter, Coming Home, Platoon, Born on the Fourth of July,* and *Full Metal Jacket.* By the 1990s, however, the situation had profoundly reversed: films with even the most tepid criticisms of the U.S. military were far less likely to receive Pentagon assistance. One recent startling exception is the powerful antiwar documentary *Why We Fight,* which did receive ample Pentagon support; the brass must have believed (no doubt correctly) that the picture would never achieve much box office success. In the context of the terrorist attack on New York and the Pentagon on September 11, 2001 (9/11), the Bush presidency, preemptive warfare, and U.S. armed interventions in Afghanistan and Iraq, the political atmosphere shifted to the right, with heightened media emphasis on patriotism, the war on terror, and rallying the population against foreign enemies—hardly an atmosphere conducive to big-budget blockbusters that might challenge any or all of this. Movies such as *Black Hawk Down, Behind Enemy Lines, Under Siege, Pearl Harbor,* and *Windtalkers* are certain to be the order of the day for at least the immediate future.

The deepening militarization of American popular and political culture corresponds to the global realities of the current period: U.S. imperial power, measured in economic, political, cultural, and above all military terms, now reaches every corner of the globe, dwarfing the scope of all previous empires. Of course ruling elites want the public to believe this power is being wielded for entirely noble ends, for universal principles of freedom, democracy, and human rights, in accordance with the long-held myth of "Manifest Destiny"—a sense of imperial entitlement—but the historical actuality has always clashed with that convenient self-image. From its beginnings the United States moved inexorably along the path of colonialism, racism, and militarism, first waging the Indian Wars and conquering vast areas of Mexico, and then, following the settlement of North America, pushing outward into Latin America and Asia at the end of the Spanish-American War. For most of the twentieth century the United States was at war (or preparing for war), across the two World Wars, Korea, Vietnam, Central America, the Balkans, Afghanistan, and Iraq, with no end in sight at the start of the twenty-first century. World War II established the permanent war economy, later bringing with it a security state of epic proportions—the kind of military-industrial complex that President Dwight Eisenhower warned about at the end of his presidency.[5] By the 1990s the U.S. had firmly established itself as an unchallenged superpower backed by the largest war machine ever, with bases in 130 nations, a growing military presence in space, and consumption of more resources than all other major armed forces in the world combined.

Continued expansion of the U.S. war machine, misleadingly labeled a "defense" system, has reconfigured every dimension of American life: economy, politics, culture, social relations, the global situation. The warnings of Eisenhower and others at the time have been validated many times over. The system is sustained ideologically by the strong tradition of national "exceptionalism" reflected in Manifest Destiny, the Monroe Doctrine, a peculiarly messianic nationalism, and a long series of presidential "doctrines" endowing U.S. leaders with the right to intervene anywhere national interests are considered to be at stake. President George W. Bush's "doctrine" of preemptive war is therefore no radical departure but follows a long pattern of imperial arrogance and righteousness, backed by military force. President Jimmy Carter's State of the Union speech in 1980 contained a passage that will suffice as a typical example: "An attempt by any outside force to gain control of the Persian Gulf Region will be regarded as an assault on the vital interests of the United States of America, and such an assault will be repelled by any means necessary, including military force." In 1986 the Christian fundamentalist Pat Robertson announced that the United States was anointed to "rule the world for God," a sentiment widely held today. While politicians and the media routinely frame exceptionalism as proof that the United States is innately democratic and peaceful, in historical reality the country has always been a warrior culture propelled by the same interests as previous empires: resources, markets, cheap labor, national chauvinism, geopolitical advantage. What makes the nation so unique today is the distinctly *global* character of its interests and ambitions at a time when leading strategists are increasingly overt and brazen about the blessings of U.S. world domination. While the new grand strategy is typically attributed to the neoconservatives, in fact the events of 9/11 and the war on terror have further legitimated this imperium in the minds of liberals and conservatives, Democrats and Republicans alike. Congress has fully endorsed every step along the road to invasion and occupation of Iraq, with the media and the bulk of academia totally compliant in this brazen exercise of militarism.

Unlimited military power appears to give the majority of Americans a sense of national pride if not grandeur, something dramatically shown at the time of the first Persian Gulf War that TV and other media outlets glorified as a combat spectacle, which mobilized widespread but ersatz feelings of community and empowerment. Military supremacy, moreover, came to be equated with *moral* and *political* supremacy; armed victory both extirpated the famous "Vietnam Syndrome" (public aversion to costly foreign interventions) and reaffirmed the legacy of exceptionalism. Further, the very real threat of terrorism after 9/11 served to reinforce the long-held myth that U.S. power (by definition benevolent) was needed to overcome the chaos and violence of a Hobbesian universe filled with evildoers intent on destroying American freedom and democracy. As the Iraq venture shows, however, U.S. militarism veered entirely out of control. Reflecting on Iraq, T.D. Allman writes that we are witnessing a "systemic dysfunction in America," a colossus that "struts the world stage...on steroids" and now "poses the greatest threat to world peace" among all countries (Allman, 2004). In Iraq, the United States has carried out brazenly illegal military aggression, occupied a sovereign nation, killed an estimated hundreds of thousands of people, tortured prisoners, and wasted untold hundreds of billions of dollars in pursuit of naked resource and geopolitical interests, all with contemptuous disregard for the United Nations and justified by an endless barrage of lies and deception.

The Iraq disaster has generated little more than moderate opposition from within the political establishment; the Bush/neocon stratagem was fully endorsed by the Democratic leadership until, by mid-2006, its abject failure could no longer be ignored. This state of affairs is no aberration from the "bipartisan" pattern that held sway throughout the Cold War era. As Floyd Rumin comments: "There is something wrong at a much deeper level in American political culture. The American addiction to military power and armed interventions extends across decades, across generations, and is so deeply rooted in the American mind that attacking another nation seems to be the natural, spontaneous reaction of choice"(Rumin, 2006). Thus, recent U.S. violations of the U.N. charter outlawing unprovoked attacks on sovereign nations (not only Iraq but Afghanistan, Yugoslavia, and Panama) simply reveal longstanding U.S. contempt for the U.N. when it refuses to go along with superpower designs. The U.S. has violated or rejected a long series of international treaties and agreements concerning, for example, the militarization of space, nuclear proliferation, chemical warfare, landmine bans, and global warming. It has dismissed the International Criminal Court, supported by some 150 nations, fearful that its jurisdiction would intrude on U.S. freedom to pursue its imperial ventures. The United States has opted to set up and finance its own tribunals in The Hague and Baghdad for the purpose of trying designated enemies.

U.S. exceptionalism has increasingly been linked to the idea of "global activism" embedded in the nineteenth century frontier push westward, Theodore Roosevelt's colonial triumphalism, Woodrow Wilson's plan to "democratize" the world, the Truman Doctrine justifying intervention anywhere on U.S. terms, John F. Kennedy's Cold War liberalism, and of course Bush's strategy of preemptive war. Bush's State of the Union address in January 2006 vigorously restated this heritage: the United States is called upon by God and History to fulfill the imperatives of a global order that "would end tyranny in our world." Citing the great unique blessings of providence, Bush said that "we accept the call of history to deliver the oppressed." In his speech the president seemed fixated on purging all lingering sentiments of "isolationism" and defeatism that might impose limits on U.S. efforts to "remap" the Middle East and dominate the globe, although where such sentiments are likely to be found among the elites was never made clear. How a country so stridently interventionist across its entire history—one now wielding unprecedented global power—could possibly embrace "isolationism" strains credulity, but the fear that public opinion, tired of the risks and costs of a fraudulent war, might turn against the Iraq disaster is surely genuine.

Despite such fears, the idea that the United States has an inalienable right to rule the world by force, to frame its own doctrines, rules, and laws, remains a durable feature of the political culture. The Iraq War is just the latest manifestation of national exceptionalism, bolstered by elevated levels of economic, technological, and military strength. The principle of universality that the United States avowedly upholds is in fact violated and subverted on a regular basis (Chomsky, 2000). Invasion and occupation of nations, aerial attacks on civilian populations, support for brutal regimes and death squads, the practice of torture—all this has come to seem acceptable and readily justifiable to elites fully convinced their mission is one of peace and democracy. According to the neocon Robert Kaplan, writing in *Warrior Politics,* the American public ought to be proud of its military tradition, for that tradition is needed as the weapon of a special nation destined to fight chaos, mob rule, terrorism, and barbarism wherever it surfaces around the world. In a Hobbesian jungle, the United States is obligated to erect a powerful Leviathan that cannot be squeamish about the use of armed force. Kaplan writes: "As Machiavelli cruelly but accurately puts it, progress often comes from hurting others" (Kaplan, 2001, p. 77). Dismissing international law as utopian, he adds: "Alas, our prize for winning the Cold War is not merely the opportunity to expand NATO, or to hold democratic elections in places that never had them, but something far broader: *We and nobody else will write the terms for international society"* (Kaplan, 2001, p. 77). It would be difficult to find a bolder contemporary reaffirmation of Manifest Destiny. Elsewhere, after insisting it is time the United States extirpated, Rambo-style, all "pacifist tendencies," Kaplan argues that it is ordinary American troops on the ground who are today's global heroes battling ubiquitous evildoers on many fronts (Kaplan, 2006, p. 99).

In neocon Donald Kagan's words, "the ambition to play a grand role on the world stage is deeply rooted in the American character" (Kagan, 2003, p. 86). Like Kaplan, he sees a world of unending chaos, violence, and anarchy that U.S. military power is uniquely equipped to counter under the banner of modern civilization. The problem with European nations today, writes Kagan, is their reluctance to use armed force toward this end, preferring instead the security of the "U.S. umbrella" and the strange preference for social over military spending. Thus: "Europeans have stepped out of the Hobbesian world of anarchy into the Kantian world of perpetual peace" (Kagan, 2003, p. 57). In other words, the Europeans have gotten mired in pure fantasy, quite at odds with the "realistic" outlook of Americans familiar with a long history of imperial expansion and military intervention. With such hubris, unfortunately, there are few psychological or military limits. In his frenzied support of the Iraq War, Christopher Hitchens refers approvingly to Bush's goal of "regime change," which "has come to mean less and less a secondhand involvement in a proxy struggle waged by other people, and more and more a direct and avowed engagement in the enterprise of invading and then remaking someone else's country" (Hitchens, 2003, p. 48). This kind of imperialist mentality, made recently fashionable by the neocons, may have been invented by Bush or even the neocons, but, as we have seen, it has the imprimatur of many Bush predecessors. In 1844 President James Polk outrageously instigated war against Mexico, lied about threats to U.S. security, and waged preemptive attacks to steal half of Mexican lands, all in the name of national progress. More than a century later, liberal icon John F. Kennedy inspired a new wave of U.S. global activism: "Other countries look to their own interests. Only the United States has obligations which stretch 10,000 miles across the Pacific, and 4000 miles across the Atlantic, and thousands of miles to the South. Only the U.S....bears that kind of burden."[6] Precisely who or what endowed the United States with such far-reaching burdens Kennedy never specified. It was Kennedy, of course, who set in motion the Vietnam War, one of the great catastrophes of modern times.

To the degree that war and orientation toward war have become a way of life in the United States, the society can be said to have grown addicted to war, above all economically but also politically and culturally. It takes little effort to see that Empire manifests itself domestically as well as internationally, all the more so since 9/11. Bush and the neocons, after all, have promised an endless, protracted war on evildoers spread around the world. As with the example of Rome and later empires, the pursuit of imperial domination has enduring consequences: vast funding for a war machine, staggering human and material costs of intervention, blowback, consolidation of a security state, subversion of democratic values and practices, widespread civic violence, and the decay of public infrastructures as recently dramatized by the Hurricane Katrina debacle. Meanwhile, an aggressive war system creates more enemies abroad (blowback), *undermining* instead of reinforcing national security. A militarized society and political system, moreover, narrows public debate, stalling any popular efforts to counter deteriorating social conditions. Neal Wood refers to the "tyranny of advanced capitalism" in the United States that "imposes its will and discipline initially in the workplace. Then it penetrates and seizes control over the political apparatus. The victim of capitalist tyranny, America is neither substantively nor procedurally a democracy in any very meaningful sense of the term" (Wood, 2004, p.141). He adds that the vacuity of national politics means "numerous fundamental questions in domestic and international politics require urgent attention, informed discussion and speedy resolution, but...little is being done" (Wood, 2004, pp. 1123–124).

Since at least the late 1970s, American elites have worked strenuously to extend the doctrine of Manifest Destiny across the entire globe, premised on a strategy of first controlling the Middle East in order to secure a resource and geopolitical foothold. This gambit was facilitated by the Soviet exit from the world scene in 1991, an epochal moment that happened to coincide with the first Gulf War. The famous "New World Order" enunciated by President George H. W. Bush at that time would be a unipolar globe dominated by the United States, with American power making the world safe for unfettered neoliberal globalization. By the 1990s the United States was indeed the first truly unrivalled imperial power, its every move calculated to negate possible future challengers: Russia, China, Europe, Japan. The goal of world domination was clearly laid out in a series of government and quasi-official documents and statements beginning in the early 1990s, with military action against Iraq a taken-for-granted priority always placed at the top of the agenda. By "remapping" the Middle East the United States would gain a stranglehold over oil and other resources at a time of both growing demand and declining supply worldwide. This "new imperialism," resting increasingly on *military* power, was taken up not only by the neocon hawks but by leaders of both major parties. Within this scenario, as the United States arrogantly pursues global hegemony in a Hobbesian cauldron of chaos and violence, the distinction between war and peace, armed engagement and politics-as-usual, begins to disintegrate, as militarism and "terrorism" now have the impetus to spread to all regions of the planet.

At a time of expanding U.S. imperial power, when the American people are asked to endure burdensome costs and sacrifices, the always-vital mechanisms of legitimation take on new meaning. All power structures need systemic ideological and cultural supports, or "hegemony" along the lines theorized by Antonio Gramsci, but the imperatives of Empire serve to ultimately intensify these ordinary requirements. Empire, a bloated war economy, constant armed interventions—all this must be made to appear "natural," routine, and desirable if not noble. Themes of national exceptionalism, superpatriotism, the glories of high-tech war, and the demands of a (global) civilizing mission help satisfy this legitimation function, as does the impenetrable hubris associated with economic, technological, and military supremacy. To translate such an ideological syndrome into popular language, to fully incorporate it into the political culture, is the task not so much of a classical propaganda apparatus but of a developed educational system and media culture appropriate to advanced capitalism. In the United States today, as we have seen, media culture is an extension of megacorporations that comprise the largest and most influential media-entertainment complex the world has ever seen. And the Hollywood War Machine has become increasingly central to this complex—a crucial instrument for the legitimation of Empire.

The U.S. plan for global domination brings with it a growing concentration of corporate, government, and military power surrounded by a refined law-enforcement and surveillance apparatus that, while in some ways indispensable, cannot by itself possibly furnish legitimation. That is the function of media culture. Hollywood filmmaking contributes admirably to this function, despite the release of pictures here and there that run counter to the dominant paradigm. Legitimation occurs not primarily by means of censorship or propaganda (though both exist) but through ordinary canons and formulas of studio production, where "conspiracies" are scarcely necessary to enforce hegemonic codes. The repetitive fantasies, illusions, myths, images, and story lines of Hollywood movies can be expected to influence mass audiences in predictable ways, much in the fashion of advertising. One popular response to the flood of violent combat, action/adventure, sci-fi, and horror films is a stronger readiness to support U.S. military operations which, in a patriotically charged milieu, will require little justification. (Indeed the popular ethical standards for what constitutes a "rational" armed intervention are scandalously loose.) This aspect of legitimation is unique to American foreign policy, the only nation in the world with a sprawling network of military bases around the world.

To be sure, complex societies have many agencies of politicization, but none today rivals the power of media culture. As Douglas Kellner points out: "Media culture spectacles demonstrate who has power and who is powerless, who is allowed to exercise force and violence, and who is not. They dramatize and legitimate the power of the forces that be and demonstrate to the powerless that if they fail to conform, they risk incarceration or death" (Kellner, 1995, p. 2). It is a culture overwhelmingly geared toward young people—not only film but TV, video games, and music—whose social views are in their formative stage and thus highly impressionable. That such views might be partial, uneven, and lacking in coherence hardly detracts from their *intensity,* which often achieves its peak around issues of patriotism and use of military force. The corporate media routinely translate U.S. imperial agendas into deeply felt popular beliefs and attitudes about the world and the American role in it, usually validating something akin to the motif of Manifest Destiny. Despite its liberal image, therefore, Hollywood tends to produce expensive, high-tech, entertaining movies that, directly or indirectly, help satisfy the ideological requirements for Empire. One might go further: Owing to powerful tendencies within the general culture, the once-prevailing liberal tradition itself appears to have lost its significant hold on public opinion as it collapses into the new conservative hegemony.[7]

We concede that it is difficult to measure the precise impact of any media form on the popular consciousness; the available instruments are much too crude and the social mediations too numerous. We can, however, identify with some specificity the particular *content* of films and other media forms, which can be investigated and decoded just as we would literature and other texts or discourses, and that is the very task we have set for ourselves in this project. We assume, further, that the societal influence of movies and related forms we subsume under the heading "Hollywood War Machine" has been, and probably will continue to be, quite substantial. We are convinced this is true for several reasons: huge audiences, the seductions of modern cinematic technology, the intersection between film content and what is conveyed by other media, including advertising, and the common-sense observation that what people are exposed to as a steady diet will inevitably shape their beliefs and attitudes. At the same time, as mentioned earlier, insofar as teenage audiences are the main target of blockbuster marketing they are more likely to psychologically *assimilate* whatever ideological motifs a film conveys than would be the case for older audiences. We have abundant indicators—increased levels of violent youth crime, gang membership, gun ownership, and civil clashes, for example—that suggest that the familiar "culture of violence" has intensified over the past two decades, a theme running through Michael Moore's documentary *Bowling for Columbine,* which also looks at the contributing role of the warfare state. We should not be surprised to find a correlation between these indicators and elevated public support for U.S. armed ventures abroad. By mid-2006, it is true, public opposition to the Iraq War had galvanized, but most questioning stemmed from the escalating *costs* of a war and occupation viewed as a failure rather than any political or moral revulsion, that is, any principled antiwar stance. While antiwar sentiment did crystallize in late 2002 and early 2003, as the Bush

Administration moved resolutely toward war, the momentum abated by the summer of 2003 and the sentiment scarcely made a dent in the armor of the political establishment.

What generalizations, then, might be formulated regarding films that we have identified as part of the Hollywood War Machine? Although the images, narratives, and ideological motifs we explore diverge enormously from one picture to another, from one genre to another, several basic themes clearly emerge from our analysis:

- U.S. military forces are innately driven by noble ends, an assumption so embedded in movie images and narratives it rarely demands much overt articulation within the script. While this is a distinctly "good war" staple, it applies to *any* combat activity (broadly defined) where it can be shown that evil demons must be vanquished by American troops. Even in films that convey the "war is hell" theme (*Black Hawk Down, Saving Private Ryan, The Thin Red Line*), we see that larger American objectives create the very *necessity* of war, justifying all the painful costs and sacrifices.

- Enemy forces are routinely shown as primitive and barbaric—Nazis and Japs in World War II, gooks in Korea and Vietnam, ragheads in the Gulf War—a cinematic portrait often infused with strong elements of racism and national chauvinism. In terrorist-themed pictures, Arabs are with few exceptions shown as subhuman agents of destruction lacking any motive or purpose.[8] Like the Indians of Western movie lore, opposition to U.S. military power is seen as the work of cartoonish, one-dimensional male warriors whose very mission is to visit evil on the world. In the form of demons, moreover, such figures are easily dehumanized, making them ready fodder for mass extermination, as graphically depicted in such films as *Sands of Iwo Jima* and *Windtalkers*).

- U.S. military forces inevitably triumph, often against insurmountable odds, even if a few lesser skirmishes are lost in the meantime. In "good war" scenarios American troops will commonly be outnumbered but manage to prevail owing to superior guile and ability, better technology, perhaps embellished by acts of John Wayne–style heroism, visible, for example, in *Hamburger Hill.* Even terrible *defeats* have been transformed by Hollywood into improbable victories—for example, *Pearl Harbor* (shifting the focus to the daring Doolittle Raid on Tokyo) and Rambo's Vietnam ("we get to win this time!").

- In contrast to typically faceless and often disheveled enemy forces, U.S. officers and enlisted men are shown as belonging to a well-organized national military structure, bound by strong leadership, discipline, order, and dedication—features that lend Americans an aura of efficiency and authority. Chaos and disarray are traits linked to backwardness, while strong organization is tied to "progress" and enlightened values. Even the most heroic actions are mediated through the military command system, as in *Saving Private Ryan* and *U-571.* One rare exception is *Behind Enemy Lines,* where a downed navy pilot is forced to survive on hostile terrain, cut off from his supporting units.

◻ Supreme military technology always prevails over weaker (though possibly more numerous) enemy troops, a maxim carried over from hundreds of combat Westerns designed to show the "primitive" character of Indians in their resistance to white-settler modernity—a motif emphatically repeated when the designated opponent is Arab. Advanced technology is equated not only with elevated moral status but with an epic victory of "civilization" over barbaric enemies—a trope permeating films about the Pacific Theater in World War II and later representations of Asians in Korea and Vietnam.[9] The Gulf War media spectacle referred to earlier fits this pattern, from the first U.S. aerial blitz in 1991 to the "shock-and-awe" campaign of 2003.

◻ Despite its horrors, war crosses the big screen as an exhilarating human activity—the most noble and even existential of all personal experiences, filtered through larger-than-life visual images made possible by the wonders of modern cinematography, including digital imaging. The more the nightmares of combat are presented as visually graphic and beautified by special effects, the more they seem to appeal to mass audiences. This aesthetic dimension of warfare is realized through several devices: dazzling technology, triumph of good over evil, exotic locales, breathtaking heroism. Here the Hollywood War Machine marks a unique culmination of the merger between war and entertainment, combat and art, which turns out to be yet another manifestation of the cinematic society.

◻ It is by now an axiom that Hollywood effortlessly turns warfare into a media spectacle—a tendency shared with TV and video games, all beneficiaries of much the same technology. Violence and bloodshed, the inevitable price of military victory, become the stuff of cinematic overkill, whether in the hands of Tony Scott or Oliver Stone, Edward Zwick or Stanley Kubrick. The war spectacle is best exemplified by the work of Steven Spielberg, the master not only of the combat genre (*Empire of the Sun, Saving Private Ryan,* etc.) but of related fare such as *Indiana Jones* and *War of the Worlds.* If scenarios of death and destruction are the inescapable fruits of Empire, they are simultaneously the stock-in-trade of Hollywood blockbusters, both mirroring and contributing to the irrepressible culture of militarism.

◻ As the war phenomenon becomes a sacralized feature of American society—that is, as violent campaigns attached to "higher" values (democracy, freedom, human rights, etc.) take on a quasi-religious meaning—cinematic heroism too comes to occupy a special niche in the culture. Hundreds of mainstream films depict glamorous, courageous military leaders able to storm the heavens and remake the world, or at least make the world "safe" for all the wonderful "American" virtues to flourish. Examples are not difficult to find: John Wayne, Patton, Rambo, the Terminator, Top Gun. Combat heroism, moreover, is often fueled by motives of vengeance as the protagonist sets out to punish wrongdoers for some earlier transgression or atrocity, as in the *Rambo* films.

◻ Patriotism, most often represented as jingoism, or ultrapatriotism, is a defining feature of the Hollywood War Machine, above all the "good war" cycle long a favorite subgenre of studio filmmakers. If, as Chris Hedges argues, "war is a force that gives us meaning," it does so mainly by virtue of the viewer's psychological attachment to the nation and its ascribed identities or missions (Hedges, 2002). Indeed, the most emotionally compelling images of patriotism usually appear with the war setting. (Think of the billowing American flag that crosses the screen at the end of *Saving Private Ryan* or the planting of the flag on Mount Suribachi in *Sands of Iwo Jima.*) The modern film experience lends itself to the kinds of psychological responses that such scenes are calculated to instill, and few are more cathartic than nationalism. Empire, the security state, the permanent war economy, the warrior mythology—none of these could be sustained in the absence of patriotic legitimation. After all, the twentieth century showed that both war and patriotism endow otherwise powerless individuals with a sense of being able to achieve something in a difficult and confining world. Hedges refers to the "plague of nationalism" as providing something of a false communal enterprise, and this must be considered one of the signal contributions of the cinematic society.

Among scores of Hollywood films dealing with military-related themes, few will exhibit *all* of these motifs; the vast majority, however, will be seen to contain most of them, with inevitable consequences for how Americans think about U.S. foreign and military policy—and about their own society. The point here is that such a wide panorama of militarized images and narratives, visible across several decades, has contributed deeply to the popular acceptance of Empire. The Hollywood War Machine, we argue, remains a dominant feature of the American landscape at the start of the twenty-first century—a logical parallel to the permanent war system, with its frightening prospects for world peace. The blockbuster as larger-than-life media spectacle takes on a special role in all this. We concede that a number of important mainstream films stand apart from the dominant pattern, witness the antiwar pictures that now and then cross the cinematic terrain—for example, *Born on the Fourth of July* and, in a different vein, *The Thin Red Line.* Some embrace the "war is hell" motif. We conclude, however, that the influence of such films is dwarfed by the much larger output of motion pictures that fit the prevailing norm, often wind up reproducing elements of the war spectacle, given their embrace of standard cinematic devices for conveying the "realism" of warfare.

Can it be said that the Hollywood War Machine, having come to fruition during an age of Empire, operates essentially as a *propaganda* apparatus that sends out crude messages to gullible mass audiences on the model of earlier authoritarian regimes? The popular consensus behind U.S. militarism, revealed again during the invasion and occupation of Iraq, might well be viewed as evidence for the propaganda model. David Robb, in his book *Operation Hollywood,* argues for this point of view, suggesting that the film industry has become a full-blown propaganda vehicle, one of the most powerful opinion-forming mechanisms ever known. (Robb's work is limited strictly to motion pictures.) We know that "propaganda" is supposed to be alien to the American experience, but Robb convincingly describes a process that is largely unseen by the public where blatant political messages in support of Pentagon interests are regularly and brazenly transmitted to viewers fully convinced they are getting nothing more than "entertainment." Thus, "...the military propaganda that is inserted into our television programs in the form of films and TV shows is done so subtly the American people don't even know it's there" (Robb, 2004, p. 365). The undeniable fact that the U.S. has grown more warlike over the past 50 years is cited by Robb as validation of a sophisticated propaganda model.

Robb is surely correct to emphasize the growth of efforts at ideological manipulation in American society over the past few decades, a trend surely accelerated by the events of 9/11 not to mention the expansion of media culture. He is also on the mark when he points to the increased public readiness to endorse U.S. military ventures, again more easily understood with the onset of Bush's war on terror. At the same time, whether the film medium as such can be described as a propaganda outlet is yet another matter. While some pictures might well fit this model, and many clearly bear the imprint of Pentagon influence, our conclusions in the following pages depart significantly from Robb's: filmmakers, most of them already immersed in the political culture and the canons of patriotism, typically do not require formal government censorship or controls as they look to produce movies that fit the contours of U.S. foreign and military policy—nor do they in fact need or prefer heavy-handed brainwashing techniques than can only run counter to entertainment values (and thus box office prospects). For producers like Jerry Bruckheimer and directors like Michael Bay, patriotic war spectacles are merely business as usual at the Hollywood studios. The motifs we have identified simply flow with the cinematic-political terrain. Many filmmakers who are ordinarily inclined toward liberal or progressive scripts on *domestic* issues often suddenly lose that same critical edge once matters reach the water's edge: Patriotism nearly always trumps progressivism when it comes to global politics. There is nothing particularly surprising or even novel about this—it is simply enough to consult the earlier cases of John Ford, Howard Hawks, and Frank Capra, all strong liberals who would never be outdone in their celebration of patriotic warrior virtues.

The expanded role of propaganda *outside* Hollywood cinema, not to be denied, actually ends up reinforcing the capacity of motion pictures to help ideologically bolster Empire and the war system. Movies could be even more effective instruments than outright propaganda. In his provocative *The War on Truth,* Nafeez Mossadeq Ahmed writes: "A massive external threat is an ideally convenient excuse to consolidate and expand U.S. hegemony, further counter Russian, Chinese, and European rivals, and to drum up the domestic consensus required to legitimate the unrelentingly interventionist character of U.S. foreign policy in the new and unlimited 'war on terror'" (Ahmed, 2005, pp. 364–365). What Ahmed describes converges with yet another trend—the corporate colonization of a political system that increasingly operates as little more than an organized machine in the service of narrow elite interests. The operation relies heavily on ideological manipulation and combines the work of diverse sectors: party elites, corporations, media, the government, lobbies, and assortment of think tanks and foundations (Brock, 2004). In this corporatist milieu what has historically been called "propaganda" extends across the entire social and political landscape. In polls conducted during and after the Bush buildup to the Iraq War, for example, a strong majority of Americans was shown to believe the repeated outlandish lies and justifications behind the invasion. In fact the whole stratagem of "regime change" was stage-managed by the government and military, with nearly total media complicity. In the field, reporters were "embedded" and muzzled, fully beholden to Pentagon agendas, while those few outside the patriotic stable were often targeted and in many cases assaulted or killed. Framing of the Iraq War as a moment of "liberation" represents the pinnacle of a media culture bringing together war and entertainment in pursuit of corporate profits, the subject of such documentaries as Robert Greenwald's *Outfoxed* and Danny Schechter's *Weapons of Mass Deception.*

James Bamford has documented the trail of propaganda that paved the way toward a war that Bush and the neocons had decided to launch months and even years before the March 2003 invasion, indeed well before 9/11. The Pentagon, CIA, and White House utilized the sprawling public relations network of The Rendon Group to carry out "perception management" of epic proportions, helping establish the ideological conditions for war against Iraq despite lack of U.N. authorization and absence of any clear threat posed by the Saddam Hussein regime. The campaign depended on large-scale saturation of the media with false reports, lies, distortions, and a variety of contrived pro-war stories with the collaboration of writers like Judith Miller of *The New York Times.* Bamford writes that "never before in history had such an extensive secret network been established to shape the entire world's perception of a war" (Bamford, 2005, p. 61). That is not all: with the U.S. occupation in full force, it was revealed that Pentagon contractors regularly paid Iraqi newspapers to publish glowing stories about the war and the role of U.S. troops as benevolent "liberators"—a propaganda enterprise, though costly, completely hidden from the American public. The Washington D.C.-based Lincoln Group was given tens of millions of dollars to infiltrate the Iraq media over a period of nearly two years. The war, from the outset unpopular around the world, was conducted within a framework of sustained domestic and international media manipulation. Its initial ideological success, at least on the home front, cannot be doubted, but the protracted occupation and insurgency—along with continuous revelations of flagrant Bush Administration deceit—began to erode even domestic supports for a costly and losing intervention.

In the aforementioned 2005 documentary *Why We Fight,* Eugene Jarecki builds his indictment of the U.S. war system on President Eisenhower's 1961 warning about the dangers of an out-of-control military-industrial complex, which by now comes across as rather understated. Neither Eisenhower nor Jarecki, however, call attention to a crucial pillar of the system—a militarized popular culture that has only deepened over the past few decades. If the Hollywood War Machine does not fully constitute a modern propaganda apparatus, its role in the legitimation process no doubt equals or even *surpasses* that of any such apparatus since its spectacular images and narratives, produced and marketed as "entertainment," probably turn out to be more effective than any heavy-handed attempts at media censorship and control. Meanwhile, the big studio productions, part of a thriving cinematic culture, have become integral to the very state-corporate order that underlies both the film industry and Eisenhower's nightmare of a military-industrial complex.

■ Postscript—2008

In the nearly three years since *The Hollywood War Machine* appeared, the main trends we identified in that book—escalating incidents of civic violence, rapid expansion of the Pentagon war machine, an imperialistic foreign policy, militarized popular culture—show no signs of receding. The markers are rather difficult to miss: two continuous, bloody wars of occupation in Iraq and Afghanistan, stepped-up "war on terrorism," threats of a U.S. armed attack on Iran, nuclear buildup, and growing security-state power at a time of recurrent domestic mass killings, sustained high levels of crime, a sprawling prison-industrial complex, and a media culture more saturated with violence than ever. Nothing here will surprise anyone vaguely familiar with the decaying American social and political scene. After all, by 2007 the United States was spending roughly $600 billion annually to feed its Pentagon colossus, not counting hundreds of billions (perhaps trillions) more on the Iraq debacle—expenditures reaching nearly *three-fifths* of the world total, dwarfing such competitors as Russia (all of $21 billion), China ($81 billion), and North Korea (a menacing five billion dollars). To maintain its unchallenged military supremacy, the Pentagon has established ten unified command structures covering most of the planet. Since no country or empire in world history has even approached this scope of military power, it would be astonishing if the system did not operate nonstop to invest that power with maximum domestic popular support, without which the burdensome risks and costs of war (and preparation for war) would surely be rejected by the general population. Lacking much in the way of a state propaganda apparatus in the United States, these ideological functions inevitably become the province of the corporate media and popular culture.

As might be expected, therefore, the militarized culture we analyzed in *The Hollywood War Machine*—transmitted not only through movies but related fare such as video games and TV—is today even more deeply entrenched in the social order. Is it a stark coincidence that the most successful and widely viewed films of 2007–08, including many nominated for Oscars, embrace dark images of savage, often relentless violence, graphic depictions of killing, and celebrations of social chaos against familiar narrative backdrops of hatred, betrayal, and revenge? Movies such as *No Country for Old Men, There Will be Blood, American Gangster,* and *Michael Clayton* highlight a violence that both *reflects* and *influences* the popular zeitgeist, the sort of dialectic we emphasize in our book. Commenting on the 2008 Academy Awards, Patrick Goldstein, writing in the *Los Angeles Times,* observes: "Today, the fallout from the war in Iraq seems to have inspired a new wave of violence-tinged films." Of course Iraq is just the latest U.S. military venture to influence the national psyche in this manner.

Mainstream cinema, today as in the past, provides an enormous public forum within which politics and culture readily converge. Not surprisingly, the Hollywood war machine has moved into full gear, capitalizing on the post-9/11 American sense of a wounded, vengeful, but still very militaristic nation prepared to take on the evildoers. A few cinematic examples will suffice here. Irwin Winkler's *Home of the Brave* (2007) tells the story of four courageous American soldiers at the end of their Iraq tours of duty, sent on one final humanitarian mission to a remote Iraqi village. The unit is ambushed, taking heavy losses—part of a narrative showing how well-intentioned U.S. troops are suddenly torn from good deeds by a scheming, ruthless enemy. In Peter Berg's *The Kingdom* (2007), we encounter a team of U.S. government agents sent to investigate the terrorist bombing of an American facility in Riyadh, Saudi Arabia, where frenetic attempts are made to locate and flush out Arab madmen from their underground cells. In a final battle between good guys and bad guys at the entrance to a hideout, it is the good guys (led by FBI agents) who prevail against impossible odds. Jesse Johnson's *The Last Sentinel* (2007) depicts a group of super-soldiers, perfect warriors, assigned to protect "civilization" against swarms of devious evildoers, although in this saga the heroes depend on electronic enhancement to ensure success. In *Terminator*-style action the good warriors learn to think and behave like machines for the epic struggle to save the human race. In Henry Crum's *Crash Point* (2006) a Strike Force team faces off against terrorists who have stolen a ground control encoder that permits someone to take over a plane by remote control. The (Muslim) terrorists plan to crash a jetliner into a secret U.S. military intelligence base in Southeast Asia. The Strike Force unit must locate and destroy the encoder to foil the terrorists and, in the process, avert a new world war. They manage to succeed. Peter Travis's box office hit *Vantage Point* (2008) depicts the assassination of a U.S. president attending (what else?) a global war-on-terrorism summit in Spain. With the evildoers mercilessly attacking the very citadel of American power, the crowd goes into shock and panic as the drama unfolds repeatedly from different angles. This Manicheistic drama was heavily promoted as a cinematic message on new threats to global order by evil forces that seem omnipresent. In *Live Free or Die Hard* (2007), Len Wiseman brings to the screen a reprise of the *Die Hard* pictures featuring Bruce Willis as New York City police detective John McClane, here taking on (and defeating) a group of sinister high-tech terrorists ready to hack into and bring down U.S. computer systems.

In our book we explored ultrapatriotic warrior motifs that go well beyond the combat genre as such—a pattern that remains visible today. In *The Hunting Party* (2007), directed by Richard Shepard, we have a documentary-style drama based on four reporters' search for an at-large war criminal in Bosnia, as they hunt down a group of Serb outlaws, those same "ethnic cleansers" whom 79 days of U.S./NATO aerial bombardments in spring 1999 were meant to neutralize. Advertised heavily by the U.S. State Department and marketed as the "story of a lifetime," the movie ends with three of the journalists, anxious for revenge, locating a Serbian war criminal and decide to inflict their own brand of justice on the spot. This formulaic plot takes us to a setting (the Balkans) where U.S. and NATO geopolitical interests happened to be threatened by the bad guys, in this case barbaric Serbs. Oliver Stone's *World Trade Center* (2006) focuses on the terror, death, and chaos following the 9/11 attacks, turning the ultimate national catastrophe into an uplifting moment of heroism and patriotism. Stone's picture, in which the erstwhile critic of U.S. militarism turns into a cheerleader of American power, won effusive praise from both mainstream and rightwing pundits.

In the popular film *Transformers* (2007), Michael Bay revisits his fascination with technowar in a movie riveted on combat between opposing robotic forces, the noble and heroic Autobats versus the evil Decepticons, repelled as they assault a U.S. military base in Qatar. A big, loud, violent film that grossed $700 million in American theaters, *Transformers* was quickly turned into another profitable combat video game. *Rescue Dawn* (2007) was released as Werner Herzog's cinematic tribute to U.S. fighter pilots shot down on a mission over Laos during the Vietnam War—a recycling of *Behind Enemy Lines* where the narrative revolves around brave U.S. military personnel taken prisoner by an enemy, in this case the faceless and brutal Vietnamese. Similarly, Tony Bill's *Flyboys* (2006) traces the adventures of American fighter pilots (the first in history) as they volunteer to help the French military defeat the Germans during World War I. While these pictures deal only peripherally with military combat, they embellish familiar militaristic themes: male heroism, battlefield camaraderie, superpatriotism, violent struggle of good against evil, noble U.S. objectives, and glorification of high-tech warfare.

Two recent films deserve special attention for their embrace of strong pro-military themes and their capacity to reach large audiences with messages celebrating U.S. imperial goals: *Rambo IV* (2008), referred to simply as *Rambo*, directed by the iconic Sylvester Stallone himself, and *Charlie Wilson's War* (2007), directed by the stalwart Mike Nichols. Revisiting the three original *Rambo* pictures (1982, 1985, 1988), it would be hard to find a warrior hero better exemplifying the virtues of American militarism and imperialism, superseding even John Wayne. Here again, the battlefield focus is Vietnam (for which "Burma" is an obvious stand-in), which the film strives mightily to transform into a "good war" that popular audiences will come to realize was a lost chance for U.S. victory. Rambo did indeed return to Hollywood after a long hiatus, ready almost singlehandedly to take on all enemies as he maneuvers through a minefield of bureaucrats, liberals, and weak patriots needing a lesson in masculine warrior politics. The renovated Rambo works to rescue Burmese medical personnel in the midst of civil war, forced to repel an enemy so barbaric that nothing less than maximum violence will suffice. Of course Rambo is more than up to the task, killing with relentless and often creative brutality. A cartoonish figure, Rambo emerges nonetheless as mythological hero, American to the core, whose efficacy (and appeal) depends on bringing continuous death and destruction to the evildoers. The film enjoyed great box office success, especially among boys, young males, and even older men frequently heard cheering every blood-soaked scene. In his review of the movie critic Peter Rainer wrote: "I saw the film on its opening night in a mostly filled theater where every splatter was greeted with whoops...When his [Stallone's] scowl hit the screen, the audiences went wild, knowing that carnage could not be very far away." The audiences had plenty of opportunities, no question. No fewer than 236 human beings were brutally killed in this *Rambo* (or 2.59 per minute of footage), compared with measly totals of 69 and 132 for episodes two and three, respectively. In one of the great movie tributes to militarized violence ever, people were bombed, blasted, stabbed, shot, blown up by grenades, incinerated by fire or flamethrowers, bludgeoned, stomped, beaten, beheaded, and tossed out of aircraft. Rambo alone killed 83 bad guys, perhaps not a record but surely enough to earn his reputation as "the beast." Some have suggested that Rambo might have returned just in the nick of time, since he is the one figure who could deliver victory out of defeat in the latest futile American imperial venture, Iraq.

Turning to *Charlie Wilson's War,* we find a somewhat more nuanced, though still blatant, rendering of well-intentioned U.S. global designs in another strategic region—this time Afghanistan, where in the 1980s the CIA gave massive aid to rightwing Mujahedeen rebels fighting the wicked Soviet Union. Based very roughly on true events, Nichols's film depicts a maverick Texas congressman, Wilson, as he boldly circumvents political and bureaucratic obstacles to provide covert support for "freedom fighters" to "liberate" their Afghan homeland. While the narrative does show American operatives dealing with fascists, tyrants, and drug traffickers in their Cold War era obsession with bringing down the Soviet regime, it also radically distorts history—and simply omits essential context— where it really matters.

Charlie Wilson's War begins by showing the Mujahedeen as idealistic fighters for all that is good and just in the world, as saviors of human freedom when in fact it was these same fighters—forerunners of the Taliban and Al Qaeda—who upheld, then as now, a virulent jihadic fascism. The Mujahedeen were championed by the U.S. simply because they opposed Communist power. The problem is that the film actually obscures this deep, and very troubling, historical connection, while the supposed beacons of liberty were shown to be childlike in their innocence and helplessness (only to be rescued by U.S. largesse). Nichols frames his narrative, consistent with Pentagon and CIA mythology, around the fiction that U.S. intervention can serve admirably to liberate or "civilize" backward peoples desperately looking for just the right tutelage and assistance. And in fact we see American personnel in the field working for humanitarian goals, while the brutal Soviets are shown deliberately blowing away retreating Afghan civilians. The operation naturally depends on the tenacity of a few good Americans, working almost Rambo-style, to overcome one hurdle after another in order to dispose of the Soviet villains. The legacy of "Charlie Wilson's War," however, has turned rather sour as Afghanistan today remains occupied by another power (the U.S.) and has degenerated into a cauldron of warlordism, chaos, drug trafficking, and violence.

As the militarization of media culture proceeds—keeping pace with similar trends in the larger society and foreign policy—some observers appear to take everything in stride, no doubt realizing that violence has been central to the American experience. Others, like the neoconservatives, might be expected to revel in such developments even as they prattle on about peace and rule of law. There are film critics who apparently "see" what is taking place but refuse to make connections between media content and social reality, as if both exist in a vacuum, disconnected from each other. One such example is a review of *The Hollywood War Machine* by Lawrence Suid and Michael Shull in the journal *Film and History* (Fall 2007). Suid is the author of *Guts and Glory,* a massive volume on war movies bursting with encyclopedic information on the filmmaking process but lacking much in the way of historical and political understanding.[10] The review scolds us for arguing that particular cycles of Hollywood films intersect with U.S. militarism, stating we "have written a polemic which accuses Hollywood of creating and perpetuating a martial spirit in the American people" and that we falsely conclude "the film industry harbors rightwing conservative patriots." Nailing down their critique, the reviewers add that "no film portraying the Vietnam War, except for perhaps *The Green Berets,* attempted to glorify or justify the conflict. *We Were Soldiers Once* [sic] saluted the bravery of the soldiers but certainly not the war."

The review appears to be part misreading of our book, part deliberate obfuscation, part ignorance about the recent developments in American politics. In fact *The Hollywood War Machine* never argues for any mechanistic cause-and-effect relationship between movies and politics, affirming rather a *dialectical* relationship between the two: media culture simultaneously *reflects* and *influences* the larger social arena. There is no compelling reason to exempt media representations of violence, warfare, and militarism that have become so endemic to American life—or, if there is, Suid and Shull ought to let us in on the secret. Moreover, we never define this phenomenon as a "martial spirit," choosing instead to address the steady diffusion of film images, narratives, and motifs that, to varying degrees, enter into popular consciousness, social life, and political behavior. Right-wing conservative patriots in Hollywood? There might well be a few such Neanderthals hanging around the studios, but the real problem is that "liberals" and even "progressives" are the main contributors to the patriotic and militaristic content we identify throughout our book. From the critical-analytical standpoint we adopt, distinctions between liberals and conservatives tend to vanish, especially on questions of foreign and military policy. Thus, war-making as such in the postwar United States has been the handiwork of liberal Democrats at least as often as "rightwing conservative patriots" such as Richard Nixon and the Bushes. The same goes for filmmaking: Suid and Shull ought to know that such directors as Steven Spielberg, Francis Ford Coppola, Oliver Stone, George Lucas, Edward Zwick, and Ridley Scott—all widely discussed in our book—are well-known Hollywood liberals. The reviewers might also recall that John Ford, director of many gung-ho, patriotic World War II films, was enough of a domestic populist to make pictures like *The Grapes of Wrath.*

In their refusal to acknowledge linkages between media and politics, between the film industry and larger society of which it is a dynamic part, Suid and Shull end up with a narrow, mechanistic, one-dimensional view of Hollywood. Do they really want to insist that movies and kindred media products (TV, video games, the Internet, advertising, etc.) have no impact on the ideas, beliefs, myths, and lifestyles of hundreds of millions of people buying these products from morning to night? Could political life be impervious to the incessant flow of visual images and social messages disseminated by the most powerful, far-reaching media complex in human history? Highly improbable, when one looks at the character of American social life today. Could it be that media representations of violence, war, and militarism enjoy a special dispensation here? Even less likely, and indeed Suid himself appears to concede this point when, in *Guts and Glory,* he notes dryly that "films can influence audiences" (Suid, 2002, p. xiii). In fact Suid goes much further in his tribute to John Wayne as the great American cinematic war hero. He writes that, largely on the basis of Wayne's role in *Sands of Iwo Jima,* Americans found a man who personified the ideal soldier, sailor, or Marine, whose "military image [continues]…to pervade American society and culture" (Suid, 2002, p. 116). According to Suid, Wayne "did become the symbol of the American fighting man, the defender of the nation," adding that "Wayne became the model of the action hero for several generations of young males, representing the traditional American ideal of the anti-intellectual doer in contrast to the thinker." Indeed Wayne "became just as much a military hero, a frontier hero, and a supporter of God, country, and motherhood" as other traditional U.S. icons, while

"Marines often cited Wayne's portrayal of [Sergeant] Stryker as the reason for their attraction to the Corps" (Suid, 2002, pp. 129–130). Suid notes that journalists covering the Vietnam War attested to the power of Wayne's influence on U.S. troops, concluding: "Wayne's influence reached not only enlisted men but also the decision makers and officers in the field" (Suid, 2002, p. 132). This is one of the finest validations we could find for our work in *The Hollywood War Machine*.

So even for such conservative reviewers as Suid and Shull the real question ought to be not whether but rather *how* and *to what extent* the content of motion pictures and other media forms influence mass publics. Contrary to the simplistic view put forth by Suid and Shull, influence moves along different lines—people might take initiative or leadership in violent behavior, they might actively participate as followers, they might lend their (ideological) support, they might simply go along out of indifference, possibly desensitized to the constant flow of violent images. There are no mechanistic causes and effects underlying any of this. In *The Hollywood War Machine* we critically analyzed dozens of mainstream films, many of them huge blockbusters, celebrating some aspect of militarism: extreme and repetitive acts of violence, male warrior heroes, gallant U.S. battlefield exploits, superpatriotism tied to noble American pursuits, the targeting of demonic enemies, and so forth. Such motifs define not only combat films but several other genres, including action/adventure, sci-fi, Westerns, and historical dramas. We argue, further, that motifs of this sort characterize the larger culture, society, and foreign policy—an argument that should draw little controversy.

Perhaps the reviewers simply choose to ignore this state of affairs, or, more likely, remain little troubled by it, even as the culture industry and U.S. global behavior have simultaneously grown increasingly militarized. Either way, their "critique" of *The Hollywood War Machine* is never substantiated. While it is impossible to measure precisely various media influences on popular consciousness (just as consciousness itself is difficult to measure), the notion that a powerful form of media culture like film has no impact whatsoever on public thought and behavior hardly follows. With American society beset with an out-of-control gun culture, recurrent acts of civic violence, killing sprees, a huge prison system, the largest war economy in history, and virtually perpetual warfare, could the striking parallels found in media culture be just a bizarre coincidence? Still another possibility is that Suid and Shull are simply indifferent to the militarization of American society. The parade of war movies, action/adventure films, and combat video games could be just harmless diversion, like sports and music, having little to do with adult behavior. Others have been less sanguine about the role of violent media culture. President Richard Nixon, managing the Vietnam carnage, said he relished seeing *Patton* again and again, moved by that and other uplifting war films, while President Ronald Reagan could not hide his enthusiasm for the1980s *Rambo* series, repeating the warrior's famous utterance (concerning Vietnam) that "we get to win this time." In his book *Ronald Reagan the Movie,* Michael Rogin quotes Reagan as saying: "Boy, I saw *Rambo* last night. Now I know what to do next time this happens" (Rogin, 1987, p. 7). Of course Reagan was able to do little about Vietnam, but he could (and did) preside over a series of proxy wars in Central America that cost tens of thousands of lives. It was ultimately left to President George H. W. Bush to finally kick the "Vietnam Syndrome" (or so he claimed) with his momentous

Desert Storm victory over the powerful Iraqis. As for the second President Bush, he derived inspiration from watching *Black Hawk Down* (2002), worth several viewings in the buildup to the *real* war against Iraq where, presumably, "we get to win this time" (finishing the job his father started in 1991). Could Goldstein be hallucinating when he writes, in his 2008 Academy Awards commentary: "Today, the fallout from the war in Iraq seems to have inspired a new wave of violence-tinged films." The most popular movies, he notes, mesh with the present "mood of America." No need here to conjure hoary visions of "rightwing conservative patriots" in a Hollywood for which most film projects are just more (liberal) business as usual.

Suid and Shull try to rescue their feeble attack by invoking the case of Vietnam War movies that, they contend, never "attempted to glorify or justify the conflict." (To frame imperialist aggression that killed more than three million human beings as a "conflict" is a rather strange Orwellian concoction, but that need not detain us here.) There is little truth to this argument which, in any event, never addresses the general thesis we formulate in *The Hollywood War Machine*. First, the reviewers seem to have forgotten that Hollywood produced an endless stream of patriotic, pro-war movies about the United States in Indochina, with *The Green Berets* (1967) just the first in a long cycle of films justifying American intervention, many focused on postwar fantasies of reversing the original national defeat and humiliation. The *Rambo* trilogy, a series of box-office hits that turned Sylvester Stallone into an American warrior icon, constitutes just this type of (more efficacious) replay of the Vietnam War, beginning with the escapades of a Vietnam avenger who says "don't forget one thing: a good supply of body bags," in *First Blood* (1982). In the second episode (1985), Rambo is released from prison to re-fight the Vietnam War, ready with every creative tool of violence at his disposal to "win this time." Few Hollywood films—at least before the 2008 recycling of *Rambo*—so powerfully fuse the warrior myths of male heroism, patriotism, stab-in-the-back revenge fantasies, and fierce combat against demonic enemies. In an absurd twist consistent with U.S. imperial arrogance, it is the Americans—not the Vietnamese—shown here to be fighting for liberation. As Michael Ryan and Douglas Kellner write, moreover: "The film [*Rambo,* 1985] rewrites history in such a way that it excuses American atrocities against the Vietnamese" (Ryan & Kellner, 1988, p. 214). This precursor to later ultrapatriotic, hypermilitaristic Hollywood films would have a far greater resonance among popular audiences than all the purportedly "antiwar" Vietnam pictures combined.

As a mythic figure in American popular culture, Rambo has come to signify the super-warrior with roots in the Western frontier, reappropriated for the Vietnam and especially post-Vietnam eras. As Bruce Franklin observes, Rambo "incorporates one of America's most distinctive cultural products, the comic-book hero who may seem to be an ordinary human being but really possesses superhuman powers that allow him to fight, like Superman, for truth, justice, and the American way, and to personify national fantasies …No wonder Rambo can stand invulnerable against the thousands of bullets fired at him, many from point-blank range, by America's enemies" (Franklin, 2000, p. 194). The *Rambo* episodes packed theaters with viewers cheering wildly at every slaying of a Vietnamese or Russian—just as they would two decades later with the new and improved Rambo. The nation was inundated with Rambo warrior goods such action dolls, walkie-talkies, water guns, pinball machines, and sportswear not to mention TV cartoons and video games. A *Rambo* TV cartoon special, designed by Family Home Entertainment for ages 5 to 12, transformed Rambo into "liberty's champion," a skilled warrior engaged in global struggles against evil. There were even "adult" video spinoffs featuring pornographic images of Rambo (Franklin, 2000, p. 195).

The *Rambo* spectacle has prevailed across a quarter-century—a larger-than-life force in American popular culture, good for patriotic rebirthing as well as corporate profit-making at a time when we were told the society was overcome by the "Vietnam Syndrome." It might be expected that the Vietnam War would eventually force a national rethinking of U.S. global behavior, but, as the present Iraq debacle shows, nothing of the sort has occurred. Nor has the Hollywood War Machine been overturned or even moderated—surely one reason that any serious rethinking process has never gotten off the ground. Nor, unfortunately, have we seen an end to silly commentaries, like those of Suid and Shull, pretending there is no linkage between war, militarism, violence, and its ceaseless, spectacular media expressions in the film industry and elsewhere.

Notes

1. Earlier seminal works on the popular media and culture industry include: Max Horkheimer, *Critical Theory* (New York: Seabury, 1972), especially pp. 273–290; Marshall McLuhan, *Understanding Media* (New York: McGraw-Hill, 1964); Guy Debord, *Society of the Spectacle*; Edward Herman and Noam Chomsky, *Manufacturing Consent* (New York: Pantheon, 1988); Jean Baudrillard, *Simulations* (New York: Semiotext(e), 1983) and *Fatal Strategies* (New York: Semiotext(e), 1990); Douglas Kellner, *Media Culture* (New York: Routledge, 1995); Robert McChesney, *Rich Media, Poor Democracy* (New York: The New Press, 1999).

2. On the profound rightward shift of the mass media, see David Brock, *The Republican Noise Machine* (New York: Crown Publishers, 2004), ch. 1.

3. See Thomas Schatz, "The Return of the Hollywood Studio System," in Erik Barnouw, et al., eds., *Conglomerates and the Media* (New York: The New Press, 1997), p. 83.

4. See "Monster Budgets," *Entertainment* (December 9, 2005).

5. For an historical overview of U.S. imperialism, see Carl Boggs, *Imperial Delusions: American Militarism and Endless War* (Lanham, MD.: Rowman and Littlefield, 2005), ch. 1.

6. Cited in Bruce Miroff, *Pragmatic Illusions* (New York: David McKay, 1976), p. 55.

7. On the decline of the liberal tradition, see H.W. Brands, *The Strange Death of American Liberalism* (New Haven: Yale University Press, 2001).

8. On negative images of Arabs in Hollywood cinema, see Jack G. Shaheen, *Reel Bad Arabs* (New York: Olive Branch Press, 2001).

9. On racist depictions of Japanese in the Pacific Theater, see John Dower, *War Without Mercy* (New York: Pantheon, 1986).

10. Suid and Shull chastise us for neglecting "primary" sources in favor of "secondary" materials (books, articles, etc.), forgetting that our basic references for viewing, criticism, and analysis—dozens of Hollywood movies—were the "primary" sources we used, supplemented (as they should be) by a range of "secondary" materials. (Suid, *Guts and Glory,* 2002).

References

Ahmed, N.M. *The war on truth.* (2005) Northampton: Olive Branch Press.

Allman, T.D. (2004) *Rogue state*. New York: Nation Books.

Bamford, J. (2005). ["The Man Who Stole the War". *Rolling Stone Magazine,* December, p. 61.

Brock, D. (2004) *The Republican noise machine: Right-wing media and how it corrupts democracy.* New York: Crown.

Chomsky, N. (2000). *Rogue states: The rule of force in world affairs.* Cambridge, MA: South End Press.

Debord, G. (1995). *The society of the spectacle.* Cambridge, MA: Zone Books.

Denzin, N.K. (1995). *The cinematic society.* Thousand Oaks: Sage.

Franklin, H.B. (2000) *Vietnam and other fantasies.* Amherst: University of Massachusetts Press, p. 194.

Gabler, N. (1988). *An empire of their own.* New York: Crown Publishers.

Hedges, C. (2002). *War is a force that gives us meaning.* New York: Public Affairs.

Hitchens, C. (2003). *A long short war.* New York: Penguin Books.

Kagan, R. (2003). *Of paradise and power.* New York: Alfred Knopf.

Kaplan, R. (2001). *Warrior politics: Why leadership demands a pagan ethos.* New York, NY: Random House.

Kaplan, R. (2006). *Imperial grunts: On the ground with the American military, from Mongolia to the Philippines to Iraq and beyond.* New York, NY: Vintage.

Kellner, D. (1995). *Media culture.* New York: Routledge.

McChesney, R. (1999). *Rich media, poor democracy.* New York: The New Press.

Ritzner, G. (1999). *Enchanting the disenchanted world: Revolutionizing the means of consumption.* Thousand Oaks, CA: Pine Forge Press.

Robb, D.L. (2004). *Operation Hollywood.* Amherst, NY: Prometheus Books.

Rogin, M. (1987). *Ronald Reagan: The movie.* Berkeley: University of California Press.

Rumin, F. (2006). *CounterPunch Newsletter,* January 1–15, p. 5.

Ryan, M. and Kellner, D. (1988). *Camera Politica.* Bloomington: University of Indiana Press.

Suid, L. (2002). *Guts and glory.* Lexington: University of Kentucky Press.

Suid, L. H. and Shull, M. S. (2007). Heroes and Patriotism. *Film & history: An interdisciplinary journal of film and television studies,* 37, 2: 99-102.

Wood, N. (2004). *Tyranny in America.* London: Verso.

28

■ Another Ethnic Autobiography?

Childhood and the Cultural Economy of Looking

Allan Luke

■ Dramatis Personae

This piece was originally written for the International Conference on Knowledge and Discourse and presented at the Run Run Shaw Theatre, Hong Kong, in 1996. A companion article on Asian masculinities was published in conference papers (Luke, 2002). My original talk included videoclips of my uncle, Keye Luke, in *Star Trek,* 'Whom Gods Destroy' (Series 3, Episode 13, 1969) and with clips of my father, Edwin Luke, in *Blood Alley* (Dir. William Wellman, Batjak Productions, 1956).

The work sat unpublished until my mother, Ahlin Wong Luke, passed in 2007. The representations of my father and uncle continue to circulate in the transnational semiotic ether—as downloads, as DVDs, and in Wikipedia. I am rereading my father's film scripts, reconnoitering his experiences and, indeed, mine.

As you read, you will notice that my discussion of ethnic narratives has been over-taken by subsequent work in film, cultural and Asian American studies. I have retained the original 1990s citations in this work, updating them only where relevant. The premise of the article stands: that in contemporary capitalist societies like those of North America and Europe, essentialist bids to reclaim originary ethnic voice and identity are invariably forged in the contexts of multi-mediated childhood. Identity and practice are shaped by media representations of 'cultures,' even where they are reproduced across generations by face-to-face and everyday exchanges between parents, community elders and youth. We learn about and constitute our cultural selves and affiliations as much through Hollywood and Bollywood, through branded toys and clothes and their affiliated corporate lifeworlds as we might through the face-to-face intergenerational passing of wisdom, habituation and logics of practice. Given the pervasive influence of new digital arts, social networking, gaming, and other emergent cultural texts—the post-war, TV-saturated childhood I describe in this chapter is, if anything, an early approximation of the hyper-mediation of childhood.

In post-modern childhood, the shifting relationships in what counts as figure/ground, authentic/inauthentic, history/nature, and, indeed, narrative and science inevitably generate new amalgams of identity and position. Just as we could see strategic bids by minority and diasporic communities as bids for new forms of solidarity and identity in the face of racism, cultural and economic marginalisation (Luke, 2008), fundamentalist and neoconservative bids for a return to a print, Anglo European 'basics' and canonical knowledges are a nostalgic essentialism built around a mythic print, Anglo American childhood lost (Luke & Luke, 2001).

In current conditions, Aristotelian concepts of mimesis, romantic concepts of authenticity, pragmatist notions of experience, and, indeed, revolutionary construals of voice are partial and unstable. His views about the possibilities of political solidarity and action aside, Baudrillard's (1995) concept of the *simulacrum* marks a key turning point in Western theories of representation, art, culture and semiotics. My aim in this chapter was to turn the concept of simulation to questions of childhood and cultural identity, albeit through the lens of my own family's idiosyncratic history. My efforts also are an attempt to reclaim that history insofar as Keye Luke's work as an actor has been the object of considerable critical analysis and speculation.[1] Because of his notoriety as Charlie Chan's 'Number One Son," he has been viewed widely as an embodiment of the stereotypical subservient Chinese.

My father, Edwin Luke (1911–1986), and his elder brother, Keye Luke (1904–1991), were children of Cantonese migrants to Seattle. When my father and uncle were young, my grandfather died as the result of a violent 'incident,' the object of speculation in Chinatown talk. The family worked its way through the next decades in Seattle, with everybody working to make ends meet. Part of our family's story is archived in Seattle's *Wing Luke Museum*. The family's folk narrative about its involvement in the movies goes something like this: Keye Luke was an excellent student and developed into a fine pen and ink artist/illustrator, modelling his drawing on that of Aubrey Beardsley. His published work includes a limited edition of the *Rubyiat of Omar Khayyam*. Keye's first involvement with cinema was as a publicity/poster artist for one of the local theatres. In Seattle, or perhaps in Los Angeles, as the story goes, he met industry contacts looking for Chinese actors with excellent spoken English diction, which his was. Keye's work in films, typical of non-white actors in the period, was an historical accident. He moved to Los Angeles in the 1930s first, followed shortly thereafter by my father, Edwin Luke.

In the 1930s, Keye signed as the first Asian contract player at MGM. Following his 1934 debut in *The Painted Veil,* he was cast as the original number one son in the Charlie

Chan series with Werner Oland who became a friend and mentor. Keye subsequently moved on to a half-century career that included over two hundred wartime and post-war movies in which he was cast as Asian soldier, scholar, politician, houseboy and servant. His corpus also included Broadway and off-Broadway leading roles in several Rogers and Hammerstein musicals such as *Flower Drum Song*. Keye was a regular on television series in the 1950s and 1960s, with featured roles in *Anna and the King* and, most notably, as Master Po in *Kung Fu*. Keye also had guest slots in everything from *Gunsmoke* to *Star Trek* to *Trapper John MD*. In his later years, he had small but notable roles in Spielberg's *Gremlins*. His final appearance was in Woody Allen's *Alice*.

My father, Edwin S. Luke, took a different route. He left Seattle in the 1930s with a journalism degree from the University of Washington. He landed a role in *The Jade Mask* (1945) as the 'number 4' son of Charlie Chan (Sydney Toler), and a feature role in the Paramount production of *Tokyo Rose* (1945). His principal work was as a featured player in the movie *Blood Alley* (1955), and over thirty minor parts in TV and cinema. From the contracts left behind in his papers, he is probably still owed residuals for his performances. The acting did not pay the bills, and by the early 1950s, parts for Asian actors had dried up considerably, with a visible shift from the portrayal of evil Japanese to evil Communist Chinese. My father worked delivering newspapers, selling insurance, and proofreading to make ends meet. He was the first Chinese member of the California printers union, and went to work in the 1940s in the press room of the *Hollywood Reporter*. A typographer and linotyper by trade, my father was a fine writer and editor. Around the time of the passage of the Civil Rights Act of 1964, he began a twenty-five year career as a social worker in Los Angeles, working closely with the Latino community in Tijunga. His life and work informed my writing, politics and world view. My father and my uncle told my sisters and me that we should never be actors.

■ Ethnic Affiliations and Visibility

One of the powerful knowledge and political effects of postcolonial and feminist intellectual work has been to open a space for other voices in the public spheres of popular and academic writing. But in attributing this 'opening' to minority voices, to feminisms and post-colonialism, it would be a mistake to overlook the long histories of underground literature that extend back to historical slave narratives, revolutionary literature, and the work of women poets and novelists, much of which was censored or suppressed from mainstream selective traditions of literature and curriculum until the last two decades. At the same time, it would be naive to think that the emergence of new narratives of ethnic identity are somehow the results of newfound political power, literary quality or suppressed genius. There are, of course, powerful political economies at work in the production and popularization of women's, ethnic migrant, diasporic and postcolonial films and literature in Sydney, Shanghai, Hollywood, New York, Hong Kong and elsewhere. Ethnic narratives, whether those of Hollywood or Hong Kong's China, have become increasingly marketable, moving from the 'foreign films' category into the mainstream.

This chapter is nominally about the construction of ethnic selves and narratives, offering an analysis of ways of portraying and narrating culturally different life histories of visible minority groups in mainstream, white-dominated cultures. It proceeds in two moves. First, I provide an overview of two genres that I provisionally term 'ethnic narratives.' These are narratives of liberation and displacement, discussing their assumptions about essence, origins, authenticity, and the place and significance of pedagogy in the formation of the self. Here I look briefly and selectively at the work of Latino, Asian American and Asian Australian writers.

I then present an alternative story, a narrative of growing up ethnic in postmodern culture. This is a more complex and complicated process than either the common 'return to the origins' or 'between two worlds' metaphors explain. My story begins to speak of ethnic childhood as *simulacrum* (Baudrillard, 1995), of identity formation as a form of channel and web surfing, and of childhood as a task of holding mirrors up to the mirrors of popular cultural texts. Along the way, I offer one such narrative, dealing at length with my family's experiences of the construction and portrayal of Asian Americans in movies and television. So, the watching and participating in the 'Hollywoodisation' of images of the Asian is what this paper is really about (Hamamoto, 1994). This is, hopefully, Orientalism and Occidentalism in technicolor, Panavision, and black and white. Or, to give you a sense of its final resting place, the subtitle should be: You thought you were constructing us as the Other, when we were busy watching and laughing at how you construct yourselves and us.[2]

I will use the shorthand terminology here of 'visible minorities' to refer to those of us who are people of color in white-dominant, so-called Western cultures like the United States, Australia, Canada and the United Kingdom. I am aware of the difficult issues of definition surrounding cultural difference, visibility and race (Luke & Luke, 1999). Whether we use the terms 'ethnic' or 'racial' or 'cultural minority' epistemological and political problems of inclusivity, exclusivity and homogeneity are bound to be raised. For the purposes of this narrative, I characterize postcolonial subjects as offspring of colonialisation, as those people of cultural and racial groups who have historically been marginalised or made diasporic by large scale political and population shifts accompanying decolonisation. This marginalization might have entailed centuries-long political and economic colonization and domestic subjugation, systematic genocide or forced relocation, as in the case of indigenous peoples, or migration as the result of the growth or collapse of European or Asian empires. The processes of marginalisation typically involve racialising practices—the discursive and institutional practices whereby people of visible differences are ascribed as an inferior, exterior, and negative Other, with curtailed or limited access to economic, political, and human rights (Luke, 2008).

There is, of course, considerable debate over the extent to which the descriptors used for diasporic and 'minority' communities refer to homogeneous communities. We can take categorizations of ethnic and cultural groups as descriptions of residual and emergent cultural affiliations defined in relation to white-dominant societies and institutions, and specific political economies. In the case of Asian Americans, who have some striking historical parallels with their counterpart Asian Australians and Asian Canadians, a range of definitional issues arise. First, the historical solidarity among Asian Americans is itself a discourse move, developed as a political strategy in the 1960s to bring together many disparate and historically autonomous groups, including Japanese Americans, Chinese Americans, Filipino Americans, and others who had been distinguished both by their own histories, and by successful 'divide and rule' strategies like the relocation policies of World War II, discriminatory housing and educational practices and citizenship legislation (cf. Kim, 1993). Second, the very term 'Asian' and such partner terms as 'Asian Pacific' are increasingly used to establish imaginary spaces that serve particular political and economic ends (Wilson, 1995; Luke & Ismail, 2007). Third, the degree to which such categories as Asian American risk totalising the class, generational, and place-bound demographic diversity of any ethnic minority group raises serious issues, as does reference to the imaginary category of a 'dominant Anglo/Australian culture.' But we've got to start somewhere.

On the other hand, to refer to Asians or, more specifically, diasporic Chinese, Caribbean migrants, African refugees and others as 'ethnic groups' comparable to other European ethnic groups, as has been the trend in Australian and Canadian legislation, immigration and multicultural literature, risks skirting the crucial issue of visibility of colour. This is a visibility, which is a biological fact, an element of the habitus that cannot be made over. However, it is reconfigured or positioned through discourse (Luke, 2008), and there is a significant critique among many of colour—African Americans, Latinos and others—that the notion of 'ethnic' or 'cultural' group does not capture the physical visibility and vulnerability that enables the practices and discourses of racism, from physical violence and exclusionary legislation to racist jokes. For their part, indigenous Australian Aborigines, Torres Strait Islanders and New Zealand Maoris have historically made the case for an essential, originary relationship to the land—one that supersedes the definitions and claims of approaches to multiculturalism.

The matter of where, when and how the 'uptake' of colour is made to count clearly is one of cultural locality and socio-political context. That is, how, when and to whom you become visible is sociologically contingent, dependent on a network of racialising practices and interpellating discourses that range from those of the mass media, to racist jokes and slurs, to actual physical violence. Yet, the issue of being a 'visible' minority becomes particularly focal when we turn to issues of representation and begin to ask who is looking at, and naming, whom, and who is looking back.

Ethnic Narratives

I will use the term *ethnic narratives* to describe those works of postcolonial writers and by marginalized minorities that attempt to provide accounts of their life-trajectories and of the intergenerational dynamics of identity, political agency and desire. Many of these have the distinctive features of minority discourses (Jan-Mohamed & Lloyd, 1991). They are oppositional, historically situated and opportunist, contradictory and hybrid texts, often drawing upon binary forms of representation. Such narratives can be provisionally classified into three broad categories: liberationist, displacement, and simulacrum.

- ❑ **Narratives of Liberation:** allegorical narratives of cultural solidarity where individual experience and struggle represent that of an oppressed collective; these works aim at the recovery of voice, authenticity and power and the documentation of oppression;
- ❑ **Narratives of Displacement:** narratives of absence, these works pivot on the theme of recovery, of cultural continuity and change; they typically aim at the recovery of self through a return to homeland and origins;
- ❑ **Narratives of Simulation:** narratives of blending, hybridity, pastiche and textual self-reconstruction; these works represent and describe the emergence of new cultural transformations, texts and identities.

These narrative structures are, of course, produced by differentially located writers and subjects, in terms of their 'outsider' status in relation to any particular cultural histories, state formations and political economies. In her analysis of *Me Llamo Rigoberta Menchu y Asi Mi Nacio la Conciencia* (Menchu & Menchu, 1990), Saldana-Portillo (2003, pp. 152–154) describes the emergence of the 'guerrilla testimonio' as a genre of liberationist literature, tracing the genre back to Che Guevara's testimonials of the early 1960s. Menchus' Mayan Quiche Indian narrative begins with the statement, 'I'd like to stress that it's not my life, it's also the testimony of the people.' Menchu's is a woman's narrative, vividly describing her work as a peasant laborer, her relationship to her mother, and the awakening of her political consciousness. The text is characterised by her move from a narrative of 'I' to the solidarity of the 'we.' This move, Saldana-Portillo (2003) argues, is different from the rhetorical constructions of male revolutionaries, who refer to the indigenous and peasant classes almost in abstract, mystical terms.

This moving from the self to the *self as embodiment of the oppressed* is a tradition from and through Fanon, Malcolm X, and others. The assumptions of the liberationist narrative return us to Freire's (1990) radical pedagogy: that through writing one's narrative, and taking oneself as an allegorical subject, one gives 'voice' to the 'voiceless,' a political act in itself. By this account, liberationist narratives are, in part, a recovery of voice and human authenticity, a realization of consciousness of material conditions and social relations, a recording of the experience of oppression and marginality, and a building of solidarity. Thus, the liberationist narrative of colonized peoples has a straightforward and valid aim: the self-production of the revolutionary self, a matter taken up in the African American literature of the 1960s and 1970s, most specifically, *The Autobiography of Malcolm X* (1987). As a genre, it has historical precedents, then, in the slave narratives of Mary Prince, Frederick Douglass, and others.

Yet, for each testimony of the emergence of voice, of power, and of identity affiliated with political analysis, other ethnic narratives reflect a sense of envy, of the experience of the colonised 'other' as characterised by intrinsic 'lack' or absence. In an influential autobiography of the 1980s that was cited as a rationale against bilingual education, Richard Rodriguez (1982), took up the issue of cultural displacement and shift.

> What I am about to say to you has taken me more than twenty years to admit: A primary reason for my success in the classroom was that I couldn't forget that schooling was changing me and separating me from the life I enjoyed before becoming a student. That simple realiza-

tion. For years I never spoke to anyone about it. Never mentioned a thing to my family or my teachers or classmates…At the end of my schooling, I needed to determine how far I had moved from my past. (1982, p. 14)

For Rodriguez, the educational issue centred on language:

> I would also hear then the high nasal tones of middle-class American speech. The air stirred with sound. Sometimes, even now, when I have been travelling abroad for several weeks, I will hear what I heard as a boy.…the high sound of American voices. For a few seconds I will hear it with pleasure, for it is now the sound of my society—a reminder of home. But inevitably—already on the flight headed for home—the sound fades with repetition. I am unable to hear it anymore. (p. 14)

Though he framed his experience by reference to Richard Hoggart's (1959) 'scholarship boy,' Rodriguez was broadly attacked for having sold out his culture, language and identity. The legacy of Rodriguez's work and the mainstream multiculturalism debate of the last three decades is the metaphor of 'between-ness' and of 'lack.'

- ◻ that we are caught between two worlds, cultures, and languages; and
- ◻ that cultural displacement is a psychological, political, and pedagogical dilemma resolvable through the restoration of 'wholeness,' equilibrium, stability.[3]

Despite the development of postcolonial and feminist models of the subaltern and marginalized subject, the dominant approach in educational and clinical settings where old style deficit, assimilationist models no longer prevail, is to treat children from visible minority groups according to the 'between two worlds' metaphors. Unlike the postcolonial narratives of liberation, the teleology of Rodriguez's work is not revolutionary but psychotherapeutic. The two worlds model operates on the basis of a binary of immigrant and dominant cultures, while presupposing the need for a 'whole,' centred individual of dominant Western culture. Narratives of psychological, intellectual, and psychic displacement hinge around themes of longing and lack, and, indeed, they search for a cure or fix for the displacement.

The theme of displacement recurs in some of the more powerful recent Asian American literature. The Chinese and Chinese American women in the Amy Tan's *Joy Luck Club* (1989) reconcile the 'two cultures' dilemma by re-narrating, reliving and mythologising a return to China. This is done principally through mother/daughter storytelling and exchange (Yu, 2002)

> My daughter wanted to go to China for her second honeymoon, but now she is afraid.
> "What if I blend in so well they think I'm one of them?" Waverly asked me. "What if they don't let me come back to the United States?"
> "When you go to China," I told her, "you don't even need to open your mouth. They already know you are an outsider." (Tan, 1989, p. 253)

Chinese Australian photographer William Yang (1994) writes

> Homesickness. What a strong emotion. What an attachment to the country. All my family's roots were in Australia. I was more Australian than the kids who told me to go back to China. I didn't even know where China was. (1994, p. 70)

In *Woman Warrior* (1994), Maxine Hong Kingston's Chinese American woman must retrace and retell her father's trip from China in search of the Gold Mountain. Hong Kingston's character quite literally loses the ability to speak until she has engaged in a historical connection with her origins.

There are, then contrasts between liberationist and displacement narratives, most obviously the move from indigenous and postcolonial narratives of political emancipation to migrant narratives of familial and biographical reconciliation. Yet, both genres are based around economies of production. They are symbolic and, at times, allegorical, productions of the self, whether as revolutionary agent, as matriarch, as literate subject, or, in Rodriguez's case, as assimilated subject.

Not surprisingly, minority representation entails the construction of a strategic essentialism as a counter-hegemonic tactic. Keesing (1992) described the discourses of identity that emerged in the Solomon Islands after decolonization, noting the construction of a discourse of authenticity, of a unitary cultural repertoire and history where none before existed. As Rey Chow (1993) argued, diasporic literature is preoccupied with a metaphoric 'return to the origins':

> …we see that in our fascination with the "authentic native," we are actually engaged in a search for the equivalent of the aura even while our search processes themselves take us farther and farther away from that 'original' point of identification. Although we act like good Communists who dream of finding and serving the "real people," we actually live and work like dirty capitalists accustomed to switching channels constantly. As we keep switching channels and browsing through different, "local" cultures, we produce an infinite number of "natives," all with predictably automaton-like features that do not so much de-universalise western hegemony as they confirm its protean capacity for infinite displacement. The "authentic" native… keeps receding from our grasp. Meanwhile our machinery churns out inauthentic and imperfect natives who are already copies. (1993, p. 46)

She goes on to redescribe Walter Benjamin's work on 'the native in the age of discursive reproduction.' Chow's point is that the search for origins, the search for authentic voice, the search for an unmediated essence and hence, political or genealogical affiliation, is finally an *in situ* act of textual self-production and self-reconstruction (cf. Ang, 2000).

Chow's work suggests the possibility of a new kind of ethnic narrative, one that is more a study in self-consciousness of how we are being represented and produced, one that moves from an economy of self-production that aims towards liberation, spiritual or psychotherapeutic redemption, and moves towards what Vicente Raphael (1995) has described as a critical 'economy of looking': looking at ourselves and Others through the critical lenses of multiple, overlapping and lived representation. In contrast to the narratives of liberation and displacement, consider this passage cited by Raphael, from *Dogeaters* (1990) by the Filipina American writer, Jessica Hagedorn:

> 1956. The air conditioned darkness of the Avenue Theatre smells of flowery pomade, sugary chocolates, cigarette smoke and sweat. "All That Heaven Allows" is playing in Cinemascope and Technicolor. Staring Jane Wyman as the rich widow, Rock Hudson as the handsome young gardener, and Agnes Moorehead as Jane's faithful friend, the movie also features the unsung starlet Gloria Talbott as Jane's spoiled teenage daughter, a feisty brunette with catlike features and an innocent ponytail.

…Huddled with our chaperone, Lorenza, my cousin Pucha Gonzaga and I sit enthralled in the upper section of the balcony in Manila's "Finest! First Run! English Movies Only!" theatre, ignoring furtive lovers stealing noisy kisses in the pitch-black darkness all around us.

Jane Wyman's soft putty face. Rock Hudson's singular, pitying expression. Flared skirts, wide cinch belts, prim white blouses, a single strand of delicate blue-white pearls. Thick pencilled eyebrows and blood red vampire lips; the virgin pastel-pink cashmere cardigan draped over Gloria Talbott's shoulders..... Her casual arrogance seems inherently American, modern and enviable. (1990, p. 3)

Hagedorn describes an economy of looking, a moment of the textual construction of desire, where issues of identity, gender, and sexuality are powerfully at work. There is a celebratory and playful tone here, altogether different from the discourses of 'lack' and displacement that dominate many of the male-authored narratives. Rodriguez's (1982) troubled search for stable male ego-identity is missing.

This is a different kind of self-production at work—where childhood, youth, and growing up becomes less a search for liberation or authenticity and more akin to cultural *bricolage*. In his early description of the 'ecstasy of communication,' Baudrillard (1995) argues that we live in a multi-mediated environment such that any longstanding analytic distinctions between figure/ground, sign/signified, truth/reality have become problematic. He argues that navigation through postmodern culture involves participation in a hall of mirrors, where image/identity are simulations. With the decay of these binary analytic categories, the dialectics of colonised/coloniser, self/Other that are at the heart of ethnic narratives of liberation and displacement also become less stable.

Following Raphael (1995), my view is that there is a politics of identity in the strategies and tactics of the practice of viewing. Hagedorn again:

We compare notes after the movie, sipping TruColas under the watchful gaze of the taciturn Lorenza. "I don't like her face," Pucha complains about Jane Wyman, " I hate when Rock starts kissing her." What's wrong with it? I want to know, irritated at my blond cousin's constant criticism. She wrinkles her mestiza nose, the nose she is so proud of because it's pointed and straight. "Ay! Que corny. .."…being corny is the worst sin you can commit in her eyes. (Hagedorn, 1990, p. 4)

Here linguistic creolization is doubled in the body: dyed blond hair and mestiza nose. We begin to see in Hagedon's text a different kind of ethnic narrative—where identity, sexuality, and politics are stitched together from popular cultural images, which are debated, mocked, critiqued, played with—without the will towards the fixity, the certainty of assumption of singular, centred identity.

This ethnic narrative of simulation provides evidence of a *stabilised for now* characteristic of ethnic identity in popular culture that is much like the channel-surfing described by Chow (1993): a multi-channelled and multi-mediated identity formation where one learns to live within the interstices and gaps of images, without a perpetual feeling of absence, loss, or lack—the absence, loss or lack presupposed in assimilationist, psycho-therapeutic and psychoanalytic analyses of difference. Rafael (1995) puts it this way:

Envy thus becomes the site from which a new kind of agency is formulated. It entails the capacity to take on diverse identities for oneself, to claim that the "I" could be other "I's" elsewhere beyond the compass of the nation state and neocolonial society. For this reason, the mestizo/a viewer can be thought of as an ideal audience whose hybridity signifies the privilege associated with collaborating with and containing the workings of power. (1995, p. 105)

With that in mind, I'll narrate as one such inauthentic and imperfect copy churned by the machinery of post-war popular culture.

■ Another Ethnic Autobiography

I was born in Los Angeles, California in 1950. Looking back, the single most important bit of my childhood was TV. When we got our first colour TV in the 1960s, we became a two-TV household because we kept the black and white TV, too. We spoke English in the home, and we swapped lunches and homework and comic books with Hispanic, Jewish, and African American kids. I learned to read from the Dick and Jane readers, recognising, sounding out, and sub-vocalising the words of Dick, Dad, and Spot, the dog (Luke, 1988). The end of each week, we would go to Chinese Schools, where our Aunt Beulah dutifully tried to teach us Cantonese and Christianity, sometimes in that order. She, like many of the aunties and uncles in our extended families, worked part time as an actor.[4]

First, there was black and white TV and, by the mid-1960s, colour, and the local theatre. When we finished playing on the streets, these were our prime-time activities. Los Angeles in the mid to late 1950s was a media mecca. There were about ten channels, showing reruns continually. Together with the neighbours, Timmy and Monica, who lived across the street and had more recently arrived from Hong Kong, I would play *Rawhide, Gunsmoke,* and *Bonanza.* When the Latino kids down the street would play war with us, we would re-divide to determine who was going to play the Japanese and the Americans, or sometimes we just split the difference and played Germans and Americans.

My father and uncle were actors. Both had raised themselves in Seattle. My two sets of grandparents had come from Canton in the 1890s. Both my father and uncle were the first educated Chinamen in our family. My uncle became MGM's first non-white contract player and first Asian featured actor, starring in the Charlie Chan series and making over 200 movies. His career culminated in Woody Allen's *Alice* and Spielberg's *Gremlins,* in which he played, surprise: a Chinese herbalist with a long Fu-Manchu beard.

They worked in an environment in which the only work they could get was playing Hollywood's Asians. As Darrell Hamamoto writes in *Monitored Peril* (1994),they were caught up playing Japanese and Chinese soldiers and generals, Pearl River peasants, Confucian scholars and, at better moments, the loyal Asian sidekick, always in supporting roles to Whites. Hamamoto's cogent analysis makes the case that Hollywood reified Asians as the Other—as objects of derision, as objects of violence, as servant and slave, or, in the case of Chinese women, as the objects of desire for Marlon Brando, Cary Grant, Gregory Peck, and just about anybody else. If this weren't enough, when the roles were featured roles, they would give them to White people playing in yellow-face, from Paul

Muni to Jennifer Jones to Lauren Bacall to Peter Sellers, playing Asians or Eurasians. This drove my father and uncle crazy.

My father's career was different. He completed a bachelor's degree in the 1930s. But his talents as a writer were unused by the Hearst-dominated Los Angeles dailies, which had invented *yellow journalism* in the 1920s. So, logically he went to Hollywood where he became a linotyper in the press room of the *Hollywood Reporter*. But, my father also worked as an actor, playing Filipino chefs, soldiers, houseboys, or anything that would pay the bills. I can remember sitting with him while he practiced his lines, dressed as a Filipino housekeeper for a White boss or as a Filipino chef for submarine movies. There were days when he would wake and leave for work early in the morning, ready to play a Japanese soldier.

My uncle would wait until everybody else upstairs was playing mah jong. He'd have a few drinks and we'd go downstairs. Always playing for an audience, he'd rehearse his lines for Rogers and Hammerstein or read Shakespeare to me from a worn set of Harvard Classics that my father had gotten from the Salvation Army store. Every time there was a casting call, whether for Rogers and Hammerstein's *South Pacific* or *Flower Drum Song,* or for TV or movies, many of my extended family's kids would go work as extras.

In 1954, the movie *Blood Alley* was cast and shot in San Rafael, California, on the north side of San Francisco Bay. This was at the height of McCarthyism, and its script by A.S. Fleischman[5] wove together two new schemata—anti-communism and the Exotic East—into a classic, but tacky action movie. Lauren Bacall was featured as Cathy, who appears in shot 37:

As she approaches the landing, we see that she is barelegged, her feet in sandals. Her hair is cut short and the South China sun has tanned her skin. She has put on her best skirt, a Tartan affair. (Fleischman, 1954, p. 8)

Blood Alley was, in many senses, an archetypal Cold War encoding of the Other, where hapless Nationalist Chinese were saved by the Duke. John Wayne plays Wilder, a reluctant American hero who takes a ferry boat of sympathetic Nationalists and peasants to safe harbour in Hong Kong. With Bacall and a cast of hundreds, namely my Dad, cousins and the entire neighbourhood, and others, they defeat the Communists. The Duke was the hero. The enemy was us.

The Duke was my father's favourite actor. Together, we went to see every John Wayne movie made. I remember sitting through *The Alamo* three times in succession at a theatre on Santa Monica Blvd. The trouble was that my father was cast as an evil communist sympathizer, the dangerous Feng Number One. His job was to take out John Wayne.

My father and many others from the Los Angeles Chinese acting fraternity went off for two months on location to shoot the movie. Here is my father's script. He has written his name in English and Chinese below the title. The cover is signed by John Wayne (in the upper right), Lauren Bacall (down the center), and the director, Bill Wellman, in the upper left. It was passed on to me as a family heirloom, as one would receive an artefact or a painting. I received a nineteenth-century gold nugget from my grandfather, and a film script from my father. I read this not as a film scholar would. I ask you to read it as you would a scrapbook or photo album.

Its story grammar is as follows: the Western hero saves diasporic people from even more diasporic bad guys. My father played First Feng, the first son of a wealthy 'Commy' as the Duke comments. Feng Senior was portrayed, in a caricature that only a McCarthy-era screenwriter could

have come up with, as part gluttonous Mandarin and part petit bourgeois, carried around by servants like an emperor. They all—noble Pearl River peasants and covert 'Commy sympathisers [sic]' alike—depart for 'freedom' on a refurbished ferry, captained by the Duke to battle hostile gunboats, disease, and a typhoon. Along the way, my father leads a cowardly attack on John Wayne on the bridge during the tempest.

On page 494 are my Father's lines.

The scribblings below the margins are his lines in Cantonese, which he hand-wrote in a Romanized notation. Hence: (1) 'We take command now, foolish captain' is transcribed as: 'ghor de yee gah fun foo ney deh, ney dey gum bungah, shoon yeung.' Now my Father could indeed speak and, though rusty, read and write Chinese characters. However, his Romanised version on the script was idiosyncratic. Actors make mnemonic notes on scripts, and his has underlines as well as exclamation and accent marks for intonation and stress.

What's more interesting here is that the scriptwriter (A. S. Fleischman) and director (William Wellman) left the translation to the Chinese American actors. Hence, First Feng's lines—(2) 'Change directions! We go back to Swatow!'—are prefaced in the script with '[In Chinese].' My father could have said anything.

Whatever he did utter was virtually inaudible in the storm and violent scuffle: 'First Feng beating to a pulp with a rifle butt,' the script explains. But not before the Duke can shout at Feng and others 'You idiots (in Chinese).' There are no diacritical marks or translations for the Duke.

My dad was knifed in the back by two anti-Communist peasants, the people who sided with the American captain. John Wayne is rescued and soothed on the deck by Lauren Bacall's character.

Blood Alley was the last feature film in which my father appeared. He returned to a career that included linotyper, proofreader, insurance salesman, and finally, social worker,

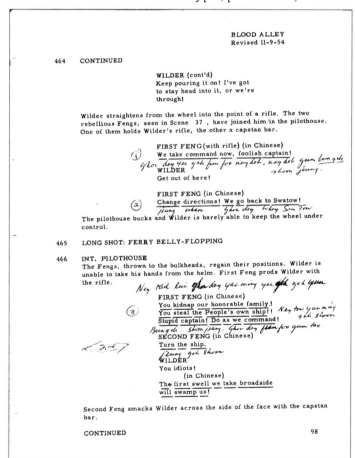

some thirty years after he received his undergraduate degree. A coffee mug autographed, 'To Ed from the Duke' sat on our mantelpiece for thirty years, an object of family debate once John Wayne's right wing politics became unbearable.

We wore his acting like a badge. I remember going to school and trying to tell the other kids that my dad had hit John Wayne. I never claimed he had beaten him to a pulp with a rifle butt. Nobody believed me. In Los Angeles at the time, KHJ was a local television station that played the same movie four times a day, morning, mid-afternoon, evening, and overnight. This meant that my sisters, cousins, neighbours, and I could stay up late and watch dad smash John Wayne, again and again. When *Blood Alley* played, we would watch it ten to twenty times a week. Like a later generation of Trekkies, we repeated each line, and watched it over and over. I even learned my dad's crowning line as First Feng, his last on big screen celluloid: 'You refuse, American Pig' ('ney ng tso, Me Gurok Gee!').

We would watch other Chinese and Japanese actors that we knew. Occasionally, Aunt Beulah or Uncle Keye, Richard Loo, or Victor Sen Yung were on programs that featured Asians playing generals, houseboys, drug barons, and constant sidekicks. We knew all the stories about the Asian actors. My parents would tell us which actors were relatives, who was divorced, who was educated, which were drunks, and which roles someone we knew *should* have had. It was like having a Chinese actor's tabloid *TV Guide* on site. We were film critics and insider traders.

We had our own folklore for viewing. My father told me that when they spoke the Chinese dialogue to the White actors, they would sometimes swear at them or insult them, sometimes when smiling. So, while the scripted speech act meant X, in Cantonese, they would deliver Y. We'd watch *Bonanza,* where we heard or imagined that Hop Sing the Cook would tell the Cartwright Brothers where to get off, and it was just that they didn't know it. So, Little Joe would ask for tea and might get called a 'running dog.' There was another story there as well. My father used to say, 'Uncle Victor has a UC Berkeley degree, but wound up playing a houseboy, how undignified.' He should speak! My grandparents had been peasants. My mother had grown up on a farm in Punalu'u, on the north shore of Oahu. Hence, there was no romanticization about rice and pig farming in our family, and no nostalgia for a China lost. My childhood goal was to watch enough TV to get into UCLA. I do not know how many times my father told me he didn't want us to be actors. He said it wasn't steady work, and that it gave you a big head. I think he was talking about himself, and my Uncle, too, about whose success everybody spoke. But I was upset when we could not be extras on movie sets like my cousins.

So, we'd sit and watch *Bonanza,* which we actually could see in colour at friends' houses. While everybody else was watching the Cartwrights, we were watching Victor Sen Yung, waiting for the day when Hop Sing would tell Little Joe where to get off in his nattering, clattering Cantonese soliloquies, or whether he might, just might, wink at the camera, since he knew we were watching. So, we learned to look for these signs of playing with the script, and we would play with the scripts, too, rethinking them, re-running them, and rehearsing them, always in our heads, sometimes physically, always among ourselves ('You refuse, American Pig!'), not with our White or Latino or African American school mates. This was our secret knowledge, our try at re-production, our indigenous Hollywood Chinese wisdom, or at least a good in-joke.

Often, the distinctions between what was ours and what was cinematic were blurred in this inter-textual and intergenerational hall of mirrors. In the 1960s, Keye Luke was featured as Master Po in the TV series *Kung Fu,* where he uttered quasi-Confucian wisdom. During that period, I remember going out to dinner with him and he'd stop and break into his TV voice and say: 'Confucius would say: Go slowly and with considered thought, Grasshopper'…or something like that. Was this the transmission of intergenerational wisdom, or the passing of another kind of wisdom, anagrams twice removed from China via blacklisted screenwriters? If, indeed, every text and utterance is already a revoicing, whose historical and cultural voices were speaking to whom?

Uncle Keye died in 1991. After a good deal of community effort, a star was put on Hollywood Boulevard in his honor. But this was not without muted controversy because my uncle remained a throwback, an anachronism, presenting an historical anomaly to a newly empowered and fully voiced Asian American acting fraternity. In his epilogue to *Monitored Peril,* Darrell Hamamoto (1994, p. 251) describes him as follows:

In a film and television career that spanned a period of fifty years, beginning with the "Charlie Chan" film series during the 1930s and running through the TV-movie reprise of Kung Fu (1986), Keye Luke (1904–1991) was probably the Asian American actor best known to the general public....With few exceptions, Keye Luke's outstanding career was predicated upon his ability to portray the stock array of Asian domestic servants, laundrymen, mystics, gangsters, and enemy soldiers. In this, Keye Luke was the prototypical "Oriental" as constructed by the implicit racism of network television standards and practices.

I share Hamamoto's analysis. But my uncle was no dupe, no sellout, no Uncle Tom, no Banana, and no Republican. He was many things. He was a mirror. He was a prism. Like my father, and perhaps, like so many migrants, he was an actor. And like my Father, he worked to survive in good faith, within and through a fundamentally racist medium.

■ Gazing Back/Looking Back

The folk wisdom that many of us were raised with in the post-war Chinese community was not to fight back but to work harder and better than whites. As my father said, when 'the White Boss tells you what to do, say yes, then just go and do what you think needs to be done.' Similarly, my mother taught us always to be polite. In the 1950s, before the Civil Rights Act had been enacted, we would sometimes dress up and go out to expensive White restaurants in order to learn how to do it properly. We couldn't afford it, but we were told that we had to learn how to use the right forks. My mother would go out of her way to show white people that she could speak their codes, that she could do their politeness protocols, sometimes making malapropisms on the phone. At the time, I resented it. I thought it was a loss of face. As an undergraduate, circa 1968, it made me angry to think she was selling out to dominant, white bourgeois culture—and I despaired at the migrant preoccupation with wealth and status that seemed to pervade many segments of the Los Angeles Chinese community. But later my mother and I have talked of what it meant to be an Asian woman in the 1930s, 1940s, and 1950s, and what it meant to be invisible. We talked about what it meant to have to avert your eyes. And I now understand better what it meant to be in that economy of looking, where unemployment, living at the fringes, the ugliness of face-to-face symbolic and physical violence always lurked just below the surface. How you looked, what you saw, how you were looked at, and what they saw were daily face-to-face and media cues and reminders. Now, I better understand and respect her historical strategies and those of my father and uncle.

Face, according to ethnographers of communication, is a premium in all intra- and intercultural communication (Scollon & Scollon, 1981). But we were taught not to confront verbally or physically. Sometimes this conferred advantage or sidestepped disadvantage. At other times, it was a cultural liability. Sometimes we fought and yelled back, but many of us who were Other growing up in White modernist cultures developed a performativity of looking, a way of reconstructing the gaze by 'staring back'—sometimes masked and covert, and at other times overt, sometimes when you were watching, sometimes when you weren't. They can't control or suppress your eyes. Even now, as sometime academic, public intellectual and state bureaucrat, I might use it in boardrooms and staffrooms, as a way of jamming the radar of the Other. This *looking back* is akin to bell hooks' (1989) 'talking back' against dominant cultures or other cultures' traditions of fighting back physically.

These moments of *looking back* are crucial to the formation of the minority subject in postmodern conditions. We regain our agency by asserting, *inter alia,* our capacity to look, stare, gaze in different ways, and to rewrite, to reconstruct texts and codes, as Hagedorn's (1990) Mestizas did. But it is not simply an economy of envy. We are also able to see absences, to see what isn't there, and to construct, on the fly, counterplots, counterpoints, and bizarre alternatives. We always wondered just what would have happened if my dad had taken out the Duke. What would Lauren Bacall have done?

I would hope that there is a simple lesson here for Hollywood, the dominant culture, talent scouts and agents within the political economy of scholarship and filmmaking, counsellors, therapists and educators who deal with children of visible minorities, and whoever is actually out there reading this text. This is a different kind of ethnic narrative, one where identity is constituted not in the binary oppositions of 'between two cultures' or in the 'finding authentic voice' argument of the liberationist and displacement narratives. These remain salient historical strategies for writing and talking back, of great efficacy and power in particular places at particular historical moments (Luke, 2004). But there are radically different stories out there as well. These are stories where cultural boundaries and exchanges are harder to pin down, where simulation suffices for something more solid, and where separating out the good guys and the bad guys is a bit more ambiguous.

Growing up different in the proto-postmodern hotbed of Hollywood left us with a different species of literacy. My parents bequeathed to me critical ways of looking. And that critical engagement with the politics of representation may be as powerful a political tool as any available today. That we really own and control the media—even when we can barely afford the light bills—is the best folk wisdom around for survival in fast capitalism that my parents could have given me—perhaps better than if I had learned Cantonese properly.

Rey Chow (1993, p. 23) asks, 'Where have all the 'natives' gone?' She answers that we are caught somewhere between what she terms the 'defiled image and the indifferent gaze.' But we are not dupes. We are no longer stuck between two cultures, two languages. We produce ourselves in many third worlds: worlds of simulation, refraction, and popular culture.

■ Postscript

I am not a novelist, or a literary critic, or a cultural studies theorist. I am a teacher, with a story to tell and, no doubt, innumerable axes to grind. I have tried here to offer yet another ethnic autobiography, but one with a slight difference. It is an attempt to mark out:

- a shift from a binary economy of production and destruction, of liberation and displacement, to an economy of looking, a notion of identity formation as channel surfing, one where you can go back, but it is back to another channel or rerun.

- a shift from a sense of the minority person as filled by lack, deficit, displacement, only to be filled up by a return to the origins myth, to a self-understanding based on the need to deal strategically with the ongoing instability and difference of a multi-mediated culture.

When you held a hegemonic mirror up to us, we held it up back at you. We saw Warner Oland, Sydney Toler, Peter Sellers, Peter Ustinov, Jennifer Jones, Marlon Brando, and David Carradine in yellowface, painted to look like us. On behalf of all of us who played your version of us, we laughed when we saw you playing us.

> First Feng, shaking off the blow, finds the rifle on the deck and grabs it by the barrel. Wilder and Second Feng are wrestling on the deck at the far end of the pilothouse. Wilder gets the Chinese to his shoulders and sends him crashing into a window. First Feng bludgeons Wilder with a rifle butt, knocking him to the deck. (*Blood Alley,* p. 99)

As a kid, I knew the layers of truths of cinema and representation. I relished my father's wondrous simulation. We were critically literate long before we invented the term. You were duped into thinking we were dupes.

Acknowledgments

This piece is dedicated to my mother, Ahlin Wong Luke (1904–2007), and to Carmen Luke and Mei-Ling Shiroishi. Thanks to Rhonda Hammer and Douglas Kellner for insisting that this tale be told.

Notes

1. For an overview, see http://en.wikipedia.org/wiki/Keye_Luke. There are numerous Charlie Chan websites describing his work and also noting Edwin Luke's role as "number 4" son. Some are laudatory, others critical, and yet others replicate, without irony, the orientalism and stereotypes of the original films.

2. There may be a salutary lesson in this for scholars focusing on the colonizing views of 'Asia' in Western literature, history and media. However intentionally, this work risks replicating the imperial assumption that the Eurocentric gaze continues to matter. Given the geopolitical and cultural shift of flows towards and from China and India, it may be strategically and critically more important to focus on how these peoples and places represent and position the 'West' (Louie, 2002).

3. In work on interethnic families in the 1990s, Carmen Luke and I found that the mainstream explanations of 'interrace' in the social sciences were also based on assumptions of lack and deficit. In social psychology, for example, the assumption was that interracial children were prime candidates for remedial intervention (Luke & Luke, 1998).

4. Beulah Quo (1902–2004) was one of the most successful Chinese-American actors of the post-war generation, appearing in over two hundred feature films and television programs. She was one of the aunties in our extended Chinatown family. See: http://de.wikipedia.org/wiki/Beulah_Quo. Lisa

See's *On Gold Mountain* (1997) is an accurate and vivid description of the post-war Los Angeles Chinatown and the social networks of our community.

5. A. S. 'Sid' Fleischman, author of numerous novels, screenplays and children's books went on to win the Newbery Medal for children's literature.

References

Ang, I. (2000) *On Not Speaking Chinese.* London: Routledge.

Baudrillard, J. (1995) *Simulacra and Simulation.* Trans. S.F. Glaser. Ann Arbor: University of Michigan Press.

Chow, R. (1993). *Writing Diaspora.* Bloomington: Indiana University Press.

Fleischman, A.S. (1954) *William A. Wellman's 'Blood Alley.'* Revised Final Script, 9 November, 1954, Hollywood, CA.

Freire, P. (1990) *Pedagogy of the Oppressed.* Trans. M.B. Ramos. New York: Continuum.

Hagedorn, J. (1990) *Dogeaters.* New York: Pantheon Press.

Hamamoto, D. (1994) *Monitored Peril.* Minneapolis: University of Minnesota Press.

Hoggart, R. (1959) *The Uses of Literacy.* Harmondsworth, UK: Penguin.

Hong Kingston, M. (1994) *The Woman Warrior.* New York: Vintage.

hooks, b. (1989) *Talking Back.* Cambridge, MA: South End Press.

Jan-Mohamed, A.R. & Lloyd, D. Eds. (1991) *The Nature and Context of Minority Discourses.* Oxford: Oxford University Press

Keesing, R. (1992) *Custom and Confrontation.* Chicago: University of Chicago Press.

Kim, E. (1993) Preface (pp. i–iv). In J. Hagedorn, Ed., *Charlie Chan Is Dead.* New York: Penguin.

Louie, K. (2002) *Theorising Chinese Masculinity.* Cambridge: Cambridge University Press.

Luke, A. (1988) *Literacy, Textbooks and Ideology.* London: Falmer Press.

Luke, A. (2002) Producing new Asian masculinities (pp. 78–90). In C. Barron, N. Bruce & D. Nunan, Eds., *Knowledge and Discourse.* London: Longman.

Luke, A. (2004) Two takes on the critical (pp. 21–30). In B. Norton & K. Toohey, Eds., *Critical Pedagogies and Language Learning.* Cambridge: Cambridge University Press.

Luke, A. (2008) Race and language as capital in school: A sociological template for language education reform. R. Kubota & A. Lin, Eds., *Race, culture and identities in second language education.* London: Routledge, 2009.

Luke, A. & Ismail, M. (2007) Urban education in the Asia Pacific (pp. 221–229). In W. Pink & G. Noblett, Eds. *International Handbook of Urban Education.* Berlin: Springer.

Luke, A., & Luke, C. (2001). Adolescence lost/childhood regained. On early intervention and the emergence of the techno-subject. *Journal of Early Childhood Literacy, 1*(1), 91–120.

Luke, C., & Luke, A. (1998). Interracial families: Difference within difference. *Ethnic and Racial Studies, 21,* 728–733.

Luke, C., & Luke, A. (1999). Theorising interracial families and hybrid identity: An Australian perspective. *Educational Theory, 49,* 223–250.

Malcolm X. (1987) *The Autobiography of Malcolm X.* (with A. Haley). New York: Ballantyne.

Menchu, R. & Menchu, E. (1992) *I, Rigoberto Menchu, An Indian Woman in Guatemala.* London: Verso.

Rafael, V. 1995. 'Taglish, or the Phantom Power of the Lingua Franca,' *Public Culture* 8(1), 101–126.

Raphael, V. L. (1994). The cultures of area studies in the United States. *Social text,* 41: 91-112.

Rodriguez, R. (1982) *Hunger of Memory.* New York: Godine.

Saldana-Portillo, M. (2003) *The Revolutionary Imagination in the Americas and the Age of Development.* Durham, NC: Duke University Press.

Scollon, R. & Scollon, S. (1981) *Narrative, Literacy and Face in Interethnic Communication.* Norwood, NJ: Ablex.

See, L. (1997) *On Gold Mountain.* New York: Vintage.

Tan, A. (1989) *The Joy Luck Club.* New York: Penguin.

Wilson, R. Ed. (1995) *Asia/Pacific as Space of Cultural Production.* Durham, NC: Duke University Press.

Yang, W. (1994) Snapshots (pp. 25–34). In B. Yahp, Ed., *Family Pictures.* Sydney: Angus & Robertson.

Yu, Y.L. (2002) Relocating maternal subjectivity: Storytelling and mother–daughter relationships in Amy Tan's *Joy Luck Club. Third Space* 1(2), retrieved 28/7/08 from http://www.thirdspace.ca/journal/article/view/yu

29

■ Ethnic Chic and the Displacement of South Asian Female Sexuality in the U.S. Media

Meenakshi Gigi Durham

"It's hard to believe that the sacred *bottu* is flaunted by goddess wannabees these days," writes Bhargavi Mandava in a reflection on her struggles growing up South Asian in the United States (1998, p. 75). She notes wryly that the *bottu,* or forehead dot, that's so trendily flaunted by chic alterna-girls now, is the very same symbol of Hindu faith that once propelled hate groups like the Dot-Busters to attack Indian women; "the same little thing that made me cringe whenever people stared and pointed at my mother in a mall" (Mandava, 1998, p. 75). Worn by Indians for religious reasons, the symbol has been construed in the West as a sinister marker of difference, but adopted by white youth it is transformed into cutting-edge fashion.

As Mandava notes, the popularity of nose-rings, mehndi, and *bottus* or bindis in U.S. and European fashion circles is a contemporary manifestation of the appropriation of elements of Asian culture, for Western amusement. This age-old phenomenon speaks to a history of colonialism, domination and exoticization that marks East-West relations, as well as to contemporary issues of global capital and cultural hybridization. South Asian-influenced style trends are now pervasive in United States mass culture, showcased in the fashion and entertainment media as consumer fads to be adopted and discarded arbitrarily, without consideration of their origins or meanings beyond the fashion statement of the moment. Moreover, these markings of South Asian femininity are not represented on South Asian women's bodies; rather, they are almost always represented in the American media as adorning white women's bodies, a phenomenon that raises potent and pressing questions about race, gender, and the politics of representation.

In this chapter, I elucidate and explore these questions as a way to understand more about the role of the mass media in articulating racial difference, with particular reference to South Asian American women. This paper seeks to account for race and national identity as part of a critical analysis of the politics of the female body in mass culture. Using notions of the gaze (Mulvey, 1975; Willemen, 1994a; Willemen, 1994b; Dixon, 1995; Rony, 1996), and its relationship to power vis-à-vis the ethnographic spectacle, my goal is to develop a theoretical framework that will allow for a complex understanding of the current media embrace of symbols of South Asian femininity, and the social, cultural, and political issues raised by it for Asian American women. Most importantly, my focus is on the way power is imbricated in the relations of looking aroused by pop culture images.

I want to make a distinction between the uses of these symbols in the mainstream media, and the "street-level" uses of these symbols in youth culture, which could be interpreted in a variety of ways including via the trope of "cultural hybridization," (García-Canclini, 1995) that hinges on creative syntheses and re-articulations of international cultural crosscurrents.

Rather, the central question of this investigation is: how is the Indian woman's body displaced/reconstituted in Western *media* texts? This analysis will focus specifically on configurations of the raced female body, and its attendant modalities of meaning in U.S. popular media. My goal is to theorize the neocolonial cultural practices that work to fix women's bodies into categories of race, gender, and sexuality. Other questions that stem from this analysis include: what sort of symbolic space does Indian femininity occupy in Western culture that requires its simultaneous appropriation and erasure? How does the dislocation of the symbols of Indian femininity contribute to the discourse of "Orientalism" that remains part of Western culture? How do relations of looking speak to issues of gender, race, and power? And, what are the implications for South Asian and white women?

These questions turn on the pivotal point that, while the artifacts of Indian femininity and sexuality are embraced and even celebrated in the U.S. mass media, they cannot, it seems, be linked with the actual bodies and cultural histories of Indian women. The ensuing study attempts to deal with these paradoxes. By engaging in a critique and analysis of these media phenomena this chapter points to resistant strategies that might progressively transform and re-imagine South Asian female sexuality; it does so in ways that have the potential to disrupt dominant relations among race, gender and nation. As Yegenoglu (1998) points out, "discourses which constitute the subject are at the same time the condition of possibility of its empowerment" (p. 21).

■ South Asian Femininities in the Media

The phenomenon of South Asian-inspired femininity as a Western media trend can be traced to February 1998, when pop icon Madonna released her video "Frozen." The (usually) blond, white-skinned singer appeared in the video adorned with mehndi, and a few months later showed up at the MTV Video Awards fully decorated with Hindu religious symbols and wearing a traditional North Indian salwar kameez outfit. Her appropriation of sacred "Vaishnava tilak" facial markings offended Hindu fundamentalist groups, who deemed her behavior blasphemous (Associated Press, 1998).

The bindi has traditionally been a symbol of Hindu femininity in India. Although its use is largely cosmetic in contemporary India, it is still understood to be a marking that indicates that a woman belongs to the Hindu faith. It is also a symbol of fertility and sexual potential: when a woman is widowed in Hindu culture, a ritual is conducted in which the bindi is ceremonially wiped away, never to be worn again. Similarly, mehndi— the henna designs on women's hands and feet—are both ceremonial and religious, applied usually during Hindu weddings, or other holy and festive celebrations.[1]

Although Madonna did not initiate the fashion for Indian beauty accessories—that had been a growing trend among youth for a couple of years prior to the video—she did propel it into the public eye by attracting the attention of the worldwide media. Following her adoption of South Asian cultural iconography, other celebrities embraced the same styles, and the fashion, beauty, and entertainment press gave it considerable coverage in the calendar year that ensued, when the craze for Indian adornment reached a peak. Religious and cultural symbols of South Asian femininity became translated in the Western media as the apex of high fashion.

In their representation in Western media, these symbols were—and continue to be—part of the decoration of highly sexualized Anglo women. Besides Madonna, adopters of Indian religious and cultural signs prominent in the mass media include Gwen Stefani of the pop group No Doubt, another fair-skinned blond woman whose use of the bindi is referred to in media texts as her "trademark," without any reference to its religious or cultural significance (in Indian culture, the bindi is worn only by women of the Hindu faith who are not widowed); actress Ashley Judd, who wore a purple sari and bindi at a charity event in November 2007; actress Angelina Jolie, who was pictured in an Indian *lehnga* skirt in a 2007 *Marie Claire* interview; actress Nicole Kidman, whose donning of sixteenth century Indian jewelry to accessorize her Dior gown at the 1998 Oscars was much ballyhooed in the press coverage; and actress Liv Tyler, who appeared in *Vanity Fair* magazine bedecked with mehndi. Lucy Lawless and Renee O'Connor, the two white women who starred in the subcultural television show "Xena, Warrior Princess," adopted pseudo-Indian clothing, studied yoga, were adorned with mehndi that turned out to have magical powers, and were visited by the Hindu god Krishna during four episodes of the series set in India. *Seventeen* magazine's 1998 back-to-school issue featured white school-girls in mehndi and bindis, and the July 1999 issue of *Cosmopolitan* carried a fashion spread in which the copy read, "Get an India jones for this hip new imported-from-the East look . . ." noting, "Bindis are for fun," and featuring white models and actresses in pseudo-Indian attire and accessories (Indian Summer, 1999, pp. 70–71). In addition, the high-fashion design houses of Giorgio Armani and Issey Miyake's 1998 shows featured Indian-inspired fabrics and designs, showcased on the willowy bodies of Western, almost all white, runway models.

Thus, at the center of all of the exultation over Indian-inspired fashion are Caucasian women, designated by the Western media as epitomizing dominant social standards of beauty and glamour. The Indian markings are strategically showcased to underscore those standards. In these images, the foreign character of the markings and the jewelry add an exotic dimension to the women's body displays. The power of the markings lies in their appropriation by white women whose bodies and sexual comportment conform to idealized Western notions of beauty. The same markings on a darker-skinned Hindu woman do not—cannot—carry the same power. Bordo (1993) offers a trenchant discussion of women's self-transformation as it is related to the concept of cultural valence, arguing that when a white woman adopts ethnic styles, the historical and contemporary significance—the symbolic weight—is different from when a woman of color adopts white/dominant styles. In these media images—and others that similarly showcase Indian markings on white women's bodies—the trope of the wildly sexual Oriental woman is conflated with the racialized sexual dominance of the white-skinned, slender, usually blond woman to create a powerful sexual image that uses symbols of South Asian femininity to achieve its authority.

The Indian adornments can therefore be understood as devices or strategies rather than objects, and these strategies are tied to issues of nation, race, and sexuality. They have historical specificity, in that they speak to the mutually constitutive categories of "East" and "West," re-circulating imperialist tropes that have taken shape over many years. These tropes engage systems of capital and dominance that intersect with discourses of sex, to position Asian women within a political order of desire, signification, and power. Reviewing the history of this positioning will provide a context for the analysis of this phenomenon.

■ Consuming the Exotic "Other"

Certainly, the presence of South Asian symbols in U.S. popular culture is not new. Since the 1960s, when the Beatles popularized Nehru jackets, sitar music and Indian religion, South Asian inflections have been a visible aspect of "alternative" culture in the United States and Europe. Yet these earlier fashion trends differ from the contemporary ones in two key ways: one, female sexuality was not a characterizing element of earlier phases of American interest in Indian culture, and two, the present historical moment is unprecedented in terms of South Asian immigration to the United States. The mediated uses of symbols of South Asian femininity speak directly to a climate of racial and sexual politics that ties gender to the nation/state—as it has in various ways at different moments in colonial history.

Commodification via the fashion and beauty industry is a key element of this strategy of appropriation. Indeed, the fashion industry operates in relation to global capital and racialized power; its constitution of beauty is inextricably bound up with the mobilization of capital. As Kondo (1997) writes, "[Q]uintessentially transnational in its dispersal and reach, [the fashion industry] is simultaneously rife with essentializing gestures that refabricate national boundaries" (p. 56). It would be naïve in the extreme to consider representation in fashion as a purely aesthetic site; its links to capital render it an arena of power and politics. "The battle ground of style is suffused, indeed constituted by, commodification. The garment industry is deeply enmeshed in an intense semiotics of distinction and a global assembly line on which many Third World women and men toil....The fashion and cosmetics industries promote aesthetic ideals that often oppressively reinscribe normative codes of gender, race, class, and sexuality. Fashion's planned obsolescence is inseparable from complicity with capitalist production and the mobilization of desire" (Kondo, 1997, p. 16).

Thus, popular culture's representations of symbols of South Asian femininity in fashion must be considered in terms of commodification. An important aspect of this commodification is its Western power base, and the East-West relations at play: the recognition that Western countries and the United States in particular, control the means of media production, and marketing must underpin any analysis of fashion and its entailments. Within this framework of capital and power, the cultural appropriation of Eastern cultures as trends, styles, or exotic sexual displays can be understood in terms of issues of imperialism and dominance.

Indeed, the role of exoticized "Oriental" female sexuality in Western consumer culture has been detailed in several studies. Thomas (1965) recounts the history of Asian influences on Western fashion beginning in the 1600s when Catherine of Braganza's dowry inspired a European, and then American, craze for "Oriental" fabrics, furnishings, and foodstuffs. Lalvani (1995) traces the strategies by which advertisers in nineteenth-century Britain exploited the allure of the Orient (particularly Oriental female sexuality) to sell products and legitimize consumer capitalism. Higashi (1994) and Studlar (1995) examine early Hollywood film representations of the Oriental tradition, again linking such representations to consumerism. "Orientalist fantasies associated with the attainment of momentary luxury were linked to the New Woman's culturally-encouraged acquisition of consumer goods," writes Studlar (p. 490). The Orient represented a sinful, luxurious world that was rhetorically and ideologically harnessed to consumerism in the pursuit of femininity; as Studlar points out, a "visual language of orientalism" in the mass media was deliberately aimed at Western female consumers.

The sexual overtones of this discourse cannot be ignored. As Yegenoglu (1998) notes, there is a "unique articulation of sexual and cultural difference as they are produced and signified in the discourse of Orientalism" (p. 1). The Orient was consistently depicted by the Western media as an arena of unleashed sexual desires and outlandish pleasures, particularly as far as women were concerned. Said (1978) first addressed the underpinnings of this ideology of Asian female sexuality when he described the Western conception of the Oriental woman as eager to be dominated, possessed of a "dumb and irreducible sexuality" (p. 187), and at the same time fascinatingly exotic. His celebrated take on Orientalism positioned these discursive formations as part of a Western rationale, "for dominating, restructuring, and having authority over the Orient" (Said, 1978, p. 3). In Said's view, the representations of Oriental sexuality that are manifested in Western texts can be read first and foremost as expressions of the hegemony of Western society over Eastern cultures; in addition, they are peculiarly patriarchal constructions that are tied to the notion of Asia as, "a deep, rich fund of female sexuality" (Said, 1978, p. 182).

While Said's explication of the racist and colonizing aspects of Orientalist discourse has considerable power, his somewhat oversimplified picture of East/West and male/female oppositions has been criticized in recent years (see Clifford, 1988; Lalvani, 1995; Lewis, 1996; Lowe, 1991; Yegenoglu, 1998). Lewis (1996) reminds us that the Orientalist gaze is not always necessarily male—a point particularly pertinent to this analysis. Bhabha (1983) points out the ambivalence in Orientalist discourses: the simultaneous allure and menace of the exoticized Eastern other, the fetishistic nature of colonial discourse that is paradoxically infused with both erotic desire and racist contempt. Lalvani (1995) builds on the idea of this ambivalence, noting that "the imaginary construction of the Other's sexuality is central to a Western politics of desire" (p. 270). The voyeuristic positioning of the "Oriental" female body in Western texts speaks to a variety of positions on sex, race, and power. Lalvani (1995) points out, "'La femme orientale' is a heterogeneous site in which a multiplicity of discourses engage and intersect, in which dominant and emergent formations may contest each other, and in which other social differences and contradictions are articulated in an ongoing hegemonic process" (p. 265).

There are definite distinctions to be made among the ways in which so-called "Oriental" female bodies circulate in Western texts. Different Eastern cultures, linked with different histories of colonization and political interactions with the West, have given rise to different exploitations of Asian, as well as Middle Eastern, women's sexuality under the broad rubric of "Orientalism." Shohat and Stam (1994) point out, "The East is divided into 'Near,' 'Middle,' and 'Far'" (p. 2), indicating a system of spatial organization that not only privileges Europe as the perspectival starting point, but also differentiates among cultures in an ideological hierarchy of relationships. Thus, women of the "far East" have been positioned as exotic sex objects, seductive and dangerous, in Western cinematic texts (Marchetti, 1993); their bodies are the sites of hegemonic expressions of domination and control in Western media culture, and these expressions rest on the Oriental woman's body as explicitly sexual.

By contrast, Yegenoglu (1998) points out that the *veiling* of the Arab woman's body is crucial in constructions of the Orient; the concealment of Arab women's bodies behind the veil is a target of colonialist discourse. She writes, "[T]he colonial subject's desire to control and dominate the foreign land is not independent from his scopic desire, from his desire to penetrate, through his surveillant eye, what is behind the veil" (p. 62). Thus, unveiling an Arab women's hidden body is a goal of colonial domination, in Yegenoglu's formulation: the female body is located at the center of the techniques of colonial control and domination.

South Asian women's bodies have a far different meaning in Western culture, argues Bannerji (1993). She observes that South Asian women—in contrast to East Asian or Middle Eastern women—are *not* sexually objectified in Western media representation; indeed, they have no sexuality, nor any other characteristic, because the lack of representation of South Asian women in Western media speaks of, and to, their complete dehumanization. "[W]hile we do not have to worry about our representation in the media, we do have to worry about the fact that, negatively or positively, we live in a vacuum, in a state of constant facelessness" she writes (Bannerji, 1993, p. 145). This visual absence is, in her words, an injunction or code of command which bids South Asian women "to be silent, to remove ourselves from areas or places where we may be seen" (p. 149).

In all of these analyses, the uses of Asian or "Oriental" female bodies in Western texts serves primarily to concretize certain colonial and postcolonial myths, and to strategically deploy Asian femininity as part of a patriarchal, heterosexist, and racially hierarchical value system. According to this considerable body of scholarship, such representations are pervasive, have taken root in our culture, and serve to inscribe Asian women's sexuality in severely limited and fixed ways that have a significant impact on society's understanding of Asian femininity, as well as Asian women's understandings of ourselves.

Such significations have brought up challenges: this formulation necessarily raises key questions about agency, representation, and non-Western subjectivity, which have moved to the forefront in recent years. In considering issues of representation, Foster (1999) writes provocatively, "by capturing the exotic Other in photographs, stereoscopes, and other visual media, men of Empire advanced the fantasies and realities of quest and Othering the subaltern. *But is the subject always the object in these cases?*" (p. 19, italics added).

This question shifts the starting point of inquiry to the other end of the camera, so to speak, moving us away from the lens of the male gaze, and its positioning of Asian womanhood as fixed, frozen, and always subordinated, to the consideration of a diametrically different point of view. In the following section, I will discuss notions of subjectivity, and the returned gaze in the context of contemporary postcolonial representation. My analysis of the present-day deployment of symbols of South Asian femininity in the U.S. mass media pivots on an interrogation and reworking of these important concepts, and a different way of considering the "ethnographic spectacle."

■ Mutual Looks and Volatile Bodies

The viewing of images involves multiple processes and multiple "looks," which is to say that constituting the viewer as active subject, and the viewed as passive object, is a simplistic and heuristically limited formulation. In cinema studies, the notion of the returned gaze or "the look back" from the performer/camera to the audience, has generated new ways of conceptualizing spectatorship and its social meanings (cf. Mulvey, 1975, with Vernet, 1989; Willemen, 1994a; Willemen, 1994b; Dixon, 1995). Willemen contends that the viewer's metacognition of his/her own act of looking creates an imaginary observer; the viewer becomes aware of the implications of being seen watching; this Willemen terms "the fourth look."

> Any articulation of images and looks which brings into play the position and activity of the viewer as a distinctly separate factor also destabilises that position and puts it at risk….When the scopic drive is brought into focus, the viewer also runs the risk of becoming the object of the look, of being overlooked in the act of looking. (Willemen, 1994b, p. 114)

This recognition challenges the viewer to consider his/her act of looking in its social context. The "fourth look" strips the act of looking of its innocence and normality, transforming into a considered action with political implications. It engenders—or perhaps demands—reflexivity in the viewer.

In Willemen's conception of "the fourth look," the viewer's observer is imaginary; the sense of being seen stems from an awareness of his/her own voyeurism. Dixon (1995) develops and concretizes this notion by asserting that while a viewer is watching a film, the film is in a sense "looking back," working to interpellate the viewer. "The film acts upon us, addressing us, viewing us as we view it, until the film itself *becomes* a gaze, rather than an object to be gazed on," he writes (Dixon, 1995, p. 2), later adding, "This 'gaze of the screen,' or 'look back,' has the power to transform our existences, to substantially change our view of our lives and of the world we inhabit" (p. 7). The look back inverts the basic premise of active viewer/passive text, revealing things about the viewer by forcing him/her to look at him/herself via his/her engagement with the text.

In a refinement of this theme, Rony (1996) brings to bear issues of race and nation, by offering us the idea of the Third Eye, that is, the gaze that the object of ethnographic spectacle turns back on the viewer, a gaze that marks the viewer and reconstitutes him from the viewpoint of the objectified Other. In this process, "[b]oth viewer and subject are captives and captors, both are involved in mediating the image of self between the known and unknown, both are co-performing a narrative of selfhood" (Foster, 1999, p. 22)—a dynamic that allows for resistance, for transgressive reinscriptions of power roles. Recognizing the power of the resistant gaze opens the possibility of a different understanding on the part of the viewer; it breaks down the traditional and familiar subject/object binary, opening the way for multiple meanings to emerge from mutual recognitions of difference.

Given these possibilities, there remains an aspect of representation that has not been adequately problematized or dealt with in the literature, and that is the notion of invisibility or erasure. As Spivak (1988) has noted, subaltern subjects, without access to cultural imperialism, are also barred from self-representation; that is, their utterances cannot achieve the status of dialogue and are thus unheard. In a similar vein, I argue here that there can be no Third Eye—no returned gaze—*if no one is really there to return the gaze.* This begets the question, "Who looks back?" when we consider representations of South Asian femininity in the Western media. On that question hinges central issues of power, national identity, and sexual subjectivity.

Williams (1980) points out the transmission of culture, involves selection and interpretation: "it is a fact about the modes of domination that they select from and consequently exclude the full range of actual and possible human practice" (p. 43). What is selected for transmission, and what is suppressed or expunged, reveals much about the politics of the social context. In this vein, certain Asian ethnicities are selected for representation and interpretation in the mass media (as injurious as this might be; see Marchetti, 1993; Bernstein and Studlar, 1997), while others—specifically, South Asian ones[2]—suffer from a curious kind of displacement. It is precisely the phenomenon of displacement that I wish to consider in detail in this chapter.

I am not referring here to outright invisibility, or total eradication; that would be easier to make sense of as a more or less straightforward case of "symbolic annihilation," to use Gerbner's familiar term (Gerbner, 1972, p. 44). Rather, in contemporary representations of Asian femininity in U.S. mass culture, the current visual strategies have the peculiar result that certain ethnic groups suffer from what I can only describe as a "semi-erasure," a simultaneous visibility and invisibility that calls to mind a phantasm or magic trick. Tajima alludes briefly to this phenomenon via the trope of the "made-up Asian," exemplified in such films as HBO's *The Far Pavilions,* where Amy Irving was cast as the Indian heroine. "Even mainstream critics had to chuckle at the brown shoe polish make-up and exaggerated boldface eyeliner worn by Irving," Tajima notes (1989, p. 313). This character was certainly not the first, or last, Asian to be portrayed by a Caucasian actor with exaggerated eyes and pancake make-up, but the issue deserves more than a dismissive giggle. What is striking here is that the bodies of Indian women in particular, are systematically displaced in the American mass media—sometimes replaced by the bodies of white women, and sometimes not replaced at all: the outline of where the body should be remains, but the lady vanishes.

■ Gender, Place, and Body Politics

In contemporary media representations of Indian body art on the bodies of iconic white female beauties, the Indian woman is Othered by stripping the traditional symbols of her femininity from her body, and using them to intensify the sexual appeal of the white woman. Thus, the political is located within the sexual, to deploy a neocolonial construction of desire. At the most basic level, these images represent a double alterity: the white female as sexual object, and the Asian Indian female as the intangible, and disembodied fetish that supports white female sexuality. Shohat and Stam (1994) discuss similar displacements in Hollywood cinema, noting, "What all these appropriations have in common is a desire for an otherness whose presence is made possible, paradoxically, only through erasure" (p. 227).

Yet the issue is a good deal more complex than that. Two distinct theoretical threads coalesce in this analysis: one tracks the idea of the Third Eye, the possibility of the object of ethnographic spectacle returning the gaze; the other, that India exists in the Western imagination as part of a neocolonial idiom that renders it a volatile metaphor used to chart difference from Western mores (see Chaudhary, 1998; Sen, 1993; Gokhale, 1992). By locating the current trendiness of Indian-inspired body art and costuming at the intersection of these discourses, I seek to create here a theoretical framework with which to interpret the displacement of the Indian woman's body, in contemporary Western popular culture.

Grosz (1994) points out, "the body must be regarded as a site of social, political, cultural, and geographical inscriptions, production, or constitution. The body is not opposed to culture, a resistant throwback to a natural past; it is itself a cultural, *the* cultural, product." White women's bodies are the dominant cultural product of popular media, in that they are deployed as sexual signifiers that serve to mobilize capital (Williamson, 1986; Faurschou, 1987; Shields, 1990; McCracken, 1993; MacCurdy, 1994). In her study of the *Sports Illustrated* swimsuit issue, Davis (1997) outlines the racial hierarchy that underpins this commodification of women's desirability, noting that "[w]omen with white skin, blonde and straight hair, blue eyes and small noses are at the top, and women with dark skin, black and curly hair, and big noses are at the bottom" (p. 92). This hierarchy always already interpellates women of color as undesirable, on the basis of phenotype.

Yet dark skin presents a paradox in this construction, since in the Western cultural idiom it signifies an exotic hypersexuality. The problem of skin color and its metaphorical link to sexuality complicates representation, necessitating a racialized layering of characteristics in media representations of ideal female sexuality. Thus, Davis (1997) notes that since the 1970s, blonde and blue-eyed *Sports Illustrated* swimsuit models have had tanned skin—although "only whites can afford to get a tan, because they do not have to (for the most part) endure racism" (p. 91). In a parallel and more pernicious construction, dark-skinned women are put to use in the mass media, "to highlight whiteness" (hooks, 1992, p. 28). In hooks' analysis of this latter phenomenon, a key theme is that whiteness is the focus of media forays into the representation of the Other. The nonwhite "exotic," is a backdrop and a foil, a contrivance that reaffirms the elements of ideal whiteness and marks the distance between white and Other. As Foster (1999) expresses it, "The definition of the clean White body is maintained by the insistent prevalence of images of an/other" (p. 3).

A corollary of this trend is white/mainstream culture's appropriation of nonwhite cultural products. hooks (1992) notes,

> Currently, the commodification of difference promotes paradigms of consumption wherein whatever difference the Other inhabits is eradicated, via exchange, by a consumer cannibalism that not only displaces the Other but denies the significance of that Other's history through a process of decontextualization. (p. 31)

Through this process, cultural products are carelessly circulated in consumer society, stripped of their meaning, and their political integrity, and converted into empty, expendable decorations. Any social consciousness, or potential for critique or disruption that these products may have held, is canceled: "As signs, their power to ignite critical consciousness is diffused when they are commodified. Communities of resistance are replaced by communities of consumption" (hooks, 1992, p. 33).

I will argue here that there is a great deal more going on than a crude process of appropriation and commodification. I believe that there is disconnect between the representation of symbols of Asian femininity in the media, and their uses at the street level. It is certainly plausible that the popularity of these symbols among Western youth speaks to more than a desire to co-opt the exotic; it seems much more likely that there are creative and complicated varieties of cultural hybridization, experimentation, and global/local intersections occurring in youth culture. But the media's showcasing of the phenomenon does not allow for these possibilities to be explored. In the mediated images, "[t]he subaltern presence…is largely inferential" (Shohat and Stam, 1994, p. 223); thus, one is left only with the insistent presence of the desirable white female body in relation to metaphors of Asian-ness that cannot "look back," in a way that might illuminate or open up what Shohat and Stam (1994) posit as, "a contrapuntal reading of a shared, conflictual history" (p. 244).

Instead, the white mainstream media's portrayal of symbols of Indian femininity speaks to a hegemonic process of disabling social critique and change. The popularity of mehndi, bindi, nose-rings, and the like, comes at a powerful political moment. This is a time when progressive social movements—affirmative action, immigrant rights, abortion rights—are under attack, and the dominant discourse is one of containing the political uprisings of marginalized members of U.S. society. It is also a time when India is making its presence felt in the West in multiple and potentially subversive, ways. Indian immigration to the West is on the rise, and the types of immigrants that are making their way into Western society challenge the traditional place of India in the Western world-view. The new Indian immigrants:

> are highly visible to Americans in professional and technical occupations, and they make an impact on the American image of India. That impact must lead to some schizophrenia in the American mind, because it contrasts with the prevailing image of Indian poverty and economic fecklessness. As against swamis and gurus, or the poverty-stricken masses of India, the American sees around him pragmatic and effective stockbrokers, financial analysts, scientists, engineers, doctors, and entrepreneurs. How the American mind will accommodate to this double vision I do not know: At least it will complicate the image of India in the American mind. (Glazer, 1990, p. 17)

Indian women—degreed, professional women with drive and independence—are among this group of immigrants, and they in particular challenge traditional views of the Oriental female, whose docility, subservience and dumb sexuality are indelible markers of her existence, in the Western construction (Mohanty, 1991). Western culture's appropriation of the symbols that inscribe Indian femininity functions, first, to disconnect them from the bodies of Indian women—bodies that threaten to subvert this essentialized construction by their potential to turn a Third Eye on viewers, second, to trivialize and delegitimize these symbols as cultural products with specific history and meaning to Indian women, and third, to re-circulate them as signs of exotic sexuality that provide a dramatic aesthetic polarity against which to position and reassert the superiority of white women in the hierarchy of appearance. The illusion is of cultural hybridization, but the underlying formulation reinforces the political notion that, "East and West form closed, mutually exclusive spaces where one term inevitably dominates the other" (Kondo, 1997, p. 49).

■ Reclaiming Meaning; Rethinking Gender, Race, and Sexuality

The mediated displacement of Indian femininity onto the white body, functions in specific ways in the context of a contemporary discourse of Orientalism. Hall (1995) argues that "how things are represented and the 'machineries' and regimes of representation in a culture do play a *constitutive,* and not merely a reflexive, after-the-event, role" (p. 224). It is clear that the use of the imaginary East in media texts has not disappeared—in fact, it is recreated in order to stabilize dominant ideologies of femininity, sexuality, and race. The U.S. mass media's presentation of Indian femininity as a substructure for white female sexuality, serves to legitimate the hegemonic construction of Western superiority over Asian culture. In a sense, it inverts the traditional objectification and exoticization of the Oriental female body—here, the South Asian body is not represented as sexually exotic; rather, it is used to supplement white female sexuality through a system of pastiche. Moreover, by privileging the white body, it suppresses counter-hegemonic discourses related to these issues of culture and national identity—for example, the use of nose-rings and mehndi by South Asian American women seeking to reestablish their connections with their heritage, in order to carve out spaces of resistance to the dominant ideology of assimilation. Such constructions are denied entry into mainstream media texts, perhaps because they threaten prevalent fantasies about the mysterious, sensuous Orient and its value to the Western politics of desire. Most importantly, they would provide Indian women with a way to look back at the West, a way to challenge and re-imagine their roles, a way to assert their sexual and political agency. As Rony (1996) points out, "the Third Eye turns on a recognition: the Other perceives the veil, the process of being visualized as an object, but returns the gaze. The gesture of being frozen into a picaresque is deflected….Open resistance…is one mode of the Third Eye" (p. 213). In the phenomenon of displacement, there is no Third Eye—no possibility for returning the gaze.

Of course, the potential exists to read these images as politically progressive. White women's embrace of these symbols could certainly connote genuine admiration, a celebration of Asian femininity. Again, though, as long as only white women are given the privilege of conferring meaning on these symbols, via popular media's representation strategies, the specificity and agency of Asian American women's relationships to these symbols are undermined. Cultural hybridization has multiple trajectories, and the interactions of these symbols as they play out among women in the Western world could tell us a great deal about sex, race, and national identity on many fronts. But as long as South Asian American women are denied symbolic access to the markers of their own heritage, this heuristic cannot be pursued.

Thus, it is vital to explore the implications of these representational issues for South Asian American women, as well as for other women of color, and for white women. DuttaAhmed (1996) writes of a "splitting" of the Asian American self—the recognition of Otherness within our intimate relationship to the "colonizing" culture. "It is in fact disrupted selves, multiple selves, that the border posits, rather than the singular, identifiable Other who is then configured in opposition to the Western subject," he writes (p. 339). Further, he argues that this disruption of the self is "actualized through the representational strategies by which the Other has been inscribed in dominant culture" (p. 340); the tensions inherent in this troubled positioning point to a need to explore our representational history in a way that might produce some kind of repositioning. Yet, DuttaAhmed cautions, visibility alone is not a sufficient goal, "because issues of difference remain ideologically valenced…and [do] not disrupt the relationships of power between observer and observed" (p. 346).

What then, is the value of cultural critique that not only exposes certain dominant core assumptions about South Asian women in America, but makes female whiteness visible as a politically motivated, ethnic/sexual construction? I believe it has the potential to open up a way of re-theorizing Asian American sexual agency. This kind of critique can situate representational stereotypes, not as dead ends or as fixed elements, but as a tool for understanding sexuality and identity as relational. This brings to bear the notion of, "articulation" developed by Hall (1995), where ideological elements are, "connected to each other, but through a specific linkage, that can be broken" (p. 53). Reflecting on the ways in which Asian American female sexuality is articulated to white female sexuality in the dominant culture, can spur us to reformulate our sexual subjectivity and explore the "splitting" that DuttaAhmed writes about: we can take into account, and also contest, the power of those articulations on the basis of our diasporic ontology, our lived experiences as South Asian American women. The next step in this analysis would necessarily be in the field, connecting with South Asian American women, as well as others, to understand more about how they negotiate these symbols, and what the meanings are in their lives. For South Asian American women, the goal would not be re-presentation, so much as social and cultural transformation: a reclaiming and reorganization of the elements of cultural practice into new discursive formations that would first, release Asian women's sexuality from bondage to whiteness, and second, catalyze the emergence of concepts of sexuality that would address the goals of South Asian women, rather than those of white men, white women, or the re-colonization of the Orient. For other women, it holds the potential to re-imagine femininity and sexuality in light of the multiple national and international contexts and cultures that traverse contemporary lives.

Notes

1. Regional variations exist in the significance and uses of these markers; mehndi also have uses in Islamic Middle Eastern and African cultures. These variations in the meanings and uses of the symbols are lost in their circulation as high-fashion accessories.

2. The term "South Asian" is used to refer to the countries of the Indian subcontinent (India, Pakistan, Bangladesh, and Sri Lanka), as well as to the neighboring countries of Nepal, Myanmar, Bhutan, and Afghanistan. Bahri and Vasudeva (1996) point out that the term in the context of the Asian American diaspora has specifically political connotations and is today deployed in Anglo-America for various purposes: to gain visibility in the sociopolitical arena, to speak against racism and misrepresentation from a position of collectivity, to initiate social action for the economically depressed and systematically alienated among the group, to open an avenue for the exploration of lost or receding cultural ties with the country of origin, to provide a forum for expressing and investigating experiences and feelings of displacement, alienation, and other forms of cultural anxiety, and to gain a more equal footing, perhaps even an advantage, in market value and economic opportunity. (p. 7)

References

Associated Press (1998, September 13). People in the news. http://wire.ap.org/APsearch/main.html

Bahri, D., & Vasudeva, M. (1996). Introduction. In D. Bahri and M. Vasudeva (Eds.), *Between the lines: South Asians and postcoloniality*, (pp. 1–34). Philadelphia: Temple University Press.

Bannerji, H. (Ed.). (1993). *The gaze: Essays on racism, feminism, and politics.* Toronto: Sister Vision Press.

Bhabha, H. (1983, November/December). The other question. *Screen 24*(6), 18–36.

Bernstein, M., and Studlar, G. (1997). *Visions of the east: Orientalism in film.* New Brunswick, NJ: Rutgers University Press.

Bordo, S. (1993). *Unbearable weight: Feminism, Western culture, and the body.* Berkeley: University of California Press.

Chaudhary, S. D. (1998). Imagi(ned)nations: The politics and ethics of representation in colonial and postcolonial narratives of India. Unpublished doctoral dissertation, University of Texas at Austin.

Clifford, J. (1988). *The predicament of culture.* Cambridge, MA: Harvard University Press.

Davis, L. R. (1997). *The swimsuit issue and sport: Hegemonic masculinity in* Sports Illustrated. Albany, NY: SUNY Press.

Dixon, W. W. (1995). *It looks at you: The returned gaze of cinema.* Albany: SUNY Press.

DuttaAhmed, S. (1996). Border crossings: Retrieval and erasure of the Self as Other. In D. Bahri and M. Vasudeva (Eds.), *Between the lines: South Asians and postcoloniality,* (pp. 337–350). Philadelphia: Temple University Press.

Faurschou, G. (1987). Fashion and the cultural logic of postmodernity. In A. Kroker and M. Kroker (Eds.), *Body invaders: Panic sex in America,* 78–93. New York: St. Martin's Press.

Foster, G. A. (1999). Captive bodies: Postcolonial subjectivity in cinema. Albany, NY: SUNY Press.

García-Canclini, N. (1995). *Hybrid cultures: Strategies for entering and leaving modernity.* Minneapolis: University of Minnesota Press.

Gerbner, G. (1972). Violence in television drama: Trends and symbolic functions. In G. A. Constock and E. A. Rubinstein (Eds.), *Media content and control.* Television and social behavior, Vol. 1 (pp. 28–287). Washington, DC: U.S. Government Printing Office.

Glazer, N. (1990). Introduction. In S.R. Glazer and N. Glazer (Eds.), *Conflicting images: India and the United States,* 1–22. Glenn Dale, MD: Riverdale.

Gokhale, B. G. (1992). *India in the American mind.* Bombay: Popular Prakashan.

Grosz, E. (1994). *Volatile bodies: Toward a corporeal feminism.* St. Leonards, Australia: Allen & Unwin.

Hall, S. (1995). New ethnicities. In B. Ashcroft, G. Griffiths, and H. Tiffin (Eds.), *The postcolonial studies reader,* (pp. 223–227). London and New York: Routledge.

Hamamoto, D. (1994). *Monitored peril : Asian Americans and the politics of TV representation.* Minneapolis: University of Minnesota Press.

Higashi, S. (1994). *Cecil B. DeMille and American culture: The silent era.* Berkeley: University of California Press.

hooks, b. (1992). *Black looks: Race and representation.* Cambridge, MA: South End Press.

Indian summer. (1999, July). *Cosmopolitan, 227,* 70–71.

Kondo, D. (1997). *About face: Performing race in fashion and theater.* New York and London: Routledge.

Lalvani, S. (1995, September). Consuming the exotic Other. *Critical Studies in Mass Communication* 12(3), 263–286.

Lewis, R. (1996). *Gendering Orientalism: Race, femininity, and representation.* New York and London: Routledge.

Ling, A. 1(989). Chinamerican women writers: Four forerunners of Maxine Hong Kingston. In A. Jaggar and S. Bordo, Eds., *Gender/body/knowledge: Feminist reconstructions of being and knowing,* (pp. 309–323). New Brunswick, NJ: Rutgers University Press,.

Lowe, L. (1991). *Critical terrains: French and British orientalisms.* Ithaca: Cornell University Press.

MacCurdy, M. (1994). The four women of the Apocalypse: Polarized feminine images in magazine advertisements. In L. Manca and A. Manca (Eds.), *Gender & utopia in advertising : A critical reader,* (pp. 31–48). Syracuse, NY: Syracuse University Press.

Mandava, B. C. (1998). To Apu, with love. In O. Edut (Ed.), *Adios Barbie: Young women write about body image and identity,* pp. 68–77. Seattle, Wash.: Seal Press.

Marchetti, G. (1993). Romance and the yellow peril: Race, sex, and discursive strategies in Hollywood fiction. Berkeley: University of California Press.

McCracken, E. (1993). *Decoding women's magazines: From "Mademoiselle" to "Ms."* London: Macmillan.

Mohanty, C. T. (1991). Under Western eyes: Feminist scholarship and colonial discourse. In C.T. Mohanty, A. Russo, and L. Torres (Eds.), *Third World women and the politics of feminism,* (pp. 51–80). Bloomington: Indiana University Press.

Mulvey, L. (1975). Visual pleasure and narrative cinema. *Screen* 16 (3), 6–18.

Rony, F. T. (1996). *The Third Eye: Race, cinema, and ethnographic spectacle.* Durham, NC: Duke University Press.

Said, E. W. (1978). *Orientalism.* New York: Vintage.

Sen, A. (1993, June 7). India and the West: Our distortions and their consequences. *The New Republic* 208 (23), 27–33.

Shields, V. R. (1990). Advertising visual images: Gendered ways of looking and seeing. *Journal of Communication Inquiry* 14 (2), 25–39.

Shohat, E., & Stam, R. (1994). *Unthinking Eurocentrism: Multiculturalism and the media.* New York and London: Routledge.

Spivak, G. C. (1988). Can the subaltern speak? In C. Nelson and L. Grossberg (Eds.), *Marxism and the interpretation of culture,* (pp. 217–313). Urbana: U of Illinois P.

Studlar, G. (1995). "Out-Salomeing Salome": Dance, the New Woman, and fan magazine Orientalism. *Michigan Quarterly Review* 34 (4), 486–510.

Tajima, R. (1989). Lotus Blossoms don't bleed: Images of Asian women. In Asian Women United of California (Eds.), *Making waves: An anthology of writings by and about Asian American women,* (pp. 308–317). Boston: Beacon.

Thomas, G. Z. (1965). *Richer than spices: how a royal bride's dowry introduced cane, lacquer, cottons, tea, and porcelain to England, and so revolutionized taste, manners, craftsmanship, and history in both England and America.* New York: Knopf.

Vernet, M. (1989). The look at the camera. *Cinema Journal* 28 (2), 48–63.

Willemen, P. (1994a). The fourth look. In *Looks and frictions: Essays in cultural studies and film theory* (pp. 99–110). Bloomington: Indiana University Press.

Willemen, P. (1994b). Letter to John. In *Looks and frictions: Essays in cultural studies and film theory* (pp. 111–123). Bloomington: Indiana University Press.

Williams, R. (1980). Base and superstructure in Marxist cultural theory. In *Problems in materialism and culture: Selected essays,* (pp. 31–49). London: Verso and NLB.

Williamson, J. (1986). *Consuming passions: The dynamics of popular culture.* London: Boyars.

Yegenoglu, M. (1998). *Colonial fantasies: Toward a feminist reading of Orientalism.* Cambridge: Cambridge University Press.

30

■ Model Minority/Honorable Eunuch

The Dual Image of Asian American Men in the Media and in Everyday Perception

Chyng Sun, Ekra Miezan, and Rachael Liberman

I know many Asian-American (and even Asian-Asian) women who shun men of their own race. Meanwhile, many Asian guys think it's impossible that they could attract women who are not Asian. What does this mean? Lots of Asian guys who aren't getting any!

> Sherng-Lee Huang, Letters of the Week, Time Out New York, *September 13–19, 2007*

The representational stereotype of Asian American men as the "model minority" is generally considered a "positive" construction; nonetheless, the characterization is a double-edged sword. On the one hand, this label represents the assumed intelligence and academic/economic success of Asian American men, but on the other hand, it refers to their silence and compliance despite the discrimination they suffer. This image of a passive and silent workhorse is coupled with popular media representations of Asian American men in confined roles such as kung fu masters, emotionless villains, restaurant workers "fresh off the boat," or nerdy computer/technical professionals. Not only are these characters depicted as socially awkward and physically unattractive by Western standards, but they are also asexual—rarely shown in romantic situations (Tajima, 1989; Xing, 1998; Cao & Novas, 1996; Chen, 1996; Zia, 2000).

The dual stereotypes of "model minority" and "honorable eunuch" appear contradictory, but are actually complementary in maintaining the status quo. The myth of Asian Americans "pulling themselves up by their bootstraps" without the need for governmental support testifies to the fairness of a race-less society and is used to blame the social and economic deprivation of other racial groups for not working hard enough. At the same time, Asian American men's supposed lack of sexual prowess, which cannot be resolved by wealth, flatters working class white men as well as other men of color, whose dominance in the sexual realm compensates for their economic or class disadvantage.

In contrast to the popular myth of the emasculated Asian American male, Asian American women are hypersexualized and always available to white men. This mythology of the different sexuality and performance of Asian American men and women has roots in colonial discourses and U.S. immigration policies. Espiritu (2000) articulates the dialectic relationship between social and ideological control and how stereotyping plays an important role:

> Racist and gendered immigration policies and labor conditions have worked together to keep Asian Americans in an assigned, subordinate place in the patriarchal economy of U.S. culture. The system of oppression in turn is maintained by a set of 'controlling images' that provides the ideological justification for the economic exploitation and social oppression of Asian Americans. (Espiritu, 2000, p. 7)

Patricia Hill Collins (1990) developed the notion of "controlling images" when she theorized about black images, contending that the ruling elite, with their dominance in the spheres of politics and economy, tends to objectify the subordinate group. Utilizing cultural institutions to disseminate images of subordinated groups as naturally violent, barbaric, and inferior, the dominant class acts to pit these marginalized groups against each other while leaving themselves unexamined (Espiritu, 2000; Hamamoto, 1994).

To solidify dominant ideology, science is often mobilized to generate, promote, and naturalize knowledge that supports the ruling elite (Gould, 1996). Using the tenets of biological determinism, Rushton (2000) claims that penis size and sexual activity correlate positively with violence, yet inversely with intelligence. Moreover, there are distinct racial differences: black males are most sexual, least intelligent, and most violent; Asian Americans are least sexual, most intelligent, and least violent; and the whites are somewhere in the middle, i.e., the normal ones. Loaded with racial and gender ideologies but lacking the social and historical analysis of the formation of racial hierarchy in North America, Rushton provides a biological endorsement for the mirror stereotype of model minority/honorable eunuch that has long permeated popular media.

Given that Asian American men are largely represented as the model minority/honorable eunuch—intelligent and successful, yet lacking masculinity and sexual charm (Chihara, 2000)—how do these representations affect people's perceptions of this group, particularly in terms of their sexuality? The research on Asian Americans and the media, however, has largely focused on the historical and ideological constructs of Asian American media representations. Comparatively few studies have attempted to investigate the ways these media images interact with and affect people's perceptions of Asian American men. Although there is anecdotal evidence that Asian American men express frustrations in the dating arena, as well as the fact that some connections have been found between media effects and perceptions of Asian American men and how they view themselves (Chan, 2001; Wong, 1993; Mok, 1998), a systematic approach to study the effects of Asian American media representation is still lacking.

Using both quantitative and qualitative research methods, the study at hand takes up the following questions: If the model minority/honorable eunuch dual image is prevalent within the mainstream media's representation of Asian American men, how does this representation affect actual perceptions of them—particularly their sexuality? How would that affect women's interests in having Asian American men as their romantic partners? How do Asian American men negotiate the complexity of their identity within these stereotypical representations affecting their self-esteem, social role, and social interactions? Such questions lead us not only to examine media effects in long-term, gradual, and nuanced ways, but also to problematize white masculinity, the marker of normativity against which yellow men are measured.

■ Literature Review

To our knowledge, no previous study has systematically addressed our research regarding potential media effects on multi-racial individuals' perception of Asian American men and their interest in dating them. Nevertheless, research from diverse disciplines informs our investigation. We broadly divide the relevant studies into two categories: media representations of Asian American men and media effects on both Asian American identities and the perceptions of Asian Americans.

Asian American Media Representations

Representations of Asian Americans are still rare in contemporary mass media. Although they represent 4.3% of the U.S. population (U.S. Census, 2005), the percentage of Asian/Pacific characters has remained the same since 2001, which is 3% of total characters and 1% of opening credits characters. In addition, Asian/Pacific characters are far less likely than characters from other racial groups to appear in primary roles (Fall Colors 2003–2004: Prime Time Diversity Report, p. 2). According to the 2005 Asian Pacific American Report Card on Television Diversity, "In some cases, network progress in providing opportunities for Asian Pacific Americans has not only slowed, but is deteriorating" (Narasaki, p. 1). However, this seeming absence is only one aspect of the force that continues to marginalize Asian Americans in the U.S. mainstream media. Ideological constructs almost always reflect, shape, and are in turn shaped by their material condition; therefore it is important to understand the historical circumstances that led to the development of particular stereotypical perceptions.

Historical Roots

Beginning in the late 1840s, Chinese men were recruited by U.S. employers as cheap labor to work as gold miners on the West Coast and later as railroad construction workers (Chen, 1996). U.S. immigration law treated those workers as temporary, disposable, and exploitable labor, and subsequently prohibited the entry of their families and unmarried Asian American women, fearing the permanent presence and growth of Asian Americans (Espiritu, 2000). During this time, the image of the emasculated Chinese male had already been developed and performed by white men in popular minstrel shows, where they were mostly depicted as lusting over white women, yet unable to compete with the white men's sexual prowess (Lee, 1999).

By the 1870s, a depression followed the completion of the Central Pacific Railroad and the decline of gold production. White laborers blamed the Chinese for driving down wages and robbing their jobs, resulting in anti-Chinese sentiment and the organization of a nativist movement. Chinese men were driven out of the industrial and agricultural job markets and forced to enter occupations such as cooks and laundrymen; jobs deemed unmanly for white workers. Moreover, thousands of these men became domestic servants in middle-class homes, doing "women's jobs" (Chen, 1996; Lee, 1999). Later, in 1882, Congress passed the Chinese Exclusion Act and eventually in 1924 barred all Asians from immigrating to the United States. This did not change until the passage of the 1965 Immigration Act (Mansfield-Richardson, 1996).

As a result of U.S. immigration policy, which excluded Asian women from entering the United States legally, and the anti-miscegenation laws, which prohibited Asian American men from marrying white women, Asian American men were forced to establish "bachelor societies" in the pre-World War II era (Espiritu, 2000). Since media are important "ideological state apparatuses" that reinforce the ruling ideology (Althusser, 1971), it is not surprising that while Asian Americans were heavily discriminated against and exploited by immigration policies and labor conditions, Chinese men were portrayed as feminine and childish. Sometimes they were even depicted as females with long queues and gowns in the popular media at that time, including cartoons, song sheet covers, and novels. The dissemination and perpetuation of these desexualized Asian American male stereotypes obscure the history that prevented them from establishing conjugal families (Espiritu, 2000). In presenting the Asian American male as natural "eunuchs," the media helped render social and cultural oppression invisible (Hamamoto, 1994).

Fu Manchu and Charlie Chan

As Snead (1994) states: "Stereotypes never completely disappear…The nature of stereotypes is to insulate themselves from historical change, or from counter-examples in the real world" (p. 140). The effemination of Asian American men in the nineteenth century media was central in constructing the two major Asian American male movie and TV stereotypes of the twentieth century: Fu Manchu and Charlie Chan. These two stereotypes are important contributions to the model minority/honorable eunuch dual image.

The character of Dr. Fu Manchu, who endlessly carried out murderous plots, was first created by novelist Sax Rohmer in *The Mystery of Dr. Fu Manchu* in 1913. It was later turned into series of popular Hollywood films from the 1920s to the 1960s. While Fu Manchu may be evil and powerful, he is still portrayed as an emasculated man, lacking "masculine heterosexual prowess." As Chin and Chan (1972) describe:

> …wearing a long dress, batting his eyelashes, surrounded by muscular black servants in loin cloths, and with his habit of caressingly touching White men on the leg, wrist, and face with his long fingernails is not so much as threat as he is a frivolous offense to White manhood. (Chin & Chan, 1972, p. 60)

In contrast to Fu Manchu's murderous plots against the West, Charlie Chan's character, a successful crime detective, has been described as a yellow-faced "house nigger" (Xing, 1998, p. 61) who speaks in a fortune-cookie style of English, walks with the "light, dainty step of a woman" (Chin, Chan, Inada & Wong, 1974, p. xvi), and overall, represents an effeminate Asian American male (Cao & Novas, 1996, p. 60). Following Charlie Chan, the distortion and emasculation of Asian American males continues today in the form of nerdy, adolescent science geniuses and socially awkward computer programmers (Cao & Novas, 1996, p. xvi; Sun, 2003). The emasculation of kung fu masters, however, is more subtle because these characters, mostly played not by Chinese American but Chinese actors such as Jet Li and Jackie Chan, are muscular and strong. Ironically, even though these Asian superstars play the roles of heroes, compared to their white counterparts such as James Bond, they are neither sexy nor romantic. To quote one critic: "Jackie Chan is a funny martial artist, but are you going to sleep with him?" (Chihara, 2000, p. 27).

On the surface, these archetypical stereotypes contradict each other: Charlie Chan is "good" and Fu Manchu is "evil." But together, they mutually reinforce the common image of the emasculated Asian American man.

Model Minority

The "model minority" myth was first publicized by William Peterson (1966) in his article, "Success story: Japanese-American style" in *The New York Times Magazine* on January, 1966 (Zia, 2000; Lee, 1999). The same concept was reinforced by *U.S. News and World Report* at the end of the same year in a story that singled out Chinese Americans' successes while criticizing African Americans' failures: "At the time when Americans are awash in worry over the plight of racial minorities, one such minority, the nation's 300,000 Chinese Americans, is winning wealth and respect by dint of its own hard work…Still being taught in Chinatown is the old idea that people should depend on their own efforts—not a welfare check—in order to reach America's 'Promised Land'" (Zia, 2000, 46). It was evident that the term "model minority" was created not as much to put Asian Americans on a pedestal, but to pit them against other minorities. As Zia (2000) states:

> …[the] news media began to distinguish between Asian Americans as the "good" minority that "strives to get ahead by dint of its own work," versus the "bad" minority that was "burning the cities and seeking to live off handouts." (p. 117)

The myth was further reinforced by profiles of overachieving Asian American children with headlines such as "Success story: Outwhiting the Whites" (*Newsweek*, 1971) and "Why do Asian Pupils Win Those Prizes?" (Graubarch, 1988). Frank Wu (2002) analyzes how that myth serves the dominant elite:

Regrettably, the model minority myth embraced by the pundits and the public alike is neither true nor truly flattering. Instead, it is a stock character that plays multiple roles in our racial drama. Like any other myth forming our collective narrative of race, it is ultimately more revealing than reassuring. Complimentary on its face, the model minority myth is disingenuous at its heart. (p. 49)

Hye Jin Paek and Hemant Shah (2003) evaluated this "model minority" myth in U.S. magazine advertising and found connections to representations of financial success, technology-savvy skills, academic excellence, problematic gender dynamics, and racial hierarchy among other minorities. Ki-Young Lee and Sung-Hee Joo (2005) updated this research by investigating the images of Asian Americans in advertising in four randomly selected months between August 2000 and August 2001, concluding that the model minority stereotype continued to dominate the representations of Asian Americans in advertising.

In summary, media stereotypes of Asian American men are reflected in both the "model minority" image depicted in the news and advertising and the "emasculated men" portrayed in the movies and on television dramas and sitcoms; together these characterizations form the model minority/honorable eunuch dual image.

Media Effects on Asian Americans

Media effects studies on racial attitudes indicate that portrayals of racial and ethnic minorities on television influence not only white Americans' perceptions of those groups, but also minorities' views of themselves (Greenberg, Mastro & Brand, 2002, p. 343). Huntemann and Morgan (2001) argue that notions of social power and hierarchy are embedded in the stereotypical images in the media. Although some people may dismiss those images and stories as "unreal" and thus not effective, Huntemann and Morgan (2001) affirm that these "mediated representations" still provide potential guidance for viewers to form their attitudes, behaviors, and construct identities (p. 310). It is also important to note that identity also takes form through interactions with other people who are additionally influenced by common media messages.

Stacey Lee and Sabina Vaught (2003) examined the way first- and second-generation Asian American girls and young women interpreted and reinterpreted popular representations of their positions in the United States. They found that their subjects largely internalized the dominant ideals of female representations in the mainstream media, resulting, in turn, in a damaging sense of self-esteem.

Wong (1993), a Chinese American professor, once asked his Chinese American students how they felt about each other. He then went on to make a connection between the students' perceptions of each other and media's portrayals of Asian American males and females. When he asked his female students, "What's wrong with Asian American men as lovers, or more simply, as dates," they responded that Asian American men were "nerdy, wishy-washy, domineering mama's boys" (paragraph 5). Using the discussion during a class on Chinese American masculinity (Chan, 2001) and interviews with college students at a psychotherapy clinic (Mok, 1998), Chan and Mok investigated the connections between media portrayals and effects on Asian American's interpretations of masculinity, dating, and white beauty standards. Their results largely supported Wong's (1993) conclusions derived from conversations with his students.

Peter Chua and Diane Fujino (1999) conducted an empirical study that examined how Asian American men constructed their own masculinities. Their analysis used survey data to analyze how college-aged Asian American and white men expressed their masculinities and how Asian American and white women perceived Asian American and white masculinities. The results suggest that although Asian American men acknowledge the white hegemonic interpretation of masculinity, they actively construct their own version of masculinity that includes politeness and obedience. While this study did not focus on the mass media as a direct influence on masculinity constructions, the respondents nonetheless acknowledged the existence of media stereotypes, which they were compelled to reject. Chua and Fujino also found that while white women considered Asian American men not masculine and not physically attractive compared to white men, they thought that personal relationships with Asian American men would be more "intimate" (p. 15). Then, how were these white women interested in dating Asian American men? This highly relevant question to our study was not asked.

■ Method

To better investigate our research concerns, this study utilized both a quantitative and a qualitative approach, each complementing the other. The quantitative approach examined patterns of perceptions and the strength to which the different variables correlate or interact, while the qualitative approach provided a rare insight into personal accounts of the issues in question. Through both methods, we obtained complementary information that shed light on our research questions at the micro and macro levels.

Quantitative Method

Using a questionnaire, the authors surveyed 538 college students of multiracial groups at two universities located on the east coast of the United States. The survey was designed with two goals in mind. The first goal was to examine respondents' perceptions of Asian American men and if those perceptions were consistent with the media stereotypes. The second goal was to detect respondents' interest in interacting with Asian Americans, especially dating them, as they would other men from other racial groups.

In the questionnaire, we listed descriptive characteristics of Asian American men and women, and asked respondents to select those characteristics that best reflected their perceptions of Asian Americans. The descriptive characteristics that we submitted to the attention of the respondents are emanated from the discussion of Asian Americans' stereotypical traits in the literature review and include those that are commonly used in the portraiture of Asian American men (such as "quiet," "hard-working," "nerdy," and "skilled in Kung Fu") and those that seldom show up (such as "sexy," "attractive," "masculine," "creative," "leader," and "aggressive"). In order to assess whether the respondents perceive Asian American men and women differently, we use the same descriptive characteristics for both groups, with the exception of the traits "masculine" and "feminine," which were used, respectively, for Asian American males and Asian American females.

We were also interested in understanding the respondents' perceptions of Asian Americans, compared to other racial groups such as whites, blacks and Latinos. (1) Did the respondents indeed see Asian Americans as the "model minority," commonly portrayed as economically successful, intelligent, hard-working, and non-violent? (2) How were the respondents interested in interacting with Asian Americans (for instance, living in their neighborhood and dating them)? For the sake of being concise, thus to reduce time in answering the questionnaire, we only asked the respondents whether they were interested in interacting/dating "people" from a particular racial group instead of "men" or "women" specifically. With the acknowledgment of an inherent heterosexual bias in the design, we assumed that, when answering the questions regarding dating, the respondents were considering the opposite sex.

Qualitative Data

In order to understand the role the media play in shaping people's impressions of Asian Americans in daily lives, we also conducted focus group interviews. As part of a larger study on media's effects on Asian American identities and perceptions of Asian Americans in the media and in everyday life, the authors recruited students from the same two universities where the survey questionnaires were administered and conducted focus group interviews. There were 7 Asian American male groups, 7 Asian American female groups, 2 black male groups, 2 black female groups, 1 white male group, and 2 white female groups. Each group had 2 to 6 respondents and there were a total of 67 respondents from 21 groups. The focus group interview questions probed the respondents' perceptions of Asian Americans in the media and everyday life, the way media images of Asian Americans inform their understanding of this group, and their interests in dating them.

■ Results

Different Perceptions about Asian American Men and Women

The respondents, as a group, viewed Asian American men and women almost identically except in the category of sexual attraction. Asian American women were considered somewhat highly, while Asian American men were not (Tables 1a and 1b). Among 18 descriptions, the six items that the respondents frequently selected to describe Asian American men were, in a descending order: *hardworking, computer whiz, quiet, skinny, con-*

servative, and *nerdy.* On the other hand, the six items that were least selected to describe Asian American men were, in an ascending order, *exotic, seductive, manipulative, angry, sexy,* and *outspoken.* In other words, the dominant image of an Asian American man is someone who is quiet, skinny, and nerdy—but not sexually attractive.

Similar to their male counterparts, Asian American women were also perceived as *quiet, hardworking, skinny, conservative, not angry, not manipulative* and *not outspoken.* What truly distinguished these two groups from one another was their perceived sexual appeal. Asian American women were considered feminine, and sexy while their male counterparts were considered nerdy and neither masculine nor sexy. Respondents' perceptions of Asian American men and women were very consistent with the representations of Asian Americans in the media.

Table 1: Perceptions of Asian American Characteristics

a. Most Perceived Characteristics of Asian Americans

Asian American Females

Variables	Mean Score	Std. Deviation
Quiet	0.65	0.478
Hardworking	0.63	0.484
Skinny	0.56	0.496
Feminine	0.45	0.498
Conservative	0.44	0.497
Sexy	0.39	0.488

Asian American Males

Variables	Mean Score	Std. Deviation
Hardworking	0.59	0.493
Computer whiz	0.44	0.496
Quiet	0.43	0.495
Skinny	0.36	0.48
Conservative	0.34	0.473
Nerdy	0.33	0.47

b. Least Perceived Characteristics of Asian Americans

Asian American Females

Variables	Mean Score	Std. Deviation
Aggressive	0.13	0.339
Athletic	0.12	0.322
Outspoken	0.12	0.326
Manipulative	0.1	0.301
Kung Fu Artist	0.1	0.303
Angry	0.07	0.26

Asian American Males

Variables	Mean Score	Std. Deviation
Outspoken	0.15	0.354
Sexy	0.14	0.343
Angry	0.13	0.335
Manipulative	0.09	0.285
Seductive	0.07	0.247
Exotic	0.05	0.226

Model Minority

The data analysis also revealed that Asian Americans were perceived in line with the concept of "model minority," that is, in terms of their economic status, intelligence, work ethics, and violent tendencies, in comparison to other racial groups (Whites, Blacks, and Latinos). Altogether, the respondents perceived Asian Americans as wealthy (right below Whites), the most intelligent, hard-working, and least violent among all racial groups (Table 2), consistent with the media discourse of "model minority."

Table 2: Model Minority Index

Dependent Variable	Whites			Blacks			Asians		
	Males	Females	Total	Males	Females	Total	Males	Females	Total
	(N = 83)	(N = 138)	(N = 221)	(N = 51)	(N = 62)	(N = 113)	(N = 57)	(N = 129)	(N = 186)
How rich are Whites	3.73	3.78	3.76 (1)	4	4.35	4.19 (1)	3.68	3.75	3.73 (1)
How rich are Blacks	2.31	2.5	2.43	2.68	2.56	2.61	2.36	2.35	2.36
How rich are Asians	3.13	3.15	3.14 (2)	3.21	3.11	3.15 (2)	3	3.03	3.02 (2)
How rich are Latinos	2.03	2.18	2.13	2.49	2.33	2.4	2.12	2.42	2.33
How intelligent are Whites	3.49	3.63	3.57	3.39	3.62	3.52	3.22	3.4	3.34
How intelligent are Blacks	2.95	3.18	3.09	3.62	3.14	3.36	2.61	2.9	2.81
How intelligent are Asians	3.69	3.92	3.83 (1)	3.72	3.33	3.51 (1)	3.4	3.68	3.59 (1)
How intelligent are Latinos	2.72	3.02	2.9	3.31	3	3.14	2.56	2.95	2.83
How hardworking are Whites	3.07	3.34	3.24	2.96	3.35	3.17	2.98	3.1	3.06
How hardworking are Blacks	2.73	2.98	2.89	3.64	3.09	3.34	2.38	2.74	2.63
How hardworking are Asians	3.67	3.91	3.82 (1)	3.94	3.38	3.63 (1)	3.77	3.77	3.77 (1)
How hardworking are Latinos	2.63	2.89	2.79	3.5	3.25	3.37	2.52	3	2.85

How violent are Whites	3.1	3.21	3.17	3.78	3.82	3.8	3.31	3.33	3.32
How violent are Blacks	3.42	3.53	3.49	3.27	3.09	3.17	3.89	3.76	3.8
How violent are Asians	2.73	2.44	2.41 (4)	2.8	2.77	2.78 (4)	2.63	2.92	2.83 (4)
How violent are Latinos	3.37	3.39	3.38	3.15	2.93	3.03	3.42	3.37	3.38

Asian Americans' Sexual Appeal and Interracial Dating

In order to find whether the perceptions of Asian Americans' sexual appeal correlated with interest in dating Asian Americans, we constructed a sex appeal index for both Asian American females and males (Table 3).

Table 3: Index of Asian Americans Sex Appeal

Asian American Males

Variables	Factor Loadings	Factors	Reliability
Asian American males are sexy	0.8	1 factor; Eigen value = 2.13; variance explained =	Cronbach alpha of internal consistency = 0.69
Asian American males are seductive	0.77	53.36%	
Asian American males are attractive	0.68		
Asian American males are exotic	0.65		

Asian American Females

Variables	Factor Loadings	Factors	Reliability
Asian American females are sexy	0.79	1 factor; Eigen value = 2.02; variance explained = 50.62%	Cronbach alpha of internal consistency = 0.67
Asian American females are seductive	0.68		
Asian American females are attractive	0.7		
Asian American females are exotic	0.66		

Pearson's correlation procedure (Table 4) indicated that there was a positive relationship between dating Asian Americans and Asian American females' sex appeal ($r = .31$, $p = .00$), and Asian American males' sex appeal ($r = .11$, $p = .01$). In other words, the more respondents perceived Asian Americans as sexy, the more they were interested in dating them.

Table 4: Correlations: Dating Asian Americans, and Asian American Sex Appeal

Independent Variables

Dependent Variable	Asian American Female Sex Appeal	Asian American Male Sex Appeal
Dating Asian Americans	0.31 p = 0.00	0.11 p = 0.00

In addition, we observed that all the racial groups involved in this study prefer self-dating (dating within their racial group) before venturing out (Table 5a). Whites had the highest tendency of self-dating, followed by Asians, then Blacks. However, Asian American men had very strong interests in dating white women, almost as equally as dating Asian American women (Table 5b).

Table 5: ANOVA Table: Race, Gender and Interracial Dating

a. Interaction of Race and Interracial Dating

Dependent Variables	F Ratio	Significance of F
Dating Whites	47.77	0
Dating Blacks	21.48	0
Dating Asians	12.94	0
Dating Latinos	6.8	0

Mean Score by Race

	Whites (N = 216)	Blacks (N = 104)	Asians (N = 177)
Dating Whites	4.8	3.3	3.46
Dating Blacks	3.34	4.12	2.63
Dating Asians	3.24	3.33	4.2
Dating Latinos	3.34	3.75	3

b. Interaction of Race and Gender with Interracial Dating

Dependent Variables	F Ratio	Significance of F
Dating Whites	7.79	0
Dating Blacks	3.21	0.02
Dating Asians	5.46	0
Dating Latinos	2.42	0.06

Mean Score by Race						
	Whites (N = 216)		Blacks (N = 104)		Asians (N = 177)	
	Male (N = 82)	Female (N = 134)	Male (N = 48)	Female (N = 56)	Male (N = 50)	Female (N = 127)
Dating Whites	4.78	4.82	3.31	3.3	4.18	3.18
Dating Blacks	3.06	3.55	4.39	3.89	2.6	2.65
Dating Asians	3.52	3.07	4	2.76	4.2	4.21
Dating Latinos	3.57	3.23	4.37	3.23	3.44	2.87

As previously indicated in the method section, because of the design limitation of the questionnaire, we could not tell whether the respondents were considering dating males or females. Acknowledging a heterosexual bias, the authors assume that respondents only considered dating the opposite sex. Since our focus is on Asian American men, we only examined the dating interests of Asian American men and all women subgroups. Black and white women both had the least interest in dating Asian American men, compared to white, black, and Latino men. Interestingly, even though those two groups of women perceived black men and Latino men as less wealthy, less intelligent, less hardworking and more violent than Asian American men, they still would rather date them over Asian American men.

The survey data indicated, at minimum, two important aspects. First, Asian American men were indeed perceived as model minority/honorable eunuchs, which was highly consistent with the images mainstream media have been propagating. Second, college women clearly considered sexual appeal, more than any other variable examined in this study, as the most important factor for becoming romantically involved with a person. Therefore, because Asian American men were not considered sexually appealing, regardless of other positive attributes, they were not "hot dates."

Focus Groups Results

The data from the focus groups were very useful in complementing and shedding light on findings from the survey. On the whole, across racial and gender focus groups, the respondents' perceptions of Asian American men in everyday life were almost identical to findings from the survey data. Furthermore, those conceptions were remarkably similar to the media stereotypes.

Three areas of the findings particularly contributed to the understanding of our research questions: (1)Women across different racial groups articulated the reasons why they don't consider Asian American men as sexually attractive or as potential dates. (2) The survey data revealed an interesting contradiction: When dating interracially, Asian American men have the highest interest in dating white women, but black and white women indicated the least interest in dating Asian American men. Why did such an inconsistency occur? (3) The respondents often used media representations of Asian

Americans to help understand, evaluate, or validate their views of real-life Asian Americans. Often, the two different kinds of experiences—perceiving Asian Americans in the media and everyday life—were conflated and confused, and were treated as if they were the same. These three areas of findings were analyzed as follows.

Failing the Beauty Standards

Psychologists have studied how women of color internalize "Caucasian-European-American ideals" and develop poor body image and low self-esteem (Hall, 1995; Milkie 1999). Comparatively speaking, there is significantly less research done on the white beauty standard effects on men of color, especially on Asian American men. Grogan (1999) maintains that the Western male beauty standard consists of an "average build with well-developed muscles on chest, arms, and shoulders…Western cultural notions of maleness as representing power, strength and aggression" (p. 58). When Asian American men are evaluated against these white male beauty standards, they are typically perceived very negatively. This idea was manifested in focus group findings when it was revealed that women respondents often linked the physical assessment of Asian American men to their interests in dating them, as indicated in the following comments:

> Jane (Asian American):…Skinny, scrawny, faked dyed hair; yeah I just never found them attractive.

> Lynn (Asian American): I would say I never look for an Asian hunk. It's always like tall, dark, and beautiful guy or a white guy. [Note: It was later clarified that "dark" meant a darker-skinned white man.]

> Terri (Asian American): When I was in high school, I was repulsed by the idea of dating Asian males…their physique.

> Emily (White): Small penis?

> Sheila (Black): Asian American males were "desexualized." They are not someone I would think of being attracted to or having a long-term relationship.

> Dean (Chinese American): If I go to a party…you look around and I am the only Asian guy… You feel somewhat less of a man.

> Sam (Cambodian American): It [the beauty standard] affects you…You look at yourself and say well, "I don't have the chiseled body like this guy does, you don't have the long legs like he does, you're not 6" 2" tall." You know, you're only 5' 6," 5' 7," and you look at yourself, you like, "Damn, maybe I'm not that beautiful," you know, "Maybe in the eyes of the people that are around me I'm not that good looking." But I mean my life was a lot easier than that, I was very accepted by the white community. I fit in with everybody, and I dated a lot of girls, so it was easy for me to get around. But for other Asian people, for other Cambodians for instance…if they look more Cambodian than I do, it's harder for them, you know. I mean, I can pass as being a mixed, you know, as being Cambodian or something else, but a lot of Cambodians are traditionally native looking, indigenous looking. It's harder for them to get around. And I also don't have an accent, so it's really easy for me to talk to people.

Sam's long comment needs to be analyzed closely. First of all, notice how he used "you" to indicate Asian American men who are negatively affected by the beauty standards that they can't meet. But he then switched to "I" when he talked about why he did not have much of a problem in being accepted by Whites. The switch of pronouns may be an indication that he tried to distance himself (by using "you" instead of "I") from the effects of the beauty standards. Second, he talked about how his look (not native Cambodian) and his lack of an accent were what got him accepted by the Whites and he was apparently pleased with that result. Third, he acknowledged the existence of the beauty standard and internalized it, so, not only did he use it to judge others (the indigenous-looking Cambodians can't get around as easily as he does), but to elevate or insulate himself from the Asian group: his look of a "mix" of white and Asian has made him more attractive.

The internalization of the notion that "White is more beautiful and better" is particularly evident when Asian American respondents consider that when "white" blood is added into Asian blood, the "mixed" ones are more attractive, as indicated by the following statements made by Asian American women:

> Lynn: Usually when they [Asian Americans] are good-looking, they're…like half white…

> Pam: I like biracial guys, because they have the nose, and they're mostly taller.

> Don: I prefer mixed.

If white beauty standards are a universal yardstick, it is not surprising why white women would find Asian American men physically unattractive. This also explains why Asian American men would find white women attractive; an asymmetrical finding that emerged strongly in the survey data.

> Bob (Asian American male): I just never had an interest really, never [in dating Asian American women]. I'm not saying that they're not beautiful, but I think it has a lot to do with media. Because you see all the beautiful white women in the media…all the babe watches and all the beautiful women that you see are white. And I've grown to love white women, and growing up that is all I ever thought of. I couldn't picture myself having an Asian counterpart.

But not all Asian American men can pursue their dream girls.

> Ken: White women aren't necessarily flocking towards Asian men; Asian men are not a sex symbol. That was one of the things that I dealt with growing up. Here you are, fed with this image of white women being beautiful and so therefore you're going to try to attain that. Meanwhile they are being fed this image of you are either a martial artist, and if you're not, then you're this socially awkward person.

Compared to white men, black and Latino men were often presented as even more hyper-masculine and with advantages over Asian American men.

> Nelson (Asian American): Look at who our competition is. We have the white men, the Hispanics—the Latin lovers—and then you have the black men who are just endowed with

every god's gift you know. So yeah, of course we are going to be squeezed out of the action.

Nelson, although stereotyping both Latinos and Blacks, echoed the sentiment of some Asian American male college students in Chan's (2001) research who called themselves "the lowest of the low" in terms of the social/dating hierarchy.

The Fusion of the Fiction and the "Real"

In all my focus group interviews, there was a common phenomenon of respondents using what they saw in the media as a reference for them to support, validate, or make intelligible what they observed of Asian Americans in everyday life.

Many non-Asian respondents recalled that when they were children they believed that Asian Americans or Asians were wise, Zen-like, and knew martial arts; most of these impressions originated from *The Karate Kid* or other popular kung fu movies that attracted children and teenagers. When asked about her impression of Asian American women, Shana, a white woman, replied that stereotypes were so readily available in her head that it had became easy for her to make certain assumptions. Then she used a book, *Memoirs of a Geisha,* to discuss her impression of Asian American women, even though that book was about a Japanese geisha, written by a white man.

> Shana (white): Yeah, I always assume, it's not [something] you think [about]...it's something that immediately pops into your head because it's like...the women are subservient. Yeah, I read *Memoirs of a Geisha*...she had to be subservient to a certain degree...Of course it was fictional, but still it was pretty good. And then you read like Amy Tan stuff, like *The Joy Luck Club*, especially you see in the movie . . .

Notice how in the same breath, Shana recalled her impressions of Asian American women being submissive—ideas gathered from *Memoirs of a Geisha.* Although she acknowledged that the book is fictional, the next example she gave, *The Joy Luck Club,* was still fictional. Ma (2000) called Amy Tan, author of *The Joy Luck Club,* "the best-paid tour guide of Chinese America" (p. xiv) because Tan, along with other well-known authors such as Maxine Hong Kingston, turned Orientalized misrepresentations into self-presentations (p. xiii). In other words, even Tan and other Asian American authors still may use the "white" lens through which to write about Asian Americans. *The Joy Luck Club* proved to be very popular among our respondents and it was the most mentioned book on Asian Americans, but it also spoke to the scarcity of the materials on Asian Americans. Todd also mentioned *The Joy Luck Club* as the source for his information.

> Todd (black): There was this woman who lived in my town and she had three kids, real bright students in our class. And I remember when we were little, we used to be like how come these kids are so smart, we take the same classes that they do, and they take piano lessons and violin, just all the renaissance type things. And she [the mother] used to come outside and be really friendly, but we swore that she was like brainwashing her kids just because they were so smart. And so that's probably what I've got in like Asian women, just that they were like really strict with their children, and wanted their children to be the best. And I

remember watching and reading *The Joy Luck Club* and how all their mothers wanted their daughters to be the absolute best that they could be, no exceptions at all.

Claude (black): I think they [Asian American women] are quiet but they also have a fire kind of temper. I finished watching *Ally McBeal* last night, and Lucy Liu, she is kind of like bitchy, that's what I kind of associate with a lot of Asian American women.

Todd attributed the academic success of neighboring Asian American "smart kids" to their mothers' "brainwashing" of them. That observation was further affirmed by the fictional mother characters in *The Joy Luck Club* who had the same attitudes toward their children, which enabled him to generalize his observation even further. Claude's comment was more ambiguous. It was not clear whether he had already observed the "quiet and fire" opposite sides within the Asian American women he knew, then, subsequently, he allowed Lucy Liu's image to confirm that dichotomy, or whether Lucy Liu's image actually helped him interpret the Asian American woman—without the balance of actual Asian American female acquaintances. Either way, the respondents' use of Asian American fictional characters as sources of information to understand Asian Americans is evidently clear.

■ Discussion

The present study utilized both large-scale survey data and focus group interviews to investigate, both at the macro and micro levels, perceptions of Asian American men, the role of the media in shaping those perceptions, and how such perceptions ultimately affect people's interaction with, and particularly, their dating interests in, Asian Americans.

We examine three sets of perceptions: Asian Americans in everyday life from the survey and the focus groups, Asian Americans in the media from the focus groups, and Asian Americans in the media from the literature review. The three sets of perceptions are remarkably similar and fit in the model minority/honorable eunuch dual stereotype that we've identified. Despite the fact that women from different racial groups think highly of Asian American men in terms of their economic success and work ethic, women still have little interest in dating Asian American men because of their perceived lack of sexual attraction, which appears to be a very important factor affecting women's dating interests.

Media studies scholars have long argued that media provide important sources from which we construct our identities and our views of others—a world view that is not individually imagined but is commonly shared by people who live in the same culture (Kellner, 2003). We acknowledge that media are not magic bullets or hypodermic needles that produce strong, direct, and visible changes. Instead, we argue that media images are neither natural nor reflecting the "real" but are ideologically constructed, often politically motivated, and subject to historical, economic, and social contingencies. This is certainly the case for the past and present representations of Asian American men. Thus, when respondents' perceptions of Asian Americans in everyday life so closely mirror media stereotypes, it is necessary to examine the process through which media images enter people's conversations, consciousness, and unconsciousness, and how they inform discursive practices and performances. The focus group interviews particularly shed light on that process.

The interview data suggest that media influence Asian American men in different aspects. First, media affect them when they perceive their marginalized position as stereotyped and ridiculed. Second, media help develop low self-esteem in Asian American men, as they perceive that they cannot measure up to the white beauty standard. Third, media foster Asian American men's sexual desire toward the dominant, specifically, white woman. The data also indicate that multi-racial college women perceived Asian American men in particular ways, often without direct contact, which were consistent with dominant media portrayals. Many of these women acknowledged that media play an important role in constructing their ideas about Asian Americans. In fact, very rarely did the female respondents, including Asian American women, actually use their understanding of Asian American men in everyday life to counter the distortion of the media stereotypes. Furthermore, since producers in the media often seek popularly circulated images for inspiration, this results in stereotypes breeding more stereotypes. Through proliferation and mutual referencing, stereotypes old and new become normalized and even gain authority.

What should be the "remedy" for the media stereotype of the asexual Asian American man? There is always an impulse to correct the "negative" stereotypes with "positive" ones. Should we promote hypermasculine Asian American male images to boost up and balance out emasculated ones? Hamamoto (2000) asserts that there should be more pornography with Asian American male performers to restore Asian American sexuality. Semiotics has taught us that a media text is always polysemic and the encoder has no control over the decoding process. Sau-Ling Wong's (1993) analysis of the "pin-up" style of muscular Asian American "manly man" images in the 1991 Asian Pacific Islander Men's Calendar proves exactly the point. If the audience already has certain stereotypes of Asian American men, how would that color their interpretation of the images? That is, although the pictures are meant for showing heterosexual prowess, why couldn't they be appreciated as gay porn?

Both Chan (2001) and Wang (1998) caution the audience about the danger of some Asian American men falling into the trap of hegemonic and misogynistic masculinity when they try to shake off the "asexual" images. Wang (1998) discussed how Asian American hip-hop artists adopted black rappers' hypermasculine images and represented themselves in hypersexual terms as cited as the following lyrics:

> I'm here today to kick some flavor/
> and to the ladies, I'm like a Lifesaver,
> A sweet Tootsie Roll, I'll last a long time.
> Gimme a minute and I'll make ya mine.
> I"ll bet you never thought about a lover that's Asian,

> Getting cozy with the yellow persuasion.
> Maybe you heard something about a small dick,
> But I'll tell you now, that that's bullshit.
> If you don't believe, follow me home,
> And find out on your own that I'm full-grown.
> Is good loving what you need?
> Well, I'll give you satisfaction guaranteed.
> (Seoul Brothers,' "Just Like Honey," cited in Wang, 1998, p. 10)

As these lyrics demonstrate, many of the Asian American hip-pop artists affirm a hegemonic masculinity: at the expense of treating women as objects.

The dilemma that these Asian American male rappers create for themselves is that while they set out to defy the hegemonic masculinity that excludes them, they end up reaffirming it. Chan (2001) further points out the importance of conceptualizing a non-hegemonic masculinity. He states,

> My contention is that Asian American archetypes have shaped the discourse on Asian American men's issues. However, in the process of debunking stereotypes, one must be willing to construct alternative models of masculinities while risking politically the stigmatization of effeminization/homosexualization...(p. 165)

In U.S. media culture, where femininity and masculinity are often rigidly defined and represented, it is certainly a daunting, but nonetheless urgent task to imagine and promote a pro-feminist and pro-queer Asian American masculinity. But merely agitating protest against some "negative" roles or adding more or "correct" minority roles on TV or in movies not only has minimal effects but it actually serves to legitimize and solidify the current commercial media system.

By challenging and opening up the media system, which is currently controlled by a handful of profit-driven, transnational media conglomerates, the public would finally expect to have media as a more democratic "public sphere" (Habermas, 1998) that facilitates the exchange of ideas and encourages diverse representations. When that happens, we will not need Asian American male porn stars or rap stars or super heroes to soothe Asian American men's injured egos. Instead, we shall expect to have such a wide array of rich and deep characters that the existence of model minority/honorable eunuch would matter very little.

References

Althusser, L. (1971). Ideology and ideological state apparatuses. In *Lenin and philosophy and other essays* (pp. 127–186). London: New Left Books.

Bordo, S. (1999). *A New Look at Men in Public and in Private.* New York: Farrar, Straus and Giroux.

Cao, L., & Novas, H. (1996). *All you need to know about Asian American history.* New York, NY: Plume Books.

Chan, J. (2001). *Chinese American masculinities: From Fu Manchu to Bruce Lee.* New York: Routledge.

Chen, C. H. (1996). Feminization of Asian (American) men in the U.S. mass media: An analysis of the *Ballad of Little Jo. Journal of Communication Inquiry, 20*(2), 57–71.

Chihara, M. (2000, February 25). Casting a cold eye on the rise of Asian starlets. *The Boston Phoenix,* p. 3.

Chin, F., Chan, J., Inada, L., & Wong, S. (Eds.). (1974). *Aiiieeeee!: An anthology of Asian American writers.* New York: Mentor.

Chin, F., & Chan, J. P. (1972). Racist love. In R. Kostelanetz (Ed.), *Seeing through shuck* (pp. 65–79). New York: Ballantine.

Chua, P., & Fujino, D. C. (1999). Negotiating new Asian-American masculinities: Attitudes and gender expectation. *Journal of Men's Studies, 7*(3), 391–413.

Collins, Patricia Hill (1990). *Black feminist thought: knowledge, consciousness, and the politics of empowerment.* Boston: Unwin Hyman.

Dening, S. (1996). *The mythology of sex.* London: Labyrinth.

Espiritu, Y. L. (2000). *Asian American women and men.* New York: Altamira.

Fall colors 2003–2004: Prime time diversity report. (2004) Oakland, CA: Children Now.

Gould, S. J. (1996). *The mismeasure of man.* New York: W. W. Norton & Company.

Graubard, S. G. (1988, January 29). Why do Asian pupils win those prizes? *New York Times,* p. A35.

Greenberg, B. S., Mastro, D., & Brand, J. E. (2002). Minorities in the mass media: Television into the 21st century. In Bryant, J. & D. Zillman (Eds.), *Media Effects: Advances in theory and research* (2nd ed., pp. 353–352). Mahwah, N.J.: Lawrence Erlbaum Associates.

Grogan, S. (1999). *Body image: Understanding body dissatisfaction in men, women, and children.* New York: Routledge.

Habermas, J. (1998). "There are alternatives," *New Left Review,* 231 (8), 3–12.

Hall, C. I. (1995). Asian eyes: Body image and eating disorders of Asian and Asian American women. *Eating Disorders, 3*(1), 8–19.

Hamamoto, D. Y. (1994). *Monitored peril: Asian Americans and the politics of TV representations.* Minneapolis, MN: University of Minnesota Press.

How to be a cool Asian. (2007). Retrieved July 13, 2007, from http://www.asianjoke.com/general/how_to_be_a_cool_asian.htm

Huang, S.-L. (2007, September 13–19). Letters of the week. *Time Out New York,* 1.

Huntemann, N., & Morgan, M. (2001). Mass media and identity development. In D. G. Singer & J. L. Singer (Eds.), *Handbook of children & the media* (pp. 309–222). Thousand Oaks, CA: Sage.

Kellner, D. (2003). Cultural studies, multiculturalism, and media culture. In G. Dines & J. M. Humez (Eds.), *Gender, race, and class in media* (Second ed., pp. 9–20). Thousand Oaks, CA: Sage Publications.

Kellner, D. (2005). *Media spectacle and the crisis of democracy.* Boulder, CO: Paradigm Press.

Lee, C. (1999). Ling Woo below: Admirably "free" or "Neo-Orientalist masturbatory fantasy figure"? *Village Voice, 44,* 65.

Lee, K.-Y., & Joo, S.-H. (2005). The portrayal of Asian Americans in mainstream magazine ads: An update. *Journalism & Mass Communication Quarterly, 82*(3), 654–671.

Lee, S. J., & Vaught, S. (2003). "You can never be too rich or too thin": Popular and consumer culture and the Americanization of Asian American girls and young women. *The Journal of Negro Education, 72*(4), 457–466.

Ma, S.-M. (2000). *Deathly embrace: Orientalism and Asian American identity.* Minneapolis: University of Minnesota Press.

Mansfield-Richardson, V. D. (1996). *Asian-Americans and the mass media: A content analysis of twenty United States newspapers and a survey of Asian-American journalists.* Unpublished doctoral dissertation, Ohio University.

Milkie, M. A. (1999). Social comparisons, reflected appraisals, and mass media: The impact of pervasive beauty images on black and white girls' self-concepts. *Social Psychology Quarterly, 62*(2), 190–210.

Mok, T. A. (1998). Getting the message: Media images and stereotypes and their effect on Asian Americans. *Cultural diversity and mental health, 4*(3), 185–202.

Narasaki, K. K. (2005). *The 2005 Asian Pacific American report card on television diversity.* Washington, DC: Asian American Justice Center.

Paek, H. J., & Shah, H. (2003). Racial ideology, model minorities, and the "not-so-silent partner": Stereotypes of Asian Americans in U.S. magazine advertising. *The Howard Journal of Communications, 14,* 225–243.

Rushton, J. P. (2000). *Race, evolution, and behavior: A life-history perspective* (3rd ed.). Port Huron, MI: Charles Darwin Research Institute.

Snead, J. (1994). *White screens, black images: Hollywood from the dark side.* New York: Routledge.

Success story: Outwhiting the whites. (1971, June 21). *Newsweek,* 24–25.

Sun, C. F. (2003). Ling Woo in historical context: The new face of Asian American stereotypes on television. In G. Dines & J. M. Humez (Eds.), *Gender, race, and class in media* (2nd ed., pp. 656–664). Thousand Oaks, CA: Sage Publications.

Tajima, R. E. (1989). Lotus blossoms don't bleed: Images of Asian women. In Asian Women for University (Ed.), *Making waves: An anthology of writings by and about Asian American women* (pp. 308–317). Boston: Beacon Press.

Takaki, R. (1989). *Strangers from a different shore: A history of Asian Americans.* Boston: Little, Brown and Company.

U.S. Census: State & County QuickFacts. (2007). Retrieved August 13, 2007, from http://quickfacts.census.gov/qfd/states/00000.html

Wang, O. (1998, November 12–28). Asian Americans and hip-hop. *Asian Week.*

Wong, S. (1993, November). Beyond Bruce Lee. *Essence, 24,* 64.

Wu, F. (2002). *Yellow.* New York, NY: Basic Books.

Xing, J. (1998). *Asia America through the lens: History, representations & identity.* Walnut Creek, California: Altamira.

Zia, H. (2000). *Asian American dreams: The emergence of an American people.* New York: Farrar, Straus and Giroux.

31

■ "Politics Is a Contact Sport"

Media, Sports Metaphors, and Presidential Masculinity

Jackson Katz

The climactic scene in *The Wizard of Oz,* where Toto pulls back the curtain to reveal a nervous, tragic man pretending to be the "Great and Powerful Oz," represents more than just a classic moment in American cinematic history. Early in the era of mass media, it gave us a powerful metaphor for looking at masculinity in a new way: not as a fixed, inevitable, natural state of being, but rather as a projection, a performance, a mask that men often wear as a means to shield our vulnerability—and to gain or exercise power.

In fact, the poses we strike and the images of masculinity that proliferate in media culture can help to illuminate a great deal about what's going on not only in individual men's lives, but in our general culture as well. That is why it is important to pull back the curtain and take a sober look at both the images themselves and their relationship to the economic, social, and historical forces that inform and produce them. These images tell a story—actually part of a story—about dynamic developments in the construction of U.S. masculinities over the past two generations.

The past half-century has been marked by rapid and seismic changes in the gender and sexual order. For example, the modern multicultural women's movement, pioneered by the enormous Baby Boom generation, must be understood as among the key transformative social movements in human history. But the work is ongoing. Men's violence against women persists at pandemic rates, and gender inequality is still deeply rooted in the DNA of myriad socioeconomic, religious, and political institutions. Notwithstanding that feminism has disparately affected the lives of women and girls based upon a multiplicity of variables that include class, ethnicity/race, and sexual orientation, what the social theorist bell hooks calls "women's movements" have utterly rewritten cultural assumptions about "femininity," or more accurately "femininities."

Less well examined than the changes women's movements brought to "women's place" are the transformations they helped catalyze in men's public and private lives and in cultural definitions of manhood. It is axiomatic that changes in women's lives—and changes in the institutional structures that are responsible for those changes—also prompt shifts in men's lives. It is also true that transformations in the gender order are both produced by and help shape other macroeconomic and macrosocial processes, such as the shift in the U.S. economy from a base of industrial manufacturing to one based in service industries as well as high technology and information systems. As Susan Faludi argued in *Stiffed: The Betrayal of the American Man* (1999), this historic economic transformation has decentered millions of men's lives and identities and has contributed to masculine anxiety and widespread confusion about what it means to be a man.

At approximately the same historical moment that women's movements were challenging traditional definitions of masculinity and femininity, the gay and lesbian liberation movements began—or accelerated—the long-term disruption of heterosexual power and privilege. These movements called into question the deeply ingrained Western belief in the normativity and inevitability of the male-led, heterosexual family as the essential building block of a healthy society. The virulence of the contemporary conservative backlash against women's sexual freedom and the civil rights of sexual minorities in the United States, as well as the rise in the past generation of fiercely patriarchal monotheistic religious fundamentalism here and around the world, is evidence that the economic, social, and family arrangements underpinning traditional justifications for (heterosexual) male dominance have encountered major opposition and are in the process of historical restructuring.

Through all of this momentous social change, an ever-expanding media culture has helped structure and guide the way we experience, think about, and react to the shifting gender and sexual terrain. As the philosopher and social theorist Douglas Kellner (2003) observes,

> We are immersed from cradle to grave in a media and consumer society...The media are a profound and often misperceived source of cultural pedagogy: they contribute to educating us how to behave and what to think, feel, believe, fear and desire—and what not to. The media are forms of pedagogy that teach us how to be men and women. They show us how to dress, look, and consume; how to react to members of different social groups; how to be popular and successful and how to avoid failure; and how to conform to the dominant system of norms, values, practices and institutions. (p. 9)

This media culture is also in the process of an epochal technological revolution, as new media and information technologies such as the Internet enable new modes of communication, including the promulgation and contestation of hegemonic and alternative gender ideologies. The post-sixties generations are immersed in a media environment that is both highly influential in the transmission of cultural ideas about masculinities (and femininities) and unprecedented in its ubiquity and global scope. Thus in order to understand what is going on with contemporary U.S. or global masculinities, it is essential that we critically examine various aspects of media culture.

Feminists who have analyzed media content have long focused on the role of media in the production and reproduction of cultural constructs of femininity. Consider the pioneering feminist media literacy work of Jean Kilbourne (1979), the work of Naomi Wolf (1992) on Western constructions of female beauty, the work of bell hooks (1992) on race and representation, or the work of Susan Bordo (1994) on women's bodies and media. As these and other feminist theorists and activists have long maintained, images of women's bodies as represented in advertising and other media are much thinner, more waifish, whiter, and younger than women's bodies in the real world. These portrayals of the "feminine ideal" function in the symbolic realm as a means of taking power away from women, because thin, waifish women literally take up less space in the world, and hence are less threatening. Not coincidentally, these images have flooded the visual landscape at a time when women have been challenging traditional male power in various areas of economic, social, and political life.

In recent years, as scholars in queer, cultural, and profeminist men's studies have taken up the subject, increased attention has been paid to media representations of masculinities. This emergent focus on masculinities and media has been part of an outpouring of scholarship—and to some extent popular discussion—over the past two decades about various aspects of multicultural masculinities. This work has contributed to the long-term feminist project of shining the spotlight not only on women as the subordinated sex-class, but on men as the dominant one. The purpose is not to push women aside and put men back on center stage but to understand the innumerable and complex ways that male dominance functions in the hope that this understanding can hasten the breaking down of gender and sexual inequality and in the process improve the lives of both women *and* men.

This chapter is a preliminary investigation of one aspect of a crucial but barely explored topic of cultural studies analysis: the role of media culture in the construction of presidential masculinity and other gendered aspects of U.S. political culture at the beginning of the twenty-first century. This line of inquiry raises a number of questions about the ideological and political functions of corporate and alternative media in the twenty-first century: to what extent are voters' electoral choices shaped by the televisual performance of candidates and politicians? How does paid political advertising on television—by far the biggest expenditure of funds in presidential campaigns—shape voters' perceptions of the relative "manliness" of candidates? What are the similarities and differences between how women and men ascertain whether male political figures measure up to the "masculine ideal" that is circulating in media culture at a given historical moment? Which mediated (white) masculine styles or archetypes have been politically successful over the past fifty years, and why? In a long political campaign that was also an unprecedented media spectacle, how did Barack Obama successfully navigate not only the racial but the masculinity politics in order to become the first African American president of the United States? What types of gendered language about leadership do journalists and other media commentators use, and how do those language choices affect who is seen as a credible—or electable—candidate? What role does right-wing talk radio play in policing the boundaries of what are considered acceptable "masculine" traits expected in a commander-in-chief? What role do popular satirical cable TV shows like *The Daily Show with Jon Stewart, The*

Colbert Report and other entertainment media play in subverting traditional constructions of presidential masculinity? In what ways are new digital media formats—including *You Tube*—creating new opportunities for the democratization of televisual images?

■ Sports Metaphors in Political Discourse

The specific focus of this study is the pervasive use of sports metaphors in political discourse and how the language of sport functions to construct a masculine ideal for leadership at the heights of political power. Sports metaphors are intimately involved in the construction of presidential masculinity in U.S. politics and media at the beginning of the twenty-first century. Metaphors are not merely figures of speech. According to the cognitive scientists and philosophers George Lakoff and Mark Johnson (1980), human thought processes themselves are largely metaphorical. Our brains use them to organize and make sense of the world. According to Lakoff and Johnson:

> Our ordinary conceptual system, in terms of which we both think and act, is fundamentally metaphorical in nature…The concepts that govern our thought are not just matters of the intellect. They also govern our everyday functioning, down to the most mundane details. Our concepts structure what we perceive, how we get around in the world, and how we relate to other people. Our conceptual system thus plays a central role in defining our everyday realities…the way we think, what we experience, and what we do every day is very much a matter of metaphor. (p.3)

This raises several questions about sports metaphors in U.S. presidential discourse: What effect does it have on our political system when mainstream commentary about politics is infused with the kind of language one hears every day on ESPN, in sports bars, and in locker rooms? To what extent can bitter partisanship in the two-party system be understood as a political manifestation of the sort of quasi-tribalism that is routinely on display in sports rivalries? What are the particularly gendered features of sports/political discourse, and how do those influence which qualities are regarded as important in potential leaders? For example, presidential debates are routinely covered by the mainstream media as if they were boxing matches. Does this subtly—or not so subtly—influence voters' perceptions of various candidates? How can a male political figure who does not embody certain traditionally masculine qualities—such as being pugnacious enough to credibly go "toe-to-toe" with our official enemies—succeed in such an environment? How can a woman? Will we get any closer to finding solutions to complex twenty-first century problems when political commentary focuses not on what candidates say or stand for, but on the fact that the "frontrunner" failed to deliver a "knockout punch"?

Social theorists have examined some of the ways the "sports-media complex" (Sut Jhally,1984) operates on an economic and an ideological level. But relatively little attention has been paid to the relationship between sports and presidential politics, especially insofar as the dominant sports culture wields enormous influence in helping to construct masculine ideals. In spite of the fact that everyone from political scientists to op-ed columnists have written about our culture's obsession with seeing the political world through the lens of sports experience and language, few academics or journalists have analyzed the particularly gendered aspects of sports metaphor. There is widespread agreement that men are more likely than women to appreciate statements like "So far, we've been waging this campaign between the forty-yard lines; we've got to begin to move downfield." In fact, much of the journalistic treatment of the topic of sports metaphors and politics highlights gender differences, with commentators frequently poking fun at men's sports obsessions and the way they creep into other areas of life.

But it is a mistake to dismiss this subject as light fare or merely fodder for pop psychological speculation. In an era when for the first time in U.S. history a woman nearly captured a major party nomination for the presidency, much more attention needs to be paid to the process by which cultural constructs of masculinity—including those shaped by the dominant male sports culture—impact voters' perceptions of the people, parties, and interests seeking to attain and exercise power at the highest levels of American government.

I intend to sketch out a number of questions about the ideological influence of male sports culture with which serious students of presidential politics, gender, media, and sport need to grapple. These questions are especially relevant in the context of a 24/7 media environment where information and propaganda come fast and furious, and notions of discrete electoral cycles have given way to the reality of a perpetual campaign. This is not a comprehensive examination of this subject; for example, there remain significant racial and ethnic dimensions to political identities and voters' preferences that are beyond the scope of this paper. It is worth noting that since men of color, especially African Americans and Latinos, tend to be much more liberal and Democratic than white men, it is possible that the masculine discourse of politics—or the masculinity of specific candidates—is less important to them than racial/ethnic issues, identities, and politics. The primary focus of this chapter, then, is on the ideological influence of sports metaphors in the political psyches of white male voters.

Today, the sports/media complex continues to grow exponentially, threatening the integrity of American democracy with a philosophy of soundbites and entertainment values. The arguments introduced here should, at the very least, be seen as a statement about the need to take this "sportspeak" seriously.

■ Sports Studies, Cultural Studies, and the Electoral Gender Gap

In an article summarizing recent developments in the study of sport sociology, Michael Messner (2005) wrote that sport scholars increasingly frame their object of study not as the "sports-world" but as "sports in the world." He located the study of sport within broader cultural studies approaches and identified the analysis of media imagery as one of the most fruitful dimensions of an interdisciplinary "cultural turn" in studies of gender and sport. As Jhally (1984) argued, most people do "the vast majority of their sports spectating via the media (largely through television), so that the cultural experience of sports is hugely mediated." (p. 41). It follows that sports culture and its many constituent parts—such as sports metaphors—are thus important sites for cultural studies critique and critical media literacy efforts.

In his book *Media Culture* (2005), Douglas Kellner provides a powerful rationale for the importance of studying media:

> A media culture has emerged in which images, sounds and spectacles help produce the fabric of everyday life, dominating leisure time, shaping political views and social behavior, and providing the materials out of which people shape their very identities…Media culture also provides the materials out of which many people construct their sense of class, of ethnicity and race, of nationality, of sexuality, of 'us' and 'them.'…For those immersed from cradle to grave in a media and consumer society, it is therefore important to learn how to understand, interpret, and criticize its meanings and messages. (pp. 1–2)

Among the media meanings and messages that are important to understand, interpret, and criticize are those—such as elements of sports culture—involved in shaping the gendered perceptions of presidential candidates. Why? Sports metaphors and other references help to define political reality for millions of men—and women. Listen to *National Review* editor Rich Lowry's analysis of former Virginia Senator George Allen, once a leading Republican hopeful for president. "Football gives Allen a conversational entree with nearly any American male," Lowry writes, "And it is one he never leaves unexploited. What Shakespeare is to the sonnet, Allen is to the football analogy. Over a period of a couple of months, I heard him compare every significant event in Washington to a football play or situation" (p. 33). But whether they're used by politicians, media pundits, or co-workers at the water cooler, sports metaphors in politics do more than provide a shared language for members of the "good ole' boys" club. They help to define key characteristics of manhood and to identify who measures up—and who does not.

It has been well-documented and often discussed that gender differences in voting patterns have been pronounced over the past few presidential elections. (Center for American Women and Politics, 2004). Consider 2004, when George W. Bush won 55% of the total male vote to John F. Kerry's 44%, while Kerry beat Bush among all female voters 51% to 48% (although he lost 55% to 44% among white women). These gender disparities offer clues to some of the differences between women's and men's political priorities, highlighting differences in their respective perceptions of the world. However, these perceptions are neither genetically predetermined nor formed in a vacuum. What is considered "common sense" in a given society at a specific time in history is actually transmitted through various institutional, cultural, and individual practices that are not fixed and immutable. Dominant ideologies, however powerful, are always subject to contestation and resistance. Precisely because media are the great pedagogical force of our time, any serious discussion about gendered patterns in political beliefs and electoral choices, as well as strategies for changing them, need to account for the breadth and depth of media's enormous influence.

Most analyses of the gender gap have focused on women: how their gendered identities impact their political choices and how their voting habits are changing the face of U.S. politics. Only recently have political scientists and journalists begun to look at the male side of the gender gap, in order to understand how men's gendered identities and sense of themselves as "men" impact their political choices. One way to frame this debate is not to ask why women tend to support Democrats, but why (white) men support Republicans in such great numbers.

Of course there are many possible explanations for this electoral gender gap. For example, Lakoff (2004) theorized that Republican ideology embodies an authoritarian "strict father" perspective, while Democrats are better characterized by the values of "nurturant parents." In political shorthand, this means the G.O.P. is perceived as the "daddy party," and the Democrats the "mommy party." In addition, since at least 1972, when the Democratic presidential nominee was the liberal Senator George McGovern, a former World War II fighter pilot who opposed the Vietnam War, polls have consistently shown that the majority of voters believe the Republican Party is more trustworthy on "national security" (Griffith, 2005). One way to interpret this belief is that for whatever reasons of substance or style, the G.O.P. is perceived to be the party that is "tougher" on communism/terrorism, meaning they are more willing to increase military spending and resort to military force to project strength and defend U.S. interests around the world. Because violence is seen as a masculine prerogative, (Katz, 2003), the Republican Party attracts a greater percentage of male votes, as men are more likely than women to prioritize "foreign policy" as an issue that determines their vote for president.

Other factors contributing to the electoral gender gap include the decline in recent decades of organized labor's political influence, white male opposition to gender and race-based affirmative action policies championed by Democrats, and "single-issue" voting on issues like gun control. A further reason to do a cultural studies analysis of how media conventions influence the political views of white males and specifically *working-class* white males is that their voting patterns over the past quarter-century confound the traditional assumption among liberal and progressive economists and political strategists that people are likely to vote their "pocketbooks," i.e., their economic/class interests. For the past couple of decades, millions of mostly non-union blue-collar white men have voted for Republican presidential candidates, who favor tax cuts for the wealthy and reduced federal spending on education and health care programs that serve middle and working-class families. Consider in 2000, when George W. Bush won the support of 63% of white men without a college degree, a stunning twenty-nine point margin over Al Gore. Pundits and writers both inside and outside of academia have sought to understand this phenomenon for years: why do so many non-wealthy white voters—men and women—consistently vote against their own economic interests? One of the most popular political books of the past decade, *What's the Matter with Kansas?: How Conservatives Won the Heart of America,* by Thomas Frank (2004), addresses this very question. Frank argues that the conservative movement has convinced millions of working-class whites that their true enemies are liberal "elites" who have contempt for good old-fashioned American values and that the solution to cultural decline is to elect conservative Republicans. The tragedy is that the economic policies pursued by these same Republicans are designed to ease the tax burden on big business and to steadily erode both the rights of workers and the social safety net that protects them from the harsh realities of economic and social inequality.

Interestingly, Frank and many others neglect to explore in any depth the role of media culture in this critical process, much less the role of sports/media culture. But it is impossible to deny the central role the media *and* sports play in contemporary presidential politics. For a long time, television advertising has been the single biggest campaign expenditure. The 2004 presidential race was at the time the most expensive in history. *USA Today* reported that the Bush and Kerry campaigns, along with "independent" groups, spent approximately $1.6 billion on the 2004 race, more than double the $771 million spent in 2000 (Memmot and Drinkard, 2004). It is estimated that in the "battleground" states alone, there were 675,000 television commercials broadcast (Anderson, 2004). Early estimates of the money spent on the presidential race in 2008 put the total at over $2.4 billion, with advertising and other expenditures shattering all previous records (Schouten, 2008). And that doesn't even begin to measure all of the *unpaid* media—the many thousands of hours of political news and talk shows on cable TV, radio, newspapers, magazines, and the Internet.

Even so, relatively little attention has been paid in scholarship or journalism to the relationship between white men's voting habits and media-driven constructions of masculinities (and femininities)—including the political impact of sports. One notable exception is a brilliant book-length social psychological study by Stephen J. Ducat, entitled *The Wimp Factor: Gender Gaps, Holy Wars, and the Politics of Anxious Masculinity* (2004), which features brief discussions of sports metaphors, talk radio, and other media phenomena. The lack of this type of analysis elsewhere is unfortunate but perhaps not surprising. It could be that the politicized use of sports metaphors is nearly invisible, even to cultural critics, precisely because they are such a part of our daily speech that they "fly under the radar" of critical consciousness. And how realistic is it to expect serious examination of this subject in media, especially when some key opinion leaders in that realm—such as MSNBC's Chris Matthews, host of the aptly-named *Hardball*—are men who are frequently caught up in the masculine mythmaking that often passes for insightful political analysis?

■ Sports Metaphors and Class Politics

What follows are some reflections about the relationship between sports metaphors and the construction of hegemonic masculinity in contemporary U.S. presidential discourse. Hegemonic masculinity is a conceptual tool, identified by the sociologist R.W. Connell (1987), which refers to the idealized and dominant form of masculinity in a given cultural context. In our culture, it is white, middle- and upper-class, and heterosexual, and is further characterized as aggressive and competitive. Not surprisingly, the qualities to date considered "presidential" track closely with those associated with hegemonic masculinity. My purpose is to sketch out some of the ways that sports metaphors help shape the perceptions of voters about the masculinity of various presidential candidates, which in turn affects male voters' propensity to positively identify with them, and both male and female voters' willingness to think they have the "right stuff" to be president. In addition, the presidency can be understood as a kind of public pedagogy, with the president as a kind of pedagogue-in-chief. He literally teaches by example what one highly influential version of dominant masculinity looks like. Since the language of sport helps define cultural expectations of what is considered "presidential," it contributes to the pedagogical influence of the presidency on the norms of masculine identity and behavior.

In this section I intend to briefly explore some of the intersections of gender and class in sports and political discourse. The language of sports in mainstream journalism and presidential campaign rhetoric not only helps shape masculine norms and presents special challenges for female candidates, it also plays a crucial role in highlighting or obfuscating class differences. It is thus an important area of study for both academics and practitioners in the field of political communication and anyone interested in gender and class politics. It should be noted that this discussion is a preliminary examination of a topic that will require a much greater degree of theory, research, and political activism in coming years.

■ The Populist Appeal of Sports Metaphors

With some variation, certain sports are identified not only with men, but with men from specific social classes. For example, racquetball in the U.S. is largely viewed as a sport primarily for middle and upper-class men in health and fitness clubs, whereas boxing and football are considered more blue-collar (although their fan base draws heavily from the middle and upper class as well). The "masculinity" of a given sport has a class dimension. As Nicholas Howe (1988) points out, American politicians "especially those of patrician background, have long appreciated that the use of sports metaphors allows them to affect a common touch or forge a bond with average voters" (p. 89). By making references to sports that are popular with working-class men, sports metaphors are surefire ways to demonstrate populist appeal. A famous example from the pre-television era is the aristocrat Teddy Roosevelt's use of boxing metaphors. More recent examples include Richard Nixon's frequent references to baseball and football or Ronald Reagan's close identification with football.

Reagan's football credentials were enhanced by his having been a college football player, and from his movie role as George Gipp in the 1940 film about a famous football coach, *Knute Rockne: All-American* (the source of the famous line, "Win one for the Gipper," which became part of Reagan lore). Reagan also effortlessly employed gridiron metaphors, such as when he stated in 1981 that European opponents of the neutron bomb were "carrying the propaganda ball for the Soviet Union," (ibid., p. 92) or when he said, in 1984, "Isn't it good to see the American team, instead of punting on third down, scoring touchdowns again?" (ibid. p. 90). Reagan's ability to talk the populist language of football while cutting programs that served working-class families and pursuing an economic policy that redistributed income upward is one of the reasons he earned the nickname the "Great Communicator."

On the other hand, politicians who get the class politics wrong—or who are characterized by their opponents as getting them wrong—run the risk of revealing themselves as elitist, out of touch, or aristocratic in a way that is not read as manly by millions of working and middle-class male voters. For example, during former Massachusetts governor Michael Dukakis's run for the White House in 1988, he repeatedly referred to his campaign as a "marathon," invoking his Greek heritage. The effectiveness of this was questionable, because while many Americans admire and in some ways are in awe of marathon runners, marathon running is not seen in the dominant U.S. culture as a "masculine" endeavor. Additionally, Dukakis's penchant for "power-walking" with the TV cameras rolling did not help bolster his masculine image, as this form of exercise is more often the object of ridicule than emulation in traditional male culture.

In the 2004 presidential campaign, news commentators and conservative media personalities had a field day with footage of John Kerry skiing and snowboarding in Sun Valley, Idaho, and windsurfing off Nantucket Island. While these visuals showed him to be athletic and adventurous and symbolically reinforced Kerry's similarities and identification with fellow Massachusetts senator and former president John F. Kennedy, they also accentuated the idea that his sports passions were upper class in nature. (The class and cultural imagery surrounding the Democratic and Republican parties in the early twenty-first century have changed dramatically since the Kennedy era. The widely-circulated images of Kennedy engaging in upper-class pastimes in the early 1960s played out very differently—and much less negatively—for him and his political persona.) This placed Kerry's constructed masculine image in sharp contrast with that of his opponent and fellow aristocrat George W. Bush, whose carefully stage-managed image was as an average guy who rides in pickup trucks and loves baseball and someone with whom plain folks could identify. The windsurfing photos also served as another kind of sports metaphor: they were the perfect visual illustration of the Republican theme of John Kerry as a "flip-flopper" who did not stand for anything and would just blow with the prevailing winds.

■ Cultural Specificity

There are no universal sports metaphors that work equally well to define manhood across national or cultural boundaries, in part because different cultures have varying definitions of what is considered "masculine." For example, in most parts of the world, soccer is considered a manly sport (even if women also play it), and male soccer stars are often national icons. This is not true in the U.S. Although soccer is our most popular youth sport in terms of athletic participation, it is not even close to American football in its cultural influence, masculine identification, or metaphorical power. It is rare to find a national-level politician in the U.S. who uses soccer metaphors, precisely because to do so would call into question the strength of their American identity, as well as their masculine credibility. Thus it is important for people who use sports metaphors in their speech or writing to know which sports are identified with the hegemonic masculinity of a given society, and to use references to those sports and avoid others. For politicians or political commentators in media, failure to do one's "homework" in this instance would be to expose oneself as either oblivious to local norms and customs, or in the case of a man, as not masculine enough because he discusses, plays or enjoys feminized—or otherwise "wrong," sports. Political professionals are well aware of this trap, which accounts for the fact that in 2004 John Kerry's presidential campaign downplayed his collegiate soccer record and emphasized his hockey credentials.

It is possible to interpret this de-emphasis on Kerry's soccer past as an attempt by his handlers to steer clear of biographical information that reinforced his European—especially French—sensibilities, as this was a line of attack that right-wing activists and media pundits used to paint him as elitist and out of touch with average (read: working class) American voters. Right-wing critics of Kerry were undoubtedly well aware of the gender and class politics that surround soccer in mainstream U.S. culture. As Franklin Foer points out in his book *How Soccer Explains the World* (2004), soccer is the province of the working class in most of the world. But in the U.S., with the exception of Latinos and recent immigrants from Asia and Africa, "the professional classes follow the game most avidly and the working class couldn't give a toss about it...half the nation's soccer participants come from households earning over $50,000...the solid middle-class and above" (p. 239). Moreover, Foer argues that when a "generation of elites" adopted soccer in the 1960s and 1970s, it gave the impression that they had "turned their backs on the stultifying conformity of what it perceived as traditional America" (p. 239). Naturally, this caused resentment toward Democratic "elites" from people in red-state America and other bastions of traditional values. Thus another sports metaphor functioned to reinforce a major tenet of right-wing propaganda, one that Republicans have used to their advantage for decades.

■ Violence in Sports Metaphors: Boxing and Football

U.S. political discourse is infused with metaphors from a range of sports. From former Central Intelligence Agency director George Tenet's infamous assertion that the presence of weapons of mass destruction in Iraq was a "slam dunk," to the criticism that some journalists are known to ask "softball" questions during presidential press conferences, to United States Supreme Court Chief Justice John Roberts' assertion during his confirmation hearings that "Judges are like umpires...They make sure everybody plays by the rules" (Roberts, 2005), to then-presidential candidate Barack Obama's statement that "A nuclear Iran would be a game-changing situation not just in the Middle East but around the world" (Zeleny, 2008), everyday speech by and about politics and politicians routinely contains sports terminology whose meaning resonates with a large number of voters.

But while metaphors from sports such as basketball and baseball regularly surface in political speech, arguably the two most metaphorically influential sports in presidential campaign rhetoric are boxing and football. Not coincidentally, both are violent sports that attract a disproportionate percentage of male participants and fans. It is not within the scope of this study to estimate how much of the white male vote is determined by impressions about the relative "manliness" or "toughness" of candidates or political parties. But there is no doubt that for several decades violence, both our individual and collective vulnerability to it, as well as questions about when and how to use the violent power of the state to protect the "national interest," has been an ominous and omnipresent factor in numerous foreign policy and domestic political issues (e.g., the Cold War, Vietnam, the "War on Terror," and the invasion of Iraq, as well as gun control, and executive, legislative and judicial responses to violent crime). The frequent use of boxing and football metaphors in political discourse did not cause violence to become such an important force in our politics, but this usage is one measure of how presidential campaigns in the mass media era are less about policy differences and complex political agendas than they are about the selling of a certain kind of executive masculinity. Until Barack Obama's election in 2008, this executive masculinity was embodied by a particular white man whom the public came to know largely through television and other mass communication technologies. What follows is a brief discussion of the role of boxing and football metaphors in this process.

Boxing metaphors

Boxing metaphors help to construct presidential campaigns as the ultimate arena for masculine competition. Boxing is a prototypical working-class or "poor man's" (or more recently, woman's) sport that strips the notion of physical combat to its barest essence: man against man ("mano a mano") in a fight to the finish. The almost exclusively white male candidates who have vied at the highest level for executive power have in effect been competing to be their party's "champion," who if victorious becomes the champion of the entire country, the man who stands in for the home team in international political competition against the champions of other countries (e.g. Saddam Hussein, Hugo Chavez, etc.)

For many decades, newspapers have covered presidential debates with language taken directly from coverage of title bouts, complete with "Tale of the Tape" features that quantify a candidate's strengths and weaknesses. To this day, the political fortunes of various candidates are in part determined by whether or not political and media elites describe them as "heavyweights." Anyone who follows contemporary U.S. politics even superficially knows that politicians and journalists constantly use boxing metaphors to describe political machinations. Before his first debate with Ronald Reagan in 1984, Walter Mondale was urged by Tip O'Neill to "come out slugging and come out fighting" (Howe, 1988, pp. 93–94). During the 2000 presidential primaries, *The Los Angeles Times* ran an article about a dramatic speech by Arizona Senator John McCain under the headline "McCain Delivers Hard Left to Christian Right" (Miller and Brownstein, 2000). In a lead-in to a jocular and substantive exchange on National Public Radio with commentator Michael Eric Dyson about the first Bush-Kerry debate in 2004, host Tavis Smiley stated: "Once the lights and cameras are off, media pundits and voters are still left to decide which punches actually landed, which political jabs will be felt throughout the rest of the campaign" (Smiley, 2004). Later in the discussion Dyson, commenting on a previous debate performance by Kerry, said "I ain't saying he was dancing like Ali, but at least he wasn't plodding like some ham-fisted contender for the crown" (Dyson, 2004).

Boxing has historically been a male bastion, and it remains so in the twenty-first century. But now, women's boxing also occupies a small—but highly visible—cultural space. It is probably too early to tell how the increased popularity of women's boxing has affected the power of masculine symbolism associated with the sport. In any case, the 2008 political season broke new linguistic ground, at first because the presence of Hillary Clinton in the ranks of political "heavyweights" complicated the boxing metaphors. Politicians and political commentators had to choose whether or not to use language that had men metaphorically hitting a woman (and vice versa). Republican Sarah Palin's entry into the race as her party's vice-presidential nominee and the second woman on a major party ticket provided another watershed cultural moment. In her first nationally televised speech, at the Republican National Convention in early September, Palin sharply attacked Barack Obama's character and record. A typical headline in the media coverage read "Defiant Sarah Palin Comes Out Swinging," (Barabak, 2008). One of Palin's most-quoted lines on the campaign trail in the fall of 2008 was "The heels are on, the gloves are off," which she typically delivered to wild cheers of approval. In coming years, when this historic campaign and those yet to come are analyzed, it will be particularly interesting to see how female and male voters respond to language where a woman throws the "knockout punch." Does this masculinize and thus help to make them more credible as potential commanders-in-chief? Or do women who are seen as "too-aggressive"—even if only in a metaphorical sense—turn voters off? What are the differences between how the sexes view a woman "throwing punches" if she's a conservative (like Palin) or a liberal feminist (like Hillary Clinton?)

Meanwhile, media commentary about Clinton's rival for the Democratic nomination, Barack Obama, repeatedly featured boxing metaphors that were used to assess his campaign strategy *and* to size him up as a man. During the primary season, one *New York Times* article entitled "Taking blows from all sides and weighing when to punch back," contained a representative paragraph:

> Counter-punching, as Mr. Obama's advisers are quick to say, is a tricky business. If Mr. Obama goes toe-to-toe too often, he risks appearing edgy and even defensive, not to mention turning off those supporters who harbor affection for his rival. But let too many blows go unmatched, and he risks appearing passive, not to mention ending up unconscious. (Powell, 2008).

In the end, Obama won the presidency after a grueling primary and general election campaign where, according to most pundits, he kept his cool in the face of relentless attacks against his character, personal associations, and readiness to lead. When this campaign is analyzed, scholars and journalists will need to examine not only the racial politics of Obama's successful run, but the masculinity politics. Obama is not just the first *person* of color to occupy the White House, he is the first *man* of color.

■ Football Metaphors

Football is a hugely popular sport across the United States, and it provides a wealth of metaphors in contemporary American politics. Journalists wonder whether a politician will do an "end run" around his/her opposition in the legislature. TV pundits preface their remarks about a candidate's debate performance by apologizing for doing a little "Monday-morning quarterbacking." Newly energized campaign volunteers claim to have been inspired to "get off the sidelines" and join the political battle. An op-ed in *USA Today* runs under the headline "Don't punt on Iran: U.S. shouldn't throw bombs or play a soft defense" (Schweizer, 2007). Interestingly, the general election campaign season—when political ads increase exponentially and political talk fills the airwaves—corresponds to the main part of the football season. In fact, Election Day is the first Tuesday in November, right in the heart of the fall football schedule. This means that it is likely a common experience for men and women who watch football on television to be at one moment watching a game, then watching a political ad during a commercial break, followed by a panel of experts analyzing the game, and perhaps moments later watching a panel of experts analyzing the political ad, with much of the rhetoric about football and politics overlapping and interchangeable.

Since football is a violent sport, football metaphors bring violent language and imagery to political discourse. They also subtly and overtly link politics to warfare. As Howe (1988) puts it, "The element of physical conflict in football...makes football metaphors effective...because it establishes that politics is a violent exercise of power with clear winners and losers" (p. 92). Football metaphors with military analogues that are used commonly by sportscasters and sportswriters, such as "throwing the bomb," "penetrating the zone," and "air game vs. ground game," ensure that the language of football and the language of war cross-reference each other. Establishment politicians of both genders who use this sort of language can prove their mastery, or at least familiarity, with two important masculine domains: football and the military. As Reagan and many others have proven, even if their economic program doesn't address the concerns or interests of working people, such language can be an effective way for wealthy candidates to show blue-collar males that they're one of the guys.

It is not difficult to find examples of football metaphors in the speech of contemporary politicians. During the 2004 Republican National Convention in New York City, Rudy Giuliani praised George W. Bush as a "great president" because "he turned around the ship of state from being solely on defense against terrorism to being on offense as well" (Giuliani, 2004). Speaking to reporters about the Iraq war several years later, Secretary of Defense Robert Gates made a similar point, with even more explicit football terminology. "It's important to defend this country on the extremists' ten-yard line, and not on our ten-yard line," he said (Richter, 2007). Republican Senator Richard Lugar compared the Bush plan for a troop "surge" in Iraq to "a draw play on third down with twenty yards to go in the first quarter. The play does have a chance of working if everything goes perfectly, but it is more likely to gain a few yards and set up a punt on the next down" (Lugar, 2007).

The 2008 campaign was also rich in football metaphors. For example, one of Obama's right-wing critics, talk radio host Hugh Hewitt, managed to combine football and boxing metaphors in this caustic dismissal: "Rolling the dice with an untried rookie might be something a desperate NFL franchise might try with a quarterback, but the world cannot afford to have its only superpower turned over to a completely unqualified and wholly inexperienced lightweight" (Hewitt, 2008).

No examination of football metaphors in politics would be complete without more discussion of former Virginia Senator George Allen. Allen, a former college quarterback and the son of the late Washington Redskins coach, has taken the political use of football metaphors to a new level. As reported by Dana Milbank in the *Washington Post,* Allen filters nearly everything political through a football lens. He once said that critics of Condoleezza Rice have used "some bump-and-run defenses and tactics against her." A couple of years ago, when the Republicans won a Senate seat in Louisiana, he said it "was like a double-reverse flea-flicker and a lateral." As head of Senate Republicans' 2004 campaign efforts, he called his candidates in the southern states the "RNC South" (Milbank, 2005).

According to Milbank, "In Allen's world, primaries are 'intrasquad scrimmages,' his Senate staff is the 'A-team,' Senate recess is 'halftime' and opponents are flagged for 'pass interference.' Allen accused the Democrats of 'Constant delay of game, constant holding, constant pass interference and, once in a while, even piling on.' Years without elections are the 'offseason.' Primaries are the 'preseason.' Senate Republicans are President Bush's 'teammates.' Big political donors join a 'Quarterback Club' or a 'Special Teams' committee" (ibid., 2005).

It is important to note that Allen's obsessive use of football metaphors did not hurt him politically. In fact, while his football language was the object of ridicule in some quarters of mainstream journalism and the blogosphere, until late in 2006 he was a major star in conservative Republican circles. Interestingly, new media contributed to the demise of George Allen's political career, which was cut short when his use of an alleged ethnic slur was caught on a hand-held video camera and broadcast widely on *YouTube,* tarnishing his reputation and contributing to the loss of his senate seat.

■ Female Candidates: Do They Play the Game?

In coming years, as more women enter presidential politics, a number of questions will arise about the role of sports in politics, including the role of sports metaphors. Will women candidates need to perfect the language and style of masculine "sportspeak" in order to succeed in a political world still dominated by men, much as female sportscasters and sportswriters have had to adjust to a male-dominated sports/media complex? It is still too early to tell. As one journalist stated in an article about Hillary Clinton's athletic credentials, "There is no playbook for a woman running for president" (Healy, 2007). Clearly, this is treacherous terrain for women candidates, in part because they are expected to be comfortable with what has been a predominantly, though not exclusively, masculine sports discourse. But they can't be too comfortable, lest they commit the unforgivable sin in politics of appearing "inauthentic."

One conundrum for women seeking the presidency is whether it is possible to talk and be talked about in the violent language of boxing and football metaphors, bolstering their image as "tough" enough to be commander-in-chief without appearing as a "wannabe" in the jock-ocratic world of male politics. One woman with some relevant experience in this regard is Condoleezza Rice, Secretary of State in the George W. Bush administration. Rice has stated publicly numerous times that she would like to be commissioner of the National Football League. In a *New York Times* article, she asserted that she is a "student of the game," but that despite her knowledge of football and her passion for it, men often underestimate what she knows because she is a woman (Freeman, 2002). However, as Rice is an appointed official who never faced the electorate as a candidate, it remains to be seen whether either male or female voters would be comfortable with a woman presidential candidate who knows more about football than many of them.

There is growing evidence that voters have become more comfortable with women in positions of political power; Hillary Clinton received over eighteen million votes in the 2008 Democratic presidential primaries. But it is still too early to tell how this new acceptance of female leadership will play out in presidential politics over the next generation, and how the language of politics might change to reflect this. Will the presence of women candidates prompt interest in a new set of (non-sports) metaphors that resonate with voters? Or will a new sort of politics emerge, where both female and male candidates come to forge and embody new kinds of gendered identities that do not fall along predictable or traditional lines?

Despite Obama's epochal victory, it is also impossible to do anything but speculate about when new styles of manhood will become acceptable presidential qualities to a majority of white male voters, especially those who in recent decades have seemed to be searching for the star quarterback to guide Team USA in our ongoing and often dangerous competitions with the rest of the world.

■ Political Complexities of Sport, Race, and Ethnicity

This article attempts to provide readers with some dimensions of a cultural studies analysis of a subject that is often discussed but infrequently taken seriously as a topic for systematic theory and research. Sports metaphors are a ubiquitous part of political speech and journalism in the United States in the twenty-first century. They help to produce and reproduce dominant constructions of masculinities (and femininities), and establish and reinforce norms both for candidates and voters. But it is premature to make broad or specific claims about exactly what effect they have on presidential politics. This study poses a number of questions about the relation between conventions of dominant male sports culture and the political beliefs and choices of white men, especially working-class white men. There are many more questions raised by this line of inquiry: What affect, if any, does political discourse filled with sports metaphors popular in *male* sports culture have on *women's* political beliefs and choices? Are there significant class dimensions to these, as well?

In addition, this study focuses on white men. What if any impact does the political use of sports metaphors have on men of color? Women of color? As increasing numbers of men and women of color enter U.S. politics, including presidential politics, what effect will race—and racism—have on the way sports metaphors are used, and discussed? For example, if an African American male politician used football metaphors as promiscuously as does former Senator George Allen, would people find it humorous, perhaps a little goofy, but still an indication that he's a "man's man"? Or is it possible that his stature would be questioned, as African Americans constantly have to fight the stereotype that they're "natural" athletes who lack intellectual heft? Barack Obama is a good basketball player and often played pick-up games on the 2008 campaign trail for exercise. Basketball is a highly popular sport in this country, yet players at the elite level in college and the pros are overwhelmingly African American. Do Obama's hoop skills reinforce his "otherness" to the white majority, his *black* masculinity? Furthermore, playing pick-up basketball has not traditionally been seen as "presidential" behavior. Could this have contributed to the perception among some white voters that he was young and inexperienced, and therefore not ready for the highest office in the land? Shared interest and experience with sports can be a catalyst for connection between a candidate and the voters—but divergent experiences can also serve as a proxy for racial/ethnic differences. "Let's not forget Barack Obama bowling," said Reuters Washington correspondent Jon Decker in a discussion of the 2008 Democratic primary in Pennsylvania. "You know, for someone who's in a bowling league in northeast central Pennsylvania, in Scranton and Wilkes-Barre, they can't identify with someone getting a thirty-seven over seven frames" (Younge, 2008). Is it overdrawn to suggest that in its own minor way, this might have been one of the reasons why Obama was slow to win the votes of working-class whites in the Democratic primaries?

In recent decades there has been a significant increase in the number of Latinos in the U.S. population and electorate, and with it growing media presence and political clout. With regard to sports metaphors, this raises a number of interesting speculations about political calculations. Will Latino politicians and Anglo politicians seeking Latino votes increasingly use soccer metaphors in their speeches or press conference banter? That might resonate with Latino soccer fans along with fans from other ethnic groups, but how will it play out in the dominant Anglo culture, especially among sports talk radio hosts and other media personalities who ridicule soccer as "wimpy" in relation to American football? As scholars and political activists alike come to understand the importance of applying media literacy theory and practice to politics, these are just a few of the countless lines of inquiry that will require further exploration.

■ Conclusion: A Call for Political Media Literacy

Finally, because media play an indisputably central role in contemporary politics, *political media literacy* should be seen as an essential part of civics and citizen education in the twenty-first century. The basic rationale for the development of a political media literacy movement is that education for democracy in this era requires citizens to be media literate. Media have become the single most important source of political information and persuasion. In order for voters to make informed choices about which parties and candidates to support, they must have the critical media literacy skills to 1) discern the underlying ideologies, class interests, and other forces that shape political discourse in a twenty-four-seven media culture dominated by corporate media, and 2) deconstruct, read critically, and contest hegemonic images of embodied power, especially white male power. There is little hope for a truly progressive politics emerging in the United States unless we address the narrow and deeply conservative ways that corporate media, in their dominance of political discourse, simultaneously reinforce hegemonic notions of "manhood," place significant obstacles in the path of women's political leadership, and frame the electoral choices available to voters.

The teaching of political media literacy in middle and high school should be seen as a fundamental component of a revitalized push for contemporary civics/government/ social studies education, and the integration of media literacy into political science curricula at the post-secondary and graduate level needs to be understood as a critical piece of a much larger progressive media reform project in the coming decade. Just as importantly, political media literacy initiatives need to emphasize new media and information technologies, as well as the implications of these technologies for civic engagement, electoral campaigns, and the very nature of democratic institutions.

References

Anderson, N. (2004). "Silence of the wolves, and their ilk, in swing states." *Los Angeles Times Online*. Nov. 2.

Barabak, M. (2008). "Defiant Sarah Palin comes out swinging," *Los Angeles Times,* Sept. 4.

Center for American Women and Politics, (2004) Rutgers, NJ Nov. 5, 2004. http://www.rci.rutgers.edu/~cawp/Facts/Elections/GG2004Facts.pdf

Connell, R.W. (1987). *Gender and Power.* Stanford, CA: Stanford University Press.

Ducat, S. (2004). *The Wimp Factor: Gender Gaps, Holy Wars, and the Politics of Anxious Masculinity.* Beacon Press: Boston.

Dyson, M.E. (2004). *The Tavis Smiley Show,* National Public Radio, www.npr.org, Sept. 30. http://www.npr.org/templates/story/story.php?storyId=4054526

Faludi, S. (1999). *Stiffed: The Betrayal of the American Man,* William Morrow and Company: New York.

Foer, F. (2004). *How Soccer Explains the World,* Harper Perennial: New York.

Frank, T. (2004). *What's the Matter with Kansas? How Conservatives Won the Heart of America.* Metropolitan Books: New York.

Freeman, M. (2002). "On pro football: dream job for Rice: N.F.L. commissioner," *New York Times,* April 17.

Giuliani, R. (2004). *www.CNN.com,* Aug 31. http://www.cnn.com/2004/ALLPOLITICS/08/30/giuliani.transcript/index.html

Griffith, L. (2005). "Where we went wrong: how the public lost faith in Democrats' ability to protect our national security, and how to stage a comeback" The Truman National Security Project, May. http://www.trumanproject.org/trumanpaper3.html

Healy, P. (2007). "Hillary Clinton searches for her inner jock," *New York Times,* June 10.

Hewitt, H. (2008). "The Obama melt." Retrieved on May 26, 2008 from http://hughhewitt.townhall. com/blog/g/e9fa1f90–2f4f-4b0d-a562–080bfe6b2f09

Howe, N. (1988). "Metaphors in Contemporary American Political Discourse." *Metaphor and Symbolic Activity,* 3(2), 87–104.

Jhally, S. (1984), "The Spectacle of Accumulation: material and cultural factors in the evolution of the sports/media complex." *Insurgent Sociologist, 12* (3).

Katz, J. (2003). "Advertising and the construction of violent white masculinity: from Eminem to Clinique for Men." In G. Dines & J. Humez (Eds.), *Gender, Race and Class in Media: A Text Reader* (Second edition). Thousand Oaks, CA: Sage Publications.

Kellner, D. (2003). "Cultural Studies, Multiculturalism and Media Culture," In G. Dines & J. Humez (Eds.), *Gender, Race and Class in Media: A Text Reader* (Second edition). Thousand Oaks, CA: Sage Publications, p.9.

Kellner, D. (2005). *Media culture.* New York: Routledge.

Kilbourne, J. (1979). *Killing Us Softly: Advertising Images of Women.* Cambridge, MA: Cambridge Documentary Films.

Lakoff, G. (2004). *Don't Think of An Elephant: Know Your Values and Frame the Debate.* White River Junction, VT: Chelsea Green Publishing Company.

Lakoff, G. and Johnson, M. (1980). *Metaphors We Live By.* Chicago: University of Chicago Press.

Lowry, R. (2005). "Buckling his chin strap: Sen. George Allen—likable, conservative, and tough—prepares to run for president." *National Review,* Nov. 7.

Lugar, R. (2007). "Beyond Baghdad," *The Washington Post,* January 30, p. A17.

Memmott, M. and Drinkard, J. (2004). "Election ad battle smashes record in 2004," *USA Today,* Nov. 25.

Messner, M. (2005). "Still a man's world: studying masculinities and sport," In *Handbook of Studies on Men and Masculinities,* eds. Kimmel, M., Hearn, J., and Connell, R.W. (pp. 313–325). Thousand Oaks, CA: Sage Publications.

Milbank, D. (2005). "Mixing politics, pigskins: when Allen talks, football jargon flows," *Washington Post,* February 6, P. C01.

Miller, T. C., and Brownstein, R. (2000). "McCain Delivers Hard Left to Christian Right," *Los Angeles Times,* Feb. 9, P. 1

Powell, M. (2008). "Taking blows from all sides and weighing when to punch back," *The New York Times,* Feb. 25.

Richter, P. (2007). "Bush sees long-term role for troops," *Los Angeles Times,* May 31.

Roberts, J. (2005). "Text of John Roberts' opening statement," www.*USAToday.com,* Sept. 12. http://www.usatoday.com/news/washington/2005–09–12-roberts-fulltext_x.htm

Schneider, W. (2007). "Presidential fundraising hits record pace," CNN.Com, July 6. http://politicalticker.blogs.cnn.com/2007/07/06/schneider-why-are-dems-winning-the-money-race/#more-729

Schouten, F. (2008). "Political spending races toward record $5.3 billion." *USA Today,* Oct. 23, p. 1.

Schweizer, P. (2007). "Don't punt on Iran." *USA Today,* June 26, 2007. p. 13A.

Smiley, T. (2004). The Tavis Smiley Show, *National Public Radio,* www.npr.org, Sept. 30. http://www.npr.org/templates/story/story.php?storyId=4054526

Wolf, N. (1992). *The Beauty Myth: How Images of Beauty Are Used Against Women,* New York: Anchor Books.

Younge, G. (2008). "Bitter fruit in Pennsylvania," *The Nation,* May 5, p. 10.

Zeleny, J. (2008). "Obama meets with Israeli and Palestinian leaders," *The New York Times,* July 24, p. A16.

Emergent Digital Cultures

■ Introduction

Part IV critically engages "emergent digital cultures." For many, the term "new media" is becoming problematic, in that it generally refers to computers and digital technology, which have now been around for decades. The notion of "new" media also suggests a rupture and a fundamental break with previous media; while computerization and digitization have enormous effects and are an important novelty, there are continuities with previous media. As McLuhan argued in *Understanding Media*, new media often absorb the format and structures of the old, just as television took up the format of previous radio genres and the same corporations dominated both, and "new media" have progressively absorbed the forms of "old media" from writing to broadcasting and video to proliferating forms of multimedia. Yet digitization is a novelty and emergent forms of digital media and culture require careful theoretical and political analysis, as the contributors to our volume carry out, pointing to distinctive and novel features of the emergent digital culture.

Leah A. Lievrouw in "The Uses of Disenchantment in New Media Pedagogy: Teaching for Remediation and Reconfiguration" provides a sweeping overview of transformations within media and digital culture over the last decades and how we need to both constantly re-theorize and analyze digital media and culture, and, as teachers, come up with new strategies for teaching critical media pedagogy. Lievrouw discusses how today's youth is growing up immersed in a digital culture environment, and thus the old strategies of critical media literacy need rethinking. Although many students have the technical skills previously taught in literacy courses, they need to reflect on the transformations and novelties of digital culture and prepare themselves more reflectively and critically as producers within the culture. Lievrouw suggests a critical "disenchantment" that aims at "re-mastering, re-purposing, and re-framing" digital culture so that students and citizens can become more informed and capable participants in their culture and society. She offers a range of pedagogical exercises that can help teachers and students better understand the emergent digital culture and how we all can participate in and shape it.

Mark Poster has long engaged the new forms of media and culture, combing postmodern with critical theories. In "Perfect Transmissions: Evil Bert Laden," Poster studies a peculiar example of global media culture that illustrates how global communication and information networks draw upon, recycle, and hybridize a wealth of cultural forms that may appear to have bizarre meanings and effects in local contexts. Poster's inquiry into the new global digital culture starts with the curious phenomenon of an American young man who demonized the cartoon figure Bert from the popular children's show *Sesame Street,* creating an "Evil Bert" website. The site was duplicated and linked throughout the world, and images of Evil Bert from the site started appearing on images and posters featuring Osama Bin Laden. Poster and various journalists researched this strange juxtaposition and came up with a variety of explanations that the reader can sort out, ranging from speculations that a group with a pro-Bin Laden website had a savvy understanding of American media culture and used the figures of Bert and Bin Laden to terrorize the West. Others speculated that the pasting-in of the Bin Laden image accidentally carried with it the "evil Bert" image, and the creators did not recognize this. In any case, it points to the globalization and hybridization of media culture and how different images can have different meanings and effects in various parts of the world.

Rebecca Stephenson's study "Doing Something That Matters: Children's Culture, Video Games, and the Politics of Representation" engages video game culture and addresses issues such as violence, commercial targeting of children, and the demonization of the culture by certain societal forces. Avoiding one-sided approaches that would either damn or uncritically celebrate gaming, Stephenson presents a cultural studies analysis that calls attention to the need for critical media literacy to engage the politics of representation in gaming culture. She discusses some representations of race and gender in the sites and warns that attention is also needed concerning how audiences actually use the sites, often in complex fashion. Yet Stephenson notes that there remains a serious problem with gender and racial stereotypes that inhabit game culture and calls for the development of games that promote more positive representations.

Alla Zollers' "Critical Perspectives on Social Network Sites" presents a cultural studies decoding of social network sites which discusses networking as a "contested terrain." Regarding gaming culture, Zollers, like Stephenson, refers to the "moral panic" associated with social networking sites, as well as the role of "consumption" in the sites. After laying out a history of the major social networking sites like MySpace and Facebook, she identifies the manner in which people construct their profiles and personal identities in terms of the products that they consume, like films or music. Yet she sees social networks as a contested terrain and discusses a variety of political uses of networking, while warning against overlooking the commercial nature of many of the sites as well as people using the sites just to promote themselves in narcissistic fashion.

Douglas Kellner and Gooyong Kim in "YouTube, Politics, and Pedagogy" explore the YouTube phenomenon and discuss how principles of critical pedagogy might help produce more democratic, enlightening, and educational forms of YouTube and other emergent digital media forms. Building on a study of YouTubers who use the medium to reflect on what they are trying to accomplish and how, based on research by Gooyong Kim, the authors argue for both the democratic, participatory potential of YouTube and ways that it might reproduce commercialism, individualism, and hegemonic forms of the consumer society. Yet, by applying a critical pedagogy to producing YouTube videos and other multimedia material, the enlargement of a democratic public sphere is possible that increases participation and social justice.

New media and social networking sites are a new and ever-expanding frontier of media and cultural studies and require novel critical approaches that assess their potential for democratization and education as well as the dangers of promoting new forms of commercialism, extreme individualism, and anti-social behavior. The chapters in this section attempt to present critical approaches to media and sites that are proliferating in often-unpredictable ways as we bring this project to a close.

32

■ The Uses of Disenchantment in New Media Pedagogy

Teaching for Remediation and Reconfiguration

Leah A. Lievrouw

> Hackers create the possibility of new things entering the world. Not always great things, or even good things, but new things. In art, in science, in philosophy and culture, in any production of knowledge where data can be gathered, where information can be extracted from it, and where in that information new possibilities for the world produced, there are hackers hacking the new out of the old.
>
> *McKenzie Wark*, A Hacker Manifesto, *(2004)*

Over the last three decades, the proliferation and hybridization of new media and information technologies have fostered a variety of new genres and forms of people's engagement with media. Media *audiences* and *consumers* are now also media *users* and *participants,* immersed in a complex ecology of divides, diversities, networks, and literacies. This changing social and technological landscape has created unprecedented opportunities for expression and interaction. But it also poses complex problems of social equity and solidarity, privacy and security, political and economic participation, and more. In such a context, the familiar "processes and effects" that motivated traditional mass communication research and scholarship, and the production-consumption dynamics of critical media studies, tell only part of the story.

In previous work, I have proposed that two particular modes of engagement distinguish new media from mass media: the *reconfiguration* of media technologies and systems, that is, the modification and adaptation of technologies as needed, to suit the users' purposes or interests; and the *remediation* of media content and forms, where existing materials are borrowed, adapted, sampled, or remixed to create new expressions, relationships, and content (Lievrouw, 2006a; 2007). Reconfiguration and remediation are hallmarks of contemporary communication, creative work, and media culture; they allow users to resist the fixity of traditional technologies and institutional systems, and to negotiate, work around, or redraw the boundaries of their communicative practices and of mediation itself, in an ongoing process of co-optation and reinvention.

Nowhere has this sensibility been more fully embraced than among young people in affluent societies like those in the United States and elsewhere around the world, many of whom are sophisticated users of new media technologies, and avid participants in online culture. Google, Facebook, del.ic.ious, SecondLife, and World of Warcraft may matter as much to young Americans, as Viacom, Disney, CNN, Murdoch, and the *New York Times* do to their parents. Instructors in media and communication studies face significant challenges as they attempt to present their students with a critical view of the new media environment, based on classic principles of media literacy and critical judgment, cultural studies, and industrial-era political economy. In the new media context, the sources and circulation of information and knowledge, as well as the standpoints of observers, critics, and participants, are often unstable or contested. Young Internet users are also widely assumed to be apathetic, self-absorbed to the point of solipsism, and politically disengaged. And as if these challenges weren't enough, mainstream media industries have waged relentless legal and public relations campaigns, in both American culture at large and in the classroom, to teach youngsters that creative engagement online is risky and that sharing information is tantamount to theft, piracy, and "trafficking" with dire legal and financial consequences (Gillespie, 2007).

Nonetheless, my students often seem frustrated by those who dismiss their engagement with new media as mere entertainment or consumption—as when they're patronizingly told that they can be "producers as well as consumers" or that "good digital citizens" avoid free downloads or file-sharing. However, recent studies indicate that young Internet users are far from apathetic. They tend to be wary of corporate media products and institutions (Pew Research Center, 2007), although they may not always be able to articulate just why "mainstream media" or "multinational corporations" cannot be trusted. In my experience, students are eager to understand and situate their experiences with new media, not only as audiences or consumers, but as active, skilled, and informed participants in a thoroughly *mediated,* networked culture, who use media and information technologies to express themselves, create relationships, and share meaning.[1]

The greatest pedagogical challenge related to new media, then, may not be students' lack of basic technical skills or literacies.[2] Nor do they need convincing that mainstream media industries wield disproportionate power, serve the interests of dominant political and economic players, or produce endless streams of distraction and junk content. Rather, the challenge for new media pedagogy is to connect students' everyday interactions and experiences with media technologies, to classic questions of equity, privacy, fairness, openness, access, power, and so on—to give students the critical vocabulary and tools to think with and to encourage them toward more active and principled media use and participation. Put differently, the challenge is to teach for reconfiguration and remediation.

In his classic book, *The Uses of Enchantment,* the psychologist Bruno Bettelheim argues that the imagery of myths and fairy tales helps the child,

> …enrich his life…stimulate his imagination; help him to develop his intellect and to clarify his emotions; be attuned to his anxieties and aspirations; give full recognition to his difficulties, while at the same time suggesting solutions to the problems which perturb him…simultaneously promoting confidence in himself and in his future.(Bettelheim, 1976, p. 5)

With respect to new media and information technologies however, there has never been a shortage of mythologizing and hype, especially directed at young people. If anything, it can be nearly impossible to disentangle facts from mythology when we talk about the "hundred-dollar laptop," "frictionless economy," "death of distance," "digital divide," "hive mind," "long tail," or "Web 2.0," for example. Often, such buzz words are no more than simplifying tokens that mask complex, socio-technical interconnections and power relationships. They serve more to obscure difficulties and possible solutions and to produce anxieties, than to make these relations and solutions intelligible.

Therefore, to encourage students toward more reflective, critical, and activist engagement with media, it is necessary to sustain the constructive, affirmative energy of the myths, while pointing the way beyond simplistic hype. At the same time, instruction must help reduce the disabling outrage and cynicism generated by ideologically driven critique that assigns simple or fixed roles to certain players and actors in the contemporary media landscape. By introducing a bit of *dis*-enchantment—for example, by drawing historical parallels between H. G. Wells's 1938 vision of an encyclopedic "world brain" and Tim Berners-Lee's vision of the World Wide Web, by demonstrating the concrete reality of Internet infrastructure and surveillance in the form of real-time maps of router traffic, the spread of e-mail viruses, or by having students keep diaries about their media uses—the way can be opened for healthy skepticism, while avoiding cynicism that shuts down engagement and commitment. Students can begin to contextualize the myths and think about new media technologies and culture less as vast, impersonal forces and more as repertoires of practices, tools, and social arrangements that they can engage and play with, intervene in, hack, reconfigure, and remediate—not just consume.

In the remainder of this chapter, I draw on my experiences teaching the social implications of ICTs (information communication technology) and new media, to reflect on a strategy for new media pedagogy that can help make this connection. It involves two main components: the first is historical contextualization that contrasts contending visions of the cultural and economic role of new media that have evolved from the days of the pre-browser Internet in the 1980s to today's Web 2.0. The second aspect is designing exercises that encourage students to assess their own media practices and to think about and critique new media culture, using a critical vocabulary that contrasts new media projects with more traditional mass media programming and content. The ultimate objective is to help students become more adept and informed participants in media culture.

■ Historical Contextualization: A Survey of the Contested New Media Landscape

The first step in creating effective new media pedagogy is setting the stage. Students are often unfamiliar with the social and economic background of the technologies and uses they take for granted in everyday life. Therefore, it is essential to demonstrate the continuity of "new" media culture with technologies, institutions, and social practices over time, as well as pointing out instances of change and discontinuity. To accomplish this, I often frame the development of media and information technologies by contrasting two rival (but in many ways interdependent and even dialectical) views of the proper role of media in society. At the risk of some simplification, these can be called the *pipeline* and *frontier* visions.

Historically, it has been well established that a handful of major firms and cultural institutions have dominated the mass media and information industries in the United States and globally, and they continue to occupy a major role in mainstream culture and politics. These "mainstream media" have tended to view the contemporary media landscape almost entirely in terms of gatekeeping and property—a "pipeline" model based in traditional mass media production and distribution that emphasizes the transmission of content and media products from a few dominant producers to large audiences of consumers.

However, these firms and institutions have been challenged, particularly since the 1990s, as growing numbers of people have turned to new media technologies for information and entertainment, to maintain and extend their networks of social relationships and interpersonal contacts, to generate and share their own self-produced content, and to resist, critique, and respond to mainstream culture and politics. These users, especially those with the skills to manipulate and play with the technology itself, tend to see new media culture more as an arena for cultivating reputation, credibility, reciprocity, trust, and voice—a "frontier" for sociality and action.

In contemporary media culture, these two visions are played out in a contested terrain where relatively concentrated, mainstream "centers" of traditional media industries and governance, organized around the pipeline model, contend with increasingly diffuse, interactive, and participatory "edges" where the frontier idea has more currency. Center and edges, pipeline and frontier—all engage in an ongoing cycle of capture, co-optation, subversion, and repurposing of information resources, content, and technological systems.

The story of these competing visions begins with the rise of networked telecommunications and computing, from the research-driven ARPANET and NSFNET in the 1960s and 1970s, to the privatized, commercialized Internet in the 1980s and 1990s (Abbate, 1999; Ceruzzi, 1998). In the early stages, the Internet was regarded as an arcane tool for experts and academics, best suited to interpersonal messaging and database manipulation, and not much of a threat to the cultural dominance of established broadcasting, cable, news, and entertainment media.[3] Before the era of browser technologies and the World Wide Web, a succession of collaborative environments for small groups, including news groups, bulletin boards, group decision support and computer conferencing systems, listservs, multi-user dungeons (MUDs), and MOOs (MUDs, Object-Oriented) emerged and flourished among skilled users with workplace or campus Internet access. E-mail, the original "killer application" of computer-mediated communication from the inception of the ARPANET, migrated into the workplace and eventually into routine personal and leisure communication settings.

However, the introduction of the World Wide Web, browsers, and inexpensive client-server network architectures in the early 1990s inaugurated a new stage in the development and spread of the Internet. Many observers confidently predicted that the Web would finally deliver on the communitarian visions of "information utilities," "wired cities," and "virtual communities," promulgated from the 1960s onward by pragmatic policy experts and utopian technophiles alike (Dutton, Blumler, & Kraemer, 1987; Greenberger, 1964, 1985; Light, 2003; Turner, 2006). Technology enthusiasts like Howard Rheingold, for example, deemed the decentralized, packet-switched architecture of the Internet to be inherently democratic and predicted that it would open a new frontier for empowerment and participation that would give marginalized communities and groups a greater role and visibility in the wider culture than had ever been possible via mass media (Rheingold, 1993). Electronic Frontier Foundation founder John Perry Barlow famously declared that "information wants to be free" and denounced government controls on encrypted personal communications as "jackboots on the Infobahn" (Barlow, 1994a, 1994b).

Certainly, the frontier vision owed a great deal to the communitarian (if intensely technocratic) "hacker ethic" that evolved among elite computer programmers and engineers in the 1960s and 1970s (Nissenbaum, 2004). Many of these bright, motivated young technologists and graduate students, deeply influenced by counterculture values and politics, were also recruited by the Department of Defense's Advanced Research Projects Agency to design and build the original ARPANET and other defense-related computing projects. The free software movement launched by Richard Stallman and his colleagues at MIT, for example, was the philosophical and ethical inspiration for today's free/libre/open source software (FLOSS) model of technological innovation and development (Moore, 2001; Raymond, 2001). The dramatic, "counterintuitive" success of the FLOSS approach, founded on broad-based information sharing instead of secrecy and restrictive patenting, has recently given rise to similar efforts across other high-technology and manufacturing industries (*Economist,* 2005a, 2005b, 2006). The hacker ethic continues to be expressed in campaigns by programmer-activists against the pervasive expansion of intellectual property rights and restrictive digital rights management (DRM) technologies, government controls on encryption, and law enforcement agencies' surveillance of individuals' private communications, particularly in the post-9/11 era (Eschenfelder & Desai, 2004; Ludlow, 2001; Wark, 2004).

By the mid-1990s, meanwhile, the mainstream media industries had begun to worry about the "frontier" of the Internet and the World Wide Web as a potential rival for the time, attention, and disposable income of mass media entertainment audiences. They viewed the theoretically limitless reproduction and circulation of digital materials as a clear threat to their traditional control over the production and distribution of media programs and products. Recasting themselves as "content industries," to emphasize their roles as cultural producers, they insisted that the Web was significant mainly as a marketing and distribution channel, in line with their existing, primarily one-way, model of production and distribution. Firms entered into mergers that would allow them to enlarge and lock in market share. In partnerships with computing firms, they bundled their content with other types of "software" and hardware platforms. They formed alliances with telecommunications operators, cable companies, and Internet service providers (e.g., AOL-Time Warner and AT&T-Comcast), to centralize and extend control over the new media infrastructure, particularly the "final mile" of cable or telephone wire into the home.

Although a glut of bandwidth had been built in the United States in the 1990s in anticipation of a surge in demand for paid online entertainment, by the end of the century most of these new networks remained dark: major media firms were reluctant to distribute their products online without ironclad copy protections and revenue guarantees. Broadband services to the home (i.e., cable modem and digital subscriber line [DSL] services) were built "asymmetrically," that is, with much more downstream capacity from the network to subscribers, than upstream from subscribers to the network, reflecting a view of subscribers primarily as consumers, rather than producers, of media.[4] The dot-com collapse at the end of the 1990s provoked further rounds of buy-outs and increased ownership concentration across the media, telecoms, and computing industries.

Media and entertainment industries also lobbied the Congress, Justice Department, Federal Communications Commission (FCC), and other relevant agencies to reshape the regulatory environment to their advantage. Limits on concentrated media ownership were substantially reduced under the 1996 Telecommunications Act and the FCC's repeal of its Financial Interest in Syndication ("Fin-Syn") rules.[5] The U.S. radio frequency spectrum, formerly considered a scarce natural resource and thus a public good, was redefined as an over-abundant commodity, and significant portions of the airwaves were put up for auction or given to private firms outright.

The traditional media and entertainment industries also enthusiastically appropriated the "intellectual property" metaphor from the invention and patenting culture of scientific research and high technology, and adopted a new and expansive view of copyright as an instrument for safeguarding and expanding their established revenue sources—a move that launched what one critic called an "intellectual property epidemic" (Litman, 1994). Historically, entertainment and media firms had placed little value on their older productions: studios, networks, music labels, and publishers were more likely to dump or destroy old films, sound recording masters, and videotaped television shows, or to let unpopular books go out of print and fall out of copyright, than to store and preserve either the works themselves, or the rights to them.[6] However, with the spread of digital technologies, the industries now saw their backlists and catalogs as potential troves of low-cost content that could be recycled, "versioned," and resold to new audiences. Extended copyright protection was one way to insure that firms would retain rights to older works, long after they would otherwise have moved into the public domain.

The 1998 Digital Millennium Copyright Act (DMCA) and the 1999 Bono Copyright Term Extension Act thus marked the beginning of a new era in American intellectual property law, extending copyright restrictions to more types of materials and rights than ever before, for unprecedented periods of time, as a hedge against the growing dominance of digital technology. Despite the fact that information technologies with significant non-infringing uses (such as VCRs) had long been legal, new "anti-circumvention" provisions of the DMCA prohibited the production or use of any new technology that *could* be used to infringe copyrights, whether the technology was in fact used that way or not. Armed with new legal doctrines and protections, in the early 2000s industry groups (notably the Recording Industry Association of America [RIAA] and Motion Picture Association of America [MPAA]) launched waves of lawsuits against student Internet users and college campuses, charging that American institutions of higher learning (where high-speed Internet access was already routine) had become willing accomplices in students' illegal downloading and file sharing.

After the attacks of 9/11, the moral panic over copyright infringement in the United States became increasingly conflated with the Bush administration's drives to expand the surveillance of citizens and foreigners in the "global war on terror." Indeed, one observer predicted that the events of September 11 would be seen in retrospect as "the iceberg [that sank] the Internet" (Meikle, 2002, p. 173). New laws abandoned the traditional regulatory principles that had underpinned telephony, postal mail, and publishing. Internet service providers (ISPs) now considered both their systems, and the content they carried, as their private property and subject to company monitoring and control.[7] In early 2007, Attorney General Alberto Gonzalez praised the proposed Intellectual Property Protection Act of 2007, which would have criminalized "attempted" infringement (previously, only actual infringement could be prosecuted), increased the punishment for use of pirated software to life imprisonment, and required the Department of Homeland Security to notify the RIAA whenever it detected the unauthorized transfer of recorded performances in the course of its surveillance sweeps of the Internet (McCullagh, 2007).

To date, established media and entertainment firms have stridently opposed any distribution scheme or technology that might threaten their gate keeping, rent-extracting role in the creation and movement of information and interpersonal communications. This stance has dovetailed neatly with the security and surveillance interests of government and law enforcement in the post-9/11 era.

Yet the frontier vision persists. Myriad community groups, cultural and political activists, artists, and others have adopted new media technologies to respond to, reflect, critique, parody, rejoin, avoid, or subvert mainstream media and culture. Ranging from volunteer indymedia news services that report on underrepresented issues and communities, to culture jamming projects that hack and ridicule images and ideas from popular culture and politics, to "folksonomies" that challenge and reorganize established institutional authority and knowledge (Lievrouw, 2006a; 2007), these projects combine the progressive hacker philosophy of early Internet proponents and visionaries, with the longer tradition of underground, alternative, and radical art and media (Atton, 2002, 2004; Bailey, Cammaerts, & Carpentier, 2007; Downing et al., 2001).

A more quotidian, but perhaps more significant, development has been the emergence of so-called "Web 2.0," as more people have turned to new media for everyday interpersonal interaction and information sharing, as well as the consumption of mass-produced content. Few of today's undergraduates even remember a time before browsers and the Web. Despite the "zero tolerance" stance of the entertainment industries and their government allies, downloads and file-sharing have become the dominant mode of engagement with media for most young Americans. Millions of Internet users routinely write blogs (see indexes and statistics at Technorati), organize and classify online materials using tagging and bookmarking sites (del.icio.us, flickr, Twitter, Pandora), interact via social networking sites (Facebook, MySpace, LinkedIn), upload home movies and more ambitious media projects on video sharing sites (YouTube), contribute to collaborative, peer-reviewed information resources (Wikipedia), and participate in "massively multi-player" games and virtual worlds (World of Warcraft, SecondLife). Nonetheless, mainstream media interests have reacted stubbornly to this shift in engagement with a mixture of derision (print journalists ridicule bloggers), co-optation (celebrating "user-generated content," *Time* magazine's 2006 "Person of the Year" cover featured the word "YOU" above a screen-shaped reflective panel), and outright capture (Rupert Murdoch's purchase of MySpace and Microsoft's stake in Facebook).

The territory of digital media culture remains contested.

■ Exercises for Participation in Digital Culture

Historical contextualization gives students some basic tools for framing and interpreting the development of media and information technologies and for forming their own views about those technologies' cultural and social significance. But the nature of contemporary digital technologies and culture suggests that effective learning *about* digital culture requires meaningful and direct participation *in* it. Therefore, once the social and cultural context of digital media has been provided, the second aspect of new media pedagogy challenges students to assess and develop their own practices and skills. The following exercises and activities range from simple research tasks to more complex team projects involving web authoring skills. Students gather and analyze information about key concepts and issues; make judgments, evaluate information, critique cases, and justify their views and conclusions; and demonstrate their knowledge and judgment in the design, production, and presentation of projects that they share with peers in class and online.

Surveillance and Privacy: "The Data Cloud"

The inspiration for this assignment is the concept of the *data cloud,* characterized by media and cultural critic Bruce Sterling as "the kind of demographic haze that surrounds the author" (Sterling, 2005). For a minimum of forty-eight hours (e.g., over a weekend), students are instructed to keep a detailed diary of all the transaction data that they generate and are captured by digital technologies as they go about their everyday activities. For example, students note every time they're in the presence of a video surveillance camera, use a credit or debit card, make a telephone call, TiVO a television program, get directions using a GPS device, send e-mail or download files online, pass a scanner at a turnpike toll booth, have purchases recorded at a store's point-of-sale scanner, swipe a card to enter a building, and so on.

At the end of the diary period, each student compiles the information into a short summary and writes up a discussion of the results. Students are asked to reflect on the significance of what they've found; for example, what does their data cloud say about them, and to whom? What are the advantages and disadvantages of data capture for them personally? Who has access to the captured information, and why might those with access be interested? How might extensive data capture affect students' speech and political rights? How might students better control the data trails they leave, if it is possible at all?

Digital Divides, Access, and Equity: The Household Media Budget

In this exercise students are instructed to prepare a "media budget" that accounts for how much the people in their households (they and their roommates or families) spend for information and communication products, services, and technologies in an average month. Expenses might include magazine and newspaper subscriptions; costs for cable television, Internet service providers, or satellite radio services; fixed-line and mobile telephone services and equipment; and spending on books, movies, games, and other entertainment programs and products. The costs of equipment and supplies should also be included (e.g., telephones, wireless routers, computers and laptops, printer paper and cartridges, and so on). Students are also allowed to include educational expenses like tuition, fees, and books.

As in the data cloud assignment, students tally their expenses, summarize and explain them in a short paper, and discuss the results with other students in class (to ensure confidentiality, students only share actual figures with the instructor). They are asked to note the most and least expensive categories in their budgets, and whether any aspect of the budget surprises them; students often find that they over- or under-estimate their actual spending on different types of goods or services. At a more general level, they are asked to think about which social groups are most or least likely to use or afford the products, services, technologies or activities they may take for granted; how cost might affect access to information and communication services for middle- or lower-income households; and what sorts of social or economic policy might help promote equitable access for different social groups.

Making Judgments about Information: "Reliable Sources"

I have used two different types of exercises to encourage students to think critically about the credibility, reliability, and authority of information retrievable from various sources. In one exercise, the class is divided into two groups, and students in both groups are given the same simple research task (e.g., finding and reporting national data on the number of households with Internet access, by demographic group; or describing and applying Marshall McLuhan's "Laws of the Media" to familiar new media technologies). The only difference between the groups is that one is restricted to using *only online sources* to complete the task, while the other is restricted to using *only non-Internet sources* (although small exceptions are allowed, such as using a library's electronic catalog on site). The students write reports that include the answer to the question as well as a detailed account of the procedures they followed to complete the task. Then the class meets as a whole to compare and discuss their experiences and the quality of the results. Students debate which methods are "easier," and which are more complete or reliable; which sources were easy to locate and retrieve, or more difficult; how they decided on the quality of the sources they found; and the skills needed to find and evaluate the information they needed to perform the task.

In an alternative exercise designed to demonstrate issues of information reliability and authority, students (either individually or in small teams of two or three) are assigned a political, cultural, or activist online website or project (that is, one that takes a particular perspective or represents an interest in an issue) as a case study (e.g., artists' projects, blogs, alternative news organizations, political parties, etc.). The students "dissect" and critique their respective cases, and present critiques for class discussion and feedback, using a simple taxonomy of characteristics of online activism (scale, interventionism, subcultural literacy, irony, perishability, collaborativeness, and separatist or heterotopic qualities; Lievrouw, 2006a). In their critiques, students must assess the sources, aims, and sponsors of the case they're assigned, the design of the site or project, including page layouts and links, the architecture of relationships among pages and links, and the graphic "look and feel" of the site or project. If possible, they should also gather information about the site's web traffic, frequency of updating, Google ranking, "tag clouds," or other indicators of audience interest and response. Students must be ready to discuss and justify their views about the effectiveness or success of the case study site/project, whether it should be considered credible or reliable, and what alternative or additional sources of information about the project or topic should be consulted.

"Be the Media": Remediation and Reconfiguration

In the most advanced exercise, small teams of students design and post simple websites for their peers that introduce a topic, issue, debate, or controversy related to new media technologies or digital culture. Examples have included copyright law and downloading; information warfare; online diasporic communities; Internet censorship and decency laws; online plagiarism; gender differences in Internet use; and the effect of the Internet on political campaigning and social movements, among other topics.

Teams must summarize all relevant aspects of their issue clearly and accessibly and design an attractive and informative site. They must locate, provide links to, and contextualize relevant and authoritative source materials, and represent different points of view or opinions about the topic. As in the reliable sources exercise, teams must justify or provide rationales for the materials they choose for their sites. The design, structure, and usability of the website are evaluated by other class members, as well as the content and presentation. Because not all students have extensive web authoring skills, students are encouraged to form teams that include strong writers, researchers, issue activists or topic experts, students with media production skills such as audio, still images, or video, as well as programmers or web authors. In past projects, students have responded to this assignment in very creative ways. Teams have contributed (or successfully revised) whole Wikipedia entries, created and posted links to PowerPoint-type instructional programs, slide shows, and short-form videos within their websites, built "spoof" sites that reproduce the design of familiar university pages to criticize institutional policies, set up collaborative wiki workspaces, and created tagging projects that link information to particular geographic locations using Google Earth.

■ Reflecting on New Media Pedagogy: The Uses of Disenchantment

To close this discussion, I want to make two general points about the pedagogical strategy that has been sketched out here.

First, historical framing and critique is a necessary element in any effective new media pedagogy. As long as mainstream media and information industries, and their regulatory allies, continue to resist any challenge to their traditional business models (and thus, political and economic power)—that is, so long as they continue to view media culture primarily in terms of industrial-era assumptions about mass media production and consumption—media critique and media literacy will continue to be essential foundations for teaching about new media. The historical, institutional perspective that applies to established industries like publishing, broadcasting, cable, and fixed and mobile telecommunications, applies as well to newer players, ranging from search engines and metadata, surveillance and cryptography, operating systems, and games, to Internet backbone operators and service providers, local wireless systems, and standards processes for Internet infrastructure.

For example, the Internet's origins in U.S. military research and development are often suggested as the underlying explanation of American dominance of new media networks. However, fewer critical scholars have attempted to explain why Americans' access to broadband systems is slower and more expensive than that enjoyed in almost any other developed society or analyzed the institutional and market conditions supporting an American mobile telephone system that is generally incompatible with, and technologically inferior to, such systems elsewhere. Classical political economy of mass media helps students understand how some kinds of messages come to dominate popular culture or political discourse while others are neglected or silenced. But political economy of new media/digital culture can help students understand why mobile telephones, rather than laptops, currently hold the most promise for bridging digital divides between the developed and developing world, or the "reputation economies" that underlie open-source technology and cultural production (Castronova, 2003; Terranova, 2000).

Moreover, historical contextualization helps to show how media law and policy have evolved over time, in parallel with technological developments. Traditional communication research and scholarship have placed speech rights, decency/censorship, and press freedoms at the center of media policy research, for example, by considering how concentrated ownership or regulatory capture by industry interests affects these rights and obligations. However, as the overview above suggests, intellectual property law, once scarcely mentioned in most texts or courses on the media law and policy, today drives debates about media access, and equity, creativity, public opinion formation, and social and political participation. Speech and press freedoms are just as critical in the new media context—indeed, they may face unprecedented challenges.

However, history and critique alone are not enough. A second point is that new media pedagogy must connect historical context and the actual practices, experiences, and tangible, material qualities and affordances that distinguish digital media and information technologies from mass media. This nexus has been suggested in a recent essay by the prominent film scholar and critic Thomas Elsaesser, who offers an intriguing way of thinking about the difference between the experience of mass media, and new media, that parallels the strategy presented here.

As noted above, Bruno Bettelheim wrote eloquently in the 1970s about "the uses of enchantment," the power of narrative and myth (in the form of fairy tales) to help children make sense of complex feelings, relationships, and events in their lives. In his essay "Cinephilia or the Uses of Disenchantment," Elsaesser (2005) makes a similar point about "cinephilia," literally the love of cinema, and the mythologizing power of Hollywood narrative film that helped fuel early, auteur-focused cinema studies in Europe and the United States. However, he argues that by the 1980s this original cinephilia had become a source of ambivalence and even embarrassment among film scholars, who (in their elaborations of "screen theory") associated it with regressive male fantasy and voyeuristic, scopophilic fandom. This ambivalence about "Hollywood as the good/bad object" led to *dis*enchantment and a new critical distance among scholars that "helped renew the legitimating enterprise at the heart of auteurism, converting 'negative' or disavowed cinephilia into one of the founding moments of Anglo-American academic film studies" (p. 32).

Elsaesser goes on to suggest that the result, "cinephilia take two," required the critic to be less of a fan and more of a

> …flâneur, prospector, [or] explorer…[it is a] post-auteur, post-theory cinephilia that has embraced the new technologies, that flourishes on the internet and finds its jouissance in an often undisguised and unapologetic fetishism of the technical prowess of the digital video disc, its sound and its image and the tactile sensations now associated with both. Three features stand out… re-mastering, re-purposing, and re-framing. (p. 36)

If cinephilia take one was a way to stabilize and even enshrine films as fixed cultural objects, Elsaesser says, cinephilia take two is more ambivalent, comfortable with new digital forms that have produced a

...non-linear, non-directional 'too much/all at once' state of permanent tension, not so much about missing the unique moment, but almost its opposite, namely about how to cope with a flow that knows no privileged points of capture at all...[a] regime of repetition, of the re-take, of the iterative, the compulsively serial, the fetishistic, the fragmented and the fractal. (p. 39)

I am certainly no film critic, and so have quoted Elsaesser's own words at length to suggest simply that the standpoint he so vividly identifies as cinephilia take two applies just as well to engagement with digital culture at large as it does to the new digital cinema of DVDs and downloads more narrowly.

Young Internet users today take the "fragmented and fractal" character of online interaction, entertainment, and learning in stride. In contemporary digital culture, what educators must do is help inform and contextualize the "re-mastering, re-purposing, and re-framing" skills that students need to become capable and effective participants in all aspects of everyday mediation. By articulating historical and institutional context, technological tools and affordances, and actual practices together, new media pedagogy can be designed that teaches for reconfiguration and remediation as well as production and consumption.

Notes

1. The idea of "mediation" as a concept bridging the traditional subfields of interpersonal and mass communication research is a perspective dating back at least as far as Katz and Lazarsfeld's *Personal Influence* (2005 [1955]). It gained momentum with the rise of new digital media and information technologies in the 1980s and 90s; see, e.g., Anderson & Meyer, 1988; Reardon & Rogers, 1988; and edited collections by Gumpert & Cathcart, 1986; Hawkins, Wiemann & Pingree, 1988; and Ruben & Lievrouw, 1990. More recent observers have begun to elaborate theories of mediation based on ethnographic studies of new media use (e.g., Licoppe & Smoreda, 2006; Silverstone, 2005). I examine this intellectual thread in communication study in another work currently in progress (Lievrouw, in preparation).

2. Obviously, basic levels of technological literacy and communicative competence are essential prerequisites for effective social, economic, cultural, and political participation in developed societies today. My point here is not that basic skills are unnecessary or that societies can or should neglect equitable access to technology and skills for their citizens. Instead, my aim is to consider the situation of students for whom the Internet and related technologies have become "banal," part of the fabric of everyday life, work and leisure (Lievrouw, 2004)—and what it takes to develop critical media pedagogy for them.

3. Among the minor exceptions was the introduction of videotex information services in the U.S., which prompted a flurry of marketing experiments by newspapers and broadcasters with interests in delivering wired news services to the home in the late 1970s and early 1980s. Though critics later charged that some trials were designed to fail, consumers' lack of enthusiasm for the new services reassured American news organizations that they had little to fear from new media technologies (see Boczkowski, 2004; Lievrouw, 2006b; Mosco, 1982).

4. In a recent report, the Organization for Economic Cooperation and Development found that the U.S. still lags most of Europe, Korea, Japan, and other nations in terms of broadband penetration, speed, and cost (OECD, 2007).

5. At the end of 2007 the FCC adopted new rules that removed virtually all remaining barriers to cross-ownership of newspapers and broadcast media in the same markets (Labaton, 2007).

6. Changing industry attitudes toward their older productions have created important problems in copyright law. One example is the problem of "orphan works," some of them classics of cinema

or recorded music, for which the rights holders cannot be located for permissions to restore and preserve decaying materials; and the publishing industry's efforts to block projects, such as those being undertaken by Google and the Internet Archive, that digitize and make available online out-of-print books whose copyrights have expired and thus have gone into the public domain (Lee, 2007).

7. Since September 11, 2001 this stance has turned out to be a particularly useful tool for the Bush administration, which has required telecommunications operators and ISPs to open their customer records—including call records and e-mail—on demand to law enforcement agencies investigating suspected terrorist activities. Firms have often been reluctant to do so, fearing lawsuits from customers whose privacy might be violated. However, in two recent legal cases, Bush administration lawyers have argued in federal appeals court that such company records are now "state secrets" and "totally classified." Thus, they say, not only would hearing the cases harm national security; the plaintiffs also have no standing to sue the telephone companies and ISPs because they are prohibited from accessing their own communications records (Liptak, 2007, p. A13).

References

Abbate, J. (1999). *Inventing the Internet.* Cambridge, MA: MIT Press.

Anderson, J. A. & Meyer, T. P. (1988). *Mediated Communication: A Social Action Perspective.* Newbury Park, CA: Sage.

Atton, C. (2004). *An Alternative Internet.* Edinburgh: Edinburgh University Press.

Atton, C. (2002). *Alternative Media.* London: Sage.

Bailey, O., Cammaerts, B., and Carpentier, N. (2007). *Understanding Alternative Media.* Maidenhead: Open University Press.

Barlow, J.P. (1994a). The economy of ideas. *Wired,* 2.03, March (n.p.). Available: http://www.wired.com/wired/archive/2.03/economy.ideas.html .

Barlow, J.P. (1994b). Jackboots on the infobahn. *Wired,* 2.04, April (n.p.). Available: http://www.wired.com/wired/archive/2.04/privacy.barlow.html .

Bettelheim, B. (1976). *The Uses of Enchantment: The Meaning and Importance of Fairy Tales.* New York: Knopf, distributed by Random House.

Boczkowski, P.J. (2004). *Digitizing the News.* Cambridge, MA: MIT Press.

Castronova, E. (2003). On virtual economies. *Game Studies, 3*(2), December, n.p.

Ceruzzi, P.E. (1998). *A Modern History of Computing.* Cambridge, MA: MIT Press.

Downing, J.D.H., with Ford, T.V., Gil, G., and Stein, L. (2001). *Radical Media: Rebellious Communication and Social Movements.* London: Sage.

Dutton, W. H., Blumler, J. G., & Kraemer, K. L. (Eds.). (1987). *Wired Cities: Shaping the Future of Communications.* Boston: G.K. Hall.

Economist. (2005a). An open secret. (Special section: A Survey of Patents and Technology.) October 22, pp. 12–14.

Economist. (2005b). The liquidity of innovation. (Special section: A Survey of Patents and Technology.) October 22, pp. 17–18.

Economist. (2006). Open, but not as usual. Online edition. March 16, n.p. Available: http://www.economist.com .

Elsaesser, T. (2005). Cinephilia, or the uses of disenchantment. In M. de Valck and M. Hagener (Eds.), *Cinephilia: Movies, Love, and Memory,* pp. 27–44. Amsterdam, Netherlands: Amsterdam University Press.

Eschenfelder, K.R. and Desai, A.C. (2004). Software as protest: The unexpected resiliency of U.S.-based DeCSS posting and linking. *The Information Society, 20*(2), 101–116.

Gillespie, T. (2007). Learning to consume culture: Copyright, technology, and participation in industry-sponsored anti-piracy campaigns. Paper presented at the annual meeting of the Society for Social Studies of Science, Montréal, Canada, October 11–13.

Greenberger, M. (1964). The computers of tomorrow. *Atlantic Monthly, 213*(5), 63–66.

Greenberger, M. (Ed.) (1985). *Electronic Publishing Plus.* White Plains, NY: Knowledge Industry Publications.

Gumpert, G. and Cathcart, R. (1986). *Inter/Media: Interpersonal Communication in a Media World* (3rd ed.). Oxford and New York: Oxford University Press.

Hawkins, R.P., Wiemann, J.M., and Pingree, S. (Eds.) (1988). *Advancing Communication Science: Merging Mass Media and Interpersonal Processes.* Newbury Park, CA: Sage.

Katz, E., Lazarsfeld, P.F., and Roper, E. (2005). *Personal Influence: The Part Played by People in the Flow of Mass Communications* (2nd ed.). New Brunswick, NJ and London: Transaction. (Originally published in 1955 by The Free Press.)

Labaton, S. (2007). FCC eases media ownership rule. *New York Times,* December 18. Available: http://www.nytimes.com/2007/12/18/business/18cnd-fcc.html.

Lee, T. (2007). Appeals court rejects challenge to "opt-out" copyright. *Ars Technica,* January 25. Available: http://arstechnica.com/news.ars/post/20070125–8704.html.

Licoppe, C. and Smoreda, Z. (2006). Rhythms and ties: Toward a pragmatics of technologically mediated sociability. In R. Kraut, M. Brynin, and S. Kiesler (Eds.), *Computers, Phones and the Internet: Domesticating Information Technology,* pp. 296–313. New York: Oxford University Press.

Lievrouw, L.A. (in preparation). Mediation: Tracing the development of new media theory in communication studies.

Lievrouw, L.A. (2007). Oppositional new media, ownership, and access: From consumption to reconfiguration and remediation. In R.E. Rice (Ed.), *Media Ownership: Research and Regulation.* Cresskill, NJ: Hampton Press.

Lievrouw, L.A. (2006a). Oppositional and activist new media: Remediation, reconfiguration, and participation. In G. Jacucci, F. Kensing, I. Wagner and J. Blomberg (Eds.), *Proceedings of the Participatory Design Conference, PDC 2006: Expanding Boundaries in Design* (pp. 115–124). Trento, Italy, July 31–August 5. Palo Alto, CA: Computer Professionals for Social Responsibility and Association for Computing Machinery.

Lievrouw, L.A. (2006b). New media design and development: Diffusion of innovations v social shaping of technology. In L.A. Lievrouw and S. Livingstone (Eds.), *Handbook of New Media* (Updated student edition), pp. 246–265. London: Sage.

Lievrouw, L.A. (2004). What's changed about new media? Introduction to the fifth anniversary issue. *New Media & Society, 6*(1), 9–15.

Light, J. S. (2003). *From Warfare to Welfare: Defense Intellectuals and Urban Problems in Cold War America.* Baltimore: Johns Hopkins University Press.

Lipinski, T.A. (1999). The commodification of information and the extension of proprietary rights into the public domain: Recent legal (case and other) developments in the United States. *Journal of Business Ethics, 22,* 63–80.

Liptak, A. (2007). U.S. defends surveillance before 3 skeptical judges. Appeals court hears challenges to N.S.A. *New York Times,* August 16, p. A 13.

Litman, J. (1994). Mickey Mouse emeritus: Character protection and the public domain. *University of Miami Entertainment and Sports Law Review, 11*(2), 429–435.

Ludlow, P. (Ed.) (2001). *Crypto Anarchy, Cyberstates, and Pirate Utopias.* Cambridge, MA: MIT Press.

McCaughey, M. & Ayers, M.D. (Eds.) (2003). *Cyberactivism: Online activism in theory and practice.* New York and London: Routledge.

McCullagh, D. (2007). Gonzalez proposes new crime: "Attempted" copyright infringement. *C|NET News,* May 15 (n.p.). URL: http://news.com.com/8301–10784_3–9719339–7.html

Meikle, G. (2002). *Future active: Media activism and the Internet.* London and New York: Routledge, in association with Pluto Press Australia.

Moore, J.T.S. (2001). *Revolution OS.* Documentary, 35mm film and video (DVD) (85 minutes). Available from Wonderview Productions, http://revolution-os.com.

Mosco, V. (1982). *Pushbutton Fantasies: Critical Perspectives on Videotex and Information Technologies.* Norwood, NJ: Ablex.

Nissenbaum, H. (2004). Hackers and the contested ontology of cyberspace. *New Media & Society, 6*(2), 195–217.

Organization for Economic Cooperation and Development. (2007, July). *OECD Communications Outlook 2007.* Paris: OECD. Available: http://www.oecd.org/document/17/0,3343,en_2649_201185_38876 369_1_1_1_1,00.html.

Pew Research Center for the People and the Press (2007, August 9). *Internet news audience highly critical of news organizations: Views of press values and performance, 1985–2007.* URL: http://people-press.org/reports/display.php3?ReportID=348.

Raymond, E.S. (2001). *The Cathedral and the Bazaar: Musings on Linux and Open Source by an Accidental Revolutionary.* Cambridge, MA: O'Reilly.

Reardon, K.M., and Rogers, E.M. (1988). Interpersonal versus mass media communication: A false dichotomy. *Human Communication Research, 15,* 284–303.

Rheingold, H. (1993). *The Virtual Community: Homesteading on the Electronic Frontier* (1st ed.). Reading, MA: Addison-Wesley.

Ruben, B.D. and Lievrouw, L.A. (Eds.) (1990). *Mediation, Information and Communication: Information and Behavior, Vol. 3.* New Brunswick, NJ: Transaction.

Rubin, A.M., and Rubin, R.C. (1985). Interface of personal and mediated communication: A research agenda. *Critical Studies in Mass Communication, 2,* 36–53.

Silverstone, R. (2005). The sociology of mediation and communication. In C. Calhoun, C. Rojek, & B. S. Turner (Eds.), *The Sage Handbook of Sociology,* pp. 188–207. Thousand Oaks, CA: Sage.

Sterling, B. (2005). Round-table discussion, Southern California Digital Culture Group. Los Angeles: Annenberg Institute for Multimedia Literacy, University of Southern California, November 18.

Terranova, T. (2000). Free labor: Producing culture for the digital economy. *Social Text, 18*(2), 33–58.

Turner, F. (2006). *From Counterculture to Cyberculture: Stewart Brand, the Whole Earth Network, and the Rise of Digital Utopianism.* Chicago, IL: University of Chicago Press.

Wark, M. (2004). *A Hacker Manifesto.* Cambridge, MA and London: Harvard University Press.

33

■ Perfect Transmissions

Evil Bert Laden

Mark Poster

In the globally networked world, strange, unexpected and sometimes amusing events occur. I shall analyze one such happening with the purpose of understanding how the global communication system affects national cultures. It is my hypothesis that the current state of globalization, of which the Internet is a major component, imposes a new and heightened level of interaction between cultures. This interactivity changes each culture in many ways, one of which I highlight: the degree of autonomy of each culture is significantly reduced as a consequence of the global information network. On the one hand, all attempts to sustain such autonomy tend to become retrograde and dangerous. Local beliefs, values, and practices can no longer be held as absolute or as exclusive, at the expense of others. On the other hand, a new opportunity arises for a practical definition and articulation of global, human or, better, posthuman culture. In short, henceforth, the local is relative and the global may become universal. This universal, unlike earlier attempts to define it or impose it, will be differential; will consist of a heterogeneity of "glocal" fragments.

Although there are significant economic and demographic components of the new level of global interactivity, I address the issue of the flow of cultural objects within cyberspace. New media contribute greatly to the quantity and quality of the planetary transmission of cultural objects. Cultural objects—texts, sounds and images—posted to the Internet exist in a digital domain that is everywhere at once. These objects are disembodied from their point of origin or production, entering immediately into a space that has no particular territorial inscription. As a result, the Internet constitutes distributed culture, a heteroglossia that is commensurate with the earth. Cultural objects in new media are thus disjunctive from their society. They are intelligible only through the medium in which they subsist. Cultural objects in cyberspace elicit a new hermeneutic, one that underscores the agency of the media, rendering defunct figures of the subject from all societies in which it persists and persisted in a position separate from objects.

For the Internet enables planetary transmissions of cultural objects (text, images and sound) to cross-cultural boundaries with little "noise." Communications now transpire with digital accuracy. The dream of the communications engineer is realized as information flows without interference from any point on the earth to any other point or points. As Claude Shannon and Warren Weaver theorize: "The fundamental problem of communication is that of reproducing at one point either exactly or approximately a message selected at another point." (Shannon and Weaver, 1949, p. 3) Cybernetic theory is fulfilled by the Internet: both machines and the human body act on the environment through "the accurate reproduction" of information or signals in an endless feedback loop that adjusts for changes and unexpected events. (Wiener, 1950) The physicist's theory of communication is realized as messages circulate around the globe in radio frequency channels, fiber optic cables, or copper cables with each element of text, image or sound being reproduced, transmitted and stored in a single, instantaneous operation.[1]

And yet, as Derrida argues in *The Postcard,* things are not so simple. (Derrida, 1987) All the bits and bytes are there alright, but the message does not always come across or get decoded. Misunderstandings abound in our new global culture, sometimes in quite pointed ways. This article is about one such miscommunication. It concerns a perfect transmission of an image halfway around the globe that somehow went awry. Indeed, one may argue that the global network, with its instantaneous, exact communications, produces systematically the effect of misrecognition as information objects are transported across cultural boundaries. Global communication, one might say, signifies transcultural confusion. At the same time, the network creates conditions of intercultural exchange that render politically noxious any culture that cannot decode the messages of others, which insists that only its transmissions have meaning or are significant. As never before, we must begin to interpret culture as multiple cacophonies of inscribed meanings as each cultural object moves between cultural differences. Let us look at one instance of the issue that I have in mind.

The second week of October 2001 was eventful with the onset of U.S. and British bombing in Afghanistan. Like many Americans, I listened intently to reports of the war and to analyses by informed commentators and academics. Driving home from work on Friday of that week, a few days after the start of the bombing, I heard, on a National Public Radio broadcast, one expert on Middle Eastern cultures explain to the interviewer and audience that among the many aspects of American society that antagonize Islamic fundamentalists the worst is American popular culture. Even more than American support for Israel or the American-led embargo of Iraq, the enemy, in the eyes of these Muslims, is, of all things, American popular culture. Samir Amin has argued to this effect for some time, pointing out that "The prodigious intensification of communication by the media, now global in scope, has both quantitatively and qualitatively modified the contradiction generated by the unequal expansion of capitalism. Yearning for access to Western models of consumption has come to penetrate large numbers of the popular masses." (Amin, 1989) In the context of the Middle East, the fundamentalist Muslims are threatened by this "yearning" for Western styles and commodities among other Middle Easterners. With some surprise, I filed this bit of knowledge in my brain's database and continued my ride home.

Much could be said about American popular culture in the age of what Michael Hardt and Antonio Negri call "the Empire" (Hardt and Negri, 2000). Here I need only note that a peculiarity of many Americans is the emotional fixation they often develop for figures in popular culture, not simply for acknowledged celebrities but for all manner of objects: clothing, food, animated figures, music, television shows, and so forth. Americans obsess about selected aspects of popular culture. One such American is Dino Ignacio, who had an extraordinary dislike for Bert, a muppet on public television's longstanding children's show *Sesame Street*. For Mr. Ignacio, Bert was evil. To satisfy his obsession, Ignacio created a Web page entitled "Bert is Evil." Here with the aid of a Web browser one finds Ignacio's "evidence" of the muppet's alleged misdeeds. Among this evidence is a series of images that Ignacio thinks prove the point: Bert is pictured with Hitler, the KKK and with Osama bin Laden, [see Figures 1, 2, and 3] and with a long list of other evil-doers.

Figure 1: Bert and Hitler   **Figure 2: Bert with the KKK**

Figure 3: Bert & Osama from Evil Bert Web page

Bert's crimes are thus detailed with fastidious and unrelenting hostile energy.[2] Perhaps Ignacio has too much time on his hands; in any case his Web design is characteristic of the commitment of many Americans to their peculiar, fetishistic attachments to popular culture figures. An understanding of this aspect of popular culture in the United States is essential to appreciate what follows. It must be noted however that Ignacio is an immigrant, a native of the Philippines who viewed *Sesame Street* from a distance, by dint of satellite television transmissions, and created the "Evil Bert" web site in Manila. This site won Ignacio a prize—"the Webby prize for best weird site in 1998," according to media historian Roy Rosenzweig[3]—and brought him to San Francisco to study art. American popular culture is thus far advanced in its global reach.

On Sunday, October 14th, a friend and colleague, Jon Wiener, e-mailed me with an urgent message to look at the *New York Times* for an incredible story concerning a protest in Bangladesh on October 8th against American bombing in Afghanistan. The story he referred to was by Amy Harmon, one of my favorite journalists writing on new media, and included a picture of the protestors in Bangladesh carrying a poster of bin Laden that was an attractive collage composed of several images of him along with a tiny picture of Bert the *Sesame Street* muppet sitting on his left shoulder and staring smugly (see Figure 4).

Figure 4: Image from *New York Times* article

Another photograph that I found on the Web indicates more clearly the face of Evil Bert (See Figure 5.)

Figure 5: Bert is highlighted

Bert is in the highlighted circle, grimacing at the viewer more fiercely than Osama. How was it possible for Bert to get into the scene in Bangladesh? Amy Harmon could not explain the inclusion of Bert in the poster, but there he was for all the world, and especially protesting Islamic militants, to see. Perhaps he truly was evil, living up to Ignacio's image of him, and siding with the Al Qaeda terrorists.

I was fascinated by Harmon's story and the accompanying photograph. Out of curiosity I searched the Web for more information about Bert's remarkable presence in Bangladesh. A simple image search for "evil Bert" in Google yielded the following photographs (see Figures 6–9) that confirm the one reproduced in the *New York Times'* article. They are also significant to understand more of the story.

Figure 6: Photo from protest in Bangladesh

Figure 7: Another photograph

Figure 8: A longer shot showing English banner

Figure 9: Poster indicates Evil Bert image in collage

Figure 9 yields the best information about how Evil Bert managed to appear in the poster. It shows that the image of Bert in the poster is taken from Ignacio's Web page. The image on the Evil Bert page has simply been set into a collage of images of Bin Laden. There are eight images of Bin Laden in the poster, including one from the Evil Bert page. In fact, the image of Bin Laden that Ignacio combined with one of Bert is the same one that is positioned centrally in the poster. Aside from noting the pleasing arrangement of the images and the visage of *Sesame Street*'s Bert, I, as a Westerner with little knowledge of Muslim culture, was able to decode the image no further.

When I presented this paper at a conference at the University of Wisconsin, Milwaukee in April 2002, Brian Larkin, a participant who is knowledgeable about the culture of Islam, pointed out that the composition of the poster contains several Islamic and Hindi references. The pattern of a central image surrounded by several smaller images, all depicting Bin Laden, is characteristic of posters for recent Bollywood films in which the star's face in the center is complemented by smaller images that depict him or her in various roles: action figure, comedian, singer, and so forth. The smaller images in the Bangladesh protest banner similarly portray Bin Laden in his many roles: religious leader, warrior, orator, and so forth. Moreover, these roles match closely the roles of Muhammed, likening the Al Qaeda leader to the founder of Islam. The images in the poster thus construct a narrative of Bin Laden, visually representing him as a great Arab leader comparable to the prophet Mohammed.

A colleague at UC Irvine, Dina Al-Kassim, a scholar of Middle Eastern culture, offered a different reading. To understand this reading we need to locate each image. If we start with the large image of Bin Laden in the center of the poster as number one, we can number the smaller images, beginning in the lower left corner and moving clockwise around the perimeter of the image number one. In Figure 2 above, the eight images are all visible, and this figure serves as a good reference for what follows. Al-Kassim reads image five, at the top left of the poster, not as a warrior but as a judge. The next image (number six) in which Bin Laden gestures by holding up a finger is typical of the religious scholar giving a lecture. Continuing clockwise, Bin Laden in number seven is holding a utility dagger with the handle visible. In image three, Bin Laden speaks into a microphone, wearing a scarf that is common to the region of the Saudi peninsula, perhaps addressing a large audience concerning political matters. Images 1, 2, and 4 are simply portraits without specific social context. Although many of the images contain contextual references, it is difficult to construct, on their basis, a clear narrative.

But what is Bert's visual function? Brian Larkin suggested that Bert, as a cuddly muppet, perhaps represents Bin Laden as a family man. This interpretation assumes that the designers of the banner recognized Bert, were willing to code him as cuddly, and include him in the main visual narrative. Each of these claims is highly dubious. As we shall see the graphics company denied recognizing Bert. Further, cute as he may be, Bert is hardly cuddly in this image as he stares at the viewer more fiercely than Bin Laden or even the protesters captured by the photographers. However one interprets Bert's inclusion in the poster, I find significant my own inability to read the visual iconography of the banner, placing me in a position of symmetrical ignorance with the designers of the banner and the protesters, none of whom could decode the image of Bert.

When I began to relate the story of Bert's appearance in a pro-Taliban demonstration to colleagues and students at UCI, I encountered another strange twist: about half the people to whom I showed the *New York Times* story and photo concluded that it indicated a sophisticated knowledge of American pop culture by the Bangladesh militants. They appropriated, as cultural studies scholars would say, the nasty image of Bert and shoved it into the face of Westerners as if to say, if you think Osama is evil, we'll take Evil Bert on our side and use him against you. Another 25% of my respondents simply did not believe the photo at all. In the age of digital images, they surmised the photo was doctored: someone in the West had added the figure of Bert to the photo that appeared in the *New York Times*. Evil Bert, they concluded, never appeared in the protest in Bangladesh. The rest of my respondents accepted the image at face value and were utterly at sea to explain it.

I next went online again to pursue the discussion. I found a flurry of comments about the photo. Some Scandinavian newspapers were convinced it was a hoax.[4] Others assumed the protesters in Bangladesh, unlike their Taliban compatriots, watched American television and were avid *Sesame Street* fans. The photo produced a variety of misunderstandings by Westerners of Bangladesh culture. The Babel-like confusion of cultural tongues only heightened with the transmission of more and more information from across the globe.

Meanwhile, Mr. Ignacio must not be left out of the picture, so to speak, for he also became a victim of information overload. His reaction to the *New York Times* story was guilt. He very quickly took down the Evil Bert Web page and posted in its place an apology. He concluded that somehow his Web page abetted terrorism. On his "apology" Web site he stated his remorse, admitting that "reality" had intruded into his fantasy. In his words, "…this has gotten too close to reality . . ." (Ignacio, 2001) Suddenly his obsession with Bert decathected and left him, shorn of his libidinal outlets, staring fixedly at his own superego-induced guilt. With a global audience presumably shocked and angered at his Web design, Ignacio now suffered from the burst bubble of his fetish.

But that was not the end of his woes. The Internet does not forget so easily the "crimes" of its producers. What Ignacio wanted to hide would not disappear. For other Web authors, admiring his work, created mirror sites. Indeed, at least nine of them were up and running at one point shortly after October 14th, all displaying boldly the full variety of Evil Bert's deeds and photographic evidence for them, including the controversial image of Bert with Osama bin Laden. The emergence of the mirror sites complicates the cultural confusion, subverting in yet another manner the power of authors to control their work. Not only did the anti-American militants of Bangladesh unknowingly and without authorization appropriate Evil Bert, but other Americans, admiring the handicraft of Ignacio, perpetuated his work for their own ends.[5]

For their part, the producers of *Sesame Street* were also not amused by the perfect transmission of the image of Bert. They are quoted in a CNN report with the following response to the event: "*Sesame Street* has always stood for mutual respect and understanding. We're outraged that our characters would be used in this unfortunate and distasteful manner. This is not humorous."(CNN)

How did the image get on that poster in Bangladesh? The answer is simpler in one sense and more complex in another than the views and imaginings of my respondents, as I reported above. A journalist discovered finally who made the poster, telephoned the company, and unraveled at least part of the mystery. A local graphics company in Bangladesh was hired by the militants to produce a poster for the demonstration. It had to be done quickly because the protest was planned for the day after the bombing commenced in Afghanistan. In these circumstances, the company did what anyone today would do. They went on the Web, did an image search for Osama bin Laden, and presto, downloaded a number of them, including, we must note, the image from the Evil Bert Web page. They also put out a request to friends, who emailed images to them as attachments. The representative of the graphics company admitted outright that the employees did not notice Bert when they put together several images of bin Laden for the poster. Here, incredible as it might seem to some, is the report on the Urban Legends Web page: "Mostafa Kamal, the production manager of Azad Products, the Dhaka shop that made the posters, told the AP he had gotten the images off the Internet. 'We did not give the pictures a second look or realize what they signified until you pointed it out to us,' he said."(Mikkelson and Mikkelson, 2001) It was as simple as that: the transmission of Bert's image went completely unnoticed in the culture of Bangladesh. Invisibly to the militants of Bangladesh, Bert snuck into the poster, where he was indeed noticed by Western journalists covering the story of the protest.

It could be that the poster company representative lied to the Western journalist, perhaps not wanting to take responsibility for the inclusion of Bert in the poster. Perhaps the company representative did not have accurate information about the image of Bert. Perhaps the company intentionally put Bert in the poster as a joke or as an ironic comment either to the West or to the protesters. Even if any of these possibilities were true, the fact remains that the protestors themselves appear not to have noticed the image of Bert and are certainly not likely to recognize his image from the *Sesame Street* program. The photos of the demonstration indeed show some banners in English. Even the notorious photo in the *New York Times* has a caption with bin Laden's name in Roman alphabet. At least some of the demonstrators were aware of Western media coverage of the event and were interested in getting a message to the West about whom they supported and what they wanted to happen.[6]

Nonetheless the circuit of transmission was closed. We may conclude that, in all likelihood, the protestors in Bangladesh did not see the image of Bert. From Ignacio's anti-cult Web site to the anti-American pop culture protest halfway around the world, and back again to the West in the medium of print journalism, Evil Bert's digital bytes circumnavigated the globe in a series of misrecognitions, perfect transmissions, confusions, blends of politics and culture that surely speaks much of our current global culture.

The conditions of global cultural transmissions in the case of Bert Laden initiate many changes in communications practices in all societies. The Internet imposes everywhere new challenges and offers new opportunities.[7] The political consequences of the response to the Internet are serious indeed. Just as the mixing of peoples within a nation renders especially noxious parochial ethnic and racial attitudes, so the mixing of cultural objects in the Internet compels each culture to acknowledge the validity, if not the moral value, of such objects that may be alien and other. With Bert Laden, the stakes are especially high in the context of the war between Al Qaeda and the American-led coalition.

Mass communications scholars tell us that the failure of recognition of Bert by the Bangladesh protesters is a case of "aberrant decoding." (Fiske and Hartley, 2002) They failed to interpret correctly the image of Bert and Osama. This omission was, however, highly motivated. The protesters cherished a pre-existing hostility toward American popular culture, even though they inadvertently displayed one of its minor icons in their demonstration. Their hostility to U.S. popular culture, like that of other fundamentalist Islamic groups, derives from a wish to maintain the autochthony of their own beliefs and values. They wish to insulate themselves against American popular culture, viewing it as a potent threat to their own way of life perhaps in part because of its popularity with other Muslims or Middle Easterners. Yet exactly this effort at insulation proved impossible in the instance at hand.

In another example of parochial attitudes, a highly respected Middle Eastern journalist, Ali Asadullah, reported in an Islamic online newspaper about the problem with American and in this case Western culture. In an article entitled "Spice Girls: Exactly the Reason Why Bin Laden Hates the West"(Asadullah, 2001), Asadullah reported that a former Spice Girl, Geri Halliwell, on October 6th, one day before the bombing began in Afghanistan, entertained British Troops in Oman. For this respected Muslim journalist, that was all the proof needed to explain, and indeed to justify, disdain by some of Islamic faith for U.S. and British society. "…the core causes for terrorist rage and aggression against the United States," he wrote, was "the Spice Girls," not "hatred of freedom, liberty and democracy . . ." Muslims, he continued, "want their cultures, traditions and religious and societal standards to be respected." We can assume that "freedom, liberty and democracy," not hallmarks of Asadullah's Muslim cultures, are not all offensive to their faith. If that is the case, one wonders why "freedom, liberty and democracy" are not more widely practiced in the Middle East, indeed, why they are completely absent from that part of the world.

I argue that Asadullah's position is exactly the logic that no longer works. With globally networked digital communications, one must be especially careful in taking as an offence the legitimate cultural practices of another even if they are on one's soil. I will not make any invidious comparisons of the practices of the Taliban with regard to women to those of the British, but you can imagine easily where my sentiments lie given my cultural context. Because cultural objects circulate everywhere, there is no longer any local soil on the earth. Moral outrage directed at the cultural practices of others, especially toward those that do no physical harm, today becomes particularly obnoxious.[8] Journalists and intellectuals such as Asadullah, with his smug air of moral repugnance at Western popular culture, do much harm in justifying the sentiments from which arose the hideous murders of September 11th.

What is more, the luxury of such a moral claim, inspired in this and many other cases not by any means limited to the world of Islam, is often grounded in versions of monotheism. It may be that in the present context the collective human intelligence embodied in the Internet is set in a deep cultural opposition to parochialism in general and to versions of monotheism in particular that refuse the condition of cultural pluralism. The one and only God will have to make way for many one and only Gods. If that is the case, then the Bert Laden incident is more than an amusing series of cross-cultural confusions; it is an allegory of changes in contemporary culture, conditions rife with profound political implications.

The main interest of my intervention is not, however, to renew a theological critique. Rather my purpose is to raise the questions of the general role of media in culture and the particular role of new media. Transmission may now, in the digital domain, be both noiseless and incoherent. Interpretive practices must accordingly recalibrate themselves to the conditions of planetary culture. Research about any cultural object in cyberspace entails an infinite series of interpretive acts. Translation is now a central dimension of any cultural study. Texts, images, and sounds now travel at the speed of electrons and may be altered at any point along their course. They are as fluid as water and simultaneously present everywhere. They mock the presuppositions of all previous hermeneutics and the subject positions associated with them. They require a discipline of study unlike any that has subsisted in academic institutions. From this vantage point, Evil Burt, the emblem I have selected to designate cyber-culture, is indeed a trouble-maker.

Notes

1. For a discussion of information and communication theory in relation to cultural theory see Mark Taylor, *The Moment of Complexity: Emerging Network Culture* (Chicago: University of Chicago Press, 2001), Chapter 4.

2. Ignacio, according to one report, denied he included this image on his page, claiming it appeared only on mirror sites. See the discussion at http:/www.fractalcow.com.

3. Rosenzweig informed me of his researches on Ignacio and "Evil Bert" in an email of July 5, 2003. He provided me with the following references: Greg Miller, "Cyberculture: The Scene/ The Webby Awards," *Los Angeles Times* (9 March 1998), D3, Peter Hartlaub, "Bert and bin Laden Poster Tied to S.F. student," *San Francisco Chronicle* (12 October 2001), A12; Gina Davidson, "Bert and Bin: How the Joke Went Too Far," *The Scotsman* (14 October 2001), 3.

4. See the Web page of Nikke Lindqvist at Nikke Lindqvist, *Mystery Solved?,* November 22, 2001 2001, Nikke Lindqvist, Available: http://www.lindqvist.com/art.php?incl=brt.php&lang=eng, December 10 2001.http://www.lindqvist.com/art.php?incl=bert.php&lang=eng for comprehensive documents relating to the incident.

5. For a discussion of the problem of disappearing web sites in relation to studying the Evil Bert/bin Laden incident see Roy Rosenzweig, "Scarcity or Abundance? Preserving the Past in a Digital Era," *American Historical Review* 108.3 (2003).

6. For those still skeptical about the incident, a similar event might be helpful. A reporter for the BBC in Kabul submitted a story about documents found in a Taliban redoubt left behind by retreating al-Qaeda forces. This document, also downloaded from the Internet, purported to outline instructions for making a thermonuclear device. It turns out however that the instructions were a hoax from a humor newsletter entitled *Annals of Improbable Research,* humor that was lost not only on the Taliban and al-Qaeda but also on the BBC reporter. See http://www.dailyrotten.com/ archive/159929.html.

   Daily Rotten, *Taliban Thwarted by Irreproducible Result,* November 16, 2001 2001, Available: http:// www.dailyrotten.com/archive/159929.html, December 10 2001.

7. One of these is the noxious intensification of surveillance. See David Lyon, *Surveillance after September 11* (London: Polity, 2003).

8. The global encounter of cultures has produced some truly bizarre responses in the West. The imposition on women of the Birkha in Afghanistan is, in some feminist circles, not the cause for critique of Afghanistan but an indication of the blindness of Western media and politicians to their own cultural assumptions. Similarly, Akhil Gupta has recently elevated superstitions about reincarnation into the status of critique of Western models of childhood. Akhil Gupta, "Reliving Childhood?

The Temporality of Childhood and Narratives of Reincarnation," *Ethnos* 67.1 (2002). While those models are certainly open to critique, narratives of reincarnation are hardly an appropriate level to enter that door. "Critique" is after all a cognitive, in the Kantian tradition, and could hardly bear the weight of modes of credulity suggested by Gupta.

References

Amin, S. (1989) *Eurocentrism.* (Russell Moore, Trans.). New York: Monthly Review Press.

Asadullah, A. (2001). Spice Girls: Exactly the Reason Why Bin Laden Hates the West. Retrieved December 10, 2001, from http://www.islamonline.net/English/ArtCulture/2001/10/article4.shtml.

Derrida, J. (1987). *The postcard: From Socrates to Freud and beyond.* Chicago: University of Chicago Press.

Fiske, J., & Hartley J. (2002). *Reading television.* London: Methuen.

Gupta, A. (2002). Reliving childhood?: The temporality of childhood and narratives of reincarnation. *Ethnos 67*(1), 1–23.

Hardt, M., & Negri, A. (2000). *Empire.* Cambridge: Harvard University Press.

Ignacio, D. (2001). *Good bye Bert.* Retrieved December 10, 2001 from http://www.fractalcow.com/bert/bert.htm.

Lindqvist, N. (2001) Mystery solved? Retrieved December 10, 2001 from http://www.lindqvist.com/art.php?incl=brt.php&lang=eng.

Lyon, D. (2003) *Surveillance after September 11.* London: Polity.

Mikkelson, B., & Mikkelson, D. (2001). Bert is evil! Retrieved December 10, 2001 from http://www.snopes.com/rumors/bert.htm.

'Muppet' Producers Miffed over Bert-Bin Laden Image. (2001, October 11). CNN. Retrieved from http://www.cnn.com/2001/US/10/11/muppets.binladen/. December 10 2001.

Rosenzweig, R. (2003). Scarcity or abundance?: Preserving the past in a digital era. *American Historical Review 108*(3), 735–62.

Shannon, C., & Weaver, W. (1949). *The mathematical theory of communication.* Urbana: University of Illinois Press.

Taliban Thwarted by Irreproducible Result. (2001). Retrieved December 10, 2001 from http://www.dailyrotten.com/archive/159929.html.

Taylor, M. (2001) *The moment of complexity: Emerging network culture.* Chicago: University of Chicago Press.

Wiener, N. (1950). *The human use of human beings: Cybernetics and society.* New York: Doubleday.

34

■ Doing Something That Matters

Children's Culture, Video Games, and the Politics of Representation

Rebecca Stephenson

> You can just hang outside in the sun all day tossing a ball around or you can sit at your computer and do something that matters.
>   *Eric Cartman, South Park Episode No. 1008, "Make Love, Not Warcraft"*

In October 2006, *South Park,* the popular (and somewhat infamous) animated series premiered an episode entitled, "Make Love, Not Warcraft." The episode was intended as a parody of gamers, and of the culture which has emerged around Massively Multiplayer Online Role Playing Games (MMORPGs), like *World of Warcraft.* In the episode, the four main characters, all preteen boys, organize friends within the game to defeat a powerful and malicious player whose enjoyment of the game comes from preventing other players from advancing. The boys decide that they must, for the sake of their own enjoyment of the game and for the safety of others in the game world, level their characters and defeat the malicious player. With assistance from paternalistic game designers concerned with the safety of their players and the father of one of the boys who ventures into the game to bring a new weapon and ends up sacrificing his avatar's life for his son, the boys defeat the player. Despite their pride at their accomplishment, the stakes in gameplay are low, and the reward for their accomplishment is the ability to continue playing.

This episode was well received by *South Park* fans as well as gamers. In addition, the episode won critical acclaim and was awarded an Emmy in the 2007 Emmy awards. Its irreverent, ironic, and tongue-in-cheek references to gamer culture also can be read as a critique of discourses about gaming, and in particular, about young people who play video games. The episode addresses a variety of current discourses about youths' use of video games—a term I will use in this chapter to encompass PC-based computer games, console games, and online games. On the one hand, it speaks to many current anxieties about gaming—from issues of violence, addiction, ignoring other responsibilities to childhood obesity, antisocial behavior, and occupation of spaces that adults do not control or understand. On the other hand, it speaks to the pleasures of gaming (and particularly online gaming)—such as socializing with friends, accomplishing goals, exploring game worlds, and even antagonizing other players (Bartle, 1996). In addition, the episode gestures toward possibilities for learning, collaboration, and collective action that are emerging as games and online communities evolve (Gee, 2003; Thomas and Brown, 2007).

The quote that began this chapter comes from a scene in "Make Love Not Warcraft" in which one of the characters begins to recruit other kids to his cause. It also strikes me as an appropriate description of the importance of video games in children's culture. As Elisabeth Hayes (2007) writes: "Videogaming is now often children's first and most compelling introduction to digital technologies and is presumed to be a door to a broader range of digital tools and applications." Gaming has been cited as a revolutionary pedagogical tool as well as a compelling site for informal learning (Gee, 2003; Salen, 2007). The assumption that media can teach contributes to children's already complex relationship with media—including, but certainly not limited to games. However, despite their importance in youth culture and newfound cachet as an educational tool, video games continue to be demonized for destroying childhood—or, at least, destroying the nostalgic version of childhood in which a child can safely and comfortably hang out outside playing with a ball all day.

This chapter will first explore the ways in which gaming has been linked to children's culture through marketing, academic research, and popular discourse, focusing on the ways in which age, gender, and race are used to construct particular audiences for gaming. It will then turn to a discussion of representation, emphasizing the role that critical media literacy can play in helping children (and adults) understand, critique, and respond to representations in game worlds. This chapter argues that games provide an important space for representation—a space in which representations are presented and preserved, protested and changed. Despite being marketed as "child's play," games are, in fact, terrain on which battles related to the politics of representation regularly are fought.

■ Gaming and Children's Culture

In our contemporary media environment, games are not just for kids. The Entertainment Software Association (ESA) reports that the average gamer in the United States is thirty-three years old. Sixty-seven percent of American heads of households play games, and the average adult gamer has been playing games for thirteen years (ESA, 2007). In addition to adults playing games alone or with peers, some parents who grew up playing video games have introduced their children to gaming. As Tews (2001) describes, "for many younger families gaming is a form of interactive family entertainment and a cultural tradition shared between generations from infancy on" (p. 171). Despite a growing adult player base, video games remain strongly associated with youth culture through marketing, academic research, and popular discourses about gaming and gamers. Early studies of gaming focused almost exclusively on young players, and many gaming studies from a psychological or media effects standpoint focus on the effect of games on youth. In addition, mass media coverage of games and gaming has contributed to moral panic over the influence of games on child behavior.

While there are more adults than ever playing video games, associating games with children and youth is certainly not incorrect. Kaiser Family Foundation's survey of American youth reported that 52% of kids, ages eight to eighteen, play some kind of videogame daily. Further, the survey results indicated that American kids spend an average of nineteen minutes each day playing computer games and forty-nine minutes playing console or hand-held video games. A surprising finding of the study is a negative relationship between gameplay and age. Sixty-five percent of kids aged eight to ten and 63% of kids aged eleven to fourteen reported playing any video or computer game, compared to only 49% of teens aged fifteen to eighteen (Roberts, Foehr, and Rideout, 2005). The lower numbers of teens playing video games could be related to a number of factors, including school pressure, competing activities, or increased mobility facilitated by getting one's driver's license. Regardless of this decrease, it is clear that gaming is an important part of many American kids' media use.

Defining children as a market for games has been essential to the success of many software and game producers. Targeting kids as consumers was particularly valuable to Nintendo, which has been described as "the first company to 'brand' the video game market" through its creation of the "Nintendo Generation," a branding campaign that made Nintendo "synonymous with video gaming, just as Xerox had once meant photocopiers . . ." (Klein, Dyer-Witheford, and De Peuter, 2003, p. 125). Recognizing simultaneously the influence children have over parent purchases (McNeal, 1992), and the need for parents to feel comfortable when purchasing an unfamiliar product for their children, Nintendo focused on being family friendly. Klein, Dyer-Witheford, and De Peuter note:

> Nintendo was very careful, at least at first, to avoid the most violent or provocative games. Promoting the Nintendo brand as a family-oriented entertainment industry was central to the company's thinking about product and market development, from the Famicom name to the resources dedicated to Donkey Kong, Mario, and later Zelda. But it couldn't allow caution to negate its appeal to children's rebellion and independence. Creating the Nintendo image was thus an exquisite balancing act. (p. 119)

In the early 1990s, Sega reinforced and expanded the association of games with the youth market as it began focusing its marketing strategy on fifteen- to seventeen-year-old boys. Sega's advertising campaigns clearly differentiated its games from Nintendo's, emphasizing an image of Sega players as more mature, cooler, and more rebellious than Nintendo's "babyish" players. The expansion of game marketing to a wider demographic of twelve- to twenty-four-year-old players was initiated by Sony in the mid-1990s with the introduction of the PlayStation. This tactic allowed Sony to differentiate itself from other game companies competing for a younger market segment. In addition, Sony "directly addressed a group with crucial disposable income, but it also appealed universally to all would-be seventeen-year-olds in the gaming world" (p. 152). Despite its targeting of a biologically older audience, marketing for the PlayStation continued to reinforce the association of gaming with youth.

Another area that has associated gaming with youth culture is the children's software industry. Mizuko Ito (2007) describes children's software as "commercial software that is targeted towards elementary aged children, and embodies these general cultural commitments to learning and developmental goals" (p. 4). Children's computer software, also known as edutainment software, emerged in the late 1970s and early 1980s as a product of educators and technology designers hoping to create alternatives to computer-based "drill and kill" instruction. Ito highlights three genres within children's software: academic, which places traditional academic content (like math) within a game; entertainment, which she describes as "family friendly, pro-social, and appropriate for young children but not necessarily academic in focus" (p. 10); and construction, which encouraged programming and authoring. According to the ESA's 2007 report, just fewer than 11% of console games sold in 2006 were categorized as children's or family entertainment, while sales of comparable genres in PC platforms came in at just over 18%. While producers of console games create a variety of titles that fit loosely within the "edutainment" category, it appears that the history of children's software has contributed to its relative dominance in the marketplace.

Video games have also become associated with youth culture through a variety of discourses about gaming and gamers. These discourses are complex, often contradictory, and reflect a general anxiety about the influence of mass media that has a long history within American culture. Discourses about kids' use of electronic media (including games) often construct young gamers within a binary of helpless victims or savvy users (Buckingham, 2000). For example, stories of violent behavior suspected to be related to game play posit kids as victims of violent media made all the more dangerous by the interactivity of the game. Games are also depicted as threats to kids' social and physical well-being. As in the case of the *South Park* episode "Make Love Not Warcraft," gamers are frequently depicted as antisocial, obsessive, nerdy, acne-ridden, lethargic, and overweight. At the same time, kids who use games sanctioned by parents, teachers, and marketers as "educational" are depicted as digital whiz kids who hold the future in the palms of their nimble, button-pushing hands.

Much of the anxiety over the effects of videogame play, particularly in relation to violence, echo past moral panics over earlier forms of media. For example, fears over the "permissive practices of reading" cultivated by wider access to books other than the Bible in the eighteenth century, or fears of crowds being manipulated by media messages in radio, film, and print in the age of industrialization, and fears about media manipulation of "passive" television audiences all represent a historical perspective on this moral panic. Now, in the twenty-first century, video games and online communities present a similar level of access to information previously carefully controlled by groups in power—parents, teachers, government, etc. (Miller, 2006).

Within youth culture, computer and video games have been largely defined as boy-dominated space. While much of this association is likely due to the fact that marketing campaigns have directly targeted boys, Jenkins (1998) points to aspects of video game culture that parallel a longer tradition of "boy culture," a movement dated around the time of the Industrial Revolution and attributed to boys' rebellion against being removed from the workplace and confined to domestic space. For example, Jenkins notes the similarities between features such as separation from parents (for gamers, this is accomplished through individualized playing in bedrooms, etc.), recognition for daring stunts, mastery of skills and self-control (for gamers, manual dexterity), hierarchy and status, violence, role playing, and social networking.

Favoring a boy audience is not unique to video games. Similar practice has been status quo in children's television, where traditional industry wisdom dictates that girls will watch boys' shows, but boys will not watch girls' shows. This led to a paucity of female characters and characters designed with girls in mind in children's television until the 1980s, when toy-based cartoons such as *The Care Bears* and *My Little Pony* began to appeal directly to the girl audience (Seiter, 1993). The same boy-centered viewpoint informed the software and videogame market until the mid-1990s when the unexpected success of *Barbie Fashion Designer* sparked increased interest in games marketed to girls (Jenkins, 1998; Beato, 1997). The resultant "girl games movement" aimed to meet girls' needs and desires in interactive media by designing titles specifically for them. The movement operated under assumptions about girls' avoidance of violence, interest in relationships, communication, and preference for problem solving rather than competitive tasks. While the girl games movement was seen as a positive step in meeting the needs of an underserved market of consumers, the software titles produced for girls suffered from incomplete attention to identity politics. Justine Cassell writes, "these narratives [in games for girls] are not about the child's own self, nor are they flexibly designed to allow a range of gendered constructions...The stories are about the lives of an imaginary character and not the user" (Cassell, 1998, pp. 301–2).

In addition to efforts by game producers and children's software manufacturers, other children's media franchises have contributed to the mainstreaming of gaming within the realm of children's culture. For example, Buckingham and Sefton-Green (2003) write about Pokemon as a key moment in bringing video games to a mainstream kid audience. Pokemon was the number one children's franchise for several years. Pokemon appealed to both boys and girls through its characters and through game functions that adhered to traditional notions about what girls and boys prefer, such as battles and social networking. Ito (2006) notes that Pokemon drew girls into hand-held gaming because of its prominence as a Game Boy game. One of the legacies of Pokemon is that the Game Boy continues to be girls' preferred gaming platform. The popularity of Pokemon and other games that show wide appeal among both boys and girls, such as Neopets or The Sims, have encouraged researchers to reconsider how they define "game" and "gamer," moving away from narrow definitions to recognize the importance of games that do not fit existing molds, such as casual web-based games, and gamers who do not fit the stereotype of White nerdy boy.

One additional initiative that has contributed to the association of gaming with children's culture is the implementation of a rating system for games. The rating system, created by the Entertainment Software Rating Board (ESRB), aims to inform consumers of the content of games, much in the way that movie ratings indicate the audience deemed appropriate for a particular film. The ESRB is a self-regulatory body within the gaming industry, and use of the ratings system by game manufacturers is voluntary. However, most major retailers of·games have agreed to carry only games that have been rated by the ESRB and to implement policies for appropriate marketing and age verification on purchases of games rated 'M' (mature) or 'AO' (adults only).[1] The ratings system was created with children in mind, as is evident from the ESRB's frequently asked questions page, which states:

> After consulting a wide range of child development and academic experts, analyzing other rating systems and conducting nationwide research with parents, the ESRB found that what parents really wanted from a video game rating system were both age-based categories and, equally if not more importantly, concise and impartial information about what type of content is in the game.[2]

The use of developmental psychology and educational theory to determine age appropriateness of game content is a strategy similar to that employed by children's television producers and toy manufacturers (Seiter, 1993). Parents are reassured that the product they are purchasing for their child is safe and beneficial to their development without having to spend a lot of time reviewing or researching the product themselves.

Through the ESRB system, games receive one of six ratings. Games can be rated "EC," (early childhood ages three and up), "E" (six years and older), "E10+" (ten years old and older), "T" (teen, thirteen years old and older), "M" (mature, seventeen and older), and "AO" (adult, eighteen and older). These ratings symbols appear on the front of the game packaging. On the back of the game are content descriptors, which indicate elements of the game that are notable or which may be of concern to parents. The ESA reports that 45% of games sold in 2006 carried the rating "E" (everyone). A rating of "E" indicates that the game content contains minimal violence and offensive language, and is thought to be suitable for players six years of age or older. Of course, the ratings system is not perfect, and children do not play only those games rated "E." Henry Jenkins notes, "…a sizable number of parents ignore game ratings because they assume that games are for kids. One quarter of children ages eleven to sixteen identify an M-rated (Mature Content) game as among their favorites."[3]

In theory, ratings systems provide an efficient way of dealing with game content. However, this protectionist approach does little to teach or encourage critical consumption or production of game representations. Introducing representations of violence or sexuality at "age appropriate" moments does not explain why certain representations are problematic, teach players to view game content with a critical eye, or reveal the underlying political/power structure of game design and distribution.

Similarly, the girls' games genre addresses girls as a market with distinct tastes and needs and creates a space for girls to play video games. However, as Cassell (1998) has pointed out, the representations in girls' games are quite often problematic in terms of agency and diversity. These representations echo female characters in mainstream games, which often are stereotypical and hyper-sexualized. Given the pedagogical undercurrent of much of children's software, it is disappointing that girls' games employ problematic representations rather than teaching girls how to question them.

Finally, a protectionist attitude toward children and gaming does little to unpack the issues of racial representations, power, and violence reproduced in games. The general invisibility of characters of color is one important issue to address in a medium in which more than two-thirds of main characters are White (Dill, et al., 2005). In addition, the widespread use of ethnic stereotypes and the overrepresentation of non-White characters as villains or targets for the hero to destroy are important, but largely overlooked, issues in videogame culture.

The continued growth of games within the children's media industry, the participation of young people in new forms of gaming, such as casual online games and MMORPGs like *Club Penguin, Whyville,* or *World of Warcraft,* and the recent surge of interest in games and learning indicate both a need and an opportunity to call increased attention to the politics of representation in video games. It is to this issue that this chapter will now turn.

■ Representation

One of the major forces behind research into representations in games is concern about the impact of particular representations on children. Such concerns are, of course, limited neither to interactive media nor to children's media. However, effects discourse relies on the construction of the audience as vulnerable—a role that children, in their assumed innocent state, easily occupy (Buckingham, 2000). The issue of representation is a complicated one that extends beyond the effects model assumed by many psychological studies of video games and children As Stuart Hall (1997) describes, there are two systems of representation involved in the production of meaning through language. The first system consists of mental representations—our thoughts about, or ways of understanding, particular concepts. Mental representations are individual, but are generally similar to mental representations of others who have had similar experiences of the world. Hall writes,

> ...we are able to communicate because we share broadly the same conceptual maps and thus make sense of or interpret the world in roughly similar ways. That is indeed what it means when we say we "belong to the same culture." (p. 18)

The second system, language, is what allows us to represent mental representations in ways that can be shared with others. Language is broadly defined to include words, symbols (indexical signs), sounds, and images (iconic signs). Meaning, then, according to a constructionist point of view, is constructed through the relationship between the conceptual system and the language system. As Edgar and Sedgwick (2002) state, "representation does not necessarily signify the representing of interests of the group or individual represented. Thus, in this context, 'representation' may be characterized as misrepresentation; as the 'presentation or construction of identity" (p. 339). The way we talk about and visually signify meaning is important.

Regardless of the specific representations one is considering, it is essential to think about representations as dynamic in that they are never consumed "as is" by an audience. Media messages are encoded with particular information by those who produce them; however, these messages are then decoded by audiences—that is, the messages are unpacked and read by audience members. There is not just one way to understand the message. Returning to Stuart Hall's (1997) writings on representation, we find that there are three possible readings of a text: dominant (as encoded), negotiated (pick and choose), and oppositional (subversive).

Negotiated and oppositional readings are possible with any text. However, within games, the element of interactivity opens up additional space for these alternative readings. Interactivity refers to the elements of the game that players can control (movement, character creation, chat, skills, etc.) Because other media, such as books, films, or television programs give much more limited opportunities (if any) for such types of interactivity, research has posited that the immersion (or "presence") felt by players as well as identification with characters (or avatars) is a unique characteristic of new media like games and virtual worlds (Schroeder, 2006). It is important to remember that interactivity is a programmed feature of games. Although players can control the game world to an extent, top-level control over meaning is maintained by the game producers. However, interactivity begins to bridge the binary between designers and players by allowing players space to customize the playing experience, an opportunity with implications for enjoyment and engagement as well as for representation.

Understanding and critiquing media representations are an essential part of critical media literacy. Critical media literacy calls attention to the constructed nature of media messages and to the embedded ideological messages in media texts and is aligned with cultural studies' understanding that audiences interpret media in multiple, diverse, and dynamic ways (Masterman, 1985; Kellner & Share, 2005; Jolls & Thoman, 2008). Representation in interactive media such as games is, in many ways, similar to representation in films, television shows, or print media—the media that have traditionally been the focus of teaching and using critical media literacy. However, interactive media have some features, such as customization of avatars, that call attention to important differences in the ways representations are crafted and used in games and virtual worlds. The following section will investigate the continuous and unique features of representation in interactive media.

■ Representing Race and Gender

On a very basic level, representation of race and gender in games can be quantified. For example, one can count how many game characters are represented as female, Asian, or Black. In 2001, the California-based children's advocacy organization, Children Now, conducted a content analysis of seventy games, and found that 64% of all game characters in the sample were male. Seventy-three percent of player-controlled characters were male. A mere 17% of characters were female, and 50% of those characters were "props or bystanders" (p. 14) that had no interaction with the player (Children Now, 2001).

The same study found imbalance in the representation of race in those games. Over 50% of player-controlled male characters and 78% of player-controlled female characters are White. African American player-controlled characters ranged from 10% (female characters) to 37% (male characters). While there were a few Asian/Pacific Islander (3% male, 7% female) and Latino (5% male) characters, there were no Latina characters and a tiny number (1%) of Native American characters (Children Now, 2001). Closer examination of the representations commonly found in games have pointed to additional markers, such as hypersexual clothing and actions of female characters, that indicate the dominance of the male gaze in video game design, as well as a limited range of female and non-White characters (Tews, 2001).

Games have a history of narrow female representations. Early games (1970s/1980s) suffered as much from technological restrictions as they did from limited narrative space for representations beyond the male hero. It was not until the 1990s that female characters were regularly represented in games. At that time (and with few exceptions, still today), female characters fell into one of three categories—the damsel in distress (e.g., Pauline in *Donkey Kong*), the villainess (e.g. Sonia in *Mortal Kombat*), or the powerful and sexy female warrior (e.g., Lara Croft in *Tomb Raider*) (Tews, 2001).

Lara Croft, the protagonist of the *Tomb Raider* series published by Eidos Interactive, is the female character that has received the most attention in the academic community. This character, who first appeared in the original *Tomb Raider* game in 1996, marked a significant change in the representation of female characters in games. An archeologist by trade and a warrior by narrative necessity, Lara is depicted quite differently from typical helpless, meaningless, or evil female characters. As Helen Kennedy (2002) writes:

> It is clear that the producers of Lara wanted to market her as a character potentially appealing to women; her arrival on the game scene dovetailed nicely with the 90's "girl power" zeitgeist and could potentially have hit a positive chord with the emergent "laddette" culture which very much centered around playing "lads at their own game(s)." (p. 2)

At the same time, Lara is a highly sexualized representation, which positions her as the object of the male gaze despite her protagonist role, rather than as a threat to the masculine order. This is demonstrated through the pairing of her hyper-feminine features—tiny waist, long hair, large breasts—with fetishistic signifiers such as her glasses, guns, and holsters. As Cassell and Jenkins write, "Lara Crofts (*sic*) exists not to empower women but to allow men to experiment with the experience of disempowerment" (1998, p. 31).

The way in which Lara is represented and marketed simultaneously as both object of sexual desire and as powerful female lead was a departure from the standards for game design and marketing at the time. Throughout the 1980s and early 1990s, games were marketed solely to young, male audiences. However, Lara's dual coding as sexy and strong can be understood as an attempt to broaden her appeal to both male and female audiences.

Despite the revolutionary nature of Lara's character, much of the analysis and debate about her has been reduced to her role as a positive or negative role model for young girls (Kennedy, 2002), a fact that speaks to the value placed on protecting children from media, but that diminishes the political stakes of female representations like Lara. Representation is far more complicated than "good" or "bad" images, a schema used in much research on stereotypes. Further, examining representations in this way has the potential to depoliticize the representation. For example, uncritical acceptance of representations that have been declared "positive" (i.e., unproblematic) or, worse, censorship of representations deemed "negative" without deeper analysis. As Kennedy points out, Lara Croft has been received with much ambivalence, particularly by feminists. However, Lara appears to set the standard for female representation in many new games, even prompting one recent study of what researchers have termed the "Lara phenomenon" ("the appearance of a strong, competent female character in a dominant position" (Jansz & Martis, 2007, p. 147).

Racial representations in games generally have received less attention from the academic community. However, in recent years, increased interest in race has been apparent, particularly in online publications and fora dedicated to game studies.[4] Paying attention to racial representations in games moves away from discourse about colorblindness, an idea reinforced by assumptions of anonymity in online and other virtual participation, and acknowledges that technological constraints that have hampered appropriate racial representations (e.g., video card capabilities), are nearly non-existent. Issues of representation in games are closely linked to representation in cyberspace in general, not just because many games exist online or use networked communication, but because both are stages for mediated interaction. As Kolko, Nakamura, and Rodman (2000) write, "race matters in cyberspace precisely because all of us who spend time online are already shaped by the ways in which race matters offline, and we can't help but bring our own knowledge, experiences, and values with us when we log on" (pp. 4–5). Similarly, Anna Everett has argued that in online spaces, representations of race and ethnicity have been problematic and that non-White people have been, for the most part, invisible. She writes:

> The overwhelming characterizations of the brave new world of cyberspace as primarily a racialized sphere of whiteness inhere in popular constructions of high-tech and low-tech spheres that too often consign black [and other minority] bodies to the latter with the latter being insignificant if not absent altogether. (Everett, 2002; qtd. in Everett 2007)

Invisibility remains a key issue in considering representations of race (as well as gender) in games. White male characters continue to have the most visibility in games. When Black, Asian, and Latino characters appear in games, they are frequently background characters or victims, particularly if they are also female.

Game characters tend to be depicted according to racial stereotypes, which, as David Leonard (2006) writes, are problematic because they "do not merely reflect ignorance or the flattening of characters through stock racial ideas but dominant ideas of race, thereby contributing to our commonsense ideas about race, acting as a compass for both daily and institutional relations" (p. 85). Writing specifically about sports games, Leonard (n.d.) discusses the politics of representation involved in representations of Black men. He writes:

Sports games represent a genre in which characters of color exist as actors (protagonists) rather than victims or aesthetic scenery. Eight out of ten black male video game characters are sports competitors; black males, thus, only find visibility in sports games. (p. 1)

While it seems that the visibility of Black males as player-controlled characters integral to the plot of a highly popular game genre is a step up from depictions as "victims or aesthetic scenery," these representations warrant examination and critique as stereotypes and reflections of dominant ideologies about race and social participation. Leonard critiques such stereotypes for glamorizing and commodifying inner-city life, ignoring the real social problems such as poverty and violence that occur there.

In virtual worlds and games in which identity is more flexible and subject to user customization, the representation of race is an essential consideration. Beth Kolko examined race in multi-user dungeons (MUDs), text-based virtual worlds created entirely by users' descriptions of people, places, things, and interactions within the world. Participation in a MUD requires the construction of an avatar, a virtual representation of self. Kolko questions why early MUDs did not have a command to allow users to define the race of their avatar along with other aspects of identity like age and gender. As text-based environments completely dependent on user-generated content, there are no technical reasons for the omission of an @race command. This indicates that the decision is ideological. Without an @race command, Kolko asserts that the default race is assumed to be White and that users resist marking race because "the MUD is an environment where racial identity is presumed to be either irrelevant or homogenous" (Kolko, 2000, p. 217).

In contrast to early MUDs, which employed the ideology of colorblindness, contemporary role playing games (RPGs) (textual and graphical) allow players to indicate racial identity. In fact, race is an important characteristic for avatars in many RPGs and MMORPGs because in-game races are designed with various characteristics, abilities, and aptitudes; for example, *World of Warcraft* players can choose from ten races for their characters: dranei, dwarves, gnomes, humans, night elves, blood elves, orcs, tauren, trolls, and undead.[5] Each race carries a set of "racial traits" that indicate strengths, weaknesses, and unique specialties assigned to characters of that race. In addition to choosing a race, players choose a class for their characters. Nine classes are available: druid, hunter, mage, paladin, priest, rogue, shaman, warlock, and warrior.[6] Each class has assigned to it a set of abilities. The choice becomes complicated by the fact that not all classes are available to all races. For example, orcs cannot be druids, mages, paladins, or priests; humans cannot be hunters, druids, or shamans. Thus, the marking of race is an essential task with real consequences for game play. Kolko writes:

...many contemporary RPG worlds have the ability to set race. While this race is tied to the fantasy of the game, participants familiar with the genre know that upon login to a new game they often will have the opportunity to choose a race for their discursive avatar. This race, in turn, will help guide their interaction in the world, providing other players with cues as to how to best approach another character and respond to actions, as well as reveal something (what, I'll not say) about how players conceptualize their virtual selves....The interface of these worlds....allows for the expression of marked race in cyberspace; rather than assuming homogeneity among participants, the political landscape of such virtual worlds takes on particular characteristics. (Kolko, 2000, pp. 225–26)

MMORPGs further complicate the issue of representation because of the way in which social interaction forms and changes gameplay. Because MMORPGs allow for (and in many cases, require) social construction of meaning and teamwork, representations within the game are constantly and synchronously shared, discussed, and altered. In addition to its role in shaping meaning within the game, the social nature of MMORPGs make them interesting sites for observing discourse about identity. T. L. Taylor writes about race, ethnicity, language, and nationality in *World of Warcraft* in light of her experiences on a server hosting players from a variety of European countries. For example, Taylor writes, "…bias, generalizations, and stereotypes about particular countries could often be heard in informal discussions ('The Brits are always logging on drunk')" (p. 321). She notes that such comments are sometimes made in jest, without any true malice. However, she notes that "they also emerge as tentative asides and explanatory devices" (p. 321) that can be problematic. MMORPGs are different from video games that one plays alone or with a few (often co-located) friends because communication within the game has a wide reach. Players in an MMORPG regularly encounter other players who possess very different worldviews. Through the persistent communication characteristic of MMORPGs, shared cultural knowledge is developed within the game. As Taylor writes, "players not only bring in existing meaning systems about their and others' national context, but may even develop (or at the minimum reify) opinions in relation to gameplay" (Taylor, 2006, p. 321). Of course, developing a new perspective through gameplay is not necessarily problematic, and Taylor emphasizes that she does not feel that a ban on discussions of nationality is necessary (or possible.)

One example of a stereotype that has emerged from within MMORPGs is that of the Chinese gold farmer. Gold farmers are players hired to earn in-game currency. In the offline world, these players often work in questionable working conditions for long hours at low pay. In the game world, gold farmers' characters can be found "grinding" in particular areas, killing the same monsters over and over again in order to accumulate gold. The in-game currency is then sold to other players. Taylor writes that the Chinese gold farmer is a "pan-game stereotype…[that] has become a kind of broad epithet, mixing the frustration some feel with real-money trade (RMT) with an overextended (and xenophobic) stereotype about which kinds of players are 'ruining the game world'" (p. 321). Like other stereotypes, the Chinese gold farmer stereotype has very little relationship to reality. Many, but certainly not all, gold farming operations are located in China, and the majority of Chinese players are not involved in RMT. However, that this stereotype persists within *World of Warcraft* and other MMORPGs is cause for concern. Taylor writes, "The issue is not only the imagined ethnic construction of the player harvesting in-game resources but that those who do not have a command of English and are hunting in a particular area may be automatically assumed to be a hired worker" (pp. 321–22). As with stereotypical representations of Black characters, the stereotype of the Chinese gold farmer contributes to players' "commonsense ideas about race" (Leonard, 2006, p. 85), shaping the way that they understand and interact with others both in game space and in offline encounters.

■ Conclusion

Acknowledging that videogame representations are complex, ideological, and frequently problematic is a necessary first step in using video games as a site for teaching and practicing critical media literacy. As was mentioned at the beginning of this chapter, there is a great deal of research emerging that investigates ways in which video games can motivate and support learning. In addition, the use of games as spaces for intervention and education about social issues is increasing. For example, the Serious Games Initiative produces games that speak to issues of education, training, health, and public policy.[7] Clearly, games are already functioning as learning spaces and have great potential for teaching players how to approach games (and other media) with a critical eye.

A second aspect of critical media literacy that could be addressed with games is the political economy of production and consumption. Projects aiming to teach game design, such as the Open Play project run by USC's School of Cinema and Television,[8] push students to consider representations and narrative from the point of view of a game designer. In this project, part of a larger Learning Games Initiative, students from a local high school created modified versions of the game Pac-Man based on their own life experiences. As researcher Katynka Martinez has noted:

> [the Pac-Man character in the games] would be a kid helping out a hotdog vendor in MacArthur Park, a kid running away from bums in his neighborhood, and an immigrant picking up trash while being chased by the minutemen. These video game protagonists have never been seen in an Xbox or PlayStation game but they were created by kids that are quite familiar with standard video game formats and themes.[9]

Projects such as this one provide opportunities for young people to be involved in the back-end of game production—in particular, in crafting representations within the game. The incorporation of games into formal learning environments presents a number of challenges but also presents an opportunity for conversations about representation to begin. Teachers trained not only in the operation of the game, but also the language of media literacy can facilitate analysis and discussion of representation and scaffold students' understanding and readings of game representations. Similarly, supervisors, mentors, and parents could use video games as an example in conversations about media representation.

David Buckingham (2000) cautions against overly celebratory attitudes toward kids' relationships with electronic media. He critiques proponents of "the electronic generation" for ignoring issues of access and class in electronic media. I reiterate this cautioning statement here and encourage game players and designers to consider very seriously the important role video games play in children's culture. Games are not inherently dangerous, nor are they ideologically neutral. However, they are important media artifacts that deserve critical attention. For the boys in *South Park,* and for a great many youth in the United States and abroad, games are very much "something that matters."

Notes

1. http://www.esrb.org/ratings/faq.jsp
2. Ibid.
3. http://www.pbs.org/kcts/videogamerevolution/impact/myths.html
4. See, for example, The International Journal of Computer Game Research, (http://gamestudies.org) and Terranova (http://terranova.blogs.com).
5. http://www.worldofwarcraft.com/info/races.
6. http://www.worldofarcraft.com/info/classes.
7. For more information, see http://www.seriousgames.org/index2.html.
8. This project was supervised by Juan Devis (Project Director), Tara McPherson (USC Faculty), and Alex Tarr (Media Director). For more information on this project, see http://iml.usc.edu/laproject/ and http://www.kcet.org/explore-ca/web-stories/ritesofpassage/maps/index.php.
9. http://digitalyouth.ischool.berkeley.edu/node/35.

References

Bartle, R. (1996). Hearts, clubs, diamonds, spades: Players who suit MUDs. *Journal of MUD Research,* 1(1). Retrieved Nov. 30, 2005 from http://mud.co.uk/richard/hcds.htm

Beato, G. (1997). Girl Games. *Wired,* 5(4). Retrieved Aug. 28, 2007 from www.wired.com/archive//5.04/es_girlgames_pr.html.

Buckingham, D. (2000). *After the death of childhood: Growing up in the age of electronic media.* Cambridge, UK and Malden, MA: Polity Press.

Buckingham, D. and Sefton-Green, J. (2003). Gotta catch 'em all: Structure, agency, and pedagogy in children's media culture. *Media, Culture, and Society,* 25(3), pp. 379–399.

Cassell, J. and Jenkins, H. (Eds.) (1998). *From Barbie to Mortal Kombat: Gender and computer games.* Cambridge, MA: MIT Press.

Cassell, J. (1998). Storytelling as nexus of change in the relationship between gender and technology: A feminist approach to software design. In J. Cassell and H. Jenkins (Eds.), *From Barbie to Mortal Kombat: Gender and computer games* (pp. 262–302). Cambridge, MA: MIT Press.

Children Now (2001). *Fair play? Violence, gender and race in video games.* Oakland, CA: Author.

Dill, K. E., Gentile, D. A., Richter, W. A., and Dill, J. C. (2005). Violence, sex, race, and age in popular video games: A content analysis. In E. Cole and J. Henderson Daniel (Eds.), *Featuring females: Feminist analyses of the media.* Washington, DC: American Psychological Association.

Edgar, A. and Sedgwick, P. (Eds.) (2002). *Cultural theory: The key concepts.* New York: Routledge.

Entertainment Software Association (2007). *Essential facts about the computer and video game industry.* Author.

Everett, A. (2007). Introduction. In A. Everett (Ed.), *Learning Race and Ethnicity: Youth and Digital Media* (pp. 1–14). Cambridge, MA: MIT Press.

Everett, A. (2002). The Revolution Will Be Digitized: Afrocentricity and the Digital Public Sphere, *Social Text,* 71(20), pp. 125–146.

Gee, J. P. (2003). *What video games have to teach us about learning and literacy.* New York: Palgrave Macmillan.

Hall, S. (Ed.) (1997). *Representation: Cultural representations and signifying practices.* Thousand Oaks, CA: Sage Publications.

Hayes, E. (2007). Gendered identities at play: Case studies of two women playing Morrowind. *Games and Culture,* 2(1), pp. 1–26.

Ito, M. (2006). The gender dynamics of the Japanese media mix. Unpublished position paper presented at Girls n' Games workshop and conference, Los Angeles, CA, May 8–9, 2006. Available: http://www.itofisher.com/mito/publications/the_gender_dyna_1.html

Ito, M. (2007). Education v. entertainment: A cultural history of children's software. In K. Salen (Ed.), *Ecology of games: Connecting Youth, Games, and Learning.* Cambridge, MA: MIT Press.

Jansz, J. and Martis, R. G. (2007). The Lara phenomenon: Powerful female characters in video games. *Sex Roles, 56*(3–4), pp. 141–148.

Jenkins, H. (1998). "Complete freedom of movement": Video games as gendered play spaces. In J. Cassell and H. Jenkins (Eds.), *From Barbie to Mortal Kombat: Gender and computer games* (pp. 232–261). Cambridge, MA: MIT Press.

Jolls, T. and Thoman, E. (2008). *Literacy for the 21ˢᵗ century: An overview and orientation guide to media literacy education.* Los Angeles, CA: Center for Media Literacy.

Kellner, D. and Share, J. (2005). Toward Critical Media Literacy: Core concepts, debates, organizations, and policy. *Discourse: Studies in the Cultural Politics of Education, 26*(3), pp. 369–386.

Kennedy, H. (2002). Lara Croft: Feminist icon or cyberbimbo? On the limits of textual analysis. *Game Studies, 2*(2). Retrieved July 7, 2007 from http://www.gamestudies.org/0202/kennedy/.

Klein, S., Dyer-Witheford, N., and De Peuter, G. (2003). *Digital play: The interaction of technology, culture, and marketing.* Montreal: McGill-Queen's University Press.

Kolko, B. E., Nakamura, L., and Rodman, G. B. (2000). *Race in Cyberspace.* New York: Routledge.

Kolko, B. E. (2000). Erasing @race: Going white in the (inter)face. In B.E. Kolko, L. Nakamura, and G.B. Rodman (Eds.), *Race in Cyberspace* (pp. 213–232). New York: Routledge.

Leonard, D. (2006). Not a hater, just keepin' it real. *Games and Culture, 1*(1), pp. 83–88.

Leonard, D. (n.d.). High tech Blackface—Race, sports video games and becoming the other. *Intelligent Agent, 4*(4).

Masterman, L. (1985). *Teaching the media.* London: Comedia/Routledge.

McNeal, J. U. (1992). *Kids as customers: A handbook of marketing to children.* New York: Lexington Books.

Miller, T. (2006). Gaming for Beginners. *Games and Culture, 1*(1), pp. 1–9.

Parker, T. (Writer, Director). (2006). Make Love, Not Warcraft [Television series episode]. In T. Parker and M. Stone (Executive Producers), *South Park.* Los Angeles: Comedy Central and Comedy Partners.

Roberts, D.F., Foehr, U.G., and Rideout, V. (2005). *Generation 'M': Media in the lives of 8–18 year olds.* Kaiser Family Foundation. Retrieved July 7, 2007 from http://www.kff.org/entmedia/7251.cfm

Salen, K. (Ed.) (2007). *Ecology of games: Connecting Youth, Games, and Learning.* Cambridge, MA: MIT Press.

Schroeder, R. (2006). Being there together and the future of connected presence. *Presence, 15*(4), pp. 438–454.

Seiter, E. (1993). *Sold separately: Parents and children in consumer culture.* New Brunswick, NJ: Rutgers University Press.

Taylor, T. L. (2003). Multiple pleasures: Women and online gaming. *Convergence, 9*(1), pp. 21–46.

Tews, R. R. (2001). Archetypes on acid: Video games and culture. In M.J.P. Wolf (Ed.), *The medium of the video game* (pp. 169–182). Austin, Texas: University of Texas Press.

Thomas, D., and Brown, J. S. (2007). The play of imagination: Extending the literary mind. *Games and Culture, 2*(2), 149–172.

35

■ Critical Perspectives on Social Network Sites

Alla Zollers

Web 2.0 technologies, adopted widely over the past few years, promise "community and collaboration on a scale never seen before," (Grossman, 2006). In fact, in 2006, with an iconic picture of a computer on the cover, *Time* magazine declared "You," the user of Web 2.0 tools, the person of the year. With this declaration, *Time* magazine acknowledged that the contributions of individuals account for the value of Web 2.0 software. Just as the telephone would lose its value if there were no one to call, Web 2.0 sites such as YouTube, MySpace, Facebook, Flickr, and Del.icio.us require the participation and volunteer labor of vast networks of users. The sites do not provide content but rather a platform where users store and share personalized information in the form of text, pictures, links, and videos. According to *Time*, "The new Web is a very different thing. It's a tool for bringing together the small contributions of millions of people and making them matter. Silicon Valley consultants call it Web 2.0, as if it were a new version of some old software. But it's really a revolution" (Grossman, 2006).

At the forefront of the Web 2.0 revolution are social network sites (SNSs) such as MySpace, and Facebook. The sites realize, create, and exhibit connections among people. For example, MySpace's[1] logo proclaims the service is "a place for friends," while Facebook[2] describes itself as "a social utility that connects you with the people around you." Due to their phenomenal popularity, especially among youth, these sites have garnered a great deal of media attention and political and legislative scrutiny as well as increasingly large sums of corporate capital. As with any new technology, the rhetoric surrounding SNSs is either utopian or dystopian in nature. The utopian rhetoric highlights the social and community aspects of the sites, whereas the dystopian view revolves around a moral panic over online predators. The challenge at hand is to begin to conceive SNSs as a contested terrain that provides a unique means of communication, while at the same time exposing people to a variety of risks.

Although SNSs enable connections among people and to some extent provide a public sphere for discourse, they are ultimately owned by corporations. With their ever-increasing popularity, the sites—and the corporations that own them—also potentially exert greater influence over a large number of people. As it stands, influence is enacted in the form of encouraging consumption of goods and services. Recently, SNSs have shifted their influence focus into the political realm. While many SNSs exist both in the United States and internationally,[3] this chapter will focus specifically on MySpace and Facebook, using the methods of cultural studies in order to illuminate the dialectical tensions present on these two particular social network sites.

■ What Is a Social Network Site?

Social network sites differentiate themselves from other social software, such as blogs, wikis, and social-tagging sites, by three distinct features: profiles, friend lists, and comments (boyd and Ellison, 2007). Unlike the "proto-social networking sites of a decade ago [that] used metaphors of *place* to organize their members: people were linked through virtual cities, communities, and homepages," today's SNSs "organize around metaphors of the *person,* with individual profiles that list hobbies and interests" (Rosen, 2007).

The fundamental feature of a social network site is the profile. A profile is constructed through a pre-defined Web form that each member completes for the purpose of describing themselves to other members of the site. boyd states that a "profile can be seen as form of *digital body* where individuals must write themselves into being" (2007). The most basic profile fields include demographics details such as age, sex, and location, followed by relationship status, educational level, political and religious affiliations, as well as tastes in music, movies, and books, a photograph, and open-ended descriptions. These fields exist because Friendster—originally designed as a dating site—was the first popular social network site and was subsequently emulated by newer SNSs.

Once the profile is created, members are then encouraged to look at others' profiles and add those people to their Friends[4] list. The creation of a Friends list is what makes up the "social network" component of the sites.

> Most social network sites require approval for two people to be linked as Friends. When someone indicates another as a Friend, the recipient receives a message asking for confirmation. If Friendship is confirmed, the two become Friends in the system and their relationship is included in the public display of connections on all profiles. (boyd, 2007; Donath and boyd, 2004)

Originally, social network theory was developed by sociologists to describe and analyze social phenomena in terms of the *relationships* between network members. Network members, or nodes, are individuals, groups, or even institutions. They are connected to each other through relationships such as friendship, kinship, support, or collegiality. When conducting social network studies, social scientists are careful to define and measure the relationships between network members. Unfortunately, SNSs failed to recognize that publicly articulated networks are not identical to the nuanced relationship data gathered by sociologists (boyd, 2004), as SNSs only allow for binary relationship indicators (friend or not friend). So users often "friend" anyone they know and do not particularly dislike. The flattening of the network removes barriers between different user networks such as work, friends, or family. This becomes problematic when people wish to represent them-selves differently in multiple social networks. Additionally, an unintended side effect to the flattening of a network concerns the removal of friends. A person only removes friends if there is an "explosive end to the relationship" instead of just a growing apart (boyd, 2004). The addition and removal of friends is a new form of social etiquette. Thus, an individual's publicly articulated network as found on SNSs is actually a poor representa-tion of their "real" complex and dynamic social network.

SNSs also provide a means for communication among Friends. This is most commonly done through comments posted on "The Wall" in Facebook or the "Friend's Comments" section in MySpace. The comments are publicly displayed and viewable to anyone with access to the individuals' profiles. According to a survey conducted by the Pew Internet & American Life Project, "the most popular way of communicating via social networking sites is to post a message to a friend's profile, page, or 'wall,'" (Lenhart and Madden, 2007). In fact, Golder, Wilkinson, and Huberman (2007) found that private Facebook messages are sent very infrequently with an average of only .97 private messages sent per user per week. Although data are not available for the average number of comments left per user per week, ethnographic data suggest that email and private messaging is minimized in favor of using the comments feature (boyd, 2007).

■ Brief History of Social Network Sites

In 1967, Harvard sociologist Stanley Milgram published results of a study about social connections called the "small world experiment." The experiment showed that any two people are connected to each other through an average number of 5.5 relations; thus popularizing the idea of "six degrees of separation." The first popular SNS launched in 1997 and was aptly named SixDegrees.com. The site allowed for the profile creation, building a Friends list, as well as traversal of the Friends network by clicking on the profiles of friends-of-friends. Although SixDegrees provided core SNS functionality, it was not widely successful and consequently went out of business in 2000. The next wave of SNSs emerged in 2001 with Ryze.com, Tribe.net, LinkedIn and Friendster. Ryze and LinkedIn both targeted business networks, Friendster was designed as a dating site, and Tribe.net targeted niche communities or "tribes." Of these startups, LinkedIn has been able to establish itself a leading provider in business networking and is thriving to this day. Friendster also quickly gained popularity, establishing a base of 300,000 users by May 2003, only three months after its beta release (O'Shea, 2003). Friendster was not able to sustain its popularity mainly due to misunderstanding of its users and the social norms and interactions that the users established on the site (boyd, 2006). According to boyd (2006), people began to create fake profiles on Friendster mainly to expand their network size and reach. "These Fakesters included characters, celebrities, objects, icons, institutions, and ideas" (boyd, 2006). Friendster was unhappy with the Fakesters and thus deleted many Fakesters in what has been coined as the "Fakester Genocide" (boyd, 2006).

The Fakester Genocide upset and alienated many users, so they began to migrate over to MySpace. In fact, "one of MySpace's early strategies was to provide a place for everyone who was rejected from Friendster" (boyd, 2006). MySpace, launched in 2003, was able to grow rapidly due to the migration of users from Friendster. The growth of MySpace was additionally spurred by bands joining the site; they in turn encouraged their fans to join. Through the use of the bulletins feature available on MySpace, bands found a way to cheaply and easily communicate with their fans, as well as spur viral marketing campaigns that utilized the strengths of the SNSs. One of MySpace's distinctive features from other SNSs is its very large community of music artists and fans. In 2004, large numbers of teenagers began joining MySpace, prompting a great deal of media attention. On July 18, 2005, the News Corporation owned by Rupert Murdoch announced its acquisition of MySpace for $580 million. (Siklos, 2005).

Facebook was created by former Harvard student Mark Zuckerberg in 2004. Facebook was conceptualized from the physical softcover class directory called "facebook" that Harvard provided to all incoming freshman. "For some time, Harvard had been planning to put the facebook online, Zuckerberg decided to do the job himself" (Cassidy, 2006). The popularity of Facebook was almost assured, as students have always been avid users of the paper version. When reminiscing about his "Class Album," Li (2007) states that

> Each page had nine black and white photographs, and each photograph had a name under it. We would flip through it, muttering things to ourselves like, 'Oh, know that person', 'Who's that?', 'Wow I nearly didn't recognize him' and the inevitable, 'Dude, she's hot.'

Much the same type of activity that once occurred around the facebook booklet translated to the online setting as "hundreds of ambitious and impressionable young people [desired] to establish themselves and make friends in an unfamiliar environment" (Cassidy, 2006). Ellison, Steinfeld, and Lampe (2007) report that students use Facebook to check out people they meet socially, to learn more about people from class, and to connect with offline contacts.

By September 2004, Facebook had one-quarter million users; by 2005, Facebook was the second fastest-growing major site on the Internet, with only MySpace outpacing its growth (Cassidy, 2006). Facebook's growth was initially limited by the fact that only college students with a valid ".edu" email account were allowed to join. Facebook subsequently opened up registration to international universities in 2004, then high schools in 2005, followed by corporations in April 2006, finally leading to an announcement of open registration on September 11, 2006 (Rosmarin, 2006). According to comScore (2007), the open registration led to an 89% increase in unique Facebook traffic from May 2005 to May 2006. The open registration did not significantly change the site's operating premise of separate networks. These new users were limited to their specific networks—be it corporate, high school, or city—thereby maintaining some network separation as well as a degree of privacy.[5]

Although corporations such as Microsoft, Viacom, and Yahoo have attempted to buy Facebook, Facebook has not been for sale. Facebook has acquired more venture capital, invested in targeted advertising on the sites, and is aiming to take the company public in the future (Cassidy, 2006). However, in October of 2007, Facebook struck a partnership with Microsoft, whereby "Microsoft will be the exclusive third-party advertising platform partner for Facebook, and will begin to sell advertising for Facebook internationally in addition to the United States" (Facebook Press Release, 2007).

■ Critical Perspectives on Social Network Sites

Social network sites have become increasingly integrated into the daily lives of millions of people around the world, especially youth. According to a Pew Internet & American Life study, 55% of online teens use SNSs, with 48% of teens visiting the sites daily (Lenhart and Madden, 2007). Although previous scholarship[6] in this area has utilized a wide range of methods to study SNSs, a critical perspective is vital in exposing the ideologies prevalent on these sites. In this section, I will utilize the methods of culture studies to demonstrate how the features of these sites perpetuate ideologies of consumption, as well as provide a contested terrain for democracy and politics.

■ A Culture of Consumption

Contemporary American culture is based on consumption; "we shop on our lunch hours, patronize outlet malls on vacation, and satisfy our latest desires with a late-night lick of the mouse," (Schor, 1999). Consumer goods and consumption pervade our daily lives and thus carry meaning beyond mere commercial value bur rather "communicate cultural meaning" (McCracken, 1986). Cultural meaning "determines how the world is seen," with each culture establishing "its own special vision of the world" (McCracken, 1986). The purpose of advertising is to encode meaning into products to encourage the consumption of both the product and the meaning, thus tying cultural consumption with cultural identity (Storey, 1999). According to Kellner, "...symbolic images in advertising attempt to create an association between the products offered and socially desirable and meaningful traits . . ." (1995); so when an individual buys the latest hip and trendy mobile phone, they are not buying the phone solely for its utilitarian value, they are also decoding and consuming the cultural meaning that the phone provides. Storey (1999) goes on to state that when we meet new people we often inquire about their consumption habits; knowing the answer to consumption questions such as musical tastes helps us "construct a cultural and social pattern and thus begin to locate the person in a particular cultural and social space—we begin, in other words, to think we know who they are." Thus, "...

cultural consumption not only 'echoes' but also actively 'reinforces' who one *can* be" (Liu, 2007, emphasis original), with class status and social differences negotiated as well as legitimated through the act of consumption (Bourdieu, 1984).

The social and public nature of SNSs creates an exaggerated social context. According to Schor (1999), consumption is a social act because "our sense of social standing and belonging comes from what we consume." Subsequently, consumption defines and facilitates the main interactions on SNSs. These interactions are expressed through (but not limited to) profile customizations, identity creation via product affiliation, and viewing placed ads.

Profile Customization

As mentioned previously, the profile is one of the defining features of SNSs because it enables users to create a digital identity. Although profile creation and customization is in itself an act of production, users are often required to define their virtual identity in terms of consumption. Many of the profile fields ask users to list favorite music, movies, and books. Storey (1999) states that "cultural consumption is perhaps one of the most significant ways we perform our sense of self." Kellner furthers the point by stating that "media culture provides resources for identity and new modes of identity in which look, style, and image replaces such thing as action and commitment as constituitives of identity" (1995).

The profile can thus be thought of as a type of "online textual performance" where the cultural signals—in the form of self-described favorite music and movies, etc.—compose a "taste statement that is 'performed' through the profile." In a study of MySpace profiles, Liu (2007) found four distinct taste statements: prestige, differentiation, authenticity, and theatrical persona, with prestige and differentiation being the most frequent type of taste statements. Prestige taste statements are those that generally identify with the popular culture or sub-culture, mainly through popular music and movie references. Differentiation statements purposefully place the individual as different from friends' tastes by including an eclectic mix of taste preferences, with the intention of expressing uniqueness. Authenticity statements provide atypical details and unique writing patterns, and are "important in the eyes of some subcultures, including rap culture and club culture" (Liu 2007). While a theatrical persona utilizes sarcasm and tongue-in-cheek responses to taste categories to demonstrate creativity (Liu, 2007), the taste statements are utilized specifically to signal belonging and create individual identity in SNSs. Interestingly, Baudrillard (1998) points out that in consumer culture there is very little individuation and differentiation, that differences in themselves have become artificial. As evidenced by those who utilize differentiation taste statements, they become "different" though conformity, and thus relinquish any real difference at all, especially since "differentiation" is one of the most popular expressions of taste.

Along with the taste statements, SNSs and MySpace in particular allow individuals to customize the look and feel of their profiles. A technical bug in the MySpace profile pages allows users to add HTML and CSS (cascading style sheets) code, thus providing a great amount of visual customizability to the profiles. "MySpace pages consist of a mish-mash of text, pictures, animated graphics, bright colors, and sound, leading a popular American business magazine to label them as 'design anarchy,'" (Perkel, in press). In fact, the value of custom profiles is so high that an entire secondary business has sprung up around MySpace layouts and code. According to Perkel (in press), "MySpace members typically use one of many third-party sites and either choose from a wide variety of 'layouts' or use a 'code generator' that presents choices of colors, fonts, font-sizes, and so forth for each aspect of the page." The custom code, along with the taste statements create a performance of individual consumption practices. The consumption practices are subsequently decoded and understood as an individual's online identity.

Because youth are the largest users of SNSs, it is not surprising to find that the constructed online identities found in SNSs are postmodern. Postmodern identities are characterized as performative, self becoming, multiple, decentered, incomplete, constituted in culture, and historical (Storey, 1999). These identities stand in opposition to traditional identities that were thought to be fixed, singular, unfolding with change, complete, and universal (Storey, 1999). The social, performative, and fluid nature of SNS profiles provides a fertile ground for constant experimentation and reinvention of self. Profiles and one's identity performance change at the click of the mouse and are perpetually being redefined. The appropriation of images from media culture, and associations with products, help complement the postmodern picture of self. As SNSs become more specialized, the identities presented on the sites are only one facet of the multiple postmodern identities that any individual possesses. For example, one can be a college student on Facebook, a musician on MySpace, and an entrepreneur on LinkedIn. Unfortunately, the identity performed on SNSs sites can be misinterpreted, with incredibly tragic results. For example, during a police raid in North Carolina, a young man named Peyton Strickland was killed by police because his Facebook profile depicted associates with guns. According to Tiemann (2007), "The police were fortified with weapons in anticipation of coming up against AR-15 firearms they had seen in the [Facebook] photograph." Although the profile photos were probably meant to identify Strickland with a "hip-hop" or "gangster" subculture, it was decoded in a significantly different manner by the authorities, underscoring the clashes in cultural meaning and performance between youth engaged in SNSs and authorities (Tiemann, 2007).

Advertisements

Both MySpace and Facebook are also littered with advertisements (Figures 1 and 2). On MySpace, even the login screen is completely cluttered by banner ads, while on Facebook the ads are surreptitiously spread out within the News Feed and side banner.

Figure 1. Facebook Login Screen

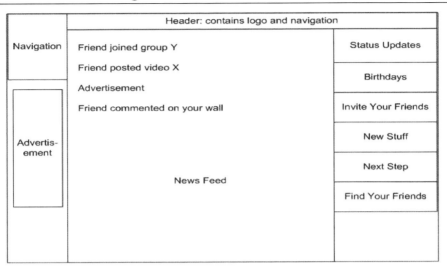

	Header: contains logo and navigation	
Navigation	Friend joined group Y	Status Updates
	Friend posted video X	Birthdays
	Advertisement	Invite Your Friends
	Friend commented on your wall	New Stuff
Advertis-ement		Next Step
	News Feed	Find Your Friends

Figure 2. MySpace Login Screen

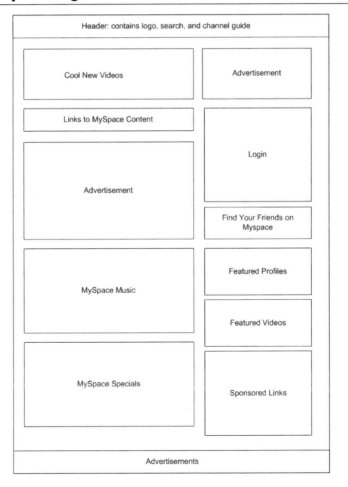

A critical reading of the ads illuminates the target audience and ideologies of SNSs. MySpace has two types of ads: featured content present on the internal site, and banners promoting outside products and companies. The internal ads encourage consumption of videos, musicians, and even other members of the site, while the external ads promote sports, upcoming movies, television shows and other content that caters to the interests of the News Corp and MySpace. A reading of the ads reveals MySpace's ideology, which centers on heterosexual, white, and affluent youth interested in traditional cultural practices such as attending sporting events, concerts, and movies. The featured videos and profiles on the login screen are mainly of young, white people, and often feature beautiful females. Additionally, the ads specifically target youth because much of the activity advertised required a significant time commitment such as constantly maintaining and personalizing profiles, discovering new bands, and viewing videos.

Facebook's interface is significantly different from MySpace's; ads take up significantly less real estate on the web page, presenting a deceptive homogenized look. The ads present on Facebook are not clearly demarcated but rather surreptitiously inserted into the main content of the site and Newsfeed, and therefore more difficult to distinguish from legitimate content.

Initially, Facebook only provided banner ads on the side of the screen, which were clearly characterized as advertisements and were targeted to specific schools or locals. If I were a student at UCLA, let's say, I would not receive advertisements meant for students at NYU. Once Facebook opened up registration and rolled out Newsfeed, they began inserting ads right into the Newsfeed. These ads are much more targeted to individuals and their respective networks because Facebook utilizes the information provided on individual's profiles to determine which ads to surface. This raises many privacy concerns, and also makes it difficult to determine Facebook's ideology, as each person only sees a specialized view of the advertising campaign. Although it is difficult to analyze Facebook's advertising campaign, many of the ads do refer back to content available on Facebook itself, further perpetuating ideologies of consumption.

In summation, consumptive practices permeate our lives and carry significant cultural meaning. The cultural meaning of goods, and their subsequent consumption, is utilized for personal identity creation and social identification. Through the personalization of profiles, consumption of ever-larger networks of friends, and advertisements, SNSs reinforce the role of consumption in identity creation. The sites are designed to incentivize individuals who engage in consumption practices because the purpose of these sites and the culture industries is to encourage and facilitate ever greater consumption.

Social Network Sites as a Contested Terrain

Aside from promoting ideologies of consumption, SNSs are uniquely suited for creating connections among people. These connections, often of the weak-tie variety (Putnam, 2001), establish wide-ranging communication channels and provide a public forum for discussion and debate not entirely unlike a Habermasian public sphere. The Internet and SNSs "make more information available to a great number of people, more easily, and from a wider array of sources, than any instrument of information and communication in history" (Kahn and Kellner, 2005).

In the last few years, SNSs have been utilized for activist and political activities. For example, in March of 2006, an estimated 14,415 high school students participated in school walkouts (Rubin and Cho, 2006), with the majority of the walkouts being advertised and coordinated on the Internet, and more specifically on MySpace. Additionally, on September 5, 2006, Facebook rolled out Newsfeed which sparked the creation of a Facebook group called the "Students Against Facebook Newsfeed (Official Petition to Facebook)," with over 13,000 people joining the group in a matter of hours. The Facebook protests were recognized and the privacy settings were quickly implemented.

According to Meikle (2002), there are three types of "Net politics" which include: "politics within the Net, politics which impacts the Net, and political uses of the Net" (p. 3). Politics within the Net refers to the social interaction in online communities, such as netiquette, flaming, spam. Politics which impacts the Net relates to "real-world politics… issues such as access, ownership and control, and censorship and regulation" (Meikle, p. 3). Political uses of the Net refer to the use of computers to effect change in the offline world. The Facebook protests can be considered politics within the Net, while protest coordination on MySpace is an example of political uses of the Net.

Meikle (2002) points out that discussion groups and messaging services such as those found on SNSs are the truly "interactive" technology because they allow anyone to take part in the creation and exchange of content and ideas. It is a space where information is not being provided by top-down organizations like the established media—where communication flows are mainly one-way—but rather opens up the "participation on a scale, and to a degree, not possible with established media" (Meikle, 2002). In theoretical terms, Jürgen Habermas coined the term "Öffentlichkeit" or "public sphere" to describe a space which is open to the public and allows debate and rational-critical exchange (Dahlberg, 2001). For Habermas, the public sphere is comprised of discourse interaction aimed at resolving political problems. Downing (2001) furthers the point by stating that "surely the essence of what is being pinpointed in the terminology of Öffentlichkeit/public sphere is information, communication, debate, media—public conversation on issues of the moment." Thus, SNSs can be conceptualized as an interactive public sphere.

The problem arises from the fact that all of the communication that takes place on SNSs is mediated through a proprietary and commercial system. The private corporations that own SNSs have control over the systems and thus can restrict, enhance, or even influence communication as they see fit. This was most aptly evidenced by the Friendster Genocide, where the company decided to remove Fakesters from their system, effectively alienating many of their users. From a critical standpoint, it is important to acknowledge that although SNSs can encourage participatory democracy, they can also extend the structures of capitalism and further hegemonic ideals (Kahn and Kellner, 2005).

Recently, Facebook and MySpace sponsored televised political debates. Additionally, they provided special areas within the sites for political action. MySpace created a new channel called "Impact"[7] where members can find news stories, videos, and blogs on a variety of political topics ranging from poverty relief to gang violence. The space also allows members to discover local volunteer opportunities. The most prominently featured aspect of the Impact page were the upcoming presidential primaries, with links to candidates' MySpace pages and the MySpace/MTV presidential video dialogs. Facebook, in conjunction with American Broadcasting Company (ABC), has created a "Politics"[8] section, which currently concentrates on the presidential primaries. The section displays the latest news from ABC, as well as news clips posted by Facebook members. It also displays the politicians supported by you or your friends, and provides debate groups that allow members to express their opinions. These questions are defined by Facebook and subsequently broadcast to your Newsfeed. The answers are then aggregated and presented on the page. Aside from the politics page, Facebook also allows politicians and supporters to create customized applications, which often provide detailed information and news on specific candidates.

As described, MySpace and Facebook have taken steps to offer specialized areas for political and democratic action. MySpace took a much broader approach to democracy than Facebook, allowing members to discuss a broad range of issues. Facebook, on the other hand, utilized the special qualities of SNSs to encourage sharing one's political views with Friends. Both SNSs have partnered with outside companies such as MTV and ABC News, providing their members a limited perspective on the issues. The featured news on the Facebook Politics page comes solely from ABC News, while the videos featured on MySpace were made in conjunction with MTV. Thus, the capitalistic nature of SNSs is exposed when the sites only serve up information provided by corporate partnerships instead of a diverse and broad range of news sources and perspectives. It is not possible to tell at this time how much control is exerted on the information exchanged within the sites, but it would not be difficult to imagine SNSs influencing members toward hegemonic ideals by featuring certain content, ideas, or perspectives, while censoring opposing or divergent views. This idea is even more frightening considering youth spend a great deal of time on the sites, and may be unduly influenced by hegemonic agendas.

Finally, SNSs are a contested terrain because they provide a unique space for connectedness and communication, while at the same time posturing to their own capitalistic interests. The "walled' nature of the sites allows for the growth of a large network, while at the same time being closing off to diverse online resources. The nature of the contested terrain is best summed up by Vaidhyanathan (2004), who states that "one side invents a device, method, algorithm, or law that moves our information ecosystem toward increased freedom of distribution and the other subsequently deploys a method to force information back into its toothpaste tube" (xii). Every time members utilize SNSs in ways which were not originally anticipated by the system designers, or companies roll out "features" that break the social norms previously established on the site, the struggle continues.

■ Conclusion

By analyzing SNSs from a critical perspective, this paper showed that even though the sites enable experimentation with postmodern identities, much of the interaction on the sites is about perpetuating consumption and capitalistic practices. From the consumption of cultural goods in identity formation, consumption of ever greater amount of Friends, to the advertising practices present on the sites, much of the interaction centers on consumptive ideals.

Additionally, although the sites facilitate connections among people and to some extent provide a public sphere, communication practices and information sources are supervised and limited by corporate entities. This chapter demonstrated that SNSs are often a contested terrain between the individuals that utilize the sites and corporations that own them. New features, changing policy practices, and featured content all work to influence the users of the sites, while perpetuating hegemonic ideologies. At the same time, members find new ways to share information, and utilize the system in unique and often unanticipated ways, going so far as lodging protests against the site itself and getting results.

It is unclear what the future holds for SNSs, and if they will continue to thrive as technology and people change. It is, however, important to continue to look at these sites from a critical perspective and illuminate the ideologies or biases that are communicated and perpetuated to millions of people worldwide.

Notes

1. http://www.myspace.com.
2. http://www.facebook.com.
3. Some other social network sites include: Orkut, popular with the Indian and Brazilian populations; Cyworld, a Koran social network site; Mixi is popular in Japan; Lunarstorm in Sweden; Hyves for Dutch; Grono in Poland; Hi5 in Latin and South America, and Bebo in the United Kingdom, New Zealand, and Australia (this list is not exhaustive).
4. Taking a cue from danah boyd, when I am talking about the Friends feature available on social network sites, I will capitalize the term.
5. For more on privacy on social network sites, see Barnes (2006).
6. See boyd and Ellison (2007) for more information on previous SNS scholarship.
7. http://impact.myspace.com.
8. http://www.facebook.com/politics/.

References

Barnes, S. (2006). A privacy paradox: Social networking in the United States. *First Monday*, 11, 9.

Baudrillard, J (1998). *The Consumer Society: Myths and Structures* . London: Sage Publications.

Bourdieu, P. (1984). *Distinction: A Social Critique of the Judgment of Taste*. Cambridge: Harvard University Press.

boyd, d. (2004). Friendster and Publicly Articulated Social Networks. *Proceedings of Conference on Human Factors and Computing Systems—CHI2004*. Vienna, Austria. New York: ACM Press.

boyd, d. (2007). Why youth (heart) social network sites: The role of networked publics in teenage social life. *MacArthur Foundation series on digital learning*. Cambridge, MA: MIT Press.

boyd, d. and Ellison, N. B. (2007). Social network sites: Definition, history, and scholarship. *Journal of Computer-Mediated Communication*, 13(1), article 11.

Cassidy, J. (2006). Me Media. *The New Yorker*, May 15.

comScore Press Release (2007). Facebook Sees Flood of New Traffic from Teenagers and Adults. Retrieved July 6, 2007 from http://www.comscore.com/press/release.asp?press=1519

Dahlberg, Lincoln. (2001, October). Computer-Mediated Communication and the Public Sphere: A Critical Analysis. *Journal of Computer Mediated Communication*, 7(1).

Donath, J., and boyd, d. (2004). Public displays of connection. *BT Technology Journal,* 22(4).

Downing, John. (2001). *Radical Media: Rebellious Communication and Social Movements.* Thousand Oaks, CA: Sage Publications.

Ellison, N., Steinfeld, C., and Lampe, C. (2007). The benefits of Facebook "friends:" Social capital and college students' use of online social network sites. *Journal of Computer-Mediated Communication,* 12(4), article 1.

Facebook Press Release. (2007). *Facebook and Microsoft Expand Strategic Alliance.* Retrieved December 25, 2007 from http://www.facebook.com/press/releases.php?p=8084

Golder, S., Wilkinson, D., and Huberman, B. (2007). "Rhythms of Social Interaction: Messaging within a Massive Online Network" *3rd International Conference on Communities and Technologies* (CT2007). East Lansing, MI. June 28–30, 2007.

Grossman, L. (2006). *Time's* Person of the Year: You. *Time.* Retrieved September 1, 2007, from http://www.time.com/time/magazine/article/0,9171,1569514,00.html

Kahn, R., and Kellner, D. (2005). Oppositional politics and the internet: A critical/ reconstructive approach. *Cultural Politics,* 1(1).

Kellner, D. (1995). *Media Culture.* New York: Routledge.

Lenhart, A., and Madden, M. (2007). Social Networking Websites and Teens: An Overview. *Pew Internet & American Life Project,* January 7.

Li, J. (2007). The Evolution of Facebook. *Adaptive Path Blog.* Retrieved September 20, 2007 from http://www.adaptivepath.com/blog/2007/09/18/the-evolution-of-a-facebook/

Liu, H. (2007). Social Network Profiles as Taste Performances. *Journal of Computer-Mediated Communication,* 13 (1), article 13.

McCracken, G. (1986). Culture and Consumption: A Theoretical Account of the Structure and Movement of the Cultural Meaning of Consumer Goods. *Journal of Consumer Research,* 13.

Meikle, Graham. (2002). *Future Active.* Annadale, Australia: Routledge.

O'Shea, W. (2003). Six Degrees of sexual frustration: Connecting the dates with Friendster.com. *Village Voice.* Retrieved September 1, 2007, from http://www.villagevoice.com/news/0323,0shea,44576,1.html.

Perkel, D. (in press). Copy and paste literacy? Literacy practices in the production of a MySpace profile. In K. Drotner, H. S. Jensen, & K. Schroeder (Eds.), *Informal Learning and Digital Media: Constructions, Contexts, Consequences.* Newcastle, UK: Cambridge Scholars Press.

Putnam, R. (2001). *Bowling Alone.* New York: Touchstone.

Rosen, C. (2007). Virtual Friendship and the New Narcissism. *The New Atlantis,* 15.

Rosmarin, R. (2006). Psst! Facebook's For Sale! *Forbes.com,* September 21. Retrieved October 3, 2007 from http://www.forbes.com/business/2006/09/21/myspace-facebook-youtube-tech-media-cx_rr_0921facebook.html.

Rubin, Joel and Cho, Cynthia. (2006, March 27). High school students extend immigration protests into 3rd day. *Los Angeles Times.*

Siklos, R. (2005). News Corp. to Acquire Owner of Myspace.com. *The New York Times,* July 18.

Schor, J. (1999). The New Politics of Consumption. *Boston Review.* Retrieved on October 28, 2007 from http://bostonreview.net/BR24.3/schor.html

Storey, J. (1999). *Cultural Consumption and Everyday Life.* New York: Arnold.

Tiemann, A. (2007). Facebook gun photos linked to fatal police shooting. *Cnet.com.* Retrieved September 1, 2007 from http://www.cnet.com/8301-13507_1-9745678-18.html.

Vaidhyanathan, S. (2004). *The Anarchist in the Library.* New York: Basic Books.

36

■ YouTube, Politics, and Pedagogy

Some Critical Reflections

Douglas Kellner and Gooyong Kim

A main goal of critical pedagogy is to facilitate simultaneously individual development and social transformation for a more egalitarian and just society. As opposed to the reproductive role of education, critical pedagogy strives for the "action of dialogical Subjects upon reality in order to transform it....[by] posing reality as a problem" (Freire, 1970, p. 168). In other words, critical pedagogy believes education to be a form of cultural politics that is fundamental to social transformation aiming to provide human agency with critical, self-directing power. With the firm belief in the "potentiality of the people," critical pedagogy equips individuals with opportunities to expose, develop and realize their potentials through "participating in the pursuit of liberation" of themselves and society at the same time (Freire, 1970, p. 169). Therefore, due to individual differences in development and abilities, genuine education is never just a matter of schooling for a certain time period. Essentially, it is a life-long process and search for self-fulfillment. As Dewey and Freire note, with critical perspectives on its role in societal as well as individual developments, education can also be a democratizing force and promote cultural revolution and social transformation.

However, education today tends to be confined to schooling, that is, getting instruction as job-training, or indoctrination into established value-systems and practices. Education in a capitalist society is a kind of voucher for politico-economic success or, at least, subsistence. Furthermore, the hidden curriculum of mass media's popular pedagogy, such as advertising and political propaganda, means that education in the United States, as a life-time process, tends to be controlled by dominant economic and political institutions. In other words, education is no longer primarily a matter of self-development, critical thought, and social progress, but is a mere matter of financial investment or ideological inculcation. Tragically, school is often no longer a live forum for liberating dialogue, but tends to be a warehouse for knowledge and skills as a matter of transmission in which "teaching for testing" becomes the norm under the banner of *No Child Left Behind*.[1] In terms of the Enlightenment project of Western civilization which promised individual freedom, social prosperity, and universal progress, an enlightened modernity has not been achieved because of education's failure to cultivate critical human agency with rationality and autonomy. Rather, schooling has promoted social conformity and striving for success in the competitive rat race.

As a main reason for the failure of the Enlightenment project, the monopoly of knowledge and the institutionalization of education have played a major role in strengthening the dominant conservative hegemony by eradicating critical consciousness, as well as by making school a crucial field for social, political, and ideological reproduction. With regard to the interconnection of power and knowledge (Foucault, 1980), schooling has become a quasi-monopoly control and dissemination of knowledge by established powers as cultural and ideological domination. Consequently, Althusser (1971) correctly identifies education as a part of the Ideological State Apparatus to produce/reproduce the dominant ruling ideology in capitalist societies.

However, the innovation of information and communication technologies (ICTs) has provided ordinary people with unprecedented opportunities to take on the dominant educational power structure and pedagogy. The uncontested monopoly of knowledge and the institutionalization of education can now be challenged by new media technologies, which make possible decentralized and interactive communication and a participatory model of culture and democracy, with multiple voices and an expanded flow of information, thus creating a new field for the conjuncture of education and democracy. In particular, dialogical two-way communication and collective "many-to-many" communication have been widely implemented with the emergence of the Internet. This technological development has amplified individual, voluntary participation in mutual education through proliferating new voices and visions, making possible the democratization of knowledge. In other words, conventional relationships between the producers and the consumers of knowledge have been productively challenged. Thus, the Internet has opened a space for individuals to realize Benjamin's (1934) belief that a "reader is at all times ready to become a writer," suggesting a new space to realize the civic engagement of a modern subject (p. 225). Consequently, individuals can become more deeply involved in the democratization of knowledge and mutual pedagogy as autonomous rational and social beings.

With regard to the potential of ICTs for reviving a more pedagogically participatory democracy, Habermas's (1989) notion of the "public sphere" is an important resource for cyber-democracy on the Internet. Grounded in an ideal of "communicative rationality," Habermas (1989) believes that individuals should strive for personal autonomy and to exchange their ideas openly and reach consensus in the "universal speech situation" of the public sphere, in which there is no domination or manipulation and the force of the better argument prevails. From this perspective, interactive and decentralized communication on the Internet can invigorate the democratic decision-making of the "public sphere." Even though Habermas's ideal of the "public sphere" is utopian without considering the "digital divide" among class, gender and race, it is still a powerful concept to examine the Internet's potential for democratization. For, in contrast to rigid notions of schooling, the Internet can provide individuals with the occasion to reclaim education as a new space for self-fulfillment and personal autonomy without any restrictions of institutional control and standardized curricula.

Yet, we must conceptualize the Internet and new media in terms of the "embeddedness in the political economy, social relations, and political environment within which they are produced, circulated, and received" for a more correct understanding about its socio/political potential as well as limitation (Kellner, 1995, p. 2). While emergent technologies provide the potential that individuals can "empower themselves in relation to dominant media and culture" (Kellner, 1995, p. 2) and can provide the oppressed with an ever more liberating forum for the counter-hegemonic politics of culture, there are also limitations that must be confronted concerning the political economy of the media and technology, their imbrications in the dominant social and political system, and the ways that media and technology generate social reproduction and can be part of an apparatus of social domination. In this chapter, we argue that new media like YouTube (hereafter, UT), combined with a transformative critical pedagogy, can help realize the Internet's potential for democratization and transformative pedagogy.

To be sure, while new media technologies allow individuals to secure unprecedented space for an alternative/counter-hegemonic politics, they also face the risks of ensnaring established social constituencies in the tentacles of the dominant culture and ideology. Emancipatory, politically progressive, and socially transformative uses of the media and technology must thus be joined with critical pedagogy to produce a viable counter-hegemonic cultural politics and pedagogy of the Internet. This requires critical insight into the important role of narrative in pedagogy. The fundamental importance of narrative in the hegemonic struggle of Internet counter-culture and critical pedagogy lies in the "discourse of plurality, difference, and multinarratives….in order to explain either the mechanics of domination or the dynamic of emancipation" (Giroux, 1992, p. 51). Giroux calls critical pedagogy to help traditionally oppressed people to acquire their voices in culture and politics as the prerequisite of developing critical human agency and a more democratic society. Therefore, by acknowledging a cultural politics of critical media pedagogy, individuals can confront the hegemonic power of domination and pursue counter-hegemonic politics of alternative pedagogy and culture. By taking over opportunities offered by the novel Internet media such as UT, individuals can organize and deploy novel strategies of self-education and social transformation.

More importantly, by providing universal points of access, the networking characteristics and the ubiquity of the new media can help the oppressed to exercise "the praxis which, as the reflection and action which truly transform reality" (Freire, 1970, p. 100). When they have an occasion and competence to address their authentic voices based on their everyday experiences of social oppression, marginalized people are likely to augment their counter-hegemonic struggle by consolidating solidarity with other social constituencies.[2] Equipped with crucial social/political consciousness and competency to make uses of the Internet, individuals can realize what Giroux (2001, p. 13) calls the "reconstruction of democratic public life." In other words, a critical media pedagogy can provide the oppressed with the revolutionary power of "praxis" by providing virtually universal points of intervention into the cultural politics of the new media. In this regard, believing that "public pedagogy represents a moral and political practice rather than merely a technical procedure" (p. 9), Giroux (2001) predicts the progressive, transformative potential of critical new media pedagogy. Giroux (2001) stresses:

> [T]he performative as a transitive act, a work in progress informed by a cultural politics that translates knowledge back into practice, places theory in the political space of the performative, and invigorates the pedagogical as a practice through which collective struggles can be waged to revive and maintain the fabric of democratic institutions. (p. 14)

From this point of view, to examine the pedagogic implications and power of UT is important because successful implementation of critical media pedagogy for social transformation requires that individuals make use of the potentially democratizing and transformative opportunities given by emergent technologies like UT. Stated differently, it is important to examine how individual UTers make use of opportunities to implement a "performative pedagogy" (Giroux, 2001, p. 7) of the new media by infusing theory and practice. On the other hand, so far, there is little academic research to investigate the transformative roles of UT in terms of its pedagogical as well as political potentials. Even though there is some research, it is essentially confined in the functionalist/instrumental paradigm to review UT's usability.[3] Consequently, this chapter will contribute to developing a critical and transformative pedagogy of new media technologies, as it examines the dialectical relationship between UT and individuals' employment of it as potential forms of critical pedagogy and democratic social transformation.

■ YouTube as the Cutting Edge of ICTs

UT has been immensely popular and influential since its inception in February 2005. *Time* magazine awarded UT the Best Invention of 2006, and Grossman (2006) describes UT's enormous impact on contemporary society:

> One year ago, this would not have been possible, but the world has changed. In the past 12 months, thousands of ordinary people have become famous. Famous people have been embarrassed...The rules are different now, and one website changed them: YouTube.

Nielsen/Net Ratings reported that users of UT grew from 7.3 million to 12.8 million by the end of July 2006. Compared to January 2006, traffic to UT almost tripled, 297% (O'Malley, 2006). According to *USA Today*, UT comprises 60% of online-served videos and 29% of market share in multimedia entertainment in the United States. There are more than 65,000 videos uploaded and 100 million videos watched daily on UT.[4]

UT has already had significant cultural, social, and political impact, beginning with producing a new form of Internet celebrity. Ordinary people can get significant attention from others in the world of the Internet and UT. For example, Geriatric1927, in his eighties, has been enjoying late-life fame as no. 6 in the "Most Subscribed Directors of All

Time" list on UT. Enjoying UT fandom, Brookers ultimately signed with a conventional mainstream medium, Carson Daly Productions, that "calls for her to help create and act in programs for television, the Internet, and portable devices" (Hardy, 2006). In terms of UT's social influences, several police departments have taken advantage of UT as a kind of press release while investigating crimes. In Massachusetts, Patrolman Brian Johnson was able to pinpoint criminal suspects through circulating a surveillance video clip on UT (Tucker, 2007).

UT's impressive popularity has created a new space for laymen to participate in traditionally restricted areas of politics. For example, Senator George Allen (R-Va) was heavily favored to win re-election to the Senate and was being touted as a 2008 Republican presidential candidate when he fell afoul of the ubiquity of digital media on the campaign trail. Baiting a young man of color who was doing oppositional video, Allen called him "macaca," the event was captured on video, put on UT, and then sent through the Internet, eventually emerging on network television. The UT footage became part of a spectacle that coded Allen as a racist and he eventually lost his re-election bid.

Furthermore, politicians have started to employ UT as a strategy to approach unde-cided and disinterested U.S. voters. Since the 2004 election, there have been studies to explore the practical viability of the Internet as a new method of political campaigning.[5] Several studies show that more than half of UTers are between thirty-five and sixty-four years old and consist of a more active voting population than other voting groups (Gueorguieva, 2007). Considering that the voting turn-out rate of the thirty-five and older population is around 70%, which is 20% more than the eighteen to twenty-four and the twenty-five to thirty-four population segments in the 2004 election (Holder, 2006), and that younger adults are more active UT users, UT's potential political impact on the 2008 election seems obvious. UT's political sites include You Choose '08, a section for potential presidential candidates, on which Hillary Clinton, Barack Obama, John Edwards, Bill Richardson, John McCain, Mitt Romney, and Rudy Giuliani signed up to have their own channels. More specifically, eight Democratic presidential candidates on July 23, 2007 and eight Republican presidential candidates on November 28, 2007 had opportunities to answer ordinary voters' questions in UT video clips hosted by CNN/UT. Even though they were preliminary and limited in terms of ordinary people's participation in the 2008 election through UT, the events substantiated the vast potential of UT's contribution to participatory democracy through individuals' deployment of the new media technologies.[6]

There was also an impressive Internet spectacle in support of Obama's presidency. Obama raised an unprecedented amount of money on the Internet; he gained over one million friends on MySpace, and mobilized youth and others through text-messaging and emails. The YouTube music video "Obama Girl," which has a young woman singing about why she supports Obama with images of his speeches interspersed, has gotten over five million hits and is one of the most seen and discussed videos in history.

In addition, grassroots campaigns for Obama illustrate the vast potential impact of UT. On behalf of Senator Obama, traditionally underrepresented youth and people of color have vigorously utilized UT and UT-style self-made videos as an innovative platform for grassroots political mobilization which contain their personal narratives and reasons they support Obama for President in order to inspire and consolidate potential Obama supporters on and offline. Among the enormous numbers of alternative media artifacts for the Obama campaign, will.I.am's *Yes, We Can* music video manifests how grassroots-initiated alternative media artifacts can mobilize individuals to support Obama as the next president.[7] This MTV style UT music video breaks with conventional ways of producing music video, as will.i.am assembled a variety of artists' grassroots participation in its production. In his words:

> I wasn't afraid to stand for "change"…it was pure inspiration…so I called my friends…and they called their friends…We made the song and video…Usually this process would take months…but we did it together in 48 hours…and instead of putting it in the hands of profit we put it in the hands of inspiration.…[8]

In addition to this avant-garde alternative media artifact made by professional musicians, there are truly grassroots-based videos made by ordinary people who have produced their own videos and narratives to support Obama, collected on the UT website.[9] There are several themes among twenty-nine self-made videos in which young people manifest their resolution to support Senator Obama for president. As a grassroots political activity, the main purpose of their production and posting is to consolidate broader popular support for Obama and to recruit undecided voters. Analyzing twenty-nine videos for Obama on the UT site, hope and dreams for a better future is the most favored reason to support Obama by eight people (27.5%). Six of the videos (20.6%) affirm that Obama is the right candidate for this time of socio-political turmoil; five (17.2%) trust Obama as the candidate who can unite people in the United States to realize the American dream. Because Senator Obama voted against the United States invasion of Iraq and helped many socially and economically marginalized people by serving community organizations, supporters express their own desire for Obama to carry on these agendas when he assumes office.

Obama is believed by his UT supporters to provide ordinary people with critical vision through which they can reflect upon their own politico-economic situation in society and realize the importance of civic/political participation. Others are moved by Obama for his ability to inspire, his possibility for being a transformative president, and his promise for carrying through significant change. The campaign validates the importance of examining how traditionally marginalized people deploy new media technologies to construct and publish their political agendas and can thus involve themselves in grassroots, participatory democracy by political agenda-setting, mobilization of supporters, and fighting for transformation of social conditions in their everyday lives.[10] In this regard, grassroots videos and campaign organizations for Obama provide highly important political as well as pedagogical implications for the future.

■ YouTube as Dialogical Learning Community

As well as practical political interventions, there have also been pedagogical discussions about UT itself via the means of self-produced videos. Based on UT's phenomenal popularity and potential, an UTer, Zakgeorge21, posted his video clip to initiate a thought-provoking discussion about the future of UT.[11] His discursive question, "Why do you tube? Why do you make a video for UT?" makes fellow UTers think over what are their motives and purposes of UTing. Further, he asked about the UT's possible effect: "What is the future of UT and how is it going to impact the world globally?" Basically, Zakgeorge21 believes that UT provides us with unique opportunities for a better future. Believing that "UT is a really cool place for serious changes to happen throughout the world," he asked UTers to discuss the desirable uses of UT for the future: "What do you think the implications of UT and what can be beneficial about it?"

It is important to examine the pedagogical values of Zakgeorge21's discursive question. First of all, the initial question substantiates the key values of critical pedagogy, that is, education as the process of problem-posing and problem-solving (Dewey, 1916; Freire, 1970; Giroux, 1992, 2001; Marcuse, 1968, 1975; Rousseau, 1764; Wollstonecraft, 1792). For Freire (1970), problem-posing pedagogy is a liberating alternative to the dehumanizing banking education in socially affirmative conventional schooling that only engages in social reproduction. Freire (1970) maintains that banking education is a hidden curriculum of dominant ideology, "for the more the oppressed can be led to adapt to that situation, the more easily they can be dominated" (p. 60).

As noted, Zakgeorge21 initiated the process of UT learning by posing questions and inviting others to engage in the mutual learning process. By posting video clips, Zakgeorge21 not only initiated dialogical learning himself by posing a discursive question about the technology which he uses, but he also induced other UTers to participate in the discursive learning process by posting their videos. Therefore, dialogues and discussion among UTers are vivid moments of learning-by-doing, learning-as-process, and learning-as-communication within the public sphere of Internet media.

Furthermore, while considering learning-by-doing presupposes an individual's own narrative as a learning process, producing video clips as a moment of realizing human agency by constructing narrative furthers transformative potential of the new media pedagogy. Further, the narrative of an individual video posting in UT elaborates the viability of the cultural politics of critical media pedagogy of learning-by-doing and establishing dialogical and pedagogical relations with others. Because it is based on the "discourse of plurality, difference, and multinarratives…in order to explain either the mechanics of domination or the dynamic of emancipation" (Giroux, 1992, p. 51), the traditionally unrepresented people can acquire their own voices in the politics of representations as the prerequisite of critical human agency for further social emancipation. While individuals are producing and posting video clips on UT, as a kind of "public pedagogy," they participate in mutually transformative pedagogy through dialogue, and can exercise the power of "performative pedagogy" for social transformation (Giroux, 2001, p. 7).

By March 5, 2007, 700,183 UTers have watched Zakgeorge21's video posting. There have been 4,062 text comments and eighty video responses since he posted his video on January 9, 2007. It is highly significant to analyze video responses of UTers because it is a dialectical learning process achieved through their active participatory communications. In other words, this discussion has provided UTers with critical moments to make meaning of their participation and reflect on their behaviors in UT, that is, moments of learning as self-reflection (Rousseau, 1764). By posting opinions on the future of UT, UTers actively involve in the pedagogic democratization through a problem-posing and problem-solving process; furthermore, they become learners-as-doers.

In this chapter, discourse analysis is used for a random sample of twenty video post-ings out of eighty video responses.[12] As discussed above, selecting the group of video postings initiated by Zakgeorge21 among many other UT video postings is justifiable in terms of its pedagogical and political potential on the Internet. Unlike other discussion forums on the Internet, video-posting and video-response are not only a unique feature of UT, but also the communicative potential of it is significant because the multi-modality of video communication presents a simulacrum of person-to-person dialogue and com-munication (Gergle, Kraut & Fussell, 2004), thus providing practical applications of "public pedagogy" and "performative pedagogy" on the Internet. Therefore, this chapter focuses on what are the UT's potential values of transformative pedagogy and how those are practically employed by UTers. Based on the arguments of classical philosophers of education,[13] this chapter critically evaluates both the pedagogical possibilities and limita-tions of UT as a form of cultural politics and its pedagogic potential for grassroots democ-racy and social transformation.

■ YouTube for Learning-by-Doing

In terms of everyday life education by both reviewing Zakgeorge21's video posting and responding to it, a UTer could experience the pedagogy of learning-by-doing motored by voluntary human agency (Dewey, 1916; Freire, 1970; Rousseau, 1764). In a two-month period, compared to the total number of 700,183 hits to Zakgeorge21's initial video post-ing, UTers who responded to it either through text comments (4,062) or video responses (80) showed highly motivated participations in the discussion. More specifically, compared to 4,062 text commenters, eighty video responders must have taken much time to think over the question, review other UTers' comments, and organize their opinions on their video postings. Furthermore, they sought to produce video clips to articulate their own ideas. Through this process of video postings as self-education, UTers thus practice the pedagogy of learning-by-doing as "performative pedagogy" that they effectively engage in everyday lives as a fundamental process of meaning-making.

Traditionally, "those under instruction are too customarily looked upon as acquiring knowledge as theoretical spectators" in conventionally socially reproductive schools, although Dewey (1916) encourages individuals to actively engage subject matters in which they are interested in everyday life for their own interests (p. 140). The Internet provides individuals today with a whole new pedagogical setting: decentralized and interactive communication, a participatory model of pedagogy, and an expanded flow of informa-tion, thus comprising a new field for the conjuncture of education and democracy. This technological development has amplified individuals' voluntary participation in mutual education through proliferating new voices and visions, making possible the democrati-zation of knowledge and learning in their daily lives. From this point of view, as opposed to rigid subject boundaries in formal education, Superangrymonkey evaluates UT's every-day life curriculum that "people can do whatever they want in UT. It is freedom; it is the closest thing to the freedom that we've got."[14] Whether they are good or bad, positive or negative, for Rousseau (1764), experiences are crucial for one to generate his or her own human potentials and life knowledge because "the Well-being of freedom makes up for many wounds" (p. 78). Therefore, LeonWestbrook appreciates UT's pedagogy of hands-on-experience and freedom for providing him with the opportunities "to express myself or trash [himself] I could not do before" for the more learner-centered pedagogy of UT.[15]

Concerning the topic of discussion, UTers are well aware that the future of UT is totally dependent upon their concrete uses of it. Stipulating individuals' active engagements, the learner-centered pedagogic value of UT, that is, learning-by-doing pedagogy, conditions the genuine potential of UT's future. A "progressive society counts individual variations as precious since it finds in them the means of its own growth" (Dewey, 1916, p. 305), UTers' varied opinions and modes of expression contribute to reviving the demo-cratic public sphere on the Internet. Owing to their active involvements in posting and responding to videos, PublicAutopsy believes that UTers are "creating a boundless com-munity where everyone can share what they feel with video and not just text."[16] The pedagogical value of learning-by-doing is clearly applied in UT; therefore, Badkid3 believes "we are the ones who make UT's future."[17] In other words, as long as UTers are posting and responding to videos discussing the future of UT, they are creating its future as they learn what is desirable or not.

The notion of learning as a lifetime process is interconnected with the pedagogic value of learning-by-doing. The real value of education as self-realization can never be confined to a classroom (Dewey, 1916; Rousseau, 1764). As long as individuals have access to the Internet and are willing to do so, the opportunities to post and watch videos are virtually unlimited. In other words, age does not restrict participation in pedagogical practices in UT. As noted, Geriatric1927, in his eighties, has been enjoying his late-life fame with no. 6 in the "Most Subscribed Directors of All Time" in UT. With learning-by-doing, Geriatric1927 engages in the life-long process of self-realization and cultivating the society. Dewey (1916) emphasizes the pedagogic value of learning as lifetime-process:

> *Life is a self-renewing process through action upon the environment...*With the renewal of physical existence goes, in the case of human beings, the re-creation of beliefs, ideals, hopes, happiness, misery and practices. The continuity of any experience, through renewing of the social group, is a literal fact. *Education, in its broadest sense, is the means of this social continuity of life* (p. 2, emphasis added).

■ YouTube for Learning as Communication

Insofar as it is part of a life-time process of self-renewal and realization, education is a continuous communication among members of society through participatory dialogue, as well as by ourselves through self-reflection. Education, as communication, simultaneously promotes individual development and a democratic society. (Dewey, 1916; Freire, 1970). For the essentially communicative nature of education, Dewey (1916) believes that "society not only continues to exist by transmission, by communication, but it may fairly to be said to exist in transmission, in communication" (p. 4). Likewise, learning as communication is a quintessential component of problem-posing pedagogy that requires dialogical communications between students and teachers where both are learning and teaching each other. In this regard, Freire (1970) further emphasizes the importance of dialogic communication among mutual-learning constituencies: "one must seek to live with others in solidarity. One cannot impose oneself, nor even merely co-exist with one's students. Solidarity [for self-learning and self-emancipation] requires true communication" (p. 63).

Through dialogical communication with others, by discussing their everyday lives and uses of technologies, individuals become active subjects of learning and their own future. Realizing the "issues of liberation and empowerment…in a mobile field of ideological and material relations" deeply embedded in run-of-the-mill things in our environments (Giroux, 1992, p. 99), individuals exercise to obtain critical human agency through communicating others in UT by posing the reality as a problem and seeking a solution by themselves. In this regard, Xanthius asserts that UTers have many opportunities to learn about different cultures by communicating with people around the world: "UT has created a milestone for so many possibilities for the Internet; in particular, context and visual abilities through saying other people throughout the world."[18] More substantially, UT's technological innovation, convergence of multimodal communications, further promotes UTers' involvement and interaction with other people for a more collective process of self-learning (Ramirez & Burgoon, 2004); therefore, it gets UTers to realize the values of learning-by-doing and to substantiate learning-as-communication at the same time. NenoBrasil accentuates UT's pedagogical contribution to real life learning through interacting with other people in the Internet: "I think the relationship will not ever be the same after UT; it is a tool that allows us to meet people all around the world to share our thought, problems, happiness, beliefs and everything."[19]

In terms of learning-as-communication, Habermas' notion of the public sphere provides UT with more solid connections between learning and democracy. Just as Dewey (1916) believes in democracy as a "mode of associated living, of conjoint communicated experience" (p. 87), Habermas (1989) stresses the importance of communicative action to reach consensus among discussion participants in public sphere. Habermas (1989) believes that individuals can achieve an expression of personal autonomy, exchange their ideas openly, and reach consensus based on "universal speech situation." Therefore, through posting video clips and exchanging their opinions, UTers practice the essential components of democracy, personal autonomy and participation. Moreover, they experience the interconnection among learning, communication and democracy.

■ YouTube for Learning Through Reflection on the Environment

As long as human beings live in a society, they are products of its influences. Marx (1845) critically assesses the dialectical relationships between human beings and their environments. As much as one's environment confines the individual, Marx states "circumstances are changed by men and that it is essential to educate the educator himself" (p. 121). Marx further demands individuals' radical intervention for learning-as-transformation: "the coincidence of the changing of circumstances and of human activity or self-change can be conceived and rationally understood only as *revolutionary practice*" (p. 121, emphasis added). Therefore, as much as one should astute the defining influence of the everyday environments, he/she has to acknowledge that human agency is the fundamental force which constructed the environmental circumstances and can transform them. It is what critical pedagogy deals with for simultaneous transformation of self and the environment.

Morrison (1970) and Wollstonecraft (1792) clearly explicate the immense influences of environments on individuals' learning and lives. Just as Althusser (1971) dissects the ubiquity of the dominant ideology's pedagogical apparatuses in everyday lives, Morrison (1970) explores how the oppressed in society are perpetually subordinated and indoctrinated by run-of-the-mill things such as the media in society:

> Adults, older girls, shops, magazines, newspapers, window sign—all the world had agreed that a blue-eyed, yellow-haired, pink-skinned doll was what every girl child treasured. "Here," they said, "this is beautiful, and if you are on this day 'worthy' you may have it." (p. 20–21)

Morrison (1970) further asserts that the oppressed are perpetually dehumanized and exploited by a mere biological marker of their body "in equating physical beauty with virtue, she stripped her mind, bound it, and collected self-contempt by the heap" (p. 122). Therefore, the hidden curriculum of banking education reproduces the dominant ideological hegemony and dehumanizes individuals to become docile objects, controlled by the established power structure.

For Wollstonecraft (1792), education for the oppressed is the very prerequisite for the re-humanization of both oppressors and the oppressed alike: "to free them from all restraint by allowing them to participate in the inherent rights of mankind…the improvement and emancipation of the whole sex" (p. 307). Emphasizing rationality as a condition for human agency, Wollstonecraft (1792) maintains that "it is the right use of reason alone which makes us independent of everything—excepting the unclouded Reason—'Whose service is perfect freedom'" (p. 235). In this regard, she advocates that "*public education,* of every denomination, should be directed to form citizens" (p. 289, emphasis added). Only through public education that everyone can participate in reciprocal pedagogy of dialogue as a basic component of constructing voluntary human agency can one realize the true value of education as the transformation of individuals and social environment at the same time.

Just as reason is a precondition for human agency (Rousseau, 1764; Wollstonecraft, 1792), a good environment is an essential condition for better education. Daily circumstances have a prescriptive power to form human developments in a given society: Dewey (1916) maintains the importance of environment which "consists of those conditions that promote or hinder, stimulate or inhibit the characteristic activities of a living being" (p. 11). However, as Marx (1845) states, although the environment exerts huge influences on individuals, it is individuals who made and can transform it (Freire, 1970; Marcuse, 1968, 1975). Considering the emancipatory use of technology for social transformation, the collective power of individuals gathered through the fundamental characteristics of the new Internet media, that is, decentralized and interactive communication, a participatory model of pedagogy, expanded flow of information, can be a good source to alter the social environment for the mutual and emancipatory pedagogy of re-humanization.

Along this vein of argument, Zakgeorge21 focuses much attention on a new learning and agency-building environment of the Internet: "Technology is the closest thing to magic so that's why we as human beings are so fascinated by it. The Internet and UT are in general really going to make a renaissance." Some of UTers highly appreciate the potential of the Internet for its emancipatory characteristics. Stating that "this is the place to be and a birthplace for something new," Superangrymonkey agrees with Zakgeorge21 concerning the transformative potential of UT's technological innovation. However, what matters most is the way individuals use technology within specific contexts because different uses of it render totally different effects of the technology (Salter, 2004). Thus, there needs to be concrete pedagogical interventions to provide ordinary people with moments to consider the vast potential of the Internet media for their cultural/social/political empowerment.

In terms of the forms of UT use, UTers utilize the technology to make use of the pedagogical potential of ICTs for its discussion forum. UTers raise generative questions about the values and potential of UT as problem-posing pedagogy[20] and facilitate interactive communications to share their ideas as learning-as-communication. From this point of view, PublicAutopsy clearly explicates the pedagogic value of UT as a learning community: UT has "already revolutionized the Internet by breaking down any border of face or religion we would have between each other. UT is creating a borderless community where everyone can share what they feel with video, not just text."[21]

■ YouTube for Learning as Self-fulfillment and Empowerment

As long as the aim of education is to bring forth individuals' many-sided potential, self-directed human agency can become a key goal for education. Further, human agency is a requirement for realizing education as a self-renewing and self-realizing process over time through continual communication with others and democratic transformation of one's environment. For Dewey, Freire, and progressive educators, education aims to achieve self-fulfillment and empowerment, as well as democratic transformation. For Dewey (1916), the main goal of public education is to achieve human agency for individuals to pursue their own interests and create a better society:

> [M]eans of transformation. The desired transformation is not difficult to define in a formal way. It signifies a society in which every person shall be occupied in something which makes the lives of others better worth living, and which accordingly makes the ties which bind persons together more perceptible—which breaks down the barriers of distance between them (p. 316).

Therefore, truly critical human agency can be obtained when individuals revolutionize their socio-political conditions by breaking through the relations of oppression (Freire, 1970). The critical process of becoming-a-subject within public education requires that individuals recognize oppressive conditions. Freire (1970) believes, as the oppressed become fully human subjects, they begin to realize their human and social potential:

> as he [sic!] breaks his "adhesion" and objectifies the reality from which he starts to emerge, he begins to integrate himself as a Subject (an *I*) confronting an object (reality). At this moment, sundering the false unity of his divided self, he becomes a true individual. (p. 174)

If a society hinders individuals from obtaining voluntary and critical human agency, it dehumanizes individuals by perpetuating a dehumanizing environment. Thus, for Freire, becoming a true subject requires and coincides with the radical transformation of society to break through the vicious circle of dehumanization and social oppression.

Considering the relationships between individuals and their learning environments, UT provides individuals with vast opportunities to form a transformative and creative learning community. In terms of Giroux (2001)'s emphasis on "performative pedagogy" (p. 7), as with Dewey's pragmatic approach to combine theory and practice, UTers can become not only theoreticians but also practitioners of the transformative pedagogy of UT. Superangrymonkey confirms the performative/pragmatic pedagogy of UT to realize human agency: "I YouTube because I want to see some proactive change and I want to be a part of it." Actually, Zakgeorge21's initial question is his attempt to achieve agency and gives UTers opportunities to obtain theirs in forming UT as their learning community by questioning and answering each other. Sabrnig confirms this point: "I want to be around people who think and share ideas while we talk. I want to be a part of using technology to make a better world."[22]

As for its accessibility and impact, the Internet/ UT can be more beneficial for the oppressed in society. Compared to the established restrictions on public self-expression in society, the oppressed become entitled to unprecedented opportunities of media access with the Internet and new forms like UT. With the universal access to the Internet as an emerging form of cultural politics, the oppressed can employ UT as a tool for proactive social changes. Therefore, focusing on "the question of social change and how people on the margins take up and use the Internet," Mehra, Merkel and Bishop (2004) substantiate how the Internet empowers the oppressed in society (p. 782). For example, sexual minorities use the Internet for constructing "positive development in their 'queer' identities" and "political empowerment via the establishment of a political agenda" (Mehra, Merkel & Bishop, 2004, p. 789).

Consequently, the Internet has opened a space for individuals to realize Benjamin's (1934) belief that readers can be writers and active producers of their culture. Individuals obtain agencies to become involved in the democratization of knowledge and pursue the transformative pedagogy of everyday lives on the Internet. Ultimately, through implementing the emancipatory potential of critical human agency, individuals become more able to secure reliable resources to revolutionize the oppressive power structure of society.

■ YouTube for Learning for Agency and Social Change

With the decentralized technological structure of the Internet, individuals have obtained a much broader space to participate in the discursive public sphere. UTers have exhibited the pedagogical power of learning-by-doing, learning-as-communication, and learning for self-fulfillment. From this point of view, the dialectic pedagogy of UTers' discussion forum can be the "vantage-point of a broader understanding of local agency" (Ridell, 2002, p. 163). In other words, UTers can actively participate in a "space of interaction" for "actual issues in actual places" and "alternative views of the lived environment" (p. 162). Superangrymonkey confirms UT's potential to realize critical human agency: "I YouTube because I want to see some proactive change and I want to be a part of it."

In view of the huge influences of education on individuals and its role of reinforcing the dominant ideology in society (Althusser, 1971), to achieve a real condition for emancipatory and democratic education means to transform everyday life and struggle against oppression (Freire, 1970; Marcuse, 1968; 1975). For Dewey (1916), the essence of education is positive transformation:

- *Knowledge is humanistic in quality* not because it is about human products in the past, but because of *what it does in liberating human intelligence and human sympathy.* Any subject matter which accomplishes this result is humane, and any subject matter which does not accomplish it is not even educational. (1916, p. 230, emphasis added)

- Criticizing the reproductive role of education in an inegalitarian capitalist society, Marcuse (1968) stresses the importance of education for human emancipation from exploitative social relations.[23] Such transformative education means that educational practice is not value-neutral or merely technical, but rather is a highly ethical engagement for political justice and transformation. In the Marcusean vision, individuals have to implement the "application of knowledge to the improvement of the human condition" and the "liberation of the mind, and of the body, from aggressive and repressive needs."

Therefore, individuals' concrete forms of UT use are important because the actual effects of it depend on their specific practices and goals. Rather than technological characteristics of UT, its practical application with specific socio-political intents renders actual value realization of UT. Admitting emancipatory uses of media technology, Freire (1970) also problematizes the effects of its concrete uses: "It is not the media themselves which I criticize, but the way they are used" (p. 136). Therefore, it is highly significant to argue the more emancipatory uses of the new Internet media for the sake of social transformation. In this regard, the Zapatista National Liberation Army (EZLN) shows how the emancipatory uses of the Internet technology are critically important for the success of revolutionary movements (Knudson, 1998).

The global demonstration in February 2003 against the U.S. invasion of Iraq clearly exemplifies the revolutionary power of individuals' transformative uses of the Internet (Hands, 2006; Kahn & Kellner, 2005a). Strategic employments of the Internet to organize the global-scale anti-war protests catalyze David Held's (1995) "double democratization," that is, "the democratization and restructuring of both civil society and the state in order to ensure active citizens and a containment of the power of global capital" (Hands, 2006, p. 236). In other words, individuals' emancipatory uses of technology can result in achieving critical agency and the transformation of a society as a learning environment. Kahn and Kellner (2005a) summarize the vast potential of the liberating uses of the Internet: "the new ICTs are revolutionary and constitute a dramatic transformation of everyday life in the direction of more participatory and democratic potentials" (p. 94).

However, the majority of discussion participants in UT forums are not aware of UT's liberating potential for social change. Though Zakgeorge21 and Superangrymonkey anticipate "serious changes" and "some proactive change" through uses of UT respectively, many other UTers seem to be satisfied to use UT as a pedagogical form of learning-by-doing, learning-as-communication or personal entertainment. As Jessebearwear articulates:

> UT is going to change, but it is not going to change the world. UT is an excellent and great place to watch videos, but it is not a place to try to change the world. UT is not going to change the political aspect or social aspect of the world.[24]

Even though UT could make some proactive changes, Retardedfolks does not believe that "it is going to change really anything, anytime soon, anything drastically."[25]

In general, UT seems to serve the liberal individualist's perspective on self-expression and education as pursuing personal needs. Based on the notion of an individual as "rational, autonomous subject who knows and can express their own best interests," Dahlberg (2001) describes the pedagogic characteristics of the prevalent uses of the Internet as "maximum information is available for private individuals to make their best possible strategic choices between competing positions" (p. 160). In other words, the pedagogic value of the Internet "means that consumers are at liberty to freely move around cyberspace and make the choices they desire without restriction found in 'real' space" (p. 163). It seems that the pedagogic uses of UT are confined within the paradigm of functionalist/instrumental rationality as the dominant ideology of a liberal/individualist society. For instance, NenoBrasil notes that being in UT means enjoying freedom: "in here we are free to watch whatever we want because there are millions of videos to watch." Sometimes, UTers enjoy other free benefits: "It is a good fun to promote my web-site for free advertising" (Nickyp0031).[26] Indeed, a causal perusal of UT reveals that much of its content expresses narcissism, rampant materialism and consumerism, and other values of the dominant capitalist society.

However, to be sure, there have been the positive pedagogical instances we have stressed, as well as concrete political effects. A telling example of how new digital technologies of everyday life are transforming contemporary U.S. politics comes from the role of UT in the debates on the U.S. invasion of Iraq. On September 1, 2007, CBS News had a report on vigorous debate over Iraq with postings getting as many as 350,000 hits. Focusing on a sixteen-year-old anti-Bush and anti-Iraq protester from a small town in New Jersey and a pro-war soldier, the segment demonstrated how ordinary people could participate in contemporary political dialogue via UT and its potential for democratization.[27]

The future of UT is open to a variety of uses and is a contested terrain like other forms of media and culture in the established society. It is up to educators and individuals to establish pedagogically and politically responsible and progressive uses of UT. In this chapter we have revealed the ways that certain practices of UT overlap with critical pedagogy, but we fear, without specific pedagogical or political goals, UT could end up a mere part of the fun-house of consumer capitalism. In conclusion, we will sum up the potential and limitations of UT, suggesting positive pedagogical and political uses but also dangers.

■ YouTube's Pedagogical Perspectives: Potential and Limitations

Ultimately, UT requires individuals' critical consciousness and active political engagement to use it pedagogically and politically. As much as the technological innovation of UT provides potentially progressive pedagogical opportunities, individual UTers' actual uses of the technology will eventually determine its practical possibilities for transformative pedagogy and social transformation. In this chapter, we have argued that UTers' progressive uses of the Internet technology substantiate the essential values of critical pedagogy, including learning-as-doing, learning-as-communication, learning-for-agency and learning-for-social transformation. Yet, without a clear critical pedagogical vision, UT could easily become a mere toy of the privileged and instrument of individual pleasure and expression.

As a communicative medium, UT is a potential exemplar of the Deweyan pedagogy of learning as communication. For Freire, the revolutionary potential of liberating communications of the oppressed can be facilitated by the ubiquitous presence of the Internet. UT could be a cradle to a critical communicative pedagogy in a multi-mediated society. For Rousseau and Wollstonecraft, education is to raise individuals' rationality to realize autonomous human agency. Posting and responding to videos in UT are fundamentally self-realizing activities of UTers because they invest their time and energy in thinking over topics, organizing ideas and producing videos. Through the video production process, UTers practice a crucial pedagogy of critical human agency, becoming a subject in Freire's sense. The oppressed traditionally are deprived of the means of expressing themselves, and self-expression on UT is consistent with the emphasis in Wollstonecraft, Toni Morrison, and Freire for self-empowerment of the oppressed.

Hence, in the society of multi-mediated and media culture, UT can provide individuals with significant opportunities to intervene in media cultural politics. However, some of the defining problems and limitations of the Internet extend to UT. The digital divide is one of the most lingering obstacles to realizing a truly transformative pedagogy of the new media.[28] Of the UT eighty-one video postings examined in the study above that analyzed how UTubers present and understand their work, seventy-seven were created and posted by whites, with only four were by non-whites. Sixty-five postings were produced by men while sixteen were by women. All the postings were in English. In short, the UT discussion forum is dominated by white-male-English-speaking users. Of course, concerning the matter of access to the Internet, it is disproportionately occupied by the dominant class in society. From this point of view, Cammaerts and Audenhove (2005) stress that "online engagement in forums is cyclical, tends to be dominated by those already politically active in the offline world and functions within a homogeneous ideological framework" (p. 193). Therefore, "the Internet reflects rather than circumvents offline power structures and relations" (Russell, 2005, p. 515).

Considering that a democratic and pedagogical public sphere can only exist without any forms of outside control, a UT takeover by major corporations is one of the most serious challenges to the potential of UT for democracy. Robins and Webster (1999) stress that a corporation's takeover of Internet sites entails "the intrusion of market and commodity relations into the public sphere, and this results in the transformation of reasoning into consumption" (p. 104). The corporate takeover of UT by Google might undermine the potential to use it as an example of Giroux's "performative pedagogy" for social transformation (2001) if its "political debate has come to be regulated by large corporate bodies" (Robins & Webster, 1999, p. 104). In this regard, Retardedfolks warns against encroachments such as censorship by Google.com as the owner of UT.

Already advertising is beginning to appear on UT,[29] and there are dangers of increasing commercialization and the expansion of a consumer and business culture, as well as possibilities of censorship and control. To protect individuals' open access to the Internet and potential for transformative pedagogy, Blumler and Gurevitch (2001) assert that "firm anti-discriminatory access policies are needed, perhaps requiring the segregation of the provision of content from the distribution channel" (p. 8). Furthermore, Blumler and Gurevitch (2001) propose "creating an authority with responsibilities for arranging, publicizing, moderating and reporting on the outcomes of a wide range of exercises in electronic democracy" (p. 9).

It is also up to individuals and groups committed to the use of emergent technologies for critical pedagogy and social transformation to develop new strategies of education and communication. Much UT production does not meet Habermas's strict criteria for rational communicative action in the public sphere (1989) due to deficits in rationality, reasoned debate, and unforced consensus. Many UT products, by contrast, exhibit silliness, narcissism, or worse. Critical pedagogical and socially transformative uses of UT and other new technologies thus require clear educational and progressive vision of social transformation.

Consequently, it is highly important and timely to examine both the potentials and the limitations of the new forms of Internet pedagogical practices. There should be extensive pedagogical endeavors to examine critically as well as incorporate the new media technologies in general education settings.[30] The new media have opened unprecedented space for individuals to exercise a performative/critical media pedagogy for self-realization and social-transformation. In terms of education as a bringing forth of individuals' many-sided potential, UT gives individuals moments of self-expression, personal empowerment, and transformative agency. In terms of education as an enlightenment project, UT provides an opportunity to exhibit the values of personal autonomy, virtuous citizenship, political participation and social justice in our everyday lives. Depending upon the form of its use and how a performative/critical pedagogy of the new media is implemented, UT can be either a reservoir of true enlightenment, or another play-pen in the capitalist fun house. Ultimately, for public educators it is highly important to develop new critical media pedagogies that will help enable students to become active subjects of emerging media technology, and for students and citizens to use new media for progressive pedagogical and political goals as well as self-expression and entertainment.

Notes

1. For critical analyses of the *No Child Left Behind* program, see Meier, D. and G. Wood (2004, eds). *Many Children Left Behind: How the* No Child Left Behind Act *Is Damaging Our Children and Our Schools.* Boston, MA: Beacon Press

2. For the Internet's potential as a social movement mobilizer, see, Bennett, W. L. (2003). Communicating Global Activism: Strengths and Vulnerabilities of Networked Politics, *Information, Communication & Society 6,* 143–68, and Kahn and Kellner (2005a).

3. For political uses of UT in the 2006 election, see, Gueorguieva, V. (2007). Voters, MySpace, and YouTube: The Impact of Alternative Communication Channels on the 2006 Election Cycle and Beyond. *Social Science Computer Review,* 1–13. For its pedagogical implications, see, Trier, J. (2007). "Cool" engagements with YouTube: Part 2. *Journal of Adolescent & Adult Literacy, 50/7,* 598–603.

4. http://www.usatoday.com/tech/news/2006-07-16-youtube-views_x.htm.

5. See, Trippi, J. (2004). *The Revolution Will Not Be Televised: Democracy, the Internet, and the Overthrow of Everything.* New York: Regan Books, and Gillmor, D. (2006). *We the Media: Grassroots Journalism by the People, for the People.* Sebastopol, CA: O'Reilly Media.

6. For more detailed transcript of the CNN/UT democratic presidential debate, see http://www.cnn.com/2007/POLITICS/07/23/debate.transcript/index.html, and http://www.cnn.com/2007/POLITICS/11/28/debate.transcript/.

7. See, http://www.dipdive.com/archives/212.

8. See, http://www.hopeactchange.com/creators/song.

9. See, http://www.dipdive.com/dip-politics/ywc/ (video #2 to 30). The following analysis was done by Gooyong Kim in summer 2008.

10. See, http://www.dipdive.com/dip-politics/ywc/ (video #2 to 30).

11. See, http://www.youtube.com/watch?v=z7JgtjeIsuY.

12. This research was undertaken by Gooyong Kim in 2007.

13. The classical philosophers of education drawn on in this chapter were the topic of Douglas Kellner's Philosophy of Education seminar at UCLA; see the web-site at http://www.gseis.ucla.edu/courses/ed206a/edphil.htm.

14. See, http://www.youtube.com/watch?v=jrH5VqOYsM8&mode=related&search.

15. See, http://www.youtube.com/watch?v=CtRVbcf4CDI.

16. See, http://www.youtube.com/watch?v=EC2A1HqPjZU.

17. See, http://www.youtube.com/watch?v=3flFRNGqY28.

18. See, http://www.youtube.com/watch?v=15053Q1L4dQ&mode=related&search.

19. See, http://www.youtube.com/watch?v=z1YHCDnuiG8.

20. For Freire, education should pose what he calls "generative questions" which "is to investigate people's thinking about reality and people's action upon reality, which is their praxis.…The more active an attitude men and women take in regard to the exploration of their thematics, the more they deepen their critical awareness of reality and, in spelling out these thematics, take possession of that reality" (p. 106). Furthermore, Freire believes that "generative questions" and liberating education are the different sides of the same coin because "every thematic investigation which deepens historical awareness is thus really educational, while all authentic educational investigates thinking.…Education and thematic investigation, in the problem-posing concept of education, are simply different moments of the same process" (p. 109).

21. See, http://www.youtube.com/watch?v=CtRVbcf4CDI.

22. See, http://www.youtube.com/watch?v=_fljRPrCYf0.

23. On Marcuse's contributions to education, see Kellner, D., T. Lewis and C. Pierce (2006). Introduction: Marcuse's Challenges to Education. *Policy Futures in Education,* 4/1 and a collection of papers on Marcuse and education at http://www.wwwords.co.uk/pfie/content/pdfs/4/issue4_1.asp.

24. See, http://www.youtube.com/watch?v=ddmieEpwDqU.

25. See, http://www.youtube.com/watch?v=2zWtSVQct9k&mode=related&search.

26. See, http://www.youtube.com/watch?v=KV2e9u-an20.

27. http://www.cbsnews.com/stories/2007/09/01/eveningnews/main3227641.shtml.

28. On the digital divide, see http://www.ntia.doc.gov/ntiahome/net2/falling.html, http://www.media.uio.no/prosjekter/ctp/papers/IAMCR-CTP04_S2–2_Lizie.pdf.

29. See Chmielewski, D. C. and J. Guynn (2007, Aug. 24). Google tests ads in YouTube videos. *Los Angeles Times,* C1 and C8.

30. On the necessity of critical technoliteracies, see Kahn & Kellner (2005b). On the necessity of incorporating critical media literacy curricular in K-12 school, see Kellner, D. and J. Share (2007). Critical Media Literacy: Crucial policy choices for a twenty-first-century democracy. *Policy Futures in Education, 5/1,* 59–69.

References

Althusser, L. (1971). Ideology and Ideological State Apparatus. *Lenin and Philosophy and Other Essays.* London: New Left Books.

Badkid3 (Jan., 11, 2007).). Re: "We" Tube: The Future of Youtube. http://www.youtube.com/watch?v=3flFRNGqY28. (Retrieved on Mar. 5, 2007).

Benjamin, W. (1934). Reflection. In Demetz, P. (Ed.), (1978), *Reflections, essays, aphorisms, autobiographical writings.* New York: Harcourt.

Blumler, J. and M. Gurevitch (2001). The New Media and Our Political Communication Discontents: Democratizing Cyberspace. *Information, Communication & Society, 4,* 1–13.

Cammaerts, B. and L. Audenhove (2005). Online Political Debate, Unbounded Citizenship, and the Problematic Nature of a Transnational Public Sphere. *Political Communication, 22,* 179–96.

Dahlberg, L. (2001). Democracy via Cyberspace. *New Media & Society, 3,* 157–177.

Dewey, J. (1916). *Democracy and Education: An Introduction to the Philosophy of Education.* New York: The Free Press.

Foucault, M. (1980). *Power/knowledge: Selected interviews and other writings.* C. Gordon (Ed.) New York: Pantheon.

Freire, P. (1970/ 2006). *Pedagogy of the Oppressed: 30ᵗʰ Anniversary Edition.* New York: Continuum.

Gergle, D., R. Kraut and S. Fussell (2004). Language Efficiency and Visual Technology: Minimizing Collaborative Effort with Visual Information. *Journal of Language and Social Psychology, 23,* 491–517.

Giroux, H. (1992). *Border crossings: Cultural workers and the politics of education.* New York: Routledge

————(2001). Cultural Studies as Performative Politics. *Cultural Studies, Critical Methodologies, 1,* 5–23.

Grossman, L. (Nov. 2006). Best Invention of 2006. *Time.* http://www.time.com/time/2006/techguide/ bestinventions/inventions/youtube.html (Retrieved on Mar. 5, 2007).

Gueorguieva, V. (2007). Voters, MySpace, and YouTube: The Impact of Alternative Communication Channels on the 2006 Election Cycle and Beyond. *Social Science Computer Review,* 1–13.

Habermas, J. (1989). *The Structural Transformation of the Public Sphere: An Inquiry into a Category of Bourgeois Society.* Cambridge: MIT Press.

Hands, J. (2006). Civil Society, Cosmopolitics and the Net: The Legacy of 15 February 2003. *Information, Communication & Society, 9,* 225–243.

Hardy, M. (June 27, 2006). The self-made star: A camcorder, a computer, and a goofy streak were all she needed to launch a career in show biz. *The Boston Globe.* http://www.boston.com/ae/movies/ articles/2006/06/27/the_self_made_star/?page=1 (Retrieved on Mar. 5, 2007).

Held, D. (1995). *Democracy and global order.* Cambridge, MA: Polity Press.

Holder, K. (2006). Voting and registration in the election of November 2004. *US Census Bureau.* URL: http://www.census.gov/prod/2006pubs/p20–556.pdf (Retrieved on August 9, 2007).

Jessebearwear (Jan. 13, 2007). Re: "We" Tube: The Future of Youtube. http://www.youtube.com/ watch?v=ddmieEpwDqU. (Retrieved on Mar. 5, 2007).

Kahn, R. and D. Kellner (2005a). Oppositional Politics and the Internet: A Critical/ Reconstructive Approach. *Cultural Politics, 1,* 75–100.

———— (2005b). Reconstructing Technoliteracy: A Multiple Literacy Approach. *E-Learning, 2/3,* 238–51.

Kellner, D. (1995). *Media culture: Cultural studies, identity and politics between the modern and the postmodern.* New York: Routledge.

Knudson, J. (1998). Rebellion in Chiapas: Insurrection by Internet and Public Relations. *Media, Culture & Society, 20,* 507–518.

LeonWestbrook (Jan., 13, 2007). Re: "We" Tube: The Future of Youtube. http://www.youtube.com/ watch?v=CtRVbcf4CDI (Retrieved on Mar. 5, 2007).

Marcuse, H. (1968). *A Lecture on Education in Brooklyn College.* Unpublished manuscript.

————. (1975). *A Lecture on Education in University of California, Berkeley.* Unpublished manuscript.

Marx, K. (1845/ 1970). Theses on Feuerbach. *The German Ideology.* C. J. Arthur (ed). International Publishers.

Mehra, B., C. Merkel, and A. Bishop (2004). The Internet for Empowerment of Minority and Marginalized Users. *New Media & Society, 6,* 781–802.

Morrison, T. (1970/ 1993). *The Bluest Eye*. New York: A Plume Book.

NenoBrasil (Jan. 12, 2007). Re: "We" Tube: The Future of Youtube. http://www.youtube.com/watch?v=z1YHCDnuiG8 (Retrieved on Mar. 5, 2007).

Nickyp0031 (Jan. 14, 2007). Re: "We" Tube: The Future of Youtube. http://www.youtube.com/watch?v=KV2e9u-an20 (Retrieved on Mar. 5, 2007).

O'Malley, G. (Jul. 21, 2006). YouTube Is the Fastest Growing Website: Traffic Grew Threefold Since January. *Advertsing Age*. http://adage.com/abstract.php?article_id=110632 (Retrieved on Mar. 5, 2007).

PublicAutopsy (Jan. 23, 2007). Re: "We" Tube: The Future of Youtube. http://www.youtube.com/watch?v=EC2A1HqPjZU (Retrieved on Mar. 5, 2007).

Ramirez, A. and J. Burgoon (2004). The Effects of Interactivity on Initial Interactions: The Influence of Information Valence and Modality and Information Richness on Computer-Mediated Interaction. *Communication Monograph, 71,* 422–447.

Retardedfolks (Jan. 11, 2007). Jan., 11, 2007). Re: "We" Tube: The Future of Youtube. http://www.youtube.com/watch?v=2zWtSVQct9k&mode=related&search. (Retrieved on Mar. 5, 2007).

Ridell, S. (2002). The Web as a Space for Local Agency. *Communications, 27,* 147–169.

Robins, K. and F. Webster (1999). *Times of the Technoculture: From the Information Society to the Virtual Life*. New York: Routledge.

Rousseau, J. (1764/ 1979). *Emile or On Education*. Basic Books.

Russell, A. (2005). Editorial: Exploring Digital Resistance. *New Media & Society, 7,* 513–15.

Sabrnig (Feb., 3, 2007). Re: "We" Tube: The Future of Youtube. http://www.youtube.com/watch?v=_fljRPrCYf0 (Retrieved on Mar. 5, 2007).

Salter, L. (2004). Structure and Forms of Use: A Contribution to Understanding the 'Effects' of the Internet on Deliberative Democracy. *Information, Communication & Society, 7,* 185–206.

Superangrymonkey (Jan. 11, 2007). Re: "We" Tube: The Future of Youtube. http://www.youtube.com/watch?v=jrH5VqOYsM8&mode=related&search (Retrieved on Mar. 5, 2007).

Tucker, E. (Mar. 5, 2007). Police departments deputize YouTube. *USA Today.* http://www.usatoday.com/tech/news/surveillance/2007–03–04-you-tube-crime_N.htm?csp=34 (Retrieved on Mar. 5, 2007).

USA Today (July 16, 2006). YouTube serves up 100 million videos a day online. http://www.usatoday.com/tech/news/2006–07–16-youtube-views_x.htm. (Retrieved on Mar. 5, 2007).

Wollstonecraft, M. (1792/ 1998). *A Vindication of the Rights of Men* and *A Vindication of the Rights of Woman*. Köln, Germany: Konemann.

Xanthius (Jan. 11, 2007). "We" Tube: The Future of Youtube. http://www.youtube.com/watch?v=15053Q1L4dQ&mode=related&search (Retrieved on Mar. 5, 2007).

Zakgeorge21 (Jan. 9, 2007). "We" Tube: The Future of Youtube. http://www.youtube.com/watch?v=z7JgtjeIsuY (Retrieved on Mar. 5, 2007).

■ Contributors

Richard Beach is Professor of English Education at the University of Minnesota. He is author or co-author of 18 books, including *Teaching Writing Using Blogs, Wikis, and Other Digital Tools; Teaching Literature to Adolescents; Teachingmedialiteracy.com: A Web-based Guide to Links and Activities;* and *High School Students' Competing Social Worlds: Negotiating Identities and Allegiances through Responding to Multicultural Literature.* He is also the organizing editor for the annual *Annotated Bibliography of Research for Research in the Teaching of English* and a member of the NCTE Commission on Media. He can be reached at rbeach@umn.edu

Carl Boggs is professor of social sciences at National University, Los Angeles. He has taught at Washington University in St. Louis, UCLA, USC, and Carleton University in Ottawa. His most recent books include *Imperial Delusions* (Rowman and Littlefield, 2005), *The Hollywood War Machine,* with Tom Pollard (Paradigm, 2007), and *The Crimes of Empire* (Pluto, 2009). He is recipient of the Charles A. McCoy Career Achievement Award from the American Political Science Association (2006).

John T. Caldwell is Professor of Cinema and Media Studies at UCLA, author of the books *Televisuality: Style, Crisis, and Authority in American Television* (Rutgers UP), *Production Culture, Industrial Reflexivity and Critical Practice in Film and Television* (Duke UP), and co-editor with Vicki Mayer and Miranda Banks of *Production Studies* (Routledge, 2009). He is also the producer/director of the award-winning films *Freak Street to Goa: Immigrants on the Rajpath* (1989), and *Rancho California (por favor)* (2002).

Meenakshi Gigi Durham is associate professor of journalism and mass communication at the University of Iowa. Her research centers on critical and cultural studies of the media, with a particular emphasis on feminist analysis. Her research has been published extensively in leading academic journals, and her books include *The Lolita Effect* and *Media and Cultural Studies: KeyWorks* (edited with Douglas M. Kellner).

Henry A. Giroux currently holds the Global TV Network Chair Professorship at McMaster University in the English and Cultural Studies Department. His most recent books include *The University in Chains: Confronting the Military-Industrial-Academic Complex,* (2007) *Against Terror of Neoliberalism* (2008), and *Youth in a Suspect Society: Democracy or Disposability?.* His primary research areas are: cultural studies, youth studies, critical pedagogy, popular culture, media studies, social theory, and the politics of higher and public education.

Larry Gross, Professor and Director, USC Annenberg School for Communication, is author of *Up From Invisibility: Lesbians and Gay Men and the Media in America* and *Contested Closets: The Politics and Ethics of Outing,* co-editor of *Image Ethics, Image Ethics in the Digital Age, The Columbia Reader on Lesbians and Gay Men in Media, Society and Politics,* and editor of the *International Journal of Communication.*

Lawrence Grossberg is an internationally renowned scholar of cultural studies and popular culture whose work focuses on popular music and the politics of youth in the United States. He is also widely known for his research in the philosophy of communication and culture. He has not only published books, such as *It's a Sin: Essays on Postmodernism, Politics and Culture* (1988), *We Gotta Get out Of This Place: Popular Conservatism and Postmodern Culture* (1992), *Dancing in Spite of Myself: Essays in Popular Culture* (1997) and *Caught in the Crossfire: Kids, Politics and America's Future* (2005), but also over one hundred articles and essays. Grossberg is co-editor (with Della Pollock) of the journal *Cultural Studies,* which is one of the longest-running and most respected academic journals in its field. He has served in that capacity since 1990. He also serves on the editorial collective of *Public Culture* among many other academic journals.

Rhonda Hammer is a Lecturer at UCLA and teaches undergraduate and graduate courses in Women's Studies; Education; Film, Television and Digital Media; and Communications. As one of the growing legions of part-time instructors, who teach the majority of undergraduate courses in many universities, she is best described as a transdisciplinary scholar. Rhonda is also a Research Scholar at the UCLA Center for the Study of Women and has co-authored *Rethinking Media Literacy* and is the author of *Anti-Feminism and Family Terrorism: A Critical Feminist Perspective,* as well as a number of articles and chapters on feminisms, globalization, media, and critical cultural studies. Her experiences in grassroots video production from the 1970s into the early 1990s has informed much of her teaching and research, and some of her courses include critical and practical media literacy, primarily in the form of student-produced short oppositional video documentaries or web sites. She firmly believes in the significance of the dialectic of theory and praxis in pedagogy, writing, and everyday life.

Myrna A. Hant is a visiting scholar at the UCLA Center for the Study of Women and teaches in the Osler Program at UCLA. Her research focus is on popular culture and the politics of representation with an emphasis on ageism, gender, race, ethnicity and class in media. Her publications include articles and chapters on portrayals of mothers on popular television programs such as *Bewitched, All in the Family, The Sopranos* and *Curb Your Enthusiasm.* Mryna is also the Chair of the Board of P.A.T.H., People Assisting the Homeless, a nationally recognized organization which has instituted innovative approaches to working with the homeless.

Felicia D. Henderson is a doctoral candidate in Cinema and Media Studies in the UCLA School of Theater, Film and Television. She was the co-executive producer on *Everybody Hates Chris, Gossip Girl, and Fringe.* Her research interests include the history of race and gender in the television comedy writers room and the relationship between new media and prime-time television authorship. She is co-creator of *Soul Food* and has worked as writer and producer in TV series such as *Gossip Girl* and *Fringe.*

Edward S. Herman is a Professor Emeritus of Finance at the Wharton School, University of Pennsylvania. He has written extensively on economics, political economy, foreign policy, and media analysis. Among his books are *The Political Economy of Human Rights* (2 vols, with Noam Chomsky, South End Press, 1979); *Corporate Control, Corporate Power* (Cambridge University Press, 1981); *The "Terrorism" Industry* (with Gerry O'Sullivan, Pantheon, 1990); *The Myth of the Liberal Media: An Edward Herman Reader* (Peter Lang, 1999); and *Manufacturing Consent* (with Noam Chomsky, Pantheon, 1988 and 2002). In addition to his regular "Fog Watch" column in *Z Magazine*, he edits a web site, inkywatch.org, that monitors the *Philadelphia Inquirer.*

Sut Jhally is a Professor of Communication at the University of Massachusetts-Amherst and a cultural studies scholar in the area of advertising, media, and consumption. He is the producer of several documentaries on media literacy topics and the founder and executive director of the *Media Education Foundation,* a non-profit established in 1992 which "produces and distributes video documentaries to encourage critical thinking and debate about the relationship between media ownership, commercial media content, and the democratic demand for free flows of information, diverse representations of ideas and people, and informed citizen participation." He is the author of numerous scholarly and popular essays and several books including *The Spectacle of Accumulation: Essays in Culture, Media, & Politics,* 2006.

MerRi Lisa Johnson is an Assistant Professor of English and Director of the Center for Women's and Gender Studies at USC Upstate and has edited three critical anthologies including *Jane Sexes It Up: True Confessions of Feminist Desire, Flesh for Fantasy: Producing and Consuming Exotic Dance* (co-edited with Danielle Egan and Katherine Frank), and *Third Wave Feminism and Television: Jane Puts It in a Box.* Her research interests include feminist media studies, sex and radical feminism, and queer theory.

Jackson Katz is a pioneer in the field of gender violence prevention education with men and boys, particularly in the sports culture and the military. Katz is co-founder of the Mentors in Violence Prevention (MVP) program, the most widely utilized sexual and domestic violence prevention initiative in college and professional athletics. He is the creator of popular educational videos including *Tough Guise: Violence, Media and the Crisis in Masculinity,* and is the author of *The Macho Paradox: Why Some Men Hurt Women and How All Men Can Help.* Katz lectures in the U.S. and around the world on violence, media, and masculinities and is completing his Ph.D. in the Graduate School of Education and Information Studies at UCLA.

Douglas Kellner is George Kneller Chair in the Philosophy of Education at UCLA and is author of many books on social theory, politics, history, and culture, including works in cultural studies such as *Media Culture* and *Media Spectacle;* a trilogy of books on postmodern theory with Steve Best; and a trilogy of books on the media and the Bush administration, encompassing *Grand Theft 2000, From 9/11 to Terror War,* and *Media Spectacle and the Crisis of Democracy.* Kellner's latest book is *Guys and Guns Amok: Domestic Terrorism and School Shootings from the Oklahoma City Bombings to the Virginia Tech Massacre,* and he has a forthcoming book *Cinema Wars: Hollywood Film and Politics in the Bush/Cheney Era.* His website is at http://www.gseis.ucla.edu/faculty/kellner/kellner.html

Gooyong Kim is a Ph.D. candidate at the Graduate School of Education & Information Studies, UCLA. He is working on his dissertation about people's grassroots mobilization for sociopolitical matters utilizing new media technologies with specific focus on YouTube videos for the Obama campaign in the 2008 U.S. presidential election. He is working on theorizing intersectionality among agency, structure, technology, pedagogy and social transformation.

Joe L. Kincheloe (1950–2008) was the Canada Research Chair of Critical Pedagogy at the McGill University Faculty of Education. He was the founder of the Paulo and Nita Freire International Project for Critical Pedagogy. He is the author of numerous books and articles about pedagogy, education and social justice, racism, class bias, and sexism, issues of cognition and cultural context, and educational reform. His books include: *The Sign of the Burger: McDonald's and the Culture of Power;* and *City Kids: Understanding Them, Appreciating Them, and Teaching Them.* His co-edited works include *White Reign: Deploying Whiteness in America* (with Shirley Steinberg et al.) and the Gustavus Myers Human Rights award winner: *Measured Lies: The Bell Curve Examined* (with Shirley Steinberg). Kincheloe was an international speaker and lead singer/keyboard player of Tony and the Hegemones.

Pepi Leistyna is an Associate Professor of Applied Linguistics Graduate Studies at the University of Massachusetts Boston, where he coordinates the research program and teaches courses in cultural studies, media literacy, and language acquisition. His books include: *Breaking Free: The Transformative Power of Critical Pedagogy; Presence of Mind: Education and the Politics of Deception; Defining and Designing Multiculturalism,* and *Cultural Studies: From Theory to Action.* His recent documentary film is called *Class Dismissed: How TV Frames the Working Class* for which he is the 2007 recipient of the Working-Class Studies Association's *Studs Terkel Award for Media and Journalism.*

Rachael Liberman is a doctoral student in the School of Journalism and Mass Communication at the University of Colorado at Boulder. She has participated in pornography studies at New York University and provided research assistance for Chyng Sun's documentary *The Price of Pleasure: Pornography, Sexuality, and Relationships.* Her research interests include mediated constructions of sexuality, the media's role in the perpetuation of female competition, and the effectiveness and relevance of media education.

Leah Lievrouw is Professor of Information Studies in the Graduate School of Education and Information Studies at UCLA. Her research and writing interests focus on the relationship between media and information technologies and social change, particularly the role of technologies in social differentiation and oppositional social and cultural movements, and intellectual freedom in pervasively mediated social settings. She is the author of over 40 journal and proceedings articles, book chapters, and other works related to new media and information society issues. With Sonia Livingstone of the London School of Economics, she is co-editor and contributor to *The Handbook of New Media* (Sage, 2006) and the four-volume *Sage Benchmarks in Communication: New Media* (2009). She is also a former co-editor of the journal *New Media & Society*. Her current projects include *Media and Meaning: Understanding Communication, Technology, and Society* (Oxford University Press) and *Alternative and Activist New Media* (Polity Press).

Allan Luke is Professor of Education at Queensland University of Technology, where he is currently working on research projects on the impacts of social class on early literacy, the capital and resources of homeless youth reentering schooling, and Aboriginal curriculum and school leadership.

Carmen Luke is Professor in Creative Industries at Queensland University of Technology, where she is currently doing research on Australian values in media and education.

Robin Mansell is Professor of New Media and the Internet, Head of the Department of Media and Communications, London School of Economics and Political Science, and Past President of the International Association for Media and Communication Research. She is internationally known for her work on the social, economic, and political issues arising from new information and communication technologies. Her publications include *The Oxford Handbook of Information and Communication Technologies* (Oxford University Press, 2007), *Trust and Crime in Information Societies* (Elgar, 2005), *Networking Knowledge for Information Societies: Institutions and Intervention* (Delft University Press, 2002), *Inside the Communication Revolution—New Patterns of Social and Technical Interaction* (Oxford University Press, 2002) and *Mobilizing the Information Society* (Oxford University Press, 2000).

Kathleen A. McHugh (mchughla@ucla.edu) directs the Center for the Study of Women (CSW) and teaches in the English Department and Cinema and Media Studies program at UCLA. She is the author of *American Domesticity: From How-To Manual to Hollywood Melodrama* (Oxford, 1999), *Jane Campion* (University of Illinois Press, 2007), the co-editor of *South Korean Golden Age Melodrama: Gender, Genre and National Cinema* (2005, 2007), and the co-editor of a special issue of SIGNS on Film Feminisms (2004). She has published articles on domesticity, feminism, melodrama, the avant-garde, and autobiography in such journals as *Cultural Studies, Jump Cut, Screen, South Atlantic Quarterly,* and *Velvet Light Trap.*

Angela McRobbie is Professor of Communication at Goldsmiths, University of London. Her earliest work on young women, sexuality, youth culture and girls magazines, was written while still a student at Birmingham University, Centre for Contemporary Cultural Studies. She is the author of many books and articles, on the UK fashion industry, on the new cultural economy, and on feminist theory. Her most recent book is *The Aftermath of Feminism: Gender, Culture and Social Change* (Sage, 2008). She is also a contributor to *The Guardian*, openDemocracy, and various Radio 4 programmes.

Ekra Miezan, Ph.D. is a lecturer at the University of Massachusetts-Amherst. His research interests include representations and cultivation effects, news and society, communication and social change, and post-colonial documentary films.

Toby Miller is chair of the Department of Media & Cultural Studies at the University of California, Riverside. His latest book is *Makeover Nation: The United States of Reinvention* and his blog is greencitizenship.blogspot.com

Ernest Morrell is Associate Professor in Urban Schooling and Associate Director for Youth Research at the Institute for Democracy, Education, and Access (IDEA) at the University of California at Los Angeles. For more than a decade he has worked with adolescents, drawing on their involvement with popular culture to promote academic literacy development. Morrell is the author of four books, *Linking Literacy and Popular Culture: Finding Connections for Lifelong Learning* (Christopher-Gordon), *Becoming Critical Researchers: Literacy and Empowerment for Urban Youth* (Peter Lang), *Critical Literacy and Urban Youth: Pedagogies of Access, Dissent, and Liberation* (Routledge) and *The Art of Critical Pedagogy: Possibilities for Moving from Theory to Practice in Urban Schools* (co-authored with Jeffrey M.R. Duncan-Andrade.

Chon A. Noriega is Professor in the UCLA Department of Film, Television, and Digital Media, Director of the UCLA Chicano Studies Research Center, and Adjunct Curator at the Los Angeles County Museum of Art. He is author of *Shot in America: Television, the State, and the Rise of Chicano Cinema* (Minnesota, 2000) and editor of nine books dealing with Latino media, performance and visual art. He is currently writing a book on Puerto Rican artist Raphael Montañez Ortiz.

Tom Pollard is professor of social sciences at National University, San Jose and a documentary filmmaker. His most recent books include *The Hollywood War Machine,* with Carl Boggs, and *Sex and Cinema* (Paradigm, 2009).

Mark Poster is Chair of the Department of Film and Media Studies and a member of the History Department at the University of California, Irvine. He has a courtesy appointment in the Department of Comparative Literature. He is a member of the Critical Theory Institute. His recent books are: *Information Please: Culture and Politics in a Digital Age* (Duke University Press, 2006); *What's the Matter with the Internet?: A Critical Theory of Cyberspace* (University of Minnesota Press, 2001); *The Information Subject* in Critical Voices Series (New York: Gordon and Breach Arts International, 2001); *Cultural History and Postmodernity* (New York: Columbia University Press, 1997); *The Second Media Age* (London: Polity and New York: Blackwell, 1995); and *The Mode of Information* (London: Blackwell and Chicago: University of Chicago Press, 1990).

Christine Quail is an assistant professor in Communication Studies at McMaster University (Canada). She is the co-author, with Kathalene Razzano and Loubna Skalli, of *Vulture Culture: The Politics and Pedagogy of Daytime Television Talk Shows*, and is a contributor to FlowTV, the critical television online journal.

Elayne Rapping is Professor of American Studies at SUNY/Buffalo and the author of *Law and Justice as Seen on TV* (2002); *The Culture of Recovery: Making Sense of the Self-Help Movement in Women's Lives* (1996), *Media-tions: Forays into the Gender and Culture Wars; The Movie of the Week: Private Stories/Public Events*, and *The Looking Glass World of Nonfiction Television,* as well as numerous articles in scholarly and mainstream publications. Her research interests include media, gender, popular culture and cultural trends.

Kathalene A. Razzano is a Ph.D. candidate in the Cultural Studies Program at George Mason University. She is co-author, with Christine Quail and Loubna Skalli, of *Vulture Culture: The Politics and Pedagogy of Daytime Television Talk Shows* (2005). Her research interests include media, gender, economics and welfare.

Chris Rojek is Professor of Sociology & Culture at Brunel University, West London and for 15 years has also been the publisher of Sociology and Cultural Studies titles at Sage Publications, London. He is the author of many books, the most recent of which are *Celebrity, Frank Sinatra,* and *Leisure Theory and Cultural Studies.* Currently, he is researching contemporary idols, neat capitalism and stateless solutions to global issues.

Jeff Share is a Faculty Advisor in the Teacher Education Program at the University of California, Los Angeles (UCLA). His research focuses on theoretical frameworks and practical applications for teaching critical media literacy in inner-city classrooms. He is the author of *Media Literacy Is Elementary: Teaching Youth to Critically Read and Create Media* (2009). Contact Email: jshare@ucla.edu.

Loubna H. Skalli is an Assistant Professor at American University's School of International Service in Washington, D.C. She specializes in gender, youth, development and communication, and has published numerous articles in these areas. She is also the author of *Through a Local Prism: Gender, Globalization and Identity in Moroccan Women's Magazines* (2006).

Shirley R. Steinberg is an Associate Professor at the McGill University Faculty of Education. She is the director of the Paulo and Nita Freire International Project for Critical Pedagogy and is the author and editor of numerous books and articles and co-edits several book series. The founding editor of *Taboo: The Journal of Culture and Education,* Steinberg's most recent books are *Christotainment: Selling Jesus Through Popular Culture* (with Joe Kincheloe); and *Media Literacy: A Reader,* edited with Donaldo Macedo. Steinberg edited *Teen Life in Europe,* and *The Encyclopedia of Contemporary Youth Culture.* With Joe Kincheloe she has edited *Kinderculture: The Corporate Construction of Childhood* and *The Miseducation of the West: How Schools and the Media Distort Our Understanding of the Islamic World.*

Rebecca Stephenson is Postdoctoral Researcher at the University of California Humanities Research Institute at UC Irvine. Her research interests include media literacy, teaching and learning with popular culture, and youth media production. She recently completed her Ph.D. in Communication at the Annenberg School for Communication at the University of Southern California. Her dissertation, *Kids as Cultural Producers: Consumption, Literacy, and Participation* investigates issues of access and media literacy through an ethnographic study of media production projects in two mixed-grade (6th, 7th, and 8th) special education classes. Previously, she was a member of the research team for the Digital Youth Project funded by the MacArthur Foundation and a graduate fellow at the Annenberg Center for Communication. Prior to beginning her graduate studies, Rebecca worked as a production manager for companies producing original content for the web and multimedia museum exhibits. Preferred contact info: bhs@hri.uci.edu.

Chyng Sun is a Master Teacher of Media Studies at McGhee Liberal Arts, School of Continuing and Professional Studies, New York University. In addition to her teaching and scholarly research on audience and the representations of gender, sexuality and race in the media, Dr. Sun is the creator of the documentaries *Mickey Mouse Monopoly: Disney, Childhood and Corporate Power* and *Beyond Good and Evil: Children, Media and Violent Times.* Her recent research projects include the documentary film *The Price of Pleasure: Pornography, Sexuality, and Relationships* and her forthcoming book, *Fantasies Matter: Pornography, Sexuality, and Relationships* (working title), to be published by Peter Lang in 2010. (chyng.sun@nyu.edu)

Alla Zollers is doctorate student at UCLA in the Information Studies department. Her research interests include social software, information architecture, critical cultural studies, and new media.